CW01433209

AIRCRAFT
of the Third Reich

VOLUME ONE
Arado to Focke-Wulf

Dedicated to William Green, 1928-2010

AIRCRAFT
of the Third Reich

VOLUME ONE
Arado to Focke-Wulf

William Green

AEROSPACE
MasterBooks

Aerospace Publishing Ltd · London

Aircraft of the Third Reich
Published by:
Aerospace Publishing ltd
179 Dalling Road
London W6 0ES, UK
www.aerospacepublishing.co.uk
Tel: +44 (0) 208 735 4200

Aircraft of the Third Reich
Volume One first published 2010

Copyright © 2010 Aerospace Publishing Ltd

Original text © William Green

ISBN: 978-1-900732-06-2

Publisher: Stan Morse
Managing Editor: Soph Moeng
Editor: David Donald

Original text by William Green

Printed in Singapore by KHL

All rights reserved. No part of this publication may be reproduced, stored in a retrieval system or transmitted, in any form or by any means, electronic, mechanical, photocopying, recording or otherwise, except brief extracts for the purpose of review, without the permission of Aerospace Publishing Ltd and the copyright holders.

Additional contributions from:
Chris Chant
Thomas Newdick
Malcolm V. Lowe
Barry Ketley

Artists:
John Weal
Dennis Punnett
Keith Fretwell
Mike Badrocke
Chris Davey
Iain Wyllie
I. Hasegawa
Petr Štepanek
Rolando Ugolini

Production Editor: Robert Vicen
Production team:
Martin Ritchie
Saliha Hamdane
Mirka Vicenova
Cloudia Castaño
Stefan Kobolka

The Publisher wishes to thank the following for their important contributions to this volume: Dennis Punnett for general arrangement line drawings; Ted Nevill of Cody Images for additional photographs; Jean-Louis Roba for additional photographs; 4+ Publications, Prague, and Petr Štepanek for the Focke-Wulf Ta 152 colour artwork

Aircraft of the Third Reich is published in three volumes, which are available from:
Aerospace Publishing Ltd,
179 Dalling Road,
London W6 0ES, UK

www.aerospacemasterbooks.com

Volume One
ISBN: 978-1-900732-06-2

Volume Two
ISBN: 978-1-900732-07-9

Volume Three
ISBN: 978-1-900732-08-6

For trade distribution enquiries please contact
Crécy Publishing Ltd at
www.crecy.co.uk

Picture credits

19: Jean-Louis Roba; **25:** Barry Ketley; **27:** Barry Ketley; **33:** Barry Ketley (two); **42:** Barry Ketley; **43:** Cody Images, Jean-Louis Roba; **45:** Jean-Louis Roba; **46:** Jean-Louis Roba; **56:** Cody Images (two); **59:** Cody Images; **63:** Cody Images; **77:** Cody Images; **79:** Cody Images; **80:** Cody Images; **81:** Jean-Louis Roba; **83:** Jean-Louis Roba; **85:** Cody Images; **86:** Cody Images; **87:** Cody Images; **90:** Cody Images; **91:** Cody Images; **92:** Jean-Louis Roba (two); **93:** Jean-Louis Roba; **94:** Jean-Louis Roba; **95:** Jean-Louis Roba (four); **96:** Jean-Louis Roba (three); **105:** Jean-Louis Roba (two); **106:** Jean-Louis Roba (three); **107:** Jean-Louis Roba (two); **108:** Jean-Louis Roba; **109:** Jean-Louis Roba (two); **110:** Jean-Louis Roba (three); **113:** Cody Images; **117:** Cody Images; **118:** Cody Images; **119:** Cody Images (three); **133:** Cody Images (two); **134:** Cody Images (three); **135:** Cody Images; **145:** Cody Images; **146:** Cody Images (three); **147:** Cody Images; **153:** Cody Images; **154:** Cody Images; **155:** Cody Images; **156:** Cody Images (two); **158:** Cody Images; **160:** Cody Images (two); **161:** Cody Images; **162:** Cody Images (three); **163:** Cody Images; **166:** Cody Images (two); **168:** Cody Images (two); **169:** Jean-Louis Roba (two); **170:** Jean-Louis Roba (three); **171:** Jean-Louis Roba; **172:** Jean-Louis Roba (two); **173:** Jean-Louis Roba (three); **174:** Cody Images; **175:** Cody Images (two); **176:** Cody Images (three); **177:** Cody Images (two); **178:** Cody Images (four); **180:** Cody Images (four); **181:** Jean-Louis Roba (two); **182:** Jean-Louis Roba; **183:** Jean-Louis Roba (three); **184:** Jean-Louis Roba (three); **185:** Jean-Louis Roba (three); **186:** Jean-Louis Roba (three); **187:** Cody Images; **191:** Cody Images; **192:** Cody Images (two); **193:** Cody Images; **194:** Cody Images (three); **200:** Cody Images; **206:** Cody Images; **208:** Cody Images; **209:** Cody Images (three); **217:** Cody Images; **220:** Cody Images; **221:** Cody Images; **222:** Cody Images; **223:** Cody Images; **224:** Cody Images; **240:** Cody Images (two); **241:** Cody Images (two); **251:** Cody Images; **260:** Cody Images; **261:** Cody Images; **280:** Cody Images; **284:** Cody Images; **288:** Cody Images; **295:** Cody Images (three); **296:** Cody Images; **297:** Cody Images; **299:** Jean-Louis Roba (three); **300:** Jean-Louis Roba (three); **301:** Jean-Louis Roba (three); **302:** Jean-Louis Roba (three); **303:** Jean-Louis Roba (two); **304:** Cody Images; **316:** Cody Images; **322:** Cody Images; **326:** Cody Images; **327:** Cody Images; **343:** Cody Images (two); **344:** Cody Images (four); **345:** Cody Images (two); **346:** Cody Images (two); **347:** Cody Images (three); **349:** Cody Images (two); **350:** Cody Images; **352:** Cody Images (two); **353:** Cody Images (five); **354:** Cody Images (three); **355:** Cody Images (four); **358:** Cody Images (two); **367:** Cody Images; **368:** Cody Images (three); **369:** Cody Images; **370:** Cody Images (three); **371:** Cody Images; **372:** Cody Images; **374:** Cody Images; **376:** Cody Images; **377:** Cody Images; **380:** Cody Images (three); **382:** Cody Images (three); **385:** Cody Images; **389:** Cody Images; **390:** Cody Images; **391:** Cody Images (two); **402:** Cody Images; **410:** Cody Images; **411:** Cody Images; **414:** Cody Images; **426:** Cody Images; **429:** Cody Images; **432:** Cody Images (two); **438:** Cody Images; **443:** Cody Images; **446:** Cody Images; **448:** Cody Images; **453:** Cody Images; **456:** Cody Images; **457:** Cody Images, Jean-Louis Roba; **458:** Cody Images (two); **459:** Jean-Louis Roba (four); **460:** Cody Images; **489:** Focke-Wulf, Bremen (via Malcolm Lowe); **491:** Focke-Wulf, Bremen (via Malcolm Lowe); **493:** Brian Nicklas via Malcolm Lowe (two); **496:** Brian Nicklas via Malcolm Lowe; **497:** Focke-Wulf, Bremen (via Malcolm Lowe); **498:** Focke-Wulf, Bremen (via Malcolm Lowe); **499:** Malcolm Lowe collection, Focke-Wulf, Bremen (via Malcolm Lowe), Peter Walter via Malcolm Lowe.

All other photographs and images from the collection of Aerospace Publishing Ltd

Contents

Preface

Extracted from the late William Green's original edition of *Warplanes of the Third Reich*, first published 1970.

"Do not take our aircraft out of the context of the requirements that they were designed to fulfil; the men who influenced the framing of those requirements, and those others whose task was the translation of the requirements into creations of steel tubing, alloy sheet and rivets. Do not confine yourself to those aircraft that were built in quantity and neglect those many others, good, bad, and indifferent, that fell by the wayside, together with their creators' hopes and aspirations.

"Some of those that advanced no further than prototype test phase contributed much to our technology, and were by no means inferior in concept or capability to those that occupied the assembly lines of our factories, their fates having been influenced, more often than not, by personal prejudices and the whims of those in authority rather than shortcomings inherent in their designs.

"Consider the technical and operational accomplishments of our aircraft without ignoring their failures, but relate both accomplishments and failures to the background against which the aircraft were designed, built, and committed to battle; the interference that we manufacturers endured from often ill-informed officialdom and successful, high-ranking young pilots whose undoubted bravery in combat could only be equated with their lack of technical knowledge; the exigencies of the times that exerted so much influence on our work, and the circumstances under which our progeny were flown with the changing fortunes of war. If you can take these many aspects into account when writing your book and I am still alive when the task is completed, I shall be more than delighted to contribute a foreword."

These comments, made by Professor Ernst Heinkel in the early 1950s when I first discussed with him my ideas for the book that was eventually to become *The Warplanes of the Third Reich*, probably influenced the form that it has taken more than any other factor. Its compilation, which, when begun, I naively envisaged taking two years, has, in fact, taken almost ten times as long, and the demise of Professor Heinkel some years ago has prevented him from fulfilling his promise to write a foreword for the work, if, indeed, after perusing the following pages, he would have considered that I had fulfilled with reasonable competence the task that we discussed so long ago.

My endeavours to follow Professor Heinkel's advice have, in fact, been responsible for the protracted gestation of this book, for I was soon to discover that, paradoxically, the more I learned the less I found that I knew. It became a work of detection, some clues leading me along paths that proved to have blind ends, and others resulting in the unravelling of one mystery only to reveal several others. But all historical research has its fascination, and if the researcher delves in sufficient depth into his chosen subject, new facts must emerge which, as often as not, explode the most cherished beliefs and theories, and reveal as fallacious information derived from what may previously have been considered impeccable sources ...

William Green (1928–20

... I found there to be little basis in fact for the numerous assertions made since World War II by high-ranking former members of the Luftwaffe and certain leaders of the wartime German aircraft industry that, but for irresolution and interference on the part of the leaders of the Third Reich, the Luftwaffe could have committed turbojet-driven fighters to combat six months earlier, with possibly dramatic effects on the course of the air war.

These and many other facts that will be found on the pages of *The Warplanes of the Third Reich* contradict much that has been published in the past, and I can only hope that my reader will not interpret this as a desire on my part to be contentious. It simply reflects the fruitfulness of the many authentic records that have been brought to light in recent years; records that have permitted reassessment and correction of what has for long been accepted as fact.

My success or failure in interpreting the advice of the late Professor Heinkel can only be adjudged by the reader.

William Green, Chislehurst, Kent, July 1970

Foreword to *The Aircraft of the Third Reich* published 2010

At New Year 2010 aviation publishing lost one of its greatest authors, William Green. There can be few aviation enthusiasts or professionals who did not fall under the spell of his wonderful publications: from the annual *Observer's Book of Aircraft* (the best five-shilling Christmas present in the world!) and his fantastic magazines *Flying Review*, *AIR Enthusiast* and *AIR International*.

I was one of those who, as a kid, woke on Christmas morning to manically leaf through the latest *Observer's*, gasping and delighting in the exciting additions to its glossy content. This magically compact volume was a superb mix of detail, accuracy, conciseness and illustration. And its author, William Green, and his works became one of the landmarks of my life. Some years later, when I became a publisher, I met up with Bill and we worked together for the next 30 years, publishing aviation books, partworks and journals throughout the world. Even though he is no longer with us, we continue to work with his famed archive of writing, photographs and artworks. Bill set an everlasting standard that we and many other publishers have sought to follow. I hope we have lived up to his demanding expectations.

His most famed book, *The Warplanes of the Third Reich*, has remained the classic work on that subject for 40 years. In the last months of Bill's life, we decided to publish a new work building on the original *Warplanes* but greatly enlarging its scope, with many more entries, illustrations and greater use of colour. This new work became more and more ambitious and is now so extensive that it is published in three separate 500-page volumes, making it by far the largest work on this fascinating and everlasting subject.

The new three-volume series *Aircraft of the Third Reich* now covers all the types flown under the swastika from 1933 until war's end, including 'civilian' aircraft flown by Lufthansa and the many foreign aircraft captured or impressed into Third Reich service.

I know that Bill was delighted with our plans for this new three-volume edition of his original work. We have great pleasure in dedicating *Aircraft of the Third Reich* to Bill, the wonderful works he produced and the enthusiasm he engendered in all those who delighted in his fantastic publications.

Stan Morse, Publisher
Aerospace Publishing Ltd, 2010

Introduction

Fallacious theories, incorrect decisions, faulty organisation, inadequacies of personnel and equipment; all allegedly conspired to defeat the Luftwaffe in World War II. Such shortcomings were, of course, suffered to a greater or lesser extent by the air arms of all the principal combatants, but whereas retrospect attaches little significance to those of the victor, the failings of the vanquished are fully exposed, and subjected to critical study and analysis. Thus, over the past 65 years, the failure of the Luftwaffe to achieve the ends for which it was conceived by the leaders of the Third Reich has been examined and re-examined in depth; the dramatic rise and decline of the German air arm over so short a span as a dozen years have provided subject matter for many treatises attributing the final debacle in which it was engulfed to a variety of factors.

The reasons for the defeat of the Luftwaffe are manifold, and do not come within the compass of this book other than in so far as the aircraft the service flew contributed to its downfall. That they did so is an indisputable fact, but one that reflects no discredit on the capabilities of German aircraft and aero engine designers, nor the industry in which they worked.

It is a widely-accepted tenet that when a new combat aircraft is introduced into service its potential successor should be on the drawing boards, and in the late 1930s, when warplane development tempo had attained an unprecedented rapidity, such was axiomatic. Yet Germany failed to ensure retention of the superiority in combat equipment that the Luftwaffe undoubtedly enjoyed when it flew its first sorties of World War II. The aircraft that fed the pyre marking the end of the air arm of the Third Reich were largely those types with which the Luftwaffe had been committed to hostilities, or, at least, their derivatives.

Apart from the Do 217, the Fw 190 and the He 177, all of pre-war origin, the first four years of the conflict saw no major combat aircraft type added to the inventory in quantity, and by the time entirely new warplanes, such as the Ar 234 and Me 262, did begin to join the ranks of the Luftwaffe, the eleventh hour had already struck; the entire German economy had begun to disintegrate and the transportation system feeding essential materials to the aircraft manufacturers had begun to break down.

Inexplicable failure

This failure to provide timely successors to the warplanes flown by the Luftwaffe during the opening phases of World War II is, at first sight, inexplicable. It was certainly not due to lethargy on the part of the design teams of the German aircraft industry, singularly well-endowed with talented, imaginative engineers. Nor was it tardiness on the part of the Technical

The Illustrirte Zeitung was an influential high-quality publication that provided an official government version of foreign and military news. Most years a Luftwaffe special was published, this example being from March 1941.

...sh from the factory, ...cke-wulf Fw 190Fs line up ...Poland on their way to the ...ssian front in 1943.

Department of the Air Ministry in framing specifications for progressively more advanced combat aircraft. It was not the result of an overly-cautious approach to aircraft procurement on the part of the Luftwaffe itself, for, while possessing its quotas of both traditionalists and visionaries, its youth and the high proportion of younger men in its upper echelons rendered it more receptive to innovations and what was widely considered the unconventional in both tactics and equipment than were its British, American, Soviet or French counterparts. Indeed, it was perhaps the hiatus of 15 years, and the lack of continuity in German service aviation in consequence, that had bred a less-bigoted approach to the new and the radical, and placed Germany's aircraft industry in a commanding position in international combat aircraft design in the late 1930s.

The seeds of this disastrous loss of technical leadership were, in fact, harboured by the personalities most closely connected with the German air arm's birth and subsequent growth. Its fate was inextricably interwoven with the qualifications, backgrounds and characters of the men whose names appear repeatedly in the narrative that follows, and who directly or indirectly influenced the types of aircraft selected for service with the Luftwaffe and the quantities in which they were produced.

The most important of these individuals was undoubtedly the Commander-in-Chief, or Oberbefehlshaber, Hermann Göring, a political revolutionary and an ambitious, flamboyant and forceful personality, whose egoism and arrogance were perhaps exceeded only by his lack of the most elementary

'Tante Ju', as the Junkers 52/3m trimotor transport was called, was the aerial workhorse of the Wehrmacht. Its offensive assault role gave way to emergency evacuation as the war situation deteriorated.

technical knowledge. Widely considered something of a buffoon outside Germany, Göring was, nevertheless, the principal architect of the Luftwaffe, displaying ruthless energy during the service's formative years when his avowed intention was the creation of the largest and most modern air arm in the world, and his target for the attainment of this goal being 1943 – four years, in fact, after his fledgeling was to be committed to battle.

Göring possessed an innate common sense which was perhaps his sole saving grace, although with the passage of years its application waned, and his effectiveness was eroded by a steadily increasing lassitude which, at times, manifested itself as complete indifference towards the Luftwaffe over protracted periods. He was intoxicated by his authority to command, regardless of the necessity or logicality of the commands that he issued, and, motivated by self-aggrandisement, he tended to arrogate everything to himself. He was incapable of imbuing his staff with any sense of common purpose, and made no attempt to discourage dissension and rivalry within the hierarchies of Air Ministry and aircraft industry. He was unable to view problems objectively or take the most elementary precautions against any danger that he personally found distasteful to contemplate; he intervened in matters that he did not possess the technical competence to understand, and he was prone to vacillation, frequently withdrawing his support from programmes that he had encouraged in the first place.

It was Göring's over-confidence, derived from the initial successes of the Luftwaffe against poorly-trained and poorly-equipped air forces, coupled with markedly lower combat attrition during these early campaigns than the most sanguine of estimates had forecast, that was primarily responsible for pushing combat aircraft development and the expansion of aircraft production well down the list of wartime priorities. His interference with aircraft planning programmes on the pretext that he was "interpreting the wishes of the Führer" did incalculable damage to the German aircraft industry's war effort, but although subjected to increasingly bitter criticism from Luftwaffe and industry alike, and a steady decline in his prestige within the Party, Göring's personal status remained unassailable almost to the end, largely owing to the intervention of the Führer on his behalf.

Clear-thinking deputy

Göring's deputy, Erhard Milch, was a man of very different ilk. From many aspects he was the exact antithesis of the Oberbefelhshaber, being essentially clearthinking and practical, although possessing something of a penchant towards making rash judgements. Göring had little fondness for Milch, who had close connections with the Party and the Führer himself, was hardworking, untiring, and, in general, highly efficient. Indeed, the only common feature in their characters was a mutual desire for power and prestige, and that antipathy existed between Göring and his deputy from an early stage in the creation of the Luftwaffe can be of little doubt; antipathy which, coupled with the unhealthy situation resulting from rivalry between Milch and successive Chiefs of the Luftwaffe General Staff, hardly augured well for the future.

While Milch's qualifications for his post as deputy to the Oberhefehlshaber were painfully few, and the limitations in his knowledge of technological matters were to result in exasperation in the aircraft industry on frequent occasions after he assumed the additional office of Generalluftzeugmeister, he had a remarkable talent for organisation that stood the Luftwaffe in good stead during the first years of its existence. Unfortunately, Göring steadily eroded Milch's authority, and the latter was thus no longer able to engender unity and singleness of purpose into his organisation, the effectiveness of which deteriorated in consequence. With the suicide of Ernst Udet and his assumption of control of the Generalluftzeugmeister-Amt, Milch jealously guarded his authority over aircraft development and procurement, and perhaps motivated by the enmity that existed between him and the Chief of the Luftwaffe General Staff, Hans Jeschonnek, ensured that no member of the General Staff had any say in technological matters.

Although there is evidence to support Milch's subsequent contention that aircraft production, which had stagnated under Udet, began to rise within eight

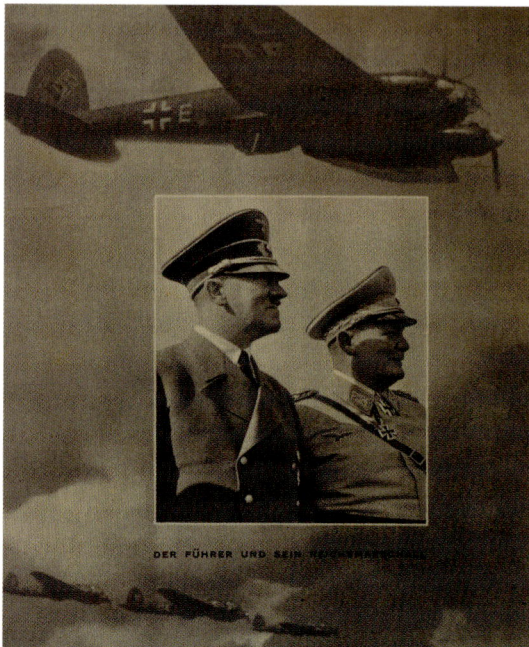

Hermann Göring took the plaudits for the creation of the Luftwaffe and its meteoric successes of the war's early months, but was also inadvertently the chief architect of its ultimate demise.

months of his becoming Generalluftzeugmeister, this relatively modest expansion was already in hand when Milch took office, and while he was fully conversant with the necessity for advanced planning, no immediate steps were taken to remedy the state of semi-stagnation in the development of new combat aircraft or to increase their priority.

Milch's predecessor as Generalluftzeugmeister, Ernst Udet, was as unfitted for his position as was Göring for that of Oberbefehlshaber. When Göring first prevailed upon Udet to take charge of the Technisches Amt he was subordinated to Erhard Milch, and the friendliest of relationships existed between the two, but, when, as part of his process of eroding Milch's authority, Göring removed Udet from Milch's supervision, friendship deteriorated into a cool, mutual acceptance, and finally into something approaching antipathy, this hardly being conducive to effective collaboration.

Udet's suicide

Udet possessed no knowledge whatsoever of the procurement side of air armament, and lacking the advice on organisation that had previously been available from Milch, neglected the production aspect almost entirely in his enthusiasm for technological development. His tendency to vacillate and his inability to provide firm leadership in the selection of aircraft to be developed for production were to prove costly, and the final accounting was not to be rendered until after Udet's suicide on 17 November 1941. Udet was subsequently to provide both Milch and Göring, equally to blame for the state of Germany's aircraft procurement and development programmes, with a useful scapegoat. Some two years after Udet's death, Göring, although hardly qualified to express an opinion on the subject, denounced him bitterly for his failure as Generalluftzeugmeister, declaiming at a conference held on 9 October 1943, "if he [Udet] was alive today I should have no alternative but to tell him that he had been responsible for destroying the Luftwaffe."

The shortcomings in Germany's aircraft production programme, for which Udet was at least technically responsible, stemmed in part from contamination by the highly-contagious over-confidence of Göring and his staff, but primarily from Udet's inability to evaluate accurately the characters and motivations of the men with whom he had to deal, to master the intrigues and rivalries that were so much a part of everyday life in the Air Ministry and aircraft industry, and to take ruthless action to keep the industrialists in line.

These then were the principal personalities that laid the foundations on which the Luftwaffe was built; foundations which time was to prove to possess all the inherent weaknesses of their creators. These seeds of disaster were destined to germinate rapidly as the war generated higher temperatures.

The industry: its rise and decline

When hostilities finally terminated in Europe, the Allies found the twisted, tangled wreckage of hundreds of aircraft in the still-smouldering ruins of factories from Augsburg to Warnemünde, from Dessau to Wiener-Neustadt. From the spring of 1943 until the early summer of 1944, the German aircraft industry, together with U-boat bases, had received pre-eminence as a target for the Combined Bomber Offensive; the RAF bombing industrial areas by night to demoralise the

labour force and destroy such factories as were located in the target area, and the USAAF bombing airfields and factories by day to destroy as many finished aircraft as possible and to cripple further production.

How much this bombing programme contributed to the end result is difficult to determine. It has been estimated that, between July 1943 and December 1944, some 25 per cent of total production, or about 18,000 aircraft, was denied to the Luftwaffe as a result of bombing, some 78 per cent of this production loss being fighters. But did this loss materially affect the issue in so far as the Luftwaffe was concerned? Had these many aircraft found their way to the Luftwaffe it is highly unlikely that the German air arm could have made effective use of them at that stage of the air war, for the Luftwaffe suffered no shortage of aircraft, but it was short of crews to man them, fuel for their powerplants, and ammunition and bombs with which to arm them.

The German aircraft industry, in fact, displayed fantastic recuperative powers, the output of aircraft being apparently stimulated rather than retarded by the Allied aerial onslaught, although it must be remembered that the immense upsurge in aircraft deliveries that took place in the spring of 1944 had been planned and provided for from mid-1943. How much higher the production curve would have risen but for the Combined Bomber Offensive can only be a matter for speculation. It was not until the autumn of 1944, after the aircraft industry *per se* had lost much of its priority as a target for the Combined Bomber Offensive that output began to lag. Airframes, powerplants and components were being produced in ever-increasing numbers by an immense network of dispersed and concealed factories, but with the progressive collapse of the transportation system and the dwindling of fuel supplies, deliveries of finished aircraft to the Luftwaffe declined rapidly.

The Air Clauses of the Treaty of Versailles, signed in June 1919, were conceived to stop once and for all

Germany's aircraft industry led the world in several key technological areas, chief among which was the jet engine. The Me 262 was the world's first operational jet warplane, although it had little influence on the war's final outcome.

Below: For a year at the start of the war the Luftwaffe was seemingly invincible. Redolent of what to the service was a glorious time is this Messerschmitt Bf 109E in France, shortly before the attack on Britain.

the development of military aircraft in Germany and remove all possibility of any resurrection of German military air power. Germany was obliged to surrender all aeronautical materials to the Allies and associated powers under the supervision of an Allied Control Commission. The surrender of more than 20,000 aircraft and 27,000 aero engines suggested that the Air Clauses of the Treaty were effective, but the Treaty had omitted to prohibit the manufacture of civil aircraft, although in 1922, it is true, certain limitations on the size and performance of civil aircraft built in Germany were imposed, only to be withdrawn four years later by the Paris Air Agreement.

Clandestine rebuilding

Those responsible for drawing up the Treaty of Versailles could hardly have been expected to anticipate the subterfuge and devious means that would be adopted by German aircraft manufacturers in order to continue the development of military aircraft. This development was undertaken both openly abroad by foreign subsidiaries of German aircraft manufacturers and clandestinely at home. This happened under the noses of the Allied Control Commission, some of whose member countries had their own reasons for instructing their representatives to turn a blind eye to infringements of the Air Clauses brought to their notice. Thus, the German aircraft industry was resurrected and, if by no means prosperous, it enabled Germany to keep abreast of aeronautical technological developments, and, indeed, initiate some of these developments itself, names such as Ernst Heinkel, Claudius Dornier, Hugo Junkers, and Willy Messerschmitt becoming increasingly familiar.

Throughout the 1920s the German aircraft industry remained small, most of its component companies experiencing financial difficulties despite subsidies from the Reichsverkehrsministerium, which, influenced in no small measure by the Reichswehr, was anxious to maintain an experienced aircraft designing and manufacturing nucleus around which a very much larger industry could grow, a vision pre-dating the accession of Adolf Hitler by a number of years. By the late 1920s, Germany was already the most air-minded nation in the world, the Deutscher Luftsportverband boasting more than 50,000 members. Thus, when in 1929, the year after his election to the Reichstag, Hermann Göring informed that body that if it did not provide the means to establish a strong air force immediately it was merely delaying the inevitable, he was stating the obvious. Few were unaware that the cadre for a new air arm was already in the process of formation.

It was to be the assumption of Germany's leadership by the National Socialist Party in January 1933, however, that provided the necessary political climate to establish an air arm on the scale envisaged by Göring, and the creation of such a force dictated immediate expansion of the aircraft industry that was to become a tool with which to attain the objectives of National Socialism. The plant and equipment of both airframe and aero engine sections of the industry were, at this time, very small indeed, with a commensurate capital investment, but funds for expansion were quickly provided, either directly by the newly-created Reichsluftfahrtministerium (RLM) or through bank credits guaranteed by this Ministry. The arrangements were liberal enough, and the close co-operation of the government and the aircraft industry enabled loans to be repaid quickly and ownership of the expanded facilities thus built up.

The development of aircraft types, the expansion of production capacity, the provision of capital investment, and the placing of production orders now depended entirely upon the government, and the keynote was 'rationalisation'; competition was discarded as a matter of policy, with the intention being to pool all patents and designs. Excellent though such a policy may have been in theory, it was not to prove itself entirely feasible in practice.

Apart from the enlarging of the facilities of existing airframe and aero engine manufacturers, the process of expansion was accelerated by encouraging concerns in other industries to establish airframe or aero engine subsidiaries. These subsidiaries were envisaged primarily as 'shadow factories' to be allocated the task of producing airframes or aero engines developed by those existing concerns possessing strong design organisations. This concept, too, was not to prove entirely practicable owing to the aspirations of some of the newcomers to the industry and, in consequence, the RLM was to be forced to accept a number of compromises.

At the outset, the foreign policy of the Führer was very much concerned with allaying the fears being evinced by neighbouring countries concerning the possibility of German rearmament. Of necessity, therefore, emphasis in the aircraft production programme had to be placed primarily on trainers and such comparatively simple military aircraft as could, if not examined too closely, pass muster as club or transport aircraft. Such requirements did not run counter to the first stage in the programme launched under the aegis of Erhard Milch in 1933, this having a twofold purpose: to provide what, initially at least, had to be a clandestine air arm with something to fly, and to afford the industry experience in mass-production techniques, this tooth-cutting demanding manufacture

The Junkers 87 was one of the key weapons of the blitzkrieg style of warfare, but its days in the dive-bomber role were numbered when it encountered modern fighter opposition. It found another niche as a close-support aircraft and killer of tanks on the Russian front.

of relatively unsophisticated aircraft. Simultaneously, the industry was to tool up for the quantity production of what were to be the first-phase combat aircraft of the Luftwaffe, all of which were flying in prototype form, while designated design bureaux were to commence work on more advanced warplanes embodying the latest state-of-the-art technology.

On 1 January 1934, with the industry tooled for producing military aircraft in substantially larger quantities, Milch instituted a new programme that provided for the manufacture of 4,021 aircraft by 30 September 1935, including 1,863 combat aircraft (excluding pre-production series of new types) and 1,760 trainers, the high proportion of the latter being dictated by the rapidity with which it was planned to expand the training programme of the still-secret Luftwaffe. By this time, Hitler's foreign policy had begun to assume a more aggressive character and demands had been placed on Milch to increase the tempo of combat aircraft deliveries to the Luftwaffe in order that the service would the sooner be ready to face the possibility of active intervention on the part of Britain and France. In the event, this initial programme was to be superseded at the end of January 1935 by a programme increasing emphasis on combat types. At that time, deliveries against the original programme totalled 2,105 aircraft, nine per cent fewer than had been scheduled for delivery by that date and representing an average monthly output of 162 aircraft over a 13-month period.

From an average monthly output of 190 aircraft during the first half of 1935, production attained 300 per month during the latter part of the year, but representing as it did an overt challenge to the western nations, the foreign policy of the Führer was becoming increasingly inconsistent with Milch's long-term development plans for both the industry and the Luftwaffe, these having been based on Göring's stated goal of 1943 as the year in which Germany's new air arm would attain the summit of its effectiveness. With German rearmament no longer a secret, the Führer made constant demands of Göring for increases in the development tempo of new combat aircraft, and for reductions in the estimates of the time that must elapse before they could attain volume production, for overriding importance was now attached to Germany emerging as the victor in the arms race against other European powers. Göring merely passed the onus of responsibility on to Milch.

A promising start

Despite the considerable amount of internal dissension, lack of co-ordination and rivalries suffered by the aircraft industry, the RLM and the Luftwaffe General Staff alike, looking at the picture as a whole, German industrial planning at the beginning of World War II was good, and was to remain so as long as Germany retained the initiative. During the late 1930s the aircraft industry had been built up to a point consistent with the supposed requirements of the Luftwaffe.

The aircraft industry was, in 1939, scattered over most of central Germany, no single region accommodating any concentration of production. The major factories lay along a roughly north-south axis from Bremen to Munich, and those built during 1934-39 were situated in open country at some distance from the nearest towns and cities. The industry thus

Der Adler *was published by the RLM and covered a wide range of Luftwaffe topics. This November 1940 edition highlights 'Tiefangriff' – low-level attacks.*

appeared to be well protected from attack. The principle of local dispersal had been applied in the design of all new factories as an additional precaution against bombing, and the RLM had restricted the total ground area covered by individual buildings, with but few exceptions, to some 7000 m² (75,000 sq ft). Each plant comprised several buildings distributed over an area of 12 to 16 hectares (30 to 40 acres), and frequently possessing an elaborate system of underground air raid shelters.

The industry was exceedingly well housed, most of the buildings having steel frames, some of them being of monitor-roof type with overhead cranes and monorail systems, and others being of hangar type with wide clearances. It was generally believed – and correctly so as events were to prove – that these types of structure were not highly vulnerable to bombing attack; that a 227-kg (500-lb) bomb would blow a section out of the roof, crater the floor, and damage equipment in the immediate vicinity of its blast, but that only a direct hit on a girder or column would result in any portion of the building collapsing.

Factories built for the aircraft industry in the years immediately preceding World War II and during the first two years of hostilities possessed sufficient capacity operating on a single-shift basis to fulfil all anticipated needs of the Luftwaffe, and thus, theoretically, half the plant capacity could be destroyed and the remaining half produce just as many aircraft by working a two-shift system. Not only was plant capacity exceptionally large, production tooling had been prepared on a commensurate scale, and could cater for operations of at least twice the extent of those being carried out when war began. In fact, for the first three years of the war a substantial excess of production capacity and tooling existed, and until at least mid-1943 the Luftwaffe general staff was to be content with aircraft production programmes that placed very light loads on the industry.

In 1939, when output was averaging 700 aircraft per month, only one shift of 40 hours per week was being worked throughout the industry, all holidays being observed, and it was not until the last years of the war that a two-shift system was to be adopted, the working week being raised from 40 to 48 hours, and subsequently to 60 hours. Eventually, in 1944, the working week was to be increased to 72 hours, all plants operating a seven-day week and employees receiving extra rations, such as an increase in meat from a half-pound to a pound-and-a-half per week, plus such luxuries as brandy, cigarettes and chocolate, which were to have a stimulating effect on production when output depended on the performance of individual workers.

Expansion of industry

At an early stage in the expansion of the aircraft industry close attention had been paid to the design of the most effective assembly tooling, and there can be little doubt that had German practices not been so well advanced in this field the manufacture of such types as the Bf 109 by several licensees simultaneously would have been rendered extremely difficult, and component interchangeability impossible. Apart from Dornier, which employed an individual system for its factories and a complex of sub-contractors minimising the use of jigs, the industry used a so-called 'standard' system of tooling in which sets of production jigs were made from a master jig, and each licensee was provided with both a set of the production jigs and a duplicate master jig, the latter being used to check the accuracy of the former. Furthermore, the principal manufacturer of the specific aircraft type retained a master control jig to which the several master jigs were sent regularly to ensure their accuracy.

The assembly tooling used by the German aircraft industry was almost entirely of the universal type, the frames being formed from heavy steel members bolted together, and the check points on the jig determining the shape of the part to be built being bolted to the frames. This type of tooling could be adjusted within limits to cater for fairly substantial design changes, and universal jigs had the advantage over special-purpose jigs that damage suffered as a result of bombing could be rectified by bolting in new sections, while, not being set permanently in the floor, they could be easily moved from one location to another.

Perhaps the most remarkable aspect of the German aircraft production programme immediately prior to

Attempts to build a heavy bomber floundered, with only Heinkel's He 177 seeing much service. It was an innovative design that proved to be troublesome.

the war and during the first years of hostilities was the strict limitation in its scope. The average monthly production of 133 fighters and 217 bombers in 1939 was only marginally increased to 150 fighters and 251 bombers per month in 1940. Even in 1941, expansion could be described as no more than modest, monthly output being raised to 244 fighters and 336 bombers. The 1939 figures are the more readily understandable when it is taken into account that some of the principal types being manufactured by the aircraft industry in that year were still low on the learning curve, and during the course of 1940 the Luftwaffe was relegated to a much lower position in the list of procurement priorities than that which the service had enjoyed when hostilities began. In fact, some aircraft manufacturers had begun to devote part of their capacity to the production of landing craft, scaling ladders, prefabricated light-alloy huts, and other non-aviation items.

This situation was in part a reflection of the overwhelming confidence and almost incredible optimism that percolated downwards from the Führer himself. The writing on the wall provided by the Battle of Britain had apparently gone unread in Germany, although in fairness to the Luftwaffe, it should be borne in mind that this operation in which the service had brought its main strength to bear over a protracted period without gaining its objective, had been broken-off prematurely by the Führer who now turned his attention towards the Soviet Union. It had not been discontinued because its aims were recognised as hopeless nor because the attrition that it incurred was considered no longer justified. There is ample evidence to support the view that Hitler considered the war in the west to be virtually over in October 1940.

Common prudence should have dictated that the period between the breaking-off of operations over Britain and the commencement of the onslaught on the Soviet Union be spent in increasing the output of combat aircraft in order to establish a cushion of reserves from which could be made good the attrition that was obviously to be suffered during the first phases of the campaign in the east, however successful this might be. But priority in the allocation of raw materials for aircraft production was, in fact, reduced, and a year later, in October 1941, with the German Army at the gates of Leningrad and Moscow, and opposition apparently crumbling in its path, the Führer believed the campaign in the east also to be almost won. It was only when

German industrial techniques allowed designs to be built in several locations, and also for the jigs to be moved to new plants. Major types, like the Heinkel He 111 depicted, were built simultaneously at several Heinkel factories.

the impetus of the German offensive in the Soviet Union had begun to slow down that the intended blitz campaign began to turn into a war of attrition with the Luftwaffe already over-extended, that it became obvious that the master plan of the Führer had gone awry, and the inadequacy of the aircraft production programme was revealed all too clearly.

Another factor directly affecting the output of the aircraft industry during this period was the weakness in leadership displayed by the RLM in production matters. This is vividly illustrated by the fact that, between 1 September 1939 and 15 November 1941, the aircraft manufacturing programme was subjected to no fewer than 16 thoroughgoing revisions, not one of which was destined to be carried through as planned, and as a result the factories affected were thoroughly bemused.

In justice to the RLM, however, it should be said that this organisation was not responsible for the weaknesses of the master planning that was the task of the Oberbefehlshaber and his staff. Furthermore, the Luftwaffe High Command was responsible for initiating all new requirements, which were then translated into specifications by the Technical Department. However, the inertia stemming from the over-confidence concerning the superiority of the combat equipment possessed by the Luftwaffe at the time combat was first joined had led to a paucity of new requirements. The warplanes equipping the air arm were good, and the old adage that the better is the enemy of the good had been accepted as a maxim, the development of new combat aircraft types having been allowed to virtually stagnate in consequence.

Development stagnation

The aircraft manufacturers were prohibited from carrying on experimental and development work not specifically requested by the Technical Department of the RLM, this being considered a vital part of the 'rationalisation' policy adopted with the expansion of the industry from the mid-1930s. In consequence, the experimental departments of the aircraft manufacturers were forced to adopt various artifices in order to pursue promising lines of research that they were aware would not, being of a long-term nature, obtain official sanction. The Technical Department of the Ministry possessed a reputation for meddling in design problems involving those developments that had been sanctioned, despite the fact that the technical staffs of the major airframe and aero engine manufacturing concerns were far more competent in so far as technological matters were concerned than were personnel of the Ministry, whose function was supposedly that of directing the desired course of development and not that of interfering in its actual fulfilment. Understandably, this meddling resulted in considerable friction between Ministry and industry.

At the beginning of the war, Udet carried on direct negotiations with the aircraft manufacturers as to production plans. The manufacturers operated, for the most part, under cost plus a percentage-of-cost contracts that did not make for efficient labour utilisation, and it was not until 1943 that fixed-price contracts began to be substituted. The complete lack of competition other than in design development was one of the greatest shortcomings of the German aircraft industry, as often the manufacturers themselves became indifferent to their factories. One of Milch's first acts when he

succeeded Udet as Generalluftzeugmeister was to set up an organisation within the RLM whose sole task was to plan the aircraft manufacturing programme. This formed a part of the Technical Office rather than the Planning Office, which was concerned with materials supply, facilities and manpower.

Planning of production programmes was now carried on with the advice and assistance of the Main Committees for airframes, engines and accessories, which, inspired by Albert Speer when he became Minister for Armaments and Munitions in 1942, were outgrowths of the Industry Advisory Council created by Milch and Udet in May 1941. The Main Committees were formed with leading people from the industry and, responsible to the RLM, they presented the industry viewpoint. The procedure now followed for programme planning called for the Luftwaffe General Staff to originate the requirement, specifying the type of aircraft, the approximate quantities in which it was required, and desirable delivery schedules, passing this requirement to the RLM whose Procurement Division planning group then initiated studies aimed at fulfilling the requirement. The planning group consulted the Main Committees and the divisions of Speer's Ministry that had jurisdiction over the supply of materials, machine tools and other matters that were basic to the procurement programme, finally sending the completed study to the General Staff for approval. Göring personally approved each programme, which thus became subject to his whims, and as he possessed little knowledge of engineering or production matters in relation to aircraft procurement, its fate was liable to be influenced more by the mood of the Oberbefehlshaber than practicability or desirability.

A complicating factor, apart from the idiosyncrasies of Göring, was the constant pressure exerted by the General Staff for the inclusion in the procurement programme of aircraft and modifications to existing aircraft resulting from the whims of famous combat

The word Stuka has come to be associated with the Ju 87, but it was an abbreviated form of Sturzkampf, or dive-bomber, and was just as applicable to the Henschel Hs 123.

pilots, who were often lacking in knowledge of the complicated industrial production and technical design considerations that their requests involved. Some of these erratic requests could, of course, be traced back to influence exerted by one or other aircraft manufacturer anxious to secure the adoption of an improved design or new technical idea. Fortunately for the industry, the Main Committees served as a useful buffer against the more unreasonable of these requests made by the General Staff in cases where Milch, because of his military position, was unable to take a firm stand.

During the first six months of 1942 the monthly output of bombers actually fell some two per cent to an average of 329 aircraft, but fighter output over the same period rose 60 per cent to 391 aircraft per month. These totals were, of course, still extremely modest, and between September 1942 and the end of the war, nine separate procurement programmes were to be set up. Prior to the establishment of the first of these programmes, the peak single-engined fighter needs had been foreseen as 465 per month as compared with 683 bombers from total monthly procurement of 1,732 aircraft of all types. This figure included such types as the He 177 and Me 210 that were still under development, and no provision had been made for the retention in production of older models as an insurance against the failure of these newer aircraft.

The procurement programmes promulgated on 21 September 1942 and 15 April 1943 gave the first indication of the growing awareness of the inadequacies of earlier programmes, but the increases in output that they prescribed were almost entirely confined to fighter types and still called for deliveries far below those of which the industry was capable. The two plans which followed, dated 8 August and 1 October 1943, provided the foundations on which the immense expansion of 1944 was to be built. The single-engined fighter requirement was raised to no fewer than 4,150 per month and twin-engined fighters to 1,750 per month, these increases being realistic maxima, bomber output being maintained at the existing rate. The next programme, dated 1 December 1943, is of special interest as it reduced output of both single- and twin-engined fighters drastically in order to provide materials for the He 177 heavy bomber, supplies being inadequate for both. This action was taken as a result of a personal directive from the Führer, and peak fighter rates were set far lower, the figure of 4,150 single-engined fighters being reduced to 2,933 and the planned output of twin-engined fighters being reduced proportionately.

In the short term this programme did not materially change output as the earlier programmes, because of

Luftwaffe aircraft fared well in the North African desert, where they were opposed by less capable types than on the Western front. Here a reconnaissance Messerschmitt Bf 110 is loaded with a camera.

the flow-time factor, controlled the flow of materials into the productive process. The following three programmes, dated 15 July, 15 September and 15 December 1944, could well be referred to as 'fantasy plans', reflecting as they did an atmosphere of sheer desperation. Fighter requirements were restored to levels even higher than those established prior to Hitler's directive regarding the He 177, and bomber production was completely abandoned. The increases in production stipulated were anything but realistic, but the final programme, dated 16 March 1945, was as realistic as it could be in conditions of disintegrating industrial economy. With the Allies crossing Germany's borders at several points all programmes were cut back drastically.

Overseeing the production complex

A distinctive feature of the organisation of the German aircraft industry was the system of complexes that was an extension of the rationalisation principle. The original was the Junkers complex, its purpose being the control of operations carried out in 'shadow factories' and in the plants of sub-contractors, rigid control being exercised over engineering design, manufacturing methods, the sequence of operations, and materials and facilities requirements. Messerschmitt and Focke-Wulf eventually built up similar complexes, but from 1942 the system was applied to any manufacturer holding a direct contract from the RLM for the production of an aircraft type under licence from the parent company. Special Committees were created for each principal design organisation to co-ordinate the several complexes engaged in the production of a particular aircraft type, these in turn being responsible to the Main Committee for Airframes. The Special Committees could draw upon expert technical staffs to handle tooling, engineering, material-expediting, and other emergencies arising out of bombing. In addition, they were authorised to arrange interchange of materials and components among the several manufacturers of the same aircraft type.

Although the location of the major components of the aircraft industry afforded them reasonable protection from bombing during the opening phases of World War II, two steps to provide additional protection soon proved necessary, the eastward movement of some factories out of range of British-based bombers, and dispersal to scattered locations that offered less concentrated bombing targets. The order to disperse the aircraft industry was not officially promulgated

While technically brilliant, the Messerschmitt Me 262 provided an excellent study in how personal interventions by those with little knowledge – in this case the Führer himself – could render a significant technological advantage almost redundant.

until February 1944, although a good many individual dispersals had already taken place. The first major aircraft factory to be dispersed had been the Focke-Wulf plant at Bremen, RAF bombing attacks on the city having convinced Kurt Tank that his manufacturing facilities should be moved eastward and broken up among several plants in different areas. The RLM had prepared a study for the dispersal of the entire aircraft industry in 1942, but this had found little favour among Germany's leaders owing to its defensive character, and it was opposed by the industrialists as inefficient and costly. However, the Combined Bomber Offensive soon forced the issue. In the summer of 1943, one of Messerschmitt's Regensburg factories suffered heavy damage from a USAAF 8th Air Force attack, and in November, when the Wiener-Neustadter-Flugzeugwerke, near Vienna, was hit by the 15th Air Force flying from Italy, the issue was no longer in doubt.

The dispersal plan provided for the breaking up of production and the establishment of multiple sources for each component part, sub-assembly, and even final assembly. Party Leader Otto Saur, who was in charge of the Jägerstab, was also responsible for the dispersal of the aircraft industry, and formulated a programme by which the 27 main aircraft-manufacturing plants were to be dispersed among 729 small factories, although when hostilities finally terminated, the actual number of small plants into which aircraft production had been moved was nearer 300. Dispersal rendered necessary a tremendous dilution of managerial and technical talent with a shortage of adequately qualified personnel as a consequence; placed an immense load on tool and jig manufacturers that soon resulted in a critical bottleneck; and placed a heavy burden on the transportation system that was already beginning to break down at the time large-scale dispersal began.

The downside of dispersal

The loss of efficiency inherent in the dispersal system of manufacture was undeniable, but it was successful from the viewpoint that potential targets were so scattered and so difficult for Allied intelligence to locate that it rendered almost impossible the reduction of the German aircraft industry's capacity to produce aircraft by means of bombing. However, it defeated its own purpose as the dispersed plants were entirely dependent on the transportation system, and rail, road and water transport were all highly vulnerable to the bombing and strafing by Allied aircraft. Manufacturers had to find their own plants to which to disperse, and a miscellany of existing structures was employed, ranging from textile mills to barns. One of the most interesting and effective dispersal methods was to hide the plants in forests, the buildings being constructed of wood, erected quickly, and easily camouflaged. Messerschmitt used this scheme extensively for the manufacture of the Me 262.

The actual dispersal operation was not accomplished smoothly by any stretch of the imagination. Operations had frequently to be resumed in dispersed locations with inadequate or unproven tooling and equipment, and in the case of such facilities as heat-treating equipment, the correct physical properties of some alloy structural components were impossible to attain. Some decline in workmanship was inevitable, and the maintenance of satisfactory inspection standards was impossible, the manufacturers not possessing sufficient competent inspectors to place them in every dispersed plant. The

This propaganda image portrays one side of the nocturnal battle over the Reich. The RAF night bomber offensive caused significant damage to the German aircraft industry, albeit not as much as could have been wrought if the factories had been more concentrated geographically, and had been planned with less inherent redundant capability.

administration problem of co-ordinating and enforcing inspection standards became enormous.

The Ministry Inspection Office had representatives in each of the main airframe, powerplant and accessory plants, the senior representative supervising the inspection of the products of both the main factory and its branches. The inspection office stamp of acceptance was held in the highest respect, but this organisation was faced with an impossible assignment when called upon by the dispersal programme to provide inspectors for several times the numbers of plants. It therefore became necessary to deputise the company inspectors to perform the detailed acceptance on behalf of the Inspection Office, further increasing the load imposed on the already inadequate inspection staffs. Otto Saur insisted that the Inspection Office discontinued the practice of deputising the manufacturers' own inspectors, and officially the practice ceased although, in fact, it was physically impossible to change the arrangements owing to the Inspection Office's lack of staff. In the circumstances, therefore, it was to be expected that the number of imperfect parts and components finding their way into the pipelines would increase.

Nevertheless, the loss in quality was surprisingly marginal, and was not a primary reason for the escalation of Luftwaffe attrition from non-operational causes, a major factor undoubtedly being the shortage of spare component parts and sub-assemblies at repair and maintenance unit level, the Jägerstab having minimised the supply of them in order to maximise the delivery of complete aircraft. A contributory factor was the reduction during the summer of 1944 in the final

Germany's aerial supremacy was first challenged, and matched, in the stalemate over Britain in 1940. After the inconclusive campaign it should have been considered by the German high command that one day it might just be the Allies that dominated the skies over Europe, and to plan accordingly.

running-in time on engines from two hours to a half-hour owing to fuel shortages, but by this time even the test-firing of guns had been discontinued owing to the shortage of ammunition, and a label was inserted in the cockpits of all newly-delivered aircraft warning pilots to exercise caution when firing the guns for the first time.

Going underground

Dispersal on the scale organised by Saur was recognised as a temporary expedient at best, however, and centralised operations underground or in huge concrete bunkers were foreseen as the ultimate solution. At the same time as the general dispersal order was issued, an agency had been established to locate suitable underground sites such as mines and railway tunnels, and prepare them for manufacturing operations. Some production of V-weapons was already being performed undergound but few of the factories created in old mine workings were regarded as ideal. Some had to be entered via vertical shafts, a limiting factor in the size of components and the handling of workers and materials thus being provided by the elevators, and ventilation, lighting, heating and sanitation presented problems. As such underground facilities were rarely located close to a source of labour, barracks had to be built in the vicinity, and adequate water and power supplies were rarely available.

One of the Daimler-Benz licensees, Bussing, moved part of its aero engine manufacturing operations into a salt mine, but humidity resulted in serious corrosion of precision machine tools. Junkers occupied about 18,580 m² (200,000 sq ft) of another salt mine at Tarthun, near Magdeburg, where sub-assembly and some final assembly

A scene repeated throughout the Reich in 1945 shows derelict and strafed Messerschmitt Bf 109s and a night-fighter Bf 110. The lack of skilled pilots, fuel and ammunition were the main factors that reduced the Luftwaffe's effectiveness in the last weeks of the war.

of Fw 190s, Ju 88s and He 162s was undertaken, but the limited capacity of the elevator impeded production efficiency. Daimler-Benz started the production of crankshafts, connecting rods and cylinder heads in a gypsum mine at Neckar-Els, near Heidelberg, but high humidity rendered working conditions almost unbearable. Junkers began producing Jumo 213 and Jumo 004 engines in tunnels at Nordhausen; BMW occupied a railway tunnel at Markirch, near Strasbourg; Skoda moved part of its DB 605 production operation into a granite quarry at Kobanya, near Budapest; Junkers made a few components in a salt mine at Stassfurt; AGO produced sub-assemblies for the Fw 190 in a small underground plant near Aschersleben; Henschel built Ju 88 sub-assemblies in an unfinished subway tunnel on the outskirts of Berlin; and Messerschmitt planned to manufacture the Me 262 entirely underground in mines at Kahla and Kammsdorf, near Weimar.

The subterranean plants obviously left much to be desired, and it was concluded that the ultimate in structures in which aircraft manufacturing operations could be conducted free of enemy bombing attack was a bunker-type factory based on the concept of the submarine pen and protected by slabs of reinforced concrete. Work therefore began at Kauffering and Muhldorf/Inn on two bunker-type structures, each of about 92,900 m² (1,000,000 sq ft), and three more were projected. These immense dome-shaped buildings, the curved surfaces of which were 6 to 9 m (20-30 ft) thick, were about 25 m (80 ft) high and comprised three or four floors. Shortages of steel and concrete delayed the completion of the first two bunker factories, and when fighting finally ended they were barely half-completed.

When the war in Europe terminated, hardly a single one of the German aircraft industry's pre-war factories had survived other than in near-devastated condition. The RAF and the USAAF had dropped more than 90,000 tons of bombs solely on primary aircraft industry targets during the Combined Bomber Offensive, blasting the aircraft industry of the Third Reich out of its well-planned factories in the vicinity of established industrial centres, forcing it to disperse to hundreds of makeshift plants all over Germany. It had fled into wooden sheds deep in forests, burrowed under the ground and, as the Third Reich finally crumbled, was endeavouring to shield itself beneath mountains of reinforced concrete, but it continued to produce aircraft for the Luftwaffe to the very last. What is more, despite all the difficulties posed by dispersal with the near-insuperable problems that it provided the inspection system, the quality of the warplanes that the German aircraft industry produced barely declined throughout.

Aero A.304

A Czechoslovak light bomber derived from a light transport for the civilian market, the A.304 was just entering service as Germany occupied Czechoslovakia. Some of the aircraft were placed in service as crew trainers, and others were transferred to Bulgaria for use as coastal patrol machines.

In 1936 Aero designed the **A.204**, a modern eight-passenger light monoplane transport with retractable main undercarriage units and powered by two 268-kW (360-hp) Walter Pollux MR radial engines. The Czechoslovak airline CSA opted instead for the Airspeed Envoy, but in 1938 Aero developed the basic design into the **A.304** light bomber, a minimum-change aircraft with an uprated powerplant and armament that included a small bomb load and a dorsal turret. Delivery of the 15 A.304 reconnaissance bombers had been completed by the time the Germans occupied Bohemia and Moravia in spring 1939, and the aircraft were promptly seized by the Luftwaffe. Several were stripped of their armament and placed in service with the Flugzeugführerschule A/B 71 training establishment at Prostejov, near Olomouc in Moravia. One was transferred to the Bulgarian air force during 1941, after Bulgaria had joined the Axis powers and used on high-speed communications duties.

The Aero A.304 was an unremarkable design, but the type proved suitable for introducing aircrew to multi-engined flying at the Prostejov school.

The A.304 had evolved from a transport into a bomber, but when impressed into Luftwaffe service they were used only as transports and trainers. Bulgaria used a few for coastal patrol duties.

Aero A.304 specification
Type: three-seat light bomber and reconnaissance aircraft
Powerplant: two Walter Super Castor I-MR air-cooled nine-cylinder radial engines each rated at 321 kW (430 hp) for take-off
Performance: maximum speed 320 km/h (199 mph) at 1750 m (5,740 ft); maximum cruising speed 290 km/h (180 mph) at 5,740 ft; climb to 2000 m (6,560 ft) in 7 minutes 30 seconds; service ceiling 5800 m (19,030 ft); range 1200 km (746 miles)
Weights: empty (reconnaissance mission) 3000 kg (6,614 lb); normal take-off 4355 kg (9,601 lb); maximum take-off 4660 kg (10,275 lb)
Dimensions: wingspan 19.20 m (62 ft 11¾ in); length 13.20 m (43 ft 3¾ in); height 3.40 m (11 ft 1¾ in); wing area 45.20 m² (486.53 sq ft)
Armament: (defensive) one 7.9-mm (0.31-in) fixed forward-firing machine-gun, one 7.9-mm trainable machine-gun in dorsal turret, and one 7.9-mm trainable machine-gun in ventral tunnel position; (offensive) up to 320 kg (705 lb) of bombs carried internally (comprising one 100- or 200-kg (220- or 441-lb) and two 50-kg (100-lb) or six 10- or 20-kg (22- or 44-lb) bombs)

AGO Flugzeugwerke GmbH

The acronym AGO (sometimes rendered Ago) was derived originally from the first letters of the company founded in 1911 by the German aviation pioneer Gustav Otto. This Aeroplanbau G. Otto und Alberti was renamed as the Aerowerke Gustav Otto in early 1912 and, later in the same year, became the Ago Flugzeugwerke GmbH. At the beginning of World War I, Ago began to design and build military aircraft. Like those of other companies, the Ago machines were intended only for the observation and communications roles because, at the start of the war, army commanders believed that they were the only tasks that could be carried out effectively by the aircraft, still a very recent invention and limited in capability factors such as range and payload. The first of the company's military aircraft carried the designation C I, and was a two-seat biplane of unusual configuration with the engine located as a pusher at the rear of the central nacelle and the empennage carried by two sizeable booms. Much of its design was contributed by a Swiss engineer, August Häfeli, who had worked earlier for the Farman brothers in France. Ago went on to produce a number of other two-seat pusher and tractor reconnaissance designs in World War I, but none of them entered large-scale production, only 70 of the company's most important type, the C IV, being built. After the end of World War I Ago

tried its hand at the manufacture of cars, but ceased trading in 1928 and was declared bankrupt two years later.

In 1934 the Nazi government resurrected Ago by refurbishing the Oschersleben plant for the licensed production of other companies' aircraft. The first orders were for 36 Arado Ar 65 fighters, 197 Arado Ar 66 trainers and 71 Heinkel He 51 fighters, of which the first Ar 65 flew in the following year. There followed 140 Henschel Hs 123 dive-bombers, 241 Gotha Go 145 and 187 Arado Ar 96 trainers, and then 150 (later increased to 390) Henschel Hs 126 reconnaissance aircraft.

Between March 1937 and March 1938, Ago manufactured 121 Focke-Wulf Fw 44 trainers. In 1938 the company embarked on the production of the Messerschmitt Bf 109 and then, from 1941, the Focke-Wulf Fw 190.

In 1935 Ago had established its own design department, resulting in the Ao 192 Kurier. A design for a heavy fighter project, the Ao 225, did not progress past the wind-tunnel stage and even the -225 designation was withdrawn by the RLM and re-assigned to Focke-Achgelis. From 1943 the Ago factory came under attack by Allied bombing raids, suffering increasingly heavy damage up to the end of the war, and in 1947 the occupying Soviet forces demolished the remnants of the factory.

AGO Ao 192

Designed for the light transport role, the Ao 192 was the only Ago aeroplane to enter production during the Third Reich's period of existence. Even so, production totalled only six aircraft as the factory was to be more usefully employed in the licensed manufacture of other companies' aircraft.

Ago's light transport design received the official designation **Ao 192**, and took shape as a clean twin-engined low-wing monoplane that incorporated a number of advanced features. Like the Heinkel He 70 Blitz, the type was optimised for a high cruising speed, and considerable attention was therefore paid to drag reduction by careful aerodynamic design and the use of flush rivetting for the light alloy skin. Accommodation in the main air-conditioned cabin was provided for five passengers, as well as mail, freight or baggage. Unusually, the flight deck was equipped with dual flying controls, thus making the Ao 192 also suitable for training.

The wing comprised a flat centre section fitted with a one-piece full-span flap, and sharply dihedralled, tapered outer

The Ao 192 was a generally unexceptional but nicely conceived light transport with a strut-braced tailplane, air-cooled engines and retractable main undercarriage units.

panels each fitted a with full-span aileron. The tailwheel undercarriage included main units that retracted outward to lie flat within the thin outer wing panels.

The powerplant comprised a pair of Argus As 10 air-cooled inverted V-8 engines installed in very small nacelles angled out from the centreline and each driving a two-bladed propeller. Alternative air-cooled engine types proposed for export customers included Hirth, de Havilland Gipsy Six and Menasco Buccaneer units.

Powered by Argus 10C engines and fitted with a low-set elliptical tailplane, the **Ao 192 V1** prototype (D-OAGO) made its maiden flight in the summer of 1935, and was soon followed by the **Ao 192 V2** second prototype (D-OCTB). This received a shorter nose, as well as a larger strut-braced tailplane which was relocated to a position about one-third of the way up the fin to correct some instability and tail flutter problems encountered by the Ao 192 V1. The first prototype was revised to the same standard as the second machine, and in the course of a protracted development period the fuselage was redesigned to accommodate six passengers. At the same time As 10E engines were fitted, and the main landing gear units were revised to retract rearward into the undersides of the enlarged engine nacelles. The Ao 192 V2 took part in the Isle of Man air races of 4-7 June 1938, and finished in seventh place.

The **Ao 192 V3** production prototype (D-ODAF) incorporated all these changes and reached flight status in 1938. Conducted mainly by Luftwaffe test pilots at Rechlin, the

Left: The Ao 192 was powered by two Argus As 10E engines, which were air-cooled inverted V-8 units each driving a two-blade propeller fitted with a neat spinner.

Below: The Ao 192 was one of the most advanced twin-engined transport designs of the mid-1930s. Ago's commitments to other projects meant that the design was not developed further, however.

flight test programme revealed that the Ao 192 had excellent flying characteristics, and the type duly entered what was planned as full-scale production. Ago planned several variants of the Ao 192 for both civil and military use, designated **Ao 192B** and **Ao 192C**, respectively.

However, the company's licence-manufacturing commitments were so extensive that only six examples of the Ao 192B were completed. They were all taken over by the German authorities for use as the personal transports of high-ranking officials. The Ago concern itself had been taken over by the giant Junkers firm in late 1936.

Above: The Ao 192 possessed good handling characteristics and offered quite impressive performance. The main undercarriage units retracted outward into bays in the underside of the wing outboard of the engine nacelles.

AGO Ao 192B specification
Type: light passenger transport
Powerplant: two Argus As 10E air-cooled inverted V-8 engines each rated at 201 kW (270 hp)
Performance: maximum speed 335 km/h (208 mph) at 200 m (6,560 ft); maximum cruising speed 288 km/h (179 mph) at 2000 m (6,560 ft); economical cruising speed 238 km/h (147 mph) at 2000 m (6,560 ft); climb to 1000 m (3,280 ft) in 3 minutes 12 seconds; service ceiling 5200 m (17,060 ft); range 1100 km (684 miles)
Weights: empty 1640 kg (3,616 lb); maximum take-off 2950 kg (6,504 lb)
Dimensions: wingspan 13.54 m (44 ft 5 in); length 10,98 m (36 ft 0¼ in); height 3.64 m (11 ft 11 ⅓ in); wing area 25.04 m² (269.54 sq ft)

A notable feature of the Ao 192 was the comparatively long span of its flat and constant-chord centre section, which carried relatively short-span dihedralled and tapered outer panels.

Airspeed AS.6 Envoy

The AS.6 Envoy was built only in moderately small numbers in the UK during the 1930s, and several aircraft seized in Germany's territorial expansion in the late 1930s, and possibly in 1940, were placed in limited and short-term Luftwaffe service as trainers and communication machines.

Airspeed's design of the **AS.6 Envoy** began late in 1933 with the object of creating an enlarged and twin-engined development of the AS.5 Courier. The prototype made its maiden flight on 26 June 1934 and a total of 49 aircraft was built. With standard accommodation for a pilot and up to eight passengers, the Envoy was of conventional all-wood construction under a covering of stressed plywood except on the fabric-covered control surfaces. A variable-incidence tailplane and tailwheel undercarriage with retractable main units were features of the design, which was built between 1934 and 1939 in three versions. The initial **AS.6 Envoy Series I** (17 examples built) had a plain wing without trailing-edge flaps; the **AS.6 Envoy Series II** (13 aircraft) introduced split flaps; and the **AS.6 Envoy Series III** (19 aircraft) was generally similar to the Series II but introduced a number of detail improvements. A wide range of radial engines could be used in the Envoy's twin-engined powerplant.

Envoy aircraft were exported to China, Czechoslovakia, France, India and Japan. The Czechoslovak national airline, CSA, took four **AS.6E** aircraft with indigenous Walter Castor engines as two Series I aircraft in 1935 and two Series II aircraft in 1936, and in December 1936 the Czechoslovak

Steel and Iron Corporation took a single Series III aircraft. All five aircraft survived to the time of Germany's annexation of the rump of Czechoslovakia in March 1939, to become the Reich Protectorate of Bohemia and Moravia. At this time the Luftwaffe impressed at least some of the aircraft, which were possibly supplemented by **AS.6J** aircraft captured in France, and used them as trainers and communication machines. The Luftwaffe gave one to Finland on 22 January 1942 as reparation for the accidental shooting down of a Finnish de Havilland Dragon Rapide, and the Finns used this machine (CM+SA/EV-1) between 1942 and 1943. The Luftwaffe donated another (OK-DOA) to Slovakia, whose air force operated the machine between 1941 to 1943.

Airspeed AS.6E Envoy specification
Type: nine-seat light transport
Powerplant: two Walter Castor II air-cooled seven-cylinder radial engines each rated at 340 hp (253.5 kW) for take-off
Performance: maximum speed 185 mph (298 km/h) at 3,450 ft (1050 m); cruising speed 165 mph (264 km/h) at 3,450 ft (1050 m); climb to 5,000 ft (1525 m) in 5 minutes 30 seconds; service ceiling 16,500 ft (5030 m); typical range 635 miles (1022 km)
Weights: empty 3,970 lb (1082 kg); maximum take-off 6,300 lb (2858 kg)
Dimensions: wingspan 52 ft 4 in (10.52 m); length 34 ft 6 in (10.53 m); height 9 ft 6 in (2.90 m); wing area 339.00 sq ft (31.49 m²)

Seen here in the form of an aircraft impressed for German service, the Envoy was one of several interim low-wing monoplane light transports built in Europe during the 1930s. The type had a wooden structure, and the main undercarriage units retracted into the underside of the nacelles for the two radial engines.

Albatros L.101

The Albatros L.101 was a two-seat trainer of the early 1930s, and in configuration was a parasol-wing monoplane with fixed tailskid undercarriage. The machine was the last production type created by the famous Albatros company before it was absorbed into Focke-Wulf.

The **L.101** was of basically all-metal construction covered with fabric. The dihedralled wing was slightly swept, braced on each side and, as on the preceding L.100, was designed to fold to the rear to facilitate hangarage and road transportation. The braced tailplane was carried on a broad-chord pylon and itself carried the elevators. The vertical tail surface included no fixed fin, and therefore comprised only a comma-type rudder.

The first of two prototypes flew in 1930 and was flown in that year's Europarundflug air rally, and manufacture totalled another 69 aircraft completed by 1934 in the form of two **A.101w** floatplanes with the As.8 engine, seven **A.101c** trainers with the As.8a engine, and 60 improved **A.101D** trainers also with the As.8a engine. With the exception of the first four, all of the aircraft were manufactured by Focke-Wulf after its 1931 amalgamation with Albatros, and all but two of the aircraft (delivered to the Deutsche Versuchsanstalt für Luftfahrt, or German Aviation Experimental Establishment), were delivered to the Deutsche Verkehrsfliegerschule (German Air Transport School), a covert military training organisation.

A parasol-wing monoplane, the L.101 had its folding wings braced to the main undercarriage, and the unusual type of vertical tail surfaces was used in several German aircraft of the 1930s.

Albatros L.101D specification
Type: two-seat training aircraft
Powerplant: one Argus As.8a air-cooled four-cylinder inverted inline engine rated at 82 kW (110 hp)
Performance: maximum speed 170 km/h (110 mph) at sea level; cruising speed 150 km/h (93 mph) at optimum altitude; initial climb rate 145 m (476 ft) per minute; service ceiling 3600 m (11,810 ft); range 670 km (416 miles); endurance 5 hours
Weights: empty 475 kg (1,047 lb); maximum take-off 795 kg (1,753 lb)
Dimensions: wingspan 12.35 m (40 ft 6¼ in); length 8.45 m (27 ft 8⅔ in); height 2.70 m (8 ft 10⅓ in); wing area 20.00 m² (215.29 sq ft)

Ambrosini S.403 Dardo

Created by the Società Aeronautica Italiana, a subsidiary of the Ambrosini industrial group from 1937, the Dardo was intended as a lightweight fighter of modern concept with a low-wing monoplane configuration and an enclosed cockpit, but on the structural basis of a largely wooden airframe under a stressed plywood skin.

The **S.403 Dardo** (dart or arrow) was essentially a more sophisticated version of the S.207 with greater power in the form of the Isotta-Fraschini Delta RC.21/60 Serie I-IV engine driving a three-blade propeller of the constant-speed type. The Dardo also featured fully retractable undercarriage, a variable-incidence tailplane, a strengthened structure including a revised rear fuselage, and provision for wing-mounted armament.

The first S.403 flew in January 1943 and revealed exceptional performance, which resulted in termination of S.207 production in favour of a planned 3,000 examples of the S.403 in three sub-variants. They were the **Dardo-A** lightweight interceptor with two 12.7-mm (0.5-in) Breda-SAFAT machine-guns, the **Dardo-B** general-purpose fighter with two 20-mm MG 151/20 cannon and two 12.7-mm (0.5-in) machine-guns, and the **Dardo-C** long-range version with two 20-mm cannon and provision for two 150-litre (33-lmp gal) drop tanks as well as internal fuel capacity increased from the 300 litres (66 Imp gal) of the Dardo-A/B to 410 litres (90.2 Imp gal).

None of these fighter developments had been delivered before the Italian armistice with the Allies in September 1943, by which time the required production tooling was still incomplete. Trials of the sole prototype were continued in German markings until the aircraft was lost in a crash after its wings had detached in flight.

Ambrosini S.403 Dardo specification
Type: single-seat lightweight fighter
Powerplant: one Isotta-Fraschini Delta RC.21/60 Serie I-IV air-cooled inverted V-12 engine rated at 560 hp (750 hp) for take-off
Performance: maximum speed 648 km/h (403 mph) at 7200 m (23,620 ft); cruising speed 490 km/h (304 mph) at optimum altitude; climb to 6000 m (19,685 ft) in 6 minutes 40 seconds; service ceiling 39,815 ft (12135 m); range 1875 km (1,165 miles) with drop tanks or 935 km (581 miles) with internal fuel
Weights: empty 1893 kg (4,372 lb); maximum take-off 2640 kg (5,820 lb)
Dimensions: wingspan 9.80 m (32 ft 1¾ in); length 8.20 m (26 ft 10¾ in); height 2.90 m (9 ft 6 in); wing area 14.46 m² (155.65 sq ft)
Armament: (planned) two 20-mm MG 151/20 fixed forward-firing cannon with 200 r.p.g. and two 12.7-mm (0.5-in) Breda-SAFAT fixed forward-firing machine-guns with 200 r.p.g.

Some testing of the Dardo was carried out in German markings. Both Heinkel and Mitsubishi wanted to build the type.

Arado Flugzeugwerke GmbH

One of the handful of small companies with aircraft design and manufacturing experience providing the nucleus around which grew the aviation industry of the Third Reich, the Arado Flugzeugwerke GmbH was fated to become one of the most important aircraft manufacturing components of the industry and one of its largest employers of labour, although the vast majority of the warplanes that were to leave its assembly lines were destined to be the design progeny of other companies. Arado's origins dated back to early 1917 and the creation of the Werft Warnemünde des Flugzeugbaus Friedrichshafen as a subsidiary of the Flugzeugbau Friedrichshafen GmbH. All aircraft manufacturing activities at the Werft Warnemünde came to a standstill in 1918, but in 1921 the factory was acquired by the industrialist Hugo Stinnes, who had aspirations of resuming aircraft design and production in the Warnemünde plant as soon as the opportunity arose.

Initially the factory confined itself to production of small boats, ice yachts and furniture, but in 1924 Stinnes acquired the services of a highly talented designer, Ing. Walter Rethel, who had served as chief designer to the Kondor Flugzeugwerke during World War I and had subsequently joined Fokker in the Netherlands. At the same time, Stinnes created a Yugoslav subsidiary, the Ikarus GmbH, with a factory at Novi Sad, near Belgrade, for the manufacture of aircraft. By 1925, when the Werft Warnemünde became the Arado-Handelsgesellschaft with Ing. Rethel as chief engineer,

Above: Period advertising for the Ar 96B trainer describes it as offering 'the characteristic traits and technical features of a modern combat aircraft'.

the newly-created design bureau was already active, and its first aircraft, the S I primary training biplane, was flown at Warnemünde in that year, to be followed in 1926 by the SC I and SC II two-seat advanced training biplanes. A refined version of the primary trainer, the S III, appeared in 1928, which proved a prolific year for the Warnemünde-based concern, also witnessing the debuts of the W 2 float trainer, the SD I single-seat fighter biplane, and the V 1 four-seat cabin monoplane. The last-mentioned type was subsequently to be used experimentally by Deutsche Lufthansa (DLH) as a mailplane, completing a number of successful long-distance flights before crashing at Neuruppin on 19 December 1929.

Clandestine support

The prolificity of the Warnemünde design bureau was even more marked in 1929, this year seeing the appearance of the SD II and SD III fighter biplanes, the SSD I float fighter, and two light sports monoplanes, the V 2

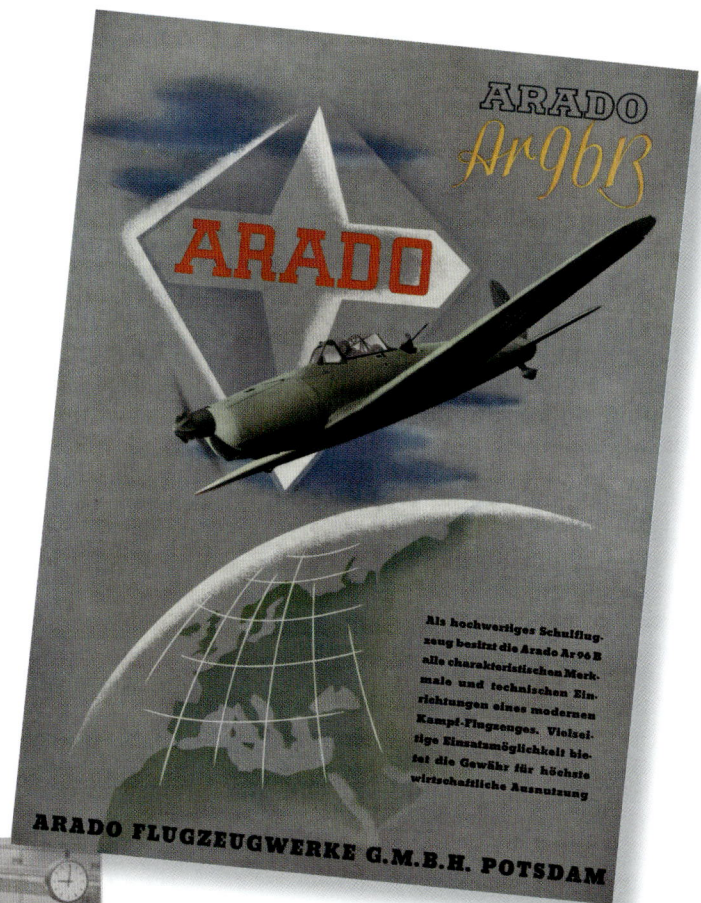

Arado first came to prominence as a manufacturer of biplane fighters and trainers. Here Ar 66s are seen in a packed hangar, with Focke-Wulf Fw 44s in the background. Both types were used extensively in the training role in the Luftwaffe's early years.

Arado Flugzeugwerke GmbH

designed by Ing. Rethel, and the L 1 designed by Dipl.-Ing. Hoffman, but Arado was now noteworthy for the profusion of its designs rather than for their proliferation, none of the company's aircraft being the recipient of series production orders. Thus the Arado-Handelsgesellschaft was still primarily concerned with non-aviation products. Its labour force numbered barely more than 100 personnel, but the wind of political change was by now blowing strongly in Germany; clandestine encouragement was being received from the Fliegerstab des Reichswehrministeriums, and occupying some 41,800 m² (450,000 sq ft) including 15,000 m² (161,000 sq ft) of covered floor space, the Arado concern was in a position to expand rapidly.

Ministerial policy was to keep pace secretly with current aviation technology abroad, and when the 1930s dawned, two new fighters were on the stocks at Warnemünde, the Ar 64 and Ar 65, together with a new training biplane, the Ar 66. Three events now took place in quick succession that were to have a profound effect on the future of the company. Hugo Stinnes died, Dipl.-Ing. Walter Blume was appointed chief engineer over Ing. Rethel (who subsequently left the company to join the Bayerische Flugzeugwerke), and Hitler assumed political leadership of Germany. Capital investment in the company had been comparatively insignificant, and the demands of the expansion programme resulted in a major infusion of funds from the government, and the company, which, on 4 March 1933, became the Arado Flugzeugwerke GmbH, came under the control of the RLM.

Luftwaffe's first fighter

The Ar 65E had been ordered into production at Warnemünde as the clandestine Luftwaffe's first fighter, and the Ar 66 trainer, which had been redesigned by Dipl.-Ing. Blume, was also ordered into production. On 6 September 1934 the company purchased a former iron foundry at Brandenburg-Neuendorf as the site for a branch factory on which work commenced on 1 December 1934. Such was the impetus placed behind the expansion programme that barely more than four months later, in April 1935, the first aircraft rolled off Arado's new assembly line. As well as manufacturing its own aircraft, Arado was soon operating as a licensee for the production of other companies' aircraft, and from 1935 onwards the Arado assembly lines were to be occupied primarily by aircraft of Heinkel, Messerschmitt, Junkers and Focke-Wulf design, while the majority of the aircraft of Arado design built in series were to be produced by licensees. Seventy-five He 51A fighters were followed by 140 He 59 and 100 He 60 floatplanes, work then commencing on a run of 300 He 111 bombers while, by the beginning of 1938, the Warnemünde factory had been phased into the Bf 109 single-seat fighter programme.

Arado's design offices produced a large array of projects but few were successful. Indeed, in terms of major types there was little of note between the pre-war Ar 196 and the Ar 234 jet bomber.

Prior to participation in this programme Arado had produced quite substantial numbers of Ar 68 fighter biplanes for the Luftwaffe, but although the Arado design bureau remained as prolific as ever, it enjoyed little success in the late 1930s in so far as series production contracts were concerned. The Ar 69 primary training biplane came off second best to the Fw 44 Stieglitz; the Ar 76 light fighter and advanced trainer was runner-up to the Fw 56 Stösser and its production limited to a small evaluation batch, and the Ar 77 twin-engined trainer and utility aircraft lost out to the Fw 58 Weihe, although some success was enjoyed in the civil field with the Ar 79 two-seat high-performance cabin tourer, which gained a number of FAI class records. The Ar 95 achieved only limited success, having been designed to a naval requirement already considered obsolescent by the time the prototypes entered the test phase, but the fortunes of Dipl.-Ing. Blume's design bureau took a sharp upward turn with the decision in 1938 to adopt as standard the highly advanced Ar 96 trainer, followed closely by the selection for series production of the Ar 196 float seaplane. In the event, relatively few of these aircraft were to be built by the parent company, AGO acting as the principal licensee for Ar 96 production until mid-1941, by which time the primary manufacturer of the trainer was Avia in Czechoslovakia, this concern being joined by Letov in 1944, and after the Warnemünde factory had delivered some 450 Ar 196s, the production of this floatplane was assigned to Fokker and the S.N.C.A. at St Nazaire.

By the beginning of World War II the Warnemünde and Brandenburg-Neuendorf factories had been supplemented by a plant at Babelsberg, near Berlin, and what was by now becoming a major factory complex soon included branch works at Eger, Rathenow, Wittenberg, Tutow, Anklam and Neubrandenburg, but apart from the Ar 196s, Arado was to undertake no large-scale production of aircraft of its own design until deliveries of the jet-powered Ar 234 began from Brandenburg-Neuendorf in mid-1944.

Almost the entire Arado organisation was engaged on assembly and sub-contract work for the aircraft of other manufacturers, and on the production of such items as gun mountings. The Warnemünde factory was largely preoccupied with the assembly of Bf 109s until this type was phased out in October 1941 in favour of the Fw 190, the first Arado-assembled fighters of the latter type being delivered in August 1941, and no fewer than 3,944 being built at Warnemünde by the end of 1944. The Brandenburg-Neuendorf facility was phased into the Ju 88 production programme at an early stage, manufacturing this bomber from 1940 until the spring of 1942, and Warnemünde and, later, Brandenburg-Neuendorf were primary manufacturing centres for the He 177, a total of 716 of these bombers having been built by Arado when further production was stopped in August 1944.

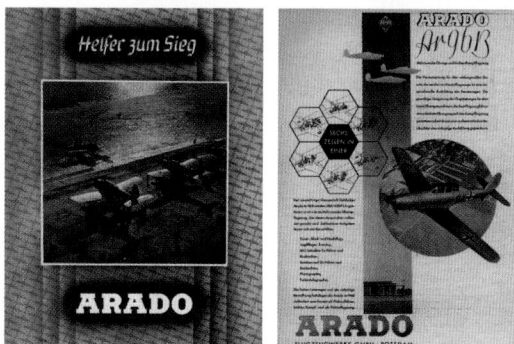

Arado Ar 64

Appearing in 1930, the Arado Ar 64 single-seat fighter was essentially a derivative of the same company's SD II and SD III, and was planned as a replacement for the Fokker D.XIII in service with Germany's military flying school in the Soviet Union. A small batch was built for clandestine use.

On the basis of his SD II and SD III fighters, which had been developed in parallel, Ing. Walter Rethel evolved the Arado Ar 64 in response to a 1929 requirement of the German war ministry for a successor to the Fokker D.XIII fighter currently equipping the Germans' clandestine flying training school at Lipetsk in the USSR. The Ar 64 was of mixed construction, with a welded steel tube fuselage and a wooden wing cellule under a covering of fabric. The **Ar 64a** first prototype that first flew in the spring of 1930 was powered by a 395-kW (530-hp) Bristol Jupiter VI radial engine built under licence by Siemens and driving a four-bladed wooden propeller. In the following year there appeared two **Ar 64b** prototypes with the 477-kW (640-hp) BMW VI 6,3 Vee engine; the sole **Ar 64c** prototype was based on the Ar 64a with some structural alterations.

Production versions

The two production models, of which 20 were delivered as the first fighters to be built in 'quantity' in Germany since the end of World War I, were the **Ar 64D** and **Ar 64E**. The Ar 64D introduced a revised main landing gear unit and an enlarged vertical tail surface, and was powered by a geared Jupiter VI engine driving a four-bladed propeller. The Ar 64E was basically similar except for its powerplant, which was based on a direct-drive Jupiter VI engine with a two-bladed propeller. Deliveries of these aircraft started in the summer of 1932, and after the first 19 had served initially at the DVS (Deutsche Verkehrsfliegerschule, German commercial pilot school) at Schleissheim, the survivors were later reallocated to

The Arado Ar 64c was a development aircraft of ungainly lines, its four-bladed propeller essentially a pair of two-bladed units bolted together. Performance was adequate, but handling problems necessitated an increase in vertical tail area in the Ar 64D, which also featured a number of structural modifications. The basic type was developed into the Ar 65.

the fighter units of the Fliegergruppen Döberitz and Damm, in which they complemented Arado Ar 65 biplane fighters.

Arado Ar 64D/E specification
Type: single-seat fighter and fighter trainer
Powerplant: one Siemens (Bristol) Jupiter VI radial engine rated at 395 kW (530 hp)
Performance: maximum speed 250 km/h (156 mph) at 5000 m (16,405 ft)
Weights: empty 1210 kg (2,667 lb); maximum take-off 1680 kg (3,704 lb)
Dimensions: wingspan 9.90 m (32 ft 5¾ in); length 8.43 m (27 ft 8 in)
Armament: two 7.92-mm (0.31-in) fixed forward-firing machine-guns

Both the Ar 64a and generally similar Ar 64c featured four-bladed propellers, which were later used on the Ar 64D production version, as seen here. The Ar 64c was the first of the series to introduce a metal propeller. The final Ar 64E model differed in its use of a two-bladed propeller, allied with the same licence-built Bristol Jupiter VI engine as the Ar 64D.

Arado Ar 65

Developed as a successor to the Ar 64, the Ar 65 appeared in 1931 and was the first fighter to enter production for the clandestine Luftwaffe. Although the type enjoyed only a relatively small production run, the Ar 65 provided the fledgling German air arm with useful interim trainers and fighters.

When the 1930s dawned, Germany was already the world's most air-minded nation, and the Luftwaffe existed in embryo. Der Deutsche Luftsportverband possessed more than 50,000 members; the branches of the Deutsche Verkehrsfliegerschule were engaged in the training of both commercial and military pilots, thus avoiding a show of open defiance of the terms of the Paris Air Agreement which placed strict limitations on the number of German military personnel permitted to fly, and the Reichswehrministerium (RWM) was, through its Fliegerstab, encouraging the small but industrious German aircraft industry to develop modern combat aircraft for a clandestine fledgling air arm.

Two companies were already actively engaged in fighter design in Germany, the Arado Handelsgesellschaft and the Ernst Heinkel Flugzeugwerke, and the chief engineer of the former concern, Ing. Walter Rethel, had been instrumental in evolving the single-seat SD I and SD II. The latter was developed into the Ar 64 fighter of 1930, a single-seat biplane powered by an air-cooled radial nine-cylinder Siemens-Halske-built Bristol Jupiter, and although thoroughly orthodox and of undistinguished performance, this warplane was to serve as a stepping stone to the still-secret Luftwaffe's first production fighter, the **Ar 65**, which made its debut in prototype form in 1931.

Flight testing

The first prototype of the new fighter, the **Ar 65a**, possessed an essentially similar airframe to that of its predecessor, but the radial engine gave place to a water-cooled 12-cylinder BMW VI 7,3 with a normal rating of 373 kW (500 hp) and offering 559 kW (750 hp) for one minute for take-off and emergency. Flight trials with this and two additional prototypes dictated a number of modifications to the basic design, and the **Ar 65d** that joined the test programme in 1932 had both the thrust line of the engine and the upper contours of the fuselage lowered, the aft fuselage deepened, and additional interplane struts. By comparison with the Ar 65a, the empty and normal loaded weights of the Ar 65d rose from 2,866 and 4,034 lb (1300 and 1830 kg) to 3,256 and 4,233 lb (1477 and 1920 kg), but both handling characteristics and performance were markedly improved, and the Fliegerstab of the RWM instructed Arado to prepare for series production of the fighter for use by the so-called Reklamefliegerabteilung, or 'Publicity Flying Department', which had activated three

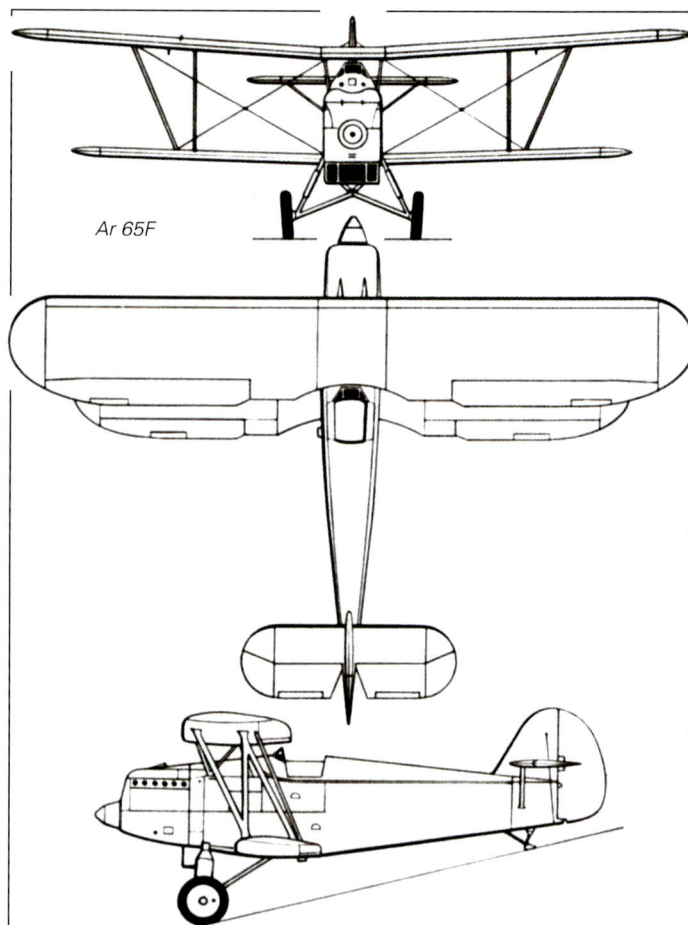

Ar 65F

Staffeln at Berlin-Staaken, Königsberg and Fürth.

With further minor modifications, the fighter entered production at Warnemünde as the **Ar 65E**, the first deliveries being made to the Reklame-Staffel at Berlin-Staaken late in 1933. Carrying an armament of two 7.9-mm (0.31-in) MG 17 machine-guns with 500 r.p.g. in the forward fuselage, the Ar 65E had a 48-Imp gal (218-litre) fuel tank located behind the firewall, and the structure comprised a rectangular welded steel-tube fuselage faired to an oval tail, wooden wings and a metal-framed tail assembly. The fuselage employed light alloy skinning forward and along the top decking, the remainder being fabric covered, and the wings were covered with plywood and fabric.

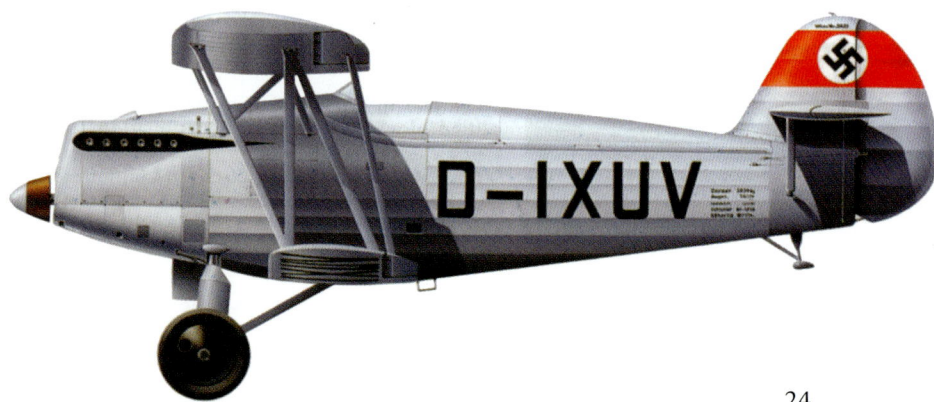

Bearing its civilian registration, this Ar 65F served with Fliegergruppe Döberitz in March 1935. Although the swastika was worn on the port side of the fin, at the time the starboard side would have carried the red, white and black stripes of Imperial Germany. The Ar 65 was the Luftwaffe's first post-war fighter, having clandestinely entered service with the Reklamestaffeln in 1933. The Döberitz unit was formed from the Reklame-Staffel Mitteldeutschland.

Based on its predecessor, the Ar 64, the Ar 65 appeared in 1931. Three prototypes, the Ar 65a, 65b and 65c that differed in minor structural details, were followed by the pre-production model, the Ar 65d, in 1933. Minor modifications resulted in the Ar 65E and 65F production models that had the previous vertical fuselage magazine for six 10-kg (22-lb) bombs deleted. This Ar 65F was used as an advanced trainer by a flying school in the Luftkreis III (Dresden) area.

The DVL Reklame-Staffel Mitteldeutschland was activated on 1 April 1934 at Döberitz with Ar 65E fighters, this unit, formed from personnel drawn from the Reklame-Staffel at Berlin-Staaken, being intended to provide the nucleus of a three-Staffel element. This unit, which was to be officially designated Jagdgeschwader 132 (and later JG 2) on 14 March 1935, began to receive the Heinkel He 51A in July 1934, operating this type alongside the Ar 65E until, in 1935, the latter was transferred to the DVS Jagdfliegerschule at Schleissheim to serve in the fighter training role, and as interim equipment for the Luftwaffe's first dive bomber unit, the Fliegergruppe Schwerin, which later became I/St.G.162. Production of the Ar 65 continued in limited numbers for the fighter trainer role until early 1936, when it was finally supplanted by the Ar 68. At a relatively early production stage, manufacture of the Ar 65E gave place to the **Ar 65F** that differed only in minor respects, the addition of slightly superior equipment increasing the aircraft's empty weight by 40 kg (88 lb).

Arado Ar 65E specification
Type: single-seat fighter
Powerplant: one BMW VI 7,3 12-cylinder liquid-cooled engine rated at 559 kW (750 hp) for take-off and 373 kW (500 hp) maximum continuous
Performance: maximum speed 300 km/h (186 mph) at 1650 m (5,415 ft); cruising speed 246 km/h (153 mph) at 1400 m (4,595 ft); initial climb

This elderly Arado Ar 65 fighter-trainer served with FFS A/B 13 at Pilsen in Czechoslovakia, and is depicted probably in late 1940. The aircraft is finished overall in well-worn L40/52 Grau or RLM 02 Grau; the spinner is white.

rate 636 m (2,086 ft) per minute; time to 1000 m (3,280 ft) 1.5 minutes, to 5000 m (16,405 ft) 10.6 minutes; service ceiling 7600 m (24,935 ft)
Weights: empty equipped 1510 kg (3,329 lb); normal loaded 930 kg (4,255 lb)
Dimensions: wingspan 11.20 m (36 ft 9 in); length 8.40 m (27 ft 6¾ in); height 3.42 m (11 ft 2¾ in); wing area 23 m² (247.58 sq ft)
Armament: two 7.9-mm (0.31-in) MG 17 machine-guns with 500 r.p.g.

Arado Ar 66

Built as a trainer, a role in which it saw extensive use between the wars, the Ar 66 ended up mounting offensive operations on the Eastern Front. The Ar 66 was also the last design completed for Arado by Ing. Walter Rethel before his transfer to the Messerschmitt organisation.

The **Ar 66** was a single-bay biplane trainer of mixed construction. Characteristic features were the swept-back wing panels, long-chord ailerons on both upper and lower wings, and the slightly anachronistic tail with the strut-braced tailplane mounted on a raised rear fuselage fairing ahead of the vertical tail surface, which comprised only a substantial rudder without any fixed fin.

The **Ar 66a** prototype first flew in 1932 as a landplane, while the **Ar 66b** second prototype was completed as a seaplane with a side-by-side pair of wooden floats, and the rudder was enlarged by an extension below the bottom of the sternpost with a ventral fin ahead of it. Ten production-standard **Ar 66B** floatplanes were subsequently built.

The Ar 66 entered series production as the **Ar 66C** that was delivered to the Luftwaffe from 1933. The Ar 66C remained in service with Luftwaffe training schools after the start of World War II. Indeed, as late as 1943 the type was pressed into service, alongside the Gotha Go 145 trainer, by the night ground-attack Störkampfstaffeln (harassing squadrons) operating on the Eastern Front. Adapted for the harassment role, the aircraft could carry 2- and 4-kg (4- and 9-lb) anti-personnel bombs.

Arado Ar 66C specification
Type: two-seat primary and basic flying trainer
Powerplant: one Argus As 10C inverted-Vee engine rated at 179 kW (240 hp)
Performance: maximum speed 210 km/h (131 mph) at sea level; cruising speed 175 km/h (109 mph) at optimum altitude; initial climb rate 260 m (853 ft) per minute; service ceiling 4500 m (14,765 ft); range 715 km (444 miles)
Weights: empty 905 kg (1,996 lb); maximum take-off 1330 kg (2,933 lb)
Dimensions: wingspan 10.00 m (32 ft 9¾ in); length 8.30 m (27 ft 2¾ in); height 2.93 m (9 ft 7½ in); wing area 29.63 m² (318.95 sq ft)

The Arado Ar 66C was widely used by military and civilian flying schools before World War II. During the war the type was pressed into service with Störkampfstaffeln (harassing squadrons) for night operations over the Eastern Front, armed with light bombs.

Arado Ar 67

The Arado Ar 67 was evolved in parallel with the Ar 68 but was considered to afford an insufficient performance improvement over the earlier Ar 65 to warrant production. Consequently, only a single example of the aerodynamically clean biplane fighter was completed.

The arrival of Dipl.-Ing. Walter Blume at the Arado Handelsgesellschaft as chief engineer in 1932 was accompanied by a marked increase in design activity, and work was initiated on two new fighters, the **Ar 67** and Ar 68. The most powerful indigenous engine available, the BMW VI installed in the Ar 65, was not the ideal fighter powerplant, so Dipl.-Ing. Blume's team at Warnemünde elected to install an imported Rolls-Royce Kestrel VI in the Ar 67, offering this fully-supercharged 12-cylinder liquid-cooled engine as an alternative to the BMW VI or the Curtiss V-1570 Conqueror in the parallel Ar 68.

Apart from the constructional methods employed and the arrangement of the tail assembly, there was little similarity between the two fighter designs. Close attention was given to aerodynamic cleanliness, and the first of the two fighters to fly, the **Ar 67a**, commenced its test programme in the late autumn of 1933. Appreciably smaller and lighter than its predecessor, the Ar 67a was a single-bay biplane with splayed N-type interplane struts, and an unusual feature was the single-piece elevator that projected aft of the tailcone, a feature destined to become virtually a trademark of Arado aircraft of the 1930s. The unequal-span wings were of wooden construction with fabric and plywood skinning, the upper wing carrying the ailerons and the lower wing the trailing-edge flaps. The fuselage was a rectangular welded steel-tube structure faired to an oval section, and covered forward and along the upper decking by detachable light alloy panels, the remainder having fabric skinning. The tail surfaces were metal-framed and fabric-covered, the tailplane being braced to the fuselage by parallel inclined struts.

Unarmed prototype

The close-cowled Kestrel VI engine, which drove a two-bladed fixed-pitch wooden airscrew, offered 391 kW (525 hp) for take-off and 447 kW (600 hp) at 3353 m (11,000 ft), and the proposed armament consisted of two 7.9-mm (0.31-in) MG 17 machine-guns with 500 r.p.g., although this was not installed in the prototype. By comparison with the Ar 65E, the Ar 67a (without armament) was substantially lighter, but wing loading was increased and power loading consequently reduced. Speed and climb were markedly superior to the

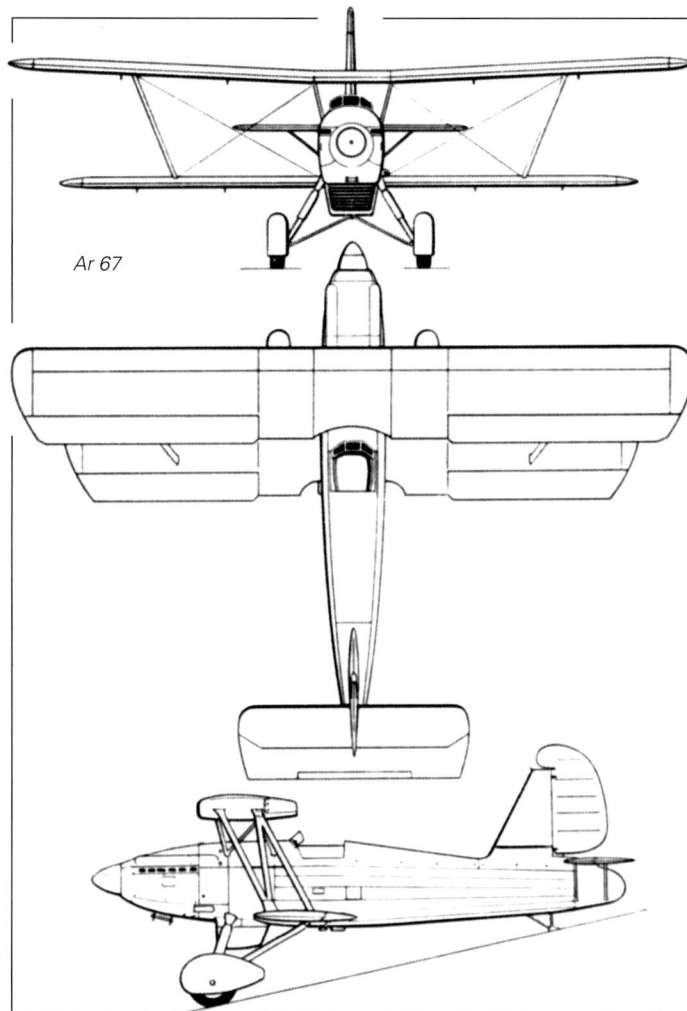

Ar 67

Ar 65E at altitude but inferior at lower altitudes, and as the C-Amt, the camouflaged Technical Department of Hermann Göring's newly-created Luftfahrtkommissariat, considered the Ar 67 to offer an insufficient advance over the earlier fighter to warrant series production, further development was abandoned in favour of the Ar 68, and only the one prototype was completed.

Arado Ar 67a specification
Type: single-seat fighter
Powerplant: one Rolls-Royce Kestrel VI 12-cylinder liquid-cooled engine rated at 391 kW (525 hp) for take-off and 477 kW (640 hp) at 4267 m (14,000 ft)
Performance: maximum speed 340 km/h (211 mph) at 3770 m (12,370 ft); initial climb rate 480 m (1,575 ft) per minute; time to 1000 m (3,280 ft) 2.1 min; service ceiling 9300 m (30,510 ft)
Weights: (without armament) empty 1270 kg (2,799 lb); loaded 1660 kg (3,660 lb)
Dimensions: wingspan 9.68 m (31 ft 9 in); length 7.90 m (25 ft 11 in); height 3.10 m (10 ft 2 in); wing area 25 m² (269.74 sq ft)
Armament: (proposed) two 7.9-mm (0.31-in) MG 17 machine-guns with 500 r.p.g.

Arado built a single prototype Ar 67. Provision was made for the aircraft to carry 1,000 rounds of ammunition for its two machine-guns which, in the event, were not fitted.

Arado Ar 68

The Ar 68 was the last biplane fighter to enter front-line sevice with the Luftwaffe. First flown in the summer of 1934, the Ar 68 was introduced in the spring of 1937. At the outbreak of World War II a small number of Ar 68 fighters survived in operational service. Thereafter, the type remained in use with Luftwaffe training schools.

Abandonment of the Ar 67 led Ing. Rethel's team, under the supervision of Dipl.-Ing. Blume, to devote its full attention to the parallel **Ar 68** design that envisaged a somewhat larger and heavier fighter. The design team was rather reluctant to use the BMW VI engine for the new fighter and, at an early stage in development, an investigation of the possibility of installing either the Rolls-Royce Kestrel or Curtiss Conqueror was conducted. However, the Luftfahrtkommissariat discouraged the adoption of a foreign powerplant as the Junkers-Motorenbau was making good progress with its new 12-cylinder inverted-Vee liquid-cooled engine, the Jumo 210, which it was anticipated would be available for series-production fighters in 1935.

Relatively low priority was attached to the development of the new Arado fighter by the Luftfahrtkommissariat for several reasons. Heinkel had already initiated series production of the He 51 which it was considered would fulfil the immediate fighter needs of the clandestine Luftwaffe for a successor to the Ar 65; the Warnemünde plant, which had, in the meantime, become the Arado Flugzeugwerke GmbH, was working to capacity on orders for training aircraft and also possessed a sub-contract for 75 He 51 fighters, and it was obvious that the new Junkers engine intended for the Ar 68 would not be available in quantity for some time. Nevertheless, the Arado team, anxious to provide the succes-

Intended as a successor to the He 51, construction of the first prototype Ar 68 commenced in summer 1933. D-IKIN was the Ar 68a, the first prototype of the new fighter, and its flight test programme began at Warnemünde in summer 1934.

sor to the He 51, had begun construction of the first prototype of the new fighter by the late summer of 1933, and this, the **Ar 68a** (D-IKIN), began flight trials at Warnemünde during the early summer of the following year with a BMW VId engine.

From the outset the Ar 68a met the most sanguine expectations held by its design team in respect of handling characteristics and manoeuvrability. Speed and climb rate were only marginally improved over the Ar 65F as a result of the retention of the BMW VI engine, although this had been anticipated by the design team. The only major criticisms voiced by the test pilots concerned the accumulation of exhaust gases in the cockpit, and the inferior forward view offered by comparison with the earlier Ar 65E, a penalty resulting from some lengthening of the nose and a reduction in fuselage depth for aerodynamic reasons. The former shortcoming was removed with the installation of the Jumo 210A, the inverted-Vee arrangement of which alleviating the latter.

'White 6' was an Arado Ar 68F assigned to the 3 Staffel of I Gruppe of JG 134 'Horst Wessel'. It wears a typical pre-war finish and markings in full accordance with then-current orders. The contrast between the glossy paint on the fuselage with the white disc suggests that it is finished in the greenish-grey RLM 02 Grau.

Arado Ar 68

By the outbreak of World War II, the Ar 68 had been largely supplanted by the Messerschmitt Bf 109 in first-line units, but a small number remained operational in a fighter capacity, these aircraft by now wearing a more warlike camouflage scheme.

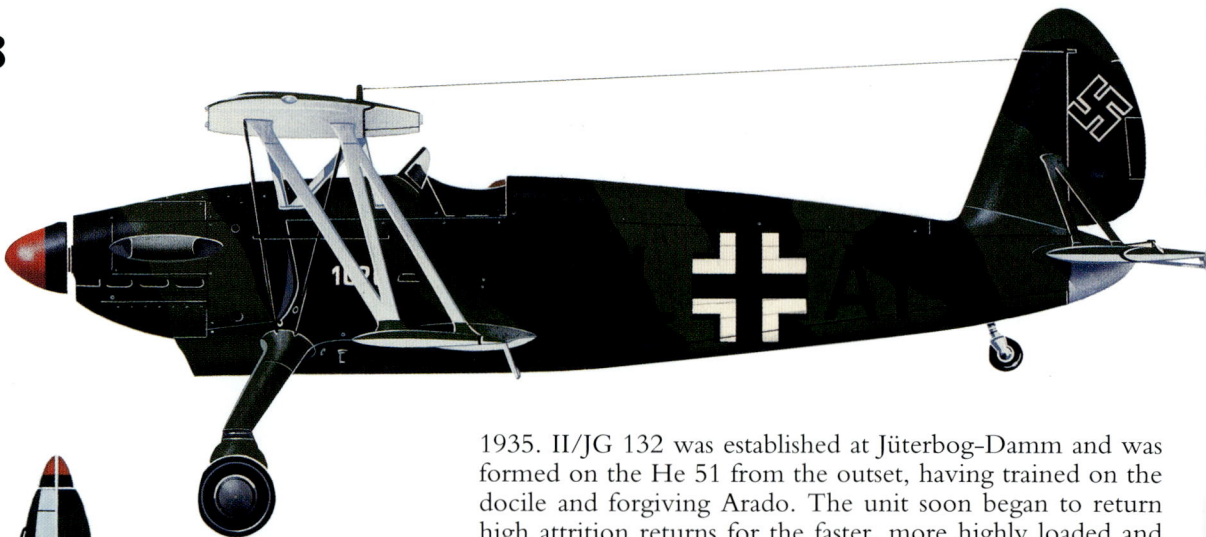

N+L

Jumo-engined prototypes

The new engine was installed in the second and third prototypes, the **Ar 68b** (D-IVUS) and **Ar 68c** (D-IBAS), which joined the flight test programme in the spring and summer of 1935, respectively. The Jumo 210A offered only 455 kW (610 hp) for take-off, but whereas the BMW VI was essentially a low-altitude engine, the supercharged Junkers engine could maintain take-off output to 3400 m (11,155 ft). The Ar 68b experienced a drag problem that resulted from a poorly designed radiator bath, but this feature had been redesigned prior to the debut of the Ar 68c, which was also the first prototype to carry the standard fighter armament of twin 7.9-mm (0.31-in) MG 17 guns with 500 r.p.g.

The Arado team fully believed its fighter to be superior to the He 51 on every count and, as additional production capacity was now available, the new plant at Brandenburg having been phased into the manufacturing programme at the end of 1934, it was assumed that the placement of series production orders for the Ar 68 was imminent. However, it was no longer the Reichsluftfahrtministerium (RLM), the successor to the Luftfahrtkommissariat, that was dragging its feet but the Luftwaffe itself. The I Gruppe of Jagdgeschwader 132 'Richthofen' at Döberitz was still equipped primarily with the ageing Ar 65E when the existence of the Luftwaffe was officially proclaimed in March

1935. II/JG 132 was established at Jüterbog-Damm and was formed on the He 51 from the outset, having trained on the docile and forgiving Arado. The unit soon began to return high attrition returns for the faster, more highly loaded and rather more temperamental Heinkel fighter. The Ar 68 was even more highly loaded than the He 51, and offered yet higher approach speeds, and the Luftwaffe had still to be convinced that the newer fighter offered any advantage. The general attitude among service pilots was 'Better the devil we know . . .!'

Early in 1936, Ernst Udet, newly appointed as Inspector of Fighter and Dive-Bomber Pilots and tiring of the Luftwaffe's vacillation over the Ar 68, decided to resolve the matter once and for all by organising a mock combat between one of the most experienced of the Luftwaffe's fighter pilots flying a production He 51A and himself flying one of the Jumo-engined Ar 68 prototypes. Shortly after the take-off of the two fighters the outcome of the contest was in little doubt, Udet in the Ar 68 out-climbing, out-turning and out-fighting the Heinkel effortlessly. In so far as level speed was concerned, the Arado fighter did not offer any noteworthy advance over the He 51, but sheer speed was not considered to be the most important criterion by which a fighter was to be judged; manoeuvrability was paramount and in this the Ar 68 excelled. Furthermore, it offered outstanding handling characteristics, coupling these with an exceptionally sturdy structure, and the future of the Ar 68 was thus assured.

Production development

In the meantime, two further prototypes had been completed, the **Ar 68d** (D-ITAR) that reverted to the BMW VI engine, and the **Ar 68e** (D-ITEP) with a Jumo 210Da equipped with a two-speed supercharger and rated at 507 kW (680 hp) for take-off. Shortly after the debut of these prototypes, the RLM instituted a standard system of Versuchs numbers for prototype aircraft, and thus the Ar 68d and 68e were redesignated **Ar 68 V4** and **V5**. The Ar 68 V5 was considered to be the production prototype for the Jumo 210Da-engined

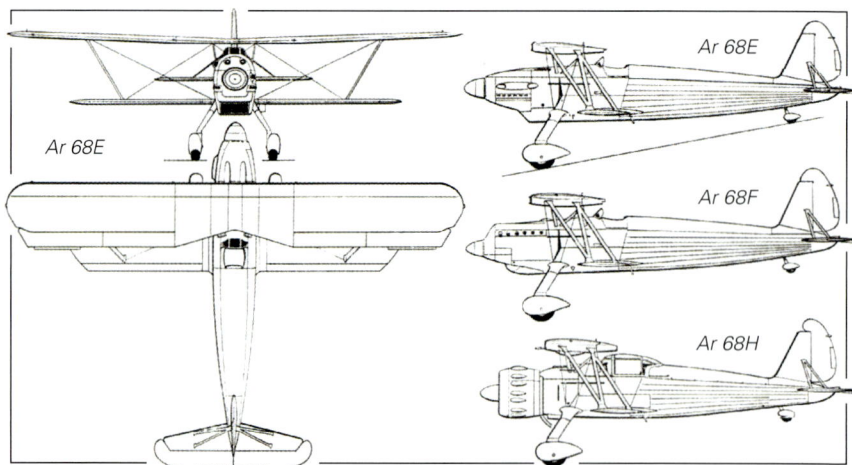

Ar 68E

Ar 68E

Ar 68E

Ar 68F

Ar 68H

This Arado Ar 68F served with 3./JG 135, based at Bad Aibling during 1937. The Geschadwer assignment was denoted by the light blue trim, while the third Staffel of any Gruppe used a white dot marking.

Ar 68E-1 fighter, and tooling had reached an advanced stage when a change in RLM priorities in the allocation of Jumo 210 engines resulted in Arado being instructed to complete the initial production series of Ar 68 fighters with BMW VI 7,3Z engines as an interim measure pending an improvement in the supply position of the Junkers powerplant.

Into service

With the BMW engine, the fighter was designated **Ar 68F-1**, and first entered service in the late summer of 1936 with the newly-formed I/JG 134 (later ZG 26) 'Horst Wessel' at Werl, the Jesau-based I/JG 131 being the next recipient, but performance of the Ar 68F-1 was virtually identical to that of the older He 51 which, during the summer of 1936, had been found inferior in almost every respect to the Soviet Polikarpov I-15 by which it was opposed over Spain. The acceptance of this unpalatable fact led to an immediate reassignment of priorities in Jumo 210 deliveries, and only relatively small numbers of BMW-engined Ar 68s had left the assembly line before, in the autumn of 1936, the Jumo 210Da was made available for installation, production immediately switching to the Ar 68E-1.

The Ar 68E-1, which was destined to be the principal production version of the Arado fighter and the Luftwaffe's last first-line fighter biplane, followed previous Arado structural practices. The wings were of wooden construction, the leading edges and under-surfaces of the upper wing back to the rear spar being plywood-covered, the remainder being fabric-covered, and the lower wing being entirely plywood-covered. The upper wing carried the ailerons and the lower wing carried the landing flaps, and the interplane struts, which were inclined and splayed, were of N-type. The fuselage was a rectangular welded steel-tube structure faired to an oval section, this being covered forward and along the upper decking by detachable light alloy panels, the aft sides and undersurfaces being fabric-covered. The tail surfaces were metal-framed, the tailplane being braced to the fin by inverted-Vee struts, and the undercarriage comprised cantilever faired legs and a swivelling tailwheel unit.

The Jumo 210Da engine, which was replaced in later production aircraft by the Jumo 210Ea possessing simi-

D-IBAS was the second Jumo-engined prototype, known as the Ar 68c. It began flight trials in the summer of 1935 and was the first prototype to carry the intended armament of two 7.9-mm (0.31-in) MG 17 machine-guns.

Arado Ar 68

Armament
Series-produced Ar 68 fighters were armed with two MG 17 machine-guns with 1,000 rounds of ammunition. They were mounted above the cowling and synchronised to fire through the propeller, in true World War I fashion. A container for six SC 10 fragmentation bombs could be carried for close-support missions.

Arado Ar 68F-1

11./JG 72, Böblingen, Germany, September 1939

The first Arado Ar 68s, BMW-powered Ar 68F-1s, entered service in 1936 with I/JG 134 at Werl. By 1938, before the Bf 109 became dominant, the Ar 68E (with the Jumo 210) was the most numerous type in the fighter arm. In 1938, two Ar 68Es were sent to Spain for operational trials and were used as night-fighters with Grupo 9 based at La Cenia. This aircraft belonged to one of two Staffeln (10. and 11./JG 72) based together at Böblingen, near Stuttgart. In 1940, the last Arados were sent to fighter-training schools.

He 51 versus Ar 68
The Heinkel He 51 beat the Ar 68 into service to be the first fighter of the rebuilt Luftwaffe. Basic performance figures of the BMW-powered He 51C and Ar 68F were almost identical, but the Heinkel was much harder to fly and suffered high training attrition. General Ernst Udet himself flew an Ar 68F in comparative flight trials with a Heinkel flown by one of the best pilots in the Luftwaffe, and so comprehensively out-fought it that Arado production was soon increased. Allocations of the Jumo 210 were made to Arado, resulting in the improved Ar 68E.

Development
The first of the Ar 68 series, the Ar 68a (D-IKIN), powered by a BMW VId engine, first flew in late summer 1934. It was followed by the Ar 68b and c (both Jumo-powered), the BMW-powered Ar 68d, and the Ar 68e, the latter with a Jumo fitted with a two-stage supercharger. When the RLM introduced Versuchs numbers, the Ar 68d and e prototypes were redesignated Ar 68 V4 and V5, respectively.

Engine

Ar 68E-1s were powered by the 515-kW (690-hp) Junkers Jumo 210Ea supercharged inverted V-12 inline engine. This powerplant offered better altitude performance than the BMW VI upright V-12, the latter being essentially a low-altitude engine.

Specification
Arado Ar 68F-1

POWERPLANT: one BMW VI 7,3Z 12-cylinder liquid-cooled engine rated at 559 kW (750 hp) at sea level for one minute and 410 kW (550 hp) at 1000 m (3,280 ft)

PERFORMANCE: maximum speed 330 km/h (205 mph) at sea level, 322 km/h (200 mph) at 2650 m (8,695 ft), 311 km/h (193 mph) at 4000 m (13,125 ft), 290 km/h (180 mph) at 6000 m (19,685 ft); initial climb rate 672 m (2,205 ft) per minute; time to 1000 m (3,280 ft) 1.35 minutes, to 5000 m (16,405 ft) 10.2 minutes; service ceiling 7400 m (24,280 ft); range 500 km (310 miles)

WEIGHTS: empty 1520 kg (3,351 lb); loaded 1950 kg (4,299 lb)

DIMENSIONS: wingspan 11.00 m (36 ft 1 in); length 9.44 m (30 ft 11⅔ in); height 3.30 m (10 ft 10 in); wing area 27.30 m² (293.86 sq ft)

ARMAMENT: two 7.9-mm (0.31-in) MG 17 machine-guns with 500 r.p.g., plus (optional) six 10-kg (22-lb) SC 10 fragmentation bombs

Structure

The Ar 68 was constructed around an oval-section framework of welded steel tubing. The fuselage was metal-skinned from the nose to the cockpit and along the spine to the tail, the remainder being fabric-covered. The wings were a fabric-covered wooden structure. The fixed tail surfaces were all metal, with fabric-covered elevators and rudder. The metal-covered landing flaps, stretching the whole length of the lower wing, were an early, if not first, use on a biplane.

Arado Ar 68

Arado Ar 68E of Leutnant Riegel, the Gruppen-adjutant of III/JG 141 based at Fürstenwalde during 1938. The Ar 68E introduced an inverted Jumo 210 in a more streamlined cowl.

'White 7' was an Ar 68F of 2./JG 131 based at Seerappen in the summer of 1937. The aircraft was finished in JG 131's black trim, with second staffel white bands. The Ar 68F was the first production version with the upright BMW VI.

lar ratings, drove a two-bladed Heine fixed-pitch wooden airscrew, and all fuel was housed in a 200-litre (44-Imp gal) capacity tank immediately aft of the firewall. Armament comprised two fuselage-mounted 7.9-mm MG 17 machine-guns with 500 r.p.g., the pilot having a Reflex-Visier IlIa reflector sight, and a cylindrical magazine for six 10-kg (22-lb) SC 10 fragmentation bombs could be fitted beneath the fuse-lage, although this was rarely carried owing to its high drag.

Re-equipment programme

Early in 1937, it was planned that seven Jagdgruppen would be formed on the Ar 68, these being I, II and III/JG 134, I/JG 135, II/JG 234, and I and II/JG 334, but the struc-ture of the fighter arm underwent numerous changes, addi-tional units were formed on the Ar 68E, such as III/JG 141 at Fürstenwalde, and various He 51-equipped Gruppen (e.g. I/JG 131) also converted to the Arado fighter which, until overtaken by the Messerschmitt Bf 109 in the spring of 1938, equipped the largest proportion of the Jagdgruppen.

Despite the imminent appearance in service of the

Luftwaffe's first fighter monoplane, Arado believed that there was still a place in the first-line inventory for the fighter biplane, and the spring of 1937 saw the appearance of the **Ar 68H** (D-ISIX). This had been preceded by the **Ar 68G** that had proved abortive owing to the non-appearance of the supercharged BMW engine for which it was intended. A radical departure from previous Arado fighter practice was the adoption of a radial air-cooled engine for the **Ar 68H**, this being the nine-cylinder BMW 132Da rated at 634 kW (850 hp) for take-off and fitted with a supercharger. As a concession to modernity, a sliding cockpit canopy was fitted, and armament was doubled by the introduction of two MG 17 machine-guns in the upper wing. The Ar 68H succeeded in attaining 400 km/h (250 mph) in level flight, and its opera-tional ceiling was boosted to some 9000 m (29,530 ft), but the Luftwaffenführungsstab had already concluded – and correctly as events were to prove – that the day of the fighter biplane was passing, and the RLM instructed Arado to aban-don all further work on the Ar 68.

In 1938, two Ar 68E-1 fighters were despatched to Spain for operational trials, these being used in the night-fighting role from La Cenia, and when World War II began in September 1939, this role was also being undertaken by the last remaining Ar 68s in the Luftwaffe's first-line strength, these being operated by 10. and 11. (Nachtjagd)/JG 72 under Luftflotte 3 in south-west Germany. Possessing 16 and 12 Ar 68E-1s, respectively, the two Staffeln were limited to nocturnal patrols

The Ar 68E (D-ITEP) was powered by a Jumo 210Da engine, complete with two-stage supercharger, and rated at 507 kW (680 hp) for take-off. The aircraft served as the production prototype for the Ar 68E-1. Aircraft were completed and delivered with closely spatted mainwheels and tailwheels. In service, these could easily clog when operating from muddy airfields during autumn and winter, and were often removed.

This Arado Ar 68F nightfighter of 10. (Nachtjagd)/ JG 53 'Pik As' was based at Oedheim/ Heilbron during September 1939. This aircraft carries the wing's famous ace of spades badge.

Fitted with the skis that allowed training to continue in the winter months, this is Ar 68E DL+VU, of Flugzeugführerschule A/B 32, seen at Chrudim, Czechoslovakia, in January 1941. This unit was headquartered at Pardubitz (today Pardubice in the Czech Republic), with Chrudim as one of its three satellite fields. It trained pilots until January 1944, employing a wide array of types. Most of the trainer types of German origin were employed, but the school also made use of captured foreign materiel, such as the Letov S.328 and Caudron C.445.

along the Franco-German border, but before many weeks had passed were re-equipped and redesignated 11./JG 2 and 5./JG 52. This was not to be the last operational service of the Arado fighter biplane, however, for shortly after the formation of III/JG 53 on Bf 109Es on 26 September 1939, the 7. Staffel was redesignated 10. (Nachtjagd)/JG 53 and, issued with Ar 68F-1s, operated as a makeshift night-fighter unit from Oedheim/Heilbronn during the winter of 1939-40. Subsequently, the surviving Ar 68s were passed to the Jagdfliegerschulen.

Arado Ar 68E-1 specification
Type: single-seat fighter
Powerplant: one Junkers Jumo 210Ea 12-cylinder liquid-cooled engine rated at 507 kW (680 hp) at sea level for five minutes and 500 kW (670 hp) at 3800 m (12,465 ft)
Performance: maximum speed 306 km/h (190 mph) at sea level, 335 km/h (208 mph) at 2650 m (8,695 ft), 325 km/h (202 mph) at 4000 m (13,125 ft), 295 km/h (183 mph) at 6000 m (19,685 ft); initial climb rate 756 m (2,480 ft) per minute; time to 6000 m (19,685 ft) 10 minutes; service ceiling 8100 m (26,575 ft); normal range 500 km (310 miles)
Weights: empty 1600 kg (3,527 lb); loaded 2020 kg (4,453 lb)
Dimensions: wingspan 11.00 m (36 ft 1 in); length 9.50 m (31 ft 2 in); height 3.30 m (10 ft 10 in); wing area 27.30 m² (293.855 sq ft)
Armament: two 7.9-mm (0.31-in) MG 17 machine-guns with 500 r.p.g., plus (optional) six 10-kg (22-lb) SC 10 fragmentation bombs

Though easy to fly, the Arado Ar 68E was no match for the Russian Polikarpov I-15 fighters it encountered in Spain, and its narrow wheel track made night operations tricky. After some ground attack trials in German hands the aircraft were passed onto the Spanish Nationalist forces, who did not like them.

Arado Ar 69

A straightforward single-bay biplane of fabric-covered mixed construction, the Arado Ar 69 was designed to satisfy training and sporting requirements in alternative versions with air-cooled radial and inverted inline engines. Characterised by open cockpits and fixed tailskid undercarriage, the Ar 69 did not enter production.

The **Ar 69** was designed in 1933 as a flying trainer with tandem open cockpits. It was, in effect, a scaled-down and lightened development of the Ar 66. Of fabric-covered wooden construction, the upper and lower wings carried long-span ailerons. The staggered wings were separated on each side by a single set of parallel interplane struts. The fuselage was based on a welded steel tube primary structure faired out to an oval shape by formers and stringers under a covering of largely fabric. The tail unit was of fabric-covered steel tube construction, and of Arado's typical type with the vertical surface set ahead of the horizontal surface. Unlike the Ar 66, however, the Ar 69 had a single-piece elevator. The undercarriage was of the fixed tailskid type.

The **Ar 69 V1** prototype (D-2821) was powered by the Hirth HM.504 air-cooled four-cylinder inverted inline engine rated at 78 kW (105 hp), and its vertical tail comprised a fin and plain rudder with straight leading and trailing edges. It was planned that the Ar 69A production model would be derived directly from the **Ar 69 V2** second prototype (D-2822) with Arado's new pattern of vertical tail with a narrower-chord fin carrying a horn-balanced rudder with a strongly curved trailing edge. The **Ar 66A** series did not enter production, so the next aeroplane was the **Ar 69 V3** prototype (D-EPYT) for the planned **Ar 69B** production model. This was basically similar to the planned Ar 69A except for its different and higher-rated BMW Bramo Sh.14a radial engine. The Ar 66B was planned as a rival to the Focke-Wulf Fw 44 Stieglitz, which was preferred, so the Ar 69B did not enter production.

Arado Ar 69 V3 specification

Type: two-seat elementary and primary trainer
Powerplant: one BMW Bramo Sh.14a air-cooled seven-cylinder radial engine rated at 112 kW (150 hp)
Performance: maximum speed 184 km/h (114 mph) at sea level; cruising speed 150 km/h (93 mph) at optimum altitude; climb to 1000 m (3,280 ft) in 3 minutes 24 seconds; service ceiling 5600 m (18,375 ft)
Weights: empty 540 kg (1,190 lb); maximum take-off 680 kg (1,499 lb)
Dimensions: wingspan 9.00 m (29 ft 6¼ in); length 7.20 m (23 ft 7½ in); height 2.70 m (8 ft 10¼ in); wing area 20.70 m² (222.82 sq ft)

Above: Developed on the basis of the Ar 66, the Ar 69 first protype was a biplane of mixed construction, and was powered by the 78-kW (105-hp) Hirth HM 504A air-cooled four-cylinder inline engine.

The Ar 69 second prototype switched to the type of tail unit that became characteristic of this manufacturer's aircraft during much of the 1930s. The engine remained unchanged.

Had it entered production, the Ar 69 would have been manufactured in two production variants. This is the prototype (V3) intended to pave the way for the Ar 69B initial variant with the 105-kW (140-hp) BMW Bramo Sh.14A air-cooled seven-cylinder radial engine, while the Ar 69A would have used the HM.504A inverted inline engine.

Arado Ar 76

Intended as an advanced trainer that could double as a lightweight 'emergency' fighter, the single-seat Ar 76 was designed by Walter Blume. Judged inferior to the rival Focke-Wulf Fw 56, a limited production run was nonetheless completed and the type served for some time with distinction at Luftwaffe flying schools.

Among the earliest specifications drawn up by the C-Amt of Göring's Luftfahrtkommissariat was one calling for an emergency Heimatschutzjäger, a 'home defence fighter'. It had also to be suitable for the role of advanced fighter trainer, and the importance attached to this specification by the Luftfahrtkommissariat may be gauged from the fact that no fewer than four aircraft manufacturers – Arado, Focke-Wulf, Heinkel and Henschel – were asked to submit proposals. The Heimatschutzjäger idea was not novel in Germany, as the Reichswehrministerium had prepared a similar specification in the 1920s, and as now envisaged by the C-Amt, the aircraft was to be a high-wing monoplane designed around the Argus As 10C eight-cylinder inverted-Vee air-cooled engine, and capable of mounting either one or two 7.9-mm (0.31-in) MG 17 machine-guns. In autumn 1934 the specification was amended to stipulate the twin-gun mounting plus the ability to carry three 10-kg (22-lb) bombs for the Heimatschutzjäger role, armament being restricted to one MG 17 for the fighter training role.

Arado's contribution to the programme, the **Ar 76** designed to the same strength factor as the Ar 67 and 68 fighters, was a parasol monoplane with a simple tubular steel fuselage with wooden formers, light alloy skinning forward and along the upper decking, and fabric covering for the aft sides and underside. The wings were of wooden construction with fabric covering and attached on each side to the fuselage mainframes by parallel bracing struts. Provision was made in the upper decking of the forward fuselage for two MG 17 machine-guns, and a bay was provided immediately aft of the fireproof bulkhead to house a magazine containing three vertically-hung 10-kg bombs.

Small production run

The first prototype, the **Ar 76a** (D-ISEN), was completed late in 1934, this being followed in the spring of 1935 by a second prototype, the **Ar 76 V2** (D-IRAS). The Ar 76 V2, like the **Ar 76 V3** completed shortly after the second prototype, differed from the original Ar 76a, which had been lost in an accident at an early stage in the flight test programme, in having some tail assembly modifications, including the elimination of all dihedral on the horizontal surfaces. The general characteristics of the Ar 76 were adjudged excellent, but in the final evaluation of the contending designs, the Arado competitor was placed second to the Focke-Wulf Fw 56 Stösser. Nevertheless, a small production series of **Ar 76A** aircraft was ordered. Delivered to the Luftwaffe in the spring of 1936, they were used by the Jagdfliegerschulen. As a result of some minor structural strengthening and certain equipment changes,

the empty and loaded weights of the Ar 76A were increased by 45 and 80 kg (99 and 176 lb), respectively, over those of the V2 and V3, these increases being accompanied by a small reduction in performance.

Ar 76A-0 specification
Type: single-seat fighter or advanced trainer
Powerplant: one Argus As 10C Series I eight-cylinder inverted-Vee air-cooled engine rated at 179 kW (240 hp) for take-off
Performance: maximum speed 267 km/h (166 mph); maximum cruising speed 220 km/h (137 mph); initial climb rate 432 m (1,417 ft) per minute; service ceiling 6400 m (21,000 ft); maximum range 470 km (292 miles)
Weights: empty 750 kg (1,653 lb); loaded 1070 kg (2,359 lb)
Dimensions: wingspan 9.50 m (31 ft 2 in); length 7.20 m (23 ft 7½ in); height 2.55 m (8 ft 4⅓ in); wing area 13.34 m² (143.59 sq ft)
Armament: (fighter) two 7.9-mm (0.31-in) MG 17 machine-guns with 250 r.p.g. plus three 10-kg (22-lb) bombs, or (trainer) one 7.9-mm MG 17 with 250 rounds

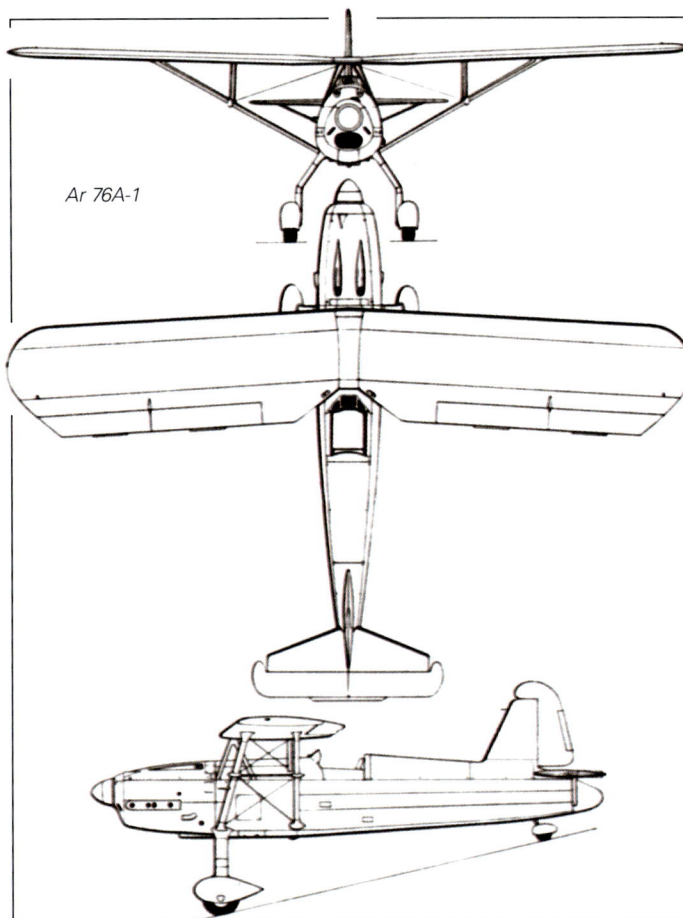
Ar 76A-1

Designed as a dual-role trainer and fighter, the Ar 76 (seen here in V2 prototype form) proved an effective trainer, with a small batch ordered as back-up to the Fw 56.

Arado Ar 77

A sleek low-wing monoplane, the Arado Ar 77 was intended to undertake training, light transport and communications duties. Although the aircraft was judged to offer useful performance and good handling, it lost out to the Focke-Wulf Fw 58 in the competition for a production order.

After it had issued its 1934 requirement for a multi-role aircraft to serve in the crew training, light transport and communications roles, the German air ministry ordered prototypes of the twin-engined **Arado Ar 77** and Focke-Wulf Fw 58 Weihe designs for a competitive evaluation. This led to the selection of a single type for series production. The Arado design team laid out the Ar 77 as a cantilever low-wing monoplane with fully enclosed accommodation in an oval-section fuselage and featuring a high-aspect-ratio wing.

The Ar 77 prototypes were produced in two forms as the **Ar 77a** and **Ar 77b**, these being differentiated largely by their structures as the Ar 77a was of mixed wood and Dural construction, whereas the Ar 77b was of wooden construction. Powered by a pair of Argus As 10C inverted-Vee engines driving two-bladed propellers, the Ar 77 was deemed to offer adequate performance and handling, but the Fw 58 was preferred for the production order.

Arado Ar 77A specification
Type: four-seat multi-role training, light transport and communications aircraft
Powerplant: two Argus As 10C inverted-Vee piston engines each rated at 179 kW (240 hp)
Performance: maximum speed 240 km/h (149 mph) at sea level; cruising speed 200 km/h (124 mph) at optimum altitude; climb to 100 m (3,280 ft) in 3 minutes 30 seconds; service ceiling 5000 m (16,405 ft); range 470 km (292 miles)
Weights: empty 1930 kg (4,255 lb); maximum take-off 2940 kg (6,481 lb)
Dimensions: wingspan 19.20 m (62 ft 11⅞ in); length 12.50 m (41 ft ⅛ in); height 3.20 m (10 ft 6 in); wing area 50.50 m² (543.60 sq ft)

A neat spatted and trousered undercarriage added to the streamlined appearance of the Ar 77. The Arado design lost out to Fock-Wulf's Fw 58, with which it shared a twin-Argus powerplant.

Arado Ar 79

Arado's first 'modern' monoplane design, the Ar 79 featured retractable undercarriage, cantilever flying surfaces and accommodation for two. The cabin monoplane was tailored to the civilian market and went on to establish a number of international records for speed and endurance.

Designed as an aerobatic two-seat training and touring aircraft intended for the civil market, the **Arado Ar 79** was the manufacturer's first 'modern' monoplane type with enclosed accommodation, cantilever flying surfaces and retractable main landing gear units. The type first appeared in prototype form during 1938 with the powerplant of one 78-kW (105-hp) Hirth HM 504A-2 inverted inline engine. The forward fuselage was of welded steel-tube construction under a covering of light alloy panels, and provided side-by-side accommodation under a rearward-sliding canopy. The rear fuselage was of light alloy semi-monocoque construction, and the wing was of single-spar wooden construction with plywood and fabric covering.

The Ar 79 set a number of international class speed

The Arado Ar 79 offered very useful endurance, as demonstrated during a non-stop flight from Libya to India in 1938. The flight was completed by pilots Oberleutnant Pulkowski and Leutnant Jennett, in this aircraft, D-EHCR, the Ar 79 V2 second prototype.

This Arado Ar 79 wears pre-war German civil markings. The Ar 79 was powered by the same 78-kW (105-hp) Hirth HM 504 engine used in the Bücker Bü 133 Jungmann and Bü 181 Bestmann two-seat primary trainers.

records during 1938, including solo 1000 km (621.4 miles) at 229.04 km/h (142.32 mph) on 15 July, and solo 2000 km (1,242.8 miles) at 227.029 km/h (141.07 mph) on 29 July. Later in the same year an Ar 79 was prepared for an attempt on the long-distance record. A jettisonable 106-litre (23.3-lmp gal) fuel tank was fitted under the fuselage and a fixed 520-litre (114.4-lmp gal) tank at the rear of the cabin. Pilots Oberleutnant Pulkowski and Leutnant Jennett ferried the aircraft from Brandenberg to Benghazi in Libya, the start-ing point for the 6303-km (3,916.5-mile) non-stop flight to Gaya in India. The flight, from 29 to 31 December, was made at an average speed of 160 km/h (99.5 mph).

Arado Ar 79 specification
Type: two-seat training and touring aircraft
Powerplant: one Hirth HM 504A-2 inverted inline engine rated at 78 kW (105 hp)
Performance: maximum speed 230 km/h (143 mph) at sea level; cruising speed 205 km/h (127 mph) at optimum altitude; initial climb rate 240 m (787 ft) per minute; climb to 1000 m (3,280 ft) in 3 minutes 48 seconds; service ceiling 5500 m (18,040 ft); range 1025 km (636 miles)
Weights: empty 460 kg (1,014 lb); maximum take-off 760 kg (1,675 lb)
Dimensions: wingspan 10.00 m (32 ft 9¾ in); length 7.60 m (24 ft 11¼ in): height 2.10 m (6 ft 10⅔ in); wing area 14.00 m² (150.70 sq ft)

Above: In a break from previous Arado tradition, the Walter Blume-designed Ar 79 featured retractable tailwheel landing gear, the mainwheels retracting sideways and inwards into the wing centre section. A total of 48 Ar 79s was completed in three sub-versions.

Above: The Ar 79's forward fuselage was of light alloy over steel tube, allied to a semi-monocoque rear fuselage assembly. The single-spar wing was of fabric-covered plywood.

Left: D-EKCX, the Ar 79 V1 prototype, was the machine used by Herr Lüber to establish a new solo speed record for its class over a distance of 1000 km on 15 July 1938.

Offering side-by-side accommodation for two in a fully enclosed cabin, the Ar 79 was a useful touring cabin monoplane. Ar 79 sub-types differed only in minor respects, such as equipment provision, and production was completed in 1941. Inevitably, a number of aircraft found their way into Luftwaffe service, where they served on liaison duties.

Arado Ar 80

During the early months of 1934, the Luftwaffenführungsstab finalised its conception of a single-seat all-metal fighter monoplane on which the C-Amt of the Luftfahrtkommissariat based its specification for issue to selected aircraft manufacturers. Recipients included the Arado Flugzeugwerke, which devised the Ar 80 in response.

The Arado team, led by Dipl.-Ing. Blume, possessed no experience in all-metal aircraft construction, nor in the design of retractable undercarriages, and in the belief that the increased drag of fixed gear would be compensated for by the reduction in weight resulting from the elimination of retraction mechanism and the cut-outs in the wing structure for wheel wells, elected to employ a cantilever low-wing configuration, with close-cowled fixed main undercarriage members, the cantilever legs being kept to minimum length by the adoption of an inverted-gull wing form. In the event,

The Ar 80 V2 was completed to a similar standard to the V1, featuring an inverted-gull wing. Here it is seen with its initial Rolls-Royce Kestrel V powerplant, subsequently changed for the intended Junkers Jumo 210C.

a miscalculation was to result in the airframe weighing in at a substantially greater weight than anticipated, this increased weight more than absorbing the saving effected by the use of a fixed undercarriage.

Alternative powerplants

Designated **Ar 80**, the fighter employed a single box-spar type wing with light alloy covering for the upper surfaces and fabric covering for the undersurfaces. As little experience existed with modern stressed-skin monocoque structures, the Ar 80 employed a welded steel-tube fuselage covered forward by detachable light metal panels and aft by lateral light metal strips riveted to the formers. The first prototype, the **Ar 80 V1**, was fitted with the Rolls-Royce Kestrel VI formerly installed in the Ar 67a fighter prototype, and commenced its flight test programme in the early spring of 1935. Unfortunately, during one of the first test flights the pilot lost control at low altitude, the aircraft crashing and being written off. A second prototype, the **Ar 80 V2** (D-ILOH), was awaiting delivery of a Jumo 210 engine, for which the fighter had been designed, but the loss of the first prototype necessitated the hurried completion of the Ar 80 V2 with a Rolls-Royce Kestrel V which, rated at 518 kW (695 hp) for take-off, drove a two-bladed fixed-pitch wooden airscrew.

Trials with the Kestrel-engined Ar 80 V2 prototype were distinctly disappointing. Structural weight was excessive, empty weight at 1630 kg (3,593 lb) being 16 per cent greater than had been anticipated, and at the normal loaded weight of 2100 kg (4,630 lb) the fighter was underpowered. Furthermore, drag was appreciably higher than calculated, with the result that maximum speed was barely 410 km/h (255 mph) at 4000 m (13,120 ft). Early in 1936, the Ar 80 V2 was re-engined with a Junkers Jumo 210C, but this resulted in only a marginal improvement in altitude performance, low-altitude performance and initial climb proving inferior. Arado estimated that the provision of a constant-speed airscrew in place of the fixed-pitch unit would boost maximum speed to 425 km/h (264 mph) at 4000 m (13,120 ft), but the Ar 80 V2 was evaluated at the test centres at Travemünde and at Rechlin and, as a result of these trials, Arado was informed that no good purpose could be served by the further development of the design.

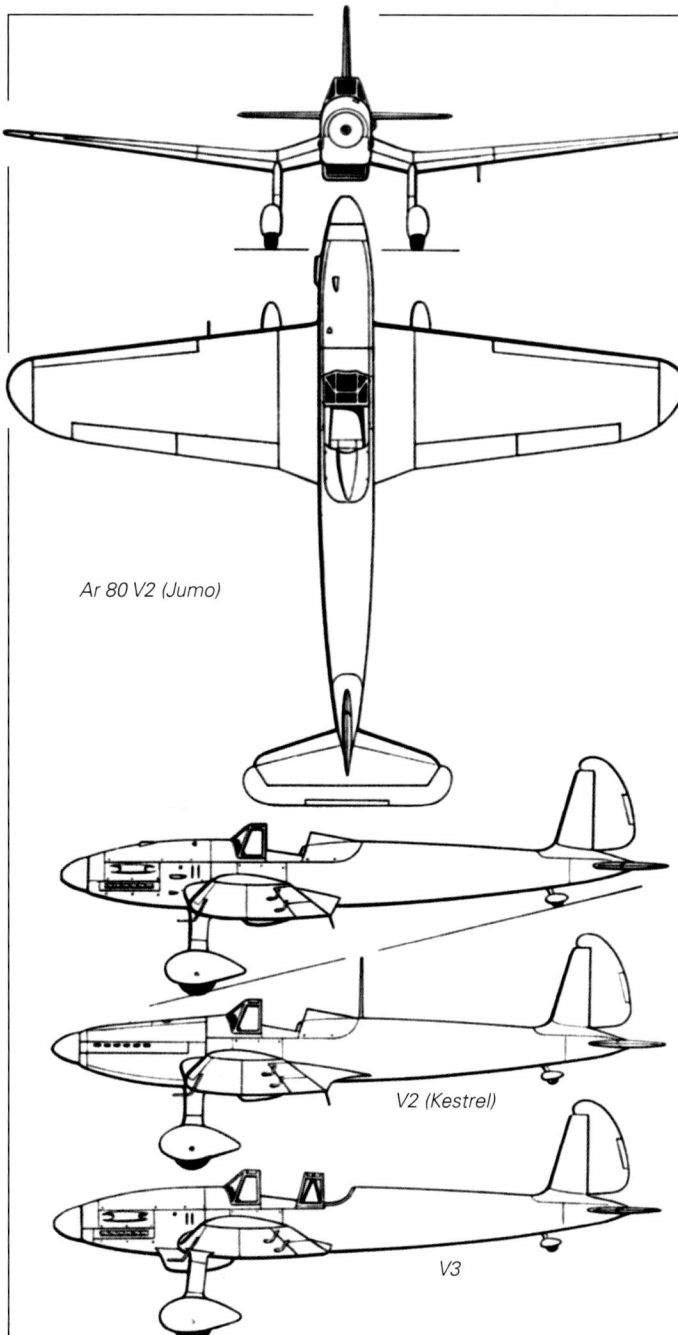

Ar 80 V2 (Jumo)

V2 (Kestrel)

V3

By this time, the construction of a third prototype, the **Ar 80 V3** (D-IPBN), had been completed. In an effort to reduce structural weight, the inverted gull wing was abandoned in favour of a simpler wing with constant dihedral from root to tip. The Ar 80 V3 was powered by the Jumo 210C, and was the first prototype to be equipped with a constant-speed airscrew.

The **Ar 80 V4** and **Ar 80 V5** were basically similar to each other, and differed from their predecessors in having an enclosed cockpit and the powerplant of one Jumo 210Ea engine with a fuel-injection system rather than a conventional carburation system. The Ar 80 V4 and Ar 80 V5 underwent extensive tests before being returned to the manufacturer for use by the defensive flight operated by the company test pilots for the protection of the Arado factory at Warnemünde.

A development of the last two prototypes with the Jumo 210Ea engine and retractable main landing gear units was proposed as a production model, but all work on this variant was terminated upon the selection of the Bf 109 to meet the Luftwaffe's needs for a monoplane fighter.

The Ar 80 V3 third prototype, *D-IPBN*, was completed with a simple wing of moderate dihedral. It was subsequently modified with a second seat for an observer to monitor the behaviour of Fowler flaps fitted to the aircraft in a test installation. The Fowler flaps were intended for use in more advanced designs, such as the Ar 198 and Ar 240. In two-seat form the Ar 80 V3 flew from 1938 onwards.

Arado 80 V2 specification
(data relates to the Jumo-engined aircraft)
Type: single-seat fighter
Powerplant: one Junkers Jumo 210C 12-cylinder liquid-cooled engine rated at 447 kW (600 hp) for take-off and 477 kW (640 hp) at 2697 m (8,850 ft)
Performance: maximum speed 349 km/h (217 mph) at sea level, 415 km/h (258 mph) at 2697 m (8,850 ft); initial climb rate 570 m (1,870 ft) per minute; time to 1000 m (3,280 ft) 1.85 minutes; time to 5000 m (16,405 ft) 7.4 minutes; time to 6000 m (19,685 ft) 9.5 minutes; service ceiling 10000 m (32,800 ft); maximum range 800 km (497 miles)
Weights: (without armament) empty 1642 kg (3,620 lb); normal loaded 2125 kg (4,684 lb)
Dimensions: wingspan 10.88 m (35 ft 8½ in); length 10.30 m (33 ft 9½ in); height 2.65 m (8 ft 8⅓ in); wing area 21.00 m² (226 sq ft)
Armament: (proposed) two 7.9-mm (0.31-in) MG 17 machine-guns

Arado Ar 81

The fledgling Luftwaffe's Sturzkampfflugzeug, or dive-bomber, programme was afforded high priority, and Arado developed its Ar 81 as a competitor to the Junkers Ju 87. Although the Arado design was superior to the Ju 87 in several key respects, its antiquated biplane configuration counted against it.

Among the most important of the new weapons forged to aid the rebirth of German military power with the creation of the Third Reich was the Sturzkampfflugzeug – the dive-bomber. Desultory interest in the potentialities of this type of warplane had been evinced in Germany from the earliest days of the embryo Luftwaffe, but it was the ardent support for the dive-bomber from the internationally-famous pilot Ernst Udet that led to the much effort placed behind the development of this type of combat aircraft in Germany.

The Sturzbomber-Programm had been initiated by the C-Amt in 1933, two stages being envisaged. The first of them, referred to as the Sofort-Programm (Immediate Programme), called for the development in the least possible time of a relatively conventional biplane as interim equipment for the planned Stukagruppen, while the next phase demanded an appreciably more advanced warplane accommodating two crew members and possessing a performance more closely comparable with those of contemporary fighters.

The first prototype of the Arado dive-bomber, the Ar 81 V1, featured marked dihedral on the horizontal tail surfaces. The tailplane also carried oval endplate vertical surfaces.

In the event, this second phase specification was not issued to the potential participants in the industry until January 1935, the Arado Flugzeugwerke being one of three manufacturers invited to compete. The specification was translated in widely varying fashion by the three competitors, and the Arado contender, the Ar 81, was somewhat surprisingly of biplane configuration. Of all-metal construction, the **Ar 81** was a single-bay staggered equi-span biplane with inclined N-type interplane struts and a fixed undercarriage. The two crew members were seated in tandem, the pilot being enclosed by

Arado Ar 81

a sliding canopy and the gunner being partly enclosed by a fixed transparent canopy. Proposed armament comprised one fixed forward-firing 7.9-mm (0.31-in) MG 17 machine-gun in the forward fuselage and an MG 15 of similar calibre on a flexible mounting in the rear cockpit, and it was intended that a single 250-kg (551-lb) would be attached to a crutch beneath the fuselage, this having swing links to lower and swing the bomb forward on release to ensure clearance of the airscrew arc.

Early trials

Powered by a Jumo 210C engine driving a three-blade fixed-pitch airscrew, the first prototype, the **Ar 81 V1** (D-UJOX), began flight trials late in 1935. An extremely sturdy aircraft despite a relatively light structure, the Ar 81 V1 featured a slim, boom-like rear fuselage that terminated in a twin fin-and-rudder tail assembly, which was, in itself, a noteworthy departure from previous Arado practice. Initial trials revealed some instability and, in consequence, the second prototype, the **Ar 81 V2** (D-UPAR), completed shortly after the first aircraft, embodied a revised tail assembly.

Trials at the Erprobungsstelle at Rechlin revealed the fact that the instability suffered by the Ar 81 V1 had not been entirely rectified, and therefore the Arado team redesigned the rear fuselage and tail assembly, introducing the modifications on the third prototype, the **Ar 81 V3** (D-UDEX). Side area aft was increased by adopting a deeper, more orthodox rear fuselage, while the twin fin-and-rudder assembly was supplanted by a single fin-and-rudder assembly of typical Arado design. The Jumo 210Ca engine of the Ar 81 V3 drove a two-blade variable-pitch airscrew, and this aircraft joined the flight test programme in the late spring of 1936. The Ar 81 V3 proved eminently satisfactory. Capable of attaining 600 km/h (373 mph) in a terminal velocity dive,

The Ar 81 V2 featured a revised tail assembly, dihedral being eliminated from the tailplane, which was now pylon-mounted above the rear fuselage and braced by inverted Vee-struts.

it was more lightly loaded than its principal competitor, the Ju 87, and its performance was superior in most respects. However, the biplane configuration of the Ar 81 was considered retrogressive and motivated against the adoption of the Arado contender. In any case, by the time the Ar 81 V3 was available for official evaluation, the decision in principle to adopt the Junkers dive-bomber had already been taken.

Arado Ar 81 V3 specification
Type: two-seat dive-bomber
Powerplant: one Junkers Jumo 210Ca 12-cylinder liquid-cooled engine rated at 447 kW (600 hp) for take-off and 477 kW (640 hp) at 2700 m (8,860 ft)
Performance: maximum speed 300 km/h (186 mph) at sea level, 344 km/h (214 mph) at 4000 m (13,120 ft); climb to 4000 m in 11 minutes; service ceiling 7698 m (25,256 ft); range 693 km (430 miles) at 4000 m
Weights: empty 1925 kg (4,244 lb); loaded 3070 kg (6,768 lb)
Dimensions: wingspan 11.00 m (36 ft 0¾ in); length 11.50 m (37 ft 8¾ in); height 3.60 m (11 ft 10 in); wing area 35.60 m² (383.2 sq ft)
Armament: (proposed) one fixed forward-firing 7.9-mm (0.31-in) MG 17 machine-gun and one 7.9-mm MG 15 machine-gun on flexible mounting in rear cockpit. (Offensive) one 250-kg (551-lb) bomb mounted externally

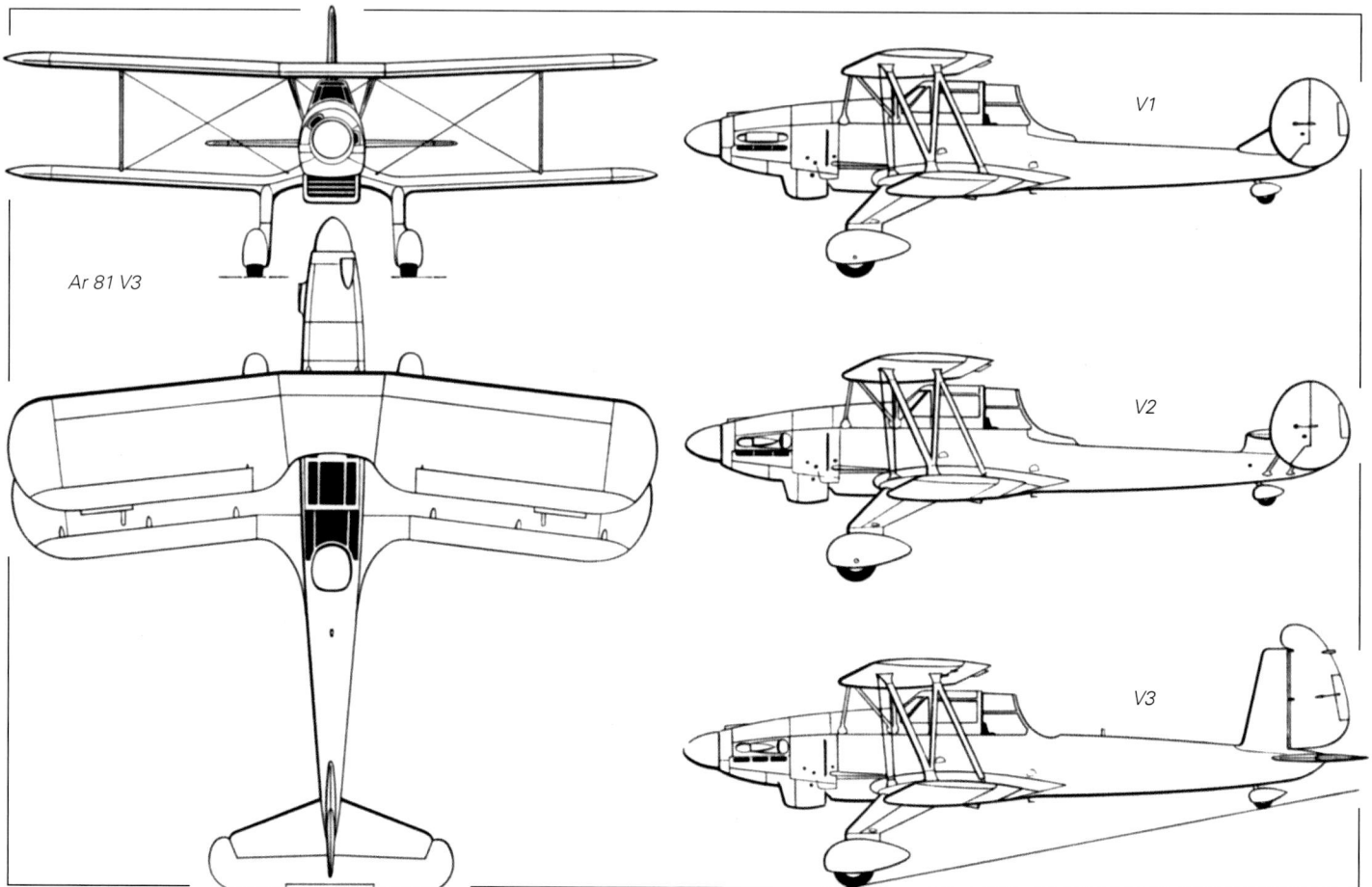

Ar 81 V3

V1

V2

V3

Arado Ar 95

The all-metal Arado Ar 95 was intended to serve in the coastal patrol, reconnaissance and light attack roles, operating from aircraft-carriers and from floats. First flown in 1937, the carrier-based version was rejected, although floatplane versions were tested by the Luftwaffe in Spain and saw limited service in World War II.

By the spring of 1935, the Construction Office of the Oberkommando der Marine, the Navy's High Command, had evolved a workable design for an aircraft-carrier, funds for which were to be included in the 1936 budget. Construction was to be assigned to the Deutsche Werke Kiel, but prior to work on the carrier commencing, the Arado Flugzeugwerke was instructed to initiate work on a torpedo-bomber/reconnaissance aircraft for shipboard use. The aircraft was intended to operate from both wheels and floats, and Dipl.-Ing. Walter Blume and his team began work on what was to be designated the **Ar 95**.

The first prototype, the **Ar 95 V1** (D-OLUO), was fitted with twin light metal floats and powered by a BMW 132 nine-cylinder air-cooled radial engine. Flown for the first time in the autumn of 1936, the Ar 95 V1 was quickly joined by the **Ar 95 V2** (D-OHEO), powered by a 12-cylinder liquid-cooled Junkers Jumo 210 Ca engine rated at 447 kW (600 hp) for take-off as compared with 630 kW (845 hp) for the BMW 132. Subsequently, the Ar 95 V2 was also re-engined with the BMW 132. Both the V1 and V2 were arranged as two-seaters, but the third prototype, the **Ar 95 V3** (D-ODGX), which joined the test programme early in 1937, was a three-seater, as was also the **Ar 95 V5** (D-OHGV), both being intended as production prototypes for the **Ar 95A** float seaplane. The **Ar 95 V4** featured a wheel undercarriage with large fairings enclosing the main members, this being the prototype for the **Ar 95B**.

Obsolesence

Trials with the five Ar 95 prototypes revealed the fact that this type fell short of the performance specified, and it was obvious that the Ar 95B would be obsolescent by the time the German Navy's first carrier was commissioned. A new specification was therefore issued in the spring of 1937, this eventually resulting in the Arado Ar 195 and the Fieseler Fi 167. In the meantime, Arado had launched a pre-production series of **Ar 95A-0** floatplanes, and had begun to solicit orders from abroad with the full backing of the RLM. The six Ar 95A-0 floatplanes were three-seaters powered by the BMW 132Dc radial rated at 656 kW (880 hp) and driving a three-blade controllable-pitch Hamilton Standard airscrew. Defensive armament comprised one fixed forward-firing 7.9-mm

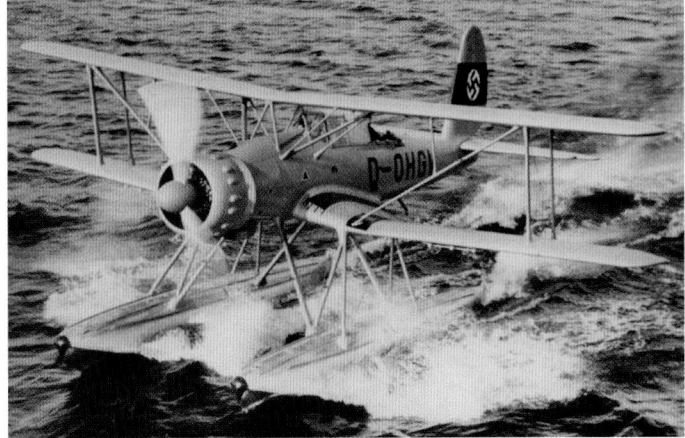

A total of five Ar 95 prototypes was completed, including two three-seaters, and the V4 that differed in being fitted with wheeled undercarriage. This is the V5, the second production prototype for the Ar 95A, limited production of which began in 1938.

(0.31-in) MG 17 with 500 rounds, and an MG 15 of similar calibre on a flexible mounting in the rear cockpit with eight 75-round drums.

All six Ar 95A-0 pre-production floatplanes were delivered to the Condor Legion in 1938, equipping what was known as Grupo 64 at Pollensa, Majorca, for reconnaissance and anti-shipping sorties. In the event, Grupo 64 undertook relatively few sorties, being disbanded in April 1939 when three of the Ar 95A-0s were transferred to the Spanish Nationalist forces, these being destined to remain in Spanish service until 1948. Limited production of the two-seat

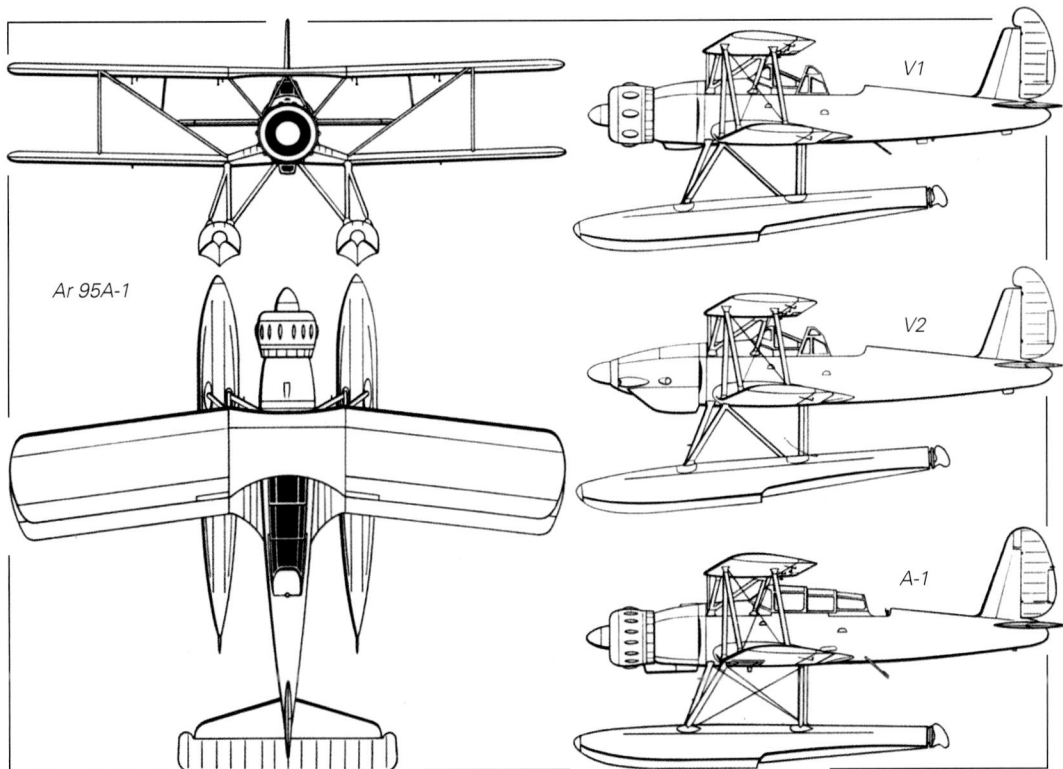

Arado Ar 95

Armed with light bombs, this Arado Ar 95A-1 of the 3rd Staffel of Seeaufklärungsgruppe 125 (3./SAGr. 125) operated in the Baltic in mid-1941 under the overall control of the Fliegerführer Ostsee. The Luftwaffe took these aircraft from an order originally destined for Turkey. Note that only a small portion of the prescribed yellow theatre fuselage band has been applied on the spine.

With a torpedo between its twin floats, D-ODGX was the first three-seat Ar 95 prototype. The V3 and V5 (D-OHGV) were built to a similar standard to serve as production prototypes for the Ar 95A float seaplane.

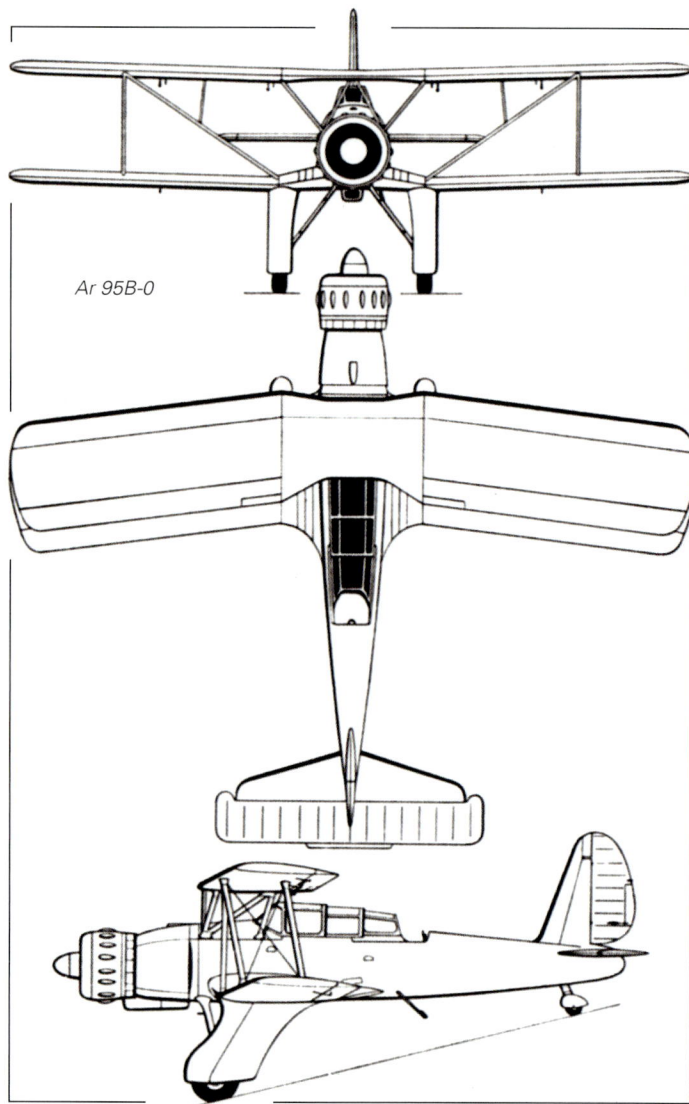

Ar 95B-0

Ar 95A-1 had begun in 1938, an order being obtained from Chile for the supply of three such floatplanes along with three Ar 95B landplanes, this order being fulfilled in 1939. Having originally been ordered by Turkey, an additional batch of Ar 95A-1s was delivered in 1939-40 to the Luftwaffe, to equip 3./SAGr. 125. The unit had a strength of eight aircraft, the other two Staffeln of the Gruppe being equipped with He 60s and He 114s, respectively.

In combat

When the invasion of the Soviet Union began on 22 June 1941, 3./SAGr. 125 was in the Baltic with its Ar 95A-1s under the Fliegerführer Ostsee. The unit followed the German advance across Latvia and Estonia, and, in October 1941, participated in the invasion of the Moon and Dägo islands off the Estonian coast. Later the unit was transferred to Finland for a brief period and, at the end of 1941, was transferred to Constanza, Romania, relinquishing its Ar 95A-1s in favour of Blohm und Voss BV 138 flying boats. The Ar 95A-1s were subsequently included on the strength of SAGr. 127, all three Staffeln initially operating a mixture of He 60s and the Arado floatplanes in the Gulf of Finland under Luftflotte 1.

Arado Ar 95A-1 specification
Type: two-seat torpedo-bomber and reconnaissance foatplane
Powerplant: one BMW 132Dc nine-cylinder radial air-cooled engine rated at 656 kW (880 hp) for take-off and 634 kW (850 hp) at 2500 m (8,200 ft)
Performance: maximum speed 275 km/h (171 mph) at sea level, 300 km/h (187 mph) at 3000 m (9,840 ft); maximum range 1094 km (680 miles); climb to 1000 m (3,280 ft) in 2.3 minutes; service ceiling 7300 m (23,950 ft)
Weights: empty 2535 kg (5,588 lb); loaded 3558 kg (7,843 lb)
Dimensions: wingspan 12.50 m (41 ft 0 in); length 11.10 m (36 ft 5 in); height 5.20 m (17 ft 0¾ in); wing area 45.38 m² (488.5 sq ft)
Armament: (defensive) one fixed forward-firing 7.9-mm (0.31-in) MG 17 machine-gun with 500 rounds and one 7.9-mm MG 15 machine-gun on flexible mounting with 600 rounds. (Offensive) one 700-kg (1,540-lb) torpedo or one 375-kg (827-lb) bomb beneath the fuselage plus six 50-kg (110-lb) bombs beneath the wings

This Ar 95A-1 (Werk Nr 952350) of 3./SAGr 125 operated in the Baltic in 1941. The overall finish appears very glossy, suggesting the aircraft has had additional clear lacquer or polish applied to give better protection in the harsh environment.

Arado Ar 96

Designed by Dipl.-Ing. Walter Blume, the Arado Ar 96 was the Luftwaffe's standard advanced trainer during World War II. The aircraft appeared in two main production versions: the initial Ar 96A and the re-engined Ar 96B with a longer fuselage for increased fuel capacity. Production was also undertaken in Czechoslovakia.

With a total production run of more than 11,500 aircraft by the end of World War II, the **Arado Ar 96** was the Luftwaffe's standard advanced flying trainer. The type was schemed as a cantilever low-wing monoplane of stressed-skin construction with fully enclosed tandem accommodation for the pupil and instructor. Designed by Dipl.-Ing. Walter Blume, the Ar 96 made its maiden flight during 1938 in the form of the **Ar 96 V1** prototype, which was powered by the 179-kW (240-hp) Argus As 10C inverted-Vee engine. It initially had outward-retracting main landing gear legs, soon replaced by inward-retracting units for greater wheel track and therefore improved stability on the ground.

The aircraft successfully completed its RLM trials, paving the way for an order for a modest number of **Ar 96A-1** initial production aircraft that were delivered in 1939 with the As 10C engine. By this time it was clear that the basic design could profitably handle a considerably higher-rated engine, so the main production model, the **Ar 96B**, was ordered in 1940 with the 347-kW (465-hp) Argus As 410A-1 inverted-Vee engine driving a two-blade propeller. Its lengthened fuselage allowed an increase in the fuel tankage.

There were several sub-variants of the Ar 96B model, known types being the **Ar 96B-1** unarmed pilot trainer, **Ar 96B-2** with a fixed forward-firing machine-gun, **Ar 96B-5** pilot gunnery trainer, and **Ar 96B-7** with provision for the external carriage of bombs in the ground-attack and dive-bomber training roles. There was also a gunner training model, probably produced in small numbers by conversion, with a trainable rearward-firing machine-gun in the modified rear of the two-seat cockpit.

Foreign manufacture

Arado itself built only a few Ar 96B aircraft, the majority being completed by a Junkers subsidiary, Ago Flugzeugwerke, and, from mid-1941, by the Czech company Avia which was joined in the programme by the Prague-based Letov organisation in 1944. Czech production continued until 1948, aircraft being supplied to the Czech air force under the designation **Avia C.2B-1**.

The **Ar 96C**, of which just one pre-production batch was built, was a development of the Ar 96B. It had the 358-kW (480-hp) Argus As 410C engine and a small transparency in the lower fuselage so that the type could be used in the bomber training role. A development of the Ar 96 that failed to reach fruition (the Ar 396 being preferred) was the **Ar 296**, with the 447.5-kW (600-hp) Argus As 411 inverted-Vee engine.

Shown here in the form of the second of four prototypes, the Ar 96 proved to be an exceptionally versatile trainer in service. The initial-production Ar 96A-1 was preceded by a batch of six pre-series Ar 96A-0 aircraft.

Arado Ar 96B-2 specification
Type: two-seat advanced flying trainer
Powerplant: one Argus As 410A-1 inverted-Vee engine rated at 347 kW (465 hp)
Performance: maximum speed 330 km/h (205 mph) at sea level; cruising speed 295 km/h (183 mph) at optimum altitude; initial climb rate 305 m (1,000 ft) per minute; service ceiling 7100 m (23,295 ft); range 990 km (615 miles)
Weights: empty 1295 kg (2,854 lb); maximum take-off 1700 kg (3,748 lb)
Dimensions: wingspan 11.00 m (36 ft 1 in); length 9.10 m (29 ft 10¼ in); height 2.60 m (8 ft 6⅓ in), wing area 17.10 m² (184.07 sq ft)
Armament: one 7.9-mm (0.31-in) fixed forward-firing machine-gun

Above: Built to the extent of 11,546 examples, the Ar 96 represented the backbone of Luftwaffe pilot training throughout World War II. In addition to Luftwaffe use, the aircraft was employed during the war by Bulgaria, Hungary and Slovakia.

The Ar 96 was one of the unsung heroes of the Luftwaffe, training countless thousands of aircrew. The type's good performance provided a good stepping stone between the basic trainers and the high-performance front-line equipment.

Arado Ar 195

One of two competing designs intended to provide Germany's new aircraft-carrier with a multi-purpose torpedo-bomber and reconnaissance aircraft, the Arado Ar 195 was afflicted by drag-related performance deficiencies and lost out to the rival Fiesler Fi 167.

On 28 December 1936, the keel of 'Carrier A' was laid on Slip Number One at the Deutsche Werke Kiel, and within a few weeks the Technisches Amt of the Reichsluftfahrtministerium had evolved a specification for a two-seat multi-purpose aircraft intended to operate from the new vessel. Issued to Arado and Fieseler, the specification called for an all-metal biplane with folding wings and stressed for diving attacks at speeds up to 600 km/h (373 mph). It had to be capable of carrying a single torpedo or a minimum bombload of 500 kg (1,100 lb) at maximum and cruising speeds of at least 300 and 250 km/h (186 and 155 mph) respectively, and it had to possess a range of not less than 1000 km (620 miles). Design accent was to be placed on maximum crew visibility; the undercarriage had to be jettisonable for emergency ditching, and provision had to be made for flotation equipment.

Both the Arado and Fieseler companies submitted propos-

Three examples of the disappointing Ar 195 were completed (the Ar 195 V1 is illustrated). The type was proposed to equip the aircraft-carrier Graf Zeppelin, *the keel of which was laid on 28 December 1936.*

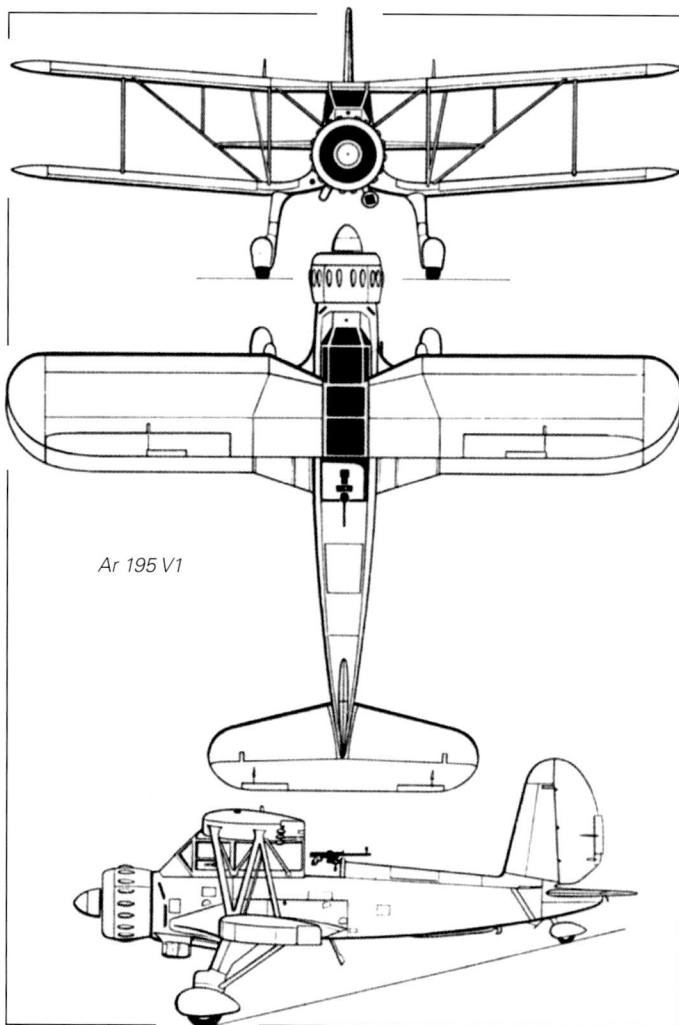

als aimed at meeting the requirements of the specification, and three prototypes were ordered from each company, the projects being allocated the designations **Ar 195** and Fi 167, respectively. Arado's offering was an equi-span, single-bay biplane with aft-folding wings. The fuselage was a welded steel-tube structure covered forward and along the upper decking by detachable light metal panels, the remainder being fabric-skinned, and the two-spar wings were of metal construction with light metal skinning. Power was provided by a BMW 132M nine-cylinder radial rated at 619 kW (830 hp) for take-off, and the first prototype, the **Ar 195 V1** (D-OCLN) began flight trials in the summer of 1938.

Limited performance

Arado devoted considerable attention to the problem of minimising structural weight, and the empty weight of the Ar 195 was substantially less than that of the earlier Ar 95B despite a major increase in fixed equipment weight. Nevertheless, initial trials quickly revealed the fact that drag had been seriously miscalculated, and that performance fell appreciably below that of the earlier warplane, failing to attain the minimum figures set by the official specification. On the other hand, the competitive Fi 167 exceeded the official requirements in every respect. The two additional prototypes were completed with minor refinements, and the **Ar 195 V3** (D-ODSO) was evaluated at the E-Stelle Rechlin, but the drag problem was too fundamental for the Arado team to effect any major improvement in performance without substantial redesign, and further development was abandoned.

Ar 195 V1

Arado Ar 195 V3 specification
Type: two-seat shipboard torpedo-bomber and reconnaissance aircraft
Powerplant: one BMW 132M nine-cylinder radial air-cooled engine rated at 619 kW (830 hp) for take-off
Performance: maximum speed 290 km/h (180 mph); maximum cruising speed 250 km/h (155 mph); climb to 4000 m (13,125 ft) in 14 minutes; service ceiling 6000 m (19,685 ft); maximum range 650 km (404 miles)
Weights: empty 2143 kg (4,275 lb); loaded 3670 kg (8,091 lb)
Dimensions: wingspan 12.50 m (41 ft 0 in); length 10.50 m (34 ft 5⅓ in); height 3.00 (11 ft 9¾ in); wing area 46.00 m² (495.14 sq ft)
Armament: (proposed) one fixed forward-firing 7.9-mm (0.31-in) MG 17 machine-gun with 500 rounds and one 7.9-mm MG 15 machine-gun on flexible mounting in rear cockpit with 600 rounds, plus one 700-kg (1,540-lb) torpedo, one 500-kg (1,102-lb) bomb, or one 250-kg (551-lb) SC 250 bomb plus four 50-kg (110-lb) SC 50 bombs

Arado Ar 196

Although it exerted only a minor influence on World War II, the Arado Ar 196 was nevertheless an important type. Evolving through a number of float configurations, the aircraft entered service in summer 1939 as a replacement for the venerable Heinkel He 60, remaining the 'eyes of the Kriegsmarine' throughout the war.

During the summer of 1936, shortly after preliminary evaluation trials with the Heinkel He 114 V1 and V2 had revealed the inadequacy of this design in its intended role as a successor to the elderly He 60 on the catapults of the surface vessels of the Kriegsmarine, the Technisches Amt of the RLM prepared a specification for yet another two-seat catapult floatplane. The specification called for the use of the BMW 132K nine-cylinder radial engine, and demanded the design of both single and twin main float arrangements, being issued to the Arado and Focke-Wulf companies in the autumn of 1936.

The biplane configuration was considered by the conventionalists to be obligatory for the small floatplane, and Dipl.-Ing. Kurt Tank of Focke-Wulf chose the conservative approach in attempting to fulfil the requirement, the Fw 62 being an orthodox biplane. However, the Arado team, not previously noteworthy for its adventurism, elected to adopt a monoplane configuration for its competing design, the **Ar 196**. In the preliminary analysis of the contenders, the latter found favour with the Technisches Amt and, accordingly, the Arado Flugzeugwerke was the recipient of an order for four prototypes, the Focke-Wulf Fw 62 being relegated to the position of a back-up programme, with only two prototypes being ordered.

Initial prototypes

The first two prototypes of the Arado design, the **Ar 196 V1** (Werk Nr 2589, D-IEHK) and **V2** (Werk Nr 2590, D-IHQI), were completed and flown during the summer of 1937. They were twin-float A-series aircraft, while the third and fourth prototypes, the **Ar 196 V3** (Werk Nr 2591, D-ILRE) and **V4** (Werk Nr 2592, D-OVMB) were B-series aircraft, each having a single central float with outrigger stabilising floats.

The prototypes were powered by the BMW 132Dc rated

The Ar 196 is perhaps best remembered as a catapult-launched spotter for German warships, but it also saw important service on coastal patrols. This aircraft was allocated to Bordfliegerstaffel 1./196, the unit that provided shipborne detachments.

at 656 kW (880 hp) for take-off and driving a two-bladed controllable-pitch airscrew. The Ar 196 V1 was initially flown with twin exhaust pipes that extended beneath the port side of the forward fuselage. They were later reduced in length and divided to port and starboard, an arrangement standardised for subsequent aircraft. Apart from some redesign of the vertical tail surfaces, the horn-balancing of the rudder being eliminated, and some modification of the water rudders, the Ar 196 V2 was similar to its predecessor, while the Ar 196 V3 differed solely in the arrangement of its float undercarriage. The Ar 196 V4 featured redesigned, low-drag stabilising floats with revised, lighter bracing, the inclined V-struts from the floats to one-third span being discarded. It also mounted fixed forward-firing armament, although this

A pleasant machine to fly, the Arado Ar 196A afforded excellent fields of vision. The type had superb water and flight handling characteristics.

Arado Ar 196

The Ar 196 V3 (illustrated) and V4 tested the single main float arrangement. Although this and the twin-float arrangement had many advantages, the water handling advantage of the twin system was deemed to be more important than the better characteristics of the single when landing on choppy water.

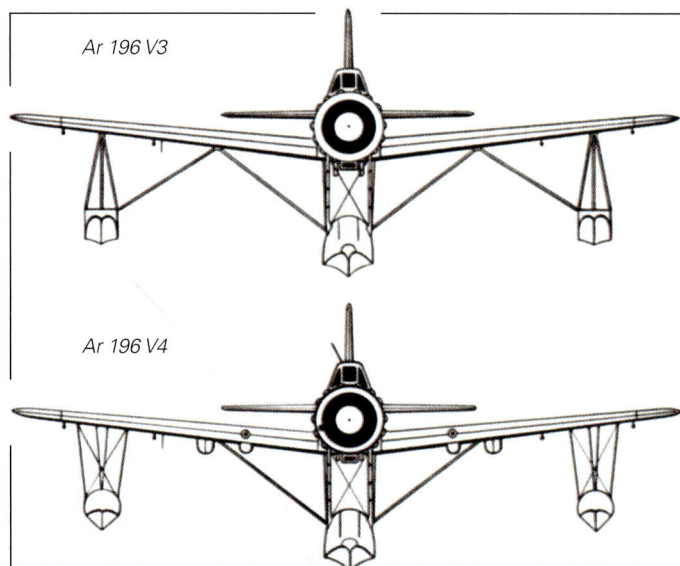

The first B-series prototype, the Ar 196 V3 D-ILRE, was joined by the second B-series prototype and together underwent comparison trials at Travemünde with the A-series twin-float prototypes.

had not been called for by the specification. It comprised two wing-mounted 20-mm MG FF cannon with 60 r.p.g., a 7.9-mm (0.31-in) MG 17 machine-gun in the starboard side of the forward fuselage with 500 rounds, and a container beneath each wing for a single 50-kg (110-lb) SC 50 bomb.

All four prototypes were tested at Travemünde where it was anticipated that a final choice would be made between the alternative float arrangements. The hydrodynamic characteristics of the floats had been thoroughly evaluated by the Aerodynamischen Versuchsanstalt Göttingen during August 1937, but neither these tests nor the trials that followed at Travemünde resulted in a clear-cut choice of float arrangement. There was little to choose between twin floats or single central float with outrigger floats in so far as weight or drag were concerned. The central float was considered preferable for landing on choppy water as the shocks were absorbed by the fuselage structure, whereas, with the twin-float arrangement, the shocks were for the most part transmitted directly to the wing. However, the twin floats offered greater stability during high-speed taxiing and taking-off, the outboard stabilising floats evincing some tendency to 'dip', with the result that, under certain conditions, the take-off run became somewhat erratic.

As no definite conclusion could be reached, Arado received instructions to proceed with preparations for a pre-production quantity of twin-float A-series aircraft, and, simultaneously, build a third B-series prototype for further trials of the central float arrangement at Travemünde. The third B-series prototype, the **Ar 196 V5** (Werk Nr 0090,

D-IPOB), was completed in the autumn of 1938. In the meantime, Arado had undertaken modifications to the Ar 196 V1 with the object of employing this aircraft for the establishment of a series of international float seaplane records. An uprated BMW 132K engine was installed, driving a three-blade variable-pitch airscrew; the cockpit canopy was refined, the hood being lowered and the rear cockpit being completely enclosed, and various other minor refinements were introduced, but at the last moment the RLM instructed Arado to abandon its record plans on the grounds of security.

Pre-production aircraft

The pre-production contract called for 10 **Ar 196A-0** floatplanes (Werk Nummern 0091-0100) powered by the BMW 132K rated at 716 kW (960 hp) for take-off, 723 kW (970 hp) at 450 m (1,480 ft), and offering a maximum cruise power of 559 kW (750 hp) at 1500 m (4,900 ft). The structure of the floatplane was strictly conventional, a rectangular-section steel-tube fuselage being faired to an oval by former ribs and covered forward by a stressed metal skin and aft by fabric, the wing being a two-spar all-metal structure with metal skinning, all movable control surfaces being fabric covered. The single-step hydronalium floats were each divided into seven watertight compartments that housed 300 litres (66 Imp gal) of fuel. Each float could also house emergency ammunition and food containers. No catapult points were provided, and armament was restricted to a single

Ar 196 V3

Ar 196 V4

In many ways the 'eyes of the Kriegsmarine' for coastal and shipborne purposes, the Ar 196 had superb water- and flight-handling characteristics. During its early career its heavy armament made it the scourge of lumbering Allied maritime patrol aircraft, although this situation was steadily reversed as the war progressed.

In the summer of 1939 the Arado Ar 196A-1 entered service as a ship-borne reconnaissance floatplane with the capital ships of the Kriegsmarine. Based initially at Wilhelmshaven and Kiel-Holtenau, the Bordfliegerstaffeln 1./196 and 5./196 acted as parent units for the Arado Ar 196s issued first to the pocket-battleship Admiral Graf Spee, and later to the Lützow, the Scharnhorst and Gneisenau, and others, to replace the ageing Heinkel He 60 aircraft.

7.9-mm MG 15 machine-gun on an Arado-designed flexible mounting in the rear cockpit with 525 rounds of ammunition, and racks for two 50-kg (110-lb) SC 50 bombs. Empty and loaded weights were 2014 kg (4,440 lb) and 2925 kg (6,448 lb), respectively.

The first Ar 196A-0 left the assembly line in November 1938 and, during the first weeks of 1939, the pre-production aircraft were intensively evaluated, the results being extremely favourable, and the only modifications requested being confined to some local structural strengthening and the repositioning of certain items of equipment.

The requested modifications were embodied in the initial production version, the **Ar 196A-1**, 20 examples of which had been ordered with deliveries commencing in June 1939. Stressed for catapult launching and equipped with catapult spools, the Ar 196A-1 began to supplant the He 60 biplane during the summer with the two shipboard units under Kriegsmarine control. Based at Wilhelmshaven and Kiel-Holtenau, these became Bordfliegerstaffeln 1./196 and 5./196. The Staffeln deployed their aircraft aboard the major surface vessels of the Kriegsmarine, among the first warships to receive the Ar 196A-1 being the *Admiral Graf Spee* that had left Germany for the Atlantic commerce routes by mid-August 1939. Other vessels to replace their He 60s with the Ar 196A-1 during the weeks immediately prior to and following the outbreak of hostilities were *Scharnhorst*, *Gneisenau*, *Deutschland* (renamed *Lützow* in February 1940), *Admiral Scheer*, and *Prinz Eugen*.

Forward-firing armament

With the completion of the 20 Ar 196A-1s, production at Warnemünde switched to the **Ar 196A-2**, deliveries of which began in November 1939. Twenty Ar 196A-1s had left the assembly line by the end of 1939, but inclement weather seriously delayed factory flight testing, and only six of the aircraft had been taken on charge. With empty and loaded weights increased from the 2044 and 2955 kg (4,506 and 6,514 lb) of the Ar 196A-1 to 2075 and 3175 kg (4,574 and 7,000 lb), respectively, the Ar 196A-2 was the first production model to be fitted with

Above and right: Ar 196A-1s were delivered for the shipborne patrol mission, and the 20 such floatplanes were followed from November 1939 by the Ar 196A-2 (illustrated). Intended for the coastal patrol mission, they were the first aircraft to feature forward-firing cannon armament for nuisance attacks against surface vessels. The cannon also gave the Ar 196 a measure of capability against any Allied maritime patrol aircraft it encountered.

Arado Ar 196

Floats

The Arado Ar 196A was fitted with braced twin floats, which offered greater stability than the single main float and stabiliser arrangement of the Ar 196B-0 and the second pair of prototypes. The single float arrangement was better for landing on choppy water, since the shocks were transmitted to the fuselage rather than the wings, which were less able to absorb them. It had the disadvantage of being less stable on the water, the outboard stabiliser floats sometimes having a tendency to dip under the water. There was little to choose between the two configurations in terms of weight, drag, complexity and cost. The unbuilt Ar 196C, with its higher all-up weight, used larger floats, and they were tested during 1941 before development work on the new version was cancelled.

Wing

The Arado Ar 196 had a broad-chord wing with an unswept leading edge and slight taper on the trailing edge. The aircraft had wide-span ailerons outboard, with relatively small flaps inboard. All control surfaces were fabric covered, the rest of the wing being a metal-skinned two-spar structure. Dihedral improved stability in roll.

Powerplant

The Ar 196 prototypes were powered by a 656-kW (880-hp) BMW 132Dc radial, driving a two-bladed variable pitch propeller. The pre-production Ar 196A-0 changed to the 716-kW (960-hp) BMW 132K that remained the standard powerplant for all subsequent variants. A nine-cylinder air-cooled radial, the BMW 132K drove a three-bladed variable pitch propeller on all production versions of the aircraft. The bulbous, broad-chord cowling had pairs of bumps over each cylinder head.

Seeaufklärungsgruppe 125

SAGr. 125 had a staff flight (Stab) and three Staffeln, of which only the staff flight and 2. Staffel operated the Ar 196. Both were based in Romania from November 1941, before 2. Staffel moved to Athens and then Souda Bay in Crete. In December 1943 2./SAGr. 125 was redesignated as 4./SAGr. 126, joining the all-Arado Seeaufklärungsgruppe 126 and remaining in Crete until it returned to Germany in September 1944. Meanwhile, a new 2./SAGr. 125 was formed at Sevastopol on the BV 138, so that by early 1944 all units of this Gruppe had standardised on the Blohm und Voss flying-boat.

Defensive guns
The MG 81Z installation, mounted in the rear cockpit of the Ar 196A-5, paired two MG 81 7.9-mm (0.31-in) machine-guns on a single mount, with a maximum load of 2,000 rounds.

Arado Ar 196A-5

2./SAGr. 125, Eastern Mediterranean, 1943

The definitive Ar 196A-5 featured improved radio equipment and improved defensive armament in the form of the MG 81Z installation. Fixed forward-firing armament remained two 20-mm MG FF cannon in the wings and one MG 17 7.9-mm (0.31-in) machine-gun in the starboard cowling. In the anti-shipping role the Ar 196 had underwing racks for a pair of SC 50 bombs. This Ar 196A-5 served with 2./ Seeaufklärungsgruppe (SAGr.) 125 in the eastern Mediterranean and Aegean Seas during 1943, alongside the Blohm und Voss BV 138. The unit later became 4./SAGr. 126 under the control of Luftwaffenkommando Südost.

Shipborne operations
The Ar 196 was designed from the start for shipboard operation, and was equipped with catapult spools and had an airframe strong enough to withstand the rigours of catapult launches. Ar 196A-1s replaced He 60 biplanes on *Graf Spee*, *Scharnhorst*, *Gneisenau*, *Lützow*, *Admiral Scheer* and *Prinz Eugen*. Ar 196A-3/4s were carried by the battleships *Bismarck* and *Tirpitz*. These vessels normally had four assigned, although could in theory each carry six.

Structure
The rectangular section steel tube fuselage was faired to an oval using former ribs and was covered by metal skinning forward and fabric aft. The single-step floats were all metal, and consisted of seven watertight compartments which accommodated 300 litres (66 Imp gal) as well as ammunition and food containers.

Iain Wyllie

Right: As befitted its shipborne role, the Ar 196 was easily winched back aboard its parent vessel by crane.

Below: The Ar 196 was as nice to fly as it was to operate from water, with good handling and adequate performance.

Below: By the beginning of 1944, the days of the Ar 196A, arguably the most successful German naval aeroplane of World War II, were obviously numbered. Its heyday, when the cannon-armed and relatively nimble floatplane was the hunter and the slow, unwieldy Whitleys of RAF Coastal Command its prey, had long passed. It was now the Ar 196 which was the prey of Coastal Command's Beaufighters, and its activities had become progressively restricted.

Der Adler

HEFT 26 / BERLIN, 28. DEZEMBER 1943

Belgien	Frs. b. 2.50
Bulgarien	Lewa 8.–
Dänemark	Øre 40
Finnland	Fmk. 4.50
Frankreich	Frs. fr. 4.–
Holland	Cents 20
Italien	Lire 7.–
Kroatien	Kuna 7.–
Norwegen	Øre 45
Protektorat	Kr. 2.–
Rumänien	Lei 30
Schweden	Öre 50
Schweiz	Rappen 40
Serbien	Dinar 5.–
Slowakei	Kr. 2.50
Türkei	Kurus 12.5
Ungarn	Fillér 46

HERAUSGEGEBEN UNTER MITWIRKUNG DES REICHS-LUFTFAHRTMINISTERIUMS

In gestaffeltem Flug

Seeaufklärer vom Baumuster Arado Ar 196, die sich bei der Überwachung der Schiffahrtswege und der Aufklärung feindlicher Geleitzüge außerordentlich bewährt haben, in gestaffeltem Flug entlang der Mittelmeerküste

PK-Aufnahme Kriegsberichter Rackhauß (Sch)

Arado Ar 196A-3 cutaway key

1 Spinner
2 Propeller hub
3 Starboard fuselage fixed 7.9-mm MG 17 gun port
4 Schwarz adjustable-pitch three-bladed propeller
5 Cowling ring
6 Cylinder head fairings
7 BMW 132K nine-cylinder air-cooled radial engine
8 Cowling panel frame
9 Quick-release catch
10 Cowling flaps
11 Engine lower bearers
12 Handholds
13 Engine accessories
14 Air louvre
15 Firewall bulkhead frame
16 Oil tank
17 Starboard MG 17 trough
18 Fuselage frame/engine support bearer attachment
19 Engine upper bearers
20 Forward fuselage decking
21 Starboard wing-skinning
22 Leading-edge rib stations
23 Starboard outer rib
24 Starboard navigation light
25 Starboard wingtip
26 Starboard aileron
27 Aileron mass balance
28 Underwing access panel
29 Aileron control linkage
30 Windscreen
31 Instrument panel
32 Forward fuselage upper frame
33 Sea rudder lever
34 Handhold
35 Sea equipment locker (incl. drag line and anchor/heaving line)
36 Rudder pedal assembly
37 Seat support frame
38 Entry footstep
39 Seat adjustment handwheel
40 Armrest and seat harness
41 Control column
42 Pilot's seat

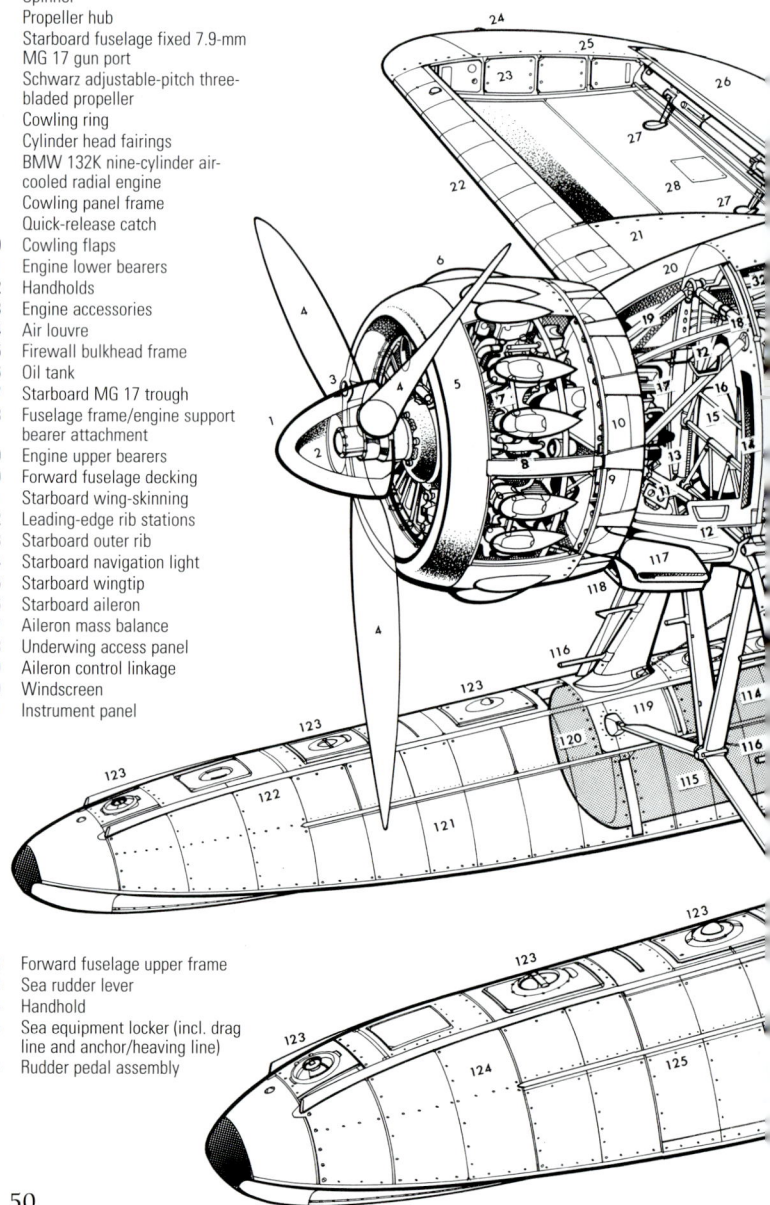

50

The very severe winter of 1939-40 delayed flight testing of the significantly improved Ar 196A-2 from Warnemünde. This version was intended for a spectrum of tasks rather than just shipborne reconnaissance. Operating from shore bases, the newer model was expected to range over the North Sea and Baltic Sea in search of Allied shipping to harass and patrol aircraft to destroy. In these tasks the Ar 196A-2 was greatly aided by its fixed forward-firing armament, in the wing's leading edges, of two 20-mm cannon.

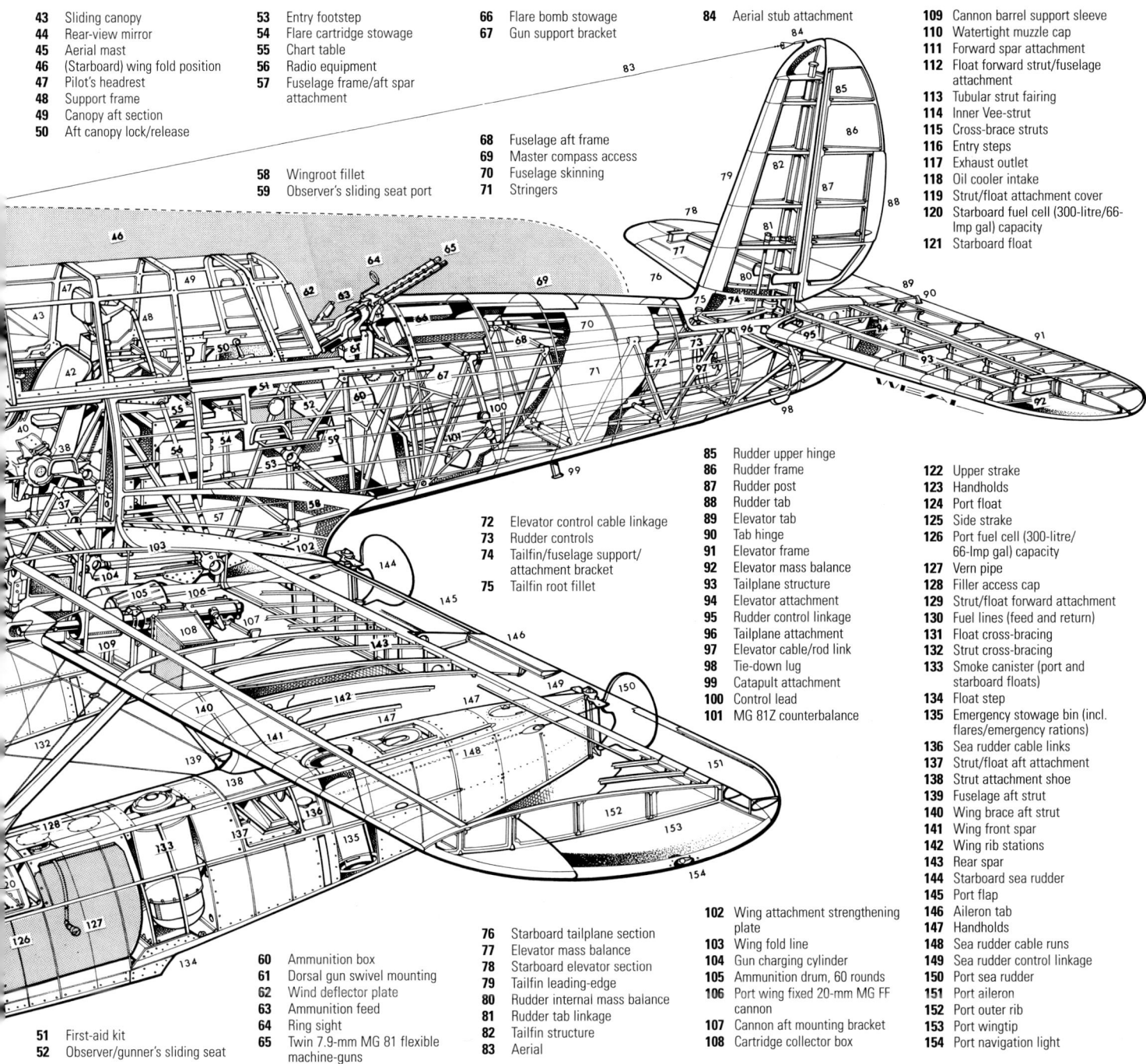

43 Sliding canopy
44 Rear-view mirror
45 Aerial mast
46 (Starboard) wing fold position
47 Pilot's headrest
48 Support frame
49 Canopy aft section
50 Aft canopy lock/release

53 Entry footstep
54 Flare cartridge stowage
55 Chart table
56 Radio equipment
57 Fuselage frame/aft spar attachment

58 Wingroot fillet
59 Observer's sliding seat port

66 Flare bomb stowage
67 Gun support bracket

68 Fuselage aft frame
69 Master compass access
70 Fuselage skinning
71 Stringers

84 Aerial stub attachment

109 Cannon barrel support sleeve
110 Watertight muzzle cap
111 Forward spar attachment
112 Float forward strut/fuselage attachment
113 Tubular strut fairing
114 Inner Vee-strut
115 Cross-brace struts
116 Entry steps
117 Exhaust outlet
118 Oil cooler intake
119 Strut/float attachment cover
120 Starboard fuel cell (300-litre/66-Imp gal) capacity
121 Starboard float

85 Rudder upper hinge
86 Rudder frame
87 Rudder post
88 Rudder tab
89 Elevator tab
90 Tab hinge
91 Elevator frame
92 Elevator mass balance
93 Tailplane structure
94 Elevator attachment
95 Rudder control linkage
96 Tailplane attachment
97 Elevator cable/rod link
98 Tie-down lug
99 Catapult attachment
100 Control lead
101 MG 81Z counterbalance

72 Elevator control cable linkage
73 Rudder controls
74 Tailfin/fuselage support/attachment bracket
75 Tailfin root fillet

122 Upper strake
123 Handholds
124 Port float
125 Side strake
126 Port fuel cell (300-litre/66-Imp gal) capacity
127 Vern pipe
128 Filler access cap
129 Strut/float forward attachment
130 Fuel lines (feed and return)
131 Float cross-bracing
132 Strut cross-bracing
133 Smoke canister (port and starboard floats)
134 Float step
135 Emergency stowage bin (incl. flares/emergency rations)
136 Sea rudder cable links
137 Strut/float aft attachment
138 Strut attachment shoe
139 Fuselage aft strut
140 Wing brace aft strut
141 Wing front spar
142 Wing rib stations
143 Rear spar
144 Starboard sea rudder
145 Port flap
146 Aileron tab
147 Handholds
148 Sea rudder cable runs
149 Sea rudder control linkage
150 Port sea rudder
151 Port aileron
152 Port outer rib
153 Port wingtip
154 Port navigation light

102 Wing attachment strengthening plate
103 Wing fold line
104 Gun charging cylinder
105 Ammunition drum, 60 rounds
106 Port wing fixed 20-mm MG FF cannon
107 Cannon aft mounting bracket
108 Cartridge collector box

76 Starboard tailplane section
77 Elevator mass balance
78 Starboard elevator section
79 Tailfin leading-edge
80 Rudder internal mass balance
81 Rudder tab linkage
82 Tailfin structure
83 Aerial

60 Ammunition box
61 Dorsal gun swivel mounting
62 Wind deflector plate
63 Ammunition feed
64 Ring sight
65 Twin 7.9-mm MG 81 flexible machine-guns

51 First-aid kit
52 Observer/gunner's sliding seat

Arado Ar 196

The compartmented floats were manufactured of Alclad light alloy, and each carried one 300-litre (66-Imp gal) tank for fuel, whose feed pipes passed up the forward struts. The latter also incorporated projecting rungs forming a ladder by which the crew could enter the cockpit and maintenance personnel could access the engine.

the fixed forward-firing armament of two 20-mm cannon and one 7.9-mm machine-gun. Production continued at Warnemünde at relatively low tempo, a total of 98 machines being delivered during the course of 1940, these being, for the most part, Ar 196A-2s but included the first few of two dozen Ar 196A-4s that began to leave the assembly line late in 1940.

Intended as a replacement for the Ar 196A-1 aboard the catapults of Kriegsmarine vessels, the **Ar 196A-4** carried similar armament to the A-2 and embodied some further structural strengthening. It was also equipped with an additional radio (FuG 16Z), and could be distinguished from the preceding production models by its airscrew spinner which had previously been fitted only to the prototypes. The **Ar 196A-3** actually succeeded the A-4 in production in the spring of 1941, and embodied similar structural improvements. The 97

floatplanes delivered from Warnemünde during the course of 1941 were mostly of this variant, which was to be built in larger numbers than any other, a further 94 being delivered by the parent company in 1942. In this year the S.N.C.A. plant at St Nazaire also began production of the Ar 196A-3, first deliveries commencing in July and a total of 13 being produced by the end of the year. However, only a further 10 had been completed at St Nazaire by March 1943 when the factory was phased out of the programme, the Warnemünde plant delivering 83 of the floatplanes in that year.

Production of the Ar 196A-3 at Warnemünde had given place, early in 1943, to the **Ar 196A-5** that differed in having improved radio equipment (FuG 16Z and FuG 25a, later supplanted by FuG 141), rearranged instrumentation, and better defensive armament, the flexibly-mounted MG 15 in the rear cockpit giving place to an MG 81Z (twin 7.9-mm MG 81s) with 2,000 rounds.

The Fokker plant at Amsterdam began production of the Ar 196A-5 in the summer of 1943, producing 11 by the end of the year and another 58 by August 1944 when further production ceased. Only 22 Ar 196A-5s were produced at Warnemünde, production being phased out in March 1944, a total of 526 having been built, excluding the 10 Ar 196A-0s and the five prototypes.

Apart from the Ar 196A twin-float seaplanes, Arado had also completed in 1940-41 a small batch of single-float **Ar 196B-0** pre-production aircraft for service evaluation. These aircraft saw brief service in 1941 with Bordfliegerstaffel 1./196 at Wilhelmshaven. In the same year project development work began on the **Ar 196C** variant. Aerodynamically refined, this was more extensively equipped and heavier than the Ar 196A, the higher loaded weights dictating the use of larger floats. Research work on these new floats was completed in 1941 by the Institut für Seeflugwesen at Hamburg, but

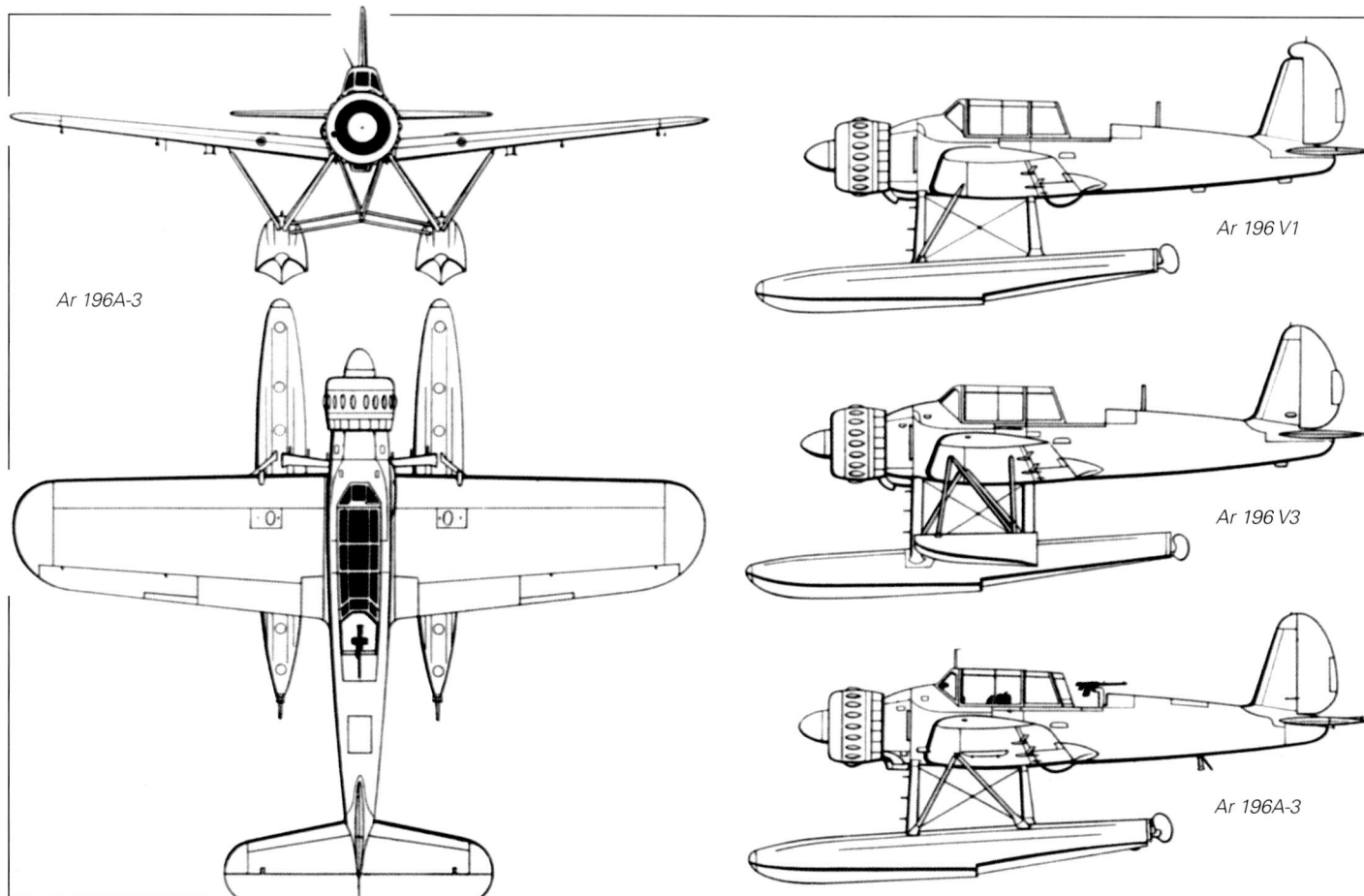

Ar 196A-3

Ar 196 V1

Ar 196 V3

Ar 196A-3

This Arado Ar 196A-3 is depicted in the markings of 1./Bordfliegerstaffel 196, operating in the Lofoten Islands off northern Norway during February 1944. Half of the unit (15 aircraft) had transferred to Stavanger from Wilhelmshaven during August 1941, with a further three aircraft operating autonomously as the Kette Arado. 1./Bordfliegerstaffel 196 returned to Germany in June 1944 and was then expanded to full Gruppe strength as Bordfliegergruppe 196.

further development of the variant was cancelled shortly afterwards.

Ar 196 in service

Apart from the previously-mentioned Bordfliegerstaffeln 1./196 and 5./196, which were the first recipients of the Ar 196A, 1./Küstenfliegergruppe 706 was formed with a mixture of Ar 196A and He 115 floatplanes and, on 5 May 1940, two Ar 196A-2s from this coastal Gruppe operating from Aalborg, Denmark, succeeded in capturing the submarine HMS *Seal* in the Kattegat. In the spring of 1941, Ar 196A-4s were launched by the *Bismarck* in an attempt to drive away the RAF Catalina flying boats shadowing the battleship during its one and only sortie into the Atlantic, and by the middle of 1941, Ar 196 units were more widespread. Bordfliegerstaffel 5./196 was based on the French Biscay coast under the Fliegerführer Atlantik with 26 Ar 196As and He 114As, hunting RAF Coastal Command's Whitleys which patrolled the routes taken by U-boats entering and leaving their pens, and necessitating the use of Beaufighters as a countermeasure.

The Bordfliegerstaffel 1./196 remained based at Wilhelmshaven until 25 August 1941, when half the Staffel with 15 aircraft was transferred to Stavanger, Norway, under Luftflotte 5, a further three aircraft from the unit operating autonomously as the Kette Arado. The 1./Kü.Fl.Gr.706 had returned to Germany from Norway by August 1941, and was in process of re-equipment, but two Seeaufklärungsgruppen

by now included Ar 196As on their strength, 2./SAGr. 131 operating in Norway with a mixture of these floatplanes and BV 138 flying boats, and 2./SAGr. 125 operating Ar 196As against the Soviets under the Fliegerführer Ostsee (Baltic) as part of Luftflotte 1.

The Bordfliegerstaffel 5./196 was subsequently redesignated 1./SAGr. 128, continuing in the sea reconnaissance role in the Bay of Biscay and Channel areas, and by summer 1943, a second Staffel, 2./SAGr. 128, had been formed. The Bordfliegerstaffel 1./196 remained in northern waters, continuing to operate from Norwegian bases until its return to Germany in 1944. By this time it was operating as part of the Bordfliegergruppe 196, which was formed in September 1943 with a Stab in Denmark, 1. Staffel in Norway and 3. Staffel in northern Germany. The Italian squadron disbanded in June 1944, and the other three components disbanded at Bug/Rugen in March 1945.

Retaining its mixture of Ar 196As and BV 138s, 2./SAGr. 131 continued to operate from Norwegian bases until December 1944. The other original Seeaufklärungsstaffeln operating Ar 196As, 2./SAGr. 125, saw service along the Baltic coast during the latter half of 1941, together with the BV 138-equipped remainder of the Gruppe, before the entire SAGr. 125 was transferred to Constanza, Romania, for Black Sea operations. Shortly after its arrival at Constanza, 2./SAGr. 125 with its Ar 196A-3s was transferred to the Aegean. The Staffel later undertook wide-scale naval co-operation duties in the Eastern Mediterranean until redes-

A pair of Ar 196A-3 floatplanes (6W+HK in foreground) of 2./SAGr. 128 flies from the base at Berre in southern France during June 1943. SAGr 128's 1. Staffel operated from Brest during this period, flying both Ar 196s and Fw 190s. Seeaufklärungsgruppen equipped with the Ar 196 operated over the Mediterranean, Norway and on the Eastern Front. The Ar 196A-3 was the most numerous of the Ar 196 subtypes, and incorporated a number of structural improvements over its predecessors. This variant was also manufactured by S.N.C.A. of St Nazaire in France. However, French production was limited to only a small number of machines.

Arado Ar 196

This Ar 196A-3 served with the Romanian Escadrilla 102, part of the Flotila de hidroaviatie operating from Odessa under the auspices of the Aufklärungsführer Schwarzes Meer West in late 1943.

This is an Ar 196A-3 of 161 Eskadra, Royal Bulgarian air force. This unit flew the Arado for Black Sea patrols from the base at Varna between autumn 1942 and summer 1944. One Ar 196 survived and is on display at a museum in Plovdiv. Two other Ar 196s from the heavy cruiser Prinz Eugen are on display in the US.

ignated 4./SAGr. 126 in September 1943. The SAGr. 126 began operations in Gruppe strength in the Mediterranean in the spring of 1943, based in Crete under the control of Luftwaffenkommando Südost. With the redesignation of 2./SAGr. 125 as 4./SAGr. 126 in September 1943, the unit operated as a four-Staffel Gruppe, all flying Ar 196s. This Gruppe operated in the eastern Mediterranean and south-east Europe until well late 1944, but by the beginning of 1945, the Ar 196As of the Stab, 1. and 2./SAGr. 126 were operating on the northern-central sector of the Eastern Front under Luftflotte 6. They ended the war at Parow.

Relatively few Ar 196As were supplied to Germany's allies, but the Romanian 101st and 102nd Coastal Reconnaissance Squadrons operated Ar 196A-3s from late 1943 under the Aufklärungsführer Schwarzes Meer West. The Ar 196A-3 was also employed by the Bulgarian 161st Coastal Squadron.

Arado Ar 196A-3 specification

Type: two-seat shipboard reconnaissance and coastal patrol float seaplane
Powerplant: one BMW 132K nine-cylinder radial air-cooled engine rated at 716 kW (960 hp) for take-off and 612 kW (820 hp) at 1000 m (3,280 ft)
Performance: maximum speed 312 km/h (194 mph) at 1000 m (3,280 ft); cruising speed 267 km/h (166 mph); initial climb rate 414 m (1,358 ft) per minute; service ceiling 7000 m (22,965 ft); range 800 km (497 miles)
Weights: empty 2335 kg (5,148 lb); empty equipped 2572 kg (5,670 lb); loaded 3303 kg (7,282 lb)
Dimensions: wingspan 12.44 m (40 ft 9¾ in); length 10.96 m (35 ft 11½ in); height 4.44 m (14 ft 7 in); wing area 28.30 m² (304.62 sq ft)
Armament: two 20-mm MG FF cannon with 60 r.p.g. and one 7.9-mm (0.31-in) MG 17 machine-gun fixed to fire forward, and one 7.9-mm MG 15 on flexible mounting with 525 rounds, plus two 50-kg (110-lb) SC 50 bombs on ETC 50/VIII wing racks

The Ar 196 served in all coastal areas of German-occupied Europe, and was also the standard floatplane carried on major surface warships of the German navy, the largest of which (the battleships Bismarck and Tirpitz) carried four each. This Ar 196A-5 of 2./SAGr. 126 (D1+FK) was operating in the eastern Mediterranean in early 1944. The unit was formed from 3./Aufklärungsgruppe 126 (See) in July 1943 at Skaramanga in Greece. In October 1944 it transferred to the Baltic theatre, based at Lochstadt near Königsberg. In December 1944 it withdrew to Parow, where it was still operational at the end of the war in Europe.

Above: One early success was the capture of the British submarine Seal by two Ar 196 floatplanes of 1. Staffel/Küstenfliegergruppe 706. The boat had been damaged by a mine and, on 5 May 1940, its crew surrendered after the Ar 196s had attacked with cannon fire and bombs.

Above: Based initially at Wilhelmshaven and Kiel-Holtenau, Bordfliegerstaffeln 1./196 and 5./196 were the two units responsible for providing aircraft for naval vessels. This aircraft is seen on board the heavy cruiser Prinz Eugen.

Above: The Ar 196 was designed to meet a requirement to replace obsolecent floatplanes aboard large ships of the Kriegsmarine. Here one of the prototypes is tested on board a ship. In operation the floatplane was catapulted into the air for take-off, and hoisted back onto the ship after landing on the sea as close as possible to its parent vessel.

Right: Designed to replace the Heinkel He 60 floatplane on board German warships, the Ar 196 was then pressed into service with Luftwaffe coastal units from 1940. Flying from French bases during 1941 and 1942, Ar 196 floatplanes intercepted anti-submarine patrols by RAF Coastal Command aircraft and claimed more than a dozen victories.

The Ar 196 was active over most European waters, from Norway to the Mediterranean. The type often scouted the area ahead of warships, spotting targets at long range and warning of possible dangers.

Arado Ar 197

Radical changes in the thinking of certain maritime powers concerning single-seat shipboard fighter design were taking place in 1936, when the Arado Flugzeugwerke initiated work on Germany's first warplane in this category, the Ar 197. Its biplane configuration counted against it, and the type was duly abandoned in 1937.

Carrier-borne fighter design concepts were lagging seriously behind those of land-based aircraft, a fact accepted in the US and Japan where it had been realised that the higher performances that would be demanded in the years ahead could only be achieved by supplanting the biplane, which had dominated naval aviation since its birth, with the monoplane. However, both the US and Japanese navies possessed a wealth of design and operating experience with carrier-based aircraft. No such experience was available in Germany, and Arado, faced with the task of evolving a fighter for 'Carrier A', the future *Graf Zeppelin*, had little choice but to adopt a thoroughly conventional approach to the problem – a biplane of traditional concept.

Destined to be Germany's last fighter biplane, the **Ar 197**, as Arado's single-seat shipboard fighter was designated, owed little to any of the company's previous designs, although the constructional methods employed were essentially similar to those of the land-based Ar 68. All other similarity between the two fighters was confined to design features common to all Arado aircraft of the period. An unequal-span single-bay staggered biplane, the Ar 197 was of all-metal construction. The wings were two-spar metal-covered structures with inclined and splayed N-type interplane struts. The welded steel-tube fuselage was covered by detachable light metal panels forward and along the upper decking, the remainder being fabric covered, and the only real concession to modernity was the sliding canopy for the pilot's cockpit.

Engine change

The **Ar 197 V1** (D-ITSE), which was flown at Warnemünde early in 1937, was powered by a 12-cylinder liquid-cooled Daimler-Benz DB 600A engine rated at 679 kW (910 hp) at 4000 m (13,120 ft) and driving a three-blade variable-pitch airscrew. This first prototype carried no armament and was not navalised. The second prototype, the **Ar 197 V2** (D-IVLE), differed from its predecessor in having a nine-cylinder radial air-cooled BMW 132J engine rated at 608 kW (815 hp) for take-off, an arrester hook and catapult spools. The reason for the engine change was simply the low priority enjoyed by the Ar 197 in the supply of the new Daimler-Benz powerplant. Indeed, very little impetus was being placed behind the development of the fighter, as the Luftwaffe had already stated its view that the development of specialised shipboard aircraft was premature. Nevertheless, construction of a third

With the DB 600 engine in some demand, D-IVLE, the Ar 197 V2 second prototype, introduced a new powerplant in the form of the BMW 132J radial, together with equipment for carrier operations.

prototype, the **Ar 197 V3**, continued, this aircraft joining the Ar 197 V2 at Travemünde in the late summer of 1937.

Considered as the production prototype, the Ar 197 V3 differed from its immediate predecessor in having a BMW 132Dc engine rated at 656 kW (880 hp) for take-off. It also carried full armament and was equipped to carry a drop tank or smoke-screen canister beneath the fuselage. Empty and loaded weights rose from the 1800 kg (3,968 lb) and 2425 kg (5,346 lb) of the Ar 197 V2 to 1840 kg (4,056 lb) and 2475 kg (5,456 lb), respectively, but the performance of the two prototypes was generally similar, apart from slight reductions in climb rate and service ceiling suffered by the third aircraft. The armament of the Ar 197 V3 comprised a pair of 7.9-mm (0.31-in) MG 17 machine-guns with 500 r.p.g. in

The Ar 197 V1 was the first prototype of what was destined to be the last fighter biplane designed and built in Germany. The first prototype was the only example with a Daimler-Benz engine.

The Ar 197 V2 was the first navalised prototype, featuring arrestor hook and catapult spools, but no armament was fitted. Compared to parallel carrier fighter developments in Japan and the US, the Ar 197 was a decidedly antiquated design.

Arado Ar 197

The Ar 197 V3 was considered as a production prototype, was fully navalised and carried full armament, but shortly after it commenced its flight test programme at Travemünde the RLM became aware of the development of shipboard fighter monoplanes abroad and further work on the Arado fighter was abandoned. Instead, attention shifted to the development of the Messerschmitt Bf 109T, which would partner the Fi 167 and Ju 87 aboard the carrier decks. When the carrier programme was revived in 1942 the intended fighter aircraft had become the Messerschmitt Me 155. In the event, Germany's on-off aircraft-carrier programme did not reach fruition, and neither Graf Zeppelin nor Peter Strasser were completed.

the forward fuselage and two 20-mm MG FF cannon with 60 r.p.g. in the upper wing. Racks were provided beneath the lower wing for a maximum of four 50-kg (110-lb) SC 50 bombs, and provision was made for explosive charges to jettison the main undercarriage for emergency ditching.

Before the end of 1937, the RLM had become aware of the development of shipboard fighter monoplanes abroad, and as it had by now become obvious that at least another two years must elapse before Germany's first carrier could be commissioned – Kriegsmarine personnel were soon to be quoting widely the play on words 'Nichts ist träger als ein Träger' (literally 'Nothing is more sluggish than a carrier') – Arado was instructed to abandon further work on its shipboard fighter biplane.

Arado Ar 197 V3 specification
Type: single-seat shipboard fighter
Powerplant: one BMW 132Dc nine-cylinder radial air-cooled engine rated at 656 kW (880 hp) for take-off
Performance: maximum speed 400 km/h (248 mph) at 2500 m (8,200 ft); maximum cruising speed 354 km/h (220 mph) at 1500 m (4,920 ft); time to 4000 m (13,120 ft) 5.3 minutes; service ceiling 8600 m (28,215 ft); normal range 695 km (432 miles); maximum range (with auxiliary fuel) 1638 km (1,018 miles)
Weights: empty 1840 kg (4,056 lb); normal loaded 2475 kg (5,456 lb); maximum loaded 2674 kg (5,896 lb)
Dimensions: wingspan 11.00 m (36 ft 1 in); length 9.20 m (30 ft 2¼ in); height 3.60 m (11 ft 9¾ in); wing area 21.30 m² (229.237 sq ft)
Armament: two 20-mm MG FF cannon with 60 r.p.g. in wings and two 7.9-mm (0.31-in) MG 17 machine-guns with 500 r.p.g. in fuselage, plus four 50-kg (110-lb) SC 50 bombs beneath lower wing

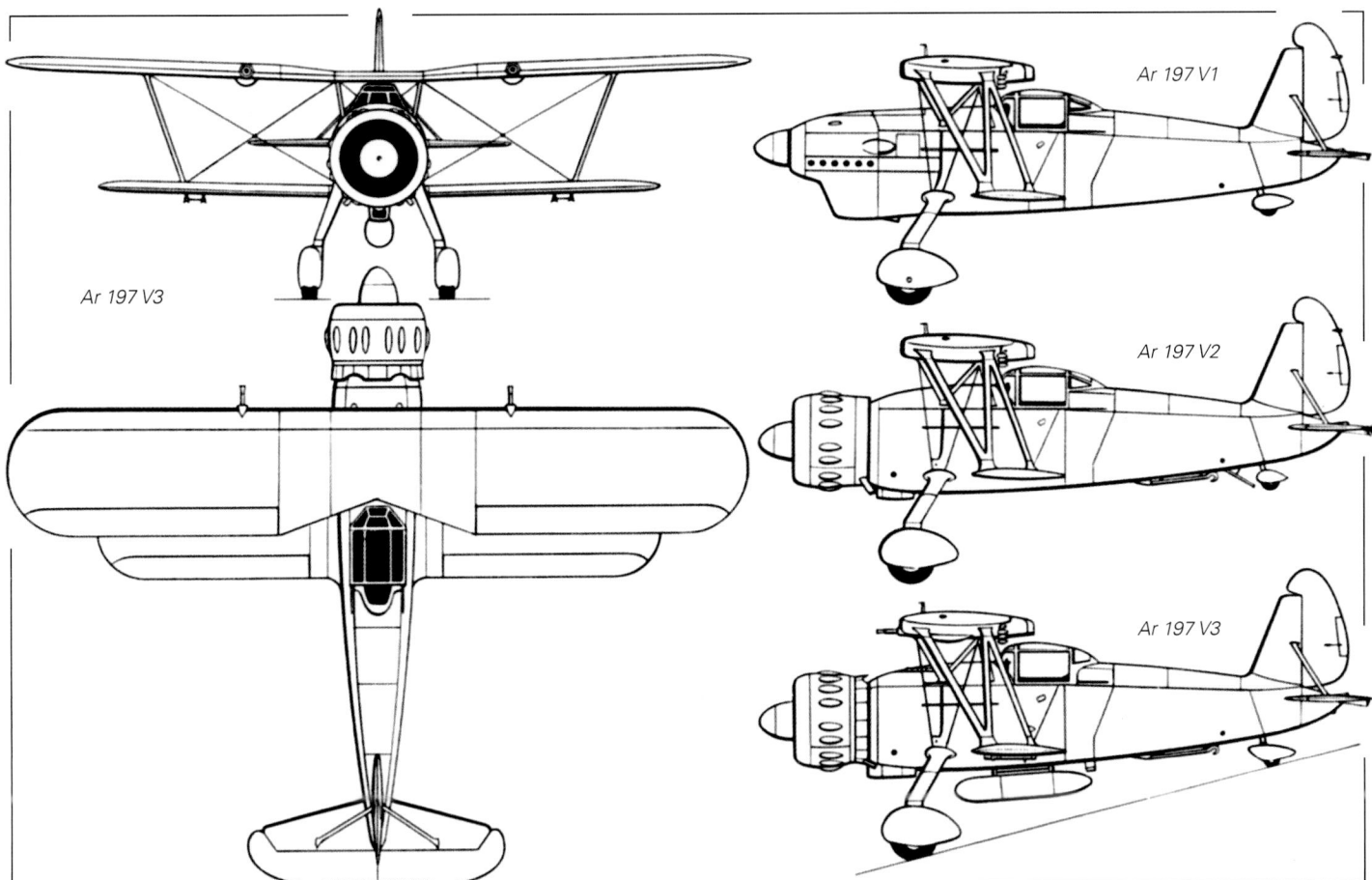

Ar 197 V3

Ar 197 V1

Ar 197 V2

Ar 197 V3

Arado Ar 198

A relatively conventional design, the Arado Ar 198 initially found favour with a Luftwaffe looking to field a new tactical reconnaissance aircraft to succeed the Henschel Hs 126. In the event, the more ambitious Ha 141 and Fw 189 projects were recipients of further contracts, and only two Ar 198s were completed.

In February 1937, the first prototype of the Henschel Hs 126 was undergoing initial trials, and bid fair to provide the Luftwaffe with the required replacement for the Heinkel He 46 in the Aufklärungsstaffeln (H) battlefield reconnaissance units, but the Technisches Amt of the RLM was already looking further ahead, and in that month issued a completely new specification that demanded an appreciably more advanced aircraft than the Henschel. This specification called for a tactical reconnaissance aircraft carrying three crewmembers, offering all-round defensive cover, and possessing a rather higher performance than anything previously envisaged for aircraft in this category.

The specification was issued to two manufacturers – Arado and Focke-Wulf – although, in the event, the Hamburger Flugzeugbau also tendered a project, and no specification could have resulted in three more dissimilar proposals to meet a single requirement. The Arado team ran true to form in proving the least venturesome of the competitors, choosing to retain the classic high-wing formula in the belief that no other acceptable arrangement could offer a comparable all-round view.

At the outset, the Technisches Amt favoured Arado's conventional approach to the requirements of the specification over the more exotic proposals of the other competitors, but, nevertheless, late in April 1937, both Arado and Focke-

First flown in spring 1938, the first prototype Ar 198 (D-ODLG) was promptly dubbed 'das fliegende Aquarium' as a result of the extensive transparent areas of the fuselage. Second and third prototypes were scrapped before they had been completed.

Wulf were recipients of contracts for three prototype aircraft. Arado's **Ar 198** contender was an all-metal cantilever shoulder-wing monoplane powered by a single BMW-Bramo 323A Fafnir nine-cylinder radial rated at 671 kW (900 hp) for take-off and 619 kW (830 hp) at 4191 m (13,750 ft). The two-spar metal-skinned wing had fabric-covered slotted ailerons and camber-changing slotted flaps. The forward portion of the fuselage was a welded steel-tube structure, the aft portion being a stressed-skin light metal monocoque. The lower forward fuselage was deepened and glazed to provide all-round vision for the observer.

Single prototype

Designated **Ar 198 V1** (D-ODLG), the first prototype was flown in March 1938. From the commencement of flying trials it was obvious that the general characteristics of the aircraft left much to be desired. Leading-edge slats were fitted to improve low-speed handling, and a lower fuselage redesign was proposed for the second and third prototypes to overcome some of the problems encountered.

While plans to adopt the Ar 198 for mass production were cancelled on the grounds of high production costs and the initially poor test results, development did continue. The **V2** second prototype was completed with the improvements, and flew well when tested by the Luftwaffe at Rechlin. However, it was damaged beyond repair in a crash. The V1 was modified to a similar standard, and continued to impress the test crews. Its excellent downward visibility led to it being employed for a while on survey tasks, operated by Weser Flugzeugbau at Bremen. The third prototype was not completed, but its airframe was used for various static trials.

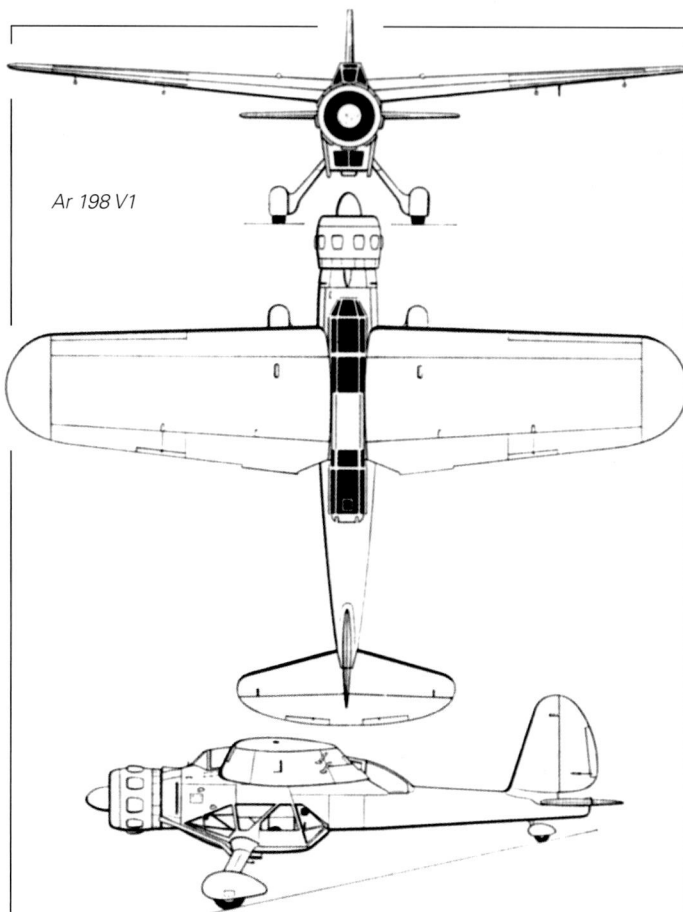

Ar 198 V1

Arado Ar 198 V1 specification
Type: three-seat tactical reconnaissance and army co-operation aircraft
Powerplant: one BMW-Bramo 323A Fafnir nine-cylinder radial air-cooled engine rated at 671 kW (900 hp) for take-off and 619 kW (830 hp) at 4191 m (13,750 ft)
Performance: maximum speed 320 km/h (197 mph) at sea level, 360 km/h (223 mph) at 3500 m (11,485 ft); maximum range 1080 km (672 miles); service ceiling 8000 m (26,250 ft)
Weights: empty 2400 kg (5,290 lb); normal loaded 3030 kg (6,683 lb)
Dimensions: wingspan 14.90 m (48 ft 10½ in); length 11.80 m (38 ft 8½ in); height 4.50 m (14ft 9½ in); wing area 35.20 m² (378.90 sq ft)
Armament: (proposed) two fixed forward-firing 7.9-mm (0.31-in) MG 17 machine-guns and two 7.9-mm MG 15 machine-guns on flexible mountings and firing aft from dorsal and ventral positions, plus four 50-kg (110-lb) SC 50 bombs on underwing racks

Arado Ar 199

Developed as a floatplane trainer for launch from a ship's catapult, the all-metal Arado Ar 199 provided accommodation for three within an enclosed cockpit. Although the type failed to enter quantity production, the two Argus-powered prototypes eventually found their way into Luftwaffe service.

Designed to meet a requirement for a floatplane trainer, the **Arado Ar 199** was a technical success, but fell victim to a change in official policy and was not ordered into production. The aircraft was of modern design and construction, being a cantilever low-wing monoplane of light alloy stressed-skin construction. Accommodation was provided for a pupil and instructor side-by-side at the front with provision for a trainee navigator or radio operator behind them in a substantial cockpit covered by a framed canopy, with a sliding section for access and egress. The trainer had a tail unit of typical Arado design, alighting gear in the form of a side-by-side pair of metal floats carried under the inner parts of the wing by a neat arrangement of wire-braced struts, and a neatly cowled engine driving a two-bladed propeller.

The first and second prototypes, **Ar 199 V1** and **Ar 199 V2**, were officially evaluated in 1939, with the design having been begun in 1938. One of the aircraft was at one time fitted with the vaned spinner associated with the Argus pitch-change mechanism for the propeller. After it had been decided not to order the type into production as the **Ar 199A**, these two machines were taken into Luftwaffe service for use as trainers.

Arado Ar 199 specification
Type: three-seat multi-role training floatplane
Powerplant: one Argus As 410C inverted-Vee engine rated at 335.5 kW (450 hp)
Performance: maximum speed 260 km/h (162 mph) at 3000 m (9,845 ft); cruising speed 212 km/h (132 mph) at optimum altitude; climb to 3000 m (9,845 ft) in 11 minutes; service ceiling 6500 m (71,325 ft); range 740 km (460 miles)
Weights: empty 1675 kg (3,693 lb); maximum take-off 2075 kg (4,575 lb)
Dimensions: wingspan 12.70 m (41 ft 8 in); length 10.57 m (34 ft 8⅛ in); height 4.36 m (14 ft 4¼ in); wing area 30.40 m² (327.23 sq ft)

Above: Pictured after its entry into Luftwaffe service, this Ar 199 displays the vaned spinner for the Argus engine's propeller pitch-change mechanism. It also shows the typical Arado arrangement of bracing struts and wires for the twin-float alighting gear.

The entire airframe of the Ar 199 was stressed for the rigours of repeated catapult launches. The cockpit had a side-by-side pair of seats at the front, with provision for a trainee navigator or radio operator in a single seat behind the pupil and instructor.

The Ar 199 was a trim machine carried on a side-by-side pair of single-step floats, and was characterised by a tail unit of typical Arado concept with the tall fin located above the fuselage and ahead of the tailplane, and carrying a rudder with a strongly curved trailing edge.

Arado Ar 231

The submarine-borne aircraft concept dated back to World War I and the Heinkel-designed Hansa-Brandenburg W 20. The Arado Ar 231, of which only six were built, was a fascinating attempt to provide the German submarine arm of World War II with a compact reconnaissance aircraft.

Prior to the advent of radar, the aircraft offered the only means of extending the effective reconnaissance range of the underwater vessel, but it possessed several distinct disadvantages. Its parent vessel was extremely vulnerable while surfaced to launch or retrieve the aircraft; it occupied valuable stowage space, and it could be launched only in calm weather. On the other hand, it enabled potential victims to be spotted while still many miles over the horizon.

The relatively small U-boats with which the Kriegsmarine entered World War II had not been designed to accommodate reconnaissance aircraft, but in 1939, with substantially larger, longer-ranging submarines planned, consideration was given in Germany once more to the possibilities of a so-called U-Bootsauge (U-boat's Eye), a small reconnaissance floatplane capable of being erected or dismantled with extreme rapidity, and stowed within the limited space available aboard a submarine. Early in 1940, the Arado Flugzeugwerke received a contract for the design of an U-Bootsauge and the construction of six prototypes under the designation **Ar 231**.

Powered by a Hirth HM 501 six-cylinder air-cooled engine, the Ar 231 employed an extremely simple light metal structure, and in order to facilitate wing folding, the small wing centre section was braced above the fuselage at an angle

*The Ar 231 was intended for use aboard the Type XI B U-boats, of which four were laid down but subsequently cancelled. Some of the water testing was undertaken from the auxiliary vessel **Stier** ('Raider J'), with two Ar 231s aboard.*

so that the root of the starboard mainplane was lower than that of the port mainplane, permitting the latter to swing over the former when they swivelled on the rear spar for stowage aboard the submarine. The twin single-step floats were detachable, and in dismantled form the entire aircraft could be housed by a tube of 2.00-m (6.56-ft) diameter. It was intended that the Ar 231 would be lowered onto the water from the submarine and subsequently retrieved after completing its mission by means of a folding crane. The process of dismantling the floatplane for insertion in the tubular hangar occupied approximately six minutes, erection taking a similar time. Sufficient fuel was provided for an endurance of nearly four hours, this being considered sufficient to enable the U-boat commander to make his attack and retrieve the floatplane a considerable distance from the scene of the action.

Limited utility

The first of six prototypes, the **Ar 231 V1**, was flown early in 1941, but trials with this and subsequent aircraft were not entirely successful, the characteristics of the aircraft both in the air and on the water being generally unacceptable. It was also ascertained that the Ar 231 could not get airborne if the surface wind exceeded 20 knots, and the idea of remaining surfaced for some 10 minutes in daylight while the floatplane was retrieved and dismantled did not appeal to U-boat commanders. In the meantime, a simpler means of providing the U-boat with an airborne observation platform, the Focke-Achgelis Fa 330 rotor-kite, had been developed successfully, and although all six Ar 231 prototypes were completed, no further development of this aircraft was undertaken.

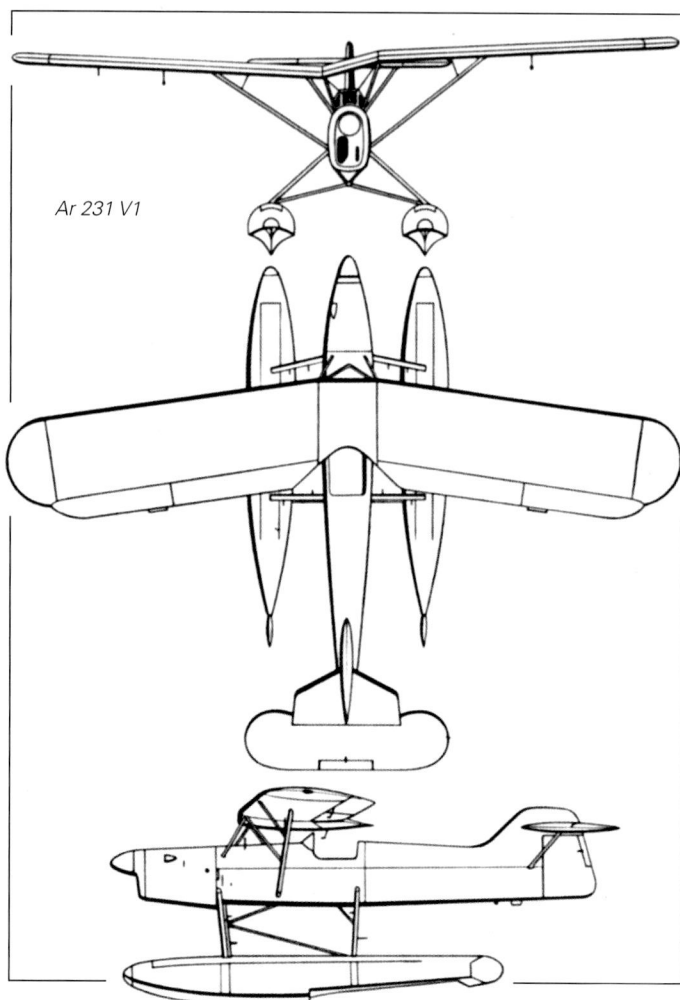

Ar 231 V1

Arado Ar 231 specification
Type: single-seat submarine-borne observation float seaplane
Powerplant: one Hirth HM 501 six-cylinder inverted inline air-cooled engine rated at 119 kW (160 hp)
Performance: maximum speed 170 km/h (106 mph) at sea level; cruising speed 130 km/h (81 mph) at sea level; service ceiling 3000 m (9,840 ft); range 500 km (310 miles)
Weights: empty 833 kg (1,836 lb); loaded 1050 kg (2,315 lb)
Dimensions: wingspan 10.20 m (33 ft 4½ in); length 7.80 m (25 ft 7½ in); height 3.12 m (10 ft 2¾ in); wing area 15.20 m² (163.61 sq ft)

Arado Ar 232

Intended to succeed the venerable Junkers Ju 52/3m, the Arado Ar 232 was an innovative transport design that switched from a twin-engined to a four-engined configuration early in its development. Characterised by its novel multi-wheel undercarriage, a limited number of the aircraft saw important action on the Eastern Front.

In the autumn of 1939, the Technisches Amt of the RLM finalised a specification calling for a medium-sized general-purpose transport successor for the ageing Junkers Ju 52/3m. Replied to by Arado and Henschel, the specification stipulated the use of two BMW 801 air-cooled radial engines, rear loading capability and truck-bed height freight floor with sufficient clearance between ground and tail assembly to permit the direct loading or discharging of cargo between aircraft hold and truck.

Both companies submitted highly original proposals embodying numerous novel features, and both projects featured a box-like rectangular-section all-metal semi-monocoque fuselage pod married to a shoulder-mounted wing, but whereas the Arado project carried its tail surfaces by means of a single circular-section boom projecting from the upper part of the fuselage pod, the Henschel concept envisaged a twin-boom arrangement.

Multi-wheel undercarriage

Another major difference between the contenders for the RLM development order was to be seen in the means by which the freight floor could be lowered to truck-bed height. The Arado project embodied a multi-wheel static undercarriage comprising 11 pairs of small idler wheels along the fuselage centreline, the aircraft resting on these for loading and unloading. The main undercarriage consisted of a semi-retractable levered-suspension nosewheel and inward-retracting single-wheel main members that could be compressed during the process of loading or unloading, and then extended by means of hydraulic rams so that the idler wheels cleared the ground for take-off. The aircraft was intended to be capable of taxiing at low speeds on its 11 pairs of small wheels with their low-pressure tyres and independently-sprung suspension legs. Henschel's approach to the variable-undercarriage problem took the form of four tandem pairs of mainwheels which retracted into lateral housings, these being partly extended for loading and unloading, and fully extended for take-off, small outrigger stabilising wheels retracting into the booms and compensating for the relatively narrow mainwheel track.

The Ar 232 V1, the first of two BMW 801A-powered prototypes began initial taxiing trials in early 1941. Production of the twin-engined version of the Ar 232 was limited, as the BMW 801 was needed for Fw 190 fighter production.

The Henschel project was eliminated after the initial evaluation of the two competing designs, and the Arado Flugzeugwerke received a contract for three prototypes which received the designation **Ar 232**. Although the BMW 801 engine had been stipulated by the Technisches Amt, by the beginning of 1941 it was realised that the inclusion of the Focke-Wulf Fw 190 in the fighter production programme would make heavy demands on available supplies of the BMW engine, and, accordingly, Arado was issued with instructions to replace the pair of BMW 801s by four BMW 323 nine-cylinder radials in its transport. At this time, the three prototypes were at an advanced stage of construction, and some work had begun on a pre-production series of BMW 801-powered **Ar 232A-0** transports at Arado's Eger factory. As the modification from twin- to four-engined configuration would have delayed the flight test programme, it was decided to complete the first two of these as originally planned, plus the small pre-series of Ar 232A-0 aircraft, with subsequent aircraft having the quartet of BMW-Bramo 323s.

Powered by two BMW 801A-series 14-cylinder radials each rated at 1193 kW (1,600 hp) for take-off and 1029 kW

The Ar 232 (one of the two twin-engined prototypes is illustrated) was an innovative transport design with a pod-and-boom fuselage to allow the incorporation of a hydraulically operated rear door for the loading/unloading of bulky freight. Another unusual feature was the retractable tricycle landing gear, whose units could be 'broken' on the ground to allow the fuselage to rest firmly on a central row of 11 pairs of independently sprung idler wheels.

The ungainly Ar 232B-0 was a four-engined development of the twin-engined Ar 232A. Nicknamed *Tausendfüssler* (millipede), several Ar 232 of both the twin-engined A-series and four-engined B-series were used by the Luftwaffe, latterly with KG 200 and Transportgeschwader 4.

(1,380 hp) at 4600 m (15,100 ft), the **Ar 232 V1** (GH+GN) was flown for the first time in early 1941, followed by the **Ar 232 V2** (VD+YA) that differed from its predecessor in being fitted with defensive armament comprising a 13-mm (0.51-in) MG 131 machine-gun with 500 rounds firing through the nose glazing, a 20-mm MG 151 cannon in a hydraulically-operated turret over the forward fuselage, and a second MG 131 fired from a position above the loading ramp. Carrying a crew of four, the aircraft could accommodate two 1000-kg (2,205-lb) PKW field cars, plus eight personnel, empty and loaded weights being 11235 and 18500 kg (24,769 and 40,785 lb), respectively. Eventually 10 pre-production Ar 232A-series examples were built, numbered up to Ar 232A-010. With fuel capacity increased from the standard 2705 litres (595 Imp gal) to 5000 litres (1,100 Imp gal), the twin-engined Ar 232A-010 (TC+EG) was used for meteorological tasks, operating from the far-north airfield at Banak in Norway with Westa 5.

Four-engined variants

The first four-engined prototype, the **Ar 232 V3** (probably Werk Nr 110013, VD+YB) was completed and flown in May 1942; by this time work was well advanced on the first genuine four-engined B-series airframes. To begin with, up to 20 **Ar 232B** were initially intended, comprising two prototypes and 18 pre-production examples. The initial four-engined Ar 232 V3 was numbered **Ar 232B-01**, with the second prototype (the **Ar 232 V4**) being the **Ar 232B-02**. The **Ar 232B-03** was the first of the genuine pre-production examples. To accommodate the additional pair of engines, the wing centre section was elongated by 1.70 m (5 ft 7 in), but few other modifications to the structure were found to be necessary. The four BMW-Bramo 323R-2 Fafnir engines were each rated at 895 kW (1,200 hp) for take-off and emergency with water-methanol injection, and performance proved closely comparable with that of the A-series prototypes. It has sometimes been claimed that one B-series aircraft flew with four Gnôme-Rhône 14M 14-cylinder radials each rated at 522 kW (700 hp), but this now appears unlikely. Similarly, claims that an Ar 232B-series aircraft was operated in Norway, with a single ski measuring 8.00 m (26 ft 2¾ in) in length by 2.40 m (7 ft 10½ in) in width beneath the fuselage, now appear to be myth rather than reality.

The Ar 232 V2 (VD+YA), the second twin-engined A-series prototype, here shows off the type's pod-and-boom layout to advantage. This aircraft was later used to fly supplies in support of German forces in Stalingrad.

One of the Ar 232B-0 aircraft was experimentally fitted with a boundary layer control (BLC) system, air being sucked from the wing leading edges and blown over the trailing edges. The pump operating the BLC system ran on hydrogen peroxide, but the system was never tested in flight as supplies of the chemical were needed for the Me 163B Komet programme. Arado used at least one Ar 232 as a company transport, latterly for the support of the Ar 234 jet bomber test programme.

The Ar 232 V1 and V2 were transferred to the Luftwaffe in the late autumn of 1942, and during the following winter the latter flew missions for the hard-pressed 6th Army in Stalingrad. This aircraft gained the distinction of being the last transport to fly out of Stalingrad before the garrison surrendered to Soviet forces, but the V1 was lost during a ferry flight in Germany. A batch of 10 Ar 232B transports was intended to follow the seven pre-production examples on the assembly line, but there is no evidence that any of these were completed.

Several other Ar 232s served with the Luftwaffe at different times, some on an *ad hoc* basis for transport units as required such as Transport Staffel 5. A number of clandestine missions were flown by Ar 232s, inserting agents behind the Russian lines, latterly for the Oberbefehlshaber der Luftwaffe by the special-operations wing KG 200. One of the Ar 232B-0 transports force-landed on Soviet-held territory in early September 1944 while carrying agents who were intending

One of the four-engined Ar 232B-0 series was surrendered to the British at Eggebek and was briefly used post-war by the RAF to ferry equipment with the captured serial number AIR MIN 17.

This detail view of the Ar 232 V2 reveals the remarkable main undercarriage. The Ar 232 series was a forward-looking attempt to provide the Luftwaffe with an advanced and flexible tactical freighter.

to assassinate Stalin. In the final months of the war several twin- and four-engined Ar 232s were concentrated in the transport wing Transportgeschwader 4, which flew various miscellaneous transport types to the end of the war. One four-engined Ar 232B-0 was surrendered to the British at the war's end and was flown by the RAF carrying equipment between Britain and the Continent.

A further development of the Ar 232 was the **Ar 432** that would have made use of wood in place of light alloys as part of the aluminium–saving programme, particularly for the outer wings. Production of the Ar 432 was initiated by Arado, and a number of major components were completed at Eger, but this transport was never assembled and flown.

Arado Ar 232B-0 specification
Type: medium-range general-purpose transport
Powerplant: four BMW-Bramo 323R-2 Fafnir nine-cylinder radial air-cooled engines each rated at 895 kW (1,200 hp) for take-off with methanol-water injection, 745 kW (1,000 hp) at sea level and 700 kW (940 hp) at 4000 m (13,120 ft)
Performance: maximum speed 307 km/h (191 mph) at 4000 m (13,120 ft); maximum cruising speed 290 km/h (180 mph) at 2000 m (6,560 ft); normal range 1336 km (830 miles) at 254 km/h (158 mph); climb to 2000 m (6,560 ft) in 7 minutes, to 4000 m (13,120 ft) in 15.8 minutes, to 6000 m (19,685 ft) in 27.5 minutes; service ceiling 6900 m (22,640 ft)
Weights: empty equipped 12780 kg (28,175 lb); normal loaded 20000 kg (44,090 lb)
Dimensions: wingspan 33.50 m (109 ft 10¾ in); length 23.50 m (77 ft 2 in); height over main gear 6.60 m (21ft 7¾ in); wing area 142.60 m² (1,534.93 sq ft)
Armament: one forward-firing 13-mm (0.51-in) MG 131 machine-gun on flexible mounting in extreme nose with 500 rounds, one 20-mm MG 151 cannon in hydraulically-operated forward dorsal turret, and either one or two aft-firing 13-mm MG 131 machine guns with 500 r.p.g.

Above: The Ar 232's 11 pairs of small wheels were fitted with low-pressure tyres and independently-sprung suspension legs, allowing the transport to negotiate small obstacles such as ditches up to 1.5 m (5 ft) in width. This is the Ar 232 V2 second prototype, with two BMW 801 radial engines as originally fitted.

This Luftwaffe-operated Ar 232 has suffered a main gear collapse, probably after a heavy landing. Several Luftwaffe units flew examples of the Ar 232 in both twin-engined and four-engined versions, some serving with the special-operations wing KG 200 on clandestine missions.

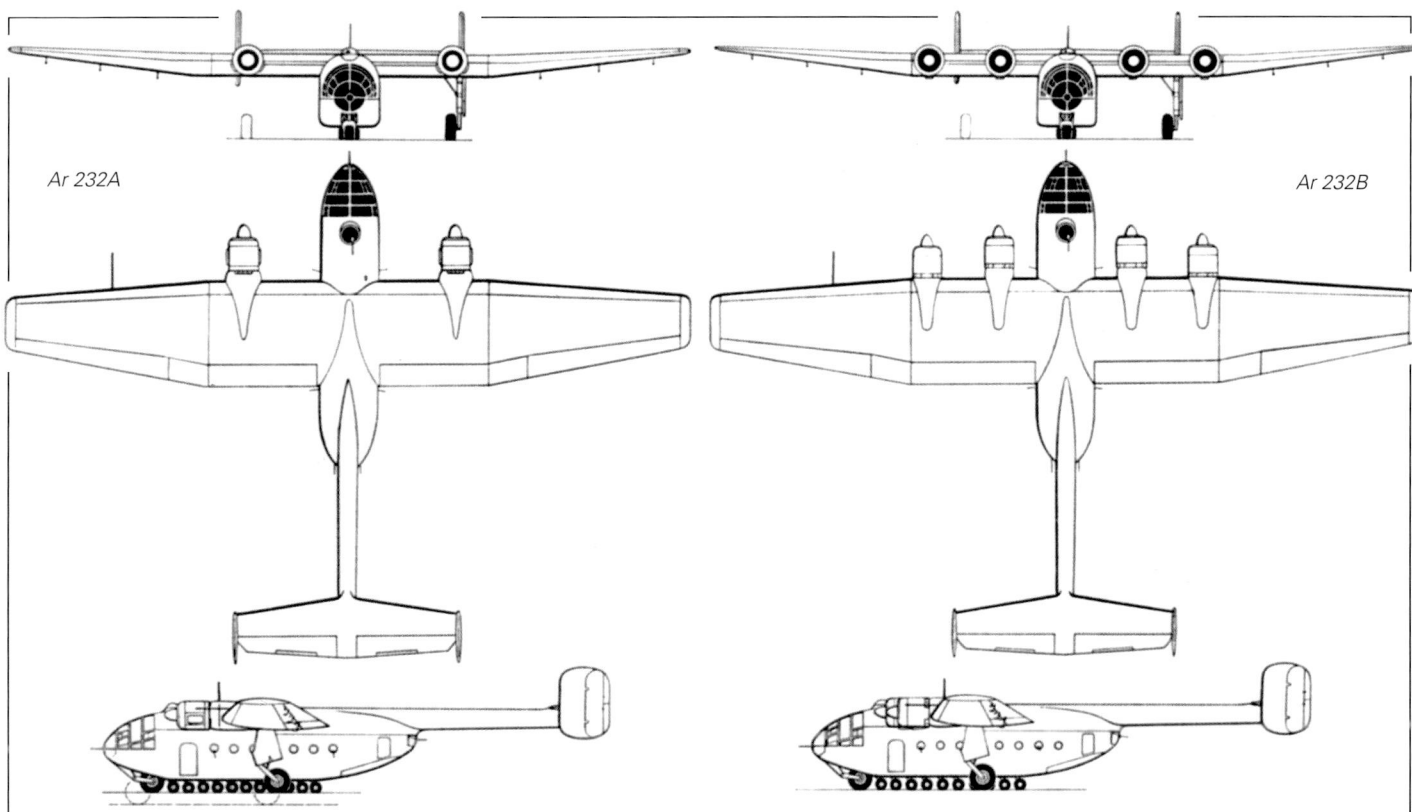

Ar 232A

Ar 232B

Arado Ar 234

By the end of World War II, Germany's aviation technology easily outstripped that of the Allies in several key areas, and if evidence of this lead is needed, look no further than the Ar 234. The world's first jet bomber, it was a sleek, fast and deftly-engineered design that was well ahead of its time.

Germany's wartime aircraft industry was responsible for prodigious advances in aeronautical research and development, and none more striking than those concerned with the evolution of turbojet-propelled combat aircraft. Lacking coordination and sound high-level directive, however, these advances saw practical application too late to affect the course of the war to any marked extent. Nevertheless, it is a remarkable fact that, at a time when the Allies were cautiously flight testing their first jet fighters, much of the German aircraft industry's manufacturing potential was already becoming concentrated on the quantity production of turbojet-driven warplanes, one of the most important of which was the **Arado Ar 234**.

During the late autumn of 1940, Dipl.-Ing. Walter Blume and Ing. Hans Rebeski of the Arado Flugzeugwerke initiated studies at the behest of the Reichsluftfahrtministerium (RLM) for a medium-range reconnaissance aircraft that was to make use of the new turbojets then being bench-run by BMW and Junkers. It was anticipated that the use of these new and revolutionary powerplants would make possible operational speeds and altitudes sufficient to endow the proposed aircraft with immunity from interception. During the months that followed, several draft proposals were submitted to the RLM, but by the beginning of 1941, one of the most orthodox of these, the **E 370**, had been selected as it promised rapid airframe development, the basic configuration being frozen shortly afterwards and the designation Ar 234 being allocated to the project.

Simple design

Basically a single-seat monoplane with a shoulder-mounted wing under which were slung two turbojets, the Ar 234 was of clean and simple aerodynamic design. The fuselage was a stressed-skin semi-monocoque with flat 'top-hat' section

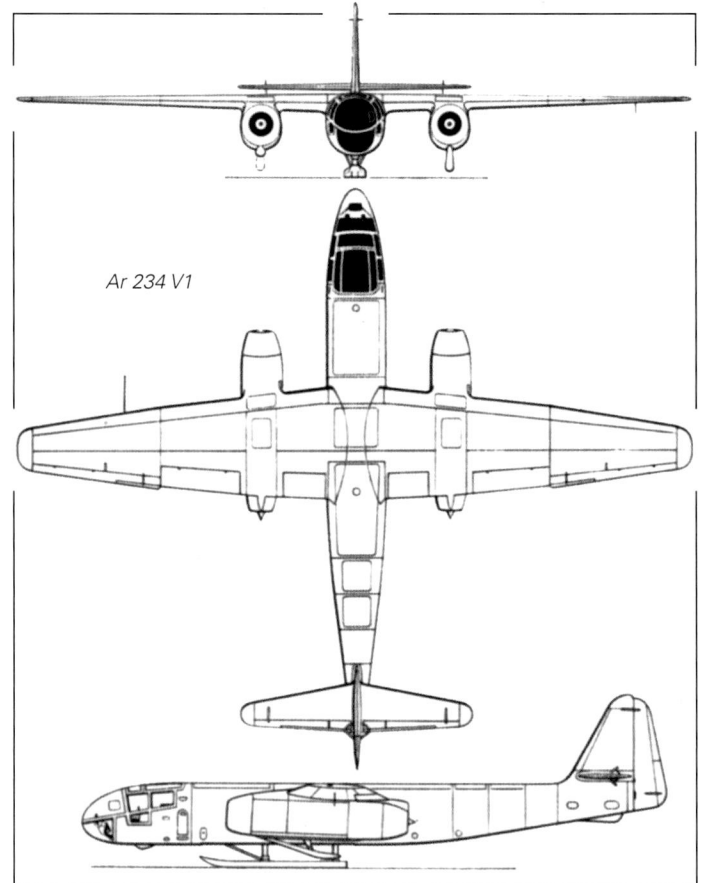

Ar 234 V1

longerons and 'Z' section formers and stringers. The two-spar stressed-skin wing rested on a reinforced box-girder section of the fuselage, being bolted to the upper longerons at four points. The pilot's cockpit, which was extensively glazed and

Just as the Me 262 was the world's first operational jet-powered fighter, so the Arado Ar 234, seen here in prototype form (probably the V5), was the first jet-powered bomber, despite having originally been designed in response to requirements for a fast reconnaissance aircraft.

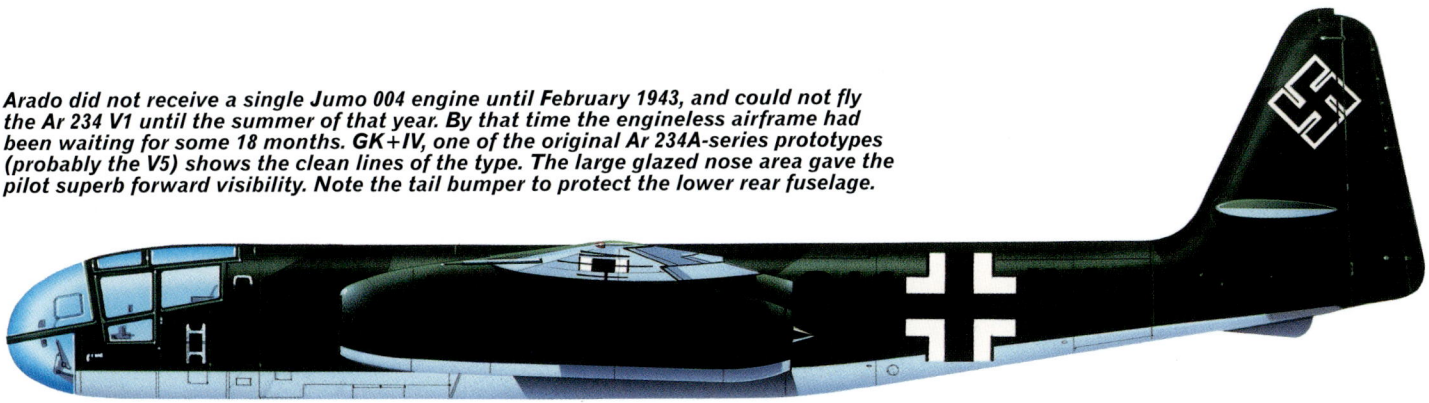

Arado did not receive a single Jumo 004 engine until February 1943, and could not fly the Ar 234 V1 until the summer of that year. By that time the engineless airframe had been waiting for some 18 months. GK+IV, one of the original Ar 234A-series prototypes (probably the V5) shows the clean lines of the type. The large glazed nose area gave the pilot superb forward visibility. Note the tail bumper to protect the lower rear fuselage.

pressurised by air tapped from the turbojet compressors, occupied the extreme nose of the fuselage, and aft of the cockpit the bulk of the fuselage was given over to fuel tanks. The wing featured dual taper on the leading edge, its trailing edge carrying Frise ailerons of exceptionally narrow chord with mass-balanced geared tabs fitted to the inboard ends adjacent to the large, hydraulically-operated plain hinged two-section flaps. The turbojets were completely underslung, and were suspended from three points, two on the front spar and one on the rear, the lower main-plane surface above the turbojets being covered with steel sheet.

Novel undercarriage

While there was little of the unorthodox about the basic design and construction of the Ar 234 airframe, the undercarriage of the aircraft was extremely novel. Undercarriage stowage had presented a major problem from the outset of design work. The thin, shoulder-mounted wing provided insufficient space to house mainwheel legs and their actuating mechanisms. In any case, the high positioning of the wing would have demanded inordinately long oleo legs which it would have been necessary to compress during retraction and extension. The fuselage cross section had been kept to a minimum and thus provided little room for a space-consuming undercarriage of orthodox type. Furthermore, such an undercarriage would have been heavy, and in view of the quantity of fuel dictated by the 2150-km (1,340-mile) range stipulated by the RLM, strict weight-consciousness had been exercised from the outset of design.

Several unorthodox approaches to the undercarriage problem were made by the Arado team at the earliest design stage, and the RLM's Technisches Amt had been offered variants of the E 370 project with various alternative and highly original landing gear arrangements, ranging from a central-ly-mounted retractable bogie comprising nine pairs of small wheels and accompanied by outrigger skids retracting into the engine nacelles, to a jettisonable take-off trolley with a centrally-mounted main skid plus outrigger skids for landing. Surprisingly, the Technisches Amt elected to adopt this last somewhat unlikely arrangement.

Prototype construction began during the spring of 1941, and it was anticipated that the first Jumo 004A turbojets would be available for trial installation in the **Ar 234 V1** towards the end of the year. The development programme was soon set awry, however, when it became obvious that Junkers' more sanguine hopes were not being fulfilled, and that turbojet development was not keeping pace with that of the airframe. The Ar 234 V1 and **V2** airframes were virtually complete during the early winter of 1941, but Junkers could not promise delivery of powerplants for at least a further 12

Above: For take-off the Arado Ar 234A, the first version, sat on a large trolley. This could be steered by the pilot using its nosewheel; brakes were fitted to the mainwheels. Once it reached flying speed the trolley was released. A retractable skid and outriggers were used for landing.

The one feature of the Ar 234A that was truly unconventional was the landing gear. With the slim fuselage full of fuel there was no room for retracted main gears as well, nor could landing gears be accommodated in the jet nacelles or wing, the high wing meaning that ordinary wing-mounted gears would have had to have been very long. The company therefore proposed various unconventional arrangements and the RLM staff selected one of the most unusual. During the first flights of the Ar 234 V1 prototype, the trolley was jettisoned at altitude, but was subsequently released on the runway, as here.

Arado Ar 234

DP+AX, the Ar 234 V3, returns to the ground in dramatic fashion, supported by its centrally-mounted main skid. Also visible is the small stabilising skid provided under the engine nacelle, and which was later replaced by a bomb shackle on the Ar 234B. The Ar 234 V3 was intended as a production prototype for the planned Ar 234A-series, which was not built.

This head-on view of an early Ar 234 on its take-off trolley reveals the location of the Rauchgeräte take-off assistance rockets underwing, outboard of the main engine nacelles.

months, and the Arado team therefore explored the possibility of installing piston engines as a temporary expedient. In this they were frustrated by the unorthodox undercarriage arrangement, insufficient ground clearance for airscrews being offered by the landing skids, and there was no alternative but to await delivery of the turbojets.

Eventually, during February 1943, a pair of pre-production Jumo 004A engines was delivered to Warnemünde, although they were only intended for static tests, Messerschmitt having priority in the delivery of flight-cleared turbojets. The engines were mounted in the Ar 234 V1 airframe (Werk Nr 130001, TG+KB) for taxiing trials, these being somewhat lengthy owing to the erratic behaviour of the 600-kg (1,325-lb) take-off trolley. This featured a steerable nosewheel, and the mainwheels were fitted with hydraulic brakes operated by the pilot's rudder pedals, a lever in the cockpit providing for the release of the trolley. It was intended that the pilot should jettison the trolley at the moment of unstick. An electrically-actuated emergency trolley-release system was also provided. Quick-release fasteners on the hydraulic brake leads were automatically disconnected as the trolley parted company with the aircraft, a braking parachute being deployed to bring the trolley to a standstill. It was decided that, until this release system had been perfected, initial flight tests would be made with the trolley attached for take-off, the pilot subsequently jettisoning this at an altitude of several hundred feet, the trolley being lowered to the ground by means of five parachutes.

The Ar 234 V1 was disassembled in the spring of 1943, and transported to Rheine, north of Münster, in Westphalia, for initial flight trials. At Rheine, flight-cleared Jumo 004A engines were substituted for the original units and, after further

taxiing, which was protracted by some oscillation of the trolley nosewheel as take-off speeds were approached, the aircraft flew for the first time on 30 July 1943 with Flugkapitän Selle at the controls (it has sometimes been claimed that the first flight date was 15 June but this is incorrect).

Selle's pre-flight briefing called for jettisoning the take-off trolley once an altitude of 60 m (200 ft) had been attained. The release system functioned successfully, but the parachutes intended to lower the trolley to the ground failed to deploy, and this was destroyed when it hit the runway. Apart from this mishap, the initial flight was entirely successful, Selle reporting extremely pleasant flying characteristics. A replacement trolley was hurriedly flown to Rheine, but the second flight of the Ar 234 V1 was a repetition of the first in so far as the trolley was concerned as this was again destroyed. On subsequent flights the trolley was released on the runway as soon as flying speed was attained. Some difficulties were encountered with the hydraulic retraction for the skids that were extended prior to take-off to provide the supports on which the aircraft rested on the trolley. On occasions the skids refused to retract, and during landing there was a tendency for one or other of the outboard skid oleo legs to subside slowly until a wingtip was ploughing up the ground.

Second prototype

The second prototype, the Ar 234 V2 (probably DP+AW), joined the V1 at Rheine in August 1943, flying on the 27th of that month, and four weeks later, on 25 August, the **Ar 234 V3** (DP+AX) was flown. Whereas the first two prototypes

An Ar 234 leaves its take-off trolley on the runway as it gets airborne during early tests. Never entirely satisfactory, the trolley and skid arrangement was replaced by conventional tricycle undercarriage for the Ar 234B production version.

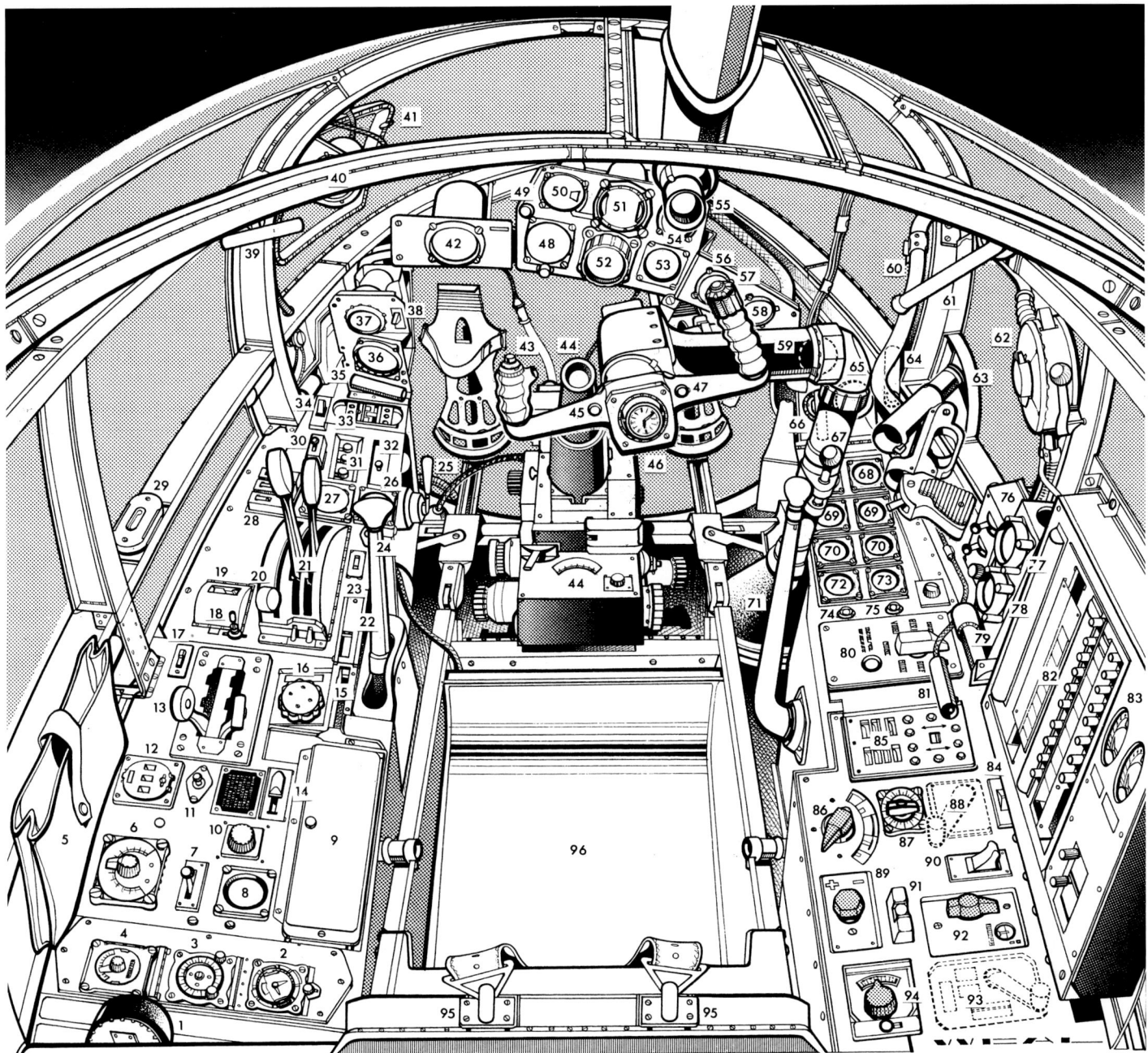

Arado Ar 234 cockpit layout

1 Undercarriage warning horn
2 Contact altimeter
3 Height corrector
4 Wind corrector
5 Map (document) case
6 Rectified airspeed corrector
7 Exhaust nozzle control switch
8 Outside air temperature gauge
9 Navigation equipment stowage
10 Cockpit lights rheostat
11 RATO jettison button
12 RATO selector panel
13 Fuel cocks
14 Engine nozzle control override switch (anti-surge)
15 Tailplane position/incidence indicator
16 Rudder trim wheel and indicator
17 Auxiliary fuel tank selector switch
18 Initial ignition switch
19 Ignition warning indicator
20 Throttle friction damper lock
21 Throttle quadrant
22 Tailplane trim actuator handle
23 Retractable landing lights (floodlights) switch
24 Emergency master electrics circuit breaker (partially obscured by 22)
25 Cockpit heating/conditioning control selector

26 Hydraulic pressure gauge (partially obscured by 22)
27 Gyro monitor (compass) switch
28 Autopilot channel selectors: elevator/aileron/rudder
29 Spirit level
30 Target approach switch
31 Three-position flap selector
32 Undercarriage selector
33 Flap and undercarriage position lights (indicators)
34 Gyro horizon erection switch
35 Braking parachute streaming handle (release)
36 Incidence indicator (artificial horizon)
37 Repeater gyro horizon (rate of climb control)
38 Autopilot master switch
39 Braking parachute jettison handle
40 Standby magnetic compass (partially obscured by canopy frame)
41 Opening direct/clear-vision panel
42 Jet tailpipe pitot pressure (combined port and starboard EPR gauge)
43 Bomb release button on left-hand control column 'horn'
44 Lotfe 7K tachometric bombsight
45 Clock illumination button

46 Clock
47 FuG 16zy (R/T) transmitter button
48 Fine-course altimeter
49 Pilot heater indicator
50 Altitude compensated airspeed indicator
51 Gyro horizon and slip indicator
52 Master compass indicator
53 FuG 16zy (AFN 2) homing indicator
54 Rate of climb and descent indicator (partially obscured by periscope eyepiece)
55 RF 2C Periscopic combined bomb/gunsight and rear mirror
56 Port RPM gauge
57 Autopilot course-setting (turn) control: fast and slow rate (right-hand 'horn')
58 Starboard RPM gauge
59 Port fuel burner pressure gauge (obscured by control column arm)
60 Oxygen hose
61 Roof canopy jettison handle
62 Oxygen regulator
63 Flare pistol mounting
64 Ultra-violet cockpit light (partially obscured by oxygen hose)

65 Starboard fuel burner pressure gauge (partially obscured by control column pivot)
66 Bomb jettison lever (partially obscured by control column mount)
67 Control column release knob (control column shown partly swivelled to expose bombsight)
68 Starboard oil pressure gauge (port gauge obscured by control column mount)
69 Port and starboard jet unit fire-warning temperature gauges
70 Jet pipe (exhaust gas) temperature gauges (port and starboard)
71 Emergency hydraulic hand-pump (see 86)
72 Front fuselage fuel tank contents gauge
73 Rear fuselage fuel tank contents gauge
74 Front tank low fuel contents warning light
75 Rear tank low fuel contents warning light
76 Riedel starter motor panel: 2-stroke engine starter switches and RPM gauge (high/low range selector button)
77 Oxygen system pressure gauge

78 Oxygen flow indicator
79 Oxygen system ON/OFF cock
80 Bomb fusing box selector panel
81 Ultra-violet cockpit light
82 Main electrical switch panel
83 Voltmeters
84 Navigation lights switch (partially hidden below electrical switch panel)
85 Bomb sequence selector panel
86 Flap and undercarriage emergency hydraulic selector switch (see 71)
87 FuG 16zy frequency selector switch
88 Ventral camera doors operating handle (not fitted on bomber variant)
89 FuG 16zy receiver fine tuning (homing aerial remote-control panel)
90 FuG 16zy MCW switch (or FuG 125 'Hermine' – bearings from ground control rotating beacon)
91 FuG 25A self-destruct switch
92 FuG 25A IFF control switch
93 Camera operating panel (not fitted on bomber variant)
94 FuG 16zy volume control and homing switch (junction box)
95 Shoulder harness anchor-points
96 Pilot's seat

Arado Ar 234B-2

Stabs-Staffel, Kampfgeschwader 76, Karstedt, 1945

The staff squadron of KG 76 was the first recipient of the Ar 234B-2 bomber version, receiving its first aircraft in October 1944. Pilots converted to the type at a training unit at Alt Lönnewitz before moving west to join the fight against the Allies. II Gruppe/KG 76 converted in November, in time to join the Ardennes counter-offensive in December and January. I Gruppe started work-up in January, followed swiftly by III Gruppe, although neither attained full status. III/KG 76 expended most of its efforts against river crossings, including the famous Remagen bridge across the Rhine. By the end of March the Ar 234 units had virtually ceased operations.

Bombsight

The Ar 234B-2 had a complex bomb-aiming system. For shallow dive attacks the PV1B sighting head was used, this being situated in the RF2C periscope above the cockpit, which could also be rotated aft to sight for the defensive cannon. The correct sighting angle was fed to the PV1B by the BZA 1 bombing computer. For level-bombing some Ar 234B-2/1 aircraft had a Lofte 7K tachometric sight located between the pilot's feet. With the aircraft on autopilot, the pilot disconnected the control column and swung it to the side to allow him to operate the Lofte 7K. After bomb release the control column was reconnected.

Powerplant and fuel

The Junkers Jumo 004B Orkan turbojet ran on J2 fuel, housed in two tanks in the fuselage either side of the wing. The forward compartment held 1800 litres (396 Imp gal) and the rear 2000 litres (440 Imp gal). A Riedel two-cylinder starter motor span the turbines up to 3,000 rpm, at which time the combustion chambers were electrically ignited. Petrol was used for the start-up sequence, fuel supply automatically switching to J2 at 6,000 rpm when the pilot activated the thrust levers.

Arado Ar 234

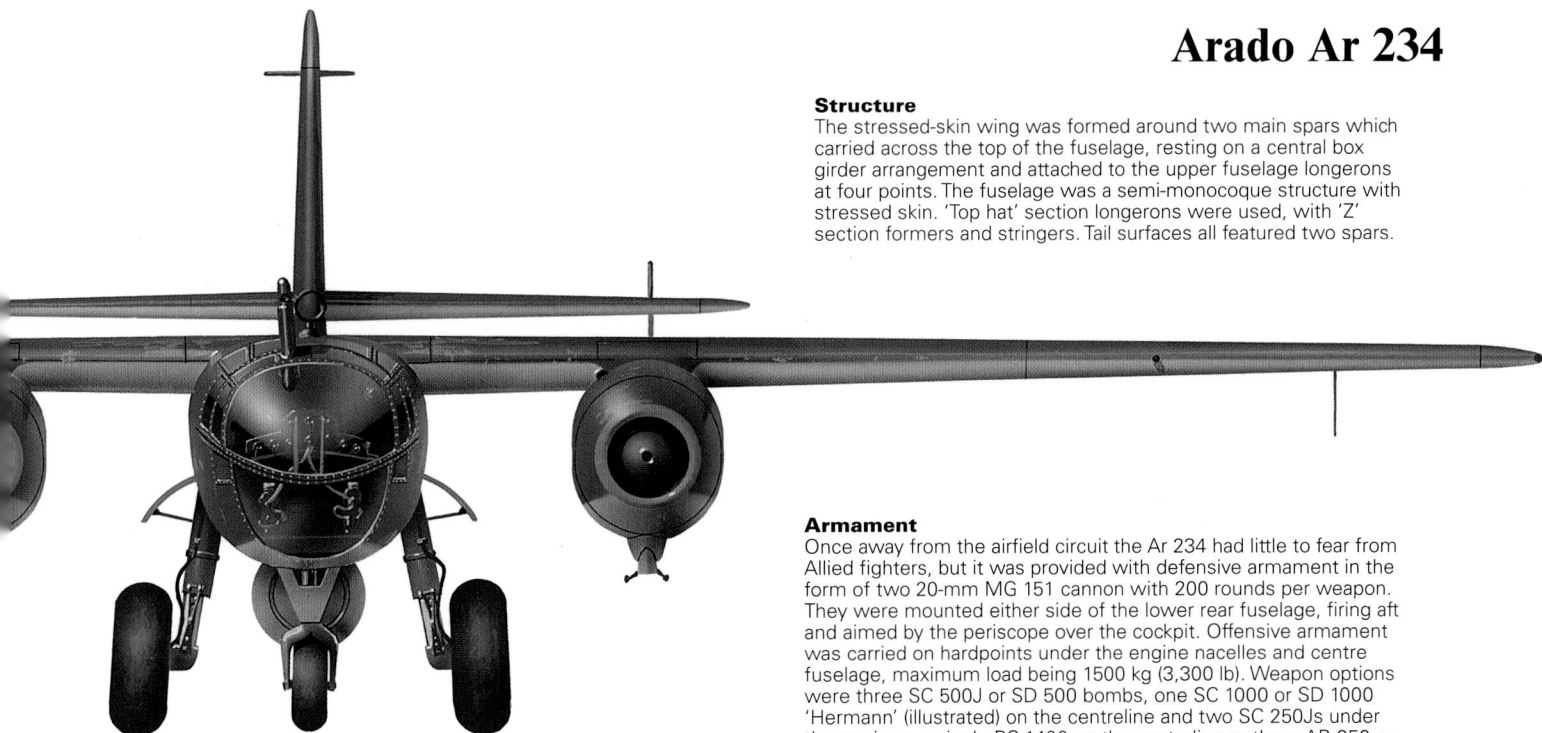

Structure

The stressed-skin wing was formed around two main spars which carried across the top of the fuselage, resting on a central box girder arrangement and attached to the upper fuselage longerons at four points. The fuselage was a semi-monocoque structure with stressed skin. 'Top hat' section longerons were used, with 'Z' section formers and stringers. Tail surfaces all featured two spars.

Armament

Once away from the airfield circuit the Ar 234 had little to fear from Allied fighters, but it was provided with defensive armament in the form of two 20-mm MG 151 cannon with 200 rounds per weapon. They were mounted either side of the lower rear fuselage, firing aft and aimed by the periscope over the cockpit. Offensive armament was carried on hardpoints under the engine nacelles and centre fuselage, maximum load being 1500 kg (3,300 lb). Weapon options were three SC 500J or SD 500 bombs, one SC 1000 or SD 1000 'Hermann' (illustrated) on the centreline and two SC 250Js under the engines, a single PC 1400 on the centreline or three AB 250 or AB 500 anti-personnel bomb clusters.

Reconnaissance operational history

The first operations were flown in July 1944 with the Ar 234 V5 and V7 by 1. Staffel/Versuchsverband Ob.d.L. Pilots from this unit then established Kommando Götz at Rheine in September, with four Ar 234B-1s, to be the first official unit. However, the original unit continued to fly the type, adding two four-engined prototypes (V6 and V7) and operating some successful missions over the British Isles. In November Kommando Hecht and Kdo.Sperling were formed, but were deactivated by December, to be replaced by 1./Fernaufklärungsgruppe 100 in January 1945, which operated from southern Germany, ending the conflict at Saalbach. Next to form was Sd.Kdo. Sommer, with three Ar 234B-1s, at Udine in northern Italy, from where it provided reconnaissance over the Italian front to great effect. By the end of the war two more units had received Ar 234B-1s – 1./FAGr. 123 and 1./FAGr. 33, the latter covering the north-western part of Germany and Denmark.

B-2 sub-variants

The Ar 234B-2 was built in several sub-variants according to equipment fit. The Ar 234B-2/b could carry cameras for the reconnaissance mission, while the Ar 234B-2/1 was fitted with Lofte 7K level-bombing sight for use in the pathfinding role. Most aircraft were fitted with Patin PDS three-axis autopilot, resulting in the 'p' suffix, while aircraft plumbed to carry long-range drop tanks had an 'r' suffix. Thus an aircraft with camera capability, drop tanks and autopilot would be designated Ar 234B-2/bpr.

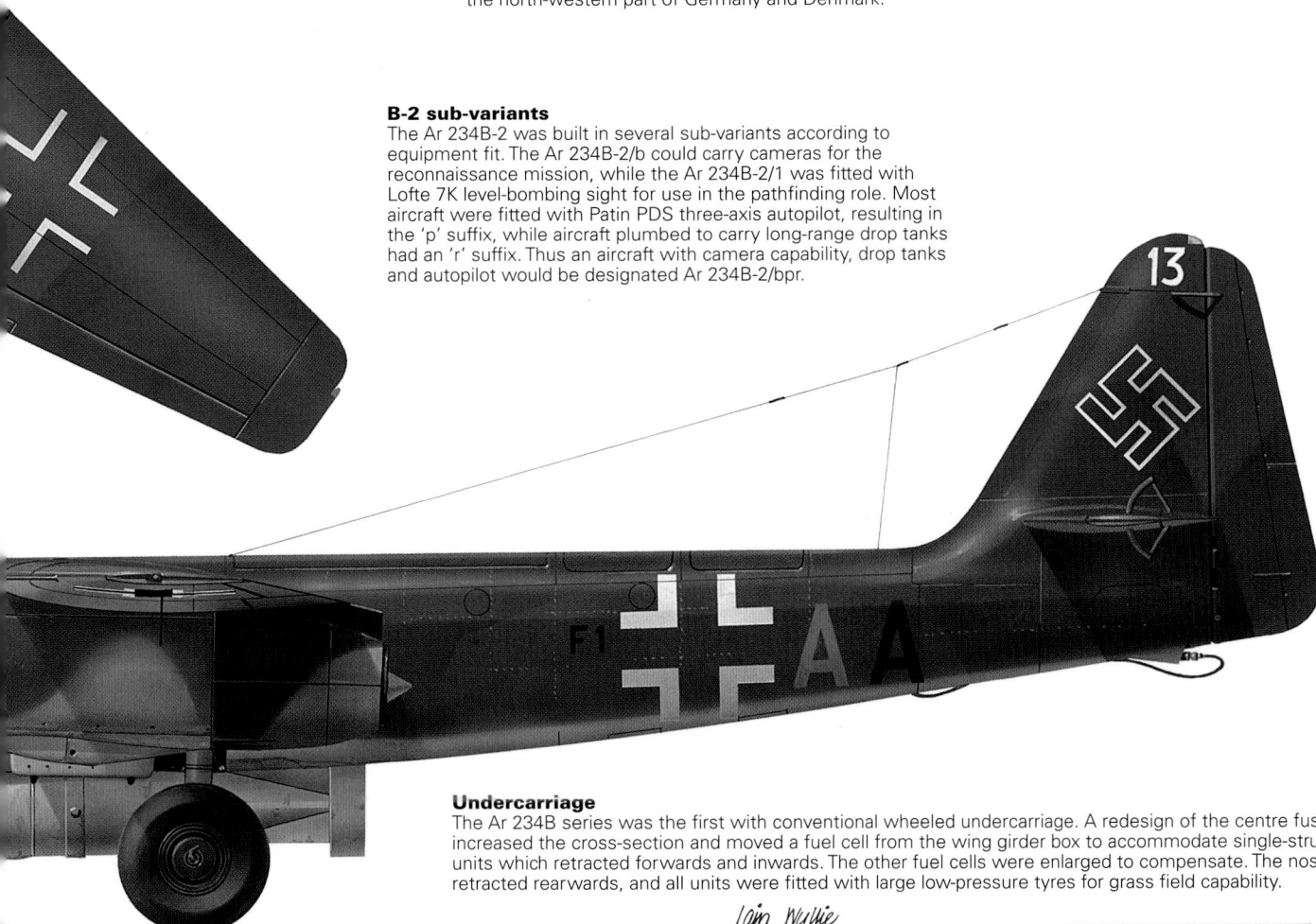

Undercarriage

The Ar 234B series was the first with conventional wheeled undercarriage. A redesign of the centre fuselage increased the cross-section and moved a fuel cell from the wing girder box to accommodate single-strut main units which retracted forwards and inwards. The other fuel cells were enlarged to compensate. The nosewheel retracted rearwards, and all units were fitted with large low-pressure tyres for grass field capability.

Iain Wyllie

Arado Ar 234

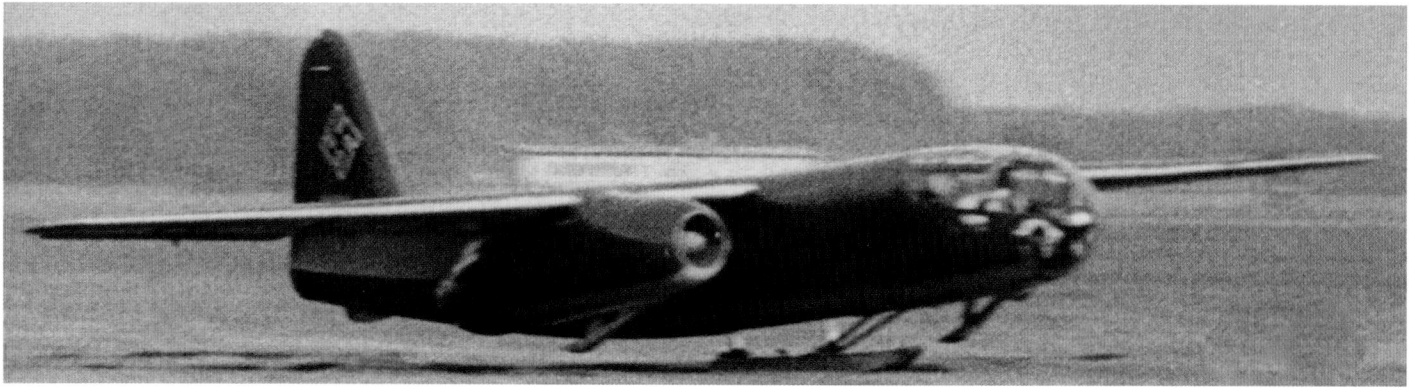

Landing the Ar 234A was accomplished on a grass strip, the aircraft resting on a central main skid and two outrigger skids that were housed in the engine nacelles. The central skid was also deployed for take-off, being used as the support to which the trolley was attached.

were, to all intents and purposes, identical, the V3 was intended initially as a production prototype for the planned **Ar 234A**, and featured an ejection seat for the pilot, cabin pressurisation, and provision for the attachment of two Rauchgeräte (take-off assistance rocket) units outboard of the engine nacelles. At this time it was anticipated that the production Ar 234A would have an empty weight of 4800 kg (10,580 lb), would carry 3000 kg (6,615 lb) of fuel, and would weigh 8000 kg (17,640 lb) fully loaded. It was anticipated that maximum speed would be 780 km/h (485 mph) at 6000 m (19,685 ft), maximum operational altitude being 11000 m (36,090 ft) and range being 2000 km (1,240 miles).

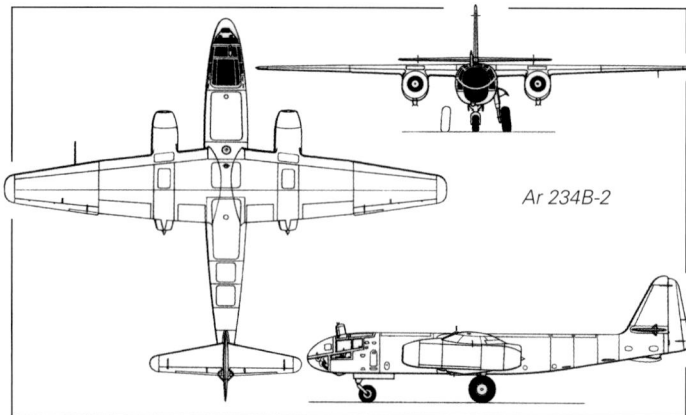

Ar 234B-2

The **Ar 234 V4**, which joined the test programme in September 1943, differed from its immediate predecessor only in certain items of test equipment, but the **Ar 234 V5** was the first prototype to receive the improved Jumo 004B-0 turbojet, this initially possessing a similar rating to the Jumo 004A at 8.23 kN (1,850 lb st), but offering a 90 kg (200 lb) decrease in engine weight. The V5 had no provision for cabin pressurisation, and was concerned with both engine development and an investigation of compressibility effects, but by this time the decision had already been taken by the Technisches Amt to abandon the proposed A-series in favour of an appreciably more versatile derivative of the design, the **Ar 234B**, which was christened the **Blitz** (Lightning). The Ar 234 V2's test career was destined to be singularly short-lived, Flugkapitän Selle experiencing a sudden fire in the port engine that burned through the control rods while the aircraft was in the landing circuit, and losing his life, his place being taken as chief test pilot and superintendent of the Alt Lönnewitz flight test division by Flugkapitän Joachim Carl. It has sometimes been claimed, incorrectly, that the aircraft in this crash was the Ar 234 V7.

One of the major drawbacks of the Ar 234A from the operational viewpoint was the fact that, after landing, the aircraft was unable to manoeuvre on its skids, having to be raised by three spiral jacks onto the take-off trolley for towing to dispersal. It was foreseen that landing areas could well be cluttered with immobile aircraft awaiting towing and, in the

In service the Ar 234B proved very difficult to catch in the reconnaissance or bombing roles, although only a small number reached operations. Visible in this view is the 'horn' above the cockpit that served as the housing for the rear weapons aiming/rear view periscope.

The first operational bomber unit in the world to be regularly equipped with jet-powered bombers was Kampfgeschwader 76 in late 1944/early 1945. This Ar 234B-2, wearing the 'F1' code of KG 76, belonged to the wing's 9th Staffel (hence the letter 'T' in the aircraft's code F1+MT).

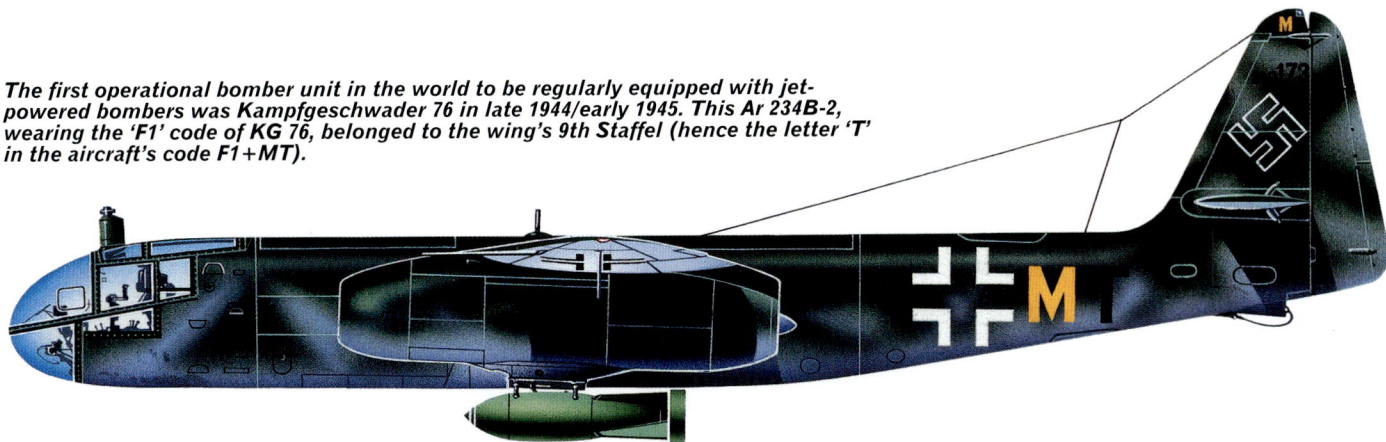

meantime, extremely vulnerable should the airfield be strafed by enemy intruders. It had become obvious, therefore, that although the trolley-and-skid scheme functioned quite efficiently, a more orthodox undercarriage was necessary, and the Arado team had undertaken some redesign to provide space for such landing gear. This space had been obtained by increasing the fuselage cross section marginally and utilising much of the bay formed by the central fuselage box girder for wheel wells, the fore and aft fuselage fuel tanks being enlarged to compensate for the loss of fuel capacity that would otherwise have resulted from the deletion of the central fuel cell.

Fitted with large, low-pressure tyres, the main undercarriage members were single-wheel units retracting forwards and inwards hydraulically by a simple but robust mechanism, and being enclosed by hydraulically-actuated doors. The heavy nosewheel fork was attached to the fuselage beneath the pilot's seat at a point slightly forward of the wheel axis, and retracted aft. This new undercarriage arrangement was first installed on the **Ar 234 V9**.

Enter the Blitz

An assembly line for the Ar 234B was set up at Alt Lönnewitz in Saxony late in 1943, and construction of the B-series prototypes and the pre-production **Ar 234B-0** reconnaissance aircraft proceeded in parallel, less than 10 weeks elapsing between the first flight of the first B-series prototype, the Ar 234 V9, in March 1944, and the first pre-production Ar 234B-0 early in the following June. In the meantime, it had been decided to complete the remaining three A-series prototypes as development aircraft for later models, the **Ar 234 V6** and **V8** being selected for the development of a definitive powerplant arrangement for the four-engined **Ar 234C**, and the **Ar 234 V7** (Werk Nr 130007, T9+MH) being fitted with production Jumo 004B-1s as part of the development programme of these units for the Ar 234B. The fact that these aircraft had A-series airframes necessitated the retention of the trolley-and-skid arrangement.

The first B-series prototype, the Ar 234 V9 (Werk Nr

Above: An Ar 234B taxies past a Siebel Si 204 liaison aircraft. Ar 234 operations were principally conducted from Rheine, although limited combat sorties were flown from bases in France and Italy.

Fitted with Rauchgeräte take-off booster rocket packs and carrying an SC 500J 500-kg (1,100-lb) bomb under the centre fuselage and under each engine nacelle, the first B-series prototype, the Ar 234 V9 (Werk Nr 130009, PH+SQ) begins its take-off run.

130009, PH+SQ) was flown on 10 March 1944, this having Jumo 004B-1 engines, an ejection seat, cockpit pressurisation and the conventional tricycle undercarriage intended for all production examples. The **Ar 234 V10** (PH+SQ), which followed on 2 April, differed initially only in having no provision for cabin pressurisation, but early in its test programme this prototype was fitted with the B2A periscopic bomb sight for use in glide and shallow dive-bombing trials. Bomb shackles were provided beneath the engine nacelles for 250-kg (550-lb) or 500-kg (1,100-lb) bombs or 300-litre

An Arado Ar 234B gets airborne with the help of a pair of Rauchgeräte boosters. They were jettisoned and recovered by parachute after take-off. Also evident in this view is the bomb carriage beneath the engine nacelle.

Arado Ar 234

Fitted with conventional wheeled undercarriage, the Ar 234B showed considerable promise, and lived up to it in service. This aircraft is one of the early Ar 234Bs, lacking the periscopic sight above the cockpit. Approximately thirteen of the 20 identified pre-production B-0 aircraft were sent to the Rechlin test centre. There was a limited production run of B-1 reconnaissance aircraft, followed by the dedicated bomber version, the B-2. Arado managed to fit normal landing gear by removing the centre fuselage tank, making the front and rear tanks bigger so that the total capacity of 3800 litres (835 Imp gal) was only slightly affected. Each undercarriage leg with a large, low-pressure tyre retracted forwards and inwards, stowing the wheel upright.

Arado Ar 234B-2/Ir Blitz cutaway key

1 Port elevator hinge
2 Tailplane skinning
3 Port elevator
4 Tab actuating rod
5 Elevator trim tab
6 Geared rudder tab (upper)
7 Rudder hinges
8 Tail navigation light
9 Plywood fin leading edge
10 T-aerial
11 Re-transmission aerial
12 Aerial matching unit
13 Tailfin structure
14 Rudder construction
15 Rudder post
16 Rudder tab (lower)
17 Lower rudder hinge
18 Rudder actuating rods
19 Parachute cable
20 Cable anchor point/tailskid
21 Starboard elevator tab
22 Elevator construction
23 Tailplane construction
24 Elevator control linkage
25 Tailplane attachment points
26 Elevator rod
27 Port side control runs
28 Internal mass balance
29 Parachute release mechanism
30 Main FuG 16zy panel (BZA computer)
31 Brake parachute container
32 Starboard MG 151 cannon muzzle
33 Brake chute door (open)
34 Mauser MG 151/20 cannon (rearward firing)
35 Cannon support yoke
36 Spent cartridge chute
37 Access panel (lowered)
38 Ammunition feed chute
39 Tail surface control rods (starboard)
40 Ammunition box
41 Bulkhead
42 Fuel vent pipe
43 Fuel pumps
44 Fuel lever gauge
45 Rear fuel cell (2000-litre/ 440-Imp gal capacity)
46 Fuselage frames
47 Fuel filler point
48 Fuel lines
49 Inner flap construction
50 Exhaust cone
51 Nacelle support fairing
52 RATO exhaust
53 Outer flap section
54 Aileron tab
55 Tab actuating rod
56 Port aileron
57 Port navigation light
58 Aileron.control linkage
59 Pitot tube
60 Front spar
61 Outer flap control linkage
62 Wing construction
63 Nacelle attachment points (front and rear spar)
64 Detachable nacelle cowling
65 FuG 25a IFF unit
66 Inner flap control linkage
67 Control rods and hydraulic activating rod
68 Rear spar
69 Hydraulic fluid tank (18-litre/ 4.4-Imp gal capacity)
70 Centre section box
71 FuG 25a ring antenna
72 Suppressed D/F antenna
73 Fuel pumps
74 Fuel level gauge
75 Fuel filler point
76 Fuel lines
77 Bulkhead
78 Port control console (throttle quadrant)

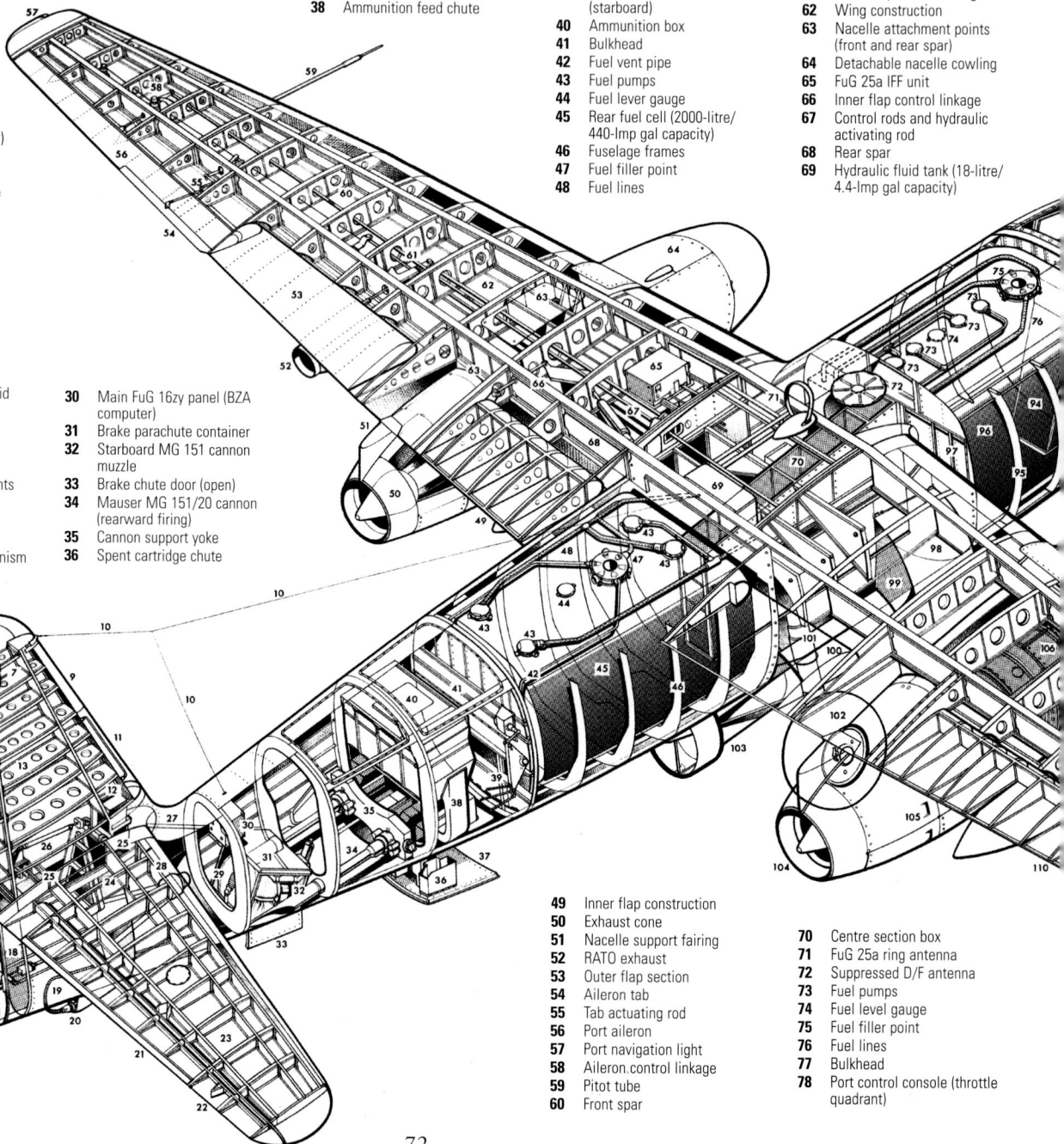

The third prototype Ar 234 featured provision for Rauchgeräte take-off assistance rockets, an ejection seat for the pilot and cockpit pressuration. Produced by Walter, the HWK 500A-1 RATO units were intended to be reused, and were recovered by parachute after they had served their purpose.

79 Pilot entry hatch (hinged to starboard)
80 Periscopic sight
81 Periscopic head (rear-view mirror/gunsight)
82 Clear-vision cockpit glazing
83 Instrument panel
84 Rudder pedal
85 Swivel-mounted control stick
86 Lotfe 7K tachometric bombsight mounting
87 Pilot's seat
88 Starboard control console (oil/temperature gauges)
89 Radio panel (FuG 16zy behind pilot's seat)
90 Oxygen bottles
91 Nosewheel door
92 Nosewheel fork
93 Rearward-retracting nosewheel
94 Nosewheel well centre section
95 Fuselage frames
96 Forward fuel cell (1800-litre/ 385-Imp gal capacity)
97 Bulkhead
98 Mainwheel door
99 Starboard mainwheel well
100 Mainwheel leg door
101 Starboard mainwheel leg
102 Forward-retracting mainwheel
103 SC 1000 'Hermann' bomb beneath fuselage
104 Engine exhaust
105 Auxiliary cooling intakes
106 Starboard Jumo 004B turbojet
107 Annular oil tank
108 Riedel starter motor on nose cone
109 Auxiliary tank (300-litre/66-Imp gal) beneath nacelle (not carried with SC 1000 bomb)
110 Flap outer section construction
111 Walter HWK 500A-1 RATO unit
112 RATO recovery parachute pack
113 Aileron tab
114 Starboard aileron construction
115 Wing skin stiffeners
116 Starboard navigation light

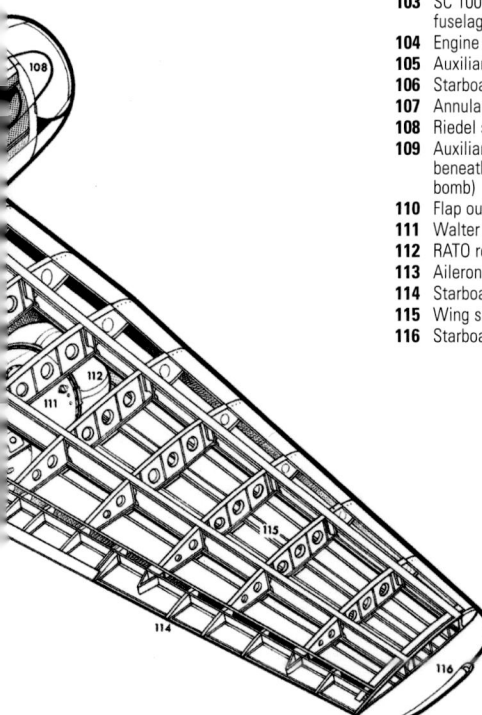

(66-Imp gal) drop tanks, and attachment points were introduced for Rauchgeräte units. The **Ar 234 V11** (PH+SR) was similar to the V9, having a pressurised cockpit and joining the test programme on 5 May, the next aircraft to fly being the first pre-production Ar 234B-0 which flew at Alt Lönnewitz on 8 June 1944, two days after the D-Day landings in Normandy, with Flugkapitän Carl at the controls.

Inauspicious debut

This first flight of the first pre-production aircraft was scheduled to be witnessed by high-ranking officials from the RLM, the Party and the Luftwaffe, but Carl decided that it would be wiser to make an unofficial first flight earlier in the day. After taking-off, the 'undercarriage up' lights failed to come on, and as the radio failed simultaneously, Carl had no means of ascertaining if the undercarriage was up or locked in the down position. Nevertheless, he decided to risk landing back at Alt Lönnewitz, and during the final approach both engines flamed out. He succeeded in getting the aircraft down safely, the troubles were traced to faulty micro-switches in the undercarriage retraction mechanism and incorrectly positioned fuel pumps, and five hours later the official first flight took place.

The pre-production Ar 234B-0 was not equipped with ejection seat or cabin pressurisation, but provision was made for a pair of Rb 50/30 or 75/30 reconnaissance cameras or a mix of one Rb 75/30 and one Rb 20/30. Thirteen of the 20 pre-production aircraft were sent to the Erprobungsstelle Rechlin, the RLM's flight test centre, to participate in an intensive flight development and evaluation programme, and one pilot, Ubbo Janssen, claimed to have attained a speed of Mach 0.86, although it is likely that there was an error in the Mach-meter as compressibility effects normally began to manifest themselves in the vicinity of Mach 0.78.

With approximately 8.83 kN (1,984 lb) of thrust available from each Jumo 004B turbojet, the Ar 234B was short on take-off power when loaded to the maximum weight of some 9800 kg (21,605 lb).

Arado Ar 234

The Ar 234 used a similar engine installation to the Messerschmitt Me 262 fighter, with long, narrow-throated nacelles slung below the inboard part of the wing. The adoption of a tricycle undercarriage on production aircraft left the engine nacelles free for weapons carriage, and bomb shackles were incorporated to take up to 500 kg (1,100 lb) of bombs beneath each wing. A third bomb shackle was located under the centreline, capable of carrying weapons of up to 1400 kg (3,000 lb), including the 1000-kg SC 1000 'Hermann', with which Ar 234s unsuccessfully attacked the bridge at Remagen during early 1945.

An Ar 234B-1 reconnaissance aircraft is prepared for a mission. Ordinary petrol was used to start the two-cylinder starter motor, which spun the turbines to 3,000 rpm, when the combustion chambers were eletronically ignited. At 6,000 rpm the throttle was opened and the petrol supply cut off, being replaced by kerosene.

For the initial test programme K1 diesel oil had been used as fuel for the Jumo turbojets, but shortages of K1 necessitated switching to the cheaper and more readily available J2 of the same calorific value. The turbines were activated by Riedel two-cylinder starter motors which ran them up to 3,000 revolutions at which the combustion chambers were electrically ignited. Petrol was used for starting purposes, and at 6,000 revolutions the pilot operated the throttle and the petrol supply was automatically replaced by J2. All fuel was housed in two flexible fuselage tanks, the forward tank, between the pilot's cockpit and the wing leading edge, being of 1800-litre (396-Imp gal) capacity, and the aft tank containing 2000 litres (440 Imp gal).

The pre-production Ar 234B-0 was followed off the Alt Lönnewitz assembly line by the **Ar 234B-1** that was essentially similar apart from being equipped with a Patin PDS three-axes automatic pilot and having provision for drop tanks as standard, but the Ar 234B-1, which was intended solely for reconnaissance, was an interim model pending the introduction of the very much more versatile **Ar 234B-2**

that was suitable for bombing and pathfinding roles as well as that of photographic reconnaissance. The Ar 234B-2s left the Alt Lönnewitz line to various equipment standards, indicated by suffix letters (however, these existed on paper but were often not used in operational documentation). For example, the **Ar 234B-2/b** was equipped for photo-reconnaissance missions with two Rb 50/30 or 75/30 cameras or a single Rb 75/30 and an Rb 20/30, while the **Ar 234B-2/1** was equipped with a Lotfe 7K bombsight for the pathfinder role. If Patin PDS equipment was installed the letter 'p' was added to the designation, while provision for long-range drop tanks resulted in the addition of the letter 'r'. Thus, reconnaissance and pathfinder versions embodying both the Patin PDS and

The wheels gave the Ar 234B better flexibility of operations. This is one of the B-series prototypes, clearly showing the Rauchgeräte take-off assistance unit beneath its starboard wing. At least one of the B-series aircraft was converted into a four-engined prototype.

Arado Ar 234

Left: An early Arado Ar 234 in flight reveals landing skids extended beneath the slender fuselage and engine nacelles. Clean, the Arado Ar 234 had a limiting Mach number of 0.78, giving the aircraft enough performance to escape from any opposing fighter, if seen in time. Despite its high speed and high altitude performance, the production Ar 234 was not invulnerable, and some fell before the guns of slower Allied fighters.

Below: Entry for the pilot into the Ar 234's comparatively roomy cockpit was by means of a glazed hatch in the upper fuselage nose. For level bombing, the control column was disconnected and swung out of the way, and the pilot used the Lotfe 7K sight that was located between his feet, flying the aircraft by overriding the Patin PDS three-axis autopilot.

drop tank attachment points became the **Ar 234B-2/bpr** and **-2/1pr**, respectively, while the standard bombing model became the **Ar 234B-2/p**, **-2/r** or **-2/pr** according to the equipment installed.

Weapons options

The Ar 234B-2 was intended to carry a 1500-kg (3,300-lb) bomb load in maximum loaded condition, comprising one 500-kg (1,100-lb) SC 500J bomb beneath the fuselage and a similar weapon beneath each engine nacelle, but alternative loads included a single 1400-kg (3,086-lb) PC 1400 bomb or 1000-kg (2,205-lb) SD 1000 bomb beneath the fuselage, or a single SC 500J and two 250-kg (550-lb) SC 250J bombs. A pair of aft-firing 20-mm MG 151 cannon was carried by some aircraft, and the PV1B sighting head of the RF2C periscope that was normally used in conjunction with the BZA 1 bombing computer could be turned to provide rearward vision for firing the cannon. The Lotfe 7K tachometric bombsight, which was located between the pilot's feet for level bombing, enabled a high degree of accuracy to be attained under good conditions. An overriding control for the automatic pilot was normally employed with this sight during the bombing run,

the pilot disconnecting the control column that then swung clear of the bombsight, being reconnected when the bombs had been released. For glide and shallow dive-bombing the BZA 1 computer fed the PV1B sighting head with the bombing angle by an electrical remote control system. The only protective armour installed comprised a 15.5-mm plate attached to the rear wall of the cockpit to provide the pilot's head and shoulders with some protection.

The Ar 234B-series prototypes, of which this is one, were used for various development trials, including work on the BZA 1 bombing computer and PV1B sighting head trials.

Arado Ar 234

Three Ar 234B have been identified as having been converted into makeshift night-fighters, with FuG 218 Neptun radar. Known as Nachtigall (Nightingale), at least one is believed to have been flown operationally by Kommando Bonow in March 1945 – this Ar 234B-2/N Werk Nr 140146 is thought to have been flown by Kurt Bonow himself.

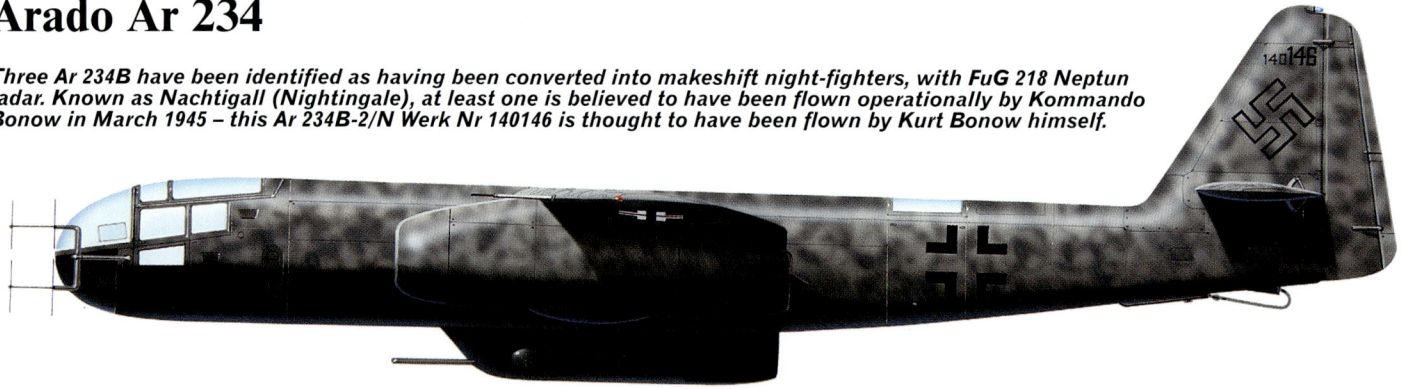

Despite the introduction of conventional tricycle undercarriage on the Ar 234B, the V6 and V8 retained the take-off trolley and landing skids of the initial prototypes and pre-production machines.

Operational career

The unit that flew the first-ever operational missions by jet-powered combat aircraft was 1. Staffel of the Versuchsverband Ob.d.L., this test and evaluation unit of the Luftwaffe High Command being largely responsible for the operational evaluation of the Ar 234. The 1. Staffel had taken delivery of the Ar 234 V5 and V7 at Juvincourt, near Reims, in July 1944 and, possessing only two aircrews conversant with the jet aircraft, the unit flew its Ar 234s from the concrete runway and landed them on a special grass strip, Rauchgeräte units being employed to assist take-offs and breaking chutes being deployed to reduce landing runs. More than 20 flying hours were accumulated by both prototypes, and a number of highly successful reconnaissance missions were flown, no difficulty being experienced in eluding Allied fighters. The first of these was made on 2 August 1944 by the Ar 234 V7, equipped with two Rb 50/30 cameras and piloted by Oberleutnant Erich Sommer over the Cherbourg peninsula. This was arguably the first jet-powered combat mission in history, and was a complete success.

In late September 1944, a Sonderkommando, Kommando Götz, was established at Rheine with several Ar 234B-1s, its

Technicians remove a film magazine from the camera of a reconnaissance-configured Ar 234 carrying the 'T9' code of the Versuchsverband Ob.d.L. The Ar 234B-0 and B-1 carried two cameras in the rear fuselage bay.

immediate task being that of reconnoitring British East Coast harbours between the Thames Estuary and Yarmouth, plus airfields in the south-east of England, to provide the German High Command with immediate warning of any sign of Allied preparations to invade the Netherlands. Kommando Götz had been formed with personnel from the 1. Staffel of

The first Ar 234 unit was 1. Staffel of Versuchsverband Ob.d.L., a test and evaluation unit, which also performed the first operational reconnaissance missions. With initial equipment comprising four Ar 234B-1s, the Sonderkommando Götz was formed from this unit at Rheine in late September 1944 to undertake reconnaissance of Britain's east coast ports and airfields, to give warning of any invasion of the Netherlands. In November 1944 Sd.Kdo. Hecht and Sd.Kdo. Sperling were formed. They were soon disbanded and incorporated into a long-range reconnaissance Staffel, 1./FAGr. 100. This Ar 234B-1 reconnaissance machine wears the 'flatulent sparrow' badge of the Sd.Kdo. Sperling ('Sparrow') on the nose.

Right: The Arado 234 V8 was powered by four BMW 003A turbojets, in paired nacelles, and acted as a prototype for the stillborn four-engined Ar 234C series. Planned production Ar 234Cs took in a range of reconnaissance, bomber, multi-purpose, night fighter and armed reconnaissance versions.

Below: The only practical way of increasing the Ar 234's engine thrust was to fit four engines. Powered by BMW 003 turbojets in four separate nacelles, the Ar 234 V6 (Werk Nr 130006, GK+IW) flew on 25 April 1944. The only Ar 234 to feature this spaced engine installation, the Ar 234 V6 was based on an A-series airframe and was intended primarily to provide a comparison with the paired nacelle arrangement of the V8.

the Versuchsverband Ob.d.L., which had arrived at Rheine in early September by way of Chièvres and Volkel. Five aircrews were now available, and the inventory comprised the Ar 234 V7 and two Ar 234B-1s. With the availability of more Ar 234B-1s Kommando Götz was formed, although the Versuchsverband Ob.d.L. continued to operate the Arado, and by the end of November, when the 1. Staffel had seven Ar 234s on strength, including the four-engined V6 and V8, and the 3. Staffel had four Ar 234s, a considerable number of photographic sorties had been flown at altitudes of the order of 8800-9000 m (29,000-30,000 ft), including several over the British Isles.

In November 1944, two other Ar 234B-1-equipped Sonderkommandos, Kdo. Hecht and Kdo. Sperling, were formed for reconnaissance tasks. Kdo. Hecht also had the Ar 234V7 at its disposal, this long-lived aircraft being the machine that flew the first-ever jet-powered sortie on 2 August 1944. In October the first Ar 234B-2 bombers had been delivered to the Stab (headquarters) of Kampfgeschwader 76, the pilots of this bomber wing receiving conversion training at a school established at Alt Lönnewitz. The first Gruppe to commence

conversion to the Ar 234B-2 was II/KG 76 in November, and operating from Achmer and Rheine, this unit undertook a number of pinpoint attacks on Allied positions during the Ardennes counter-offensive during December 1944 and January 1945. In January 1945, I/KG 76 was also working up to operational status, being followed by III/KG 76, although neither Gruppe was destined ever to attain full strength.

Kommandos Hecht and Sperling had been disbanded by the end of 1944, but in January 1945, 1./FAGr. 100, a long-range reconnaissance Staffel, was operating a combination of Ar 234B-1s and Me 262As in southern Germany under Luftflotte 6. The Ar 234B-2s of III/KG 76 were assigned to Luftwaffenkommando West under Jagdkorps II, this organisation being disbanded in February when the Gruppe became a component of the 16 Fliegerdivision, but flying activities were restricted owing to the severe fuel shortages. However, on 24 February, an Ar 234B-2 from this unit suffered a flame-out in one engine and was forced down by P-47 Thunderbolts near the village of Segelsdorf. On the following day the village was captured by the 9th US Army and, with it, the first example of the Blitz to fall virtually intact into Allied hands. Early in March, improvements in fuel supplies enabled the Ar 234B-2s of III/KG 76 to increase operational missions up to some 50 per day, most of them being directed against Allied river crossings and spearheads. Between 7 March when it was captured by the Allies and 17 March when it finally collapsed, the Remagen Bridge was often attacked by Ar 234s of III/KG 76 carrying 1000-kg (2,205-lb) bombs, operating in concert with Me 262As that attempted to strafe surrounding flak emplacements.

Several Ar 234Bs were captured intact by the Allies at the war's end, often in a relatively pristine condition. Naturally, they became the subject of much interest and were extensively tested in both Britain and the United States, although the type's limited engine life (and a high level of sabotage) proved a major handicap.

Another captured Ar 234B, named Snafu 1, sits on the ramp awaiting testing. British test pilot Eric Brown praised the Ar 234 for its range and speed. However, Brown considered the immature turbojets to be the aircraft's Achilles' heel and himself suffered an engine explosion shortly before taking off for a test flight.

Arado Ar 234

Arado Ar 234s line up in the snow awaiting another mission during the Ardennes counter-offensive of December 1944 and January 1945. The Ar 234s were used for pinpoint attacks on the advancing Allies positions.

In the spring of 1945, the Sd.Kdo. Sommer was activated with three Ar 234Bs at Udine, north-west of Trieste, as a result of constant complaints concerning the inadequacy of aerial reconnaissance reports made by German forces in northern Italy. The arrival of these aircraft radically changed the situation for, operating at altitudes between 9000 and 12000 m (29,500 and 39,000 ft), they maintained regular reconnaissance over the Ancona and Leghorn sectors of the front, and had the situation developed differently it was proposed to raise this unit in the Italian theatre to full Staffel strength.

By the end of March 1945, most surviving Ar 234B-2s of III/KG 76 had been gathered at Marx, Oldenburg, where they were virtually immobilised through lack of fuel and spare parts, and KG 76's other Gruppen were in no better situation, their remnants being gathered on airfields in Schleswig-Holstein, I/KG 76 being at Leck, II/KG 76 being at Scheppern, and the Stab (headquarters) being at Karstedt. The Ar 234Bs of 1./FAGr. 100 ended the war at Saalbach, and two other reccce units that had received the Blitz in small numbers were 1./FAGr. 123 and 1./FAGr. 33, the latter having a mixture of Ar 234Bs and Ju 188s, and being under the control of Luftwaffe General Denmark. A total of 210 Ar 234Bs are recorded as having been completed at Alt Lönnewitz when production was finally halted, but owing to fuel shortages and the confusion reigning during the closing months of the war, at least a third of them failed to reach operational units.

At least three Ar 234B-series aircraft are known to have been converted into improvised night-fighters. This was to satisfy the increasing awareness that defensive jet-powered night-fighters had become by mid-1944 an absolute necessity, and beginning in September 1944 the first of them, Ar 234B-2 Werk Nr 140145, was converted with the addition of FuG 218 Neptun radar and a radar operator's crew station in the rear fuselage where cameras were normally fitted in reconnaissance Ar 234s. At least two other conversions are known to have been made, and one of them is thought to have carried out several unsuccessful combat evaluation missions.

The Ar 234 has the accolade of having flown the final sorties made by the Luftwaffe over the British Isles in World War II. On 4 April 1945 an Ar 234B of reconnaissance unit 1./FAGr. 33 piloted by Oberleutnant Planck set off from Wittmundhafen and overflew Hull. Although this is generally regarded as the last such sortie, there is evidence also of a later flight, on 10 April 1945, of a Stavanger-based Ar 234B making a reconnaissance sortie over the east coast of England.

From the cockpit

In Luftwaffe service, the Ar 234B proved a relatively pleasant aircraft to fly, although directional stability left something to be desired. Without the Rauchgeräte units and with half-full tanks, it could take-off within 1000 m (1,100 yards) but demanded between 1800 and 2000 m (2,000 and 2,200 yards) fully laden. The shape of the sharp-nosed Frise ailerons had been determined in the Adlershof wind tunnel,

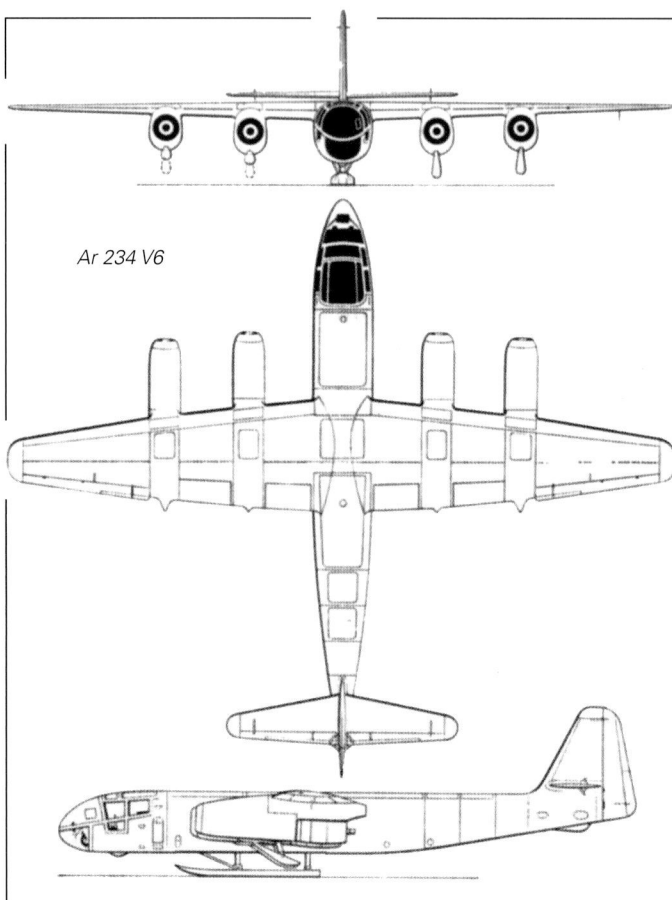

Ar 234 V6

Ar 234 V8

The Ar 234 V8 first flight tested the paired four-BMW 003A-0 turbojet layout as part of the C-series development programme

although they did not prove entirely satisfactory in service. Unless extreme care was exercised in rigging and in adjusting hinge shroud distances and the like, the ailerons misbehaved violently at speeds greater than 590 km/h (370 mph), and a common fault was rapid oscillation accompanied by the stick thrashing from side to side. Sometimes as many as 10 flights were demanded by each production aircraft before the ailerons were adjusted correctly. On prototypes where the fin and rudder were hand-made no bad directional unsteadiness was experienced, but on production aircraft the fin profile rarely carried on smoothly to the rudder, resulting in decidedly poor directional stability.

Diving speeds were restricted owing to jet surge and sensitivity of lateral trim, the latter rendering it difficult for a pilot not well versed in the idiosyncrasies of the aircraft to keep it straight in dives. Normal production testing involved a dive from 3000 m (10,000 ft) up to a true air speed of 850 km/h (530 mph), and no Mach effects were noticeable on longitudinal trim at this speed, but above 900 km/h (560 mph) the aircraft became nose heavy and the elevators sloppy. In 'over-pulled' condition, the aircraft simply stalled through, the nose

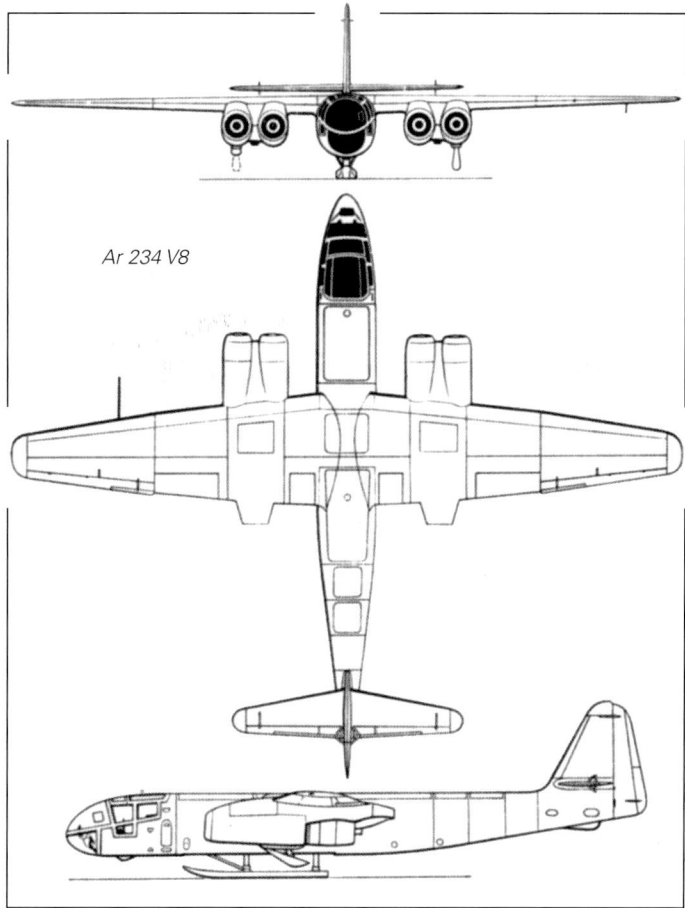

dropping and speed being picked up. A spin following a stall lasted for only one full turn, and the aircraft was immediately fully controllable again. All aerobatic manoeuvres could be executed, and the landing approach speed (at 6000 kg/ 13,200 lb) with 25° flap was of the order of 250 km/h (155 mph), decreasing to 200 km/h (130 mph) with 45° flap at which stalling speed was about 175 km/h (110 mph). The lowering of the undercarriage and flaps had very little effect on trim, and a baulked landing with undercarriage and flaps down presented no difficulties as the forces could easily be held with one hand while retrimming with the other.

The Ar 234's need for more power resulted in the installation of four BMW 003A turbojets instead of the two Junkers Jumo 004Bs. The revised aircraft received the new designation of Ar 234C.

Arado Ar 234

In addition to its revised power plant, the Ar 234C introduced a new cockpit, with pressurisation that had been tried out on the Ar 234 V3 and some Ar 234B-series development aircraft. Illustrated is one of the pre-production examples of the planned Ar 234C-3 bomber.

The Ar 234B was very stable on landing and unaffected by normal cross winds, but at least 1000 m (1,100 yards) were required for the landing run with the brakes held on continuously. In consequence, the brakes were frequently burned out after two or three landings. A braking parachute was provided, however. It was not difficult to relight one of the Jumo 004Bs after a flame-out at altitudes below 4000 m (13,000 ft) and at speeds between 400 and 500 km/h (250 and 310 mph), but above this altitude and at higher speeds a relight was impossible. In the event of a flame-out at higher altitudes the pilot had to close the fuel cock immediately as, failure to do so resulted in flooding the engine, which was usually followed by a fire.

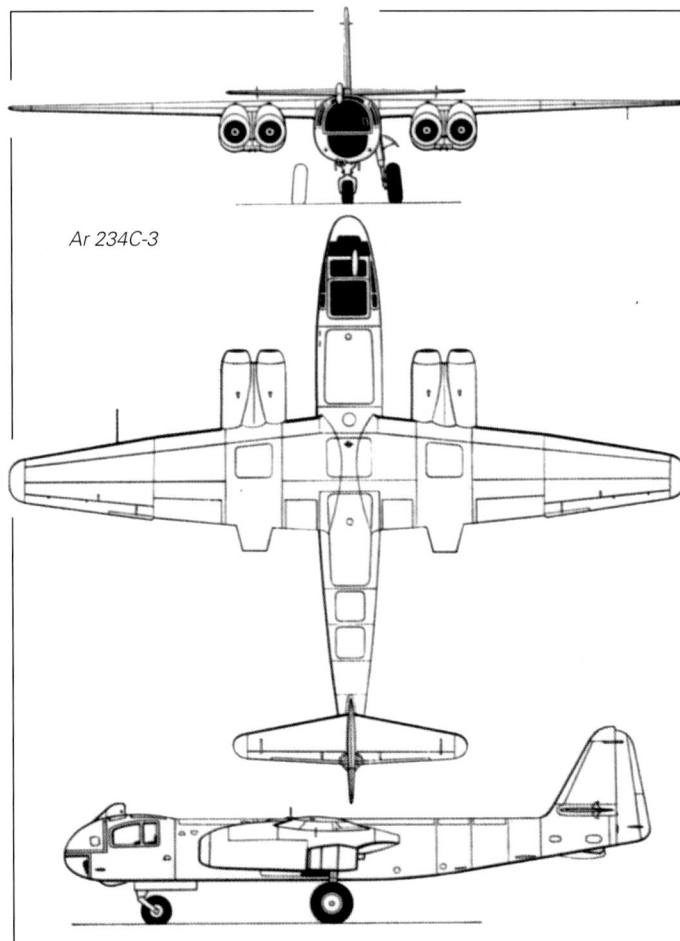

Ar 234C-3

Ar 234C series

At an early stage in the development of the Blitz it had become obvious that the basic airframe could absorb substantially more power than that provided by a pair of Jumo 004Bs, and a further derivative was proposed, this, the **Ar 234C**, utilising four of the smaller and lighter BMW 003A turbojets. In order to arrive at a definitive engine arrangement, two A-series prototypes were adapted to take four BMW 003A-0 turbojets, the first of them to fly being the Ar 234 V8 (Werk Nr 130008, GK+IY) that began trials on 4 February 1944, thus becoming the first four-engined jet-powered aircraft in the world to fly. It was followed two months later, on 25 April, by the Ar 234 V6 (Werk Nr 130006, GK+IW). Whereas the V6 had four individual and widely spaced turbojet nacelles, the V8 had its engines paired in two nacelles, this arrangement subsequently proving the most efficient and being adopted for the C-series.

A B-series prototype, the **Ar 234 V13** (Werk Nr 130023, PH+SU) was fitted with four production BMW 003A-1 turbojets to participate in the Ar 234C development programme, this being readied for flight testing at the end of August 1944, one month before the debut of the first genuine Ar 234C prototype, the **V19**. Another B-series prototype airframe, the **Ar 234 V15**, was fitted with two BMW 003A-1s primarily for engine development purposes as considerable difficulties were initially encountered with this powerplant. Problems of regulating the BMW 003 were resolved by adapting the Jumo 004B regulator to the new powerplant, but not so easily overcome was the problem of relighting after a flame-out. Petrol had been used for fuel throughout the entire test programme of the BMW 003, and it did not take kindly to the use of J2 necessitated by the general fuel situation that existed by mid-1944. For starting petrol was used, as with the Jumo 004B, but a relight with J2 in flight proved virtually impossible. In fact, the problem of relighting the BMW 003 in flight was not finally solved until a few weeks before all development finally terminated and, in the meantime, production of the Ar 234C had been initiated at Alt Lönnewitz.

Apart from its powerplants, the Ar 234C differed from the B-series in having a redesigned cockpit. Cabin pressurisation had been applied to the Ar 234 V3 and several of the B-series prototypes, the glazed cockpit panels being sealed by synthetic rubber strips, washers of similar material being interposed between the flush-fitting retaining screws and the panels, but the Ar 234C featured a double-glazed cockpit, and the first C-series prototype to embody cabin pressuri-

An unusual proposal for the Ar 234C-3 was its use as a launch platform for the Arado E 381 Julia series of prone-pilot rocket-powered midget parasite fighters. A number of mock-ups were constructed for tests.

sation was the **Ar 234 V20** that made its debut late in October 1944. During the previous month the similarly-powered Ar 234 V13 succeeded in attaining an altitude of 7300 m (42,000 ft). By comparison with the Ar 234B, the Ar 234C embodied several detail modifications, such as a certain amount of skin re-contouring, some changes in aileron design, and an enlarged nosewheel, but apart from relighting the BMW 003 engines in flight, the principal problem was provided by the hermetic sealing of the control rods and leads.

Range of variants

Development of the C-series was considerably hampered by the fact that the experimental assembly plant had to be dispersed several times, and was complicated by the fact that several sub-variants were being evolved simultaneously. The initial model, the **Ar 234C-1**, was intended solely for reconnaissance tasks with a similar camera array to the Ar 234B-1, but two aft-firing 20-mm MG 151 cannon with 250 r.p.g. were to be housed in a ventral pack. The **Ar 234C-2** was an essentially similar machine intended for the bombing role and carrying no defensive armament. With a single 1000-kg (2,205-lb) bomb and two 500-kg (1,100-lb) bombs, the Ar 234C-2 took off within 890 m (972 yards), but this distance could be reduced to 600 m (667 yards) with two 4.9-kN (1,100-lb) thrust Rauchgeräte units. The **Ar 234C-3** was intended as a multi-purpose model suitable for use as a bomber, night fighter or ground attack aircraft, and it was originally proposed that this version should receive the BMW 003C turbojets, which, with Brown-Boveri compressors, offered 8.8 kN (1,980 lb st) as compared with 7.8 kN

(1,760 lb) for the BMW 003A. The non-availability of this powerplant, however, necessitated the retention of the BMW 003A. At an early stage, the pair of aft-firing 20-mm MG 151 cannon was supplemented by a pair of similar weapons fixed to fire forward, also with 250 r.p.g.

A proposed BMW 003C-powered reconnaissance model was the **Ar 234C-4**, while the **Ar 234C-5** bomber was to have been the first two-seat variant, the pilot and navigator/bombardier being accommodated in staggered seats, and the **Ar 234C-6** was an equivalent long-range reconnaissance version. In view of Germany's concentration on fighter production during the closing months of the war, it is hardly surprising that the Ar 234 should be considered for this role, and proposals were prepared for a specialised night fighting version of the C-series, the **Ar 234C-7**. Armament was to have comprised one 20-mm MG 151 cannon with 300 rounds in the forward fuselage and a ventral pack housing two 30-mm MK 108 cannon with 100 r.p.g. The radar was intended to be the FuG 245 Bremen O. Yet a further C-series proposal was the **Ar 234C-8** single-seat bomber with a fixed forward-firing armament of two 20-mm MG 151 cannon with 250 r.p.g., a bomb load of 1000 kg (2,205 lb), and a pair of 10.3-kN (2,310-lb st) Jumo 004D turbojets.

Several C-series prototypes either joined or were close to joining the test programme before Germany's collapse. The first to fly was the Ar 234 V19 (PI+WX) on 16 October 1944. Also included was the **Ar 234 V21** that was intended

Arado built prototype/development aircraft of the Ar 234 up to the Ar 234 V30 (although further were under construction at the war's end). The first true prototype for the four-engined Ar 234C-series was the V19, which first flew on 16 October 1944.

Arado Ar 234

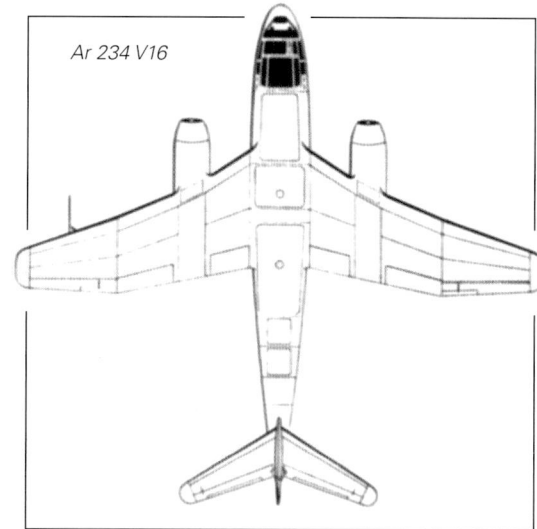
Ar 234 V16

Left: The pilot entered the aircraft by pulling down a retractable step on the left side, using kick-in steps up the left side and entering via the outwards-opening roof hatch. The hatch was jettisoned if a rapid exit was needed.

as a production prototype for the Ar 234C-3 multi-purpose variant, and the basically similar **V22**, **V23**, **V24** and **V25**, the **Ar 234 V28** prototype for Ar 234C-5, the **Ar 234 V29** prototype for the Ar 234C-6, and the **Ar 234 V27** that was intended primarily to evaluate various types of air brakes. Two further C-series prototypes, the **V26** and **V30** with laminar flow aerofoils, were virtually complete when development terminated. In addition to the 10 C-series prototypes completed before VE-Day, 14 Ar 234C-3 pre-production multi-purpose aircraft and Ar 234C-1 production reconnaissance machines were essentially completed, but few received powerplants. Preparations were under way to form an operational test squadron.

Throughout its development career, the Ar 234 was the subject of numerous development programmes concerned with various aerodynamic innovations, powerplant, armament and other tests. Mention has already been made of the Ar 234 V26 and V30, the former having a thick-section laminar flow wing of wooden construction and the latter a slim laminar flow section wing of metal construction, both proto-

types being destroyed when virtually completed to prevent them falling into Soviet hands, but an even more interesting prototype intended for aerofoil research was the **Ar 234 V16**. The eighth B-series prototype, the Ar 234 V16 was intended to test the revolutionary crescent wing planform evolved by Dipl.-Ing. R. E. Kosin, Arado's chief aerodynamicist.

The design of the crescent wing was partly a compromise to maintain the existing Ar 234 undercarriage/fuselage by utilising the existing wing attachment points, but its primary purpose was that of maintaining a constant critical Mach number from root to tip by means of graded sweepback. The leading edge sweep angle was 37° inboard decreasing in two steps to 25° outboard, and the wing carried leading edge flaps. Power was to have been provided by a pair of BMW 003R units, each comprising a normal BMW 003A turbojet coupled with a BMW 718 bi-fuel rocket motor that augmented thrust for take-off and climb by 12 kN (2,700 lb) for three minutes. The experimental crescent wing was ready for attachment to the fuselage of the Ar 234 V16 in April 1945, but before this could be effected, the experimental assembly plant was

Towards the end of the war many Arado Ar 234s were captured intact by the advancing Allied armies and several more were used by their crews to escape to neutral nations. One even got as far as Ireland, arriving on the last day of the war. The majority of these aircraft survived to become objects of study for British, American and Soviet scientists.

An RAF officer and airmen clamp their hands over their ears as the engines of a captured Ar 234 are run up. British test pilots found the Ar 234 the most effective and pleasant of the German jets to handle.

occupied by British troops and the wing was scrapped. However, some two years later, this wing planform was to be resurrected by Handley Page in the UK, tested in 1951 on the H.P.88 and subsequently adopted for the Victor V-bomber.

The Ar 234 was also involved in Deichselschlepp, or 'Air Trailer', trials that were initially aimed at providing the aircraft with an expendable and jettisonable long-range tank. Arado specified a 2800-litre (616-Imp gal) towed tank for the Ar 234B and a 4000-litre (880-Imp gal) tank for the Ar 234C, these being attached to the aircraft by means of a semi-rigid tube that acted as tow bar and fuel feed pipe.

Missile-carrier

From the towed fuel tank was evolved various schemes for an offensive Deichselschlepp, and it was proposed that a 1400-kg (3,086-lb) bomb with rudimentary wing surfaces be towed behind the Ar 234C-2. Alternatively, a Fieseler Fi 103 flying bomb could be towed, the bomb being fitted with a two-wheel undercarriage and a tow bar attachment. It was proposed that the undercarriage be jettisoned after take-off and the tow bar detached when the bomb had been directed at its target. Extensive trials were undertaken at the Erprobungsstelle Rechlin with an Ar 234B towing an Fi 103 from which the athodyd propulsion unit had been detached, but the definitive system involved the use of a cradle to which auxiliary wings and undercarriage were attached, the intention being that the cradle would be discarded after take-off, and glide to the ground for recovery and re-use. Yet a further Deichselschlepp scheme involved towing a Henschel Hs 294 missile behind

an Ar 234C. With the Hs 294 on tow, the Ar 234C attained maximum speeds of 760 km/h (470 mph) at sea level and 820 km/h (510 mph) at 8000 m (26,250 ft), range at the latter altitude being 760 km (475 miles) and reducing to 400 km (250 miles) at sea level. A rather more elaborate scheme was evolved for launching an Fi 103 from the back of an Ar 234C. This involved a special cradle on which the Fi 103 sat until the parent aircraft reached the vicinity of the target, a series of hydraulically-operated arms then raising the missile clear of the top of the aircraft for launching.

At the time the experimental assembly plant was occupied by the Allies, construction of a further batch of 10 prototypes,

A mixed bag of Ar 234s was surrendered to the British at Stavanger-Sola in Norway at the war's end, including reconnaissance and KG 76 machines. Others were surrendered at Grove in Denmark.

Illustrated by a captured example in the United States, the Ar 234 was a spearhead of Germany's introduction of jet aircraft but was never produced in sufficient numbers to avert the Reich's inevitable defeat. The Luftwaffe's first and only jet-powered bomber in service, it exhibited great potential and was of significant influence on jet bomber design in the immediate post-war years.

Arado Ar 234

Fuel capacity had been a concern of the designers of the Ar 234 from the outset, and the most ambitious method of providing additional fuel was the development of the Deichselschlepp, an expendable long-range tank that was towed behind the aircraft, attached by means of a combined tow bar/fuel pipe.

the Ar 234 V31 to V40, was in hand, these being intended for the D-series. A two-seater powered by a pair of 12.7-kN (2,860 lb st) Heinkel-Hirth HeS 011 turbojets, the **Ar 234D** was projected in two versions, the **Ar 234D-1** reconnaissance aircraft and the **Ar 234D-2** bomber. At an advanced design stage was the P-series intended for the night fighting role and featuring a lengthened fuselage nose accommodating centimetric intercept radar, increasing overall length to 13.25 m (43 ft 6 in). Four versions were projected: the **Ar 234P-1** powered by four BMW 003A turbojets and carrying two crew and an armament of one 20-mm MG 151 cannon with 300 rounds and one 30-mm MK 108 cannon with 100 rounds; the **Ar 234P-3** powered by two HeS 011 turbojets and carrying two crew and a fixed forward-firing armament of two MG 151 cannon with 125 r.p.g. and two MK 108 cannon with 100 r.p.g.; the **Ar 234P-4** differing from the –3 only in having Jumo 004D engines, and the three-seat **Ar 234P-5** with two HeS 011A turbojets, reduced fuel capacity (from 3700 to 3000 litres/815 to 660 Imp gal), and an armament comprising one forward-firing MG 151 with 300 rounds and two MK 108s with 100 r.p.g., and an additional pair of MK 108s with 100 r.p.g. fixed to fire upward at an oblique angle.

The Ar 234 was undoubtedly an extremely advanced warplane by any standard, and it was perhaps fortunate for the Allies that the numbers produced were sufficient to provide only an annoying thorn in their side.

Arado Ar 234B-2 Blitz specification

Type: single-seat bomber and ground-attack aircraft
Powerplant: two Junkers Jumo 004B-1 axial-flow turbojets each rated at 8.83 kN (1,984 lb)
Performance: maximum speed 742 km/h (461 mph) at 6000 m (19685 ft); cruising speed 700 km/h (435 mph) at 1000 m (32,810 ft); service ceiling 10000 m (32,810 ft); range with 500-kg (1,100-lb) bomb load 1556 km (967 miles)
Weights: empty equipped 5200 kg (11,464 lb); maximum bomb load 1500 kg (3,300 lb); maximum take-off 9800 kg (21,605 lb)
Dimensions: wingspan 14.10 m (46 ft 3½ in); length 12.64 m (41 ft 5 in); height 4.29 m (14 ft 1 in); wing area 26.40 m² (284.17 sq ft)
Armament: two fixed aft-firing 20-mm MG 151 cannon with 200 r.p.g. plus offensive loads of up to 1500 kg (3,000 lb) and including three 500-kg (1,100-lb) SC 500J or SD 500 bombs, one 1,000-kg (2,205-lb) SC 1000 or SD 1000 bomb and two 250-kg (550-lb) SC 250J bombs, one 1400-kg (3,086-lb) PC 1400, or three AB 250 or AB 500 anti-personnel bomb clusters

Arado Ar 234C-3 Blitz specification

Type: single-seat bomber and ground-attack aircraft
Powerplant: four BMW 003A-1 Sturm axial-flow turbojets each rated at 7.83 kN (1,760 lb st)
Performance: maximum speed (without external load and half fuel), 800 km/h (496 mph) at sea level, 853 km/h (530 mph) at 6000 m (19,700 ft); range with maximum internal fuel 1230 km (765 miles); climb to 10000 m (32,810 ft) 16.7 min; service ceiling 12000 m (39,370 ft)
Weights: empty equipped 6532 kg (14,400 lb), loaded 11000 kg (24,250 lb); loaded with two 300-litre (66-Imp gal) auxiliary tanks 10000 kg (21,800 lb)
Dimensions: wingspan 14.10 m (46 ft 3½ in); length 12.64 m (41 ft 5½ in); height 4.29 m (14 ft 1 in); wing area 26.40 m² (284.17 sq ft)
Armament: two 20-mm MG 151 cannon with 250 r.p.g. fixed to fire aft and two 20-mm MG 151 cannon with 250 r.p.g. fixed to fire forward and three 500-kg (1,100-lb) SC 500J or SD 500 bombs, one 1000-kg (2,205-lb) SC 1000 or SD 1000 bomb and two 250-kg (550-lb) SC 250J bombs, or three AB 250 or 500 anti-personnel bomb clusters

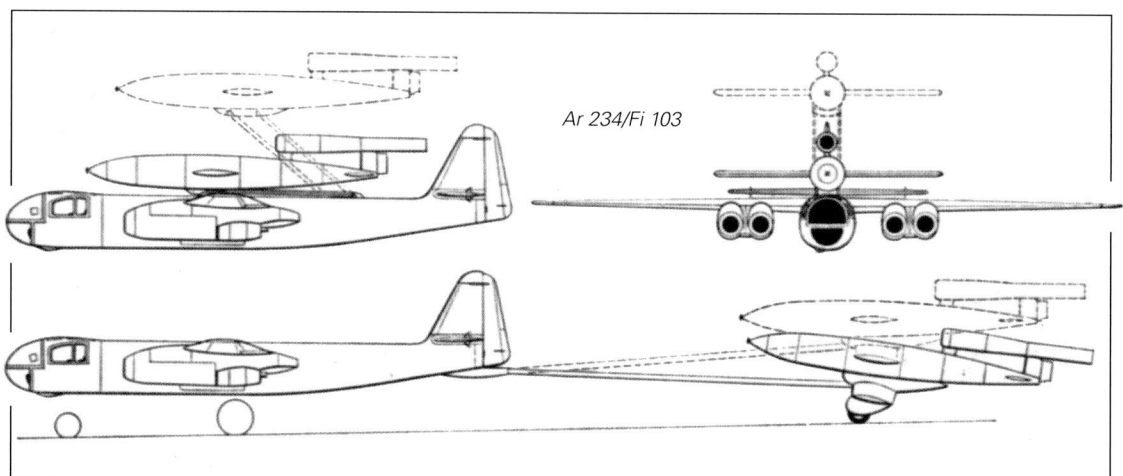

Ar 234/Fi 103

Right: A further extrapolation of the Deichselschlepp concept allied the Ar 234C to a Fieseler Fi 103 flying bomb. The flying bomb was adapted with a twin-wheel undercarriage that could be jettisoned after take-off, while another scheme saw the missile carried pick-a-back on an Ar 234C.

Left: The original Deichselschlepp ('Air Trailer') provided the Ar 234 with an auxiliary fuel tank, attached to the rear of the aircraft. The winged fuel tank was intended to be discarded when the fuel supply was exhausted.

Arado Ar 240

Requested as a fast twin-engined warplane equipped with an advanced remotely-controlled defensive gun system, the Arado Ar 240 suffered from early instability problems. After design revisions, early aircraft underwent operational trials and saw some service in the reconnaissance role before the project was halted in late 1942.

During the late 1930s, the technical director of the Arado Flugzeugbau, Dipl.-Ing. Walter Blume, working in collaboration with the Rheinmetall-Borsig organisation, evolved what was for its time a revolutionary defensive system for aircraft comprising remotely-controlled low-drag gun barbettes directed by means of a periscopic sight. Although such barbettes were considered by many to be too futuristic, the Technisches Amt of the Reichsluftfahrtministerium (RLM) encouraged Blume to submit proposals for a fast Kampfzerstörer embodying his new concept for defence; an aircraft possessing advanced performance capability and suitable for use with equal facility in the heavy fighter, fast reconnaissance, dive-bombing and attack roles.

Thus, early in 1938, the Arado team initiated studies against an RLM development order for a highly sophisticated multi-purpose aircraft which was allocated the project designation **E 240**. The company's finalised proposal submitted to the RLM early in the following year took advantage of the very latest developments in aeronautical technology, and was basically a highly-loaded tandem two-seater of all-metal construction with pressurised accommodation for the crew, remotely-controlled gun barbettes for defence, high-lift devices in the form of automatic leading-edge slats and double-slotted trailing-edge flaps, and a radical form of dive brake working in a similar fashion to a parachute and acting as a tail cone when closed.

In 1938 the German air ministry requested proposals for a fast twin-engined warplane fitted with two FA 13 armament system installations. The contenders were the AGO Ao 225, and the E 240 designed by Hans Rebeski and redesignated as the Arado Ar 240 (above) when awarded a contract.

Dipl.-Ing. van Nes was appointed overall project engineer for the E 240, Oberingenieur Hans Rebeski being structural supervisor. The Technisches Amt drew up an official requirement which, in essence, merely outlined the salient features of the E 240, and during the summer of 1939, work began on prototype construction. The first two prototypes, the **Ar 240 V1** and **V2**, were intended to serve primarily as aerodynamic test vehicles, neither having provision for cabin pressurisation or the hydraulic control system for defensive barbettes, although the second aircraft featured forward-firing armament (comprising a fuselage-mounted pair of 20-mm MG 151 cannon and a 7.9-mm/0.31-in MG 17 machine-gun in each wing root). The barbette control system, which,

A number of major airframe changes, as well as the FA 9 remotely controlled armament system, were incorporated in the marginally improved Ar 240 V3 third prototype, which first flew in the early summer of 1941 and differed in many respects from the first two prototypes.

Above: A notable feature of the Ar 240's design was the length and depth of the engine nacelles, which also provided accommodation inside door-covered bays for the twin-wheel main units of the fully retractable tailwheel undercarriage.

Above: Visible in this photograph of the Ar 240A-01 is the remotely-controlled dorsal barbette, part of the FA 13 defensive system. Each of the two FA 13 installations (dorsal and ventral) was fitted wih a pair of 13-mm (0.51-in) MG 131 machine-guns.

One of the innovations employed in the Ar 240 was a cabin pressurisation system, although this was absent from the first two prototypes. The Ar 240A-01, flown in October 1942, was a reconnaissance version.

evolved by Arado in co-operation with the DVL as a successor to the totally unworkable LGW-developed FA 4 system, was at this time being flight tested on the Messerschmitt Bf 162 V3 and was proving to be fairly reliable during air firing trials, but development of the accompanying periscopic sight had fallen badly behind schedule.

One problem was target detection by the gunner and subsequent tracking, despite 1.6 times magnification by the viewfinder, and an even more serious problem was presented by the icing-up of the periscopic heads when tested under simulated high-altitude conditions at Göttingen. After much experimentation, the latter difficulty was finally solved by means of pumping pre-dried air into the sighting head through a chlorine-calcium filter, and it was ascertained that by this method it was possible to keep the sights free of ice up to an altitude of 9800 m (32,150 ft).

Instability issues

These tests were still under way when, on 25 June 1940, the Ar 240 V1 was flown for the first time, and from the outset of flight trials it was obvious that the new Kampfzerstörer was unstable about all three axes. The V2 second prototype flew shortly after. Some redesign of the basic aircraft had already been undertaken, and the third prototype, the **Ar 240 V3** (KK+CD), then under construction as the first dive-bomber and reconnaissance model, featured radical changes in the forward and centre fuselage, the entire pressure cabin having been moved forward to the extreme nose.

As a result of the unsatisfactory characteristics revealed by the first two prototypes, further changes were made in the Ar 240 V3, the principal being the introduction of an additional 1.25 m (4 ft 1½ in) section in the rear fuselage. The tail-mounted dive brake was removed and replaced by a short cone carrying auxiliary fins, and the wing leading-edge slats were eliminated. Like its predecessors, the Ar 240 V3 was powered by a pair of DB 601A engines each rated at 802 kW (1,075 hp) for take-off, and was the first aircraft to embody the FA 9 hydraulic barbette control system with dorsal and ventral barbettes each intended to house a pair of 7.9-mm MG 81 machine-guns. A similar fixed forward-firing armament to that of the Ar 240 V2 was installed.

These modifications delayed the completion of the Ar 240 V3 until the late spring of 1941. Flight tests began on 6 April and revealed that, although markedly improved over those of the Ar 240 V1 and V2, flying characteristics still left much to be desired, and further modifications had to be made, including the provision of new ailerons. During the late summer months, the Ar 240 V3 was delivered to the Aufklärungsgruppe of the Oberbefehlshaber der Luftwaffe for operational evaluation. The FA 9 system, which had proved reasonably reliable under test conditions but unsatisfactory in the field, was removed, together with the fixed forward-firing armament, a pair of Rb 50/30 cameras was installed, and Colonel Knemeyer of the Aufkl.Gr.Ob.d.L. flew the aircraft as an unarmed reconnaissance machine, flying several sorties over Britain, its high-performance and high-altitude capabilities enabling the prototype to evade interception.

A fourth prototype, the **Ar 240 V4**, had, in the meantime, been completed by Arado, and the AGO Flugzeugwerke at Oschersleben had been designated subcontractor for the manufacture of a pre-production series of **Ar 240A-0** aircraft for the reconnaissance role, having begun the necessary tooling. The Ar 240 V4 was primarily a dive-bomber with secondary reconnaissance capability, and forward-firing and defensive armament were similar to those initially installed in the V3, but racks were provided beneath the fuselage for eight 50-kg (110-lb) bombs, the tail-mounted dive brake was reinstated, increasing overall length from 2.32 m (40 ft 7⅓ in) to 13.00 m (42 ft 8 in), and power was provided by two DB 603A engines each rated at 1305 kW (1,750 hp) for take-off. Prior to the completion of dive-bombing trials, it had been concluded that the armed reconnaissance mission was of greater immediate importance than that of dive-bombing, priority being given to this role, and thus the first pre-production machines to be completed by AGO, the **Ar 240A-01** and **-02** (GL+QA and QB) which also received the Versuchs numbers **V5** and **V6**, were intended solely for reconnaissance. They were the first to be fitted with the FA 13 armament system, with twin MG 131 13-mm (0.51-in) machine-guns replacing the twin MG 81s.

Pre-production batch

The Ar 240A-01 and -02, both flown in October 1942, embodied still more aerodynamic changes aimed at eradicating the poor handling characteristics that had continually plagued the development of the aircraft.

Although unchanged in outline or dimensions, the wing was, in fact, entirely new. The revised wing section was of near-laminar type with the deepest point approaching mid-chord, and the characteristics of the aircraft were immeasurably improved as a result. The dive brake was finally dispensed with, and yet another Daimler-Benz engine variant was employed, the DB 601E rated at 876 kW (1,175 hp) for take-off. Forward-firing armament was restricted to the pair of wingroot-mounted 7.9-mm MG 17 machine-guns, but the FA 13 system with its paired MG 131 gun barbettes was retained. The two crew members were seated back-to-back in the pressurised forward section of the fuselage, the double-glazed canopy being sealed by inflatable rubber strips. Eight self-sealing fuel tanks housed 2273 litres (500 Imp gal), and this could be augmented by a 600-litre (132-Imp gal) drop tank beneath the fuselage. An automatic Rb 50/30 vertical

Above: The two crew members of the Ar 240 were seated in tandem, and back-to-back. The heavy-duty rubber canopy seals associated with the cabin pressurisation are evident in this view.

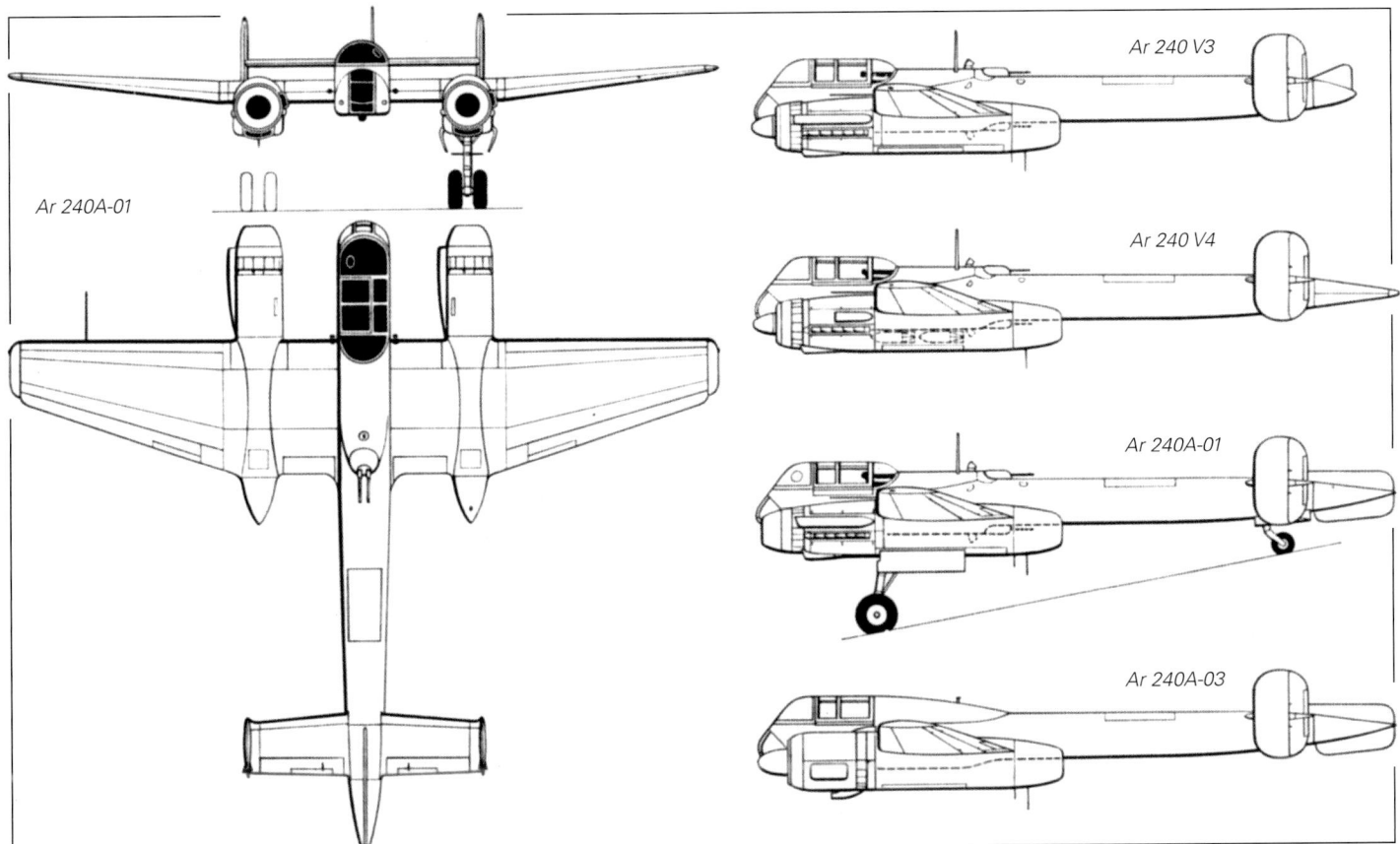

Ar 240A-01

Ar 240 V3

Ar 240 V4

Ar 240A-01

Ar 240A-03

Arado Ar 240

Above and below: Features of the Ar 240 V1 included the radical tail-mounted air brake shown deployed (above left) and retracted (above right). The parachute-type air brake was intended to permit the aircraft's use as a dive-bomber, but this feature was deleted from the reconnaissance aircraft and from the C-series Zerstörer. The Ar 240 was provided with high-lift automatic leading-edge slats (below left) and double-slotted trailing-edge 'travelling' flaps (below right).

camera was mounted in the tail of each engine nacelle. By this time, loaded weight had grown to 9450 kg (20,834 lb).

A further three Ar 240A-0 reconnaissance aircraft were completed and flown by AGO in October 1942, the first of these, the **Ar 240A-03**, flying initially with the DB 601E engines but subsequently being converted to take a pair of BMW 801TJ 14-cylinder air-cooled radials with turbo-superchargers and rated at 1402 kW (1,880 hp) for take-off and 1133 kW (1,520 hp) at 10790 m (35,400 ft). The **Ar 240A-04** and **-05** (alias **Ar 240A-0/U1** and **U2**), which were completed without defensive armament, were powered by DB 603A engines, and Ago had 80 per cent of the jigs and tools set up at Oschersleben in December 1942 for an initial production batch of 40 Ar 240As when a directive issued by Erhard Milch stopped the entire programme

Despite the termination of the Ar 240 programme, the pre-production aircraft were promptly issued to service units. The Ar 240A-01 and -02 were delivered to Jagdgeschwader 5, the 'Eismeergeschwader', which, dispersed around Petsamo in the

north of Finland, used the Arados for reconnaissance of the Murmansk railway. Another Ar 240 was operated alongside the Ju 88s of 3.(F)/100 from February 1943 under Lw.Kdo. Ostland, from July 1943, under Lw.Kdo. Don. During June 1943, 1.(F)/100 was also operating an Ar 240 under Luftflotte 6. During the summer of 1943, the Ar 240A-02 was transferred from JG 5 to 2.(F)/122 based at Frosinone, south-east of Rome. After a few test flights the aircraft performed its first operational reconnaissance mission but was written off after a bad landing. Shortly afterwards, the unit took over from 1.(F)/123 at Perugia, north of Rome, the Ar 240A-04 (A-0/U1), but before any operational missions could be flown with this aircraft, troubles developed with its DB 603A engines, and, after temporary repairs, it was flown back to Germany.

This aircraft, together with the Ar 240A-05 (A-0/U2), the BMW 801TJ-powered Ar 204A-03, and the **Ar 240 V7** and **V8**, later served on the southern Russian Front with Aufklärungsgruppe 10 and on the eastern Russian Front with 1. Staffel of the Aufkl.Gr.Ob.d.L.

The Ar 240A-01 on a compass-swinging platform. Otherwise known as the Ar 240 V5, this aeroplane was a result of Luftwaffe's need for a reconnaissance aircraft rather than a heavy fighter-bomber. From 1943 the type served with JG 5 in northern Finland.

A number of Ar 240 pre-production aircraft were completed, and the AGO factory at Oschersleben was tasked with manufacture of 40 production aircraft. In December 1942, however, the programme was discontinued as a result of continued teething problems.

Ar 240C-01

Ar 240C-01

Ar 240C-02

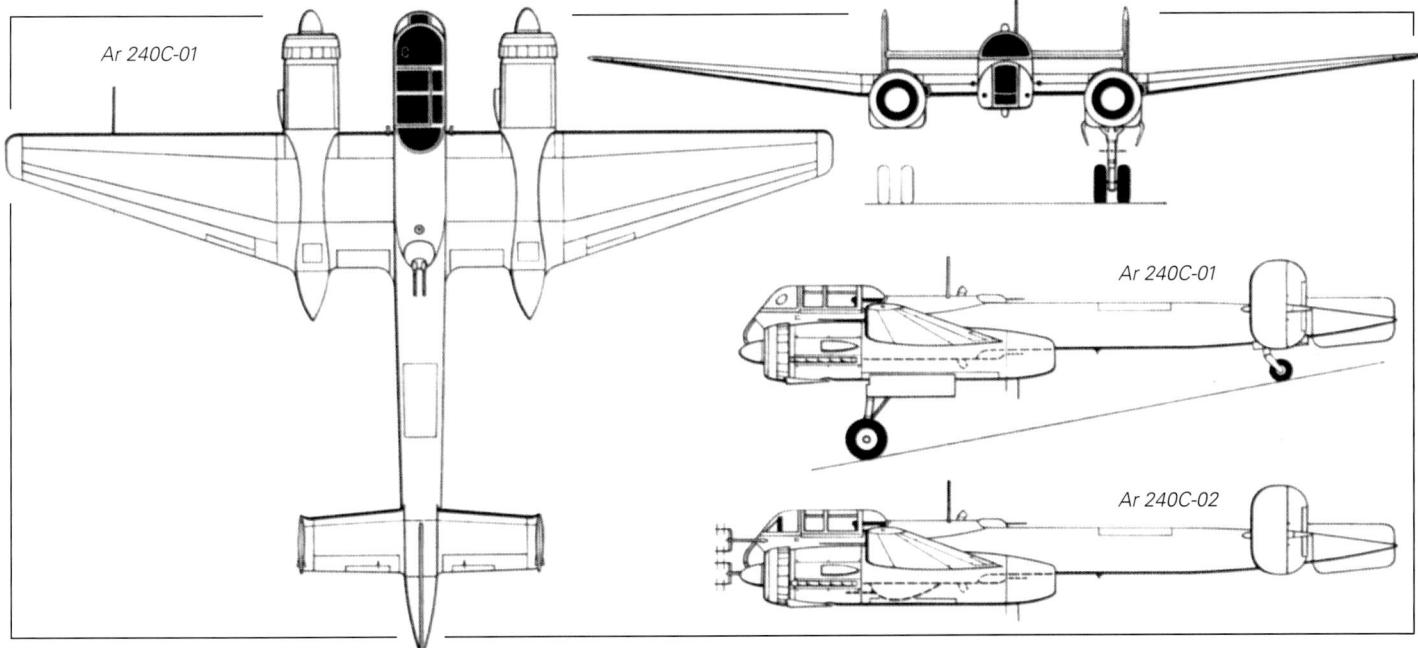

The Ar 240 V7 and V8, which had been completed before Milch's edict and had flown in October and December 1942 respectively, were pre-production examples of the **Ar 240B** reconnaissance aircraft, and were also known as the **Ar 240B-01** and **-02** respectively. They were essentially similar to the Ar 240A-0 apart from having DB 605AM engines which, normally rated at 1100 kW (1,475 hp) for take-off, had an MW 50 methanol-water injection system which could be used to boost take-off power to 1342 kW (1,800 hp). Both the V7 and V8 were completed with the twin forward-firing MG 17 machine-guns and the paired remotely-controlled barbettes, and the latter also had a fixed aft-firing 20-mm MG 151 cannon.

Zerstörer prototype

The development of reconnaissance versions of the Ar 240 had taken precedence over other versions of this multi-purpose aircraft, and the first Zerstörer prototype, the **Ar 240 V9** (alias **Ar 240C-01**), did not commence its flight test programme until March 1943, some three months after

the programme had been officially abandoned. Powered by DB 603A-2 engines rated at 1305 kW (1,750 hp) for take-off and 1380 kW (1,850 hp) at 2100 m (6,900 ft), the Ar 240 V9 possessed an essentially similar airframe to those of the A- and B-series prototypes, but the wingtips were extended to result in an overall span of 16.60 m (54 ft 5⅛ in), and the lengthened engine nacelles increased overall length to 13.35-m (43 ft 9½ in). A forward-firing armament of four 20-mm MG 151 cannon was installed, and the remotely-controlled dorsal and ventral barbettes each mounted a pair of 13-mm (0.51-in) MG 131 machine-guns. Both empty and loaded weights were markedly increased, the former to 8480 kg (18,695 lb) and the latter to 10550 kg (23,258 lb), and thus, despite some 3.72 m² (40 sq ft) increase in gross wing area, the wing loading remained virtually unchanged, and trials revealed no improvement in flying characteristics.

Three further C-series prototypes had been built in parallel with the Ar 240 V9, the **V10** (**Ar 240C-02**) being a night-fighter with two additional 20-mm MG 151 cannon in a ventral WT 151A housing, and an FuG 202 Lichtenstein

Operational use of the Ar 240 was very limited, but a handful of the aircraft did see unofficial service with front-line units. This is the second Ar 240A-0, seen while being flown by JG 5 'Eismeer' in northern Finland. Together with the first Ar 240A-0, this aircraft flew reconnaissance missions along the Murmansk railway. Its speed and altitude performance rendered it relatively immune to interception.

Arado Ar 240

radar array, and the **V11** and **V12** (**Ar 240C-03** and **-04**) Kampfzerstörer prototypes which, capable of carrying a 1800-kg (3,968-lb) bombload, were equipped with a GM 1 (nitrous oxide injection) system that boosted maximum level speed in clean condition by 56 km/h (35 mph).

Numerous proposals existed for further versions of Arado's basic design. They included the DB 603G-powered **Ar 240C-1** Kampfzerstörer, **Ar 240C-2** night-fighter, and **Ar 240C-3** and **-4** high-speed bomber and reconnaissance models; the multi-purpose **Ar 240D** with Daimler-Benz DB 614 engines (DB 603s with three-speed superchargers); the enlarged **Ar 240E** bomber with DB 603G engines, and an equivalent fighter variant, the **Ar 240F**. However, the Technisches Amt of the RLM refused to reinstate the Ar 240 programme, a decision undoubtedly motivated in part by the still imperfect flying characteristics of which pilots complained during operational trials, and the numerous small teething troubles that, when production was halted at the end of 1942, remained unresolved.

Arado Ar 240A-0 specification
Type: two-seat long-range reconnaissance aircraft
Powerplant: two Daimler-Benz DB 601E 12-cylinder liquid-cooled engines

each rated at 876 kW (1,175 hp) for take-off
Performance: maximum speed 618 km/h (384 mph) at 6000 m (19,685 ft); maximum cruising speed 555 km/h (345 mph) at 6000 m; maximum range at 555 km/h at 6000 m with 600-litre (132-Imp gal) auxiliary tank 2000 km (1,242 miles); climb to 6000 m in 11 minutes; service ceiling 10500 m (34,450 ft)
Weights: empty 6200 kg (13,669 lb); empty equipped 7285 kg (16,060 lb); loaded 9450 kg (20,834 lb); maximum overload 10297 kg (22,700 lb)
Dimensions: wingspan 13.34 m (43 ft 9 in); length 12.81 m (42 ft 0⅓ in); height 3.95 m (12ft 11½ in); wing area 31.30 m² (336.91 sq ft)
Armament: (optional) two fixed forward-firing 7.9-mm (0.31-in) MG 17 machine-guns and two 13-mm MG 131 machine-guns in each of dorsal and ventral remotely-controlled barbettes

Arado Ar 240C-03 specification
Type: two-seat heavy fighter-bomber
Powerplant: two Daimler-Benz DB 603A-2 12-cylinder liquid-cooled engines each rated at 1305 kW (1,750 hp) for take-off, 1380 kW (1,850 hp) at 2100 m (6,900 ft), and 1212 kW (1,625 hp) at 5700 m (18,700 ft)
Performance: maximum speed 674 km/h (419 mph) at 6000 m (19,685 ft) (with GM 1 boost), 576 km/h (358 mph) at sea level, 731 km/h (454 mph) at 11186 m (36,700 ft); normal range 1870 km (1,162 miles) at 6000 m; service ceiling 10500 m (34,450 ft)
Weights: empty 8460 kg (18,650 lb); maximum loaded 11726 kg (25,850 lb)
Dimensions: wingspan 16.60 m (54 ft 5⅛ in); length 13.35 m (43 ft 9½ in); height 3.95 m (12 ft 11½ in); wing area 35.00 m² (376.73 sq ft)
Armament: four 20-mm MG 151 cannon (two in wingroots and two in fuselage) fixed to fire forward, and two 13-mm (0.51-in) MG 131 machine-guns in each of two (dorsal and ventral) remotely-controlled barbettes, plus maximum external bombload of 1800 kg (3,968 lb)

Arado Ar 396

Arado planned to follow its prolific Arado Ar 96 advanced trainer with the Ar 296 with an uprated engine, although this was soon abandoned in favour of the Ar 396, which placed reduced demands on strategic materials. Development of the trainer was undertaken in France, but the type was too late for wartime service.

The Arado Ar 96 trainer was to have been developed further as the Ar 296 with the higher-rated Argus As 411 engine, but shortages of strategic materials led instead to the introduction of the Arado Ar 396 with an airframe revised with the minimum amount of metal. At the same time, the aircraft's systems were simplified in features such as manually- rather than power-operated flaps and main landing gear units that were only semi-retractable. Development of this cheaper variant was entrusted to the Société Industrielle pour l'Aéronautique (SIPA) in occupied France, and the first of three prototypes flew on 29 December 1944, after France's liberation. Letov in Czechoslovakia was also to have built the Ar 396, but none reached the Luftwaffe before the cessation of hostilities. SIPA subsequently built more than 200 examples for the French armed forces in **S.10**, **S.11** and **S.12** variants, the last of them with an all-metal structure.

Variants for the Luftwaffe were the **Ar 396A-1** advanced flying trainer also operated in the single-seat gunnery trainer role, and the **Ar 396A-2** unarmed instrument flying trainer.

The Ar 396 was a derivative of the concept first embodied in the Ar 96, in this instance re-engineered to produce a trainer whose manufacture made minimal demands on strategic building materials such as light alloys. This example was Czech-built.

Arado Ar 396A-1 specification
Type: two-seat advanced flying trainer
Powerplant: one Argus As 411 MA inverted-Vee engine rated at 433 kW (580 hp)
Performance: maximum speed 355 km/h (220 mph) at 2400 m (7,870 ft); cruising speed 275 km/h (171 mph) at sea level; climb to 4000 m (13,125 ft) in 10 minutes 18 seconds; service ceiling 6900 m (22,960 ft); range 600 km (373 miles)
Weights: empty 1643 kg (3,623 lb); maximum take-off 2060 kg (4,541 lb)
Dimensions: wingspan 11.00 m (36 ft 1 in); length 9.30 m (30 ft 5¾ in); height 2.45 m (8 ft 0½ in); wing area 18.30 m² (196.99 sq ft)
Armament: one 7.9-mm (0.31-in) fixed forward-firing machine-gun, plus two 50-kg (110-lb) bombs carried on underwing racks

A tandem two-seat advanced flying and armament trainer, the Ar 396 was developed in France. The aircraft was of orthodox low-wing monoplane layout with the pupil and instructor seated in tandem under a framed canopy, and the powerplant was based on the As 411, an inverted V-12 engine with air- rather than liquid cooling.

Arado Ar 440

The generally unsatisfactory characteristics revealed by the early Ar 240 prototypes, and the difficulties experienced by the manufacturer in its attempts to rectify the shortcomings of the aircraft, led the Arado design team to consider, at the beginning of 1942, more drastic measures, resulting in the promising Ar 440.

While every effort was expended in endeavouring to eradicate the defects suffered by the Ar 240, the design team initiated parallel work on a progressive development of the basic design as a safeguard against the total failure of the existing aircraft.

Designated **Ar 440**, this development was considered as an entirely separate programme, despite the fact that it made use of modified Ar 240 basic components. Based on the use of DB 603G engines that differed from the DB 603A in having increased-speed supercharger and increased compression ratio, and offered 1417 kW (1,900 hp) for take-off, the Ar 440 differed from the Ar 240 principally in having additional sections inserted immediately aft of the cockpit and in the rear fuselage, an increase in the span of the wing centre section that resulted in the engine nacelles being positioned further outboard from the fuselage, extended wing outer panels, a longer-span tailplane, and lengthened engine nacelles. The DB 603G engines were provided with GM 1 boost equipment, and it was proposed that they should be supplanted in the production Ar 440 by DB 627s which, based on the DB 603G, were fitted with two-stage mechanical superchargers and aftercoolers, and offered 1491 kW (2,000 hp) for take-off. Intended in its initial form as a Kampfzerstörer, the

Arado's original design for the Ar 240 was unstable. The first attempt at a cure was this aircraft, the Ar 240 V3, which had a redesigned nose and lengthened rear fuselage. This did not solve the problem, so the Ar 440 had an even longer rear fuselage, plus extended wings, nacelles and tail surfaces.

Ar 440 carried a forward-firing 30-mm MK 108 cannon in each wing root, two forward-firing 20-mm MG 151 cannon in the fuselage, and a pair of 13-mm (0.51-in) MG 131 machine-guns in each of the dorsal and ventral barbettes. Provision was also made for a fixed aft-firing MG 151 beneath the fuselage, and for an external bombload.

Improved handling

The first prototype, which bore the designation **Ar 440A-01**, was flown for the first time in the early summer of 1942, and initial factory trials gave extremely encouraging results – none of the defects in handling characteristics that were still plaguing the parallel Ar 240 programme were displayed by the Ar 440. Three additional **Ar 440A-0**s had joined the test programme by the end of November and, during the following month and in January 1943, they were delivered to the Erprobungsstelle Rechlin and to the Luftwaffe for evaluation. On 24 January 1943 the **Ar 440A-04** was flight tested by one of the Luftwaffe's most experienced Zerstörer pilots, Oberleutnant Thierfelder, who was thoroughly enthusiastic about the characteristics of the aircraft. Despite this and excellent reports from Rechlin, the Technisches Amt of the RLM refused to sanction series production of the Ar 440. Production of the aircraft was to be considered once again some 18 months later, following the initiation of the so-called Jägernotprogramm (Emergency Fighter Programme), but by this time the Dornier Do 335 had attained an advanced stage of development, and as this offered an even higher performance than that of the Ar 440, the Arado fighter was once more discarded.

Arado Ar 440A-0 specification
Type: two-seat heavy fighter-bomber
Powerplant: two Daimler-Benz DB 603G 12-cylinder liquid-cooled engines each rated at 1417 kW (1,900 hp) for take-off
Performance: maximum speed 700 km/h (435 mph) at 8290 m (27,200 ft), 750 km/h (467 mph) at 11190 m (36,700 ft) with GM 1 boost; maximum range with two 670-litre (147.5-Imp gal) drop tanks 2700 km (1,680 miles)
Weights: empty 9200 kg (20,282 lb); normal loaded 12200 m (26,896 lb)
Dimensions: wingspan 16.25 m (53 ft 4½ in); length 14.30 m (46 ft 10¼ in); height 4.00 m (13 ft 1½ in); wing area 35.00 m² (377 sq ft)
Armament: two 30-mm MK 108 and two 20-mm MG 151 cannon fixed to fire forward, two 13-mm (0.51-in) MG 131 machine-guns in each of two (dorsal and ventral) remotely-controlled barbettes, and one fixed aft-firing 20-mm MG 151 cannon, plus a maximum bombload of 1000 kg (2,205 lb)

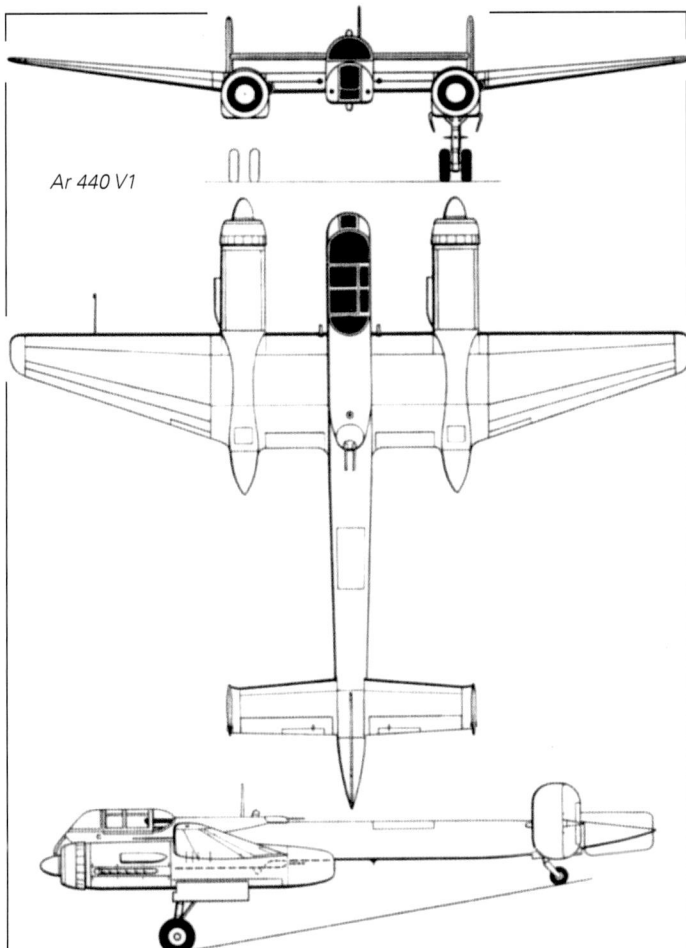

Ar 440 V1

Avia B.71

The Avia B.71 was the Czech military designation for the Soviet Tupolev SB-2 twin-engined medium bomber first flown in October 1934. Aircraft of this type seized by the Germans when they occupied the rump of Czechoslovakia in March 1939 were pressed into service as crew trainers and target-tugs.

In late 1936 the Czechoslovak government decided to procure the Tupolev SB-2 in quantity, and during March 1937 contracted with the Soviet government to import 61 aircraft and licence-manufacture another 160. By the time of the Munich crisis in September 1938, the aircraft from the USSR, with different equipment and weapons as well as French engines, had entered service with three air regiments, and plans were in hand for the other 160 to be built in Czechoslovakia. None of these aircraft had been delivered before the German occupation of the rump in March 1939, but 129 **B.71** aircraft were then completed (45 by Aero and 84 by Avia, respectively). Eventually 184 were used by the Luftwaffe in the training and target-towing roles: the latter was undertaken by Fliegerzeilgeschwader 1, among other units. A batch was exported to Bulgaria (24 or 32 machines, according to Czech or Bulgarian sources, respectively), and material for 16 others was delivered to Finland, where they were completed with M-103 engines for use in the coastal patrol task. Some B.71s were adapted as target-tugs, and were fitted with a chute under the fuselage for the deployment of the cable-towed target.

Avia B.71 specification
Type: three/four-seat medium bomber
Powerplant: two Avia (Hispano-Suiza) 12Ydrs liquid-cooled V-12 engines each rated at 860 hp (641 kW)
Performance: maximum speed 430 km/h (267 mph) at 3000 m (9,845 ft); service ceiling 9000 m (29,525 ft); range 1000 km (621 miles)
Weights: maximum take-off 6000 kg (13,228 lb)
Dimensions: wingspan 20.33 m (66 ft 8½ in); length 12.27 m (40 ft 3 in); height 4.10 m (13 ft 5½ in); wing area 56.70 m² (610.33 sq ft)
Armament: (defensive) one 7.9-mm (0.31-in) trainable machine-gun in each of the nose, dorsal and ventral positions; (offensive) up to 1,323 lb (600 kg) of bombs carried internally

Obsolecent, if not actually obsolete, in the bomber role, the B.71 proved nonetheless useful to the Germans as a trainer (right) and as a target tug (left).

Avia B.135

The B.135 was the last important fighter developed and flown by Czechoslovakia before its absorption into the new German empire, and for its time was an effective warplane with good armament and adequate performance. Only a few such fighters were completed, and they were used by the Bulgarian air force.

Flown for the first time in September 1938, the **B.35/1** low-wing monoplane fighter prototype was of moderately advanced concept but with fixed tailwheel undercarriage. The aircraft was of mixed construction, and initially flew with the Hispano-Suiza 12Ydrs engine rated at 641 kW (860 hp), but this was later replaced by an identically rated Hispano-Suiza 12Ycrs with provision between the cylinder banks for a 20-mm cannon. The B.35/1 was very impressive but crashed in November 1938. The **B.35/2**, with revised ailerons and flaps as well as a fuselage of increased cross section, first flew in February 1939, a month before the German occupation of the rump of Czechoslovakia. Continued development under German control resulted in the **B.35/3** that first flew in August 1939 with a revised wing, retractable main undercarriage units and the armament of one 20-mm Oerlikon cannon and two 7.9-mm (0.31-in) machine-guns. A new all-metal wing was added to create the **B.135**, which appeared in 1940 and caught the attention of a Bulgarian mission. Bulgaria ordered 12 examples as a lead-in to licensed manufacture of 50 **DAR 11 Ljastuvka** fighters. The B.135s were built in the summer of 1942 and entered service with the Bulgarian air force's fighter school, although they also saw some operational service in 1944. The DAR 11 did not enter production.

Avia B.135 specification
Type: single-seat fighter
Powerplant: one Avia (Hispano-Suiza) 12Ycrs liquid-cooled V-12 engine rated at 641 kW (860 hp)
Performance: maximum speed 535 km/h (332 mph) at 4000 m (13,125 ft); cruising speed 460 km/h (286 mph) at optimum altitude; initial climb rate 810 m (2,657 ft) per minute; service ceiling 8500 m (27,890 ft); range 550 km (342 miles)
Weights: empty 2063 kg (4,548 lb); maximum take-off 2547 kg (5,615 lb)
Dimensions: wingspan 10.85 m (35 ft 7⅛ in); length 8.50 m (27 ft 10⅔ in); height 1.60 m (8 ft 6⅓ in); wing area 17.00 m² (182.99 sq ft)
Armament: one 20-mm cannon and two 7.9-mm (0.31-in) machine-guns

The B.35 prototypes and B.135 production type were worthy examples of the last stage of Czechoslovak fighter design.

This Avia advertisement appeared in a German magazine.

Avia B.158

Built only in prototype form, the B.158 medium bomber was one of the several Czechoslovak warplane types that were evaluated, somewhat cursorily, by the Luftwaffe following the German seizure of the rump of Czechoslovakia in March 1939.

Projected by Robert Nebesar in 1935, the **Avia B.58** medium bomber was to have been powered by a pair of 420-hp (313-kW) Avia Rk 17 air-cooled nine-cylinder radial engines and had fixed tailwheel undercarriage. In the following year it was decided to use Hispano-Suiza 12Ydrs liquid-cooled V-12 powerplants offering double the output of the radial engines, and this improvement led to the revised **B.158** design.

This all-metal type incorporated other changes, including the replacement of the original single centreline vertical tail surface with twin endplate vertical tail surfaces, and a change from the fixed spatted undercarriage to a more modern type in which the main units retracted into the lower portions of the engine nacelles. The B.158 had an inverted-gull wing, extensively glazed but heavily framed crew accommodation and somewhat ungainly nacelles for the engines, which drove three-blade propellers.

The B.158 prototype was completed during the early summer of 1938. The flight test programme was still being undertaken when, in March 1939, the Germans occupied the rump of Czechoslovakia surviving from the loss of the Sudetenland as a result of the Munich agreement of September 1938. Revised with German markings, the sole prototype continued its test programme in the summer of 1939, but testing appears then to have been halted and the aircraft appears to have been scrapped soon after this. Nothing came of the planned **B.158B** development of the B.158

Avia B.158 specification
Type: three-seat medium bomber
Powerplant: two Avia (Hispano-Suiza) 12Ydrs liquid-cooled V-12 engines each rated at 860 hp (641 kW)
Performance: maximum speed 435 km/h (270 mph) at optimum altitude; cruising speed of 365 km/h (227 mph) at optimum altitude; initial climb rate 420 m (1,378 ft) per minute; service ceiling 8500 m (27,885 ft); range 1100 km (684 miles)
Weights: empty 4300 kg (9,480 lb); maximum take-off 7260 kg (16,005 lb)
Dimensions: wingspan 16.00 m (52 ft 6 in); length 12.00 m (39 ft 4½ in); wing area 43.00 m² (462.86 sq ft)
Armament: (proposed) one 7.9-mm (0.31-in) trainable machine-gun in each of the nose, dorsal and ventral positions, plus up to 2,205 lb (1000 kg) of bombs carried internally

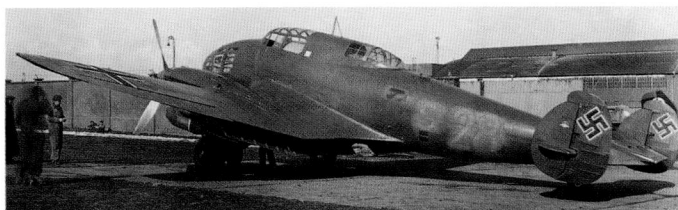

The B.158 prototype (right) used Hispano-Suiza engines built under licence by Avia. A potentially useful though unremarkable bomber design, the B.158 was overtaken by invading German forces and test-flown in Luftwaffe markings (above).

Avia B.534

The B.534 was the culmination of a long series of fighter biplanes from the Avia company, and as such represented one of the high points in the development of warplanes of this type anywhere in the world. The Luftwaffe used comparatively large numbers of B.534 aircraft seized in 1939 as fighter trainers.

Avia's **B.534** was the most important Czechoslovak warplane between the world wars, as reflected in a production total of 536 aircraft. The type may be regarded as a fine example of the penultimate stage in the fighter biplane's evolution as it was of clean design, carried moderately heavy armament, had an enclosed cockpit, and missed being a member of the ultimate fighter biplane family only in its lack of retractable main undercarriage units.

The B.534 stemmed from the open-cockpit **B.34**, which first flew in 1932 with the 552-kW (740-hp) Hispano-Suiza 12Nbr liquid-cooled V-12 engine, and was later built in small numbers as the **B.34/1** with a revised engine cowling, a larger empennage, and unspatted wheels. From the beginning of the programme the use of different engines had been planned, and they were projected in the B.134 to B.434 proposals that did not fly. Further extrapolation led to the

B.534, whose prototype was in fact the sole **B.234**, which had been completed but not flown. This was now revised as the **B.34/2** with the 559-kW (750-hp) Hispano-Suiza 12Ydrs engine. This first flew in August 1933 with other changes including the armament relocated from the wings to the fuselage, and was later redesignated as the **B.534/1**.

The B.534 was the most important warplane in service with the Czechoslovak air force in 1938, equipping some 21 squadrons. Occupation of the country by German forces in March 1939 led to some 450 examples of all variants being acquired by the Luftwaffe.

Avia B.534

Above: In the B.534-IV the powerplant was a licence-built Hispano-Suiza 12Ydrs V-12 unit with provision for a cannon or machine-gun firing through the hollow shaft of the metal propeller, which was a two-blade unit of the fixed-pitch type.

Above: Removal of the fuselage skinning reveals some the cockpit details of the B.534, as well as the location of the fixed forward-firing machine-guns with their 300-round ammunition boxes extending across the cockpit above the pilot's legs.

The B.534 was obsolete by the start of World War II in September 1939, but its agility and generally good performance nonetheless gave the type – which was available to the Germans in large numbers – a continued utility in the fighter trainer role.

The **B.534/2** second prototype differed in having an enclosed cockpit and other detail changes. However, development was delayed by damage to both prototypes in crash landings during 1934, but the Czechoslovak air arm had already decided to order the type as the **B.534-I** based on the B.534/2 but with a licence-built version of the French engine driving a wooden rather than metal propeller, an open cockpit, unspatted wheels, and the gun armament doubled to four 7.9-in (0.31-in) vz.28 or vz.30 machine-guns installed as two on the fuselage sides and two on the upper surface of the lower wing, although the latter were often not fitted as their maintenance presented problems and their accuracy was considerably inferior to that of the two more rigidly mounted fuselage guns.

An initial order was placed in July 1934 for 148 aircraft, including the two prototypes upgraded to the B.534-I initial production standard. Production of 46 B.534-I fighters then followed, and the aircraft entered service from the second half of 1934 with the 4th Air Regiment and the fighter squadrons of the 1st, 2nd and 3rd Air Regiments. The **B.534-II** second production model, of which 100 entered service, differed from the B.534-I in having all four machine-guns grouped on the fuselage sides. This eliminated the problems associated with the earlier variant's wing-mounted guns, and allowed the installation of two underwing racks for a maximum of six light bombs, giving this fighter a limited although still useful close-support capability. The **B.534-III** third production model was built to the extent of 26 aircraft, and differed from the B.534-II in the more forward location of the carburettor air inlet under the nose, the enlargement of the supercharger air inlet, and the adoption for the first time on a production model of the spatted wheels tested on the B.534/2 second prototype. Another 20 aircraft were built for export to Greece (six) and Yugoslavia (14).

Definitive model

The **B.534-IV** was the last and definitive production model, and production totalled 272 aircraft that differed from the B.534-III in the adoption of a metal propeller in place of the original wooden type and an enclosed cockpit. The **Bk.534** was the last model, and was produced by the construction of 54 aircraft, as well as the conversion of 35 B.534-IIs, with the Hispano-Suiza 12Ycrs engine to allow the incorporation of one 20-mm Oerlikon FFS cannon in a moteur-canon installation. There were shortages of the Oerlikon cannon and difficulties with the type's ammunition feed system, however, and most of these fighters were fitted with a machine-gun rather than a cannon in this engine installation, for a total of three 7.9-mm (0.31-in) vz.30 machine-guns.

By the time of the Munich crisis of September 1938, when France and the UK agreed to the German annexation of Czechoslovakia's Sudetenland border regions, the Czechoslovak air force had 21 squadrons operational with the B.534, which had been one of the outstanding biplane fighters of its time but was now obsolescent against the threat posed by monoplane fighters such as the Luftwaffe's Messerschmitt Bf 109. In March 1939 Germany took over the rump of Czechoslovakia, and thereby gained some 450 examples of the B.534 and Bk.534.

Most of the B.534 and Bk.534 fighters in German service were, for the most part, assigned to the Jagdfliegerschulen as advanced trainers and to training Jagdgeschwadern (operational training units), serving with these well into the second half of World War II. Another important role for the B.534 was the towing of DFS 230 assault transport gliders. Together with Henschel Hs 123s, the B.534s were assigned to 1. to

This B.534-IV flew with 3. Staffel of Jagdgeschwader 71 based at Eutingen near Stuttgart late in 1939. German use of such captured aircraft in first-line service was limited, and in the following month this Luftwaffe unit was redesignated 6./JG 51 and equipped with the Messerschmitt Bf 109 monoplane fighter.

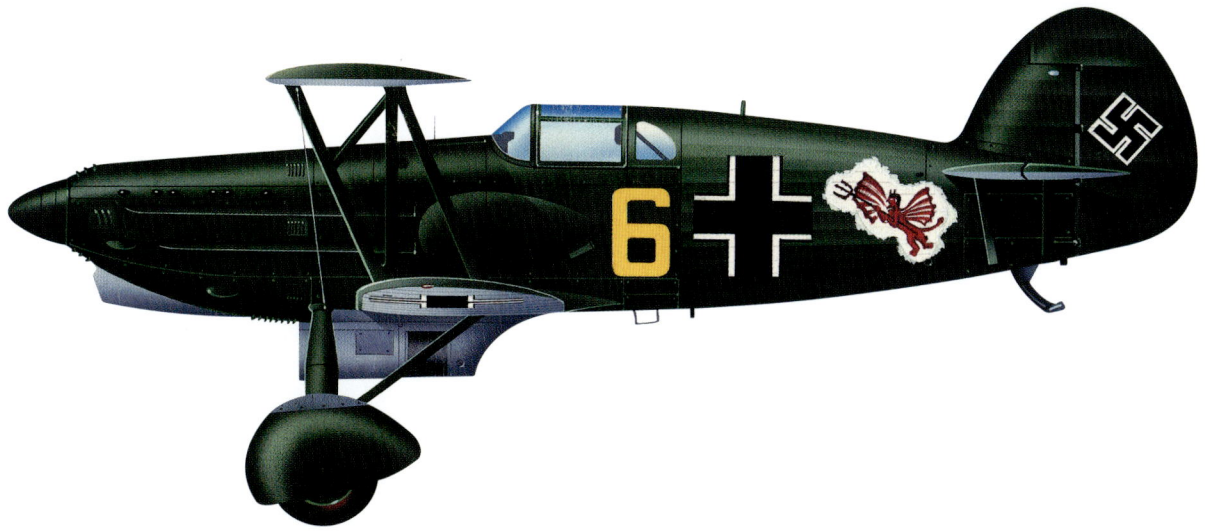

10./DFS 230 Staffeln der Luftwaffe. The B.534 tugs were not employed on operations, being initially restricted to training operations in France and then, during 1942-43, supply runs to forward or encircled units on the Eastern Front. The 10 Staffeln were gradually incorporated into the three Schleppgruppen, and the B.534s were replaced in the tug role by more powerful aircraft.

Only one fighter unit of the Luftwaffe flew the B.534, this being 3./Jagdgeschwader 71. Intended primarily for the nocturnal interception role, I/JG 71 was formed in July 1939 at Friedrichshafen, its 1. and 2. Staffeln flying the Bf 109C, but the B.534 was never employed in combat. Three B.534s were fitted with catapult spools and arrester hook for deck landing trials, and a number of B.534-Is and -IIs were fitted with all-round vision cockpit canopies, some of them being supplied to the Slovak air arm as attrition replacements.

The B.534 was first used in combat by the German puppet state of Slovakia, which inherited 79 B.534 and 11 Bk.534 fighters and soon used them against Hungary during the border war of 1939. Later, two B.534 squadrons assisted the

Right: This B.534-IV in German markings reveals the enclosed cockpit, which was a modern feature, but the main undercarriage lacked the cantilever legs that would have reduced drag.

Below: Supervised by the pilot. no doubt anxious about his charge, ground crew manhandle a B.534-IV. Note that the spinner is missing the section ahead of the propeller hub.

Right: Watched by a member of his aircraft's ground crew, the pilot of a B.534-IV runs up the engine before taxiing the machine out for a training flight.

Below: Pilots of the Luftwaffe's fighter training Jagdgeschwadern appreciated the B.534-IV's excellent handling qualities, developed through the type's predecessor line.

Below: A Bk.534 in Slovak markings taxis on Nitra airfield in the winter of 1941-42 with the alternative ski undercarriage that provided continued operability in snow-covered conditions.

Having learned to fly in low-powered biplanes, prospective Luftwaffe pilots went through basic training before moving on to fighter school. Obsolete fighters such as the B.534 provided a useful stepping stone to the Bf 109 or Fw 190.

Luftwaffe during the invasion of Poland in September 1939. The same squadrons served under German control against the Soviets in the southern USSR during summer 1941, with one squadron returning in 1942 for anti-partisan duty. Obsolescence, spares shortages and the need for an unusual fuel mixture finally relegated the surviving B.534s to training. This would have been the last of the B.534 in Slovak markings but for the Slovak National Uprising of September and October 1944. The bulk of the Slovak air arm did not turn against the Germans, as had been expected, and the uprising's leadership had to use a mix of obsolescent aircraft, including at least three B.534 machines. On 2 September

1944, Master Sergeant František Cyprich downed a Junkers Ju 52/3m transport in Hungarian markings: this was the first aerial victory for the uprising and at the same time the last recorded air-to-air victory by a biplane.

Bulgaria acquired 78 B.534s in 1939–42; these were used by five home-defence squadrons until the late autumn of 1943. On 1 August 1943, seven aircraft attacked Consolidated B-24 Liberator heavy bombers of the USAAF returning from a raid on the Romanian oilfields at Ploesti. The fighters scored hits but shot down no B-24s, and some of the B.534s were damaged so badly that they crashed on landing. After the anti-German coup of 9 September 1944, Bulgaria switched sides overnight and its B.534s were thereafter used in attacks on German ground forces. On 10 September 1944, six B.534s blundered into a brief dogfight with six Bf 109 fighters at low altitude: one B.534 was lost, but the Germans quickly broke away, wary of the B.534's manoeuvrability, especially at lower altitude.

Avia B.534-IV specification
Type: single-seat fighter
Powerplant: one Avia (Hispano-Suiza) 12Ydrs liquid-cooled V-12 engine rated at 850 hp (634 kW)
Performance: maximum speed 405 km/h (252 mph) at 4400 m (14,435 ft); cruising speed 345 km/h (214 mph) at optimum altitude, initial climb rate 900 m (2,953 ft) per minute; service ceiling 10600 m (34,775 ft); range 580 km (360 miles)
Weights: empty 1460 kg (3,219 lb); normal take-off 1985 kg (4,376 lb); maximum take-off 2120 kg (4,674 lb)
Dimensions: wingspan 9.40 m (30 ft 10 in); length 8.20 m (26 ft 10⅞ in); height 3.10 m (10 ft 2 in); wing area 23.56 m² (253.61 sq ft)
Armament: four 7.9-mm (0.31-in) fixed forward-firing machine-guns, plus up to six 20-kg (44-lb) bombs on underwing hardpoints

Avions Tipsy

The Tipsy aircraft were designed by E. O. Tips, manager of Fairey's Belgian subsidiary. Tips appreciated the advantages of the of the low-set cantilever wing, which he incorporated in his lightplanes with cantilever main undercarriage units. Several Tipsy aircraft were seized by the Germans when they overran Belgium in 1940.

Avions Tipsy was established in Belgium during the late 1930s to build monoplane aircraft designed by Ernest Oscar Tips and manufactured initially by Avions Fairey, of which he was manager. Built in only small numbers, these aircraft included the **Tipsy S.2** single-seat ultralight of 1934 with the 12-kW (16-hp) Douglas Sprite engine, the **Tipsy B** and **B.2** of 1937 with two-seat side-by-side seating in an open cockpit or, in the **BC**, an enclosed cockpit with a number of engine types including the 24-kW (32-hp) Sarolea or 30-kW (40-hp) Train units, and the **Tipsy M** military trainer of 1939 with tandem seating under a continuous canopy and powered by a 97-kW (130-hp) de Havilland Gipsy Major engine. A number of aircraft captured in Belgium in 1940 were impressed as 'hacks' by the Luftwaffe.

Tipsy B specification
Type: two-seat light aircraft
Powerplant: one Walter Mikron II air-cooled four-cylinder inverted inline engine rated at 46 kW (62 hp)
Performance: maximum speed 200 km/h (124 mph) at sea level; cruising speed 170 km/h (106 mph) at optimum altitude; initial climb rate 137 m (450 ft) per minute; service ceiling 6000 m (19,685 ft); range 725 km (450 miles)
Weights: empty 225 kg (496 lb); maximum take-off 450 kg (992 lb)
Dimensions: wing span 9.50 m (31 ft 2 in); length 6.60 m (21 ft 8 in); height 1.73 m (5 ft 8 in); wing area 12.00 m² (129.17 sq ft)
Dimensions: wingspan 9.50 m (31 ft 2 in); length 6.60 m (21 ft 8 in); height 1.73 m (5 ft 8 in); wing area 12.00 m² (129.17 sq ft)

Luftwaffe personnel cast an interested and slightly amused look over a seized example of the S.2 single-seater, which was powered by an air-cooled flat-two engine.

Above: Some of the Tipsy aircraft were later revised to a more comfortable standard with a simple enclosure over the original open cockpit. With a low-powered engine driving a small-diameter propeller, the aircraft needed only short undercarriage legs.

Left: A pilotless Ba 349 is prepared for the first vertical launching on 18 December 1944. This had been preceded by piloted gliding trials, with the Ba 349 being towed aloft behind a Heinkel He 111. The glider trials revealed the Natter to have good handling and controllability.

Right: Only the first 50 Natters were to be built in the Ba 349A configuration with the Walter 509A main engine and original Schmidding booster packs, as illustrated here. The 'definitive' Ba 349 had the longer endurance Walter 509C engine and improved boosters, which were located further aft on the fuselage to maintain centre of gravity in the correct position.

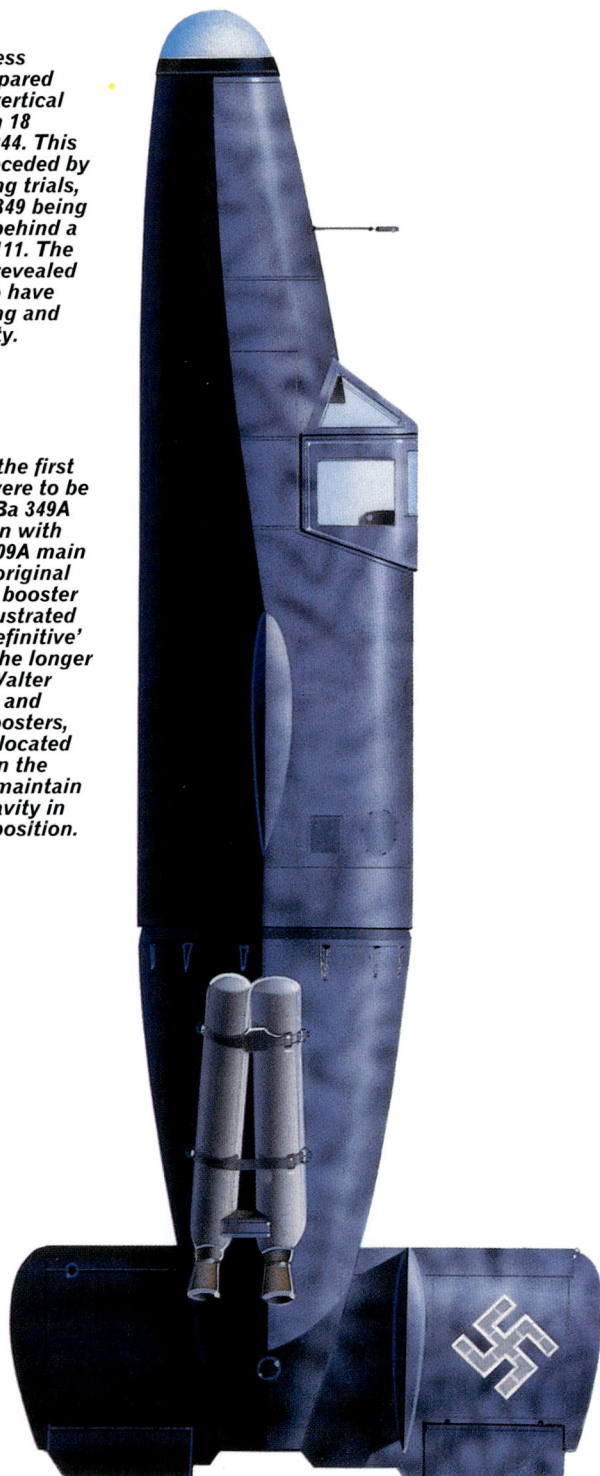

the scheme was discarded as impracticable by the RLM, the concept captured the imagination of Dipl.-Ing. Bachem, then technical director of the Gerhard Fieseler Werke, who prepared a series of interceptor design studies under the generic designation Fi 166. They, too, were rejected by the RLM, but Dipl.-Ing. Bachem maintained close contact with Dr von Braun and bi-fuel rocket motor development at Peenemünde, and when, in the late spring of 1944, the RLM issued a requirement for a small and inexpensive target-defence interceptor, he submitted a proposal which he designated the **BP 20 Natter**.

Himmler's intervention

Numerous projects were submitted to the Technisches Amt of the RLM to meet the demands of the new requirement and, in the final evaluation during the early summer, a Heinkel proposal, the Projekt 1077 Julia, was selected as the winning contender, while the Natter was rejected out of hand, Dipl.-Ing. Bachem's proposal having been uninvited and, in any case, submitted for consideration through abnormal channels. Dipl.-Ing. Bachem had enlisted the aid of the General der Jagdflieger Adolf Galland who had himself passed the Natter project to the RLM, but in defence of the Technisches Amt it should be stated that Dipl.-Ing. Bachem's project did not meet the demands of the requirement, which did not envisage partial loss of the interceptor after each mission. However, convinced of the feasibility of his project, Bachem had no intention of accepting defeat in this fashion, and promptly applied for and was granted an interview with no lesser personage than Heinrich Himmler.

Himmler displayed immediate interest in the Natter project, promised his full personal support and, within 24 hours, Dipl.-Ing. Bachem had been informed by the Technisches Amt that it had reconsidered its earlier rejection of the Natter project, which was now to receive the highest development priority. A small factory had been acquired at Waldsee in the

Black Forest, Dipl.-Ing. Bachem was joined by Dipl.-Ing. H. Bethbeder, formerly a technical director of the Dornier-Werke, while the Walter-Werke at Kiel provided a rocket motor specialist, Ing. Grassow. In August 1944 work on the BP 20 Natter began in earnest, this development coming within the orbit of the Jägernotprogramm (Emergency Fighter Programme) of the Technisches Amt under Oberst Knemeyer, and receiving the official designation **Ba 349**.

Operational concept

The definitive Natter differed in some respects to that originally proposed by Dipl.-Ing. Bachem. The first scheme envisaged an initial attack on the bomber formation during which the Natter would expend its battery of rockets, the pilot then using the remaining kinetic energy to gain sufficient

Extreme simplicity lay at the heart of the BP 20 (Ba 349) design. This allowed the airframe to be built by semi-skilled woodworkers, reducing the programme's reliance on strategic materials. It also allowed the Natter to be built rapidly in quantity, although the factory was overtaken before this could become a reality.

Bachem Ba 349B cutaway key

1　Jettisonable plastic nosecone
2　Honeycomb arrangement of hexagonal tubes for 24 Hs 217 Föhn rockets
3　Ring sight
4　Armoured bulkhead
5　Missile control and fusing box
6　Nose/cockpit attachment frame (nose section jettisonable by means of explosive bolts)
7　Rudder pedal

8　Control column
9　Instrument panel
10　Armoured windscreen (jettisoned with nose section)
11　Seat pan
12　Seat harness
13　Padded seat back
14　Headrest
15　Rear armour
16　Aft-hinging armoured canopy
17　T-stoff tank (435-litre/95.6-Imp gal capacity)
18　Filler cap
19　C-stoff tank (190-litre/41.8-Imp gal capacity)
20　Filler cap
21　Walter HWK 509C-1 rocket motor
22　Rear fuselage separation frame

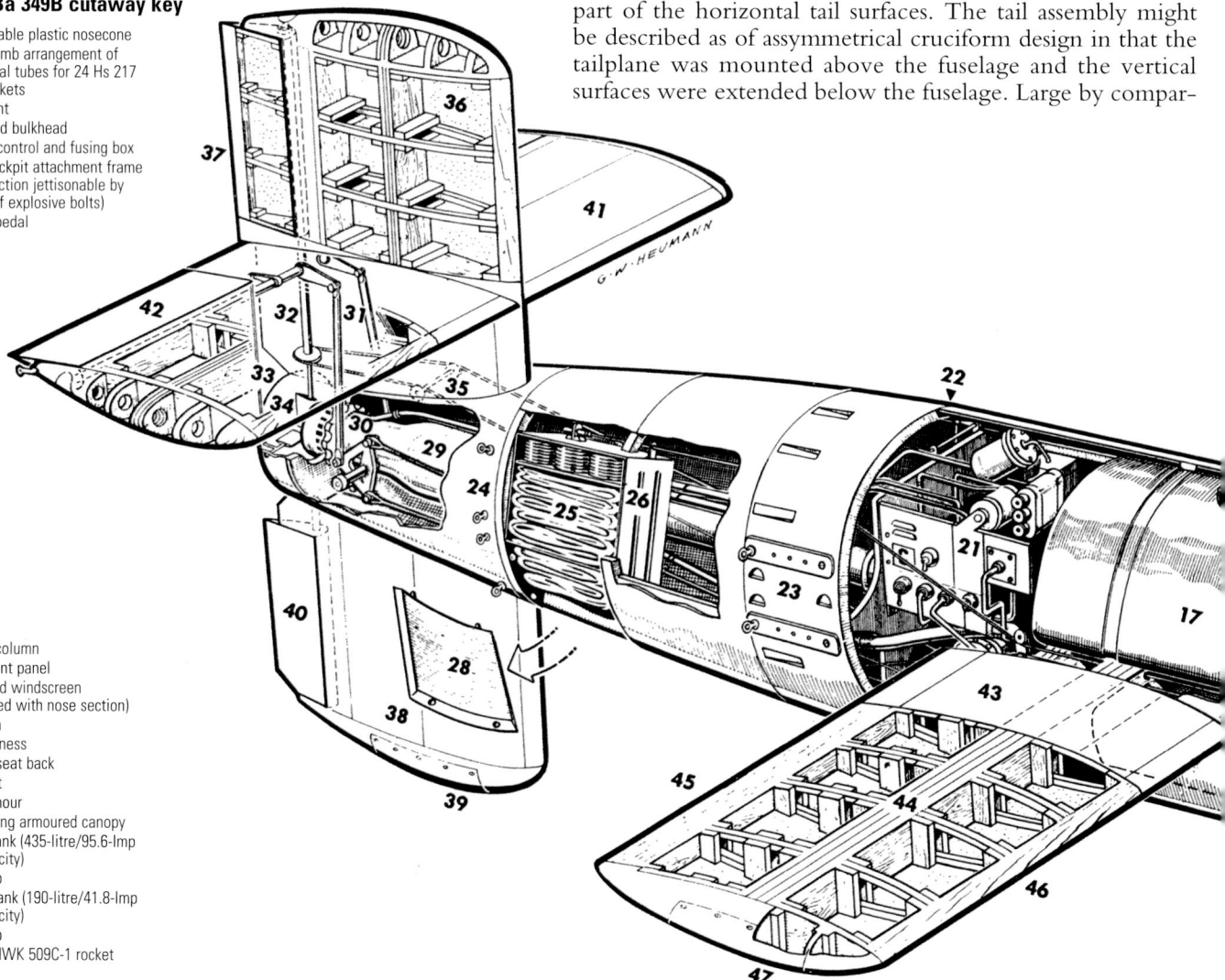

height to perform a ramming attack in a dive. Immediately before impact the pilot was to eject himself from the cockpit of the Natter, activation of the ejection seat triggering explosive bolts that would detach the aft fuselage housing the rocket motor, a parachute being automatically deployed to lower this to the ground for retrieval and re-use. Dipl.-Ing. Bethbeder concluded that the cockpit of the Natter was too small to permit the installation of an effective ejection seat. Furthermore, its provision would only serve to complicate a design that was intended to provide the essence of simplicity, and it was decided, therefore, to dispense with the ramming attack, the pilot jettisoning the forward fuselage complete with windscreen after discharging his rockets, this action releasing the parachute housing cover and deploying the parachute.

During the weeks that followed, detailed design was pursued in parallel with wind tunnel trials at Braunschweig. During tunnel testing speeds in excess of Mach 0.95 were simulated without the appearance of any adverse stability or compressibility effects. The entire airframe was of wooden construction, metal being used only for control push-rods, hinges and load-supporting attachment points. The fuselage was of semi-monocoque construction with laminated skin, stringers and formers, and the wing possessed a single laminated wooden spar that was continuous from wingtip to wingtip and passed between the fuselage fuel tanks. The wing incorporated no movable surfaces, rolling control being obtained by differential operation of the elevons that formed part of the horizontal tail surfaces. The tail assembly might be described as of assymmetrical cruciform design in that the tailplane was mounted above the fuselage and the vertical surfaces were extended below the fuselage. Large by compar-

Bachem Ba 349

The central fuselage housed the tanks for the rocket fuel, comprising C-Stoff in the upper tank and T-Stoff below. The rocket motor was located immediately aft of the tanks with a simple duct leading to the tail nozzle. The four Schmidding booster rockets only burned for around 10 seconds during launch before being jettisoned.

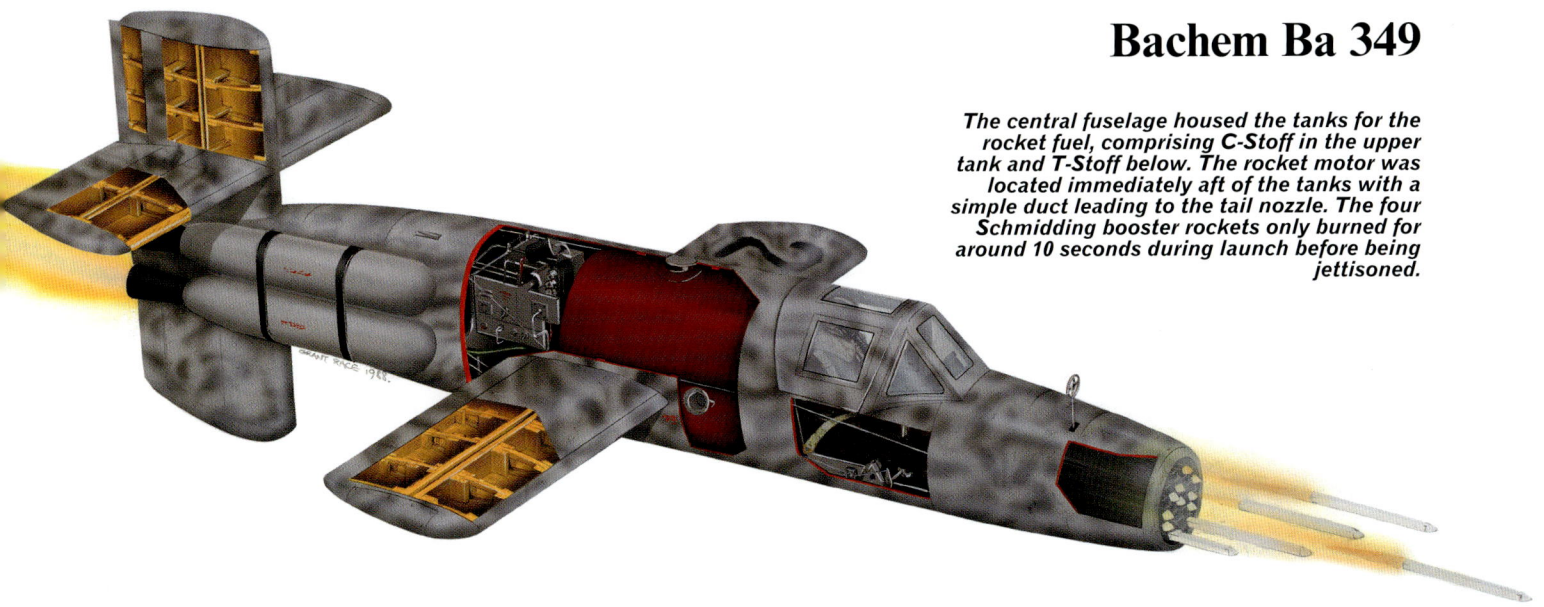

ison with the wing, the tailplane contributed an important proportion of the total lift, both wing and tailplane being of rectangular planform without dihedral, taper or sweep. The wing utilised a symmetrical aerofoil, thickness to chord being 12 per cent and maximum thickness being located at 50 per cent chord.

Rocket battery

Alternative forms of armament considered during the initial development stage included a Rohrbatterie of 49 30-mm (1.18-in) SG 119 rocket shells, and the cylindrical semi-automatic Trommelgerät with 40 30-mm shells, but eventually a Bienenwabe (Honeycomb) arrangement of hexagonal tubes for 73-mm (2.87-in) Hs 217 Föhn (Storm) rockets or quadrangular tubes for 55-mm (2.17-in) R4M rockets was adopted. Whereas the Bienenwabe for the smaller rockets comprised 33 tubes, that for the larger rockets consisted of

24 tubes, an earlier arrangement of 28 Föhn tubes being discarded owing to the inadequacy of exhaust gas venting arrangements which resulted in an explosion during the test firing. A jettisonable plastic fairing enclosed the forward end of the Bienenwabe prior to firing.

Considerable importance was attached to the provision of adequate armour protection for the pilot, and the forward cockpit bulkhead was provided by an armour plate which was cut away at the base in order that the pilot's feet could reach the rudder pedals which were positioned one on each side of the Bienenwabe. Sandwich-type armour was provided on each side of the pilot's seat, and aft protection was provided by the rear armour bulkhead dividing the cockpit from the fuel tanks. Instrumentation was spartan, and the rocket firing sight consisted solely of a ring sight projecting from the nose ahead of the cockpit. Immediately aft of the rear cockpit bulkhead were the two fuel tanks, the tank above the wing spar accommodating 435 litres (95.6 Imp gal) of T-Stoff (80 per cent hydrogen peroxide plus oxyquinoline as a stabiliser) and the tank below the spar housing 190 litres (41.8 Imp gal) of C-Stoff (a 30 per cent hydrazine hydrate solution in methanol), and the Walter 509A-1 rocket motor.

For launching, the Ba 349 was to be mounted on a near-vertical 24.00-m (80-ft) ramp, the wingtips and the tip of the lower fin being strengthened to run in the three guide rails. The ramp itself was pivoted at its base to enable the aircraft to be 'loaded' in the horizontal position. As the thrust

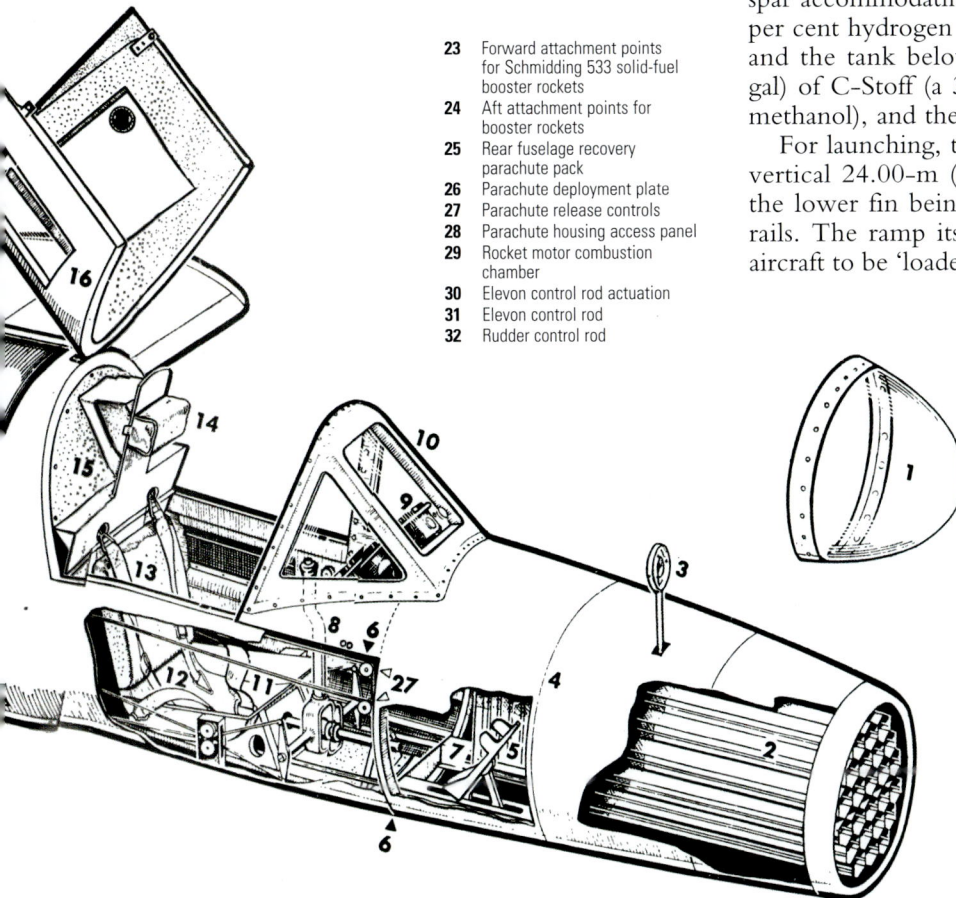

23 Forward attachment points for Schmidding 533 solid-fuel booster rockets
24 Aft attachment points for booster rockets
25 Rear fuselage recovery parachute pack
26 Parachute deployment plate
27 Parachute release controls
28 Parachute housing access panel
29 Rocket motor combustion chamber
30 Elevon control rod actuation
31 Elevon control rod
32 Rudder control rod

33 Fixed fin extension
34 Exhaust orifice
35 Rudder control cables
36 Laminated wood tail structure
37 Upper rudder
38 Lower fin
39 Strengthened tip (to run in guide rail during take-off)
40 Lower rudder
41 Port tailplane
42 Starboard elevon
43 Symmetrical aerofoil
44 Laminated wooden mainspar
45 Single-piece wooden trailing edge
46 Single-piece edge
47 Strengthened tip (to run in guide rail during take-off)

Bachem Ba 349

to weight ratio was marginally short of 1:1 and therefore insufficient for vertical take-off, it was proposed to attach four 4.9-kN (1,102-lb) thrust Schmidding solid-fuel booster rockets to the rear fuselage, these firing for 10 seconds after which they were to be jettisoned. It was calculated that the initial acceleration would not exceed 2.2 g but the possibility of the pilot blacking out was safeguarded against by pre-setting the elevons for the required flight path while the Ba 349 was still on the ramp, a three-axis autopilot ground-controlled by radio link assuming guidance of the interceptor at an altitude of 170-180 m (550-600 ft), at which point the booster rockets would theoretically be jettisoned. At a range of 1.6-3.2 km (1-2 miles) from the target formation it was intended that the pilot would override the autopilot control, jettison the nosecone to expose the rockets, close with the bombers, fire the entire complement of missiles in one salvo, turn away from the formation and bale out. As the sole purpose of the pilot was to direct the aircraft during the final phase of the attack the scheme offered the possibility of employing personnel without any training other than that which could be provided on a rudimentary ground rig. After completing his attack the pilot was to release his seat harness, uncouple the control column, and release the safety catches and mechanical connections holding the nose section. This would then fall away from the aircraft, complete with windscreen, instrument panel, forward bulkhead and rudder pedals, simultaneously releasing a parachute housed in the rear fuselage. The sudden deceleration resulting from the deployment of this chute would throw the pilot forward and clear of the aircraft, and he would then descend by parachute in the normal way.

Gliding trials

Such was the impetus placed behind the Ba 349 programme that the first of an initial series of 50 Versuchs models was completed at Waldsee within three months of the launching of the Natter project. At this stage it was proposed to expend all 50 of the first batch of aircraft on the 'unpowered' test phase, and the first gliding trials were performed near Heuberg in November 1944, the Ba 349 being ballasted to a weight of 1700 kg (3,748 lb) and then towed to an altitude of approximately 5500 m (18,000 ft) behind an He 111. The test pilot, Zübert, subsequently reported that stability was excellent and the controls light and effective at all speeds between 200 and 680 km/h (125 and 425 mph). The first vertical launching with a pilotless Ba 349 was attempted on 18 December 1944, the empty airframe being fitted with the four Schmidding booster rockets. This test proved a complete failure, the Ba 349 failing to leave the ramp as a result of the booster rockets burning through the release cables. A second attempt was made four days later, and on this occasion the Ba 349 left the ramp as planned and disappeared into the cloud base at an altitude of 750 m (2,460 ft).

Ten more unmanned Ba 349s were launched successfully, although it was ascertained that climbing speed attained by

Left: The launch gantry devised for the Natter could be pivoted to facilitate loading of the interceptor. The launcher ensured that the Natter left the ground in a near-vertical trajectory, after which a simple autopilot took control for the first stages of the climbout.

Above: The Ba 349 is prepared for its first piloted launch, which took place on 28 February 1945. During the launch the aircraft reached around 500 m (1,650 ft) before the canopy was seen to detach, after which it crashed.

Above: Lothar Siebert boards the Ba 349 for its first piloted flight. The accident that followed was never entirely explained, but it was assumed that the canopy had not been properly locked prior to take-off and that Siebert had been knocked out.

Right: A Ba 349 takes to the skies with the Schmidding boosters adding their thrust to that from the main Walter engine. The boosters were required to provide a positive thrust-to-weight ratio for liftoff and acceleration to a controllable flying speed.

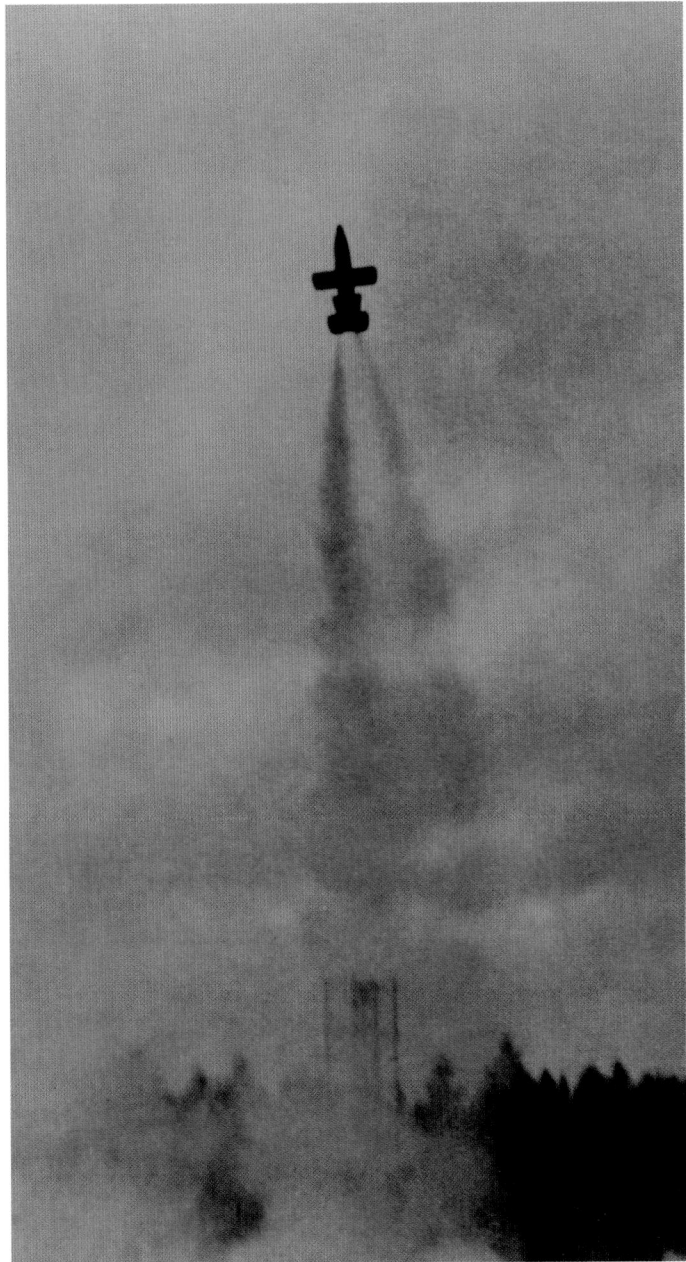

the time the booster rockets were jettisoned was insufficient to result in full control surface effectiveness. To remedy this defect the vertical tail surfaces were substantially redesigned, both upper and lower rudder portions being almost doubled in chord, the lower portion also being substantially reduced in depth as was also the elongated ventral fin. The chord of the elevons was also increased, and small water-cooled control vanes were introduced in the rocket exhaust orifice, these having a life of approximately 30 seconds by which time sufficient speed had been attained to render the normal control surfaces fully effective. These changes were introduced on the **Ba 349A V16** and all subsequent Natters.

The original idea of using the first 50 airframes for gliding trials and pilotless launchings had by this time been abandoned owing to the time factor, and something of the impetus placed behind the Natter programme as a result of Heinrich Himmler's support had diminished. In fact, on 22 December 1944, the day on which the first successful pilotless launching was made, a meeting in Berlin of the Entwicklungs Hauptkommission (Chief Development Commission) for aircraft concluded that neither the Ba 349 or Projekt 1077 Julia held promise; that development of the Me 263 should be expedited by all means, and that tests of the Me 262 with supplementary rocket propulsion should be pursued as this aircraft might render all other target-defence interceptors superfluous. It was recommended that all work on Julia be suspended, and that development of the Ba 349, although opposed on technical and tactical grounds, should be continued in view of the imminence of powered trials, but that all preparations for series production should be discontinued.

Powerplant troubles

These pronouncements of the Entwicklungs Hauptkommission were no more than recommendations and, in so far as the Ba 349 was concerned, never implemented, but the Natter programme was encountering problems unrelated to the disapproval of the Hauptkommission. It had been ascertained that construction of the airframe demanded only 250 man-

hours, and the interceptor could be built for the most part by semi-skilled and unskilled labour. A number of small wood-working shops in and around the Black Forest were producing laminated wooden components for the Ba 349, but the behaviour of the Schmidding booster rockets was proving unreliable, burning time and thrust varying and several units exploding under test. The Patin three-axis autopilot tended to be erratic and was proving difficult to synchronise, and promised deliveries of the Walter 509A rocket motor failed to materialise. In fact, the first Walter powerplant did not reach Bachem until February 1945. Thus, the first complete Natter could not be launched until the 25th of that month.

For the initial test with the Walter 509A installed a dummy pilot was seated in the cockpit. The Ba 349 was launched successfully and, at a predetermined altitude, the nose section and powerplant section broke away, and both the dummy pilot and the powerplant descended safely by parachute. The RLM, impressed by the results of the test, demanded that piloted trials with the Walter 509A installed should commence immediately. Dipl.-Ing. Bachem voiced his opinion that such tests were still premature, and in this he was supported by Professor Ruff of the DVL, but all objections were dismissed,

Bachem Ba 349

and on 28 February Oberleutnant Lothar Siebert, who had volunteered to perform the first fully-powered flight trials, was launched in a Ba 349. The aircraft climbed to an altitude of approximately 500 m (1,650 ft) when the cockpit canopy suddenly detached itself, the aircraft turning over on its back and continuing to climb at a shallow angle to an altitude of some 1460 m (4,800 ft), then nosing down and diving into the ground, exploding on impact.

Despite the accident, tests continued, and other pilots volunteered to replace Siebert. Three successful manned tests were performed in rapid succession, and it was decided that the Ba 349 had reached a sufficiently advanced stage in its trials for operational evaluation. Meanwhile, Bachem and Bethbeder, dissatisfied with the powered endurance of the Natter, had adapted the interceptor to take the Walter 509C featuring an auxiliary cruising chamber. This necessitated some revision of the aft fuselage to take the vertically-disposed rocket pipes of the new powerplant, and, for aerodynamic reasons, the lower contours of the fuselage were deepened marginally, this having the incidental advantage of providing space for the installation of two 30-mm cannon which had been proposed as an alternative armament to the Föhn or R4M rockets. No attempt was made to increase fuel capacity, but for C of G reasons the attachment points of the booster rockets were moved aft, and provision was made for the replacement of the 4.9-kN (1,102-lb) units by two Schmidding 533 solid-fuel rockets each providing 9.8-kN (2,205-lb) thrust.

This development, designated **BP 20B** by the Bachem-Werke and **Ba 349B** by the RLM, was intended to supplant the initial model, the **Ba 349A**, with the 51st aircraft, the A-series of the Natter thus being restricted to the original batch of Versuchs machines and the Ba 349B becoming the actual production version. The B-series offered a powered endurance of 4.36 minutes at 800 km/h (495 mph) at 3000 m (9,840 ft) as compared with 2.23 minutes at this altitude for the A-series, but launching weight was only 58 kg (127 lb) greater and flying weight was virtually unchanged. In the event, only three Versuchs Ba 349B interceptors were completed before work came to a standstill at Waldsee, one of them actually being flown, although non-availability of the definitive booster rockets necessitated the retention of the 4.9-kN (1,102-lb) thrust units.

A total of 36 Natter interceptors was actually completed at Waldsee of which 25 were flown, although only seven of them with pilots and, in April 1945, 10 A-series Natters were set up at Kirchheim, near Stuttgart, to await the arrival of USAAF bombers. In the event, Bachem's ingenious weapon was never to be blooded in action, for Allied tanks arrived in

the vicinity of the launching site before the expected bombers, and the Natters were destroyed on their ramps to prevent them falling into enemy hands.

Bachem Ba 349B-1 specification
(based on manufacturer's data)

Type: single-seat semi-expendable interceptor fighter
Powerplant: one Walter HWK 509C-1 bi-fuel rocket motor with a maximum thrust of 19.6 kN (4,410 lb) (11.2 kN/3,750 lb from main chamber and 2.9 kN/660 lb from auxiliary chamber), plus (for take-off) four 4.9-kN (1,102-lb) thrust or two 9.8-kN (2,205-lb) thrust solid-fuel rockets
Performance: maximum speed 1000 km/h (620 mph) at 5000 m (16,400 ft); cruising speed 800 km/h (495 mph); initial climb rate 11400 m (37,400 ft) per minute; range after climb 60 km (36 miles) at 3000 m (9,840 ft), 55 km (34 miles) at 6000 m (19,685 ft), 42 km (26 miles) at 9000 m (29,530 ft), 40 km (24 miles) at 10000 m (32,810 ft); endurance 4.36 minutes at 3000 m, 4.13 minutes at 6000 m, 3.15 minutes at 9000 m
Weights: take-off (including booster rockets) 2232 kg (4,920 lb), (with boosters jettisoned) 1769 kg (3,900 lb), (fuel expended) 880 kg (1,940 lb)
Dimensions: wingspan 4.00 m (13 ft 1½ in); length 6.00 m (19 ft 9 in); height (fin base to tip) 2.25 m (7 ft 4½ in); wing area 4.70 m² (50.59 sq ft)
Armament: 24 73-mm (2.87-in) Hs 217 Föhn or 33 55-mm (2.17-in) R4M rockets, or (proposed) two 30-mm MK 108 cannon with 30 r.p.g.

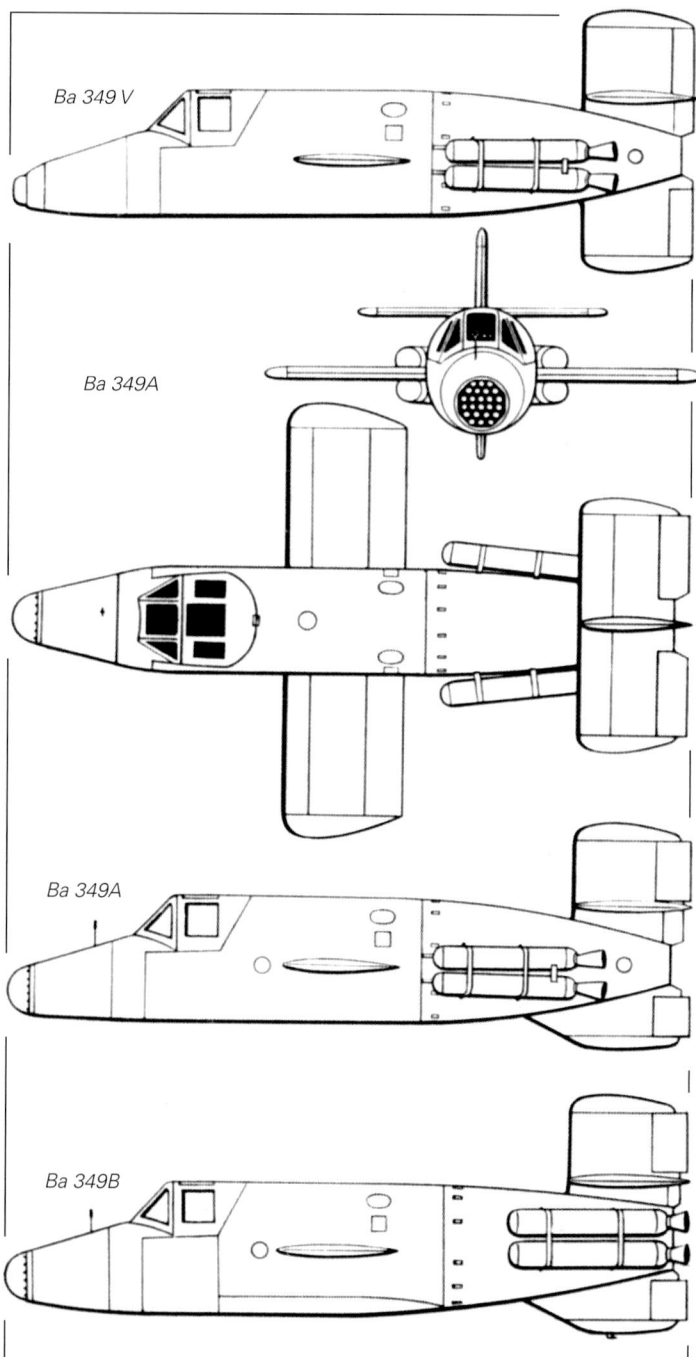

Ba 349 V

Ba 349A

Ba 349A

Ba 349B

A Ba 349A is seen mounted on the trailer on which it was towed to the launching ramp. One of the Schmidding solid-fuel booster rockets is visible in the foreground. These units were found to be unreliable and were to be replaced in the Ba 349B.

Beneš-Mráz Be.50 and Be.51 Beta-Minor

Not notably attractive as a result of the high decking that faired the cockpit into the tail unit, the Be.50 and Be.51 were nonetheless highly effective trainers, and aircraft of these two types seized in the German occupation of Czechoslovakia were gratefully impressed for Luftwaffe service as trainers and 'hacks'.

Beneš & Mráz Továrna na Letadla was formed in 1935 to design and manufacture a series of lightplanes. The **Be.50 Beta-Minor** was a low-wing cantilever monoplane of ply-covered wooden construction with fixed tailskid undercarriage, and accommodation for two in open cockpits with dual controls as standard. The **Be.51 Beta-Minor** followed the same general lines, but had a wing of slightly reduced span and a modified fuselage with an enclosed cabin: as with the Be.50, this accommodated two in tandem with dual controls. The Beta Minor proved popular in the immediate pre-war years, with the Be.51 being more extensively built. After the March 1939 annexation of Czechoslovakia, a number aircraft, almost all of them Be.51s,

were seized by Germany, being used by the Luftwaffe in the communication and training roles, the latter including the Flugzeugführerschulen A/B 4, 14, 23, 62, 71, 114 and 119.

Beneš-Mráz Be.51 Beta-Minor specification
Type: two-seat training and touring light aeroplane
Powerplant: one Walter Minor air-cooled four-cylinder inverted inline engine rated at 71 kW (95 hp) for take-off
Performance: maximum speed 205 km/h (127 mph) at sea level; cruising speed 180 km/h (112 mph) at optimum altitude; climb to 1000 m (3,280 ft) in 6 minutes; service ceiling 5000 m (16,405 ft); range 800 km (497 miles)
Weights: empty 480 kg (1,058 lb); maximum take-off 760 kg (1,676 lb)
Dimensions: wingspan 11.44 m (37 ft 6¼ in); length 7.76 m (25 ft 5½ in); height 2.05 m (6 ft 8¾ in); wing area 15.30 m² (164.69 sq ft)

Left and below: The Be.51 Beta-Minor was operated in modest numbers by the Luftwaffe. The main gear fairings and wheel spats were often removed as they proved to be traps for mud and grass.

Beneš-Mráz Be.252 Beta-Scolar

The Be.252 was a logical step up from the Be.50 and Be.51 series for the advanced training role with improved fields of vision from the fully glazed cockpit and higher performance from the more powerful engine. Like its predecessors, the Be.252 was readily taken into useful German service.

The **Be.252 Beta-Scolar** was designed as an advanced flying trainer with aerobatic capability, and was in essence a development of the Be.50 with internal changes to provide a more robust structure. This was needed not only to cater for the installation of a more powerful engine, but also because of the additional stresses resulting from aerobatic usage. Most of the aircraft seized after the German occupation of Czechoslovakia in March 1939 were impressed into Luftwaffe service in the training role.

Beneš-Mráz Be.252 Beta-Scolar specification
Type: two-seat advanced trainer
Powerplant: one Walter Scolar air-cooled seven-cylinder radial engine rated at 134 kW (180 hp) for take-off
Performance: maximum speed 250 km/h (155 mph) at sea level; cruising speed 215 km/h (134 mph); at optimum altitude; initial climb rate 252 m (827 ft) per minute; service ceiling 7000 m (22,965 ft); range 500 km (311 miles)
Weights: empty 610 kg (1,345 lb); maximum take-off 890 kg (1,962 lb)
Dimensions: wingspan 10.966 m (34 ft 11¾ in); length 7.45 m (24 ft 7½ in); height 2.02 m (6 ft 7½ in); wing area 14.00 m² (150.70 sq ft)

The Be.252 offered a number of aerodynamic refinements over the Be.50 and Be.51, and possessed higher performance as well as better fields of vision for the front-seat pupil and rear-seat instructor.

Bloch MB.151 and MB.152

In its MB.150 Bloch had created the basis for an excellent fighter that began to mature in the MB.151 and MB.152. But development was slow, and production hampered by the nationalisation and reorganisation of the French aero industry in the late 1930s. A few were pressed into service by Germany as fighter trainers.

By revising the MB.150 with a wing of greater span and area, taller main undercarriage units and the 686-kW (920-hp) Gnome-Rhône 14N-11 radial engine, later replaced by the identically rated 14N-35 unit, Bloch produced the **MB.151.01** prototype. This first flew on 18 August 1938. Work on a pre-production batch of 25 aircraft had already started by this time, but only four had been delivered by April 1939. At the same time the design team of the Société Nationale de Constructions Aéronautiques de Sud-Ouest (SNCASO), of which the nationalised Bloch company was now a part, had been working on an improved version with the 768-kW (1,030-hp) 14N-21 engine and belt- rather than magazine-fed machine-guns. First flown on 15 December 1938, the **MB.152.01** prototype was, in the event, powered by the 746-kW (1,000-hp) 14N-25 engine, and entered high-priority flight testing in February 1939. The improved performance of this version led to an initial order for 400 aircraft, of which 60 and 340 were to be completed to the **MB.151C.1** and **MB.152C.1** production standards, respectively. Orders for the MB.151C.1 eventually reached 144, the first of them being accepted on 7 March 1939. The type was inferior to the MB.152C.1, and used mainly for conversion and fighter training, although some machines were flown in combat by the Armée de l'Air and Aéronavale.

Production of the series was very slow, however, and by the outbreak of World War II a combined total of only 120 MB.151C.1 and MB.152C.1 fighters had been delivered, the first MB.152C.1 having been accepted in April 1939. Not one of them could be used operationally for lack of reflector gun sights, and 95 of the total could not even be flown as they had been delivered without propellers. Even by the end of November, at which time 358 aircraft had been

Above: Deliveries of the MB.152C.1, seen here in the form of an aircraft under German evaluation, began in April 1939. The type was powered by either of two Gnome-Rhône 14N engine models.

Below: The MB.152C.1 was evaluated by the Germans after the Franco-German armistice of June 1940. The Germans assessed the French fighter as of only indifferent overall capability.

After assessing the MB.152C.1, the Germans were happy to allocate available numbers to the air arm of the collaborationist Vichy French regime. By April 1941 the Germans had agreed that the Vichy French fighter arm should be equipped with only the superior Dewoitine D.520C.1 fighter. The surplus MB.152C.1s were placed in storage, and many were seized by the Germans in November 1942.

This MB.152C.1 carries limited German markings over its French camuflage and yellow/red Vichy French markings.

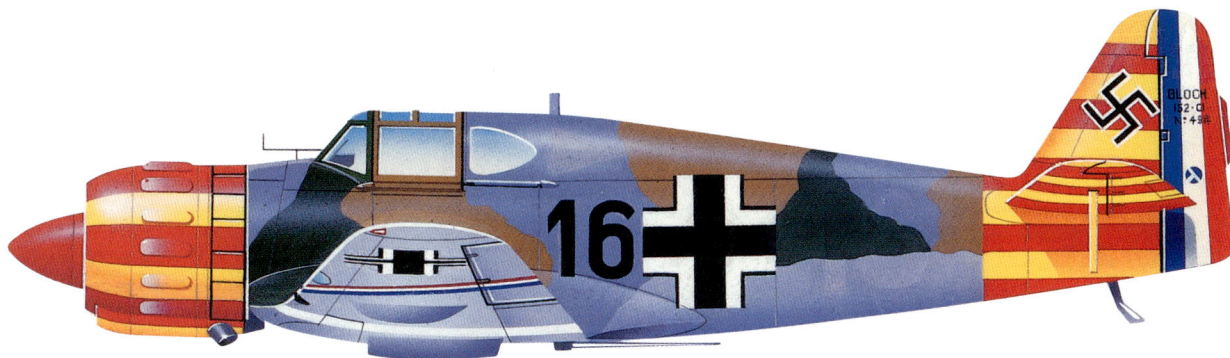

This was an example of the MB.152C.1 as evaluated by the Germans. The machine carries no evidence of Vichy French markings.

delivered, 157 were still without propellers and there were serious problems with engine overheating. The only immediate development of the MB.152 was the sole **MB.153.01** prototype, which was an MB.152 taken from the production line and re-engined with the 783-kW (1,050-hp) Pratt & Whitney R-1830-SC3-G Twin Wasp air-cooled 14-cylinder radial engine.

Despite the problems it faced, the Armée de l'Air did all in its power to speed the introduction of what was potentially a valuable addition to its fighter inventory. The fighter groups soon realised that their MB.151C.1 and MB.152C.1 fighters were adequate warplanes, though not fully a match for the opposing Messerschmitt Bf 109E fighter, and it was tragic that indifference and political intrigue cost so many French pilots their lives in totally obsolete aircraft, instead of being able to fight the Luftwaffe on more equal terms with capable machines such as the MB.152C.1.

Nine MB.151 fighters were supplied to the Greek air force and, after the collapse of France, six groups of the Vichy French air force were permitted to fly the MB.151C.1 and MB.152C.1. When manufacture by the SNCASO ended in May 1940, 144 MB.151C.1 and 482 MB.152C.1 fighters had been built. Three of these groups were later re-equipped with Dewoitine D.520C.1 fighters.

At the time of the armistice which ended Germany's campaign against France in June 1940, the Luftwaffe seized 173 Bloch fighters of all types, of which only 83 were immediately serviceable and the rest in varying states of disrepair. There is no evidence that the type saw significant service in German colours, but a small number of MB.151C.1 and a larger number of MB.152C.1 machines (seized in 1940 and later in 1942 after the German had occupied Vichy France) were revised with German markings over their French camouflage, and it is therefore very likely that they saw limited service as fighter trainers until increasing maintenance requirements made it uneconomical to persevere with the type.

Above: Seen to the right of a Focke-Wulf Fw 190 fighter, an MB.152C.1 has the appearance of belonging to a slightly earlier and less capable generation.

Bloch MB.152C.1 specification
Type: single-seat fighter
Powerplant: one Gnome-Rhône 14N-25 air-cooled 14-cylinder radial engine rated at 805 kW (1,080 hp), or one Gnome-Rhône 14N-49 engine rated at 820 kW (1,100 hp)
Performance: maximum speed 509 km/h (316 mph) at 4500 m (14,765 ft); cruising speed 450 km/h (280 mph) at optimum altitude; climb to 2000 m (6,560 ft) in 3 minutes 24 seconds; service ceiling 10000 m (32,810 ft); range 600 km (373 miles)
Weights: empty 2158 kg (4,757 lb); maximum take-off 2800 kg (6,173 lb)
Dimensions: wingspan 10.54 m (34 ft 7 in); length 9.10 m (29 ft 10¼ in); height 3.03 m (9 ft 11⅓ in); wing area 17.32 m² (186.43 sq ft)
Armament: two 20-mm Hispano-Suiza HS 404 fixed forward-firing cannon with 60 r.p.g and two 7.5-mm (0.295-in) MAC 1934 M39 fixed forward-firing machine-guns with 500 r.p.g., or four 7.5-mm (0.295-in) MAC 1934 M39 fixed forward-firing machine-guns with 500 r.p.g.

An MB.152C.1 in German markings is seen after coming to grief in a landing accident. The ring-and-bead sight in front of the cockpit is evidence of the French air force's pre-war equipment shortages.

Bloch MB.155

With the MB.155 the French fighter family initiated by the MB.150 began to achieve a real combat capability, and it was a tragedy for France that development of this effective warplane took so long. Only a few aircraft were completed, and Germany later used some of them as fighter trainers.

With production of the MB.151/MB.152 in progress, SNCASO started development of an improved version, for both company and official testing had suggested that the MB.152, while flawed, had considerable potential. Once again pressure of circumstance intervened to prevent any really significant improvement except in range, by a redesign of the fuselage to move the cockpit aft and allow the incorporation of an enlarged fuel tank. Thus most of the MB.152's jigs and tooling could be used and so speed the start of production. Other modifications introduced in the **MB.155.01** prototype (an MB.152 conversion) that first flew on 3 December 1939 included increased wing chord and a lower-drag engine cowling. The type entered production in early May 1940 as the **MB.155C.1**, and other improvements on production aircraft included extra armour and an armoured windscreen. The French capitulation of 25 June came before any of the new fighters, of which 10 had been completed, had been delivered. Another 19 aircraft, incomplete at the time of the armistice, were finished and delivered to the Vichy French air force. On German occupation of Vichy France in November 1942, the Luftwaffe seized the surviving MB.155C.1s for service as fighter trainers.

Bloch MB.155C.1 specification
Type: single-seat fighter
Powerplant: one Gnome-Rhône 14N-49 air-cooled 14-cylinder radial engine rated at 820 kW (1,100 hp)
Performance: maximum speed 520 km/h (323 mph) at 4500 m (14,765 ft); climb to 4000 m (13,125 ft) in 6 minutes 55 seconds; service ceiling 10000m (32,810 ft); range 1050 km (652 miles)
Weights: empty 2140 kg (4,718 lb); maximum take-off 2900 kg (6,393 lb)
Dimensions: wingspan 10.54 m (34 ft 7 in); length 9.05 m (29 ft 8⅓ in); height 3.21 m (10 ft 6 in); wing area 17.32 m² (186.43 sq ft)
Armament: two 20-mm Hispano-Suiza HS-404 cannon and two or four 7.5-mm (0.295-in) MAC 1934 M39 machine-guns, or six 7.5-mm (0.295-in) MAC 1934 M39 fixed forward-firing machine-guns

This MB.155C.1 fighter seized by the Germans was pressed into service by the Luftwaffe as a fighter trainer during 1942.

Above: Seen here in German markings, the MB.155C.1 had its cockpit moved to a location farther to the rear than that of the MB.152, and this allowed the installation of a larger fuselage fuel tank.

Bloch MB.157

The MB.157 was undoubtedly the best fighter developed in France before that country's defeat by Germany in June 1940. However, only a single prototype had been completed, and this was quickly appropriated by the Germans for an evaluation centred on the fighter's excellent, low-drag powerplant installation.

The **MB.157** was to combine the MB.152's airframe with a far more powerful Gnome-Rhône 14R engine offering a supercharged rating of 1268 kW (1,700 hp) at 8000 m (26,245 ft), but the engine's greater size and weight meant that the MB.152 airframe could not be modified to suit, so the SNCASO designed a new fighter retaining the same basic concepts. In just more than six months the components of the prototype were ready for assembly. With German forces by then closing on Paris, the components were loaded for movement to a secure site, but the vehicle was seized by the Germans.

The MB.157 was assembled and, in March 1942, first flew under German supervision, demonstrating superb perform-

Potentially the best fighter produced by France in World War II, the MB.157 offered superb combat capability and had the potential for great reliability. The prototype was extensively tested by the Luftwaffe after its components had been captured by advancing German forces in 1940.

ance. The prototype was then flown to Orly, where the powerplant was removed for bench testing. This was the most interesting feature of the fighter as far as the Germans were concerned, and the engine was later transported to Germany. The airframe was destroyed during an Allied air raid.

Bloch MB.157 specification
Type: single-seat fighter
Powerplant: one Gnome-Rhône 14R-4 air-cooled 14-cylinder radial engine

rated at 1186 kW (1,590 hp) for take-off
Performance: maximum speed 710 km/h (441 mph) at 7850 m (25,755 ft); cruising speed 400 km/h (249 mph) at optimum altitude; climb to 8000 m (26,245 ft) in 11 minutes; range 1095 km (680 miles)
Weights: empty 2388 kg (5,265 lb); normal take-off 3250 kg (7,165 lb)
Dimensions: wingspan 10.70 m (35 ft 1¼ in); length 9.15 m (30 ft 1¼ in); height 4.30 m (14 ft 1¼ in); wing area 19.40 m² (208.82 sq ft)
Armament: (proposed) two 20-mm Hispano-Suiza HS-404 fixed forward-firing cannon and four 7.5-mm (0.295-in) MAC 1934 M39 fixed forward-firing machine-guns

Bloch MB.175

A three-seat light bomber and attack warplane, the Bloch MB.175 was one of the best military aircraft developed by France before World War II. Yet again, though, the aircraft was developed too late, and then built too slowly, to play a decisive part in May and June 1940. The Germans subsequently used the type as an operational trainer.

The **MB.175** was developed as an improved version of the MB.174A.3 reconnaissance bomber for the light and attack bomber roles. The primary change was a larger bomb bay, which was a problem easy to identify but difficult to solve, for the length of the MB.174's bomb bay had been determined by the position of the wing spars, which continued through the fuselage. The new version's creation thus entailed the design of a new wing centre section that introduced a greater gap between the spars. In other respects the **MB.175.01** prototype, first flown in December 1939, differed little from its predecessor. Testing showed that the MB.175 retained the MB.174's excellent performance and flying characteristics, and the type was put into production to meet outstanding orders for more than 1,100 aircraft.

While the development of the MB.175 was progressing, the SNCASO had also been working on the revised powerplant of two 783-kw (1,050-hp) Pratt & Whitney R-1830-SC3G Twin Wasp air-cooled 14-cylinder radial engines in an MB.174 airframe, with a view to easing the pressure on French engine manufacturing capability. The resulting **MB.176.01** prototype had, in fact, been flown before the MB.175.01, in September 1939, but offered markedly reduced performance. Even so, this version was ordered into production, but on the basis of the new MB.175 airframe. Thus the first production examples of these new aircraft, the **MB.175B.3** and **MB.176B.3**, initially flew in April and May 1940, respectively, but only 23 of the former and five of the latter had been completed when production ended on 25 June 1940 with the fall of France.

The MB.175B.3 entered service first with the Groupe de Reconnaissance II/52 in May 1940, and the group's aircraft, plus additional MB.175s and one MB.176, were subsequently flown to North Africa, the majority being destroyed during an Allied ground attack on the airfield at Oran-La Sénia in November 1942.

At the time of France's defeat, about 200 airframes remained on the production lines, and a large proportion of the components for an additional batch of 200 had been manufactured. In July 1940, the SNCASO's Bordeaux group of factories came under Focke-Wulf control, and production of the MB.175 was resumed, in a form without armament, after a German evaluation had found it acceptable for Luftwaffe use as an operational trainer. The Bordeaux-Mérignac factory was therefore instructed to complete the 200 aircraft that were already well advanced. Between October 1940 and June 1941, just 56 examples of the MB.175 were completed and despatched to Germany for service, while a considerable

Fast and comparatively agile, with good handling characteristics, aircraft of this type were flown by the Germans in the operational training role, such as these MB.175B.3s.

number of additional machines were almost complete, or had been completed and merely awaited collection. At this point instructions were received at Mérignac that the Gnome-Rhône engines, complete with propellers, radiators, cowlings and all wiring were to be removed from the MB.175 airframes, and immediately sent to Messerschmitt for used in its Me 323 Gigant heavy transport programme. No further production of the MB.175 took place until after the end of World War II, when 80 **MB.175T** torpedo-bombers were built for the Aéronavale.

Bloch MB.175B.3 specification
Type: three-seat light bomber
Powerplant: two Gnome-Rhône 14N-48/49 radial engines each rated at 850 kW (1,140 hp) for take-off and 772 kW (1,035 hp) at 4800 m (15,750 ft)
Performance: maximum speed 540 km/h (335 mph) at 5200 m (17,060 ft); cruising speed 395 km/h (245 mph) at 4000 m (13,125 ft); climb to 8000 m (26,245 ft) in 13 minutes 30 seconds; range 1600 km (994 miles)
Weights: empty 5660 m (12,478 lb); maximum take-off 8023 kg (17,688 lb)
Dimensions: wingspan 17.95 m (58 ft 10⅓ in); length 12.43 m (40 ft 9½ in); height 3.55 m (11 ft 7¾ in); wing area 38.29 m² (413.29 sq ft)
Armament: two 7.5-mm (0.295-in) MAC 1934 fixed forward-firing machine-guns in the leading edge of the wing, two 7.5-mm (0.295-in) MAC 1934 trainable rearward-firing machine-guns in the dorsal position, and three 7.5-mm (0.295-in) MAC 1934 trainable rearward-firing machine-guns on wobble mounts in the ventral position, plus up to 600 kg (1,323 lb) of bombs carried internally

This was one of 56 examples of the MB.175 delivered to the Luftwaffe between October 1940 and June 1941 for use in the operational bomber trainer role.

Bloch MB.200 and MB.210

The MB.200 and MB.210 were useful bombers by the standards of the early 1930s, but by the outbreak of World War II were obsolete for operational purposes. The Germans used some of the aircraft they seized in Czechoslovakia and France as trainers in Luftwaffe service, and also passed many aircraft to their allies.

Designed to a 1932 requirement for a night bomber, the **MB.200** was a four-seat aircraft with a high-set cantilever wing, all-metal construction and fixed tailwheel undercarriage. The **MB.200.01** prototype was powered by two 567-kW (760-hp) Gnome-Rhône 14Krsd engines and first flew in July 1933. Despite the fact that the prototype's speed was 18 per cent below estimate, an initial order for 25 aircraft was placed in January 1934. When the **MB.200B.4** production model began to enter service towards the end of the year, it was found to be both reliable and viceless. Some 208 aircraft were completed.

At the beginning of World War II seven front-line Groupes de Bombardement were still equipped with these obsolete aircraft but, at the time of the German offensive in May 1940, all had been relegated to the training role. Another 74 aircraft had also been built under licence by Aero and Avia for the Czechoslovak air arm. These aircraft differed from the French aircraft primarily in their lower-rated licence-built Gnome-Rhône 14K engines. After the German take-over of Czechoslovakia in March 1939, the aircraft were used by the Luftwaffe for crew training as well as a number of trials purposes, and twelve aircraft were later passed to Germany's ally Bulgaria. The Luftwaffe also used captured French aircraft as crew trainers, and passed some to German satellites.

The same, but different

Although developed from the MB.200, the MB.210 was in general appearance a very different machine as a result of the switch from a high- to low-set wing. The **MB.210.01** prototype first flew on 23 November 1934 with two 596-kW (800-hp) Gnome-Rhône 14Kdrs/Kgrs engines and fixed undercarriage, but the first **MB.210BN.4** production model had retractable main units and 649-kW (870-hp) Gnome-Rhône 14Kirs/Kjrs engines. First flown on 12 December 1935, the second production example introduced increased dihedral on the outer wing panels and this became standard

The Luftwaffe made limited use of captured MB.210 bombers as crew trainers, but passed most of the aircraft to allies, who made little but probably no operational use of the aircraft.

on subsequent aircraft. One more change came before the definitive model was realised, this resulting from the type's modification from BN.4 four-seat to **MB 210BN.5** five-seat standard, and the first of them flew in November 1936. Contracts were placed with nine companies for 257 aircraft, and another 10 MB.210s were built for Romania and delivered by mid-1938. The MB.210 entered service late in 1936, and soon revealed an engine overheating tendency and a number of related problems. All aircraft then in service were grounded pending installation of Gnome-Rhône 14N-10/11 engines, which became the standard powerplant.

At the outbreak of World War II, 12 groupes were equipped with the MB.210, but its speed of about 320 km/h (199 mph) meant that the type could be regarded as little more than a sitting target for Luftwaffe fighters. However, the type's replacement by more advanced aircraft was so slow that the MB.210's relegation to the training role was nowhere near complete when the German campaign against France began on 10 May 1940. Thus, nine bomber groupes still flew the MB.210, and made night attacks on German targets before all surviving airworthy aircraft were flown to North Africa on 17 June 1940. In November 1942 the Germans occupied Vichy France and seized 37 MB.210 aircraft.

Left: Though it seemed markedly different to the low-wing MB.210, the earlier MB.200 was basically similar and also saw German use for crew training.

Bloch MB.210BN.5 specification
Type: five-seat night bomber
Powerplant: two Gnome-Rhône 14N-10/11 air-cooled 14-cylinder radial engines each rated at 679 kW (910 hp) for take-off
Performance: maximum speed 320 km/h (199 mph) at 3500 m (11,485 ft); cruising speed 240 km/h (149 mph) at 3500 m; climb to 4000 m (13,125 ft) in 12 minutes; service ceiling 9900 m (32,480 ft); range 1700 km (1,056 miles)
Weights: empty 6400 kg (14,109 lb); maximum take-off 10200 kg (22,487 lb)
Dimensions: wingspan 22.80 m (74 ft 9½ in); length 18.90 m (62 ft 0 in); height 6.69 m (21 ft 11¾ in); wing area 62.50 m² (672.76 sq ft)
Armament: (defensive) one 7.5-mm (0.295-in) MAC 1934 trainable machine-gun in each of the nose position and the retractable dorsal and ventral turrets; (offensive) up to 1600 kg (3,527 lb) of bombs carried internally

German markings cannot conceal the fact that the Bloch MB.200 belonged to the era of the late 1920s and early 1930s, when French aircraft were notable for their almost complete lack of grace.

Blohm und Voss Schiffswerft, Abteilung Flugzeugbau

Established as Hamburger Flugzeugbau in 1933, only one Blohm und Voss aircraft design, the BV 138, was destined to be built in significant numbers, but the company was to produce some of the most ambitious and far-sighted aircraft to emerge from the Third Reich, culminating in the remarkable BV 238 flying boat.

The accession of Adolf Hitler marked the beginning of a period of great expansion for the German aircraft industry; expansion achieved both by the granting of liberal government-guaranteed bank credits to existing concerns and by encouraging other industries to participate in the production of aircraft. The keynote of the programme was rationalisation. Free-for-all competition was discarded as a matter of policy, patents and designs were to be pooled, and it was intended that only experienced companies with development teams of proven capability would be encouraged to undertake design work, the aircraft-manufacturing subsidiaries established by companies in heavy industry being regarded as potential shadow factories for the products of those concerns with strong design organisations.

It was soon to be discovered that this concept, despite its undeniable logic, was not acceptable to some of the newcomers to the aircraft industry, particularly those subsidiaries representing substantial financial investment on the part of their parent concerns. Some persisted in establishing their own design bureaux, and one such was the Hamburger Flugzeugbau GmbH created on 4 July 1933 as a subsidiary of Germany's largest shipbuilder, the Blohm und Voss Schiffswerft of Hamburg, originally established in 1877. The contribution of this company to the Luftwaffe solely in terms of numbers of aircraft produced was to be insignificant; its contribution to German aviation technology, however, was to be considerable.

Limited experience

In 1932 Blohm und Voss had had some slight contact with aircraft manufacture as a sub-contractor to Junkers in producing sub-assemblies for the Ju 52/3m. This contact had aroused the interest of Walther Blohm in commercial air transportation, and as a result of his influence the Blohm und Voss management responded with alacrity to the proposal that the shipbuilding industry should be among those establishing subsidiaries for the manufacture of aircraft. Blohm's motivation was

Nineteen prototypes and 200 production examples of the BV 40 glider interceptor were ordered, the BV 40 V1 first prototype making its initial flight in May 1944. The first two test flights of the BV 40 V2 second prototype, seen here as it was being completed, were carried out on 5 June. Altogether, some seven or, according to some sources six, prototypes had been completed before the BV 40 programme was finally abandoned in the autumn of 1944.

rather different to that of Göring's Luftfahrtkommissariat in encouraging this development, being provided by a conviction that commercial aviation must eventually make inroads into the domain of shipping in the long-distance transportation of passengers.

The design bureau of the Hamburger Flugzeugbau was formed under the leadership of Reinhold Mewes, and before the concern celebrated its first anniversary, its initial product, the Ha 135 primary training biplane, had been rolled out. Mewes' tenure of office at Hamburg had been short-lived, however, as he had left to join the Fieseler Flugzeugbau before completion of the Ha 135, his place being taken by Dr.-Ing. Richard Vogt, who, having worked in Japan with Kawasaki since the early 1920s, was rich in experience and, as events were to prove, even richer in ideas.

The first of several projects initiated by Vogt to be built was the Ha 136 single-seat all-metal advanced training monoplane that, flown in 1934, was confined to two prototypes. The more ambitious Ha 137 dive-bomber embodying the novel form of wing construction evolved by Vogt while working in Japan was to fare little better, but before this flew the Hamburger Flugzeugbau had received a development contract for an ocean-going reconnaissance flying-boat. This, the Ha 138 (later BV 138), was destined to be the only aircraft conceived on the Hamburg drawing boards to be built in fairly substantial numbers.

Flight trials of the Ha 138 were not to commence until three years later, by which time Vogt had been joined by Dipl.-Ing. Hermann Pohlmann, the designer of the Ju 87, and although the Hamburger Flugzeugbau was heavily committed to military projects, Vogt had decided that his team, which included Hans Amtmann in charge of prelimi-

BLOHM & VOSS

Blohm und Voss Schiffswerft, Abteilung Flugzeugbau

Left: The BV 246 Hagelkorn was a long-range glide bomb with with a passive guidance system designed to home on the emissions of British long-range radio navigation transmitters. Seen here are BV 246 weapons in storage at Karlshagen in the early months of 1944. Note the unusual nose of the missile in the foreground, which probably houses the Radieschen passive homing equipment. When the German missile programme was cut back at the beginning of 1944, the BV 246 glide bombs that had entered production over the previous eight or so weeks were cancelled, although the time was sufficiently long for 1,100 to have been produced. Some of the weapons were then expended in an experimental programme.

Below left: As suggested by this publicity material, Blohm und Voss was primarily a ship builder.

nary design and Richard Schubert as Chief of Aerodynamics, was now strong enough to launch the development of the long-range commercial aircraft that had been the primary objective of the Blohm und Voss management in the first place. The Ha 139 float seaplane, designed to meet a DLH requirement, was the first commercial project to see fruition, using, like its land-based derivative, the Ha 142, Vogt's fuel-carrying tubular wing spar arrangement. More unusual in design concept than the company's commercial progeny, however, was the assymetrical Ha 141 short-range reconnaissance aircraft on which work began in 1937. Simultaneously, the Hamburger Flugzeugbau design team was working on its most ambitious project to that time, the Ha 222 flying boat intended for use on regular passenger services across the North and South Atlantic.

By mid-September 1937, when DLH placed a contract for the Ha 222, the Hamburger Flugzeugbau had assumed the title of Abteilung Flugzeugbau der Schiffswerft Blohm und Voss. The future of the company now seemed assured, and during the course of 1937 assembly shops and an airfield were completed at Wenzendorf, near Hamburg. It was here that final assembly of the Ha 138 prototypes was performed, the flying boats being flown from the nearby River Elbe. It was soon obvious that

more spacious facilities would be demanded by the construction of the BV 222 (as the Ha 222 had by now been redesignated), and work commenced on a large, modern factory at Hamburg-Finkenwerder, which, with accompanying airfield and seaplane facilities, was completed in 1940. Today Finkenwerder is a key assembly site for Airbus Industrie.

Licence production

It was anticipated that the newly established Finkenwerder factory would be fully occupied by series production of the BV 138 and construction of the BV 222 prototypes, but events were to restrict the proportion of the new plant available for production of Blohm und Voss aircraft. Delays in deliveries of powerplants, instrumentation, etc., for the BV 138 resulted in the Finkenwerder factory temporarily finding itself with excess capacity. In January 1941, dispersal of the Focke-Wulf factory housing the principal Fw 200 assembly line resulted in the available capacity at Finkenwerder being assigned to this aircraft, the Fw 200 assembly line soon occupying some 80 per cent of the factory, and necessitating the Weser Flugzeugbau becoming a BV 138 licensee.

Apart from the BV 222, barely more than a dozen of which were built, no further aircraft of Blohm und Voss design was to attain production status. Nevertheless, Vogt's design bureau remained extremely active, producing numerous projects, many of which embodied considerable ingenuity, but only three of them were to reach the prototype stage, the BV 238 that was the world's heaviest aircraft at the time of its debut, the unique BV 40 interceptor glider, and the BV 144 transport with variable-incidence wing, two examples of this aircraft being completed in France shortly after the German withdrawal but neither being tested in flight.

In addition to the design of aircraft, the wartime activities of the Abteilung Flugzeugbau der Schiffswerft Blohm und Voss included the development of a variety of air-launched weapons, the principal example of which being the BV 246 Hagelkorn (Hailstone) gliding bomb, some 1,100 examples of which were manufactured, and the L 10 Friedensengel (Angel of Peace) torpedo-carrying glider, about 450 of which were produced. More advanced weapons, such as the L 11 Schneewittchen (Snow White), were under test when hostilities in Europe came to an end and Dr.-Ing. Vogt's design bureau disbanded.

Blohm und Voss BV 40

An interesting example of the strange lengths to which the Germans were compelled to go in their search for an effective counter to the USAAF's bomber fleets, the Blohm und Voss BV 40 glider fighter offered low frontal area and good pilot protection coupled with heavy gun armament.

From the earliest days of Blohm und Voss's aircraft division, its chief designer and technical director, Dr.-Ing. Richard Vogt, had displayed a marked penchant for the unorthodox in aircraft design; a radical approach to design problems that resulted in many of his less conservative projects being regarded as degenerate expressions of the designer's art by the more conservative elements within the RLM. In view of this hard core of traditionalists in the RLM and its Technisches Amt, it is perhaps surprising, therefore, that Vogt's most original proposal – a small and heavily armoured glider for attacking enemy bomber formations – should have received official support.

In January 1943, USAAF day bomber formations of B-17 Flying Fortresses began to penetrate Germany for the first time, flying in tight formations known as combat boxes to afford maximum defensive power. Early battle experience indicated that the frontal area of an Fw 190's radial engine – some 1.60 m² (17 sq ft) – afforded a target capable of being hit by an average B-17 gunner at a range of more than 914 m (3,000 ft), and it was axiomatic that the only means by which the frontal area of a fighter could be substantially reduced was by eliminating the engine altogether. After pondering this problem, Dr.-Ing. Vogt proposed to the Technisches Amt the idea of an unpowered interceptor; a 'glide-fighter' manufactured largely from non-strategic materials and towed to attack altitude by an orthodox fighter. It was suggested that in a head-on attack such an aircraft would be virtually invisible to the bomber's gunners before it had actually opened fire with its own 30-mm cannon armament.

Official approval

It was obvious that all possible means, both conventional and unconventional, of stemming the USAAF day bomber tide were worth exploring, and Dr.-Ing. Vogt was invited to submit firm proposals for an interceptor such as he envisaged,

The BV 40 glider, represented here by the first prototype, was a novel attempt to stem the daylight USAAF bomber attacks. The pilot lay in a prone position, allowing the aircraft to be made very small in terms of frontal cross-section, and thus making it difficult to see and aim at for the gunners protecting the bombers.

the project being allocated for some inexplicable reason the designation **BV 40**.

The keynote of the BV 40 was simplicity, and it was designed for construction primarily from non-strategic materials by carpenters, joiners, locksmiths and welders having no previous experience of aircraft construction. The cockpit, in which the pilot reclined on a padded couch, was constructed of welded sheet metal, the front panels being

Above: The cockpit of the BV 40 had 120-mm (4.72-in) armour glass windscreen and very simple instrumentation.

Left: The very compact BV 40 V1 prototype is seen before flight testing. The twin-wheel take-off dolly was jettisoned after lift-off, a semi-retractable skid being provided for landing. The structure was comparatively simple, facilitating manufacture by craftsmen inexperienced in aircraft construction. A further advantage was an apparent requirement for little more than glider training for the single pilot, who lay in a prone position in the diminutive cockpit.

113

Blohm und Voss BV 40

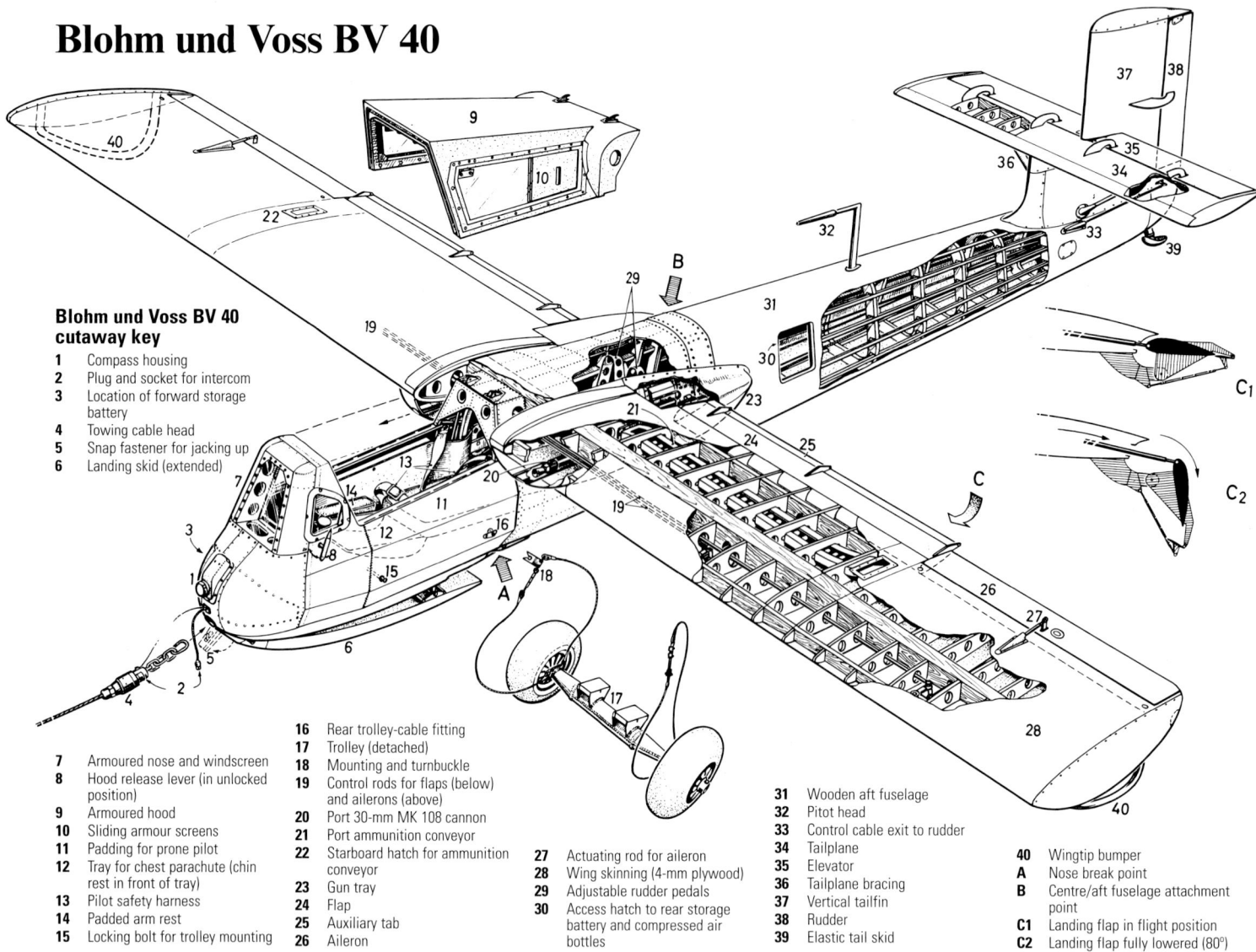

Blohm und Voss BV 40 cutaway key

1. Compass housing
2. Plug and socket for intercom
3. Location of forward storage battery
4. Towing cable head
5. Snap fastener for jacking up
6. Landing skid (extended)
7. Armoured nose and windscreen
8. Hood release lever (in unlocked position)
9. Armoured hood
10. Sliding armour screens
11. Padding for prone pilot
12. Tray for chest parachute (chin rest in front of tray)
13. Pilot safety harness
14. Padded arm rest
15. Locking bolt for trolley mounting
16. Rear trolley-cable fitting
17. Trolley (detached)
18. Mounting and turnbuckle
19. Control rods for flaps (below) and ailerons (above)
20. Port 30-mm MK 108 cannon
21. Port ammunition conveyor
22. Starboard hatch for ammunition conveyor
23. Gun tray
24. Flap
25. Auxiliary tab
26. Aileron
27. Actuating rod for aileron
28. Wing skinning (4-mm plywood)
29. Adjustable rudder pedals
30. Access hatch to rear storage battery and compressed air bottles
31. Wooden aft fuselage
32. Pitot head
33. Control cable exit to rudder
34. Tailplane
35. Elevator
36. Tailplane bracing
37. Vertical tailfin
38. Rudder
39. Elastic tail skid
40. Wingtip bumper
A. Nose break point
B. Centre/aft fuselage attachment point
C1. Landing flap in flight position
C2. Landing flap fully lowered (80°)

of 20-mm thickness, the side panels and jettisonable roof hatch being of 8-mm thickness, and the floor being of 5-mm thickness. The windshield was of 120-mm armour glass, and two sliding armour panels could seal off the side windows to provide additional protection for the pilot's head, his legs being protected by 8-mm armour plate. The centre fuselage was constructed of riveted sheet metal and was bolted to the wooden aft fuselage. The wings and tailplane were also of wooden construction, the former having a single plywood box mainspar with fore and aft auxiliary spars. The wings were covered by 4-mm plywood and attached to the centre fuselage by four bolts.

A two-wheel jettisonable trolley was adopted for take-off, and a semi-retractable skid served for landing. Flaps capable of being lowered 80 degrees enabled pinpoint landings to be effected. Originally, Dr.-Ing. Vogt had planned to restrict the gun armament to one 30-mm MK 108 cannon with

Designed by Dr.Ing. Richard Vogt, the BV 40 was of mixed metal and wood construction. The entire cockpit section was fabricated of welded sheet steel and armour, and in this the pilot lay in a prone position on a padded bench.

The port landing flap of the BV 40 V1 is seen is its fully lowered position. For normal landing a 50-degree flap deflection was standard, but for pin-point landings the full 80-degree setting was employed.

70 rounds, and he proposed that, if the BV 40 still possessed sufficient altitude after its initial firing pass against the bomber formation, a second attack should be made with a device known as the Gerät Schlinge (sling equipment) – a wire cable suspended from the glider and carrying a small explosive charge. However, the general consensus of opinion was that the BV 40, making a head-on attack at some 400 km/h (250 mph), would close with its target at some 800 km/h (500 mph), and its pilot would therefore have time for only one burst of cannonfire that should represent the maximum possible weight of fire. Thus it was desirable to divide the total available ammunition capacity between two cannon, and as no satisfactory means of accommodating the Gerät Schlinge could be found once two MK 108 cannon had been installed, this device was abandoned.

For take-off, the BV 40, mounted on its two-wheel trolley, was attached to a Bf 109G or Fw 190 fighter by means of a 30-m (98-ft) cable, the pilot of the glider jettisoning the trolley immediately upon leaving the ground. For a normal landing the skid was extended and the flaps lowered 50 degrees, the maximum deflection of 80 degrees being adopted only in an emergency.

During the last days of May 1944, the first prototype glider, the **BV 40 V1**, was towed off the ground behind a Bf 110 for its first flight test. Its pilot reported that, in general, the characteristics of the glider were good, and it handled well in the turbulent slipstream from its tug. A second flight test was conducted on 2 June 1944 at Wenzendorf, the track of the take-off trolley having by now been increased marginally to improve stability during the take-off run, and the tyre pressures lowered. The pilot cast-off from the towplane at an altitude of 790 m (2,600 ft) and a speed of 240 km/h (150 mph). He then reduced speed to 150 km/h (93 mph) and found that he still possessed good rudder control but, to his surprise, at 140 km/h (87 mph) the glider virtually fell out of the sky, crashed through the airfield boundary fence, and came to rest within 25 m (75 ft). The prototype was left badly damaged.

Additional prototypes

The second prototype, the **BV 40 V2**, had already been completed, and the first two test flights with this machine were carried out on 5 June, two further test flights following three days later, releases being performed at 2195 m (7,200 ft) and a maximum speed of 330 km/h (205 mph) being attained. The **BV 40 V3** was tested to destruction, the **BV 40 V4** was severely damaged after a test flight late in June, being replaced in the test programme at Wenzendorf by the **BV 40 V5**. On 27 July 1944, the **BV 40 V6** was towed from Stade to Wenzendorf behind a Bf 110, this being the first 'long-distance' flight, and its test pilot reported that the journey imposed a considerable strain, the prone position with chin resting on a padded stick proving tiring. By this time, the handling characteristics of the glider had proven acceptable, and a total of 19 prototypes had been ordered for completion by March 1945, together with an initial production batch of 200 BV 40A 'glide-fighters', but the Technisches Amt had now begun to propose changes in armament and equipment, the application of small pulse jets and rockets, and even alternative roles. It was suggested by Flieger-Stabsingenieur Tilenius that the BV 40 should carry a variety of small bombs

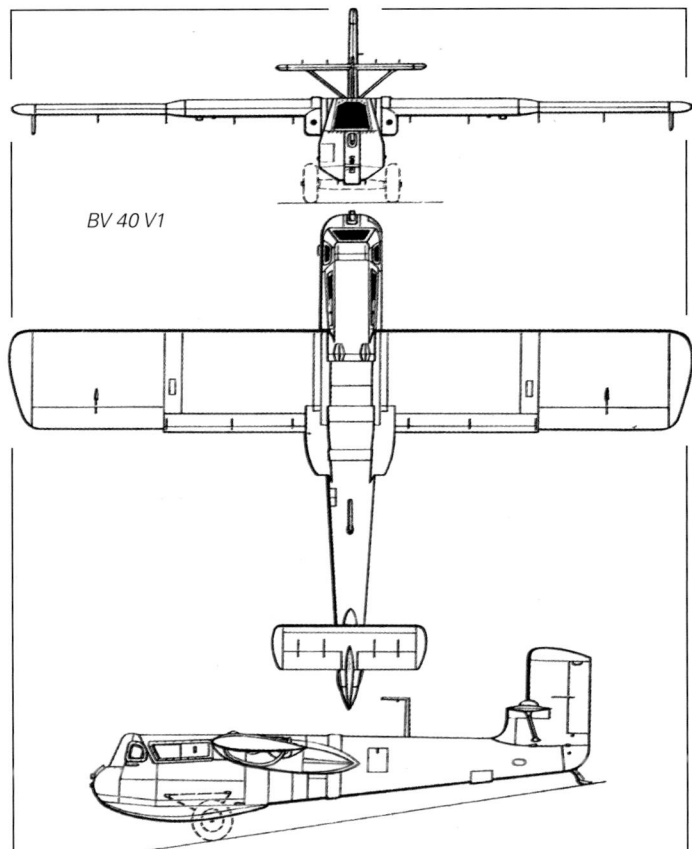

BV 40 V1

Blohm und Voss BV 40

The BV 40 glider fighter was armed with two 30-mm cannon, one in each wing root with 35 rounds of ammunition. The aircraft incorporated a heavily armoured cockpit section and centre fuselage of metal construction and a rear fuselage, wing and tail surfaces of wooden construction.

that, fitted with proximity fuses, could be dropped on enemy bomber formations. The heaviest load suggested comprised four 700-kg (1,543-lb) BT 700 bombs that were to be carried beneath the wings. It was also suggested that two BV 40s should be carried beneath He 177A-5 or B-5 bombers, that automatic control devices, rockets and pulse-jets should be fitted, and that the glider should be adapted for use as a towed fuel tank. In mid-July 1944, the basic flight test programme had been completed. A speed of 470 km/h (292 mph) had been attained at 2000 m (6,560 ft), and it was believed that 900 km/h (560 mph) could be attained by the BV 40 in a dive, although it would have been impossible to use the ailerons at such speeds owing to flutter. It was suggested that a 40 per cent reduction in aileron area would permit their use at such speeds, and investigation of this possibility was being undertaken in the autumn of 1944, but the entire programme

was halted by the bombing of Wenzendorf in October.

The **BV 40 V7** had been completed in August 1944, and it had been planned to have the **V8** and **V9** ready in September and October respectively, the remaining 10 prototypes being completed at a rate of two per month.

Blohm und Voss BV 40A specification
Type: single-seat glider interceptor-fighter
Powerplant: none
Performance: maximum speed estimated to be attainable in a dive 900 km/h (560 mph); maximum speed of Bf 109G towing one BV 40 554 km/h (344 mph) at 5790 m (19,000 ft), towing two BV 40s 507 km/h (315 mph); time to climb to 7010 m (23,000 ft) with one BV 40 12 minutes, with two BV 40s 16.8 minutes
Weights: empty 836 kg (1,844 lb); loaded 950 kg (2,094 lb)
Dimensions: wingspan 7.90 m (25 ft 11 in); length 5.70 m (18 ft 8½ in); height 1.63 m (5 ft 4⅛ in); wing area 8.70 m² (93.65 sq ft)
Armament: two 30-mm MK 108 cannon with 35 r.p.g.

Blohm und Voss Ha 135

Designed by Reinhold Mewes and Viktor Maugsch, the Ha 135 was the first aircraft to emerge from the design offices of the Hamburger Flugzeugbau after its creation in July 1933. An unexceptional biplane, the Bramo-powered Ha 135 was intended for use as a primary trainer, but only a handful of examples were completed.

The first aircraft designed by the Hamburger Flugzeugbau was the Ha 135, created under the initial supervision of Reinhold Mewes before his departure to Fieseler. The unremarkable **Ha 135** was a primary flying trainer of equal-span biplane layout, offering tandem accommodation for the pupil and instructor in open cockpits. First flown in the late spring of 1934, the prototype was the only example to be completed and was of mixed metal and wood structure, covered largely with fabric.

A total of six Ha 135s was completed during 1934-35, five of them serving with the Fliegerübungsstelle Hamburg-Fuhlsbüttel, part of the Deutsche Luftsportverband (DLV). The sixth was operated by the Flugabteilung der Deutsche Versuchsanstalt für Luftfahrt (DVL) at Berlin-Adlershof.

Blohm und Voss Ha 135 specification
Type: two-seat primary flying trainer
Powerplant: one BMW-Bramo Sh 14A radial engine rated at 119 kW (160 hp)
Performance: maximum speed 205 km/h (127 mph) at sea level; service ceiling 5750 m (18,865 ft); range 795 km (494 miles)
Weights: empty 520 kg (1,146 lb); maximum take-off 860 kg (1,896 lb)
Dimensions: wingspan 9.00 m (29 ft 3½ in); length 9.60 m (31 ft 6 in)

Key features of the Ha 135 were its staggered single-bay wing cellule, sturdy main undercarriage arrangement, and air-cooled radial engine with its cylinders heading exposed for improved cooling.

Blohm und Voss Ha 137

With the establishment of the Hamburger Flugzeugbau on 4 July 1933, the fledgling company initiated design work on two training aircraft, subsequently designated Ha 135 and Ha 136, as a means of cutting its teeth, following them with an ultimately abortive dive-bomber, the Ha 137 with its characteristic inverted gull wing.

Dr.-Ing. Richard Vogt, who had been appointed chief designer at Blohm und Voss upon his return to Germany from Japan where he had been working with Kawasaki, was anxious to inaugurate a more ambitious project than the Ha 135 and Ha 136 trainers, embodying an entirely new form of wing construction that he had evolved while working at Kobe. This wing, which had been incorporated in the last aircraft that Vogt had designed for Kawasaki, the Ki-5 fighter, prior to his return to Germany, was of inverted-gull form and featured one main load-carrying tubular spar located at the thickest point of the wing section and sealed to form a fuel tank.

Almost simultaneously with the creation of the Hamburger Flugzeugbau, the Sturzbomber-Programm had been initiated by the C-Amt, this being a two-phase programme intended to provide the still-clandestine Luftwaffe with interim and, subsequently, definitive dive-bombing equipment. The immediate, or Sofort, phase called for a conventional state-of-the-art biplane, the second phase being intended to provide an appreciably more sophisticated warplane, and in view of its total lack of combat aircraft design experience, the new company was excluded from those invited to participate in the later phase. Nevertheless, Dr.-Ing. Vogt was confident that his new ideas on wing construction offered an extremely rugged structure ideally suited to withstand the stresses of dive-bombing, and that the Sturzbomber-Programm offered the opportunity to demonstrate to the full the advantages of his tubular-spar wing. He therefore initiated a design study for a dive-bomber designated **Projekt 6**, and submitted this as a private venture to the C-Amt.

The Projekt 6 was essentially an aerodynamically improved and slightly scaled-up development of the Kawasaki Ki-5, and was intended to employ the BMW XV engine then being developed by the Bayerische Motoren Werke. As the future

Above and below: Preceding the Ha 137 dive-bomber was the Ha 136, a design for an all-metal, single-seat monoplane advanced trainer. Two prototypes were constructed, this being the first. It took to the air in 1934.

A crowd surrounds the Ha 137 V6 prototype, one of three to be completed with Junkers Jumo 210Aa engines. They were also known as Ha 137B-0s. The design was too small to accommodate a second seat, as demanded by the official specification, but showed sufficient promise to be continued as a fallback should the Junkers Ju 87 have failed to meet expectations.

of the BMW XV was in doubt, the C-Amt requested modification of the project to take the Pratt & Whitney Hornet nine-cylinder radial air-cooled engine that was being manufactured under licence by the Bayerische Motoren Werke. Accordingly, Dr.-Ing. Vogt's proposal was re-submitted as the **Projekt 6a**, together with a study for an alternative version with a Rolls-Royce Kestrel engine as the **Projekt 6b**. The C-Amt was sufficiently impressed to award the Hamburger Flugzeugbau a contract for three prototypes under the designation **Ha 137**. It is of interest to note that Dr.-Ing. Vogt's team had prepared an alternative design study for a Wright Cyclone-powered biplane dive-bomber, the **Projekt 7**, for submission to the C-Amt in the event that the tubular-spar wing of the Projekt 6 was considered too radical for official acceptance.

Blohm und Voss Ha 137

This is the first Ha 137 prototype, D-IXAX, which was completed with a BMW 132A-3 radial engine, a licence-built version of the Pratt & Whitney Hornet. The second machine also had this powerplant, and any production aircraft would have been designated Ha 137A. The apertures in the top of the undercarriage fairings showed where machine-gun or cannon armament could have been fitted.

Design details

A low-wing cantilever monoplane of all-metal construction, the Ha 137 featured Vogt's tubular main load-carrying spar, the centre portion of which was of welded chrome-molybdenum steel sheet and sealed to accommodate 270 litres (59.4 Imp gal) of fuel, the outer portions being of riveted duralumin. Hydraulically-operated trailing-edge flaps were carried by the centre section and the inboard portions of the outer panels. The fixed main undercarriage members were attached to the extremities of the wing centre section which was set at a course anhedral angle, a sharp dihedral angle being adopted for the outboard panels to result in an inverted-gull configuration. Each wheel was mounted between two vertical pneumatic shock-absorbers and enclosed by detachable streamlined fairings. The rectangular-section fuselage was a semi-monocoque structure, and the pilot was seated in an open cockpit over the wing trailing edge. Provision was made for a built-in armament of two 7.9-mm (0.31-in) MG 17 machine-guns in the upper decking of the forward fuselage and a similar weapon in each undercarriage fairing, space being available to permit the replacement of the latter by a 20-mm MG FF cannon. The BMW 132A-3 (licence-built Hornet) engine had a normal rating of 485 kW (650 hp), and offered 537 kW (720 hp) for take-off.

The final mock-up inspection was performed on 9 October 1934, and the first prototype, the **Ha 137 V1** (D-IXAX), was completed and flown at Hamburg in April 1935, this being closely followed by the second proto-type, the **Ha 137 V2** (D-IBGI). In the meantime, however, the definitive second-phase Sturzbomber specification had been

issued by the RLM, this stipulating a two-seater. Dr.-Ing. Vogt had been aware from the outset that a two-seater dive-bomber was preferred in order that rear defence could be provided, but the provision of a second seat would have necessitated a somewhat larger aircraft than he considered desirable if the outline performance requirement was to be fulfilled. The specification had, in fact, been drawn up around one of the Ha 137's competitors, the Junkers Ju 87, which, favoured by the RLM from the outset, thus possessed a considerable advantage over the other contending designs. Apart from being a single-seater, the Ha 137 was remarkably similar in overall concept to the Ju 87, but this similarity was purely coincidental, although some years later, in 1940, the designer of the Junkers dive-bomber, Dipl.-Ing. Hermann Pohlmann, was to join Blohm und Voss.

Despite the fact that, as a single-seater, the Ha 137 no longer met the Sturzbomber specification, the RLM elected to continue development of the aircraft as a back-up programme and as a possible close-support aircraft, or Schlachtflugzeug, and three further prototypes were ordered with the new Junkers Jumo 210 liquid-cooled engine. Whereas the radial-engined first and second aircraft were considered as proto-

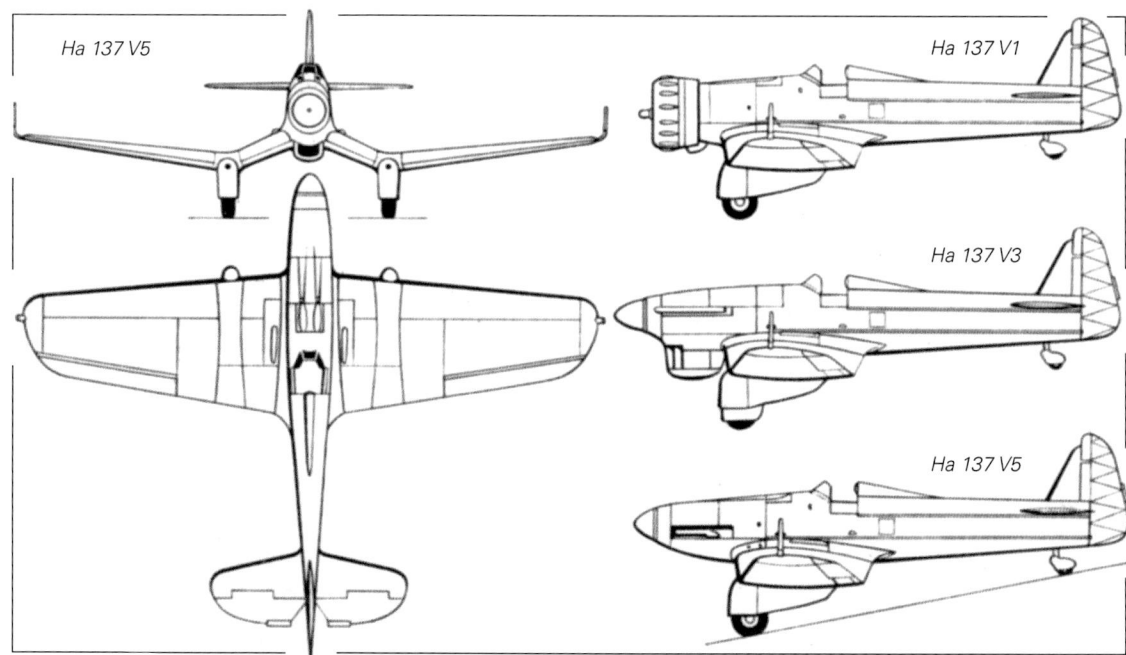

118

The Ha 137's main spar was installed in the thickest part of the wing and naturally conformed to the wing's front elevation. The latter was of inverted gull shape to reduce the length of the main units of the fixed tailwheel landing gear.

The Ha 137 was an outsider in the definitive phase of the contest to provide the Luftwaffe with a new dive-bomber, and the fourth prototype, the Ha 137 V4 (D-IFOE), was employed as a testbed in several experimental programmes.

Above left and right: The last Ha 137 to fly was the V5 (D-IUXU), which was delivered in October 1937. With the dive-bomber project moribund, the V4 and V5 were used for various armament trials, including the firing of unguided rockets.

types for the **Ha 137A**, the third prototype, the **Ha 137 V3** (D-IZIQ), was now completed with a Rolls-Royce Kestrel V 12-cylinder liquid-cooled engine as the first **Ha 137B**. This fully-supercharged powerplant was rated at 391 kW (525 hp) for take-off, offered 477 kW (640 hp) at 4267 m (14,000 ft), and drove a two-bladed fixed-pitch wooden airscrew, this replacing the three-bladed adjustable-pitch metal airscrew of the V1 and V2. Testing of the first two prototypes had begun at Travemünde during the summer of 1935, the Ha 137 V1 being damaged during October of that year when, in the course of armament trials, ammunition exploded in the starboard side of the wing centre section. The Ha 137 proved to be an exceptionally sturdy aircraft with a good performance and pleasant handling characteristics, although view for take-off and landing came in for some criticism.

Dive-bomber trials

The Ha 137 V3 participated in the dive-bomber trials held at the Rechlin Erprobungsstelle in June 1936, but the replacement of Oberst Wolfram von Richthofen, who favoured the continued development of the Ha 137 for the Schlachtflieger, by Ernst Udet as chief of the Development Section of the RLM's Technisches Amt during the same month did not augur well for Dr.-Ing. Vogt's design. While an ardent supporter of the dive-bomber, Udet attached little importance to close-support aircraft, and promptly informed Dr.-Ing. Vogt that no production contract would be awarded to the Ha 137.

Meanwhile, Hamburger Flugzeugbau had evolved a navalised version of the BMW 132-powered Ha 137A that was offered for operation from the aircraft-carrier for which

funds had been included in the 1936 budget. In navalised form the aircraft was known as the **Projekt 11** with wheel undercarriage and **Projekt 11a** with floats, but the limited tactical radius and single-seat configuration prevented any serious interest being shown in these proposals.

Work continued on the batch of three additional prototypes powered by the Jumo 210Aa rated at 440 kW (590 hp) for take-off and 455 kW (610 hp) at 2600 m (8,550 ft), these being the **Ha 137 V4** (D-IFOE), the **V5** (D-IUXU), and the **V6** (D-IJJE). The Ha 137 V6 actually preceded the V5, and was completely destroyed in a crash early in July 1937, the Ha 137 V5 not being delivered until 26 October 1937. The two surviving Jumo-engined prototypes subsequently served in various experimental trials, one of them performing some of the first firing tests with the Rheinmetall-Borsig 65-mm (2.56-in) Rauchzylinder 65 (RZ 65) unguided rocket.

Blohm und Voss Ha 137 V4 specification
Type: single-seat dive-bomber and close-support aircraft
Powerplant: one Junkers Jumo 210Aa 12-cylinder liquid-cooled engine rated at 440 kW (590 hp) for take-off and 455 kW (610 hp) at 2600 m (8,550 ft)
Performance: maximum speed 330 km/h (205 mph) at 2000 m (6,560 ft), 300 km/h (186 mph) at sea level; maximum cruising speed 290 km/h (180 mph) at 2000 m (6,560 ft); climb (without external load) to 2000 m in 4 minutes, to 4000 m (13,120 ft) in 9 minutes; service ceiling 7000 m (22,965 ft); range 580 km (360 miles)
Weights: empty 1814 kg (4,000 lb); loaded 2415 kg (5,324 lb)
Dimensions: wingspan 11.15 m (36 ft 7 in); length 9.45 m (31 ft 0¾ in); height 2.80 m (9 ft 2¼ in); wing area 23.50 m² (252.95 sq ft)
Armament: two 7.9-mm (0.31-in) MG 17 machine-guns in fuselage and one 7.9-mm MG 17 (or 20-mm MG FF cannon) in each main undercarriage fairing, plus four 50-kg (110-lb) SC 50 bombs on underwing racks

In July 1937 the Ha 137 V6 was written off in a crash. Here a technician sifts through the wreckage after several components such as tail surfaces and ailerons have already been removed. With the Ju 87 proving itself in the dive-bomber role, the Ha 137 stood little chance of a production order, despite proposals for it to be tailored to close support and carrierborne roles.

Blohm und Voss BV 138

The first flying-boat design to be built by Hamburger Flugzeugbau under the direction of chief engineer Dr.-Ing. Richard Vogt, the Blohm und Voss BV 138 was a stalwart of the Luftwaffe's coastal patrol and anti-convoy efforts in the hostile waters of the Arctic Ocean and North Atlantic, remaining in use until the end of the war in Europe.

Officially called **Seedrache** (Sea Dragon), the **BV 138** was promptly nicknamed 'Der Fliegende Holzschuh' ('The Flying Clog') when it made its debut in prototype form in the summer of 1937. Dr.-Ing. Richard Vogt's first flying-boat was unique in configuration among the large waterborne maritime patrol and reconnaissance aircraft of its era. The inter-

As first schemed, the Ha 138 V1 was to have been powered by two Jumo 206 diesel engines, but was in fact completed with the revised powerplant of three lower-rated Jumo 205C engines.

est of the Hamburger Flugzeugbau in waterborne aircraft was to be expected in view of the company's Blohm und Voss shipbuilding parentage, and when, in the winter of 1933-34, the C-Amt prepared a rather vague specification for a Hochseefähiger Fernaufklärungsflugboot, an ocean-going reconnaissance flying-boat, Dr.-Ing. Vogt's fledgeling design team was anxious to fulfil the requirement.

After a careful study of flying-boat development abroad, Vogt submitted three proposals to the C-Amt, all featuring the single load-carrying tubular wing spar. The **Projekt 8** envisaged an abbreviated central hull, tail surfaces carried by twin tubular booms, a gull wing spanning 25.00 m (82 ft 0 in) and possessing a gross area of 100.00 m² (1,076.39 sq ft), and a pair of BMW XV engines. The **Projekt 12** proposed a conventional central hull, a wing spanning 27.00 m (88 ft 8 in) and having a gross area of 120.00 m² (1,291.67 sq ft), and a trio of Junkers Jumo 205 diesel engines, and the **Projekt 13** utilised a similar wing but was of twin-hull configuration and was intended to have four Jumo 205 engines.

None of the three project studies proved acceptable in the form presented, but the C-Amt favoured the novel Projekt 8 configuration, and a fresh presentation was made after this had been scaled up to approximately the dimensions of the Projekt 12, a development contract calling for three proto-types being awarded to the Hamburger Flugzeugbau in the late spring of 1934, the flying-boat receiving the official designation **Ha 138**. By the time detailed design began it had become obvious that development of the BMW XV engine was to be abandoned, and therefore Dr.-Ing. Vogt proposed that the first prototype should be powered by a pair of Jumo 206 diesel engines, that the second prototype should have three Jumo 205s, and that the third prototype should receive two Daimler-Benz DB 600 engines.

Low priority

The definitive mock-up of the first prototype was completed in March 1935 and, after several official inspections that resulted in minor modifications, the first metal was cut. Work on the prototypes proceeded relatively slowly as little urgency

The BV 138A-01 demonstrates its sprightly take-off performance. In reality, though, the type was not strong enough to withstand the rigours of prolonged open-sea operations. The BV 138A had a hydraulically-powered LB 204 bow turret fitted with a 20-mm MG 204 cannon. Both the turret and its cannon proved extremely troublesome, and the turret was replaced by a simpler type carrying the well-proved and reliable 20-mm MG 151/20 cannon.

was attached to the Hochseefähigen Fernaufklärer, and in the autumn of 1936, by which time assembly of the first airframe had reached an advanced stage, Dr.-Ing. Vogt was informed by the Junkers Flugzeug-und-Motorenwerke that further development of the Jumo 206 engine was being abandoned. As no other engine in the power category anticipated for the Jumo 206 presented itself, the Hamburger Flugzeugbau had no recourse but to rebuild the aircraft to take three Jumo 205s. In consequence, the first prototype was not completed until July 1937, 27 months after the commencement of construction, by which time the second prototype, which had been built from the outset for three Jumo 205s and possessed a suitably redesigned wing centre section from which the sharp dihedral angle had been eliminated, was virtually complete. The first prototype, the **Ha 138 V1** (D-ARAK), was flown for the first time on 15 July 1937, being followed from the Wenzendorf factory within four weeks by the second prototype, the **Ha 138 V2** (D-AMOR). From the outset it was obvious that the hydrodynamic characteristics of the short central hull left much to be desired, and once airborne the flying-boat proved directionally unstable. A partial solution to the stability problem was provided by redesigning and enlarging the vertical tail surfaces of the Ha 138 V2, this prototype being transferred to Travemünde for official evaluation on 6 November 1937.

Sea trials were undertaken in the Baltic under a variety of conditions, and in the spring of 1938, the Hamburger Flugzeugbau was informed by the Technisches Amt that hull drag was excessive and the planing bottom inefficient; that the hull needed extensive reinforcement in order to withstand the stresses imposed by rough water under conditions of maximum load; that the tubular tailbooms were prone to vibration, and that the crew accommodation was inadequate for long-endurance patrols. Furthermore, it was recommended that a complete redesign be undertaken.

Redesign

Further work on the **Ha 138 V3** had been held in abeyance at Wenzendorf pending the results of the Travemünde trials, and this third prototype was now scrapped and work begun on a redesign retaining little but the basic configuration. The wing remained little changed, being of metal construction with a tubular main spar and built in three sections, the leading edges being dural-covered and the remainder fabric-covered. The centre section attached directly to the hull and carried the outboard engines and tailbooms, the tubular spar housing three self-sealing fuel cells. All-metal stabilising floats were strut-braced to the outboard wing panels, and the hull itself was of all-metal construction with a shallow Vee planing bottom and inclined flat sides. Divided into 10 watertight compartments, the hull bore little similarity to that of the first two prototypes, its length being increased from

Above: The Ha 138 V2 (D-AMOR) is seen during initial trials on the Elbe river. It will be noted that the engines' thrust line had been reduced by comparison with that of the first prototype, and the hull deepened to mate with the revised wing's new centre section.

Defensive fire to the rear was provided by two 7.9-mm (0.31-in) MG 15 machine-guns, one on the rear of the centreline engine nacelle on an Arado mounting, and one in the rear of the hull on a D 30 ring mounting. The hulls of the Ha 138 V1 and V2 were shorter than those of later boats.

12.20 m (40 ft 0⅓ in) to 15.10 m (49 ft 8 in), and the step in the planing bottom being moved forward. Rectangular all-metal stressed-skin tailbooms supplanted the earlier tubular booms, these terminating in integral metal fins. All movable control surfaces were fabric-covered, and the controls themselves were hydraulically assisted.

Power was provided by three Jumo 205C-4 diesel engines, one mounted in a nacelle above the fuselage centreline and two in nacelles at the extremities of the centre section as extensions of the tailbooms, all three engines driving three-bladed metal controllable-pitch airscrews. Provision was made for a standard crew complement of five members, and the flight deck

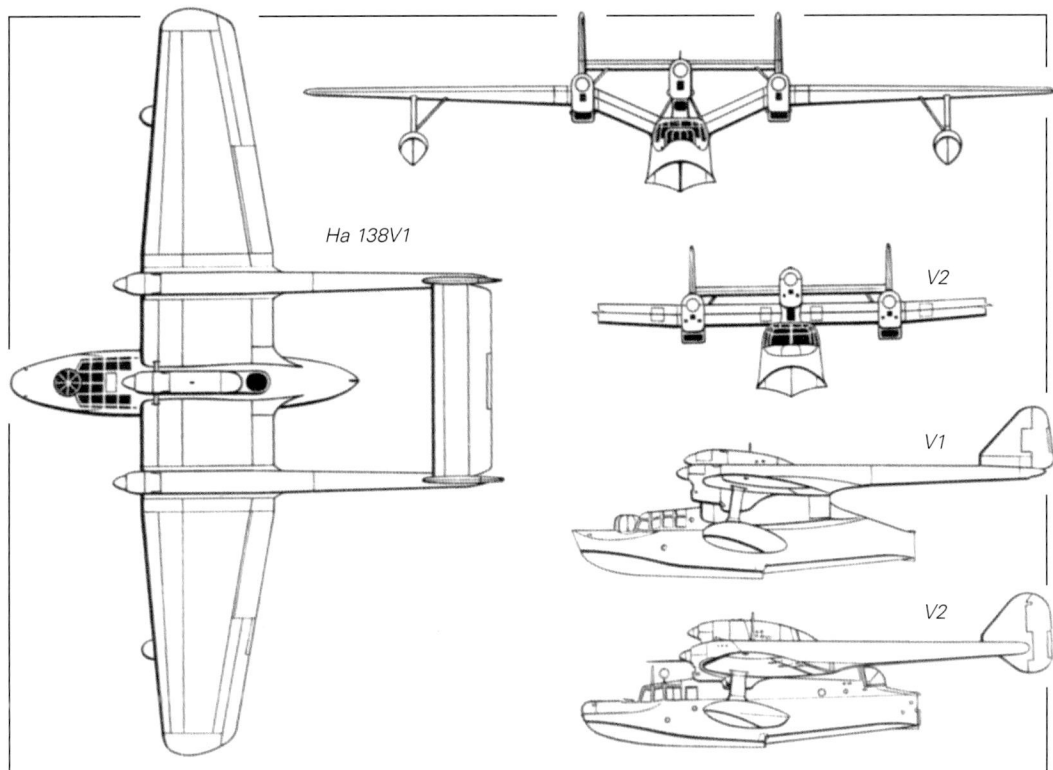

Ha 138V1

V2

V1

V2

Blohm und Voss BV 138

Right: The Ha 138 V2 introduced a modified hull design, but this was insufficient to overcome the many aero- and hydrodynamic problems suffered by the type. A complete hull redesign, with greater length, resulted in the BV 138A production version.

Below: In all but the first boat, the BV 138 had a flat rather than gulled centre section. This located the centreline engine somewhat higher than the two outer units at the front of the booms carrying the tail unit.

was equipped with full dual controls. The central portion of the hull was occupied by the radio compartment, the galley and a rest room containing three bunks. Three defensive gun positions were provided, all possessing an excellent field of fire. The bow gunner was provided with an hydraulically-operated LB 204 turret mounting a 20-mm MG 204 cannon, and the two open gun positions aft of the wing, one in the tail of the central engine nacelle and the other in the tail of the hull to give fields of fire above and below the tailplane, were each provided with a 7.9-mm (0.31-in) MG 15 machine-gun, the upper position having an Arado mounting and the lower position having a D 30-type ring mounting. Offensive armament comprised three 50-kg (110-lb) bombs on ETC 50 racks beneath the starboard side of the wing centre section.

Production development

The first example of the redesigned flying-boat, the **BV 138A-01** (Werk Nr 148, D-ADJE), was flown for the first time in February 1939, the Hamburger Flugzeugbau having meanwhile become the Abteilung Flugzeugbau der Schiftswerft Blohm und Voss, and initial water and flying trials were as encouraging as those with the initial proto-types had been discouraging. Work on five additional **BV 138A-0** pre-production flying-boats had already begun at Wenzendorf, and an initial production order for 25 **BV 138A-1** flying-boats was confirmed by the RLM.

Testing of the six pre-production BV 138A-0 flying-boats by Blohm und Voss and at the Erprobungsstelle at Travemünde proved the efficacy of the redesign, but it was considered that structural strength was still inadequate for safe operation in heavy seas and, accordingly, the **BV 138A-04** (Werk Nr 152, BI+AT) was eventually sent to Blohm und Voss's new factory at Finkenwerder for major strengthening of the structure, the extent of which may be gauged from the fact that, when the aircraft re-emerged as the first **BV 138B-0**, the normal loaded weight of the flying-boat had risen from 13750 kg (30,313 lb) to 14480 kg (31,930 lb) with the equipment unchanged. A pre-production batch of 10 BV 138B-0 flying-boats had been ordered, and the Technisches Amt instructed Blohm und Voss to modify three additional BV 138A-0s to B-0 standard, but the urgency now attached to the delivery of the flying-boat to the coastal units, the Küstenfliegergruppen, led to the decision to complete the 25 BV 138A-1s unmodified in order to avoid the delay that would inevitably result from any attempt to apply the struc-

tural strengthening on the assembly line. Thus construction of the BV 138A-1 ran parallel with that of the BV 138B-0.

Flight testing of the first BV 138A-1 had to await the melting of the ice in the River Elbe and, in consequence, did not commence until April 1940, when Operation Weserübung, the invasion of Denmark and Norway, was about to be launched. The shortage of waterborne aircraft suitable for logistic support tasks resulted in the first and second BV 138A-1s from the Finkenwerder line being impressed by the Luftwaffe after only cursory flight testing, and delivered to KG.z.b.V 108 See (Kampfgeschwader zur besonderen Verwendung 108 See, or Battle Geschwader for special duties 108 Sea), the three Gruppen of which operated a miscellany of float seaplanes and flying-boats from Nordeney under the Lufttransportchef See. The two BV 138A-1s flew supply missions into Stavanger, Åndalsnes, Trondheim and Bodø.

Subsequent BV 138A-1s were flown from Hamburg to Travemünde for acceptance trials as they came off the Finkenwerder line, and in June 1940, 1./Kü.Fl.Gr.506 at Hörnum took delivery of 10 BV 138A-1s and began working up to operational status. Apart from some difficulties with the Jumo 205C-4 diesel engines that demanded exceptionally careful maintenance by specially trained personnel, serious problems arose with the LB 204 bow turret and its MG 204 cannon. Designed by Rheinmetall-Borsig as a potential replacement for the MG FF (Oerlikon), the MG 204 was intended primarily for fixed installation. The weapon's teething troubles, which still had to be overcome, were aggravated by its adaptation for turret mounting, and the turret mechanism itself was so unreliable that a team of Blohm und Voss personnel was sent to Hörnum solely to maintain the bow turret and its cannon. Despite the failure to eradicate the bow armament problems, which led to the decision to abandon further production of both the MG 204 cannon and the LB 204 turret, 1./Kü.Fl.Gr. 506 was deployed operationally in the Biscay area from October 1940, being joined before the end of the year by 2./Kü.Fl.Gr. 906 also equipped with the BV 138A-1.

Poor serviceability

The serviceability of the BV 138A-1 flying-boats operated by the two Küstenfliegerstaffeln was extremely low, primarily owing to recurrent troubles with both engines and airscrews, and as the weather deteriorated towards the end of the year the inadequacy of the hull and float structures when pounded by heavy Biscay seas became increasingly apparent. The centrally-mounted Jumo 205C-4 proved particularly troublesome, frequently suffering a loss of power on take-off as a result of blockages in the exhaust pipes, and operations were increasingly restricted. However, by this time, tests with the strengthened BV 138B-0s at Travemünde indicated that the most serious shortcomings revealed by the flying-boat in service had been overcome, and although the appreciably heavier model was rather underpowered, this fault was being rectified

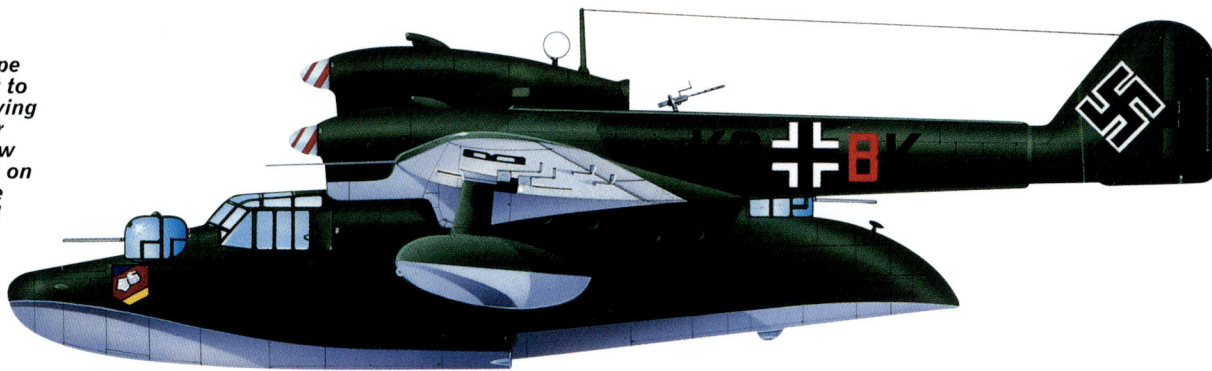

2. Staffel/Küstenfliegergruppe 406 was the first BV 138 unit to operate from Norway, receiving its first boats in the summer of 1941. The unit initially flew from Stavanger and Tromsø on convoy search duties. These were highly successful until the British introduced the Hawker Sea Hurricane as protection in September 1942. From that time, only long-distance surveillance of the convoys could be maintained.

on the production **BV 138B-1** by the installation of the more powerful Jumo 205D engine.

During conversion of the BV 138A-04 as the first BV 138B-0, the LB 204 bow turret was removed and replaced by a similarly-shaped metal fairing pending availability of a new turret mounting a 20-mm MG 151 cannon. The first production BV 138B-1 left the Finkenwerder assembly line in December 1940, and 14 had been completed by the end of the year, but heavy icing on the River Elbe delayed both acceptance and the initiation of the planned training programme, and acceptances could not be resumed until March 1941 when a further seven BV 138B-1s were taken on charge by the Luftwaffe, together with a similar number of the definitive **BV 138C-1** version that had succeeded the B-series on the assembly line.

Stronger and more powerful

Embodying the structural strengthening introduced by the pre-production B-0, the BV 138B-1 differed in having Jumo 205D diesel engines rated at 656 kW (880 hp) for take-off, and improved defensive armament which comprised a 20-mm MG 151 cannon in the bow turret, a similar weapon mounted in a turret in the elongated tail of the hull, and a 7.9-mm MG 15 in the open position aft of the central engine. The offensive load remained unchanged initially, but prior to acceptance by the Luftwaffe, an Umrüst-Bausatz (factory conversion set) was fitted which enabled the offensive load to be increased to six 50-kg (110-lb) bombs or four 150-kg (331-lb) depth charges. In this form the flying-boat was designated **BV 138B-1/U1**.

The BV 138C-1 featured still more structural strengthening resulting in further weight escalation, auxiliary intakes on the upper decking of the engine nacelles, and a 13-mm (0.51-in) MG 131 machine-gun in place of the 7.9-mm weapon in the open upper gun position. A four-bladed airscrew replaced the three-blader driven by the central engine, this later being applied as a retrospective modification to the BV 138B-1, and provision was made for an optional 7.9-mm MG 15 machine-gun which could be fired by the radio-operator from a position in the starboard side of the hull. The **BV 138C-1/U1** featured a similar Umrüst-Bausatz to that of the BV 138B-1/U1.

With the availability of the BV 138B-1 and C-1, the

The BV 138A-0 is seen after conversion as the first BV 138B-0. This boat had only a metal fairing forward of the cockpit pending the advent of a new turret armed with the 20-mm MG 151 cannon.

surviving BV 138A-1s were withdrawn from the operational Küstenfliegergruppen in France, and returned to Germany for modification to the latest standards, but although the BV 138 programme now enjoyed considerable priority, production began to run into difficulties in the late spring, and whereas 15 BV 138C-1s were accepted by the Luftwaffe in April 1941, the monthly output had dropped to 11 in May and a mere five in June, this being due to shortages in the supply of weapons, powerplants, airscrews, instruments and radio equipment. Arrangements had been made for the licence production of the BV 138C-1 by the Weser Flugzeugbau, but only one example of the flying-boat was completed by the factory in 1941, and this from components supplied from Finkenwerder, and it was not until April 1942 that regular deliveries could commence, Weser eventually contributing 67 flying-boats to the programme, production terminating in September 1943. The parent company completed 59 BV 138C-1 flying-boats in 1942, compared with 79 in 1941, and only a further 30 were delivered from Finkenwerder before production was finally phased out in December 1943, the total number of BV 138C flying-boats produced being 227.

Minesweeping aircraft

A limited number of BV 138C flying-boats were modified for the task of minesweeping during 1942-43 under the designation **BV 138 MS** (the suffix letters indicating Minensuche or Mine-search), aircraft so modified soon acquiring the nickname of 'Mausi-Flugzeuge', or 'Mouse-catching aircraft'. Used to sweep magnetic mines from canals, rivers and coastal

The BV 138A-01 (D-ADJE) was the first of the pre-series flying-boats, and retained little more than the overall configuration of the prototypes. This machine began its flight test programme in February 1939. Water and air trials quickly confirmed that the worst characteristics of the prototypes had been overcome.

Blohm und Voss BV 138

waters, the BV 138 MS had all armament removed and a Dural hoop braced to the hull and to the wings outboard of the engine nacelles, this hoop being energised by an auxiliary motor mounted in the position previously occupied by the bow turret. Other BV 138C flying-boats were equipped with FuG 200 Hohentwiel radar for convoy shadowing, operating in collaboration with U-boats, and on occasions the aircraft was even pressed into service as a troop transport, accommodating up to 10 fully-equipped troops.

All BV 138Bs and Cs could be fitted with a pair of 4.9-kN (1,100-lb) thrust take-off assistance rockets, and 70 BV 138Cs were fitted with catapult points for operation from the Luftwaffe's seaplane tenders, *Bussard*, *Falke*, *Ostmark*, *Sperber* and *Westfalen*. These catapult-and-recovery crane-equipped vessels were frequently used as floating bases for BV 138 Ketten deployed in northern waters away from the principal seaborne aircraft bases.

Once its teething troubles had been overcome, the BV 138 proved itself an effective maritime patrol aircraft and an exceptionally sturdy warplane capable of absorbing a considerable amount of punishment, both from nature and from the enemy. Its seagoing capabilities coupled with its ability to withstand the pounding of rough seas for protracted periods led to consideration being given to proposals that flying-boats of this type should be flown out into the Atlantic, descend on the sea and float on station for periods as long as two or three days until, informed of the approach of an Allied convoy by a prowling U-boat or a search aircraft, the BV 138s would take-off and attack in concert with U-boat packs. Considerable attention had been given to the problems of maintenance away from shore facilities, and in an emergency even relatively major repairs could be effected at sea by its crew.

The BV 138 formed a stable firing platform, its three defensive gun positions had good fields of fire, and the long-ranging cannon armament proved effective. The crew complement had been increased to six with the BV 138C-1, but most normal operations were flown with only five crew members. With maximum auxiliary fuel, the BV 138C-1 could stay aloft for as long as 18 hours, although normal endurance was 6.5 hours, and at its normal loaded weight of

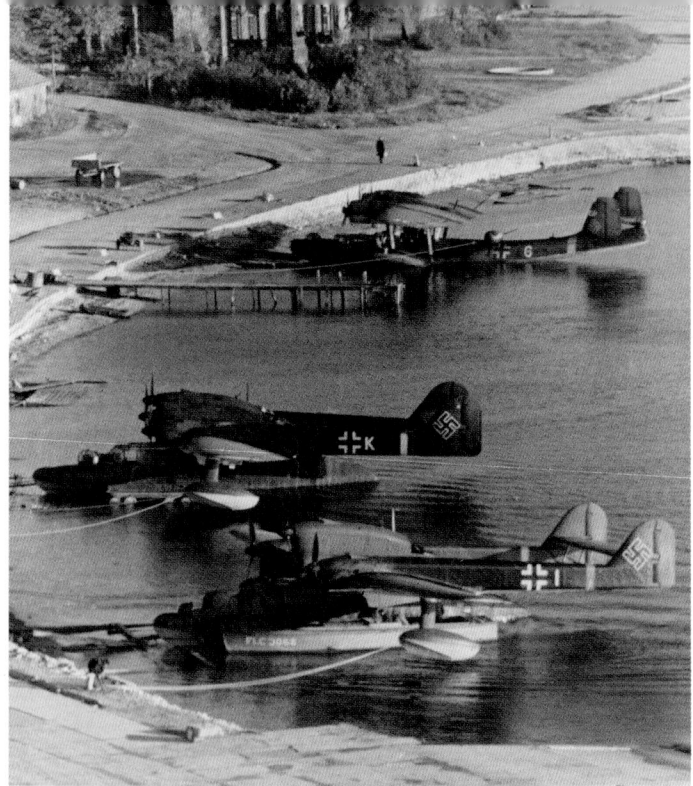

Two BV 138 flying-boats rest at their moorings alongside a Do 24. The boats carried their fuel in the company's patented type of tubular main spar, and by comparison with the first two prototypes, which had tubular booms, the later boats had sturdier stressed-skin booms of rectangular section.

14500 kg (31,967 lb) and from relatively smooth water, the boat would unstick within 30 seconds after a run of 650 m (710 yards), take-off speed being 110 km/h (68 mph) and landing speed being 115 km/h (71 mph).

As early as the spring of 1940, the Technisches Amt, realising the immense value of long-range flying-boats, began to consider a successor to the BV 138, placing a development contract with Blohm and Voss for what was simply referred to as an 'Ersatz (Replacement) BV 138', and suggesting that the existing concept should be scaled up to provide an aircraft with a take-off weight of 24000 kg (52,910 lb), a defensive armament of remotely-controlled gun barbettes, an offensive load of up to 2600 kg (5,730 lb), and the ability to accommodate 60 fully-equipped troops when necessary. Blohm und Voss submitted no fewer than eight project studies all of which envisaged the use of Jumo 208 diesel engines rated at 820 kW (1,100 hp) for take-off. These were the **Projekt 110** which was essentially a slightly scaled up BV 138 with either two or three engines; the **Projekt 111** which was a three-engined asymmetrical variant of the P 110; the **Projekt 112** which was similar to the P 111 but featured an enlarged hull; the **Projekt 113** which was a three-engined twin-hull boat similar in size and weight to the P 112; the **Projekt 122** which was a four-engined twin-boom boat; the **Projekt 123** which was a twin-hull equivalent to the P 122; the **Projekt 124**

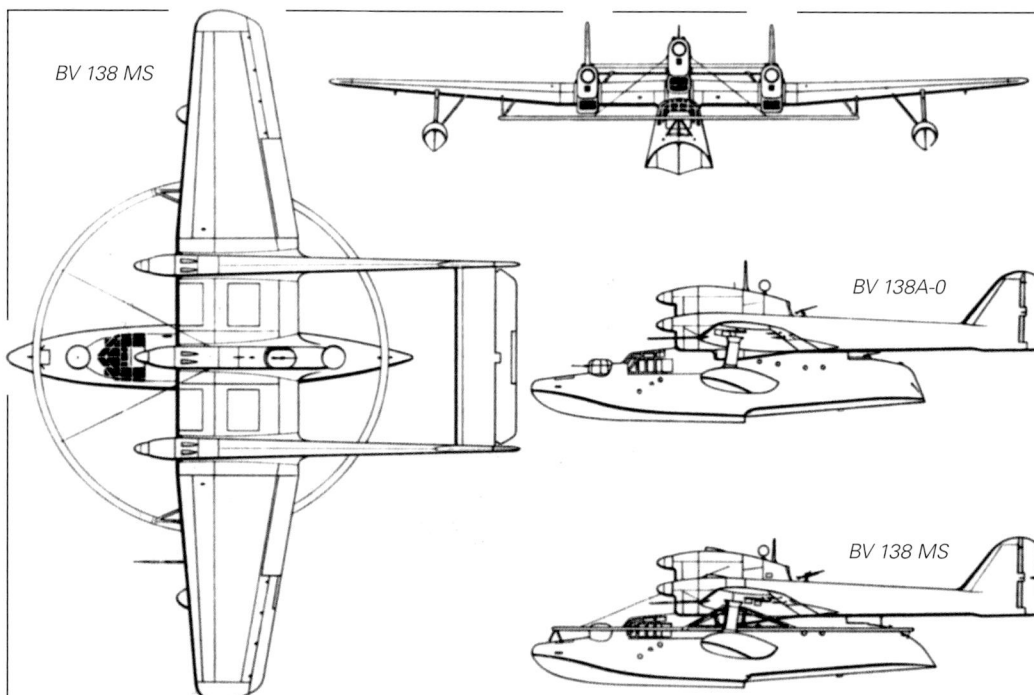

BV 138 MS

BV 138A-0

BV 138 MS

Wearing the customary two-tone splinter camouflage and yellow theatre bands, this BV 138C-1 served with 3. (Fern) Staffel of Seeaufklärungsgruppe 125, based at Constanza, Romania, in April 1943 for service over the Black Sea.

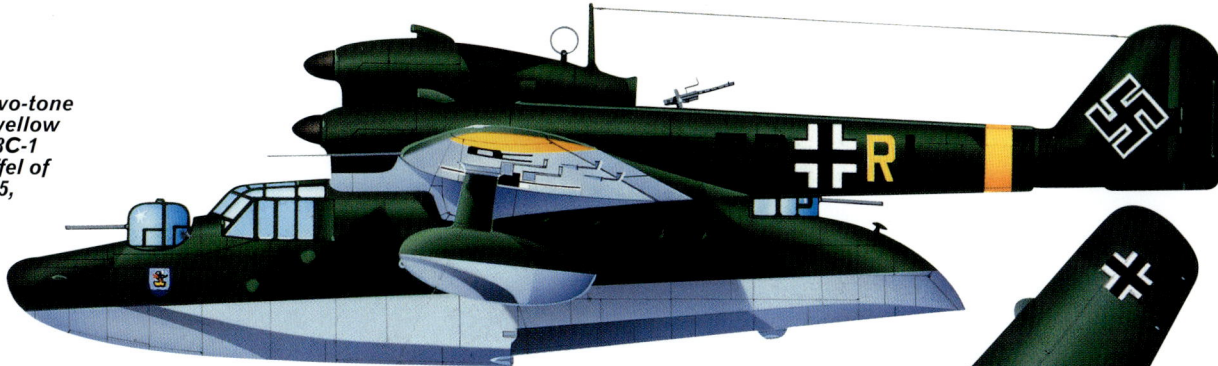

which was similar to the P 122 but embodied a retractable roller-type undercarriage, and the **Projekt 125** which was a similarly-equipped version of the P 123. In the event, none of these projects materialised, the Jumo 208 engine never progressed further than the test bench, and the BV 138 soldiered on until the end of the war.

'The Flying Clog' in service

Owing to the teething troubles suffered by the BV 138A-1, the two Küstenfliegerstaffeln that had re-equipped with the flying-boat for operations in the Biscay area during the closing months of 1940, 1./Kü.Fl.Gr. 506 and 2./Kü.Fl.Gr. 906, saw only limited active service, and both Staffeln had been withdrawn from France for re-equipment with the BV 138B and C before the establishment of the Fliegerführer Atlantik in March 1941. The Kü.Fl.Erg. Staffel 138 was formed as a replacement and training unit, but the conversion of existing units and the formation of additional units on the BV 138 was seriously delayed owing to severe icing on the River Elbe. However, the programme was accelerated during the late spring, and during the summer 2./Kü.Fl.Gr. 406 had converted to the BV 138B-1 and had begun convoy search operations from Stavanger and Tromsø under the Fliegerführer Nordost and the Fliegerführer Lofoten.

The two BV 138 Staffeln formerly based in France, 1./Kü.Fl.Gr. 506 and 2./Kü.Fl.Gr. 906, had been transferred to the Baltic for operations under the Fliegerführer Ostsee, and during the remaining months of 1941, additional BV 138-equipped units joined operations over the North Atlantic and the Arctic Ocean, based on Banak, Tromsø and Trondheim, including 3./Kü.Fl.Gr. 906 that operated the flying-boat in concert with He 115 float seaplanes, and

Above: The curious three-engined BV 138C-1 suffered lengthy development problems but eventually emerged as an effective flying-boat. The type was employed primarily in the Baltic Sea and against the Allied convoys passing round the North Cape to the Soviet Union's northern ports.

Right: The BV 138 was dubbed 'The Flying Clog' on account of the shape of its hull. This BV 138C-1/U1 was operated by 1.(F)/SAGr. 130 in the Trondheim area of northern Norway in April 1944. Note the application of temporary winter camouflage.

Seeaufklärungsstaffeln 1. and 2.(F)/SAGr. 130 and 1. and 2.(F)/SAGr. 131, the last-mentioned Staffel operating both BV 138s and Ar 196s.

During October 1941, one Staffel of BV 138B-1s with 10 aircraft on strength amassed more than 500 flying hours on long-range search tasks, representing some 104600 km (65,000 miles), and the reliability of the Blohm und Voss flying-boat was considered proven. Furthermore, the BV 138 had also proved its ability to defend itself, and soon after its Norwegian debut had accounted for a Blenheim fighter over the Skagerrak, and a Catalina over the North Sea.

At the end of 1941, 3.(F)/SAGr. 125, which had been operating Ar 95A-1s under the Fliegerführer Ostsee, converted to the BV 138C-1, and with some 20 flying-boats on strength was transferred to Constanza, Romania, to form the nucleus of the Black Sea patrol force. By the end of 1943 all BV 138 operations in the region were controlled by SAGr. 125, with three Staffeln and the Gruppenstab operating the type. Operating under the Aufklärungsführer Schwarzes Meer West and frequently escorted by Romanian fighters, the BV 138s of SAGr. 125 performed reconnaissance

Blohm und Voss BV 138

The BV 138 MS was a conversion of the BV 138C. Intended for the destruction of magnetic mines, the BV 138 MS had no armament but carried a large Dural ring that was energised by an auxiliary engine in the location previously occupied by the bow turret.

and anti-shipping strikes until the late summer of 1944. That year the BV 138 force was briefly swelled by the arrival of 2./SAGr. 131 from Norway.

The principal areas of activity remained the Baltic, the North Atlantic and the Arctic Ocean for the BV 138, and once the danger to Germany of the Allied PQ convoys via the Arctic to Murmansk and Archangelsk was fully appreciated, the convoy search and shadowing activities of the Norwegian-based flying-boat Staffeln were given new impetus, and at the climax of the anti-convoy operations, in mid-1942, 44 BV 138s were operating from northern Norwegian bases. The BV 138s were responsible for most of the initial convoy sightings and subsequent shadowing, and losses to enemy action were few, but on 8 September 1942, when a Tromsø-based BV 138 sighted PQ 18 in the vicinity of Jan Mayen Island, the event heralded a new chapter in the story of the PQ convoys. From the initial sighting PQ 18 was kept under continuous observation by relays of BV 138s, but on the morning of the 9th the warships escorting the convoy were joined by the escort-carrier HMS *Avenger* carrying 12 Sea Hurricane IIC fighters of Nos 802 and 883 Squadrons. For the first time a PQ convoy had brought its own fighter cover, and the ponderous BV 138s were now hard put to maintain contact with the convoy at maximum visual range, one flying-boat fighting a 90-minute running battle with the Sea Hurricanes yet, surprisingly, regaining its base, though sorely damaged.

Kara Sea operations

During 1942, the Norwegian-based BV 138s frequently rendezvoused with U-boats in the Arctic Ocean and were refuelled at sea to enable them to reconnoitre the Siberian

Whereas most BV 138 boats operated in the harsh environment of Arctic waters from their Norwegian bases, the BV 138C-1 boats of 3. (Fern)/Seeaufklärungsgruppe 125 patrolled the comparatively balmy Black Sea coast from Constanta, moving to Varna in Bulgaria in March 1942. A forward base was established in the Crimea at Sevastopol.

Blohm und Voss BV 138C-1 cutaway key

1 Towing lug
2 Nose light
3 Mooring clamps
4 Anchor attachment
5 Nose entry hatch
6 Crawlway
7 Forward bulkhead sections
8 Bow turret mechanism
9 Bow cannon (MG 151)
10 Bow turret
11 Turret/hull cut-out
12 Bulkhead door
13 Ammunition stand
14 Flight deck bulkhead
15 Instrument panel
16 Windscreen
17 Naval observer/co-pilot's seat
18 Central console
19 Underfloor crawlway
20 Pilot's seat
21 Rudder pedals
22 Control linkage
23 Floor support member
24 Bulkhead
25 Navigator's station
26 Crew deck bulkhead
27 Wireless-operator's station
28 Bulkhead door
29 Fuselage upper skinning
30 Radiator intake
31 Chin intake
32 Centre engine four-bladed propeller
33 Engine nacelle
34 Intakes
35 Access panels
36 Engine tubular mount
37 Tubular main spar
38 Radar antenna
39 Auxiliary engine room (flight engineer's position)
40 Portholes
41 Ladder to dorsal position
42 Bulkhead
43 Crew off-duty bunks (three)
44 Aft bulkhead door
45 Aft turret mechanism
46 Aft decking
47 Mooring hook
48 Boat tail
49 Mooring clamp
50 Stern cannon (MG 151)
51 Stern turret
52 Dorsal fairing
53 Dorsal machine-gun mounting (MG 131)
54 Ring-and-bead sight
55 Wind deflector
56 Turret ring
57 Antenna winch
58 Entry/exit hatchway
59 Aerial mast
60 D/F loop
61 Firewall bulkhead
62 Wing fillet
63 Starboard inner wing section
64 Oil tank

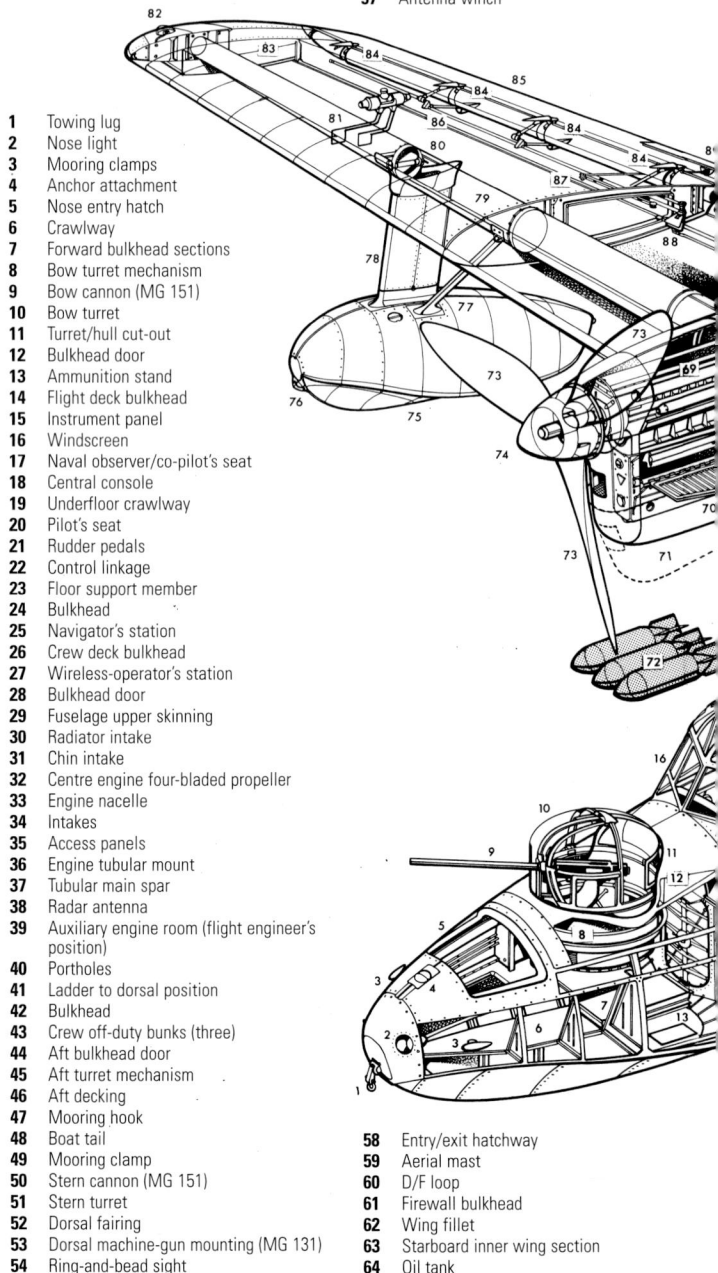

This BV 138C-1 was redeployed south from Norway in January 1944 to operate over the Black Sea, based at Varna in Bulgaria with 1.(F)/SAGr. 131.

seaways, such refuelling operations continuing as late as August 1943. At this time, in the late summer of 1943, the BV 138 also participated in a spectacular operation for which they were supplied from a base within Soviet-controlled territory. In order to enable the flying-boats to reconnoitre the Kara Sea in which important convoy activity had been

reported, two U-boats established a forward supply base for the BV 138s on the Soviet Arctic island of Novaya Zemlya from which they operated for three weeks, undertaking eight reconnaissance flights which took them far to the east of Bely Island, off the Yamal Peninsula, north-east of the Urals.

By 1943, the BV 138 had reappeared in some numbers in

65	Engine access panels	86	Control rod linkage	130	Step	
66	Intakes	87	Tab linkage	131	Radiator intake	
67	Engine mounting blocks	88	Control quadrant	132	Tubular spar inner/outer section flange	
68	Radiator	89	Aileron tab	133	Wing leading-edge	
69	Junkers Jumo 205D diesel engine	90	Flap mechanism	134	Spar outer section	
70	Hinged inspection/maintenance panel	91	Starboard flap	135	Wing structure	
		92	Tailboom join capping strake	136	Port flaps	
71	Hinged cowling lower section	93	Aerials	137	Aileron trim tab	
72	Underwing (starboard) bomb-load (three 50-kg/110-lb bombs also applicable to port wing on BV138C-1/U1)	94	Tailboom skinning			
		95	Rudder cables			
73	Three-bladed (paddle) VDM propeller					

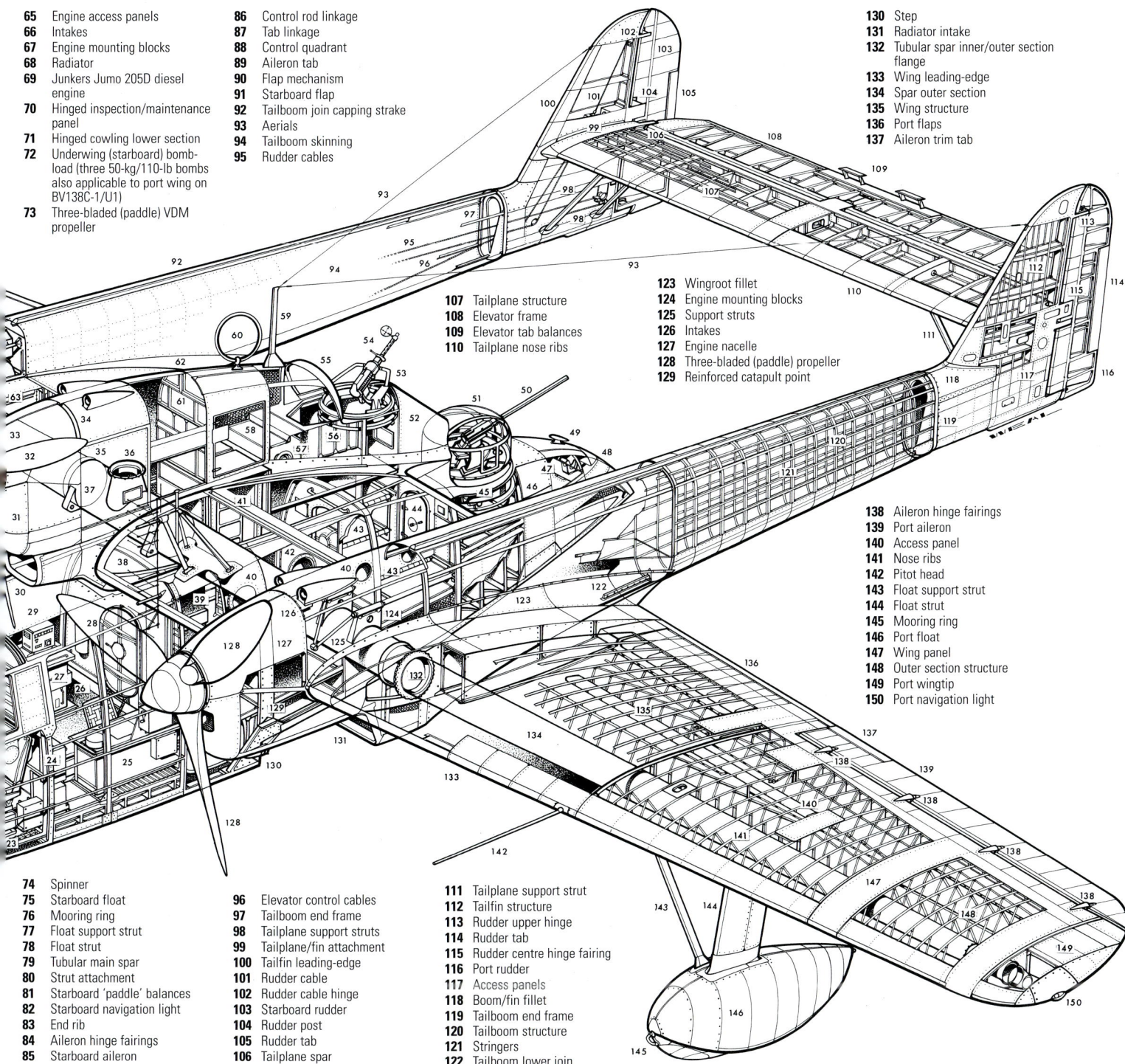

107	Tailplane structure
108	Elevator frame
109	Elevator tab balances
110	Tailplane nose ribs

123	Wingroot fillet
124	Engine mounting blocks
125	Support struts
126	Intakes
127	Engine nacelle
128	Three-bladed (paddle) propeller
129	Reinforced catapult point

138	Aileron hinge fairings
139	Port aileron
140	Access panel
141	Nose ribs
142	Pitot head
143	Float support strut
144	Float strut
145	Mooring ring
146	Port float
147	Wing panel
148	Outer section structure
149	Port wingtip
150	Port navigation light

74	Spinner	96	Elevator control cables	111	Tailplane support strut
75	Starboard float	97	Tailboom end frame	112	Tailfin structure
76	Mooring ring	98	Tailplane support struts	113	Rudder upper hinge
77	Float support strut	99	Tailplane/fin attachment	114	Rudder tab
78	Float strut	100	Tailfin leading-edge	115	Rudder centre hinge fairing
79	Tubular main spar	101	Rudder cable	116	Port rudder
80	Strut attachment	102	Rudder cable hinge	117	Access panels
81	Starboard 'paddle' balances	103	Starboard rudder	118	Boom/fin fillet
82	Starboard navigation light	104	Rudder post	119	Tailboom end frame
83	End rib	105	Rudder tab	120	Tailboom structure
84	Aileron hinge fairings	106	Tailplane spar	121	Stringers
85	Starboard aileron			122	Tailboom lower join

127

Blohm und Voss BV 138

the Biscay area and had also appeared in the Mediterranean. In May 1943, 3./Kü.Fl.Gr. 406 was based at Biscarosse for operations under the Fliegerführer Atlantik with seven BV 138C-1s and the BV 222 V3 on strength. In the following month, by which time the strength of the Staffel had been augmented by the arrival of the BV 222 V2, V4 and V5, the flying-boats of 3./Kü.Fl.Gr. 406 were strafed and bombed at their moorings in Biscarosse harbour by RAF fighter-bombers, a number of the boats (including the BV 222 V3 and V5) being sunk and others being seriously damaged, operational strength falling to two BV 138C-1s and two BV 222s. By the following October, the unit had been redesignated 1.(F)/SAGr. 129, strength later being augmented by a small number of replacement BV 138C-1s and by the BV 222 V7 and pre-production BV 222C-09 and -010, the Staffel continuing to operate over the Biscay area and the Atlantic until Biscarosse was vacated in 1944. In the Mediterranean, the Gruppenstab of See Aufklärungsgruppe 126 briefly operated the BV 138, based on Crete under the control of the Luftwaffenkommando Südost.

By May 1944, the number of BV 138s in service had markedly diminished, the continued operation of slow flying-boats in the face of almost total enemy air supe-riority having become extremely hazardous, but northern waters remained the principal venue of the BV 138, and Norwegian-based Staffeln still operating this type were 1. and 2.(F)/SAGr. 130 at Trondheim with six and five BV 138s, respectively, 3.(F)/SAGr. 130 (originally 2./Kü.Fl.Gr. 406 and subsequently 1.(F)/SAGr. 131) with eight BV 138s at Tromsø. The Gruppenstab of SAGr. 131 flew BV 138s alongside 2. Staffel, with a mixture of BV 138s and Ar 196s at Stavanger, until July 1944, 2. Staffel remaining until the end of the year.

A few BV 138 MS minesweeping aircraft were operated by Minensuch-Gruppe 1 der Luftwaffe, but the only remaining BV 138-equipped Staffeln listed in the Luftwaffe Quarter Master General's returns of 10 January 1945 were 1. and 3.(F)/SAGr. 130 under Luftflotte 5 (Ost). However, although no longer appearing in the official strength lists, that elements of other BV 138 units still existed is indicated by the fact that, on 1 May 1945, Oberleutnant Wolfgang Klemusch of 3.(F)/SAGr. 130 based at Copenhagen received instructions to fly his BV 138 to Berlin, land on a lake after midnight, and ferry out two vitally important couriers. Oblt Klemusch landed successfully on the lake under heavy shell-fire, but as the couriers could not produce any identification papers he refused to take them on board and, instead, picked up 10 wounded troops and then flew the BV 138 back to Copenhagen. Subsequently, it was reported that the couriers that should have been ferried out of Berlin in the BV 138 had been entrusted with Adolf Hitler's last will and testament.

Blohm und Voss BV 138A-1 specification
Type: long-range maritime reconnaissance flying-boat
Powerplant: three Junkers Jumo 205C-4 six-cylinder vertical opposed-piston compression-ignition two-stroke engines each rated at 447 kW (600 hp) for take-off
Performance: maximum speed at 13750 kg (30,313 lb) 265 km/h (165 mph) at sea level; maximum cruising speed 250 km/h (155 mph) at 1000 m (3,280 ft); normal range 1250 km (778 miles) at 245 km/h (151 mph); maximum range (with overload fuel) 3930 km (2,442 miles) at 240 km/h (148 mph); climb (at 13750 kg) to 2000 m (6,560 ft) in 8.5 minutes; service ceiling (at 13750 kg) 3600 m (11,810 ft), at (16200 kg/35,715 lb) 800 m (2,625 ft); normal endurance 5.2 hours; maximum endurance 16.5 hours
Weights: empty 10800 kg (23,810 lb); normal loaded 13750 kg (30,313 lb); maximum loaded 16200 kg (35,715 lb)
Dimensions: wingspan 26.90 m (88 ft 4¼ in); length 19.85 m (65 ft 1½ in); height 5.90 m (19 ft 4¼ in); wing area 112.00 m² (1,205.56 sq ft)
Armament: one 20-mm MG 204 cannon in hydraulically-operated bow turret and one 7.9-mm (0.31-in) MG 15 machine-gun in each of two open turrets, plus three 50-kg (110-lb) bombs on racks beneath the starboard wing centre section

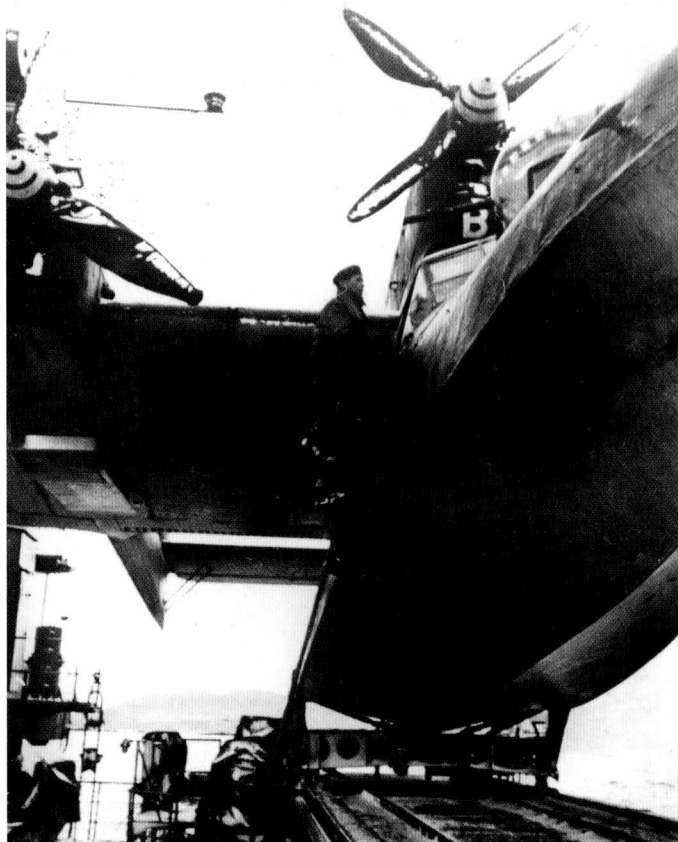

Above: Production examples of the BV 138 had a designed hull of greater length with the step moved farther forward. The centreline engine drove a four-blade propeller, and the two outer engines had three-blade units. The new propeller was introduced by the BV 138C-1, but was retrofitted to the BV 138B-1 as well.

Right: A few BV 138 MS minesweeper conversions were operated by the Luftwaffe's Minensuch-Gruppe to clear rivers, canals and coastal waters. This variant featured a large-diameter Dural degaussing loop for countering magnetic mines. The armament was deleted, a simple fairing replacing the bow turret, underneath which was an auxiliary motor for the magnetic field-generation equipment.

Although the majority of the BV 138 boats served on standard coastal patrol duties, a small number were converted for minehunting tasks. This aircraft served with 6. Staffel/ Minensuchgruppe 1 at Grossenbrode in the last year of the war.

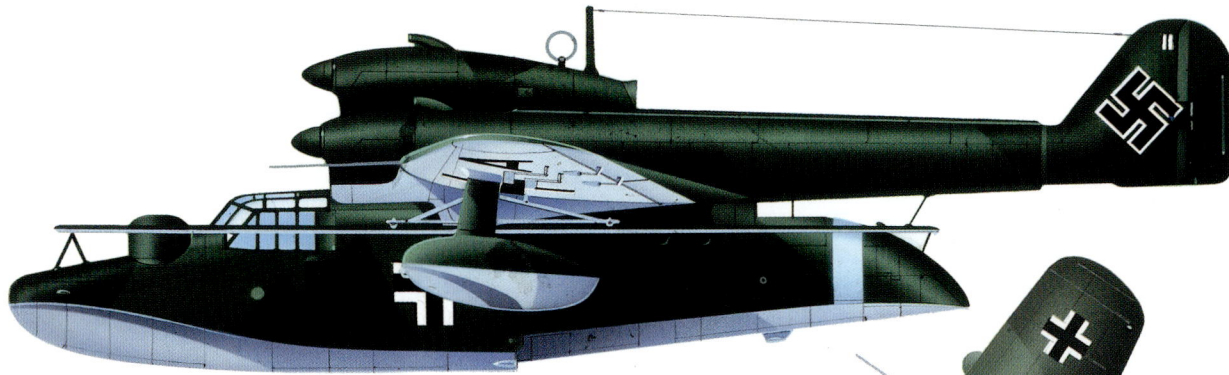

Blohm und Voss BV 138C-1 specification

Type: long-range maritime reconnaissance flying-boat
Powerplant: three Junkers Jumo 205D six-cylinder vertical opposed-piston compression-ignition two-stroke engines each rated at 656 kW (880 hp) for take-off
Performance: maximum speed at 14500 kg (31,967 lb) 285 km/h (177 mph) at sea level; normal cruising speed 235 km/h (146 mph) at 1000 m (3,280 ft); normal range 1220 km (758 miles) at 195 km/h (122 mph); maximum range with 3750 litres (825 Imp gal) fuel 4300 km (2,670 miles); climb to 3170 m (10,390 ft) in 24 minutes; service ceiling at 14500 kg (31,967 lb) 5000 m (16,400 ft), at 17650 kg (38,912 lb) 2800 m (9,185 ft); normal endurance 6.5 hours; maximum endurance 18 hours
Weights: empty 11770 kg (25,948 lb); normal loaded 14500 kg (31,967 lb); maximum loaded 17650 kg (38,912 lb)
Dimensions: wingspan 26.90 m (88 ft 4¼ in); length 19.85 m (65 ft 1½ in); height 5.90 m (19 ft 4¼ in); wing area 112.00 m² (1,205.56 sq ft)
Armament: one 20-mm MG 151 cannon in bow turret, one 20-mm MG 151 mounted in turret in hull tail, and one 13-mm (0.51-in) MG 131 machine-gun in open position aft of central engine, plus (optional) one 7.9-mm MG 15 machine-gun firing through hatch in starboard side of hull; (offensive) three 50-kg (110-lb) bombs on racks beneath the starboard wing centre section, or (U1) six 50-kg bombs or four 150-kg (331-lb) depth charges

Left: The BV 138's defensive armament was steadily improved, and in the war's later stages comprised two 20-mm turreted cannon in the front and rear of the hull, one 13-mm (0.51-in) machine-gun behind the centreline engine, and provision for one 7.9-mm (0.31-in) machine-gun in a hull hatch.

Below: A BV 138 awash and on its way to the bottom. The lower part of the hull, including the shallow V-type planing bottom, was divided into 10 watertight compartments.

Left: A BV 138C-1 of Seeaufklärungsgruppe 130 makes a rendezvous with a U-boat in the Arctic Ocean. Note the hastily-applied white distemper for Arctic camouflage, and the Hohentwiel search radar antennas on the wing's leading edges.

Blohm und Voss Ha 139

The Blohm und Voss Ha 139 was designed as a mailplane for Deutsche Lufthansa's routes across the Atlantic, and was also stressed for catapult launches. Only three examples were completed, and all went on to serve during World War II, two of them as transports and the third as a minesweeper.

Although the Hamburger Flugzeugbau's design office at Hamburg was heavily committed to military projects, notably the Ha 137 and Ha 138, early in 1935 the company prepared a proposal to meet a Deutsche Lufthansa (DLH) requirement for a long-range seaplane for transocean operations. One of the initial objectives of the Hamburger Flugzeugbau management team had been the development of long-haul intercontinental transport aircraft, and the DLH requirement provided the opportunity to enter the civil field. The DLH specification called for an aircraft stressed for catapult launching, capable of taking off from and alighting on rough water with sufficient fuel for a 1000-km (620-mile) range, and possessing the ability to carry a 500-kg (1,102-lb) payload over a distance of 5000 km (3,106 miles) at a minimum cruising speed of 250 km/h (155 mph).

To meet this specification, Dr.-Ing. Richard Vogt evolved **Projekt 15** which, aesthetically, was one of the most attractive multi-engined float seaplanes envisaged at that time. Of all-metal construction, the Projekt 15 featured a slim, circular-section monocoque fuselage and an inverted-gull wing incorporating Vogt's fuel-carrying tubular main spar. The two single-step floats were attached to the centre section spar at the point of transition between negative and positive dihedral by vertical steel stubs enclosed by streamlined fairings. Accepted by DLH, which ordered three prototypes, the Projekt 15 was allocated the designation **Ha 139**, and construction began during the autumn of 1935. Detail design and construction of the first two prototypes progressed extremely rapidly, and at the end of 1935, a study of a reconnaissance-bomber variant, the **Projekt 20**, was submitted to the RLM but failed to arouse official interest.

Maiden flight

The first prototype, the **Ha 139 V1** (Werk Nr 181, D-AMIE), was flown for the first time in the late autumn of 1936, and delivered to DLH in March 1937 as the **Ha 139A** *Nordmeer*, this being followed in June by the **Ha 139 V2** (Werk Nr 182, D-AJEY) dubbed by DLH as Ha 139A *Nordwind*. Operating from the depot ships *Friesenland* and *Schwabenland*, the two aircraft made seven return flights between Horta, in the Azores, and New York between mid-August and the

Above: The Ha 139 was of generally elegant overall configuration, perhaps spoiled by the thick section its its wing and the fact that this wing was untapered in either thickness or chord.

Above: The Ha 139 V1 is seen at high speed. The circular endplate fin-and-rudder units provided inadequate directional authority, and the vertical tail area was steadily increased .

Above: In service with Lufthansa, the Ha 139 V2 was designated as the Ha 139A and named **Nordwind***. This and the preceding* **Nordmeer** *were operated from the catapult-equipped depot ships* **Friesenland** *and* **Schwabenland** *for experimental services.*

This view from straight ahead of the Ha 139B/MS minesweeper conversion highlights the unsual contours of the magnetic mine degaussing loop, which extended on each side from the tail to attachments under the outer wing panels and thence, via the bows of the two floats, to the underside of the nose.

From the outset the Ha 139 was designed to operate from depot ships, covering long transoceanic distances with the aid of mid-ocean refuelling stops. Here the V1 is seen being winched up from a company-owned vessel with its four Jumo 205C engines running.

The Ha 139 V3 was the prototype for the Ha 139B series. Externally the main difference was the enlarged vertical fins being mounted further inboard on the tailplanes. Note the additional cooling intakes above the engine nacelles.

end of November 1937, average speeds being 230 km/h (143 mph) westbound and 250 km/h (155 mph) eastbound.

The two A-series prototypes were each powered by four Jumo 205C diesel engines driving three-blade variable-pitch Junkers-Hamilton airscrews. The sliding shutter-controlled radiators were mounted in pairs in the float-stub fairings, and the tubular centre-section spar was divided into five separate tanks with a total capacity of 6000 litres (1,320 Imp gal). A mooring compartment and stowage for marine gear was provided in the extreme nose, and the flight deck provided side-by-side seats with dual controls for the two pilots and positions immediately aft for the flight engineer to starboard and the radio-operator to port. The mail and freight compartment was separated from the flight deck by the main spar, and no access was possible in flight.

Poor directional stability with the original circular endplate fin-and-rudder assemblies dictated a substantial increase in the size of the rudders, and subsequently inadequate cooling

necessitated the introduction of auxiliary intakes in the upper decking of the engine cowlings, the original radiators simultaneously being removed from the float-stub fairings owing to the corrosive effect of salt water spray during take-offs and landings, and replaced by a separate radiator for each engine beneath the wings.

In the spring of 1938, the two A-series prototypes were joined by the B-series prototype, the **Ha 139 V3** (Werk Nr 217, D-ASTA), which entered DLH service as the **Ha 139B** *Nordstern*. Retaining the Jumo 205C engines, the Ha 139 V3 was somewhat heavier than its predecessors, empty and loaded weights being increased from 10360 kg and 16970 kg (22,840 lb and 37,412 lb) to 10940 kg and 17550 kg (24,118 lb and 38,691 lb) respectively. The overall dimensions were greater, these comprising a wing span increased to 29.50 m (96 ft 9⅜ in) from 27.00 m (88 ft 7 in), length to 19.65 m (64 ft 5⅝ in) from 19.50 m (63 ft 11¾ in), height to 4.80 m (15 ft 9 in) from 4.50 m (14 ft 9⅛ in), and wing area

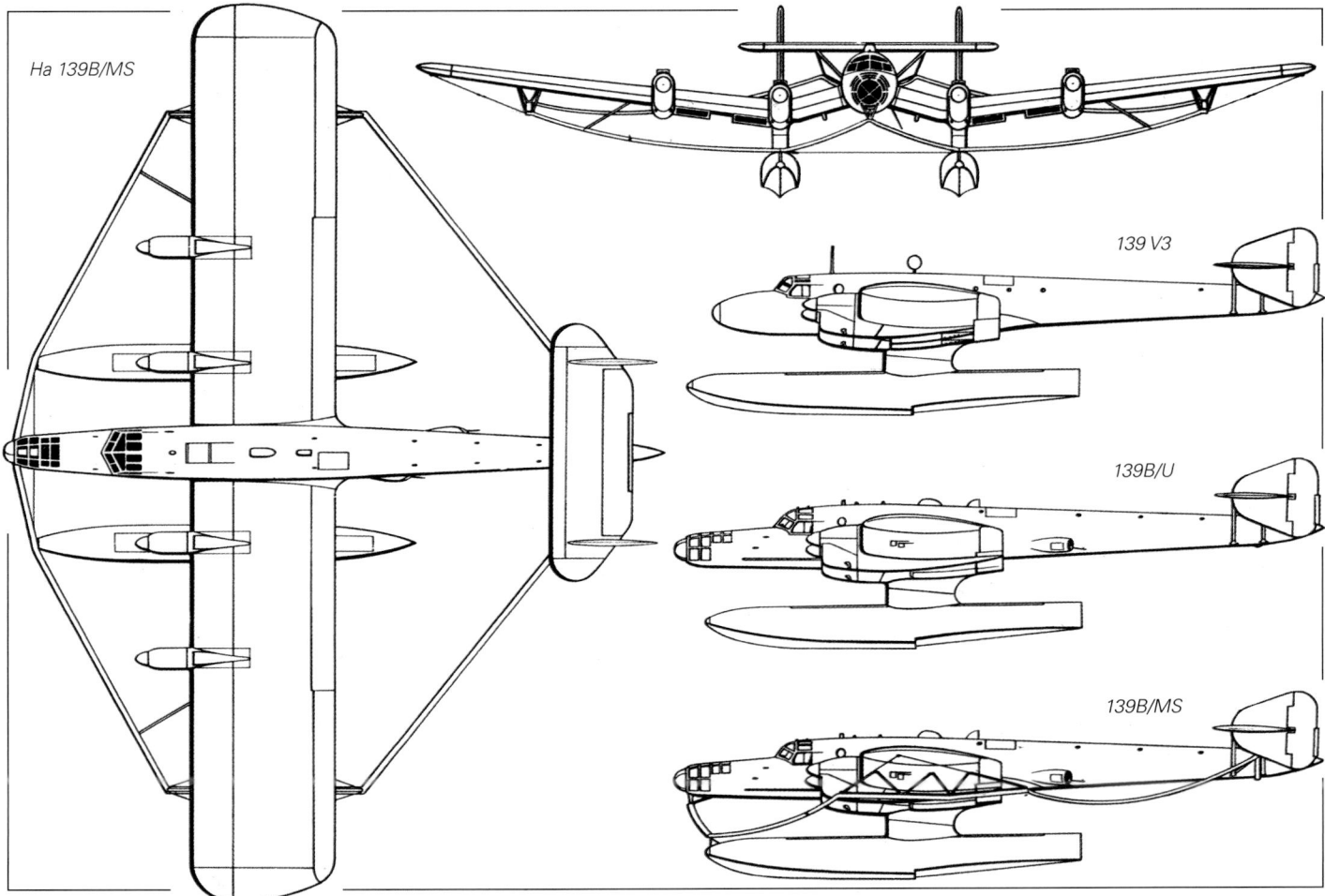

Ha 139B/MS

139 V3

139B/U

139B/MS

Blohm und Voss Ha 139

Above and right: The Ha 139 V1 became the Ha 139A Nordmeer in Lufthansa service, and is here seen on its launching trolley on the steam-powered catapult of its mother ship.

to 130.00 m² (1,399.31 sq ft) from 117.00 m² (1,259.37 sq ft). The engine nacelles were deepened, and the vertical tail surfaces were again enlarged and inset.

Between 21 July and 19 October 1938, the Ha 139 V3 made several return flights between Horta and New York, the North Atlantic trials being shared by the Ha 139 V1 and V2, a total of 597 hours being logged in the air, and subsequently the three aircraft were operated over the Bathurst, Gambia, and Natal, Brazil, sector of the South Atlantic service flown by DLH until shortly before World War II.

From September 1939 DLH had little use for the Ha 139 floatplanes, and thought was given to their adaptation for long-range maritime reconnaissance, the Ha 139 V3 being returned to Wenzendorf for experimental conversion. The fuselage nose was extended and glazed to provide a position for an observer, an Ikaria spherical mounting for a single 7.9-mm (0.31-in) MG 15 machine-gun forming the extremity of the nose. A second MG 15 was provided for the radio-operator to fire from a hatch in the roof of the flight deck, and a pair of similar weapons could be fired from staggered lateral lens-type mountings. Radio and navigational aids were substantially increased, loaded weight rising to 19000 kg (41,888 lb), and as the **Ha 139B/Umbau**, the modified floatplane was flown for the first time on 19 January 1940 after a catapult take-off from the *Friesenland* in the Baltic, the crew comprising Oberleutnant Graf Schack and Flugkapitän Schuster.

The Ha 139B/Umbau was later delivered to 1. Staffel of Küstenfliegergruppe 406, a general-purpose reconnaissance unit primarily equipped with the Do 18 flying boat, and which, by the time it participated in the Norwegian campaign, had taken five Do 26s on strength. 1./Kü.Fl.Gr. 406 performed reconnaissance and transport missions during the Norwegian operation, the Ha 139B/Umbau serving primarily in the arctic weather reconnaissance role. In the meantime, the two Ha 139A prototypes had been modified in a similar fashion to the Ha 139B, and they, too, participated in the Norwegian campaign, serving in the logistic support role with KG.z.b.V 108 See, operating from Norderney and landing in Norwegian fjords with ammunition and other

This is the Ha 139 V3 in its final form as the Ha 139B/MS. The enormous degaussing loop required considerable bracing. This configuration was not used operationally.

Lack of adequate direction authority meant that the vertical tail surfaces of the Ha 139 were increased in size and eventually in shape. Depicted here is the V3, with the final vertical fin configuration.

supplies for isolated German units.

Shortage of spares limited the Luftwaffe service of the Ha 139s, but the V1 and V2 are known to have served with Flugzeugführerschule C 17 at Pütnitz. In 1942, the Ha 139B/Umbau (alias Ha 139 V3) saw further modification as the **Ha 139B/MS** (Minensuche) minesweeper. A most unusual magnetic degaussing structure was looped from the fuselage nose to the float tips and from there to the outer wing panels and, finally, to the tailplane. There is no record of the Ha 139B/MS having seen service with any of the Staffeln of the Minensuch-Gruppe.

Blohm und Voss Ha 139B/Umbau specification
Type: long-range maritime reconnaissance float seaplane
Powerplant: four Junkers Jumo 205C liquid-cooled six-cylinder vertically opposed-piston compression-ignition diesel engines each rated at 447 kW (600 hp) for take-off
Performance: maximum speed 288 km/h (179 mph) at 3000 m (9,840 ft); maximum cruising speed 238 km/h (148 mph) at 2000 m (6,560 ft); economical cruising speed 200 km/h (124 mph); service ceiling 5000 m (16,405 ft); maximum range 4600 km (2,858 miles) at 238 km/h, 4950 km (3,075 miles) at 200 km/h
Weight: loaded 19000 kg (41,888 lb)
Dimensions: wingspan 29.50 m (96 ft 9⅜ in); length 20.07 m (65 ft 10¼ in); height 4.80 m (15 ft 9 in); wing area 130.00 m² (1,399.31 sq ft)
Armament: single 7.9-mm (0.31-in) MG 15 machine-guns in the nose, flight deck roof hatch and two staggered rear-fuselage lateral mountings

Blohm und Voss Ha 140

Designed in response to an official requirement calling for a twin-engined floatplane to meet the Luftwaffe's maritime torpedo-bombing and reconnaissance needs, the Ha 140 was designed by Dr.-Ing. Vogt. Only three examples were completed, with the rival Heinkel He 115 being selected for service instead.

During the summer of 1935 the Hamburger Flugzeugbau and the Ernst Heinkel Flugzeugwerke were invited to submit proposals to meet a specification for a twin-engined maritime reconnaissance and torpedo-bombing float seaplane, and in September 1935, Dr.-Ing. Vogt's team submitted its **Projekt 19** to the Reichsluftfahrtministerium, together wih a parallel proposal for a land-based version, the **Projekt 19a** with a fully-retractable undercarriage. Once more displaying Dr.-Ing. Vogt's predilection for wings of inverted-gull form, the Projekt 19 envisaged the use of two Junkers Jumo 210 12-cylinder liquid-cooled engines, and on 1 November 1935 an official order was placed for three prototypes under the designation **Ha 140**.

Created to meet a maritime reconnaissance and torpedo bombing requirement, the Ha 140 was designed with a gun turret and observation blister in the nose. Although with its streamlined float pylons it looked the part, the type's water and flight handling characteristics were poor.

Early revisions

At an early stage in the design development of the aircraft, wingspan was increased from 20.00 m to 21.20 m (65 ft 7½ in to 69 ft 6⅜ in), and model tests revealed the desirability of eliminating the course anhedral angle of the inboard wing panels, a straight centre section being adopted and the dihedral of the outer panels being markedly reduced. As some weight escalation proved unavoidable, more powerful engines than the proposed Jumo 210s were desirable if the specified performance was to be attained, and by the time the final mock-up was ready for inspection on 3 December

1936, it had been decided to adopt the nine-cylinder radial BMW 132K (licence-built Pratt & Whitney Hornet).

The first prototype, the **Ha 140 V1** (D-AUTO), flew for the first time on 30 September 1937, a month after its Heinkel competitor, the He 115, and was flown to the Erprobungsstelle at Travemünde late in December for official trials. Shortly after its arrival at Travemünde, the Ha 140 V1 suffered an accident when, while alighting on rough water, the starboard float dipped, its forward structure failing and the tip bending upwards, striking the airscrew. The impact partly tore the starboard engine from its bearers, and debris flung up by the airscrew punctured the fuselage nose. The Ha 140 V1 was replaced in the Travemünde test programme by the second prototype, the **Ha 140 V2**, completed in December 1937, and the damaged aircraft was returned to Wenzendorf for repair.

Three prototypes of Ha 140 were ordered. As the design was finalised, the wing was altered in size and configuration, and the need for greater power was reflected in the switch to the powerplant of two BMW 132K radial engines. The Ha 140 V1 first prototype (D-AUTO) made its maiden flight on 30 September 1937, about one month later than the rival Heinkel He 115.

133

Blohm und Voss Ha 140

Seen in standard configuration, the clean lines of the Ha 140 are readily apparent. Later experimental tasks included testing a scaled version of the BV 222's empennage, and flying with a variable-incidence wing arrangement in a test programme for the BV 144.

The Ha 140 V1 and V2 differed in no major respect, and both were powered by the BMW 132K rated at 597 kW (800 hp) for take-off and 619 kW (830 hp) at 1000 m (3,280 ft). All-metal construction was employed and flush-riveted metal skinning. The cantilever wing had a single main load-carrying tubular spar, the centre portion of which was sealed and divided into five individual fuel tanks, the centre and smallest of these being the reserve tank. The fuselage was a monocoque built up of cross-frames and longitudinal stringers, the main bulkheads being heavy box frames, and the two all-metal cantilever floats were attached to the extremities of the centre-section portion of the main spar by vertical tubular steel stubs enclosed by streamlined fairings. Each float had a central Wagner beam extending almost its entire length, and was divided by seven watertight bulkheads. Proposed armament comprised a 7.9-mm (0.31-in) MG 15 machine-gun in the nose, this possessing somewhat limited traverse and firing

through a slot in a small glazed cupola, and a similar weapon for rear defence fired by the radio-operator from a sliding dorsal hatch. The internal weapons bay could accommodate a single torpedo or four 250-kg (551-lb) bombs, and the crew comprised three members.

Final prototype

The third prototype, the **Ha 140 V3** (D-AMME), was not completed until late in 1938, this differing from its predecessors in embodying slats that occupied the entire leading edges of the wing outer panels, some local structural reinforcement, and deletion of the nose gun cupola. The Ha 140 V3 was delivered to Travemünde on 11 May 1939, but Blohm und Voss was already aware that no production contract was forthcoming, the Technisches Amt having selected the He 115 to fulfil its specification as early as the spring of 1938, Ha 140 development continuing only as a back-up programme. The performance of the two aircraft was closely comparable, but whereas the He 115 possessed exceptionally fine water handling qualities and good stability throughout its speed range, the characteristics of the Ha 140 both on the water and in the air left something to be desired, and on 21 September

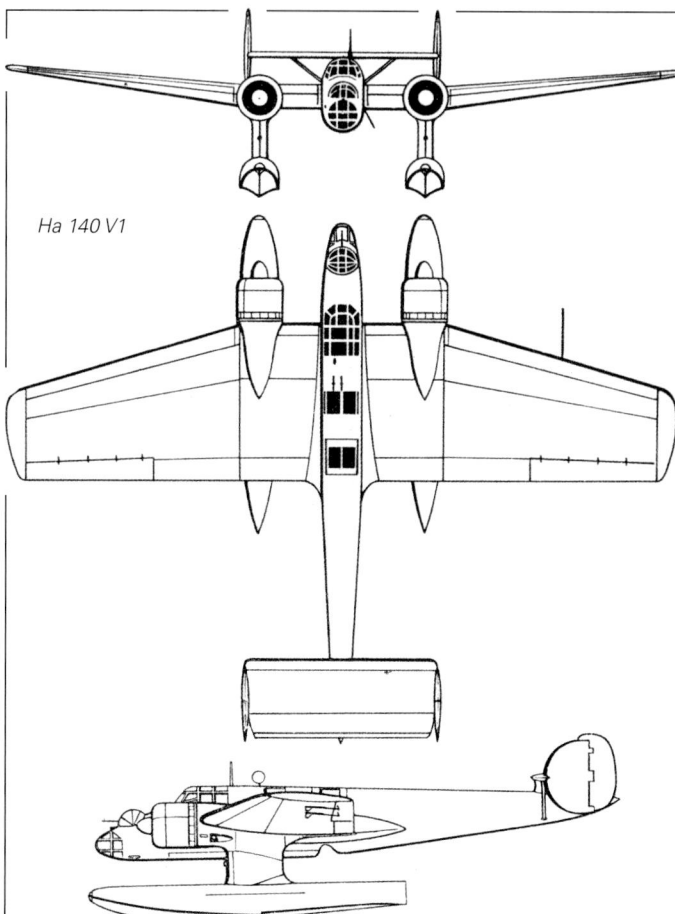

Above: The Ha 140 V3 third prototype (D-AMME), which was completed late in 1938, differed from its predecessors in having a strengthened airframe and slats along the full span of the outer wing panels' leading edges.

Below: The Ha 140 V3 omitted the gun cupola that had been a characteristic feature above the nose of the two earlier prototypes.

Ha 140 V1

The Ha 140 programme was officially ended in September 1939 with the selection of the He 115 for service. The Ha 140 prototypes were then operated by Blohm und Voss for a number of experimental tasks.

1939, the Ha 140 programme was officially terminated.

The Ha 140 V3 was returned to Blohm und Voss for use as an aerodynamic testbed, and before the end of 1939 the aircraft was flying with a reduced-scale model of the vertical tail surfaces of the BV 222 mounted above the fuselage. During the course of 1940, the same aircraft was once again modified, this time to test the novel variable-incidence wing, this venturesome feature being intended for application to the BV 144 medium-range transport under development for DLH. The tubular main load-carrying spar concept of Dr.-Ing. Vogt lent itself admirably to the pivoting of the wing, and the Ha 140 V3 was adapted so that the outboard wing panels could be pivoted through nine degrees by means of two electrically-operated screw jacks. The variable-incidence wing tests conducted with the Ha 140 V3 must

The Ha 140 V1 is seen after being rescued from the water following its mishap. The photograph shows clearly the extent of the damage suffered by the float and engine mounting.

Above: The Ha 140 V1 is seen at Travemünde after the accident in which the forward part of its starboard float buckled upward while the floatplane was alighting on rough water.

have enjoyed a measure of success, as indicated by the placing of an order for two BV 144 prototypes in 1942.

Blohm und Voss Ha 140 V2 specification

Type: three-seat reconnaissance and torpedo-bomber float seaplane
Powerplant: two BMW 132K nine-cylinder radial air-cooled engines each rated at 597 kW (800 hp) for take-off and 619 kW (830 hp) at 1000 m (3,280 ft)
Performance: maximum speed 320 km/h (199 mph) at sea level, 333 km/h (207 mph) at 3000 m (9,840 ft); maximum cruising speed (80 per cent power) 295 km/h (183 mph) at sea level; normal range with 1390 litres (306 Imp gal) fuel 1150 km (715 miles); maximum range with 2365 litres (520 Imp gal) fuel 2000 km (1,242 miles); climb to 3000 m in 11.5 minutes, to 5000 m (16,400 ft) in 39 minutes; service ceiling 5000 m
Weights: empty 6300 kg (13,889 lb); normal loaded 8500 kg (18,739 lb); maximum overload 9230 kg (20,342 lb)
Dimensions: wingspan 22.00 m (72 ft 2⅛ in); length 16.75 m (54 ft 11½ in); height 3.05 m (10 ft 0¼ in); wing area 92.00 m² (990.280 sq ft)
Armament: one 7.9-mm (0.31-in) MG 15 machine-gun in nose cupola and one 7.9-mm MG 15 firing aft from dorsal hatch, plus one 950-kg (2,095-lb) torpedo or four 250-kg (551-lb) bombs housed internally

Blohm und Voss BV 141

Every decade in the history of military aviation has seen its share of the unconventional in aircraft design; warplanes that, in concept or configuration, markedly deviated from what was considered to be orthodox at the time of their debut. One such example was the remarkable BV 141 battlefield reconnaissance aircraft.

Few more unorthodox aircraft appeared in the 1930s than Dr.-Ing. Richard Vogt's asymmetrical **BV 141** short-range reconnaissance and army co-operation machine, which represented a highly novel approach to the problem of endowing a single-engined aircraft with outstanding all-round vision.

Early in 1937, the Reichsluftfahrtministerium (RLM) issued to Arado and Focke-Wulf a specification that called for a short-range reconnaissance aircraft capable of fulfilling the light bomber, low-level attack and smokescreen-laying roles in an emergency. The specification stipulated a three-seat machine, emphasised the need for an outstanding all-round view for the crew members, and demanded 634-671 kW (850-900 hp) for take-off. From an early stage the Arado company's proposal was favoured by the RLM's Technisches Amt, this concern eventually being awarded a development contract for what was to be the totally unsuccessful Ar 198. The Hamburger Flugzeugbau had not been invited by the RLM to tender a proposal, but its technical director, Dr.-Ing. Vogt, had some revolutionary ideas concerning the best way to fulfil the RLM's specification, and accordingly submitted a private-venture proposal.

Radical configuration

The RLM's Technisches Amt had not stipulated that total power should be confined to one engine, but it was tacitly assumed that, for the army co-operation role, no designer would consider using more than one powerplant. Vogt believed that the only way in which adequate all-round vision for reconnaissance purposes could be provided in a single-engined aircraft was to adopt an asymmetrical configuration, the crew being housed in an extensively-glazed nacelle offset to starboard. He also believed that virtue could be derived from necessity, the asymmetrically-mounted crew nacelle cancelling out the airscrew torque that provided every designer of a single-engined aircraft with something of a headache. His proposal to the RLM was, therefore, for an asymmetric

Above: Two of the pre-production batch of BV 141B-0s pose for the camera, the upper aircraft being the seventh aircraft in the series (also known as V15).

The BV 141 was an extremely unorthodox reconnaissance/army co-operation aircraft, its asymmetric configuration being designed to provide the crew with first-class fields of vision. The BV 141 V9 illustrated was the first of the pre-production BV 141B-0 series, which was redesigned and structurally revised, and also had the uprated BMW 801 engine. The whole programme foundered on the type's persistent hydraulic problems. This aircraft was tested at the E-Stelle at Rechlin from May 1941 onwards, joined by other prototypes.

Above: The Ha 141-0 is shown in its original configuration, with a small, stepped crew nacelle. The RLM considered this as not offering sufficient all-round visibility for the battlefield reconnaissance role and a redesign was ordered.

A close-up displays the extensive glazing of the BV 141's crew nacelle, which was increased yet further as the design progressed. The pilot and observer sat side-by-side, with the observer positioned to starboard.

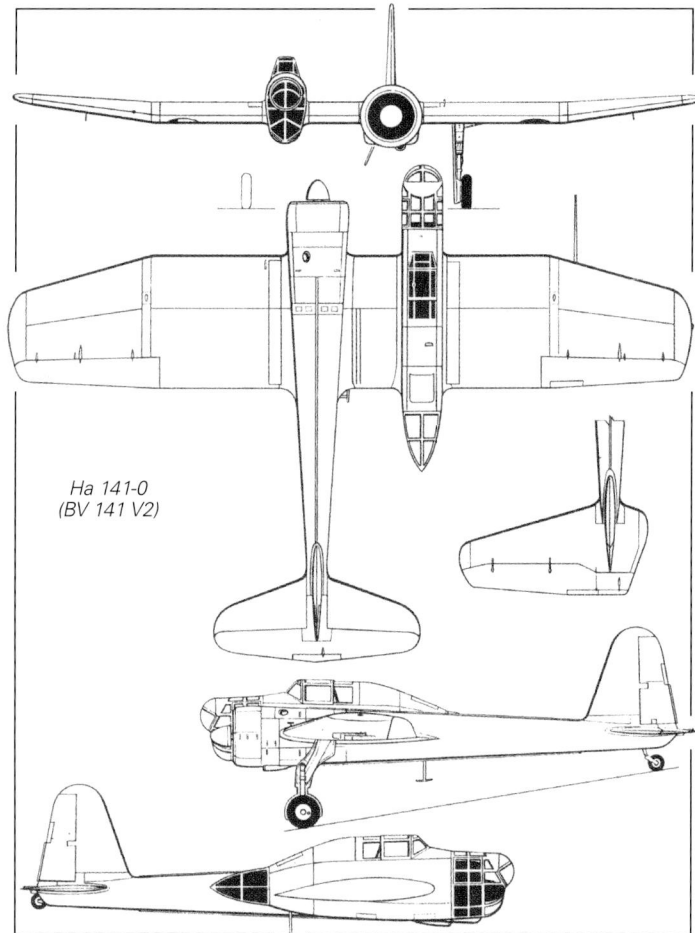

Ha 141-0
(BV 141 V2)

aircraft, but as Arado had already begun construction of the Ar 198, it was hardly surprising that little official interest was evinced in this unconventional design. However, Ernst Udet, newly-appointed chief of the Development Section of the Technisches Amt, showed Vogt some encouragement and, the Hamburger Flugzeugbau management having agreed to finance the project, work began on the strange prototype that, designated **Ha 141-0** and registered D-ORJE, flew for the first time on 25 February 1938.

Apart from slight over-sensitivity of the control surfaces and minor undercarriage oscillation, the unorthodox Ha 141-0 proved singularly trouble-free and, after Udet himself had flight tested the prototype, an official contract was placed for three prototypes. The existing prototype was not covered by the contract, but after somewhat protracted negotiations, the RLM agreed to accept the machine as one of the three for which it had contracted, and D-ORJE was promptly allocated Werk Nummer 172 and eventually redesignated **BV 141 V2** when the name of the company was changed from Hamburger Flugzeugbau to Abteilung Flugzeugbau der Schiffswerft Blohm und Voss, while the second prototype became the first official prototype as the **BV 141 V1** (Werk Nr 171).

The stepped cockpit of the BV 141 V2 (alias Ha 141-0) did not prove acceptable to the RLM and, in consequence, the entire crew nacelle was redesigned for the BV 141 V1, the new nacelle following closely the design of that of the Focke-Wulf Fw 189 that was under development simultaneously, and featuring copious glazing comprising a multitude of flat panels. Provision was made for two fixed forward-firing 7.9-mm (0.31-in) machine-guns and two hand-held aft-firing guns of similar calibre (although the first aircraft actually to feature armament was the **BV 141 V3**), and underwing racks were provided for four 50-kg (110-lb) bombs. The overall dimensions of the BV 141 V1 were slightly increased by comparison with the V2, span being extended from 15.00 m to 15.10 m (49 ft 2½ in to 49 ft 6½ in),

The Ha 141-0 prototype looked quite different from the aircraft that followed. The stepped crew nacelle seated the pilot above, with the observer in the nose. Although the aircraft flew well, the German authorities were wary of this oddity, but nonetheless allowed the programme to continue in a significantly revised form.

Blohm und Voss BV 141

*Although **D-OTTO** followed the Ha 141-0, it was deemed to be the 'official' prototype, and was given the **BV 141 V1** designation. It first flew in September 1938 but soon encountered hydraulics problems.*

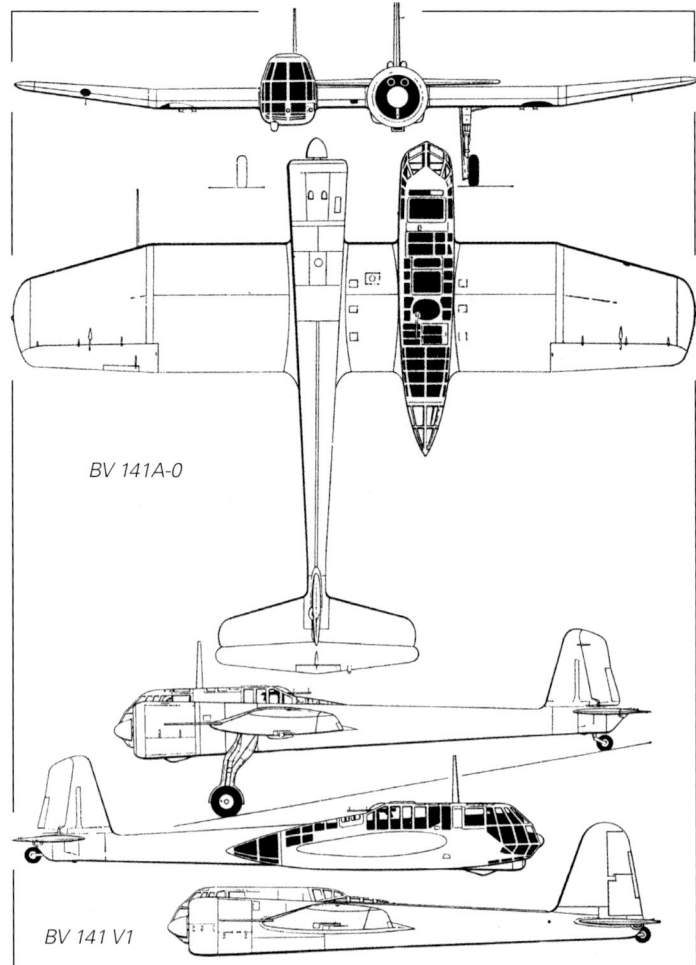

BV 141A-0

BV 141 V1

resulting in a wing area of 41.80 m² (449.93 sq ft) compared with 41.50 m² (446.7 sq ft), while length was raised from 11.10 m to 11.40 m (36 ft 5 in to 37 ft 4¾ in).

Registered D-OTTO, the BV 141 V1 weighed 3090 kg (6,812 lb) empty and 3830 kg (8,441 lb) in normal loaded condition, and was rolled out for initial flight trials in September 1938. Early in its test programme problems with the hydraulic system were encountered, and on 5 October 1938 a forced landing was made in a ploughed field with the mainwheel legs only half extended, the starboard wing suffering considerable damage. Fortunately, the BV 141 V3 (D-OLGA) was available to participate in the flight test programme shortly after the V1 had come to grief, and this aircraft (Werk Nr 359) was considered to all intents and purposes a production prototype.

Pre-production changes

In order to improve directional stability, the BV 141 V3's fuselage had been lengthened to 12.15 m (39 ft 10⅓ in), and overall span was once more increased slightly to 15.35 m (50 ft 4⅓ in), while to improve ground stability the wheel track was widened from 4.90 to 5.15 m (16 ft 1 in to 16 ft 10¾ in). The crew nacelle accommodated the pilot to port with the observer to starboard, and the observer's seat was attached to a track so that when pushed to its forward extremity it enabled him to operate the bomb sight, the radio equipment being situated at the aft end of the seat track. The observer also operated the camera and, in an emergency, the upper aft-firing machine-gun. The entire nacelle was of minimum section, measuring only 1.20 m (3 ft 11¼ in) from side to side, and 1.50 m (4 ft 11 in) from top to bottom, and terminated in a pointed cone housing a similar 7.9-mm MG 15 machine-gun to that mounted in the upper position. Of Focke-Wulf design, this rear position could be rotated through 360 degrees, the gunner being prone over the wing trailing edge.

The tailplane was almost symmetrical, and trim tabs were fitted in the elevators, rudder and port aileron, and the ailerons were balanced by means of two spoilers on each outer wing section, these being interconnected with the ailerons. All control surfaces were actuated by rods, the flaps and undercarriage being hydraulically operated. Power was provided by

*Above: **D-OLGA** was the third **BV 141** prototype, and was considered a production-representative article for the **BV 141A** series. It embodied a number of new features, including an increased-span wing and wider-track undercarriage.*

*Left: Seen in full warpaint and '**BL+AA**' codes, the **BV 141 V3** was demonstrated to the RLM, exhibiting the type's excellent handling qualities. Following these successful trials the RLM was persuaded, possibly against its better judgment, to continue with the **BV 141**, resulting in a further five pre-series **BV 141As** being ordered. This raised production of BMW 132-powered aircraft to eight.*

One of the BV 141A prototypes shows off its unique configuration. The A series was fitted with the BMW 132N, which the RLM thought underpowered. The BMW 801 that was introduced for the BV 141B brought with it unpleasant vibration.

a nine-cylinder BMW 132N radial air-cooled engine offering maximum power of 645 kW (865 hp) for one minute at sea level and 716 kW (960 hp) at 3000 m (9,842 ft), and this was fed from a 490-litre (108-Imp gal) fuel tank immediately aft of the engine firewall. Apart from the two fixed forward-firing MG 17s and two aft-firing MG 15s on flexible mountings, the BV 141 V3 had four FTC 50 bomb racks and an automatic camera (Rb 20/30, 21/18, 50/18 or 50/30).

Even the RLM, which had viewed the BV 141 with the utmost suspicion from the outset, was forced to admit that, despite its highly unorthodox appearance, the aircraft possessed extremely docile handling characteristics and fully met the original specification. Somewhat reluctantly, an order was placed for a pre-series of five aircraft (BV 141A-01 to 05), but these machines were also allocated Versuchs numbers, and thus the **BV 141A-01**, which was registered D-OLLE, was also known as the **BV 141 V4**. This aircraft (Werk Nr 360) joined the test programme early in 1939. Wingspan and area were slightly increased, from 15.35 m to 15.45 m (50 ft 4⅓ in to 50 ft 8¼ in) and from 42.50 m² to 42.85 m² (457.47 sq ft to 461.23 sq ft), but empty weight was actually reduced from 3200 to 3105 kg (7,064 to 6,845 lb), normal loaded weight remaining constant at 3900 kg (8,598 lb). The Achilles' heel of the BV 141 remained its hydraulic system, however, and shortly after commencing flight testing the BV 141 V4 suffered an accident when one mainwheel leg locked down and the other remained up during a landing. As this aircraft was intended for trials at the Erprobungsstelle Rechlin there was an inevitable delay in the initiation of the official evaluation programme.

The remaining four BV 141A-0 pre-series aircraft, the **V5** (Werk Nr 361), the **V6** (Werk Nr 362), the **V7** (Werk Nr 363), and the **V8** (Werk Nr 364), were completed to schedule and were virtually identical to the V4, the only change of any importance being the provision of a new upper defensive position that replaced the sliding hatch.

The official flight test programme was completed at Rechlin with the BV 141 V5 in January 1940, and the E-Stelle pilots' reports were generally favourable. For low-level bombing a special bomb sight had been developed and installed in the V5, and 13 bombing trials were undertaken, a total of 58 bombs being dropped from various altitudes. The BV 141 V3 also participated in bombing trials at Rechlin and Tarnewitz. The Luftwaffe's High Command, the OKT, displayed little enthusiasm for this 'oddity', and on 4 April 1940 succeeded in persuading the RLM to cancel its plans for large-scale production of the BV 141A.

Re-engined version

The OKL's lack of enthusiasm for the BV 141 resulted primarily from the unorthodox appearance of the aircraft, and in casting around for a valid technical reason for the rejection of the Blohm und Voss machine, it decided to base its decision on the fact that the BV 141A-0 was marginally

Above: D-OLLE was the first of the BV 141A-0 pre-production machines, featuring a slight increase in wingspan. The aircraft is seen after a hydraulics failure on landing, a problem that dogged the BV 141. The aircraft later received the codes 'GL+AH'.

Below: The adoption of the BMW 801 radial of greater power required considerable redesign in the BV 141B series. Among the most notable features was the tailplane offset to port. This is the prototype of the B series (V9), which first flew on 9 January 1941.

Blohm und Voss Bv 141

Blohm und Voss BV 141A-0
This is the BV 141A-04, the seventh prototype of the BV 141A series, depicted carrying four SC 50 bombs on the underwing racks. From the side the A could be recognised by its large vertical tail, as opposed to the smaller unit adopted for the BV 141B. The most obvious differences, however, were the horizontal tailplanes, which were symmetrical in the earlier aircraft, and the outer wing panels, which had pronounced taper on the leading-edge only in the BV 141A.

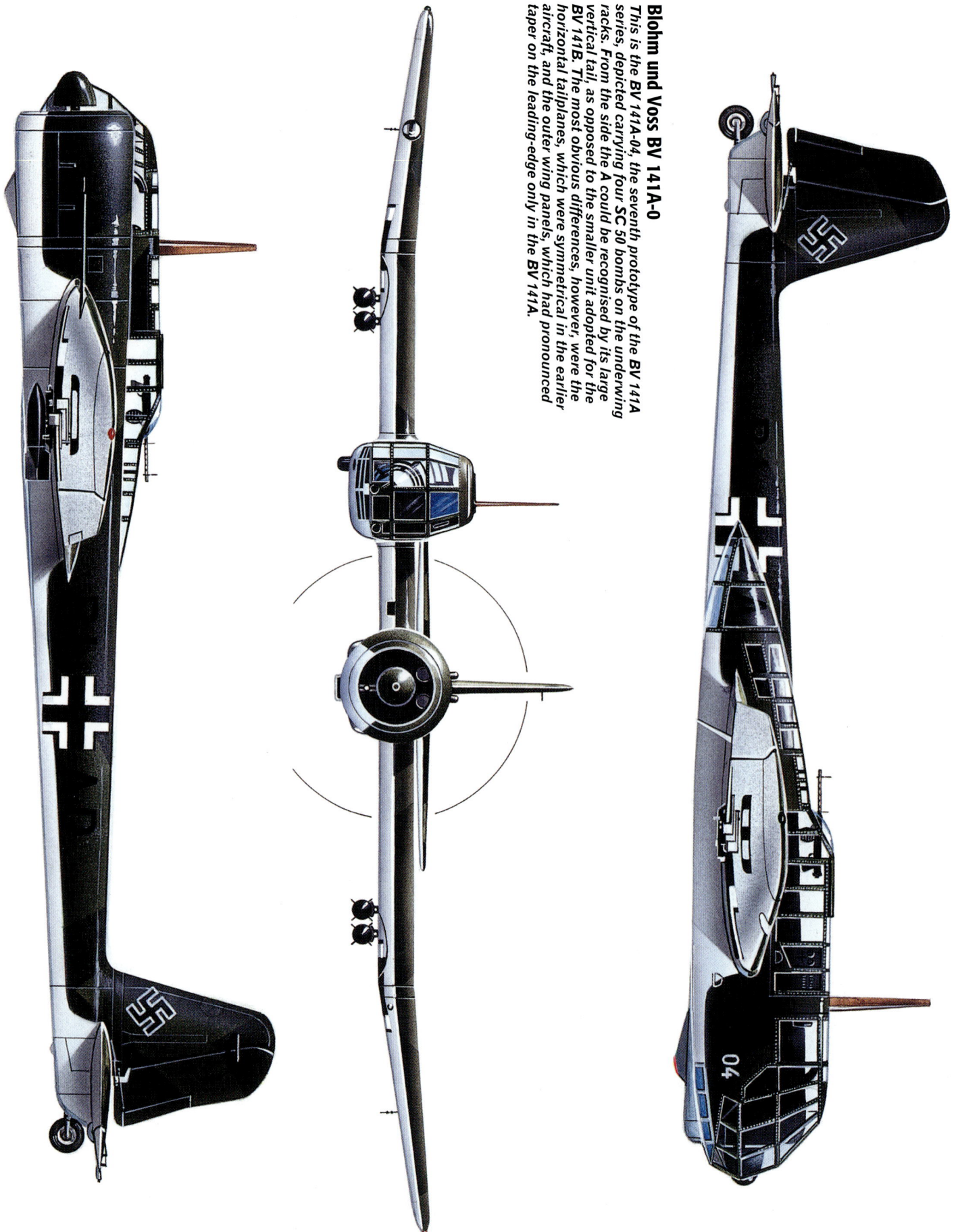

140

The BV 141B was nowhere near as pleasant to fly as the A series, with heavy vibration levels showing up under static tests. The offset tailplane had first been tested on the V2, and was introduced to increase the field of fire available to the rear gunner.

underpowered. Dr. Vogt had already foreseen the possibility that more power would be demanded, and as early as January 1939, his team had begun the redesign of the basic aircraft to take the more powerful BMW 801. A complete structural redesign was undertaken, and the final mock-up of what was to be designated the **BV 141B** was inspected and approved by an RLM commission on 14 February 1940. Less than a year later, on 9 January 1941, the first of five pre-series **BV 141B-0** aircraft, the **BV 141 V9** (NC+QZ), flew for the first time. At this time, Blohm und Voss held a firm contract for only five BV 141B-0 aircraft, but the RLM had taken options on a further five pre-production machines and 10 production **BV 141B-1**s.

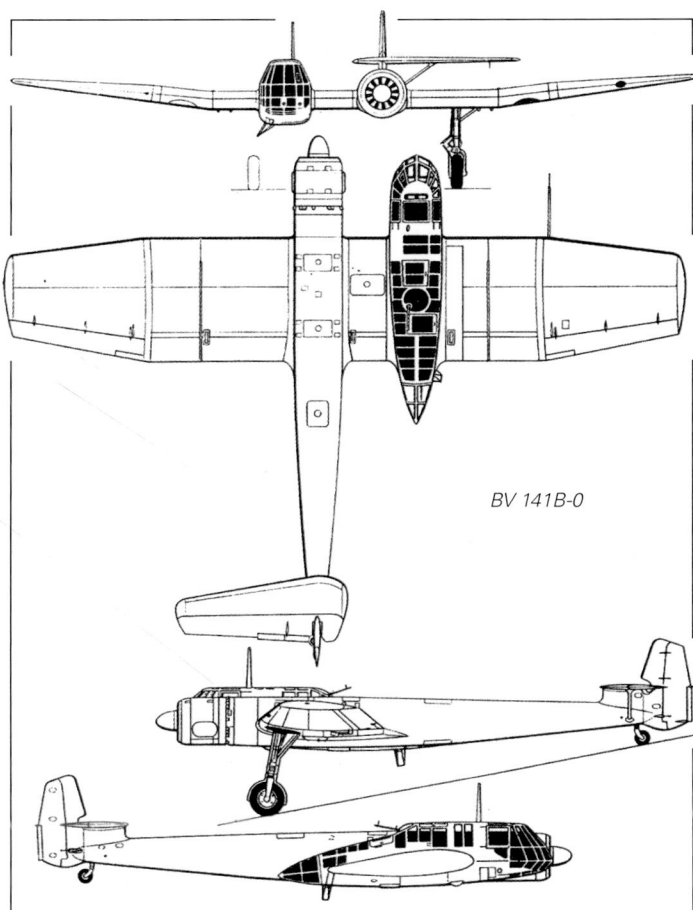

BV 141B-0

It was soon obvious that the BV 141B did not share the pleasant characteristics of its predecessor. Static vibration trials in November 1940 had revealed the fact that substantial strengthening of certain components was called for, and it had been found that major modifications had to be made to the tail assembly supports, the undercarriage and the control system. Static tests had been continuously plagued by hydraulic troubles, problems with the undercarriage actuating mechanism and when engine runs had begun, with the BMW 801 powerplant itself. By the time that flight trials began, the results of vibration tests had still to be fully evaluated and, in consequence, the BV 141 V9 had to be limited to a maximum speed of 450 km/h (280 mph). Aileron trimming proved ineffective, the ailerons themselves proved oversensitive, while functional defects in the hydraulic system and numerous other troubles disrupted the entire test schedule.

Completion of the remaining four BV 141B-0 aircraft was slowed pending the satisfactory outcome of modifications to the BV 141 V9. By comparison with the BV 141 A, B-series aircraft featured enlarged dimensions, equi-tapered outboard wing panels were introduced, the oval section of the fuselage gave place to a circular section over its entire length, and the tail surfaces were entirely redesigned. Earlier, the BV 141 V2 had tested a further innovation – an asymmetric tailplane. In order to improve the rear gunner's field of fire, the starboard half of the tailplane had been removed and the port half increased in size, and as this modification resulted in no noticeable deterioration in handling qualities, the asymmetric tailplane was adopted for the BV 141B.

Official testing

The BV 141 V9 was eventually delivered to the E-Stelle at Rechlin in May 1941, and it was joined there by the **V10** (NC+RA) that had finally flown on 1 June 1941 after having gathered dust for some three months in the Blohm und Voss plant while the delivery of an airscrew was awaited. Constant minor failures troubled the official evaluation programme, and when the seventh BV 141B, the **V15** (NC+RF), was delivered to Tarnewitz for armament trials, it was discovered that the gun ports were too short, and that cordite fumes filled the cockpit when the guns were fired. As might be gathered, Blohm und Voss had received approval to build a further five pre-production aircraft (V14 to V18; NC+RE to NC+RI). The last was not delivered until 15 May 1943.

In the autumn of 1941, the second BV 141B, the V10,

Blohm und Voss BV 141

Tailplane
The entire tail surfaces of the BV 141B were redesigned, including the adoption of an asymmetric taiplane. A vestigial section was retained on the starboard side. This configuration was tested on the BV 141 V2 (the original Ha 141-0 prototype), and showed no detriment in handling. However, when tests of the BV 141B got under way the supporting strut was found to require strengthening.

Blohm und Voss BV 141B-0

This is the seventh BV 141B-0 pre-production aircraft (BV 141 V15), as seen when it was delivered to Tarnewitz for armament trials. During gun-firing tests, it was discovered that the gun ports were too short, meaning the cockpit rapidly filled up with cordite smoke. The B series was considerably different to the A series, with a bigger engine, redesigned fuselage structure, larger dimensions, equi-taper outboard wing sections and the tailplane offset to port. This last improvement had been introduced to provide the gunner with an almost uninterrupted field of fire from the rear of the cockpit. The gun smoke and other problems haunted the BV 141B programme throughout, and by the time the BV 141 was ready to enter service its role was being adequately filled by the Fw 189.

Configuration
The remarkable configuration of the BV 141 was adopted to provide the best possible view for a battlefield reconnaissance aircraft with a single-engined aircraft. It also negated much of the effect of propeller torque, making landing and takeoff easier for the pilot.

Bombload
BV 141s were fitted with two bomb racks under each wing just inboard of the outer panel joint. Each could carry a single 50-kg (110-lb) SC 50 general-purpose bomb.

Forward-firing guns
For strafing of ground targets and providing a measure of air-to-air capability against other observation aircraft, the BV 141 had two MG 17 7.9-mm machine-guns firing forward from the crew nacelle.

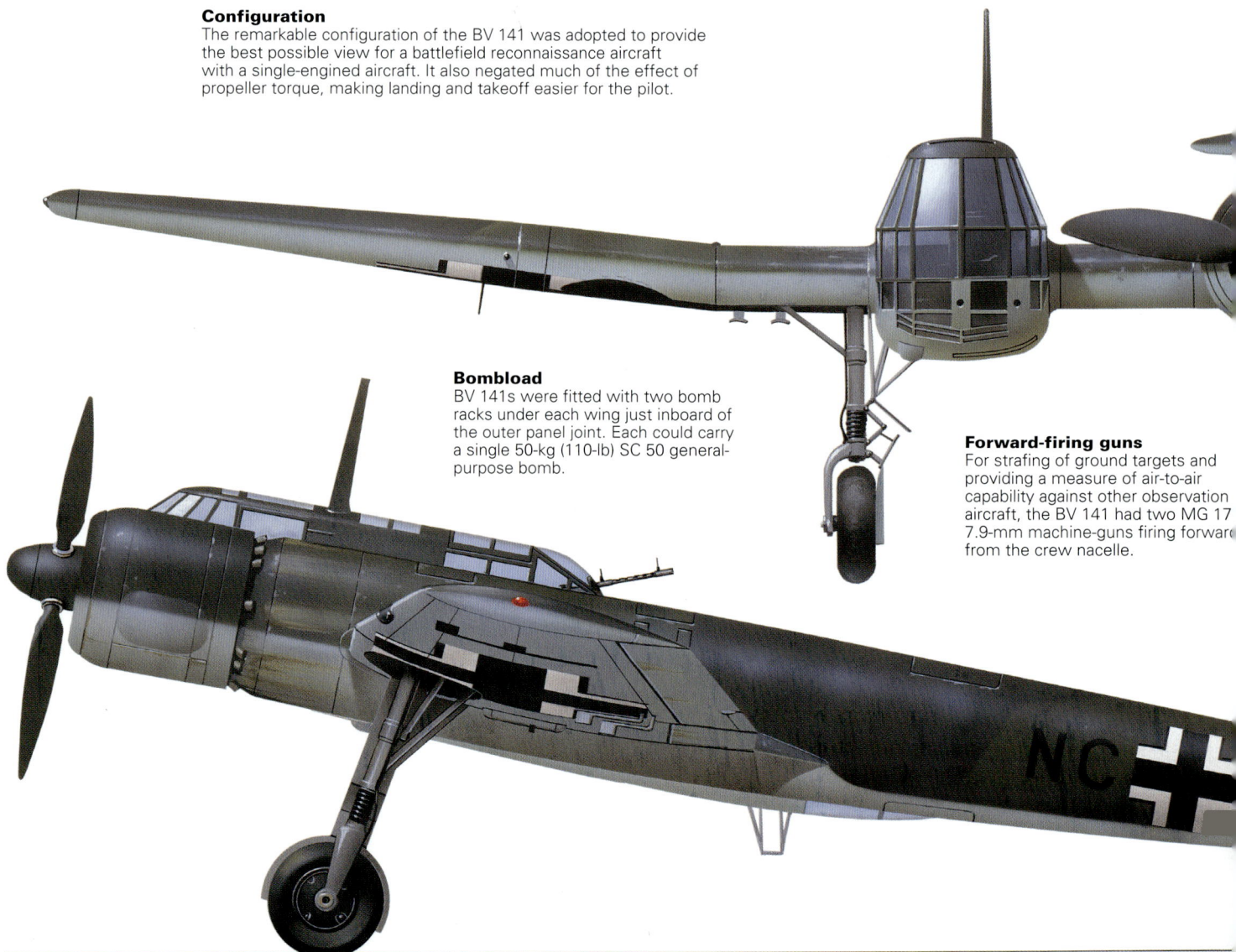

Fuselage redesign

As well as the more obvious redesigns, the BV 141B introduced a circular-section fuselage instead of the oval-section structure of the BV 141A. The vertical fin was also changed to a smaller surface incorporating a cut-out for the asymmetric elevator section.

Powerplant

BMW received a licence to build the nine-cylinder Pratt & Whitney Hornet radial in 1928 and soon began its own development. The BMW 132 was the result, which entered production in 1933. The engine's best-known application was in the Junkers Ju 52/3m transport.

Defensive armament

The BV 141 had two rear-facing weapons, both MG 15 7.9-mm machine-guns. One was mounted in a dorsal dome and the other in the rear of the nacelle. The whole tailcone of the nacelle could be rotated through 360°.

Crew nacelle

The BV 141's nacelle was based on the design of the Focke-Wulf Fw 189. It accommodated a crew of three, comprising pilot, observer/dorsal gunner and radio operator/rear gunner.

Wing planform

In its original A-series form the BV 141 had a taperless centre-section and marked taper on the leading edge of the outer, dihedralled panels. In the BV 141B the outer panels were replaced with new equi-taper units and revised ailerons. The new layout ruined the sweet handling of the earlier variant, in particular the ailerons, which were found to be over-sensitive.

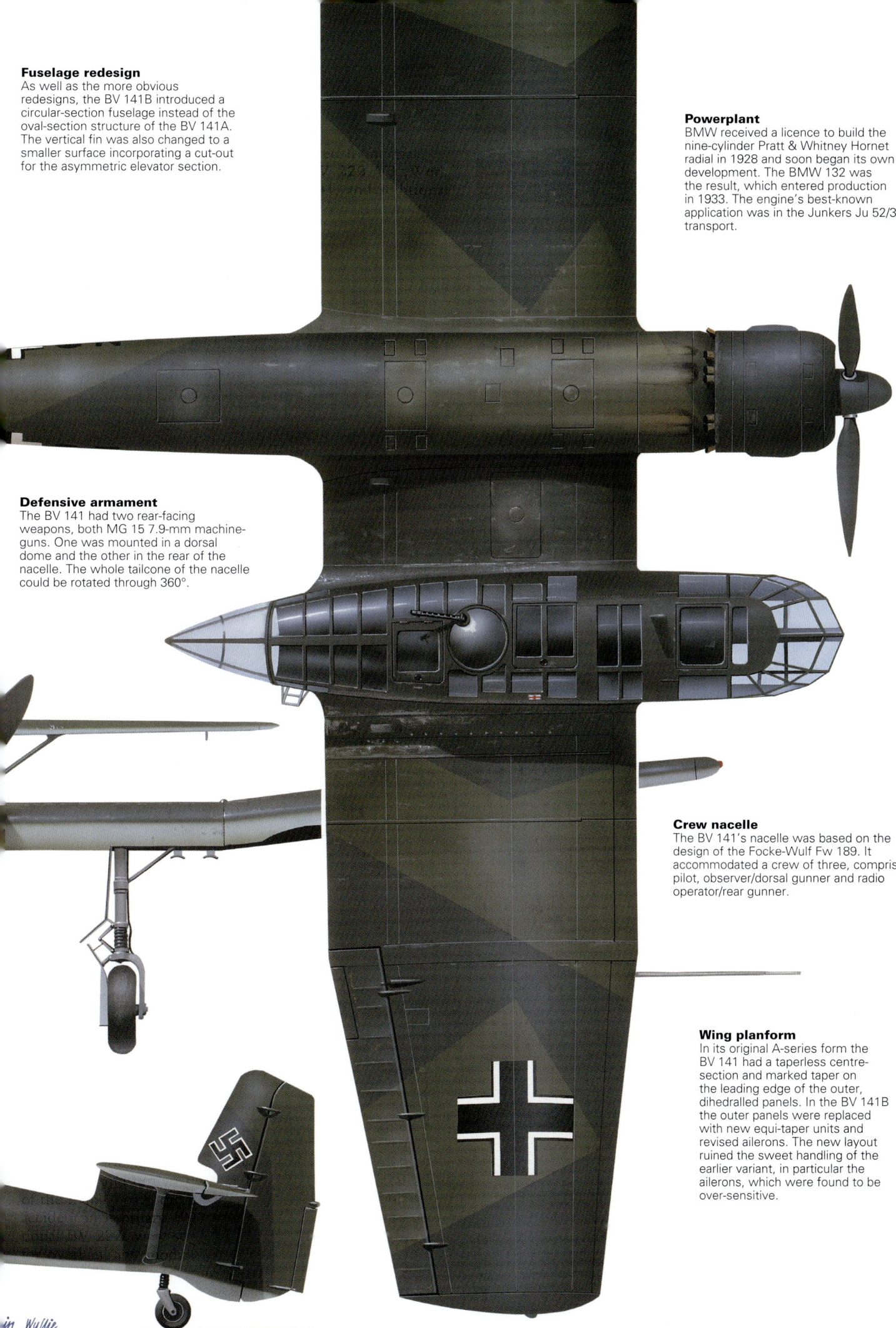

in Wyllie

Blohm und Voss BV 141

Above: The crew nacelle culminated in a slender glazed cone in which the rear gun was housed. In the battlefield reconnaissance role the BV 141 used visual observation by the crew, and also had a photo-reconnaissance capability.

Right: The front end of the crew nacelle incorporated the apertures for the two forward-firing guns. Note the pilot's seat and the passage to the aft of the nacelle that allowed the observer to access the dorsal gun.

had been delivered to Aufklärungsschule 1 at Grossenhain, Saxony, for trials under service conditions, and shortly afterwards, the General-Luftzeugmeister issued instructions that sufficient BV 141Bs should be delivered to form at least one operational squadron on the Eastern Front.

Plans for the Sonderstaffel BV 141 were finally cancelled by the General Staff in the spring of 1942, as, by that time, the role for which the BV 141B had been foreseen was being adequately fulfilled by the reliable twin-engined Focke-Wulf Fw 189. This decision was undoubtedly also influenced by the teething troubles being suffered by the BV 141, and a third motivation was probably the desire to ensure deliveries of the Focke-Wulf Fw 200 Condor, some 80 per cent of available Blohm und Voss assembly shop space at Hamburg-Finkenwerder having been taken over for the Fw 200 after damage to the Focke-Wulf plant in a bombing raid. Nevertheless, eight of the 10 planned BV 141B-1 production aircraft were completed, although they were not used operationally.

Blohm und Voss BV 141A-04 (V7) specification
Type: three-seat tactical reconnaissance and army co-operation aircraft
Powerplant: one BMW 132N nine-cylinder radial air-cooled engine rated at 645 kW (865 hp) at sea level and 716 kW (960 hp) at 3000 m (9,840 ft)
Performance: maximum speed 340 km/h (211 mph) at sea level, 400 km/h (248 mph) at 3800 m (12,467 ft); maximum cruising speed 310 km/h (193 mph) at sea level, 365 km/h (227 mph) at 4500 m (14,765 ft); maximum range 1140 km (708 miles); service ceiling 9000 m (29,530 ft)
Weights: empty equipped 3167 kg (6,982 lb); loaded 3900 kg (8,598 lb)
Dimensions: wingspan 15.45 m (50 ft 8¼ in); length 12.15 m (39 ft 10½ in); height 4.10 m (13 ft 5½ in); wing area 42.85 m² (461.23 sq ft)
Armament: two fixed forward-firing 7.9-mm (0.31-in) MG 17 machine-guns and two aft-firing 7.9-mm. MG 15 machine-guns on flexible mountings; (offensive) four 50-kg (110-lb) bombs on underwing racks

Blohm und Voss BV 141B-02 (V10) specification
Type: three-seat tactical reconnaissance and army co-operation aircraft
Powerplant: one BMW 801A-0 14-cylinder radial air-cooled engine rated at 1163 kW (1,560 hp) for take-off
Performance: maximum speed 368 km/h (229 mph) at sea level, 438 km/h (272 mph) at 5000 m (16,400 ft); normal range 1200 km (745 miles); maximum range 1900 km (1,180 miles); service ceiling 10000 m (32,810 ft)
Weights: empty equipped 4700 kg (10,362 lb); normal loaded 5700 kg (12,566 lb); maximum take-off 6100 kg (13,448 lb)
Dimensions: wingspan 17.45 m (57 ft 3⅓ in); length 13.95 m (45 ft 9¼ in); height 3.60 m (11 ft 9¾ in); wing area 52.90 m² (569.41 sq ft)
Armament: two fixed forward firing 7.9-mm (0.31-in) MG 17 machine-guns and two aft-firing 7.9-mm MG 15 machine-guns on flexible mountings; (offensive) four 50-kg (110-lb) SC 50 bombs on underwing racks

The BV 141 programme was cut short before the type could be used in combat, but sufficient BV 141B-1s were built to begin the equipment of a special trials unit. In the meantime, the Luftwaffe had adopted the Focke Wulf Fw 189 for battlefield reconnaissance.

A small number of BV 141s were found by the Allies when they occupied Germany, and one was returned to the United Kingdom for examination, although it was not flown. This wrecked example is the eighth and final production BV 141B-1.

Blohm und Voss BV 142

The BV 142 was schemed as a long-range mailplane, but was then adapted as a strategic and maritime reconnaissance aircraft. With military equipment the BV 142 was underpowered, however, and therefore offered only indifferent performance. The type was withdrawn from service in 1942.

The success that attended the initial flight trials of the Ha 139 long-range floatplane in 1937 prompted the Hamburger Flugzeugbau to evolve a land-based version of the basic design using as many components of the floatplane as was feasible.

Intended as a long-range mailplane to operate over distances up to 4400 km (2,735 miles), this **Ha 142** landplane was of all-metal construction, and employed a circular-section semi-monocoque fuselage and an inverted-gull wing similar to those of the Ha 139. The parallel-chord wing was of the extended-span type applied to the Ha 139 V3. It was built up on the usual large-diameter tubular load-carrying spar tapered in thickness to meet the required loads, and its centre section was sealed to form five tanks carrying 6360 litres (1,399 Imp gal) of fuel. The centre section, which featured marked anhedral between the fuselage and inboard engine nacelles, had flush-riveted metal skinning and carried the four sections of the hydraulically operated flaps, and the outboard wing panels were fabric-covered. The crew comprised the pilot, co-pilot, navigator and radio operator, and the flight deck was separated from the small mail compartment by the centre-section spar. The twin floats of the Ha 139 were replaced by hydraulically operated rearward-retracting twin-wheel main undercarriage members and a retractable twin-wheel tail member.

No commercial success

The **Ha 142 V1** first prototype (D-AHFB *Pollux*) was first flown on 11 October 1938, and was followed within a few weeks by the **BV 142 V2** second prototype (D-ABUV *Kastor*), the name Hamburger Flugzeugbau having been abandoned by this time. Two further prototypes joined the test programme in the spring and summer of 1939, it being intended that all four aircraft would be operated on transatlantic mail-carrying flights by Deutsche Lufthansa (DLH). After the provision of additional air intakes beneath the engines and the replacement of the single-piece undercarriage doors by three-piece doors, the Ha 142 V1 was delivered to DLH. However, after a few exploratory flights DLH returned the

The origins of the BV 142 in the Ha 139 seaplane can be seen in the inverted gull wing, whose lower angles carried the twin float alighting gear in the original seaplane model.

BV 142s to Blohm und Voss, plans for the commercial operation of the aircraft being abandoned.

Shortly after the beginning of World War II, the idea of adapting the BV 142 for the long-range maritime and strategic reconnaissance tasks was conceived, and the second prototype was selected for trial adaption. As the BV 142 was intended to operate far outside the range of fighter protection in its new role, emphasis was placed on defensive armament. The fuselage nose was elongated, terminating in an extensively glazed compartment for the bombardier and a mounting for a single 7.9-mm (0.31-in) MG 15 machine-gun. An electrically operated dorsal turret, also mounting a single MG 15 gun, was introduced aft of the wing trailing

Above: With heavy, drag-producing armament grafted onto an airframe designed for civil purposes, the BV 142 conversions were overloaded and offered only indifferent performance.

The BV 142 V2/U1 was a six-seat maritime and strategic reconnaissance conversion of the BV 142 V2 mailplane with a longer, glazed nose, a dorsal gun turret, two beam guns and a ventral gun gondola.

Blohm Und Voss BV 142

Left: Both the first and second prototypes were evaluated briefly by DLH for the mailplane role. Here the V2 is seen with engines running and the upper hatch open. The latter provided a ready-made position for upper defensive armament when the aircraft was militarised for Luftwaffe service.

Above: The Ha 142 V1 prototype was initially evaluated by DLH with the civil registration D-AHFB and name Pollux, but was later adapted as a long-range reconnaissance platform for use by 2./Aufklärungsstaffel Oberbefehlshaber der Luftwaffe.

Above: As with other aircraft designed by Richard Vogt, the BV 142 had a tubular main spar whose central part was sealed to create five tanks carrying 6360 litres (1,399 Imp gal) of fuel.

edge, and the ventral cupola of an He 111H-6 was fitted, this providing a housing for a similar weapon. Ports were provided in the waist of the fuselage for two MG 15 beam-firing guns, although MG 81Z twin guns were later fitted to the beam positions. The mail compartment immediately aft of the main spar was adapted as a bomb bay, dictating the provision of a number of external stiffeners on the forward fuselage.

As there was no provision for access to the rear fuselage from the flight deck, a trap in the upper fuselage decking provided entry and egress for the dorsal and ventral gunners. The crew complement was increased to six, the navigator doubling in the role of bombardier, and the remainder of the crew comprising the pilot, co-pilot, radio operator and two gunners. The rudimentary bomb bay carried only an extremely modest load — around 500 kg (1,102 lb) maximum — and extensive radio and navigational equipment, the so-called Transozean-Funkanlage, was installed.

Designated **BV 142 V2/U1** (PC+BC), the first conversion was completed in the spring of 1940 and delivered during the following autumn to 2./Aufkl.St.Ob.d.L., being attached directly to the Headquarters of Luftflotte 3. The first prototype was converted in a similar fashion to become the **BV 142 V1/U1** (PC+BB), and plans existed to convert the remaining two prototypes. In the meantime, however, limited transport capacity had necessitated the use of these aircraft in the invasion of Denmark and Norway, the **BV 142**

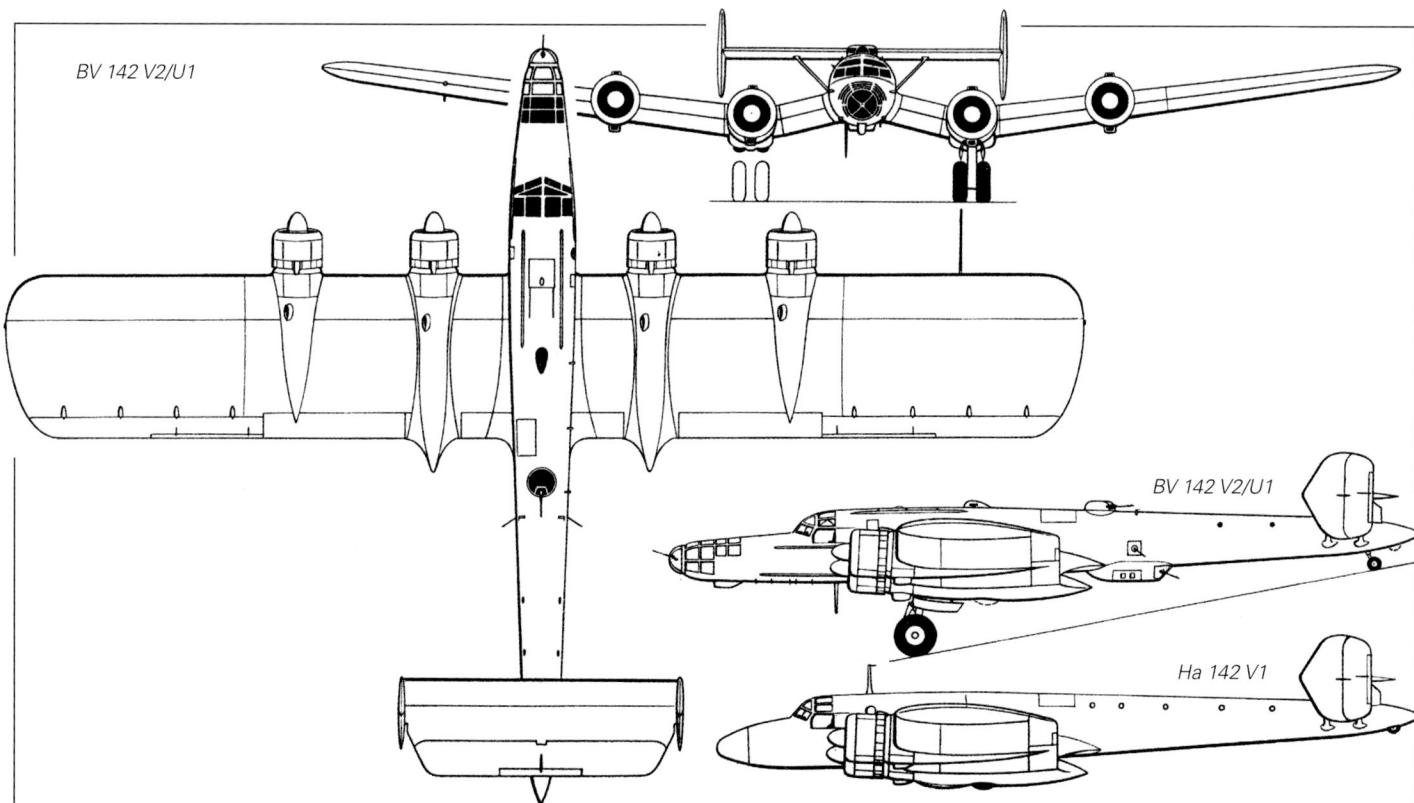

BV 142 V2/U1

BV 142 V2/U1

Ha 142 V1

Left: The BV 142 was not successful in the maritime patrol role for which it was subsequently modified. Its performance was insufficient and its overall structure – particularly the undercarriage – was not strong enough to permit operations with a full load.

V3 (D-ATTA *Burgenland*) and **BV 142 V4** operating in concert with a miscellany of other types (e.g. Ju 89, Ju 90 and Fw 200B) with K.Gr.z.b.V. 105 under Fliegerkorps X, and their ultimate fate is uncertain. The number of sorties operated by the two converted BV 142s was limited by their vulnerability, their performance when carrying a full warload being appreciably below that originally anticipated, and by 1942 the aircraft had been withdrawn from service. A scheme existed to employ these aircraft as launching platforms for the Blohm und Voss GT 1200C guided torpedo, but there is no evidence to indicate that this proposal saw fruition.

Blohm und Voss BV 142 V2/U1 specification
Type: six-seat maritime and strategic reconnaissance aircraft
Powerplant: four BMW 13H-1 air-cooled nine-cylinder radial engines each rated at 656 kW (880 hp) for take-off
Performance: maximum speed 373 km/h (232 mph) at sea level; maximum cruising speed 325 km/h (202 mph) at 2000 m (6,560 ft); initial climb rate 400 m (1,312 ft) per minute; service ceiling 9000 m (29,5230 ft); maximum range 3900 km (2,425 miles) without bomb load
Weights: empty equipped 11080 kg (24,427 lb); maximum take-off 16560 kg (36,508 lb)
Dimensions: wingspan 29.53 m (96 ft 10¾ in); length 20.48 m (67 ft 2¼ in); height 4.44 m (14 ft 6¾ in); wing area 130.0 m² (1,399.3 sq ft)
Armament: (defensive) one 7.9-mm (0.31-in) MG 15 trainable machine-gun in each of nose, ventral and two beam positions, and one 7.9-mm (0.31-in) MG 15 trainable machine-gun in the electrically operated dorsal turret; (offensive) four 100-kg (220-lb) or eight 50-kg (110-lb) bombs carried internally

Below: All four BV 142s served with the Luftwaffe, two as transports and two for reconnaissance. Any hopes of developing the type further for a military career were dashed by the successful transformation of the Fw 200 Condor into a viable military aircraft. As early as January 1940 Blohm und Voss concluded that the BV 142 was not up to a military task. The aircraft were probably all scrapped during 1942.

Blohm und Voss BV 144

The BV 144 was designed as a medium airliner for service after Germany's supposed victory in World War II. With development and prototype entrusted to the Breguet factory at Bayonne in occupied France, progress was slow, and only the first prototype had been flown by the time of the Allied liberation of France.

In 1940, when German fortunes in World War II were very much in the ascendant, Deutsche Lufthansa began to plan its post-war operations and foresaw a requirement for an 18-seat airliner to replace the Junkers Ju 52/3m. Developed to meet such a specification, the **BV 144** was a high-wing monoplane of all-metal construction with retractable tricycle landing gear and the powerplant of two BMW 801MA radial engines. Its internal layout provided accommodation for two pilots, a radio operator and 18 to 23 passengers. The cabin included a toilet compartment, and there were forward and aft cargo holds.

The design featured a number of innovative features, of which the most notable was the variable-incidence wing.

This could be rotated about its tubular main spar to change the angle of attack by up to 9°.

Two prototypes were ordered and, after the surrender of France in June 1940, the project was transferred to Breguet's factory near Bayonne, where the **BV 144 V1** initial prototype was completed and flown for the first time before the liberation of France. Although French development continued for a while after the German withdrawal, the project was eventually discontinued.

Blohm und Voss BV 144 V1 specification
Type: medium-range airliner
Powerplant: two BMW 801MA air-cooled 14-cylinder radial engines each rated at 1193 kW (1,600 hp) for take-off
Performance: maximum speed 470 km/h (292 mph) at optimum altitude; service ceiling 9100 m (29,855 ft); range 1500 km (932 miles)
Weight: maximum take-off 13000 kg (28,660 lb)
Dimensions: wingspan 27.00 m (88 ft 7 in); length 21.80 m (71 ft 6¼ in); wing area 88.00 m² (947.25 sq ft)

The Blohm und Voss BV 144 medium-range airliner for Lufthansa had an ingenious variable-incidence wing to improve passenger comfort and aircraft control at take-off and landing. The sole prototype was evaluated in French markings after the liberation.

Blohm und Voss BV 155

Following the cancellation of the German carrier programme, the Messerschmitt Me 155 naval fighter was reworked as a land-based warplane, ultimately providing the basis for a high-altitude interceptor. The project was taken over and adapted by Blohm und Voss, which completed one prototype with two more nearly finished.

Perhaps the most bizarre piston-engined fighter to be flown in Germany during the life of the Third Reich was the ungainly **BV 155** high-altitude interceptor, with its inordinate wing span and, in its B-series, uniquely-situated coolant radiators. The development history of the Blohm und Voss BV 155 was no less curious than its appearance, for it commenced its career not on the drawing boards of Dr.-Ing. Vogt's team at Hamburg-Finkenwerder, but in the project office of Ing. Waldemar Voigt of the Messerschmitt AG at Augsburg. Furthermore, its type number had been previously applied to a single-seat shipboard fighter, being resurrected when the RLM's Technisches Amt conceived a requirement for what was, by the standards of the day, an ultra-high-altitude interceptor.

In the spring of 1942, Grossadmiral Erich Raeder made repeated demands for the completion of the carrier *Graf Zeppelin* to escort commerce raiders. Construction of this vessel had been halted in May 1940, and it had subsequently languished at Gotenhafen and Stettin, its future undecided. Finally, on 13 May 1942, the Ob.d.M. issued instructions for work to be resumed on the carrier, which it was now decided should carry an air group comprising 28 bombers and 12 fighters. However, the Bf 109T fighter originally developed for operation from the *Graf Zeppelin* had become obsolescent, and the Messerschmitt AG was invited to prepare proposals for a new shipboard fighter that was allocated the designation **Me 155**, the RLM having now abandoned its earlier practice of allocating sequences of type numbers to individual aircraft manufacturers, using numbers previously included in issued sequences that had remained unused ('155' having originally been included in the sequence reserved for Klemm).

The Technisches Amt stressed both the urgency of the requirement and the importance of adapting existing Bf 109 components for the new design in so far as was possible for ease of manufacture and to limit the added workload placed on the already overloaded Messerschmitt design staff. The response to the requirement was extremely rapid;

With its huge underwing radiators and wide wheeltrack, the BV 155 V1 was one of the most unusual aircraft to fly during World War II. These features were to have disappeared from production aircraft.

outline proposals had been submitted to and accepted by the Technisches Amt within three weeks, and by late September 1942, detail design of the Me 155 was complete. Powered by a DB 605A-1 rated at 1100 kW (1,475 hp) for take-off, the Me 155 employed an essentially standard Bf 109G fuselage complete with tail surfaces, these being married to an entirely new wing, the overall span and gross area of which were 11.00 m (36 ft 3½ in) and 19.40 m² (208.82 sq ft), respectively. The main undercarriage members retracted inwards into wing wells, provision was made for wing folding, catapult spools and arrester gear, and the proposed armament comprised an engine-mounted 20-mm MG 151 cannon with 220 rounds, and two 20-mm MG 151s with 240 r.p.g. and two 13-mm (0.51-in) MG 131 machine-guns with 250 r.p.g. in the wings. With empty and loaded weights of 2900 and 3530 kg (6,398 and 7,784 lb), the Me 155 had an estimated maximum speed of 650 km/h (404 mph), endurance being calculated at 1.16 hours.

Carrier project abandoned

By the time detail design of the Me 155 was complete, it had been realised that so many changes to the *Graf Zeppelin* had become necessary that it would be at least two years before the vessel could become operational. Enthusiasm waned and it was tacitly admitted that there was little likelihood of the

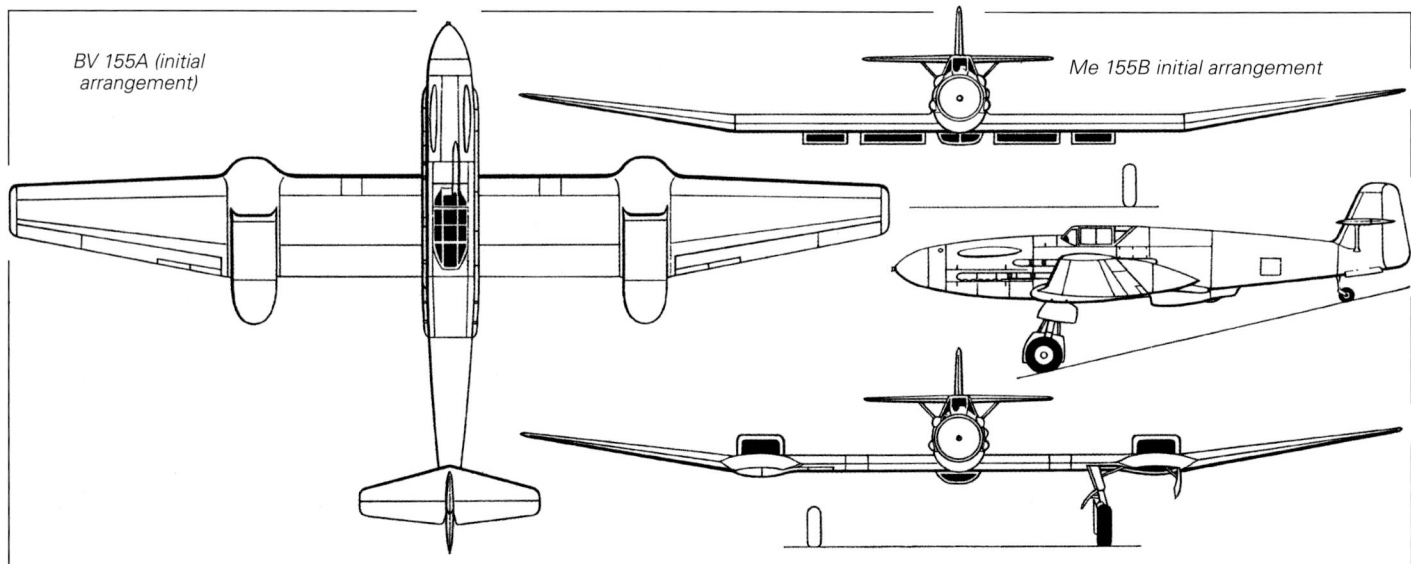

BV 155A (initial arrangement)

Me 155B initial arrangement

The initial design for the Me 155 high-altitude fighter used many components from the Bf 109G, but when Blohm und Voss took over the project many of them were redesigned. This is the first prototype, with the huge wing radiators relocated to under the trailing edge of the wing to solve cooling problems encountered on takeoff. The radiator fairings also provided space for the mainwheel wells.

carrier joining the Kriegsmarine in the foreseeable future, Messerschmitt being instructed unofficially to shelve the Me 155. The *Graf Zeppelin* was, in fact, towed to Kiel early in December 1942 for work to recommence, but during the following February, the Ob.d.M. ordered the termination of all work on surface vessels, the decision having been taken that the Kriegsmarine should concentrate on submarines.

Loath to waste the design work undertaken on the Me 155, Messerschmitt re-submitted the project in modified form to the Technisches Amt in November 1942 to fulfil a requirement for a fast single-seat aircraft suitable for pinpoint bombing attacks with a single 1000-kg (2,205-lb) SC 1000 bomb. As the **Me 155A**, the design was stripped of its carrier equipment together with most of its armament, and was provided with additional fuel cells and an elongated, non-retractable, faired tailwheel leg to provide sufficient clearance for the bomb during take-off. With a maximum loaded weight of 4500 kg (9,932 lb), the Me 155A was expected to attain maximum speeds of 650 km/h (404 mph) in clean condition and 510 km/h (317 mph) carrying an SC 1000 bomb at an altitude of 7000 m (22,965 ft).

With the steady escalation of USAAF bomber strength in Europe during the closing months of 1942, and the fear that the Luftwaffe would soon find itself confronted by bombers cruising above the effective combat ceilings of its existing interceptors, priorities had changed from the pinpoint bomber to the high-altitude fighter, and as a matter of extreme urgency, Messerschmitt was asked to tender proposals for such an aircraft. Thus, the Me 155 once again underwent redesign to emerge as the **Me 155B** interceptor with an estimated service ceiling of 14100 m (46,250 ft). Wingspan was extended to 13.00 m (42 ft 8½ in), a pressure cabin was introduced, and it

was proposed that the Daimler-Benz DB 628 engine should be adopted, this being similar in general arrangement to the DB 605A but fitted with a two-stage mechanical supercharger with an induction cooler.

In May 1943, a Bf 109G adapted to take the DB 628 completed two 30-hour tests and attained an altitude of 15500 m (50,850 ft), but the Technisches Amt concluded that the DB 603 engine with the exhaust-driven TKL 15 turbo-supercharger developed by the Deutschen Versuchsanstalt für Luftfahrt (DVL) possessed greater potential. Accordingly, the fuselage was elongated to house the TKL 15 turbo-supercharger aft of the pressure cabin, exhaust gases being carried along the fuselage by external ducts to drive the turbine, this being coupled through an hydraulic drive to the two-stage centrifugal impeller. Motor induction air was drawn in through a ventral trough immediately aft of the wing, passed to the turbo-driven supercharger, from there to the engine-driven supercharger via the first intercooler, and finally reached the engine induction manifold by way of the second intercooler. Overall wingspan was further extended, and four shallow coolant radiators were slung beneath the centre section.

In August 1943, the Technisches Amt, concluding that Messerschmitt was already committed to too many major development programmes to devote adequate attention to the Me 155B, issued instructions that all calculations and drawings were to be transferred to Blohm und Voss. By this time, the finalised Messerschmitt design, the **Me 155B-1**, embodied standard Bf 109G wings married to a new, long-span untapered centre section, Bf 109G horizontal tail surfaces, Me 209 vertical tail surfaces, and Bf 109G main undercarriage members. The fuselage was still essentially that of the

To maintain power in the thin air of high altitude the BV 155 had a TKL 15 turbo-supercharger installed in the rear fuselage. This required extensive ducting either side of the cockpit to link the system, via intercoolers, to the DB 603 engine's exhaust and inlet manifolds. The British forces that occupied Hamburg and its surroundings on 3 May 1945 captured all three BV 155 prototypes.

Blohm und Voss BV 155

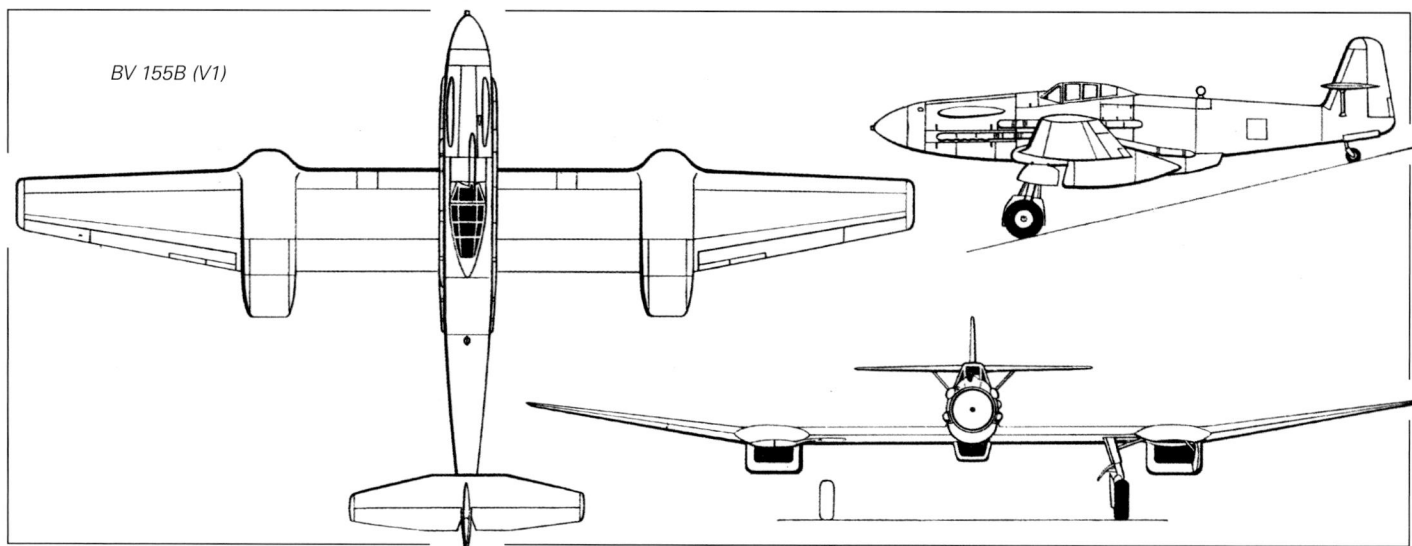

BV 155B (V1)

Bf 109G with an additional section inserted aft, and Me 209 engine bearers.

After careful examination of the calculations and drawings, Dr.-Ing. Vogt and his team were convinced that the project possessed too many inherent weaknesses to result in a successful high-altitude fighter, and friction between the Blohm und Voss team and Messerschmitt personnel steadily increased. Instructions issued by the RLM were that Blohm und Voss should implement construction of the Messerschmitt design as expeditiously as possible, and it was necessary for Dr.-Ing. Vogt to obtain Messerschmitt sanction before incorporating any major changes in the existing design. As a result of failure to reach agreement with Messerschmitt, Vogt reported to the RLM: 'After careful investigation we feel it necessary to undertake the redesign of the Me 155B-1's major components. The following features call for complete redesign: (1) the structure of the wing centre section; (2) arrangements for housing the fuel; (3) the undercarriage and its accommodation; (4) the radiators; (5) the wing profile; (6) the installation of the supercharger, and (7) the horizontal tail surfaces.'

Revised contract

A series of abortive meetings between Blohm und Voss and Messerschmitt personnel and representatives of the Technisches Amt failed to resolve the situation amicably, the RLM eventually overruling Messerschmitt and allocating complete design responsibility to Blohm und Voss, and awarding the company a contract for three prototypes.

Redesign of the Me 155B-1 continued at Finkenwerder

The BV 155's derivation from the Bf 109 is apparent in this view of the front fuselage. The initial Messerschmitt design retained the Bf 109's cockpit, but Blohm und Voss redesigned the rear fuselage to provide the pilot with a much better all-round view.

throughout the remainder of 1943. Dr.-Ing. Vogt elected to adopt a laminar-flow aerofoil section, abandoning Messerschmitt's scheme of utilising standard Bf 109G wings for the outer panels, claiming that it would be cheaper to design entirely new panels as the undercarriage well and radiator cut-outs of the Bf 109G wing would have to be covered, the leading-edge slots removed and the flaps replaced by ailerons. The wing centre section structure was entirely redesigned, the original Messerschmitt main spar situated at 45 per cent chord with six separate fuel tanks in the forward portion of the wing was supplanted by a hollow rectangular-section spar of 5-mm welded sheet steel, accommodating 1200 litres (264 Imp gal) of fuel and being armoured by 8-mm sheet steel on its front profile. Wind tunnel tests proved that two immense radiators mounted over the trailing edges of the wing at the extremities of the centre section were more efficacious than the four independent radiators beneath the centre section proposed by Messerschmitt, Ju 87D-6 undercarriage legs and wheels replaced the Bf 109G units, the aft fuselage was substantially reinforced, the Bf 109G horizontal tail surfaces were replaced, area being increased from 2.80 to 4.00 m² (30.14 to 43.05 sq ft), and the vertical tail surfaces were also enlarged.

Powered by a DB 603A engine with a TKL 15 turbo-supercharger offering an output of 1081 kW (1,450 hp) at 15000 m (49,210 ft), and driving a four-bladed wooden airscrew with a diameter of 3.90 m (12 ft 9 in), the **BV 155 V1** had provision for MW 50 injection, an Rb 50/30 camera aft of the pilot's seat, FuG 16ZY with direction and range-measuring facilities, and FuG 25a IFF equipment. Normal internal fuel capacity was 595 litres (131 Imp gal), but total fuel capacity when using the full main spar volume was 1200 litres (264 Imp gal). The pressurised cockpit was a welded steel plate box to which were attached the engine and turbo-supercharger mountings, and the folding canopy was fitted with an inflatable rubber seal. The engine supercharger was tapped for cockpit pressurisation, and supplemented by a special blower, a pressure equivalent to 7620 m (25,000 ft) being maintained at all altitudes up to the absolute ceiling of the fighter.

Revised intakes

Siting of intakes overwing had originally been adopted to avoid the disruption of airflow to the radiators by the retracting mainwheels at the most critical moment of take-off, but tunnel tests revealed that the wing blanked the radiators at high angles-of-attack, notably during the critical moments of the take-off run. The same tests suggested that, if an exceptionally powerful actuating jack be provided, the momentary interruption of flow into the radiator intakes should not prove serious if they were mounted beneath the wing.

The intakes were therefore substantially enlarged and underslung, but this change presented a CG problem which could only be resolved by moving the pressurised cockpit forward. Making a virtue of necessity, Dr.-Ing. Vogt took the opportunity to introduce an aft-sliding all-round vision canopy for the cockpit, cutting down the rear fuselage decking and compensating for this by enlarging the vertical fin. This necessitated some redesign of the rudder and, simultaneously, enlarged horizontal surfaces were applied, these, introducing a parallel-chord centre section, were increased in span from 4.20 to 5.00 m (13 ft 9⅓ in to 16 ft 4¾ in). Another modification concerned the ventral radiator bath which was deepened.

Above: This is the turbo-supercharger housing of the BV 155 V2, with the starboard duct leading from the engine's exhaust.

BV 155B and C series

All these changes were incorporated in the BV 155 V1 that was considered to be the first genuine B-series prototype, but Dr.-Ing. Vogt and his team were dissatisfied with the fighter, the design of which revealed some of the inevitable shortcomings of an aircraft that had undergone a succession of modifications to rectify failings in the basic concept. Thus, before the **BV 155 V2** commenced flight trials, Blohm und Voss submitted to the Technisches Amt proposals for yet another revision of the design as the **Projekt 205**. It was suggested that the Projekt 205 should employ the DB 603U engine, this powerplant having the larger mechanically-driven supercharger of the DB 603E and a reduction gear ratio of 2.07:1. The TKL 15 turbo-supercharger was to be retained.

Having been redesignated as the BV 155 V1, the first prototype was completed at Finkenwerder around January 1945. It first flew on 8 February with Helmut 'Wasa' Rodig at the controls. The right radiator leaked badly and Rodig was forced to cut short the flight. It flew again on the 10th, and then on the 26th.

In view of the parlous state in which the Third Reich now found itself, it was somewhat surprising that the Technisches Amt accepted Blohm und Voss's proposals, agreeing to the abandonment of further development of the **BV 155B** in favour of the revised design that was designated **BV 155C**, a pre-production batch of 30 aircraft being ordered.

Construction of two more BV 155 prototypes, the **BV 155 V2** and **V3**, continued at Finkenwerder in parallel with detail design of the BV 155C and preparations for construction of the pre-production batch of the definitive model. The BV 155 V2 differed from its immediate predecessor solely in having the DB 603U intended for the BV 155C, the engine cowling and TKL 15 turbo-supercharger being

Above: The huge underwing radiator assemblies were only fitted to the second and third prototypes. The fourth machine was to have had an annular radiator arrangement around the engine.

unchanged. The BV 155C was rather less bizarre in appearance than the BV 155B, a radical alteration being the discarding of the clumsy wing-mounted radiators. The basic wing structure remained unchanged, the outer panels simply attaching directly to the centre section instead of to the carry-through structure of the radiator housings, gross area being reduced accordingly but the loss in lifting surface being mitigated to some extent by the forward extension of the wingroot leading edge. The elimination of the wing-mounted radiator housings, which had also provided convenient housings for the mainwheels, led to the accommodation of the mainwheels in the wingroot extensions, the main leg attachment points being moved inboard to retract inwards into the new wells, undercarriage track being reduced from 6.70 to 3.90 m (22 ft 0½ in to 12 ft 9½ in).

By the time the BV 155 V1 emerged the aircraft showed none of its original genesis as a Messerschmitt-designed carrier fighter. In German hands the aircraft probably only flew three times in early 1945. An attempt to fly it after capture by British forces ended in tragedy when the aircraft crashed soon after take-off, killing the test pilot.

Blohm und Voss BV 155

The second and third prototypes was captured in semi-complete form by British forces and were returned to the Royal Aircraft Establishment at Farnborough for analysis. The British considered completing the V2 for flight testing, but in the event the aircraft went on display in late 1945 before being transferred to the United States.

A much more compact liquid cooling system was provided by means of an annular frontal radiator similar to that of the Ta 152, and two large circular intakes were attached to the fuselage sides above the wingroot trailing edges. The starboard intake served the turbo-supercharger, and air from the port intake passed through a heat exchanger and was discharged through an efflux in the starboard intake fairing. After being finally compressed in the engine supercharger, the intake air was directed to an intercooler in the ventral bath before passing to the induction manifold. The pressurised cockpit and fuselage remained virtually unchanged, as did also the horizontal tail surfaces, although the tail bracing struts were eliminated and the vertical surfaces were redesigned and enlarged.

The development schedule called for the completion of the **BV 155C-01** (**V4**) in April 1945, with the **C-02** (**V5**) in May and the **C-03** and **-04** (**V6** and **V7**) in June, but assembly had not commenced when the Allies occupied the Blohm und Voss factory at Finkenwerder on 3 May 1945. The V1 was intact, and the British decided to fly it back to England for detailed examination. An RAF pilot was detailed to fly it, but the aircraft crashed shortly after take-off. The incomplete second and third prototypes were subsequently transported to the United Kingdom's Royal Aircraft Establishment at Farnborough. Immediately after the end of the war there were plans to fly one of the aircraft, but they were shelved and the the aircraft put on display. The V2 was virtually complete, with just a few wiring harnesses remaining to be connected, whereas the V3 was around 75 percent finished.

Soon after being displayed at Farnborough in late 1945, one BV 155 was shipped to the United States for evaluation, gaining the foreign equipment serial FE-505. It currently resides in the Paul F. Garber restoration facility of the National Air & Space Museum. For many years it was assumed to be the third prototype, but recent examination revealed that it was, in fact, the V2.

One of the three BV 155s survived and is with the National Air & Space Museum, though not on display. The BV 155 V3 was the last aircraft product of the Blohm und Voss company.

Blohm und Voss BV 155B specification
(manufacturer's estimated performance figures)
Type: single-seat high-altitude interceptor
Powerplant: one Daimler-Benz DB 603A 12-cylinder inverted-Vee liquid-cooled engine with TKL 15 turbo-supercharger rated at 1200 kW (1,610 hp) for take-off and 10000 m at (32,810 ft), and 1081 kW (1,450 hp) at 15000 m (49,210 ft)
Performance: maximum speed 420 km/h (261 mph) at sea level, 520 km/h (325 mph) at 6000 m (19,685 ft), 600 km/h (373 mph) at 10000 m (32,810 ft), 650 km/h (404 mph) at 12000 m (39,370 ft), 690 km/h (429 mph) at 16000 m (52,490 ft); range at maximum continuous power (with 595 litres/131 Imp gal) 460 km (285 miles) at sea level, 560 km (347 miles) at 10000 m, 590 km (366 miles) at 16000 m, (with 1200 litres/264 Imp gal) 1080 km (670 miles) at sea level, 1350 km (838 miles) at 10000 m, 1440 km (895 miles) at 16000 m; initial climb rate 690 m (2,260 ft) per minute; climb at 16000 m 235 m (770 ft) per minute; time to 16000 m in 29 minutes; service ceiling 16950 m (55,610 ft); maximum ceiling 17100 m (56,100 ft)
Weights: empty 4870 kg (10,734 lb); normal loaded (Armament A) 5520 kg (12,172 lb), (B) 5125 kg (11,299 lb), (C) 5100 kg (11,237 lb), (D) 5440 kg (11,991 lb); maximum loaded 6020 kg (13,263 lb)
Dimensions: wingspan 20.50 m (67 ft 3 in); length 12.00 m (39 ft 4½ in); height 3.00 m (9 ft 9½ in); wing area 39.00 m² (419.8 sq ft)
Armament: (Proposal A) one engine-mounted 30-mm MK 108 cannon with 60 rounds plus two wing-mounted 20-mm MG 151 cannon, or (Proposal B) one 30-mm MK 103 cannon with 60 rounds and two 15-mm MG 151 cannon with 200 r.p.g., or (Proposal C) three 30-mm MK 108 cannon with 60 r.p.g., or (Proposal D) three 30-mm MK 103 cannon (two mounted in underwing fairings) with 60 r.p.g.

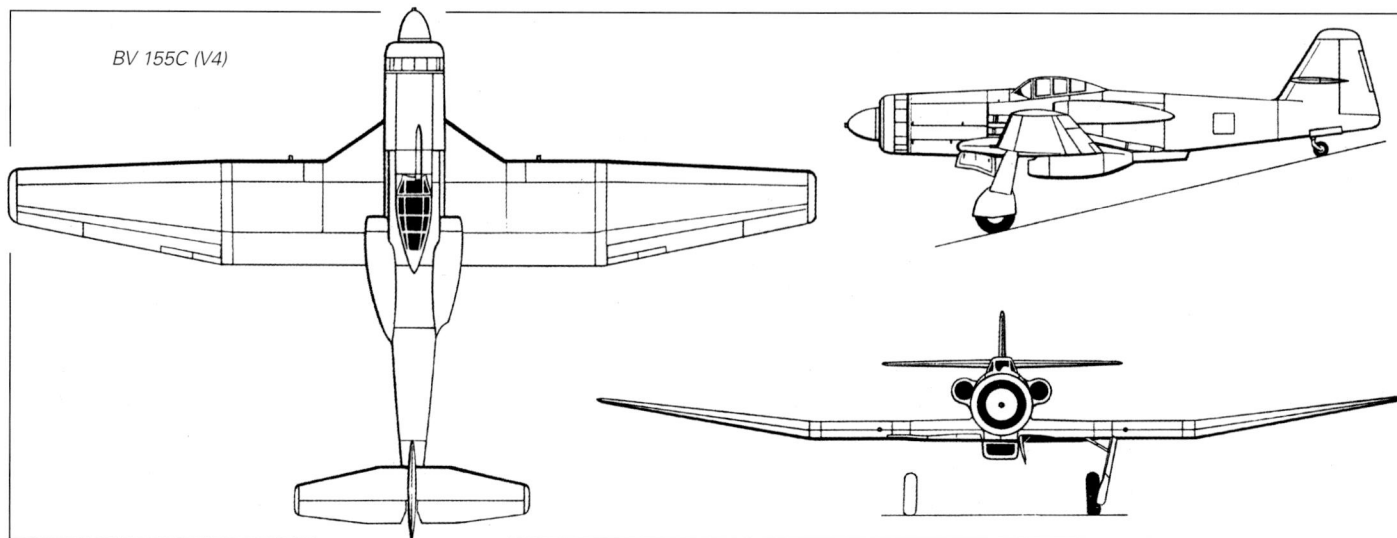

BV 155C (V4)

Blohm und Voss BV 222 Wiking

The largest flying-boat to achieve operational status during World War II, the Blohm und Voss BV 222 was originally designed to meet a Lufthansa requirement for a long-range passenger transport, but went on to see wartime service conveying both cargo and troops, as well as undertaking convoy-hunting patrols in the Atlantic.

On 31 May 1937, the Hamburger Flugzeugbau had still to celebrate the fourth anniversary of its existence; by internationally recognised standards the company was still in its infancy. Yet, on that date, this youthful and relatively inexperienced organisation submitted to Deutsche Lufthansa (DLH) its definitive design proposals for a transatlantic flying-boat only marginally smaller than the largest waterborne aircraft in existence, the Dornier Do X; proposals that were to be accepted in preference to competitive studies prepared by the more experienced Dornier and Heinkel concerns.

The Hamburger Flugzeugbau design team led by Dr.-Ing. Vogt had displayed a measure of daring from its earliest projects, but to initiate studies for so advanced a requirement as that prepared by DLH late in 1936, at a time when a mere handful of dive-bomber prototypes and a single prototype of a float seaplane designed by the Hamburg-based company had flown, called for either remarkable courage or singular temerity. DLH was anxious to inaugurate regular passenger services across the North and South Atlantic, over which only small amounts of mail and freight had previously been flown, framing a broad specification and informing Dornier, Heinkel and the Hamburger Flugzeugbau of its requirements. Dornier already possessed a project, the Do 20 based broadly on experience gained with the Do X, which the company considered to fulfil the DLH specification, this being a 50000-kg (110,230-lb) flying-boat powered by eight diesel engines coupled in pairs to drive four airscrews via extension shafts, and both Heinkel and the Hamburger Flugzeugbau initiated rival developments.

Through a series of project studies for flying-boats of various sizes and configurations, including the twin-hulled Projekt 42 and the single-hulled Projekt 43, both powered by

The largest flying-boat to achieve operational status during World War II, the BV 222 was also the largest aircraft to shoot down another during the conflict, scoring a kill over a US Navy PB4Y Liberator in October 1943. On the other hand, the BV 222 was also the largest aircraft of the war to be shot down, with three of the giants falling to the guns of RAF fighters.

six engines, Dr.-Ing. Vogt's team arrived at what was considered to be the definitive proposal, the Projekt 54 powered by six BMW 132B radial air-cooled engines, weighing some 45000 kg (99,200 lb) and featuring retractable outboard stabilising floats. The Heinkel team was less ambitious, its finalised proposal envisaging a smaller, 29000-kg (63,930-lb) flying-boat powered by four Junkers Jumo 205 diesel engines and having fixed stabilising floats. Both Heinkel and Hamburger Flugzeugbau design studies were submitted on 31 May 1937, the RLM simultaneously allocating the designations He 120 and **Ha 222** to the respective projects.

Definitive specification

After careful analysis of the competing studies, DLH concluded that the Ha 222 was the most promising, confirming its choice on 19 September 1937 with an order for three aircraft, and while the airline finalised its detailed requirements, a thorough evaluation of the hydrodynamic characteristics of the proposed Ha 222 planing bottom was undertaken with models by the Deutschen Schiffsbau–Versuchsanstalt (DSV). In December, Dr.-Ing. Vogt's team received the definitive DLH specification, which called for luxurious and spacious

On 7 September 1940, after two and a half years' work, the BV 222 V1 (D-ANTE) lifted off on its maiden flight from the River Elbe at Finkenwerder in the hands of Flugkapitän Helmut Wasa Rodig. The flight lasted for 20 minutes. There were only minor complaints about the boat's handling characteristics and behaviour, though it was also discovered that there was a slight lack of directional stability and a tendency to porpoise on the water while taxiing.

153

Blohm und Voss BV 222 Wiking

Above: Armament was introduced on the second and third prototypes, which were first flown on 7 August and 28 November 1941, respectively. The BV 222 V3 third prototype carried only a 7.9-mm (0.31-in) MG 81 machine-gun in the bow, but the BV 222 V2 second prototype was fitted additionally with a similar weapon in each of four waist positions and in two upper turrets, as well as a pair of 13-mm (0.51-in) MG 131 guns in two gondolas located beneath the wing's centre section.

accommodation for 24 passengers by day and an alternative arrangement for 16 sleeping berths. Detailed structural design began in January 1938 at Wenzendorf, and the first drawings reached the machine shops six months later.

Conventional in structural design, apart from its fuel-carrying tubular single main spar, the Ha 222 nevertheless embodied several novelties, the principal of them being the length-to-beam ratio of the planing bottom, the stabilising floats and the control system. Whereas the generally accepted flying-boat hull planing bottom length-to-beam ratio was of the order of 6, Dr.-Ing. Vogt chose to use a ratio of 8.4 to reduce both hydrodynamic and aerodynamic drag. The electrically-actuated retractable floats were arranged so that they split vertically, each half retracting outward from the main attachment point to lie flush with the outer wing panel under-surfaces.

The control system, which, at first sight, appeared extraordinarily complex, was part-servo and part-manual. Each aileron was split into two unequal parts, the larger inboard section being driven by a servo tab, the smaller outboard section being driven by a servo motor, the tab on the latter being operated directly through rod linkage by the pilot. A patented so-called 'paddle balance' under the wing comprising two aerofoil sections added lift to produce a moment that assisted the aileron. Each elevator was divided into three sections, the outboard section being operated by an electric motor and used for trimming, the similarly-operated central portion which, not connected to the stick, could be controlled by the autopilot or disconnected and allowed to float, and the servo tab-operated inboard or main section. The single-

The BV 222's first operational flight for the Luftwaffe was flown by a civilian crew between Hamburg and Kirkenes, in the extreme north-east of Norway, on 10 July 1941. The boat then received military camouflage and the registration CC+EQ, and by 19 August 1941 had completed seven supply flights to Kirkenes, carrying 65 tons of goods and evacuating 221 wounded soldiers. It had flown a total distance of 30000 km (18,640 miles). The generally satisfactory performances included a maximum speed of almost 385 km/h (239 mph) and a range of 7000 km (4,350 miles). Service also revealed that the instability troubles had still not been wholly solved, and the engine type, the BMW-Bramo 323 instead of the original BMW 132, was found somewhat troublesome.

piece rudder was operated by two interconnected tabs driven by the main circuit. A spring-box beneath the pilot's seat provided a certain amount of control feel.

The all-metal mainplane structure was built up around the tubular 1.45-m (4-ft 9-in) diameter spar, which was sub-divided by bulkheads to form six 3450-litre (759-Imp gal) capacity fuel tanks. The spar was situated at 30 per cent chord, welded steel-tube extensions carrying the six Bramo Fafnir 323R-2 nine-cylinder radial engines each offering 746 kW (1,000 hp) for take-off, 597 kW (800 hp) for climb to cruise altitude and a continuous output of 477 kW (640 hp). The parallel-chord wing centre section carried electrically-operated flaps, and a catwalk ahead of the main spar provided access to the engines in flight. The hull, which was a two-step all-metal structure covered by corrosion-resisting alloy sheet varying from 3 mm to 5 mm in thickness, was divided

The BV 222 V1 first prototype (D-ANTE) was rolled out in civil markings. After its successful test flights in September 1940, it was revised with a camouflage finish and used by the Luftwaffe for long-range heavy transport tasks.

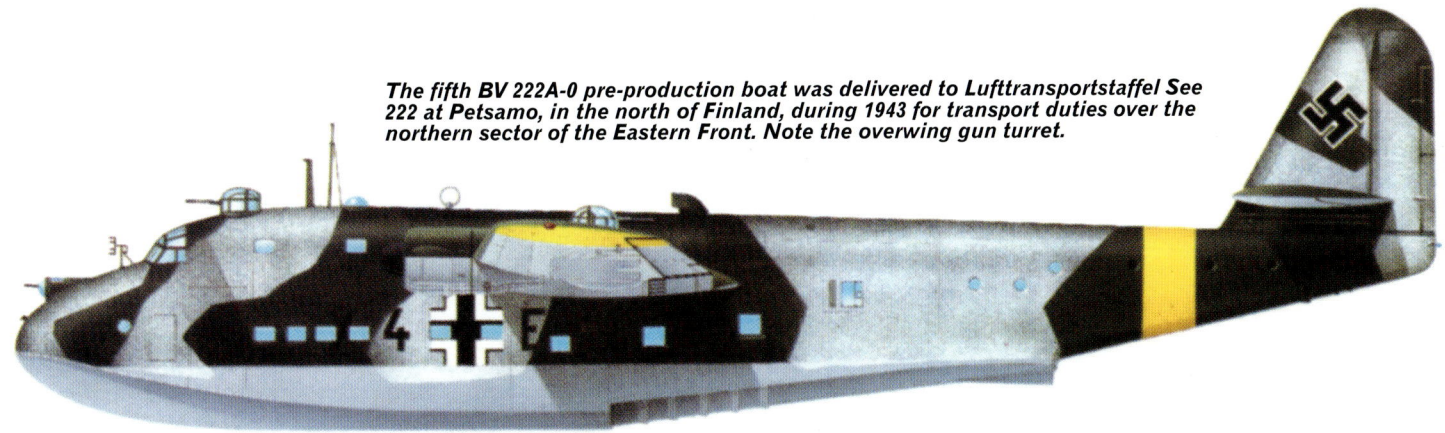

The fifth BV 222A-0 pre-production boat was delivered to Lufttransportstaffel See 222 at Petsamo, in the north of Finland, during 1943 for transport duties over the northern sector of the Eastern Front. Note the overwing gun turret.

into two decks, passenger accommodation being provided on the lower deck, and the crew consisting of two pilots, two flight engineers, a navigator and a wireless operator.

With the commencement of hostilities in September 1939, some specialist manpower was diverted to the BV 138 programme, but work on the three flying-boats for DLH, by this time redesignated BV 222s, continued, and on 16 July 1940, DLH representatives inspected a full-scale mock-up of the interior, although it was already apparent that the airline stood little chance of adding the flying-boat to its fleet. The first example, the **BV 222 V1** (D-ANTE), was completed late in August 1940, flying for the first time on 7 September with Flugkapitän Helmut Wasa Rodig at the controls. The initial flight test of 20 minutes duration was generally satisfactory, the flying-boat responding well to all control movements, but the pilot complained of a slight tendency towards directional instability, and on the water the BV 222 V1 was inclined to porpoise to some degree while taxiing.

Long-range cargo flights

Flight testing progressed steadily throughout the autumn and early winter, being interrupted between December 1940 and February 1941 by the icing of the River Elbe, and with the spring plans were made for a series of long-distance flights. At this stage, the Luftwaffe proposed that these flights should in fact be useful supply missions, and Blohm und Voss agreed to modify the prototype by cutting cargo doors in the side of the hull and rearranging the interior to accommodate bulky freight. In Luftwaffe insignia and the civil registra-

Above: A distinctive feature of the BV 222 was provided by the pair of underwing floats to provide waterborne stability. Each float was divided vertically, and in flight the halves were electrically retracted into wells in the underside of the outer wing panels, thereby reducing drag.

Above: The BV 222 V8 was the last of the A-series Wiking flying-boats, and enjoyed a singularly short operational career, being delivered to the Luftwaffe in the late autumn of 1942 and falling victim to RAF fighters before the end of the year.

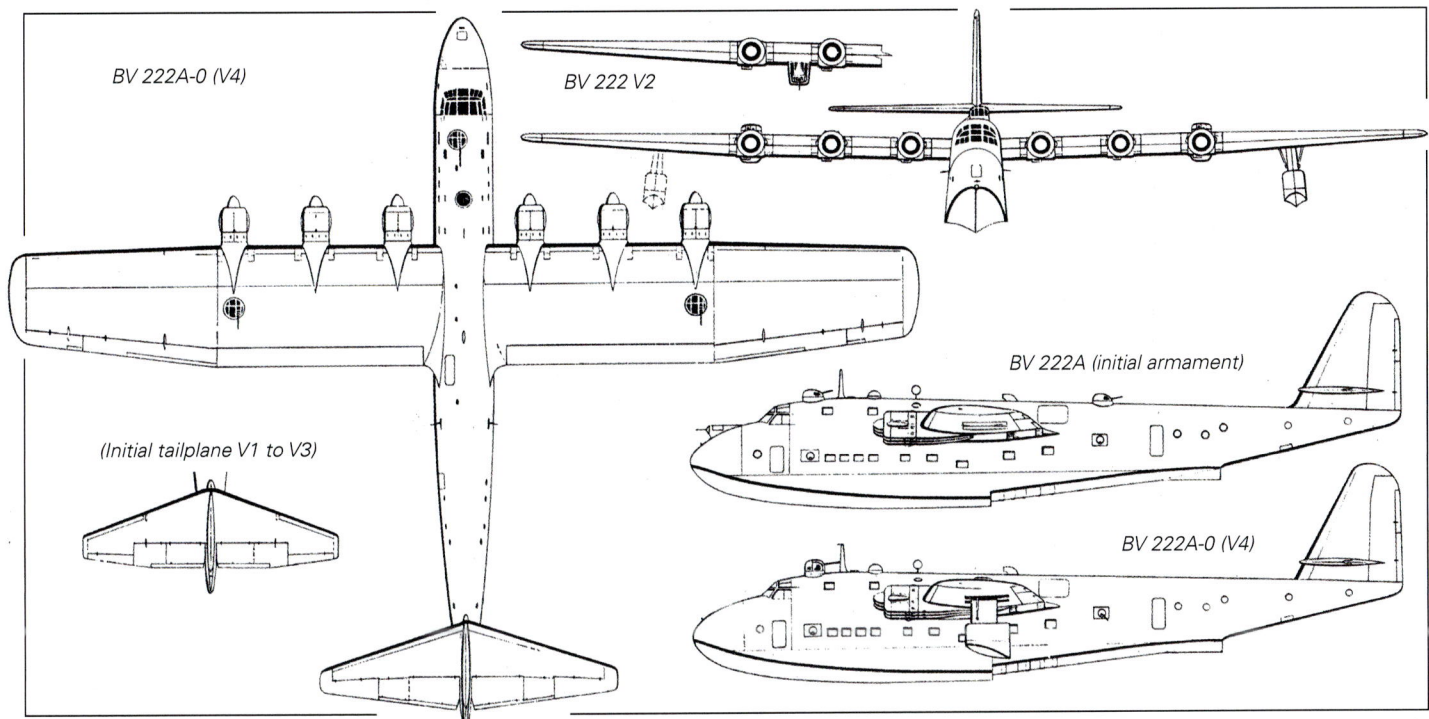

BV 222A-0 (V4)

BV 222 V2

(Initial tailplane V1 to V3)

BV 222A (initial armament)

BV 222A-0 (V4)

155

Blohm und Voss BV 222 Wiking

Totally devoid of defensive armament, the BV 222 V1 was normally escorted by two Bf 110 heavy fighters, but if the escort missed the rendezvous then the flying-boat had to continue its mission alone. On one such occasion, the lone BV 222 encountered two patrolling RAF Beauforts, but for some inexplicable reason they did not attack the defenceless flying-boat.

tion replaced by the radio call-sign CC+EQ, the BV 222 V1 performed its first mission on behalf of the Luftwaffe on 10 July 1941, flying from Hamburg to Kirkenes, on the Barents Sea. Seven flights between Hamburg and Kirkenes had been made by 19 August, some 30,000 km (18,600 miles) being flown, approximately 65,000 kg (143,300 lb) of freight being carried to Kirkenes and 221 casualties being ferried back to Hamburg.

After overhaul at Finkenwerder, the BV 222 V1 resumed its long-distance flights on 10 September 1941 with a mission to Athens from where it was supposed to operate a shuttle service to Derna, Libya. However, before this service could begin, the flying-boat was forced to return to Finkenwerder to have a thick layer of shellfish scraped from its hull. During the period 16 October-6 November 1941, the BV 222 V1 made 17 return flights between Athens and Derna, carrying

30,000 kg (66,140 lb) of freight and evacuating 515 casualties. During these flights a maximum speed of 385 km/h (239 mph) was recorded at 4500 m (14,765 ft), the maximum range was calculated at 7000 km (4,350 miles), and it was found that up to 72 casualty stretchers or 92 fully-equipped troops could be accommodated.

The BV 222 V1 was totally unarmed and was normally escorted by two Bf 110s, but on occasions the fighters missed the rendezvous and the flying-boat had to fulfil its mission unescorted. During one such flight, the lone flying-boat encountered two patrolling RAF Beauforts which, for some inexplicable reason, did not attack the defenceless transport. In November 1941, the BV 222 V1 was returned to Blohm und Voss for the installation of defensive armament, this comprising a single 7.9-mm (0.31-in) MG 81 machine-gun in the bow, fore and aft upper turrets each mounting a single

Lufttransportstaffel See 222 used the 'X4' unit code. The V1, having earlier been coded 'CC+EQ', became 'X4+AH'.

13-mm (0.51-in) MG 131 machine-gun, and four MG 81s firing from beam positions in the hull.

Meanwhile, the second prototype, the **BV 222 V2** (Werk Nr 366, CC+ER), had commenced flight trials on 7 August 1941, and was joined by the **BV 222 V3** (Werk Nr 439, DM+SD) on 28 November 1941, and additional hulls had been laid at Finkenwerder. The BV 222 V2, which it had been decided should be placed at the disposal of the Fliegerführer Atlantik for long-range reconnaissance tasks in co-operation with U-boats, was completed with full defensive armament that was similar to that installed in the V1 apart from the addition of four 13-mm MG 131s shared between two gondolas slung beneath the wing and between the outer engine pairs, each gondola mounting one forward-firing and one aft-firing weapon. Trials at Travemünde revealed that the drag penalty incurred by the addition of the underwing gondolas was greater than could be accepted, and the appendages were promptly removed.

Other modifications resulting from the Travemünde trials included the introduction of five short auxiliary steps immediately aft of the first main step in the planing bottom, the deepening of the rear step by the simple expedient of adding a wedge-shaped auxiliary structure, and some structural strengthening. In the event, the BV 222 V2 was to serve initially in the transport role for which the V3 was intended for the outset, the latter being delivered with a defensive armament consisting solely of the MG 81 machine-gun in the bow position.

Pre-production series

Additional BV 222s had been laid down early in 1941, and it was envisaged that they would serve in both transport and long-range maritime reconnaissance roles. The initial batch of five pre-production flying-boats were intended to retain the Bramo Fafnir 323R-2 radials and were considered as A-series machines although allocated Versuchs numbers, and in the event, the fourth of them, the BV 222 V7, was modified during construction to take the diesel engines intended for the planned C-series.

The **BV 222 V4** (X4+DH), **BV 222 V5** (X4+EH), **BV 222 V6** (X4+FH) and **BV 222 V8** (X4+HH) were handed over to the Luftwaffe between 20 April and 26 October 1942, and embodying the structural strengthening and planing bottom modifications earlier applied to the V2, the aircraft were fitted with similar defensive armament, and commenced their service career as transports, the V4 and V5 initially as the Luftverkehrsstaffel 'C' and subsequently as components of its successor, the Lufttransportstaffel See 222, in the Mediterranean. Along with two of the first three prototypes, the V1 and V2, these flying-boats were engaged on supply missions from Italian and Greek bases to Rommel's Afrika Korps, landing at Tobruk and Derna, and returning with casualties. The two further boats delivered to LTS See 222, the BV 222 V6 and V8, fell victim to RAF fighters before the end of 1942.

As a result of the action in which the BV 222 V8 was lost, the V4, which had suffered serious damage at the same time, was temporarily repaired and returned to Blohm und Voss for the installation of more effective, longer-ranging defensive armament, and further structural strengthening. Yet another of the flying-boats, the BV 222 V1, was lost as a result of an accident in February 1943, and LTS 222's remaining operational BV 222s were stood down and returned to Germany for overhaul and modification, the V2 and V5 going to the Lufthansa-Werft at Travemünde.

The new defensive armament standardised by the surviving

Above: In the transport role the BV 222 could carry about 92 fully armed troops, or alternatively up to 72 casualties on litters.

Left: The underwing floats, each of which split vertically to hinge upward into inboard and outboard wells to rest flat within the wing, had to be retracted as soon as the boat had lifted off since the electrically powered retraction process occupied about 20 seconds, and had to be completed before the airspeed reached 225 km/h (140 mph).

On 9 December 1941 the BV 222 V3 was officially taken on strength by the Luftwaffe and, as the entire aircraft complement of Lufttransportstaffel See 222, V3 undertook 21 flights from bases in Italy to Tripoli during the period between January and March 1942. The aircraft delivered vital supplies to the Axis forces fighting in North Africa.

Blohm und Voss BV 222 Wiking

The BV 222 A-series boats were not equipped with the planned MW 50 methanol-water injection system for boosting take-off power until the summer of 1942, and then the maximum permissible take-off weight was raised from 45000 kg (99,206 lb) to 48000 kg (105,820 lb). The Bramo Fafnir 323R-2 engines each afforded 746 kW (1,000 hp) at 2,500 rpm, 596 kW (800 hp) at 2,250 rpm and 477 kW (640 hp) at 2,100 rpm, MW 50 boosting the take-off power to 895 kW (1,200 hp).

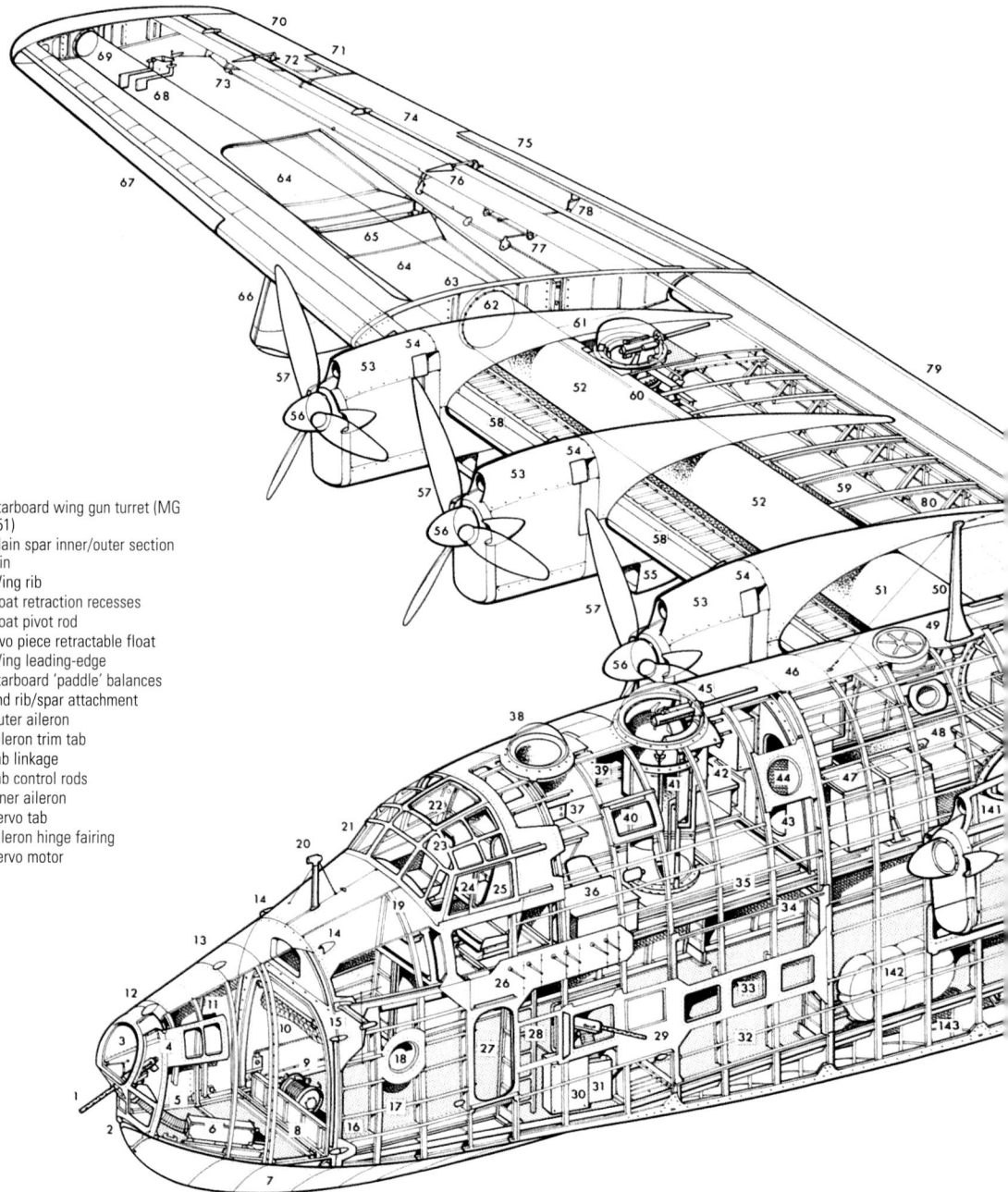

Blohm und Voss BV 222C Wiking cutaway key

1 MG 131 nose machine-gun
2 Mooring ring
3 Nose glazing
4 Nose section side windows
5 Cartridge link chute
6 Cartridge link collector box
7 Forward hull
8 Bulkhead step
9 Winch
10 Forward cargo net
11 Ammunition boxes
12 Nose front section (upward hinging)
13 Nose section (hinged to port)
14 Air scoops
15 Radar array
16 Nose hinge fairings
17 Main cargo hold floor
18 Porthole
19 Instrument panel
20 Mast sight
21 Windscreen panels
22 Canopy emergency jettison section
23 Co-pilot's seat
24 Flight engineer's jump seat
25 Pilot's moulded armour seat
26 Side aerial array
27 Forward entry door
28 Ladder to flight deck
29 Forward port machine-gun (MG 131)
30 Ammunition box
31 Cartridge link collector box
32 Cargo hold
33 Hold side windows
34 Bulkhead frame
35 Crew-deck floor support frame
36 Navigator's position
37 Wireless operator's station
38 Astro-hatch
39 Ammunition boxes
40 Crew-deck window
41 Dorsal turret support/mechanism
42 Engineer's station
43 Bulkhead
44 Porthole
45 Dorsal turret (MG 151)
46 Fuselage skinning
47 Galley
48 Galley section port
49 D/F antenna
50 Aerial mast
51 Aerial lead in
52 Tubular main spar (fuel carrying)
53 Engine nacelles
54 Exhaust gills
55 Radiator intake
56 Three-blade VDM-Schwarz propellers
57 Spinner
58 Engine access forward crawlway
59 Aft crawlway
60 Wing turret mechanism

61 Starboard wing gun turret (MG 151)
62 Main spar inner/outer section join
63 Wing rib
64 Float retraction recesses
65 Float pivot rod
66 Two piece retractable float
67 Wing leading-edge
68 Starboard 'paddle' balances
69 End rib/spar attachment
70 Outer aileron
71 Aileron trim tab
72 Tab linkage
73 Tab control rods
74 Inner aileron
75 Servo tab
76 Aileron hinge fairing
77 Servo motor
78 Tab linkage
79 Starboard flaps
80 Wing rib structure
81 Wing surface skinning
82 Aerial
83 Fuselage skin panels

84 Entry to aft crawlway
85 Tubular spar centre section
86 Over-spar steps
87 Forward port crawlway entry (rectangular)
88 Centre-section fuel tanks (six)
89 Aft port crawlway entry (circular)

90 Bulkhead frame
91 Stepped upper baggage hold
92 Intake
93 Pitot mast
94 Bulkhead
95 Fuselage structure
96 Aft hold bulkhead
97 Aft fuselage structure
98 Portholes

99 Fin leading-edge
100 Tailplane centre section
101 Tailplane tubular spar
102 Starboard tailplane
103 Elevator balance
104 Trimmer elevator section
105 Elevator centre section
106 Servo tab
107 Starboard main elevator
108 Tailfin nose ribs

The BV 222 V1 made a large number of transport flights, carrying both cargo and personnel, including the repatriation of wounded soldiers from Norway and North Africa. Blohm und Voss modified the aircraft for its new role by adding this large door in the fuselage side so that bulky cargo could be admitted at water level from lighters or temporary jetties.

109 Tailfin spar/fuselage attachment
110 Tailfin structure
111 Tailfin tubular spar
112 Rudder post
113 Rudder frame
114 Rudder upper hinge
115 Rudder servo tabs
116 Tab linkage

125 Aft fuselage frames
126 Tailfin spar support pillar
127 Hull ventral skinning
128 Tail inspection crawlway

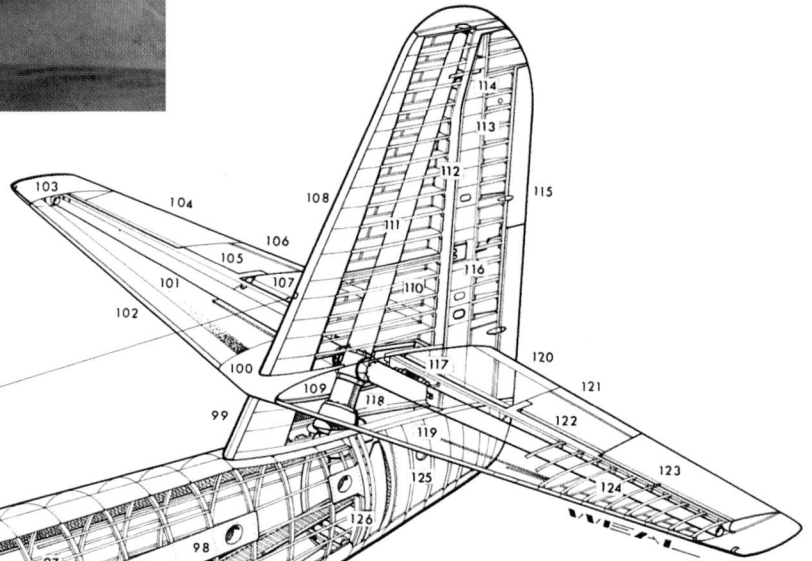

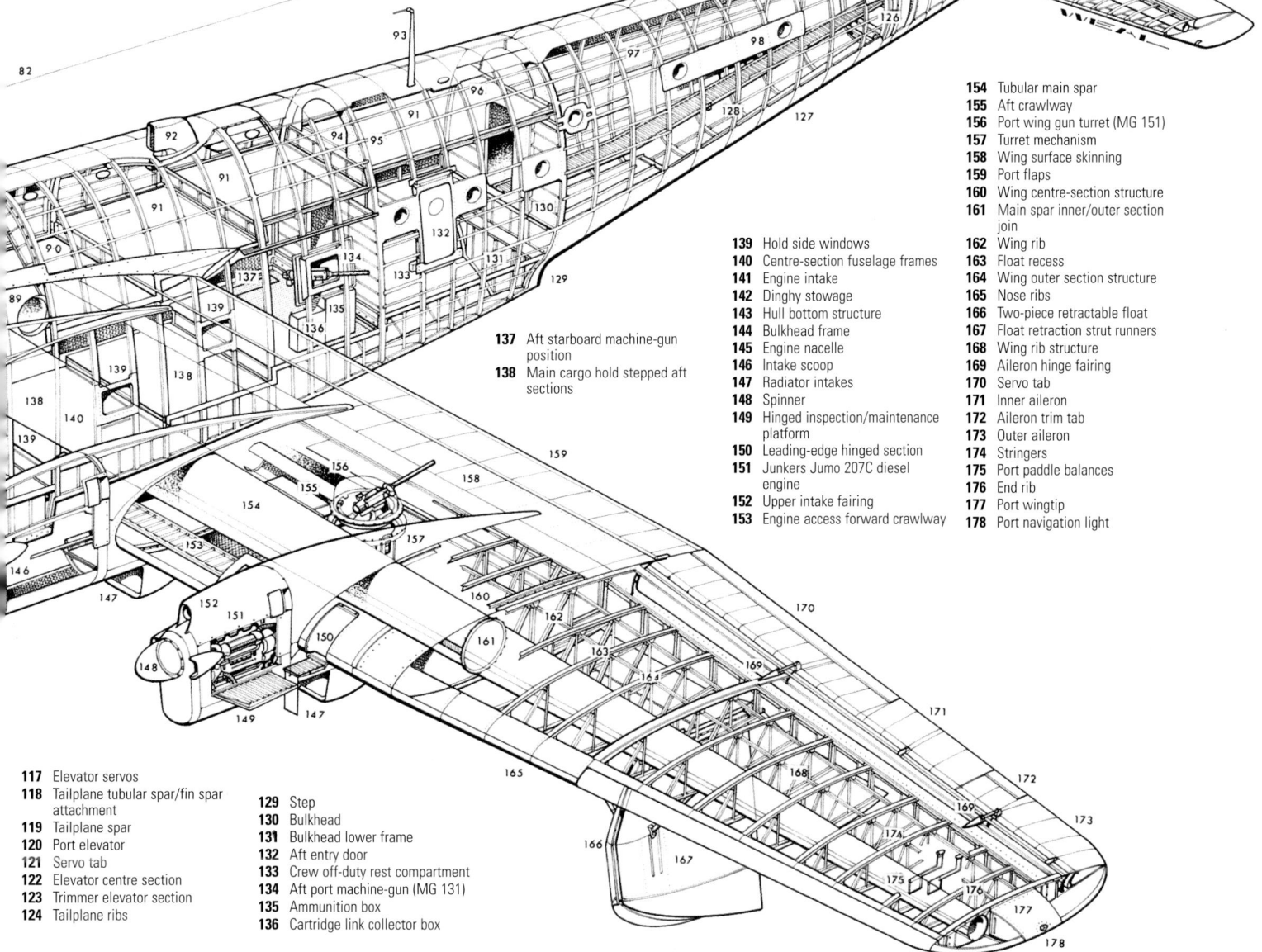

137 Aft starboard machine-gun position
138 Main cargo hold stepped aft sections

139 Hold side windows
140 Centre-section fuselage frames
141 Engine intake
142 Dinghy stowage
143 Hull bottom structure
144 Bulkhead frame
145 Engine nacelle
146 Intake scoop
147 Radiator intakes
148 Spinner
149 Hinged inspection/maintenance platform
150 Leading-edge hinged section
151 Junkers Jumo 207C diesel engine
152 Upper intake fairing
153 Engine access forward crawlway

154 Tubular main spar
155 Aft crawlway
156 Port wing gun turret (MG 151)
157 Turret mechanism
158 Wing surface skinning
159 Port flaps
160 Wing centre-section structure
161 Main spar inner/outer section join
162 Wing rib
163 Float recess
164 Wing outer section structure
165 Nose ribs
166 Two-piece retractable float
167 Float retraction strut runners
168 Wing rib structure
169 Aileron hinge fairing
170 Servo tab
171 Inner aileron
172 Aileron trim tab
173 Outer aileron
174 Stringers
175 Port paddle balances
176 End rib
177 Port wingtip
178 Port navigation light

117 Elevator servos
118 Tailplane tubular spar/fin spar attachment
119 Tailplane spar
120 Port elevator
121 Servo tab
122 Elevator centre section
123 Trimmer elevator section
124 Tailplane ribs

129 Step
130 Bulkhead
131 Bulkhead lower frame
132 Aft entry door
133 Crew off-duty rest compartment
134 Aft port machine-gun (MG 131)
135 Ammunition box
136 Cartridge link collector box

159

Blohm und Voss BV 222 Wiking

Entering Luftwaffe service in the autumn of 1942, BV 222 V8 had only a brief career, being shot down by RAF fighters later in the year. It was the last of the A-series aircraft.

Above: The BV 222 V7 was intended from the outset primarily for the long-range reconnaissance role. It featured repositioned wing turrets that were now situated in the rear of engine nacelles numbers two and five.

four flying-boats comprised a forward dorsal turret mounting a single 20-mm MG 151 cannon, a similar weapon in each of two turrets mounted in the wings immediately aft of the extreme outer engine nacelles, a 13-mm MG 131 machine-gun firing from a forward beam position, and two 7.9-mm MG 81s firing from aft beam positions, the aft dorsal turret and the bow gun position being deleted. A methanol-water injection system was introduced to boost take-off power from each engine to 895 kW (1,200 hp) but while modifications were in progress it became obvious that Axis resistance in North Africa was collapsing. As the task of co-operating with the U-boat fleet in the Atlantic had become as vital as the transport role, it was decided to transfer all four BV 222s

to the control of the Fliegerführer Atlantik. In consequence, the flying-boats were fitted with search radar and additional radio aids, including FuG 200 Hohentwiel, FuG 16Z VHF radio with direction and range measuring facilities, FuG 25a IFF, and a FuG 101a radio altimeter. An ETC 501 rack was fitted to carry a FuG 302c Schwan (Swan) beacon.

The BV 222 V3 had already joined the 3. Staffel of Küstenfliegergruppe 406, a BV 138-equipped unit based at Biscarosse, early in May 1942, the remaining three BV 222s joined it at Biscarosse during the course of May 1943, forming Aufklärungsstaffel See 222 which subsequently operated as a component part of 3./Kü.Fl.Gr. 406. During the following month, the BV222 V3 and V5 were strafed and sunk at their moorings.

Production version

Early in 1939, Blohm und Voss had begun to consider the application of diesel engines to the company's new flying-boat, and proposals were made to DLH for the **BV 222B** powered by six Junkers Jumo 208 engines. However, the B-series progressed no further than the proposal stage owing to Junkers's failure to persist with the development of the Jumo 208. Consideration was once more given to the possible use of diesel engines in 1941, the Technisches Amt accepting Blohm und Voss's proposals and agreeing to the installation of Jumo 207C diesel engines in the fourth BV 222A-0 airframe

One of the small number of BV 222 C-series boats completed shows the gun turret just inboard of the outer nacelle on the port wing.

Blohm und Voss BV 222 Wiking

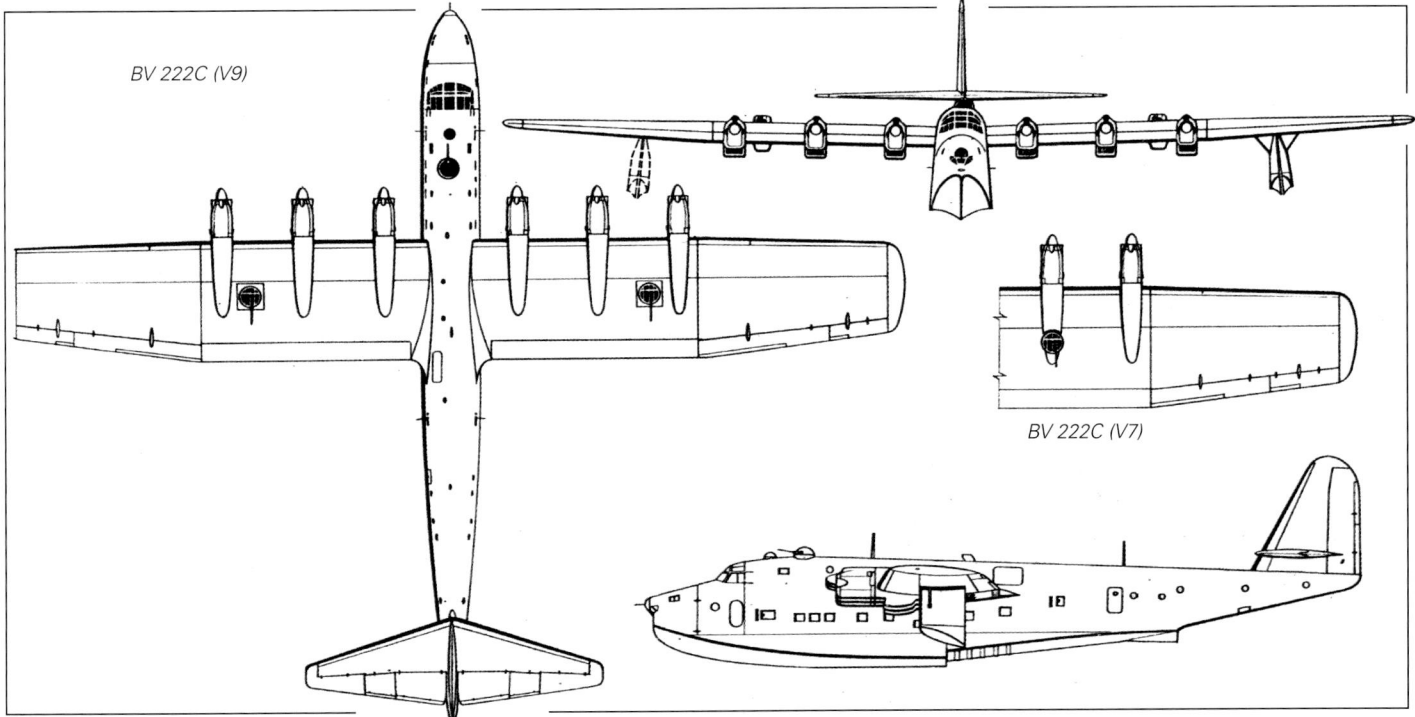

BV 222C (V9)

BV 222C (V7)

which, as the BV 222 V7 (TB+QL), flew for the first time on 1 April 1943 as the prototype of the **BV 222C**.

Possessing an essentially similar airframe to the A-series aircraft, the BV 222 V7 was intended from the outset primarily for the long-range reconnaissance role. Fuel tank capacity was decreased, each of the six mainspar tanks accommodating 2878 litres (633 Imp gal) as compared with 3450 litres (759 Imp gal) in A-series aircraft. Six 173-litre (38-Imp gal) oil tanks replaced the six 86-litre (19-Imp gal) tanks and one 480-litre (105.6-Imp gal) tank, and defensive armament was again revised, the bow position being reinstated and mounting a 13-mm MG 131, an additional forward beam MG 131 being provided, and the rear beam MG 81s being supplanted by MG 131s. Furthermore, the wing turrets were repositioned, being placed aft of engine nacelles two and five. Normal loaded weight was increased to 45990 kg (101,390 lb), and maximum overload to 49000 kg (108,026 lb) at which the

Jumo 207C engines delivered insufficient power for normal take-off, provision being made for the attachment of four solid-fuel take-off rockets beneath the wings, to be fired after 10 seconds at full throttle and burning for 30 seconds. The stabilising floats, which were retracted at 225 km/h (140 mph), a process taking approximately 20 seconds, were redesigned. The BV 222C's standard crew comprised 11 members – two pilots, two flight engineers, a navigator, a radio-operator, and five gunners.

Prior to the completion of the last A-series flying-boat, work had begun on several pre-production C-series flying-boats, the first of them, the **BV 222C-09**, being completed some six weeks after the Jumo-powered V7 prototype, and actually preceding this aircraft into service under the Fliegerführer Atlantik. The BV 222C-09, which was taken on strength by the Aufklärungsstaffel See 222 on 23 July 1943, differed from the V7 in that the wing turrets were

The BV 222's structure was essentially conventional except for the incorporation of the typical Blohm und Voss welded steel tubular main wing spar, which had a diameter of 1.45 m (4 ft 9 in) and was sub-divided by bulkheads into six separate fuel compartments. In the A-series each had a capacity of 3450 litres (759 Imp gal), although this was reduced in the diesel-powered C-series aircraft. The fuel tanks were pressure-filled from the front wing catwalk, which also gave access to the rear of the engines, and the tanks had to be filled in staggered sequence one, six, two, five, three and four, and with 1000 litres (220 Imp gal) at a time so as to avoid the risk of capsizing. If either tanks one or six was emptied separately the boat would capsize.

Blohm und Voss BV 222 Wiking

Above: This view of a beached BV 222 A-series boat gives an idea of the high length-to-beam ratio that gave the aircraft such good aerodynamic and hydrodynamic qualities.

Above: In the winter of 1941-42, the BV 222 V1 underwent a major overhaul in Hamburg to add defensive armament.

Below: Carrying one MG 131 in a dorsal turret, one MG 81 in a nose station and four MG 81s in waist positions, the BV 222 V1 performed the basic operations of LTS 222 and served in the Mediterranean theatre.

again changed in position, being relocated slightly further forward and between the outboard engine pairs. The BV 222 V7 joined the C-09 in service on 16 August 1943, and was followed at short intervals by the **BV 222C-010, BV 222C-011** and **BV 222C-012**.

The **BV 222C-013** was intended to receive Jumo 207D engines rated at 1119 kW (1,500 hp) for take-off and proposed for the **BV 222D** series. Four additional hulls had been laid for what were to be pre-production D-series flying-boats, but after a protracted delay, Junkers failed to deliver the Jumo 207D engines required for the BV 222C-013, and this was finally completed with Jumo 207C diesels, it being decided that similar powerplants would be installed in the four additional aircraft under construction which would thus become the **BV 222C-014** to **BV 222C-017**. In the meantime, the RLM ordered the abandoning of all further production and development of diesel engines owing to the maintenance and fuel problems that they provided. Prolonged discussions were conducted between Blohm und Voss and the RLM in order to decide what powerplants would replace the diesels in the four flying-boats under construction. Blohm und Voss made proposals for the installation of either four or six BMW 801s, thus resurrecting proposals made to the RLM in 1939, which included **Projekt 97** with six BMW 801s and **Projekt 98** with four BMW 801s, but the Technisches Amt remained adamant that this 14-cylinder radial must be reserved for other aircraft. Thus, Blohm und Voss had no recourse but to revert to the Fafnir 323R-2 with which the flying-boat was to be designated **BV 222E**. In the event, the production programme was cancelled early in 1944 in order that Blohm und Voss could devote all production to more urgently required aircraft, and the BV 222s already on the assembly line were scrapped.

Wiking at war

After successful operational trials, the BV 222 V1 returned to Blohm und Voss in November 1941 for the installation of defensive armament. Its place in the Mediterranean was taken by the BV 222 V3. This became the first of the type to be officially taken on strength by the Luftwaffe, the event occurring on 9 December 1941. The flying-boat was now dubbed **Wiking** (Viking), and the BV 222 V3 operated as the entire aircraft complement of Lufttransportstaffel See 222 V3, flying 21 supply missions between Italian bases and Tripoli from January to March 1942.

On 20 April and 7 July 1942 respectively, the BV 222 V4 and V5 were taken on strength, and with the transfer of the BV 222 V3 to the Biscay area in May for long-range reconnaissance tasks under the control of the Fliegerführer Atlantik, the two boats operated as Luftverkehrsstaffel 'C' until they were joined by the BV 222 V1, which had been returned to service on 10 May 1942, to continue operations as Lufttransportstaffel See 222. During the course of the summer, the strength of LTS See 222 was augmented by the BV 222 V2, which had been undergoing protracted trials at Travemünde, and the BV 222 V6, which were added to the inventory on 10 August and 21 August 1942, respectively. A sixth Wiking joined the unit on 26 October with the arrival of the BV 222 V8.

By the end of 1942, Wiking flying-boats operating in the transport role in the Mediterranean theatre had carried 1,453 tons of supplies, 17,778 fully-equipped troops and 2,491 casualties, and with missions outside the Mediterranean total loads carried were 2,043 tons of supplies, 19,750 troops and 2,678 casualties.

In service, the Wiking had presented few serious problems,

One of LTS See 222's Wikings rides at anchor in the Mediterranean, a sheet having been draped over its frame in an attempt to keep the flight deck and upper deck cool in the heat of the sun. The BV 222 compiled significant achievements in the theatre through its ability to haul large amounts of cargo or troops, but it was always vulnerable to Commonwealth fighters, both in the air and while moored. Only 13 of the giants were completed, all of which were used operationally. A further four hulls were laid down, but they were scrapped before completion as the German industry became involved in more pressing matters.

although considerable care had to be exercised in ensuring that the tanks were refuelled in the correct sequence. Filling was undertaken in staggered fashion in the tank sequence 1, 6, 2, 5, 3 and 4, and if this was not adhered to there was a serious danger of capsizing. It was standard practice for the flight engineers to examine each engine from the wing catwalk immediately after take-off, then again after 30 minutes and subsequently every hour.

Defensive armament was insufficient for unescorted missions in areas where enemy fighters were likely to be encountered, and the first casualty was suffered by LTS See 222 on 21 August 1942, when the BV 222 V6 was intercepted and shot down by RAF Beaufighters when flying unescorted south of Pantelleria. This loss resulted in orders being issued by KG.z.b.V 2, to which LTS See 222 was subordinated, to the effect that BV 222s would subsequently fly all missions in formation at low altitude. Despite this precaution, on 10 December 1942, the BV 222 V1, V4 and V8 flying in formation at low altitude over the Mediterranean en route for Tripoli were intercepted by a trio of RAF Beaufighters, the V8 being shot down and the V4 being seriously damaged, although the latter succeeded in reaching Tripoli in company with the V1.

In his report concerning the incident, the Staffelkapitän of LTS See 222 stated, 'It has now been proven that the defensive armament of the BV 222 is totally inadequate. Low-level flying, accepted hitherto as the best means of defence, is now seen to be of little value as any fighter can position itself behind the tail so that it is flying a good three metres lower than the flying-boat, and once so positioned it cannot be hit by any of the existing defensive guns. Furthermore, while flying in formation it is almost impossible for the BV 222 to take evasive action.'

This report led to the decision to conduct all future supply operations by night until effective defensive armament could be provided, but it was soon discovered that such nocturnal operations were subjected to hazards equally as danger-

This is a A BV 222 in its militarised version complete with defensive gun turrets. Although there were several reports of BV 222 six-motor boats in the Mediterranean theatre during the Tunisian campaign, some of them may have been Messerschmitt Me 323 six-engined heavy land-based transports. Only a few BV 222 boats had been built by this time.

ous as that of encountering enemy fighters during a daylight mission. As the North African ports at which the BV 222s were intended to descend were being attacked by Allied bombers virtually every night, no lights could be displayed to guide the flying-boats, and the risk of striking floating debris or submerged obstacles while taxiing was severe. Indeed, in February 1943, the BV 222 V1 foundered in Athens harbour when it struck a marker buoy while taxiing at speed, the buoy ripping several yards of skinning from the planing bottom. Thus, LTS See 222 stood down, and its surviving Wikings returned to Germany for re-arming and other modifications.

With the completion of modifications, the BV 222s were transferred to the control of the Fliegerführer Atlantik, joining the BV 222 V3 in the Aufklärungsstaffel See 222 at Biscarosse, this being subordinated to 3./Kü.Fl.Gr. 406. However, on 20 June 1943, two Wiking flying-boats, the BV 222 V3 and V5, were sunk at their moorings in Biscarosse harbour by RAF Mosquitoes from No. 264 Squadron, leaving the BV 222 V2 and V4 as the sole survivors. They were augmented by the BV 222C-09 on 23 July, and the

The fourth BV 222A-0 airframe was later revised with Jumo 207C diesel engines as the BV 222 V7, the prototype for the C-series.

Blohm und Voss BV 222 Wiking

BV 222 V7 on 16 August 1943, to which had been added the BV 222C-010 by October 1943 when the unit was redesignated 1.(F)/SAGr. 129. Flying far out over the Atlantic on U-boat co-operation tasks, the five BV 222s continued sorties from Biscarosse until shortly before the evacuation of the port. On 22 October 1943, the BV 222 V4 encountered and destroyed a US Navy PB4Y Liberator from VB-105, and early in 1944, the BV 222C-010 was shot down in the vicinity of Biscarosse by RAF night-fighters.

As the war situation deteriorated, the remaining BV 222s were progressively returned to transport tasks, 1.(F)/SAGr. 129 being disbanded in July 1944 and the survivors transferred to 3./KG 200, mainly for duties in the Baltic. The fate of those Wiking flying-boats that survived until the end of the war in Europe was as follows: the BV 222 V2 was discovered in Norway and blown up by British forces; the BV 222 V4 was destroyed by its own crew at Kiel-Holtenau; the BV 222 V7 was destroyed by its own crew at Travemünde; the BV 222C-09 was damaged beyond repair in a strafing attack by a Canadian Typhoon on Seedorf; the BV 222C-011 and -013 were captured intact by US forces and flown to the US, and the BV 222C-012 was captured by British forces in Norway and flown to the UK for examination.

Blohm und Voss BV 222A-0 (V4) Wiking specification
Type: long-range maritime patrol and reconnaissance flying-boat
Powerplant: six Bramo Fafnir 323R-2 nine-cylinder radial air-cooled engines each rated at 895 kW (1,200 hp) for take-off with methanol-water injection
Performance: maximum speed at sea level (at 45600 kg/100,530 lb) 300 km/h (184 mph), (at 35000 kg/77,162 lb) 310 km/h (193 mph); maximum continuous cruising speed at sea level (at 45600 kg) 254 km/h (158 mph), (at 35000 kg) 278 km/h (173 mph); economical cruising speed (at 45600 kg) 250 km/h (155 mph), (at 40000 kg/88,185 lb) 260 km/h (160 mph); maximum range 7000 km (4,350 miles) at sea level, 7450 km (4,630 miles) at 4900 m (16,075 ft); optimum flight endurance 33 hours at sea level, 23 hours at 4900 m; climb to 6000 m (19,685 ft) in 49 minutes; service ceiling 6500 m (21,325 ft)
Weights: empty equipped 28550 kg (62,941 lb); maximum loaded 45600 kg (100,530 lb)
Dimensions: wingspan 46.00 m (150 ft 11 in); length 36.50 m (119 ft 9 in); height 10.90 m (35 ft 9 in); wing area 255.00 m² (2,744.80 sq ft)
Armament: one 20-mm MG 151 cannon in forward dorsal turret, one 20-mm MG 151 cannon in each of two wing-mounted turrets, and one 13-mm (0.51-in) MG 131 and two 7.9-mm (0.31-in) MG 81 machine-guns firing from beam positions

Blohm und Voss BV 222C-09 Wiking specification
Type: long-range maritime patrol and reconnaissance flyingboat
Powerplant: six Junkers Jumo 207C six-cylinder vertical opposed-piston compression-ignition two-stroke engines each rated at 745 kW (1,000 hp) for take-off
Performance: maximum speed (at 46000 kg/101,390 lb) 330 km/h (205 mph) at sea level, 390 km/h (242 mph) at 5000 m (16,400 ft); continuous economical cruising speed 300 km/h (189 mph) at sea level, 344 km/h (214 mph) at 5550 m (18,210 ft); optimum endurance 28 hours at 245 km/h (152 mph) at sea level; maximum range 6100 km (3,790 miles); initial climb rate (at 46000 kg) 144 m (473 ft) per minute; time to 6000 m (19,700 ft) in 52 minutes; service ceiling 7300 m (23,950 ft)
Weights: empty 30650 kg (67,572 lb); normal loaded 45990 kg (101,390 lb); maximum overload 49000 kg (108,026 lb)
Dimensions: wingspan 46.00 m (150 ft 11 in); length 37.00 m (121 ft 4⅔ in); height 10.90 m (35 ft 9 in); wing area 255.00 m² (2,744.80 sq ft)
Armament: one 13-mm (0.51-in) MG 131 machine-gun in bow position, one 20-mm MG 151 cannon in forward dorsal turret, one 20-mm MG 151 cannon in each of two wing turrets, and four 13-mm MG 131 machine-guns firing from beam positions

BV 222 operations taxed the ingenuity of those tasked with servicing the big boats. Jury-rigged jetties and pontoons were constructed to ensure men and materiel could be loaded and unloaded quickly and safely.

Left: When it was conceived, the BV 222 was intended to enjoy a peaceful career as a transatlantic airliner, as evidenced by the V1 here wearing DLH colours. It soon adopted warpaint and embarked on an altogether different career.

Blohm und Voss BV 238

The BV 238 was not the world's largest aircraft to have flown at the time of its maiden flight, this distinction belonging to the Tupolev ANT-20, but it was certainly the heaviest. Although very costly, such an aircraft if available in numbers would have given the Luftwaffe a prodigious long-range and multi-role maritime capability.

During the spring of 1940, the Technisches Amt of the RLM had placed a study contract with Blohm und Voss for what was referred to as an 'Ersatz BV 138'; a combined See-Fernaufklärer and Langstreckentransporter successor to the BV 138 flying-boat that was on the point of entering Luftwaffe service. Dr.-Ing. Vogt's team, now joined by Dipl.-Ing. Hermann Pohlmann from Junkers, submitted eight project studies for flying-boats varying widely in configuration, and each potentially capable of meeting the new requirement. In the meantime, however, the Technisches Amt had set its sights somewhat higher.

Flying-boat hull planing bottom design had remained virtually static for two decades, and a length-to-beam ratio of the order of 6 had become traditional. Largely as a result of water tank tests conducted at the Deutsche Schiffsbau-Versuchsanstalt (DSV), the planing bottom of the BV 222, the first prototype of which was being readied for its initial trials, displayed a noteworthy advance in utilising a length-to-beam ratio of 8.4, the idea being to reduce both hydrodynamic and aerodynamic drag, and simultaneously permit operation in rough seas by cushioning landing loads. There was some uncertainty concerning the waterborne behaviour of the slender planing surface, and it was feared that it would prove to be somewhat less stable longitudinally and directionally. The first tests of the BV 222 V1 in September 1940 resolved doubts concerning the practicability of slender planing bottoms, and as DSV tests indicated that even greater increases in length-to-beam ratio could be advantageous, the Technisches Amt completely revised its 'Ersatz BV 138' requirement.

In November 1940, Blohm und Voss was instructed to submit new proposals which, to embody the latest developments in planing bottom design, were to be based on the

Experimental work on a water tank showed that a flying-boat's planing bottom could be considerably narrower than was traditional, allowing the construction of a much larger boat. Armed with these results, Dr.-Ing. Richard Vogt's team began work on a new design in November 1940, the result being designated as the Blohm und Voss BV 238.

use of four Jumo 223 diesels providing a total of 7457 kW (10,000 hp) for take-off. The Jumo 223 was a 24-cylinder 'box' diesel comprising four Jumo 205s with a single gear casing connecting the four crank-cases, the four crankshafts driving a single airscrew shaft gear. The project study finally submitted in mid-February 1941 envisaged a flying-boat spanning 53.00 m (173 ft 10⅔ in) and possessing an overall length of 39.65 m (130 ft 1 in). Normal and maximum loaded weights were estimated at 56000 and 74500 kg (123,459 and 164,244 lb), the proposed gross wing area was 186.00 m² (2,002 sq ft), and the length-to-beam ratio of the planing bottom was 10. This project made interesting comparison with the Martin XPB2M-1, or Model 170 Mars, then under construction at Baltimore, the American flying-boat having a length-to-beam ratio of 6.3, and a 61-m (200-ft) span wing of 342.15 m² (3,683 sq ft) gross area.

Armament and performance

Proposed defensive armament comprised 12 20-mm MG 151 cannon, mostly mounted in remotely-controlled barbettes, and estimated performance included maximum speeds of 344 km/h (214 mph) at sea level and 400 km/h (248 mph) at 6000 m (19,685 ft), maximum range being 4900 km (3,045 miles) at 380 km/h (236 mph) at normal loaded

The V1 was the only example of the huge BV 238 to fly. It was not fitted with any armament, and was still undergoing initial flight tests when it was sunk at its moorings and the programme cancelled.

Blohm und Voss BV 238

The Bv 238 V1 was the world's heaviest aircraft when first flown. Apart from the slender planing hull, other noteworthy features were the fully-retracting outrigger floats and large trailing-edge flaps.

weight, and 9400 km (5,840 miles) at 325 km/h (202 mph) at maximum loaded weight. Blohm und Voss was instructed to proceed with detail design, and the RLM allocated the project, appropriately enough, the designation **BV 238**.

By July 1941, it had become obvious that expectations for the Jumo 223 were not to be fulfilled, and as no alternative offering sufficient power presented itself, Dr.-Ing. Vogt's team was forced to redesign the BV 238 to take six engines, this change being accompanied by increases in overall dimensions, wingspan and gross area becoming 57.75 m (189 ft 5⅔ in) and 347.00 m² (3,735 sq ft), respectively, and length being extended to 45.50 m (149 ft 3⅓ in). At this juncture the intended roles of the BV 238 were augmented to include that of bombing.

During the autumn of 1941, Blohm und Voss was awarded a contract by the RLM for four prototypes, comprising three A-series aircraft powered by Daimler-Benz DB 603 liquid-cooled engines, and one B-series aircraft with BMW 801 air-cooled radials. The Weser Flugzeugbau was instructed to assist Blohm und Voss in the design of the BV 238, some component design was allocated to the French Louis Breguet drawing office, and the Flugtechnisches Fertigungsgemeinschaft

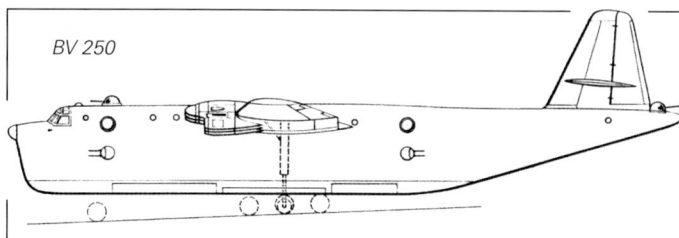

Prag in Czechoslovakia received an order to build a 1:3.75 scale wooden flying model of the boat.

The BV 238 followed what had become by this time traditional Blohm und Voss constructional methods, with the typical fuel-carrying welded tubular wing spar at 30 per cent chord. The entire trailing edge of the parallel-chord wing centre section was occupied by electrically-operated flaps, and a catwalk was provided ahead of the centre-section main spar to provide access to the engines in flight. The hull, which was an all-metal structure covered by corrosion-resistant alloy, featured power-operated bow doors permitting direct loading and unloading of the lower deck, and was basically a two-step design, the forward step being extremely shallow and augmented by a series of eight small auxiliary steps. The control system followed that of the BV 222, being part-servo and part-manual.

Landplane version

Before the end of 1941, Blohm und Voss had submitted a proposal to the Technisches Amt for what was referred to as the **BV 238-Land**, this being essentially a land-based derivative of the flying-boat with the planing bottom replaced by bomb-bays and accommodation for a multi-wheel main undercarriage bogie that was used in conjunction with a retractable twin nosewheel member and inward-retracting stabilising outrigger members. The BV 238-Land was intended for use as a heavy transport, carrying a 40000-kg (88,185-lb) freight load over a 2000-km (1,240-mile) distance; as a heavy bomber carrying a 20000-kg (44,090-lb) bombload over a distance of 7000 km (4,350 miles) or an 4000-kg (8,818-lb) load over a distance of 10000 km (6,215 miles), and as a long-range

Although considerably larger than the BV 222, the BV 238 was generally similar in configuration to the earlier boat. It differed primarily by having a high- rather than shoulder-mounted wing, a modified tail unit, and one-piece rather than split retractable stabilising floats. Flown successfully in the spring of 1944, the BV 238 V1, which was the only prototype to be completed, was strafed and destroyed on Lake Schaal by North American P-51 Mustang fighters in September 1944.

strategic reconnaissance aircraft possessing a tactical radius sufficient to enable it to reconnoitre a considerable proportion of the US Atlantic seaboard. Early in 1942, this project was allocated the designation **BV 250**, four prototypes being ordered for construction in parallel with the four BV 238 prototypes. Apart from the deletion of the planing bottom and the provision of bomb-bays and a wheel undercarriage, the land-based BV 250 was identical to the waterborne aircraft and retained the system of defensive twin-cannon barbettes.

This defensive system comprised a forward dorsal barbette and two forward lateral barbettes, sighting stations being provided in the fuselage sides immediately aft of the flight deck, two additional lateral barbettes were mounted on the aft fuselage with sighting stations immediately above from which the tail barbette was also directed. In April 1942, the four lateral barbettes were abandoned in favour of manned positions each mounting either paired 13-mm (0.51-in) MG 131 machine-guns or a single 20-mm MG 151 cannon, and a year later Blohm und Voss was instructed to discard the two remaining barbettes. The definitive BV 238 armament now envisaged comprised a forward dorsal HD 151Z turret mounting twin 20-mm MG 151s with 2,800 rounds, nose and tail HL 131V turrets each with four 13-mm MG 131s and 7,200 rounds, two pairs of MG 131s with 500 r.p.g. firing from beam positions, and two HL 131V four-gun turrets with 3,600 rounds per turret projecting aft of the wing trailing edges at the outer extremities of the centre section.

The wing-mounted turrets demanded a special 1.20-m (3.97-ft) wide reinforced component inserted between the centre and outboard wing panels to transfer turret loads to the main spar, the new components increasing overall wing-span and gross area to 60.17 m (197 ft 4¾ in) and 360.16 m² (3,876.84 sq ft). However, the main spars for the first three prototypes had already been completed, and it was therefore decided to introduce the modified main spar, suitably reinforced to support the turret extensions, on the first B-series flying-boat, the **BV 238 V4**, which was also to be the first aircraft to carry the definitive defensive armament, the removal of the elongated tailcone with its barbette and replacement by a manned turret reducing overall length from 45.50 m to 43.35 m (149 ft 3⅓ in to 142 ft 3 in).

Flying scale model

In the meantime, work had continued on the wooden flying scale model, designated **FGP 227**. Powered by six 15.7-kW (21-hp) ILO F 12/400 two-stroke air-cooled engines, this weighed 1250 kg (2,756 lb) empty and 1640 kg (3,615 lb) loaded, and had accommodation for a crew of two. Overall dimensions included a span of 15.25 m (50 ft 0⅓ in) and a length of 11.95 m (39 ft 2⅔ in), gross wing area being 24.24 m² (260.920 sq ft).

Finally completed early in 1944, the FGP 227 (BQ+UZ) was provided with a rudimentary wheel undercarriage of 10 small wheels with low-pressure tyres, the intention being to perform initial flying trials from a grass field in the vicinity of the factory in which the model had been built. As the FGP 227 resolutely refused to take-off, it was dismantled and loaded aboard a train for the journey to Travemünde, suffering some damage in the process when French prisoners-of-war manhandling the flying model onto flatbed trucks, and believing it to be some sort of secret weapon, allowed the wing, complete with its six diminutive engines, to fall 4.50 m (15 ft) from a hoist. Repairs were not completed until September 1944, when the FGP 227 was flown for the first time at Travemünde. Shortly after the small flying-boat took-off all six engines seized as a result of fuel starvation, and

Above: The FGP 227 scale model intended to aid development of the BV 238 was discovered by the Allies at Travemünde in May 1945. It was eventually taken for examination to Felixstowe, and was later broken up.

Completion of the FGP 227 was delayed by several factors and, in the event, the model was to play no part in the BV 238 development programme.

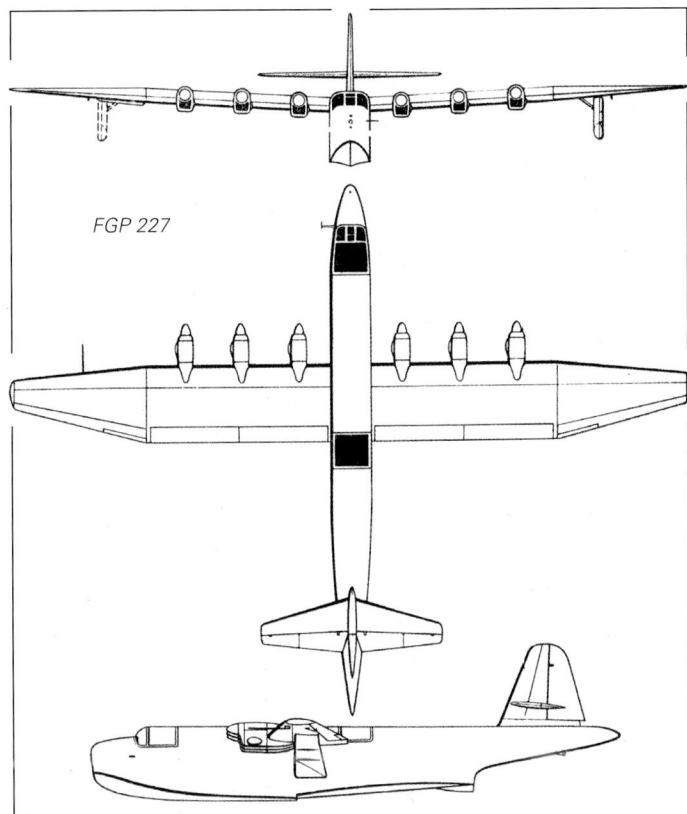

FGP 227

Blohm und Voss BV 238

Tests had shown the BV 238 to be suitable for service use, but this did not materialise and the BV 238's claim to fame lay in the fact that it was the largest military flying-boat to be built and flown during World War II.

The BV 238 V1 is seen during the taxi trial period that preceded flight testing from Lake Schaal in April 1944.

further damage was suffered in the ensuing heavy landing. Repaired once more, the FGP 227 was flown several times.

The **BV 238 V1** (RO+EZ) was completed early in 1944, commencing its flight trials in April. Lacking all defensive armament and powered by six DB 603A engines each rated at 1305 kW (1,750 hp) for take-off, the BV 238 V1 was the world's heaviest aircraft to have flown at that time, being flown at weights of up to 80000 kg (176,370 lb), the intended maximum take-off weight being as high as 90000 kg (198,416 lb) with the aid of four 14.7-kN (3,307-lb) thrust R–Geräte (take-off assistance rockets). Empty weight was 50800 kg (111,984 lb), maximum fuel capacity being 49000 litres (10,779 Imp gal), and provision was made for a crew complement of 10.

Initial flight trials of the BV 238 V1 were still in progress when the flying-boat was sunk at its moorings in September on Lake Schaal by three strafing P-51 Mustangs from the 361st Fighter Group, including one flown by the renowned ace Lieutenant Urban Drew. At this time, the second prototype, the **BV 238 V2**, was virtually complete, and construction of the **BV 238 V3** was well advanced, both machines being scheduled to receive DB 603Gs rated at 1417 kW (1,900 hp) for take-off. The BV 238 V4 and **BV 238 V5**, which were considered as pre-production aircraft for the B- and A-series respectively, had reached the pre-assembly stage, as had also

three of the four prototypes of the land-based BV 250, but during the late summer of 1944, the entire programme was cancelled and the semi-completed prototypes scrapped.

Blohm und Voss BV 238A-02 (V6, projected) specification
(manufacturer's estimated data)

Type: long-range transport, maritime patrol and bomber flying-boat
Powerplant: six Daimler-Benz DB 603G 12-cylinder liquid-cooled engines each rated at 1417 kW (1,900 hp) for take-off and 1163 kW (1,560 hp) at 7375 m (24,200 ft)
Performance: maximum speed at 60000 kg (132,277 lb) 350 km/h (216 mph) at sea level, 425 km/h (264 mph) at 6000 m (19,685 ft); maximum speed at 70000 kg (154,324 lb) 340 km/h (212 mph) at sea level, 405 km/h (253 mph) at 6000 m; maximum speed at 80000 kg (176,370 lb) 335 km/h (208 mph) at sea level, 380 km/h (237 mph) at 6000 m; maximum speed at 90000 kg (198,416 lb) 320 km/h (200 mph) at sea level, 360 km/h (223 mph) at 5000 m (16,405 ft); range 6620 km (4,113 miles) at 92000 kg (202,825 lb) at 365 km/h (227 mph) at 2000 m (6,560 ft), 7850 km (4,878 miles) at 92000 kg at 320 km/h (198 mph) at 10560 m (6,560 ft)
Weights: empty 54780 kg (120,769 lb), normal loaded (reconnaissance) 90000 kg (198,460 lb), (bomber) 95000 kg (209,439 lb); maximum overload 100000 kg (220,460 lb)
Dimensions: wingspan 60.17 m (197 ft 4¾ in); length 43.35 m (142 ft 3 in); height 12.80 m (42 ft 0 in); wing area 360.16 m² (3,876.84 sq ft)
Armament: (defensive) four 13-mm (0.51-in) MG 131 machine-guns with 1,800 r.p.g. in each of nose and tail turrets, and with 900 r.p.g. in two wing-mounted turrets, two pairs of MG 131 machine-guns with 500 r.p.g. firing from beam positions, and two 20-mm MG 151 cannon with 1,400 r.p.g. in forward dorsal turret; (offensive) wing bays housing 20 250-kg (551-lb) SC 250 bombs plus the following alternative external loads: four 1200-kg (2,645-lb) LD 1200 torpedoes, four 1000-kg (2,205-lb) SC 1000 bombs, four Henschel Hs 293 missiles or two 1000-kg BV 143 glide bombs

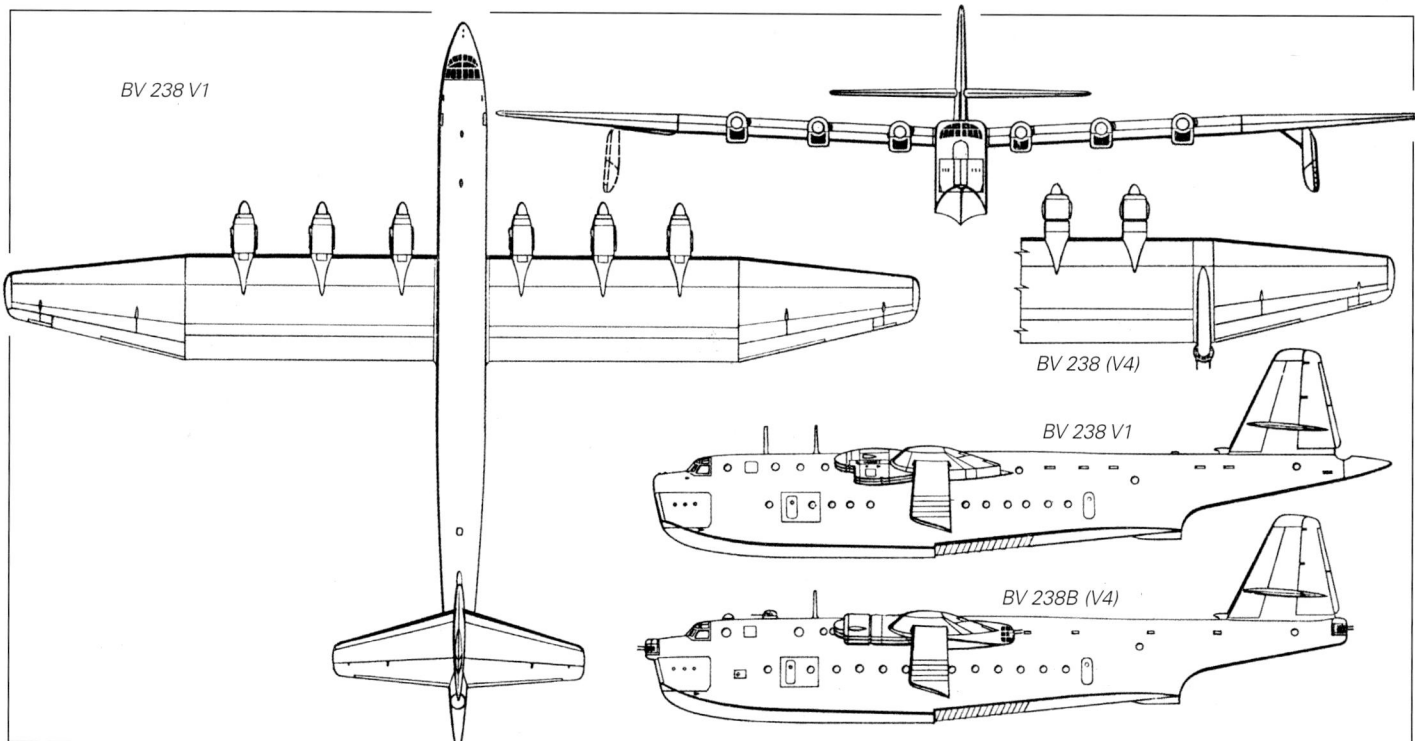

BV 238 V1

BV 238 (V4)

BV 238 V1

BV 238B (V4)

Boeing B-17 Flying Fortress

A mainstay of the US bombing campaign in Europe, the B-17 was flown in large numbers and on occasion suffered heavy losses. Of the many such bombers which crash-landed or were brought down by mechanical problems, about 40 were restored by the Germans for special purposes and development of anti-bomber tactics.

In May 1934 the US Army Air Corps issued its specification for an advanced multi-engined bomber able to haul a 2,000-lb (907-kg) bomb load over a range of between 1,020 miles (1640 km) and, somewhat optimistically, 2,200 miles (3540 km) at speeds of between 200 and 250 mph (322 and 402 km/h). Boeing responded with its **Model 299** design, and built a private-venture prototype that first flew on 28 July 1935. There followed a number of pre-production and limited-production variants of what was now the **B-17** before the advent of **B-17E** as the first large-scale production model (512 built), followed by the **B-17F** (3,405) and final **B-17G** (8,680) within an overall total of 12,731 aircraft. All three had a redesigned and enlarged vertical tail surface that was easily distinguishable from that of their predecessors by its large dorsal fin.

The B-17E and B-17F were the first of these bombers to serve with the 8th Army Air Force in Europe, and differed from each other primarily in armament and equipment. The B-17E and B-17F were then the most advanced developments of the B-17, but in two major operations against German strategic targets, made on 17 August and 14 October 1943, 120 bombers were lost. Clearly the B-17 could not mount an adequate defence against determined and skilled fighter interception, no matter how cleverly devised was the box formation in which the type flew. The following B-17G therefore introduced a 'chin' turret housing two 12.7-mm (0.5-in) machine-guns, which meant that this version carried a total of 13 such guns. To increase the type's operational ceiling, later production examples had an improved turbocharger for its Wright R-1820-97 radial engines.

After crash-landing or being forced down, about 20 B-17s were recovered and refurbished by the Luftwaffe, and about 12 of them were also placed into operational use. Some of them were used for overt tasks such as the familiarisation of fighter pilots with one of their primary targets and the development of the best possible tactics for attacks on Flying Fortress formations, but most were given German markings. For covert tasks such as long-range reconnaissance missions that could not be undertaken by German aircraft as a result of their inadequate range, these aircraft ranged across Europe and the Middle East from Norway to Jordan and the Western Desert in north Africa.

Another task was the delivery and support of secret agents. In this covert role the best known unit was Kampfgeschwader 200, one of the Luftwaffe's most highly specialised units that undertook a considerable spectrum of tasks. One of this unit's B-17s, possibly B-17G 42-39969 of the 401st Bomb Group, was interned by Spain when it landed at Valencia airport on 27 June 1944 and remained there for the rest of the war. Starting

Above: Carrying German markings in place of its original US colours, this B-17F, 42-30336, was used by the Luftwaffe primarily for technical evaluation and the development of fighter tactics.

*B-17F **Wulfe Hound** is examined by Germans (above) after its capture. The 'Fort' (serial 41-24585) was delivered to the USAAF's 303rd Bomb Group's 360th Bomb Squadron, and at the very start of operations on 12 December 1942, came down almost undamaged in France. Markings were added by the Germans on the wing's upper surface to indicate the position of fuel tanks, along with the codes DL+XC (right).*

*The career of **Wulfe Hound** after its capture by the Germans was extremely active. The bomber initially served as a 'target' for developing anti-B-17 tactics and finally carried out clandestine missions with I/KG200, in whose service it was coded A3+KB*

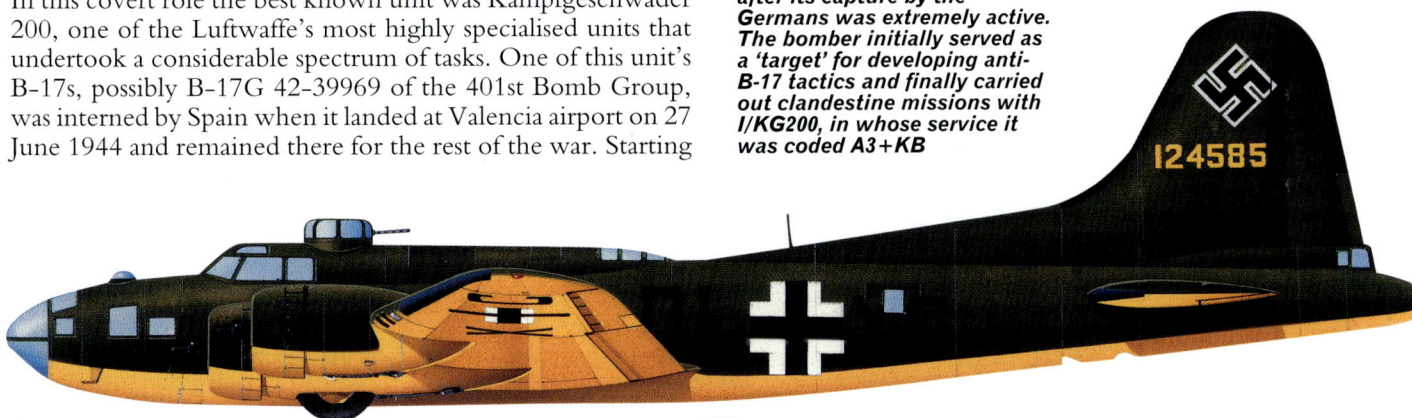

Boeing B-17

Right: Subjected to a technical evaluation at Rechlin, DL+XC Wulfe Hound was flown in demonstrations to the Jagdgruppen. For this role it was flown by the Zirkus Rosarius, formed in 1943 as part of 2./Versuchsverband Ob.d.L.

Below: The use of DL+XC in German skies allowed fighter pilots to gain a thorough knowledge of the Flying Fortress's nature in the air, in terms of both performance and manoeuvring capability.

Below left: Flight demonstrations and the wide circulation of detail images, such as this photograph of a B-17 tail gun installation on 42-5714, were important to the improvement of fighter tactics.

This photo detail of Wulfe Hound was used to teach German fighter pilots about the B-17's beam defence, which included one 12.7-mm (0.5-in) machine-gun in each of two waist positions.

from autumn 1943, the 2.Versuchsverband and, later I/KG 200 operated across the Mediterranean and Gulf of Sirte to establish secret bases inland at Al Mukaram and Wadi Tamet in the Western Desert, and also Shott al Jerid behind the Mareth Line. These undertakings involved one Messerschmitt Bf 108, two Heinkel He 111, and one B-17 aircraft. The last was badly damaged during a raid on Al Mukaram on 16 May 1944 by a Sudan Defence Force detachment watching the base, but was flown as far as Kalamata Bay where it crashed. In addition to local intelligence and meteorological work, the detachment ferried agents via French West Africa to Cairo, Freetown and Durban. One such operation delivered two German agents to Liberia: a Bf 108 staged ahead of the B-17 to find an area where its personnel could clear an airstrip on which the B-17 landed, the light aircraft then being refuelled to range ahead once more and locate the next airstrip location. The largest undertaking by I/KG 200, which was controlled by the Sicherheitsdienst, took place in July 1944, when 260 agents dropped, mainly by automatic parachute, in northern France.

One aircraft probably B-17F (US serial 42-3190) 'Mr Five by Five', German-coded A3+BB, was shot down by an US-flown Beaufighter on the evening of 2/3 March 1945. Six members of the Luftwaffe crew survived, but remainder of those on board, including nine secret agents, all died.

Some B-17s were kept in their Allied markings and were used in attempts to infiltrate B-17 formations and report on their position and altitude. The practice was initially successful, but the USAAF's crews quickly learned of the tactics and developed procedures to warn off or, if this failed, fire upon any aircraft trying to join a group's formation.

Boeing B-17F Flying Fortress specification
Type: 8/10-crew heavy bomber
Powerplant: four Wright R-1820-97 air-cooled nine-cylinder radial engines each rated at 1,200 hp (895 kW)
Performance: maximum speed 325 mph (523 km/h) at 25,000 ft (7620 m); economical cruising speed 160 mph (257 km/h) at 5,000 ft (1525 m); initial climb rate 900 ft (274 m) per minute; service ceiling 36,000 ft (10975 m); range 4,420 miles (7113 km)
Weights: empty (typical) 35,728 lb (16206 kg); normal take-off 56,000 lb (25402 kg); maximum overload take-off 72,000 lb (32659 kg)
Dimensions: wing span 103 ft 9 in (31.62 m); length 74 ft 9 in (22.78 m); height 19 ft 2½ in (5.85 m); wing area 1,420.00 sq ft (131.92 m²)
Armament: (defensive) one 0.3-in (7.62-mm) and up to 12 0.5-in (12.7-mm) trainable machine-guns; (offensive) bombload of up to 9,600 lb (4355 kg) later increased to 17,600 lb (7983 kg)

The 1.Staffel of KG 200 was responsible for long-range operations, including the dropping of agents behind enemy lines, for which the B-17 was ideal. The unit had around three B-17Fs and this single B-17G on strength, but also had a number of non-flying aircraft that could be raided for spares. This aircraft was acquired in early 1944, and was inadvertently shot down on 6 April 1945 by German flak gunners.

Breda Ba 88 Lince

Trumpeted as a world-beater on its debut, the Ba 88 quickly emerged as a type of wholly indifferent capability once equipment and armament had been added. Perhaps the Lince's greatest controbution to the Italian war effort was its use as a ground decoy for Allied aircraft that might have attacked more useful warplanes.

A propaganda triumph when its appearance as a record-breaker was trumpeted by Benito Mussolini's Italian Fascist regime in 1936, the **Ba 88 Lince** (lynx) was a sleek shoulder-wing monoplane of all-metal construction, but the addition of military equipment and armament then led to an immediate and drastic degradation of performance. By this time 155 production aircraft were being built. They proved to have dismal combat capability, and by mid-November 1940 most survivors had been stripped of useful equipment and scattered on operational airfields as decoys.

In 1942 Agusta modified three Ba 88s as **Ba 88M** ground-attack aircraft. The wingspan was increased by 2.00 m (6 ft 6¾ in) to alleviate wing loading problems, the Piaggio engines were replaced by 742-kW (840-hp) Fiat A.74 RC.38 air-cooled 14-cylinder radial units, the nose armament was increased to four 12.7-mm (0.5-in) machine-guns, and dive brakes were installed. The aircraft were evaluated at Guidonia and then delivered to a unit at Lonate Pozzolo on 7 September 1943. Two days later the Italian armistice with the Allies came into effect, and the aircraft were seized by the Luftwaffe for evaluation, and this was the last heard of the type.

Underpowered and with too great a wing loading, three Ba 88s were upgraded to Ba 88M standard and evaluated by the Luftwaffe, but disappeared into the fog of history.

Breda Ba 88 Lince specification
Type: two-seat ground-attack and reconnaissance aircraft
Powerplant: two Piaggio P.XI RC.40 Stella air-cooled 14-cylinder radial engines each rated at 746 kW (1,000 hp) for take-off
Performance: maximum speed 490 km/h (304 mph) at 4000 m (13,125 ft); climb to 3000 m (9,845 ft) in 7 minutes 30 seconds; service ceiling 8000 m (26,245 ft); range 1640 km (1,019 miles)
Weights: empty 4650 kg (10,252 lb); maximum take-off 6750 kg (14,881 lb)
Dimensions: wingspan 15.60 m (51 ft 2⅛ in); length 10.79 m (35 ft 4¾ in); height 3.10 m (10 ft 2 in); wing area 33.34 m² (358.88 sq ft)
Armament: three 12.7-mm (0.5-in) Breda-SAFAT machine-guns fixed forward-firing machine-guns in nose and one 7.7-mm (0.303-in) Breda-SAFAT trainable machine-gun in rear cockpit, plus up to 1000 kg (2,204 lb) of bombs in fuselage bomb-bay or, alternatively, three 200-kg (441-lb) bombs carried semi-exposed in individual recesses in the fuselage belly

Breguet Bre.521 Bizerte

A French biplane flying-boat based on a British type, the Bre.531 was typical of seaplane design in the early 1930s. The Bizerte was rugged and reliable, however, and the Germans took into service as many as they could for the air-sea rescue role in the waters round north-western France and in the Mediterranean.

In 1931 Breguet obtained a licence from Short Brothers for construction of the British company's Calcutta biplane flying-boat. Breguet then responded to a 1932 requirement of the Aéronautique Maritime for a long-range maritime reconnaissance flying-boat, and this **Bre.520** proposal based on the Calcutta became the **Bre.521 Bizerte** in its definitive form. The Bizerte was thus a large biplane (almost sesquiplane) based on an all-metal structure with stabilising floats strut-mounted beneath the lower wing, a strut-braced tail unit, and a powerplant of three engines strut-mounted between the upper and lower wings, which were separated and braced by Warren-type struts. The powerplant of the **Bre.521.01** prototype, which first flew on 11 September 1933, was three 630-kW (845-hp) Gnome-Rhône 14Kdrs radial engines in uncowled mountings. Official trials began in January 1934, by which time revised engines had been enclosed in NACA-type cowlings. The navy ordered three pre-production examples of the Bre.521 before the trials had been completed, and the first of these flew during 1935.

The second of the pre-production aircraft introduced a number of modifications that became standard on subsequent boats. They included deletion of the open bow gun position, a forward extension of the cockpit canopy, the provision of two new gun positions in blisters on the hull sides, and a new tail position. Deliveries of production boats began in 1935 and continued at a steady pace into 1940, by which time 31 (including the prototype) had been built. By October 1939

This Bre.521 flying boat served with the 1.Seenotstaffel, which appreciated the strength, reliability and range of this boat for the taxing air-sea rescue role round the Brittany peninsula.

The Luftwaffe's 1.Seenotstaffel was based at Brest-Hourtin in north-west France during the winter of 1943-44. It operated this Bre.521.

Below: The Warren-type strut arrangement of the Bre.521's biplane wing cellule provided good mountings for the nacelles for the three engines, which were fully cowled and drove tractor propellers.

five squadrons were equipped with the type, but only two survived to serve with the Vichy French naval air arm, the other three being disbanded in June 1940.

Between June 1940 and November 1942, the Luftwaffe acquired an eventual 17 Bizerte flying-boats, some of them bought from the Vichy French government as surplus to requirement. In mid-August 1940 eight of the boats were flown to Brest-Poulmic, from where they were allocated to the 1.Seenotstaffel for air/sea rescue operations between the Bay of Biscay and the South-Western Approaches to the UK. When they occupied Vichy France on 8 November 1942, the Germans discovered two or three boats in service with Flottille 9E at Berre, and others in storage. This allowed the Germans to operate a detachment of 1.Seenotstaffel from Lorient and St Mandrier, operating over the Bay of Biscay and western Mediterranean, respectively. The fate of the boats remains obscure except in the case of one, which was found on the Mediterranean coast by the allies in August 1944 and placed in service with Flottille 9F Tr until withdrawn in 1946 for lack of spares.

Breguet Bre.521 Bizerte specification

Type: eight-seat long-range maritime reconnaissance or, in German service, air/sea rescue flying-boat
Powerplant: three Gnome-Rhône 14Kirs or 14N-11 air-cooled 14-cylinder radial engines each rated at 671 kW (900 hp)
Performance: maximum speed 245 km/h (152 mph) at 1000 m (3,280 ft); cruising speed 200 km/h (124 mph) at optimum altitude; climb to 2000 m (6,560 ft) in 8 minutes 46 seconds; service ceiling 6000 m (19,685 ft); range 3000 km (1,864 miles)
Weights: empty 9470 kg (20,878 lb); maximum take-off 16600 kg (36,597 lb)
Dimensions: wingspan 35.15 m (115 ft 4 in); length 20.50 m (67 ft 3 in); height 7.45 m (24 ft 5¼ in); wing area 162.50 m² (1,750.27 sq ft)
Armament: (defensive) two 7.5-mm (0.295-in) Darne trainable machine-guns in each of the port and starboard dorsal positions, and one 7.5-mm (0.295-in) Darne trainable rearward-firing machine-gun in the tail position; (offensive) up to 300 kg (661 lb) of bombs carried under the lower wing

Breguet Bre.693

Had it appeared earlier for lengthier development, greater production and more time for training and the evolution of the right tactics, the Bre.693 could have been invaluable to France's air effort in 1940. Late in 1942 the Germans seized all Vichy French aircraft, and after short evaluation passed the Bre.693s to the Italians.

The **Bre.690.01** multi-role warplane prototype first flew on 23 March 1938 with two 507-kW (680-hp) Hispano-Suiza 14AB-02/03 radial engines. Thereafter development switched to an AB.2 two-seat assault bomber with an internal bomb bay. Developed via the **Bre.691** with Hispano-Suiza engines, the **Bre.693.01** prototype switched to more reliable Gnome-Rhône engines and first flew on 25 October 1939. The **Bre.693AB.2** model was the only production variant, with 234 built. The type's combat debut, on 12 May 1940 in attacks on German columns advancing through Belgium, was disastrous: 10 out of 11 aircraft were

shot down or written off. By 25 June almost half of the 106 Bre.693AB.2s delivered by that time had been destroyed. After the Franco-German armistice, the type remained in Vichy French service, but in November 1942 the Germans occupied Vichy France and seized the aircraft, which were then transferred to Italy for service as operational trainers.

Breguet Bre.693AB.2 specification

Type: two-seat attack bomber
Powerplant: two Gnome-Rhône 14M-6/7 air-cooled 14-cylinder radial engines each rated at 522 kW (700 hp) for take-off
Performance: maximum speed 490 km/h (304 mph) at 5000 m (16,405 ft); cruising speed 400 km/h (249 mph) at 4000 m (13,125 ft); climb to 4000 m in 7 minutes 12 seconds; range 1350 km (839 miles)
Weights: empty 3010 kg (6,636 lb); maximum take-off 4900 kg (10,803 lb)
Dimensions: wingspan 15.37 m (50 ft 5 in); length 9.67 m (31 ft 8¼ in); height 3.19 m (10 ft 5¾ in); wing area 29.20 m² (314.32 sq ft)
Armament: one 20-mm Hispano-Suiza fixed cannon and two 7.5-mm (0.295-in) MAC 1934 fixed machine-guns in the nose, one 7.5-mm MAC 1934 trainable machine-gun in the rear cockpit, one 7.5-mm MAC 1934 fixed rearward-firing machine-gun in the ventral position and (late aircraft) one 7.5-mm MAC 1934 fixed rearward-firing machine-gun in the rear of each engine nacelle, plus up to 400 kg (882 lb) of bombs

Here an ex-Vichy French example of the Bre.693 is seen in German markings, late in 1942 or early in 1943, before all the aircraft were transferred to the Regia Aeronautica as trainers.

Bristol Blenheim and Beaufighter

As the RAF's main light bomber of the early war years the Bristol Blenheim came into widespread conflict with German forces, and it is no surprise that a number were captured and evaluated by the Luftwaffe. The Beaufighter also operated over Europe and the Mediterranean, and at least one was captured intact.

Named after a village in Germany, where a Grand Alliance army led by the Duke of Marlborough had defeated a Franco-Bavarian army in 1704, the **Bristol Blenheim** was the RAF's principal light bomber in the early years of the war. It also undertook reconnaissance, maritime patrol and night-fighting duties, and saw action in all Allied theatres. It had largely been withdrawn from front-line duties by late 1942 in Europe, and by mid-1943 in the Middle East.

By far the most numerous variant was the **Blenheim Mk IV**, of which over 3,000 were built, the majority by Rootes Securities at Speke and Blythe Bridge. Ten were also built by Valtion Lentokonetehdas in Finland using parts sold by Germany from Yugoslav stocks. The Mk IV featured a lengthened nose to provide the navigator with a more comfortable working area, and also to provide the mounting for rear-facing ventral armament.

A number of Blenheim Mk IVs were captured by the Germans, the type being evaluated and probably demonstrated to front-line units. The first main opportunity to acquire Blenheims came during the Battle of France in May 1940, as the type was one of the main RAF protagonists in the desperate campaign to stem the German advance. Aircraft from Nos 21 and 114 Squadrons were captured, if not others. It is from this campaign that the Luftwaffe is thought to have acquired the Mk IV that appeared with dark undersides, mottled upper surfaces and the codes '5-5'. Another opportunity came in 1941 with the Battle of Greece, in which a No. 11 Squadron aircraft was captured. Blenheims were also widely used by the Commonwealth and Free French in North Africa. One aircraft depicted in Luftwaffe insignia has a kangaroo nose marking, and almost certainly had previously operated with an Australian unit flying in the theatre.

As well as their limited Luftwaffe service, Blenheims also fought on the Axis side with Romania and Croatia. Romania received 37 **Blenheim Mk I** aircraft (of 40 purchased) to equip four long-range reconnaissance units. They served alongside Luftwaffe units during Operation Barbarossa, but suffered heavy losses, and were withdrawn in December 1942, thereafter flying Black Sea patrols. By August 1944 only three aircraft were still operational.

Croatia's aircraft came from the former Royal Yugoslav air force, which bought 20 Mk Is from the UK and had acquired a licence for Ikarus to build a further 50. Around 16 of them had been completed by the time of the German invasion in April 1941. After the battle three were sold to Romania, and

Above: A crowd gathers round the possibly damaged front end of a captured Blenheim Mk IV. The fuselage markings are the original RAF codes (YH-F) and signify previous allocation to No. 21 Squadron, which was involved in cross-Channel operations for the first two years of the war.

Below: This Blenheim Mk IV carries a kangaroo nose marking, and was probably captured in North Africa.

eight were given to the newly formed Croatian Air Force Legion, which established the 12th Bomber Squadron within the 5th Bomber Wing to operate them. They operated alongside Luftwaffe units on the Russian front for a while.

Bristol Beaufighter

To the Luftwaffe the **Bristol Beaufighter** would have been of considerably more interest than the Blenheim. The RAF's night-fighter versions were an effective defence against nocturnal Luftwaffe raids over Britain, especially when equipped with airborne interception radar, and the type also exacted a heavy toll from Axis coastal shipping in its strike versions. It appears that at least one Beaufighter was flown by the Luftwaffe, based on a reference to the type having been flown by KG 200, and a single poor-quality photograph.

This is most likely the Beaufighter Mk I which landed in error at Syracuse in 1942, and was captured by the Italians, as indicated by the white fuselage band and the overpainted rudder.

Bristol Blenheim Mk IV specification
Type: three-seat light bomber
Powerplant: two 905-hp (675-kW) Bristol Mercury XV radial piston engines
Performance: maximum speed 266 mph (428 km/h) at 11,800 ft (3595 m); cruising speed 198 mph (319 km/h); service ceiling 27,260 ft (8310 m); maximum range 1,460 miles (2350 km)
Weights: empty 9,790 lb (4441 kg); maximum take-off 14,400 lb (6532 kg)
Dimensions: wingspan 56 ft 4 in (17.17 m); length 42 ft 7 in (12.98 m); height 9 ft 10 in (3.00 m); wing area 469.00 sq ft (43.57 m²)
Armament: five 0.303-in (7.7-mm) machine-guns (one forward-firing in port wing, two in power-operated dorsal turret, and two remotely controlled in mounting beneath nose and firing aft), plus up to 1,000 lb (454 kg) of bombs internally and 320 lb (145 kg) of bombs externally

Bücker Flugzeugbau GmbH

Bücker was established in 1933 as the manufacturer of compact but agile light aircraft for the aerobatic and training roles, and swiftly became one of the most important designers and builders of training aircraft for the newly emerged Luftwaffe. This situation remained true to the end of World War II.

The Bücker Flugzeugbau GmbH was established in Germany during 1933 as a designer and manufacturer of light aircraft, and soon became well known for its sporting aircraft, which gained high plaudits for their good performance and fuel economy. The company also created a series of biplane, and later monoplane, aircraft that offered superb capabilities as trainers, and several of them entered large-scale production for the Luftwaffe before and during World War II.

The company was founded by Carl Clemens Bücker, who had been born on 11 February 1895, served as an officer in the Imperial German navy's air arm during World War I, and after that war's end spent some years in Sweden. Here he was involved in the development of the Swedish navy's air arm and, from 1921, in the creation of Svenska

The Bü 180 Student was something of a departure for the company: it was the first Bücker monoplane, and also introduced a composite structure with wood/plywood flying surfaces and a steel-tube fuselage. Designed only for civil use, the Student was not a commercial success.

Aero. When this company merged with ASJA in 1930, Bücker resigned his managing directorship and returned to Germany, where in October 1933 he used financial backing from a car coach-building company to establish the Bücker Flugzeugbau in the premises of his backer in Johannisthal, just outside Berlin. In 1935 the company moved to a new and bigger factory in Rangsdorf.

The company's chief designer was Anders J. Andersson, a Swede who had worked with Bücker in Sweden. As the company grew it expanded to another factory, at Wernigerode. Bücker's three great successes were the Bü 131 Jungmann of 1934, the Bü 133 Jungmeister of 1935 and the Bü 181 Bestmann of 1939. Bücker was also involved in the manufacture of other companies' designs, including the Focke-Wulf Fw 44 and DFS 230, as well as components for the Focke-Wulf Fw 190, Junkers Ju 87 and Henschel Hs 293.

At the end of World War II, the company's premises fell into the Soviet occupation zone, and were seized. The company then went out of business.

Bücker
Bestmann

Bü 181

das neue deutsche
Einheitsflugzeug
für Anfangs- und
Kunstflugschulung

BÜCKER · FLUGZEUGBAU GMBH / RANGSDORF BEI BERLIN

Left: When the Bü 181 Bestmann prototype (D-ERBV) first flew in February 1939, it immediately became the key product on factory advertisements. The RLM responded by making this model a standard primary trainer for the Luftwaffe.

Anders Andersson was the Bücker company's Swedish chief engineer, and arguably his greatest creation was the Bü 133 Jungmeister. Bücker himself had worked in Sweden, initially as a navy test pilot, before establishing the Svenska Aero-aktiebolaget (not to be confused with today's Saab organisation). Svenska Aero's main initial business was the manufacture of Heinkel designs.

Bücker Bü 131 Jungmann

The Jungmann was designed by a Swede, Anders Andersson, and was the Bücker company's first production aircraft. The type proved immensely successful and became Germany's most important primary trainer of World War II, with fairly large numbers being exported or built under licence, notably in Japan.

The first product of the Bücker Flugzeugbau GmbH, established at Johannisthal, Germany, during 1932, was a two-seat light trainer known as the **Bü 131 Jungmann** (Youth). Designed by Anders Andersson, the company's Swedish chief engineer, the Jungmann was a conventional single-bay biplane with a staggered, swept and single-bay biplane wing cellule of fabric-covered wooden construction, a welded steel-tube fuselage that, with the exception of light alloy around the engine and cockpit, was also fabric-covered, and a wire-braced tail unit of similar construction to the fuselage. The fixed tailwheel type landing gear had rather stalky divided main units, and the prototype first flew on 27 April 1934, powered by a Hirth HM 60K inverted inline engine rated at 60 kW (80 hp).

The **Bü 131A**, as the initial production version was designated, proved to be very successful. The type was manufactured not only for civil flying schools in Germany, but was also built very extensively for the Luftwaffe, although production figures do not appear to have survived. Examples were also exported for service in some eight European countries, with the largest numbers going to Hungary (100) and Romania (150), and in addition 75 aircraft were licence-built in Switzerland.

The **Bü 131B** was an improved version with the uprated Hirth HM 504A-2 engine, while the **Bü 131C** was an experimental model, of which only a single example was built power provided by a Cirrus Minor inverted inline engine rated at 68 kW (90 hp).

Japanese manufacture

The most extensive licensed construction was undertaken in Japan, where 1,037 **Nippon Kokusai Ki-86a** aircraft were built for service with the Imperial Japanese army air force under the service designation **Type 4 Primary Trainer**.

The Bü 131 became Germany's most important primary trainer of World War II, and fairly large numbers were exported or built under licence in countries including Czechoslovakia, Japan, Spain and Switzerland.

This followed the initiation of production for the Imperial Japanese navy air force, which operated the type as the **Navy Type 2 Trainer Model 11** (otherwise **K9W1 Momiji**, or Maple), built by Hitachi and Kyushu. Production figures for the naval version differ according to source at between 217 and 339, but it seems reasonably certain that more than 200 were used as the navy's standard trainer. The engine

Designed by Anders Andersson, the Jungmann was Bücker's first aircraft to enter production. The prototype first flew in April 1934 with a 60-kW (80-hp) Hirth HM 60R air-cooled four-cylinder inverted inline engine, and proved immensely successful. It was docile enough to provide ab initio *training, but also proved a good mount for aerobatics training.*

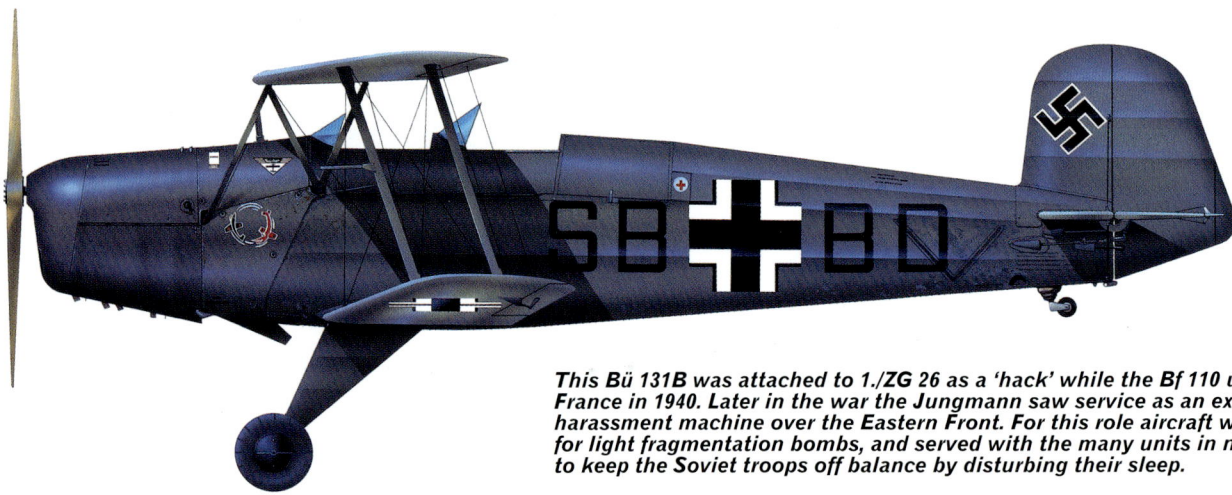

This Bü 131B was attached to 1./ZG 26 as a 'hack' while the Bf 110 unit was based in France in 1940. Later in the war the Jungmann saw service as an extemporised night harassment machine over the Eastern Front. For this role aircraft were fitted with racks for light fragmentation bombs, and served with the many units in nuisance raids designed to keep the Soviet troops off balance by disturbing their sleep.

used in the two Japanese variants, which each had the Allied reporting name **'Cypress'**, was the 82-kW (110-hp) inverted inline engine known to the army as the Hitachi (Ha-47) 11 and to the navy as the Hitachi GK4A Hatsukaze 11. The sole

Ki-86B was an experimental development with an all-wood airframe, but was somewhat heavier than the Ki-86a, with inferior performance.

Used throughout World War II by the Luftwaffe, the Bü 131A was later displaced by the superior Bü 181, and many of the aircraft also saw service with auxiliary ground-attack squadrons. Carrying 1- and 2-kg (2.2- and 4.4-lb) bombs, they were used by night to maintain non-stop harassment over the Soviet lines. Like other classic trainers, many Bü 131 aircraft survived the war, and were even built by Aero in Czechoslovakia during the 1950s under the local designation **C-4**.

Above: The Jungmann could be adapted with ski undercarriage so that operations continued in the winter months. The Bü 131 proved to be an excellent trainer, with handling characteristics superior to those of its Allied counterparts, the Tiger Moth and Stearman. Production continued after the war, and Spain retained the type as its standard basic trainer until 1968, a testament to its sound design.

Bucker Bü 131B Jungmann specification
Type: two-seat primary flying trainer with a secondary tasking for night harassment
Powerplant: one Hirth HM 504A-2 inverted inline engine rated at 78 kW (105 hp)
Performance: maximum speed 183 km/h (114 mph) at sea level; cruising speed 170 km/h (106 mph) at optimum altitude; climb to 1000 m (3,280 ft) in 6 minutes 18 seconds; service ceiling 3000 m (9,845 ft); range 650 km (404 miles)
Weights: empty 390 kg (860 lb); maximum take-off 680 kg (1,499 lb)
Dimensions: wingspan 7.40 m (24 ft 3⅓ in); length 6.60 m (21 ft 8 in); height 2.25 m (7 ft 4½ in); wing area 13.50 m² (145.32 sq ft)
Armament: generally none, although provision was later added for the occupant of the rear seat to drop light fragmentation bomblets, and finally for such weapons to be dropped from racks under the lower wing

Left: The Bü 131 Jungmann is most easily distinguished from the later single-seat Bü 133 Jungmeister by its inverted inline rather than radial engine.

Below: The Bü 131 could be used for aerobatic and sport flying as well as flying training. Among the type's attributes were interchangeable upper and lower wooden wings, and a steel tube fuselage and tail unit.

Above: The Bü 131 possessed all the attributes required of any successful basic trainer, for it was viceless in its handling and had the ruggedness to survive nearly all that was thrown at it by trainee pilots.

Right: Vics of Bü 131s are seen at a training base of the Deutscher Luftsportverband (German Aviation Sport Union). The photograph was taken between autumn 1935 and spring 1936 over Adlershof airfield, near Berlin.

Bücker Bü 133 Jungmeister

A robust, aerobatic derivative of the Jungmann, the Bü 133 Jungmeister single-seat biplane was slightly smaller and, fitted with a more powerful engine, offered excellent flying characteristics and performance. The Bü 133 served as an advanced trainer with the Luftwaffe, and licence production took place in Spain and Switzerland.

Demand for the Bü 131 Jungmann was so great that Bücker's production facilities at Johannisthal were soon overwhelmed. A new factory was therefore established at Rangsdorf and there, where it would be possible to expand production facilities, the company began development of a single-seat trainer based on the Bü 131 design. Generally similar in overall configuration and construction, this **Bü 133 Jungmeister** (Young Champion) differed primarily in its smaller overall dimensions, which meant that the prototype, with power from a Hirth HM506 inverted inline engine rated at 104 kW (140 hp), possessed excellent aerobatic performance.

The prototype Bü 133 (D-EVEO) was first flown on 21 August 1935 by Luise Hoffmann, Europe's first female works test pilot. Hoffmann died later that year after being seriously injured in a crash of a Bü 131 Jungmann while returning from a demonstration tour of the Balkans and Turkey.

In 1935 the Jungmeister made its first public appearance at a rally in Lausanne, Switzerland. The following year it appeared at the International Aerobatic Championship held at Rangsdorf, just to the north of Berlin and home to the Bücker factory. Despite displaying extraordinary agility, no orders were forthcoming for the Hirth-powered version. There followed two **Bü 133B** aircraft that switched to Siemens-Bramo Sh 14A radial power; one Bü 133B was exported to the United States, arriving on board the airship *Hindenburg*. The definitive version of the Jungmeister was the **Bü 133C**, which had the Sh 14A radial engine as standard, covered by a characteristic cowling with bulges over the cylinder heads. The fuselage was shortened by 13 cm (5 in), which further improved the type's agility, and new elevators were fitted.

Bü 133Cs were initially inducted into service by civilian Luftsportverband clubs and the Nationalsozialistisches Fliegerkorps (NSFK), organisations that purported to operate for sport-flying purposes, but in reality acted as flying schools for the nascent Luftwaffe. By 1938 the Luftwaffe

The success of the Jungmann led Bücker to open a second factory where a single-seat derivative could be produced in parallel with the original two-seater. Seen here in use with Jagdfliegerschule 2 of the Luftwaffe, the Jungmeister single-seat advanced trainer was essentially a scaled-down Jungmann.

itself had chosen the Bü 133 to be its main advanced trainer, but it is thought that only 72 were acquired for air force service. In 1938 a three-aircraft Luftwaffe team astonished the crowds at the Brussels flying meet, and the following year a nine-ship formation team attended the event. From

Above: D-EAKE was the first of the radial-engined Bü 133Bs, and was powered by the Siemens Sh 14A-4 engine. Like the Bü 131, primarily construction was of wood and tubular steel, and many parts were interchangeable.

Based on the initial Bü 133A version seen in the foreground, the Bü 133B (represented by D-EAKE) was created once the Siemens Sh 14A engine became available. More compact and more powerful, the Sh 14A engine served to enhance the aircraft's extraordinary flying qualities.

Bücker Bü 133 Jungmeister

The Bü 133 V1, with the registration D-EVEO, was equipped with a six-cylinder inline Hirth HM 506-A engine and was flown for the first time in early 1935, with Luise Hoffman at the controls.

January 1937 Jungmeisters were exported to Spain, acquiring the Nationalists' type designator '35'. At least one is believed to have been operated by the Republicans, who assigned the type designator 'EX'.

Luftwaffe operations

In Luftwaffe service the Jungmeister was issued in small numbers to a number of training units, including Jagdfliegerschulen 2, 5 and 6 (fighter schools), and at least five of the general flying schools (Flugzeugführerschulen A/B 5, 9, 11, 116 and 120) and their predecessors. The Jungmeister was used for advanced aerobatic training. By September 1944 18 are recorded as still being in Luftwaffe service.

Around 280 Jungmeisters were built, including 46 Bü 133Bs that were manufactured by Dornier-Werke in Altenrhein for the Swiss air force, and 25 Bü 133Cs built by CASA in Spain for the Spanish air force. Known as 'Pepino' in Spanish service, the Jungmeister survived into the 1960s, when the lack of Sh 14A spares forced its retirement. In civilian hands, the Bü 133 has remained a sought-after recreational aircraft. Several have been re-engined, including one that flew with a 299-kW (400-hp) Allison turboprop. A re-engined Jungmeister was also the favoured mount of Colonel José Luis de Aresti Aguirre, who devised the Aresti notation system for describing aerobatic manoeuvres.

Bücker Bü 133C Jungmeister specification
Type: single-seat advanced flying and aerobatic trainer
Powerplant: one Siemens Sh 14A-4 radial engine rated at 119 kW (160 hp)
Performance: maximum speed 220 km/h (137 mph) at sea level; cruising speed 200 km/h (124 mph) at optimum altitude; climb to 1000 m (3,280 ft) in 2 minutes 48 seconds; service ceiling 4500 m (14,765 ft); range 500 km (311 miles)
Weights: empty 425 kg (937 lb); maximum take-off 585 kg (1,290 lb)
Dimensions: wingspan 6.60 m (21 ft 7¾ in); length 6.00 m (19 ft 9 in); height 2.20 m (7 ft 2½ in); wing area 12.00 m² (129.17 sq ft)

Below: By 1938 the Bü 133 was the Luftwaffe's standard advanced trainer. A nine-aircraft display team was formed in 1939 to display at the Brussels international air meet.

Above: The definitive Bü 133C was powered by a radial engine. The aircraft offered excellent agility and performance, and was used as a lead-in fighter trainer and for advanced flying training.

Below: A number of Bü 133s were supplied to Spain from the Bücker factory. After the Civil War the type was built at Sevilla-Tablada for the Spanish air force as the CASA 1.133.

Arguably the finest inter-war aerobatic aircraft, the Jungmeister was designed by Carl Bücker for the Luftsportsbund, which employed the type for aerobatic competitions and display flying. This radial-engined Bü 133 is fitted with ski undercarriage.

Bücker Bü 180 Student

The Bücker Bü 180 Student represented something of a departure for the company: it was the first Bücker monoplane, and also introduced a composite structure with wood/plywood flying surfaces and a fuselage of steel-tube construction. Designed for civil use, the Student was not a commercial success.

After it had designed the successful Bü 133 Jungmeister and got this type into production, Bücker Flugzeugbau turned its attention to the development of the Bü 134 as a two-seat cabin monoplane of high-wing configuration. The single prototype of this aircraft proved to be unsuccessful when tested, and its development was abandoned. Convinced that future trainers would need to be of monoplane configuration, the company persevered and now designed another two-seat trainer of cantilever low-wing layout.

Designated **Bü 180**, and later named **Student**, this had a monoplane wing of wooden construction, covered partially with plywood and partially with fabric, and the tail unit was of similar construction. The forward fuselage was fabricated of welded steel tube and the rear fuselage was a wooden monocoque, all covered by fabric except for light alloy panels around the engine. The fixed landing gear was of the tailskid type with divided main units, the powerplant was based on one 45-kW (60-hp) Walter Mikron II or Zundapp 9-092 inverted inline engine, and the two-seat accommodation was provided in a tandem arrangement of open cockpits. The prototype first flew in the autumn of 1937, and there then followed a small number of production aircraft intended for civil use.

Bücker Bü 180 Student specification
Type: two-seat sporting and training aircraft
Powerplant: one Walter Mikron II or Zundapp 9-092 inverted inline engine rated at 45 kW (60 hp)
Performance: maximum speed 175 km/h (109 mph) at sea level; cruising speed 160 km/h (99 mph) at optimum altitude; climb to 1000 m (3,280 ft) in 8 minutes 54 seconds; service ceiling 4500 m (14,765 ft); range 650 km (404 miles)
Weights: empty 295 kg (650 lb); maximum take-off 540 kg (1,190 lb)
Dimensions: wingspan 11.50 m (37 ft 8¼ in); length 7.10 m (23 ft 3½ in); height 1.85 m (6 ft ¾ in); wing area 15.00 m² (161.46 sq ft)

Generally similar in design to the British Miles Magister, the Bü 180 Student seated the instructor and pupil in tandem. The first prototype of the Bü 180 flew in 1937.

Bücker Bü 181 Bestmann

A development of the Bü 180 Student, the Bü 181 low-wing monoplane trainer featured enclosed side-by-side accommodation for the crew of two. The production version for the Luftwaffe was the Bü 181A, of which several thousand were built in Germany, with further wartime production taking place in the Netherlands and Sweden.

Experience with the Bü 180 showed Bücker that, even with an engine of small power output, the two-seat monoplane could offer surprisingly good performance. With this encouragement the company began the design of a new trainer that adopted the construction of the Bü 180 in combination with side-by-side seating in an enclosed cabin to provide ideal conditions for primary training. Identified as the **Bü 181** and later named **Bestmann** (mate), the new aircraft had wings of wooden basic construction with plywood and fabric covering, a tail unit of similar structure, and a fuselage with steel-tube forward section and a wooden monocoque rear section. The landing gear was of the fixed tailwheel type with divided main units, and power was provided by a Hirth HM 504 inverted inline engine. The prototype made its first flight early in 1939 and, following testing by the Luftwaffe, the type was ordered into full production as the **Bü 181A** for service as a standard basic trainer.

Details of the number of Bü 181s constructed for the

Several thousand examples of the Bü 181 were built. Aircraft not required for training were utilised most usefully in the liaison, glider-towing and anti-tank weapon transportation roles.

Bucker Bü 181 Bestmann

The Bü 181 low-wing monoplane trainer was a development of the Bü 180 Student with enclosed side-by-side accommodation for the crew of two, and was of typical mixed construction (ply/fabric-covered wooden flying surfaces, aluminium alloy-covered steel-tube forward fuselage and wooden monocoque rear fuselage) with fixed tailwheel undercarriage. In addition to its designed role, the Bu 181 was used as a communications aeroplane and, in small numbers, as a tug for light training gliders.

Luftwaffe are not accurately known, but it has been estimated that production must have run into several thousands. As the type became available in large numbers it was also used as a communications aircraft and, in smaller numbers, as a glider tug. The **Bü 181D** was a later production version with a number of detail improvements.

In addition to production by Bücker, 708 aircraft of this type were built by Fokker in the Netherlands during the war, and in 1944-46 125 machines were built in Sweden for that nation's air force under the designation **Sk 25**. Wartime production for German requirements had also been launched in occupied Czechoslovakia, where it continued after the war

Below: The Bü 181B NF+IR can still be seen in the Luftwaffe Museum at Gatow, Berlin.

Below: The Bü 131's cockpit featured side-by-side seats and dual controls behind a simple instrument panel with the key elements grouped on the left in front of the pupil's seat.

to yield the **Zlin Z-281** and **Z-381** for civil use as well as the **C-6** and **C-106** for military service. Under licence from Czechoslovakia, Egypt also manufactured a derivative of the Z-381 as the **Heliopolis Gomhouria** that was exported to several other Arab states.

Bücker Bü 181A Bestmann specification
Type: two-seat primary flying trainer
Powerplant: one Hirth HM 504A inverted inline engine rated at 87 kW (105 hp)
Performance: maximum speed 215 km/h (134 mph) at sea level; cruising speed 195 km/h (121 mph) at optimum altitude; climb to 1000 m (3,280 ft) in 5 minutes 18 seconds; service ceiling 5000 m (16,405 ft); range 800 km (497 miles)
Weights: empty 480 kg (1,058 lb); maximum take-off 750 kg (1,653 lb)
Dimensions: wingspan 10.60 m (34 ft 9¼ in); length 7.85 m (25 ft 9 in); height 2.05 m (6 ft 8¼ in); wing area 13.50 m² (145.32 sq ft)

Above: With side-by-side enclosed seating, the Bü 181 was adopted as the Luftwaffe's basic trainer to succeed earlier biplane types.

Above: Large-scale production followed the Bü 181's selection by the Luftwaffe as a basic flying trainer. Thus the Bestmann, which had been designed primarily as a sporting aircraft, came to succeed many earlier Bücker types in German military service. The fairings inside the wheels were often removed as they trapped mud and other debris.

Bücker Bü 182 Kornett

One of the company's least successful lightplanes, in commercial terms, the Bü 182 was intended only for the civil market, and was a very light low-wing monoplane with a single-seat open cockpit and fixed tailskid undercarriage. Production was limited to just a handful of aircraft.

First flown late in 1938, the single-seat **Bü 182 Kornett** (cornet) was a marginally smaller aircraft than the two-seat Bü 181, but like that aircraft was based on the Bü 180 in terms of its configuration and structure as a low-wing cantilever monoplane of basically all-wooden construction with fixed tailwheel undercarriage. The aircraft was evaluated by the Luftwaffe in the advanced flying trainer role with limited armament training capability (four light bombs), but was not ordered. Only a handful of aircraft were built for civil purchasers before the start of World War II.

Bücker Bü 182 Kornett specification
Type: single-seat light aircraft
Powerplant: one Bücker Bü M700 air-cooled 4-cylinder inverted inline engine rated at 60 kW (80 hp) for take-off
Performance: maximum speed 205 km/h (127 mph) at sea level; cruising speed 195 km/h (121 mph) at optimum altitude; initial climb rate 275 m (902 ft) per minute; service ceiling 5000 m (16,405 ft); range 850 km (528 miles)

Weights: empty 315 kg (694 lb); normal take-off 510 kg (1,124 lb)
Dimensions: wingspan 8.60 m (28 ft 2½ in); length 6.67 m (21 ft 10½ in); height 1.85 m (6 ft 0¾ in); wing area 9.80 m² (105.49 sq ft)

The Bü 182 was an attractive light aircraft intended largely for the sporting role, and perhaps as few as four had been delivered before the outbreak of World War II ended production.

CANT Z.501 and Z.506

The Z.501 single-engined flying-boat and much larger Z.506 three-engined floatplane were intended for the maritime reconnaissance bomber role in Italian service. The Germans seized numbers of these seaplanes in September 1943, and retained them in service for the rest of the war for the air-sea rescue role.

The **Z.501 Gabbiano** (seagull) reconnaissance flying-boat prototype, powered by a 671-kW (900-hp) Isotta-Fraschini Asso XI R2C liquid-cooled V-12 engine, first flew on 7 February 1934. The type entered Italian service in 1937, and by the time Italy entered World War II in June 1940 more than 200 were in service. Protected by three 7.7-mm (0.303-in) machine-guns and carrying a 640-kg (1,411-lb) bomb load, the Z.501 remained in production (455 machines) to 1943, and very small numbers were seized by Germany after Italy's armistice with the Allies.

The **Z.506B Airone** (heron) was a large twin-float seaplane that entered service in 1938, and was built to the extent of 324 machines, including two prototypes. The Z.506B featured a stepped tandem two-seat cockpit, and a ventral gondola for the bombardier and bomb bay. The sole variant was the **Z.506S** air-sea rescue version, whose total included 20 Z.506B conversions in 1948. The Germans seized several Z.506s in September 1943, and flew them to 1945.

CANT Z.506B Airone specification
Type: five-crew reconnaissance bomber and rescue floatplane
Powerplant: three Alfa Romeo 126 RC.34 air-cooled nine-cylinder radial engines each rated at 559 kW (750 hp)
Performance: maximum speed 365 km/h (227 mph) at optimum altitude;

German casualties are loaded into a Z.506 floatplane operated by the Luftwaffe in an overall white colour scheme with red crosses to indicate its humanitarian role.

cruising speed 325 km/h (202 mph) at optimum altitude; climb to 4000 m (13,125 ft) in 14 minutes; service ceiling 8000 m (26,245 ft); range 2745 km (1,705 miles)
Weights: empty 8300 kg (18,298 lb); maximum take-off 12300 kg (27,117 lb)
Dimensions: wingspan 26.50 m (86 ft 0⅓ in); length 19.25 m (63 ft 1⅔ in); height 7.45 m (24 ft 5½ in); wing area 87.00 m² (936.49 sq ft)
Armament: one or two 7.7-mm (0.303-in) Breda-SAFAT trainable machine-guns and one 12.7-mm (0.5-in) Breda-SAFAT trainable machine-gun, plus up to 1200 kg (2,646 lb) of bombs or one torpedo

A Z.506 floatplane wears the markings of the Luftwaffe, which operated seized examples for the air-sea rescue role in the waters off the east and west coasts of northern Italy.

The Z.501 was a parasol-wing flying-boat with a wing centre section supported over the hull by stalky N-struts. There was a gunner's position above the nacelle.

CANT Z.1007 Alcione

The Z.1007 exemplified Italy's penchant for the three-engined bomber, and was an adequate medium bomber in terms of performance, albeit with a comparatively light bomb load. After Italy's September 1943 armistice with the Allies, many surviving Z.1007 aircraft were operated in German markings.

A derivative of the Z.506 seaplane, the **Z.1007** prototype, powered by three 825-hp (615-kW) Isotta-Fraschini Asso XI liquid-cooled engines, first flew in March 1937. Some 34 interim aircraft paved the way to the **Z.1007bis** with Piaggio P.XI radial engines. This variant was put into quantity production and was followed by the **Z.1007ter** variant with 858-kW (1,150-hp) Piaggio P.XIX radial engines and bomb load reduced to 1000 kg (2,205 lb). Some 561 Z.1007s of all variants were completed, and in September 1943 72 aircraft survived, 32 remaining in Fascist hands. Several of them were impressed into service with the ANR, the Italian air arm that flew alongside the Luftwaffe.

CANT Z.1007bis Alcione specification
Type: five-crew medium bomber
Powerplant: three Piaggio P.XI R2C.40 air-cooled 14-cylinder radial engines each rated at 746 kW (1,000 hp)
Performance: maximum speed 465 km/h (289 mph) at 4000 m (13,125 ft); climb to 6000 m (19,685 ft) in 16 minutes 8 seconds; service ceiling 7500 m (24,605 ft); range 1795 km (1,115 miles)
Weights: empty 9395 kg (20,712 lb); maximum take-off 13620 kg (30,027 lb)
Dimensions: wing span 24.80 m (81 ft 4⅓ in); length 18.35 m (60 ft 2¼ in); height 5.22 m (17 ft 1½ in); wing area 75.00 m² (807.32 sq ft)
Armament: two 12.7-mm (0.5-in) trainable machine-guns and two 7.7-mm (0.303-in) trainable machine-guns, plus up to 1200 kg (2,646 lb) of bombs

MM24248 served with the Aviazione Nazionale Republicana during 1944. It was one of only four Z.1007bis aircraft to wear Luftwaffe markings.

Caudron C.445 Goéland

The C.445 Goéland was one of the definitive variants of a very successful series of French civil light transport and military communications aircraft, and was built in large numbers during the late 1930s. The Germans ordered continued production after June 1940 and made extensive use of the aircraft for a host of roles.

D eveloped as a fast, economical and comfortable transport, the **C.440 Goéland** (seagull) appeared in 1934 as a conventional low-wing monoplane. Construction was of wood throughout, with plywood skinning everywhere but the forward and upper fuselage sections, which were skinned in metal. As usually configured, the cabin seated six passengers with baggage compartments fore and aft, and a lavatory aft.

The Goéland series remained in production up to the outbreak of World War II, the principal model being the **C.445** (114 built), which was adopted by the Armée de l'Air as the **C.445M** military version (404 aircraft) for service in a variety of tasks, including communications duties and crew training. Some C.445Ms were also used by the Aéronavale.

Production continued during World War II and, after the German occupation of France, 44 C.445 and 10 C.445M aircraft were impressed for German use, some flying on Lufthansa routes and others being operated by the Luftwaffe. Considerable numbers of C.445Ms and improved **C.449** aircraft (more than 349 eventually built) were manufactured specifically for German service by Renault and Caudron. The

Germans used the Goéland as a pilot, radio and navigational trainer, and also for the communications role, and a small number of the aircraft had glazed noses to permit their use in the bomb-aimer training task. The other Axis operator of the C.445M was the Slovak air force, which ordered 10 such aircraft in 1942.

Caudron C.445M Goéland specification
Type: two-crew military transport and trainer
Powerplant: two Renault 60-00/01 or 6Q-08/09 Bengali 6 air-cooled six-cylinder inverted inline engines each rated at 164 kW (220 hp)
Performance: maximum speed 300 km/h (186 mph) at sea level; cruising speed 261 km/h (162 mph) at optimum altitude; climb to 2000 m (6,560 ft) in 10 minutes 15 seconds; service ceiling 7000 m (22,965 ft); range 1000 km (621 miles)
Weights: empty 2292 kg (5,053 lb); maximum take-off 3500 kg (7,716 lb)
Dimensions: wingspan 17.59 m (57 ft 8½ in); length 13.68 m (44 ft 10½ in); height 3.40 m (11 ft 1¾ in); wing area 42.00 m² (452.10 sq ft)
Payload: up to six passengers

The C.445M had good performance, and offered ready availability. As it was built of wood, it did not impose on the supply of strategic materials. The type was much favoured by the Luftwaffe as a communications aircraft and also as a trainer offering capabilities in several technical disciplines.

Consolidated B-24 Liberator

Though not as numerous as the B-17 over Europe, the B-24 was nonetheless operated in significant quantities. Many were shot down, and many others were forced down relatively intact. Some of the latter were repaired and pressed into German service for clandestine operations and to familiarise fighter pilots with the type.

In January 1939 the US Army Air Corps asked Consolidated to design a heavy bomber with performance superior to that of the B-17. Consolidated wasted little time in submitting its **Model 32** design, which first flew in **XB-24** prototype form on 29 December 1939. There followed seven **YB-24** service test aircraft, and then a number of development types until the very similar **B-24D** and **B-24E**, which were the first major production models with 2,838 and 801 built, respectively. The B-24 soon proved itself capable of undertaking a multitude of tasks including transport and maritime patrol and, with 18,482 completed, became the most numerous US warplane type of World War II. Other major models were the **B-24G** that introduced a nose turret, **B-24H** with a different nose turret, **B-24J** improved version of the B-24H, **B-24L** with manually operated tail guns in place of a turret, and the **B-24M** improved B-24J variant.

Of the many Liberators that crash-landed or were forced down over Axis-controlled territory, the Germans repaired several for an overall evaluation of their capabilities, the development of tactics that could by used by German fighters and anti-aircraft gunners to tackle this long-range bomber, and several types of special mission.

A selection of specific instances provides some illumination of these tasks. A B-24D captured by the Italians and then transferred to the Germans, but not given a German code, was used for evaluation until wrecked in a landing accident, and another B-24D was operated for a time by KG 200, which also flew a B-24G with the code NF+FL and at least one B-24H with the code KO-XA. A B-24G (CL+XZ) was used for the testing of radar and other electronics. A B-24H (A3+KB) was flown on supply missions to the isolated German garrison of Rhodes late in 1944, and another B-24H was flown without any fuselage code for the infiltration of British night bomber

The serial 252106 (42-2106) identifies this as B-24H Sunshine from the 449th Bomb Group. It landed intact at Venegono airfield in April 1944, and was soon on the strength of KG 200.

streams, whose location and course were then reported, until the aircraft was shot down in error by German AA guns over Bavaria in April 1945.

Consolidated B-24H/J Liberator specification
Type: 10-crew long-range heavy bomber
Powerplant: four Pratt & Whitney R-1830-65 air-cooled 14-cylinder radial engines each rated at 1,200 hp (895 kW) for take-off
Performance: maximum speed 300 mph (483 km/h) at 30,000 ft (9145 m); cruising speed 215 mph (346 km/h) at optimum altitude; climb to 20,000 ft (6095 m) in 25 minutes; service ceiling 28,000 ft (8535 m); range 2,100 miles (3380 km)
Weights: empty 36,500 lb (16556 kg); maximum take-off 71,200 lb (32296 kg)
Dimensions: wingspan 110 ft 0 in (33.53 m); length 67 ft 2 in (20.47 m); height 18 ft 0 in (5.49 m); wing area 1,048.00 sq ft (97.36 m²)
Armament: two 0.5-in (12.7-mm) Browning trainable machine-guns in each of the nose, dorsal, ventral and tail turrets, and a 0.5-in (12.7-mm) Browning trainable machine-gun in each of two beam positions, plus bombload of up to 12,800 lb (5806 kg)

Above: Another view of B-24H Sunshine shows its original nose art. This aircraft was used for making propaganda films of a mock 'forced' landing featuring the actual US crew. However, nose-gunner Orel Harper sabotaged the filming by flashing the 'V' sign upon disembarking from the aircraft.

Right: This B-24H, 41-28641 (coded A3+KB), was the aircraft used to fly supplies into Rhodes in late 1944. It was an ex-453rd BG aircraft that was previously used by the Zirkus Rosarius that evaluated Allied aircraft and demonstrated them to front-line units.

Curtiss Hawk 75

The Model 75 was an early-generation monoplane fighter, and proved successful on the export market as the Hawk 75. The French were so short of modern fighters that they placed large orders for the H75, not all of which had been delivered by June 1940. The Germans seized the aircraft for training and redelivery to Finland.

In 1934 Curtiss undertook the private-venture development of the **Model 75** monoplane fighter, whose prototype first flew in May 1935 with the 671-kW (900-hp) Wright XR-1670-5 radial engine, replaced in 1936 by a 634-kW (850-hp) Wright XR-1820-39 unit to create the **Model 75B**. Curtiss later received USAAC orders for the P-36, which was built in modest numbers, but the type proved more successful as the **Hawk 75A** for export.

In May 1938 France ordered 100 **H75A-1** fighters with the 783-kW (1,050-hp) R-1830-SC3-G Twin Wasp and differences to the P-36A standard such as an armament of four 7.5-mm (0.295-in) FN-built Browning guns, a throttle operating in the reverse direction to that of the US types, metric instrumentation and French equipment. The first two aircraft reached France on 24 December 1938, and in 1939 orders were placed for 100 **H75A-2** and 135 **H75A-3** fighters, the former with six machine-guns, and the latter with

the same guns but the 895-kW (1,200-hp) R-1830-S1C3-G engine. There followed an order for 395 **H75A-4** fighters with the 895-kW GR-1820-G205A engine. Only 291 H75A fighters were taken on strength by the Armée de l'Air before the collapse of France in June 1940, but a number were lost en route to French ports. All 200 H75A-1 and -2 fighters reached France, and most of the others taken on strength were H75A-3s and a small number of H75A-4s.

A number of H75As were captured in France by the Germans, some still in their delivery crates, and they were transported to Germany for assembly by Espenlaub Flugzeugbau with German instrumentation, and then sold to Finland, which received 31 H75A-1, -2, -3 and A-4 French aircraft and 13 A-6 ex-Norwegian model.

A small number of H75A aircraft were also flown in Germany, at least six by the Erprobungsstelle Rechlin for evaluation, and others by the Jadgfliegerschule 4 and III/Jagdgeschwader 77 as fighter trainers.

This H75A-4 fighter was seized from the French in 1940 and repainted in German markings (KQ+ZA) for use as a fighter trainer.

Curtiss H75A-4 specification
Type: single-seat fighter
Powerplant: one Wright GR-1820-G205A Cyclone air-cooled nine-cylinder radial engine rated at 1,200 hp (895 kW) for take-off
Performance: maximum speed 323 mph (520 km/h) at 15,100 ft (4602 m); cruising speed 262 mph (422 km/h) at optimum altitude; climb to 15,000 ft (4570 m) in 4 minutes 54 seconds; service ceiling 32,700 ft (9965 m); range 603 miles (970 km)
Weights: empty 4,541 lb (2060 kg); maximum take-off 6,662 lb (3022 kg)
Dimensions: wingspan 37 ft 4 in (11.38 m); length 28 ft 6 in (8.69 m); height 9 ft 6 in (2.90 m); wing area 236.00 sq ft (21.92 m²)
Armament: six 0.30-in (7.5-mm) FN-Browning fixed forward-firing machine-guns

de Havilland D.H.89 Dragon Rapide

A neat two-bay biplane of extremely elegant apperance, the D.H.89 Dragon Rapide sold well on the civil market and also formed the basis of military communications and navigation/radio trainers. The Germans seized several civil aircraft in 1940, and operated them in the communications role.

Of largely fabric-covered wooden construction, the **D.H.89 Dragon Six** prototype first flew on 17 April 1934. Production aircraft, which had the revised name **Dragon Rapide**, were delivered from July 1934, and **D.H.89A** aircraft delivered from March 1937 switched from the Gipsy Six to Gipsy Queen engine, had

cabin heating and introduced small trailing-edge flaps. The type's reliability and economy generated significant sales for the mid- and late 1930s, and by the outbreak of World War II almost 200 examples of this eight-passenger transport had been delivered to civil operators around the world.

Aircraft were sold to Belgium, France and the Netherlands, and some of them were captured intact by the Germans in 1940 and pressed into service by the Luftwaffe as communications aircraft for as long as they could be maintained.

The Luftwaffe operated the simple yet effective Dragon Rapide in the communications role until it ran out of spares, especially for the Gipsy Queen engines.

de Havilland D.H.89A Dragon Rapide specification
Type: one/two-crew light transport aeroplane
Powerplant: two de Havilland Gipsy Queen 3 air-cooled six-cylinder inverted inline engines each rated at 200 hp (149 kW) for take-off
Performance: maximum speed 157 mph (253 km/h) at optimum altitude; cruising speed 132 mph (212 km/h) at optimum altitude; initial climb

rate 687 ft (209 m) per minute; service ceiling 19,500 ft (5945 m); range 578 miles (930 km)
Weights: empty 3,276 lb (1486 kg); maximum take-off 5,500 lb (2495 kg)
Dimensions: wingspan 48 ft 0 in (14.63 m); length 34 ft 6 in (10.52 m); height 10 ft 3 in (3.12 m); wing area 336.00 sq ft (31.21 m²)

Dewoitine D.520

The D.520 was the best fighter available to the French air force in 1939, but had been delivered in only modest numbers before France's defeat. The aircraft then served with the Vichy French air force, which received more machines, but they were seized by the Luftwaffe in November 1942 as trainers and for delivery to allies.

In 1920 Dewoitine developed the D.1 parasol-wing fighter, and retained this layout until 1932, when the D.500 was developed as a low-wing monoplane. This had an open cockpit and fixed tailskid undercarriage including wide-track divided main units. The fighter entered French service in 1935, when its basic concept was already obsolescent, and led to a series of steadily improving fighters of the same layout. The last of them was the **D.510**, which entered service late in 1936. Via some largely unsuccessful prototypes with spatted undercarriage and then the combination of an enclosed cockpit and retractable main undercarriage units, this paved the way to the **D.520**, which first flew on 2 October 1938, and was an altogether more modern fighter of low-wing monoplane layout with an enclosed cockpit, tailwheel undercarriage with retractable main units, and a notably clean engine installation.

Before the last of the three prototypes had flown, on 5 May 1939, Dewoitine had received an order for 200 **D.520C.1** single-seat fighters, and two months later this number had risen to 710. By then, the last details had been finalised for production aircraft, which were to be powered by the Hispano-Suiza 12Y-45 liquid-cooled V-12 engine fitted with a Szydlowski supercharger, and the first of these D.520C.1 machines flew on 31 October 1939. Without doubt the most capable fighter of French origin available to the Armée de l'Air early in World War II, the D.520C.1 had been delivered to the extent of only some 300 aircraft by mid-June 1940 and just 403 machines had been taken on charge by the time of the French armistice with Germany on 25 June 1940. Continued production of the D.520 was authorised in Vichy France, 474 being built before and after the German occupation of Vichy France in November 1942.

In response to the Allied landings in French North Africa

Above: The Luftwaffe made only the smallest use of obsolescent D.510 fighters, and then only for training, after capturing small numbers from the French in 1940.

Possessing good performance and excellent agility, the D.520 was a very useful fighter trainer, but caused losses among German pilots lacking experience of French aircraft.

in November 1942, German forces seized the previously unoccupied zone of France. On 27 November the Vichy French air force was demobilised, and its 1,876 aircraft seized by the Germans included 246 D.520s, 13 of them awaiting

D.520 fighters seized in unoccupied France from November 1941 found ready and useful employment in the Luftwaffe's fighter training wings based in France, where the aircraft could be readily maintained and supplied with spares.

Dewoitine D.520

This D.520 wears the marki... of the JG 105 fighter trainin... wing, at Chartres in 1944. Command of these training units often served to provi... a rest period for high-scori... middle-ranking fighter pilo... JG 105 was headed by Majo... Richard Leppla, a Knight's Cross holder with 68 air combat victories.

The Luftwaffe used the D.520 as a fighter trainer with Jagdfliegerschulen and fighter training Geschwadern in France. This machine flew with JG 101 at Pau-Nord in the Pyrenees in March 1944. The unit was at that time commanded by the great ace Major Walter Nowotny.

Above: Small, light and nicely balanced for very crisp handling in the air, the D.520 was much favoured by the Luftwaffe as a fighter trainer paving the way to German first-line fighters.

Accidents were common among inexperienced pilots operating from poorly maintained airfields, but propeller damage was a situation that could easily be repaired.

Left: Part of a line-up of D.520 fighters in Luftwaffe service are seen on an airfield in German-occupied France.

repair and four damaged irreparably. In the Toulouse plant of the SNCASE the Germans seized a further 169 D.520s in varying stages of manufacture and assembly, 19 of them in flyable condition. In March 1943, the first D.520 to be taken on charge by a German pilot stalled and crashed immediately after take-off. However, the SNCASE factory, which had just been reactivated, received a contract to continue the construction of 192 partly-completed machines. By summer 1944 all of them had been delivered, bringing the final total of D.520 production to 905 aircraft.

A few D.520s were at first used as fighter trainers (and in a few cases operationally) by several of the Jagdgeschwadern engaged in the USSR, and the French fighter's exceptional manoeuvrability was highly praised by Luftwaffe veterans. When the JG 105 training wing was moved to Chartres and various airfields around Paris, it was entirely re-equipped with D.520s. So too, at least in part, was JG 103 at Zeltweg in Austria. A third training wing, JG 101, flew D.520s alongside its Focke-Wulf Fw 190As at Pau-Long and its satellite airstrips. The rate of losses was fairly high, largely as a result of the great differences between it and the German fighter aircraft to which the pilots were accustomed.

A total of 72 D.520s was also transferred to the Regia Aeronautica, and served for a limited period as trainers and second-line fighters with one squadriglia each of the 13°, 22°, 24° and 167° Gruppi. A further 96 D.520s constituted the main strength of the Bulgarian 6th Air Force: most of these imported fighters were destroyed in combat with the Lockheed P-38 Lightning fighters and Consolidated B-24 Liberator bombers of the US 9th Army Air Force in the American attacks on the oil installations at Ploiesti.

Dewoitine D.520C.1 specification

Type: single-seat fighter
Powerplant: one Hispano-Suiza 12Y-45 liquid-cooled V-12 engine rated at 697 kW (935 hp) for take-off
Performance: maximum speed 534 km/h (332 mph) at 5500 m (18,045 ft); cruising speed 370 km/h (230 mph) at optimum altitude; climb to 4000 m (13,125 ft) in 5 minutes 48 seconds; service ceiling 10500 m (34,450 ft); range 1530 km (950 miles)
Weights: empty 2036 kg (4,449 lb); maximum take-off 2677 kg (5,902 lb)
Dimensions: wingspan 10.20 m (33 ft 5½ in); length 8.60 m (28 ft 2½ in); height 2.57 m (8 ft 5¼ in); wing area 15.97 m² (171.91 sq ft)
Armament: one 20-mm Hispano-Suiza 404 fixed forward-firing cannon between the engine's cylinder banks, and four 7.5-mm (0.295-in) MAC 34 M39 fixed forward-firing machine-guns in the leading edges of the wing

Deutsche Forschungsanstalt für Segelflug

From some aspects the title of Deutsches Forschungsanstalt für Segelflug (DFS, German Research Institute for Gliding) was to appear in retrospect a misnomer, for this organisation concerned itself with aspects of aeronautical research and development seemingly remote from the glider. The Me 163 rocket-driven interceptor owed its existence to work originally undertaken at the DFS, and the practicability of the Mistel composite was first demonstrated by the DFS, which designed the superstructure attaching the piloted upper component to the pilotless lower component. The DFS was also responsible for evolving a piloted version of the Fieseler Fi 103 missile, but it was the development of the assault glider that made the most significant DFS contribution to the war effort of the Third Reich, while DFS work on what was, in effect, a powered sailplane to perform reconnaissance missions from altitudes endowing it with immunity from interception was, more than a decade after the war, to be seen as a basis for such types as the Lockheed U-2.

Humble origins

The DFS grew from the Rhön-Rossitten Gesellschaft established at the Wasserkuppe in 1925 by a group of gliding enthusiasts. This provided the nucleus for the DFS which, after moving to Darmstadt-Griesheim in 1933 and being placed under the directorship of Prof. Walter Georgii, expanded its activities rapidly. Initially the DFS devoted itself exclusively to glider and sailplane research, its design department, led by Ing. Hans Jacobs, evolving a variety of sailplanes such as the Kranich and Seeadler, and also a novel freight-carrying glider, which, originally conceived for meteorological research, was to provide the inspiration for the military assault glide

Ing. Jacobs was also responsible for the design of a highly-successful spoiler-type automatic airbrake, and it was as a result of an impressive demonstration of this device that the DFS test pilot, Hanna Reitsch, received the honorary title of Flugkapitän, the first woman to enjoy this distinction.

The DFS had, by the mid-1930s, been divided into a number of separate departments, each of which was devoted to one specific field of research. The Meteorological Department was headed by Prof. Georgii and the Glider Development Department by Ing. Jacobs, and to these had been added departments concerned with aerodynamics, instrument development and, after Dr. Alexander M. Lippisch joined the DFS, experimentation with tailless aircraft. In the last-mentioned category was the DFS 39 Delta IVb derived from the Fieseler F-3 Vespe, this being followed by the Delta IVc and Delta V, the former providing the basis for the rocket-powered DFS 194 which, in turn, was the forerunner of the Messerschmitt Me 163.

Apart from prototype construction, the DFS workshops at Darmstadt-Greisheim and Ainring, where a branch development bureau was established, were not responsible for the manufacture of DFS designs, this being undertaken by the Gothaer Waggonfabrik and others. Apart from such experimental programmes as the Huckepack (Pick-a-back) trials, the DFS was responsible for a number of advanced designs, including the DFS 332 powered glider intended to test full-scale wing sections at high speeds, and the DFS 346 supersonic reconnaissance aircraft intended to follow the DFS 228.

Following military interest in a research glider developed by DFS, a contract was awarded for the construction of three prototypes of the DFS 230 assault glider, the company's most successful design.

DFS 228

The outbreak of World War II saw DFS become involved in more advanced programmes, and it was realised that research that had been undertaken in relation to glider flight at high altitude could possibly be associated with a rocket motor powerplant, leading to development of a high-performance reconnaissance aircraft.

From the beginning of World War II, the German General Staff attached great importance to reconnaissance aircraft, and considerable ingenuity was displayed by the German aircraft industry in evolving aircraft for the reconnaissance role capable of operating at altitudes endowing them with a measure of immunity from interception. The most revolutionary of these aircraft was undoubtedly the **DFS 228** which, developed by the DFS, was in effect a rocket-propelled sailplane. The idea of developing an aircraft that could be propelled to extreme altitudes by means of a rocket motor and subsequently soar for considerable distances was conceived in 1940, and in the following year, an outline specification was issued to the DFS by the Technisches Amt of the RLM. Although design work was initiated immediately,

The DFS 228 V1 was experimentally launched from the back of the Dornier Do 217K V3 some 40 times, though the controllable rocket motor was never used to sustain the DFS 228's flight.

DFS 228

more pressing commitments necessitated shelving the project until, in 1943, it was revived by orders from the RLM.

Designated DFS 228, the aircraft was intended to be carried or towed to an altitude of some 10000 m (32,808 ft) at which it would be released or cast off from the parent aircraft or tug, the rocket then being lit and the service ceiling of 22860 m (75,000 ft) being attained. From this altitude the rocket motor was to be used intermittently for a series of steep climbs interspersed between shallow glides, maximum ceiling being maintained for 45 minutes. At the end of this time the rocket fuels were expected to be exhausted and a long glide commenced during which reconnaissance photographs were to be taken with infra-red cameras. By the time an altitude of 12000 m (39,400 ft) was reached it was estimated that the aircraft would have travelled a total distance of 750 km (466 miles). A further 300 km (186 miles) could be covered during the glide from 12000 m, although this distance could be increased by making use of thermals in the fashion of a high-performance sailplane, the aircraft landing on a retractable skid.

Wooden construction

Wood was employed wherever possible in the construction of the DFS 228, and the simple semi-monocoque fuselage was built in three sections; the pressurised nose compartment, the fuselage centre section and the tail cone. The wing employed a single laminated wooden spar extending from tip to tip, with wooden ribs and plywood skinning. The fabric-covered ailerons extended over half the span and operated in two sections, the inner sections serving as flaps during landing. Lift spoilers were fitted to both upper and lower wing surfaces. The pressurised nose compartment was a metal two-skin structure sealed by a rear bulkhead and three Plexiglas panels, and maintained a pressure equivalent to an altitude of 7925 m (26,000 ft). Provision was made for the circulation of hot air between the Plexiglas panels, and temperature and humidity were maintained at a constant level by means of an electrically-driven air-conditioning unit. No mechanical load was imposed on the nose compartment shell, the inner skin withstanding air pressure loads inside the cabin and the outer skin contending with external pressures, insulation being provided by aluminium foil between the skins.

The pilot, who, supported in a prone position by a couch arrangement attached to the rear bulkhead, breathed pure oxygen. The entire nose compartment was jettisonable and was attached to the main fuselage by means of four explosive bolts, being stabilised after jettisoning by means of an automatically-

Unpowered trials with the DFS 228 carried above the Do 217K V3 showed the pressure cabin to be unsuitable, while gliding flight revealed some minor limitations in the flight control systems.

deployed parachute. After reaching a predetermined height it was proposed that the pilot's couch would be ejected from the compartment by compressed air, his oxygen and R/T leads and safety harness being disconnected simultaneously with his parachute opening.

The wooden fuselage centre section also had two skins, and housed two Zeiss infra-red cameras, and the C-Stoff and T-Stoff tanks, together with the Walter HWK 109-509 bi-fuel liquid rocket motor. A retractable metal landing skid was housed in the lower part of the centre fuselage, and the tail cone merely carried the rocket combustion chamber.

The **DFS 228 V1** was completed in 1943 with a conventional seated pilot position, and extensive trials were carried out by the DFS at Hörsching, near Linz, and at the Erprobungsstelle Rechlin, the Do 217K V3 being employed as a carrier aircraft. A second prototype, the **DFS 228 V2**, was completed with the intended prone pilot position, and handling trials, without the rocket motor installed, were generally satisfactory, although test pilots found the aircraft to be unusually sensitive to elevator movements and reported that aileron effectiveness was poor at altitude. Although powered flight had not been attempted at the time of Germany's collapse, the construction of a pre-production batch of 10 **DFS 228A-0** aircraft had begun at Griesheim, near Darmstadt, and the DFS was working on the design of a more advanced successor, the supersonic DFS 346 that was expected to attain a speed of Mach 1.9 at 20120 m (66,000 ft). The DFS 228 V2 was destroyed in May 1945, but the V1 survived to be taken to the UK, where it was believed to have been scrapped in 1947.

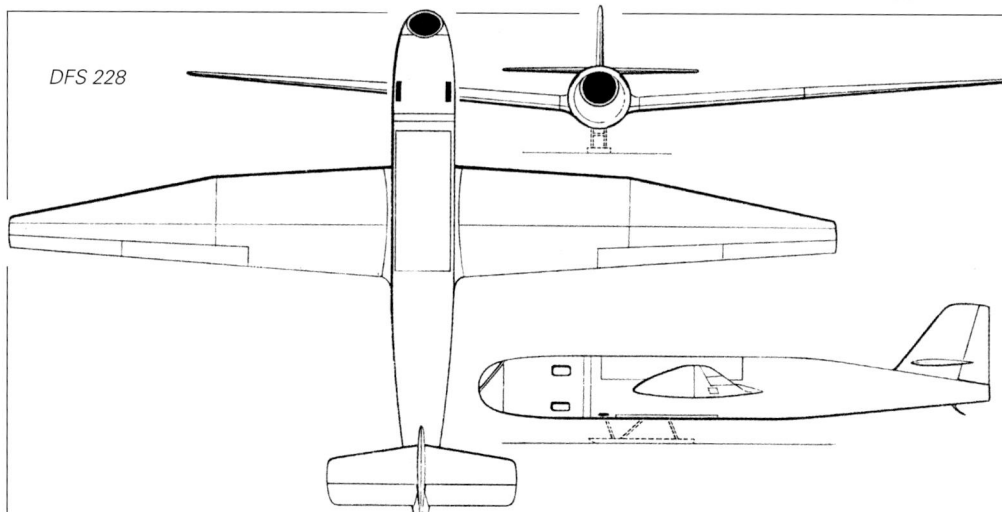

DFS 228

DFS 228 specification
Type: high-altitude reconnaissance aircraft
Powerplant: one Walter HWK 109-509 hi-fuel liquid rocket motor rated at 14.71 kN (3,307 lb st) at sea level and 16.18 kN (3,638 lb) at altitude
Performance: maximum speed 900 km/h (559 mph) at sea level; maximum range 1050 km (652 miles) comprising 750 km (466 miles) of intermittent powered flight and 300 km (186 miles) continuous gliding; launching altitude 10000 m (32,808 ft); service ceiling 22860 m (75,000 ft); design absolute ceiling 25000 m (82,021 ft); glide descent altitude 12000 m (39,370 ft)
Weights: empty equipped 1650 kg (3,638 lb); loaded 4200 kg (9,259 lb)
Dimensions: wingspan 17.56 m (57 ft 7¼ in); length 10.58 m (34 ft 8½ in); wing area 30.00 m² (323 sq ft)

DFS 230

The DFS 230 became Germany's chief troop glider for a substantial part of the war years. The type was designed before 1937, when the DFS 230 was demonstrated to senior officers who were impressed by its capabilities. The result was the first assault glider to be used by any air force, and which took part in various notable operations.

At 04.30 on 10 May 1940, 82 aircraft began to take off from Ostheim and Butzweilerhof, on the outskirts of Cologne, to initiate what was to be one of the most audacious aerial operations of World War II; an operation depending for its success on an entirely new weapon of war – the assault glider. Forty-one of the aircraft taking off from the two Cologne airfields were **DFS 230A** assault gliders, the first of their kind in the history of aerial warfare, the remainder being their Ju 52/3m towplanes. Belonging to the Luftlandegeschwader 1, the Luftwaffe's first 'air-landing' Geschwader and the first unit of its kind in the world, each DFS 230A carried paratroops whose tasks were the storming of the Eben-Emael fortifications and the capture of the Kanne, Veldwezelt and Vroenhoven bridges that were to be held until the arrival of ground forces. So successful was this operational initiation of the assault glider that virtually every aircraft-manufacturing nation immediately followed Germany's lead and began the design and development of troop and freight-carrying gliders, while the Reichsluftfahrtministerium, which had previously expressed doubts concerning the operational value of the Lastensegler (cargo glider), promptly demanded that the highest priority be awarded the development and manufacture of larger aircraft in this category.

Designed by Hans Jacobs, the DFS 230, which was developed in the greatest secrecy and began flight tests late in 1937, stemmed from trials conducted in the mid-1930s by the Deutsche Forschungsinstitut für Segelflug (DFS) with a large glider intended primarily for high-altitude meteorological research and originally conceived by Rhön-Rossitten Gesellschaft. During a visit to Griesheim, Ernst Udet watched the flight testing of the glider which was towed into the air behind a Ju 52/3m, and was particularly impressed by its pinpoint landing capabilities. Afterwards Udet remarked to his World War I comrade Oberstleutnant Robert Ritter von

The DFS 230B-1 and dual-control DFS 230B-2 introduced an air-deployable brake parachute to allow the glider to dive steeply if it came under attack from ground fire.

Greim that large gliders such as that he had seen at Griesheim would, if suitably modified, provide a modern equivalent of the Trojan Horse, depositing troops silently and unnoticed behind an enemy's defences. Within a few weeks of this conversation, the DFS had received instructions to design and build a glider capable of accommodating a pilot and nine fully-equipped troops.

DFS 230 anatomy

The structural design of the DFS 230 was thoroughly conventional. The wing comprised a single main spar at approximately one-third chord with plywood covering forward and fabric aft, the long-span ailerons with inset tabs were fabric

A DFS 230A-1 tests the Starrschlepp or rigid-tow arrangement with a Ju 52/3m three-engined transport and tug aeroplane. The system proved workable, but presented a number of of piloting problems and was not used operationally.

DFS 230

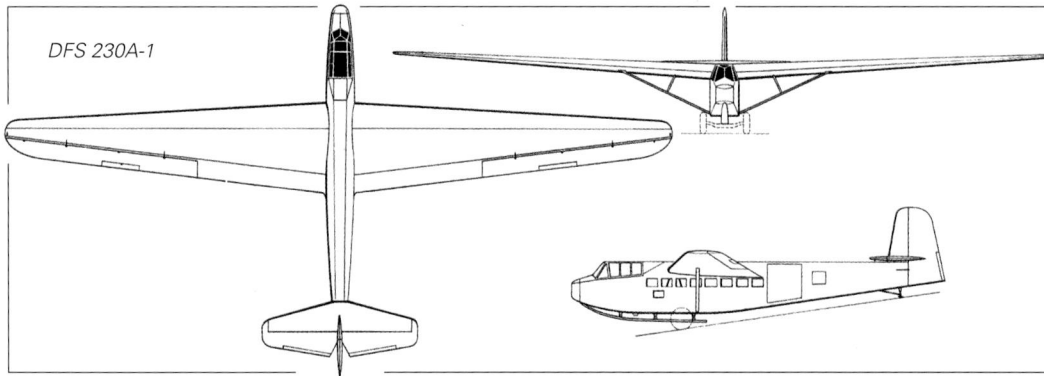

DFS 230A-1

covered, and the wing was braced to the fuselage at quarter-span by light metal struts. The fabric-covered welded steel-tube fuselage was of rectangular section, and built up on a central keel member or boom intended to absorb the impact loads transmitted to it from the sprung steel skid. Provision was made for either single or dual control, and, in addition to the pilot, accommodation was provided for nine men who were seated on the central boom. As the maximum permissible flying weight of 2100 kg (4,630 lb) included 1240 kg (2,734 lb) disposable load, some 275 kg (606 lb) of freight could be carried in addition to the full complement of 10 men. A large loading door was provided at the rear of the cabin in the fuselage port side, and the loading of bulky items of freight was facilitated by a detachable panel beneath the wing in the starboard side of the fuselage.

Launch procedure

For take-off a two-wheel dolly was provided, this being jettisoned once the glider was airborne, and early trials revealed a gliding angle of 1:18 in fully loaded condition. All initial trials were performed with the Ju 52/3m serving as a tug, but as testing progressed various other aircraft were employed in this role, including the He 46, the Hs 126, and the Ju 87B, and some trials were performed with a fully-laden DFS 230 towed by a team of five He 72 Kadett training biplanes. Various alternatives to the normal flexible towline were also investigated, these including the Starrschlepp, or rigid-

Above: Towable by a variety of Luftwaffe aircraft, the DFS 230 used jettisonable wheels for take-off, and landing was accomplished on a central skid mounted beneath the fuselage.

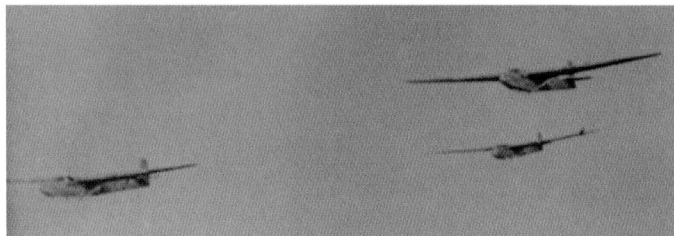

The DFS 230 mounted the world's first operation by glider-borne troops when the Belgian fort of Eben Emael was captured on 10 May 1940. DFS 230s were used also in the invasion of Crete and on many other airborne operations.

tow arrangement, the DFS 230 being coupled to its tug by a 1.20-m (4-ft) rigid connection. The practicability of the Starrschlepp was demonstrated by the DFS with a Ju 52/3m towing a DFS 230 on a nocturnal flight Darmstadt-Hamburg-Munich-Darmstadt.

From the outset of the DFS 230 development programme the Institute collaborated closely with the Gothaer Waggonfabrik (GWF) that was to have initial responsibility for the quantity production of the glider, although this was slow to gather tempo in part due to lingering doubts within the RLM regarding the tactical value of such aircraft, a vociferous faction declaiming that the glider offered nothing not already offered by the appreciably less expensive parachute. Three prototypes, the **DFS 230 V1**, **V2** and **V3** assembled and tested by the Institute, were followed by a small series of GWF-built pre-production **DFS 230A-0** gliders, and deliveries of the production **DFS 230A-1** and **DFS 230A-2**, the latter having dual controls, finally commenced in October 1939, a total of 28 of the gliders having been accepted by the Luftwaffe by the end of the year.

During the autumn of 1938, a small glider-borne commando had been formed with the pre-production DFS 230s and, as part of 7. Fliegerdivision, developed assault techniques before combining with the existing paratroop cadres in the XI Fliegerkorps. With the rapid increase in DFS 230 output from the beginning of 1940, the I Gruppe of Luftlandegeschwader 1 was formed, its operational successes in May being followed by the establishment of II and III Gruppen, and the Gothaer Waggonfabrik being joined in the manufacture of the DFS 230 by several other concerns, including Hartwig at Sonneburg, Erla at Leipzig, and a factory in Prague. During the course of 1940 a total of 455 of the assault gliders was accepted by the Luftwaffe, the majority of these being the initial DFS 230A-1 sub-type. This version had been succeeded on the assembly lines in the late autumn by the **DFS 230B-1** and dual-control **DFS 230B-2** embodying modifications resulting from experience gained during the first glider assault operations.

It had been realised that glider operations were hazardous once the enemy's ground defences had been alerted, the DFS230 providing an excellent target for small arms fire during its slow, shallow landing approach. The DFS 230B was therefore fitted with an external parachute pack beneath the rear fuselage, this chute being intended for deployment in the event of a rapid, diving descent necessary to avoid ground fire. The addition of the braking chute was accompanied by some local structural strengthening and the provision of a sturdier landing skid.

Provision was also made for the mounting of a single 7.9-mm (0.31-in) MG 15 machine-gun immediately aft of the sideways-hinging cockpit canopy, this having the dual task of providing a measure of defence while the glider was airborne, and supplying suppressive fire once the glider had landed and while its occupants were leaving their transport and establishing themselves under cover. Some units augmented this armament with a pair of 7.9-mm (0.31-in) MG 34 infantry machine-guns that was attached to the nose of the glider and intended to provide suppressive fire during the landing approach.

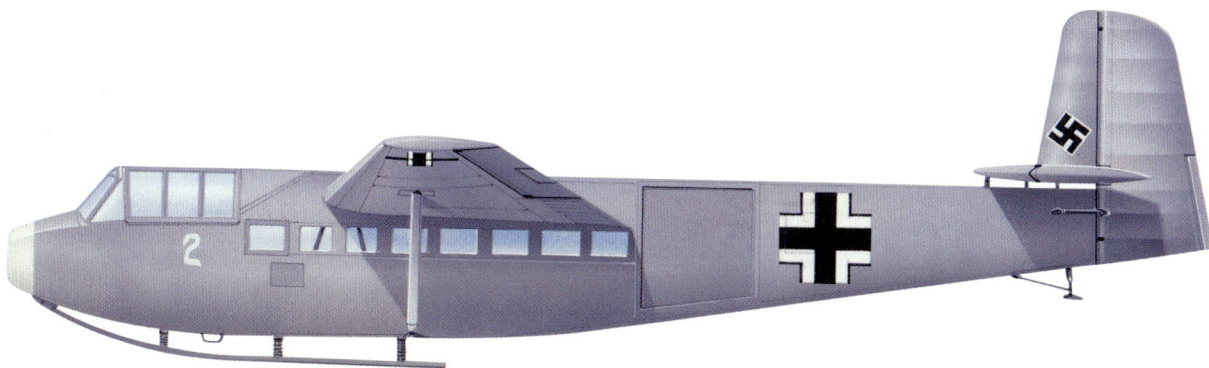

This is a DFS 230A assault glider of the I Gruppe of Luftlandgeschwader 1. Each such glider (80 were allocated to the Crete operation) could carry up to 10 men (including the pilot) as well as a useful freight load of 275 kg (606 lb), loaded through the port-side door or a detachable starboard-side panel under the wing.

For nearly a year after their operational debut in the offensive against France and the Low Countries the DFS 230-equipped Lastenseglerstaffeln were restricted to freight-carrying tasks using a variety of tugs, but they reappeared in the assault role on 26 April 1941 when they participated in an attempt to capture the bridge over the Corinth Canal. This operation was only a prelude to the most ambitious airborne assault to be mounted by German forces and in which gliders were to be employed, the invasion of Crete. The assault, in which the Luftlandegeschwader 1 again participated, began on 20 May 1941, and no fewer than 493 Ju 52/3m transports with some 80 DFS 230 gliders were employed to carry 15,750 men to the island. Although this operation was ultimately successful, it was something of a Pyrrhic victory as it was achieved at the cost of crippling losses by the airborne forces.

Production ends

Although production of the DFS 230 continued in Czechoslovakia throughout 1941, the Gothaer Waggonfabrik had virtually phased out of the programme by the beginning of the year, delivering three in January and one in February, although a further 28 were produced in June. Nevertheless, no fewer than 1,022 DFS 230 gliders were accepted from five assembly lines, 322 of them being manufactured in Czechoslovakia, and from the summer of 1941 the Lastenseglerstaffeln had begun to augment their strength with the larger Go 242. By the beginning of 1942, only the

Prague factory was still producing the DFS 230, and this, too, phased the glider out of production in April after delivering a further 74 aircraft.

The principal DFS 230 Lastenseglerstaffeln were 1. to 10./DFS 230 Staffeln der Luftwaffe, most of which, together with 1. to 6./Go 242 Staffeln, were soon incorporated in Schleppgruppen 1, 2 and 3. There were also the two Luftlandegeschwadern, LLG 1 and LLG 2, and a number of semi-autonomous Schleppstaffeln. The DFS 230 saw considerable use in the supply role both in the Mediterranean theatre and on the Eastern Front, its first large-scale operation on the latter being the supply of German forces encircled in Kholm between January and May 1942. For this task the DFS 230s were used in concert with Go 242s, and during the final stages of the battle, shortly before the town was relieved, the gliders were having to land in the streets under heavy fire, the losses in both gliders and trained personnel being heavy.

The DFS 230s usually employed the Seilschlepp, or cable-tow, being attached to a cable of 40-m (131-ft) length, but for night and bad-weather missions the Starrschlepp arrangement was used. Yet another arrangement that Fritz Stamer and his group at the DFS began to investigate in 1942 was the so-called Mistelschlepp in which a powered aircraft was attached to the DFS 230 in a Huckepack (pick-a-back) configuration. Preliminary tests were made with a Klemm Kl 35B as the Huckepack component of a DFS 230B-2, the combination being towed off the ground by a Ju 52/3m,

Above: More than 1,000 DFS 230s were built by several factories to become the Luftwaffe's standard assault glider.

Above: The DFS 230 design began life as the basis for a meteorological glider able to carry a useful load of instruments. It found fame, however, as a troop and cargo transport. This is the initial production version, the DFS 230A-1.

The DFS 230 was based on a boxy fuselage of basically rectangular section, and was carried in the air by a strut-braced high-set wing that had long-span ailerons but no flaps.

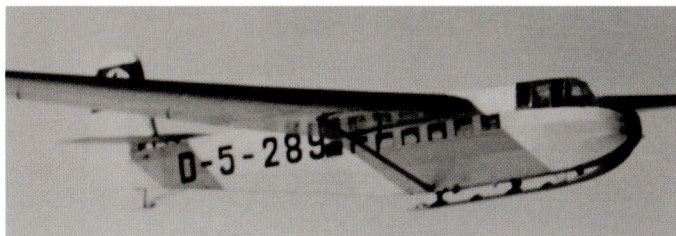

The DFS 230 was simple to build and based on a structure that made no major demands on Germany's stocks of strategic light alloys. The glider was also straightforward to fly.

Above: An unpowered aircraft intended for short-endurance flights in good weather, the DFS 230 had only basic instruments, which also accorded with the type's semi-expendable nature,

Above: Light armament is seen attached to a DFS 230B-1 to provide suppressive fire during the landing approach. The machine-guns in this instance are MG 34 infantry weapons.

Accommodation was provided for nine soldiers on a longitudinal row of seats along the length of the cabin, and also had volume for weapons and supplies. The DFS 230 was flown by a single pilot.

the powerplant of the Kl 35B being sufficient to sustain both upper and lower components in flight once operational altitude had been attained. A further series of tests were conducted with the Kl 35B replaced by an Fw 56 Stösser, these leading up to testing in 1943 of the definitive composite in which a Bf 109E-1 was attached to a more sophisticated superstructure above a DFS 230B fitted with a special under-carriage, the landing skid being removed. This Huckepack combination was tested with considerable success, being capable of taking off and maintaining flight on the power of the Bf 109E-1's engine, but the Mistelschlepp scheme was not adopted for general use with the DFS 230.

Rotary-wing trials

Various experiments were also conducted to find means of landing the DFS 230 in extremely confined spaces, and a DFS 230B airframe minus wings but with a similar under-carriage to that later utilised for the Huckepack experiments with the Bf 109E-1 was delivered to Focke-Achgelis, which fitted a simple rotor pylon carrying the tilting rotor head and 12-m (39-ft 4¾-in) diameter three-blade rotor of the Fa 223 helicopter. With rotor replacing fixed wing, the DFS 230B was redesignated **Fa 225**, and was intended as a pinpoint-landing assault rotor-glider, being towed in the normal fashion by Seilschlepp at speeds of 185-250 km/h (115-155 mph) with the rotor free-wheeling. Weighing 2000 kg (4,409 lb) of which disposable load was 1000 kg (2,205 lb), the Fa 225 could land in a space only 14-18 m (46-59 ft) in length. However, controllability of the Fa 225, which was designed and built within seven weeks, left something to be desired, and preference was shown for a totally different scheme proposed and developed by the DFS in which braking rock-ets were fired in sequence during the landing run.

In the **DFS 230C-1** Rheinmetall-Borsig powder rock-ets were mounted in a specially-modified nose cone, and the pilot made a fast diving approach to the landing area, deployed his braking chute and, at the moment of touching down fired the first of the three braking rockets, the remain-ing rockets being fired in rapid sequence. The trio of rockets had a dramatic effect on deceleration, the glider coming to a standstill within around 15 m (49 ft), and an incidental advantage in their use was the dense cloud of smoke that they generated, which completely hid the glider as it came to a standstill.

DFS was prompted to design a new nose section which it was proposed to fit retrospectively to existing DFS 230B-1 gliders. The new nose embodying an improved braking rocket installation with a device to fire the rockets automatically in sequence was fitted to the **DFS 230 V6**, and with this modification the DFS 230B-1 would have become the **DFS 230D-1**, although it was not, in the event, to be adopted.

Braking rockets were not available for the September 1943 rescue of the deposed Italian dictator, Benito Mussolini, from his prison at the peak of the Gran Sasso Massif in the Abruzzi e Molise. For the raid DFS 230B-1 gliders were accompanied by an Fi 156 Storch in which Mussolini was to be flown to safely. Twelve DFS 230 gliders of the III/LLG 2 carried 108 assault troops from the I/Fallschirmjägerregiment 7, led by the redoubtable SS-Hauptsturmführer Otto Skorzeny. They landed on rocky ground close to the mountain-top hotel, achieving suprise and allowing the assault force to take over the hotel from the carabinieri that were guarding it. This extremely tricky operation was performed with complete success by the gliders, requiring precise flying. To shorten the landing run the glider pilots had wrapped barbed wire around the landing skids.

The losses suffered by the Schleppgruppen and the Luftlandegeschwadern during the supply of the Kholm pocket in the early months of 1942 resulted in the decision not to employ gliders to supply the similarly-besieged Stalingrad at the end of the same year, but the situation had become so precarious by the beginning of 1943 that the three Gruppen of LLG 1 were sent to Luftflotte 4's sector, although they were not to be used to carry supplies to the Stalingrad garrison, being transferred in January 1943 to the Kerch peninsula to participate in the supply of the Kuban bridgehead. At this time LLG 1 comprised I/LLG 1 with DFS 230s and Do 17 towplanes, and II and III/LLG 1 with DFS 230s and a mixture of He 45s, He 46s and Hs 126s for use as towplanes, plus an attached Gruppe of Go 242s and He 111 towplanes, and a few Me 321s with He 111Z tugs. During the course of the Kuban operations, from January to October 1943, LLG l's Lastenseglerstaffeln suffered serious losses, particularly during the winter months and periods of bad weather for which they had neither the necessary experience or equipment.

A DFS 230-equipped unit that took part in the supply of the 1. Panzer-Armee was the Schleppgruppe 2, operating with He 111 towplanes from Lemberg. After flying two missions to the 1. Panzer-Armee, Schleppgruppe 2 concentrated solely on supplying forces within encircled Tarnopol. This was surrounded by such concentrated Soviet anti-aircraft artillery that supply missions could only be carried out at dawn and dusk, the DFS 230s being released at altitudes from 2000 and 2500 m (6,560 and 8,200 ft) and making their approach while the Soviet flak positions were subjected to diversionary bombing attacks. Despite the efforts of Schleppgruppe 2, however, Tarnopol fell to Soviet forces on 15 April 1944.

The next such DFS 230 re-supply operation was that of Budapest between 28 December 1944 and 15 February 1945, the unit concerned being I/LLG 2. Do 17s were employed as towplanes but were of limited use as they were equipped only with the Seilschlepp attachment that was unsuited for night or bad weather operations. In the event, the He 111Hs of KG 4, which were fitted with the Starrschlepp attachment, were placed at the disposal of I/LLG 2's Lastenseglerstaffeln, experienced towing crews being seconded to KG 4 and taking over the aircraft as glider tugs after completion of bombing sorties. By 9 February the Budapest airfield had to be abandoned, and supplies could only be air-dropped. These operations had cost I/LLG 2 36 DFS 230s and 12 Go 242s that had landed and could not be retrieved.

Final actions

One of the last operations of the DFS 230 in World War II took place on the night of 23 March 1945 when an attempt was made to land six gliders at Breslau, which was under Soviet siege. Unbeknown to the Wehrmacht commander, Gauleiter Hanke had personally radioed Martin Bormann in the Reichskanzlei with a request that heavy artillery be airlifted to Breslau to dislodge Soviet forces already established in city blocks. The Führer personally ordered the despatch of six 15-cm (5.91-in) s.I.G.33 heavy infantry guns, but even dismantled they could not be loaded into Ju 52/3m transports. Three

Above: The definitive version of the Huckepack (pick-a-back) combination saw a Bf 109E-1 attached to a superstructure above a DFS 230B fitted with a special undercarriage, the landing skid being removed. Tests were notably sucessful.

Above: DFS 230 assault gliders were often flown alongside Ju 52/3m transports. The gliders themselves also relied on Dornier Do 17, Heinkel He 45 and He 46, and Henschel Hs 126 tugs.

In common with the assault gliders used by other nations, the DFS 230 suffered a very high operational attrition rate in opposed landings on rough ground.

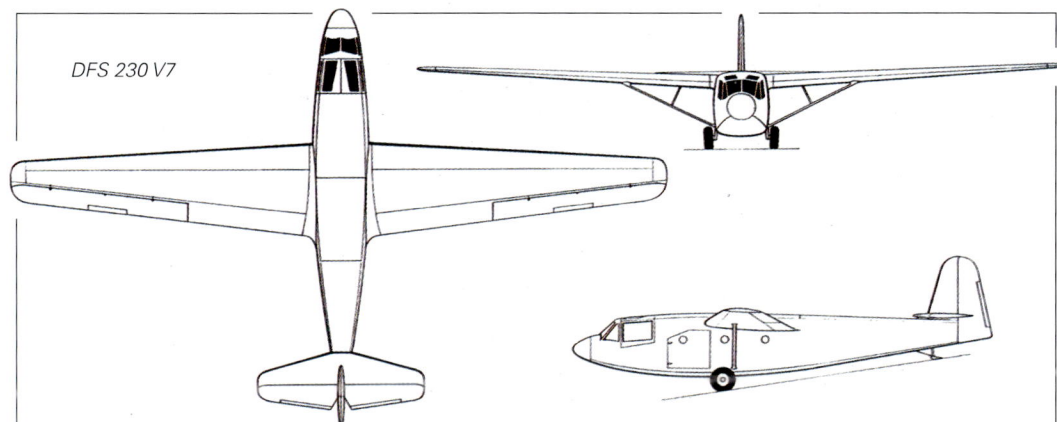

DFS 230 V7

Above: Trials were made of the DFS 230 assault glider on twin-float alighting gear, but they were not notably successful and no attempt was made to place the type in production.

Above: A cloud of smoke envelops a DFS 230C-1 during trials of the powder rocket brakes. Combined with the brake chute which allowed a steep approach, the rockets could bring the glider to a stop in a very short distance, typically around 15 m (49 ft).

Above and below: The DFS 230 V7 was an entirely new design which, apart from the general configuration, bore no resemblance to earlier versions of the DFS 230.

Below: The sole DFS 230 V7 prototype would have eventually led to production DFS 230F-1 aircraft. The type was intended for higher towing speeds and significantly greater payloads, carrying up to 15 troops.

of the guns were, therefore, loaded into Go 242 gliders, their ammunition being carried by DFS 230s. One of the Go 242s and two of the DFS 230s were shot down, but two of the guns were landed, and were supplied intermittently with ammunition by DFS 230s until the capitulation.

At the beginning of 1945 five Lastenseglerstaffeln had still been operational, but by 25 April the Luftwaffe's remaining glider force comprised only 1, 2, and 3. Staffeln of Schleppgruppe 1 based at Königgrätz with 13 DFS 230s and six Go 242s, their tugs comprising three Ju 87s, 11 Do 17s and 15 He 111s. Slightly more than 1,500 DFS 230 gliders had been manufactured, these including 14 assembled in 1944 by the Mráz factory at Chocen.

DFS 230 V7 – entirely new design

Despite its designation, the **DFS 230 V7** in fact bore no relationship to the earlier design, and was the appellation for an entirely new transport glider designed by Ing. Hünerjäger of the Gothaer Waggonfabrik Konstruktionsbüro. Although the DFS 230 had been designed in 1937, and was, by 1941, somewhat dated in view of the progress made in glider development in Germany, the RLM issued a directive that no effort was to be expended in designing and developing further assault gliders in this weight category. The reason for this directive would seem to have been a desire to avoid the development of new designs in a class that was considered to be adequately filled by the existing DFS 230.

Despite this directive, Ing. Hünerjäger believed that higher permissible towing speeds and substantially greater useful loads could be achieved by gliders in the DFS 230 category without any appreciable increase in overall size. However, the GWF was anxious to avoid being accused of openly ignoring the RLM directive, and thus the prototype of the new design was given the designation DFS 230 V7 and the proposed production model was referred to as the **DFS 230F-1**.

Completed late in 1943, the DFS 230 V7 had a freight hold measuring 4.50 m by 1.50 m by 1.50 m (14 ft 9 in by 4 ft 11 in by 4 ft 11 in), and in addition to large freight-loading hatches in the fuselage sides forward of the wing to port and beneath the wing to starboard, a large section of the upper decking was removable so that bulky items could be loaded directly into the cargo hold from above. As an assault glider the DFS 230 V7 could carry a crew of two and 15 troops, disposable load ranged from 1150 to 1750 kg (2,529 to 3,852 lb) in overload condition, and landing speed in normal loaded condition was 95 km/h (59 mph). Although flight trials with the DFS 230 V7 were successful, no production order was forthcoming and no further examples were built.

DFS 230B-1 specification
Type: 10-seat light assault transport glider
Performance: maximum gliding speed 290 km/h (180 mph); maximum towing speed 209 km/h (130 mph); normal towing speed 180 km/h (112 mph); glide ratio (empty) 1:11, (fully loaded), 1:18
Weights: empty 860 kg (1,896 lb); maximum loaded 2100 kg (4,630 lb)
Dimensions: wingspan 21.98 m (72 ft 1⅓ in); length 11.24 m (36 ft 10½ in); height 2.74 m (8 ft 11¾ in); wing area 41.30 m² (444.12 sq ft)
Armament: (optional) one 7.9-mm (0.31-in) MG 15 machine-gun on a trainable mounting in the upper decking of forward fuselage and two 7.9-mm MG 34 machine-guns attached to the forward fuselage sides and fixed to fire forward

DFS 230 V7 specification
Type: 17-seat light assault transport glider
Performance: maximum gliding speed 330 km/h (205 mph); maximum towing speed 300 km/h (186 mph); landing speed 95 km/h (59 mph)
Weights: empty 1253 kg (2,762 lb); normal loaded 2400 kg (5,291 lb); maximum overload 3000 kg (6,614 lb)
Dimensions: wingspan 19.40 m (63 ft 7¾ in); length 12.50 m (41 ft 0⅛ in); height 2.90 m (9 ft 6 in); wing area 39.50 m² (425.17 sq ft)
Armament: none

DFS 331

Developed as a collaborative venture by DFS and Gotha, the DFS 331 assault glider was designed by Hans Jacobs, who had gained experience with the earlier DFS 230. Its wide fuselage would have permitted the carriage of light vehicles and artillery, but the single prototype was eventually rejected in favour of the larger Gotha Go 242.

The success enjoyed by the DFS 230 assault transport glider during the offensive in the West in May 1940 led to an immediate demand for larger-capacity gliders, and Hans Jacobs of the DFS responded by designing the DFS 331. Unusual in featuring an exceptionally broad fuselage that contributed in some measure to the total lift, the DFS 331 featured single-spar wooden wings and a welded steel-tube fuselage with plywood and fabric skinning. The capacious hold could accommodate loads including light military vehicles or light anti-aircraft guns. The fuselage nose was extensively glazed and a raised canopy for the pilot was offset to port, providing excellent visibility.

A single prototype, the **DFS 331 V1**, was built by the Gothaer Waggonfabrik in 1941, but the RLM required appreciably more capacity than was afforded by this type, and although the DFS 331 was evolved in parallel with the more capacious Go 242, the Gothaer Waggonfabrik had received instructions to embark on series production of the latter type before its prototypes had actually commenced their flight test programme, so no further development of the DFS design was undertaken.

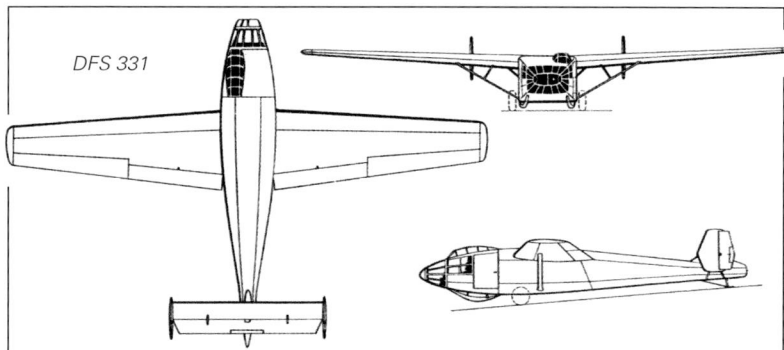

DFS 331 V1 specification
Type: medium transport glider
Performance: maximum gliding speed 330 km/h (205 mph); maximum towing speed 270 km/h (170 mph); gliding ratio 1:17.5
Weights: empty 2270 kg (5,004 lb); maximum loaded 4770 kg (10,516 lb)
Dimensions: wingspan 23.00 m (75 ft 5¼ in); length 15.81 m (51 ft 10¼ in); height 3.55 m (11 ft 7¾ in); wing area 60.00 m² (645.83 sq ft)
Armament: (proposed) one 7.9-mm (0.31-in) MG 15 machine-gun on flexible mounting in extreme nose

Above: These two views show the only example of the DFS 331 to be built and tested. A noteworthy feature was the aerofoil-section fuselage that was intended to contribute a measure of lift.

Below: Designed by Hans Jacobs of the DFS and built by the Gothaer Waggonfabrik, the DFS 331 was evolved to meet a requirement for a more capacious transport glider than the DFS 230. The boxy fuselage offered good capacity, and would also have been cheap to produce.

Dornier-Werke GmbH

The progeny of the Dornier drawing boards did more to gain international recognition of German capabilities in the field of aircraft design and development in the 1920s and early 1930s than did the products of any design team of the resurrected German aircraft industry, with the possible exception of those of the Junkers organisation. From inconspicuous beginnings as an experimental division of the Zeppelin-Werke, the Dornier company, headed by Prof.-Dr. Claudius Dornier, a singularly gifted designer and a pioneer of metal construction for aircraft, established a pre-eminent position between the two world wars, and became one of the most important components of the aircraft industry of the Third Reich.

Claudius Dornier first joined the Zeppelin Luftschiffbau in 1910. After undertaking aerodynamic research work for an all-metal rigid airship and initiating the design of an airship intended for transatlantic operation, he had sufficiently impressed Ferdinand Graf von Zeppelin with his capabilities for a separate design and research branch to be created at Lindau-Reutin as the Zeppelin-Werke Lindau GmbH, specifically for the design and construction of aircraft embodying his highly original theories. The first of Dornier's aircraft built at Reutin by Zeppelin-Lindau was a large multi-engined flying-boat, the Rs I, which was noteworthy both

For Dr Claudius Dornier the dream was a multi-engined passenger-carrying flying-boat that could operate on commercial transatlantic routes, and the dream began to turn into reality with the important Do J Wal.

In the years after World War I, when Germany was prohibited from the manufacture of all but the smallest aircraft, Dr Claudius Dornier of the Zeppelin-Werke Lindau GmbH (from 1922 the Dornier Metallbauten GmbH to reflect the name of the chief designer and its emphasis on aircraft of all-metal construction) maintained a design capability in Germany.

for its size and in being the first German aircraft to embody duralumin in its construction.

Launched in October 1915, the Rs I was wrecked before it could be tested in flight, but three other metal flying-boat prototypes, the Rs II, III and IV, were built by Zeppelin-Lindau over the next three years, and contributed much to Dornier's subsequent developments in the field of water-borne aircraft. Dornier's design bureau, which had been transferred to Seemoos, near Friedrichshafen, during 1916, did not confine itself exclusively to seaplanes, however, for 1917 witnessed the debut of the CL I two-seat escort and ground attack aircraft built to test Dornier's theories on metal stressed-skin construction, while the D I single-seat fighter of 1918 embodied stressed fuselage skinning, cantilever wings of torsion-box construction, and a jettisonable fuel tank beneath the fuselage – all features ahead of the contemporary state of the art.

Both waterborne and land-based aircraft from Dornier's drawing boards had been considered as essays in technique rather than serious production aircraft, none being manufactured in quantity, but Zeppelin-Lindau continued after the Armistice of 1918, using the old Flugzeugbau I Friedrichshafen GmbH works at Manzell, where the primary activity was initially the completion of a batch of 20 Zeppelin C II observation biplanes, of which 19 were supplied to the Swiss Fliegertruppe. Dornier had meanwhile turned his attention to commercial aviation, and the six-passenger Gs I flying-boat was flown on 31 July 1919. Featuring the inherently stable broadbeam-hull and sponsons, or Stummel, that were to characterise Dornier flying-boats in the years that followed, the Gs I was a great success, but after a demonstration in the Netherlands, the Allies demanded its destruc-

tion as it came within a category of aircraft forbidden by the Control Commission. The Gs I was duly sunk off Kiel on 25 April 1920, and the completion of two examples of a nine-passenger derivative, the Gs II, was not permitted.

Evading Allied scrutiny

Dornier thus began to investigate the possibility of evading the restrictions imposed by the Allies – as did also several of his contemporaries – by establishing foreign subsidiaries, meanwhile confining aircraft actually built at Manzell to a size permitted by the Control Commission. These included the small Cs II Delphin five-passenger flying-boat first flown on 24 November 1920 and, in the following year, a land-plane counterpart, the C III Komet, and a two-seat flying-boat, the Libelle I. While these aircraft, suffering the limitations in size and performance imposed by the Allies, were noteworthy only for their extensive use of steel and duralumin, far more ambitious projects had reached detail design on Dornier's drawing boards. In 1922, in which year the Zeppelin-Werke Lindau GmbH changed its title to Dornier Metallbauten GmbH, an Italian subsidiary was formed at Marina di Pisa as the Societa di Construzioni Meccaniche Aeronautiche (CMASA) specifically for the construction of a development of the forbidden Gs II flying-boat. Dubbed the Wal, the CMASA-built prototype flew on 6 November 1922, and such was the success of initial trials that the majority of the shares in the Italian subsidiary were transferred to an Italian syndicate to finance immediate tooling for series production of the Wal, which, in the years that followed, was to gain international acclaim for its sturdiness and efficiency. It was also manufactured under licence in Japan, the Netherlands and Spain.

Work at the Manzell factory was largely confined to the small commercial Delphin and Komet and, from 1925, the six-passenger Merkur, although some clandestine military aircraft development was undertaken, including the Do H Falke and Seefalke all-metal cantilever single-seat fighter monoplanes with wheeled undercarriage and float alighting gear, respectively. The prototype of the Falke flew on 1 November 1922, and a licence was acquired by Kawasaki although, in the event, it was never taken up. Another warplane evolved in the mid-1920s was the Do D twin-float torpedo-bomber monoplane that flew in July 1926 and was later adopted by the Yugoslav naval air service.

Relocation to Switzerland

The limitations imposed on the German aircraft industry by the 'Nine Rules' that were, in fact, waived during 1926, had been particularly embarrassing to Dornier, anxious to capitalise on the international reputation of the Dornier Metallbauten GmbH established by the Wal. The associated Italian company, CMASA, was occupied in fulfilling the constantly increasing orders for the Wal, and thus, by 1926, Dornier had elected to transfer his main centre of activities across Lake Constance from Manzell to Altenrhein in Switzerland, and by the following year the AG für Dornier-Flugzeuge had begun activities at Altenrhein, near Rorschach. The Swiss subsidiary immediately began preparations for the construction of what was to be the largest aircraft in existence, the Do X 12-engined flying-boat designed for transatlantic operations.

The prototype of this immense aeroplane was flown from Lake Constance for the first time on 25 July 1929, but by now design emphasis had already begun to switch from commercial to military aircraft, and to the bomber in particular. Dornier had previously designed a twin-engined night

To meet Dutch requirements of 1935 for a general-purpose military flying boat to replace the Dornier Wal, Dornier laid out plans for a boat in keeping with its earlier projects and making use of a broad-beamed, shallow hull, a semi-cantilever high wing and sponsons for stability on the water. This became the Do 24.

bomber, the Do N, which had been built by Kawasaki in Japan, and on 31 March 1930 the first of two prototypes of a four-engined heavy bomber, the Do P, was flown. It was followed some 18 months later, on 17 October 1931, by the first of two prototypes for the Do Y three-engined heavy bomber. Both types were demonstrated in Germany in the guise of commercial freight aircraft, but they were only stepping stones to the Do F, the prototype of what was to become the clandestine Luftwaffe's first heavy bomber.

Plans were already being secretly prepared for the expansion of the German aircraft industry, the Dornier concern being seen as a part of the nucleus around which the growth was to take place. Initially expansion of the Dornier Metallbauten GmbH itself was to centre on Friedrichshafen, and preparations began to supplement the capacity of the old Manzell works with facilities at Löwenthal and Allmansweiler. In 1932, Dornier once again began the construction of large aircraft on the German side of Lake Constance, production of the Militär-Wal 33 commencing, while, late in 1933 the first Do 11 bomber, the production version of the Do F, rolled off the German assembly line.

Another change of name

The company now again changed its title, becoming the Dornier-Werke GmbH, and a state-financed associate company was created at Wismar-Aldorf as the Dornier-Werke Wismar GmbH. The quantity manufacture of the Do 17 resulted in the parent company's output being supplemented by Siebel at Halle, and Henschel at Berlin-Schönefeld. The Dornier-Werke continued to expand, establishing a new factory at Oberpfaffenhofen in 1938, but by this time the Wismar-Aldorf associate company, which was to be renamed the Norddeutsche Dornier-Werke GmbH, had begun production of 300 He 111s, and, in so far as the Luftwaffe

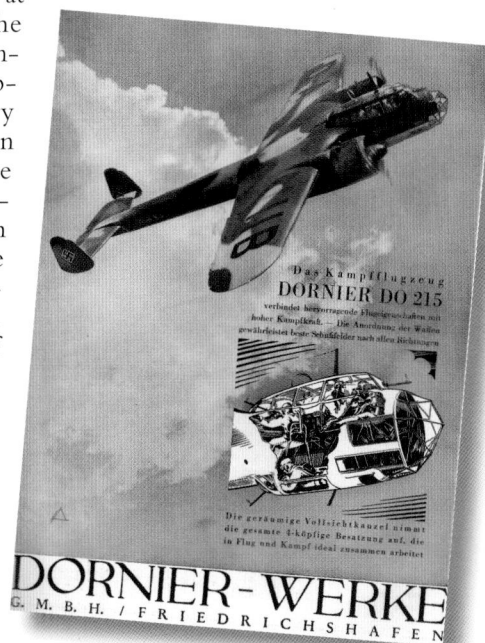

Dornier designs formed an important part of the Luftwaffe's bomber forces during the early part of the war, but the company's influence declined as the war progressed.

Dornier-Werke GmbH

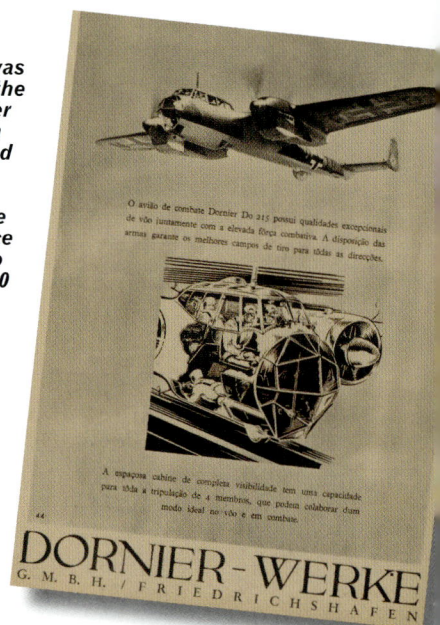

The Do 215 designation was applied to the Do 17Z on the orders of the RLM to cover a proposed export version for Yugoslavia. Embargoed before delivery, the 18 aircraft were modified on the production line for the long-range reconnaissance role and were delivered to the Luftwaffe as Do 215B-0 and Do 215B-1 machines. Dornier was ordered to continue production of the type for the Luftwaffe, and produced a succession of sub-variants.

was concerned, the Dornier star was soon to be on the wane. After the phase-out of the Do 17 series in 1940, only one other Dornier design was to see large-scale production, the Do 217 that was built by the Friedrichshafen group of factories and at a plant established at Munich, although this factory switched to the Me 410 in 1943. The Norddeutsche Dornier-Werke, which expanded during the war years to incorporate factories at Lübeck, Reinickendorf and Sternberg, was destined to produce relatively few aircraft of Dornier design, the Wismar-Aldorf plant, after completing the He 111 contract, switching to the Ju 88 until the beginning of 1942, then phasing into the Do 217 programme until September 1943, and subsequently producing Fw 190s. The last Dornier design to be ordered into production, the Do 335, the most audacious piston-engined fighter of World War II, was to be too late to have any impact on the course of the conflict.

Dornier Do 11

The Do 11 from the Dornier company was one of the Third Reich's first attempts at the creation of a heavy day and night bomber, and was a thoroughly indifferent warplane with a number of serious problems. The type was phased out of German first-line service, and a number were transferred to the Bulgarian air force.

When the existence of the previously clandestine Luftwaffe was officially proclaimed on 1 March 1935, the world at large, lethargic and blasé, evinced little surprise or concern that such a force should have been created and was now flaunted in direct contravention to the Treaty of Versailles, nor that this fledgling 'defensive' air arm already possessed a bombing component. Few governments, interested or disinterested, were unaware of the fact that bomber development had been undertaken by the foreign subsidiaries of German aircraft manufacturers since the mid-1920s as a means of evading the restrictions placed on military aircraft production in Germany. Indeed, the bombers that now equipped the Luftwaffe's first Kampfstaffeln had already been revealed to the world, albeit in more pacific guises.

The Dornier Metallbauten GmbH at Friedrichshafen am Bodensee had founded subsidiary companies in Italy and Switzerland, the Swiss branch at Altenrhein, established in 1927, being involved in multi-engined heavy bomber development at an early stage in its history, producing the **Do P**, a 12000-kg (26,455-lb) shoulder-wing monoplane powered by four 500-hp (373-kW) Bristol Jupiter engines mounted in tandem pairs above the wings. Two prototypes were completed, the first of them (CH-302) being flown on 31 March 1930, and the second, which flew during the following summer, having bomb racks removed and gun positions faired over for delivery to Germany, where (as D-1982) it was presented as a freighter.

Within 18 months of the debut of the first Do P, a second Dornier multi-engined bomber, the **Do Y**, was rolled out

An advanced design for its era, the Do 11 (seen here in Do F prototype form) featured a retractable undercarriage and all-metal construction. The type was beset by structural problems, however.

at Altenrhein, this following the general configuration of its predecessor but having three 500-hp (373-kW) Jupiter VI engines, of which two were mounted on the leading edge of the wing's centre section and the third on a pylon above the fuselage. The first of two Do Y prototypes was flown on 17 October 1931, and both were subsequently demonstrated in Germany as freighters, but the Do Y was little more than a stepping stone to an appreciably more advanced bomber, the **Do F**, which was destined to serve as the prototype for the Luftwaffe's first genuine multi-engined bomber.

Retaining all the angularity of earlier large Dornier aircraft, the Do F, which flew at Altenrhein on 7 May 1932, was a twin-engined semi-cantilever monoplane with a metal three-spar wing covered with fabric, a rectangular-section metal-skinned fuselage, and retractable main undercarriage units. The last-mentioned feature represented an innovation in so far as European heavy bomber design was concerned, although the Douglas XB-7 and Fokker YB-8 bomber monoplanes with retractable undercarriages had flown in the USA

*Carrying Lufthansa markings (later **D-ABEL**) to conceal its real nature, the Do F was later redesignated Do 11a and was the first European heavy bomber with retractable main undercarriage units.*

during the previous year. The main wheels were hinged to the bottom of the fuselage by means of V-struts, with shock-absorber legs running vertically down from the main spar, and turned through 90 degrees to lie flat in engine nacelle wells, the upper extremities of the vertical legs running along tracks to lie flat within the wing. The retraction process was intended to be electrically operated, but in practice the electrical system proved inadequate for the task and was discarded in favour of manual retraction.

The Do F was powered by two Siemens-manufactured Jupiter air-cooled nine-cylinder radial engines each rated at 410 kW (550 hp), enclosed by Townend rings and driving Dornier four-blade, fixed-pitch wooden propellers. Provision was made for a crew of five comprising the pilot, co-pilot/engineer, bombardier/nose gunner, radio operator and dorsal gunner, and a bomb bay was provided in the fuselage beneath the wing. Possessing a maximum speed of 250 km/h (155 mph) at sea level, and cruising at 220 km/h (137 mph) over a 1200-km (746-mile) range, the Do F compared favourably in performance with any bomber in its category, and the Fliegerstab of the Reichswehrministerium recommended immediate preparations for series production at Friedrichshafen. Manufacture started late in 1932, and the first aeroplane came off the assembly line a year later.

Designation change

The designation Do F was changed to **Do 11** in 1933. The first production model, the **Do 11C**, which appeared late that year, introduced Siemens Sh.22B-2 radial engines driving three-blade metal propellers. In October 1933, the newly-created Luftfahrtkommissariat established a Behelfsbombergeschwader (auxiliary bomber group) as the nucleus of the future Luftwaffe's bombing force, the Deutsche Lufthansa (DLH) assisting the Luftkommando-Amt in this task. For deception purposes the unit was known as the Verkehrsinspektion der DLH (Traffic Inspectorate of the DLH). Shortly afterwards, on 1 November 1933, the Deutsche Reichsbahn (German State Railway) began operating an air freight service, although in reality these Reichsbahn-Strecken had the sole task of providing navigational and night flying training for multi-engined bomber pilots, the organisation coming under the Inspektion der Fliegerschulen, and the pupils being seconded from the Behelfsbombergeschwader. Thus, the first production

D-AHOS *was an example of the Do 11D, the designation applied to aircraft built to the revised version of the Do 11C standard, and the main production standard for the Do 11 series. Production of the Do 11C and Do 11D totalled only 150 aircraft, the programme being curtailed because of continued problems, including main landing gear retraction difficulties.*

Do 11C bombers were delivered ostensibly to the Deutsche Reichsbahn.

Although the lethal intent of the Do 11C was patently obvious, the new regime in Germany did not consider the time yet opportune to flout openly the restrictions imposed by the Allies, and therefore a freight hatch was cut in the upper decking of the fuselage of the first few production aircraft, this providing access to a small cargo compartment, and the gun positions and glazed bomb-aiming position in the nose were faired in, providing at least a surface veneer of commercial respectability. Thus, in the guise of a commercial freighter and bearing the insignia of the Reichsbahn, the Do 11C was publicly displayed on 1 May 1934, and began operating a night freight and mail service between Berlin, Danzig and Königsberg. What was not publicly revealed was the fact that each Do 11 delivered to the Reichsbahn was accompanied by an assortment of crates which, labelled as spares, in fact contained an interchangeable fuselage nose section complete with a glazed bomb-aiming position and machine-gun mounting, dorsal and ventral mounts, and bomb racks.

It had been anticipated that quantity deliveries of the Do 11 would commence during the late autumn of 1933, but Siemens und Halske failed to maintain the schedules agreed with the Luftfahrtkommissariat for the full flight clearance of the Sh.22B-2 engine, and only a limited number of pre-production engines could be made available to Dornier before January 1934. Thus, by 1 March 1934, the Behelfsbombergeschwader, by now redesignated the Behelfskampfgeschwader, had received only three Do 11Cs as compared with 24 Ju 52/3m ge interim bomber/transports.

This Do 11C was probably on the strength of the Behelfskampfgeschwader in 1934. This individual aircraft was subsequently modified to Do 11D standard.

Dornier Do 11

The importance attached to the Do 11 may be gauged from the fact that the Luftfahrtkommissariat expansion programme called for the delivery of no fewer than 372 aircraft of this type during 1934.

Unfortunately for the fledgling Luftwaffe, development of the Do 11 proceeded anything but smoothly, and Reichswehr and DLH pilots were highly critical of the flying characteristics of the bomber. Under certain conditions the wings of the Do 11C vibrated alarmingly, and the risk of a structural failure necessitated restricting the Do 11C to angles of bank no greater than 45 degrees. Poor stability had already necessitated redesign of the vertical tail surfaces, including provision of a substantially enlarged rudder and small auxiliary fins beneath the tailplane, and the wingspan was now reduced from 28.00 m (91 ft 10¼ in) to 26.30 m (86 ft 3¼ in), and the wingtips were redesigned. The wing modifications markedly alleviated vibration without eliminating the problem, but the flying characteristics were now considered acceptable, and the shorter-span wing was introduced on the assembly line to result in the **Do 11D**, the few Do 11Cs already delivered being modified retrospectively.

Undercarriage difficulties

A troublesome feature of the Do 11 from the outset had been its retractable undercarriage, and it had been found necessary to lock this permanently in the down position on all service aircraft. Dornier's early acceptance of the shortcomings of this undercarriage is indicated by the fact that, before the end of 1932, the company had begun work on a simplified version of the basic design with fixed, spatted undercarriage and Junkers-type 'double-wing' flaps, the prototype of this variant, the **Do 13**, having flown for the first time on 13 February 1933. Initial trials with the Do 13 had revealed structural weaknesses and dangerously unstable flying characteristics coupled with the wing vibration already suffered by the Do 11. Various modifications were made, and two further prototypes, the **Do 13b** and **Do 13c**, were produced, the latter switching from the Sh.22B-2 radial engine to the BMW VI liquid-cooled V-12 engine offering 559 kW (750 hp) for one minute at take-off and having a maximum continuous rating of 373 kW (500 hp). The BMW VI-powered prototype, with similar wing modifications to those of the Do 11D, displayed a sufficient improvement in performance to warrant the Luftfahrtkommissariat transferring orders for 222 Do 11s to the **Do 13C**, as the production model with BMW VI engines was designated.

Production tempo of the Do 11D increased slowly, and by the end of 1934, a total of 77 was being operated by the Behelfskampfgeschwader, the strength of which included those Do 11Ds registered to the Reichsbahn, two new bomber units, the Fliegergruppen Tutow and Fassberg, and the Kampffliegerschulen at Lechfeld and Prenzlau. However, the flying characteristics of the bomber still left much to be desired, and training attrition was high, while the Do 13, which had barely attained service status, had already acquired an even less enviable reputation. Delays in initiating production of the Do 13C had resulted initially from difficulties

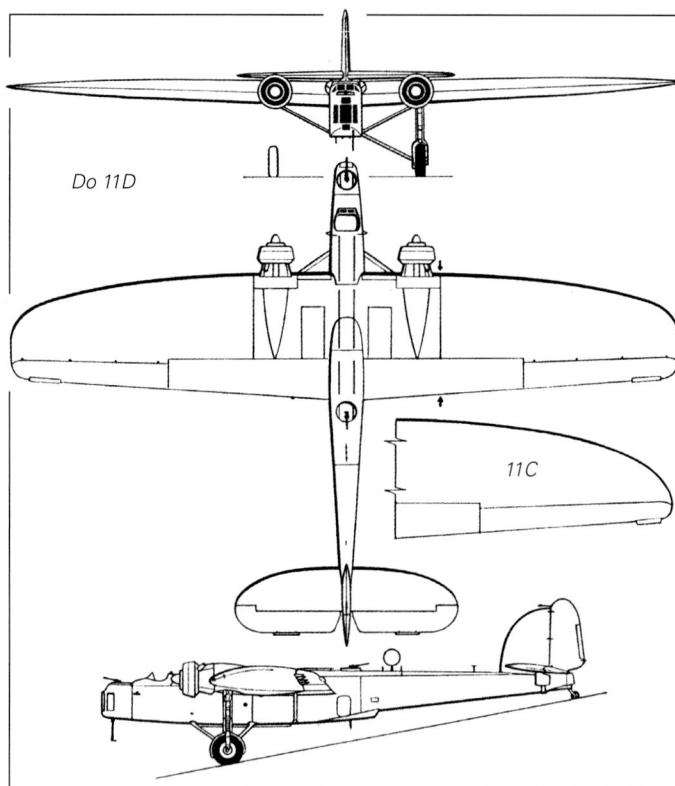

in cooling the BMW VI engines. Supplementary radiators beneath the wing outboard of the engines created so much drag that performance suffered, the problem finally being solved by the application of flush radiators in the lower engine cowling panels. The first Do 13Cs had been delivered during the late autumn, but within the space of a few weeks several had been lost as a result of structural failures. The remaining Do 13Cs were therefore placed under severe restrictions, and production was halted while the entire airframe was restressed. When the bomber once again began to leave the Friedrichshafen factory, the designation had been changed for psychological reasons to **Do 23**.

From the autumn of 1935, the Do 11D began to give place to the Do 23, the earlier aircraft being progressively relegated to the training role and other second-line duties, and a small number being transferred to the Bulgarian government which was in process of forming a clandestine air arm in contravention of the terms of the Treaty of Neuilly.

Dornier Do 11D specification
Type: four-seat heavy day and night bomber
Powerplant: two Siemens Sh.22B-2 air-cooled nine-cylinder radial engines each rated at 485 kW (650 hp) for take-off and 447 kW (600 hp) at 1500 m (4,920 ft)
Performance: maximum speed 260 km/h (161 mph) at sea level; normal cruising speed 225 km/h (140 mph) at 1000 m (3,280 ft); climb to 1000 m (3,280 ft) in 7 minutes, and to 3000 m (9,845 ft) in 36 minutes; service ceiling 4100 m (13,450 ft); maximum range 960 km (596 miles) with 1545 litres (340 Imp gal) of fuel
Weights: empty 5975 kg (13,173 lb); maximum take-off 8200 kg (18,078 kg)
Dimensions: wingspan 26.30 m (86 ft 3⅓ in); length 18.80 m (61 ft 8 in); height 5.49 m (18 ft 0 in); wing area 107.80 m² (1,160.30 sq ft)
Armament: (defensive) one 7.9-mm (0.31-in) MG 15 trainable machine-gun in each of open nose, dorsal and ventral positions; (offensive) 1000 kg (2,205 lb) of bombs carried internally in vertical cells

The Do 11 enjoyed only a short operational career, being phased out of German service from the autumn of 1935 as the improved Do 23 became available. The type was then relegated to training and other second-line tasks for a short time longer, and 12 of the surplus aircraft were transferred in 1937 to Bulgaria.

Dornier Do 16

The Do 16 definitive version of the Wal flying-boat, whose basic design dated from the early 1920s, was an important aircraft in the development of the Luftwaffe's long-range maritime reconnaissance capabilities, but was phased out of first-line service in the late 1930s, shortly before the start of World War II.

From its earliest days, the Dornier Metallbauten GmbH specialised, as the company's name implied, in metal construction, but although a variety of all-metal landplanes was born on Dornier's Friedrichshafen drawing boards, it was for its sturdy and efficient all-metal seaplanes that the company achieved international fame in the 1920s and early 1930s, and for the **Wal** (whale) series of flying-boats in particular. The Wal, whose first prototype flew on 6 November 1922, employed many of the features first embodied in flying-boats designed by Dipl.-Ing. Claudius Dornier during World War I, including the inherently stable broad-beam hull and sponsons, or Stummel, and was destined to be manufactured under licence in several countries over more than a dozen years.

The restrictions placed by the Treaty of Versailles on the German aircraft industry had necessitated the construction of the first prototype by Dornier's Italian subsidiary, the Construzioni Meccaniche Aeronautiche (CMASA) at Marina di Pisa, this concern initiating production deliveries of the flying-boat in the following year. During the years that elapsed between CMASA completing the first production Wal in 1923 and Dornier Metallbauten starting production of the **Militär-Wal 33** at Friedrichshafen in 1932, the basic design underwent a succession of changes: its wingspan was increased four times, it was fitted with more than a score of different engine types ranging from 224 to 559 kW (300 to 750 hp), its loaded weight rose from 4000 kg (8,818 lb) to more than 10000 kg (22,046 lb), and it was produced for a variety of tasks, both military and civil. It was hardly surprising, therefore, that the Fliegerstab of the Reichswehrministerium should elect

The Wal was a parasol-wing monoplane with its wing braced from the outboard ends of the sponsons by a pair of parallel struts on each side. Somewhat unusually for a long-range type, the Wal's wing was of comparatively low aspect ratio.

to adopt this proven flying-boat as a Seefernaufklärer (long-range maritime reconnaissance) type for the planned operational elements of the Seefliegertruppe. The **Wal 33** was, in fact, the ultimate refinement of this flying-boat type and, flown for the first time on 3 May 1933, it was usually known as the **'10 Tonnen-Wal'** because of its gross weight of 10 metric tons, but the Militär-Wal 33, which also appeared in 1933 and was subsequently designated **Do 16**, was based on the earlier **'8 Tonnen-Wal'** which had flown as a prototype on 27 January 1931. Several '8 Tonnen-Wal' boats had been delivered to Deutsche Lufthansa for operation over the airline's proposed South Atlantic mail service at a time before the delivery of the first examples of the Militär-Wal 33 to the Seefliegertruppen late in 1933, and there were few differences between the commercial and military models apart from the provision of defensive armament and other military equipment in the latter.

Before 1933, the Reichsmarine ostensibly possessed no aircraft, naval co-operation and target-towing tasks

The Wal's tandem push/pull engine arrangement was enclosed in a long nacelle above the wing centre section, itself supported above the hull by two pairs of sturdy inward-canted N-struts. The large sponsons provided excellent waterborne stability, and in flight supplemented the lift provided by the wing.

Dornier Do 16

Above: The Wal was important in pioneering South American air services and, operating from depot ships, established Lufthansa's south Atlantic mail service, making some 328 crossings.

being performed by aircraft officially hired from the Severa GmbH, a company clandestinely financed by the Reichswehrministerium, with bases at Kiel-Holtenau and Norderney. Personnel and aircraft from this company and its successor, the Luftdienst GmbH, provided the nucleus for the so-called Seefliegerübungsstaffel (coastal flying practice squadron) formed during the second half of 1934, but naval and mercantile marine personnel had already received flying training at the Deutsche Verkehrsfliegerschule (DVS) establishments at Warnemünde and Travemünde: these were camouflaged naval aviation schools that were soon to come under the open control of the Kommando der Fliegerschulen (See). It was to these schools that the first few Do 16 (Militär-Wal 33) flying-boats were delivered late in 1933, but no more than four were on strength by 1 March 1934.

Small but steady growth in numbers

By the late, 16 Do 16s were on the strength of the Seefliegerstaffeln, and the production programme finalised in mid-1934 envisaged the delivery of 21 Do 16s between July of that year and September 1935, by which time the first operational long-range reconnaissance unit had been formed on these boats, this being known as the Fliegerstaffel (F) List. In July

With its large and capacious hull, the Wal was ideally suited for the low-volume air services of its time. It was therefore possible to create spacious and well appointed passenger accommodation with high-quality service.

1936, when the coastal flying units, or Küstenfliegergruppen, were formed, the Fliegerstaffel (F) List, now redesignated 2./ Kü.Fl.Gr. 106, remained the only operational flying-boat unit as, although four Fernaufklärungsstaffeln were envisaged, it had been decided to await delivery of the Do 18 before forming the remaining three of these units. Thus, in 1935, production of the Do 16 was phased out at Friedrichshafen, some 30 flying-boats of this type having been delivered to the Luftwaffe.

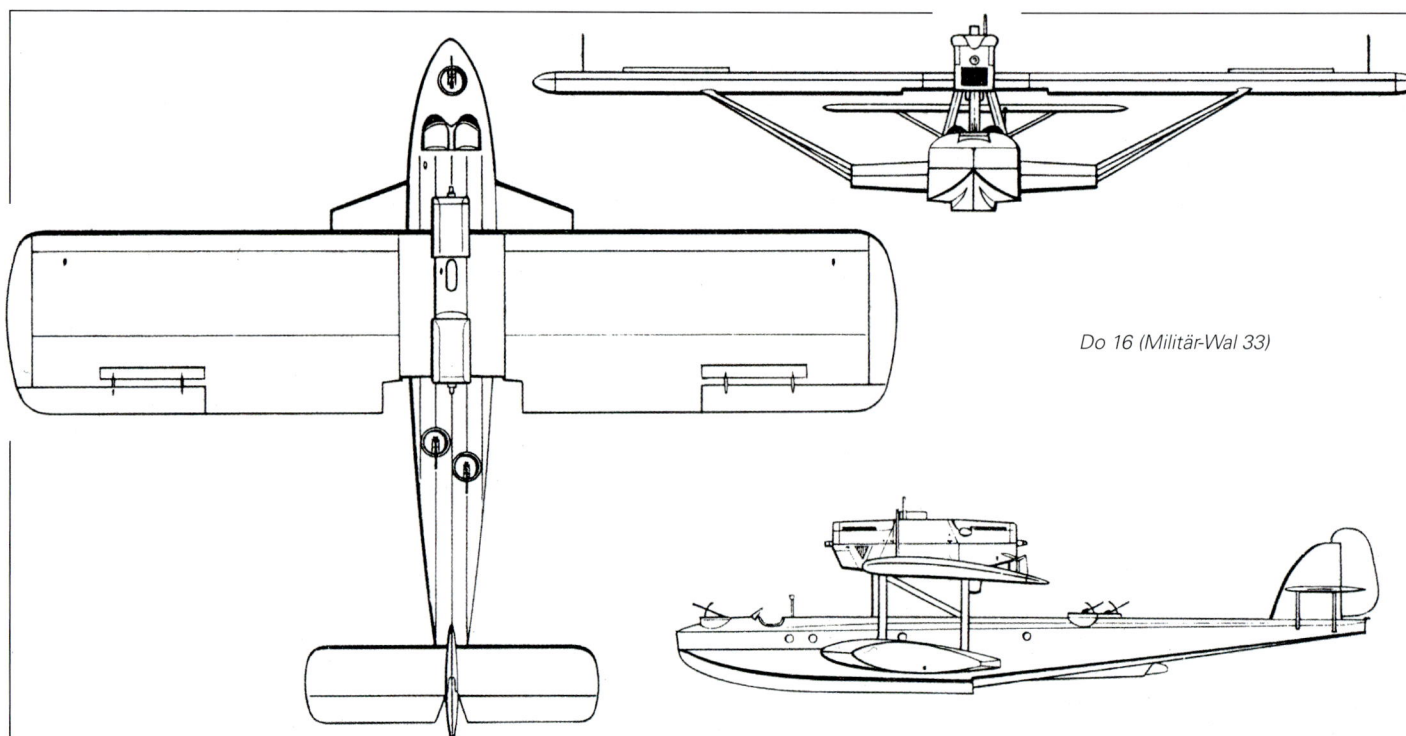

Do 16 (Militär-Wal 33)

Above: **This modified Do J Wal was one of two used during the Amundsen expedition. It has been re-engined with BMW VI engines for the first transatlantic flight by Wolfgang von Grönau in 1930. In 1932 von Grönau flew another Do J (D-2053) around the world.**

Above: **Careful maintenance of the Wal, as well as the catapult and the trolley on which the boat sat for launch, was essential for safe operations over long oceanic passages.**

Above: **The Wal flying boat made much of the crossing on the catapult of its mother ship, and was catapulted into the air with mail and a few passengers for the last stage of the service.**

Above: **G-EBQO was a Do J Wal with Rolls-Royce Eagle IX engines, and in 1925 was used by the Amundsen-Ellsworth polar expedition to fly farther north than any other aircraft of the time.**

Above: **The Wal is readied for launch from the steam-powered catapult as the mother ship turns into the wind to provide greater air speed over the wing as the boat leaves the catapult.**

Right: **The mother ship's catapult officer checks that all is ready before the Wal's engines are started and the flying-boat is launched into the air.**

Dornier Do 16

This example is a Do 16 Militär-Wal 33 of 2./Kü.Fl. Gr.106. The military Wal had more powerful engines than its civilian counterpart, and served with the Agrupación Española (Spanish nationalist air force) during the Spanish Civil War.

The Do 16's hull displayed typical Dornier practice of the period, the sharp V-bottom at the bow changing to a flat bottom at the main step, the rear step fairing into a vertical knife edge. Both hull and sponsons were divided into watertight compartments, and the two-spar wing was carried above the hull on sloping N-struts, being braced outboard by inclined parallel struts to the sponsons. Provision was made for a crew of four (pilot and co-pilot seated side-by-side with navigator and radio-operator immediately aft to port and starboard, respectively). Three open gun positions were provided, each with a single 7.9-mm (0.31-in) MG 15 machine-gun on a Scarff-type mounting, these being disposed in the extreme bow (for operation by the co-pilot) and staggered to port and starboard (for use by the navigator and radio-operator) in the hull above the rear step. Racks could be fitted for four 50-kg (110-lb) bombs.

The Do 16 remained in service with 2./Kü.Fl.Gr. 106 until 1938, when the Militär-Wal was finally supplanted by the Do 18, subsequently serving in the training role and for test purposes. The latter included weapons trials, the first seven 13-mm (0.51-in) MG 131 machine-guns being fitted on Militär-Wals for firing trials that began on 1 July 1938.

Dornier Do 16 (Militär-Wal 33) specification

Type: four-seat long-range maritime reconnaissance flying-boat
Powerplant: two BMW VI 7.3 liquid-cooled V-12 engines each rated at 559 kW (750 hp) for take-off and 373 kW (500 hp) maximum for continuous cruising
Performance: maximum speed 220 km/h (137 mph) at sea level; normal cruising speed 190 km/h (118 mph) at 1000 m (3,280 ft); climb to 3000 m (9,845 ft) in 35 minutes; service ceiling 3000 m (9,845 ft); normal range 2200 km (1,367 miles)
Weights: empty equipped 5385 kg (11,872 lb); normal loaded 7600 kg (16,755 lb); maximum take-off 8000 kg (17,637 lb)
Dimensions: wingspan 23.20 m (76 ft 1½ in); length 18.20 m (59 ft 8½ in); height 5.50 m (18 ft 0½ in); wing area 95.97 m² (1,033.00 sq ft)
Armament: one bow and two dorsal positions each with one 7.9-mm (0.31-in) MG 15 trainable machine-gun, and provision for two or four 50-kg (110-lb) bombs on external racks

D-AGAT was named 'Boreas', and was one of the Do J IIfBos boats operated by Lufthansa on its South American service. The boat is seen here on the catapult of Schwabenland.

Above: Many nations operated Wals in military roles, including Argentina, Chile, Colombia, Italy, Netherlands East Indies, Norway, Portugal, the Soviet Union, Spain, Uruguay and Yugoslavia.

Above: In the Do R4 Super Wal the Do J Wal's powerplant of two engines in a centreline arrangement was replaced by four engines, still in tandem push/pull pairs, above the wing outboard of the centreline and approximately above the junction of the hull and sponsons.

Above: As indicated by the row of circular portholes, the passenger accommodation of the Wal was located in the forward section of the hull. The boat was flown from an open cockpit above the forward part of the cabin.

Above: Spain led the way in acquiring the Wal for military purposes, procuring an eventual 14 early Wals from the CMASA production line at Pisa, Italy. The initial order was placed based on the blueprints alone, before a single Wal had been completed. CASA later built 27 Militär-Wals for the Spanish forces, as well as a pair of mailplanes. Other Wals were built in the Netherlands by Aviolanda, which manufactured 38, primarily for service with the Netherlands East Indies air arm.

A Do R4 Super Wal flies low over the water. The type was, in essence, an enlarged and four-engined extrapolation of the Do J Wal. A notable change was the enclosed cockpit, which was set farther back than on the Wal and offset to port below the leading edge of the wing. A water rudder was hinged to the rear of the skeg under the after part of the hull.

Dornier Do 17

The Do 17 series of medium bombers marked the apogee of Dornier's design and large-scale manufacture of tactical warplanes in World War II, but by 1942 the type was obsolescent as a first-line warplane and was steadily relegated to less taxing roles in which it would not face high-quality fighter opposition.

In the mid-1930s the first rumours of a very fast and efficient *Schulterdecker-Kampfflugzeug* began to percolate through to the British and French air ministries: they suggested a graceful shoulder-wing bomber faster than any single-seat fighter extant. Confirmation of the existence of this advanced warplane came in October 1935 when one of the prototypes was demonstrated at Bückeberg, but it was not until nearly two years later, in July 1937, when the **Do 17 V8** participated in the International Military Aircraft Competition at Zürich, winning the 'Circuit of the Alps' and displaying a clean pair of heels to the fighters of every country represented in the contests, that it became generally known that this graceful aircraft had been developed. The slender new bomber was promptly dubbed the 'Flying Pencil'.

What was not known at Zürich was the fact that the **Do 17** owed its existence as a bomber solely to chance, or that the Do 17 V8 embodied aerodynamic improvements and substantially more powerful engines than those of the production model then being delivered to the Luftwaffe, resulting in a speed 90 km/h (56 mph) superior to that of the bomber entering service with the Kampfgruppen.

The Do 17 had been evolved at a time when German theories of air strategy relegated the fighter to a secondary role, the bomber possessing sufficient speed to elude interceptors. Although this was to prove a fallacy, the theory was reinforced by the debut of the Do 17, which initiated the German trend towards relatively small, highly-loaded and high-powered but versatile aircraft that was to be maintained throughout World War II. Perhaps the most remarkable feature of the Do 17's development, however, was that, unlike the He 111 which was designed from the outset primarily as a bomber although first revealed as a commercial transport, the Do 17 had been designed as a commercial transport.

The Deutsche Lufthansa had conceived a requirement for a high-speed mailplane also able to carry six passengers. To

A Do 17Z medium bomber unloads its bombs over its target. In this variant a new and completely revised forward fuselage was introduced to increase crew volume and also allow the addition of a machine-gun providing ventral protection.

meet this requirement, Dornier created a design setting new standards in aerodynamic cleanliness and intended for the powerplant of two 492-kW (660-hp) BMW VI liquid-cooled V-12 engines, which were the most powerful aero engines then available in Germany. The most characteristic feature of the design was the exceptional slenderness of the fuselage in side profile, this being accentuated by a long, pointed nose cone. The Do 17, as the design was designated, was by no means so slender in planform, however, the centre fuselage being, abnormally broad, the section starting more or less as an oval, changing rapidly to what may best be described as

These two Dornier Do 17Zs of KG 2 are seen during the campaign against the Low Countries. The type faired well in these early battles, but when a higher level of defence was encountered, such as that over England in 1940, the Do 17 was found to be lacking and was soon relegated to less demanding roles.

A Do 17E-1 of III/KG 255 'Alpen' wears the Geschwader's Edelweiss badge below the cockpit. The fuselage cross was partially obscured to indicate the machine was an 'enemy' in the 1938 war games.

an inverted triangle, about twice as wide at the top as at the bottom, and then reverting once more to an ellipse.

Orthodox construction

The fuselage structure comprised built-up frames and intermediate stiffeners with channel-section stringers, the whole being covered by light metal panels. The shoulder-mounted wing was of two-spar design with part metal and part fabric skinning. The spar booms were thick duralumin extrusions of asymmetrical section, the primary ribs being built up of duralumin channel sections, and the intermediate ribs having tubular bracing. The fabric skinning was confined to the wing undersurfaces between the spars, slotted flaps extended between the ailerons and the fuselage, and all fuel was housed between the inboard section spars. The main undercarriage members retracted rearwards into the engine nacelles, and the tailwheel was also retractable.

The **Do 17 V1** first of three prototypes was flown in the autumn of 1934, and before the end of the year the **Do 17 V2** and **Do 17 V3** had joined the test programme, all three aircraft being passed to Lufthansa for evaluation early in 1935. Although the Do 17 fully met the airline's performance demands, Lufthansa rapidly concluded that the Do 17 was unsuited for service as the passenger accommodation was impracticable. The Do 17's slim fuselage contained two tiny cabins: one accommodating two passengers was situated immediately aft of the two-seat flight deck, and the other, seating four passengers, was positioned aft of the wing.

The passengers thus had to perform virtual acrobatics to enter these diminutive compartments, so Lufthansa decided that such accommodation would have strictly limited commercial appeal. The trio of prototypes was therefore returned to Dornier, and it is probable that the career of the Do 17 would have ended there had it not been for a casual visit to Dornier's Löwenthal plant by a former Dornier employee, Flugkapitän Untucht. After leaving Dornier, Untucht had joined Lufthansa and also acted as liaison officer between the airline and the Reichsluftfahrtmimsterium (RLM). Untucht decided to fly one of the Do 17 prototypes himself. Impressed

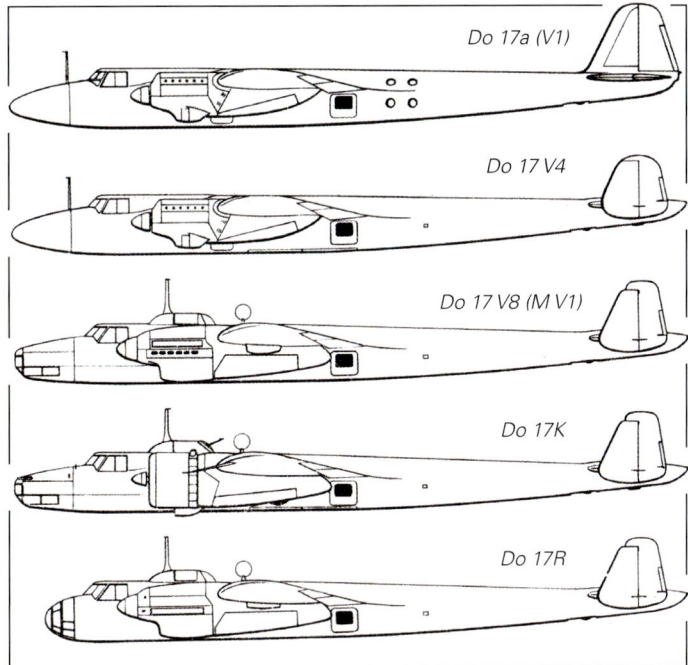

by the aircraft's handling qualities and performance, Untucht suggested that, with some additional keel area to provide a stable bombing platform, the Do 17 could well be amenable to the bombing role. Although Dornier personnel were sceptical, the Technisches Amt of the RLM proved receptive to Untucht's proposal, and after RLM test pilots had completed a preliminary flight evaluation of the aircraft, the company received instructions to produce a fourth prototype that was to embody the minimum modifications necessary for military trials. Thus, during the late summer of 1935, the **Do 17 V4** made its appearance. This prototype differed externally from its predecessor solely in having the cabin portholes eliminated and a twin fin-and-rudder assembly in place of the original single fin-and-rudder arrangement to eliminate the tendency to yaw. Internal changes included provision of a radio operator's compartment in the space previously occupied by the

The first of Dornier's 'flying pencils' was the Do 17 V1 prototype for a fast mailplane. This caused much anxiety in France and the UK when it appeared late in 1934, for its military potential was both obvious and frightening.

Dornier Do 17

D-AHAK was the registration allocated to the Do 17 V9 prototype for the Do 17E bomber model. The machine was later converted as a high-speed liaison aeroplane with a longer and nicely tapered 'solid' nose. The aircraft lasted in service into 1944.

passenger cabin, and the introduction of a bomb bay in the bottom of the fuselage behind the plane of the front spar. By comparison with the transport prototypes, the overall length of the Do 17 V4 was reduced from 17.70 m (58 ft 1 in) to 17.15 m (56 ft 3¼ in), but the BMW V1 engines were retained.

Two further prototypes, the **Do 17 V5** and **Do 17 V6**, were built in parallel with the Do 17 V4, these joining the flight test programme during the autumn of 1935. Whereas the V6 was virtually identical to the V4, the Do 17 V5 was powered by two Hispano-Suiza 12Ybrs liquid-cooled V-12 engines each rated at 578 kW (775 hp) at sea level and 641 kW (860 hp) at 4000 m (13,125 ft), and with these

Above: Few aircraft come off better in a collision with a hangar, and this Do 17 was no exception. The shape of the nose in early Do 17 variants precluded the addition of a machine-gun for ventral defence, a deficiency noted during the Spanish Civil War.

engines attained a speed of 390 km/h (243 mph). At this time, the Gloster Gauntlet fighter, which was just entering RAF service, could barely reach 230 mph (370 km/h). No provision had been made for defensive armament in the Do 17, but wiser councils prevailed over the factions in the Luftwaffe that believed that speed alone would enable the bomber to evade interception, and a further prototype, the **Do 17 V7**, was completed with provision for a single 7.9-mm (0.31-in) MG 15 rearward-firing machine-gun in a blister fairing above the forward fuselage and fired by the radio operator. This prototype also featured a hemispherical glazed nose cap and flat glazed panels in the lower portion of the nose. The Do 17 V8 was retained by Dornier as a development aircraft, and the **Do 17 V9**, which appeared in the spring of 1936, was to all intents and purposes the prototype for the initial production bomber, the **Do 17E-1**.

The Do 17 V9, registered D-AHAK, differed from its predecessors in several respects. The fuselage nose was reduced in length by nearly 1 m (3 ft 3 in), overall length reducing to 16.24 m (53 ft 3¼ in); the glazed nose cone was substantially enlarged and introduced optically flat panels for the bombardier; additional glazed panels were inserted in the starboard side of the forward fuselage; the blister fairing aft of the flight deck was refined; the vertical tail surfaces were redesigned and enlarged, and full military equipment was installed. Two years later, the Do 17 V9 was adapted for the high-speed liaison and communications role in which it was to serve until 1944. The **Do 17 V10** (D-AKUZ) was completed for engine development purposes and, lacking the glazed nose and provision for defensive armament, was initially flown with uprated BMW VI 7,3 engines in place of the BMW VI 6,0 units of earlier prototypes. Featuring increased compres-

The first three Do 17 prototypes had a single fin-and-rudder unit, but revealed a tendency to yaw, so from the Do 17 V4 a revised tail unit, with endplate vertical surfaces, was introduced. This also improved the field of fire from upper rear of the cockpit.

In common with other German medium bombers of World War II, the Do 17 concentrated its crew in the foward part of the nose. Here they were able to communicate easily with each other, but were also very vulnerable to decimation in a single attack.

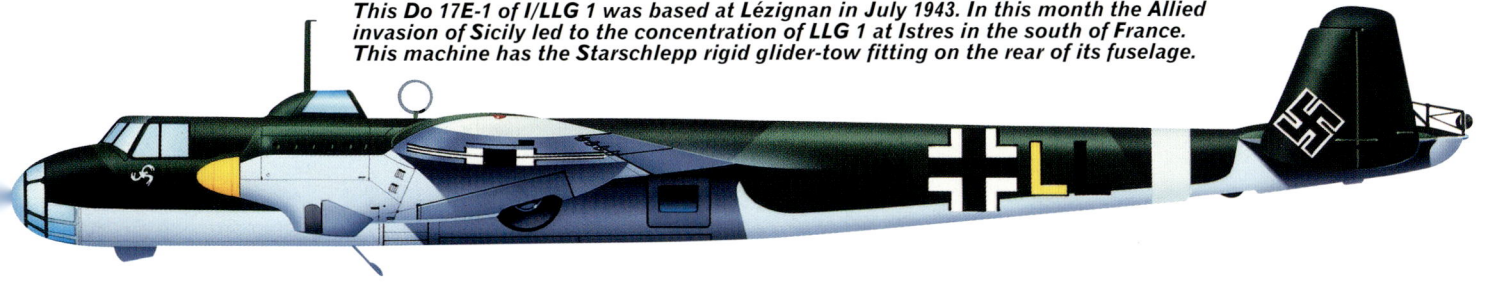

This Do 17E-1 of I/LLG 1 was based at Lézignan in July 1943. In this month the Allied invasion of Sicily led to the concentration of LLG 1 at Istres in the south of France. This machine has the Starschlepp rigid glider-tow fitting on the rear of its fuselage.

sion ratio, the BMW VI 7,3 offered a maximum output of 559 kW (750 hp) as compared with 492 kW (660 hp), but normal output remained 373 kW (500 hp).

Do 17E and Do 17F series

Preparations for the quantity manufacture of the Do 17 for the Luftwaffe had begun at Dornier's plants at Allmansweiler, Löwenthal and Manzell early in 1936, the initial production models being the Do 17E-1 bomber and the **Do 17F-1** long-range reconnaissance aircraft. Produced in parallel, the two models were essentially similar, the latter having the bomb sight and bomb-release mechanism removed, provision made for an auxiliary fuselage fuel tank, and a pair of automatic vertical cameras mounted in the bomb bay. Both the Do 17E-1 and F-1 were powered by BMW V1 7,3 engines and carried a defensive armament of one MG 15 machine-gun, although this was soon augmented by a second MG 15 mounted in the floor forward of the bomb-bay to fire downward through a hatch. The bomb bay of the Do 17E-1 normally accommodated a 500-kg (1,102-lb) load of horizontally stowed bombs, typical loads comprising 10 50-kg (110-lb) SC 50 bombs, four 100-kg (220-lb) SD 100 bombs, or two 250-kg (550-lb) SD 250 bombs, but for reduced-range missions the load

could be increased to 750 kg (1,653 lb). Shortly after the Technisches Amt of the RLM had begun to display interest in the potentialities of the Do 17 as a bomber, Dornier had initiated the 'productionisation' of the design, breaking a considerable proportion of the basic airframe down into component form readily amenable for sub-contract. This also had the advantage of enabling relatively major components to be replaced at unit level, and with the decision to adopt the Do 17 on a large scale the German aircraft industry's first major dispersed production programme was initiated, this forming a pattern for programmes that were to follow.

Before the end of 1936 the first production aircraft had left the assembly lines. Some difficulties were experienced with the first subcontracted components, but the production tempo built up rapidly, and by the beginning of 1937 a number of aircraft were undergoing service trials with the Luftwaffe.

A small fuel bowser moves up toward a Do 17F bomber as part of the process to make the warplane ready for its next operational mission. Note the two guns for forward hemisphere defence.

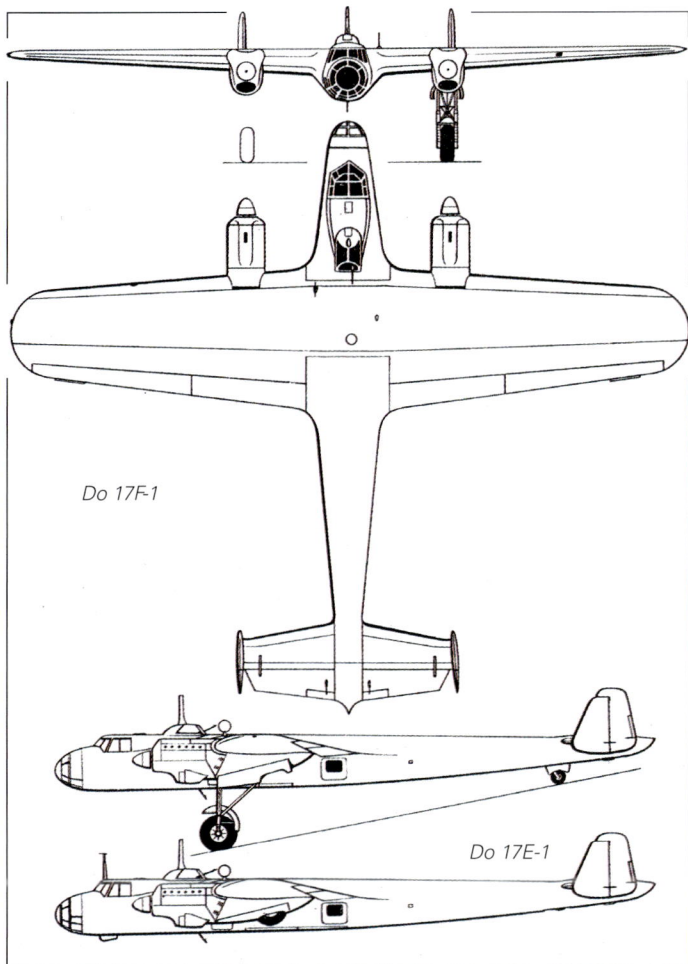

Dornier Do 17

The initial production model of the bomber series was the Do 17E-1, which began equipping the Kampfgeschwadern in 1937. The Do 17E-1 soon received its baptism of fire in Spanish skies, alongside the similar Do 17F-1 reconnaissance version. This Do 17E-1 of 7./KG 255 is seen with national insignia obscured for involvment in the 1938 war games, in which it was operating as part of the 'enemy' forces.

During the early months of 1937, I/KG 153 at Merseburg and I/KG 155 at Giebelstadt, these being the Luftwaffe's original Kampffliegergruppen, began conversion to the Do 17E-1 bomber and, almost simultaneously, the first long-range reconnaissance Gruppe, Aufkl.Gr.(F)/122, began to receive the Do 17F-1. This unit, which was to be redesignated Aufkl.Gr.(F)/22 in the following October, attained full strength with 36 aircraft by April 1937. During the course of 1937, II and III Gruppen of KG 153 followed I Gruppe and converted to the Do 17E-1 at Finsterwalde and Altenburg, respectively, together with II and III Gruppen of KG 155. This last-mentioned Kampfgeschwader became KG 158 in October 1937 (KG 155 was subsequently re-formed with He 111s), and in the same month, IV/KG 153 was activated on Do 17E-1s at Liegnitz as the eventual nucleus of KG 252, the Gruppe becoming II/KG 252 during 1938, and I/KG 252 was formed at Cottbus in November of that year. A fourth Kampfgeschwader, KG 255, had begun forming on the Do 17E-1 before the end of 1937, and by that time plans had already been initiated to evaluate the Luftwaffe's newest warplane under operational conditions in Spain.

The importance placed by the Oberkommando der Luftwaffe (OKL) on gaining actual operational experience may be gauged from the fact that, as early as the spring of 1937,

The Do 17 pilot's position was offset slightly to port to provide sufficient room for the bombardier to reach his position in the extensively glazed nose.

Dornier Do 17E-1 cutaway key

1 Port rudder
2 Rudder balance
3 Aerial attachments
4 Port tailfin
5 Fin/tailplane fairing
6 Tailfin lower section
7 Elevator balance
8 Rudder tab
9 Port elevator
10 Port tailplane
11 Elevator torque tube
12 Tailplane centre-section fairing
13 Elevator control horns
14 Elevator tab
15 Tail navigation light
16 Starboard elevator tab
17 Aerial
18 Starboard elevator
19 Tailfin structure
20 Rudder frame
21 Rudder tab
22 Tab hinge fairing
23 Rudder balance
24 Elevator balance
25 Tailplane structure
26 Tail bumper
27 Tailplane attachment
28 Rudder control linkage
29 Fuselage aft skinning
30 Tailwheel door
31 Retractable tailwheel
32 Tailwheel leg forging
33 Retraction mechanism
34 Control linkage
35 Frame
36 Fuselage structure
37 Compass
38 Stringers
39 Wing root/fuselage fairing fillet
40 Control linkage
41 First-aid equipment (port side access)
42 Fuselage/wing upper skin
43 Slotted flap profile
44 Starboard fuel tank (700 litre/154 Imp gal capacity)
45 2x 250-kg/ 550-lb bomb load
46 Bomb rack
47 Aft entry/inspection door
48 Wing/fuselage former
49 Rear spar
50 Horizontal stowage bomb magazine
51 Bomb electrical release switches
52 Front spar
53 Dorsal flexible 7.9-mm MG 15 machine gun
54 D/F loop
55 Fuel filler cap
56 Port fuel tank (700 litre/154 Imp gal capacity)

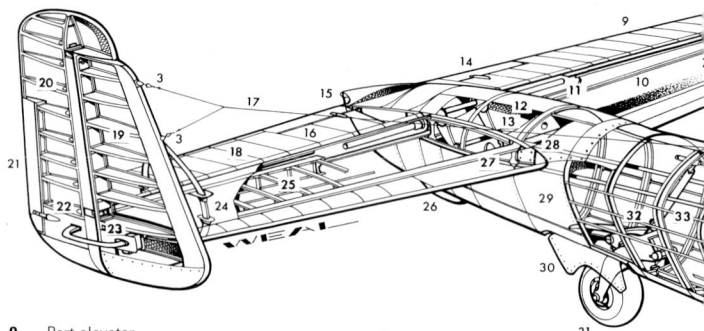

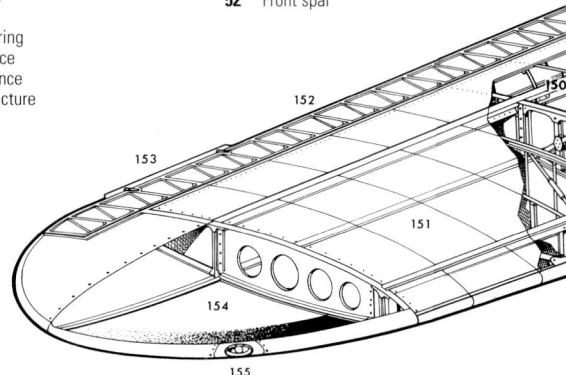

Dornier Do 17

A close-up view shows the Do 17's upper rearward defence of a 7.9-mm (0.31-in) MG 15 machine-gun with its ammunition in a saddle drum magazine. Offset to port is the antenna loop for the radio direction-finding system.

An open-air final briefing is held for Do 17F crews, framed by an aircraft of III/KG 255 (later III/KG 51), before their departure on a training flight.

57 Flap track rod
58 Aerials
59 Aileron profile
60 Aerial mast
61 Port engine oil tank
62 Oil filler cap
63 Aileron rod
64 Aileron hinge fairings
65 Port Aileron

78 Spinner boss
79 Crew emergency escape roof hatch
80 Exhaust stubs
81 Leading-edge fillet
82 Dorsal blister front glazing
83 Dorsal blister
84 Tailwheel manual retraction
85 Spent cartridge net attachment
86 Ammunition magazine stowage
87 Bomb magazine front face
88 Dorsal gunner's fire step

89 FuG III aU radio transmitter/receiver equipment (starboard wall)
90 Crew forward entry door
91 Ventral sliding hatch
92 Bomb-aimer's convertible
93 D/F control equipment
94 Control linkage
95 Oxygen bottles
96 Crew emergency escape roof hatch
97 Pilot's seat (offset port)
98 Autopilot
99 Bomb selector panel
100 Bomb switch panel
101 Bomb-aimer's convertible sliding/folding seat (horizontal)
102 Control column
103 Instrument panel

109 Nose glazing
110 Optically-flat lower panels
111 Side windows
112 Zeiss bombsight
113 Bombsight fairing
114 Port mainwheel
115 Ventral flexible 7.9 mm MG 15 machine gun
116 Spinner boss
117 Three-blade VDM
118 Trailing aerial lead in
119 Nacelle front panel
120 Bomb-bay doors
121 Exhaust stubs
122 Starboard engine
123 Engine bearer assembly

133 Mudguard strut
134 Retraction strut
135 Cross-brace
136 Mainwheel door
137 Mainwheel pivot
138 Louvres
139 Leading-edge structure
140 Front spar
141 Starboard engine oil tank
142 Starboard mainwheel well
143 Oil filler cap
144 Slotted flap profile
145 Flap track rod

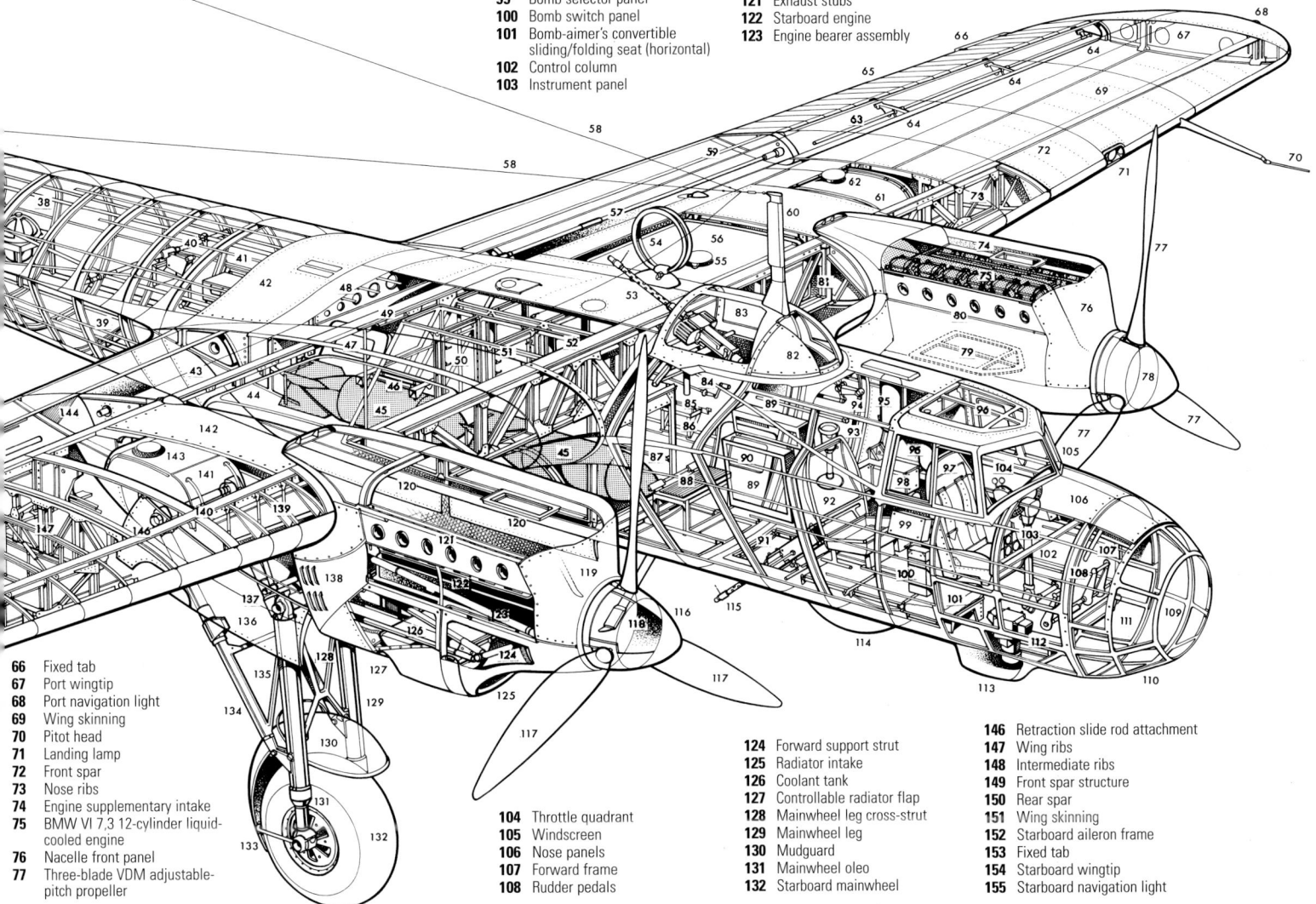

66 Fixed tab
67 Port wingtip
68 Port navigation light
69 Wing skinning
70 Pitot head
71 Landing lamp
72 Front spar
73 Nose ribs
74 Engine supplementary intake
75 BMW VI 7,3 12-cylinder liquid-cooled engine
76 Nacelle front panel
77 Three-blade VDM adjustable-pitch propeller

104 Throttle quadrant
105 Windscreen
106 Nose panels
107 Forward frame
108 Rudder pedals

124 Forward support strut
125 Radiator intake
126 Coolant tank
127 Controllable radiator flap
128 Mainwheel leg cross-strut
129 Mainwheel leg
130 Mudguard
131 Mainwheel oleo
132 Starboard mainwheel

146 Retraction slide rod attachment
147 Wing ribs
148 Intermediate ribs
149 Front spar structure
150 Rear spar
151 Wing skinning
152 Starboard aileron frame
153 Fixed tab
154 Starboard wingtip
155 Starboard navigation light

Do 17E-1 bombers fly over an airfield with their main undercarriage units lowered and slotted inboard flaps slightly depressed. The main units retracted to the rear into nacelle bays that were then covered by two doors.

Above: Do 17E-1s from III/KG 255 form a neat line-up. The code for the aircraft translated as '5' for Luftkreis 5, '4' for the fourth geschadwer in that region, 'J' for individual aircraft, '3' for the III Gruppe and '8' for 8. Staffel.

Do 17E-1 bombers of III/KG 255 are seen with temporary special codes applied. The unit transitioned to the Heinkel He 111H in August 1939. KG 51 spent most of the summer training and recruiting personnel from flight schools.

one Staffel from Aufkl.Gr.(F)/122 was despatched to Spain with 15 Do 17F-1s, joining the Condor Legion as 1.A/88. The Do 17F-1s supplanted He 70F-2s that were transferred to the Spanish Nationalist forces, and soon proved capable of evading Republican fighters, apparently vindicating the theories earlier formulated by the OKL. The virtual immunity to interception enjoyed by the Do 17F-1 in Spanish skies so impressed the Luftwaffe that high priority was allocated to the re-equipment of all long-range reconnaissance units with this type, the He 70F quickly being retired from first-line service. During the course of 1937-38, the Do 17F-1s of Aufkl.Gr. (F)/122 based at Prenzlau were progressively supplemented in Luftwaffe service as Staffeln of the other five existing Aufklärungsgruppen (Aufkl.Gr.(F)/121 at Neuhausen, /123 at Grossenhain, /124 at Kassel, /125 at Würzburg, and /127 at Goslar) converted to the Dornier.

Bombers to Spain

In the meantime, the Do 17F-1 reconnaissance aircraft of 1.A/88 had been joined in Spain by Do 17E-1 bombers, 20 aircraft of this type supplementing the He 111B in 1. and 2.K/88. Like the Do 17F-1s, the bombers initially

Part of a flight of Do 17 warplanes is framed in the hatch of a dorsal air-to-air gunner, complete with the sight and mounting for his 7.9-mm (0.31-in) MG 15 trainable machine-gun.

enjoyed virtual immunity from interception, but this was lost as increasing numbers of modern Soviet fighters made their appearance in Republican service, and in August 1938, the surviving Do 17E and Do 17F aircraft, together with a number of **Do 17P** machines (10 of which had earlier been delivered to 1.A/88 to supplement the unit's Do 17F-1s), were passed to the Spanish Nationalists, Grupo 8-G-27 being formed on them at La Cenia with both Spanish and German personnel. In Spanish service the Do 17 was known as the **Bacalao**, and when the Civil War ended, 8-G-27 was based at Logroño with 13 Do 17Es and Do 17Ps, these remaining in Spanish service for a number of years.

Dornier built 328 Do 17Es and 77 Do 17Fs at its Oberpfaffenhofen site. Three Do 17E-1s were converted for special reconnaissance missions as the **Do 17E-2** and **Do 17E-3**. The two E-2s were further modified to have BMW 132F radial engines, becoming the **Do 17J-1** and **Do 17J-2** in the process. They served on various trials programmes. Another 'special' variant was the **Do 17F-2**, of which one was built for camera trials with Carl Zeiss-Jena, appropriately registered D-ACZJ.

Even when operating in formation, the Do 17 proved somewhat vulnerable through its lack of armour protection and indifferent defensive firepower, which was based on rifle-calibre machine-guns that lacked range and penetrative power.

Dornier Do 17E-1 specification
(figures in square brackets relate to the Do 17F-1)
Type: three-seat medium bomber [long-range reconnaissance aircraft]
Powerplant: two BMW V1 7,3 liquid-cooled V-12 engines each rated at 559 kW (750 hp) for take-off
Performance: maximum speed 355 km/h (220 mph) [357 km/h (222 mph)] at sea level, 193 km/h (390 km/h) [315 km/h (196 mph)] at 4000 m (13,125 ft); maximum cruising speed both 315 km/h (196 mph) at sea level, 262 km/h (163 mph) [265 km/h (165 mph)] at 4000 m; service ceiling 5100 m (16,730 ft) [6000 m (19,685 ft)]; tactical radius 500 km (311 miles) [680 km (422 miles)] with maximum military load; maximum range 1500 km (932 miles) [2050 km (1,274 miles)] without military load
Weights: empty 4500 kg (9,921 lb); maximum take-off 7040 kg (15,520 lb) [7000 kg (15,430 lb)]
Dimensions: wingspan 18.00 m (59 ft 0⅔ in); length 16.25 m (53 ft 3¾ in); height 4.32 m (14 ft 2 in); wing area 55.00 m² (592.01 sq ft)
Armament: one 7.9-mm (0.31-in) MG 15 machine-gun firing downward through ventral hatch, and one MG 15 machine-gun on pillar-type mounting at rear of flight deck to fire to the rear; (offensive) 750 kg (1,653 lb) of bombs carried internally

Do 17M and Do 17P series

Before the first production Do 17s had left the assembly line, the Dornier team had turned its attention to developing the basic design, and the Do 17 V8, which was also known as the **Do 17M V1** (D-ABVD) and which gave such a startling demonstration of its performance capabilities in July 1937 at Zürich, was completed with Daimler-Benz DB 600A liquid-cooled V-12 engines each rated at 746 kW (1,000 hp) for take-off and driving three-blade VDM controllable-pitch propellers. The Do 17M V1 attained a maximum level speed of 425 km/h (264 mph). It was proposed that the DB 600A-powered Do 17M be placed in production for the Luftwaffe, but priority in the supply of the Daimler-Benz engine was allocated to fighter production and, in consequence, Dornier was forced to investigate the possibility of installing alternative engines. The choice eventually fell on the Bramo 323A-1 Fafnir, an air-cooled nine-cylinder radial engine with two-speed supercharger offering 671 kW (900 hp) for take-off and 746 kW (1,000 hp) at 3100 m (10,170 ft). The conversion from liquid-cooled to air-cooled

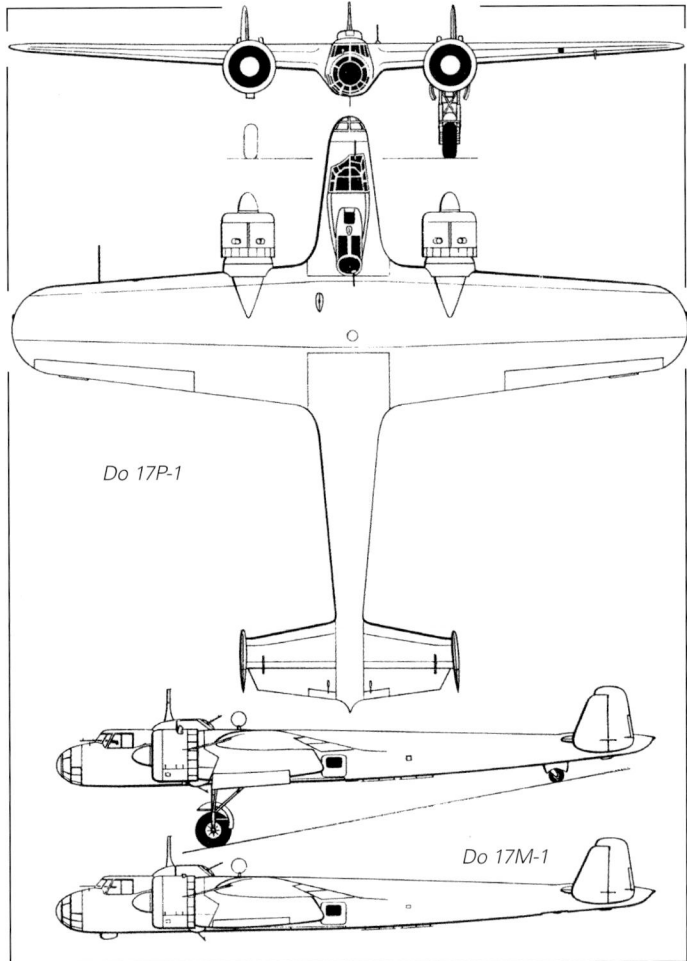

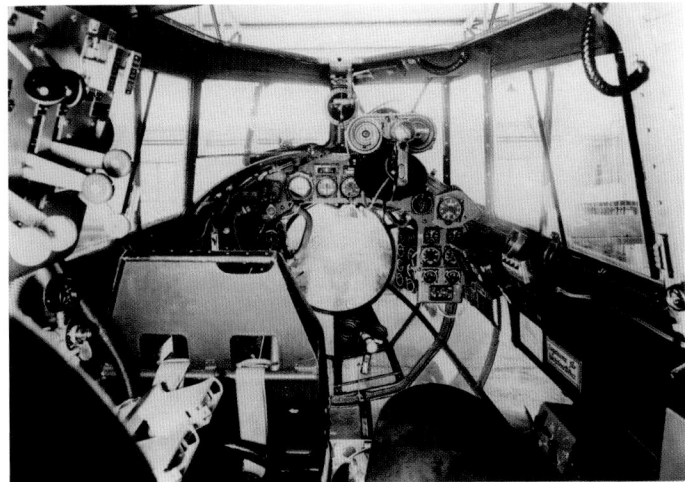

Do 17P-1

Do 17M-1

Above: The Do 17P-1 was the reconnaissance counterpart of the Do 17M-1 bomber, and its extensive area of framed glazing provided the bombardier/camera operator with good forward and downward fields of vision. The engines are BMW 132N radial units.

Above: The cockpit of the Do 17 was always cramped, especially in the first production variants. On the credit side the crew had good fields of vision and ease of communication, but on the debit side was horribly vulnerable to a single concerted firing pass.

The Do 17 series reflected the technical and tactical thinking of the 1930s in its modest bomb load and the three-man crew grouped tightly in the nose. The limitations of the concept had started to become evident as early as the Spanish Civil War.

The BMW air-cooled radial engines which powered the Do 17M bomber and Do 17P reconnaissance type were each enclosed in a full circular-section cowling and drove a three-blade VDM propeller of the controllable-pitch type.

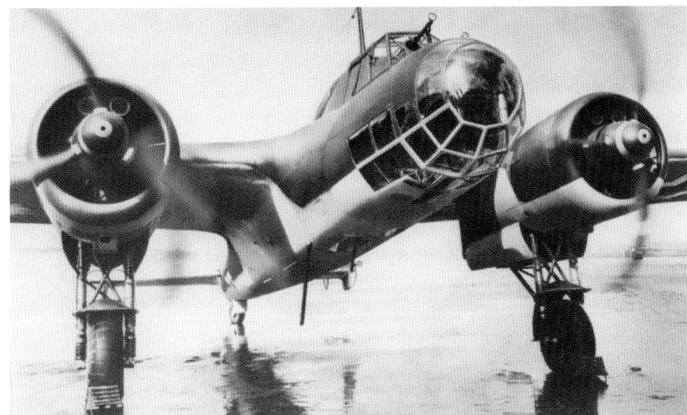

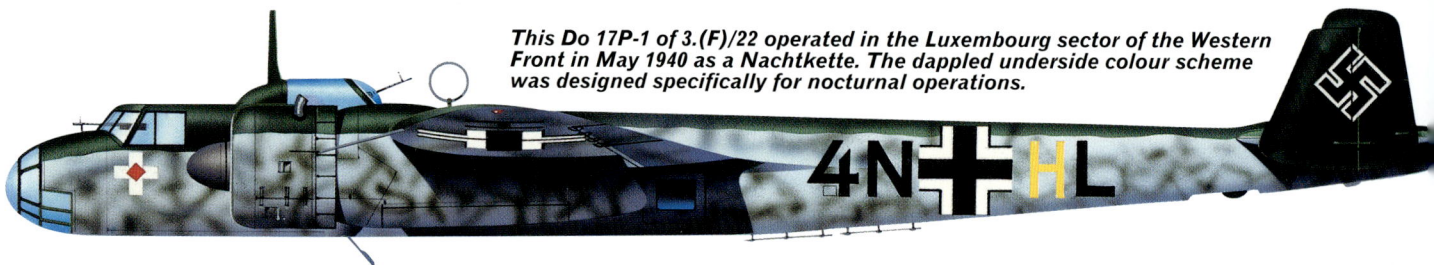

This Do 17P-1 of 3.(F)/22 operated in the Luxembourg sector of the Western Front in May 1940 as a Nachtkette. The dappled underside colour scheme was designed specifically for nocturnal operations.

engine presented no problem, the Do 17 taking both power-plant types with equal facility, and thus, late in 1937, the assembly lines began to turn over from the Do 17E and F to the **Do 17M** and **Do 17P**.

The Do 17M and Do 17P were parallel developments,

Above: The raised cupola behing the cockpit of the Do 17 accommodated a single 7.9-mm (0.31-in) MG 15 trainable machine-gun on a pillar mounting for defence against stern attacks in the upper hemisphere.

being respectively bomber and long-range reconnaissance aircraft, but as it was not possible to meet the range demands of the Luftwaffe for the latter with the Bramo 323A-1 Fafnir, Dornier elected to power the Do 17P with another nine-cylinder radial air-cooled engine, the less powerful but smaller, lighter and rather more economical BMW 132N, which, rated at 645 kW (865 hp) for take-off and 496 kW (665 hp) at 4500 m (14,765 ft), provided the aircraft with the depth of penetration specified.

Production of the new models was preceded by two Bramo-powered prototypes, the **Do 17M V2** and **Do 17M V3** (alias **Do 17 V13** and **Do 17 V14**), and a BMW 132N-powered prototype, the **Do 17P V1** (alias **Do 17 V15**), and apart from some local structural strengthening to accommodate the increased power and higher loaded weights, the airframes of these variants remained virtually unchanged from those of their predecessors. A change was made in defensive armament which, initially at least, comprised a trio of MG 15s, a forward-firing weapon being added which, normally clamped in position and fired by the pilot with the aid of a ring-and-bead sight, could also be operated as a free gun by the navigator/bombardier, although its traverse was strictly limited. Do 17Ms and Do 17Ps surviving in Luftwaffe service after the first few months of World War II had a pair of additional MG 15s installed by forward maintenance units. The bomb bay of the Do 17M was extended aft, enabling maximum bomb load to be raised to 1000 kg (2,205 lb), and towards the end of the production run, a housing was introduced ahead of the upper gun position for an inflatable dinghy, aircraft so fitted being designated **Do 17M-1/U1**. The provision of sand filters and desert survival equipment by forward maintenance units resulted in the **Do 17M-1/Trop** and **Do 17P-1/Trop**. Apart from their powerplants,

Left: The prototypes and initial Do 17E and Do 17F production models were powered by BMW VI liquid-cooled V-12 engines, but the Do 17M and Do 17P models switched to an air-cooled radial engine in the form of the BMW 323 and 132, respectively.

This is a late-production example of the Do 17P-1 as it undergoes pre-acceptance testing in the winter of 1939-40. Little more than obsolescent even as it entered service, the Do 17P had been largely phased out of first-line service by the middle of 1941.

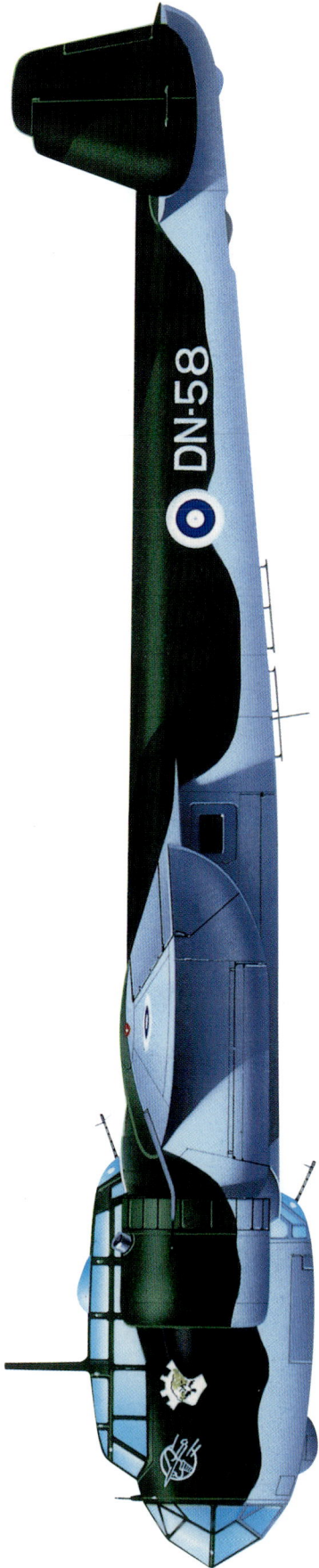

This Do 17Z-3 flew with the Finnish air force's *PLeLv 43* (formerly *PLeLv 44*) at Mami in July 1948. Early in 1942, Hermann Göring presented 15 ex-Luftwaffe Do 17Zs to the Finnish air force, in whose service they supplanted Bristol Blenheims with PLeLv 46 and enjoyed considerable success against Soviet forces. This example survived the war and was flown for several years after by PLeLv 43 on reconnaissance duties.

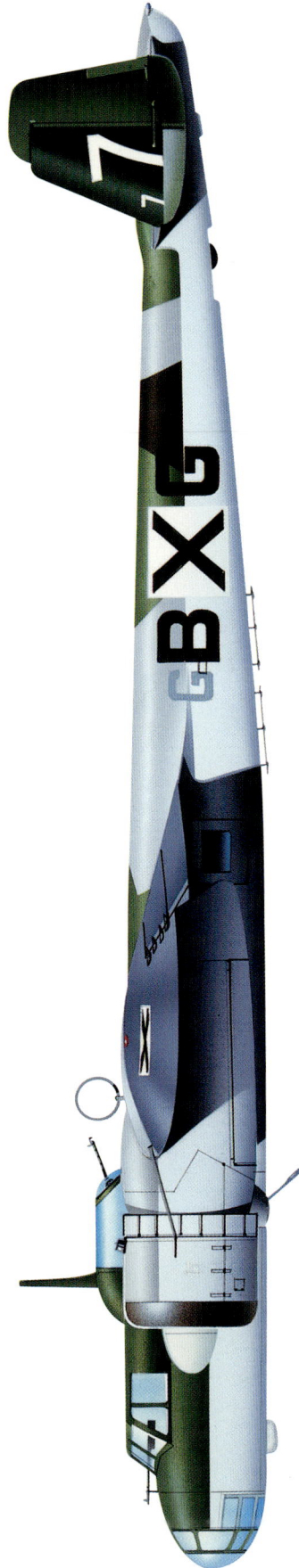

This is a Do 17M-1 bomber of the Bulgarian air force based at Molai in occupied Greece in about May 1941. The first batch of Do 17M bombers for Bulgaria was withdrawn from Luftwaffe stocks and delivered in 1940, another batch following in August 1943. After Bulgaria had changed sides, the surviving aircraft were operated from September 1944 in support of the Soviet forces advancing through the Balkans toward Hungary and Austria.

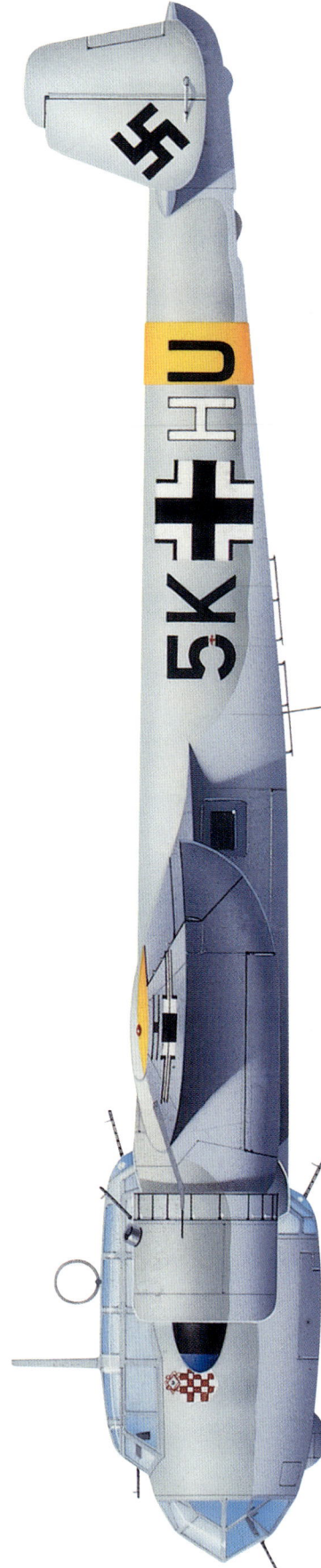

The Croat-manned 10. Staffel of Kampfgeschwader 3 operated this Do 17Z-2 on the central sector of the Eastern Front in December 1941: the Croat Ustachi emblem is carried below the flight deck. The whole of KG 3 was committed to Operation Barbarossa in June 1941, under Fliegerkorps II.

Dornier Do 17

Above: This 1938 production BMW Bramo-powered Do 17M-1 sets a scene which reflects the primitive conditions in which many German warplanes had to operate, especially in winter.

The pilot of a Do 17M medium bomber takes a look out of his open port cockpit window before starting the BMW Bramo 323 engines. Note the simple ring and bead sight that was provided to aim forward-firing armament, if fitted.

the Do 17M and Do 17P differed solely in that the latter had bomb sight and release gear removed and provision made in the bomb bay for a pair of Rb 50/30 or 75/30 reconnaissance cameras.

In 1938, the Do 17M and Do 17P began to supplant the Do 17E and Do 17F in the Kampfgruppen and Aufklärungsgruppen, respectively, and, as previously mentioned, 10 early production Do 17P-1 reconnaissance aircraft were sent to 1.A/88 with the Condor Legion in Spain, those surviving the Civil War subsequently serving with the Ejercito del Aire. According to OKL strength returns for 19

September 1938, the Luftwaffe had 479 Do 17s (E, F, M and P variants) on strength from a total of 580 delivered at that time by Dornier, and production of an improved bomber model, the **Do 17Z**, had already been initiated. Thus, the production life of the Do 17M was relatively short and, in the event, this bomber was to be outlived in first-line Luftwaffe service by its long-range reconnaissance counterpart, the Do 17P. Dornier built 200 Do 17Ms at Oberpfaffenhofen, while 230 Do 17Ps were built by Henschel, Siebel and Hamburger Flugzeugbau.

Dornier Do 17M-1 specification
(figures in square brackets relate to Do 17P-1)
Type: three-seat medium bomber [long-range reconnaissance aeroplane)
Powerplant: two BMW-Bramo 323/4-1 Fafnir air-cooled nine-cylinder radial engines each rated at 671 kW (900 hp) for take-off and 746 kW (1,000 hp) at 3100 m (10,170 ft) [two BMW 132N air-cooled nine-cylinder radial engines each rated at 645 kW (865 hp) for take-off and 496 kW (665 hp) at 4500 m (14,765 ft)]
Performance: maximum speed 345 km/h (214 mph) [350 km/h (217 mph)] at sea level, 410 km/h (255 mph) [395 km/h (246 mph)] at 4000 m (13,125 ft); maximum cruising speed 350 km/h (218 mph) at 3250 m (10,665 ft) [332 km/h (206 mph)] at 2800 m (9,185 ft)]; service ceiling 7000 m (22,965 ft) [6200 m (20,340 ft)]; tactical radius 500 km (311 miles) [730 km (454 miles)] with maximum military load; maximum range 1360 km (845 miles) [2200 km (1,367 miles)] without military load
Weight: loaded 8000 kg (17,637 lb) [7660 kg (16,887 lb)]
Dimensions: wingspan 18.00 m (59 ft 0⅔ in); length 16.10 m (52 ft 9¾ in); height 4.55 m (14 ft 11 in); wing area 55.00 m² (592.01 sq ft)
Armament: (defensive) three 7.9-mm (0.31-in) MG 15 machine-guns comprising one forward-firing gun in starboard side of windscreen, one gun firing downward through ventral hatch, and one rearward-firing gun on pillar-type mounting at rear of flight deck; (offensive) 1000 kg (2,205 lb) of bombs carried internally

This Do 17M-1 bomber built in 1938, and powered by BMW-Bramo 323 radial engines, appears to be factory-fresh. The gills round the rear of the engine nacelles were opened and closed to provide the right degree of cooling.

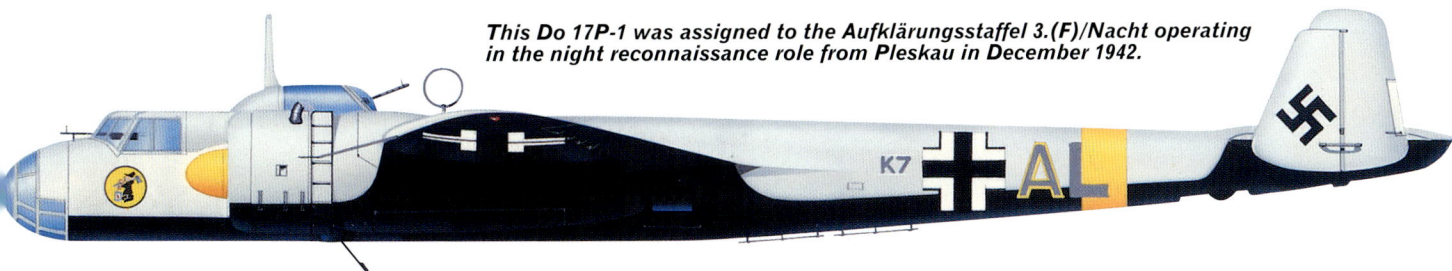

Export and experimental models

Manufactured in parallel with the Do 17M was an export version for Yugoslavia, the **Do 17K**. Yugoslav pilots had flown the third prototype as early as November 1935, while the Yugoslav delegation to the Zürich meeting in the summer of 1937 had been so impressed by the showing of the Do 17M V1 that the Yugoslav government had immediately approached Dornier with a view to acquiring this advanced warplane for the Royal Yugoslav air force. Official approval was immediately given for the negotiations, and within two months a contract had been placed by Yugoslavia for 20 aircraft, a licence for manufacture also being purchased at the same time.

At that time, licensed manufacture of the Gnome-Rhône 14N-1/2 engine had begun at Rakovica, near Belgrade, and the Yugoslav-manufactured engines were supplied to Dornier for installation in the Do 17K, the first example of which was flown to Yugoslavia in October 1937. The export model did not feature the short nose with hemispherical glazed cap characteristic of the Do 17s supplied to the Luftwaffe, retaining the longer, more angular nose of the Do 17M V1, and the 20 aircraft delivered to Yugoslavia consisted of three versions, the **Do 17Kb-1** intended solely for the bombing role, and the **Do 17Ka-2** and **Do 17Ka-3** which, differing in camera arrangements and equipment, were primarily reconnaissance aircraft with secondary bombing and attack capability.

Powered by two Gnome-Rhône 14Na-2 air-cooled 14-cylinder radial engines each rated at 731 kW (980 hp) at 4525 m (14,850 ft), the Do 17K attained maximum speeds of 357 km/h (222 mph) at sea level and 417 km/h (259 mph) at 3450 m (11,320 ft), and maximum range in the reconnaissance role was 2400 km (1,491 miles). The maximum bomb load of the Do 17Kb-1 variant was 1000 kg (2,205 lb), and maximum defensive armament comprised a 20-mm Hispano-Suiza 404 cannon (not in the Do 17Ka-3) and one 7.92-mm (0.31-in) FN-Browning machine-gun in the forward fuselage nose, one free-mounted 7.9-mm machine-gun in the starboard side of the cockpit, and single 7.9-mm machine-guns firing from a ventral trap ahead of the bomb and firing aft from the upper position.

Production of the Do 17K started at the State Aircraft Factory, the Državna Fabrika Aviona, at Kraljevo in 1939, deliveries to the Royal Yugoslav air force starting early in 1940, and when the German forces invaded Yugoslavia on 6 April 1941, a total of 70 Do 17Ks was on strength, equipping the 3rd Bomber Wing whose bases were prime targets for the Luftwaffe from the outset of the campaign. No fewer than 26 of the Do 17Ks were destroyed in the initial assault, but those that survived the Luftwaffe's bombing and strafing made attacks on Sofia and other targets in Bulgaria, and were also used for strafing attacks on German armour and troop concentrations. Relatively few Do 17Ks survived, but on 19 April two escaped to Heliopolis in Egypt with cargoes of gold (they were allocated the RAF serial numbers AX706/707 but were struck off charge a few months after their arrival in Egypt), and those captured by the German forces were repaired and issued to the newly-formed Croatian air force early in 1942. Supplemented by a small number of Do 17E-1s passed to the Croat air arm by the Luftwaffe, the Do 17Ks equipped the Croat Gruppen I and IV based at Agram and Banja Luka, respectively, their activities being confined largely to sorties against partisan groups.

Evolved simultaneously with the Do 17M, the **Do 17L** was a similarly powered (Bramo Fafnir 323A-1) pathfinder version with provision made for a fourth crew member. Two prototypes were completed, the **Do 17 V11** and **Do 17 V12** (alias **Do 17L V1** and **Do 17L V2**), but no production was undertaken. Two further experimental aircraft were the **Do 17R V1** and **Do 17R V2** that were essentially test-beds. Initially flown with BMW VI engines and subsequently re-engined with 708-kW (950-hp) Daimler-Benz DB 600Gs, the Do 17R V1 (D-ABEE) was employed principally as a test-bed for new bomb-aiming devices but, like the Do 17R V2 (D-ATJU) which was powered by two 820-kW (1,100-hp) DB 601A engines, also served as a power plant development aircraft.

Do 17Z series

During the early months of 1939, the Kampfgruppen began to convert to a markedly improved development of the basic Dornier design, the Do 17Z, and this model was entering service when extensive redesignation and reorganisation of the Kampfgeschwader took place, three of the four existing Do 17-equipped Geschwadern being reduced in strength from three to two Gruppen, and the fourth converting to He 111s, although an additional Kampfgeschwader was formed with Do 17s by transferring three Gruppen from existing units. Under this rearrangement II and III/KG 153 became II and III/KG 3, I and III/KG 158 became I and III/KG 76, I and III/KG 252 became I and II/KG 2, and I and III/KG 255 converted to He 111s and became I and III/KG 51. The I/KG 153, II/KG 158 and II/KG 255 Gruppen became

Here the Starrschlepp rigid tow is seen in operation with a Do 17 towing a DFS 230 assault glider. This type of towing arrangement, often undertaken with the Junkers Ju 52/3m transport as the tug, was especially useful in adverse weather conditions, especially at night.

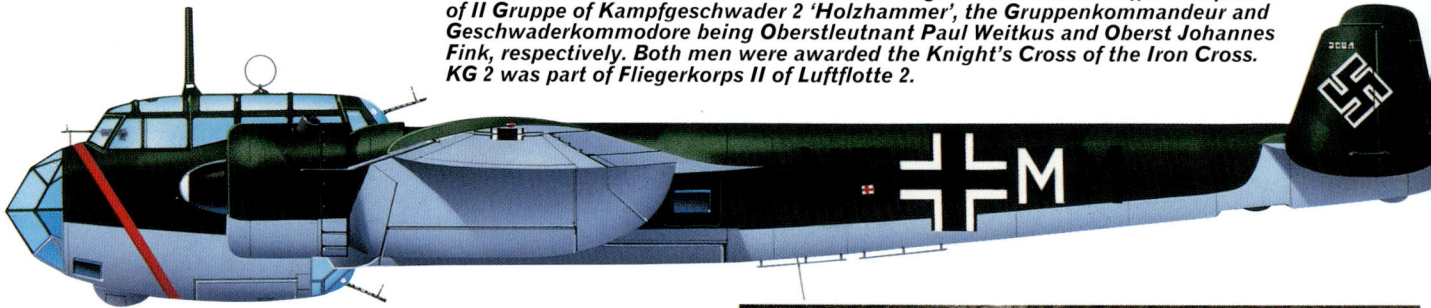

This Do 17Z of 4./KG 2 was based at Arras in August 1940. The 4. Staffel was part of II Gruppe of Kampfgeschwader 2 'Holzhammer', the Gruppenkommandeur and Geschwaderkommodore being Oberstleutnant Paul Weitkus and Oberst Johannes Fink, respectively. Both men were awarded the Knight's Cross of the Iron Cross. KG 2 was part of Fliegerkorps II of Luftflotte 2.

respectively the I, II and III Gruppen of the newly formed KG 77, and the first-line strength of the Luftwaffe thus comprised nine Kampfgruppen operating the Do 17.

During the Spanish Civil War, it had become obvious that better protection would have to be afforded the Do 17's belly. The downward-firing MG 15 machine-gun in the floor hatch had too limited a field of fire to provide anything approaching satisfactory protection, and thus the Dornier team had begun, early in 1938, to design an entirely new forward fuselage that owed everything to the dictates of operational efficiency and nothing to aerodynamic refinement. Crew accommodation provided by the Do 17 had always been somewhat cramped for maximum operational efficiency, and thus the cockpit roof was raised and fully glazed. The nose containing the bombardier's station was also fully glazed with a series of small flat panels, or facets, and the lower part was bulged and extended aft to a point just forward of the wing leading edge, terminating in a position for a rearward- and downward-firing MG 15.

This new forward fuselage was first applied to a high-speed reconnaissance model, the **Do 17S-0** powered by DB 600G engines and providing accommodation for four crew members. The first of three examples of the Do 17S-0 (D-AFFY) was flown early in 1938 and delivered to the Luftwaffe for service evaluation, but no further aircraft of this model were ordered. Evolved simultaneously with the Do 17S-0 was the **Do 17U** pathfinder that accommodated a crew of five, including two radio operators, and was powered by DB 600A engines. Three pre-production **Do 17U-0** aircraft were followed by 12 **Do 17U-1** production aircraft, and they were distributed among the Kampfgruppen designated to receive what was by this time considered to be the definitive Do 17 development, the Do 17Z that followed the Do 17U on the assembly line in the autumn of 1938. Two of the Do 17U pathfinders were delivered to 7 Kompanie of the Luftnachrichten Abteilung (Air Signals Detachment) 100, or Ln.Abt. 100, this being absorbed by Kampfgruppe 100 in November 1939, the two Do 17Us being retained on the Gruppe Stab.

The Do 17Z was essentially similar to the Do 17S and U, but owing to the uncertainty of supplies of the Daimler-Benz V-12 engines, which were in considerable demand for the fighter programme, switched to the Bramo 323A-1 radial engine. The pre-production **Do 17Z-0**, which appeared

Illustrating the broad slab wing of the Do 17 is this early Z-1, the first bomber variant with a redesigned cabin. This version was markedly underpowered and had a reduced bomb load to compensate.

late in 1938, was a four-seat bomber. Armament remained three MG 15 machine-guns (one on a pillar-type mounting in the rear of the flight deck, a second protruding through the starboard panels of the windscreen, and the third in a hemispherical mounting firing below the fuselage), but this was augmented by a fourth MG 15 protruding through the nose cone of the production **Do 17Z-1**, which had also made its appearance before the end of 1938.

The Do 17Z-1 possessed an airframe similar to that of the Do 17M-1, apart from the forward fuselage, and performance remained virtually unchanged despite the increased aerodynamic drag. It retained the good handling qualities and manoeuvrability of its predecessor, but with the additional crew member and increased armament and equipment, the Do 17Z-1 was decidedly underpowered with the full 1000-kg (2,205-lb) bomb load. Accordingly, bomb load was reduced to 500 kg (1,102 lb), but was restored to 1000 kg early in 1939 with the appearance of the **Do 17Z-2** fitted with Bramo 323P Fafnir engines with two-speed superchargers and developing 746 kW (1,000 hp) for take-off and 701 kW (940 hp) at 4000 m (13,125 ft). The restoration of the full bomb load necessitated some reduction in fuel capacity, however, and depth of penetration in maximum loaded condition was reduced to only 330 km (205 miles). The Do 17Z-2 could accommodate an additional crew member for certain missions, and produced in some numbers

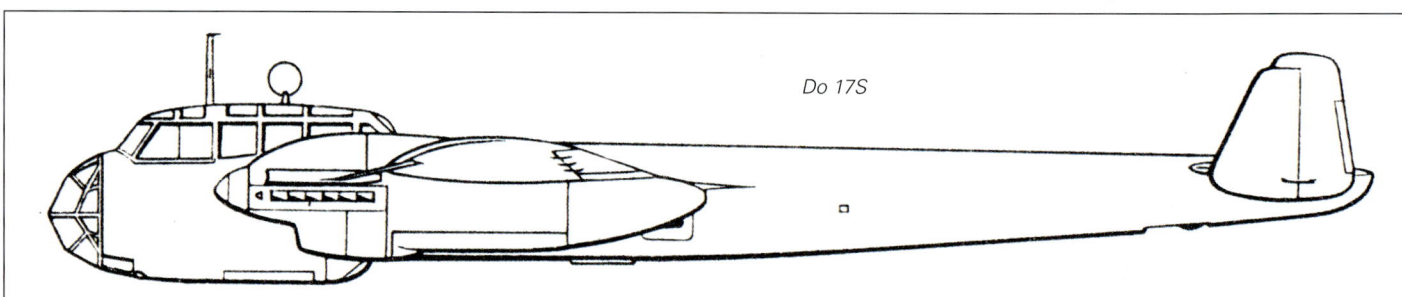

Do 17S

Above: A Luftwaffe dedication ceremony is performed in front of a Do 17Z. This final production variant introduced a larger and altogether more practical crew compartment with heavier defensive armament. However, the crew remained very vulnerable.

Left: This classic World War II image shows two Do 17 bombers over London during the evening air assault of 7 September 1940. The painted rectangles on the wingtips were to indicate the particular Gruppe's station in the bombing formation.

was a reconnaissance-bomber variant, the **Do 17Z-3**, which carried automatic Rb 20/30 cameras in the entry hatch and a 500-kg (1,102-lb) bomb load. The lower nose gun was replaced by the harder-hitting MG 151/15 cannon, and the aircraft was powered by the Bramo 323P-2 engine.

Modifications carried out by Luftwaffe maintenance units resulted in the **Do 17Z-4** dual-control trainer, and the **Do 17Z-5** fitted with inflatable flotation bags and additional life-saving equipment to suit it for long-range over-water reconnaissance missions. A single **Do 17Z-6** prototype was built, this aircraft being intended for the long-range weather reconnaissance mission. A handful of earlier aircraft were modified to this version, with offensive armament capability deleted and extra fuel tankage. For long overwater missions they also carried the larger emergency dinghy and rescue kit developed for the Z-5.

Two further variants that were not built were the **Do 17Z-8** ground attack aircraft and the **Do 17Z-9** with specialist low-level bombing equipment for close support duties.

The Do 17Z was popular with both flying and ground personnel, and was the most reliable of the Luftwaffe's bombers, but it lacked the load-carrying capability of the He 111 and the speed of the Ju 88, and by the end of 1939 production was already tapering off, finally terminating during the early summer of 1940, by which time some 500 Do 17Z-1 and -2 bombers and 22 Do 17Z-3 reconnaissance-bombers had been delivered.

Kauz night-fighters

Until the early summer of 1940 there was a marked reluctance on the part of the Oberkommando der Luftwaffe in general and the Oberbefehlshaber, Hermann Göring, in particular to accept the possibility that the Luftwaffe might find itself in need of a substantial night-fighter force. None of Germany's leaders was thinking defensively. Yet to be told of the Führer's resolve to launch Operation Barbarossa against the USSR by mid-1941, and engaged in a fantastically successful offensive westward with its dazzling prospect of a lightning decision in what they believed to be a single-front war, they viewed the Luftwaffe as a purely offensive force.

Desultory thought had been given to night-fighting, and in September 1939, some of the last remaining operational Ar 68 biplanes had been organised as makeshift night-fighter units for nocturnal patrols along the Franco-German border. A rudimentary system of collaboration with searchlights known as *helle Nachtjagd* had been evolved, and 10./JG 26 had been formed on Bf 109E fighters for experimental nocturnal intercept tasks, but the night defence of the Third Reich depended first and foremost on the Flak regiments; the undeniably efficient force of anti-aircraft artillery and searchlight batteries that had prompted Göring's famous boast that no foreign aircraft would ever penetrate the Ruhr.

On the night of 15-16 May 1940, the complacency of the Ob.d.L. was markedly weakened, though by no means disintegrated, by the opening of RAF Bomber Command's strategic offensive. Ninety-nine Wellingtons, Whitleys and Hampdens from Nos 3, 4 and 5 Groups were despatched to bomb Ruhr industrial and railway targets, a ground haze

This Do 17Z-10 Kauz II of I/NJG 2 was based at Gilze-Rijen in the occupied Netherlands during October 1940 for operations in the night intruder role over the southern part of the UK.

R4+AK

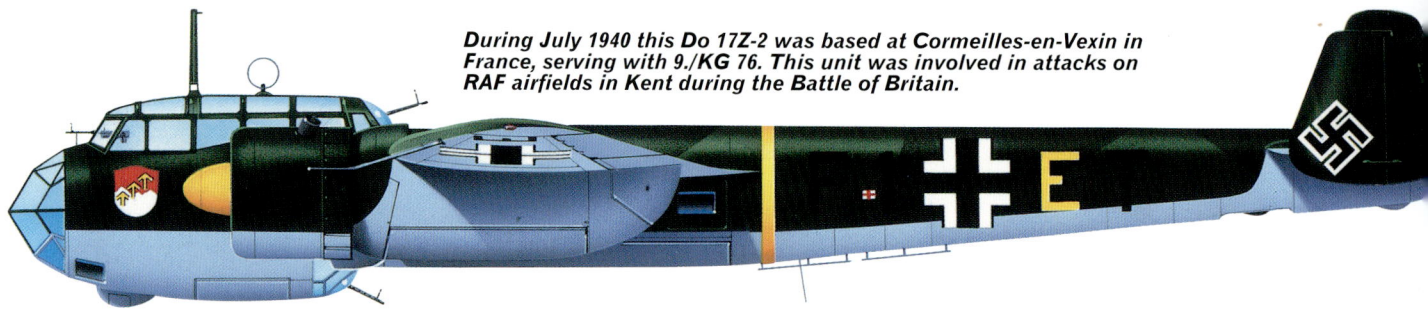

During July 1940 this Do 17Z-2 was based at Cormeilles-en-Vexin in France, serving with 9./KG 76. This unit was involved in attacks on RAF airfields in Kent during the Battle of Britain.

rendering the searchlights and, in consequence, the anti-aircraft batteries impotent. The creation of a night-fighter arm was hastily initiated, two Staffeln of I/ZG 1 on Bf 110Cs being immediately transferred to Düsseldorf for instruction in nocturnal fighting tactics to become, on 20 July 1940, I/NJG 1 and moving to Venlo in the occupied Netherlands.

The night-fighter division that Göring had instructed Oberst Josef Kammhuber to create was not considered solely as a defensive force, however, as such was believed quite unrealistic with France out of the war, and the first phase of what was to become the Battle of Britain about to be launched as a prelude to invasion. Thus, II/NJG 1 was envisaged from

Above: The Do 17Z's ventral hatch provided the crew with its means of access to and egress from the nose compartment, and in the closed position gave the ventral gunner access to his rearward-firing 7.9-mm (0.31-in) MG 15 trainable machine-gun.

the outset as a Fernnachtjagd-Gruppe, a long-range unit for nocturnal intruder missions over Bomber Command's East Anglian bases, and the Dornier-Werke was instructed to investigate the adaptation of the Do 17Z-3 reconnaissance-bomber as a long-range night-fighter and intruder for interim use, this aircraft possessing the necessary endurance to loiter in the vicinity of the RAF's bomber bases and pounce on returning aircraft during their final approach when they would have little reserve speed to evade attack.

The initial conversion, designated **Do 17Z-7** and dubbed **Kauz** (screech owl), was essentially a Do 17Z-3 with the nose cone of the Ju 88C-2, complete with circular 11-mm (0.43-in) armour bulkhead and fixed forward-firing armament of three 7.9-mm (0.31-in) MG 17 machine-guns and one 20-mm MG FF (Oerlikon) cannon, replacing the standard glazed nose. The crew was reduced to the pilot, radio operator and engineer. The radio operator was responsible for firing the upper and lower aft-firing MG 15 machine-guns, and it was the engineer's responsibility to reload the drum-fed MG FF cannon, the breech of which protruded into the crew compartment. The aft bomb bay was retained, this accommodating 10 50-kg (110-lb) SD 50 or two 250-kg (551-lb) SD 250 bombs, the forward bay housing a 895 litre (197-Imp gal) fuel tank.

Three Do 17Z-7 prototypes were modified from earlier variants, powered by Bramo 323P-1 engines. Although the fuselage cross-section of the Ju 88C-2 was almost identical to that of the Do 17Z-3, Dornier did not consider this marriage of convenience to be entirely satisfactory, and an entirely new nose cone was designed to be applied to the **Do 17Z-10 Kauz II**. The last ten (or nine, according to some sources) Do 17Z-3s on the assembly line were completed in this form.

Fitted with BMW-Bramo 323P Fafnir engines each rated at 746 kW (1,000 hp) for take-off, the Do 17Z-2 appeared in 1939 and was able to carry a 1000-kg (2,205-lb) bomb load. This example was one of the last in front-line service, fighting on the Eastern Front in 1942 with 15.(Kroat)/KG 53.

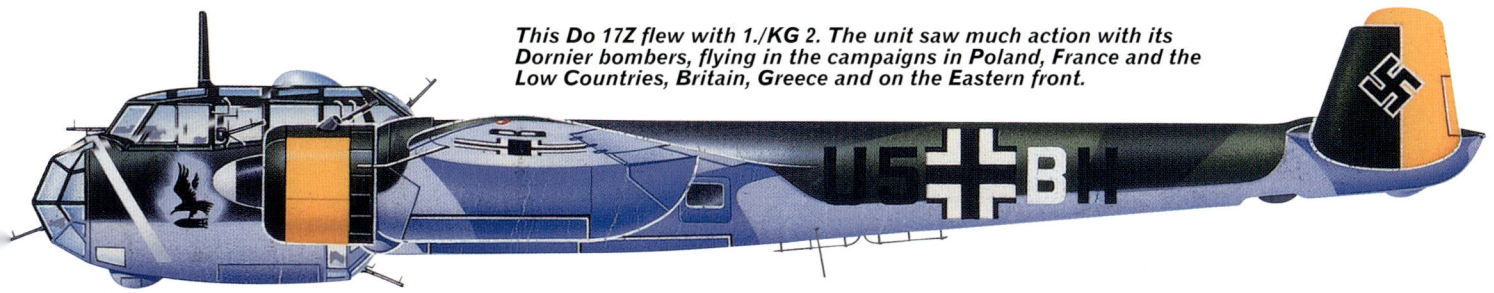

This Do 17Z flew with 1./KG 2. The unit saw much action with its Dornier bombers, flying in the campaigns in Poland, France and the Low Countries, Britain, Greece and on the Eastern front.

Aerodynamically, the new nose cone was markedly improved, and housed four MG 17 machine-guns in its upper section with a pair of MG FF cannon below. The cannon shell drums were still replaced by the engineer, but the machine-gun ammunition boxes slotted into position like the magazine of an automatic pistol. The extreme tip of the nose cone was occupied by the infra-red sensor of the so-called Spanner-Anlage, which reacted to the hot exhaust gases emitted by any aircraft flying immediately ahead of the fighter, the presence of the aircraft being registered on a small screen known as the Q-Rohr (Q-tube) mounted aft of the starboard front window. The device could not differentiate between friend and foe, and the pilot had the responsibility of deciding if the aircraft was a legitimate target, subsequently relying on his Revi C 12/D sight. One Kauz II aircraft was used to test the FuG 202 Lichtenstein B/C airborne intercept radar system.

Kauz operational service

II/NJG 1, which had been formed as the Fernnachtjagd-Gruppe, drew its nucleus from the Zerstörerstaffel/KG 30, which had been performing coastal and anti-shipping patrols from Trondheim, Norway, with a mixture of Ju 88As and Bf 110Cs. Issued with the first 20 Ju 88C-2 heavy fighters converted on the assembly line from Ju 88A-1 bombers, II/NJG 1 was redesignated I/NJG 2 in September 1940, and began intruder operations over East Anglia, a new II/NJG 1 being formed on Bf 110D-1/U1 fighters from the three Staffeln of I/ZG 76 in the same month, and based at Deelen in the Netherlands. In the meantime, 3. Staffel of NJG 1 had been formed on the Do 17Z-10 Kauz II as a Fernnachtjagdstaffel, this now being transferred to II/NJG 1 as 4. Staffel, the former Bf 110-equipped 4. Staffel being absorbed by I Gruppe simultaneously as its

This Do 17Z-2 served with the Gruppenstab of KG 2. The Do 17Z series was easily identified by its deeper nose section and lower gondola.

new 3. Staffel. Operating from Deelen as an autonomous unit under the control of the Sonderkommando Schiphol, 4./NJG 1 gained its first 'kill' (also the Gruppe's first victory) on the night of 18-19 October 1940, when the Spanner-Anlage of the Do 17Z-10 flown by Oberleutnant Ludwig Becker picked up a Wellington, which was then despatched into the Zuider Zee.

Two days earlier, on 16 October, Kammhuber had been promoted to Generalmajor and designated General der Nachtjagd, the force at his disposal comprising four understrength Gruppen, one-third of the Staffeln of which were concerned primarily with offensive nocturnal intruder sorties. For these I/NJG 2 operated from Gilze-Rijen and 4./NJG 1 from Deelen, the Ju 88C and Do 17Z-10 pilots evolving a technique of infiltrating the approach circuit of returning RAF bombers, effecting some kills. However, their greatest success was an indirect effect resulting from their mere presence, many bombers being badly damaged in

Ground personnel prepare to refuel a Do 17Z-2 of KG 77 on what is clearly an extemporised airstrip. The fuel is carried in drums in the flatbed part of the truck, and a pump is to be used to transfer the fuel from the drums to the starboard wing tank. Like its counterpart in the port wing, this held 700 litres (154 Imp gal). This Geschwader converted to the Ju 88 in mid-1940.

Dornier Do 17

Above: A loose formation of KG 3 Do 17Z-2 bombers heads towards its target somewhere over the Eastern Front, probably at a time late in 1941 or early in 1942.

Above: The Do 17Z-2's defensive armament comprised six 7.9-mm (0.31-in) MG 15 machine-guns: two fixed or trainable forward-firing, two trainable side-firing and two trainable rearward-firing.

By the time the Do 17 appeared over Britain the type's speed was no longer sufficient for it to survive in the face of fighter opposition, and its weak defensive armament was no deterrent.

Above: Groundcrew consider the task ahead of them in bringing this Do 17Z-2 back into fully serviceable condition. There were fixed tabs on the ailerons, and trimmable tabs on the tail surfaces.

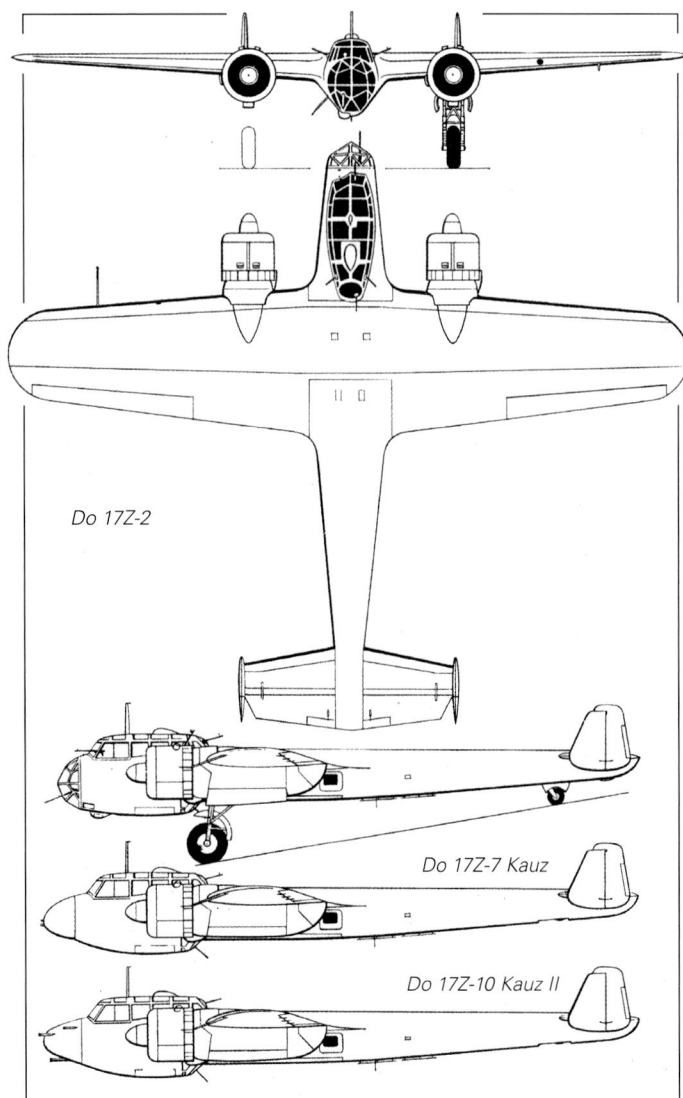

Do 17Z-2

Do 17Z-7 Kauz

Do 17Z-10 Kauz II

heavy landings stemming from their pilots' anxiety to get down, no matter how poor their approach. Less success was enjoyed in the defensive role, however, as RAF bombers soon learned to avoid the searchlight batteries necessary for the *helle Nachtjagd* system of interception.

In addition to its operational activities, 4./NJG 1 was also occupied with the development of new night-fighting techniques. Late in December 1940, by which time the Staffel was in process of exchanging its Do 17Z-10s for Do 215B-5s and had been transferred from Deelen to Leeuwarden, a team arrived from the Erprobungsstelle Rechlin with two Würzburg-A radar sets. They were to test an improvised fighter control unit, one set plotting the fighter and the other its target, the former being vectored towards the latter by the ground controller. This system, which had already been dubbed Himmelbett (four-poster bed) in allusion to the four components of the system (i.e. the Freya early warning set, the two Würzburg sets, and the Seeburg plotting table), completed successful operational trials at Leeuwarden with the co-operation of 4./NJG 1, and was subsequently adopted on a large scale, a chain of Himmelbett control stations being established.

With the delivery of Do 215B-5s, the surviving Do 17Z-10 Kauz II fighters of 4./NJG 1 were passed to I/NJG 2, which continued to operate them in concert with Ju 88Cs on intruder missions over RAF bomber bases until 12 October 1941, when Leutnant Hans Hahn, a popular night-fighter 'ace', failed to return from such a mission. All such nocturnal intruder operations were subsequently cancelled by the direct order of the Führer. Two months later, I/NJG 2 was transferred to Catania, Sicily, having been equipped entirely with the Ju 88C by this time, relinquishing the few remaining Do 17Z-10s to 4./NJG 2, a II/NJG 2 having been formed on 1 November 1941.

During the early months of 1942, the Do 17Z-10 Kauz II finally disappeared from the Nachtjagd organisation. In view of the small number of aircraft of this type delivered and the hazardous type of operations on which it was engaged, its service life had been surprisingly long. It was popular with

Stab III Gruppe, KG 3 flew this Do 17Z-2 from Heiligenbeil in East Prussia during September 1939. Such aircraft were heavily committed to the assault on Poland alongside Junkers Ju 87 dive-bombers.

its crews, and its performance, if inadequate for chasing RAF bombers, was sufficient for night intrusion when it could lay in wait for its quarry, and its armament was effective. Some aircraft of this type were fitted with a supplementary MG 15 machine-gun in the roof aft of the pilot. This could be operated as a free weapon or fixed to fire upward at an oblique forward angle, a scheme conceived by Oberleutnant Schönert of I/NJG 2, and the forerunner of the later 'schräge Musik' (oblique or jazz music) installation, although there is no record of this weapon actually being used in combat by the Kauz II.

Dornier Do 17Z-2 specification

Type: four-seat medium bomber
Powerplant: two BMW-Bramo 323P Fafnir air-cooled nine-cylinder radial engines each rated at 746 kW (1,000 hp) for take-off and 701 kW (940 hp) at 4000 m (13,125 ft).
Performance: (at maximum loaded weight) maximum speed, 300 km/h (186 mph) at sea level, 360 km/h (224 mph) at 4000 m (13,125 ft) or (at 8040 kg/17,730 lb) 345 km/h (214 mph) at sea level, 410 km/h (255 mph) at 4000 m; cruising speed (at maximum loaded weight) 270 km/h (168 mph) at sea level, 300 km/h (186 mph) at 4000 m; service ceiling 7000 m (22,965 ft) at 8540 kg (18,827 lb), 8200 m (26,900 ft) at 8040 kg (17,725 lb); tactical radius with standard fuel (two 775-litre/170.5-Imp gal wing tanks) and 1000-kg bomb load 330 km (205 miles); maximum range with auxiliary fuselage tank (895 litres [197 Imp gal]) and 500-kg bomb load 1160 km (720 miles)
Weights: empty 5210 kg (11,484 lb); empty equipped 5888-5963 kg (12,958-13,145 lb); maximum loaded 8587 kg (18,931 lb); maximum overload 8837 kg (19,481 lb)
Dimensions: wingspan 18.00 m (59 ft 0⅓ in); length 15.80 m (51 ft 9⅔ in); height 4.56 m (14 ft 11½ in); wing area 55.00 m² (592.01 sq ft)
Armament: (defensive) two 7.9-mm. (0.31-in) MG 15 fixed or trainable machine-guns, two MG 15 machine-guns firing from side windows, and two MG 15 machine-guns firing aft, one above and one below the fuselage; (offensive) up to 1000 kg (2,205 lb0 of bombs carried internally, and typically comprising 20 50-kg (110-lb) SD 50 or four 250-kg (551-lb) SD 250 bombs

Operational career

On 2 September 1939, the nine Kampfgruppen of KG 2, 3, 76 and 77 equipped with Do 17s possessed a first-line strength of 370 aircraft, of which 319 were serviceable. Of these, 212 were Do 17Z-1s and -2s (of which 188 were serviceable), the remainder being Do 17M-1s plus a small number of Do 17F-1s awaiting imminent replacement. There were 23 long-range reconnaissance Staffeln with a total strength of 262 Do 17s (of which 235 were serviceable), all but one Staffel being equipped with the Do 17P-1, the remaining Staffel having Do 17F-1s. In addition, the Stab of each of the nine Ju 87-equipped Stuka-Gruppen had three Do 17M-1s on strength, as did also the Geschwaderstab of the otherwise He 111-equipped KG 51.

The Do 17-equipped Aufklärungsstaffeln were distributed among the four Luftflotten; nine Staffeln [3.(F)110, 2, 3, and 4.(F)/11, 1.(F)/120, and 1, 2, 3, and 4.(F)/121] being attached to Luftflotte 1 in north-east Germany; three Staffeln [1, 2, and 3.(F)/122] being attached to Luftflotte 2 in north-west Germany; six Staffeln [1, 2 and 3.(F)/22 and 1, 2 and 3.(F)/123] being attached to Luftflotte 3 in south Germany, and three Staffeln [4.(F)/I4, 3.(F)/31 and 1.(F)/124] being attached to Luftflotte A in Austria, Silesia and Czechoslovakia. Two other Do 17 Aufklärungsstaffeln [7 and 8.(F)/LF 2] were on the strength of Luftwaffe Lehr Geschwader 2.

The Do 17's first operational sortie of World War II was undertaken by a Staffel of Do 17Z-2s from III/KG 3, which

Above: In common with the men of all the armed forces involved in World War II, the flight and ground crews of the Luftwaffe, here of a Do 17Z unit, wasted no opportunity to rest in the sun when the pace of operations permitted it. The wing provided pleasant shade.

This Do 17Z medium bomber is seen around the time of the Polish campaign. Even after they had been considered obsolete for active service over hotly contested sectors of the front, these ageing aircraft retained a limited capability for offensive operations over quieter sections, and also performed sterling work as glider-tugs.

Dornier Do 17

Below: Do 17 bombers over a patchwork of agricultural land indicate how difficult it could be at times for fighters to pick up possible targets by visual means alone.

Above: Operating under the aerial umbrella of the Luftwaffe's fighters units, the Do 17Z squadrons proved quite effective during the Polish campaign, and again in the opening assault on Russia.

Below: Luftwaffe crew discuss the forthcoming mission in front of a Do 17Z of III/KG 3. This Gruppe had the distinction of flying the first combat mission of the war when it attacked railway bridges in Poland. It was also the last German-manned bomber unit to operate the 'Flying Pencil', not converting to the Ju 88 until late 1941, when its aircraft were handed over to the Croats.

Above: From his position in the nose glazing the bombardier had a good view over the frontal hemisphere, as evidenced here during a formation raid. The bombardier operated the lower nose gun, while the pilot could fire another from the upper window.

took off from Heiligenbeil in East Prussia at 05.30, 45 minutes after the official outbreak of war, to bomb the approaches to the important railway bridge at Dirschau, a major link across the Polish 'corridor', but for the most part all four Do 17 Kampfgeschwadern (KG 2 and 3 in the north and KG 76 and 77 in the south) concentrating primarily on attacking Polish airfields, ammunition dumps, troop concentrations, and targets of opportunity throughout the Polish campaign.

The Do 17 Kampfgeschwadern did not participate in the Norwegian campaign in April 1940, but all had been transferred to the Western Front to participate in the fighting over France, their efforts culminating on 27 May in attacks by the Do 17Zs of KG 2 and KG 3 on Dunkirk. The Battle of Britain opened with attacks on Channel convoys early in July 1940, and the Kommodore of KG 2, Oberst Fink, was given the title of Kanalkampfführer (Channel battle leader) and entrusted with the task of clearing the Channel with a battle group comprising the Do 17Zs of his own KG 2, plus two Stuka-Gruppen and one Zerstörergeschwader, the first attack being made on a convoy off Dover on 10 July. On Adlertag, 13 August, at 07.00-07.30, the Do 17Zs of the Stab and III/KG 2 bombed Eastchurch, having not received Göring's postponement order and lost five Do 17Zs in the process. Two days later, 88 Do 17Zs representing the entire serviceable strength of KG 3 bombed Eastchurch and Rochester, and on 16 August the Dorniers of I/KG 2 and III/KG 76 attacked West Malling, I and III/KG 75 following this with attacks on Kenley and Biggin Hill on 18 August.

Alternative attack capability

Apart from its good manoeuvrability, the Do 17Z was able to exploit its high structural strength in shallow diving attacks at speeds exceeding 500 km/h (370 mph), and was thus the

This Do 17Z-2 was used by the DFS from 1941 as a testbed for the Lorin series of ramjets designed by Dr Eugen Sänger. The increasingly powerful engines began to place too much strain on the Do 17's airframe, so trials migrated to a Do 217.

Above: The Do 17Z proved effective in the Balkans theatre where, during the conquests of Yugoslavia and Greece in April 1941, the Dornier bombers could operate against only limited fighter defences and achieve major results.

Do 17Z-2 medium bombers of I/Kampfgeschwader 2 head out on a raid. The bomb-carrying eagle below the cockpit was the emblem of this group's 1. Staffel.

most successful of German bombers employed during the Battle of Britain in evading RAF fighters. Despite the fact that it carried no armour protection for its crew members, the Do 17Z proved capable of absorbing a considerable amount of punishment but, whereas it had encountered virtually no fighter opposition over Poland, its incursions over the UK soon revealed the fact that its defensive armament was lamentably weak, and in consequence forward maintenance units added two 7.9-mm (0.31-in) MG 15s that could be fired laterally from the radio operator's position. Soon afterwards they were supplemented by yet another pair of MG 15s to provide a total defensive armament of eight machine-guns. In their operations against the UK, the Do 17Z formations specialised in low-level, terrain-following attacks, making maximum use of the element of surprise, but their numerical importance in the Luftwaffe's first-line operational strength was already dwindling.

II/KG 76 had been formed from the outset on the Ju 88A, and by the end of 1940, I and III Gruppen had converted from the Do 17Z to the Junkers type. Before the start of the Battle of Britain proper, KG 77, which had suffered some losses in July, had been withdrawn from operations to exchange its Do 17Zs for Ju 88As, and KG 3, after participating in concert with KG 2 in some of the first night attacks mounted against London in September 1940, began to exchange its Do 17Zs for Ju 88As, although III/KG 3 retained the Dornier bombers. Thus, when the assault on the USSR began on 22 June 1941, KG 2 was the sole remaining Kampfgeschwader fully equipped with the Do 17Z, and even II and III/KG 2 were on the verge of conversion to the Do 217E.

During the spring of 1941, the Do 17Zs of KG 2 had been transferred south-east to participate in the offensive against Greece and the Balkan countries under Luftflotte 4, and by the end of May were based at Tatoi in Greece for anti-shipping sorties in the eastern Mediterranean. In the following month, the Do 17Zs of I and III/KG 2, together with those of III/KG 3, began operations on the Eastern Front, II/KG 2 remaining in the West to complete conversion to the Do 217E, to which type the other two Gruppen of the Geschwader converted progressively during the remaining months of 1941. Thus, apart from III/KG 3, the Do 17Z disappeared from the Luftwaffe's bomber strength.

End of the line

This last Do 17Z-equipped Gruppe operated on the central sector of the Eastern Front, where it was joined in October 1941 by a Staffel of the Croat air force that had undergone conversion training on the Do 17Z at Greifswald. The Croat contingent began operations from Vitebsk shortly before Christmas, and as III/KG 3 returned to Germany for conversion to the Ju 88, its Do 17Zs were passed to the Croats who, by the beginning of 1942, were operating as

IV/KG 3, although the unit was at hardly more than Staffel strength. After losing six crews on operations, this unit was withdrawn to Croatia, returning to the Eastern Front, still with Do 17Zs, in July 1942, by which time the unit had been redesignated as 15.(kroat.)/KG 53. The Croat Staffel finally left the Eastern Front in November 1942, subsequently being confined to anti-partisan operations in Croatia.

Early in 1942, Göring made a gift of 15 ex-Luftwaffe Do 17Z-2s to the Finnish Air Force, and these, supplanting the Blenheims of PLeLv 46, joined operations in April 1942, subsequently undertaking both day and night sorties with considerable success. By the time that the final Soviet offensive began in June 1944, only five serviceable and four unserviceable Do 17Zs remained on PLeLv 46's strength.

With the final withdrawal of the Do 17 from the Luftwaffe's bombing elements, the Dornier was adapted for the glider-tug role. At the beginning of 1943, the Do 17 was serving as a tug for DFS 230 gliders with I/Luftlandegeschwader 1, which participated in the supply, and later evacuation, of the German 17th Army fighting in the Kuban bridgehead. These operations lasted from February until October 1943, after which came the evacuation of Crimea, and by March 1944 the unit had converted to the He 111/Go 242 combination. The Do 17 continued to soldier on in the glider-tug role until the last days of the war in Europe, however, serving with the Schleppgruppen, one of its last operations being the aerial supply of Budapest early in 1945.

Armourers manhandle SC 50 bombs to a Do 17Z. Although its bombload was limited, the Do 17 achieved significant success during the Blitz on the Low Countries in May 1940.

Dornier Do 18

At the time it was designed in the mid-1930s, the Do 18 was seen as an elegant, almost 'state of the art' flying-boat for civil and military serice. Most of the production boats were delivered to the Luftwaffe, but were already obsolescent as they entered service, for they lacked high performance and possessed only limited armament.

In the winter of 1933-34 the C-Amt, the camouflaged technical department of the Luftfahrtkommissariat, began to consider the long-term requirements of the planned Seefliegerstaffeln. Of the two specifications which resulted, one called for a Fernaufklärungsflugboot (long-range reconnaissance flying-boat) to succeed the Do 16 Militär-Wal that was just entering service with the Reichsmarine, and the other a Hochseefähiger-Fernaufklärungsflugboot (ocean-going reconnaissance flying-boat). As more urgency was attached to the former, a development contract was awarded to the experienced Dornier Metallbauten, and the newly established Hamburger Flugzeugbau was invited to tender for the flying-boat.

During the spring of 1934, Dornier discussed with the Deutsche Lufthansa the airline's possible requirement for a Wal replacement on the recently inaugurated scheduled mail service across the South Atlantic, the aim being to combine both military and civil requirements in one design. DLH evinced interest in Dornier's proposal, which had already proved acceptable to the C-Amt, and in the summer work began on the construction of four **Do 18** prototypes.

Retaining the Wal's layout, with the characteristic Stummeln, as the sponsons providing lateral stability were known, the Do 18 was in aerodynamical terms probably the most advanced waterborne aircraft conceived up to that time.

The registration D-AHIS identifies this boat as the Do 18a first prototype. Also evident are the Junkers type of 'double wing' flaps and ailerons over almost the full span of the wing's trailing edge.

The finely contoured hull was of typical Dornier two-step design, the rear step faired into a vertical knife-edge carrying a water rudder. The hull was divided into seven watertight compartments, any two of which could be filled with water without the boat sinking or losing its stability. The lateral sponsons were also divided into watertight compartments. The two-spar wing was mounted above the hull on a streamlined pylon and braced to the sponsons by pairs of inclined parallel struts. The hull had flush-riveted metal skinning, and the wing was fabric-covered apart from the area of the centre section bathed by the propeller slipstream, where metal was employed. The bow could house either an open gun position

The Do 18 had a classic Dornier configuration, with a narrow, two-step hull, waterline sponsons, and a parasol wing. The latter was carried by a centreline pylon that also incorporated the engine coolant radiators, and braced from the sponsons by pairs of parallel struts.

Do 18D-1 of FFS (See) in
colours. Developed from
ries of long-range light
sport and mail carriers,
Do 18D-1 was employed
econnaissance and attack
sions over the North Sea
off Norway during 1939
early 1940.

A direct descendant of the distinguished Wal family of inter-war military and commercial flying boats, the tandem-engined Do 18 parasol
monoplane first flew in 1935. At the outbreak of war the Do 18D was being replaced by the Do 18G-1 in the maritime reconnaissance role,
and a similar unarmed trainer with dual controls was designated Do 18H. Production ran out in 1940 when many Do 18G-1s were modified
for air-sea rescue work under the designation Do 18N-1. Do 18s were frequently encountered over the North Sea in the early months of
the war and over the English Channel, particularly during the Battle of Britain. Production totalled 170 Do 18s, of which 79 were Do 18Gs.
Shown here is the Do 18c, the third prototype. It was delivered to DLH as a Do 18E.

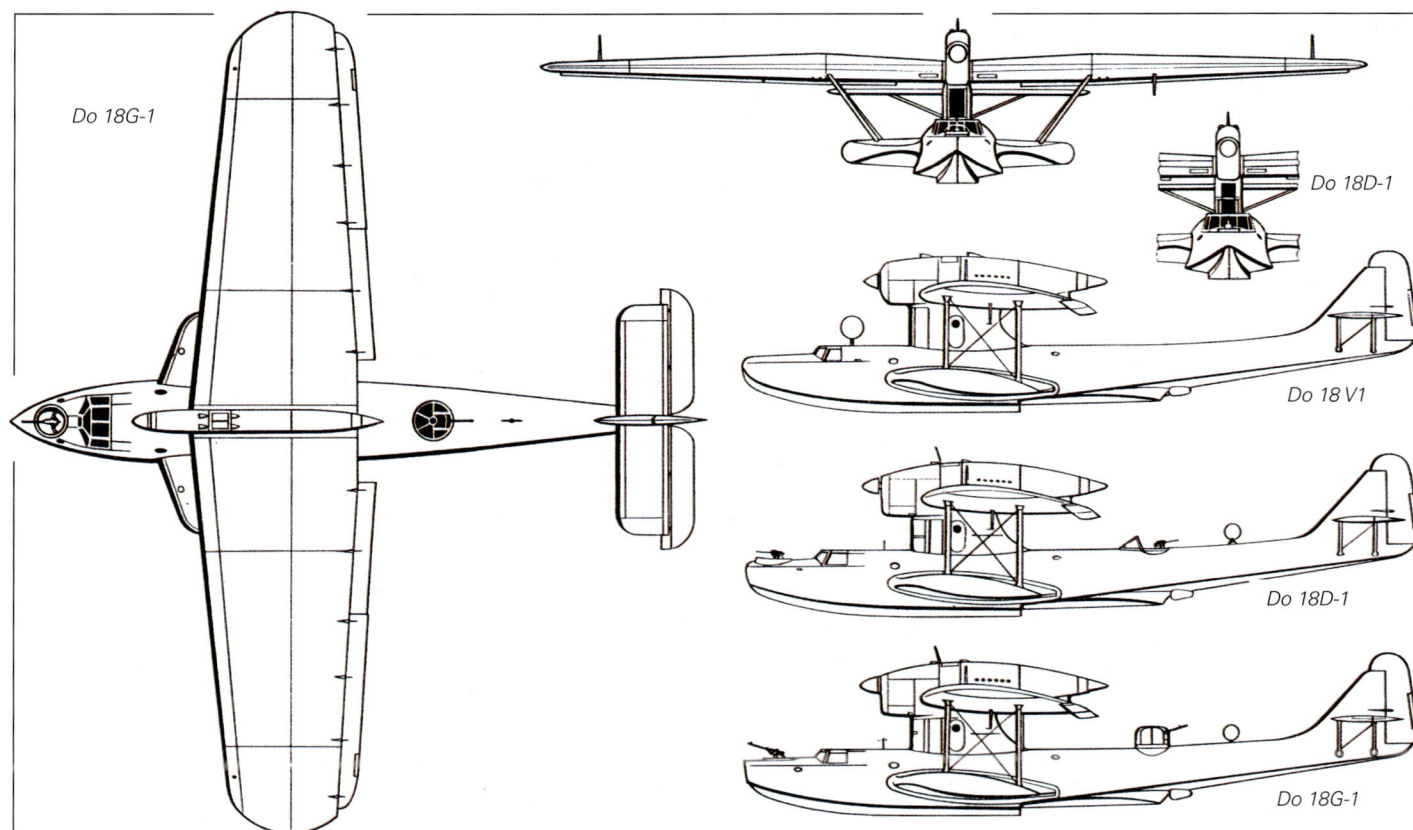

Do 18G-1

Do 18D-1

Do 18 V1

Do 18D-1

Do 18G-1

Dornier Do 18

Above and left: The Do 18 was ordered by Deutsche Lufthansa in 1934 to replace the Wal and was of similar configuration, though greatly refined aerodynamically. The prototype was powered by two Junkers Jumo 5 diesel engines mounted back-to-back, and first flew on 15 March 1935. Four further DLH aircraft, powered by Jumo 6C engines and named Zyklon, Aeolus, Pampero and Zephir, were designated Do 18E. The sole Do 18F, first flown on 11 June 1937, was a specially equipped version with a larger wing. It established a straight-line non-stop distance record for seaplanes during 27-29 March 1938, flying 8392 km (5,214 miles) in 43 hours. With a crew of two pilots and a radio operator, the Do 18s were used for high-speed transatlantic mail flights.

or a compartment for mooring and the stowage of marine gear. The enclosed cockpit provided accommodation for the pilot and co-pilot side by side with the radio operator and navigator immediately aft, and a compartment over the rear step accommodated equipment in the civil version and provided space for a gun position in the military version.

Diesel power

The Junkers Motorenbau had been engaged in the development of diesel heavy oil engines for aircraft installation since the mid-1920s, and by 1933 had evolved the Jumo 205 six-cylinder compression-ignition unit offering appreciably lower fuel consumption than contemporary petrol engines of comparable power output. From the outset of Do 18 development Dornier had planned to use this engine, mounting two in tandem above the wing, the forward engine driving a three-blade metal tractor propeller and the rear engine driving a similar propeller via an extension shaft as a pusher unit. The engine radiators were installed in the pylon. The Jumo 205 engine was not available in time for installation in the first prototype, the **Do 18a** (D-AHIS), which therefore flew for the first time on 15 March 1935 with two of the earlier Jumo 5 diesels with a maximum rating of 403 kW (540 hp).

Completion of the remaining three prototypes was delayed by the inability of Junkers to provide the necessary Jumo 205C engines, priority having been allocated to the Ju 86 bomber programme, and the next prototype to fly was the **Do 18d** fourth machine, which was the prototype Seefernaufklärer and began flight trials late in 1935. By this time tooling for production of the **Do 18D** military version had already begun. The second and third prototypes had originally been designated **Do 18b** and **Do 18c**, but the former was completed to a standard similar to that of the Do 18d and delivered for trials to Fliegerstaffel (F) List as a production Do 18D, and as by this time a uniform system of Versuchs numbers had been adopted for experimental aircraft, the latter became the **Do 18 V3** (Werk Nr 661), this being delivered to DLH as D-ABYM *Aeolus*. DLH had already taken the Do 18a, now redesignated **Do 18 V1** and named *Monsun*, but this was lost in late 1935. A third boat (Werk Nr 677) was converted on the Do 18D assembly line to DLH requirements as the **Do 18 V2** (D-AANE) and named *Zyklon*.

During July 1936 DLH performed endurance tests over the Baltic with its Do 18s, one flight exceeding 31 hours. Another early production Do 18D (Werk Nr 663) had by this time been modified and delivered to DLH as D-ARUN *Zephir*,

The Jumo 5C-engined Do 18a (D-AHIS Monsun) first prototype taxis at speed on Lake Constance. The aircraft was lost in November 1935 during high-speed trials over the Baltic.

This Do 18D served with 2./Kü.Fl.Gr 906, which was based at Hörnum in the Frisian islands during the winter of 1939-40, before participation in the Norwegian campaign. The unit badge (depicting three fish) was worn on the forward engine cowling. Topside markings consisted of standard black crosses, a repeat of the individual aircraft letter (red 'C') and giant white crosses for identification.

and together with D-ABYM *Aeolus*, this boat participated in North Atlantic trials. On 11 September 1936, the *Zephir* flew from Horta in the Azores to New York, the *Aeolus* flying simultaneously from Horta to Hamilton, Bermuda, continuing to New York on the following day. All three boats were modified to similar standards and operated by DLH under the designation **Do 18E**, and the fleet was increased to four by the addition of a 'Weser'-built example (Werk Nr 255) registered D-AROZ and named *Pampero*. After the North Atlantic trials, the Do 18E flying-boats were transferred to the South Atlantic route, and by the time hostilities began, 65 crossings were to have been flown. Two had been lost: *Aeolus* was badly damaged in a landing in heavy water and the subsequent recovery attempt, while *Pampero* was lost on 1 October 1938 between Natal and Bathurst.

In the meantime, Dornier's Friedrichshafen production capacity was expanding, new plants being under construction at Allmansweiler and Löwenthal, and a large associate factory at Wismar, the Dornier-Werke Wismar GmbH, had already delivered its first boat, but the volume of orders for the Do 17 bomber necessitated transfer of Do 18D production to the Einswarden and Nordenham factories of the 'Weser' Flugzeugbau, which had been formed as a branch of the Schiffs- und Machinenbau of Bremen.

Military deliveries

Deliveries of the Do 18D to the Luftwaffe began in the summer of 1936, the first boats being produced by the parent company. Powered by two Jumo 205C diesels each rated at 447 kW (600 hp) for take-off, the **Do 18D-1** carried four crew members, defensive armament comprised one 7.9-mm (0.31-in) MG 15 trainable machine-gun in an open bow position and a similar weapon in an open position in the hull aft of the wing, and two ETC 50 racks could be fitted beneath the starboard wing for a pair of 50-kg (110-hp) bombs. The recipients of the Do 18D were the 2.Staffeln of each of the four Küstenfliegergruppen, these being the long-range reconnaissance components of the three-Staffeln coastal units, 1. and 3.Staffeln being the short-range and general-purpose components, respectively.

As a result of the transfer of production to 'Weser', deliveries of the Do 18D to the Luftwaffe did not really get into their stride until 1938, only two Staffeln being completely equipped with the flying-boat by the beginning of that year. Various modifications were introduced at an early production stage, the single water rudder giving place to twin rudders, and changes being made to the controllable radiator shutters, while equipment updating resulted in the **Do 18D-2** and **Do 18D-3**. One other commercial example had been produced, the **Do 18F** (D-ANHR), which first flew on 11 June 1937. Featuring an extended wing spanning 26.30 m (86 ft 3½ in) and offering a 13.20-m² (142.08-sq ft) increase in area, the sole Do 18F was delivered to DLH, and on 27-29 March 1938 established an international distance

record for seaplanes by flying 8390 km (5,214 miles) after being catapulted from the tender *Westfalen*.

By the summer of 1939, the Do 18D equipped the 2.Staffeln of Küstenfliegergruppen 106, 406, 506, 806 and 906, but was all too obviously obsolescent. A thoroughly reliable boat with pleasant handling characteristics both on the water and in the air, it had otherwise only a respectable endurance to commend it, its defensive armament being totally inadequate and both maximum and cruising speeds leaving much to be desired. Production was scheduled to be phased out during the course of 1939, in which year the Do 18's intended successor, the BV 138, was expected to join the Küstenfliegergruppen, but the protracted development of the Blohm und Voss boat necessitated the extension

Above: Dornier developed the Do 18 ostensibly to replace the successful Wal, and Lufthansa took delivery of its first Do 18s in 1936. Aeolus was the third prototype Do 18, and after North Atlantic trials transferred to the South Atlantic run.

A view along the interior of a Do 18's hull shows the suspended seat for the dorsal gunner and, beyond it, one of the boat's several watertight hatches.

One of DLH's Do 18E boats waits for launch from the type of catapult installed on a few ocean-going tenders to extend the range of commercial flying-boat services. Tender vessels were stationed in Bathurst in the Gambia, and at Fernando de Noronha in Brazil to support the South Atlantic route.

Dornier Do 18D cutaway key

1 Starboard navigation light
2 Junkers-type 'double-wing' aileron
3 Aileron tab
4 Aileron attachment hinges
5 Aileron actuating hinge fairings
6 Inboard flap section
7 Flap attachment hinges
8 Wing aft section impregnated fabric skinning
9 Rear spar
10 Wing forward section metal skinning
11 Starboard aerial mast
12 Front spar
13 Wing main ribs
14 Wing intermediate ribs
15 Leading-edge aerial mast/separator
16 Underwing (starboard) optional bomb load (2 x 220 lb/100 kg)
17 Aerial
18 Starboard sponson/wing struts
19 Starboard sponson squared-off trailing-edge
20 Sponson rear spar
21 Sponson strut/spar attachment points
22 Hull step
23 Catapult launch dolly rear attachment
24 Fuel lines
25 Sponson/fuselage main frame member
26 Sponson fuel cells
27 Fuel filler/access panels
28 Starboard sponson mooring lug
29 Sponson end rib
30 Sponson leading-edge
31 Sponson/fuselage fairing panels
32 Hull sidewall
33 Catapult launch dolly front attachment
34 Squared planning hull bottom
35 Bulkhead
36 Fuselage frame
37 Flight deck step
38 Jump seat support (provision for dual pilot control Do 18H blind-flying trainer)
39 Control link tunnel
40 Forward hull mooring lugs
41 Hull 'Vee' bottom structure
42 Nose compartment/flight deck bulkhead door (starboard side)
43 Gunner's step
44 Nose compartment (sea equipment stowage)
45 'Vee' bottom bow

46 Bow frame member
47 Bow mooring ring
48 Retractable mooring/towing bollard
49 Ammunition magazines
50 Bow turret
51 Gun mounting ring
52 7.92-mm MG 15 bow machine-gun
53 Nose decking
54 Windscreen panels
55 Compass
56 Instrument panel coaming
57 Pilot's seat
58 Flight deck bulkhead door
59 Hinged roof glazing (crew entry)
60 Roof structure/external strakes
61 Bulkhead frame
62 Port sponson
63 Fuel filler/access panels
64 Port sponson mooring lug
65 Port sponson/wing strut
66 Diagonal brace wires
67 Three-blade variable-pitch metal tractor propeller
68 Spinner
69 Propeller hub
70 Wing centre-section front spar
71 Centre/outer-section spar joint/strut attachment point
72 Outer-section front spar structure

73 Main rib stations
74 Port aerial mast
75 Port navigation light
76 Aerial
77 Aileron tab
78 Junkers-type 'double-wing' aileron
79 Aileron attachment hinges
80 Aileron actuating hinge fairings
81 Rear spar
82 Control rods
83 Centre/outer-section rear spar joint/strut attachment point
84 Inboard flap section
85 Flap attachment hinges
86 Handgrip rail

87 Aft engine intake scoops
88 Oil tank
89 Hoist attachment forward lug
90 Wing front spar/nacelle main frame
91 Forward engine bearers
92 Forward engine water header tank
93 Forward engine intake scoops
94 Nacelle aerial mast
95 Port sponson/wing rear strut
96 Exhaust outlet
97 Inner wing exhaust pipe
98 Forward engine nacelle
99 Exhaust manifold

100 Junkers Jumo 205C forward diesel engine
101 Nacelle hinged inspection/servicing side panels
102 Hull/wing support superstructure
103 Leading-edge intake controllable radiator shutters
104 Oil cooler radiators (upper to aft engine, lower to forward engine)
105 Aerial leads-ins
106 Bulkhead door
107 Crew deck porthole
108 Navigator/wireless-operator's station

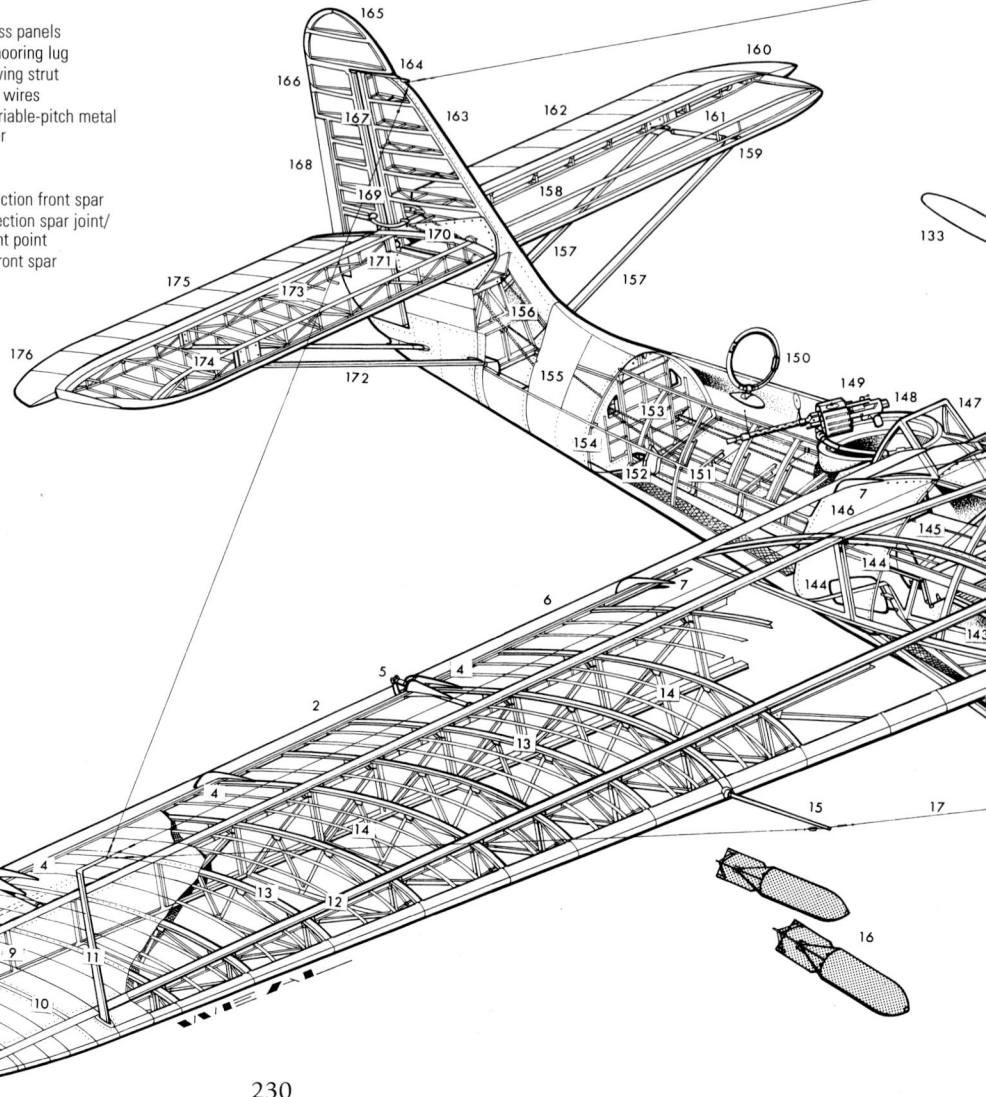

D-ANHR flies in its original form as the Do 18F. This was a special extended-range model with an enlarged wing, and was one of the last Do 18s off the Manzell assembly line.

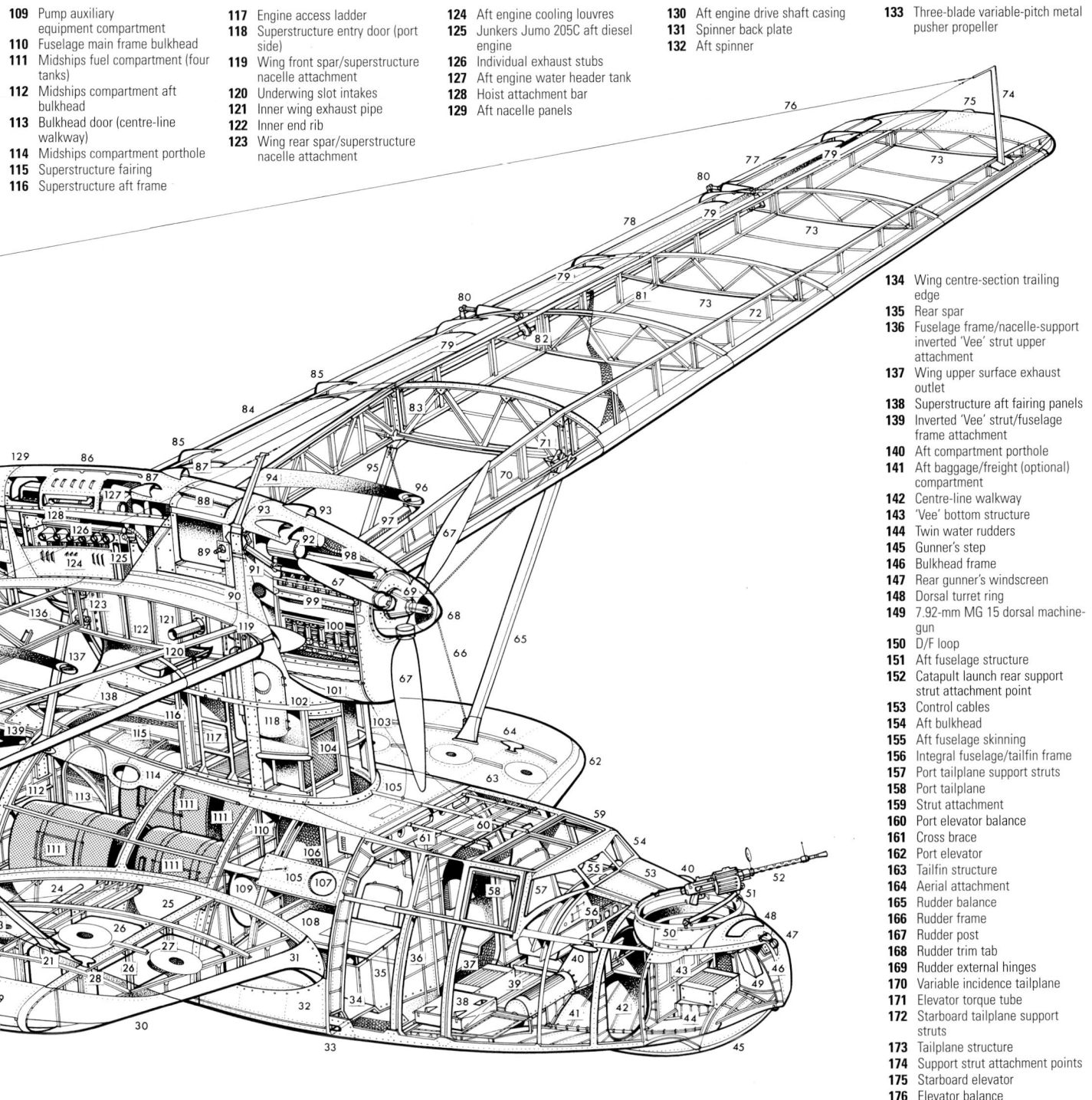

109 Pump auxiliary equipment compartment
110 Fuselage main frame bulkhead
111 Midships fuel compartment (four tanks)
112 Midships compartment aft bulkhead
113 Bulkhead door (centre-line walkway)
114 Midships compartment porthole
115 Superstructure fairing
116 Superstructure aft frame
117 Engine access ladder
118 Superstructure entry door (port side)
119 Wing front spar/superstructure nacelle attachment
120 Underwing slot intakes
121 Inner wing exhaust pipe
122 Inner end rib
123 Wing rear spar/superstructure nacelle attachment
124 Aft engine cooling louvres
125 Junkers Jumo 205C aft diesel engine
126 Individual exhaust stubs
127 Aft engine water header tank
128 Hoist attachment bar
129 Aft nacelle panels
130 Aft engine drive shaft casing
131 Spinner back plate
132 Aft spinner
133 Three-blade variable-pitch metal pusher propeller

134 Wing centre-section trailing edge
135 Rear spar
136 Fuselage frame/nacelle-support inverted 'Vee' strut upper attachment
137 Wing upper surface exhaust outlet
138 Superstructure aft fairing panels
139 Inverted 'Vee' strut/fuselage frame attachment
140 Aft compartment porthole
141 Aft baggage/freight (optional) compartment
142 Centre-line walkway
143 'Vee' bottom structure
144 Twin water rudders
145 Gunner's step
146 Bulkhead frame
147 Rear gunner's windscreen
148 Dorsal turret ring
149 7.92-mm MG 15 dorsal machine-gun
150 D/F loop
151 Aft fuselage structure
152 Catapult launch rear support strut attachment point
153 Control cables
154 Aft bulkhead
155 Aft fuselage skinning
156 Integral fuselage/tailfin frame
157 Port tailplane support struts
158 Port tailplane
159 Strut attachment
160 Port elevator balance
161 Cross brace
162 Port elevator
163 Tailfin structure
164 Aerial attachment
165 Rudder balance
166 Rudder frame
167 Rudder post
168 Rudder trim tab
169 Rudder external hinges
170 Variable incidence tailplane
171 Elevator torque tube
172 Starboard tailplane support struts
173 Tailplane structure
174 Support strut attachment points
175 Starboard elevator
176 Elevator balance

This Do 18D (K6+HL) was flown by 3./Kü.Fl.Gr. 406 in the maritime reconnaissance and air-sea rescue roles. The unit was renumbered from 2./Kü.Fl.Gr. 306 and served in the North Sea area from various bases, including spells in Norway.

Developed from successful commercial mail-carrying flying boats, the Do 18D entered Luftwaffe service in 1938. This boat served with 3./Kü.Fl.Gr. 406 at Hörnum in the Frisian islands, in August 1939. Note the open bow and midships gun positions.

of the production life of the Do 18, and during the summer of 1939, consideration had to be given to improving both performance and armament.

The result was the **Do 18G-1** with Jumo 205D engines rated at 656 kW (880 hp) for take-off, revised bow contours and heavier defensive armament, a 13-mm (0.51-in) MG 131 machine-gun being mounted in the open bow position, and a

hydraulically-operated turret with a 20-mm MG 151 cannon being provided aft. Attachment points were provided for R-Geräte (take-off assistance rockets). The first Do 18G-1s had not reached the Küstenfliegergruppen by the outbreak of war when the Luftwaffe's first-line Do 18D strength comprised 36 flying-boats in the North Sea area and 27 in the Baltic.

On 26 September 1939, a Do 18D of 2./Kü.Fl.Gr. 106 operating from Norderney on patrol north of the Great Fisher Bank encountered the carrier *Ark Royal*, accompanied by the battleships *Nelson* and *Rodney*, and the battle-cruisers *Hood* and *Renown*. The Do 18D was destroyed by a Blackburn Skua scrambled from the carrier, but not before it had reported the position of the force. Do 18Ds of 2./Kü.Fl. Gr. 506 were engaged on naval co-operation tasks during the invasion of Poland and, based on List, this unit participated in the invasion of Norway during the following year. Other Do 18s participating in the Norwegian campaign included the nine boats of 1./Kü.Fl.Gr. 406.

Continued service

By 11 May 1940 five Staffeln were still equipped entirely with the Do 18, these being 2./Kü.Fl.Gr. 106 with nine boats (six serviceable); 1., 2. and 3./Kü.Fl.Gr. 406 with 29 boats (10 serviceable); and 2./Kü.Fl.Gr. 906 with 10 boats (eight serviceable). The 2./Kü.Fl.Gr. 106 was deployed to Brest and then Cherbourg during the Battle of Britain until November 1940, until BV 138s arrived in the Biscay area. The Do 18s were temporarily employed in the Seenotdienst (air-sea rescue) role.

Production of the Do 18 had ended during the early summer of 1940, and of the 44 flying-boats of this type accepted by the Luftwaffe

Above: A characteristic feature of the Do 18, and other Dornier flying boats, was the large-area sponsons that added lifting area and also provided attachments for the wing-bracing struts.

The Do 18D-01 (D-AJII) was the first pre-production example of the Do 18's initial military variant. Most of the Do 18D's production was undertaken by the 'Weser' Flugzeugbau.

This Do 18G served with the Luftwaffe's Seenotstaffel 6, operating in the central Mediterranean in 1941-42. Given the number of flights over and across the Mediterranean by German aircraft, an effective air-sea rescue service was essential, though this was never developed as fully as its British equivalent.

in 1939 and 50 accepted in 1940, 84 were completed to the Do 18G and Do 18H standards. The **Do 18H-1** was an unarmed crew training version of the **Do 18G-1** with provision for a crew of six. From early 1941, the Do 18G-1, which had by now supplanted the Do 18D in service with the first-line Küstenfliegergruppen, was progressively relegated to the increasingly important Seenotdienst role, being modified for this task as the **Do 18N-1** before transfer to the Seenotstaffeln. At the beginning of 1941, the 2. and 3./Kü.Fl.Gr. 406 were still operating the Do 18 from Norwegian and north German bases under the control of the Oberkommando der Marine, together with 3./Kü.Fl.Gr. 906 under Luftwaffe control. A few Do 18s were also included on the strength of 1./Kü.Fl.Gr. 506 based at Biscarosse in western France, but by 16 August 1941, the only remaining first-line Küstenfliegergruppen operating the Do 18 were the Norwegian-based 3.Staffeln of Kü.Fl.Gr. 406 and 906, and even they had re-equipped during the following weeks, the Dornier boat subsequently confining its activities to training and air-sea rescue.

Production of the boat reached about 170, including some 79 Do 18Ds, 62 Do 18Gs and 22 Do 18Hs. It was widely believed that a version powered by two 645-kW (865-hp) BMW 132N air-cooled radial engines had also been produced in series, but in fact only one example of the boat was so powered, this being the Do 18F (D-ANHR) which was re-engined with BMW 132Ns and, redesignated **Do 18L**, was flown on 21 November 1939.

Dornier Do 18G-1 specification

Type: four-seat maritime patrol and reconnaissance flying-boat
Powerplant: two Junkers Jumo 205D liquid-cooled six-cylinder vertical opposed-piston compression-ignition two-stroke engines each rated at 656 kW (880 hp) for take-off
Performance: maximum speed 267 km/h (166 mph) at 2000 m (6,560 ft); normal cruising speed 230 km/h (143 mph) at 1000 m (3,280 ft); long-range cruising speed 165 km/h (102 mph) at optimum altitude; climb to 1000 m in 7 minutes 48 seconds; 2000 m in 17 minutes 30 seconds; service ceiling 4200 m (13,780 ft); maximum range 3500 km (2,175 miles)
Weights: empty equipped 5980 kg (13,183 lb); maximum take-off 10800 kg (23,810 lb)
Dimensions: wingspan 23.70 m (77 ft 9 in); length 19.23 m (63 ft 1 in); height 5.32 m (17 ft 5½ in); wing area (including sponsons) 98.00 m² (1,054.86 sq ft)
Armament: (defensive) one 13-mm (0.51-in) MG 131 trainable machine-gun on a D 30/131 mount in the open nose position and one 20-mm MG 151 trainable cannon in the hydraulically operated HD 151/1 dorsal turret; (offensive) two 50-kg (110-lb) bombs on LTC 50 racks beneath the starboard wing

Above: This Do 18D was operated by 2./Kü.Fl.Gr.506, which was formed at Kamp in early 1939 before moving to Hörnum. In October it renumbered as 1./Kü.Fl.Gr. 406, while a new 2./Kü.Fl.Gr. 506 formed at List with the He 115.

Above: Photographed in 1940, this Do 18D-3 shows the revised bow line by comparison with that of the Do 18D-2, and the large windscreen protecting the dorsal gunner against the worst effects of the slipstream.

Above: Preparations are made to lift a Do 18D onto a tender by an attachment between the engines.

Right: D-ARUN was a pre-production Do 18D completed to Do 18E standard and flown non-stop between Horta and New York.

Dornier Do 18

Above: Showing the open bow position to advantage, this was the pre-production Do 18D-01. The Stummel sponsons were a Dornier trademark.

Above: This Do 18D-2 carries the emblem of of 2./Kü.Fl.Gr. 506 on the side of the forward engine cowling.

Above: A Do 18 prepares to taxi out onto the water from the slipway of a German seaplane base in preparation for take-off on a sortie.

Above and below: The Do 18d, the prototype of the maritime reconnaissance version of the Dornier flying-boat, is seen alighting during early flight trials. This was the only example of the Do 18 to feature a twin fin-and-rudder tail assembly, this being discarded in favour of a single unit by the series model. Note the bombs under the starboard wing.

Above: A pre-production Do 18D was tested with a cut-down fin, braced tailplane and endplate auxiliary fins. A different layout was finally adopted by the boats of the production series.

Above: Aeolus, the Do 18 V3, is hoisted from the water.

Above: The Do 18G differed from its predecessors by having a power-operated dorsal turret, although the type remained very vulnerable to enemy fighters. This Do 18G-1 of 6. Seenotstaffel is being hoisted on to a launching trolley that would then be wheeled down the slipway into the water.

Above: Despite the compartmentation of the hull and sponsons, there was a limit to the amount of damage which a Do 18's structure could survive, as this sinking boat testifies.

Dornier Do 19

Hindsight suggests forcibly that the Luftwaffe's 'Ural Bomber' concept of the mid-1930s was a case of 'too much, too soon' for Germany's emergent aero industry. Nevertheless, the Do 19 was built and tested, and revealed that it would have lacked a real strategic capability even if the Luftwaffe had been able to bring it into service.

During 1934, the Führungsstab der Luftwaffe (Luftwaffe operations staff) was already thinking in terms of a Langstrecken-Grossbomber (long-range heavy bomber) capable of carrying an effective bomb load over a radius that would allow it to attack strategic targets as far distant as the north of Scotland and the Urals from air bases in Germany. Despite the fact that this concept was most certainly some years ahead of the contemporary political situation and, in some respects, the state-of-the-art in so far as the fledgling German aircraft industry was concerned, the Langstrecken-Grossbomber had the full support of Generalleutnant Walther Wever, who, convinced of the importance of the heavy bomber by Oberstleutnant Wilhelm Wimmer in charge of the Technisches Amt (technical office of the RLM), was to become the Luftwaffe's first chief-of-staff. Wever was a far-sighted and competent officer, and soon an ardent protagonist of the long-range strategic bomber, and it was largely as a result of his pressure exerted on the Reichsluftfahrtministerium that the Technisches Amt finalised a specification for a four-engined heavy bomber, which it unofficially called the 'Ural Bomber'.

From the outset the 'Ural Bomber' concept had numerous opponents who protested that the industry lacked the technical skills and capabilities for the successful development of such a warplane; that its introduction would impose an insupportable strain on the Luftwaffe's training organisation; and that a strategic bombing force was a luxury that it was far too early to contemplate. Nevertheless, under Wever's aegis the specification was issued to Dornier and Junkers during the summer of 1935, these companies having already undertaken preliminary studies upon which the Technisches Amt had based its specification, and then during the early autumn of the same year, three prototypes were ordered of the respective designs, which were allocated the designations **Do 19** and Ju 89.

Inelegant design

Totally lacking in the elegance that characterised the contemporary Do 17, the Do 19 featured a slab-sided fuselage of rectangular cross section, and a thick-section broad-chord

Potentially a useful long-range bomber, though more for tactical use, the Do 19 took to the air only in the form of the Do 19 V1 first prototype, and the project was cancelled after the death of Generalleutnant Wever. Note the lack of turreted armament.

wing in the mid-set position and offering much evidence of its flying-boat ancestry. The fuselage structure was a flush-riveted metal semi-monocoque, and the wing's structure was based on two steel girder-type spars and covered by flush-riveted light alloy. The inset twin vertical tail surfaces were braced to the fuselage by single inclined struts, and all three members of the undercarriage retracted aft, the main members into door-covered bays in the undersides of the two inboard engine nacelles. Provision was made for a crew of nine, comprising the pilot, co-pilot/navigator, radio operator, bombardier and five gunners. The proposed defensive armament comprised a nose turret manned by the bombardier and mounting a single 7.9-mm (0.31-in) MG 15 trainable forward-firing machine gun, a similar trainable rearward-firing weapon in an open tail position, and immense hydraulically operated two-man

The construction of the Do 19 V1 prototype revealed that Germany was perhaps pushing the cutting edge of its technical capabilities a little too far, especially in aspects such as the hydraulically-operated cannon turrets for the production model.

Dornier Do 19

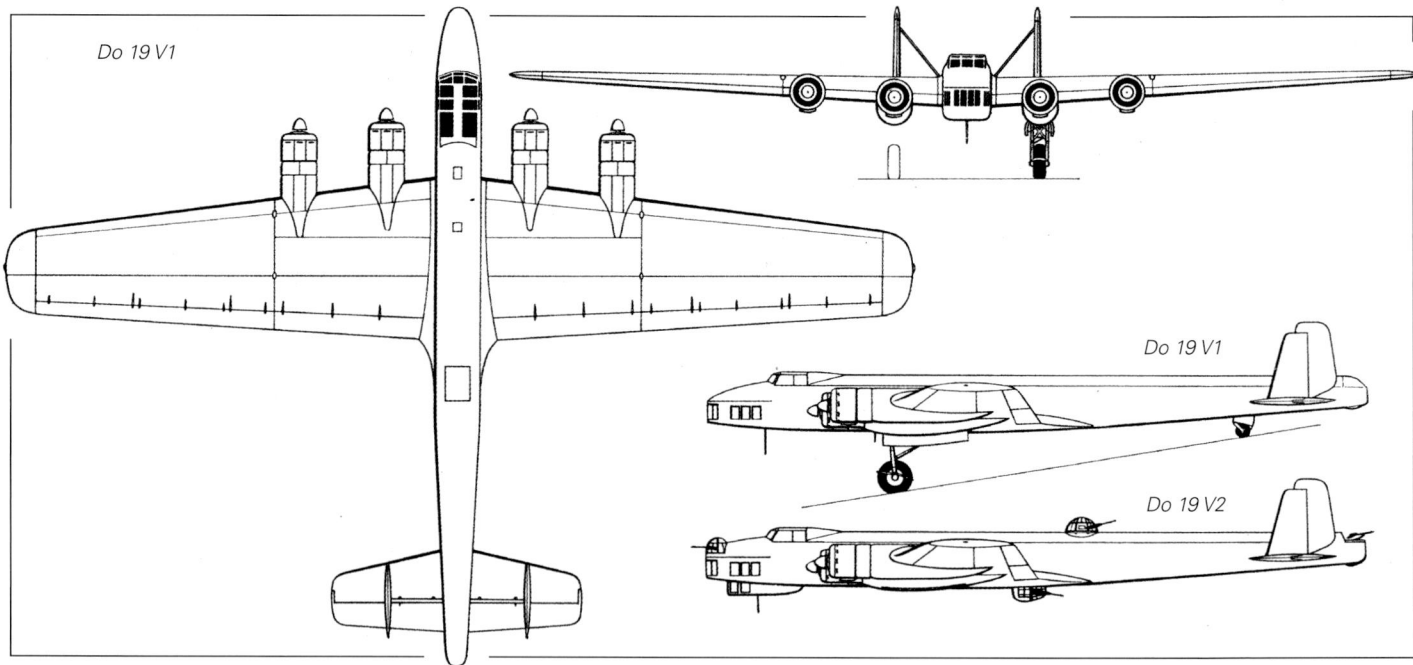

Do 19 V1

Do 19 V1

Do 19 V2

dorsal and ventral trainable turrets each mounting a single 20-mm cannon. The bomb bays were intended to accommodate up to 1600 kg (3,527 lb) of bombs in the form of 16 100-kg (220-lb) SC 100 or 32 50-kg (110-lb) SC 50 weapons. The entire fuel capacity was housed in tanks built into the centre section of the wing.

Into the air

The **Do 19 V1** first prototype (D-AGAI) flew on 28 October 1936, powered by four Bramo (Siemens) 322H air-cooled nine-cylinder radial engines, each rated at 533 kW (715 hp) for take-off and having a maximum continuous output of 447 kW (600 hp). No armament was installed. The second prototype, the **Do 19 V2**, was scheduled to be powered by BMW 132F air-cooled nine-cylinder radials each rated at 604 kW (810 hp) for take-off and having a maximum continuous output of 485 kW (650 hp), and it was planned that the similarly powered **Do 19 V3** would be the first aircraft with defensive armament. However, the two-man cannon

Above: The Do 19 was lacking in elegance, and it is doubtful whether the type would have offered any significant development potential even if it had been ordered into production and service.

The full span of the Do 19 wing's trailing edge was occupied by outboard ailerons and inboard flaps, and all of the tail unit's fixed surfaces carried balanced control surfaces.

turret (with one man controlling traverse and the other elevation), whose design had been proceeding in parallel with the construction of the prototypes, was found to be considerably heavier and more cumbersome than had been anticipated: static tests indicated that the installation of the two such turrets would demand considerable structural strengthening of the centre fuselage, and as weight had escalated during construction, the Do 19 was already underpowered.

At this juncture no alternative turret was available for installation, but Dornier proposed powering the initial production model, the **Do 19A**, with four Bramo 323A-1 Fafnir air-cooled nine-cylinder radial engines each rated at 671 kW (900 hp) for take-off and 746 kW (1,000 hp) at 3100 m (10,170 ft), and on the assumption that lighter, lower-drag dorsal and ventral turrets would be provided, it was estimated that the loaded weight could be limited to 19000 kg (41,887 lb), and that performance would include a maximum speed of 370 km/h (230 mph), climb to 3000 m (9,845 ft) in 10 minutes, service ceiling of 8000 m (26,245 ft), and range of 2000 km (1,243 miles).

The project is reappraised and cancelled

In the meantime, Wever had been killed on 3 June 1936 in an air accident, and his successor, Generalleutnant Albert Kesselring, began a reappraisal of the 'Ural Bomber' programme. The Führungsstab der Luftwaffe had already established the basic performance parameters for an appreciably more advanced heavy bomber, evolving its 'Bomber A' requirement to which Heinkel had begun work on the Projekt 1041 (to emerge as the He 177). Kesselring concluded that the smaller, twin-engined bomber would suffice for any war such as was envisaged in western Europe, with its implicit limitations on air strategy; that the primary role of the Luftwaffe must remain tactical rather than strategic, and that, in view of the limited capacity of the German aircraft industry at that time, the heavy strategic bomber could be produced only at the expense of more urgently-needed fighters and tactical bombers. Thus, despite some protests from the Technisches Amt, on 29 April 1937 all further development of the 'Ural Bomber' was officially terminated.

The Do 19 V2, which had been virtually complete at the time of contract cancellation, and the semi-completed Do 19 V3 were scrapped. The Do 19 V1 remained in existence, however, and in 1939 was modified as a troop transport and taken on charge by the Luftwaffe, seeing service during the Polish campaign.

The decision to terminate the 'Ural Bomber' programme in 1937 has provided a subject for controversy ever since, but in view of the contemporary situation within the German aircraft industry, its envisaged rate of growth, and its existing commitments, there can be little doubt that any serious effort at that time to establish a force of heavy strategic bombers would have been totally unrealistic. In the circumstances, therefore, the abandoning of the 'Ural Bomber' in favour of the longer-term 'Bomber A' programme appeared sound.

Dornier Do 19 V1 specification
Type: nine-crew long-range heavy bomber
Powerplant: four Bramo (Siemens) 322H-2 air-cooled nine-cylinder radial engines each rated at 533 kW (715 hp) for take-off and 447 kW (600 hp) for continuous running
Performance: [at 18000 kg/39,683 lb] maximum speed 315 km/h (196 mph) at sea level; cruising speed 250 km/h (155 mph) at 2000 m (6,560 ft); climb to 1000 m (3,280 ft) in 3 minutes 24 seconds and to 5000 m (16,405 ft) in 30 minutes 30 seconds; service ceiling 5600 m (18,375 ft); maximum range 1600 km (994 miles)
Weights: empty 11865 kg (26,158 lb); maximum take-off 18500 kg (40,785 lb)
Dimensions: wingspan 35.00 m (114 ft 9¾ in); length 25.45 m (83 ft 5¾ in); height 5.78 m (18 ft 11½ in); wing area 160.20 m² (1,724.38 sq ft)
Armament: (proposed defensive for production model) one 7.9-mm

It was planned that any production model of the Do 19 would have had a ventral 20-mm cannon turret under the fuselage in lines with the roots of the wing's trailing edge, and a dorsal 20-mm turret above the fuselage slightly farther to the rear.

(0.31-in) MG 15 machine-gun in nose turret, one 7.9-mm (0.31-in) MG 15 machine-gun in open tail position, and one 20-mm cannon in each of the power-operated dorsal and ventral turrets; (proposed offensive for production model) up to 1600 kg (3,527 lb) of bombs in the form of 16 100-kg (220-lb) SC 100 or 32 50-kg (110-lb) SC 50 weapons

Dornier Do 22

The Do 22 was designed and built for the export market, orders being received from Greece, Latvia and Yugoslavia. No aircraft reached Latvia, some of these machines probably being delivered to Finland, and several of the Yugoslav aircraft escaped to Egypt in Aptil 1941 for service under British control.

Although from the mid-1930s Dornier's design activity was devoted largely to meeting specific requirements of the Luftwaffe and, to a lesser extent, Deutsche Lufthansa, the company had established a thriving export business and, in 1934, began work on a three-seat multipurpose military monoplane suitable for operation with float, wheel or ski undercarriages, and intended solely for export. Designated **Do 22**, the prototype was built by the AG für Dornier-Flugzeuge at Altenrhein, and flown for the first time in 1935 as a twin-float seaplane.

A three-seat high-wing braced monoplane, the Do 22 had a two-spar fabric-covered metal wing braced to a tubular structure on the sides of the fuselage to which could be attached wheels, floats or skis, and the fabric-covered oval-section welded steel-tube fuselage incorporated a tunnel beneath the rear cockpit from which a ventral machine-gun could be fired. Single or twin machine-guns could be mounted on a Scarff ring over the rear cockpit, and a fixed gun could be provided to fire through the propeller disc. The three cockpits were mounted in tandem, the pilot's cockpit being situated beneath a cut-out in the wing centre section, and a folding transparent cover being provided for the centre cockpit that housed the observer with dual controls.

Export orders
The Do 22 soon attracted orders, and production machines were manufactured at Friedrichshafen with some components being provided from Altenrhein. The first order for 12 examples of the twin-float version was placed on behalf of the Royal Yugoslav naval air service, a similar order being received from Greece, and further aircraft being ordered by

The first Do 22L landplane was built as part of a Latvian order, but there is no evidence that any delivery was made to Latvia, and it seems likely that four were later supplied to Finland.

the Latvian government. The first production Do 22 floatplane was flown on 15 July 1938, and deliveries to Yugoslavia began before the end of the year, being followed in 1939 by deliveries to Greece. The first production landplane, the **Do 22L** (D-OXWD), flew on 10 March 1939, but no export orders for this version were fulfilled, and there is no evidence to indicate that Do 22s built against the Latvian order, although completed, were delivered to that country before its incorporation into the USSR.

A suffix letter was applied by Dornier to the designation of the floatplane in order to differentiate between examples built against different contracts (i.e. **Do 22Kg** indicating a Greek contract machine and **Do 22Kj** and **Do 22Kl** indicating Yugoslav and Latvian contract machines, respectively). The aircraft delivered to Greece equipped the 12th Naval Co-operation Squadron, which had 10 Do 22s on strength

Dornier Do 22

The structures extending laterally from the Do 22's fuselage provided attachment points for the wing-bracing struts, and also allowed a straightforward switch between landplane undercarriage with wheels and seaplane alighting gear with floats.

when that country was invaded by Italian forces. Most Royal Hellenic air force Do 22s were lost in action during the weeks that followed, but eight of the 12 Yugoslav machines reached Egypt in April 1941, equipping No. 2 (Yugoslav) Squadron that began patrol operations over the Mediterranean from Aboukir under the control of the RAF's No. 230 Squadron on 3 June 1941. One of the Do 22s was used as a source of spares and the remainder continued their patrol activities until the unit was disbanded on 23 April 1942. Four Do 22s were supplied to Finland in 1941, and these, presumably ex-Latvian contract machines, were employed by T/LeLv 6 on both floats and skis for coastal reconnaissance and anti-submarine patrols.

Dornier Do 22 specification
(Figures in parentheses relate to the Do 22L)
Type: three-seat light reconnaissance and torpedo bomber
Powerplant: one Hispano-Suiza 12Ybrs liquid-cooled V-12 engine rated at 578 kW (775 hp) for take-off and 641 kW (860 hp) at 4000 m (13,125 ft)
Performance: maximum speed 350 km/h (217 mph) [360 km/h (224 mph)] at 4000 m (13,125 ft); cruising speed 300 km/h (186 mph) [310 km/h (193 mph)] at 4000 m; climb to 1000 m (3,280ft) in 2 minutes 6 seconds [1 minute 48 seconds], and to 5000 m (16,405 ft) in 15 [13] minutes; service ceiling 8000 m (26,245 ft [8200 m (26,905 ft)]; normal range with 990 [635] litres (218 [140] Imp gal) of fuel 2300 km (1,430) [1500 km (932) miles]
Weights: empty 2545 kg (5,610 lb) [2295 kg (5,060 lb)]; empty equipped 3100 kg (6,834 lb) [2780 kg (6,129 lb)]; loaded 3990 kg (8,800 lb) [3690 kg (8,135 lb)]
Dimensions: wingspan 16.20 m (53 ft 2 in); length 13.15 m (43 ft 1¾ in) [12.90 m (42 ft 3¾ in)]; height 4.85 m (15 ft 11 in) [4.65 m (15 ft 3 in)]; wing area 44.98 m² (484.20 sq ft)
Armament: (defensive) one 7.62- or 7.9-mm (0.3 or 0.31-in) fixed forward-firing machine-gun, one or two machine-guns of similar calibre on Scarff ring mounting in rear cockpit, and one machine-gun firing aft below fuselage from ventral tunnel; (offensive) one 800 kg (1,764-lb) torpedo when flown as two-seater, or four 50-kg (110-lb) bombs on external fuselage racks

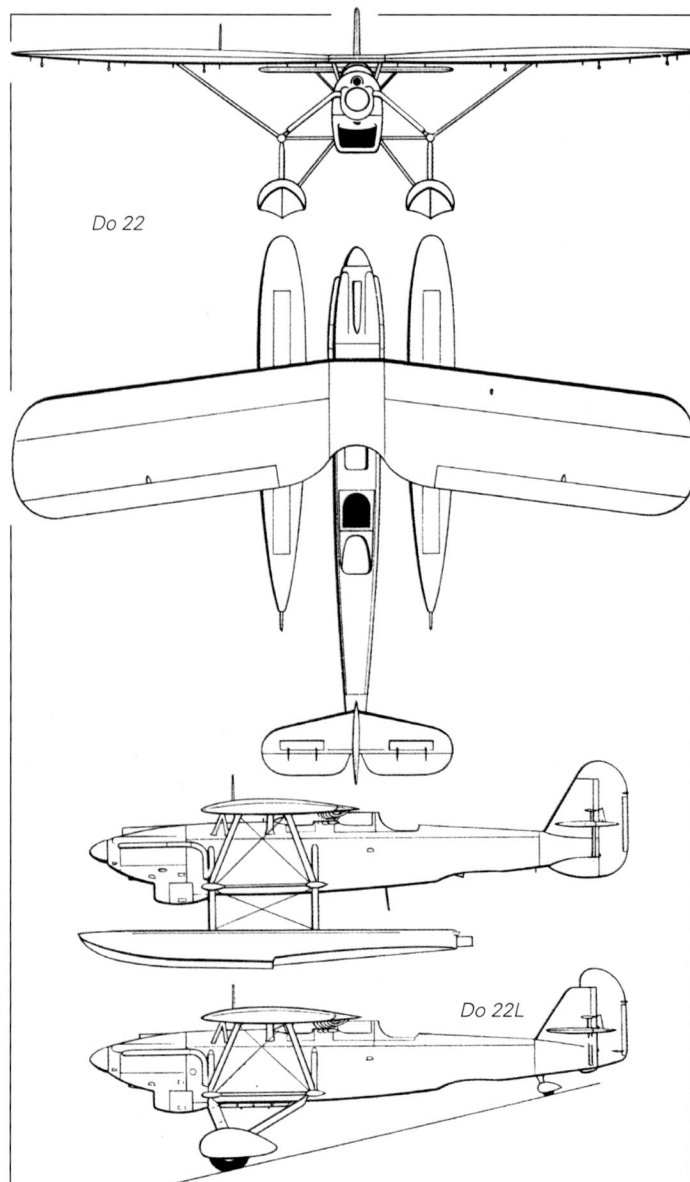

Do 22

Do 22L

Deliveries of the Do 22 floatplane were made to Greece and Yugoslavia for operations in the Mediteranean Sea. Most of the Greek seaplanes were destroyed in the German invasion of April 1941, while some of the Yugoslav seaplanes escaped to Egypt.

Dornier Do 23

The Do 23 was certainly an improvement over the preceding Do 13, and proved an important element of German air strength propaganda, but in reality it was still a very limited warplane by the standards prevailing in the mid-1930s, with even the bomber version of the Ju 52/3m transport exceeding it in general capability.

In so far as other nations were concerned, Dornier's first tangible contribution to German rearmament was the **Do 23** bomber which, when the Luftwaffe was finally revealed to the world as a force in being, provided the material for propaganda films to promote abroad a somewhat exaggerated picture of the Third Reich's new-found air strength. Thus it was widely believed that the Do 23 was the Luftwaffe's first bomber. What was not revealed, understandably enough, was the fact that the Do 23 was the definitive development of an earlier bomber, the Do 11, which had acquired so unenviable a reputation as a result of accidents stemming from structural weaknesses and execrable handling that it had been dubbed the Fliegender Sarg (flying coffin) by the crews unfortunate enough to fly it.

An attempt to eradicate the undesirable characteristics of the Do 11 had led to the Do 13 which, in its **Do 13C** production form, was found to have even fewer endearing features than its predecessor, the Luftfahrtkommissariat being forced to halt production while the airframe was completely restressed and modications made to the wing. These changes were embodied in the **Do 13e** prototype, which first flew on 1 September 1934. While retaining the Do 13C's basic structure, the Do 13e was extensively strengthened, the fuselage having additional supporting frame members and internal cross-bracing, and 1.20 m (3 ft 11¼ in) being lopped from each wingtip, reducing overall span from 28.00 m (91 ft 10¼ in) to 25.60 m (83 ft 11¾ in). The Junkers type of so-called 'double-wing' flaps introduced by the Do 13 were retained, these occupying the entire wing trailing edge and being used to vary the camber and so increase the lift, the mass-balanced outer sections being operated differentially as ailerons. The auxiliary vertical surfaces beneath the tailplane already adopted for the Do 11 were retained.

Structural weight had risen by some 445 kg (981 lb), but the Do 13e now offered the desired strength, and its handling characteristics were at last considered acceptable. Thus, after load tests to assure the C-Amt (technical department of the Luftfahrtkommissariat) of the structural integrity of the modi-

Final development of the Do F series, the Do 23G was an ungainly machine of indifferent performance, but it permitted the Luftwaffe to start formal development of bombing tactics in the 1930s. This quartet was on the strength of 4./KG 253.

fied bomber, production was reinstated at Friedrichshafen early in 1935. However, in view of the evil reputation of the Do 11 and the superstition of many concerning the number '13', it was agreed that the modified bomber should be redesignated **Do 23**.

Well-proved structural design

The construction of the Do 23 followed closely that of the earlier Dornier bombers, the semi-cantilever high wing being a three-spar duralumin structure with fabric covering, and the rectangular-section fuselage having a framework of duralumin profiles with light alloy skinning. The metal-framed tail surfaces were fabric-covered, and the braced tailplane was adjustable on the ground. The fixed undercarriage was of the divided type, each unit comprising a vertical shock-absorber strut attached to the engine mount with the lower end hinged to the fuselage by a steel-tube axle and radius rod, the wheel being enclosed by a large streamlined fairing.

The initial production model was the **Do 23F** with two

The Do 23's defensive armament was based on three open positions each carrying a single 7.9-mm (0.31-in) trainable machine-gun. The ventral gun was located in a tunnel position in the underside of the fuselage to the rear of the bomb bay.

Dornier Do 23

A clearly evident feature of the Do 23 was the Junkers type of 'double-wing' flaps along the full span of the wing's trailing edge. The outboard ends were operated differentially as ailerons.

BMW VId water-cooled V-12 engines, but at an early production stage the ethyl glycol-cooled BMW VIU was substituted to result in the **Do 23G**, both models having a generally similar performance. Defensive armament comprised three 7.9-mm (0.31-in) MG 15 trainable machine-guns in single nose, dorsal and ventral positions, and the bomb load totalled 1000 kg (2,205 lb), this being made up of 50- or 100-kg (110- or 220-lb) bombs stowed in vertical cells.

Do 13 orders inherited

All unfulfilled orders for the Do 13 under the 1934 expan-

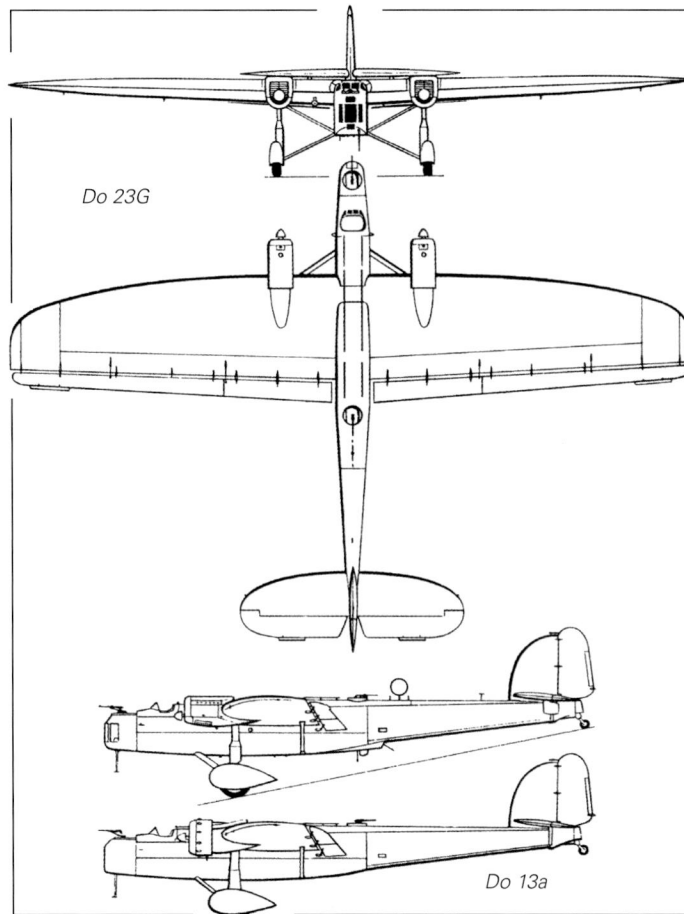

Do 23G

Do 13a

sion programme had been transferred to the Do 23, the first production examples of which began to leave the Friedrichshafen assembly line in the spring of 1935, alongside the last of 150 Do 11s. Contracts for the Do 13 had called for 222 aircraft, but barely a dozen of them had been delivered when production was halted. The Do 11 was rapidly transferred to the Kampffliegerschulen as it was replaced by the Do 23 during the summer and autumn of 1935, and by October of that year the new bomber had been delivered to Staffeln of the Fliegergruppen Merseburg, Finsterwalde, Gotha, Fassberg and Giebelstadt. The capabilities of the Do 23 had proved disappointing, and thus no additional orders for the bomber were placed by the Luftfahrtkommissariat, the type being phased out of production late in 1935 after delivery of 200–210 aircraft.

In the meantime, production of the Ju 52/3m ge, considered only as a Behelfs-Kampfflugzeug (auxiliary bomber) but untroubled by the difficulties that had plagued the Dornier, had increased rapidly, and thus, by October 1936 (by which time the bomber-equipped Fliegergruppen had been redesignated Kampfgruppen and increased in number from five to 12) there were two Ju 52/3m Kampfstaffeln for every one equipped with the Do 23G. The Kampfflieger now comprised I/KG 153 at Merseburg, II/KG 153 at Finsterwalde, III/KG 153 at Altenburg, I/KG 154 at Hanover, II/KG 154 at Wunstorf, I/KG 155 at Giebelstadt, II/KG 155 at

Above: The Do 23 can be described only as ungainly, and characteristic features included the auxiliary fins under the tailplane, the large wheel spats and the four-blade propellers.

Among the Do 23's several obsolescent features was the largely open accommodation, including the pilot's cockpit located on the upper part of the fuselage ahead of the wing. The gunners sat in open turrets not appreciably advanced from those of World War I.

Ansbach, III/KG 155 at Schwabisch Hall, I/KG 253 at Gotha, II/KG 253 at Erfurt, III/KG 253 at Nordhausen, and I/KG 254 at Delmenhorst.

The first-line operational career of the Do 23G was destined to be short-lived, and by the summer of 1936, the first steps had been taken to phase it out of Kampfflieger service for relegation to the bombing and gunnery schools. Other Do 23Gs were passed to the Luftwaffe branch of the Fliegerforstschutz (forest service) for aerial spraying and other tasks, and the first aerial mine-detector units, the Minensuchstaffeln, flew the elderly Dornier until more suitable aircraft had become available.

Dornier Do 23G specification
Type: four-seat heavy day and night bomber
Powerplant: two BMW VIU liquid-cooled V-12 engines each rated at 559 kW (750 hp) for take-off and 410 kW (550 hp) for continuous running
Performance: maximum speed 260 km/h (161 mph) at optimum altitude; cruising speed 210 km/h (130 mph) at optimum altitude; initial climb rate (at 8750 kg/19,290 lb) 270 m (886 ft) per minute; climb to 1000 m (3,280 ft) in 4 minutes; service ceiling 4200 m (13,780 ft); maximum range 1350 km (840 miles) at 187 km/h (116 mph) at 2500 m (8,200 ft); endurance 7 hours 30 minutes
Weights: empty 5600 kg (12,346 lb); empty equipped 6480 kg (14,286 lb); normal loaded 8750 kg (19,290 lb); maximum take-off 9200 kg (20,282 lb)
Dimensions: wingspan 25.60 m (83 ft 11¾in); length 18.80 m (61 ft 8¼ in); height 5.40 m (17 ft 8½ in); wing area 106.60 m² (1,147.43 sq ft)
Armament: One 7.9-mm (0.31-in) MG 15 trainable machine-gun in each of the nose, dorsal and ventral open positions, and up to 1000 kg (2,205 lb) of bombs carried internally

Like many other German bombers of the period, the Do 23 carried its bombs in vertical cells built into the lower fuselage. In the case of the Do 23 this stowage took the form of four groups of cells arranged as two on each side of the centreline. Vertical release of the bombs was conducive to poor bombing accuracy.

Below: Clearly evident on this Do 23 are the 'double-wing' flaps and ailerons, which were carried behind and slightly below the trailing edge of the wing. This arrangement had been pioneered by Junkers, and proved an effective yet simple method of providing extra lift at low speed and improved control.

Below: Indifferent though it was as a warplane, the Do 23 was delivered in numbers sufficient for the Luftwaffe to establish a large number of bomber units and to embark on the development of the operational procedures and tactics that would be refined in the Spanish Civil War and result in a notably capable bomber arm by the beginning of World War II.

Dornier Do 24

Designed to meet a Dutch requirement, and later built in France, Germany and the Netherlands, the Do 24 was a first-class patrol flying-boat that the Germans later pressed into invaluable service for the air-sea rescue and and emergency transport roles right round the coasts of occupied Europe.

The Dutch government had been among the first customers for the military version of the Wal flying-boat, and after purchasing six Wals from CMASA, Dornier's Italian subsidiary, ordered licensed manufacture from Aviolanda for the Marine Luchtvaartdienst (MLD). Thus another 40 Wals had been delivered when Dutch production ended in 1931. The Wals performed invaluable service in the Netherlands East Indies, and in 1934 the MLD began to consider its requirements for a successor. At this time, Dornier Metallbauten was engaged in the construction of prototypes of the Do 18, which it saw as a Wal successor, but the MLD wanted a larger, heavier and more powerful boat possessing full seagoing capability and retaining the Wal's robustness. Discussions were held between the MLD and Dornier, and in 1935 design of a suitable flying-boat was initiated.

Close liaison was maintained between the MLD and Dornier, mock-up inspections were completed before the end of 1935, and the Netherlands government contracted with the Friedrichshafen factory for an initial six **Do 24** flying-boats to a pattern that followed the general configuration of earlier Dornier designs, with a broad-beamed, shallow hull, a semi-cantilever high-set parasol wing, and sponsons.

At around this time the RLM showed interest in the Do 24, and two prototypes were ordered as competition to the Blohm und Voss Ha 138. The first metal was cut on two prototypes and the first two of the boats ordered for the MLD. Dornier believed the use of diesel engines to be extremely advantageous owing to their economy, and proposed the Jumo 205 for the Do 24, but in July 1936 the USA released the Martin Model 139 bomber for export, and with the decision to adopt this type for the Air Division of the Royal Netherlands Indies Army, the MLD elected to employ an engine basically similar to that of the bomber. The Do 24 was intended essentially for East Indies service, and uniformity of engine was attractive from the viewpoint of spares and servicing.

Most of the Do 24s built by Dornier were ferried to the Netherlands with the same registration – D-AYWI. This is thought to be the second aircraft, the Do 24 V4.

The initial version of the Martin bomber ordered for use in the East Indies was the Model 139WH-1 with Wright Cyclone R-1820-F52 air-cooled nine-cylinder radial engines rated at 875 hp (652 kW) for take-off. These engines were some 15% lighter and almost 50% more powerful than the Jumo 205, a fact which required the restressing of the wing centre section and supporting structure. As construction of the two Do 24 prototypes was by now well advanced, it was decided to modify the first two production aircraft against the Dutch contract to take the Cyclone engines, using them for prototype and acceptance trials. In order to meet the original test schedule, work on the first two Jumo-powered prototypes for the RLM, the **Do 24 V1** and **Do 24 V2** (D-AIBE), was shelved in order to accelerate completion of the first two production machines as the **Do 24 V3** (D-AYWI) and **Do 24 V4** (D-ADLP), the former performing its initial flight from the Bodensee on 3 July 1937, flown by Erich Gundermann.

Intensive air and water trials were conducted with the

*The first example of the type to fly, the Dornier Do 24 V4 was tested from Lake Constance as **D-ADLP** as pictured here, before being delivered to the Dutch Marine Luchtvaartdienst as one of 30 built for the Netherlands by Dornier.*

This Do 24T-2 flew with the 7.Seenotstaffel/SBK XI in the Aegean during 1942. The boat carries white Mediterranean theatre bands.

Do 24 V3, open water trials in extremely heavy seas being performed with the Do 24 V4, which had joined the test programme in the autumn of 1937, and the MLD confirmed that the boat fully met its requirements, the Dutch government taking up its option on a production licensing agreement. Original planning had called for the manufacture of 72 Do 24s in the Netherlands by Aviolanda at Papendrecht, with De Schelde at Dordrecht contributing the wings. While preparations were made for licence production, the Dutch bought more aircraft from Dornier, eventually taking 30.

Production in Switzerland

The parent company's other commitments had necessitated transfer of the Dutch order to the Swiss subsidiary, and with the delivery of the Do 24 V3 and Do 24 V4 to the Netherlands late in 1937 under the export designation **Do 24K-1**, the MLD began to make preparations for the service introduction of the X-boats, having allocated serial numbers with an X prefix. The first Swiss deliveries followed within a few months, continuing throughout 1938, with the 28th and last Do 18K-1 reaching the Netherlands early in 1939.

One further German-built aircraft was delivered, the only **Do 24K-2** to be built. Whereas the Do 24K-ls were powered by Cyclone R-1820-F52 engines, the K-2 had Cyclone R-1820-G102s rated at 1,000 hp (746 kW) for take-off and 900 hp (671 kW) at 6,700 ft (2040 m), the more powerful G-series engines having been chosen to conform with those

being installed in the Martin 166 (Model 139WH-3) bombers that had been ordered for the Royal Netherlands Indies Army. With the registration X-37, the sole Do 24K-2 was shipped to the Dutch East Indies on 8 May 1940, just two days before the German invasion. By that time the Aviolanda factory had begun to produce Do 24K-1s, seven having been delivered to the MLD by the time of the invasion. Orders had been received for 43, of which the final 25 were to have been Do 24K-2s.

The Do 24K's wing was a two-spar structure built in three parts. The rectangular centre-section, which carried the engines, was supported above the hull by two sets of inverted-V struts and single forward-inclined central struts, and braced to the sponsons by parallel sloping struts, the trapezoidal outer panels being attached to the extremities of the centre section. A single split flap spanned the centre section, and was used to increase camber for take-off and landing, and the outer panels carried high aspect ratio slotted ailerons that also functioned as flaps for landing. The hull, which was of normal Dornier two-step design with sponsons for lateral stability, was divided by seven bulkheads into eight water-tight compartments. The braced tailplane carried endplate fins and rudders, the latter being statically and aerodynamically balanced with servo tabs. All fixed surfaces were covered by light alloy, the movable surfaces being fabric covered.

The two main fuel tanks, each of 1000-litre (220-Imp gal) capacity, were housed in the wing centre section, and were

Above: The Jumo 205-engined Do 24 V1 was actually the third example of this Dornier flying-boat to start on its test programme, and did not fly until 10 January 1938.

Right: This Do 24T-2 entered service with the Seenotdienst as CM+IU and was soon reallocated to Seenotstaffel 8 at Mamaia in Romania in June 1942. After a year it was damaged in the waters of the Black Sea near Sevastopol.

This is another of the popular Do 24T-2 variant operating in Greece from the summer 1942, in the hands of Seenotstaffeln 6 and 7, with the markings CM+IT.

Most, but not all, of the Do 24T-2 boats were fitted with a 20-mm MG 151 cannon in the dorsal turret in place of the French HS 404 weapon of the Do 24T-1. The bow and stern turrets retained the ubiquitous 7.9-mm (0.31-in) MG 15 gun.

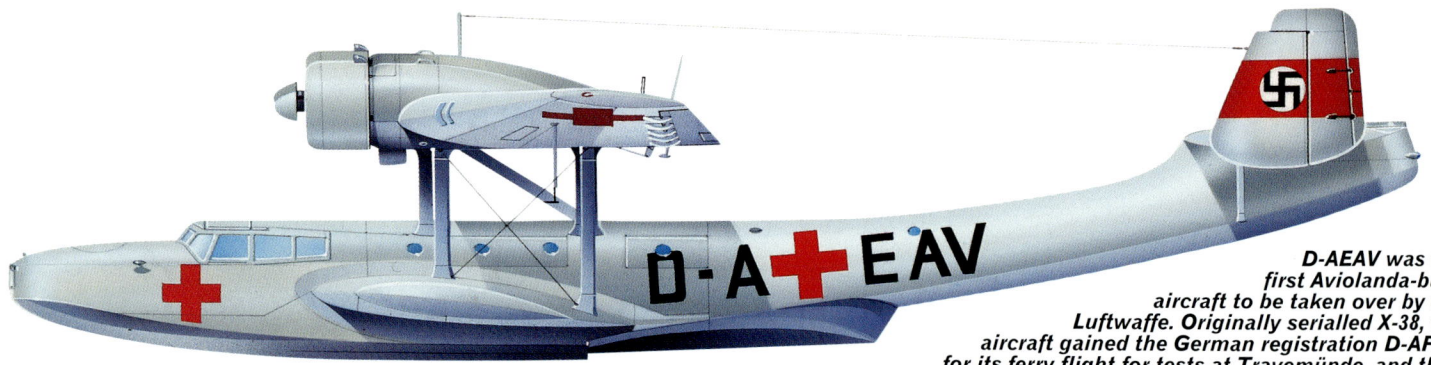

D-AEAV was the first Aviolanda-built aircraft to be taken over by the Luftwaffe. Originally serialled X-38, the aircraft gained the German registration D-AFBT for its ferry flight for tests at Travemünde, and then received D-AEAV. It was tested as the prototype for the Do 24N-1.

supplemented by six tanks in each sponson that raised total fuel capacity to 5300 litres (1,166 Imp gal). Accommodation was provided for six crew members, the portion of the hull below the wing centre section offering full living and sleeping facilities to enable the flying-boat to operate for extended periods away from its base. Defensive armament comprised a 7.9-mm (0.31-in) FN-Browning machine-gun in bow and stern turrets, and a 20-mm Solothurn cannon in a dorsal turret, and racks were provided for 12 50- or 100-kg (110- or 220-lb) bombs.

Little early German interest

While the Dutch dominated the early history of the Do 24, the Technisches Amt of the RLM evinced little interest in the Dornier flying-boat, which was in a similar category to the BV 138 to which it was already committed as a successor to the Do 18 with the Küstenfliegergruppen. The first and second prototypes had been completed at Friedrichshafen with Junkers Jumo 205C diesel engines each rated at 447 kW (600 hp) for take-off, the Do 24 V1 flying for the first time on 10 January 1938 and being followed shortly by the Do 24 V2. After the completion of factory flight testing, the two prototypes languished at Friedrichshafen until 1940, when, with the formulation of plans for the 'Weserübung' inva-

sion of Denmark and Norway, they were hastily fitted with defensive armament comprising an HD 151/1 dorsal turret with a 20-mm MG 151 cannon, an open bow position with a single 7.9-mm MG 15 machine gun, and a similar weapon in a turret in the stern. The Do 24 V1 and Do 24 V2 were then taken over by the Luftwaffe and delivered to KG.z.b.V. 108 See, whose three Gruppen flew a miscellany of seaplanes from Norderney under the Lufttransportchef See. Used for the logistic support of isolated pockets of German troops, the Do 24s made numerous hazardous flights into and out of narrow Norwegian fjords, performing missions as far north as the Narvikfjord and both sustaining damage during the campaign.

With the occupation of the Netherlands in May 1940, German forces found the Do 24K manufacturing facilities at Papendrecht and Dordrecht to be intact, with 13 Do 24K-2s in various states of assembly. During the months that followed, the vital importance of an efficient air-sea rescue service, first appreciated during 'Weserübung', was emphasised by the Battle of Britain, as was also the inadequacy of the elderly He 59 floatplane for the air-sea rescue role. One air-sea rescue unit, Seenotstaffel 1, had been formed as early as the summer of 1939, but no serious attempt to establish an effective Seenotdienst (air-sea rescue service) was made

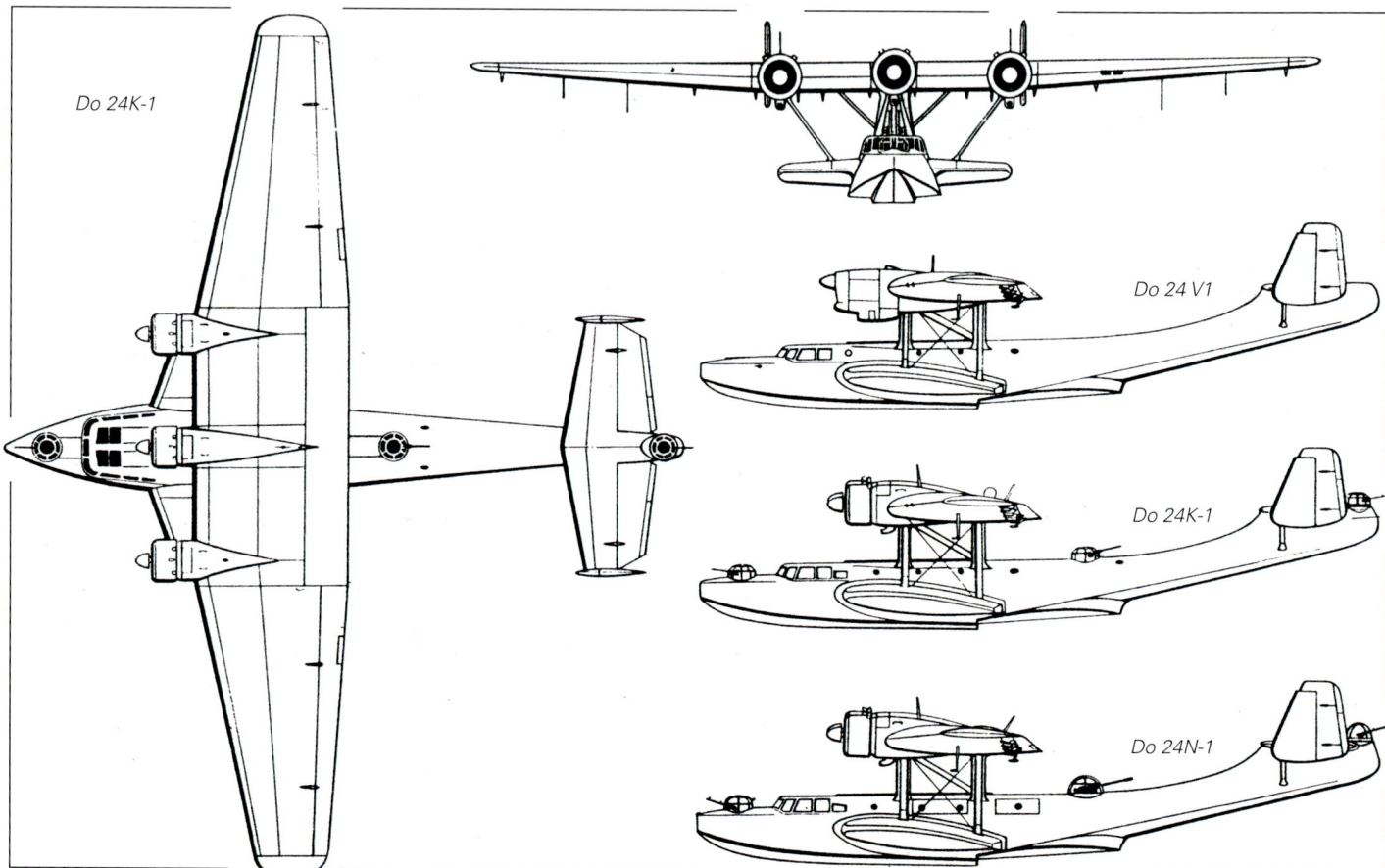

Do 24K-1

Do 24 V1

Do 24K-1

Do 24N-1

Above: The Do 24 was of typical Dornier concept and all-metal construction, with a parasol wing and a comparatively narrow hull stabilised on the water by large sponsons.

Above: This aircraft was built as a Cyclone-engined Do 24N-1 by Aviolanda, but became the prototype for the Do 24T-1.

Above: Derived for German service from the Do 24K-2, the Do 24N-1 had a dorsal turret fitted with a 20-mm Hispano-Suiza HS 404 cannon, of which large stocks had been seized in 1940.

Above: Manufactured in the Netherlands, the Do 24T-1 was used extensively by the Seenotstaffeln.

The pilot and co-pilot occupied a roomy flight deck. The hatch between them provided access to the bow compartment with its simple gun turret, and stowage for specialised maritime equipment for mooring and anchoring.

The Do 24 excelled in the rescue role. Two hatches were cut into the port side of the hull at approximately dinghy level, while the cabin had six bunks for survivors and stowage for emergency medical equipment.

until the summer of 1940, and this was hampered by lack of suitable seaplanes, leading, during the autumn, to the deployment of the Do 18s of 2./Kü.Fl.Gr. 106 in the air-sea rescue role. With a view to their possible suitability for use by the Seenotstaffeln, one of the completed Do 24K-2 flying-boats acquired in the Netherlands was therefore flown to Travemünde for evaluation.

The trials were an outstanding success, and it was considered that, with its seagoing capability, relatively high cruising speed, considerable endurance and substantial internal capacity, the Do 24K-2 was 'made to measure' for the Seenotdienst role. Accordingly, in the spring of 1941, the Dutch production organisation was reactivated under the supervision of personnel from the 'Weser' Flugzeugbau, Aviolanda and De Schelde receiving instructions to resume production of hulls and wings, respectively, and Fokker being ordered to undertake final assembly and flight testing.

To adapt the Do 24K-2 for its new task, German instrumentation and radio equipment were fitted; the bomb-release mechanism and bomb racks were removed; two large rescue hatches were cut in the upper port decking of the hull, these hinging upward and their sills being little above waist-height for a man standing upright in a dinghy; six bunks were provided for rescued personnel, together with the necessary emergency medical equipment, and defensive armament was modified to comprise a 7.9-mm MG 15 machine gun in the

...ng the savage fighter battles ... the English Channel during ...ummer of 1940, the Luftwaffe ...e good use of Heinkel He 59 ...Dornier Do 24 seaplanes in air-...escue work. This is a Dornier ...4T-1 of 3.Staffel/Seenotgruppe ...ogne-Wimereux. Dorsal sting ...provided by a single 20-mm ...ano-Suiza 404 cannon.

Dornier Do 24

On one occasion a Do 24T lost its entire tail unit and part of the rear fuselage after landing to pick up survivors, but taxied back to the Kjøllefjord after sealing all the watertight bulkheads and crowding everyone into the bows to lift the rear hull stump clear of the water.

Above: The three Fafnir radial engines of the Do 24T were installed in neat nacelles along the leding edges of the centre section, and drove three-blade propellers of the variable-pitch type.

Access to the engines of large parasol-wing aircraft always offered problems for maintenance, but in the Do 24 were reduced by large hinge-down panels allowing engineers to service the engines without undue difficulty.

bow and stern turrets, and a turret amidships mounting a 20-mm Hispano-Suiza 404 cannon from captured French stocks. With these modifications the Do 24K-2 became the **Do 24N-1**, and the first two such boats were accepted by the Luftwaffe in August 1941, followed by three in September and four in October.

Available stocks of Cyclone R-1820-G102 engines were limited, however, and a suitable German engine had already been selected for use as soon as supplies of the American engine became exhausted, this being the BMW-Bramo 323R-2 Fafnir air-cooled nine-cylinder radial unit rated at 746 kW (1,000 hp) for take-off and 701 kW (940 hp) at 4000 m (13,125 ft), and already in production for the Fw 200C Condor. Sufficient Cyclones were available for 13 Do 24N-ls, the last of which was accepted in November 1941, in which month the first two Fafnir-powered examples were also accepted. With the BMW-Bramo engines the boat became the **Do 24T-1**, and although equipment remained unchanged and the type was still considered primarily as an air-sea rescue machine, it was now allocated secondary transport and maritime patrol roles.

Continued Dutch production

Five Do 24Ts had been accepted from the Dutch assembly line by the end of 1941, a further 44 being accepted by the end of the following year. After 11 Do 24T-1s had been built a new subtype, the **Do 24T-2**, made its appearance, this differing only in having improved radio and navigational equipment, some examples also having a 20-mm MG 151

cannon amidships in place of the French HS 404. After 37 had been built, further detail changes led to the **Do 24T-3**. The production tempo in the Netherlands rose slowly, 61 boats being accepted during 1943.

During the spring of 1944, the German government offered to supply Spain with 12 Do 24s to enable that country to establish its own air-sea rescue service. The establishment of such a service was in the interests of Germany, for the Seenotgruppen were seriously over-extended, and with the loss of its Sicilian bases, the Seenotbereichskommando X (Syrakus) was no longer capable of offering adequate air-sea rescue coverage of the western Mediterranean. The Spanish government accepted the German offer, Spanish personnel were trained at Berre, France, and early in June the first flying-boat arrived at Pollensa, Majorca, from where the rescue service was to operate.

By the end of 1942 the increasing demands of the Seenotbereichskommandos, which extended in an almost unbroken chain around German-occupied Europe, had necessitated an expansion of Do 24T production, and during the summer of 1942, the former CAMS factory at Sartrouville in France was phased into the programme, delivering its first

Do 24 flying-boat proved ideal [for] the air-sea rescue role, with [good] seagoing capability and long [end]urance. This particular example is [Do] 24T-2 of Seenotstaffel 8, which [was] sunk in 1943 while trying to [resc]ue two downed English pilots. Its [crew], and the downed Allied pilots, [were] rescued by other Do 24s.

Do 24T-3 in mid-1943. Under the control of SNCAN, the factory contributed 40 Do 24T-3s.

A further 26 Sartrouville-built machines were to have been accepted by the Luftwaffe by mid-1944, but the approach of Allied forces necessitated the evacuation of the plant. Unfinished Do 24Ts at Sartrouville were subsequently completed for France's Aéronavale, the Flottille 9F Tr being formed on 5 December 1944 to operate these flying-boats as a transport unit from St Mandrier, the first two aircraft being taken on strength on 29 December. Altogether, 40 Do 24Ts were completed at Sartrouville for service with the post-war Aéronautique Navale.

One other nation was destined to employ the Dornier flying-boat in the air-sea rescue role. Sweden acquired an example when Do 24T-1 (Werk Nr 3343, CM+RY) of Seenotgruppe 81 landed at Hällevik on 31 October 1944. As Sweden possessed no air-sea rescue flying-boats at this time, the Do 24T-1 was purchased from Germany, overhauled and placed in Flygvapnet service on 10 May 1945 under the designation **Tp 24**. It was retired in mid-1951 and scrapped the following year.

Although the Do 24 remained essentially unchanged throughout its production life, 'Weser' adapted one example to take an Arado-designed boundary layer control system, with which it was redesignated **Do 318 V1**. This was tested at Friedrichshafen in 1944 with encouraging results, but early in 1945 this interesting experimental flying-boat was scuttled on Lake Constance to prevent it falling into Allied hands.

Operational career

As the first Do 24N-1 flying-boats were entering service with the Seenotstaffeln in Europe, the MLD's Do 24Ks had already undertaken their first operational missions against the Japanese. On 8 December 1941 (Tokyo time), when war began in the Pacific, many of the Do 24Ks were on detached patrols, and were soon engaged in attacks on Japanese troop transports singly and in small groups, but fighters and anti-aircraft defences took their toll of the flying-boats which dwindled steadily in number. In February 1942, five of the older Do 24K-1s (X-5, 7, 8, 9 and 10) that had been used for training at Morokrembangan, near Surabaya, were evacuated to Australia, and on 2 March 1942, six days before the Dutch forces in East Indies capitulated, the surviving operational Do 24K-1s took-off from Lake Grati, Java, for Broome, Western Australia, where the four that completed the journey were destroyed at their moorings on the following day in a Japanese attack. Two of them had failed to reach Broome, making forced landings off the Australian coast, one (X-36) being destroyed and X-24 refuelling and flying on to Perth. This latter was retained by the MLD and used for clandestine operations on behalf of the Netherlands Forces Intelligence Service until October 1943, when it was handed over to the Royal Australian Air Force. Five Do 24K-1s were taken on strength by No. 41 Squadron, and were operated until lack of spares rendered their further use impracticable.

During 1940, various emergency Seenotstaffeln had been formed on the He 59, these being directed by a central command, the Seenotdienstführer, and not subordinated to the local air commanders. By the beginning of 1942, the He 59s had been supplemented by Fokker T.VIII-W float-planes and Do 18 flying-boats in the Seenotstaffeln, which had been progressively increased in number and allocated to specially activated air-sea rescue area commands, the Seenotbereichskommandos, and for the first months of 1942, the older aircraft were supplemented and eventually supplanted by the Do 24.

The Black Sea saw perhaps the most varied and extensive operational use of the Do 24, which first appeared in the area in May 1942 when the Seenotkommando Varna transferred to Eupatoria on the Crimean coast with two He 59s and three Do 24s. When air-sea rescue commitments permitted, the Do 24s flew reconnaissance sorties and performed escort missions for Axis convoys to and from

Above (all three photos): In the air-rescue role, the Do 24T served in the Arctic, Mediterranean, English Channel, North Sea, Atlantic and Black Sea, epic rescues including the recovery of a fighter pilot who ditched just off the Scillies, and the rescue of the crew of a meteorological aircraft 560 km (350 miles) out into the Atlantic. Perhaps the Do 24's greatest advantage was its ruggedness, allowing it to operate in high sea states, as shown here by the V3.

Dornier Do 24

This Dutch-built example of the Do 24 has a dorsal turret armed with a 20-mm Mauser MG 151/20 cannon as opposed to the French HS 404 cannon of the Do 24T-1. The boat served with Seenotstaffel 7 in the Aegean Sea, and carries the name of a well-known brandy.

Dornier Do 24T cutaway key

1 Bow navigation light
2 Towing/mooring ring
3 Fore hull structure
4 Retractable mast
5 Ammunition magazine racks
6 Spent cartridge chute
7 Bow compartment (sea equipment stowage)
8 Turret mechanism
9 Bow 7.92-mm MG 15 machine-gun
10 Bow turret
11 Removable turret dome
12 Nose decking
13 Nose mooring lug
14 Mooring rope stowage
15 Bulkhead
16 Crawlway
17 Rudder pedal assembly
18 Bulkhead door frame
19 Instrument panel shroud
20 Co-pilot's control column
21 Compass
22 Windscreen panels
23 Cockpit roof glazing
24 Sliding entry panels
25 Hatch runners
26 Flight deck windows
27 Navigator's station
28 Co-pilot's seat
29 Pilot's seat
30 Seat adjustment lever
31 Side-mounted control column
32 Floor support frame
33 Radio-operator's position
34 "Vee" bottom hull structure
35 Fuselage/sponson fairing
36 Access panels

37 Sponson nose ribs
38 Sponson main fuel cells (four, approx 350 litres/77 Imp gal capacity each)
39 Sponson abbreviated fuel cell (180-liter/39.6-Imp gal capacity)
40 Port sponson mooring lug
41 Rib reinforcement
42 Sponson main spar/ fuselage frame

43 Sponson/ forward wing strut lower attachment
44 Fuel collector tank (210 litres/46 Imp gal)
45 Access panels
46 Fuselage hull step
47 Sponson rear spar/fuselage frame
48 Sponson/aft wing strut lower attachment
49 Mooring lug
50 Non-slip sponson walkway
51 Forward midships bay (two stretcher accommodation; 28 oxygen bottles stowed along centre-line walkway)
52 Forward bay hinged entry hatch
53 Sponson/forward wing strut,
54 Fuselage main frame bulkhead

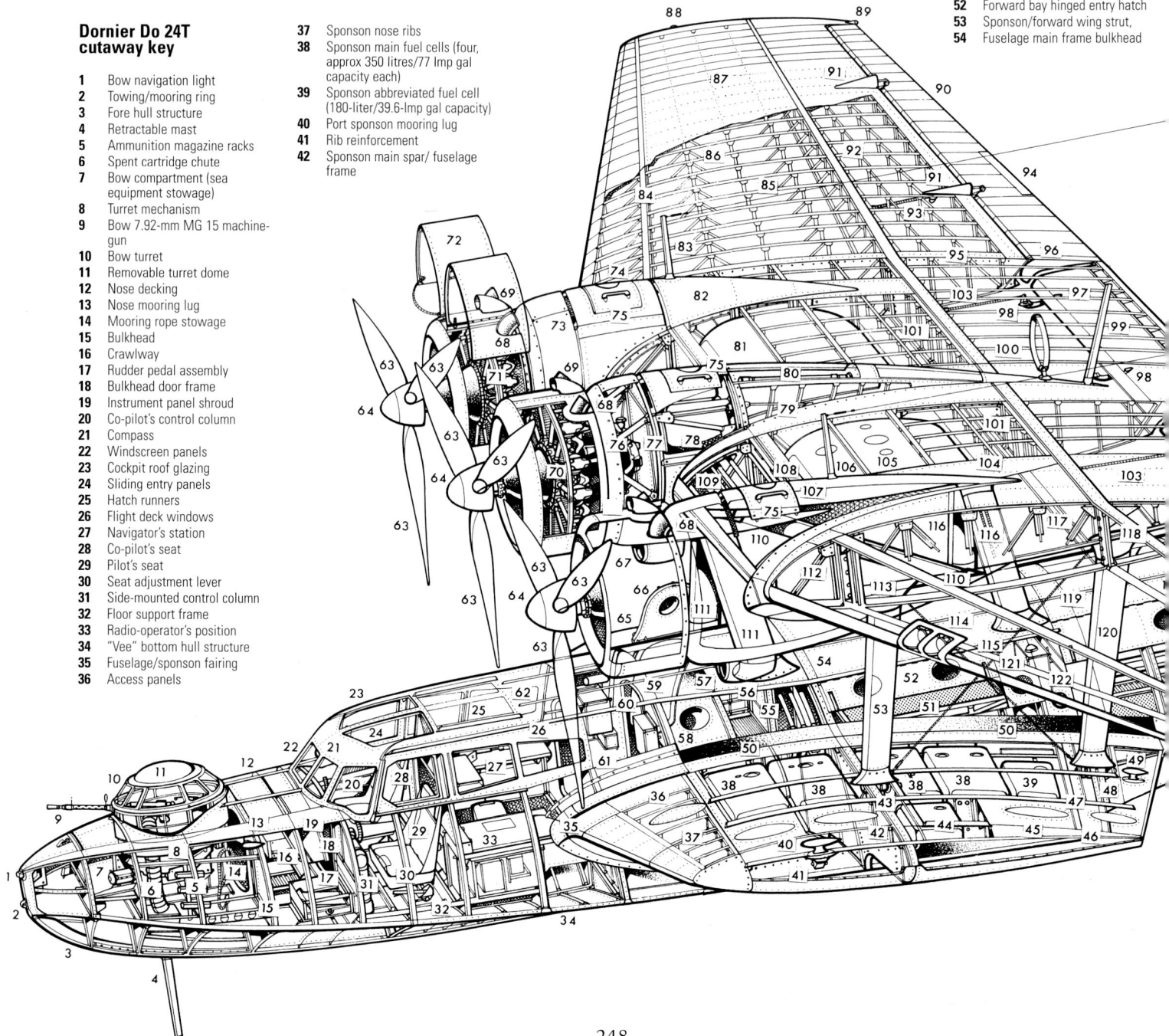

55 Medical attendant: station
56 Fuselage/wing strut attachment fairing
57 Port engine nacelle intake
58 Fuselage porthole
59 Starboard crew entry door
60 Bulkhead
61 Radio equipment installation
62 Roof external strakes
63 Three-blade VDM metal propellers
64 Spinners
65 Starboard sponson
66 Roof (starboard) entry hatch
67 Centre engine nacelle intake
68 Engine exhausts
69 Engine upper air intakes
70 746-kW (1,000-hp) Bramo 323R-2 radial engine
71 Cowling ring
72 Hinged engine inspection/maintenance panels
73 Cooling louvre
74 Oil tank cover
75 Servicing handgrip
76 Engine bearers
77 Firewall/bulkhead
78 Centre engine oil tank
79 Centre nacelle frames
80 Centre nacelle pick-up/hoist bar
81 Starboard wing fuel tank

82 Starboard engine nacelle fairing
83 Starboard aerial mast
84 Wing frontspar
85 Aerial
86 Wing ribs
87 Wing metal skinning
88 Starboard navigation light
89 Starboard formation/identification light

90 Starboard aileron
91 Aileron hinge fairings
92 Wing rear spar
93 Aileron control runs
94 Aileron trim tab
95 Wing centre/outer section join
96 Aileron inboard profile
97 Centre-section underwing flap
98 Flap actuating hinges
99 Antenna
100 D/F loop
101 Rear spar structure
102 Wing rib/flap cut-out
103 Flap control runs
104 Port engine nacelle fairing
105 Port wing fuel tank
106 Port aerial mast
107 Oil tank cover
108 Front spar
109 Hinged leading-edge (inspection/maintenance access)
110 Fuselage/wing centre-line diagonal brace strut
111 Fuselage/wing forward inverted "Vee" struts (housing control runs)
112 Wing centre/outer section front spar join

113 Sponson/forward wing strut upper attachment
114 Twin landing lights
115 Sponson/wing strut diagonal bracing
116 Fuselage/wing aft inverted "Vee" struts (housing fuel lines from sponsons)
117 Wing centre/outer section join rib

118 Sponson/aft wing strut upper attachment
119 Midships dorsal decking
120 Sponson/aft wing strut
121 Fuselage air ventilation plant
122 Fuselage main frame bulkhead
123 Centre-line walkway
124 Aft bay hinged entry hatch
125 Aft midships bay (four x stretcher accommodation)
126 Hull "Vee" bottom structure
127 Galley/hot plate (port)
128 Blanket/survival clothing cupboard (starboard)
129 Fuselage midships mooring lug
130 Aileron hinge fairings
131 Bulkhead door
132 Aileron underwing mass balances
133 Wing rear spar
134 Port navigation light

135 Port formation/identification light
136 Port aileron
137 Hull aft step
138 "Vee" bottom sternpost frame
139 Reinforced fuselage frame
140 Turret support
141 Compressed air bottles
142 Turret ring
143 Dorsal turret
144 20-mm MG 151 cannon
145 Toilet
146 Peat bag (toilet sanitary refill)
147 Porthole
148 Master compass
149 Aft fuselage centre-line catwalk
150 Tail surface control rod linkage
151 Fuselage aft frames

152 Fuselage skinning
153 Ventral stringers
154 Control rods
155 Fuselage/tailplane fairing
156 Tailplane front spar
157 Elevator control rod
158 Elevator hinges
159 Tailplane ribs

160 Tailplane rear spar/tailfin attachment
161 Starboard tailfin structure
162 Aerial attachment
163 Rudder balance
164 Rudder frame
165 Rudder upper trim tab
166 Starboard rudder post
167 Rudder lower trim tab
168 Trim tab actuating linkage
169 Starboard elevator tab
170 Port rudder balance
171 Starboard elevator structure
172 Elevator control linkage
173 Rudder linkage
174 Port aerial attachment
175 Tailplane inboard end rib structure
176 Tailplane front spar/fuselage frame attachment
177 Fuselage aft main frame
178 Control linkage
179 Stern mooring rope stowage
180 Tailplane brace struts
181 Port tailfin
182 Tailplane/fin attachment
183 Port elevator hinge

184 Rear turret ammunition stowage
185 Port rudder post
186 Rear turret
187 Turret ring
188 Tail gunner's armour plating
189 Port rudder
190 Rudder lower trim tab hinge fairing
191 Port rudder lower trim tab
192 Tail navigation light
193 Tail mooring ring
194 7.92-mm MG stern machine-gun

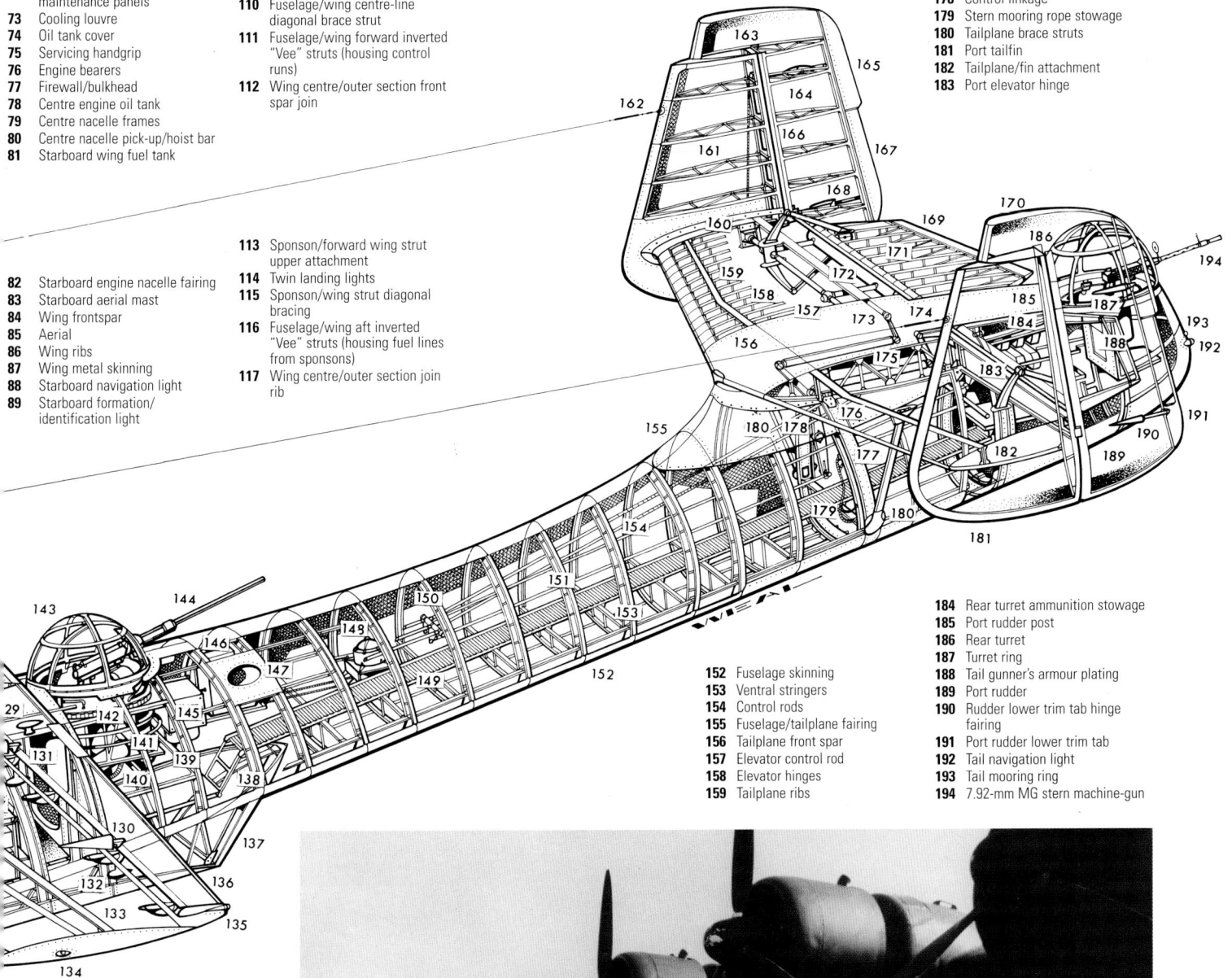

This Do 24T-2 served with Seenotstaffel 7, whose badge appears below the flight deck, in the Aegean Sea area, during 1942. The unit was subordinate to SBK XI.

Extending the successful parasol-wing flying-boat concept, the three-engined Do 24 first flew in July 1937 and a production manufacturing licence was negotiated with the Dutch. After the German conquest of the Netherlands in May 1940, Dutch production continued for the Luftwaffe. Production amounted to around 270 examples, with Dornier building the first 32. SNCAN produced 40 in France, the remainder being built by Aviolanda/Fokker in the Netherlands.

Odessa and Sevastopol. At the end of February 1943, when the thaw set in and mud made it impossible for landplanes to fly supplies into the Kuban bridgehead, floatplanes and flying-boats had to be pressed into service, and Do 24Ts were collected from all air-sea rescue areas and gathered at Sevastopol, where they formed two 11-aircraft Staffeln, 1. and 2.Seetransportstaffeln Sewastopol. The Do 24Ts carried about 1,000 tons of supplies into the bridgehead between 5 and 25 March 1943, these being unloaded in shallow water off Kuban and the boats then being loaded with wounded for the return flights. When the Soviet offensive against Crimea began, Seenotbereichskommando XII transferred some of the Do 24Ts back to Constanza, and later Varna. Those flying-boats remaining to the Seenotkommandos Sewastopol and Sultan-Eli continued to provide both rescue and transport facilities. As late as April 1944, just before the recapture of Odessa by Soviet forces, the Do 24Ts were flying supply and evacuation missions between Odessa harbour and Galatz on the Danube, and the last Luftwaffe aircraft to leave Crimea was a Do 24T that took-off on two engines with no fewer than 40 troops on board. In August, the eight Do 24Ts of Seenotstaffel 8, which formed a component of Seenotbereichskommando XI, were hurriedly evacuated from Mamaia in Romania to Varna in Bulgaria, and then via Salonika to Athens where, by 1 September, they had joined the surviving Do 24Ts of

Seenotstaffeln 6 and 7 to form a single 19-aircraft unit with the primary task of evacuating German personnel from Crete and the Dodecanese, standard load being 24 men, each with 30 kg (66 lb) of equipment. In mid-October, the evacuation of Athens necessitated the transfer of the unit to Salonika, and by the night of 23-24 October, when the surviving six Do 24s were flown to Vienna, some 3,000 troops had been evacuated from the islands.

The Do 24 had made its Mediterranean debut almost simultaneously with its appearance in the Black Sea, but few flying-boats of this type were available until the spring of 1943, when they were subordinated to the Seenotzentrale Syrakus (Air-Sea Rescue Centre Syracuse) that performed its 1,000th rescue at the height of the Malta convoy battles. Following the sinking of the Italian battleship *Roma* in September 1943, five Do 24Ts were despatched to pick up survivors. One returned with 19 sailors but the remaining four were shot down by Allied aircraft, and the crews themselves had to be rescued during the night by a tender.

Farther-flung operations

Only limited operations were performed with Do 24s in the Arctic, although flying-boats of this type did play an important part in the anti-convoy measures taken by the Luftwaffe in 1942. On one occasion during the PQ convoy battles,

This moored Do 24 is caught by the camera with all the engine access panels opened for major maintenance to be undertaken on two of the powerplants. There was just enough space to stand on the upper decking immediately behind the cockpit.

two He 115s ran out of fuel and ditched. One of the three Do 24Ts sent to search the area spotted a dinghy containing three men, and despite extremely heavy seas landed alongside the dinghy, the complete tail unit and part of the rear fuselage of the flying-boat promptly breaking off and sinking. The crew gathered in the bows after securing all watertight bulkheads, picked up the survivors in the dinghy, and taxied all the way back to the Kjøllefjord, which the Do 24T reached on the following day.

Operations in the Channel and Baltic

Boulogne and Cherbourg were used by the Do 24T-equipped Seenotstaffeln for English Channel rescue missions, Brest being used as a base for operations over the Atlantic and Western Approaches. On one occasion, a Do 24T from Brest rescued the crew of a meteorological reconnaissance aircraft some 560 km (350 miles) out in the Atlantic, and on another occasion a fighter pilot was picked up off the Scilly Isles by night. In the Baltic air-sea rescue missions did not play so large a part as they did elsewhere, and the few Do 24Ts stationed in the area were called upon to perform many other duties, including the evacuation of wounded from the Eastern Front.

By 1944, many of the Seenotstaffeln bore the numbers of the surface flotilla with which they co-operated, the air and surface units together forming a Seenotgruppe. For example, the Seenotgruppen 50 and 51, based respectively on Oslo and Bodø in Norway, comprised Seenotstaffel 50 at Stavanger-Sola and Seenotflottille 50 at Oslo in the case of the former, and Seenotstaffel 51 at Bodø and Seenotflottille 51 at Tromsø in the case of the latter. With the invasion of Normandy, the western-based Do 24T units were gradually withdrawn eastwards along the Dutch and north German coastlines, and in the summer of 1944, the increasingly heavy losses being suffered to Allied fighters resulted in the Seenotdienst organisation being given permission to form its own 'search and defence' Staffel with Me 410s.

With the evacuation of north-west Germany, the Do 24Ts and their escorting Me 410s left Norderney and Jever, respectively, the 10 remaining flying-boats going to List on the island of Sylt, and by the war's end the only two Do 24T-equipped Seenotgruppen were 80 and 81 based at

This Do 24T was found unserviceable in Grossenbrode on the Baltic Sea on 25 April 1945, and had previously served for six months with Seenotgruppe 81.

Grossenbrode under Luftwaffe Division See. The surviving Do 24Ts were dismantled and scrapped, and the last example, which had been used for a number of test flights in the summer of 1946, was towed out to sea off Sylt and used as a target for British fighters. Despite taking on a heavy list, the flying-boat refused to sink and, finally, had to be scuttled by a charge the following day, this incident being indicative of the exceptional sturdiness displayed by the Do 24 which, at the peak of its Luftwaffe career, had equipped some 15 Seenotstaffeln. In the post-war era the Do 24 survived longest with Spain, flying in the air-sea rescue role until at least the late 1960s.

Dornier Do 24T-1 specification

Type: air-sea rescue and transport flying-boat
Powerplant: three BMW-Bramo 323R-2 Fafnir air-cooled nine-cylinder radial engines each rated at 746 kW (1,000 hp) for take-off and 701 kW (940 hp) at 4000 m (13,125 ft)
Performance: maximum speed 330 km/h (205 mph) at 2600 m (8,530 ft), 290 km/h (180 mph) at sea level; maximum continuous cruising speed 295 km/h (183 mph) at 2600 m, 250 km/h (155 mph) at sea level; maximum endurance cruising speed 220 km/h (137 mph); normal range 2900 km (1,800 miles); maximum range 4700 km (2,920 miles); climb to 2000 m (6,560ft) in 6 minutes, 4000 m (13,125 ft) in 13 minutes 12 seconds; service ceiling 7500 m (24,605 ft)
Weights: empty 9400 kg (20,723 lb); normal loaded 13700 kg (30,203 lb); maximum loaded 16200 kg (35,714 lb); maximum overload 18400 kg (40,564 lb)
Dimensions: wingspan 27.00 m (88 ft 6⅞ in); length 22.05 m (72 ft 4 in); height 5.75 m (18 ft 10⅓ in); wing area 108.00 m² (1,162.50 sq ft)
Armament: one 7.9-mm (0.31-in) MG 15 machine-gun each in bow and stern turrets, and one 20-mm HS 404 cannon in dorsal turret

It is believed that only two boats were modified to the Do 24MS standard for mine-sweeping, these being fitted with a dural hoop and onboard field-generating equipment. They may have served operationally with the Minensuchgruppe.

Dornier Do 26

There was nothing wholly radical in the design or construction of the Do 26, but the boat was nevertheless an attractive and effective combination of modern elements. The type appeared too late in the 1930s for significant use in its intended commercial role, but was then taken over by the Luftwaffe for a short military career.

The combination of broad-beamed shallow hull, stabilising sponsons and pylon-mounted wing had become almost synonymous with the design of Dornier flying-boat by the mid-1930s, and the debut of the **Do 26** in 1938 was greeted with some surprise as it revealed a complete departure from traditional Dornier flying-boat design. Without a doubt the most shapely and attractive waterborne aircraft of its period, the Do 26 did not embody any particularly noteworthy innovations in flying-boat design or display any features previously untried, and the length/beam ratio of its planing bottom was a thoroughly conventional 6.2/1, but it carried aerodynamic cleanliness to what was widely considered the ultimate for aircraft in its category.

Appealing combination of novel features

Work on the design of the Do 26 had been started in 1936 after discussions with Deutsche Lufthansa (DLH) had produced a specification for a flying-boat capable of operating non-stop services across the North Atlantic between Lisbon on the western extremity of Europe and New York on the eastern seaboard of the United States of America. For the first time, Dornier adopted a completely cantilever wing, whose rectangular centre section, built integral with the hull, was set at a coarse dihedral angle with the engines mounted in tandem push/pull pairs at its outboard ends. The forward engines drove tractor propellers and the rear engines drove pusher propellers via hinged extension shafts that enabled them to be raised 10 degrees during take-off so that the lower arcs of their swept discs were clear of the water spray generated by the hull. The tapered outer wing panels carried the stabilising floats, which retracted inwards into bays in the underside of the outer wing panels. The essentially rectangular-section hull, which was of normal Dornier two-step design, with a vertical rear step, and divided by bulkheads into eight watertight compartments, provided accommodation for the four members of the flight crew and a compartment for up to 500 kg (1,102 lb) of mail. The sector distance for which the

This view of the Do 26 V2 'Seefalke' highlights the boat's clean lines and reveals the interesting upward tilting of the rear propellers to keep them clear of water spray.

Do 26 was designed was 5800 km (3,605 miles), but allowance for headwinds resulted in provision being made for a maximum range of 9000 km (5,590 miles).

Three orders and three options

In 1937, DLH placed an order with Dornier Metallbauten for three examples of the Do 26, and took an option on three more of the boats. The first of them, the **Do 26 V1** (D-AGNT *Seeadler*), recorded its maiden flight on 21 May 1938, powered by four Jumo 205C diesel engines each rated at 447 kW (600 hp) for take-off and driving a Junkers-Hamilton three-blade propeller of the variable-pitch type. The second prototype was the **Do 26 V2** (D-AWDS *Seefalke*), which differed from its predecessor only in having Jumo 205D engines each rated at 656 kW (880 hp) for take-off, and this first flew in February 1939. By this time the Do 26 V1 had been delivered to DLH for route-proving trials,

An unusual feature of the Do 26, seen here in the form of the Do 26 V1 on the step during its take-off run, was the upward inclination of the rear propellers at take-off and alighting. Another interesting feature was the retractable nature of the underwing stabilising floats, which hinged upward and inward after take-off to come to rest in bays in the underside of the outer wing panels.

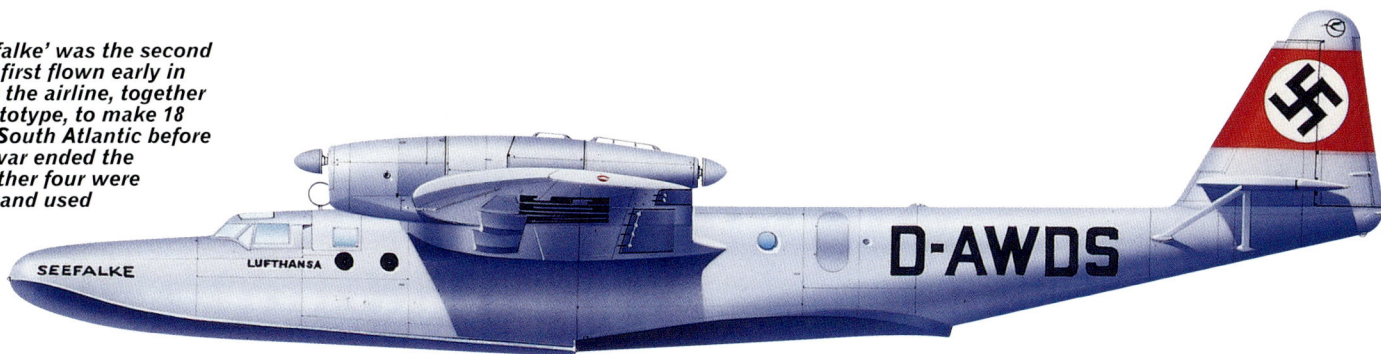

Lufthansa's 'Seefalke' was the second prototype Do 26, first flown early in 1939 and used by the airline, together with the first prototype, to make 18 crossings of the South Atlantic before the outbreak of war ended the programme. Another four were built as Do 26Ds and used by the Luftwaffe transports.

and in that month made a 20600-km (12,800-mile) round trip to Chile carrying medical supplies for the assistance of the victims of an earthquake.

Success in initial service

The Do 26 V2 followed the Do 26 V1 into service with DLH in the late spring of 1939, by which time the airline had taken up its option for a second batch of three boats. Considered as boats of the **Do 26A** series, the first two prototypes made a total of 18 crossing of the South Atlantic

in the mailplane role before the outbreak of World War II in September 1939 halted any attempt at further operations, but the type did not enter service on its intended route across the North Atlantic.

The third prototype was the Do 26 V3 (D-ASRA *Seemöwe*), and this was intended as the first boat of the **Do 26B** series. The new standard differed from that of the first and second flying-boats in having VDM propellers and a cabin for four passengers. However, this boat was still under construction when hostilities began in September 1939, at which time

In common with other Deutsche Lufthansa long-range seaplanes, the Do 26 was designed for the taxing demands of catapult launches from specially equipped tenders. This is the V1.

Above: The Do 26 V1 'Seeadler' underwent route-proving trials across the South Atlantic in the hands of Deutsche Lufthansa, and proved eminently suitable for the task.

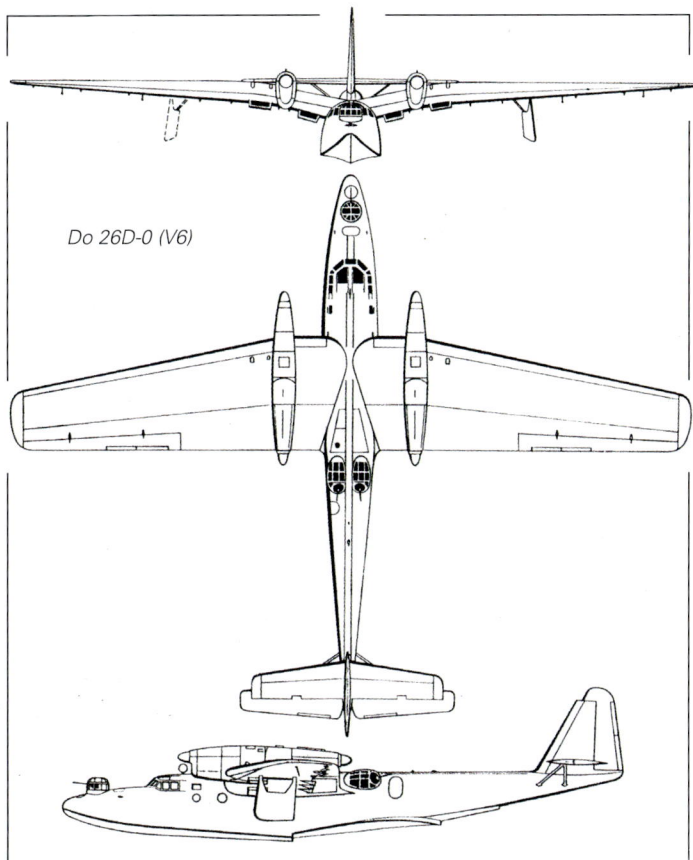

Do 26D-0 (V6)

Above: The Do 26 V2 'Seefalke' taxis on the water. To allow for transatlantic crossings against strong headwinds, the boats had a maximum fuel capacity offering very great still-air range.

The Do 26D – this is the V4 – had provision for a 20-mm cannon in a bow turret, and three rearward-firing machine-guns in a watertight ventral position and a blister fairing on each beam.

Dornier Do 26

the three remaining DLH boats had just reached the initial assembly stage.

The second batch of three flying-boats had been laid down as **Do 26C** series machines with the passenger capacity increased to eight persons, and bore the Versuchs numbers **Do 26 V4**, **Do 26 V5** and **Do 26 V6**. In view of the Do 26's exceptional range capability, the Reichsluftfahrtministerium now instructed Dornier to adapt all four of the boats still under construction for the twin tasks of long-range oceanic reconnaissance and transport. The conversion process involved the installation of military instrumentation and radio equipment, as well as the addition of defensive armament in the form of a Blohm und Voss BV 138B-type bow turret mounting a 20-mm MG 151 trainable cannon, lateral glazed blisters amidships each mounting a 7.9-mm (0.31-in) MG 15 trainable machine-gun, and a weapon of the same type firing aft from a water-tight position behind the rear hull step.

Limited military service

The four Do 26C boats, together with the Do 26 V1 and V2 that had been taken over from DLH and also modified to Do 26C standard, were allocated to the Trans-Ozean Staffel, formed at Travemünde in March 1940. Attached to Kampfgruppe zur besondere Verwendung 108, this unit, which participated in the 'Weserübung' operation to take Denmark and Norway from April 1940, was intended to fulfil both the reconnaissance and transport tasks, but during the Norwegian campaign the Do 26s were confined largely to the latter role, operating into and out of the narrow fjords along Norway's western coastline on troop transportation and re-supply missions.

On 8 May 1940 the V2 was shot down in a fight with Royal Navy Blackburn Skuas, while on 28 May 1940, Hawker Hurricane single-engined fighters of No. 46 (F) Squadron encountered the V1 and V3 at moorings at Sildvik in the Rombaksfjord. Both flying-boats were destroyed. With the completion of the occupation of Norway, the three surviving Do 26s were withdrawn to France in August, the Trans-Ozean Staffel operating from Brest-Hourtin as part of Marinegruppe West until February 1941. During this period the V5 was lost on 16 November 1940, having been launched from the tender *Friesenland*. The Trans-Ozean Staffel and its two remaining Do 26s were absorbed into the Stab/Küstenfliegergruppe 406 at Brest-Sud. The fate of the V4 and V6 is unknown, although both were at Travemünde with the trials unit as late as 1944.

Dornier Do 26C-0 (V6) specification
Type: long-range maritime reconnaissance and transport flying-boat
Powerplant: four Junkers Jumo 205D liquid-cooled six-cylinder vertical opposed-piston compression-ignition two-stroke engines each rated at 656 kW (880 hp) for take-off
Performance: maximum speed 325 km/h (202 mph) at 2600 m (8,530 ft); 295 km/h (183 mph) at sea level; maximum cruising speed 305 km/h (190 mph) at optimum altitude; long-range cruising speed 257 km/h (160 mph) at optimum altitude; normal range 4800 km (2,983 miles); maximum range 7100 km (4,412 miles); climb to 1000 m (3,280 ft) in 8 minutes 12 seconds, to 2000 m (6,560 ft) in 16 minutes 30 seconds; service ceiling 4500 m (14,765 ft)
Weights: empty 11300 kg (24,912 lb); normal loaded 20965 kg (46,217 lb); maximum overload 22500 kg (49,603 lb)
Dimensions: wingspan 30.00 m (98 ft 5⅛ in); length 24.60 m (80 ft 8½ in); height 6.85 m (22 ft 5¾ in); wing area 120.00 m² (1,291.67 sq ft)
Armament: one 20-mm MG 151 trainable cannon in bow turret, one 7.9-mm (0.31-in) MG 15 trainable machine-gun firing aft from each of two lateral amidships blisters, and one 7.9-mm (0.31-in) MG 15 trainable machine-gun firing aft from position behind rear planing bottom step

Above: A Do 26D seen at speed on the water reveals the rationale for the upward inclination of the pusher propellers, a feature designed to keep the propellers' lower arcs clear of the spray rising upward and outward from the hull.

Radically different from earlier Dornier flying boats as it had neither sponsons nor a parasol wing, the Do 26 was a thoroughbred machine, seen here in the form of the Do 26 V4 wearing the codes of the Trans-Ozean Staffel while assigned to KGr.z.b.V. 108. This aircraft was one of two to survive service with the unit in Norway and France.

Dornier Do 215

The Do 215 was developed as the export counterpart of the Do 17, but in fact was operated only by Germany and Hungary. The type was a little better than the Do 17, and operated primarily as a reconnaissance bomber with a glazed nose and, later, as a radar-equipped night fighter with a 'solid' armament-carrying nose.

The interest aroused in the Do 17 in July 1937 by its success at Zürich was renewed in 1938 by the debut of the improved Do 17Z, and at an early stage of the new model's development Yugoslavia began to consider it as a potential production successor to the Do 17K for which the Državna Fabrika Aviona (State Aircraft Factory) was in the process of tooling up. Dornier obtained permission to solicit export orders for the Do 17Z and, although the model to be offered on the export market was in effect identical to that manufactured for the Luftwaffe, except for equipment, the RLM imposed a new type designation on export aircraft.

A pre-production Do 17Z-0 was given the civil registration D-AIIB, and served as the **Do 215 V1** demonstration machine. In view of the interest displayed by Yugoslavia, a second Do 17Z-0 airframe was re-engined with a pair of Gnome-Rhône 14N-1/2 air-cooled 14-cylinder radial engines in place of the Bramo 323A-1 Fafnir air-cooled nine-cylinder radial engines to become the **Do 215 V2**, which was demonstrated to the Royal Yugoslav air force. However, the Do 215 V2 did not offer a sufficient performance advance over the Do 17K already in production in Yugoslavia, and therefore a third airframe was allocated to the Do 215 development programme, and this **Do 215 V3** was powered by two Daimler-Benz DB 601A liquid-cooled inverted V-12 engines each rated at 802 kW (1,075 hp) for take-off. Demonstrated during the late spring of 1939, the Do 215 V3 offered a noteworthy improvement in performance.

Foreign orders

The Do 215 V3 was demonstrated to several foreign missions and, in the autumn of 1939, after the French government had cancelled a Swedish contract for the Breguet Bre.694, the Swedish government placed an order with Dornier for 18 **Do 215A-1** bombers, these being essentially similar to the Do 215 V3 and carrying a crew of four and a 1000-kg (2,205-lb) bomb load. Production of the Do 215A-1 against the Swedish contract began late in 1939, but before the first delivery could be effected an embargo was placed on the export of the bomber, which was adapted on the production line for long-range reconnaissance tasks with the Luftwaffe as the **Do 215B-0** and **Do 215B-1**. These aircraft reached the Luftwaffe in January and February 1940, and were promptly issued to 3.(Fern) Aufkl.St./Ob.d.L., one of the Staffeln of the reconnaissance Gruppe attached to the Oberbefehlshaber der Luftwaffe. This unit was operating from Stavanger, Norway, shortly after the airfield's capture in April 1940, with 13 Do 215B-0 and Do 215B-1 aircraft and three He 111s on strength.

Above: The Do 215 V1 (D-AIIB) was originally a Do 17Z-0.

The most obvious difference between the production Do 215 and the Do 17 from which it was derived was the later type's Daimler-Benz 601A liquid-cooled engines; these were installed in boxy nacelles with a deep chin intake.

The revised powerplant offered the Do 215 better performance than the Do 17. The bomb load could not be increased, however, so the Do215 series was most gainfully employed in the reconnaissance bomber role, most especially for the Luftwaffe high command.

The first two prototypes of the Do 215 retained an air-cooled radial powerplant, as in the Do 17, in the form of the Bramo 323 Fafnir and Gnome-Rhône 14N, respectively.

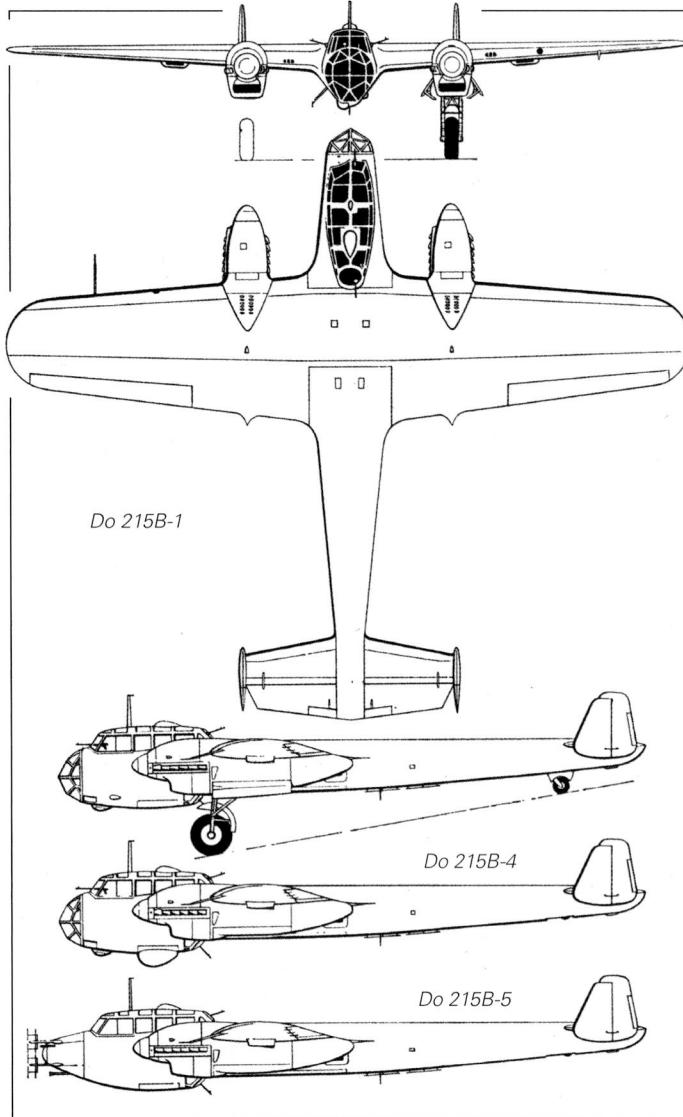

Do 215B-1

Do 215B-4

Do 215B-5

Below: The Do 215B-1 began life on the production line as a Do 215A-1 bomber for the Swedish air force, but was completed in this form as a long-range reconnaissance machine for service with the Aufklärungsgruppe/Ob.d.L.

By this time, Dornier had been ordered to continue Do 215 production for the Luftwaffe, and in March 1940 began delivery of the **Do 215B-4**. This differed from the Do 215B-l in its camera equipment, with an Rb 50/30 camera mounted beneath the lower gun position and an Rb 20/30 camera installed in the crew entry hatch. For combined bombing and reconnaissance missions five 50-kg (110-lb) bombs were normally carried, but up to 10 such bombs could be carried on short-range missions, and for long-range and ferry missions the two 775-litre (170.5- Imp gal) standard fuel tanks in the wing between the fuselage and engine nacelles could be augmented by a 900-litre (198-Imp gal) auxiliary tank in the bomb bay. Defensive armament comprised two 7.9-mm (0.31-in) MG 15 forward-firing machine-guns, two similar weapons firing to port and starboard from the rear of the cockpit, and a further pair of these guns firing aft from above and below the fuselage. The designation Do 215B-2 had been allocated to a pure bomber variant that was not proceeded with, while **Do 215B-3** was the designation applied to the two examples supplied early in 1940 to the USSR under the Soviet-German agreement of August 1939.

By May 1940, all three Staffeln of the Aufkl.Gr./ Ob.d.L. had Do 215Bs on strength, 1.Staffel operating three Do 215Bs, two Bf 110Ds and seven He 111s, and 2. and 3. Staffeln both being equipped entirely with Do 215B, with 10 and 11 aircraft, respectively. Limited production was continued by Dornier until early 1941 when the 101st and last example left the assembly line. At that time, apart from 4./NJG 1, the only Luftwaffe unit operating the Do 215B was still the Aufkl.Gr./Ob.d.L., and the 1.Staffel was operating a mixture of Do 215B-4s and Do 217A-0s on long-range reconnaissance sorties, and the 2. and 3.Staffeln operated the Do 215B-4 alongside other types.

The successful conversion of the Do 17Z-3 for the night fighting role as the Do 17Z-10 Kauz II prompted, in the

The flight deck of a Do 215B had the pilot's seat and primary controls on the port side, with access to the nose compartment on the starboard side.

A rare Luftwaffe night-fighter, and one of the first equipped with FuG 202 Lichtenstein radar, the Do 215B-5 became operational in early 1941. This example was flown by Helmut Lent, Gruppenkommandeur of II/NJG 2, and a pioneer of airborne radar interception, from Leeuwarden during the summer of 1942.

late autumn of 1940, a similar conversion of the Do 215B-4 primarily for the nocturnal intruder role. The performance of the DB 601A-powered Do 215B was markedly superior to that of the BMW-Bramo 323-powered Do 17Z, and thus offered considerable advantages for both offensive and defensive night operations. Designated **Do 215B-5** and known as the **Kauz III**, the converted aircraft began to enter service late in 1940 with 4./NJG 1 at Leeuwarden, this unit becoming part of II/NJG 2 in late 1941. In October 1942 the Gruppe became IV/NJG 1, with a few Do 215B-5s still assigned.

Night-fighter equipment

The Do 215B-5 used a nose cone similar to that of the Do 17Z-10 (this mounted four 7.9-mm (0.31-in) MG 17 machine-guns and two 20-mm MG FF cannon) plus the infra-red sensor for the Spanner-Anlage, with the Q-Rohr screen in the cockpit. The Spanner-Anlage had limited operational capability, its range being short and its reliability poor. Fortunately for the Nachtjagdflieger, Telefunken had designed a radar set of a size suiting it for installation in a twin-engined night fighter, this being known as Lichtenstein-Gerät. Working on a 490-megacycle frequency, it had a minimum range of 200 m (220 yards) and a maximum range of 4000 m (4,375 yards), and provided useful direction-finding in azimuth and elevation by the use of a rotating phase switch that actuated the different antennas in rapid succession.

This radar unit underwent its first flight trials in July 1939, and as a result of lack of interest on the part of the Technisches Amt, it was not until July two years later that a pre-production FuG 202 Lichtenstein BC set was mounted in a Do 215B-5 of 4./NJG 1 at Leeuwarden. The cumbersome Matratzen (mattress) aerial array reduced the speed of the Do 215B-5 by some 25 km/h (15½ mph), but on 9 August 1941 Oberleutnant Ludwig Becker, who nine months earlier had scored the first 'kill' of his Gruppe with a Spanner-Anlage-equipped Do 17Z-10, effected the first Lichtenstein interception, shooting down an RAF bomber. Becker scored additional 'kills' with the aid of the Lichtenstein on 15 and 23 August, 11 September and 2 October, the last being obtained at a range of 2800 m (3,060 yards), by which time the potential was considered proven, and preparations went ahead for a full-scale operational test, known as 'Adler', with Bf 110E-1/U1 fighters of I/NJG 1 at Venlo.

A full year elapsed before the whole of I/NJG 1 had

Obsolete Do 215B aircraft were used for test and instructional purposes. This machine has four-blade propellers.

Lichtenstein, and successful interceptions increased proportionately with the number of radar-equipped aircraft available. Production of the Do 215B had been finally phased out early in 1941 with 105 having been built. Twenty of the last Do 215B-4s on the assembly line were completed as Do 215B-5 night fighters, and they served in steadily dwindling numbers with NJG 1 until late 1943.

Early in 1942, four of the Luftwaffe's Do 215B-4s were transferred to the Hungarian Légierö to supplement the six He 111P-6s with the 1st Long-Range Reconnaissance Squadron operating on the Eastern Front from July until supplanted by the Junkers Ju 88. In Luftwaffe service, the Do 215B had virtually disappeared from first-line service by 1942, and survivors were mostly relegated to test roles.

Dornier Do 215B-1 specification
Type: four-seat medium reconnaissance-bomber
Powerplant: two Daimler-Benz DB 601Aa liquid-cooled inverted V-12 engines each rated at 820 kW (1,100 hp) for take-off
Performance: maximum speed 385 km/h (239 mph) at sea level, 465 km/h (289 mph) at 4000 m (13,125 ft), 470 km/h (292 mph) at 5000 m (16,405 ft); maximum cruising speed 410 km/h (255 mph) at 4000 m (13,125 ft); initial climb rate 364 m (1,195 ft) per minute; service ceiling 9000 m (29,530 ft); tactical radius with standard fuel and 1000-kg (2,205-lb) bomb load 380 km (236 miles); maximum range with 875-litre (192-lmp gal) auxiliary bomb bay tank 2445 km (1,519 miles)
Weights: empty equipped 5775 kg (12,731 lb); maximum loaded 8800 kg (19,400 lb)
Dimensions: wingspan 18.00 m (59 ft 0½ in); length 15.80 m (51 ft 9½ in); height 4.56 m (14 ft 11½ in); wing area 55.00 m² (592.01 sq ft)
Armament: (defensive) two 7.9-mm (0.31-in) MG 15 forward-firing machine-guns (either fixed or trainable), two 7.9-mm (0.31-in) MG 15 trainable machine-guns firing to port and starboard, and two 7.9-mm (0.3-in) MG 15 trainable aft-firing machine-guns, one above and one below the fuselage; (offensive) maximum internal bomb load 1000 kg (2,205 lb), typical loads including 20 50-kg (110-lb) SD 50 or four 250-kg (551-lb) SD 250 bombs

Above: The very close relationship between the Do 17 and Do 215 included the short-span wing of considerable thickness.

Dornier Do 217

The Do 217 was an extrapolation from the Do 17, and was a type from which much was expected. However, the type consistently failed to meet expectations, although some successes were achieved. As a bomber the Do 217 achieved little, but it was an important pioneer as a launch platform for early air-to-surface missiles.

The success achieved by the Do 17 bomber and reconnaissance aircraft led, in 1937, to Dornier's proposal for a scaled-up development to meet a requirement for a longer-ranged, heavier and more versatile warplane capable of lifting substantially larger offensive loads and delivering them in level or diving attack.

Classified as a heavy bomber, the project received the Reichsluftfahrtministerium designation **Do 217**. Prototypes were ordered in the early summer of 1937, and the structure of the new warplane was optimised for mass production, and to take air-cooled and liquid-cooled engines with equal facility. In general, the Do 217 followed the lines established by the Do 17 models then under development with a deepened forward fuselage, but apart from this strong external family resemblance the Do 217 was structurally and aerodynamically an entirely new design.

The Do 217 featured an all-metal two-spar wing with a stressed metal skin. Slotted ailerons were carried by the outer sections, these being linked with electrically operated split flaps on the inboard section. The structural design of the fuselage differed to a more marked degree from earlier Dornier practice. The fuselage was an all-metal structure built in three sections, of which the centre portion was integral with the wing centre section, and each section was joined to the next by 25 bolts passing through flanges riveted to the skin. All four (initially three) members of the crew were grouped together ahead of the wing leading edge, with pilot seated to port and bombardier to starboard, the radio operator behind the pilot, and the gunner, who was intended to operate the lower aft-firing trainable weapon, between the bombardier and the radio operator.

As well as using the Hs 293 missile and FX 1400 Fritz-X guided bomb operationally, the Do 217 was also used for development trials associated with other weapons.

One of the most novel features of the Do 217's design was the dive brake, which was attached to the extreme rear fuselage. This brake operated somewhat after the fashion of a parachute, or a four-ribbed umbrella, the 'ribs' when closed forming the four sides of the tail extension. The brake was operated by a threaded collar and spindle, the movement of the collar pulling the 'ribs' open against four short hinged struts. This air brake had been tested exhaustively on a Do 17M-1, and the trials had given promising results.

Powered by two Daimler-Benz DB 601A liquid-cooled inverted V-12 engines each rated at 802 kW (1,075 hp) for take-off, the **Do 217 V1** first prototype made its initial flight on 4 October 1938, and it was immediately apparent that the new bomber did not retain its predecessor's good handling. There was a marked tendency to swing during take-off, directional stability left much to be desired, and control response was sluggish. Seven days after its first flight

It was the complete reworking of the fuselage, introduced by the V9, which gave the Do 217 its distinctive appearance and respectable bomb load. The Do 217E was the first bomber version and in its later sub-variants could launch the Hs 293 guided missile and Fritz-X guided bomb, which were used to good effect against shipping, notably sinking the Italian battleship Roma on 9 September 1943.

the V1 was totally destroyed while engaged in single-engined low-altitude trials.

On 5 November 1938, Dornier flew the **Do 217 V2** second prototype. It was intended to fit DB 603 engines for high-altitude trials, but they did not materialise and the aircraft was later scrapped. The **Do 217 V3** flew on 25 February 1939, similar to the first prototype apart from having Junkers Jumo 211A liquid-cooled inverted V-12 engines rated at 708 kW (950 hp) for take-off. This prototype continued the flight development programme, including diving trials during which it was discovered that the tail brake was unsatisfactory. The brake proved unreliable in operation and exerted severe strain on the rear fuselage, resulting in the distortion of stringers and the buckling of the stressed skin.

In April 1939, another Jumo-engined prototype, the **Do 217 V4** (D-AMSD), joined the test programme, this being intended as the production prototype and the first aircraft of the series to carry armament, a single 7.9-mm (0.31-in) MG 15 trainable forward-firing machine-gun protruding through the starboard side of the nose glazing, and similar aft-firing weapons being mounted above and below the fuselage. The Do 217 V4 also had a dorsal strake in an attempt to rectify the stability problem, a redesigned tail brake, enlarged rudder trim tabs and more minor changes, and was delivered to the Erprobungsstelle Rechlin for official evaluation. In general, the Rechlin reports were unfavourable, highlighting poor stability and performance falling short of requirement. The Technisches Amt considered that the Do 217 V4 made inadequate provision for new systems and equipment then under development, and with fuel for extended-range operations insufficient space was available for large-calibre bombs, torpedoes or mines.

While the RLM evaluation was proceeding, Dornier was building further prototypes and starting construction of a batch of pre-production aircraft, and the next prototype to fly was a replacement for the original Do 217 V1 and thus designated **Do 217 V1E**, the suffix letter indicating Ersatz (replacement). The Do 217 V1E substituted rods and

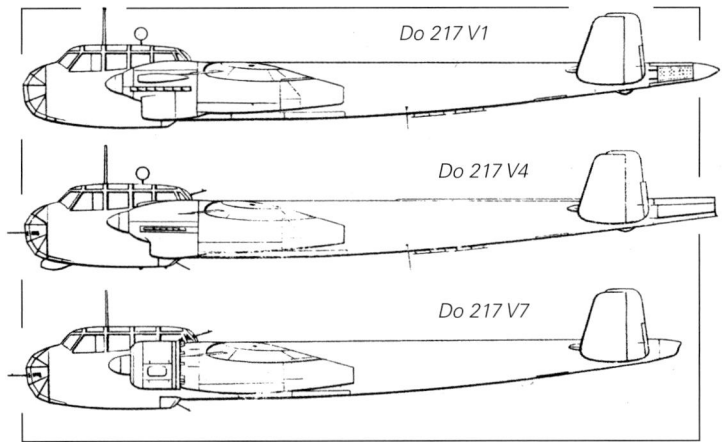

pulleys for the cable-type control runs of its predecessors, and fixed slots were attached to the leading edges of the fins, these effectively improving stability. The **Do 217 V5** and **Do 217 V6** were similar to the Do 217 V1E and were tested throughout the summer months of 1939, the latter with various underwing loads such as 900-litre (198-Imp gal) auxiliary fuel tanks. Both were completed with Jumo 211B-1s, but later re-engined with DB 601As. The test programme was frequently interrupted by mechanical failures, and as a result of the phenomenally high effective wing loading, by the standards then appertaining, of 308.6 kg/m² (63.2 lb/sq ft), the test pilots compared the Do 217's manoeuvrability very

Above: The family relationship between the Do 217, seen here in the form of the V4 prototype, and the smaller Do 17 and Do 215 is readily evident.

Left: The Do 217 V4 was the first prototype with defensive armament. It first flew in April 1939 at Friedrichshafen, before being transferred to Rechlin for trials. As well as trials of the airbrake, it also tested a chute system for short landings.

As originally designed, the Do 217 retained the slim, pencil-like fuselage of the Do 17 and Do 215, as displayed here by the Do 217 V4 fourth prototype. This was the first of the series to feature armament, and was powered by Jumo 211B engines.

Dornier Do 217

The requirement to which the Do 217 was created demanded a limited dive-bombing capability in addition to the standard type of level bombing. It was in response to the dive-bombing requirement that Dornier's design included a lengthened rear fuselage incorporating an umbrella-like dive brake which, as trials proved, served its primary purpose but was also unreliable and imposed very severe, indeed almost intolerable, stresses on the structure of the rear fuselage. Nevertheless, following trials of numerous configurations, the dive brake did make an appearance in the Do 217E-2 version, although it appears it was wired shut for most operations. Other versions were constructed with the dive brake as an option.

unfavourably with that of other current aircraft. Little further success had attended protracted trials with the tail-mounted air brake and the Technisches Amt finally agreed to the tempo- rary waiving of the dive-bombing requirement, permitting Dornier to concentrate on developing the Do 217 for the level bombing and armed anti-shipping reconnaissance tasks. It was stated categorically, though, that work on a suitable dive brake had to continue, and this would be incorporated in the bomber as soon as perfected. Before this decision was

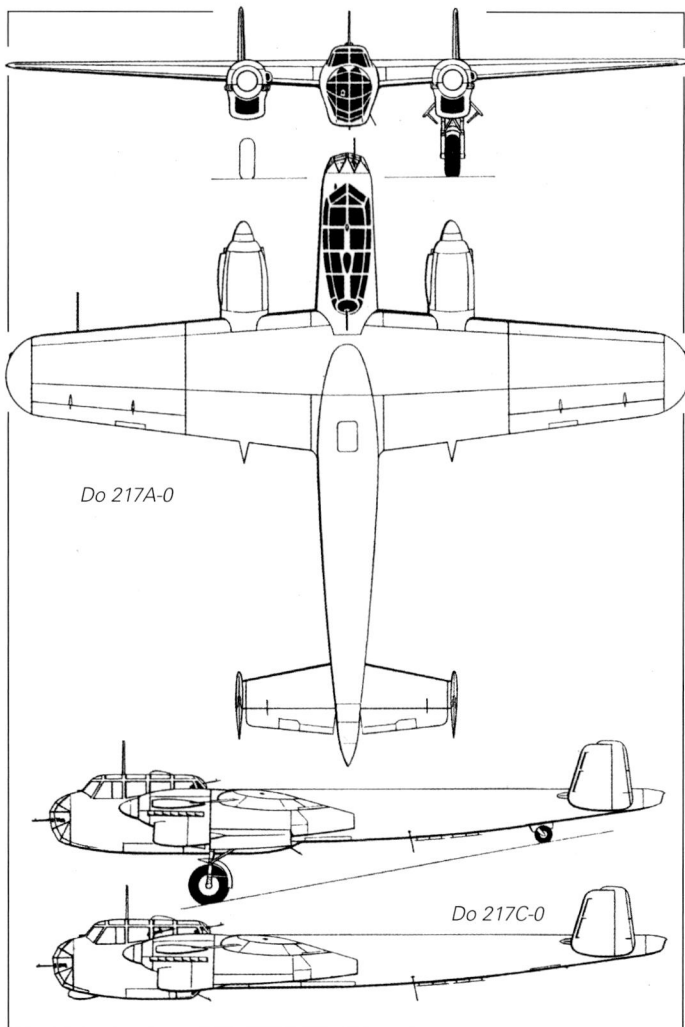

taken, Dornier had begun to look further afield for engines suitable for the Do 217 as it had become obvious that the bomber would never attain the specified performance with either the DB 601A or Jumo 211B. Early in 1939, BMW was engaged in the development of a compact, small–diam- eter, high-performance 14-cylinder radial air-cooled engine, the BMW 139, offering 1156 kW (1,550 hp) for take-off, and Dornier elected to power the **Do 217 V7** (D-ACBF) with the new engines, which were enclosed by a long-chord cowling and featured a cooling fan geared to propeller speed. The BMW 139-engined prototype featured the tail brake extension, but by the time the aircraft started flight trials in the late autumn of 1939, it had already been decided to abandon the BMW 139 in favour of the potentially more powerful BMW 801. The additional power promised by the new engine enabled the Dornier team to initiate the redesign of the fuselage of the bomber to accommodate substantially larger and heavier internal loads, and thus overcome one of the RLM's principal objections to the Do 217. BMW 801s were first tested in the **Do 217 V8** (D-AHJE).

Do 217A series

In the meantime, Dornier was engaged in completing a pre- production batch of six **Do 217A-0** long-range reconnais- sance aircraft and nine **Do 217C-0** bombers powered by the DB 601A. They were, in fact, preceded by a Jumo 211B- engined bomber prototype, the **Do 217C V4** (Werk Nr 690, CN+HL). The Do 217A-0 differed from the proto- types primarily in having the bulged lower contour of the forward fuselage extended aft to provide accommodation for two downward-facing cameras. Power was provided by the DB 601B, although two were subsequently given DB 601Ns. The defensive armament remained a trio of 7.9-mm (0.31-in) MG 15 trainable machine-guns, and the six aircraft were delivered to the Aufklärungsgruppe/Oberbefehlshaber der Luftwaffe (Kommando Rowehl), the special long- range reconnaissance Gruppe attached to the Luftwaffe high command, during the early spring of 1940. In the early winter of 1940-41, the Do 217A-0s, in concert with other aircraft operated by 1. and 3.Aufkl.St./Ob.d.L., flew clandestine photographic missions over Soviet territory in preparation for the imminent German invasion of the USSR, and also saw some use from bases in the Netherlands. A related project was the **Do 217B**, a high-altitude reconnaissance aircraft with dedicated film stowage, but this was not proceeded with.

Do 217A-0

Do 217C-0

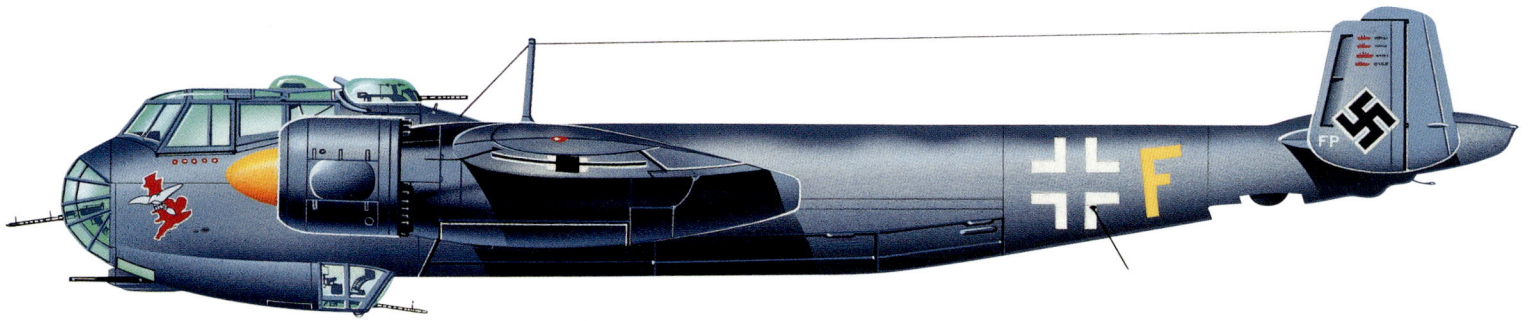

A maritime grey livery was adopted by the Do 217E-2 bombers used on anti-shipping missions by 6./KG 40, which operated with this type from Soesterberg until March 1943. This example has an anti-ship cannon under the left side of the nose.

The Do 217C-0 bomber was generally similar to the Do 217A-0 reconnaissance aircraft, but the lower contour of its fuselage reverted to that of the prototypes, provision was made for a 3000-kg (6,614-lb) offensive load, and the defensive armament was increased by the introduction of two gimbal-mounted 7.9-mm (0.31-in) MG 15 machine-guns firing laterally through the rear upper side windows and operated by the wireless operator. In addition, a 15-mm MG 151 cannon was mounted in the lower port side of the nose and fired by the pilot using a Revi 12 gun sight. As all effort was concentrated on the markedly improved **Do 217E** by the spring of 1940, no further examples of the Do 217C were manufactured, and the Do 217C V1 and four pre-production Do 217C-0 aircraft were relegated to the role of equipment and armament test beds.

Do 217E series

During the first weeks of 1940, a radically modified prototype, the **Do 217 V9**, was undergoing its initial trials. Powered by two BMW 801MA air-cooled 14-cylinder two-row radial engines, each rated at 1178 kW (1,580 hp) for take-off, this was the prototype for the Do 217E. The principal changes introduced by the Do 217 V9 were a substantial deepening of the fuselage throughout its length and the introduction of a four-man crew. The centre and rear fuselage were divided on the horizontal plane to within a short distance of the tail, the lower half of the fuselage forming the bomb bay and the remainder containing transverse bracing frames to support the weight of the bomb load, a fuel tank and dinghy stowage. The bomb bay itself was 4.52 m (14 ft 10 in) long, and a 1.73-m (68-in) extension was provided to enable a torpedo to be accommodated, the whole weapons bay being enclosed by three sets of doors. The BMW 801MA engines drove three-blade Schwarz propellers of wooden construction, and were supplied as 'power eggs', their mountings attaching by four ball-and-socket joints to the forward spar. All services were electrically powered, including undercarriage actuation and bomb bay door operation.

Preparations for quantity production continued throughout the early months of 1940, and the first **Do 217E-0/ Do 217E-1** pre-production bombers left the assembly line in the autumn, followed by the first examples of the production model before the end of the year. Essentially similar to the Do 217 V9, the Do 217E-1 was intended for level bombing and anti-shipping tasks, and was not initially fitted with the tail dive brake. The bomb bay provided accommodation for four 250-kg (551-lb), three 500-kg (1,102-lb) or one 1000-kg (2,205-lb) bombs. For strafing a single 15-mm MG 151 cannon, fired by the pilot, was mounted in the lower port side of the forward fuselage with 250 rounds, and the defensive armament comprised three 7.9-mm (0.31-in) MG 15 machine-guns on gimbal mountings.

Kampfgeschwader 40 was the first unit to take the Do 217E-1 into action, II/KG 40 forming on the type in May

Above: From the Do 217E onwards, the main production variants of the Do 217 family were powered by BMW 801 radial engines. In all variants, the high wing loading was an impediment to agility.

Above: Throughout the Do 217's early development and production, the Reichsluftfahrtministerium demanded that trials with a dive brake arrangement be concluded satisfactorily.

One of the important tasks demanded of the Do 217's forward-firing armament, in addition to defence against head-on fighter attack, was the suppression of light AA fire from ships.

Dornier Do 217

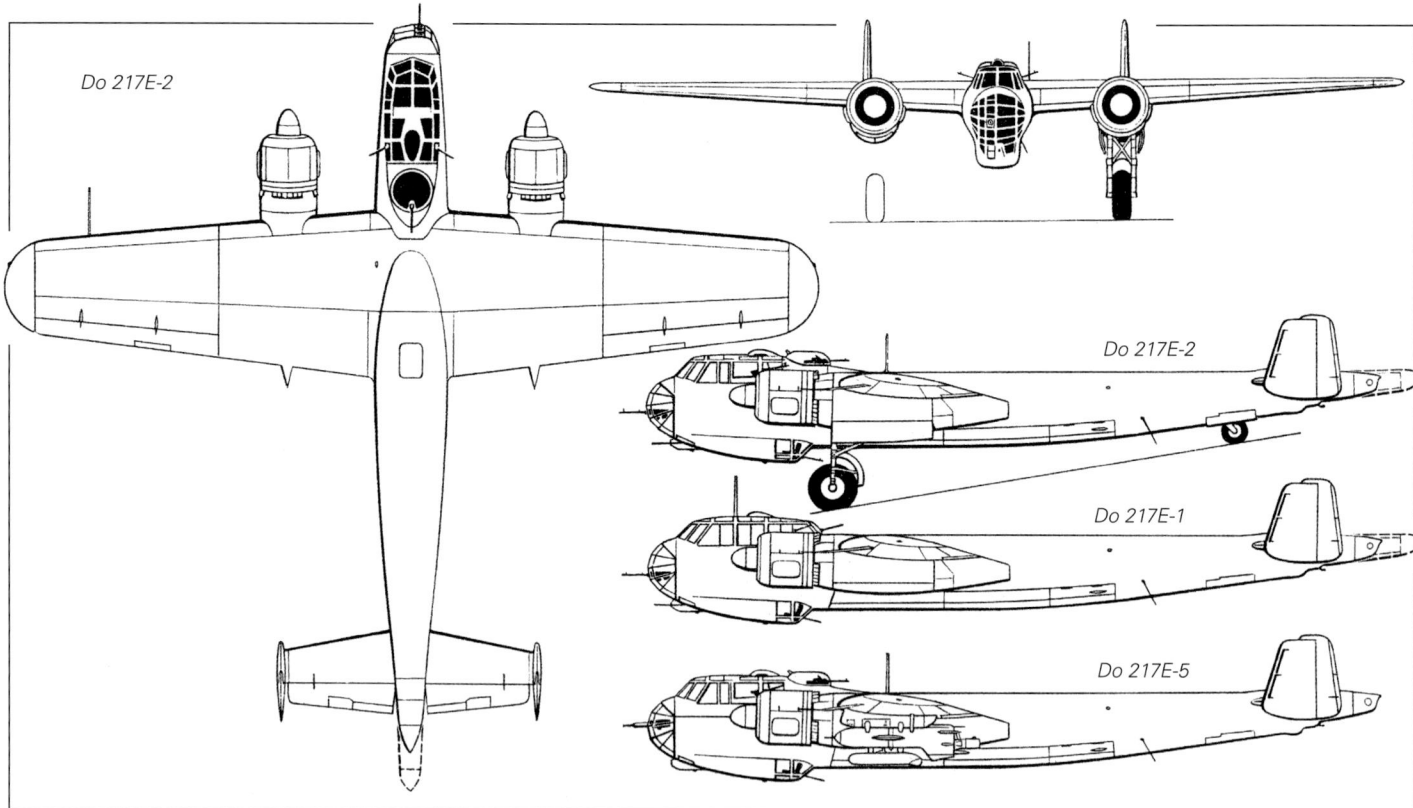

Do 217E-2

Do 217E-2

Do 217E-1

Do 217E-5

Above: The Do 217 V7 was a prototype completed with the BMW 139 fan-cooled radial engine driving a four-blade propeller. Termination of this engine led to the adoption of the BMW 801 engine and a three-blade propeller.

The ETC 2000/XII carrier allowed Do 217 bombers so equipped to operate with the Hs 293 air-to-surface guided missile, most typically in the anti-ship role.

1941 for anti-shipping operations, which commenced from Cognac in July, before the Gruppe moved to Soesterberg in the Netherlands in September.

Although the Do 217E-1 proved relatively effective during early operations, experience dictated increases in both offensive and defensive armament, the provision of some armour protection for the crew, and other changes aimed at increasing the versatility of the basic aircraft.

Do 217E-3 variant

These modifications led to a change in designation to **Do 217E-3**. A 20-mm MG FF trainable cannon was installed in the lower starboard side of the nose for use in anti-ship attacks, and two additional gimbal-mounted 7.9-mm (0.31-in) MG 15 machine-guns were added to fire laterally from the cockpit windows immediately aft of the pilot. The Do 217E-3 thus had an imposing array of no fewer than seven 7.9-mm (0.31-in) weapons but, in fact, only a comparatively light weight of fire could be brought to bear as five of the guns were intended to be fired by the radio-operator alone. Nevertheless, a wide field of fire was covered. Protection for the crew was provided by 5- and 8.5-mm plates on the rear cockpit cover, on the top of the fuselage immediately aft of the cockpit and beneath the lower gunner's position. The pilot's seat was armoured, and side plates were added at the lateral-firing gun positions. The aircraft's versatility was also substantially increased by the development of a series of standard Rüstsätze (field conversion sets) which were, for the most part, applicable to the Do 217E-3 and to other variants of the basic design. The most important of these Rüstsätze were as follows:

R1: special 1800 bomb carrier for a single 1800-kg (3,968-lb) SC 1800 bomb with annular fin (applicable to Do 217E-2 and E-3)

R2: two external racks under outer panels for a pair of 250-kg (551-lb) SC 250 bombs (applicable to Do 217E-2 and E-3)

Do 217E-4

This Do 217E-4 wears a typical two-tone splinter camouflage on the upper surfaces. The national insignia have been crudely painted over so that the white outlines do not show up during night operations.

Do 217E-2

For operations at night, and over the sea, the Wellenmüster wave pattern was applied over a mid-grey base, breaking up the aircraft's outline when viewed from above.

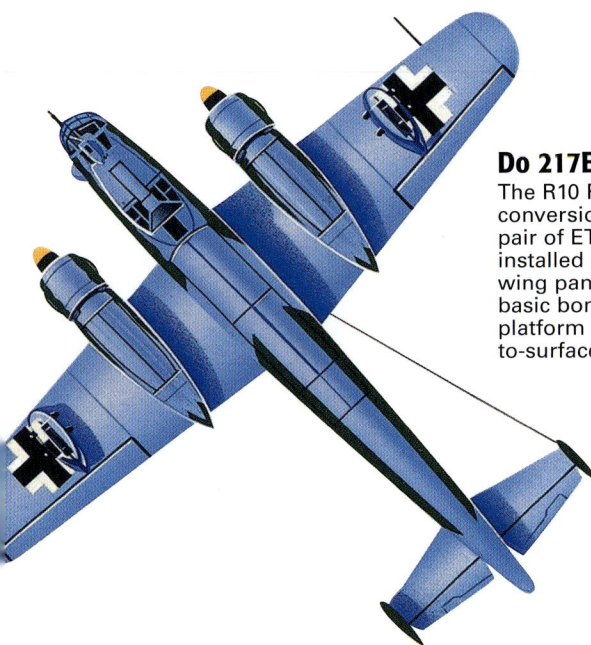

Do 217E-4/R10

The R10 Rüstsatz (field conversion set) comprised a pair of ETC 2000/XII carriers installed under the outer wing panels to turned the basic bomber into the launch platform for two Hs 293 air-to-surface missiles.

Do 217E-2

This was an aircraft (U5+LT) of KG 2 based in the German-occupied Netherlands during 1942. Note the yellow fuselage band and propeller spinners. On the fuselage sides the Geshwader code was obliterated with black paint, leaving only the individual letter (L) in black-outlined yellow.

R3: two internal racks in bomb bay for a total of 16 50-kg (110-lb) stores (applicable to Do 217E-2 and E-3)

R4: PVC 1006 carrier for single L5 torpedo (applicable to Do 217E-1, E-2, E-3, E-4 and K-1)

R5: one 30-mm MK 101 cannon in lower port side of forward fuselage (applicable to Do 217E-2 and E-3)

R6: bomb-bay camera installation (Do 217E-1, E-2, E-4, K-1 and M-1)

R7: four-man dinghy pack for installation above bomb bay, aft of wings (applicable to Do 217E-1, E-2, E-4 and K-1)

R8: auxiliary 750-litre (165-Imp gal) fuel tank for installation in the forward bomb bay (applicable to Do 217E-1)

R9: auxiliary 750-litre (165-Imp gal) fuel tank for installation in the aft bomb bay (applicable to Do 217E-1)

R10: two ETC 2000/XII carriers for Hs 293 stand-off weapons under outer wing panels (applicable to Do 217E-2, E-4 and K-1)

R11: same as R3 (applicable to Do 217E-5, J-1, K-1, M-1, M-9 and N-1)

R12: similar to R1; special PVC 1006B bomb carrier rated at 1,800 kg (3,968 lb) (applicable to Do 217E-4, K-1, M-1, M-3 and M-9)

R13: alternative auxiliary fuel tank of unspecified capacity in forward bomb bay (applicable to Do 217E-2, E-4 and K-1)

R14: alternative auxiliary fuel tank of unspecified capacity in aft bomb bay (applicable to Do 217E-2, E-4 and K-1)

R15: two ETC 2000/XII carriers for Hs 293 stand-off weapon under wing centre section between fuselage and engine nacelles (applicable to Do 217E-4 and K-2)

R16: provision for one exterior ETC 2000/XIIA carrier under either portion of inner wings for missile or long-range fuel tank (applicable to Do 217E-4, K and M)

R17: one auxiliary 1160-litre (255-Imp gal) fuel tank for installation in forward bomb bay (applicable to Do 217E-4 and K-2)

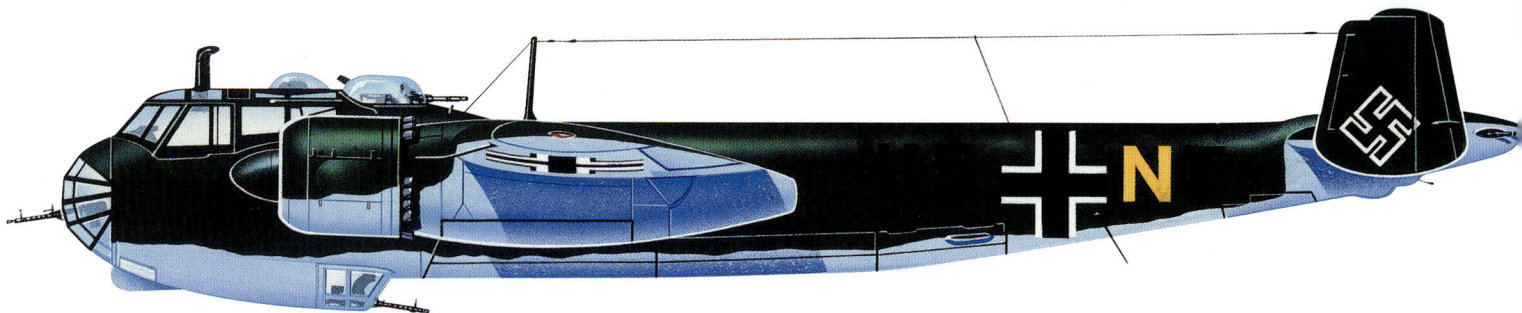

KG 2 'Holzhammer' was the only Geschwader ever wholly equipped with the Do 217. Originally beginning replacement of the Do 17Z in 1941, KG 2 pulled back from the Eastern Front and relocated to the Netherlands for bombing and anti-shipping attacks over the North Sea. This is a Do 217E-2/R19 of 9./KG 2 with two MG 81 machine-guns in the tailcone.

R19: frame in bomb compartment holding a rack for eight 50-kg (110-lb) stores (applicable to Do 217E-4, K-1 and M-1)

R20: four racks for 500/100/XI gun mounts, presumably tail-mounted (applicable to Do 217M-3)

R21: similar to R20, except two racks for 500/100/XI gun mounts, presumably tail-mounted (applicable to Do 217M-3 and M-9)

R22: one rack for a single 500/100/XI or 2000/XI gun mount (applicable to Do 217M-3)

R23: tail-mounted, four-gun weapons unit for two MG 81Z twin-guns (applicable to Do 217E-2, K-2, K-3 and M-9)

R25: Perlon tail braking chute (applicable to Do 217E-4, K-1, K-2, M-1, M-11 and P)

R25: alternative R25 designation applied to aircraft with attachment for 300-litre (66-Imp gal) or 900-litre (198-Imp gal) external fuel tanks, similar to R10 (applicable to Do 217E-4, K-1 and M-1)

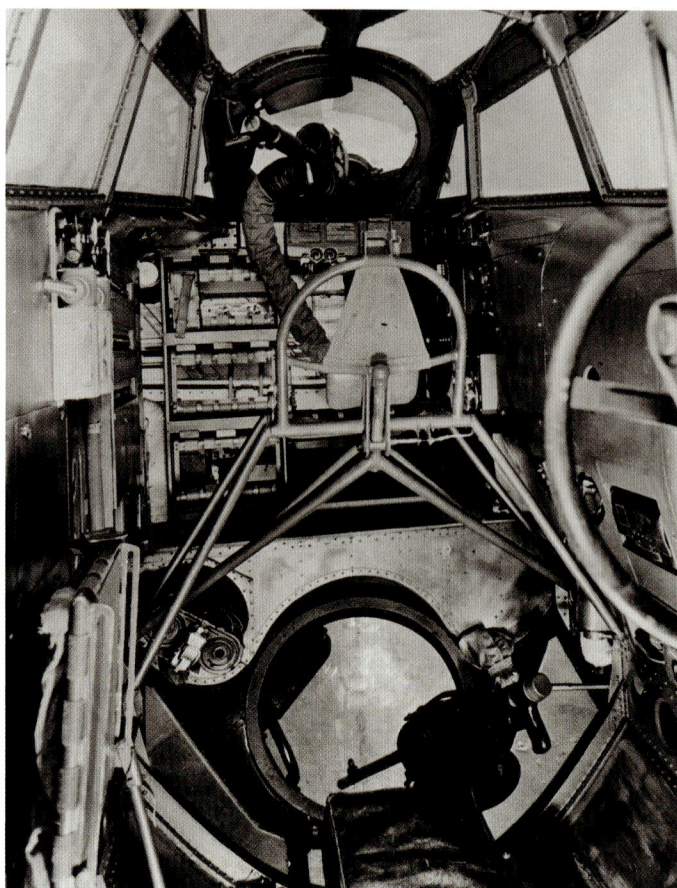

Above: The rear of a Do 217E-2's crew compartment, looking aft, shows the positions of the single 7.9-mm (0.31-in) MG 15 trainable dorsal and ventral machine-guns.

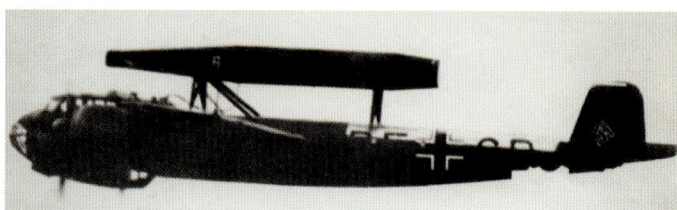

Above: This is a Do 217E-2 with gun armament including a 20-mm trainable cannon in the nose, and a 13-mm (0.51-in) MG 131 machine-gun in the electrically operated dorsal turret.

Above: This Do 217 has come to grief during a landing. With its high wing loading, the Do 217 had very poor gliding capability and a high sink rate after engine failure.

Taking over from a Do 17Z, this Do 217E-2 (RE+CD) was used to test various ramjet designs from Dr Eugen Sänger. This is a 500-mm diameter design tested in 1942.

There was nothing truly exceptional about the Do 217, which offered worthy performance wth a moderately heavy bomb load. The type was never very popular with its crews.

Despite teething troubles with the tail-mounted dive brake, the RLM was still determined that dive bombing should be added to the repertoire of the Do 217 and, in October 1940, the **Do 217 V11** prototype of a further variant of the bomber, the **Do 217E-2**, had started its flight trials, this being intended primarily for the dive-bombing role. In fact, although not fitted with the dive brake, the torsion rod extending from the cockpit to the tail of the fuselage, and to which the screw jack operating the dive brake was attached, had been retained by the Do 217E-1 for some inexplicable reason and was thus to be retained by the Do 217E-2. As fitted to the E-2, the dive brake embodied some improvements, but the most important modification was the introduction of an electrically operated dorsal turret housing one 13-mm (0.51-in) MG 131 trainable machine-gun with 500 rounds, this effectively improving defensive capability. Simultaneously, the 7.9-mm (0.31-in) MG 15 in the ventral step was replaced by an MG 131 with 1,000 rounds. Two MG 15s fired laterally from the cockpit, a similar weapon for the bombardier was provided in the extreme nose, and the fixed forward-firing 15-mm MG 151 cannon was replaced by a 20-mm MG FF. Power was supplied by two BMW 801ML radial engines that possessed ratings similar to those of the BMW 801MA engines of the Do 217E-1 and differed only in the type of propeller control fitted, the wooden Schwarz-type blades on the VDM hub being supplanted by metal blades and the propeller diameter being increased from 3.80 m (12 ft 5½ in) to 3.90 m (12 ft 9½ in).

The RLM gave high priority to the introduction of the Do 217E-2 on the Dornier assembly line and, by the spring of 1941, production of this model was running in parallel with that of the Do 217E-3. A small number of early production Do 217E-2s were issued to Stab/St.G.2, part of a Ju 87-equipped Geschwader, for operational evaluation during the early summer of 1941, but results proved unfavourable. Although the operating mechanism of the dive brake was now efficient, the rear fuselage still suffered severe strain and sometimes structural distortion during a dive in which the brake was fully extended, and on occasions the torsion rod actuating the brake was itself distorted, the brake

Above: The most important innovation pioneered on the Do 217E-2 was the electrically operated dorsal turret. This was a very neat, low-drag installation with one 13-mm (0.51-in) MG 131 machine-gun and 500 rounds of ammunition.

Below: The 12th pre-production Do 217E-0 (Werk Nr 1012) was employed on an assortment of development tasks as well as the establishment of the operational concepts appropriate for the forthcoming production aircraft.

Dornier Do 217

Missile armament
The missile armament of the Do 217E-5 was a pair of Hs 293A anti-ship missiles carried under the outer wing panels on ETC 2000/XII carriers. The missile was powered by a ventrally-mounted Walter 109-507B liquid-propellant rocket motor, which exhausted downward and to the rear. The guidance was based on radio command to line of sight, and the 295-kg (649-lb) warhead was delivered to a maximujm range of 5 km (3.1 miles).

Engine
The Do 217E-5 was powered by two BMW 801C air-cooled 14-cylinder two-row radial engines each rated at 1178 kW (1,580 hp) for take-off. Unlike the 801MA/ML engine of earlier aircraft, this unit was not delivered as a 'power egg' that had merely to be bolted to the airframe and have its fuel and control connections completed.

Missile warming
Trials revealed that the Hs 293A misisle suffered from icing problems, and Do 217E aircraft destined for the missile-carrier role had to be completed with hoses in their wing to deliver hot air from the engines to the missile carriers, so that the missile's internal temperature could be maintained at a constant level.

Dorsal armament
The Do 217E-5's electrically powered dorsal turret was a man unit fitted with a 13-mm (0.51-in) MG 131 machine-gu This belt-fed weapon weighe 16.6 kg (36.6 lb) and fired at rated of 900 rounds per minu the bullet leaving the muzzle 750 m (2,461 ft) per second a possessing an effective rang 1800 m (1,970 yards).

Gun armament
The Do 217E-5's gun armament comprised 20-mm MG FF fixed forward-firing cannon i lower port side of the nose, one 13-mm (0.5 MG 131 trainable machine-gun in the ventra step position, and three 7.9-mm (0.31-in) M trainable machine guns mounted individuall the nose and two beam positions.

Dornier Do 217E-5

6./Kampfgeschwader 100 based at Marseilles-Istres

The Geschwaderkommodore of KG 100 between May and September 1943 was Major Fritz Auffhammer, succeeded on 10 September 1943 by Oberstleutnant Bernhard Jope. The 6. Staffel was a component of KG 100's II Gruppe, whose Gruppenkommandeure in 1943 were Auffhammer, Major Franz Hollweg, Hauptmann Heinz Molinnus and Hauptmann Heinz-Emil Middermann. The Gruppe was based at Istres and Foggia during July 1943 under the control of the 2nd Fliegerdivision for the anti-ship role with the new Hs 293 air-to-surface guided missile. It then spent two months with Fliegerführer Atlantik at Cognac, before returning to Istres.

Missile guidance
The guidance package for the Hs 293A comprised the FuG 203b Kehl III transmitter for the missile's FuG 230b Strassburg receiver, with commands passed to the FuG 203b from the Knüppel joystick unit operated by the bombardier, who had to keep the misisle superimposed on his visual image of the target.

Crew accommodation
In the fashion typical of most German bombers of its period, the Do 217E-5 was operated by a four-man crew grouped closely together in the forward part of the fuselage in an extensively glazed two-level compartment.

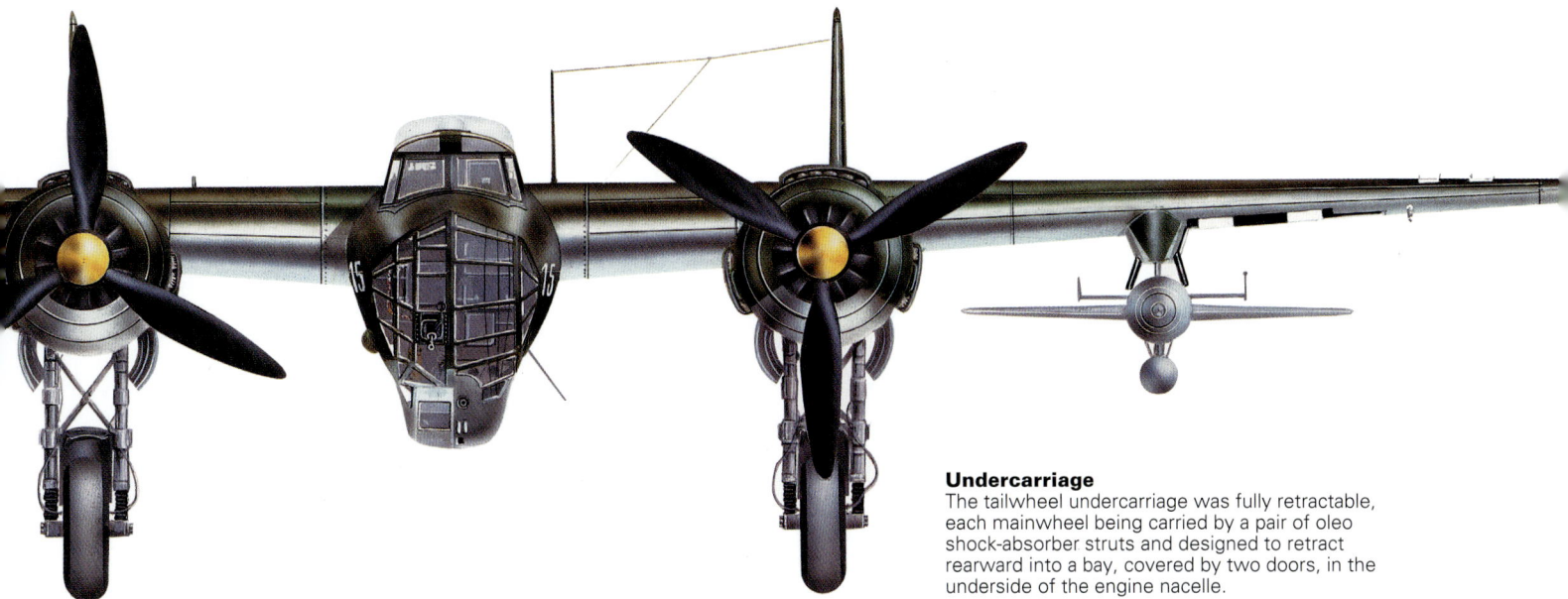

Undercarriage
The tailwheel undercarriage was fully retractable, each mainwheel being carried by a pair of oleo shock-absorber struts and designed to retract rearward into a bay, covered by two doors, in the underside of the engine nacelle.

Dornier Do 217

being jammed open after the aircraft had pulled out of the dive, and having to be jettisoned. However, because of its preoccupation with the concept of dive-bombing, and the accuracy of delivery against pinpoint targets that it offered, the Technisches Amt chose to ignore the lack of success that attended evaluation trials.

In an attempt to overcome the problem, during the summer of 1941, Dornier fitted the 36th production Do 217E-2 with new dive brakes that took the form of slotted plates which, mounted between the fuselage and the engine nacelles, turned through 90 degrees. A series of diving tests were carried out near Friedrichshafen, but after one test, the pilot levelled out at some 760 m (2,500 ft) and retracted the dive brakes, whereupon the interlinked elevator tabs should have returned to their normal flight position. However, the tabs jammed and the aircraft crashed. In the meantime, Dornier had been delivering the Do 217E-2 to service units with an alternative tail cone packed in the bomb bay. On arrival at their destination, Luftwaffe personnel had simply removed the tail brake and substituted the tail cone. By the late summer of 1941, the RLM admitted defeat, and all further attempts to employ the Do 217 in the dive-bombing role were abandoned.

Throughout 1941, deliveries of the Do 217E-2 and Do 217E-3 continued to the three Gruppen of Kampfgeschwader 2 which, by the autumn, were all based along the channel coast for operations against the UK and, in concert with II/KG 40, attacks on Allied shipping in the North Sea. The 20-mm MG FF cannon was useful for anti-shipping operations, and various minor modifications were introduced by forward maintenance units to improve operational effectiveness. By the end of 1941, approximately 300 Do 217E bombers had been delivered to the Luftwaffe. They included the pre-production aircraft and first few production Do 217E-1s completed in 1940, plus 100 Do 217E-3s, the remainder of the total being made up almost equally of Do 217E-1s and Do 217E-2s.

Late in 1941, the assembly lines had begun to switch from the Do 217E-2 to the **Do 217E-4**, which came into operational use late in 1942. The Do 217E-4 differed from its predecessor in only minor respects, having BMW 801C engines that, unlike the BMW 801MA and ML, were supplied as bare powerplants rather than as complete 'power eggs', but possessed similar ratings. The aircraft were fitted with the Kuto-Nase balloon-cable cutter in the wing leading edges. Around 70 late-production examples of this model were modified on the assembly line to **Do 217E-5** standard as parent aircraft for the Henschel Hs 293A stand-off missile. These aircraft were fitted with an ETC 2000/XII carrier under each outboard wing panel, a Telefunken FuG 203b Kehl III transmitter for the missile's FuG 230b Strassburg receiver, a Knüppel (joystick) control box manipulated by the bombardier for line-of-sight guidance, and the necessary warm air hoses in the wings to maintain the missile's interior temperature at a constant level. A number of Do 217E-5s were subsequently used by the Lehr und Erprobungskommando 36 at Garz, Usedom, on the Baltic Sea coast, this unit having the task of bringing the Hs 293 and FX 1400 missiles up to operational status and training personnel in their use, and others operated by II/KG 100 launched the first Hs 293As operationally against Allied destroyers in the Bay of Biscay on 25 August 1943.

Right: The grouping of the Do 217 crew in the forward fuselage offered good inter-communication, but left the entire crew vulnerable to a single AA hit or fighter attack. This is a Do 217E.

Below: A Do 217E-2 starts to run up its engines before a pre-delivery test flight. The E-2 standard added an MG 131 in an electrically operated dorsal turret behind the flight deck, and a weapon of the same type was installed in the ventral step.

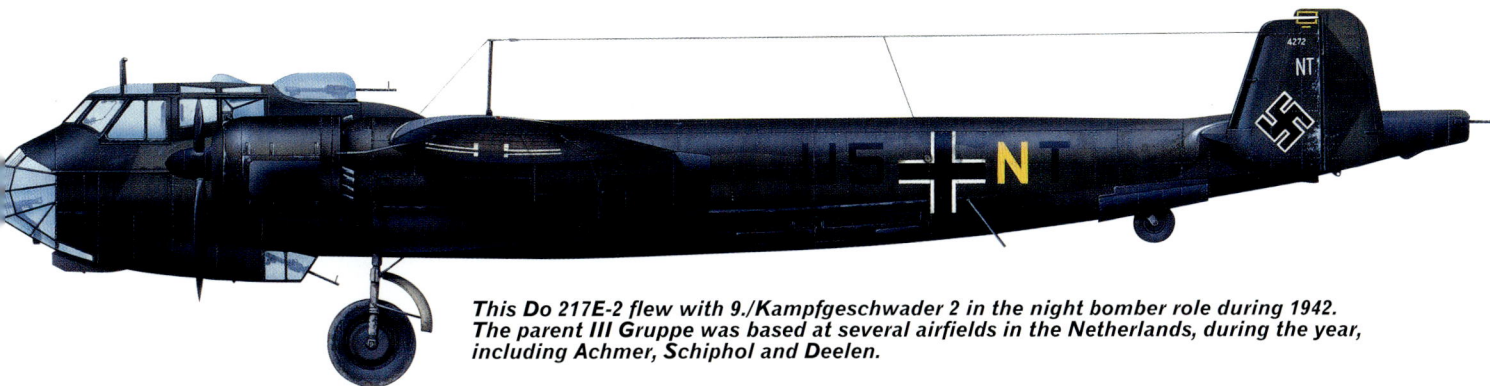

This Do 217E-2 flew with 9./Kampfgeschwader 2 in the night bomber role during 1942. The parent III Gruppe was based at several airfields in the Netherlands, during the year, including Achmer, Schiphol and Deelen.

Dornier Do 217E-2 specification

Type: four-seat heavy bomber
Powerplant: two BMW 801ML air-cooled 14-cylinder two-row radial engines each rated at 1178 kW (1,580 hp) for take-off and 1029 kW (1,380 hp) at 4600 m (15,0900 ft)
Performance: maximum speed 440 km/h (273 mph) at sea level, 515 km/h (320 mph) at 5200 m (17,060 ft); cruising speed with maximum internal bomb load 415 km/h (258 mph) at 5200 m (17,060 ft); economical cruising speed 395 km/h (245 mph) at optimum altitude; maximum range on standard internal fuel 2300 km (1,420 miles), with auxiliary fuel 2800 km (1,740 miles); initial climb rate with maximum internal bomb load 216 m (710 ft) per minute; service ceiling with maximum internal bomb load 7500 m (24,605 ft), without bomb load 9000 m (29,530 ft)
Weights: empty 8855 kg (19,522 lb); empty equipped 10535 kg (23,225 lb); normal loaded 10080 kg (33,070 lb); maximum overload 16465 kg (36,299 lb)
Dimensions: wingspan 19.00 m (62 ft 4 in); length 18.20 m (59 ft 8½ in); height 5.03 m (16 ft 6 in); wing area 57.00 m² (613.542 sq ft)
Armament: one 15-mm MG 151 fixed forward-firing cannon in lower port side of nose, one 13-mm (0.51-in) MG 131 machine-gun with 500 rounds in electrically operated dorsal turret, one 13-mm (0.31-in) MG 131 trainable machine-gun in ventral step with 1,000 rounds, one 7.9-mm (0.31-in) MG 15 trainable forward-firing machine-gun and two 7.9-mm (0.31-in) MG 15 trainable lateral-firing machine guns, plus (Do 211E-2/R19) two remotely controlled 7.9-mm (0.31-in) aft-firing MG 81 machine-guns in tail cone, and (offensive) maximum bomb load of 4000 kg (8,818 lb) including 2520 kg (5,555 lb) internally, and comprising typical internal loads of eight 250-kg (551-lb), four 500-kg (1,102-lb) or two 100-kg (2,205-lb) plus two 250-kg (551-lb) bombs

Do 217J and Do 217N

During the closing months of 1941 and the early months of 1942, the General der Nachtjagd steadily added links to the defensive chain that had become known as the 'Kammhuber Line'. This comprised a searchlight belt some 35 km (22 miles) in depth for illuminated interceptions and a closely integrated series of circular zones in which individual night fighters were vectored towards their targets by the Himmelbett system of ground control. By May 1942, Generalmajor Josef Kammhuber had at his disposal three Nachtjagdgeschwadern (NJG 1, 2 and 3) each with three Gruppen, and a fourth (NJG 4) of which two Gruppen had been activated.

RAF Bomber Command attacks, which had previously been little more than nuisance raids, were now beginning to mount in intensity. The slow, poorly defended bombers with which Bomber Command had entered World War II were giving place to more potent warplanes, such as the Avro Lancaster that had made its debut in German skies on the night of 10-11 March when No. 44 Squadron attacked Essen, which had also being the target two nights earlier when the Gee navigational and target-identification aid was used on a large scale for the first time. On the night of 10-11 April, Essen had been the recipient of the first 3629-kg (8,000-lb) bomb and, if there was still any lingering doubt concerning the vital importance of the Nachtjagd within the Oberkommando der Luftwaffe, this was to be dispelled on the night of 30-31 May, when Bomber Command launched Operation 'Millennium', the first 'Thousand Bomber' raid, against Cologne.

The Ju 88 was generally conceded to be the best type available for night fighting: it was a sturdy, stable warplane with potent fixed forward-firing armament and excellent performance that included the endurance necessary for standing patrols. Equipped with FuG 202 Lichtenstein BC or the

Above: The Do 217E-4 began to supplant the Do 217E-2 in production late in 1941, but differed only in powerplant details and balloon cable cutters in the wing's leading edge.

Above: During operations the bomb-aimer moved into the aircraft's nose to operate the bomb release mechanism, while the engineer/ventral gunner moved into the rear of the lower gondola.

Fixed slots in the leading edges of the Do 217's fins helped to cure the yawing tendency evident in the prototypes, and thus improved the aircraft's stability for bombing.

All three units of the Do 217E's undercarriage were fully retractable into door-covered bays in the undersides of the engine nacelles and rear fuselage.

Dornier Do 217

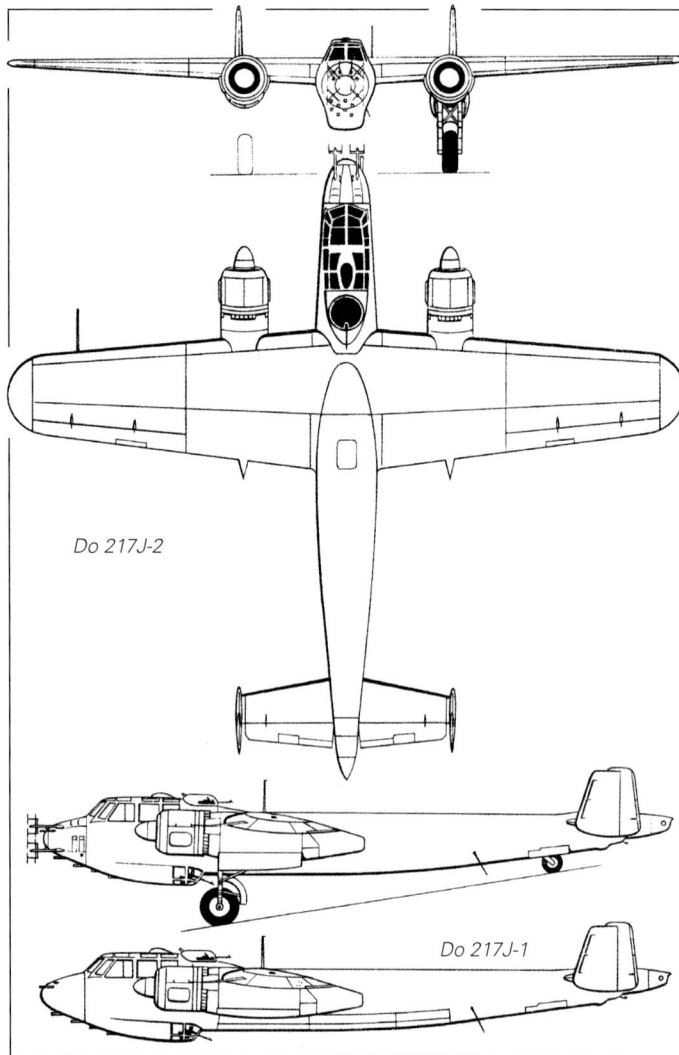

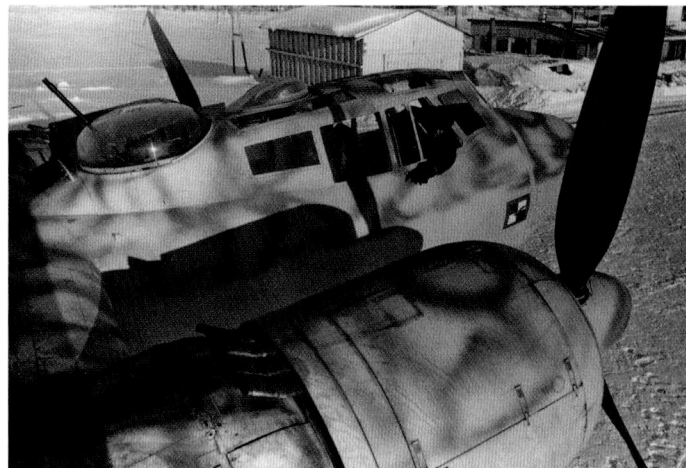

Do 217J-2

Do 217J-1

The **EDL** 131 powered dorsal turret and 13-mm (0.51-in) machine-gun of later **Do** 217E bombers did much to enhance the type's defensive capability. The gun was supplied with 500 rounds.

simplified FuG 212 Lichtenstein C radar, the Ju 88C-6b, which attained service status at the beginning of 1942, was unquestionably the most capable night fighter available to the Luftwaffe. Unfortunately for the Nachtjagdflieger, of the 2,619 Ju 88s accepted by the Luftwaffe during 1941, only 66 were completed as fighters and the bulk of them went to the Zerstörergeschwadern. The situation barely improved in 1942 when the 3,094 Ju 88s accepted included a mere 257 fighters, few of which mounted Lichtenstein for nocturnal operations.

Thus the Bf 110, by no means ideal for night fighting, had to soldier on as the backbone of the Nachtjagdflieger, and even this warplane was in short supply.

In the circumstances, and in view of the fair measure of success that had attended the conversion of the Do 17Z and Do 215 bombers as night fighters, the suggestion that the Do 217E-2 heavy bomber should, despite its size and weight, be adapted as an interim night fighter was approved readily by the Technisches Amt of the RLM, as was also the parallel proposal that the forthcoming DB 603A-powered version of the bomber should be developed in both bomber and night fighter forms from the outset. Consequently, within six months of II/KG 40 taking the Do 217E-1 into action for the first time in March 1941, work had begun on a night fighter version of the Do 217E-2 bomber under the designation **Do 217J-1**, and the DB 603A-powered Do 217M bomber was being developed in parallel with its night fighter counterpart, the **Do 217N**.

The first Do 217J-1 night fighter conversion of the Do 217E-2 bomber had flown in January 1942. Intended for both the interceptor and intruder roles, the Do 217J-1 differed from the standard bomber only in having a redesigned nose cone in which was mounted an armament of four 20-mm MG FF cannon and four 7.9-mm (0.31-in) MG 17 machine-guns. The aft bomb bay was retained, this accommodating up to eight 50-kg (110-lb) SC 50X bombs, the forward bomb bay having provision for a 1160-litre (255-Imp gal) auxiliary tank supplementing the standard internal fuel capacity of 2960 litres (651 Imp gal).

The Rüstsatz 23 twin MG 81Z four-gun tail 'stinger' installation was of dubious value, its sighting system including a periscope that presented an inverted image to the pilot. He then had to hold the aircraft steady before firing the guns at an attacker that was directly behind the Do 217, at a time when evasive manoeuvring may have been a more prudent means of defence. Although the kit may not have caused much damage to Allied aircraft, a warning burst was certainly a useful deterrent.

The electrically operated upper turret mounting a 13-mm (0.51-in) MG 131 machine-gun with 500 rounds and the MG 131 trainable aft-firing machine gun in the ventral step with 1,000 rounds were retained.

Deliveries of the Do 217J-1 began early in 1942, the first aircraft for operational evaluation by II/NJG 1 reaching Gilze-Rijen at the beginning of March 1942. The 4.Staffel pilots to whom the Do 217J-ls were entrusted compared the aircraft unfavourably with the Do 215B-5 from which they had converted, considering the poor manoeuvrability and inadequate reserve of speed to be major disadvantages in the helle Nachtjagd searchlight-illuminated system of night fighting to which the type was confined by its lack of intercept radar. Furthermore, the high wing loading was disliked as it was considered to restrict the number of night fighter fields from which the Do 217J-1 could operate with safety.

Most of the Do 217J-1s were relegated to the training role during the summer of 1942, the availability of FuG 202 Lichtenstein BC radar permitting production to switch to the **Do 217J-2**. Apart from the installation of the Lichtenstein with its Matratzen aerial array on the nose, and the deletion of the aft bomb bay, the Do 217J-2 was similar to its predecessor. Despite its admitted shortcomings in speed and manoeuvrability, it was considered an adequate nocturnal interceptor, and although the rate-of-fire and ballistic trajectory of its drum-fed MG FF cannon left something to be desired, the battery of four of these weapons proved extremely effective. During firing trials, the four MG FF cannon of one Do 217J-2 fired 125,000 shells without a single stoppage. Weighing 9350 kg (20,616 lb) in empty equipped and 13180 kg (29,059 lb) loaded conditions, it was powered by two BMW 801ML engines, that provided a speed of 490 km/h (304 mph) at 5500 m (18,045 ft).

Do 217 night fighter operations

The first recorded operation of the Do 217 night fighter took place on the night of 29-30 May 1943, when Bomber Command attacked Wuppertal. Some 150 bombers were reported in II/NJG l's sector, the Gruppe putting up 13 Bf 110Es and three Do 217J-2s that claimed 11 'kills', one of the Do 217J-2s being attacked and destroyed by an RAF intruder during take-off, but by this time the Do 217J-2 and its DB 603A-powered equivalent, the Do 217N, were serving with several Nachtjagdgeschwadern, although no single Gruppe was ever to be equipped wholly with this type, which usually operated in concert with Bf 110s in mixed units.

The Do 217N had flown for the first time on 31 July 1942, and apart from its engines and the retention of the aft bomb bay, the **Do 217N-1** initial model was similar to the

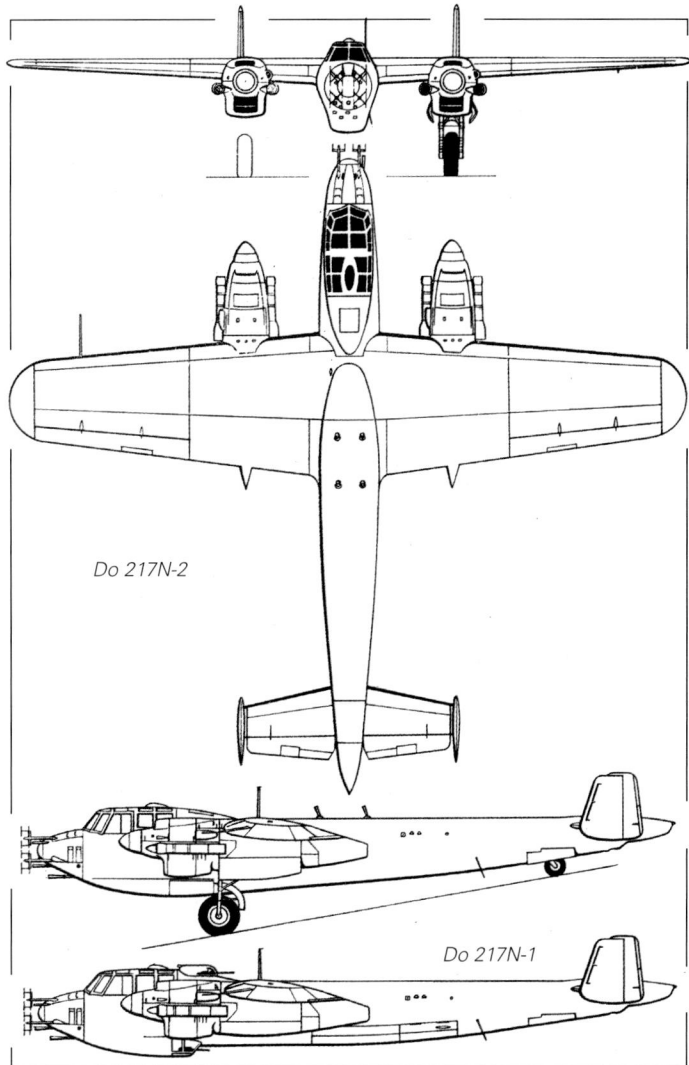

Do 217N-2

Do 217N-1

Do 217J-2 and began to reach the Nachtjagdgeschwadern during the winter of 1942-43. At first, armament remained the same as that of the early night fighter models, and the Do 217N-1 was delivered with either FuG 202 or FuG 212 Lichtenstein intercept radar, other equipment including FuG 25 that provided the Flak batteries with identification and also acted as a direction indicator for the Himmelbett controller, FuG 101 radio altimeter, and FuG 10 HF communications receiver/transmitter. From April 1943, by which time the RAF was jamming radio communications between the night fighters and the Himmelbett stations, FuG 16 VHF radio, operating over a part of the spectrum not covered by

Featuring a redesigned nose packed with guns, the Do 217J was the night fighter/intruder version of the Do 217E. This example, a Do 217J-2, differed from the Do 217J-1 by having radar installed and no rear bomb bay. Do 217Js often operated in concert with Messerschmitt Bf 110s, whose manoeuvrability and speed were greater than those of the Do 217.

Dornier Do 217

Radar
Do 217 night-fighters were routinely fitted with FuG 202 or 212 Lichtenstein C-1 radar, with a characteristic Matratzen array. Later aircraft also had the FuG 220 Lichtenstein SN-2, but retained the earlier set to cover the shortfall in minimum range of the FuG 220.

Powerplant
Late production Do 217s were available with two powerplants, either the BMW 801 radial (Do 217J and K) or the Daimler-Benz DB 603A V-12 (Do 217M and N). The V-12 engine had a higher rating, but did not fully address the lack of power suffered by all Do 217s.

Markings
This aircraft wears typical night fighter markings, consisting of mottled light greys. It wears factory codes (used as radio call-signs) before delivery to an operational unit.

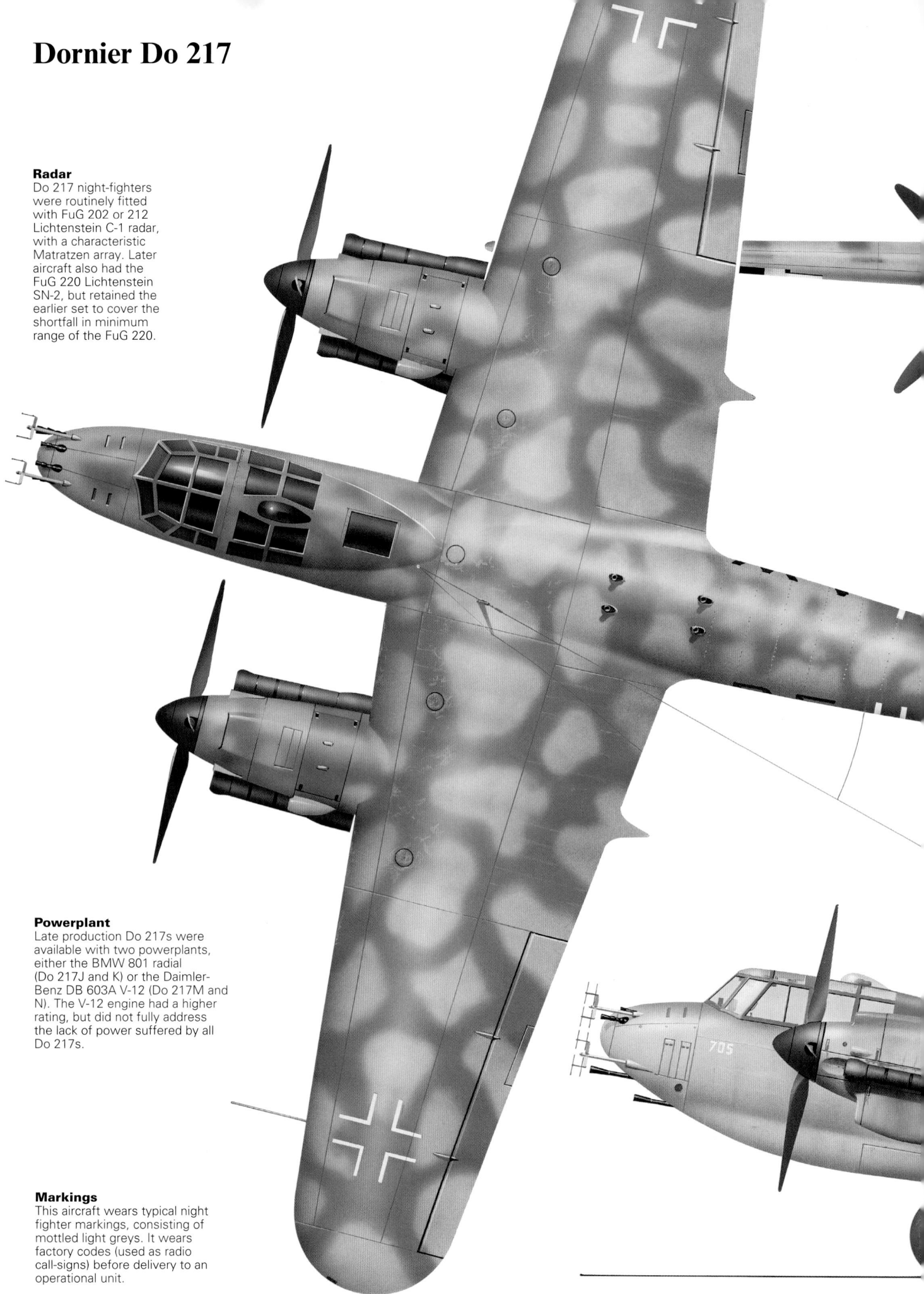

Radio equipment

The Do 217N carried an FuG 25 beacon that allowed the ground-based Himmelbett system controllers to identify the aircraft as friendly and provide guidance. An FuG 101 radio altimeter and FuG 10 HF communications were also fitted. When the RAF began jamming communications, the FuG 16 VHF radio was fitted.

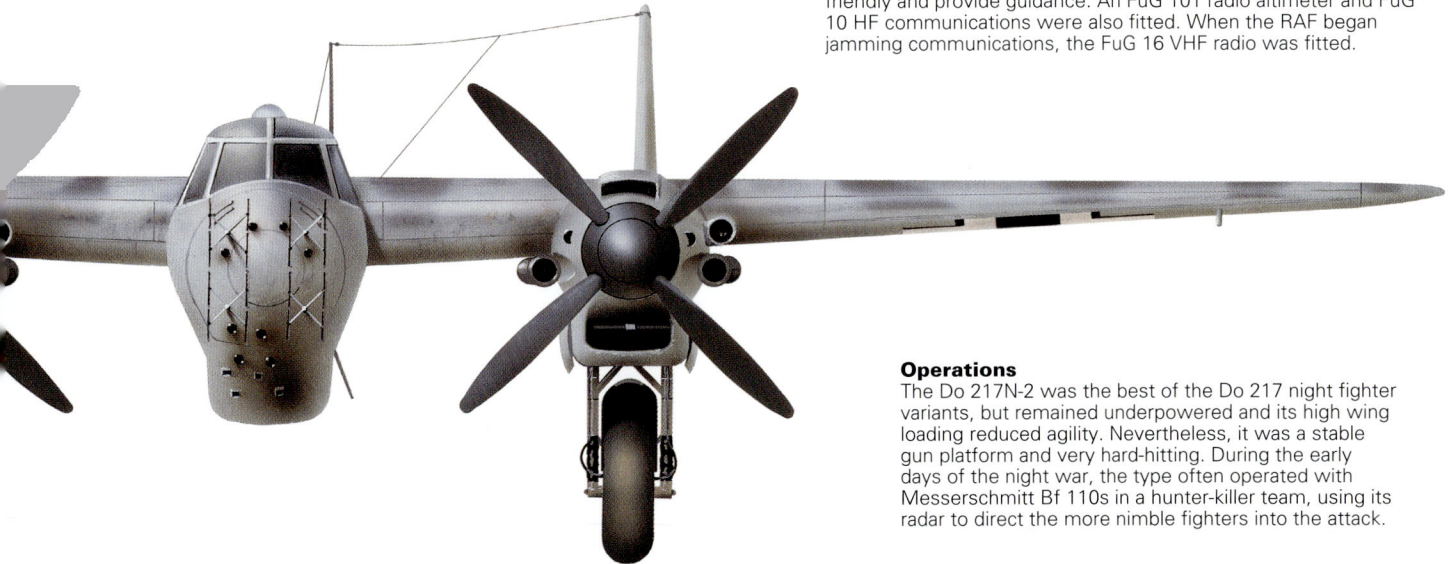

Operations

The Do 217N-2 was the best of the Do 217 night fighter variants, but remained underpowered and its high wing loading reduced agility. Nevertheless, it was a stable gun platform and very hard-hitting. During the early days of the night war, the type often operated with Messerschmitt Bf 110s in a hunter-killer team, using its radar to direct the more nimble fighters into the attack.

Dornier Do 217N-2/R22

Pre-delivery markings

In production from the spring of 1943 until late in that year, the Do 217N-2 embodied as standard all the production developments made to the N-1. Many aircraft were modified like this to Do 217N-2/R22 standard, with four cannon in a schräge Musik installation in the fuselage. As well as subsequently gaining Lichtenstein SN-2 radar, the Do 217N-2 also later featured the FuG 227 Flensburg set, which homed in on the emissions of the RAF's Monica tail-warning radar, and the FuG 350 Naxos tuned to H_2S bombing radar frequencies.

Armament

The Do 217N-2 dispensed with the rearward-firing armament (saving much weight), and relied on the nose armament of four machine-guns and four cannon in the nose, and the schräge Musik installation. The original MG FF cannon were very reliable, but were later replaced by MG 151/20s offering higher muzzle velocity and better rate of fire.

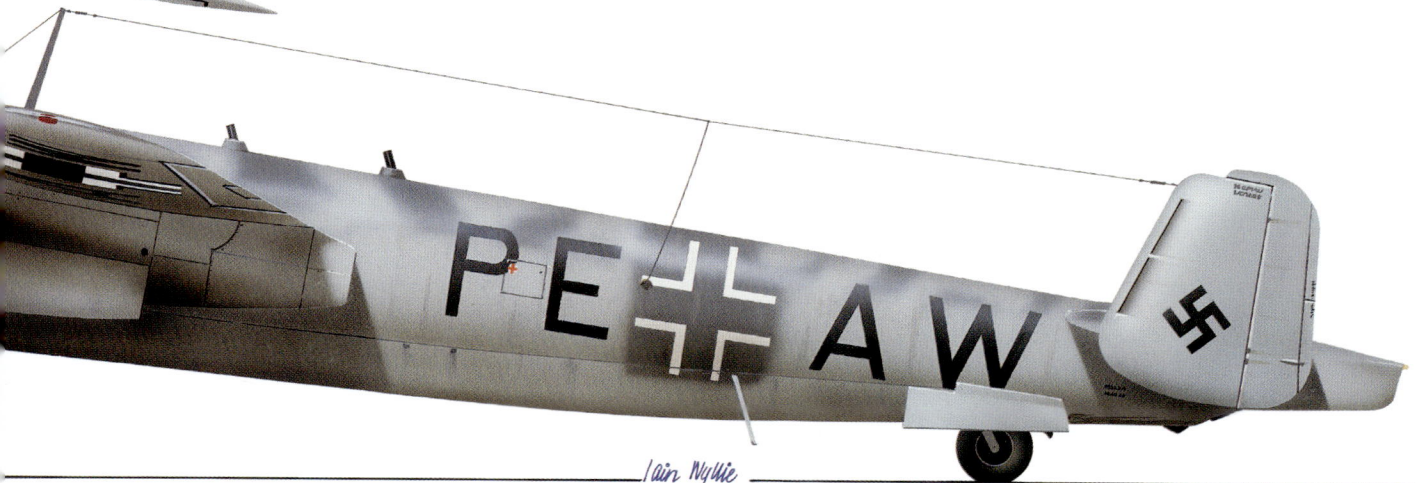

Iain Wyllie

Dornier Do 217

*The nose of a **Do 217J-2** displays the main equipment of the night fighter variants. Four **MG 17** machine-guns were mounted in the nose, with four **MG 151** 20-mm cannon beneath them. The Matratzen aerial array was for the **FuG 202** Lichtenstein BC or simplified **FuG 212** Lichtenstein C radar.*

The DB 603A engine fitted to the Do 217N addressed some of the performance shortfalls of the Do 217J, but the type remained underpowered and sluggish. This aircraft does not have the Matratzen antenna array fitted, but the mounting posts are present.

British jamming, was added, and to increase the weight of fire some aircraft had the battery of MG FF cannon replaced by a quartet of MG 151 cannon of the same calibre but offering a higher velocity and better trajectory. Simultaneously, the upper turret was removed, together with the aft-firing ventral position, the latter being covered by a long wooden fairing that marginally reduced aerodynamic drag. With these modifications, which were undertaken with the aid of Umrüst-Bausätze (factory conversion sets) by forward repair depots, the type became the **Do 217N-1/U1**.

Schräge Musik

Another modification introduced on the Do 217N-1 was supplementary cannon armament arranged to fire upward at an oblique angle, this installation being dubbed schräge Musik (oblique or jazz music). Credit for this development was subsequently to be claimed by various individuals, but there is evidence to suggest that its originator was Oberleutnant Rudolf Schönert who, as Staffelkapitän of 4./NJG 2, had experimented with machine-guns fixed to fire upward from the cockpit decking of the Do 17Z-10. When receiving the Ritterkreuz (Knight's Cross of the Iron Cross) from Kammhuber in July 1942, Schönert suggested to Kammhuber the mounting of cannon in the Do 217 fixed to fire upward so that the night fighter could attack the virtually unprotected belly of a bomber from a position in which it would be virtually immune from defensive fire. As a result of this conversation, Kammhuber ordered the modification of three Do 217 night fighters to take upward-firing cannon armament, two 20-mm MG 151 cannon being mounted in the centre of the fuselage to fire forward and upward at an angle of 70 degrees, the weapons being sighted by means of a reflector sight attached to the cockpit roof above and slightly in front of the pilot's head.

The three modified aircraft were delivered for operational testing in the spring of 1943, by which time Schönert had been promoted to Hauptmann and appointed Gruppenkommandeur of II/NJG 5 which, formed in December 1942, was a Bf 110-equipped unit at Parchim. The first schräge Musik 'kill' was obtained by Hauptmann Schönert himself during a Bomber Command attack on Berlin in May 1943. Subsequently, the Bf 110s of II/NJG 5 were fitted with the oblique armament, and between August 17 and the end of September 1943 attributed 18 'kills' to the schräge

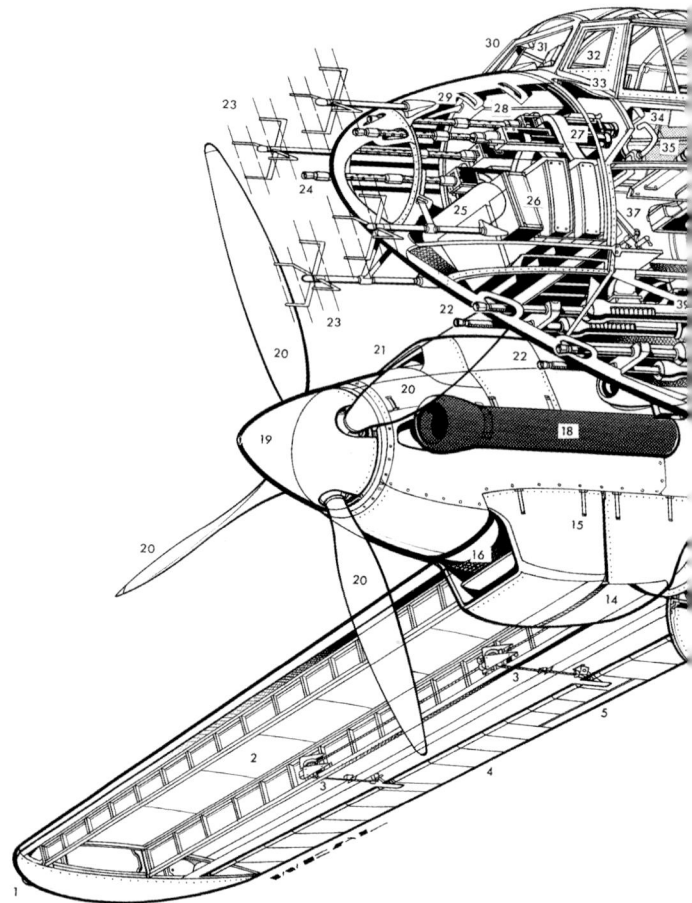

Dornier Do 217N-2/R22 cutaway key

1 Starboard navigation light
2 Wing skinning
3 Control linkage
4 Starboard aileron
5 Aileron trim tab
6 Starboard mainwheel
7 Mudguard
8 Mainwheel doors
9 Engine nacelle fairing
10 FuG 101 radio altimeter
11 FuG 25a (IFF)
12 Entry ladder
13 Entry hatch (open)
14 Radiator outlet gill
15 Quick-release catches
16 Radiator intake
17 Cartridge ejector chutes
18 Flame damping exhaust shroud
19 Propeller boss
20 Four-bladed VDM propeller
21 Oil cooler intake
22 Cannon muzzles
23 FuG 202 Lichtenstein BC radar array
24 Machine-gun muzzles
25 Aerial tuner

Dornier Do 217

26 MG 17 machine-gun ammunition boxes
27 Ammunition feed chute
28 Four 7.9-mm MG 17 machine-guns
29 Gun cooling intakes
30 Armoured windscreen
31 Revi C12D gunsight
32 Armourglass side panel
33 Additional extent armour
34 Control home
35 Engine controls
36 Pilot's seat

54 Control run conduit
55 Flanked off ventral gun position
56 Wooden belly fairing
57 Wooden formers
58 Fuselage lower fuel tank 1160-litre (255-Imp gal/) capacity
59 Longeron
60 Wing strengthening plate
61 Fuselage upper fuel tank 1050-litre (231-Imp gal) capacity
62 Port innerfuel tank 795-litre (175-Imp gal) capacity
63 Schräge Musik gun muzzles
64 Radiator outlet gill

92 Aerial (FuG 16 VHF)
93 Outer section split flaps
94 Engine nacelle fairing
95 Mainwheel well
96 Engine manual starter
97 Mainwheel retraction mechanism
98 Mainwheel tog
99 Mudguard
100 Schräge Musik mounting with four 20-mm MG 151 cannon
101 Cannon magazines
102 Entry/inspection hatch
103 Walkway

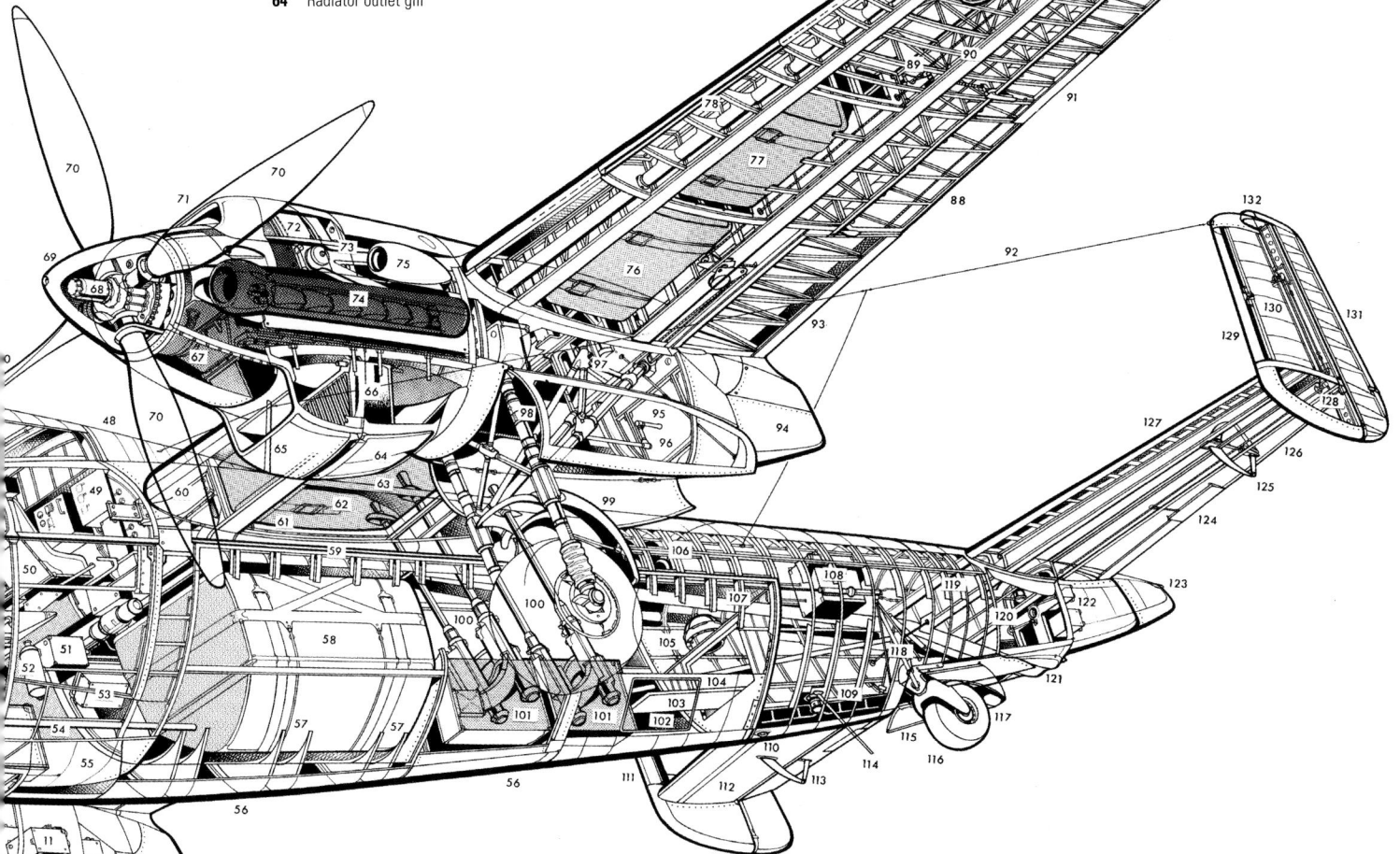

37 Rudder pedals
38 Folding seat
39 Upper pair of 20-mm MG 151 cannon (offset to starboard)
40 Compressed air bottles
41 Lower pair of 20-mm MG 151 cannon
42 Entry hatch
43 Four cannon magazines (each of 200 rounds) – three to starboard and one (deleted) to port
44 Folding map table
45 Side armour
46 D/F blister (in jettisonable roof panel)
47 Wireless operator's ceiling window
48 Wooden dorsal fairing
49 Radio equipment
50 Wireless operator's seat
51 Aircraft self-destruct
52 Fire extinguisher
53 Flare cartridges

65 Aerial mast
66 Radiator
67 Daimler-Benz DB 603A 12-cylinder liquid-cooled engine
68 Propeller mechanism
69 Propeller boss
70 Four-bladed propeller
71 Oil cooler intake
72 Armoured oil cooler
73 Engine bearer
74 Flame-damping exhaust shroud
75 Supercharger air intake
76 Port oil tank 235-litre (51.5-Imp gal) capacity
77 Port outer fuel tank 160-litre (35-Imp gal) capacity
78 Balloon-cable cutter in leading edge
79 Leading-edge hot-air de-icing
80 Hot air duct
81 Landing light (swiveling)
82 Front spar
83 Pilot head
84 Braced wing ribs
85 Intermediate ribs
86 Port navigation light
87 Port wingtip
88 Aileron structure
89 Control linkage
90 Rear spar
91 Aileron trim tab

104 Aft bulkhead inspection hatch
105 Master compass
106 Spherical oxygen cylinders
107 Emergency fuel jettison
108 Batteries
109 Dipole antenna
110 Dorsal anti-collision beacon
111 Leading-edge slot
112 Starboard tailplane
113 Elevator mass balance
114 Trailing aerial
115 Tailwheel doors
116 Tailwheel
117 Mudguard
118 Tailwheel retraction mechanism
119 Tailplane carry-through
120 Tailcone attachment
121 Fuel dump
122 Tail counter weights
123 Rear navigation light
124 Fixed tab
125 Elevator mass balance
126 Port elevator
127 Tailplane leading-edge structure
128 Tailplane/fin attachment
129 Tailfin leading-edge slot
130 Tailfin
131 Rudder tab
132 Rudder mass balance (lead insert)

Lack of airborne radar on the Do 217J-1 was rectified by the introduction of the related J-2 model (as seen here). This introduced the FuG 202 Lichenstein BC radar and its associated Matrazen array. Both sub-types were powered by BMW 801L engines

Dornier Do 217

The Do 217N night-fighter may have been underpowered, but it certainly packed a heavy punch, as evidenced in this view. Noteworthy are the flame-dampers covering the exhausts, which further degraded the already sluggish performance.

Musik. The success resulted in the design of a Rüstsatz (field conversion set) for installation in the **Do 217N-2** fighter, this comprising four 20-mm MG 151 cannon firing upward at an angle of 70 degrees above the horizontal, the installation creating the **Do 217N-2/R22** that had an empty equipped weight 500 kg (1,102 lb) heavier than that of the baseline type, so reducing the service ceiling by 500 m (1,640 ft) and the maximum speed by 5 km/h (3 mph) at sea level and 14 km/h (9 mph) at 6000 m (19,685 ft).

Radar equipment

The Do 217N-2, which had supplanted the Do 217N-l in production during the spring of 1943, adopted all the modifications introduced by the Do 217N-1/U1 as standard, production being finally phased out late in 1943. By this time some aircraft were being modified to carry FuG 220 Lichtenstein SN-2 as well as FuG 202 or 212 radar, this having been necessitated by the extensive use by the RAF of strips of metal foil known as Window, a device that cut to one half the wavelength of both the earlier Lichtenstein and the Würzburg fighter control radar by reflecting the search impulses, thus paralysing the Himmelbett system. The SN-2 operated on part of the spectrum not covered by the Window then being dropped by the RAF, but had a minimum range of 365 m (400 yards), and it was for this reason that the FuG 202 or 212, with its minimum range of 180 m (200 yards), was normally carried by the Do 217N-2 in addition to the FuG 220 SN-2. Some Do 217K-2s and Do 217N-2s were also eventually

fitted with FuG 227 Flensburg for homing onto the emissions of the Monica tail-warning sets of RAF bombers, and FuG 350 Naxos which was tuned to the frequency of the H_2S radar of RAF pathfinder aircraft.

Do 217 night fighters began to appear over a wide area in 1943. NJG 4, which had been formed with three Gruppen during the previous year, was based in the Frankfurt sector, being occasionally deployed to Eindhoven under Luftflotte 3, with both Bf 110s and Do 217s, the bulk of the latter being concentrated in two Staffeln of II/NJG 4, although both I and III Gruppen included Do 217s in their strength from time to time. NJG 3, which was operating under the Oberbefehlshaber Mitte (High Command Central) included Do 217s in its inventory from mid-1942, and between August and November 1943, the Do 217 saw service on the Eastern Front with I/NJG 100, an independent Gruppe known as the 'railway night fighters' as its ground control operated from trains. I/NJG 100 first appeared in the USSR on the central sector under Luftflotte 6 at the end of August 1943, its strength at that time comprising 16 Do 217s and 16 Ju 88Cs. The Gruppe performed nocturnal intercept and intruder missions, but by mid-October, when it was transferred to the southern sector where it operated under both Luftflotten 4 and 6, the number of Do 217s on strength had diminished to three, of which only one was serviceable, and in November the Gruppe converted completely to the Ju 88C.

The operational service of the Do 217 night fighter was not restricted entirely to the Luftwaffe as, with the increase

Retaining the BMW 801 powerplant of the Do 217E, the Do 217K bomber introduced an entirely new forward fuselage without the stepped cockpit line of the earlier aircraft.

Defence against attack from below and the rear was vested in the ventral gun position fitted with one 13-mm (0.51-in) MG 131 machine-gun with 1,000 rounds of ammunition.

Do 217K-1

Do 217K-2

Do 217K V1

Do 217K-1

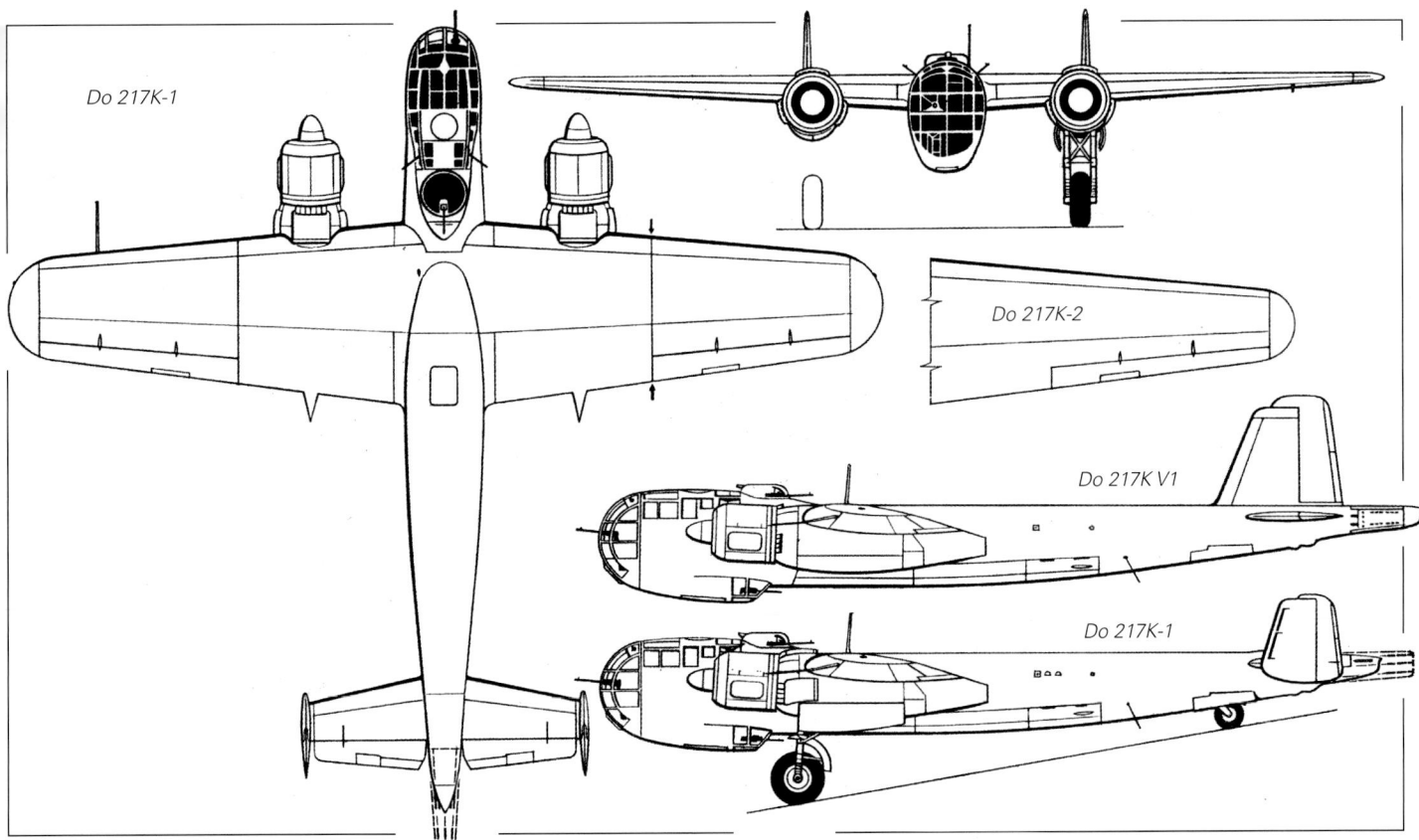

Right: Do 217E-4s from III/KG 2 taxi out for take-off. The trailing edge of the wing was occupied by outboard slotted ailerons and inboard electrically actuated split flaps.

of Allied air attacks on the industrial centres of northern Italy, the Italian high command had decided to establish a special defence force, the Forza Aerea Intercettatori, headquartered at Tortona and based on night fighting techniques evolved in Germany. Intended primarily for the night defence of Milan, Genoa and Turin, this force initially comprised the 2°, 59° and 60° Gruppi Intercettatori equipped with Fiat CR.42 and Caproni-Reggiane Re.2001 single-seat fighters with exhaust flame–dampers and other minor modifications to render them more suitable for use as interim night fighters. Radar-equipped fighters had been requested from Germany, and during the spring of 1943, the Regia Aeronautica began to receive Lichtenstein-equipped Bf 110G-4/U5 and Do 217J-2 fighters, the former entering service with the 60° Gruppo and the latter with both the 59° and 60° Gruppi. However, by the eve of Italy's capitulation in September 1943, only two Bf 110G-4s and eight Do 217J-2s remained with the Forza Aerea Intercettatori.

During the early months of 1944, the Do 217J and Do 217N began to disappear from the Nachtjagdgeschwadern, and the process had been completed by the middle of the year. Production of all versions of the Do 217 night fighter had totalled 130 Do 217J and 325 Do 217N aircraft.

Dornier Do 217N-2 specification
(figures in square brackets apply to the Do 217N-2/R22)
Type: four-seat night interceptor and intruder fighter
Powerplant: two Daimler-Benz DB 603A liquid-cooled inverted V-12 engines each rated at 1305 kW (1,750 hp) for take-off and 1379 kW (1,850 hp) at 2100 m (6,890 ft)
Performance: maximum speed 430 km/h (267 mph) [425 km/h (264 mph)] at sea level, 515 km/h (320 mph) [500 km/h (311 mph)] at 6000 m (19,685 ft); maximum cruising speed 470 km/h (292 mph) [465 km/h (289 mph)] at 5400 m (17,715 ft); economical cruising speed 425 km/h (264 mph) [420 km/h (261 mph)] at 5400 m (17,715 ft); climb to 4000 m (13,125 ft) in 9 [11] minutes, to 6000 m (19,685 ft) in 15 [17] minutes; service ceiling 8900 m (29,200 ft) [8400 m (27,560 ft)]; normal range 1755 km (1,090 miles)
Weights: empty equipped 10280 kg (22,665 lb) [10780 kg (23,767 lb)]; loaded 13200 kg (29,101 lb) [13700 kg (30,203 lb)]
Dimensions: wingspan 19.00 m (62 ft 4 in); length including aerial array 18.90 m (62 ft 0 in); height 5.00 m (16 ft 4¾ in); wing area 57.00 m² (613.54 sq ft)
Armament: four 20-mm MG 151 cannon and four 7.9-mm (0.31-in) MG 17 fixed forward-firing machine-guns in the nose [and four 20-mm MG 151 fixed cannon firing upward and forward in the centre of the fuselage]

This head-on view of a Do 217M-1 bomber emphasises the comparatively short span (and thus the small area and high wing loading) of all the early-generation Do 217s.

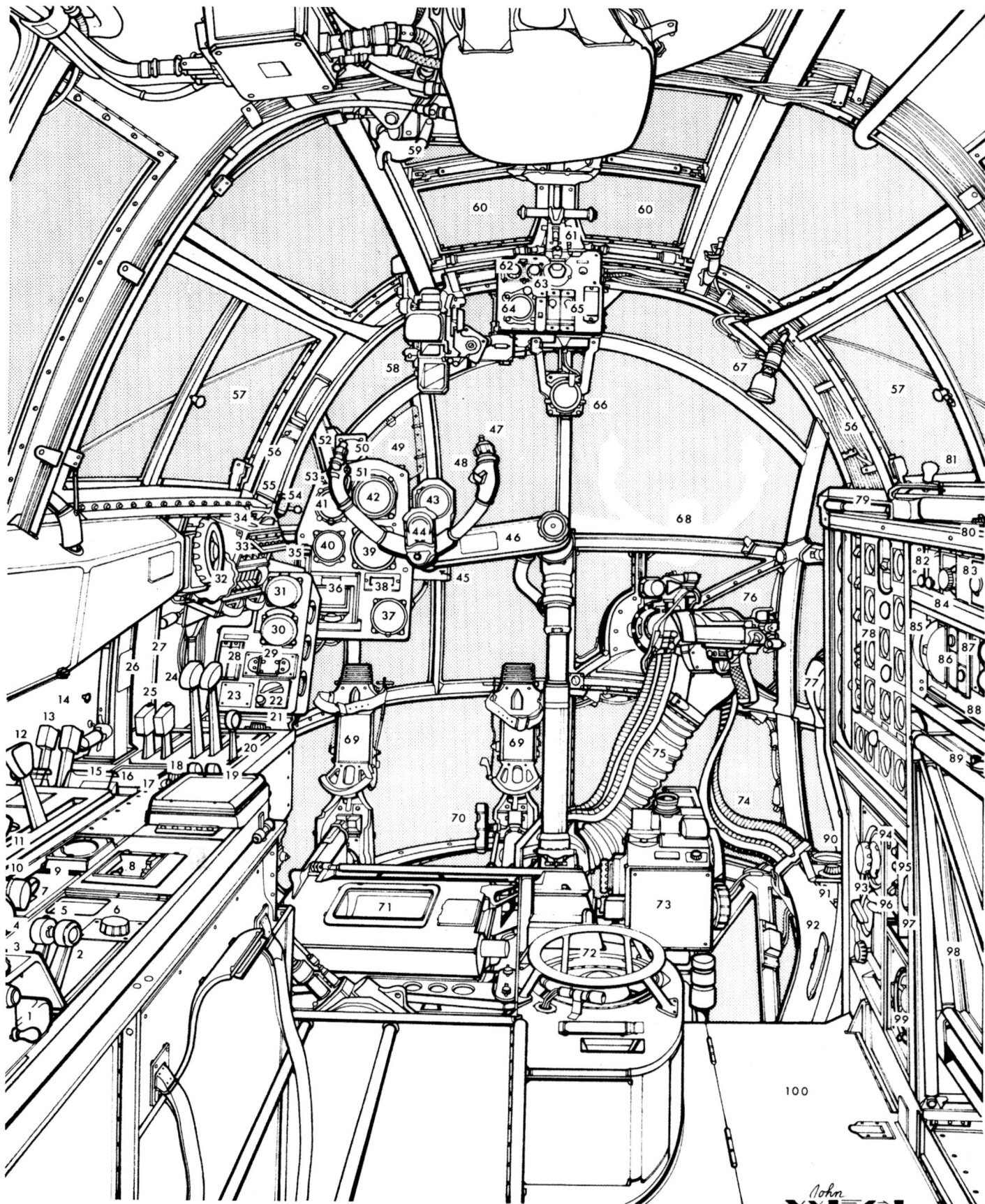

Dornier Do 217M-1 cockpit layout

1	Auxiliary external stores release knob (Rüstsatz 16)	**9**	FBG 16 remote-control panel	**17**	Ignition switch	
2	Fuselage heating lever	**10**	Cooler intakes emergency lever	**18**	Emergency fuel jettison knob	
3	Wing leading-edge heating lever	**11**	Starter switch	**19**	Propeller pitch control levers	
4	Oil cooler flaps actuating lever .	**12**	Auxiliary external stores release lever (Rüstsatz 10)	**20**	Throttle locking lever	
5	Propeller de-icing switch	**13**	Ignition advance levers (cold-weather starting)	**21**	ADb 11 junction box	
6	EiV contact breaker (Fzf)	**14**	Stores box	**22**	Autopilot switch	
7	Spark plug cleanser/tropical filter activation	**15**	Plexiglass protective cover	**23**	SZKK1 panel	
8	Emergency-stop switch panel	**16**	Main line switch	**24**	Throttle levers	
				25	Fuel cock levers	
				26	Operating instructions table	

27	Engine data plate	**36**	Directional gyro
28	Propeller setting switch	**37**	Radio altimeter
29	Twelve-lamp indicator	**38**	Course setting
30	Dual pressure gauge	**39**	Repeater compass
31	Dual RPM counter	**40**	Airspeed indicator
32	Aileron/elevator/rudder trim knobs and indicators	**41**	Fine-coarse altimeter
33	Ultra-violet lighting/pitot head heating/instrument panel lighting switches	**42**	Artificial horizon
		43	Variometer
34	Course correction / autopilot / compass switches	**44**	Clock
		45	AFN 2 radio navigation homing indicator
35	Deviation tables	**46**	Control column swing-over arm
		47	LRi 2 autopilot turn switch

Above: Intended primarily as a night bomber, the Do 217K-1 introduced BMW 801D engines and a redesigned forward fuselage, giving a bulbous look by eliminating the stepped cockpit. This aircraft carries Luftflotte 2's badge on its nose.

Right: The extensive glazing of the fuselage nose of the Do 217K and M series produced something of a 'goldfish bowl' effect for the pilot, the large areas of transparent panelling being seen in this photograph of a Do 217K. The RF2C periscope with its PV1B sighting head for the tail-mounted battery of fixed guns can be seen above the flight deck.

Do 217K and Do 217M

The designations Do 217F and Do 217G had been reserved for two 1941 derivatives of the basic design that were not proceeded with, and the **Do 217H** was a conversion of the 21st production Do 217E with DB 601 engines fitted with experimental turbochargers undertaken in September 1941 by Daimler-Benz at the Erprobungsstelle Echterdingen for high-altitude trials.

Thus the next production bomber version was the **Do 217K-1** that began flight trials on 31 March 1942. This differed markedly from its predecessors, the most noteworthy innovation being an entirely redesigned forward fuselage from which the stepped windscreen was eliminated, the glazed panelling being extended forward to the extreme nose. The BMW 801C engines were supplanted by BMW 801A or 801ML units which, operating on 96-octane fuel, each offered 1163 kW (1,560 hp) for take-off and 1074 kW (1,440 hp) at 5700 m (18,700 ft). The defensive armament comprised one 7.9-mm (0.31-in) MG 81Z (twin MG 81 machine-guns) with 1,000 rounds in the nose, one 13-mm (0.51-in) MG 131 machine-gun with 500 rounds in the electrically operated dorsal turret, a similar weapon with 1,000 rounds in the lower rear position, and two (later four) MG 81s with 750 r.p.g. in lateral positions.

The Do 217K series was intended primarily for the night bombing role, and the Do 217K-1 initial production model, which began to leave the assembly line in the late summer of 1942 and entered service with Kampfgeschwader 2 in the autumn, was preceded by three prototypes, the first of which, the **Do 217K V1**, was briefly flown with an experimental single fin-and-rudder assembly, and the third, the **Do 217K V3**, was later used as a carrier aircraft for the DFS 228 V1 high-altitude reconnaissance sailplane. The Do 217K-l was used for trials with the R25 tail fairing housing a Perlon braking chute, and in 1944 experiments were conducted with a Do 217K-1 fitted with ETC 2000/XII carriers both under the outboard wing panels (R10) and between the fuselage and engine nacelles.

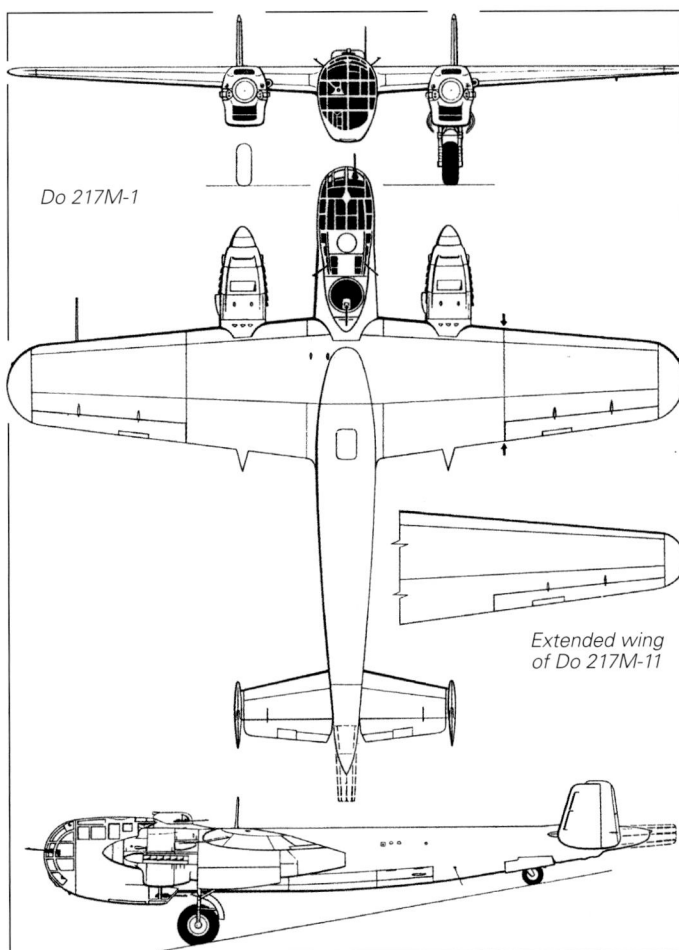

Do 217M-1

Extended wing of Do 217M-11

48 Fixed weapon firing button	**58** Stuvi 5B dive-bombing sight	**69** Rudder pedals	**81** Bomb-arming crank	**92** Ammunition box
49 Clear-vision panel	**59** Landing flap manual coupling lever	**70** Rudder adjustment screw	**82** ZH-and OFF transmitter (BZA 1)	**93** RAB 14d automatic sequence bomb release
50 Emergency turn-and-bank indicator	**60** Jettisonable canopy roof section	**71** Pilot's seat mount	**83** ADb 11 junction box	**94** Bomb door position indicator switch
51 BK XI bomb-release button	**61** Canopy jettison lever	**72** D/EF controls	**84** Wind-speed indicator (BZA 1)	**95** Bomb door indicator lights
52 FuG 16 transmission button	**62** Dimmer switch	**73** Lotfe 7D bombsight	**85** External bomb rack switches	**96** Bomb door closing switch
53 Pitot head heating indicator (obscured by control horn)	**63** Illuminator button	**74** Ammunition feed	**86** BG25	**97** ZSK244A ignition switch box
54 Lever for hinged section of blind-flying panel (Nos 43 and 45)	**64** Trim indicator	**75** Link and casing collector chute	**87** ASK-N smoke discharge switch box	**98** Observer's foldaway seat
55 Ultra-violet light	**65** Trim levers	**76** MG 81Z machine-gun	**88** Dimmer switches	**99** Angled delivery setting control
56 No. 4 fuselage frame	**66** Standby compass	**77** Oxygen supply	**89** Observer's seat release	**100** Bomb aimer's well
57 Sliding window panels	**67** Cockpit light	**78** Engine instrument nel/temperature/pressure gauges	**90** Height-compensated airspeed indicator	
	68 Control column swing-over position	**79** Bomb jettison lever	**91** BZA 1 true-speed indicator	
		80 EiV contact breaker		

The Dornier Do 217K-1 bomber was much altered in comparison with its predecessors. The type featured prominently in the Operation 'Steinbock' raids against England in early 1944, flying alongside Do 217Ms.

Missile carrier

In December 1942, a version of the bomber intended specifically to carry the FX 1400 Fritz-X stand-off missile, the **Do 217K-2**, made its debut. Equipped with the FuG 203a Kehl I transmitter for the missile's FuG 230a Strassburg receiver, and ETC 2000/XII carriers between the fuselage and the engine nacelles, the Do 217K-2 introduced extended wing outer panels increasing overall span from 19.00 m (62 ft 4 in) to 24.80 m (81 ft 4½ in), and the gross wing area from 57.00 m² (613.54 sq ft) to 67.00 m² (721.18 sq ft). A 1160-litre (255-Imp gal) auxiliary fuel tank was mounted in the forward bomb bay (R17) as standard, and the tail cone housed four 7.9-mm (0.31-in) MG 81 aft-firing machine-guns (R23). The entire battery of fixed guns was fired by the pilot, aided by an RF2C periscope with the PV1B sighting head.

Do 217K-2s operated by III/KG 100 based at Marseilles-Istres launched their first Fritz-X missiles in action over the Mediterranean on 29 August 1943, only four days after the operational debut of the Hs 293A with II/KG 100. The

The radial-engined Do 217K was produced in two forms as the Do 217K-1 bomber and the Do 217K-2 carrier for the Fritz-X guided bomb. The latter introduced a longer-span wing.

Do 217K-3 was essentially similar to the Do 217K-2 but was fitted with the later FuG 203c or 203d Kehl IV transmitter enabling it to carry either the Hs 293A or Fritz-X with equal facility.

During the spring of 1943, two prototypes of a modified version of the Do 217K with rearranged cockpit and defensive armament were tested at Dornier's Lowenthal plant as the **Do 217L V1** and **Do 217L V2**, but no production of this variant was undertaken, the last bomber model of the basic design to be built in any quantity being the **Do 217M** manufactured in parallel with the Do 217K. During 1942, in order to safeguard against production delays resulting from shortages of BMW 801D engines, Dornier adapted the Do 217K-1 airframe to take Daimler-Benz DB 603A engines as the **Do 217M-1**, the two models being manufactured in parallel and entering service virtually simultaneously. The DB 603A was rated at 1305 kW (1,750 hp) for take-off and 1208 kW (1,620 hp) at 5700 m (18,700 ft), and provided the Do 217M-1 with performance generally similar to that of the BMW 801D-powered model, offensive loads and defensive armament also being similar. An example of the Do 217M-1 (Werk Nr 56051) fell into Allied hands on the night of 23-24 February 1944 when an aircraft of 2./KG 2 attacking London received minor damage from anti-aircraft fire over the north-west suburbs, the crew promptly baling out at 3000 m (9,845 m) and the abandoned aircraft flying on to make an excellent belly landing in Cambridge.

Minor variants

Consideration was given to mounting a turbocharged engine on the Do 217M, and two prototypes, the **Do 217 V13** and **Do 217 V14**, were tested with such an installation, but it was not adopted for production models. A single prototype was built of the **Do 217M-2** torpedo-carrier, but this was abandoned in favour of the Ju 88. Another sub-variant that did not enter production was the **Do 217M-5** missile carrier, with a single Hs 293 mounted semi-externally beneath the fuselage. A single **Do 217M-8** was built with DB 603 engines, TK11 booster and triangular tail fins. The **Do 217M-11** embodied similar extended outer wing panels to those of the Do 217K-2 and was intended as a long-range missile carrier with either an FX 1400 Fritz-X or Hs 293A missile mounted semi-externally beneath the fuselage. A few (37) were built, but the pressing need for additional night fighters early in 1943 resulted in the majority of the Do 217M being completed as Do 217N, relatively few Do 217M-ls thus reaching the Kampfgruppen.

Series production of the Do 217 finally terminated in June 1944. Sources differ as to how many were built, some claiming 1,730 and others suggesting as many as 1,905.

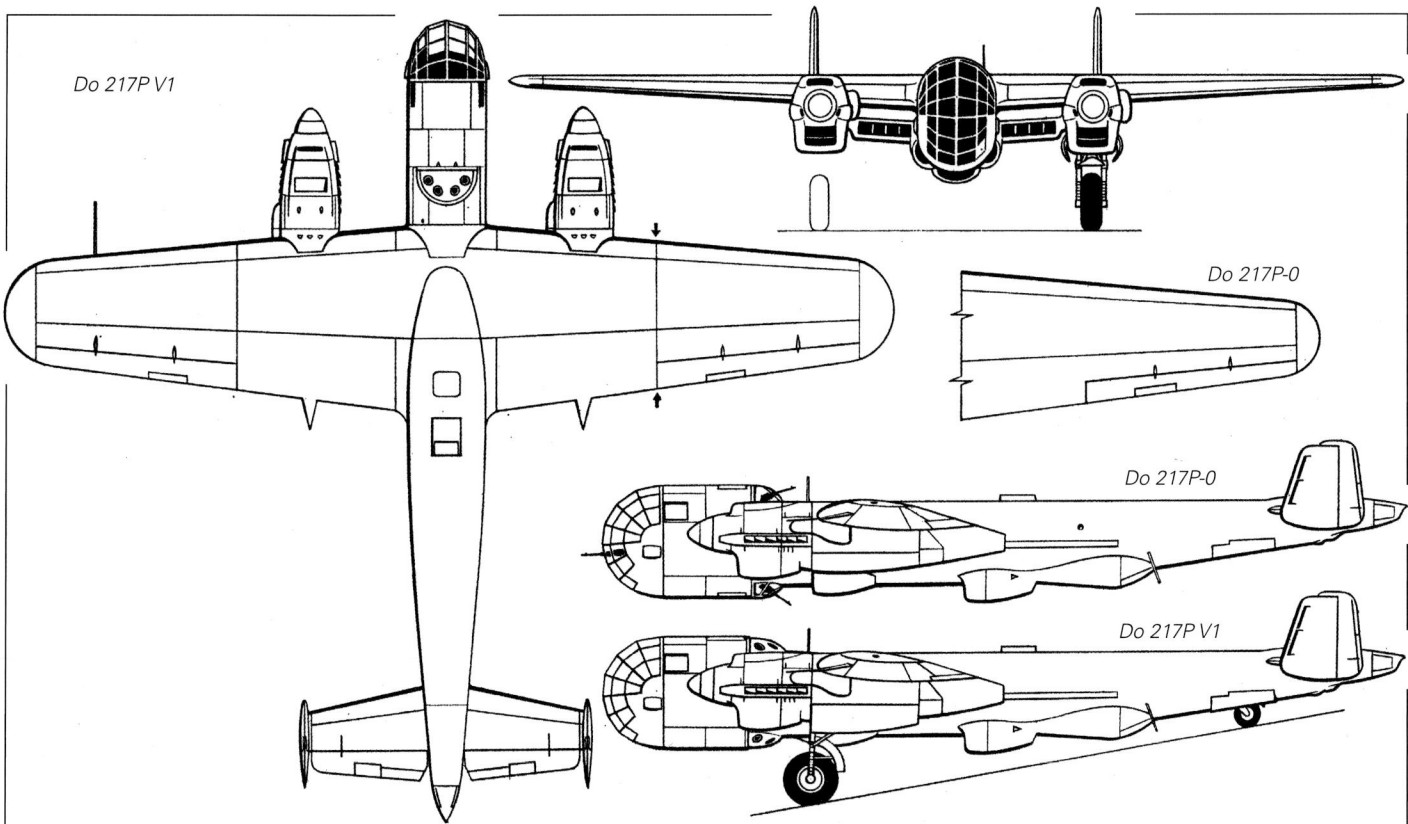

Do 217P V1

Do 217P-0

Do 217P-0

Do 217P V1

Dornier Do 217M-1 specification

Type: four-seat heavy night bomber
Powerplant: two Daimler-Benz DB 603A liquid-cooled inverted V-12 engines each rated at 1305 kW (1,750 hp) for take-off and 1379 kW (1,850 hp) at 2100 m (6,890 ft)
Performance: maximum speed 475 km/h (295 mph) at sea level, 560 km/h (348 mph) at 5700 m (18,700 ft); economical cruising speed 400 km/h (249 mph) at optimum altitude; initial climb rate at normal loaded weight 210 m (690 ft) per minute; climb to 1000 m (3,280 ft) 3 minutes 18 seconds, to 2000 m (6,560 ft) 6 minutes 42 seconds; service ceiling with maximum internal bomb load 7370 m (24,180 ft) and without bomb load 9500 m (31,170 ft); maximum range on internal fuel 2180 km (1,335 miles) or with auxiliary fuel 2500 km (1,553 miles)
Weights: empty 9065 lb (19,985 lb); empty equipped 10950 kg (24,140 lb), maximum overload 16700 kg (36,817 lb)
Dimensions: wingspan 19.00 m (62 ft 4 in); length 17.00 m (55 ft 9¼ in) or for the Do 217M-1/R25 17.88 m (58 ft 8 in); height 4.97 m (16 ft 3½ in); wing area 57.00 m² (613.54 sq ft)
Armament: two 7.9-mm (0.31-in) MG 81 machine-guns with 500 r.p.g. in nose, one 13-mm (0.51-in) MG 131 machine-gun with 500 rounds in electrically operated dorsal turret, one 13-mm (0.51-in) MG 131 machine-gun with 1,000 rounds in ventral step, and two 7.9-mm (0.31-in) MG 81 machine-guns with 750 r.p.g. in lateral positions; (offensive) maximum bomb load 4000 kg (8,818 lb) of which 2520 kg (5,555 lb) were carried internally

Do 217P

Before the phasing out of Do 217 production late in 1943, Dornier had adapted the basic airframe for operation at extreme altitudes as both a bomber and reconnaissance aircraft under the designation **Do 217P**. Retaining the wing, tail assembly, basic fuselage structure and undercarriage of the Do 217E-2, the **Do 217P V1** first prototype was powered by two Daimler-Benz DB 603B engines supercharged by a DB 605T engine, this arrangement being known as an HZ-Anlage and offering a total of 2610 kW (3,500 hp) for take-off, 2774 kW (3,720 hp) at 2100 m (6,890 ft), and 2416 kW (3,240 hp) at 5700 m (18,700 ft). For climb and combat a total of 2147 kW (2,880 hp) was available at 13700 m (44,950 ft), and maximum cruising power at the same altitude was 1968 kW (2,640 hp).

The DB 605T, which drove a two-stage supercharger, was installed in the centre fuselage. Large intercooler radiators

were slung beneath the wing, between the fuselage and the engine nacelles, and air scoops for the blower and DB 605T engine were located below the fuselage, just aft of the wing trailing edge. The four crew members were housed ahead of the wing in a pressure cabin built in the form of a detachable compartment, this being extensively glazed by flat panels, and a Perlon tail braking chute was fitted.

The Do 217P V1 was flown for the first time in June 1942, and during the course of flight trials attained an altitude of 13400 m (43,960 ft). Two additional prototypes, the **Do 217P V2** and **Do 217P V3**, joined the test programme during the summer and autumn of 1942. These differed from the Do 217P V1 primarily in having extended outer wing panels that increased overall wingspan to 24.50 m (80 ft 4½ in) and gross wing area to 66.90 m² (720.13 sq ft). By the beginning of 1943, work was in hand on the manufacture of three additional prototypes, but these were never completed.

The Do 217P-0 was primarily a reconnaissance aircraft intended to operate at altitudes at which it would be immune from interception, and its defensive armament, which comprised a pair of 7/9-mm (0.31-in) MG 81 forward-firing machine-guns and a similar pair of weapons firing aft above and below the fuselage, was intended for use only at lower altitudes owing to the problem of sealing the gun openings. A single Rb 20/30 camera was installed in the fuselage immediately aft of the pressurised compartment, and two automatic Rb 75/30 cameras were mounted in the aft end of the centre fuselage. For the bombing role it was proposed that two 500-kg (1,102-lb) bombs should be slung from racks under the outboard wing panels, and for long-range reconnaissance sorties these racks were to be occupied by 900-litre (198-Imp gal) auxiliary tanks.

The trio of Do 217P-0 aircraft was exhaustively tested at Rechlin, but plans for putting the type into quantity production failed to materialise.

Dornier Do 217

The Do 217P V1 first flew in July 1942 and featured a fuselage-mounted DB 605T engine to drive the large supercharger installation supplying the DB 603G flight engines essential for good performance at very high altitude.

Dornier Do 217P-0 specification
Type: three-seat high-altitude reconnaissance-bomber
Powerplant: two Daimler-Benz DB 603B liquid-cooled inverted V-12 engines (supercharged by a Daimler-Benz DB 605T) each rated at 1305 kW (1,750 hp) for take-off, 1387 kW (1,860 hp) at 2100 m (6,890 ft) and 1074 kW (1,440 hp) at 13715 m (45,000 ft)
Performance: maximum speed at 13265 kg (29,244 lb) 585 km/h (364 mph) at 14000 m (45,930 ft); initial climb rate at 14335 kg (31,603 lb) 290 m (9510 ft) per minute; climb to 8960 m (29,395 ft) in 19 minutes 49 seconds; service ceiling at 13265 kg (29,244 lb) 16155 m (53,000 ft), and at 13925 kg (30,700 lb) 15485 m (50,805 ft).
Weights: normal loaded 14335 kg (31,603 lb); maximum overload 15965 kg (35,195 lb)
Dimensions: wingspan 24.50 m (80 ft 4½ in); length 17.95 m (58 ft 10½ in); wing area 66.90 m² (720.13 sq ft)
Armament: two 7.9-mm (0.31-in) MG 81 forward-firing machine-guns, and two 7.9-mm (0.31-in) MG 81 machine-guns in each of two aft-firing positions above and below fuselage; (offensive) two 500-kg (1,102-lb) bombs on underwing racks

The **Do 217R** was intended as long–wingspan dive–bomber with a similar fuselage to the Do 217K series; it was to be fitted with DB 603 engines and dive brakes in the wings and was to be capable of carrying various ordnance loads, including torpedos or even SC 1800 bombs. In the event, testing of the only two prototypes built revealed serious performance shortcomings and the project was cancelled in late 1942/early 1943.

Operational career

Only one complete Kampfgeschwader was ever equipped with the Do 217, this being KG 2 of which II Gruppe had remained in the west when the assault on the USSR began on 22 June 1941 in order to complete conversion from the Do 17Z to the Do 217E. III/KG 2 actually began conversion from the Do 17Z to the Do 217E while still in the USSR, but was pulled back during the autumn of 1941 to complete re-equipment, and was followed by KG 2's remaining component, I Gruppe. During the remaining months of 1941 the entire Kampfgeschwader converted and was based

The ungainly underfuselage excrescences of the Do 217P-0 indicated the fitment of a third engine used to drive the two-stage supercharger installation.

**Dornier Do 217K-1
cutaway key**

1 Starboard rudder tab
2 Rudder controls
3 Rudder mass balance (lead insert)
4 Starboard tailfin
5 Leading-edge slot
6 Tailplane/tailfin attachment
7 Elevator
8 Elevator mass balance
9 Fixed tab
10 Trim tab
11 Tailplane construction
12 Elevator controls
13 Rear navigation light
14 Four aft-firing 7.9-mm MG 81 machine-guns (Rüstsatz [field conversion set] 19)
15 Ammunition boxes
16 Tailplane trim control
17 Fuel emergency jettison
18 Mudguard
19 Tailwheel
20 Tailwheel doors
21 Tailwheel retraction mechanism
22 Tailplane carry-through
23 Fuselage skinning
24 Master compass
25 Dipole antenna
26 Anti-collision beacon
27 Elevator mass balance
28 Port tailfin
29 Leading-edge slot
30 Bomb bay division
31 Bomb bay hinge line
32 Bomb bay rear bulkhead entry/ inspection hatch
33 Spherical oxygen cylinder
34 Starboard mainwheel
35 Mudguard
36 Mainwheel doors
37 Mainwheel retraction mechanism
38 Mainwheel well
39 FuG 25 (A-A recognition)
40 FuG 101 radio altimeter
41 Outer section split flaps
42 Starboard aileron
43 Aileron tab
44 Control lines
45 Rear spar
46 Braced wing ribs

Dornier Do 217

The large units between the fuselage and engines of the Do 217P were intercooler radiators to cool and thereby further compress the air delivered from the supercharger installation (supplied with air through a ventral inlet) to the two flight engines.

47 Intermediate ribs
48 EGS101 antenna
49 Starboard navigation light
50 Front spar
51 Leading-edge hot-air de-icing
52 Hot-air duct
53 Balloon-cable cutter in loading-edge
54 Starboard outer fuel tank 160-litre (35-Imp gal) capacity
55 Starboard oil tank 235-litre (51.7-Imp gal) capacity
56 Flame-damping exhaust pipes
57 Sliding-ring cooling air exit
58 BMW 801D 14-cylinder two-row radial engine

59 Annular oil cooler
60 VDM three-blade metal propeller of 3.90 m (12.8 ft) diameter
61 Cooling fan
62 Cowling sliding nose-ring
63 Propeller boss
64 Starboard inner fuel tank 795-litre (175-Imp gal) capacity
65 Fuselage main fuel tank 1050-litre (231-Imp gal) capacity
66 Wing spar carry-through
67 Bomb bay top hinge line
68 Load-bearing beam
69 Bomb shackle
70 Bomb bay centre hinge line
71 Typical bomb load: two 1000-kg (2,250-lb) SC 1000 bombs
72 Forward bomb doors
73 13-mm MG 131 machine-gun in ventral position (1,000 rounds)
74 Ammunition ejection chute
75 Ventral gunner's station
76 Armoured bulkhead
77 Cartridge collector box
78 Batteries (two 24-volt)
79 Radio equipment

80 Dorsal gunner's seat support
81 Cabin hot air
82 Dorsal gunner's station
83 Armoured turret ring
84 Aerial mast
85 Gun safety guard
86 Starboard beam-mounted 7.9-mm MG 81 machine-gun (750 rounds)
87 13-mm MG 131 machine-gun (500 rounds)
88 Electrically-operated dorsal turret
89 Revi gunsight
90 Angled side windows
91 Jettisonable decking
92 Bomb-aimer's folding seat
93 Navigator's station
94 Pilot's contoured table seat
95 Rear view gunsight
96 Upper instrument panel
97 Nose glazing
98 Control horns

99 Engine controls
100 One 13-mm MG 131 in strengthened nose glazing (alternatively twin 7.9-mm MG 81Z)
101 Balloon-cable cutter in nose horizontal frame
102 Cartridge ejection chute
103 Ammunition feed
104 Lotfe 7D bombsight
105 Bomb aimer's flat panel
106 Control column counterweight
107 Nose armour
108 Ventral gunner's quilt
109 Ammunition box (nose MG 131)
110 Cartridge collector box
111 Entry hatch
112 Entry hatch (open)
113 Entry ladder
114 Port mainwheel doors
115 Mudguard
116 Port mainwheel
117 Mainwheel leg cross struts
118 Port engine cowling
119 Landing light (swivelling)
120 Control linkage
121 Pilot head
122 Port navigation light
123 Port aileron
124 Aileron trim tab

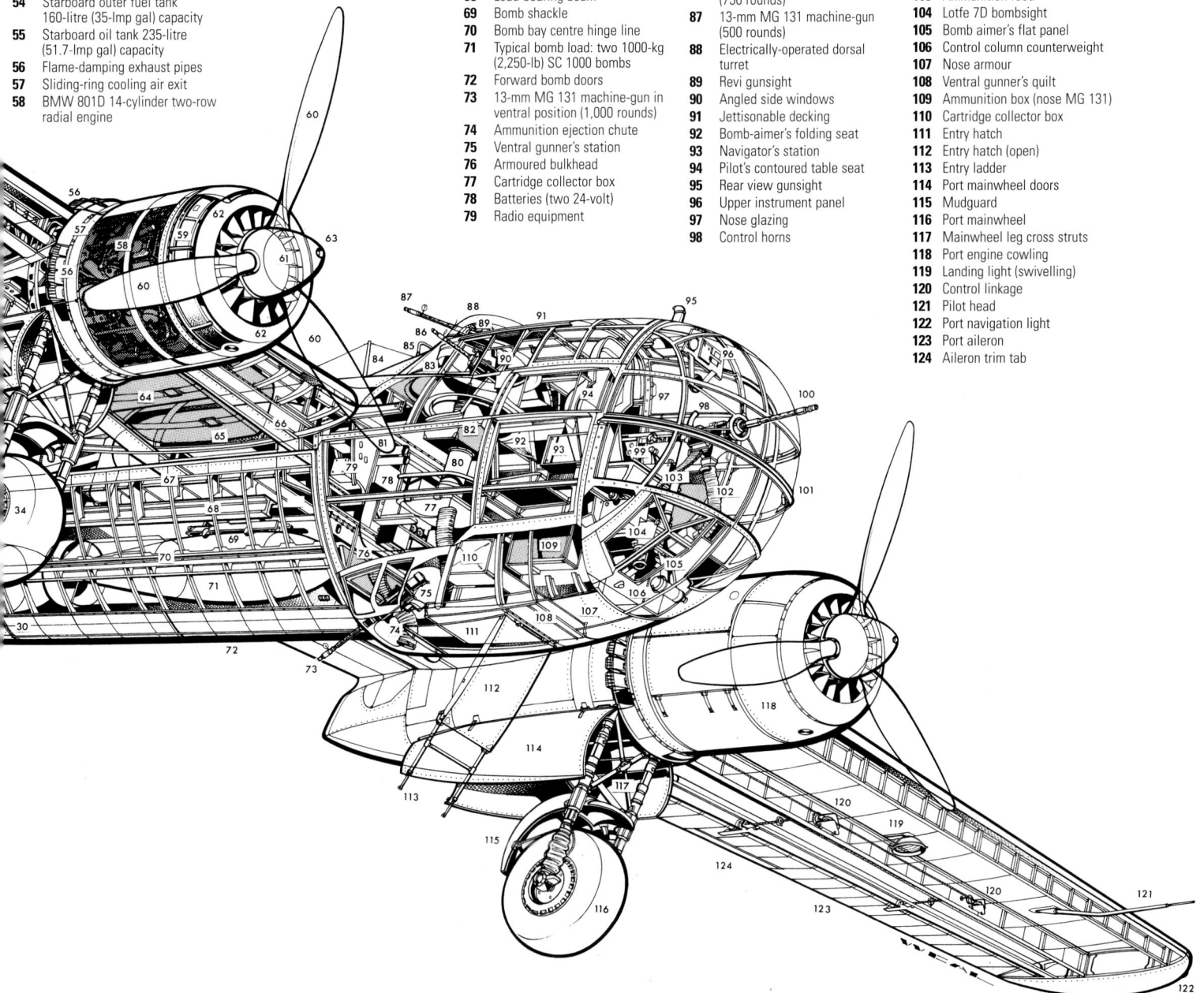

Left: Seen in late 1942, this Do 217E-4 served with II/KG 40. This group had been the first to take the Do 217E into combat, primarily on anti-shipping duties against the British. Note the lateral-firing MG 15 in the aft portion of the flight deck.

Left: The combination of the dorsal turret and lateral-firing weapons provided good fields of fire, but all these weapons had to be operated by just the radio operator.

in the Netherlands, at Gilze-Rijen, Deelen, Soesterberg and Eindhoven, by early 1942 for bombing raids over England and anti-shipping strikes in the North Sea. KG 2 remained in the Netherlands with its Do 217s until July 1944, participating in the 'Little Blitz' in that year under the direction of the Angriffsführer England.

Kampfgeschwader 40 had, in fact, preceded KG 2 into action with the Do 217E, II/KG 40 starting operations against North Sea shipping under the tactical command of the Fliegerführer Atlantik in July 1941 from Cognac, the remaining two Gruppen operating the Fw 200C Condor. In the first half of 1943 II/KG 40 began to give up its Do 217s and convert to the Me 410, being redesignated as V/KG 2 in June. A new II/KG 40 was formed at Bordeaux-Mérignac on He 177As. Meanwhile, at Achmer, IV/KG 2 had converted the previous year to the Do 217, so that by mid-1943 Kampfgeschwader 2 comprised four Do 217-equipped Gruppen and one with the Me 410. KG 2's Gruppen were equipped with a succession of Do 217 variants, including the E-1, E-2, E-3, K-1 and M-1, undertaking sporadic day and night attacks on the UK but concentrating their efforts primarily against Allied shipping.

Missile carrier operations

In April 1943, II/KG 100 re-equipped with Hs 293-carrying Do 217E-5s while III/KG 100, formed from the Lehr- und Erprobungskommando 21, equipped with the Fritz-X-carrying Do 217K-2, these Gruppen starting operations in the Bay of Biscay on 25 August 1943 and the Mediterranean on 29 August 1943, respectively. The Do 217K-2s succeeded in hitting the battleships *Roma* and *Italia* on 9 September 1943 with Fritz-X missiles, and III/KG 100's aircraft were active in opposing the Salerno landings throughout the following week, scoring hits on the US cruiser *Savannah* and several supply vessels, and subsequently damaging the British battleship *Warspite* with Fritz-X missiles. In January 1944 III/KG 100's Do 217K-2s sank two British warships, the cruiser *Spartan* and the destroyer *Janus*. III/KG 100 was active over the Allied beachhead in Normandy but without major success. In August the Gruppe attacked bridges on the Cherbourg peninsula in the first use of the Hs 293 missile in the overland role.

Other operators of the Do 217 included one that employed Do 217s and He 111Hs for pathfinder duties over the British Isles. Based at Chartres, the Lehr- und Erprobungskommando 17 was redesignated as 15./KG 6 in September 1942, and then became 1./KG 66 in April 1943. Operations came to an end in early 1944. It fell to the Versuchskommando of KG 200 to undertake the last missile attack with Do 217s, 12 aircraft from this unit launching their Hs 293s against the Oder bridges on 12 April 1945.

Left: The Do 217 was tested with a brake chute, intended to reduce landing roll but also as a means to stabilise the aircraft in the dive-bombing role, or to rapidly decelerate it to disrupt a fighter attack.

Left: This KG 2 Do 217E is seen after sliding into a ditch. Note the blacked out fuselage markings, a common feature of this unit, which regularly operated over England at night.

Above: A Do 217 peels away to port, probably in the course of a training flight. Bomber Do 217s normally sported black undersides for night sorties.

Below: The basic tactical unit of the Kampfverbände was the Kette (literally chain) of three bombers. Here one of the three breaks away to port.

Above: Luftwaffe personnel consider a Do 217E, possibly as part of the initial instruction of ground crew to this limited but nonetheless essential heavy bomber.

Above: Preparations for engine start-up on a Do 217E included the moving up of a starter trolley to provide essential services until at least one of the engines was running.

Below: Men of the Luftwaffe in the forward section of a Do 217's flight deck, where the pilot and bombardier were accommodated to port and starboard, respectively.

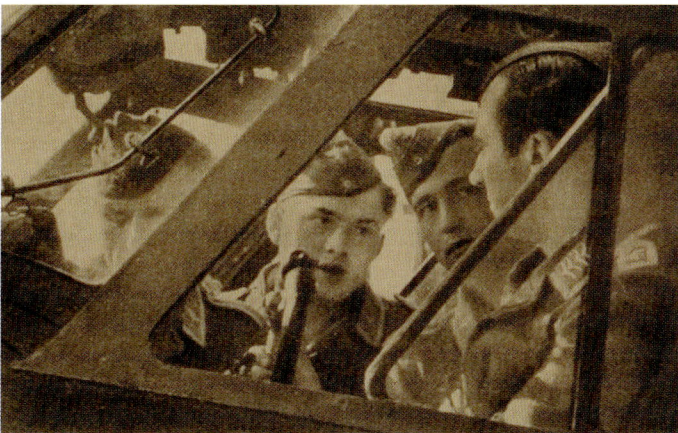

Above right: Seen from the Kette's third aircraft, two Do 217Es enter a shallow dive. The RLM had hoped that the Do 217 could be developed for the heavyweight dive-bomber role.

Below: A German magazine emphasises the fact that the Do 217's preferred operational medium was the night sky over enemy territory.

Left: There were a host of aerodynamic and, more importantly, structural problems associated with the petal-type dive brake developed by Dornier for the Do 217, and eventually the Reichsluftfahrtministrium conceded defeat and the bomber was operated ony in the level role.

Dornier Do 317

The Do 317 was schemed as a high-altitude bomber in response to the 'Bomber B' strategic bomber requirement, but after rejection was re-offered in two somewhat different forms. Only the less ambitious Do 317A was ordered, and then only in prototype form, though five of the six aircraft saw some service as missile-carriers.

When the Führungsstab der Luftwaffe drafted its so-called 'Bomber B' requirement, which was translated into a specification for issue to selected airframe manufacturers in July 1939 by the Technisches Amt of the Reichsluftfahrtministerium (RLM), the intention was not merely to create successors to the Junkers Ju 88 and Heinkel He 111, but also to carry the state of the art in medium bomber design a significant step forward.

The specification was noteworthy in the performance advances it demanded, and equally so in the design innovations it required. The 'Bomber B' had to possess a range of 3600 km (2,237 miles) to endow it with an operational radius sufficient to encompass the entire British Isles from bases that it was assumed would be available in France and Norway; a maximum speed of 600 km/h (373 mph) at 6000-7000 m (19,685-22,965 ft), which compared favourably with the speeds of the best contemporary fighters; and a bomb load of 2000 kg (4,409 lb). It had to carry three or four crew, possess a loaded weight in the order of 20000 kg (44,092 lb), and be of twin-engined configuration using the extremely advanced Daimler-Benz DB 604 or Junkers Jumo 222 liquid-cooled 24-cylinder engines then at an early stage in development, but the really radical demands of the specification were its insistence on pressurised crew accommodation and remotely controlled barbettes to carry the defensive armament.

Multi-company approach

The specification was first issued to Arado, Dornier, Focke-Wulf and Junkers, although the scope of the contest was later broadened to include Henschel when the RLM came to appreciate that this company had more pressure cabin experience than any of the other contestants, with the possible exception of Junkers. The final proposals of the original four competitors were submitted to the Technisches Amt in July 1940. Evaluation eliminated the Arado Ar 340, and prototypes were ordered of the **Do 317**, Fw 191 and Ju 288.

The Do 317 V1 was the first of Dornier's contributions to the 'Bomber B' programme, but revealed an insufficient performance advance over current concepts to warrant continued development.

Dornier's proposal was based broadly on the design of the Do 217 then undergoing prototype trials. The four crew were housed ahead of the wing in a pressure cabin which, taking the form of a detachable compartment pressurised by air tapped from the the DB 604 engines' superchargers, was extensively glazed by a series of curved panels. The Technisches Amt considered the technically more advanced projects tendered by Focke-Wulf and Junkers more promising than the Do 317, and Dornier was instructed to embody some of the features proposed for its 'Bomber B' in a new high-altitude version of the Do 217. Some design development of the Do 317 continued without priority as a possible back-up for the Fw 191 and Ju 288, but after attaining the mock-up stage in 1940, further work was stopped to allow efforts to be concentrated on the Do 217P high-altitude reconnaissance bomber.

In 1941, the Do 317 was resurrected and offered to the RLM as a potential production successor to the Do 217. Two versions were proposed: the simplified and less ambitious **Do 317A** powered by two DB 603A engines and featuring conventional defensive armament, and the more advanced **Do 317B** with DB 610 engines, remotely controlled defensive barbettes, and an extended wing. Six prototypes of the Do 317A were ordered, and the first of them the **Do 317 V1**

Of the six protoypes, the Do 317 V1 was the only machine to be completed with the cabin pressurisation equipment originally specified to provide good high-altitude conditions for the four-man crew.

Triangular endplate fin-and-rudder units characterised the Do 317 V1, although this was otherwise little more than a pressurised Do 217M. The few completed aircraft were Do 217R machines used as unpressurised Hs 293 missile-carriers.

(VK+IY), started its flight test programme in 1943. Following closely the structural design of the Do 217, the Do 317 V1 featured an all-metal two-spar wing carrying slotted ailerons interlinked with electrically operated split flaps, and housing a 1560-litre (343-Imp gal) fuel tank between the spars on each side of the fuselage, inboard of the engine nacelles, and a 215-litre (47-Imp gal) tank immediately outboard of each nacelle. The oval-section fuselage housed a further 2100 litres (462 Imp gal) of fuel in a main tank immediately aft of the pressure cabin and above the bomb bay, which was designed to accept up to six 500-kg (1,102-lb) bombs. Power came from two DB 603A liquid-cooled V-12 engines, and though no provision for defensive armament was made in the Do 317 V1, the production Do 317A was to have featured a single 13-mm (0.51-in) MG 131 machine-gun in an electrically operated turret in the roof of the pressure cabin, a 15-mm MG 151 fixed forward-firing cannon in the lower port side of the forward fuselage, a pair of 7.9-mm (0.31-in) MG 81 trainable machine-guns projecting from the starboard side of the nose glazing, and two 13-mm MG 131 trainable rearward-firing machine-guns as one above and the other below the fuselage.

No performance increase

Trials with the Do 317 V1 revealed no real performance advance over the Do 217P-0, and the decision was taken, therefore, to complete the remaining five prototypes without cabin pressurisation for use as Hs 293A missile-carriers. In this form the prototypes were redesignated **Do 217R**, and subsequently saw service with III/KG 100 at Orléans-Bricy. At this time, the Do 317B project had attained the full-scale mock-up stage, but the Technisches Amt concluded that it lacked sufficient promise to warrant further development, and thus the entire Do 317 programme was cancelled. Using the same basic airframe as the Do 317A, the Do 317B would have had a wing with span increased by 5.35 m (17 ft 6½ in), increased wing fuel tankage, maximum bomb load raised to 5600 kg (12,346 lb), and defensive armament also substantially enhanced.

Above: In this view the Do 317 V1 clearly shows its derivation from the Do 217, sharing the same wings and fuselage structure. The entire front end was a pressurised capsule. The V1 was powered by DB 603 engines, from which air was tapped to drive the pressurisation system.

Dornier Do 317B specification
(based on manufacturer's estimates, and data in square brackets applying specifically to the Do 317A)
Type: four-seat high-altitude heavy bomber
Powerplant: two Daimler-Benz DB 610A/B liquid-cooled double V-12 engines each rated at 2150 kW (2,870 hp) for take-off and 1909 kW (2,560 hp) at 25,000 ft (7620 m) [DB 603 liquid-cooled inverted V-12 engines each rated at 1305 kW (1,750 hp) for take-off and 1212 kW (1,625 hp) at 5700 m (18,700 ft)]
Performance: maximum speed 670 km/h (416 mph) at 7620 m (25,000 ft); maximum cruising speed 540 km/h (336 mph) at optimum altitude; service ceiling 10500 m (34,450 ft) maximum range on standard internal fuel 3600 km (2,237 miles), with auxiliary tank in forward bomb bay 4000 km (2,485 miles)
Weight: maximum take-off 24000 kg (52,910 lb)
Dimensions: wingspan 26.00 m (85 ft 3½ in) [20.65 m (67 ft 8½ in)]; length 16.80 m (55 ft 1½ in); height 5.45 m (17 ft 10½ in)
Armament: (defensive) two 13-mm (0.51-in) MG 131 machine-guns in electrically operated upper turret, two 7.9-mm (0.31-in) MG 81 machine-guns in remotely controlled chin barbette, two 13-mm MG 131 machine-guns in remotely controlled dorsal barbette, and one 20-mm MG 151/20 cannon in remotely controlled tail position; (offensive) maximum bomb load 5600 kg (12,346 lb) internally plus two 1800-kg (3,968-lb) bombs on underwing racks; typical internal loads were four 1400-kg (3,086-lb) or two 1800-kg) bombs, or two 1400-kg bombs and a 1600-litre (352-Imp gal) auxiliary fuel tank in forward bomb bay

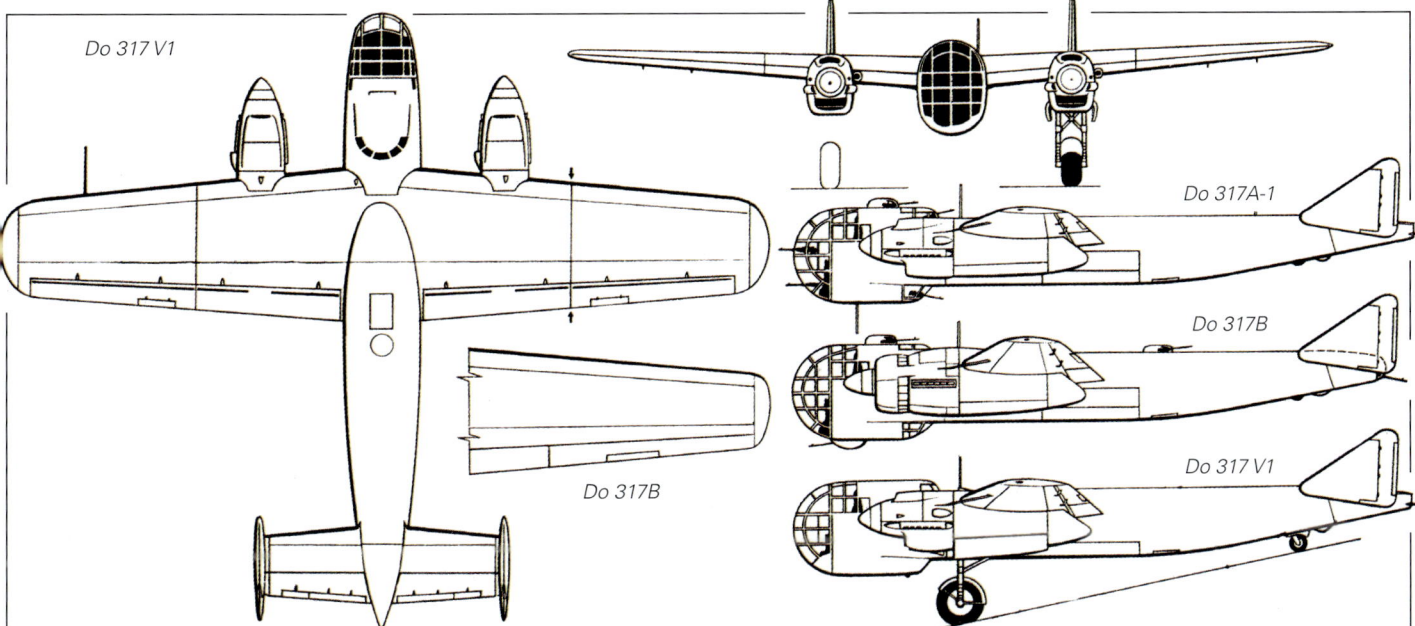

Do 317 V1

Do 317B

Do 317A-1

Do 317B

Do 317V1

Do 317B

Dornier Do 335

With its tandem push/pull arrangement of propellers at the ends of the single fuselage, the Do 335 was unique among piston-engined fighters. The type was full of potential for several roles, but development and production were slow, and the Do 335 had not entered operational service before the end of World War II.

Throughout the history of military aircraft design, few successful warplanes justifiably claiming to be unique at their birth have retained this status for any great length of time, the features rendering them unique invariably being plagiarised by their competitors. An exception among piston-engined fighters was the **Do 335**, which was unique at conception and remained so.

Named by Adolf Hitler himself on 26 March 1945 as the **Pfeil** (arrow), but also nicknamed 'Ameisenbär' (ant-eater), the Do 335 was radical rather than revolutionary. Its centreline thrust concept was not new in itself. The tandem fore-and-aft engine arrangement for twin-engined fighters stemmed, in fact, from World War I, when the notion was embodied in the Fokker K I and Siemens-Schuckert DDr I, both twin-boom aircraft with the engines mounted fore and aft of a pilot seated in a central nacelle. Between the wars a similar arrangement was adopted for the Chernyshov-designed ANT-23 and the Fokker D.XXIII, while in France, Messrs Vernisse and Galtier working at the Arsenal de l'Aéronautique displayed rather more ingenuity in achieving the same end with their VG 20 (later VB 10) fighter which, dispensing with the twin booms, employed contra-rotating propellers driven through concentric shafts.

The Do 335 offered yet a third variation on the centreline thrust theme, the rear engine driving a propeller aft of a cruciform tail. This unusual propeller position again was not new in itself, for the Tatin-Paulhan Aéro-Torpille of 1911 had employed just such an arrangement, but until the debut of the Do 335 no aircraft had coupled this oddly situated propeller with an orthodox tractor propeller, the Pfeil thus being rendered unique among combat aircraft.

Maximum power with minimum wetted area

The periodic revival of the centreline thrust concept was understandable in view of the fighter designer's constant demand for more power than was afforded by contemporary engines and the penalties exacted in the form of increased drag and reduced manoeuvrability by the adoption of two

The Do 335A-0 pre-production fighter was armed with a hub-firing 30-mm MK 103 cannon and two cowling-mounted 15-mm MG 151 cannon. This is the seventh of an initial batch of 10 Do 335A-0s.

engines in an orthodox wing-mounted arrangement. With the power from both engines delivered along the centreline, the desired attributes of minimal frontal area and a clean wing could be obtained, these being coupled with the elimination of power asymmetry in the event of an engine failure.

Prof.-Dr. Claudius Dornier had revealed an interest in the centreline thrust concept early in his career, using a tandem arrangement of one tractor and one pusher engine for his Gs 1 flying-boat of 1919, and retaining this for many of his subsequent designs. However, it was not until the mid-1930s that he gave active consideration to its adaptation for high-speed combat aircraft. Dornier patented the layout in 1937, and to prove the practicability of the aft-mounted propeller with its long extension shaft he commissioned Ulrich Hütter to design a small test-bed.

This Göppingen Gö 9 was built by Schempp-Hirth, and its data included a wingspan of 7.20 m (23 ft 7½ in), length of 6.80 m (22 ft 3¾ in) and gross weight of 720 kg (1,587 lb).

During initial tests at Oberpfaffenhofen and Rechlin, the Do 335 V1 demonstrated superb acceleration and generally very good handling. However, problems were found with the landing gear doors, which were removed for most of the aircraft's flying career. The unique propulsion arrangement is fully evident in this side view.

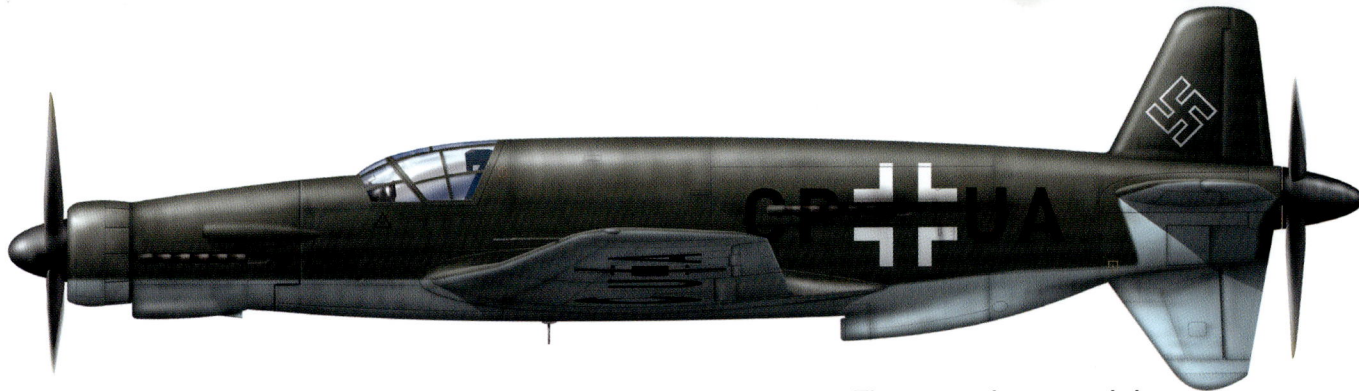

This is the Do 335 V1, depicted in the scheme it wore for its first flight in October 1943. The nose engine was cooled by air passing through an annular radiator, and the rear engine by air ducted through a ventral radiator installation.

Power was provided by a 60-kW (80-hp) Hirth HM 60R air-cooled engine mounted beneath the wing at the centre of gravity and driving a four-blade wooden propeller aft of a cruciform tail by means of a long transmission shaft. After protracted ground trials, the Gö 9 was eventually flown early in 1940, and during subsequent testing attained 220 km/h (137 mph) in level flight, the pusher propeller and its extension shaft proving extremely efficient.

By this time Dornier had prepared several project studies for fighters embodying the radical propulsion arrangement, but although the Technisches Amt of the RLM evinced some interest, the Dornier-Werke's assigned types were bombers and flying boats. However, in 1942 the Technisches Amt issued a requirement for a single-seat unarmed intruder capable of carrying a 500-kg (1,102-lb) bomb load at speeds of the order of 800 km/h (497 mph). Arado, Dornier and Junkers submitted proposals to meet this requirement, and in the subsequent competitive evaluation Dornier's **Projekt 231**, employing the fore-and-aft engine arrangement, was the winner.

Many variants ordered

A development contract was promptly awarded, and the Projekt 231 was assigned the RLM designation Do 335, but shortly after the start of detail design the Dornier team was informed that the unarmed intruder requirement had been overtaken by a demand for a multi-purpose fighter of broadly similar performance, and was therefore instructed to investigate the possibility of adapting the Do 335 as a single-seat fighter-bomber, high-speed reconnaissance aircraft and heavy Zerstörer, and two-seat night fighter and all-weather interceptor. The redesign had been completed and the first metal had been cut on the prototypes by the end of 1942 at Oberpfaffenhofen, and when the **Do 335 V1** first prototype (CP+UA) made its initial flight on 26 October 1943 with Flugkapitän Hans Dieterle at the controls, contracts had been placed with Dornier for 14 Versuchs aircraft, 10 pre-production **Do 335A-0** and 11 production **Do 335A-1** single-seat fighter-bombers, and three **Do 335A-10** and **Do 335A-12** tandem two-seat dual-control conversion trainers.

After preliminary handling trials at Oberpfaffenhofen, the Do 335 V1 was ferried to the Erprobungsstelle Rechlin for official trials. Although they discovered some snaking and porpoising at high speeds, the Rechlin pilots were generally enthusiastic over the characteristics of the Do 335 V1, commenting favourably on its general handling behaviour, manoeuvrability and, in particular, high acceleration and small turning circle. The aircraft was flown on the power of the forward engine alone and on the aft engine alone, and with forward engine cut and propeller feathered a speed of 560 km/h (348 mph) was clocked in level flight.

During the winter of 1943-44, the first prototype was

The Do 335's wide-track undercarriage units retracted into bays in the underside of the wing. In the V1 the bays were left uncovered while new doors were redesigned for subsequent aircraft.

joined in the test programme by several more aircraft. The **Do 335 V2** (CP+UB) was powered by the DB 603A-2 engine rated at 1305 kW (1,750 hp) for take-off at 2,700 r.p.m. and 1379 kW (1,850 hp) at 2100 m (6,890 ft), and first flew on the last day of 1943, again with Dieterle as pilot. The **Do 335 V3** (Werk Nr 230003, CP+UC) with 1417-kW (1,900-hp) DB 603G-0 engines, was first flown on

Above: Despite the Do 335's tricycle undercarriage, pilots were advised to land in a tail-down attitude on the mainwheels and bumper wheel built into the bottom of the lower fin.

Above: This was the seventh Do 335A-0 pre-production fighter. The low-drag installation of the forward engine meant that the nosewheel had to be accommodated under the cockpit.

Dornier Do 335

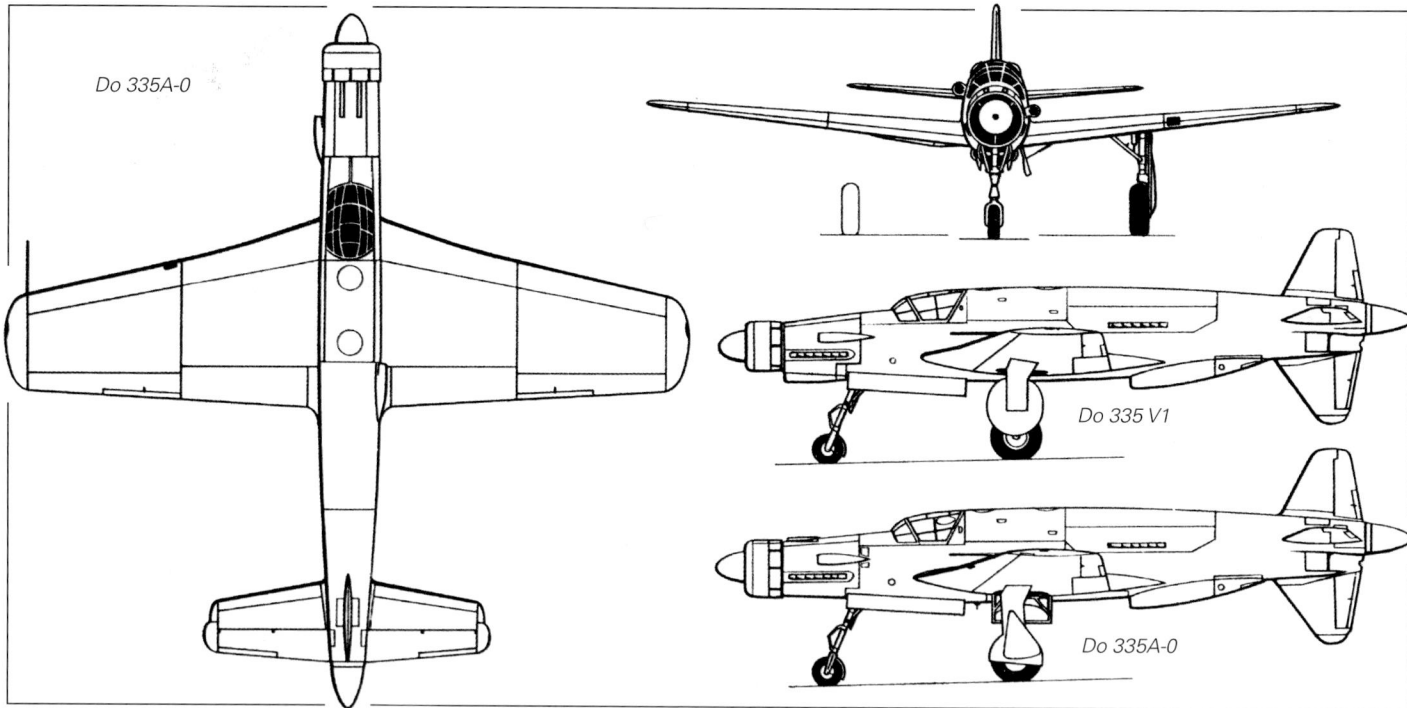

Do 335A-0

Do 335 V1

Do 335A-0

flew on 20 January 1944 by Werner Altrogge. The V2 and V3 were retained for flight trials at Oberpfaffenhofen, and differed from the initial prototype in several minor respects. The external oil cooler intake was deleted and incorporated in an enlarged annular cowling; criticisms of poor rear vision were overcome by the provision of blisters, fitted with rear-view mirrors, in the cockpit canopy, and the mainwheel well covers were redesigned, the one-piece circular plates giving place to divided covers whose inboard portions were attached to the wing roots.

In the autumn of 1943, Dornier proposed the **Do 435** as a night/all-weather interceptor development of the Do 335. The Do 435 was to have featured a simplified structure and

Above: A number of Do 335s were captured by the Allies, of which at least two were shipped to the United States. One of these aircraft is now on display at the National Air & Space Museum.

Seen in US markings while under evaluation, this is now the sole Do 335 survivor. In the 1970s it was restored by Dornier at the factory where it had been completed as the second Do 335A-0.

side-by-side seating for its two crew members, with cabin pressurisation and long-span wooden outer wing panels. The **Do 335 V4** (CP+UD) was fitted with larger wings in connection with the programme. The Do 335 V4 crashed on 24 December 1944, killing its pilot.

Potent armament

The **Do 335 V5** was the second prototype to be fitted with armament, in the form of one 30-mm engine-mounted MK 103 cannon with 70 rounds and two 15-mm MG 151 cannon with 200 r.p.g. mounted in the upper decking of the forward fuselage. This prototype was delivered to the Waffenerprobungsstelle at Tarnewitz for firing trials in late September 1944.

The **Do 335 V6** and **Do 335 V7** were assigned to equipment trials, the Do 335 V6 later being transferred to Junkers at Dessau, where it was employed through the summer of 1944 for ground tests to solve the various problems with the rear engine. The **Do 335 V8** was fitted with the definitive DB 603E-1 engines and was used for night-flying trials with flame-dampers. The **Do 335 V9** was completed to pre-production standard and was the first aircraft to be fitted with full armament. It was delivered to the Erprobungsstelle Rechlin in August 1944.

The Do 335 V9 was followed off the line by the first **Do 335A-0** (Werk Nr 240101, VG+PG) intended for service evaluation as a single-seat fighter-bomber. The aircraft was, however, destroyed during a US bombing raid on Friedrichshafen on 20 July 1944.

Powered by two DB 603A-2 engines, the Do 335A-0 was an all-metal low-wing cantilever monoplane. The trapezoidal stressed-skin wing featured 13-degree taper on the leading edge and was built round a single box spar. Forward of the spar the centre section housed a 310-litre (68-Imp gal) self-sealing fuel tank on each side of the fuselage, and the trailing edges carried variable-camber flaps inboard of the ailerons. The wing also accommodated the master compass, armoured hydraulic fluid reservoir, and compressed air bottles. The tail assembly was of cruciform type with a cantilever tailplane and upper and lower fins and rudders, the lower fin incorporating a tail bumper with an oleo leg. The tail assembly was covered

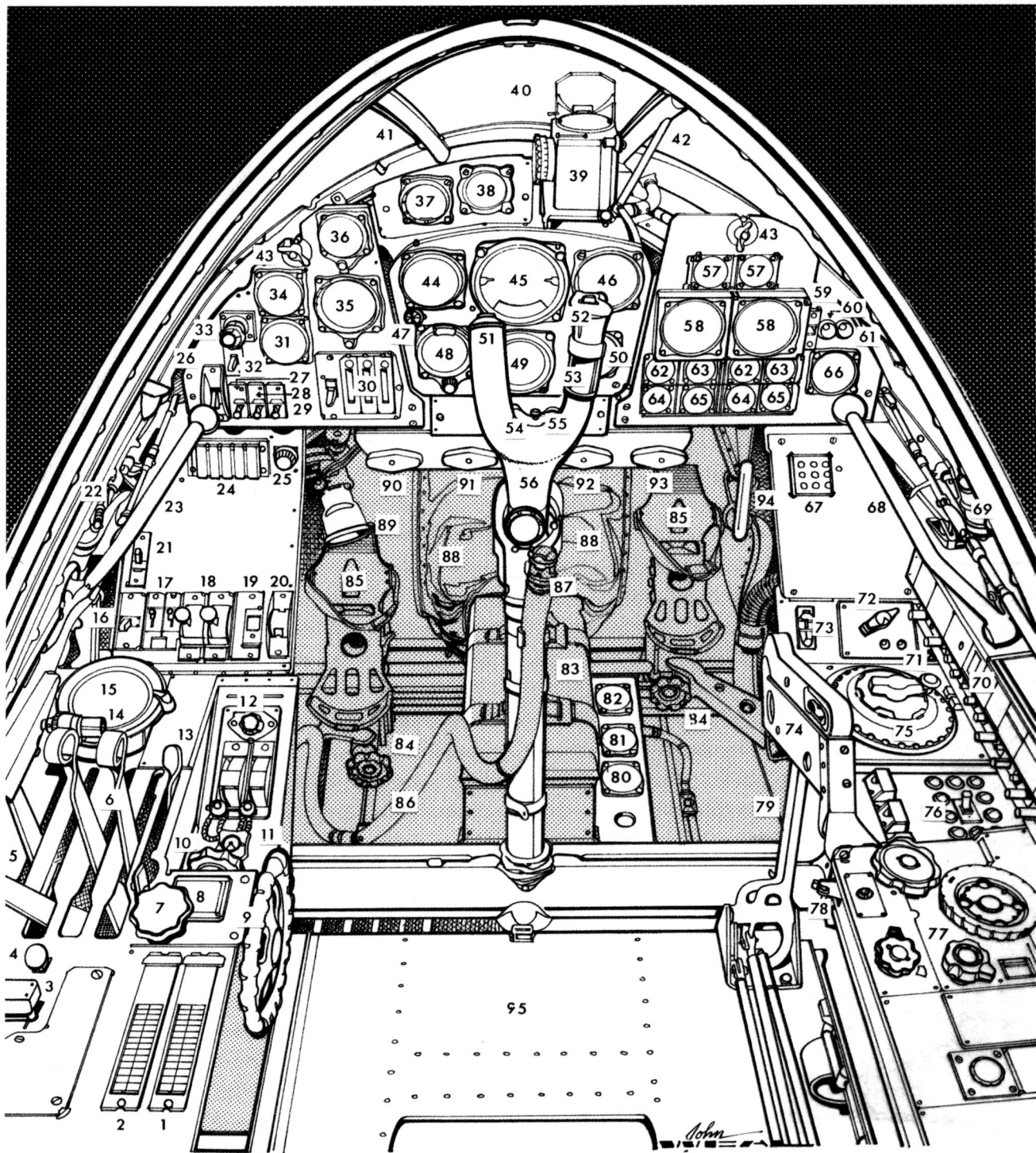

Dornier Do 335A cockpit layout

1   Deviation tables (master compass)
2   Deviation tables (standby compass)
3   Rear engine fire-extinguisher button (covered)
4   Front engine fire-extinguisher knob
5   Fuel safety cock levers
6   Throttle levers
7   Rudder trim handwheel
8   Trim indicator
9   Elevator trim handwheel
10 Aileron trim handwheel
11 Oxygen flow valve
12 Main electrics emergency switch
13 Throttle lock
14 Compass lamp
15 Standby (emergency) compass
16 Steering switch
17 Propeller selector switches (2)
18 Propeller manual control switches (2)
19 Landing flaps switch
20 Undercarriage switch

21 Explosives charge switch (belly landing)
22 UV light
23 Canopy release lever
24 Undercarriage position indicator
25 Compass lamp dimmer switch
26 Searchlight switch
27 Identification/navigation lights switch
28 Instrument panel lighting switch
29 Pitot heating switch
30 Armament control panel (SZKK3)
31 Gyro control switch
32 Auxiliary identification lights switch
33 UV lights dimmer switch
34 External air temperature indicator
35 Radio altimeter
36 Clock
37 Oxygen pressure gauge
38 Oxygen regulator
39 Revi 16D gunsight
40 Windshield
41 Windshield frame

42 Gunsight brace
43 Hinged panel sections retaining screws
44 Airspeed indicator
45 Artificial horizon
46 Variometer
47 Pitot heating indicator
48 Altimeter
49 Master (repeater) compass
50 AFN2 radio navigation
51 Bomb release button (left horn of control column)
52 Fuselage cannon firing button (right horn of control column; MG 151 firing button on forward face of horn)
53 Course setting (autopilot)
54 Autopilot switch
55 R/T transmit button
56 Control column
57 Propeller pitch indicators
58 Combined pressure/RPM indicators
59 Fuel transfer pump switch (nose auxiliary tank)

60 Rate-of-use fuel warning lamp
61 Fuel contents warning lamp
62 Coolant temperature gauges
63 Oil temperature gauges
64 Fuel pressure gauges
65 Oil pressure gauges
66 Fuel contents gauge
67 Fire warning lamps
68 Canopy emergency jettison lever
69 UV light
70 Electrics switch panel
71 Explosives charge switch (abandon aircraft)
72 BG 25a control panel
73 'Kurs' (Course) axial-switch
74 Ejector seat activating mechanism
75 ZSK 246 fuse box and selector switch
76 ASK 335 bomb release switch panel
77 FuG 16Z(Y) control panel
78 Radio selector switch
79 Provision for FBG 2 installation

80 Ejector seat system pressure gauge
81 Emergency compressed air pressure gauge
82 Pressure oil pressure gauge
83 Battery casing
84 Rudder pedal adjustment starwheels
85 Rudder pedals
86 Oxygen hose
87 Oxygen connection
88 Cannon breech cover
89 Spotlamp
90 Undercarriage emergency switch
91 Landing flaps emergency switch
92 Steering emergency switch
93 Bomb-bay doors emergency switch
94 Bomb-bay doors emergency lever
95 Ejector seat base

Dornier Do 335

Structure

An all-metal cantilever monoplane, the Do 335 had a dihedralled trapezoidal stressed-skin wing with a leading-edge sweep of 13 degrees, and was built round a single box spar. The cantilever tailplane was of similar construction, but the vertical fins had wooden leading edges. The all-metal monocoque fuselage incorporated an internal weapons bay immediately aft of the nosewheel bay.

Cockpit

The cockpit was of extremely low drag design, and this necessitated the addition of small blisters in the canopy sides, housing rear-view mirrors. On the prototypes the canopy slid aft, but on the Do 335A-0 and subsequent types it opened to starboard. In emergency, the canopy was jettisoned, and the upper fin and rear propeller were explosively separated. The pilot sat on a primitive ejection seat, in front of an armoured bulkhead that separated him from the 1230-litre (270.5-Imp gal) main fuel tank.

Two-seaters

The Do 335 V10, as prototype for the Do 335A-6 two-seat night fighter, introduced a second cockpit, aft of the first, for the radar operator. The Do 335 V11 was the prototype for the Do 335A-10 two-seat trainer, and as such had a rear cockpit accommodating an instructor pilot. The Do 335 V12 was similar, although powered by the DB 603E-1.

Tail unit

The Do 335 had a cruciform tail unit, with the conventional (dorsal) fin augmented by a ventral fin of similar size and shape, and fitted with a second rudder and trim tab. This lower fin could be jettisoned in the event of a belly landing. The fixed horizontal tailplane was conventional, with full-span elevators and outboard trim tabs.

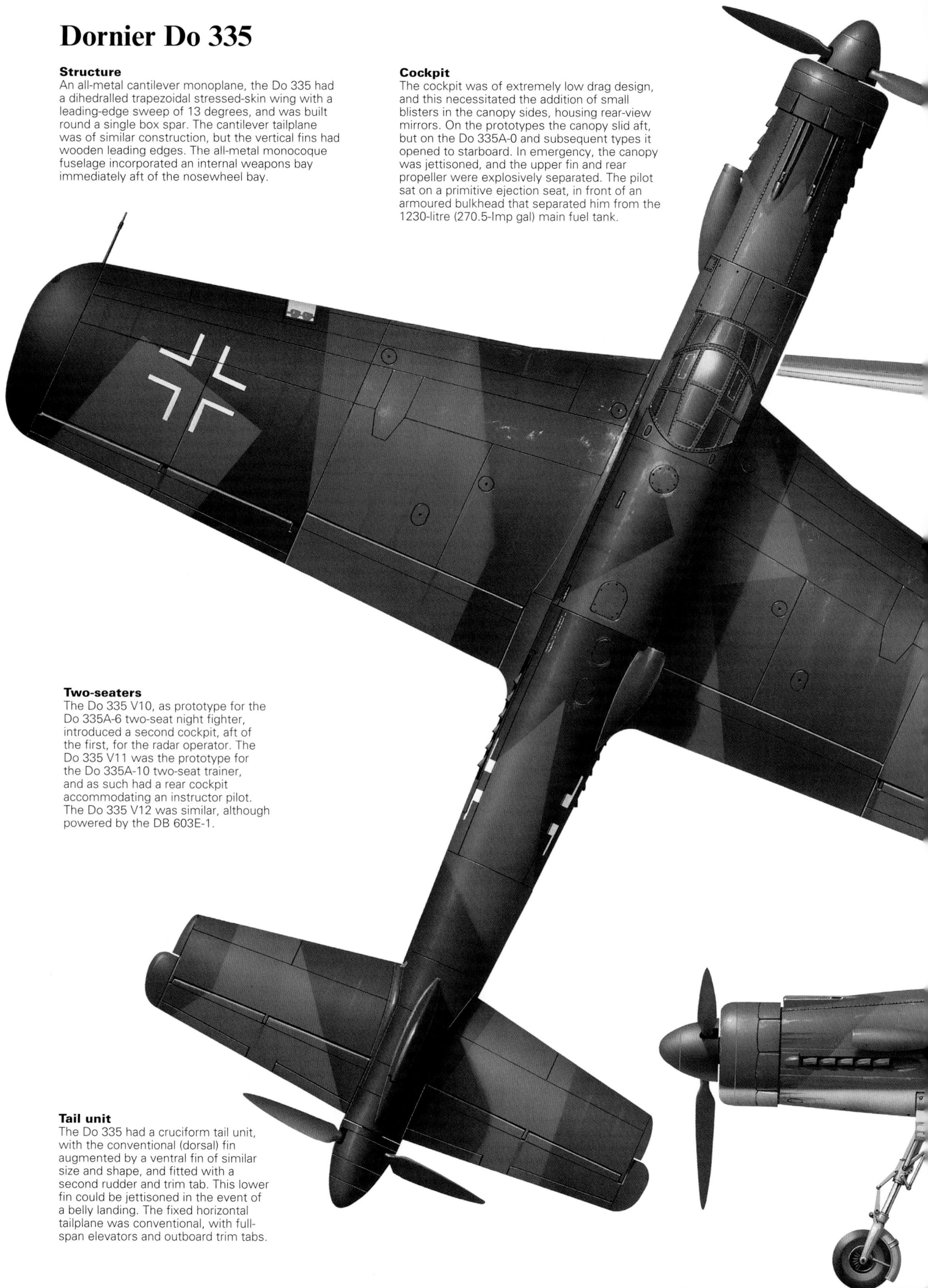

Intake
The underslung airscoop below the aft fuselage provided ram air to the aft engine's radiator, the forward engine having an annular radiator in the circular cowling.

Powerplant
Installed engine power increased in each successive Do 335 sub-variant. The Do 335 V1 was powered by a pair of Daimler-Benz DB 603A-2 engines, each rated at 1305 kW (1,750 hp), while the production Do 335A-1 introduced the more powerful 1342-kW (1,800-hp) DB 603E-1 with an enlarged supercharger. Planned later variants featured the 1417-kW (1,900-hp) DB 603G with high-speed superchargers and increased compression ratio, or the DB 603E with water-methanol injection. The Do 335B would have had the DB 603LA, with two-stage superchargers. A single prototype (the Do 335 V7) was fitted with Jumo 213A and 213E engines which were at one time considered as an alternative powerplant to the DB 603. The aircraft did not fly with Jumo engines, however.

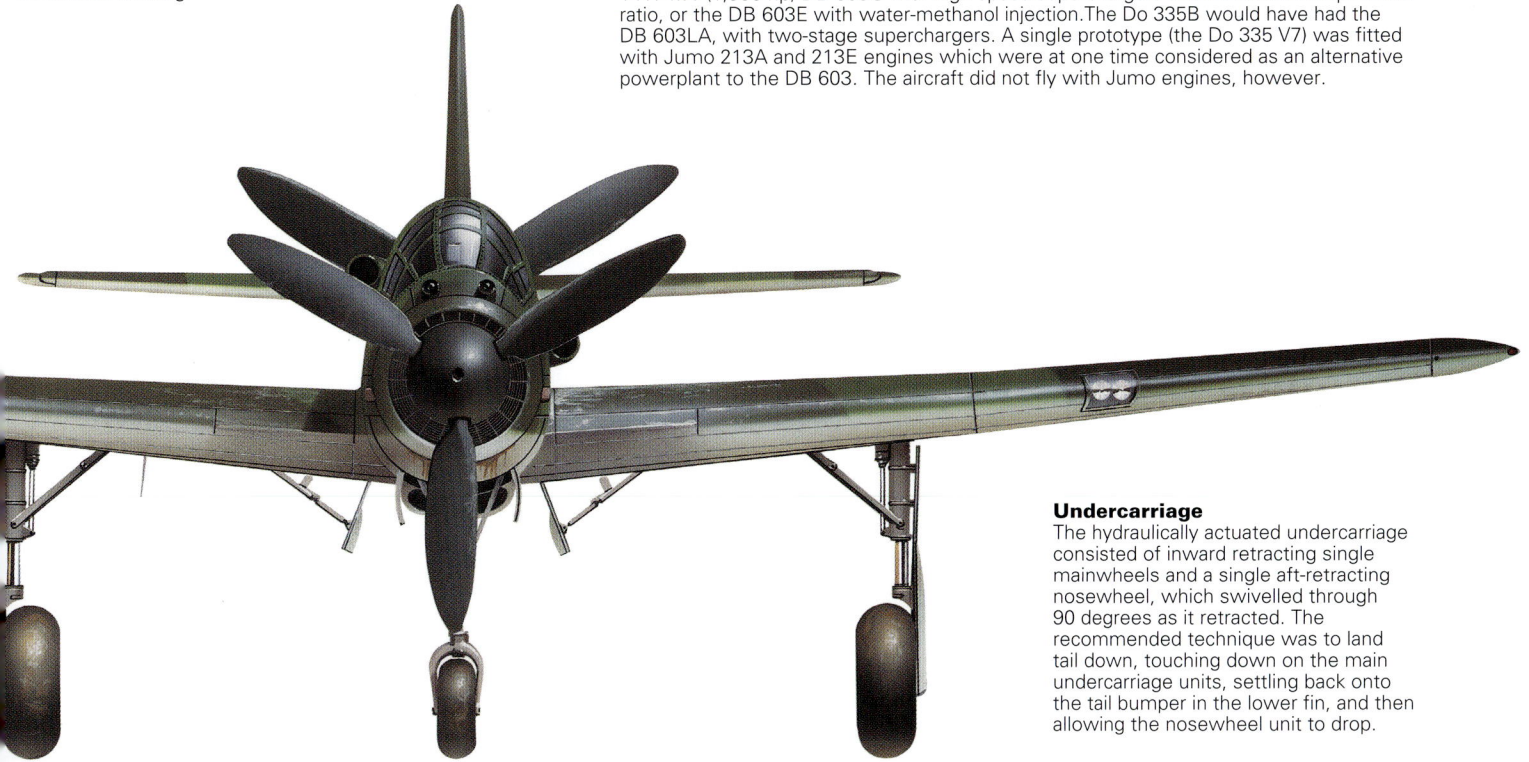

Undercarriage
The hydraulically actuated undercarriage consisted of inward retracting single mainwheels and a single aft-retracting nosewheel, which swivelled through 90 degrees as it retracted. The recommended technique was to land tail down, touching down on the main undercarriage units, settling back onto the tail bumper in the lower fin, and then allowing the nosewheel unit to drop.

Dornier Do 335A-0

Erprobungskommando 335
Oberpfaffenhofen, May 1945

This is the seventh of 10 Do 335A-0 pre-production aircraft, most of which were used by Erprobungskommando 335 for service evaluation. This was as close as the Do 335 came to Luftwaffe service. Even had the type reached front-line units it would have done little to stem the tide of the Allied advances from east and west, and its unusual layout did nothing to lessen its in-built obsolescence at the dawn of the jet age.

Iain Wyllie

Dornier Do 335

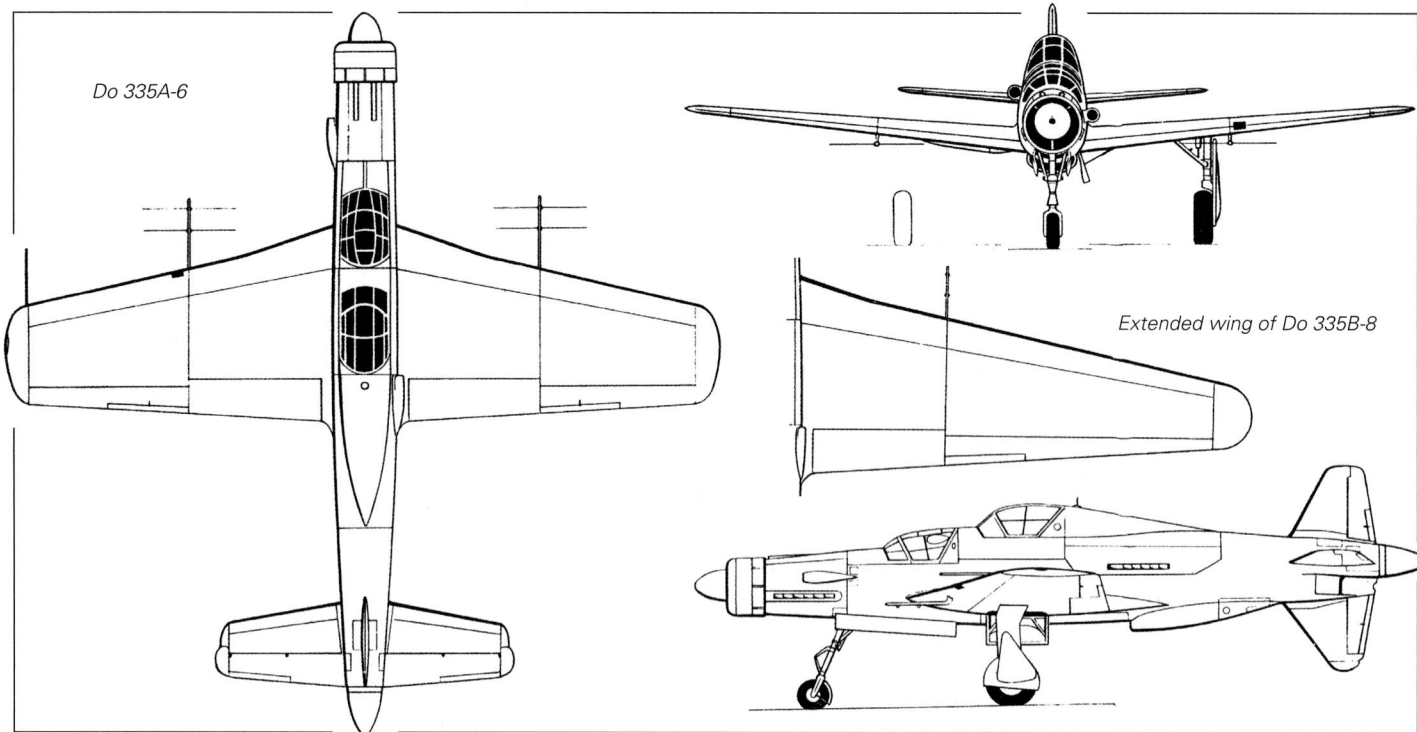

Do 335A-6

Extended wing of Do 335B-8

by a stressed metal skin except for the leading edges of the fins, which were of wood and housed radio aerials.

The fuselage was an all-metal monocoque. The nose-mounted DB 603A-2's coolant passed through an annular nose radiator, and the aft-mounted engine had a ventral scoop radiator. The tractor propeller was of reversible-pitch type, and the pusher propeller was driven via a hollow extension shaft supported by three thrust races. The main fuel tank of 1230-litre (270.5-Imp gal) capacity was installed aft of the cockpit, together with two 102-litre (22.4-Imp gal) oil tanks, and the weapons bay beneath the tank bay could house either one 500-kg (1,102-lb) PC 500 or SD 500 bomb, or two 250-kg (551-lb) SC 250 bombs. The cockpit was enclosed by a jettisonable canopy that, unlike the aft-sliding canopies of the prototypes, hinged to starboard, and was separated from the tank bay by an armour bulkhead. The pilot was provided with an ejection seat and provision was made for the upper vertical tail surface and rear propeller to be jettisoned by means of explosive bolts that were actuated with the ejection seat. The pilot was provided with a Revi C 12/D reflector sight which, mounted on a Schwenkplatte (swivel-plate) SP 1, could be used both as a gun sight and as a dive-bombing sight, and the radio equipment included FuG 16ZY R/T, FuG 25a IFF, and an FuG 125a blind-landing receiver. All three members of the undercarriage were hydraulically operated, the mainwheels being raised inwards and the nose-wheel turning through 90 degrees and retracting backwards. Despite the provision of a tricycle undercarriage, pilots were recommended to land tail-down, using the mainwheels and the tail bumper for the initial impact before allowing the nose to drop onto the nosewheel. In the event that a wheels-up landing proved necessary provision was made for jettisoning the lower vertical surfaces.

Operational evaluation

Several of the Do 335A-0 pre-production aircraft were used by the Erprobungskommando 335 formed in September 1944 for service evaluation of the Pfeil and for the development of operational tactics. Before the establishment of this unit, however, the Do 335 V3, which had been undergoing RLM trials at Rechlin and Mengen, was transferred to the 1. Staffel of the Versuchsverband der Oberkommando der Luftwaffe (acquiring the new code T9+ZH) for service trials after the installation of a photo-reconnaissance camera in the bomb bay.

None of the intended initial production model, the **Do 335A-1**, that appeared on the production lines during autumn of 1944, were completed before the end of

This is the Do 335 V11, prototype for the DB 603A-powered Do 335A-10 two-seat dual-control trainer. The extra cockpit radically reduced the available fuel tankage, which resulted in the deletion of the weapon bay to provide revised fuel tanks.

The Do 335 V11 was the prototype for the Do 335A-10 two-seat trainer. Both this and the V12 prototype for the Do 335A-12 were delivered unarmed, but the intention was to complete the production model with the armament of the Do 335A-1.

the war. The **Do 335A-2** was a proposed bomber variant, while the **Do 335A-3** was intended to be a photo-reconnaissance version, modified in small numbers from the A-1. The **Do 335A-4** was also intended as a single-seat photo-reconnaissance conversion, equipped with one or two cameras in the fuselage bay; this apparently remained only a project.

The **Do 335 V10** served as the first prototype for the **Do 335A-6**, a radar-equipped, two-seat, all-weather and night interceptor. A second cockpit for the radar operator was inserted behind and above the normal cockpit. In order to provide space for the additional cockpit the fuel tankage was drastically revised, the weapons bay being used to accommodate a jettisonable 500-litre (110-Imp gal) fuel tank. The aircraft retained the capability to carry bombs instead of the extra tank. Additionally a 310-litre (68-Imp gal) fuel tank was installed in each wing leading edge, plus a hard point on

each wing could carry a 300-litre (66-Imp gal) drop tank, giving a total capacity of 2,320 litres (510 Imp gal).

Cannon armament remained unchanged, but an FuG 101a radio altimeter was introduced, along with FuG 218 Neptun intercept radar with wing-mounted antennas. Exhaust flame-damping tubes for the fore and aft engines added their measure of drag to that provided by the second cockpit and the radar antennas, yet the normal loaded weight was only increased by 90 kg (198 lb) over that of the A-1. Performance fell by some 10 per cent, but the addition of 75 litres (16.5 Imp gal) in small tanks in each wing for MW 50 methanol-water injection for power boosting below the rated altitude of the engines made the performance acceptable. The only modification additionally required to the engines by the MW 50 installation was special spark plugs. Use of the MW 50 increased engine power to 1491 kW (2,000 hp) for short periods, although it did eventually reduce engine life. It was intended that all A-6 models be converted from A-1 production aircraft.

Conversion trainers

Two further two-seaters were the **Do 335 V11** and **Do 335 V12** prototype dual control conversion trainers, powered respectively by the DB 603A-2 and DB 603E-1 engines. It was the intention that those with the DB 603A engines were to be converted from A-0 models to **A-10** trainers, while **A-12** variants were to be converted from A-1s. In the event no A-12 trainers were ever built. Having a raised second cockpit similar to that of the Do 335 V10, but equipped with full instrumentation and controls, and occupied by the instructor, the Do 335 V11 and V12 were delivered without armament, but weapons similar to those of the Do 335A-1 may have been specified for production models.

Left: This is possibly the Do 335 V12, prototype for the Do 335A-12 tandem two-seat dual-control trainer. The Do 335A-12 had DB 603E power and was a conversion of a Do 335A-1 airframe, whereas the similar Do 335A-10 was a converted Do 335A-0 and had the DB 603A-2.

Below: Dornier and test personnel cluster round a two-seat trainer. Note the starboard-hinged canopy. The two-seat layout was also employed in the night-fighter variants, providing a second seat for a radar operator.

When US forces over-ran the Oberpfaffenhofen factory some 22 Do 335A-0 single-seaters had been completed. Of these some 11 had been converted to Do 335A-10 trainers, and nine or ten further A-1/A-12 models were in final assembly. Components for nearly 30 additional aircraft had been completed. Production of the Do 335A-6 night and all-weather fighter had been transferred to Heinkel's factory at Vienna, but despite the high priority allocated to this pro-gramme, circumstances prevented the necessary jigs and tools being assembled.

With the worsening of Germany's war situation, development emphasis in the Pfeil programme switched from the Do 335A fighter-bomber to the more heavily armed **Do 335B** Zerstörer, and during the winter of 1944-45 the first Do 335B

Dornier Do 335B-2 cutaway key

This head-on view emphasises the drag advantages of placing the two engines almost in longitudinal line with each other.

1 Upper rudder trim tab
2 Upper rudder
3 Upper tailfin (jettisonable by means of explosive bolts)
4 VDM airscrew of 3.30 m (10.83 ft) diameter
5 Airscrew spinner
6 Airscrew pitch mechanism
7 Starboard elevator

8 Elevator tab
9 Metal stressed-skin tailplane structure
10 Ventral rudder
11 Tail bumper
12 Tail bumper oleo shock-absorber
13 Ventral tailfin (jettisonable for belly landing)
14 Coolant outlet
15 Rear navigation light
16 Explosive bolt seatings
17 Rudder and elevator tab controls
18 Hollow airscrew extension shaft
19 Rear airscrew lubricant feeds
20 Aft bulkhead
21 Coolant trunking
22 Oil cooler radiator

33 Aft Daimler-Benz DB 603E-1 12-cylinder inverted-Vee liquid-cooled engine rated at 1340 kW (1,800 hp) for take-off and 1415 kW (1,900 hp) at 1800 m (5,905 ft)

23 Coolant radiator
24 Fire extinguisher
25 Ventral air intake
26 FuG 25a IFF
27 FuG 125a blind landing receiver
28 Rear engine access cover latches
29 Exhaust stubs
30 Supercharger intake
31 Coolant tank
32 Engine bearer

34 Supercharger
35 Aft firewall
36 FuG 25a ring antenna
37 Fuel filler cap
38 Main fuel tank (1230-litre/270-Imp gal capacity)
39 Secondary ventral fuel tank
40 Two (45-litre/9.9-Imp gal capacity) lubricant tanks (port for forward engine and starboard for rear engine)
41 Pilot's back armour

42 Rearview mirror in glazed teardrop

43 Headrest
44 Pilot's armoured ejection seat

45 Clear-vision panel
46 Jettisonable canopy (hinged to starboard)
47 Protected hydraulic fluid tank (45-litre/9.9-Imp gal capacity)
48 Undercarriage hydraulics cylinder

49 Oxygen bottles
50 Port flaps

51 Aileron tab
52 Port wing fuel tank
53 Port aileron
54 Master compass
55 Pitot head

56 Twin landing lights
57 Cannon muzzle of 30-mm Rheinmetall Borsig MK 103
58 Cannon fairing
59 Ammunition tray
60 Windscreen

61 Port control console (trim settings)
62 Control column
63 Twin 20-mm Mauser MG 151/20 cannon
64 Ammunition box
65 Forward firewall
66 Breech of nose-mounted MK 103 cannon
67 Engine bearer
68 Forward DB 603E-1 engine
69 MG 151 cannon blast tubes
70 Gun trough
71 Hydraulically-operated cooling gills
72 Coolant radiator (upper segment)
73 Oil cooler radiator (lower segment)

74 VDM airscrew of 3.50 m (11.48 ft) diameter
75 Airscrew spinner
76 MK 103 cannon port
77 Armoured radiator ring
78 Coolant tank (15-litre/3.3-Imp gal capacity)
79 Exhaust stubs
80 Nosewheel oleo leg
81 Nosewheel scissors
82 Damper
83 Nosewheel

Dornier Do 335

The Do 335 V9 ninth prototype was completed to full pre-production standard and delivered to the Erprobungsstelle Rechlin for evaluation. The armament consisted of a single 30-mm MK 103 cannon firing forward through the hollow shaft of the tractor propeller, and a pair of 15-mm MG 151 cannon, aimed by a Revi C 12/D reflector gun sight. This was mounted on a swivel plate and could function as either a gunsight or as a dive-bombing sight.

84 Mudguard
85 Retraction strut
86 Nosewheel door
87 MK 103 cannon ammunition tray
88 Collector tray
89 Accumulator
90 Electric systems panel
91 Ejection seat compressed air bottles
92 Rudder pedals
93 Ammunition tray
94 Armour
95 Cannon fairing
96 MK 103 barrel
97 Muzzle brake
98 Ammunition feed chute
99 Starboard MK 103 wing cannon
100 Mainwheel retraction strut
101 Oleo leg
102 Starboard mainwheel
103 Mainwheel door
104 Forward face of box spar

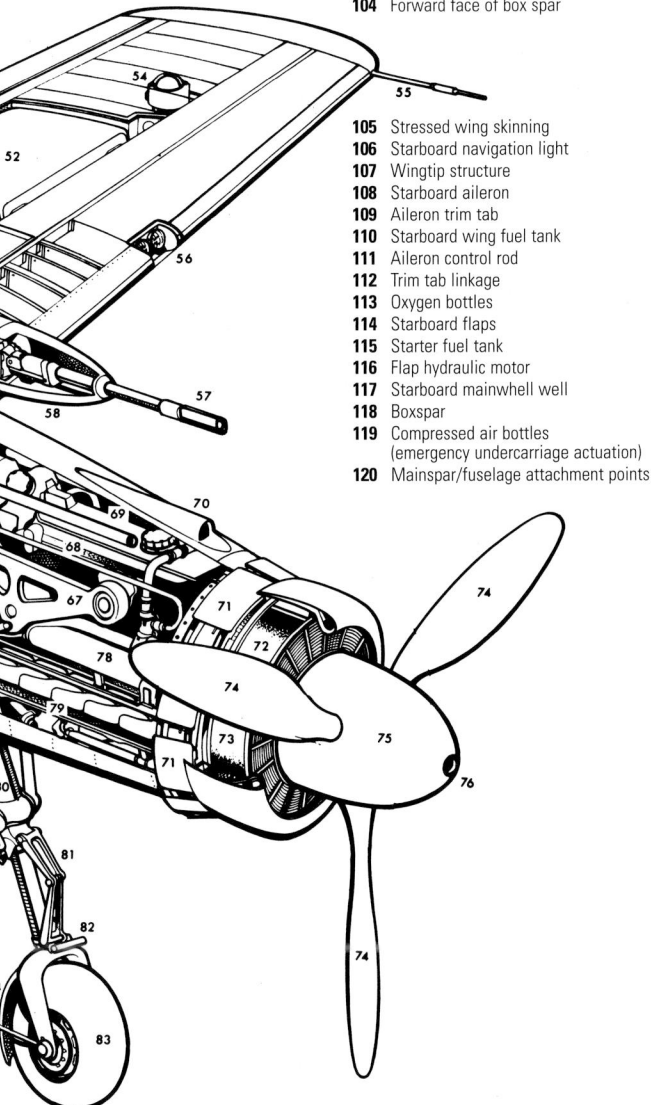

105 Stressed wing skinning
106 Starboard navigation light
107 Wingtip structure
108 Starboard aileron
109 Aileron trim tab
110 Starboard wing fuel tank
111 Aileron control rod
112 Trim tab linkage
113 Oxygen bottles
114 Starboard flaps
115 Starter fuel tank
116 Flap hydraulic motor
117 Starboard mainwhell well
118 Boxspar
119 Compressed air bottles (emergency undercarriage actuation)
120 Mainspar/fuselage attachment points

prototypes were completed at Oberpfaffenhofen. The initial B-series heavy fighters were essentially similar to the Do 335A-1 apart from armament and the deletion of the internal weapons bay, the latter's volume being used for a supplementary fuel tank.

The **Do 335 V13** served as a prototype for the **Do 335B-2** Zerstörer (which was in essence a strengthened Do 335A) and had two 30-mm MK 103 cannon in the wings, an armoured windscreen, a redesigned nose wheel and new wingtips to give an area of 41 m² (441.32 sq ft). The **Do 335 V14** (Werk Nr 230014) was also equipped with wing-mounted MK 103 cannon as a Do 335B-2 prototype. Two two-seat night-fighter prototypes, the **V15** and **V16**, were also flown, their exact sub-type being uncertain. The **Do 335 V17** was a B-series airframe intended as a two-seat night and all-weather fighter that was captured by French forces and completed and flown by them in 1947; the **Do 335 V18**, **Do 335 V19** and **Do 335 V20** were all intended to be fitted with long-span wings, possibly in connection with **Do 335B-6** development, but were destroyed before completion. There is some evidence that a few Do 335B-6s were produced by Heinkel at Oranienburg before the war's end.

Heinkel had been entrusted with the task of improving the altitude capability of both the single-seat Zerstörer and the two-seat night and all-weather fighter, and accordingly designed new wing outer panels that would have increased the overall span and gross area to 18.40 m (60 ft 4½ in) and

This captured Do 335A-0 (the fifth example) is pockmarked with small calibre bullet holes, probably inflicted by a bored Allied soldier in the aftermath of victory, or perhaps a reminder of the battle to capture this anonymous airfield. The Do 335 did not enter service before the Third Reich's defeat.

297

Dornier Do 335

Though large and heavy for a fighter, the Do 335 went through its development programme with few problems and revealed excellent performance and generally good handling.

Above: The Do 335A-1 initial production version appeared in the autumn of 1944. Emphasis soon switched to the more heavily armed Do 335B Zerstörer single-seat heavy fighter.

Below: Maintenance personnel work on a Do 335. The large intake on the port side of the forward engine cowling allowed ingress of air to the supercharger installation.

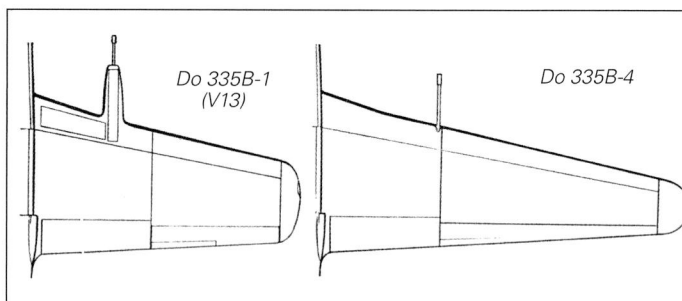

43.00 m² (462.848 sq ft). The new outer panels were to be fitted to the **Do 335B-4** single-seat Zerstörer (equivalent to the Do 335B-3), the **Do 335B-5** tandem two-seat conversion trainer, and the **Do 335B-8** two-seat night and all-weather fighter (equivalent to the Do 335B-7) but, like various other proposed derivatives of the basic Pfeil, the end of hostilities in Europe found these sub-types still on Dornier's drawing boards.

Dornier Do 335A-1 Pfeil specification
(data in square brackets relate to the Do 335A-6)
Type: single-seat fighter-bomber (two-seat night and all-weather interceptor)
Powerplant: two Daimler-Benz DB 603E-1 liquid-cooled inverted V-12 engines each rated at 1342 kW (1,800 hp) for take-off and 1417 kW (1,900 hp) at 1800 m (5,905 ft)
Performance: maximum speed 763 km/h (474 mph) at 6500 m (21,325 ft) [690 km/h (429 mph) at 5300 m (17,380 ft)]; maximum cruising speed 685 km/h (426 mph) [597 km/h (371 mph)] at 7200 m (23,620 ft); economical cruising speed 452 km/h (281 mph) [445 km/h (276 mph)] at 6000 m (19,685 ft); climb to 1000 m (3,280 ft) in 55 seconds, to 8000 m (26,245 ft) in 14 minutes 30 seconds; service ceiling 11400 m (37,400 ft) [10400 m (34,120 ft)]; range on internal fuel at maximum continuous power 1395 km (867 miles [1425 km (886 miles)], at economical cruise power 2060 km (1,280 miles) [2100 km (1,305 miles)]
Weights: empty equipped 7260 kg (16,005 lb); normal loaded 9600 kg (21,164 lb) [10085 kg (22,233 lb)]
Dimensions: wingspan 13.80 m (45 ft 3¼ in); length 13.85 m (45 ft 5¼ in); height 5.00 m (16 ft 4¾ in); wing area 38.50 m² (414.41 sq ft)
Armament: one 30-mm MK 103 fixed forward-firing cannon with 70 rounds and two 15-mm MG 151 fixed forward-firing cannon with 200 r.p.g., plus (A-1) one 500-kg (1,102-lb) PC 500 or SD 500 bomb or two 250-kg (551-lb) SC 250 bombs internally and two 250-kg (551-lb) SC 250 bombs externally

Above: The Do 335 in flight reveals the slightly unusual appearance resulting from the use of a cruciform tail unit trailed by the VDM three-blade pusher propeller, which was jettisoned when the pilot had to eject.

Left: A partly completed Do 335A-10 is examined by US troops after they overran the factory at Oberpfaffenhofen. The resources dedicated to the Do 335's development were wasted, for the warplane did not enter service.

Douglas DC-3

More than any other airliner of its time, the DC-3 characterised the emergence of the all-metal 'modern' airliner, and paved the way to the current pattern of airline operations. The Germans seized a few of the aircraft in 1939-40, and used them as standard transports, as well as for clandestine operations.

Undoubtedly a classic airliner that helped to establish the nature of modern air transport in the 1930s, the **DC-3** was the logical successor to the **DC-2**, and first flew as the **DST** (Douglas Sleeper Transport) on 17 December 1935 as a 'sleeper' that could be used on transcontinental flights within the USA. The DST led to the DC-3 with day seating, and civil production totalled 430 aircraft before manufacture switched to military models. The variants were the DST with accommodation for 28 day or 14 night passengers, and powered by Wright Cyclone radial engines (21 built); the **DST-A** similar to the DST but powered by Pratt & Whitney Twin Wasp radial engines (19 built); the DC-3 basic day passenger transport with accommodation for between 21 and 28 passengers, and power provided by Cyclones (266 built); the **DC-3A** basic day passenger transport similar to the DC-3 but powered by Twin Wasp engines (114 built); and **DC-3B** convertible model with seat/berths in the forward cabin and seats in the after cabin for 28 day passengers and fewer night passengers (10 built).

During World War II, in addition to 10 DC-2s, Lufthansa flew 10 DC-3s (one Belgian initially seized by Italy, four Czechoslovak and five Dutch), one of the Dutch aircraft probably being operated for a time by III/KG 200. At least six of the aircraft were lost.

Douglas DC-3A specification
Type: two-crew medium transport aeroplane
Powerplant: two Pratt & Whitney S1C3G Twin Wasp air-cooled 14-cylinder radial engines each rated at 1,200 hp (895 kW) for take-off and 1,050 hp (783 kW) at 7500 ft (2285 m)
Performance: maximum speed 230 mph (370 km/h) at 8,500 ft (2590 m); cruising speed 207 mph (307 km/h) at optimum altitude; initial climb rate 1,130 ft (344 m) per minute; service ceiling 23,200 ft (7070 m); range 2,125 miles (3420 km)
Weights: empty 16,865 lb (7650 kg); maximum take-off 11431 kg (25,200 lb)
Dimensions: wingspan 95 ft 0 in (28.96 m); length 64 ft 5½ in (19.65 m); height 16 ft 0⅛ in (5.16 m); wing area 987.00 sq ft (91.69 m²)

The Germans made only limited use of the Belgian, Czechoslovak and Dutch DC-3 transports they obtained.

Fiat CR.20

A thoroughly obsolete biplane fighter designed by Celestino Rosatelli and built in Italy, and of which Germany inherited small numbers with its annexation of Austria, the CR.20 was used only for very limited short-term training purposes by the Luftwaffe.

The **CR.20** single-seat biplane fighter with fixed tailskid undercarriage was produced in considerable numbers for its time. The first of four prototypes flew on 19 June 1926, the type entered production in 1927, and 124 had been delivered by 1929. There were also floatplane and two-seat trainer models, the latter securing an Austrian order for four. The **CR.20bis** that appeared in 1929 had a new divided main undercarriage arrangement, and production between 1920 and 1921 reached 211, including an unknown number of the **CR.20AQ** sub-variant with the 317-kW (425-hp) A.20AQ engine for increased ceiling. Sales were also made to Austria (16 CR.20bis and 16 CR.20AQ aircraft), Hungary and Paraguay. Flown only by Italy, the final version was the **CR.Asso** with the 336-kW (450-hp) Isotta-Fraschini Asso Caccia engine.

The CR.20bis and CR.20AQ were still in Austrian service at the time of the German annexation of 1938, after which some of the aircraft were painted in Luftwaffe markings and used briefly at German training schools.

Fiat CR.20bis specification
Type: single-seat fighter
Powerplant: one Fiat A.20 liquid-cooled V-12 engine rated at 306 kW (410 hp) for take-off
Performance: maximum speed 270 km/h (168 mph) at sea level; climb to 5000 m (16,405 ft) in 13 minutes 37 seconds; service ceiling 8500 m (27,885 ft); endurance 3 hours
Weights: empty 980 kg (2,160 lb); maximum take-off 1400 kg (3,086 lb)
Dimensions: wingspan 9.80 m (32 ft 1¾ in); length 6.70 m (21 ft 11¾ in); height 2.75 m (9 ft 0¼ in); wing area 25.65 m² (276.10 sq ft)
Armament: two 7.7-mm (0.303-in) Vickers fixed forward-firing machine-guns in the upper part of the forward fuselage

One of the CR.20 biplane's most striking features was the Warren-type truss interplane bracing that removed all need for wires.

A CR.20 fighter wears German markings during 1938-39 after Austria's forces were absorbed by those of Germany.

Fiat CR.30 and CR.32

The CR.30 and CR.32 designed for the Italian air force were among the last of the classic biplane fighters, and proved to be very useful by the standards of their day. Germany inherited a number of the fighters in its annexation of Austria, and made limited use of them as trainers before passing 36 aircraft to Hungary.

The first of four **CR.30** prototypes flew in March 1932. The Italian air force ordered 121 examples of the production-standard CR.30, and production of 176 aircraft for all customers lasted from 1932 to 1935. Italy retired its last CR.30 fighters from first-line service in 1938. The conversion of a pair of prototypes to two-seat configuration proved a great success, and many single-seat aircraft were later converted to this **CR.30B** standard as 'refresher' trainers and station hacks. The most important export customer for the CR.30 was Hungary, which received three CR.30 single-seaters and 10 CR.30B two-seaters. The Germans later passed to Hungary two of the five CR.30s that had come into their hands when they took over Austria, which had received three CR.30s and three CR.30Bs in 1936 and later served with I/138 at Aspern and I/135 at Aibling.

Above: The Luftwaffe made brief use of the CR.32 fighters it gained from the annexation of Austria, and then passed 36 of the survivors to the Hungarian air force.

Above: Luftwaffe pilots discuss the day's flying in front of an ex-Austrian CR.32, a type which the Germans found to be of limited value even for advanced training.

Despite the CR.30's agility, the designer Celestino Rosatelli wished to achieve an overall improvement in performance, and this led to the more refined and slightly smaller **CR.32**, which first flew in prototype form on 28 April 1933. It was an instant success, the first production order being received in March 1934. Production aircraft had variable-pitch propellers and could carry a radio transmitter/receiver, panoramic camera or bomb racks. Modified versions for Italy were built up to 1939, each designed to reduce all-up weight and improve performance.

In addition, the CR.32 was demonstrated widely abroad and attracted considerable export orders. The original CR.32 was supplied to the Regia Aeronautica (291, including prototypes), Hungary (76) and China (16). The **CR.32bis** was produced from 1935 with provision for two forward-firing 0.303-in (7.7-mm) SAFAT machine-guns in the leading edges of the lower wing in addition to the standard pair of fuselage-mounted guns, but the additional weight meant that the wing-mounted weapons were often removed. Total production was 328, Italy and Austria receiving 283 and 45, respectively. The **CR.32ter** had only the two 12.7-mm (0.5-in) fuselage-mounted weapons. Some 103 were built and all served in Spain, 60 of them with the Spanish air arm. Finally there was the **CR.32quater** that was lighter than any version other than the original CR.32 but with the same armament as the CR.32ter. Some 398 were built, of which 105 served with the Italian Aviazione Legionaria in Spain, 27 went directly to Spain, about 14 in all to Paraguay and Venezuela, and the balance to the Regia Aeronautica. Total Italian production was 1,212 aircraft.

Austria ordered 45 CR.32bis fighters in the spring of 1936 to equip 4., 5. and 6. Jagdstaffeln of Fliegerregiment Nr 2 Wiener-Neustadt. In March 1938 the Austrian units were absorbed into Luftwaffe fighter groups, but after a brief period with I/138 at Aspern and I/135 at Aibling, the 36 remaining aircraft were handed over to Hungary.

Fiat CR.32bis specification
Type: single-seat fighter
Powerplant: one Fiat A.30 RA bis liquid-cooled V-12 engine rated at 447 kW (600 hp) for take-off
Performance: maximum speed 360 km/h (224 mph) at 3000 m (9,845 ft); cruising speed 315 km/h (196 mph) at optimum altitude; climb to 3000 m in 4 minutes 45 seconds; service ceiling 8800 m (28,870 ft); range 750 km (466 miles)
Weights: empty 1380 kg (3,042 lb); maximum take-off 1950 kg (4,299 kg)
Dimensions: wingspan 9.50 m (31 ft 2 in); length 7.45 m (24 ft 5¼ in); height 2.63 m (8 ft 7½ in); wing area 22.10 m² (237.89 sq ft)
Armament: two 12.7-mm (0.5-in) Breda-SAFAT fixed forward-firing machine-guns in the upper part of the forward fuselage and two 7.7-mm (0.303-in) Breda-SAFAT fixed forward-firing machine guns in the leading edges of the lower wing, plus up to 100 kg (220 lb) of bombs carried externally

This line-up of ex-Austrian CR.32bis aircraft is seen just after the Anschluss, when Luftwaffe markings had been applied.

Fiat CR.42 Falco

The CR.42 was one of the definitive last-generation biplane fighters, and offered an appealing combination of performance, agility and strength. Designed for Italian service and the export market, the CR.42 was seized in some numbers by the Germans in September 1943, and remained in limited but useful service into 1945.

Extremely light on the controls, universally viewed as a delight to fly, superbly agile and innately robust, the **CR.42 Falco** (falcon) synthesised 15 years of continuous fighter development. It was a thoroughbred with a distinguished pedigree carrying fighter biplane evolution to its apex. However, its intrinsic qualities were those demanded of an era in air warfare earlier than that in which it was to find itself. Developed by Celestino Rosatelli, the CR.42 resulted from the Italian belief, stemming from the success of biplanes in the early stages of the Spanish Civil War, that there was still a role for the highly manoeuvrable fighter biplane. The prototype of the new type first flew on 23 May 1938 as a type derived from the CR.32 with a radial engine, in this instance the Fiat A.74 R1C.38 unit in a long-chord cowling.

Into production

Italy ordered an initial 200 production machines, and the first of them was completed in February 1939. The final figure for CR.42 production in all versions, according to the manufacturer, was 1,781 aircraft, although there are some discrepancies. In addition to the baseline CR.42, the other service models for Italian service were the tropicalised **CR.42AS** for North African use as an assault fighter with provision for two 100-kg (220-1b) underwing bombs; the **CR.42CN** night-fighter with two searchlights in underwing fairings, radio equipment and exhaust flame dampers; and the **CR.42ter** development of the Swedish-ordered **CR.42bis** with two additional 12.7-mm (0.5-in) guns underwing.

Nine Belgian CR.42s seized by the Germans in northern France were probably flown as fighter trainers by Jagdgeschwader 107 at Toul. Production continued after the completion of the final Italian contract in 1943 to meet a German order for 200 **CR.42LW** anti-partisan and night harassment aircraft with only minor changes from the Italian standard. In February 1944 the first of them were placed in service by 1./Nachtschlachtgruppe 9 based at Rieli, north of Rome, for nocturnal operations against the Allied forces in the 'Shingle' beach-head at Anzio. 1./NSGr. 9 flew its first operations with the CR.42LW on 24 March, by which

Right: Much of the sturdiness inherent in the CR.42's biplane (almost sequiplane) wing cellule derived from the use of Warren-type truss bracing.

Above: Evident on the lower part of the CR.42's cowling is one of the two exhausts through which the engine's spent gases were discharged from the collector ring.

Above: German-marked CR.42s are lined up on an airfield, probably somewhere in the Balkans. Here Luftwaffe-operated CR.42s were active and effective in the anti-partisan role.

This was a CR.42 operated by 1./NSGr. 7 based at Banya-Luka, Croatia, during May 1944 under the Fliegerführer Kroatien. Note the all-black undersurfaces and lack of underwing crosses and tail swastika. The Italian rudder marking can still be seen beneath the camouflage, and the outer ring of the original Italian upper wing markings was retained after the application of German insignia.

Based in the Rimini area for night harassment and anti-partisan duties early in 1944, this CR.42 Falco was assigned to the 2.Staffel, Nachtschlachtgruppe 9.

formed a 3.Staffel with the CR.42LW, and in September the 5.Staffel also began to convert to the CR.42LW. Production of the CR.42LW had been seriously disrupted by US air attacks, and plans to convert at least part of another Nachtschlachtgruppe to the CR.42LW were abandoned. However, NSGr. 7 did not experience serious shortages of aircraft until the final stages of hostilities, for about 150 aircraft were completed and 112 of them accepted by the Germans.

time 2./NSGr. 9 had been formed with the same type. The two Staffeln operated against the Anzio beach-head and the Allied forces round Cassino. With their small warloads, the CR.42LW aircraft proved to be comparatively ineffectual, and NSGr. 9 therefore started to convert to the Ju 87.

In April 1944 NSGr. 7, which had been activated in the Balkans with a mix of German types in two Staffeln,

Fiat CR.42AS Falco specification
Type: single-seat fighter and fighter-bomber
Powerplant: one Fiat A.74 R1C.38 air-cooled 14-cylinder radial engine rated at 626 kW (840 hp) for take-off
Performance: maximum speed 430 km/h (267 mph) at 5000 m (16,405 ft); cruising speed 378 km/h (235 mph) at 6000 m (19,685 ft); climb to 4000 m (13,125 ft) in 5 minutes 26 seconds; service ceiling 10150 m (33,300 ft); range 785 km (488 miles)
Weights: empty 1708 kg (3,765 lb); maximum take-off 2405 kg (5,302 lb)
Dimensions: wingspan 9.70 m (31 ft 10 in); length 8.27 m (27 ft 1⅝ in); height 3.59 m (11 ft 9⅓ in); wing area 22.40 m² (241.12 sq ft)
Armament: two 12.7-mm (0.5-in) Breda-SAFAT machine-guns in the forward fuselage and, in some aircraft, two 12.7-mm Breda-SAFAT in blister fairings under the lower-wing leading edges, plus up to 441 lb (200 kg) of bombs

While the main undercarriage's faired legs and spatted wheels reduced drag, they also increased maintenance and trapped both grass and mud, and therefore were often removed.

The CR.42 constituted a fitting end to the history of the biplane fighter, and was still a useful weapon in the low-level close-support and counter-partisan roles in 1945.

Fiat G.50 Freccia

The G.50 Freccia low-wing fighter was designed by Giuseppe Gabrielli from April 1935, and the first of two prototypes made its initial flight on 26 February 1937. The type was obsolescent on entering service, and was manufactured in only modest numbers. Some aircraft survived to fight in German markings later in the war.

The **G.50 Freccia** (arrow) was an all-metal aircraft, only the control surfaces being fabric-covered, with tailwheel undercarriage including retractable main units. The prototypes and first pre-production batch of 45 aircraft had an enclosed cockpit with a rear-sliding canopy but, as a result of pilot pressure, later machines had either an open or partially enclosed cockpit. After the two proto-types, a total of 778 machines was built. The final production aircraft left the Fiat assembly lines in the spring of 1942.

When Italy entered World War II there were 97 G.50s in service, and they took part in the fighting in southern France in June 1940 and then flew with the Corpo Aereo Italiano in Belgium for operations against the UK between September 1940 and January 1941, a campaign in which the type's lack of range proved a severe impediment. The G.50-equipped 24° and 154° Gruppi later moved to Albania for operations against Greece. The **G.50bis**, the first example of which was tested from 9 September 1940, incorporated increased fuel tankage and redesigned vertical tail surfaces, and had glazed

cockpit side panels to protect the pilot from the slipstream. Some G.50bis fighters were used in Croatia, but most were tropicalised for North African service with two Gruppi. Some Freccias were converted as fighter-bombers with underwing

Italian fighter pilots appreciated the open cockpits of the biplanes from which they transitioned onto the Freccia, and many demanded a return to an open or semi-enclosed cockpit.

bomb racks, and this version equipped the 50° Stormo in North Africa. In early 1943 the G.50bis was in service with the 24° Gruppo in Sardinia, the 151° Gruppo in Greece, and the 154° Gruppo in the Aegean. After the September 1943 armistice between Italy and the Allies, there were only 48 Freccias left, a mere 17 of them serviceable, and they were flown by units of both the revived Fascist republic and of co-belligerent forces.

Ten G.50s (nine single-seaters and one **G.50B** two-seat trainer) were supplied to Croatia in the winter of 1941-42. After the Italian armistice of 9 September 1943, the Germans seized a number of Italian airfields in the Balkans. The Germans had no need for obsolete fighters of this type and, after a short evaluation, transferred 20 to 25 of the aircraft to the Croat air force to equip two units collaborating with the Germans on anti-partisan operations. The only other aircraft to be exported were 35 G.50s sold to Finland in 1939.

Above: A decidedly war-weary and German-marked example of the G.50 reveals one of the two lateral hinged panels by which the pilot gained access to the cockpit.

Fiat G.50bis Freccia specification
Type: single-seat fighter and fighter-bomber
Powerplant: one 840-hp (626-kW) Fiat A.74 RC.38 air-cooled 14-cylinder radial engine rated at 626 kW (840 kW) for take-off
Performance: maximum speed 472 mph (293 mph) at 5000 m (16,405 ft); cruising speed 415 km/h (258 mph) at optimum altitude; climb to 6000 m (19,685 ft) in 7 minutes 30 seconds; service ceiling 9835 m (32,265 ft); range 670 km (416 miles)
Weights: empty 1975 kg (4,354 lb); maximum take-off 2415 kg (5,324 lb)
Dimensions: wingspan 10.96 m (35 ft 11⅞ in); length 7.79 m (25 ft 6⅞ in); height 2.96 m (9 ft 8½ in); wing area 18.15 m² (195.37 sq ft)
Armament: two 12.7-mm (0.5-in) Breda-SAFAT fixed forward-firing machine-guns, and up to 300 kg (661 lb) of bombs carried externally

A few German-marked G.50 fighters, for the most part unserviceable, were seized by the Allies late in World War II. Here a US soldier poses in the cockpit of one such machine.

Fiat G.55 Centauro

Produced in only the smallest of numbers, the G.55 could have been a major asset to the Regia Aeronautica had it been created sooner and placed speedily in high-volume production. The type exhibited excellent performance, especially at the higher altitudes at which US heavy bombers generally operated.

The **G.55 Centauro** (centaur) constituted a major improvement over the G.50, for it benefited from the great care that had been taken to combine an Italian-made version of a classic German liquid-cooled engine with an aerodynamically advanced airframe. The first of three prototypes flew on 30 April 1942. Pre-production **G.55/0** fighters left the assembly line during the spring of 1943, two of them being for evaluation in the hands of Italian and German pilots in mock combat with the Bf 109G and the Fw 190A. The G.55 was found superior to its opponents in most respects, with better manoeuvrability, handling and acceleration. This was the only direct German involvement in G.55 flight operations.

Only 16 G.55/0 pre-production and 15 **G.55/1** initial production aircraft had been delivered by September 1943, when Italy signed an armistice with the Allies, and subsequent production was undertaken under German supervision for the Fascist air arm flying alongside the Luftwaffe in efforts

to hold the northern half of Italy. Before wartime production ended, 274 more G.55s had been completed and a further 37 were abandoned at an advanced stage of their construction.

Fiat G.55/1 Centauro specification
Type: single-seat fighter and fighter-bomber
Powerplant: one Fiat RA.1050 RC.58 Tifone (licence-built DB 605A) liquid-cooled inverted V-12 engine rated at 1100 kW (1,475 hp) for take-off
Performance: maximum speed 630 km/h (391 mph) at 8000 m (26,245 ft); cruising speed 560 km/h (348 mph) at optimum altitude; climb to 6000 m (19,685 ft) in 7 minutes 12 seconds; service ceiling 12700 m (41,665 ft); range 1200 km (746 miles)
Weights: empty 2630 kg (5,798 lb); maximum take-off 3718 kg (8,197 lb)
Dimensions: wingspan 11.85 m (38 ft 10½ in); length 9.37 m (30 ft 9 in); height 3.13 m (10 ft 3¼ in); wing area 21.11 m² (227.23 sq ft)
Armament: three 20-mm MG 151/20 fixed forward-firing cannon and two 12.7-mm (0.5-in) Breda-SAFAT fixed forward-firing machine-guns, plus up to 705 lb (320 kg) of bombs

Seen in German markings during evaluation, the G.55 combined the best of Axis capabilities in its Italian airframe and German engine.

Gerhard Fieseler Werke GmbH

The aircraft manufacturing concern headed by and bearing the name of Gerhard Fieseler is remembered primarily for its part in two widely diverse fields of aeronautical development: the creation of an aircraft which, for many years, was the pattern for what was eventually to become known as the STOL type, and the design of a pilotless aircraft that played a major role in ushering in the era of the guided missile. The former, the Fi 156 Storch, with its outstanding short take-off and landing characteristics and slow-flying capabilities, gained international recognition for Fieseler; the latter, the Fi 103 (Vergeltungswaffe Eins, or 'reprisal weapon one') acquired for the company some notoriety.

Gerhard Fieseler was undoubtedly the greatest aerobatic pilot of pre-World War II Germany and, perhaps, the world. The international acclaim that he received was of a different nature to that of his contemporary, Ernst Udet. Fieseler practised the *haute école* of flying whereas 'Udlinger', though brilliant, acted the clown, his performances having little relationship to classic aerobatic flying. Fieseler gained distinction as a fighter pilot on the Macedonian Front in World War I, his 22 'kills' earning for him the nickname of 'Tiger'. In May 1926 he acquired a shareholding in the Raab-Katzenstein-Flugzeugwerke GmbH, which had been established in the previous November at Kassel-Bettenhausen to design and manufacture light aircraft and to operate a flying school. The company developed such types as the Schwalbe and Grasmücke light biplanes, Fieseler participating as an instructor in the school.

Fieseler's mastery of aerobatics soon earned him widespread fame, and to his requirements the Raab-

The Fi 156 Storch ranks as one of the truly outstanding aircraft of World War II, and no Allied aircraft could match its winning combination of slow-speed capability and sturdiness. With little more than a breath of wind it could fly in and out of tiny strips, and in a good breeze could virtually hover. Its strong undercarriage could absorb the punishment from the roughest of surfaces, as demonstrated when one was used in September 1943 to lift Benito Mussolini from the rocky slope adjacent to the mountain-top hotel where he was being held prisoner.

Katzenstein-Flugzeugwerke built a more powerful derivative of the Schwalbe specifically for aerobatic flying as the F 1 Tigerschwalbe. Shortly after this, on 1 April 1930, Fieseler purchased from Fritz Ackermann the Segel-Flugzeugbau-Kassel that also operated at Bettenhausen. This concern specialised in the design and construction of high-performance sailplanes, and continued to concentrate its efforts in this sphere, producing the Wien for Robert Kronfeld, the Musterle for Wolf Hirth, and the largest sailplane in the world, the 30-m (98.43-ft) span Austria, among others. In 1932, when the name of the company was changed to Fieseler-Flugzeugbau, the first powered aircraft was built to the designs of Ing. Schüttkowsky. It was while flying this machine, the F 2 Tiger aerobatic biplane, that Fieseler was to win the world aerobatic championship and a prize of 80,000 gold marks in 1934, but in the meantime the Fieseler-Flugzeugbau had begun to expand.

Carefully calculated risk-taking

In 1932 the Kassel-Bettenhausen factory had also built the tailless two-seat Delta IV monoplane to the designs of Alexander M. Lippisch as the F 3 Vespe, and the more orthodox F 4 and F 5 tandem two-seat light monoplanes, but only the last-mentioned type proved an unqualified success. Such was its promise that, with the completion of flight trials in the early summer of 1933, Fieseler took a tremendous financial risk, more than doubling his work force to some 200 men, and in the seven weeks remaining before the start of the Deutschlandflug in August, succeeded in building a further eight F 5s to participate in the event.

At this time the Fieseler-Flugzeugbau was joined by Dipl.-Ing. Erich Bachem as technical director and, shortly afterward, by Reinhold Mewes as chief designer. Series production of the F 5R was launched, and the ideas of Fieseler and Mewes on the possibilities of high-lift devices, which led to the development of the so-called Fieseler-Rollflügel, gained prompt recognition from the Reichsluftfahrtministerium, which supported the design and construction of the four-seat Fi 97 embodying these ideas and intended for participation

Uberaus lange schon lag die kleine deutsche Truppe einer feindlichen Ubermacht gegenüber. Es schien ziemlich aussichtslos. Da plötzlich erscheint ein „Storch", und wie ein Aufatmen geht es durch die Reihen: General Rommel kommt! Panzer greifen an, sprungauf geht es vorwärts, bis der Feind geworfen ist.

GERHARD FIESELER WERKE

in the 1934 Europarundflug. Simultaneously, the company launched the design of its first combat aircraft, the Fi 98 dive-bomber, although this was not destined to emulate the success of the Fi 97.

By 1935, the Fieseler-Flugzeugbau, like other components of the German aircraft industry, was immersed in the early phases of a major expansion programme, and had begun to manufacture under licence the designs of other companies on behalf of the Luftwaffe, starting with a batch of 12 He 46s, and following them in 1936-37 with 200 He 51 fighters and 30 He 72 trainers. Meanwhile, Reinhold Mewes's design team had carried its ideas on slow-flying aircraft a stage further with the development of the Fi 156 Storch, and had been engaged simultaneously on the design and construction of a high-performance pilotless drone for use as a target for anti-aircraft artillery. The drone received the designation Fi 157, and three prototypes were ordered, all of which crashed during trials. Nevertheless, the company persisted with a piloted derivative, the Fi 158, intended primarily for experiments in remote radio control, which was flown in 1938.

Dipl.-Ing. Bachem, whose imagination had been captured by the concept of a rocket-powered vertically launched target-defence interceptor, was engaged in a series of studies for such a warplane under the designation Fi 166, although this radical scheme was not to materialise until Bachem left Fieseler in order to devote his full attention to the concept, his place as technical director being taken by Dr.-Ing. Banzhof. The Fieseler-Flugzeugbau was also working on a multi-purpose shipboard aircraft, the Fi 167, which, despite evincing truly outstanding capabilities, achieved only pre-production status owing to delays in the construction of the carrier from which it was intended to operate.

Continued expansion

By the beginning of World War II, the much-expanded Fieseler concern, which had changed its title to Gerhard Fieseler Werke GmbH on 1 April 1939, was largely preoccupied with production of the Fi 156 and the licensed manufacture of the Messerschmitt Bf 109, having been phased in to this fighter programme in 1938, and continuing to build this type until June 1941. An additional factory had been built at Kassel-Waldau, this being phased into the Focke-Wulf Fw 190 programme early in 1942, being joined by the Bettenhausen works in the autumn of 1943, the combined Fw 190 output of the two factories totalling 2,155 by the end of 1944. Production of the Fi 156 at Bettenhausen ended during the first week of October 1943, all jigs and tools being transferred to the Mráz plant at Chocen in Czechoslovakia, manufacture of the Storch also taking place in France where the former Morane-Saulnier factory at Puteaux had commenced deliveries of the Fi 156 in April 1942.

With one notable exception, no other aircraft from the

Fieseler drawing boards was to achieve series production. A light side-by-side two-seat sports monoplane, the Fi 253 Spatz, had been flown in 1940 but had progressed no further than the prototype stage, and in 1941 a potential four-seat successor to the Storch, the Fi 256, had been designed, but its development was to be restricted to two prototypes built in 1943-44 at the Puteaux factory in France. A rather more novel product of the Fieseler design team was the Fi 333 general-purpose monoplane conceived in 1942. This embodied the highly original 'Pack Plane' concept that was to be resurrected some years later in the USA by Fairchild with the XC-120: an aircraft intended to carry its entire payload in a detachable pack or pod. The Fi 333 was to be capable of lifting interchangeable packs to accommodate troops, casualty litters or freight, a lifeboat, or a dismantled fighter beneath its slender fuselage, ground clearance being assured by an exceptionally tall undercarriage, each member possessing two independently sprung wheels in tandem. Three prototypes of the Fi 333 were built and tested, although the tandem-wheel undercarriage was never fitted.

The one aircraft of Fieseler design evolved during World War II to be manufactured in quantity was noteworthy enough, being the Fi 103 guided missile driven by a pulsejet unit under development by the Argus-Motoren-Gesellschaft mbH. Fieseler's proposals for the missile were accepted in 1941, a team led by Dipl.-Ing. Robert Lüsser, a former Heinkel technical director, being primarily responsible for the airframe design. Emphasis was placed on suitability for mass production with strict limits imposed on precision work and the use of critical materials. The weapon that resulted demanded only 800 production manhours, excluding the warhead, and more than 30,000 Fi 103s were to be built, although few of them were actually manufactured by the Gerhard Fieseler Werke, quantity production being the responsibility of Volkswagen at Fallersleben and Schönbeck, near Magdeburg, and Mittelwerke at Nordhausen.

The Fieseler concern achieved neither the growth nor fame of several of its contemporaries of the early 1930s, and its principal contribution to the war effort was the production of Bf 109 and Fw 190 fighters. At their peak, the Gerhard Fieseler factories in the Kassel area employed a direct labour force of 5,467 persons, almost as many again being employed by Fieseler-controlled dispersal factories engaged in the manufacture of components with which to feed the main Bettenhausen and Waldau assembly lines.

Fieseler's most notorious product was the Fi 103/V-1 flying bomb. Around 10,000 were launched against southeast England, and another 2,500 hit the Antwerp region. Their use caused thousands of casualties and much destruction, and brought back the grim feeling of terror in the population that had not been experienced since the 1940 Blitz.

Fieseler F 5

The Fieseler F 5 was designed primarily for the sporting and touring roles, and was a light aircraft with open cockpits, a low-mounted cantilever wing and fixed tailskid undercarriage. The type was not suitable for inexperienced pilots, but proved moderately popular with those of greater experience.

Gerhard Fieseler became Germany's leading aerobatic pilot during the inter-war years, and in 1926 acquired an interest in the Raab-Katzenstein-Flugzeugwerke GmbH at Kassel, a manufacturer of lightplanes and the operator of a flying school. Fieseler was involved as a flying instructor, and induced the company to build to his specification one of the Schwalbe biplanes that it produced. A more powerful version, and constructed specifically for aerobatic flight, it was designated Fieseler F 1 Tigerschwalbe.

In 1930 Fieseler acquired the sailplane-building company Segel-Flugzeugbau-Kassel and continued to build sailplanes, but in 1932 began the construction of powered aircraft under the new name Fieseler-Flugzeugbau. First came a new aerobatic biplane for use by Fieseler. This aircraft, designated F 2 Tiger, enabled Fieseler to win the world aerobatic championship in 1934. Two comparatively unsuccessful machines followed, a tailless two-seat delta-wing monoplane designed by Dr Alexander Lippisch and known as the F 3 Vespe, and a conventional two-seat lightplane known as the F 4. The real beginning of the company's success came with design of the **F 5** two-seat trainer/tourer, a cantilever low-wing monoplane of mixed construction with some fabric covering. Its tail unit was of conventional braced construction and the landing gear of fixed tailskid type, while power was provided by a Hirth HM.60 inline engine. The fuselage incorporated tandem enclosed cockpits, dual controls being provided as standard. Even this early aircraft provided a hint of the company's interest in high-lift devices, the trailing edge of the wing

The thoroughbred lines of the F 5 were clear proof that its designer was not only a world-class aerobatic pilot, but also a talented aeronautical engineer. The wing carried full-span trailing-edge flaps whose outer portions were used differentially as ailerons. In April 1946, the F 5R improved model seen here with enclosed accommodation was registered in Switzerland as HB-ELF.

having full-span flaps, the outboard sections of which could be operated differentially to act as ailerons.

Fieseler F 5R specification
Type: two-seat touring and training lightplane
Powerplant: one Hirth HM.60R air-cooled four-cylinder inverted inline engine rated at 60 kW (80 hp) for take-off
Performance: maximum speed 200 km/h (124 mph) at sea level; cruising speed 175 km/h (109 mph) at optimum altitude; initial climb rate 220 m (722 ft) per minute; service ceiling 4200 m (13,780 ft); range 1000 km (622 miles)
Weights: empty 871 lb (395 kg); maximum take-off 1,455 lb (660 kg)
Dimensions: wingspan 10.00 m (32 ft 9¾ in); length 6.60 m (21 ft 7¾ in); height 2.30 m (7 ft 6½ in); wing area 13.60 m² (146.39 sq ft)

First flying in 1932, the Fieseler F 5 was a two-seat lightplane powered by a 60-kW (80-hp) Hirth HM.60 engine. It became popular as a sporting and touring aeroplane. D-ENAZ was flown as a trainer by the Fliegerlandesgruppe IV, a Sportfliegerschule located at Berlin-Johannisthal.

Fieseler Fi 97

Designed for the touring role with four-seat accommodation in a large cabin under a heavily framed canopy, the Fieseler Fi 97 was not an attractive aircraft. However, the type offered a good blend of flying and performance characteristics, and proved itself a successful competition machine.

The F 5 was able to demonstrate good short-field performance and a low stalling speed thanks to a combination of good wing design and the incorporation of full-span trailing-edge flaps, and this type's capabilities brought Reichsluftfahrtministerium support for the development of a more advanced four-seater to take part in the Europarundflug of 1934. This **Fi 97** was also a low-wing cantilever monoplane of mixed construction, and differed from the F 5 in its enclosed cabin for its pilot and passengers and more powerful Hirth HM.8U engine, with the 157-kW (210-hp) Argus As.17 air-cooled six-cylinder inverted inline engine as an option.

However, the most significant feature of the Fi 97 was the high-lift devices incorporated in the wing, reflecting the interests of Gerhard Fieseler and his chief designer, Reinhold Mewes, in the creation of aircraft combining high performance with safety and ease of handling at low speeds. The leading edge had automatic slats of the Handley Page type extending over more than 50 per cent of the span, and the trailing edge incorporated the Fieseler-designed Ausrollflügel, a Fowler-type flap that extended aft and down to increase the wing area by nearly 20 per cent. As a result, the Fi 97 had a controllable speed range extending from 58 to 245 km/h (36 to 152 mph).

Designed by Kurt Arnolt and of mixed construction, the Fi 97 was a low-wing cantilever monoplane with a conventional tail unit. The fuselage had a steel tube frame covered with fabric, while the wing had a wooden structure covered with plywood and fabric. The wing's outer panels could be folded to the rear to facilitate hangarage and ground transport. The fixed undercarriage was of the tailskid type, and accommodation was provided for the pilot and three passengers in an enclosed cabin.

Fieseler Fi 97 Specification
Type: four-seat cabin monoplane
Powerplant: one Hirth HM.8U air-cooled inverted V-8 engine rated at 168 hp (225 hp) for take-off
Performance: maximum speed 152 mph (245 km/h) at 1000 m (3,280 ft); cruising speed 220 km/h (137 mph) at optimum altitude; initial climb rate 335 m (1,165 ft) per minute; service ceiling 7300 m (23,950 ft); range 1200 km (746 miles)
Weights: empty 560 kg (1,235 lb); maximum take-off 1050 kg (2,315 lb)
Dimensions: wingspan 10.70 m (35 ft 1¼ in); length 8.04 m (26 ft 4½ in); height 2.36 m (7 ft 9 in); wing area 15.30 m² (164.69 sq ft)

In 1934 this Fi 97 was one of five such aircraft that took part in the fourth and last FAI Challenge International de Tourisme, a touring aircraft contest that took place between 28 August and 16 September at Warsaw, Poland. Apart from the Germans and a home team, Czechoslovak and Italian teams competed. The pilot of D-IVIF (race number 17) was Wolf Hirth, who finished in 13th place, but the Fi 97 proved to be the best German entrant in aspects such as short take-off and landing, and average speed. In fuel consumption and maximum speed, the Messerschmitt Bf 108 was dominant, while the worst of the German aircraft, the Klemm Kl 36, received the best results only in the minimum-speed trials. The entire competition was won by the Polish team, while the best German aircraft was the Fi 97 that claimed third place. All five Fi 97 aircraft finished the competition.

Fieseler Fi 98

The Fi 98 was designed for the dive-bomber role, and emerged as a notably sturdy two-bay biplane. From the beginning of the programme, however, the rival Henschel Hs 123 had a greater degree of official support, and the Fieseler offering was not ordered into production. The type also failed to find any export customer.

On 19 October 1933, two crates were unloaded from a freighter that had just arrived in Bremerhaven from New York. Each crate contained a dismantled Curtiss Hawk II, a sturdy single-seat fighter biplane capable of dive-bombing. The aircraft were ostensibly the property of the internationally famous German pilot Ernst Udet, an ardent protagonist of dive-bombing, but they had in fact been purchased with funds supplied by the government of the fledgling Third Reich.

Sinister motives were later to be ascribed to the acquisition of these warplanes: the Hawk IIs and their demonstration by Udet were to be held responsible by some historians for convincing the embryo German planning staff that the dive-bomber was a practical weapon rather than merely an intriguing novelty. On the contrary, the Curtiss biplanes played no role in convincing the Luftkommandoamt or the Technical Department of the Reichsluftfahrtministerium of the potential of dive-bombing.

The dive-bomber had occupied the minds of German military and technical experts since the end of World War I. The Fliegergeräte-inspektion (Inspectorate for Aircraft Equipment) of the Luftschutzamt (Air Defence Office), and the Technisches Amt of the Luftkommandoamt had evolved dive-bomber requirements well before the last-mentioned organisation was transferred to the Reichsluftfahrtministerium with its creation on 15 May 1933, and a dive-bomber development programme had been formulated before the arrival of the Hawk IIs in Bremerhaven. In fact, the purchase of the Curtiss biplanes was nothing more than a whim of Hermann Göring, a new convert of the dive-bombing concept.

Worthy but obsolescent concept

The dive-bomber programme envisaged two stages. The first of them, or Sofort-Programm, called for a single-seat all-metal biplane which, embodying no radical or advanced features, would be suitable for rapid development and production. With the encouragement of Ernst Udet, the Fieseler Flugzeugbau, owned and operated by the well-known aero-

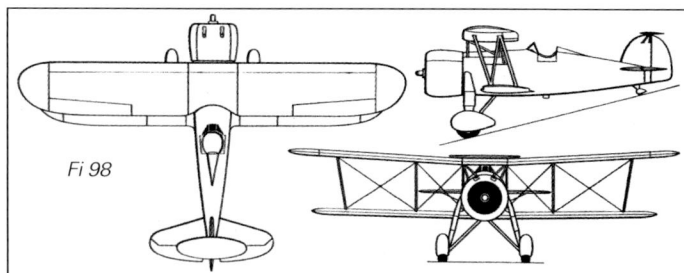

Fi 98

batic pilot Gerhard Fieseler, submitted design proposals intended to meet the official requirement, these proposals being tendered in competition with a submission from the newly established Henschel Flugzeugwerke.

The contending designs were both aerodynamically clean biplanes with light-metal semi-monocoque fuselages and fixed undercarriages, but while the somewhat less elegant Henschel study was a single-bay sesquiplane with interplane bracing reduced to a minimum, and cantilever, closely faired undercarriage legs, its Fieseler competitor adopted a more traditional approach to structural integrity, being a two-bay biplane with a profusion of bracing struts and wires. From the outset the Henschel design was favoured and, allocated the designation Hs 123, was awarded a three-prototype contract, while the Fieseler design, the **Fi 98**, was considered as a back-up programme, and two prototypes were ordered.

Designed by Reinhold Mewes, the first prototype, the **Fi 98a**, was flown for the first time early in 1935. Provision was made for a forward-firing armament of two 7.9-mm (0.31-in) MG 17 machine-guns in the upper decking of the forward fuselage, and it was intended to provide racks beneath the wings for four 50-kg (110-lb) bombs. Some diving trials were performed at Rechlin but little official interest was shown in the Fieseler dive-bomber, and development was discontinued before completion of the second prototype, the **Fi 98b**. An attempt was made to sell the design to the Japanese navy's air arm, but this met with no success.

Fieseler Fi 98a specification
Type: single-seat dive-bomber
Powerplant: one BMW 132A-3 air-cooled nine-cylinder radial engine rated at 485 kW (650 hp) for take-off
Performance: maximum speed 295 km/h (183 mph) at 2000 m (6,560 ft); maximum continuous cruising speed 270 km/h (168 mph) at optimum altitude; climb to 1000 m (3,280 ft) in 1 minute 7 seconds; service ceiling 9000 m (29,530 ft); maximum range 470 km (292 miles)
Weights: empty 1450 kg (3,197 lb); normal take-off 2160 kg (4,762 lb)
Dimensions: wingspan 11.50 m (37 ft 8¾ in); length 7.40 m (24 ft 3⅓ in); height 3.00 m (9 ft 10 in); wing area 25.50 m² (274.48 sq ft)
Armament: (proposed) two 7.9-mm (0.31-in) MG 17 fixed forward-firing machine-guns and four 50-kg (110-lb) bombs

The Fi 98a was first flown early in 1935, and adopted a more traditional approach towards structural integrity than the competing Hs 123 in which interplane bracing was reduced to the minimum. Only one prototype Fi 98 was built although the original contract called for two.

Fieseler Fi 103

Such were the straits in which Germany found itself from the middle of 1944 that approval was given to the development of the Fi 103 unpiloted missile, otherwise known as the V-1 'buzz-bomb' and 'doodlebug', into a piloted version for attacks on high-value targets. The 'Reichenberg' programme moved with great speed, but none of the Fi 103R machines, essentially suicide weapons, was used operationally.

Of the many unorthodox weapons proposed for the Luftwaffe during the last 18 months of World War II, one of the most remarkable was a piloted version of the **Fi 103** unpiloted missile, the so-called Vergeltungswaffe Eins (reprisal weapon 1) that was launched in large numbers against the British Isles and Antwerp. Intended for use against shipping or heavily defended ground targets, the Fi 103 piloted missile was developed under the codename **'Reichenberg'**, and its progenitors were primarily the celebrated pilot Flugkapitän Hanna Reitsch and SS-Hauptsturmführer Otto Skorzeny, one of Germany's leading exponents of unconventional warfare. Earlier, Hauptmann Heinrich Lange had urged the recruitment of a cadre of pilots willing to sacrifice their lives if necessary by crashing their aircraft on to important targets. Although this scheme met with little favourable response from any but a few fanatics, it was pursued in modified form on a limited scale.

Various aircraft types were considered for adaptation as piloted missiles, but the Fi 103 was initially discarded in favour of the Me 328, which, in turn, gave place to a modified version of the Fw 190 fighter carrying a large bomb. The intention was that the fighter should be aimed at the target by its pilot, who would bail out after ensuring himself that the objective of the attack could not escape. Meanwhile, an experimental unit, 5./KG 200, had been formed, with Lange as Staffelkapitän, to investigate unconventional methods of attacking heavily defended targets, but its unofficial appellation of Leonidas Staffel, after the king of Sparta who fought a suicidal battle against the Persians at Thermopylae, was indicative of the unit's true purpose.

Very difficult piloting task

Trials with Fw 190s carrying large-calibre bombs soon confirmed that the chances of these heavily laden aircraft penetrating Allied fighter screens and reaching their targets were negligible. It was obvious that desperate measures were demanded, and independently of Reitsch's proposals, Skorzeny suggested the adaptation of the Fi 103 to accommodate a pilot. As the scheme gave the pilot some chance of survival it was adopted in the summer of 1944, and the Deutsche Forschungsinstitut für Segelflug at Ainring was

Above: The development and deployment of the Fi 103 flying bomb, better known as the V-1 reprisal weapon, is well recorded in aviation history. A small fixed-wing pilotless aircraft, it was powered by a pulsejet engine mounted above the rear fuselage, incorporated a simple flight-control system to guide it to its target, an air log device to measure the distance flown, and a warhead packed with high explosive.

Above: The first guided missile to be used operationally in large numbers, the Fi 103 was a pilotless flying bomb, seen here in the form of a development machine.

Left: Development of the Fi 103 was ordered in June 1942, and the design began to take shape under the leadership of Dipl.-Ing. Robert Lusser as an aircraft-configured weapon with a circular-section fuselage. Operational weapons had, on the nose, a small air-log propeller whose rotation measured the distance flown and, at a pre-set range, commanded a dive (cutting the fuel supply to the engine) toward the ground, where an impact fuse triggered the warhead.

Fieseler Fi 103

More than 30,000 Fi 103s, known for deception purposes as the FZG 76 (anti-aircraft target device 76), were manufactured. The long-range Fi 103 F-1 version had a smaller warhead but larger tank inside the otherwise unchanged body.

instructed to evolve a piloted version of the missile. Such was the impetus behind the project that, within 14 days of the Reichenberg programme being authorised, both training and operational variants had been completed and testing initiated. Simultaneously, a line for adapting the Fi 103 from pilotless to piloted configuration was prepared near Dannenburg.

Initial piloted trials were conducted at Lärz in September 1944, an unpowered airframe being launched from beneath the port wing of an He 111 bomber but crashing when the pilot lost control after inadvertently jettisoning his cockpit canopy. The second flight test on the following day also ended in the loss of the aircraft, but subsequent testing was taken over by Reitsch with more success, although on one occasion the tail of the Fi 103 was damaged as a result of striking the He 111 carrier during release, and on another, sand ballast broke loose and the Fi 103 crashed, but Reitsch emerged unscathed from the wreckage. German propaganda reports later stated that Reitsch suffered severe injuries during the testing of the Fi 103, but they were, in fact, suffered earlier when the take-off dolly of an Me 163B in which she was performing gliding trials could not be dislodged and she attempted a landing with the dolly still attached.

Four piloted models of the manned **Fi 103R** were evolved under the Reichenberg programme, three of them being training variants. They were the **Reichenberg I** single-

The first of the V-1 weapons struck the London area in the early hours of 13 June 1944. Long before that, in late 1943, German officials were considering the use of piloted missiles to make precision attacks on high-priority targets, a policy that was developed quite independently of the Japanese Kamikaze attacks.

seater with landing skid and flaps; the **Reichenberg II** with a second cockpit in the position normally occupied by the warhead in the operational version, and the **Reichenberg III** single-seater with a similar arrangement of landing skid and flaps but with the Argus As 014 pulsejet duct fitted and ballast compensating for the weight of the warhead.

Planned operational model

The proposed operational model was the **Reichenberg IV**, and its conversion from the standard Fi 103 missile was the essence of simplicity. The basic Fi 103 fuselage was divided into six compartments accommodating the magnetic compass, 850-kg (1,874-lb) Amatol warhead, fuel tank, two circular compressed air bottles, autopilot and height and range setting controls, and servo mechanisms controlling the rudder and elevators. The Reichenberg IV conversion included the insertion of a small cockpit ahead of the propulsive duct. The instrument panel comprised an arming switch, a clock, an airspeed indicator, an altimeter, and a turn-and-bank indicator, a gyrocompass being carried by a floor-mounted bracket which also provided a mounting for a three-phase inverter and a small 24-volt wet battery. Flight controls were of the conventional stick-and-rudder bar type, and the pilot was accommodated on a plywood bucket seat with a padded headrest. The single-piece hood, which incorporated an armour-glass windscreen, hinged to starboard, and guidelines were provided for calculating diving angles.

The cockpit occupied the space taken in the pilotless version by the compressed air bottles, and the Reichenberg IV was provided with only one compressed air bottle, this being housed in the aft compartment normally occupied by the missile's autopilot. The entire trailing edge of the wing was occupied by the ailerons.

It was intended that the Reichenberg IV would be carried to the vicinity of its target beneath an He 111 bomber in a fashion similar to that used for the pilotless Fi 103s launched against the British Isles by Kampfgeschwader 53, communication between pilot and launching aircraft being maintained via a four-channel connector in the top of the fuselage ahead of the cockpit. In theory the pilot was intended to jettison the cockpit canopy and bail out after aiming his aircraft at the target, but it was calculated that his chance of survival was little better than one in a hundred. To release the canopy it was necessary to operate a lever on the port side of the

The V-1 (Vergeltungswaffe-1, or reprisal weapon-1) was launched from a fixed 'ski site' by means of launcher ramp, about 50 m (164 ft) long, in which a powered piston accelerated the weapon to flying speed. The V-1 had a range of 240 km (149 miles) with an 850-kg (1,874-lb) HE warhead.

To overcome the probable loss of the 'ski jump' launch sites as the Allies overran them, the Germans adapted Heinkel He 111H bombers to be flown as He 111H-22s by III/KG 3 (later I/KG 53) for the carriage and air-launch of the V-1. Operating initially from Venlo in the Netherlands, this unit began operations in July 1944, and was later supplemented by two other Gruppen.

Above left: The offensive that followed a number of trials saw the Luftwaffe launch 8,617 standard missiles against London and other British targets in the period up to the end of August 1944, when the programme was taken over by the German army, which fired 11,988 weapons against a range of European targets in the period up to the end of March 1945. Another version of the weapon had a wooden wing and a smaller warhead for longer-range attacks, and 275 of these weapons were fired by the SS against British targets between January and March 1945. Finally, the Luftwaffe fired 865 missiles from adapted He 111 bombers between September 1944 and March 1945.

Above right: An Fi 103 is hunted by Spitfire fighter, whose pilot is trying to use the proximity of the wing tips to roll the V-1 beyond the limit controllable by its autopilot, causing it to crash before reaching its intended range.

cockpit, the canopy having to swing through an angle of 45 degrees before the forward-hinged connection on the starboard side could be detached, and at the estimated target approach speeds of 790-850 km/h (491-528 mph) it is highly improbable that this method of jettisoning the canopy would have proved practical.

The training of a nucleus of instructors on the Reichenberg I and II was started, and although a successful landing called for considerable skill, the unpowered Reichenberg presented no insurmountable problems, and it was anticipated that 5./KG 200 would employ the Reichenberg IV operationally. Hanna Reitsch was instrumental in developing landing

The Argus 014 pulsejet was very simple in mechanical terms, and on the ground was started with compressed air before the missile was launched. The engine pulsed at 47 cycles/second, resulting in a distinctive sound that led the Allies to nickname the weapon as the 'buzzbomb' or 'doodlebug'.

Fieseler Fi 103

Derived from the V-1 flying bomb, the Fieseler Fi 103R was intended as a piloted bomb from which the pilot bailed out after aiming the bomb at its target. In practice, this would have been unlikely as the canopy would foul on the pulsejet mounted above the cockpit. This variant was the Reichenberg IV operational version, which was not used.

Above: A pilot demonstrates the narrow confines of the Fi 103R-IV's cockpit. The aircraft has a warhead fitted, but not the characteristic pimple for the nose-mounted impact fuse.

techniques for the Fi 103R. Following a number of landing crashes, she recommended a higher landing speed to overcome stall prolems. In November 1944 Oberstleutnant Werner Baumbach took over as Geschwaderkommodore of KG 200, and instigated a reorganisation in which 5./KG 200 became 15.Staffel as part of a new IV Gruppe at Prenzlau. At the same time the Fi 103R programme was terminated. By then some 175 Fi 103s had been adapted for the Reichenberg programme but none had been used operationally.

Fieseler Fi 103R Reichenberg IV specification
Type: single-seat expendable attack aircraft
Powerplant: one Argus As 014 pulsejet rated at 2.94 kN (661 lb st) at sea level
Performance: maximum speed 800 km/h (497 mph) at 2450 m (8,040 ft); range 330 km (205 miles) from point of launch at 2500 m (8,200 ft); powered endurance 32 minutes
Weight: loaded 2250 kg (4,960 lb)
Dimensions: wingspan 5.71 m (18 ft 9 in); length 8.00 m (26 ft 3 in)
Warhead: 850 kg (1,874 lb) HE

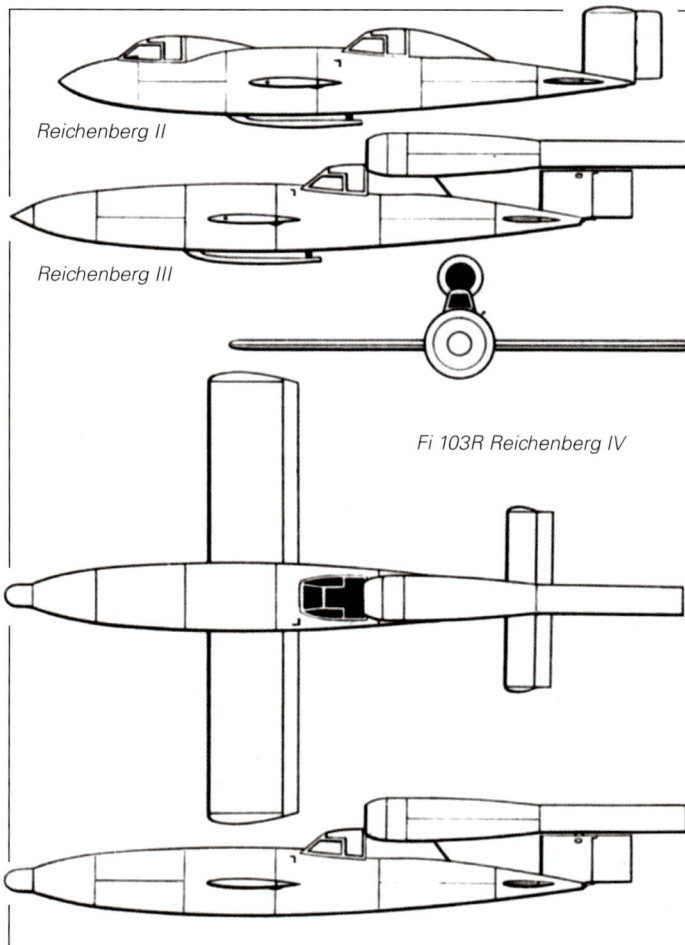

Reichenberg II

Reichenberg III

Fi 103R Reichenberg IV

Allied soldiers examine a near-complete Fi 103R (left) and a camouflaged V-1 launch ramp (right). Pilot survival for the Fi 103R was rated as being most unlikely, yet the Germans steadfastly claimed a subtle distinction between their Selbstopfermänner (self-sacrifice men) and the Japanese Kamikaze pilots who were sealed into their cockpits before take-off. Operational manned missions would most likely have been air-launched from converted He 111 bombers.

Fieseler Fi 156 Storch

The Storch was the product of one man's ambition to develop an aircraft that could fly like no other. The Fi 156 that followed was a STOL design that had no equal. Born in the dark days of Germany in the 1930s, it was not long before its military potential was noticed. In the hands of the Luftwaffe, its wartime exploits became legend.

It has been said of World War II that wherever the German army was to be found so too would be the **Storch** (stork), as Gerhard Fieseler's remarkable slow-flying **Fi 156** was so appropriately named. An unpretentious, somewhat bizarre braced monoplane, with extensive high-lift devices, bulged transparent 'conservatory', and stalky, long-stroke main undercarriage units designed to absorb the impact of high vertical descent rattes, the Fi 156 perhaps most completely represented army co-operation and observation aircraft ideas of the mid-1930s, establishing a pattern that was to be followed for many years. Of all the aircraft of the Luftwaffe, the Storch was omnipresent. With a light wind it demanded a negligible forward run either taking off or landing. Indeed, it could land in a length no greater than its wingspan, and wartime feats were legion in which its short take-off and landing characteristics were employed to the full.

The ideas of Gerhard Fieseler and his chief designer, Reinhold Mewes, on the use of high-lift devices to achieve exceptionally short take-off and landing distances, and extremely low stalling speeds received early recognition and support from the Reichsluftfahrtministerium, under whose aegis the Fieseler Flugzeugbau designed and built the four-seat Fi 97 for participation in the 1934 Europarundflug rally. With Handley Page automatic slots over some 55 per cent of each half span and so-called Fieseler-Rollflügel (extendable flaps moving aft and downward to increase gross wing area by some 18 per cent), the Fi 97 offered an exceptional slow-flying performance and remarkably short take-off and landing runs.

Refined design

In 1935, the Fieseler Flugzeugbau carried its ideas on slow-flying aircraft a stage further with the design of the Fi 156 which, with military considerations uppermost, was nevertheless intended to fulfil a variety of civil roles. Of thoroughly conventional construction, comprising a rectangular-section welded steel-tube fabric-skinned fuselage, two-spar fabric-covered wooden wing, and plywood-covered wooden tail

A Fieseler Storch brings a senior officer into the Place de la Concorde in Paris following the fall of France in June 1940. Not many aircraft could land safely even in so large an urban open space, but it was little problem to a Storch pilot.

surfaces, the Fi 156 featured an undercarriage possessing two compression legs incorporating long-stroke steel-spring oil-damping shock absorbers, the upper ends of which were attached to the apices of two pyramid structures built out from the sides of the fuselage, with the lower ends hinged to the underside of the fuselage centreline by steel-tube V-struts. The cabin, which could accommodate up to three persons, afforded an exceptional view, the entire sides and roof being glazed, and the side panels sloping outward at an acute angle. An Argus As 10C air-cooled inverted V-8 engine was carried by a welded steel-tube mount, and the entire fuel capacity was located in the wing roots, the two tanks having a total capacity of 145 litres (32 Imp gal).

The entire trailing edge of the wing was hinged, the outer portions acting as statically balanced and slotted ailerons, and the inner portions as slotted, camber-changing flaps. Two

In the summer of 1935, Gerhard Fieseler, Reinhold Mewes and technical director Erich Bachem (later creator of the Ba 349 Natter) designed the ultimate in practical STOL aircraft, the Fieseler Fi 156. The Storch made its public debut in the summer of 1937, when one of the 10 pre-production Fi 156A-0 aircraft was demonstrated at the 4th International Flying Meeting held at Zürich-Dübendorf.

Fieseler Fi 156 Storch

Above and below: The Fi 156 V1 (D-IKVN) first flew in May 1936, fitted with a metal adjustable-pitch propeller. The V2 (D-IDVS) differed in that it had a fixed-pitch wooden propeller, while the V3 (D-IGLI) introduced military equipment.

The Fi 156 V4 (the fourth prototype), D-IFMR, had ski undercarriage and a drop tank fitted for test purposes.

Below: One of the A-0 pre-production machines, D-IJFN, put on a dazzling show at the Zürich meeting in July 1937, during which the Storch repeatedly demonstrated full-load take-offs after a ground run of never more than 45 m (148 ft), and a fully controllable speed range of 50-175 km/h (32-108 mph).

versions were envisaged as the **Fi 156A** with a fixed light-metal slot occupying the whole of the wing leading edge, and the **Fi 156B** with movable slots, the latter avoiding the penalty imposed at the upper end of the speed range by the fixed slot. Three A-series prototypes were completed during the spring and early summer of 1936, the **Fi 156 V1** (D-IKVN) and **Fi 156 V2** (D-IDVS) having a metal adjustable-pitch propeller and a fixed-pitched wooden propeller, respectively, and the **Fi 156 V3** (D-IGLI) having military equipment. The results of initial flight testing exceeded the most sanguine expectations, the speed range proving to be 50-175 km/h (32-108 mph). The potential of the Fi 156 for the short-range reconnaissance, observation, and army co-operation roles was obvious, and during the autumn of 1936 the Fieseler Flugzeugbau was instructed to build further prototypes for military evaluation and initiate preparations for a pre-production series of aircraft.

Official requirement

Simultaneously, the Technisches Amt of the RLM issued a requirement to the industry for an army co-operation and observation aircraft, the performance parameters for which were provided by the Fi 156. The only stipulations made by the requirement other than those relating to performance concerned the use of a single Argus As 10 engine and the need to emphasise short take-off and landing and slow-flying characteristics in combination with the provision of the greatest possible fields of vision for the crew.

The issue of this requirement reflected no dissatisfaction with the capabilities of the Fi 156, which by this time had become known as the Storch, but adherence to the standard RLM procedure of encouraging competitive development by placing design and prototype contracts with two or more manufacturers for each specification.

To compete with the Fi 156 the Bayerische Flugzeugwerke tendered the Bf 163, essentially similar in concept to the Storch; the Siebel Flugzeugwerke, which had just changed its name from the Flugzeugwerke Halle, submitted the rather more radical Si 201 with the engine mounted to the rear of the cockpit and driving a pusher propeller above a slim tail-boom, and Focke-Wulf, which had acquired Cierva licence rights in 1933, proposed the Fw 186 jump-start gyroplane. Focke-Wulf's gyroplane was eliminated from the contest from the outset as the Technisches Amt believed that the advantages offered by rotorcraft at that stage in their development were far outweighed by their disadvantages, although, in the event, the company elected to proceed with prototype development as a private venture, and the Fw 186 was tested in 1938. The Bayerische Flugzeugwerke was preoccupied with the Bf 109 fighter and, in consequence, prototype construction was transferred to the 'Weser' Flugzeugbau with the result that trials with the sole Bf 163 prototype were not begun until 1938, and in the same year the first prototype trials of the Si 201 also started. By this time, the Storch had already attained production status and no direct comparison trials between this and its BFW and Siebel competitors were therefore undertaken.

By a time early in 1937, the first three prototypes of the Fi 156 had been joined by the **Fi 156 V4** (D-IFMR) which, fitted with skis, was used for winter trials, and the **Fi 156 V5** (D-IYZQ) completed to pre-production standards, these being followed in the early spring of 1937 by 10 **Fi 156A-0** machines for evaluation and demonstration purposes, one of them (D-IJFN) being demonstrated at the 4th International Flying Meeting held at Zürich-Dübendorf between 23 July and 1 August 1937, this marking the public debut of the Storch. The Storch had by this time already attained series production status as the **Fi 156A-1**, this being a general util-ity model suitable for both civil and military roles, and the Fieseler Flugzeugbau envisaged the series manufacture of the **Fi 156B-1** from the beginning of 1938, this having movable slots and various other refinements with which maximum speed was expected to be raised to 210 km/h (130 mph). In the event, the Fi 156B, which was intended primarily for the commercial market, was not to materialise. By mid-1937, the Storch had been fully evaluated by the Luftwaffe and its considerable potential appreciated.

During trials it had been ascertained that, at a loaded weight of 1240 kg (2,734 lb) the Storch could be flown under full control at 50 km/h (32 mph) in still air, and with a fair headwind could virtually hover. It could take off into a 13-km/h (8-mph) wind within 45 m (148 ft) and land within 15 m (49 ft), and during trials with a medium-strength wind blowing the Storch landed in a ploughed field within 4.5 m (15 ft). Its unique attributes obviously rendered the Storch suitable for a variety of tasks other than short-range recon-naissance and army co-operation with the Nah-(Heeres-)Aufklärungsstaffeln originally foreseen, and the Storch was tested with external smoke canisters, in the supply-dropping role, as a coastal patrol aircraft with a 135-kg (298-lb) depth charge attached to a rack beneath the fuselage, and even as a bomber, with a 50-kg (110-lb) bomb beneath the fuselage and two similar bombs beneath the wing, the pilot using aiming guidelines on the cockpit perspex and bracing struts to attack his target in a shallow dive.

Deliveries begin

Fieseler was instructed to expand production facilities for the Storch, and as it was obvious that some consider-able time must of necessity elapse before any deliveries could be diverted to fulfil commercial orders. As the RLM had no requirement for a higher performance, development of the Fi 156B was abandoned, production then being concentrating on the Fi 156A-1. Deliveries to the Luftwaffe began in the winter of 1937-38, and several of the first production examples were despatched to Spain for use as staff transports and utility aircraft

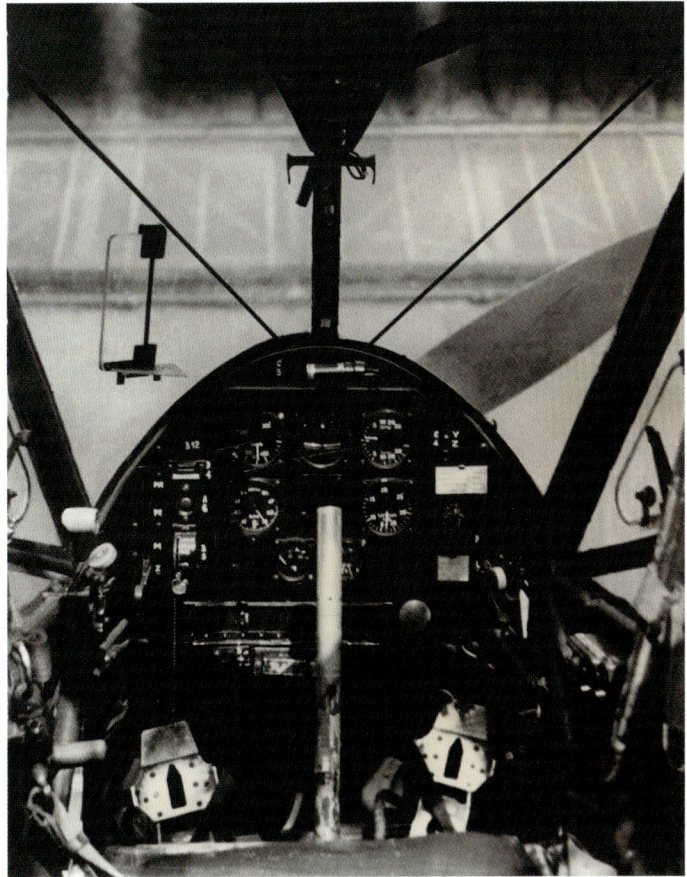

Above: Preparation for take-off involved lowering the flaps 20 degrees (which was observed on the gauge mounted just above the pilot's head), selecting the elevator trim one division tail heavy, and setting the ignition to 'früh' (advance). The Storch could be held on the hydraulic foot brakes until virtually the full 2,000 r.p.m. was reached.

The first production version of the Storch was the Fi 156A-1 utility and liaison machine. By mid-1937, the company had flown the ski-equipped V4, the military V5 and 10 Fi 156A-0 pre-production machines.

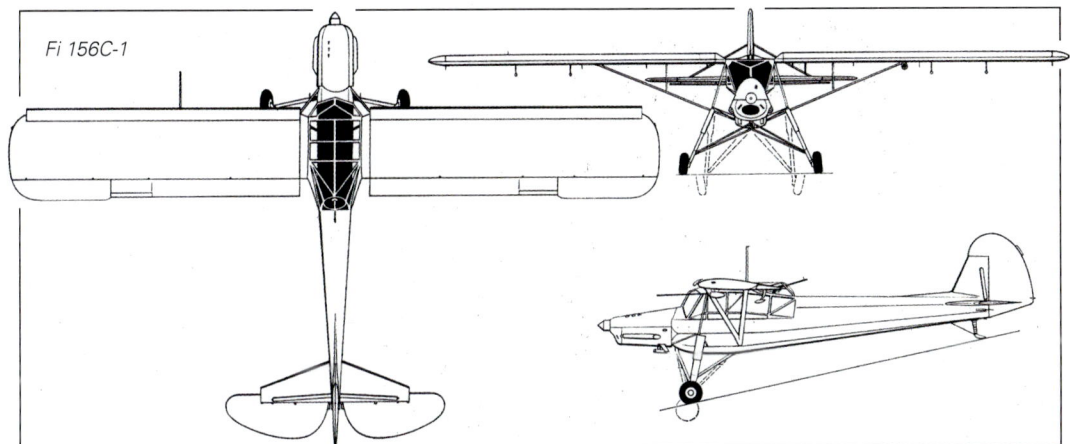

Fi 156C-1

Fieseler Fi 156 Storch

This Fi 156C Storch of the Kurierstaffel Oberkommando der Luftwaffe (Luftwaffe High Command Liaison Squadron) operated on the Don section of the Eastern Front during the drive for the Caucasus in August 1942. This unit operated throughout the war in several theatres, although its headquarters was in Berlin. The L2 codes were assigned to Lehrgeschwader 2.

with the Legion Condor. Production tempo built up steadily during the course of 1938, attaining a rate of three per week by the end of the year when work had begun on the improved C-series. The **Fi 156C** embodied minor equipment changes dictated by service experience with the Fi 156A-1, and introduced light defensive armament in the shape of a single 7.9-mm (0.31-in) MG 15 trainable machine-gun that fired aft from a lens–type mounting inserted in a raised section of the glazed aft decking. This weapon was considered primarily as 'respect armament', the principal defence of the Storch being its remarkable slow speed capabilities which, it was believed, would enable it to elude any fighter.

The aft-firing MG 15 appeared late in 1938 on the pre-production, but was not standardised on the **Fi 156C-1**, which was primarily a light staff transport and liaison aircraft that was to be issued, at the rate of one or two examples, to almost every Gruppe of the Luftwaffe. The Fi 156C-1 began to leave the Kassel line early in 1939, alongside the **Fi 156C–2** that was intended primarily for the Nah-(Heeres-) Aufklärungsstaffeln. The Fi 156C-2 was fitted with the aft-firing MG 15 machine-gun as standard, had provision for a single vertical camera in the rear of the cabin, and carried

only two crew members in its standard production version. Some late production examples were modified so that a casualty litter could be accommodated.

A total of 227 Fi 156s was accepted by the Luftwaffe during the course of 1939, and small numbers were exported to

Key to the Fi 156 Storch's exceptionally short take-off and landing performance and slow-flying characteristics were the high-lift devices across the wing leading and trailing edges. Fixed slats occupied the entire leading edge of the wing, while extendable flaps moved aft and downward to increase gross wing area by approximately 18 per cent.

Fieseler Fi 156C-2 Storch cutaway key

1	Fixed tab
2	Rudder construction
3	Rudder balance
4	Navigation light
5	Tailplane bracing strut
6	Tailplane tab
7	Elevator construction
8	Wooden tailplane construction
9	Lower surface elevator slat
10	Elevator bell crank
11	Tailplane pivot mounting
12	Fin construction
13	Fin leading edge
14	Elevator fabric covering
15	Port tailplane
16	Elevator balance
17	Tailplane trim jack
18	Tailskid strut cuff
19	Tailskid

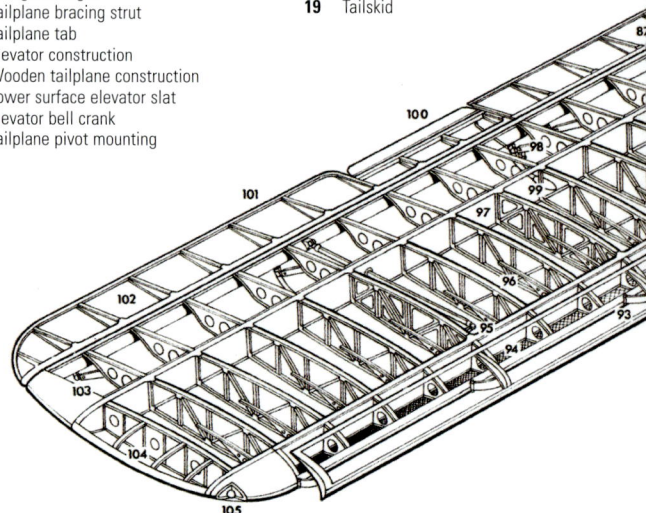

Stalin was so impressed wth the capabilities of the Storch that he issued instructions for the design to be adapted for Soviet production. The task was assigned to Oleg K. Antonov, who was later to achieve an international reputation for his own designs. However, deliveries had still to start from an assembly line established at Kaunas, Lithuania, when the Germany invaded the USSR. The factory was turned over to MiG-3 repairs, and shortly thereafter was overrun by the German forces.

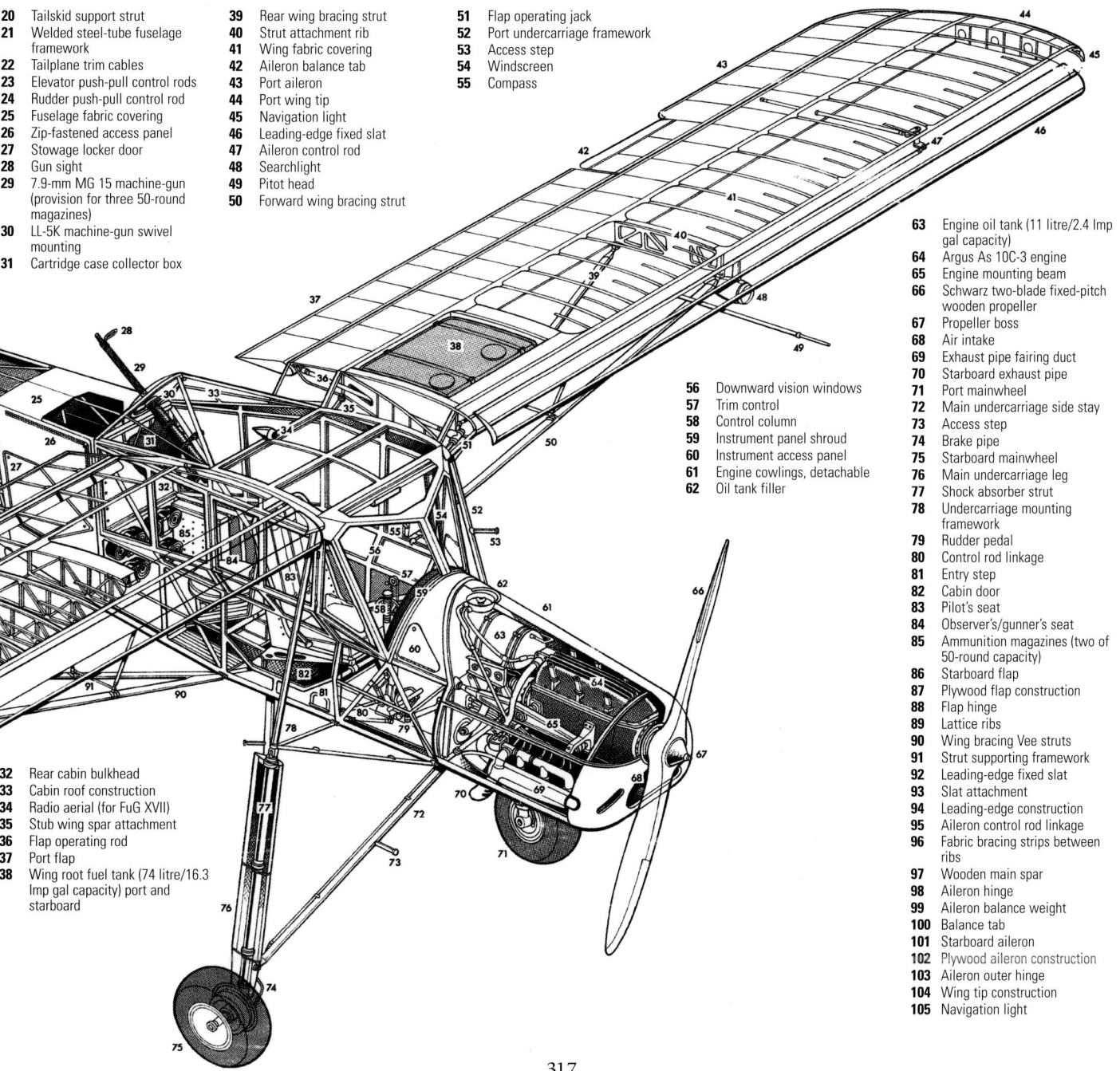

20 Tailskid support strut
21 Welded steel-tube fuselage framework
22 Tailplane trim cables
23 Elevator push-pull control rods
24 Rudder push-pull control rod
25 Fuselage fabric covering
26 Zip-fastened access panel
27 Stowage locker door
28 Gun sight
29 7.9-mm MG 15 machine-gun (provision for three 50-round magazines)
30 LL-5K machine-gun swivel mounting
31 Cartridge case collector box

39 Rear wing bracing strut
40 Strut attachment rib
41 Wing fabric covering
42 Aileron balance tab
43 Port aileron
44 Port wing tip
45 Navigation light
46 Leading-edge fixed slat
47 Aileron control rod
48 Searchlight
49 Pitot head
50 Forward wing bracing strut

51 Flap operating jack
52 Port undercarriage framework
53 Access step
54 Windscreen
55 Compass

56 Downward vision windows
57 Trim control
58 Control column
59 Instrument panel shroud
60 Instrument access panel
61 Engine cowlings, detachable
62 Oil tank filler

63 Engine oil tank (11 litre/2.4 Imp gal capacity)
64 Argus As 10C-3 engine
65 Engine mounting beam
66 Schwarz two-blade fixed-pitch wooden propeller
67 Propeller boss
68 Air intake
69 Exhaust pipe fairing duct
70 Starboard exhaust pipe
71 Port mainwheel
72 Main undercarriage side stay
73 Access step
74 Brake pipe
75 Starboard mainwheel
76 Main undercarriage leg
77 Shock absorber strut
78 Undercarriage mounting framework
79 Rudder pedal
80 Control rod linkage
81 Entry step
82 Cabin door
83 Pilot's seat
84 Observer's/gunner's seat
85 Ammunition magazines (two of 50-round capacity)
86 Starboard flap
87 Plywood flap construction
88 Flap hinge
89 Lattice ribs
90 Wing bracing Vee struts
91 Strut supporting framework
92 Leading-edge fixed slat
93 Slat attachment
94 Leading-edge construction
95 Aileron control rod linkage
96 Fabric bracing strips between ribs
97 Wooden main spar
98 Aileron hinge
99 Aileron balance weight
100 Balance tab
101 Starboard aileron
102 Plywood aileron construction
103 Aileron outer hinge
104 Wing tip construction
105 Navigation light

32 Rear cabin bulkhead
33 Cabin roof construction
34 Radio aerial (for FuG XVII)
35 Stub wing spar attachment
36 Flap operating rod
37 Port flap
38 Wing root fuel tank (74 litre/16.3 Imp gal capacity) port and starboard

Fieseler Fi 156 Storch

Finland, Switzerland, and even the USSR. Hermann Göring presented examples of the Storch to both Benito Mussolini and Josef Stalin. The latter was so impressed by the capabilities of the Storch that he issued instructions that the design be adapted for Soviet manufacture and placed in production. This task was given to Oleg K. Antonov, and a factory was established in Lithuania for the series production of the **OKA-38** aircraft with a licence-built Renault 6Q air-cooled six-cylinder inverted inline as the **ShS** (Shtabny Samolyot, or staff aircraft). Prototypes of the Soviet version of the Storch were completed and tested, but before series deliveries could be made in 1941, the assembly plant was overrun by the advancing German forces.

Medical evacuation

With the German offensive in the West during the summer of 1940, the Storch began to be used extensively both as an ambulance and rescue aircraft. In the latter role it frequently rescued fighter pilots under the most arduous conditions, landing and taking-off in confined spaces under enemy fire, and with the creation of the specialised rescue units, including the Wüstennotstaffeln in the desert, the Storch was employed for this task throughout the remainder of the war. Experience gained in France also led to the testing of the Storch as a tug for the so-called 'airborne infantry pontoon bridge', trials being conducted in January 1941 by Pionier-Bataillon 32 at Altrhein, near Darmstadt. It was proposed that gangplanks of 0.6-m (2-ft) width and of varying length complete with 3-m (9.8-ft) pontoons should be fitted with sets of wings and towed by Fi 156s to the site of the pontoon bridge. Towing tests with gangplanks 16 m (52 ft 6 in), 24 m (78 ft 10 in), and 28 m (91 ft 10 in) long were conducted, these weighing 380, 540 and 880 kg (838, 1,190 and 1,944 lb), but it was eventually concluded that the Storch was insufficiently powerful for this task, and better results were obtained with the Henschel Hs 126.

Production of the Storch totalled 216 in 1940, and was almost doubled in 1941 when Fieseler delivered 430 aircraft of this type, small numbers of which were supplied to Bulgaria, Croatia, Hungary, Romania and Slovakia, the assembly line concentrating primarily on the **Fi 156C-3** and **Fi 156C-5**. The Fi 156C-3 was a multi-purpose model, suitable for short-range reconnaissance, communications, ambulance and rescue missions, late production examples having the As 10C-3 engine replaced by the improved As 10P, and the Fi 156C-5 was generally similar but standardised on the As 10P engine, and had provision for a drum-like camera container or a drop tank beneath the fuselage. With the latter fitted, the range of the Fi 156C-5 could be extended from 385 to 1010 km (239 to 628 miles). With dust filters and desert survival equipment both the Fi 156C-3 and Fi 156C-5 saw extensive use in the Mediterranean theatre and North Africa as the **Fi 156C-3/Trop** and **Fi 156C-5/Trop**. The Storch was favoured by Generalfeldmarschall Erwin Rommel as his personal transport in North Africa, and also by Generalfeldmarschall Albert Kesselring until his Storch was shot down and he elected to use the faster Fw 189.

Produced in parallel with the C-series Storch from late

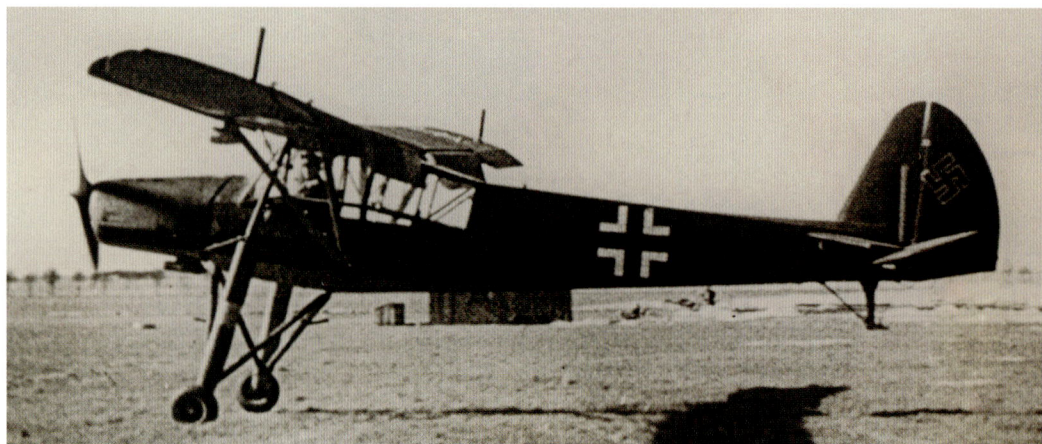

Right: Structurally there was little unconventional about the Storch, with its rectangular-section welded steel-tube fabric-skinned fuselage, two-spar fabric-covered wooden wing and plywood-covered wooden tail surfaces, but its main undercarriage members, designed to absorb the impact of high vertical descent rates, appeared inordinately long at first sight.

Below: The Fi 156 starred in the North African campaign, especially the Fi 156C-5/Trop long-range version that often flew deep into the desert to rescue Luftwaffe aircrew.

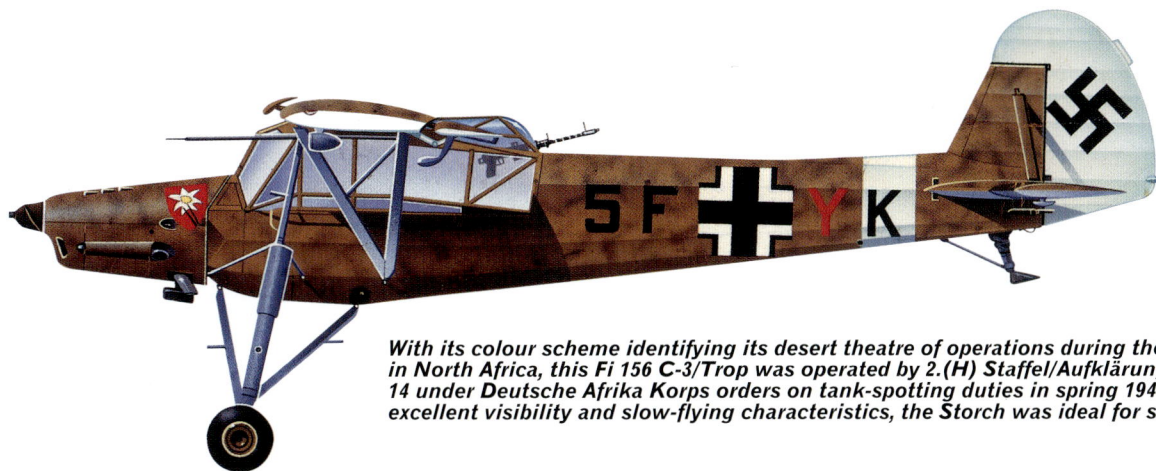

With its colour scheme identifying its desert theatre of operations during the conflict in North Africa, this Fi 156 C-3/Trop was operated by 2.(H) Staffel/Aufklärungsgruppe 14 under Deutsche Afrika Korps orders on tank-spotting duties in spring 1941. With excellent visibility and slow-flying characteristics, the Storch was ideal for such duties.

1941 was the D-series intended primarily for use by the Wüstennotstaffeln. This featured an enlarged upward-hinging loading hatch in the starboard side of the fuselage aft of the cockpit, and extended aft-fuselage glazing, part of which could be hinged downward. These features, coupled with relocation of some interior equipment, eased litter accommodation. The pre-production **Fi 156D-0** appeared in the autumn of 1941, being followed by the **Fi 156D-1** that was manufactured concurrently with the C-series until 1944. One other sub-variant of the Storch that appeared late in 1941 was the **Fi 156E** with a form of track undercarriage intended to increase the aircraft's independence of prepared landing surfaces. Each main undercarriage member comprised two independently-sprung wheels in tandem with a contin-

uous tubular pneumatic rubber track which, by increasing the area in contact with the ground, reduced the risk of the Storch coming to grief as a result of concealed ruts, furrows or stones. A pre-production batch of 10 aircraft was completed with this undercarriage as **Fi 156E-0** machines and delivered to the Luftwaffe for operational evaluation, but although the tracked landing gear was considered generally successful, no further E-series aircraft were produced.

Despite increased emphasis by Fieseler on the licence manufacture of the Bf 109 fighter, production of the Storch at Kassel continued to increase, averaging 40.3 per month during 1942, in which year the parent company delivered 484 aircraft, production being supplemented from April by the former Morane-Saulnier factory at Puteaux, from which

Generalfeldmarschall Erwin Rommel confers with a captain of the Luftwaffe, the pilot of a reconnaissance Storch. Rommel made extensive use of this versatile aircraft, as did those Allied commanders whose forces captured them in operating order.

Although tested at an early stage for a variety of specialist tasks, including smoke-laying, coastal patrol and supply-dropping, it was in its primary army-support role that the Storch found fame. Most Luftwaffe Gruppen also used the type as a 'hack'.

Above: Some Fi 156s were built at the captured Morane-Saulnier factory in France, where post-war production continued as the MS.500 series. This particular example (G-AZMH) can be seen in Berlin's Luftwaffe Museum.

Above: An early production Fi 156C-1 lands with its large flaps and fully extended. Combined with the fixed slats, they gave the Storch its phenomenally low stalling speed. The fully-extended oleos are also noteworthy.

Fieseler Fi 156 Storch

Fieseler Fi 156C-3 Storch
Eastern Front, 1943

Without doubt, the Fieseler Storch was the prime example of a wartime army co-operation and observation aircraft, and certainly the design by which other types operating in these roles were judged. This anonymous Fi 156C-3, which retains four-letter factory radio codes instead of any unit identification, clearly illustrates the purposeful design of the undercarriage with the long compression legs incorporating long-stroke, oil-damping shock absorbers capable of coping with very high vertical descent rates. Such was the success of the Storch in its intended role that trials were conducted around supply-dropping, coastal patrol and light bombing roles, although only as secondary operations.

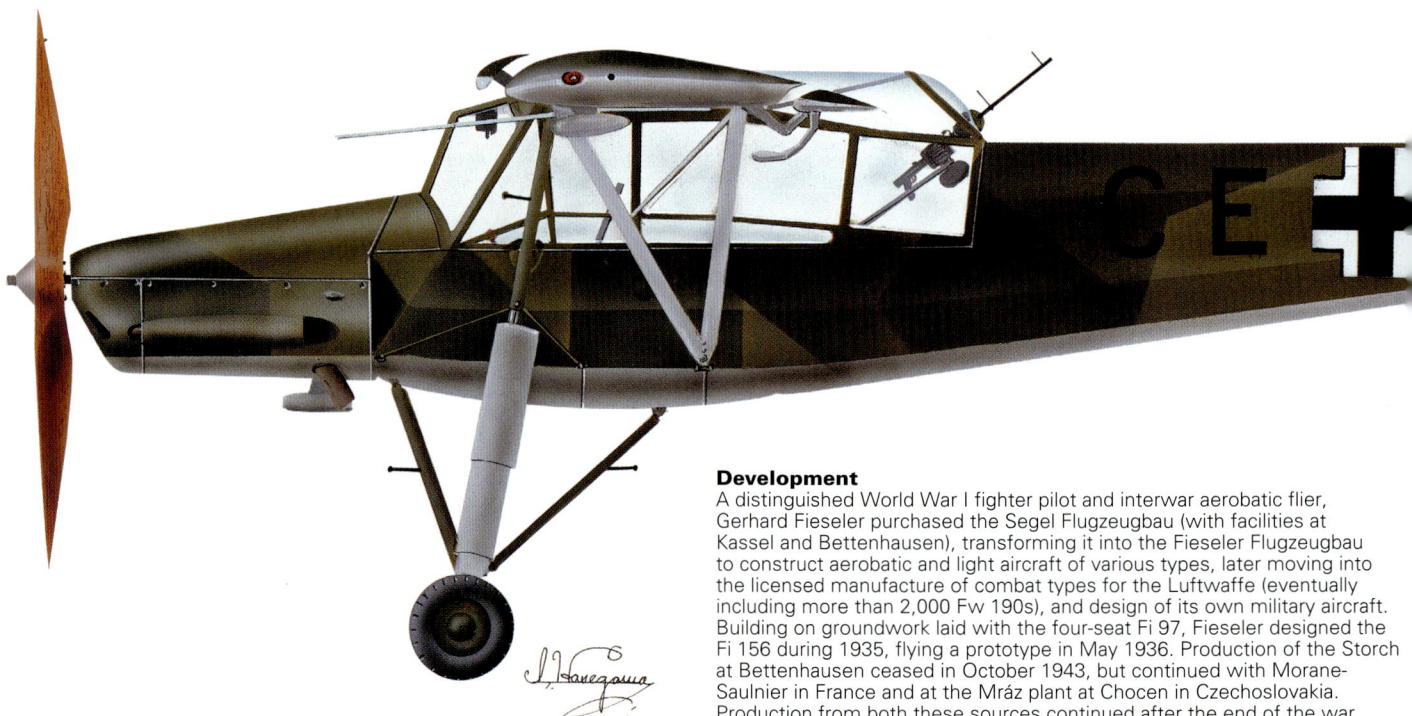

Development
A distinguished World War I fighter pilot and interwar aerobatic flier, Gerhard Fieseler purchased the Segel Flugzeugbau (with facilities at Kassel and Bettenhausen), transforming it into the Fieseler Flugzeugbau to construct aerobatic and light aircraft of various types, later moving into the licensed manufacture of combat types for the Luftwaffe (eventually including more than 2,000 Fw 190s), and design of its own military aircraft. Building on groundwork laid with the four-seat Fi 97, Fieseler designed the Fi 156 during 1935, flying a prototype in May 1936. Production of the Storch at Bettenhausen ceased in October 1943, but continued with Morane-Saulnier in France and at the Mráz plant at Chocen in Czechoslovakia. Production from both these sources continued after the end of the war.

Powerplant
The Storch prototype was powered by an Argus As 10C eight-cylinder, air-cooled piston engine, of inverted Vee configuration, with the similar As 10P adopted on the multi-role Fi 156C-3. Although a metal, variable-pitch propeller was fitted to the second Storch prototype, production aircraft had a fixed-pitch, wooden Schwarz airscrew.

Structure
The Fi 156 had a fuselage of welded steel tube construction, with fabric covering, while the folding wings were of wooden construction, with fabric covering. The bracing struts were steel tubes, the leading-edge slats were aluminium, and the trailing-edge flaps were wooden.

Performance characteristics
At a loaded weight of 1242 kg (2,740 lb), it was demonstrated that a Storch could be flown down to 50 km/h (32 mph). With a 13-km/h (8-mph) headwind, the Storch required a take-off run of 45 m (149 ft) and a landing run of 15 m (49 ft). With a stronger wind, a Storch landed within 4.5 m (15 ft) on a ploughed surface. Carrying an auxiliary fuel tank under the centreline, the Fi 156C-5 had a range of 1010 km (628 miles), by comparison with the 386-km (240-mile) range of the basic aircraft. The Storch's incredible slow-flying capabilities were its best form of defence against attacks by enemy fighters, but the aircraft could also carry a single 7.9-mm (0.31-in) MG 15 machine-gun firing aft through a transparent panel in the top decking.

Undercarriage
The Storch's STOL capability was enhanced by its enormously strong undercarriage, whose energy-absorbing oleos could withstand the high vertical sink rates imposed by very steep approaches. With a decent wind to land into, the Storch could land within the length of its own wingspan.

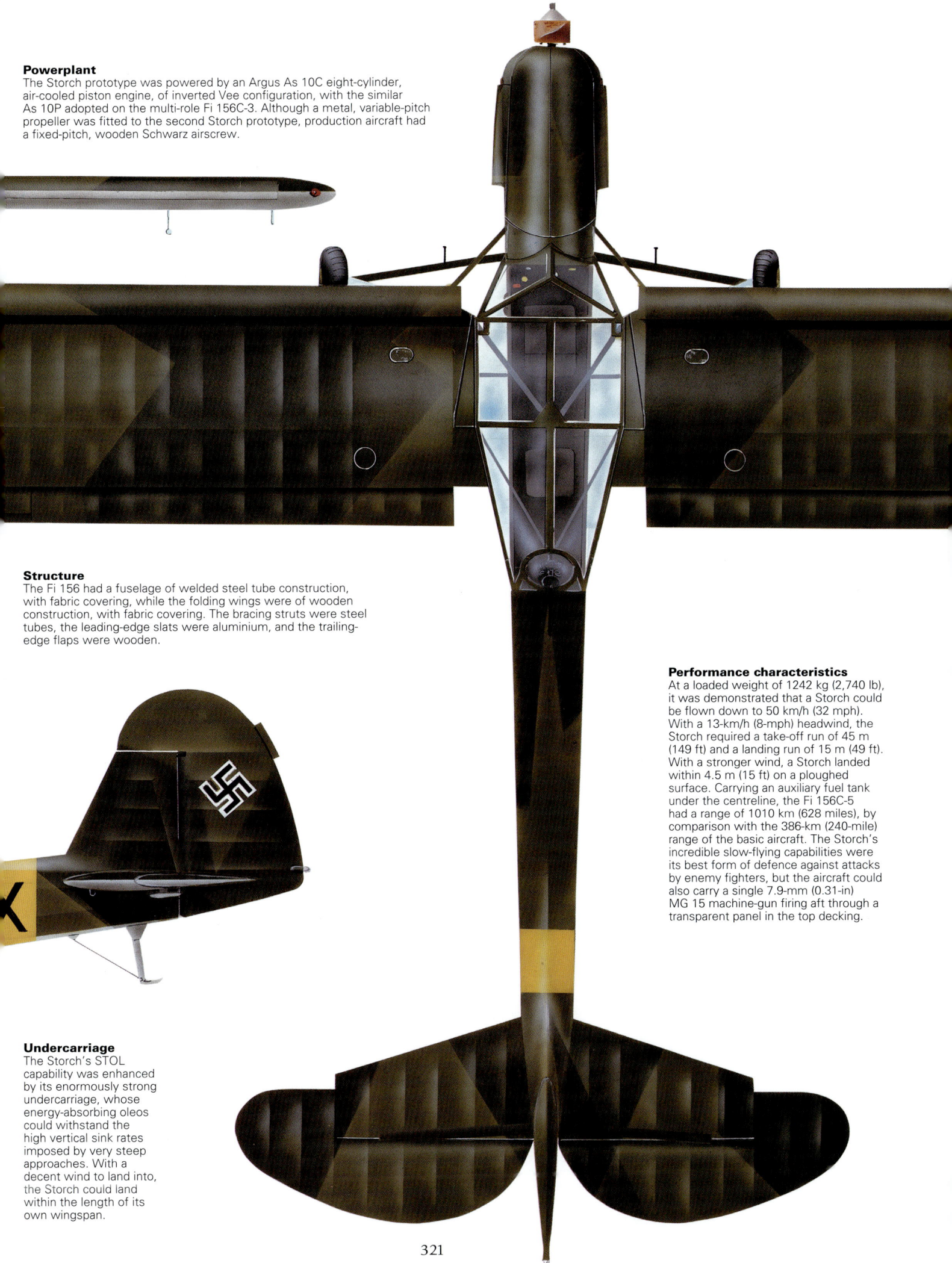

Above: A Storch of the Kurierstaffel Ob.d.L. (Courier Squadron, Luftwaffe High Command) takes off from a landing strip on the Don sector of the Eastern Front, 13 August 1942. In 10 days' time, the 6th Army would reach the Volga and attack Stalingrad.

Left: Last of the Fi 156C series was the Fi 156C-5, an Fi 156C-3 with a belly hardpoint for a camera pod or drop tank. Some were fitted with skis, rather than wheels, for operation on snow.

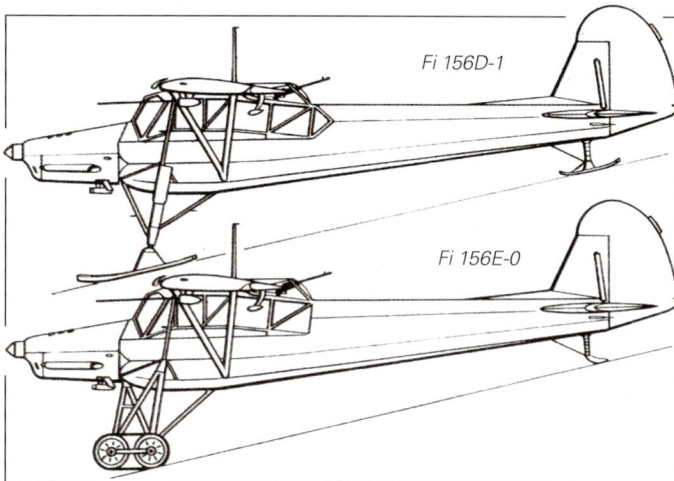

Fi 156D-1

Fi 156E-0

Above: The Fi 156D-1 was the main air ambulance variant, with two hatches in the starboard side to admit a stretcher case. Here, the patient is transferred to a Ju 52/3m in Tunisia during 1943.

Left: The badge on the cowling of this Storch identifies it as an aircraft of 1. Wüstennotstaffel. Tasked with rescuing downed pilots, this unit accompanied the Afrika Korps throughout North Africa, and then back to Sicily and Italy. In June 1943 it was renamed Verbindungsstaffel 400.

121 aircraft had been delivered by the end of the year. Fieseler production of the C- and D-series Storch continued at a high rate until August 1943, in which month 60 Fi 156s left the Kassel line, but the need to devote the space occupied by the Storch assembly line to the Fw 190 resulted in a tapering off of production in September, in which month only 30 left Kassel, the last two Fi 156s to be built by the parent company leaving the plant in October when all jigs and tools were transferred to the Mráz factory at Chocen in Czechoslovakia. The parent company had delivered 480 Fi 156s during the course of 1943, a total nearly equalled by the Puteaux factory which produced 403, and in December 1943 the Chocen plant delivered its first Storch.

Rescuing Il Duce

It was in 1943 that the Storch was involved in the exploit for which it is best remembered, namely the liberation of Benito Mussolini, the deposed Italian dictator. The Führer had assigned the task of tracing and rescuing Il Duce to SS-Hauptsturmführer Otto Skorzeny, who eventually located Mussolini's place of imprisonment as the hotel at the peak of the Gran Sasso massif in the Abruzzi e Molise. Accessible only by cable car, the hotel was situated at an altitude of 2760 m (9,050 ft). Skorzeny had intended to fly out Mussolini in a Storch that landed at the lower cable car station, but it was damaged on arrival. There was no alternative but to hastily clear the larger boulders from an area close to the hotel. Skorzeny's personal pilot, Hauptmann Heinrich Gerlach, landed in a second Storch (Fi 156C-3 SU+LL). Carrying both Skorzeny and Mussolini, the Fi 156 was overweight and was damaged on takeoff, but made it safely to Rome.

Production of the Storch for the Luftwaffe continued at Puteaux until mid-August 1944, by which time a further 260 French-built aircraft had been accepted, and in Czechoslovakia throughout 1944, 137 Fi 156s being delivered from Chocen during the year. Fewer than a dozen additional Fi 156s were accepted by the Luftwaffe in 1945. Production continued post-war in both Czechoslovakia (as the **Mraz K-65 Cap**) and France (as the **Morane-Saulnier MS 500** series).

During the period 1937-45, the Luftwaffe accepted just short of 2,900 Storch monoplanes, of which about 8 per cent were diverted to Germany's allies, and the story of the wartime development of this aircraft would be incomplete without reference to the **Fi 256** designed by Fieseler in 1941 as a civil four-passenger successor to the abandoned Fi 156B.

322

Fieseler Fi 156 Storch

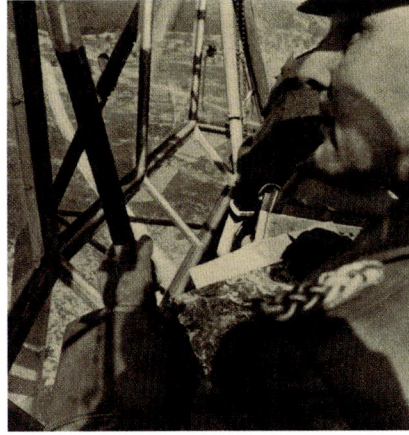

Above and left: As evidenced by this series of wartime propaganda photographs, the Storch became a familiar sight wherever German forces were operating. The Fieseler design was to perform some remarkable feats, not least of which was the retrieval of Mussolini from imprisonment in the hotel at the peak of the Gran Sasso massif. In the evening of 28 April 1945 and with Red Army troops in the streets of Berlin, Hanna Reitsch flew the last German aircraft out of the city through a barrage of flak, her Storch carrying newly appointed Luftwaffe chief – and her lover – Robert Ritter von Greim on a futile mission from the Führer to rally a last counter-attack.

Although the Fi 256 was of essentially similar concept to the Storch, it was, in fact, an entirely new design without any interchangeable components. Aerodynamically refined and featuring automatic wing leading-edge slats, the Fi 256 had a larger cabin in which the pilot was seated centrally with the passengers accommodated in two side-by-side pairs of seats. The Fi 256 was proposed by Fieseler to the Technisches Amt of the RLM as a potential successor to the Storch but was not accepted. However, two prototypes were built at the Puteaux factory in 1943-44.

Fieseler Fi 156C-2 specification
Type: two-seat light air observation post and army co-operation aircraft
Powerplant: one Argus As 10C-3 air-cooled inverted V-8 engine rated at 179 kW (240 hp) for take-off
Performance: maximum speed 175 km/h (109 mph) at sea level; maximum continuous cruising speed 150 km/h (93 mph) at 1000 m (3,280 ft); economical cruising speed 130 km/h (81 mph); initial climb rate 275 m (905 ft) per minute; time to 1000 m 4 minutes 6 seconds; service ceiling 4600 m (15,090 ft); range 386 km (240 miles) at 150 km/h at 1000 m
Weights: empty 930 kg (2,050 lb); normal loaded 1325 kg (2,920 lb)
Dimensions: wingspan 14.25 m (46 ft 9 in); length 9.90 m (32 ft 5⅔ in); height 3.00 m (10 ft 0 in); wing area 26.00 m² (279.86 sq ft)
Armament: one 7.9-mm (0.31-in) MG 15 trainable machine-gun firing aft from the rear of cabin

Right: The cabin of the Fi 156 was roomy and comfortable, and was entered via an automobile-style door. The entire sides and roof of the cabin were glazed and the side panels sloped outwards at an acute angle as an aid to downward vision.

Above: The Storch's original role was as an army co-operation platform, and as such provided valuable service in the German campaign in the West, scouting ahead of the highly mobile mechanised formations. Here, a Storch overflies a convoy of halftrack-towed artillery.

Right: A common sight wherever German forces were operating, the Storch could perform in several valuable roles. Here, a photo-montage illustrates a Storch using its impressive STOL capability to take off from a short strip of road.

Fieseler Fi 157 and Fi 158

The Fi 157 and Fi 158 were pilotless and piloted half-brothers of the same basic concept. The Fi 157 drone proved unsuccessful, and while the Fi 158 offered good performance with a low-powered engine, there was little requirement for the type and only limited trials were undertaken before the programme was terminated.

During the mid-1930s Fieseler received an order for a radio-controlled target drone. Fieseler's proposal was accepted and three **Fi 157** prototypes were ordered. Fieseler also proposed an **Fi 158** experimental piloted version. All three Fi 157s crashed. The Fi 158 appeared in 1938, differing from the drone primarily in its single-seat cockpit and retractable tailskid undercarriage. The **Fi 158 V1** was of wooden construction, and completed only limited trials.

Fieseler Fi 158 specification
Type: single-seat experimental aircraft
Powerplant: one Hirth HM 506A air-cooled six-cylinder inverted inline engine rated at 119 kW (160 hp) for take-off
Performance: maximum speed 350 km/h (217 mph) at sea level; cruising speed 300 km/h (186 mph) at optimum altitude; climb to 1000 m (3,280 ft) in 2 minutes; service ceiling 6700 m (21,980 ft); range 370 km (230 miles)
Weight: empty 494 kg (1,089 lb); normal take-off 646 kg (1,424 lb)
Dimensions: wingspan 7.00 m (22 ft 11¾ in); length 6.60 m (21 ft 7¾ in); height 1.70 m (5 ft 7 in); wing area 7.00 m² (75.35 sq ft)

Left and below: Fieseler built a single prototype Fi 158 (D-EAEN). It flew in 1938 and was eventually destroyed in an air raid. Its Fi 157 counterpart was designed for artillery target practice.

Fieseler Fi 167

Designed to meet a requirement for a ship-based two-seat torpedo-bomber and reconnaissance aircraft, the Fieseler Fi 167 possessed exceptional low-speed characteristics, but suspension of the German carrier-building programme put an end to its development and, when the carrier was resurrected, the Ju 87 was selected instead.

Both the Arado and Fieseler companies submitted proposals aimed at meeting the requirements of a specification issued in 1937 for a two-seat multi-purpose shipboard aircraft, and three prototypes were ordered from each company, the projects being designated Ar 195 and **Fi 167**, respectively. The prototypes of both aircraft were completed during the summer of 1938, but the Ar 195 was soon found to be incapable of meeting the performance demands of the specification. The Fi 167, on the other hand, exceeded the the specification in every respect.

Designed by Reinhold Mewes, who placed emphasis on ease of manufacture and maintenance, the Fi 167 was a somewhat angular two-bay biplane. The entire engine installation could be exposed for servicing by the removal of a series of light metal panels; the centre fuselage was covered by light alloy sheet, and the rear fuselage was a stressed-skin semi-monocoque. The staggered two-spar wings were braced on each side by two pairs of N-struts, a pair of splayed N-struts supported the upper mainplane centre section above the fuselage, and the wings were hinged to fold aft immediately outboard of the inner pair of interplane struts. Full-span leading-edge automatic slats were fitted to both upper and lower wings, the latter also carrying large-area trailing-edge

The Fi 167 V1 is seen with its biplane wings folded, outboard of the main undercarriage units, for shipboard stowage.

This Fieseler Fi 167A-0 was assigned to the Erprobungsstaffel 167. The unit used the Fi 167A-0 aircraft on various test duties in the Netherlands from summer 1940.

Below: The Fi 167 V1 carried out its initial trials in 1938. Flight testing proved the aircraft to be an instant technical success.

Below: Differing little from the two prototypes, the first pre-production Fi 167A-0 began its test programme early in 1940.

Despite its awkward looks, the Fi 167 displayed outstanding low-speed flying qualities. The ungainly undercarriage could be jettisoned for emergency ditching.

flaps, and the undercarriage featured long-stroke shock-absorber legs to cater for high descent rates.

Flight trials revealed the fact that the **Fi 167 V1** possessed truly exceptional low-speed characteristics, and throttled back and with elevators fully up, the aircraft simply sank slowly and almost vertically. On one occasion, with Gerhard Fieseler at the controls, the aircraft 'sank' around 3000 m (9,845 ft) to an altitude of 30 m (100 ft) above the ground while remaining continuously over one spot. At the other end of the performance scale, the Fi 167 V1 improved on the stipulated maximum speed, and proved capable of carrying double the offensive load demanded by the specification. Indeed, so successful were initial trials that Fieseler decided that it was unnecessary to complete the third prototype, and immediately initiated preparation for the construction of the 12 pre-production **Fi 167A-0** aircraft.

Pre-production Fi 167s

The pre-production aircraft differed little from the Fi 167 V1 and **Fi 167 V2** prototypes, the primary changes resulting from tests at the Erprobungsstelle at Rechlin being the introduction of larger low-pressure tyres, new flame-damper exhausts, outlets and modified supercharger air intake for the DB 601B engine, and the provision of Flettner tabs on the rudder and elevators. Other changes included an improved emergency release mechanism for the main undercarriage members, spring-loaded bolts being released electrically, and the provision of an inflatable two-man dinghy in the wing.

In the meantime, 'Carrier A' had been christened *Graf Zeppelin* and launched on 8 December 1938, but as it was not anticipated that this vessel would be commissioned before the summer of 1940, construction of the Fi 167A-0 received no special priority, and the **Fi 167A-01** (TJ+AJ) did not start its flight test programme until the early months of that year. By this time, the Technisches Amt had decided that the shipboard dive-bomber role would be performed by the Junkers Ju 87C-0, thus restricting the Fi 167A to the tasks of torpedo-bombing and reconnaissance, and a further blow was dealt the Fieseler biplane's prospects when, in May 1940, construction of the *Graf Zeppelin* was halted. Nevertheless, the manufacture of the 12 Fi 167A-0 aircraft was continued, and all the aircraft of the batch were accepted by the

Fieseler Fi 167

Below: As with the Fi 156, Fieseler's new aircraft possessed exceptional low-speed handling characteristics, achieved in this case by the provision on both the upper and lower wings of large ailerons on the outboard ends of the trailing edges and automatic slats on the leading edges of the outer panels, and large-area flaps on the inboard parts of the lower wing's trailing edges.

Right: These Fi 167s served with Erprobungsstaffel 167, which employed the type on various test duties. The divided main undercarriage units allowed carriage of a centreline bomb.

Luftwaffe during the summer of 1940, the Erprobungsstaffel 167 being formed for operational suitability trials. Late in September 1941, the 11th Fi 167A-0 (KG+QE) was loaned to the Daimler-Benz Erprobungsstelle at Echterdingen for various engine trials, and by 13 May 1942, when the order was given to resume construction of the *Graf Zeppelin*, the Erprobungsstaffel 167 with nine Fi 167s on strength had been transferred to the Netherlands for what were referred to as 'advanced service trials' in Dutch coastal areas. However, the Fieseler biplane, despite its unique qualities, was no longer considered as potential equipment for Germany's first carrier, for by the time the Luftwaffe resumed the training of shipboard squadrons, a decision had been taken to adapt the Ju 87D as a torpedo-bomber under the designation Ju 87E.

The Fi 167s remained in the Netherlands until early in 1943, participating in several experimental programmes, including one intended to evolve the most effective camouflage pattern for aircraft operating over the sea, the Erprobungsstaffel 167 then returning to Germany where it was disbanded. The Fi 167s were returned to Fieseler for overhaul, three subsequently being delivered to the Fahrwerkserprobungsstelle der DVL, the DVL's undercarriage test centre at Budweis, where they were used for measuring landing shocks under various load conditions, flying both in standard biplane configuration and as highly-loaded sesquiplanes, the lower mainplanes being detached immediately outboard of the undercarriage and additional struts supporting the upper mainplanes.

Nine of the surviving Fi 167s were sold to Croatia, arriving in September 1944. Their load-carrying ability and short-field performance made them ideal for supplying Croatian army garrisons. On 10 October 1944 a Croatian Fi 167 was attacked by five RAF Mustangs, shooting one down before it succumbed to its attackers.

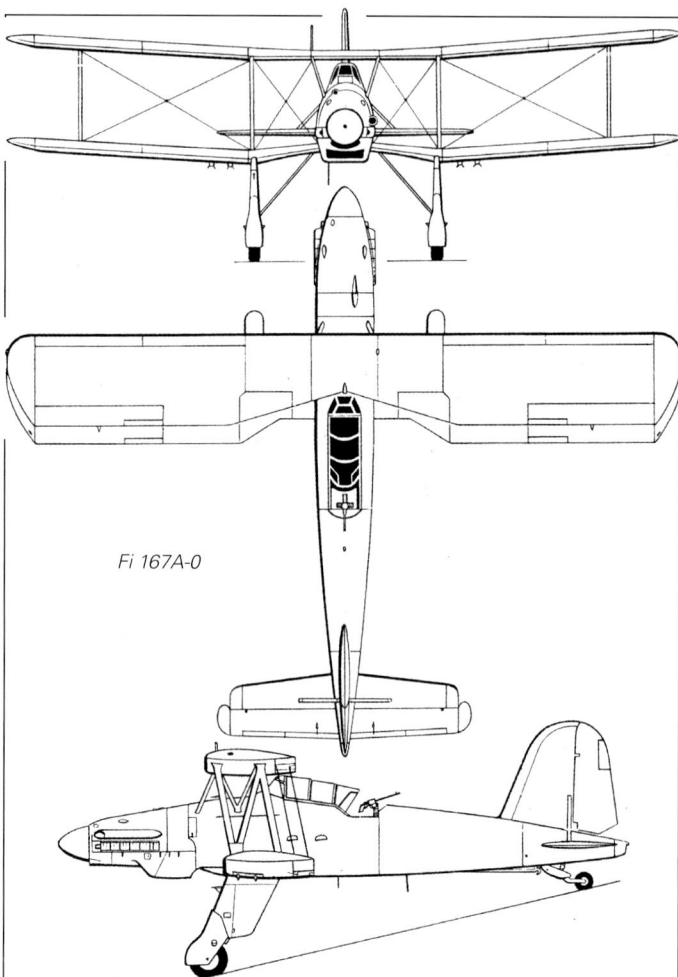

Fi 167A-0

Fieseler Fi 167A-0 specification

Type: two-seat shipboard torpedo-bomber and reconnaissance aircraft
Powerplant: one Daimler-Benz DB 601B liquid-cooled inverted V-12 engine rated at 820 kW (1,100 hp) for take-off
Performance: maximum speed in bomber role 320 km/h (199 mph), in reconnaissance role 325 km/h (202 mph); normal cruising speed 250 km/h (155 mph); maximum cruising speed 270 km/h (168 mph); service ceiling 7500-8200 m (24,605-26,905 ft); range 1300 m (808 miles) or in reconnaissance role with a 300-litre (66-Imp gal) drop tank 1500 km (932 miles)
Weights: empty 2800 kg (6,173 lb); normal loaded 4500 kg (9,920 lb); maximum take-off 4850 kg (10,690 lb)
Dimensions: wingspan 13.50 m (44 ft 3½ in); length 11.40 m (37 ft 4¾ in); height 4.80 m (15 ft 9 in); wing area 45.50 m² (489.76 sq ft)
Armament: (defensive) one 7.9-mm (0.31-in) MG 17 fixed forward-firing machine-gun with 500 rounds in starboard side of forward fuselage and one 7.9-mm (0.31-in) MG 15 machine-gun on a trainable mounting in observer's cockpit with 600 rounds; (offensive) normal load comprising four 50-kg (110-lb) SC 50 bombs plus one 250-kg (551-lb) SC 250 or 500-kg (1,102-lb) bomb, or maximum load comprising one 1000-kg (2,205-lb) SD 1000 bomb or one 765-kg (1,687-lb) LT F5b torpedo.

Below: The Fi 167's two-man crew was accommodated in tandem, beneath a long canopy that was designed to allow for operation of a machine-gun on a pivoted mount at the rear.

Left and above: The Fi 167A-0 (TJ+AN) was the fifth pre-production aircraft. When some of the fleet were used for generic undercarriage trials, the Fi 167's landing characteristics were too benign for some tasks, and so the aircraft were operated with most of the lower wing removed to increase the landing forces.

Below: The Fi 167 was a two-bay biplane with rearward-folding outer wing panels, metal construction with a measure of fabric in the covering, fixed tailwheel undercarriage with jettisonable main units, and a conventional braced tail unit.

Anton Flettner GmbH

Anton Flettner is associated with several aerodynamic fields. In World War I, for example, he created the Flettner servo-tab, and soon after the war he bought a schooner and modified this to be propelled by two rotating cylinders to exploit the Magnus effect: this vessel made a transatlantic crossing in 1926. In the mid-1920s Flettner became fascinated by rotary-wing flight, and used the profits of his highly successful company, which made rotary ventilators also based on Flettner's interest in the movement of air, to develop in his new enthusiasm. His first design was a small helicopter with a rotor powered by a small propeller, driven by a 15-kW (20-hp) Blattenden engine, on each blade.

Flettner established the Flettner GmbH in 1935 with premises at Berlin-Johannisthal and later at Bad Tölz. The company received considerable support from the German navy, which appreciated the potential of the helicopter for shipborne reconnaissance and gunnery spotting. The company's first design was the Fl 184 autogyro, which was followed in 1936 by the Fl 185 helicopter with the main rotor's torque reaction offset by a small propeller on a port-side pylon. Success finally came in the form of the Fl 265 with a side-by-side pair of intermeshing rotors, which turned in opposite directions so that each rotor's torque reaction cancelled that of the other. This in turn led to the Fl 282 Kolibri, which

was the first helicopter ordered into large-scale production anywhere in the world. Orders were placed with BMW to manufacture 1,000 Kolibris, but Flettner insisted that his company was the only one able to assemble the complex intermeshing rotor gearbox.

Anton Flettner stands in front of a line-up of his company's most significant product, the Fl 282 Kolibri that was the world's first helicopter to receive certification and enter mass production. The Kolibri was ready for production in 1940 but, as a result of Allied bombing, only 25 had been built before the end of the war. However, no other helicopter saw such extensive wartime use.

Flettner Fl 184, Fl 185 and Fl 265

The autogyros and helicopters designed under the leadership of Anton Flettner were among the most advanced examples of their types to be created in World War II, and only Allied bombing prevented the widespread adoption of the Fl 282 with its side-by-side pair of intermeshing rotors.

Seeking a way to overcome the torque induced when a rotor is driven from an airframe-mounted power source, the German rotary-wing pioneer Anton Flettner explored the idea of putting a 22-kW (30-hp) Anzani engine and tractor propeller on the leading edge of each blade of a two-blade rotor with a diameter of some 29.90 m (98 ft 1¼ in). This prototype made a successful tethered flight in 1932, but was soon destroyed on the ground when it overturned during a gale.

Flettner then built the two-seat **Fl 184** autogyro with enclosed accommodation, a three-blade auto-rotating rotor on a pylon above the cockpit, and a 104-kW (140-hp) Siemens-Halske Sh.14 engine driving a two-blade tractor propeller. This, too, was destroyed before it could be evaluated. Next came the prototype of the **Fl 185**, which was a combined autogyro and helicopter. Its Sh.14A engine, mounted in the nose, could be used to drive two propellers on outriggers, one on each side, but the main rotor was powered only when required for the helicopter mode. When the Fl 185 was flown as an autogyro, the propellers on the outriggers both acted as pusher units and the main rotor auto-rotated, but for helicopter flight the main rotor was powered from the engine and the outrigger propellers set so that one acted as a tractor and the other as a pusher to offset rotor torque.

Technically successful

Though technically successful, the Fl 185 was obviously not the starting point for an operational type, and was flown only a few times before Flettner began construction, in 1937, of his **Fl 265 V1** pure helicopter prototype. This had an airframe configuration similar to that of the Fl 185, but dispensed with the outriggers and propellers and introduced a counter-rotating assembly of a pair of side-by-side two-blade rotors whose rotations were synchronised to ensure that the blades intermeshed without touching. As the rotors turned in opposite directions, each cancelled the effects of the

The Fl 184, was a two-seat autogyro with an enclosed cabin and a three-blade rotor. D-EDVE, the only example built, caught fire during a test flight and was completely destroyed.

other's torque. To simplify control problems there was a tail unit that incorporated an adjustable tailplane for longitudinal trimming, and for directional stability and control a large fin-and-rudder assembly was incorporated to augment the use of differential collective-pitch change on the two rotors.

The Fl 265 V1 first flew in May 1939, with autorotation trials starting in August. Later it was lost in an accident when the counter-rotating blades struck each other. However, the **Fl 265 V2** second prototype was used successfully for a variety of military trials. They were conducted from the decks of vessels operating in the Baltic and Mediterranean Seas. As

The Fl 265 prototype (D-EFLV) made its first flight in May 1939, and its first auto-rotative descents were completed during the following August, but this machine was eventually destroyed in flight when the blades of the two rotors struck each other.

Above and right: The Fl 265 V2 was the first of the prototypes to be used in a series of naval trials in the Baltic and Mediterranean. It is seen above undergoing tests in a wind tunnel, and at right operating from a platform mounted on a Kriegsmarine cruiser. The Fl 265 exhibited excellent stability and controllability during these trials, its safe landing being aided by the widely spaced main undercarriage units.

well as deck landings, the Fl 265 demonstrated its ability to land on a surfaced U-boat. During one of these sea trials the V2 was lost after running out of fuel following an oversight on behalf of its pilot.

Altogether six prototypes were built for the German navy. They flew a number of trials, including demonstration of the type's utility in the army support role. Fl 265s were tested as spotters for land forces, and for unusual roles such as the towing of dinghies across rivers and as an aid to combat bridge construction. One was also later tested in air combat with Luftwaffe fighters to evaluate the type's vulnerability. Bf 109s and Fw 190s tried their hardest to score camera gun 'kills' on the little Flettner, but its astonishing agility meant that they returned to base without a single frame to suggest that they could shoot it down with real ammunition.

On the basis of the original naval trials, an order was placed for quantity production in 1940. By that time, however, Flettner had designed a more advanced two-seat helicopter, so it was decided to proceed with the development and manufacture of this improved machine, which became the two-seat Fl 282 Kolibri (humming bird).

Flettner Fl 265 specification
Type: single-seat helicopter
Powerplant: one Bramo Sh.14A air-cooled seven-cylinder radial engine rated at 160 hp (119 kW)
Performance: maximum speed 140 km/h (87 mph) at sea level; range 300 km (186 miles); ceiling 4100 m (13,450 ft)
Weights: empty 800 kg (1,764 lb); maximum take-off 1000 kg (2,205 lb)
Dimensions: rotor diameter, each 12.30 m (40 ft 4¼ in); length 6.16 m (20 ft 2½ in); height 2.82 m (9 ft 3 in); total rotor disc area, total 237.6 m² (2,558 sq ft)

Above and right: All six Fl 265 prototypes were trialled extensively by the German navy and army for a variety of roles. This is the Fl 265 V3 (TK+AN) which was tested in a large wind tunnel at Chalais-Meudon, near Paris, in mid-1940.

Flettner Fl 282 Kolibri

Designed as a follow-on to the Fl 265, the Fl 282 was a considerably more advanced design. The helicopter's ability to take off from, and land on, very small flat surfaces made it of immediate interest to the German navy, and the Fl 282 was among the very first rotorcraft to go into any kind of useful service, with the Kriegsmarine.

Above: Dispatched for trials aboard German vessels, the Fl 282 was employed operationally on spotting duties. Here, Fl 282 V6 is seen on board the Luftwaffe's air-sea rescue ship Greif.

Above: Flettner demonstrated that the little Fl 282 could safely land on a ship, even in heavy seas. The Kriegsmarine (German navy) was impressed with the Kolibri and wanted to evaluate its capabilities in the submarine-spotting role.

Flettner's next helicopter was the two-seat **Fl 282 Kolibri** (humming bird), and to speed the development of a helicopter that could prove valuable for naval use a total of 30 prototypes and 15 pre-production examples was ordered early in 1940. Although the basic fuselage configuration was similar to that of its Fl 265 predecessor, the new machine differed in one important respect. Its engine was mounted in the centre fuselage and the pilot was accommodated in the nose, with enclosed, semi-enclosed and open cockpits in the 24 prototypes that were completed. Not all of them were two-seaters, but those that were accommodated an observer behind the rotor pylon looking to the rear.

Naval trials

In 1942 the German navy began its Fl 282 trials, finding the type extremely manoeuvrable, stable in poor weather conditions, and so reliable that in 1943 about 20 of the 24 prototypes were operating from warships in the Aegean and Mediterranean for convoy protection duties. It was discovered that, as pilots gained experience, the Fl 282 could be flown in really bad weather, leading to an order for 1,000 production helicopters. As a result of Allied bombing attacks on the BMW and Flettner works, these helicopters were not built, and only three of the prototypes survived to VE-Day, the remainder having been destroyed to prevent them being captured.

Flettner Fl 282 V21 specification
Type: single-seat helicopter
Powerplant: one BMW Bramo Sh.14A air-cooled seven-cylinder radial engine rated at 119 kW (160 hp)
Performance: maximum speed 150 km/h (93 mph) at sea level; initial vertical climb rate 91 m (300 ft) per minute; service ceiling 3300 m (10,825 ft); hovering ceiling 300 m (985 ft); range 170 km (106 miles)
Weights: empty 760 kg (1,676 lb); maximum take-off 1000 kg (2,205 lb)
Dimensions: rotor diameter, each 11.96 m (39 ft 2¾ in); fuselage length 6.56 m (21 ft 6¼ in); height 2.20 m (7 ft 2½ in); rotor disc area, total 224.69 m² (2,418.61 sq ft)

Below: The Fl 282 V11 (CJ+SE.) was the 11th prototype. The Fl 282 did not have a tail rotor to counteract the torque reaction associated with a single main rotor's rotation, but instead it had a pair of counter-rotating rotors whose blades intermeshed, each rotor's torque offsetting that of the other.

The Fl 282 V21 (also known as the Fl 282B) is illustrated as it appeared while under evaluation in 1943.

Above: The 24 Kolibri prototypes displayed a variety of different noses, incorporating enclosed, semi-enclosed and open cockpits. Fl 282 V7 was fitted with a glazed nose surrounding the cockpit.

Above: The helicopter pilot could match the speed and course of any submarine he spotted, and radio the position to a warship. He could also mark the submarine's position with a smoke bomb. The helicopter was too small to carry a useful weapons load, although tests were conducted with small anti-submarine bombs.

Above: In 1942, the Kriegsmarine started shipboard evaluation of the Kolibri. Special platforms were built on the after sections of either minelayers or cruisers. The Kolibris had to operate from these platforms, which were 5.0 m (16 ft 5 in) square, while the ship was under way.

Right: Not all Kolibris were two-seaters. The Fl 282 V6 (GF+YF) was a single-seat variant, here demonstrating its controllability.

Below: Compact but eminently serviceable, the Fl 282 was widely evaluated as this line-up of prototypes (with the Fl 282 V14 in the foreground) suggests. Ambitious production plans were thwarted by Allied bombing.

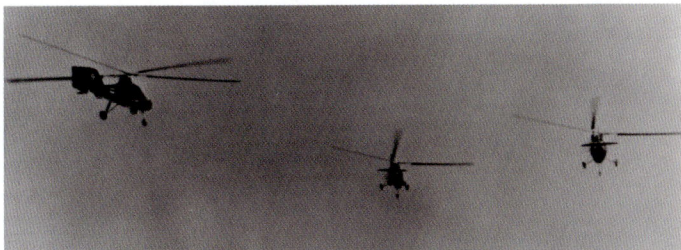

Above: Trials quickly proved that the Kolibri was an agile craft and very reliable, and also possessed good stability under bad weather conditions. Some 20 of the 24 prototypes were used by the Kriegsmarine in the Mediterranean and Aegean Seas, mainly for the protection of convoys.

Above: FI 282As were intensively tested by the Kriegsmarine. GF+YF, the V6 protype, is seen aboard the minelayer **Drache**, operating in the Aegean Sea during the winter of 1942-43.

Above: Captured by US Army troops at Ainring, Bavaria, FI 282B-1 V15 took part in a 'Victory Tour' of America soon after the war.

Above: Another US-captured FI 282 wears the registration FE-4613. An FI 282B-2, V23 previously wore the Luftwaffe registration CI+TW and was tested at Wright Field, Ohio, after the war.

Above: Luftwaffe materiel captured by the US originally received the registration prefix FE. This was subsequently changed to T2, although the original inventory numbers were retained.

Focke, Achgelis & Co, GmbH

In 1936 Professor Heinrich Karl Focke had left the Focke-Wulf company, of which he had been a co-founder in 1924, as a result of shareholder pressure. Though the declared reason for Focke's departure from the company was ostensibly that he was considered 'politically unreliable' by the Nazi regime now ruling Germany, it is probable that the change was forced through by the German government to ensure that the Focke-Wulf company's manufacturing capacity would be available for manufacture of the new Messerschmitt Bf 109 single-engined fighter on which the Luftwaffe had placed very high expectations. The company was then taken over by the AEG industrial group, but soon after this the Reichsluftfahrtministerium, which had been highly impressed by the potential hinted at by the Fw 61 helicopter, suggested that Focke establish a new company dedicated to the development of rotary-wing aircraft. This paved the way for Focke, Achgelis & Co GmbH, located at Delmenhorst, which almost immediately received a requirement for a helicopter able to lift a 700-kg (1,543-lb) payload.

It was on 27 April 1937 that Focke formally established his new company in partnership with the celebrated and gifted pilot Gerd Achgelis, and Focke-Achgelis embarked on development work in the following year, subsequently producing several designs including the closely related Fa 266 Hornisse civil and Fa 223 Drache military helicopters, the

Fa 225 development of the DFS 230 assault glider with a rotor replacing the standard wing, and the Fa 330 Bachstelze kite autogyro. All were created before the end of the war in 1945 and proved to be technically successful, but none of the company's designs entered either large-scale manufacture or extensive operational service.

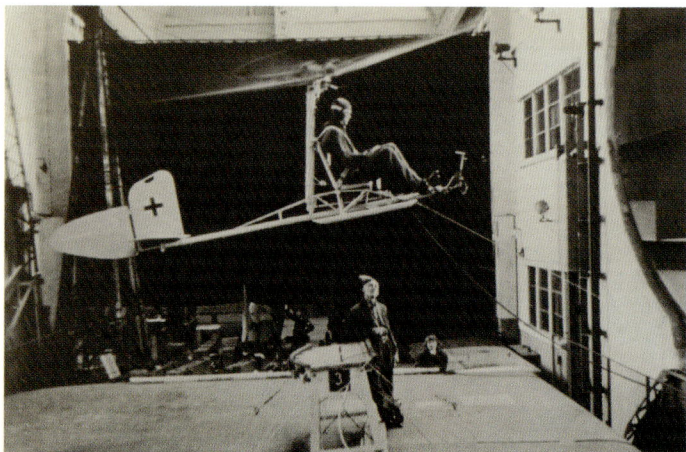

Developed as a kite autogyro towed as an 'aerial eye' by surface-running U-boats, the Focke-Achgelis Fa 330 was workable as an aircraft, but was of limited use in operational terms. Here an Fa 330 is seen in the wind tunnel at Chalais Meudon, France.

Focke-Achgelis Fa 223 Drache

Ungainly it most certainly was, but the Fa 223 Drache was in reality a practical helicopter. Had they been able to push forward the development and production programme, the Germans could have been able to field a new type of military aircraft offering a host of novel and wide-ranging applications.

At an early stage Professor Heinrich Focke appreciated that one of the most acute problems to be overcome in a helicopter was the torque reaction resulting from the delivery of power from a fuselage-mounted engine to the lifting rotor, which tended to turn the fuselage in the opposite direction to the rotor. Focke's solution to this problem was highly practical: a lifting element of two rotors that turned in opposite directions so that each rotor's torque reaction cancelled that of the other. The solution was practical but hardly elegant, for Focke did not opt for superimposed or even intermeshing rotors, but rather two large-diameter rotors installed side-by-side at the ends of long-span outriggers extending from the fuselage and giving the whole machine great overall span as well as a distinctly ungainly appearance.

The Fw 61 (later Fa 61) was Focke's first helicopter, and had a fuselage very similar to that of many current light-planes with the exception that the empennage was of the T-tail type with a strut-braced tailplane on top of the vertical surface and the fixed tailwheel undercarriage was augmneted by a small wheeled nose unit to prevent nosing over. The nose-mounted Siemens-Halske (later Bramo and finally BMW-Bramo) Sh.14A radial engine drove a small propeller used for engine cooling rather than propulsion. The major difference between the Fw 61 and any conventional aircraft was, of course, the lifting system based on two three-blade rotors. The rotors were driven via a gearbox, long extension shafts and angle-changing bevelled drives: the blades were attached to the hubs by fully articulated hinges, and employed cyclic pitch, differential pitch and differential collective pitch for control in the longitudinal, directional and lateral planes, respectively. The Fw 61 climbed or descended through an increase or decrease in rotor speed for greater or lesser lift.

The technical success of the Fw 61, which first flew in June

The inelegant layout of the Fa 223 (here the V14), with the combination of two rotors at the tips of long lateral outriggers producing a great overall width, is clearly evident in this view.

1936, prompted Deutsche Lufthansa to order a passenger-carrying development. This was the six-passenger **Fa 226 Hornisse** (hornet), which retained the Fa 61's layout. The **Fa 226 V1** (D-OCEB), one of the three prototypes ordered by Deutsche Lufthansa, completed its ground running and 100-hour tethered hovering programme in the summer of 1940, and made its first free flight in August of the same year. The Fa 266 V1 was powered by a BMW-Bramo 323 air-cooled nine-cylinder radial engine rated at 626 kW (840 hp) for take-off, and in its flight trials revealed good performance

One of the primary tasks envisaged for the planned Fa 223E production model was the resupply of mountain troops, who could not readily be reached by fixed-wing aircraft other than light types such as the Fieseler Fi 156, which had only a very small payload. The Fa 223E would also have been able to undertake the casualty evacuation role.

Focke-Achgelis Fa 223 Drache

The Drache's lifting system comprised a side-by-side pair of counter-rotating three-blade rotors, which were powered by a drive chain extending from the radial engine buried in the fuselage close to the centre of gravity position. The undercarriage was of the fixed tricycle type, and under the fuselage were the attachments for a drop tank or the cable carrying a slung load.

and generally satisfactory handling except at the lower end of the speed range, where there was slight instability; downwind turns at low speed also caused problems as the rotors lost lift rapidly in these conditions. In February 1941, the Fa 266 V1 was lost in an accident after an engine failure at an altitude too low for an auto-rotative landing.

Switch to a military emphasis

By this time World War II was already well under way, so work on the civil Fa 226 was abandoned in favour of the military **Fa 223 Drache** (kite), of which 39 had been ordered by the Reichsluftfahrtministerium for evaluation in diverse military roles. The variants planned at this time were the **Fa 223A** anti-submarine model with two 250-kg (551-lb) bombs or depth charges, **Fa 223B** reconnaissance model with a jettisonable fuel tank, **Fa 223C** search and rescue model fitted with a winch and cable, **Fa 223D** freight variant for resupplying mountain troops, and **Fa 223E** dual-control trainer.

The oval-section fuselage was of welded steel tube construction covered with fabric except in the area around the engine installation, which had a light alloy skinning. This fuselage was divided into four compartments accommodating, from front to rear: the cockpit; the hold that carried the self-sealing fuel tankage as well as the payload, and was accessed by a starboard-side door; the engine; and the empennage that was of the T-tail type with a moving rudder and a trimmable tailplane. Extending from the sides of the fuselage on the centre of gravity position were the two upward-angled outriggers

The Fa 223E V2 (D-OGAW) was the first Drache to feature the 'beetle-eye' nose that was subsequently standardised. In most other respects, this second prototype was similar to its predecessor, but the aerofoil-section fairings enclosing some of the bracing struts of the rotor pylons were noteworthy.

Focke-Achgelis Fa 223E cutaway key

1. MG 15 nose armament
2. Circular mounting frame
3. Cartridge collector chute
4. Tie-down eye
5. Towing lug
6. Pitot head
7. Optically-flat observer's ventral panel (starboard)
8. Rudder pedal/brake assembly
9. Observer's (hinged) seat
10. Angled forward frame
11. Double-drum magazine stowage
12. Hinged instrument panel (flying instruments)
13. Sliding window
14. Fixed forward glazing
15. Windscreen panels
16. Panel light
17. Fixed instrument panel (fuel/engine gauges)
18. Roof panels
19. Overhead console
20. Emergency exit panels (port/starboard)
21. Sliding side panel
22. Entry door (starboard)
23. Control column
24. Trim handwheel
25. Pilot's seat
26. Side console
27. Control linkage
28. Nosewheel mounting
29. Nosewheel leg
30. Axle fork
31. Nosewheel
32. Entry step (cockpit)
33. Forward fuselage frame
34. Side formers
35. Rotor control cables
36. Cable-laying drum assembly (provisional)
37. Cable feed
38. Entry step (load compartment emergency exit door)
39. Cable release/runner
40. Load compartment ventral hatch (secured)
41. Rescue cradle entry flap
42. Rescue cradle (stowed)
43. Cradle emergency hand-crank
44. Cradle upper hoop frame and attachment
45. Cables
46. Load compartment side windows
47. Switch panel

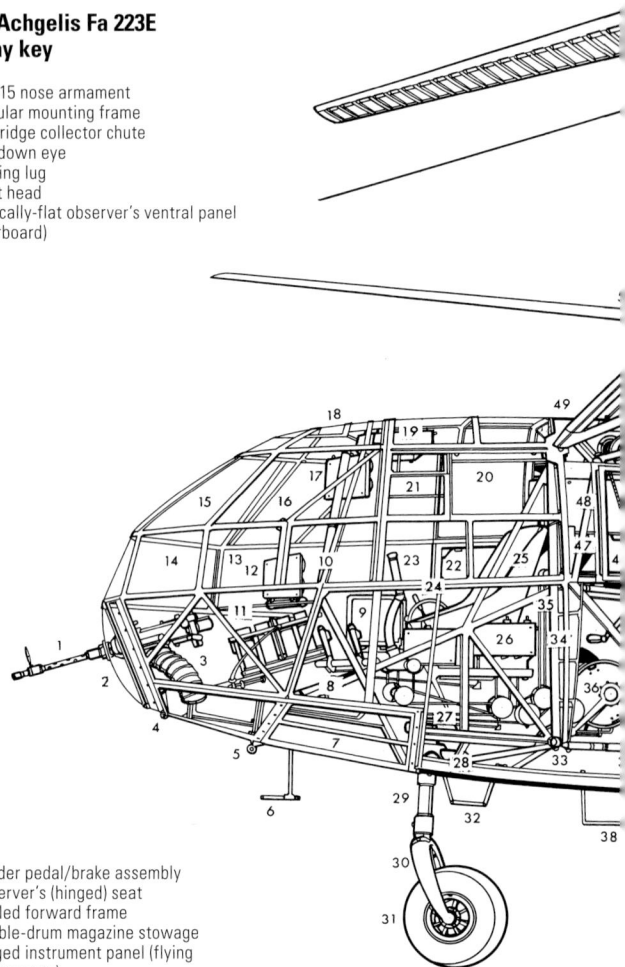

73 Starboard mainwheel
74 Port mainwheel tyre
75 Axle hub
76 Brake drum
77 Torque links
78 Port mainwheel oleo leg
79 Mainwheel leg/sponson attachment
80 Engine bay frame
81 Nine-cylinder BMW 323 radial engine
82 Universal joint
83 Transmission shaft main bevel gears
84 Undercarriage leg extension
85 Main sponson strut attachment
86 Outer strut
87 Transmission shaft whip damper
88 Transmission shaft ball bearing/universal joint
89 Dorsal exhaust stub
90 Cool air
91 Engine aft mounting ring (rubber-sprung)
92 Engine accessories
93 Mounting ring support strut
94 Engine bay aft frame

95 Fuselage break cold air outlet
96 Aft fuselage section forward wall
97 Antenna mast
98 Dinghy stowage
99 Dinghy release/CO_2 bottle
100 Handhold
101 Fuselage formers
102 Aft fuselage steel frame
103 Control cables
104 Lower longeron
105 Ventral skinning
106 Access/service panel
107 Trim adjustment chains
108 Tailfin/fuselage root fairing
109 Tailfin forward spar attachment
110 Tailskid upper mounting
111 Tailskid shock leg
112 Tailskid
113 Rudder lower balance
114 Rudder actuating cable
115 Trim control wheel
116 Rudder structure
117 Tail navigation light
118 Rudder centre hinge
119 Tailplane port support strut
120 Tailfin structure
121 Trim actuating rod

122 Tailfin leading-edge
123 Rudder upper hinge
124 Tailplane strut upper attachment
125 Tailplane pivot point
126 Upper-mounted tailplane/trim stabiliser
127 Cargo sling net
128 16/30-m (approx. 52/98-ft) cargo cable
129 Port rotor blades
130 Blade ribs
131 Aft outer strut
132 Diagonal brace
133 Inertia damper assembly
134 Collective/cyclic pitch control pulleys
135 Splined transmission outer shaft
136 Control rocker arm casing
137 Bevel gear
138 Blade root housings
139 Control cables
140 Drag hinges
141 Blade push rods
142 Rotor head axle casing

48 R/T installation (FuG 17)
49 Forward strut attachment (rotor setting control cables)
50 Rescue cradle electric winch motors
51 Cable rollers
52 Port sponson inner brace wire
53 Cross strut
54 Starboard sponson assembly
55 Starboard rotor blades
56 Starboard rotorhead
57 Fuel filler cap
58 Safety belt
59 Main fuel tank (490-litre/ 108-Imp gal capacity)
60 Handhold

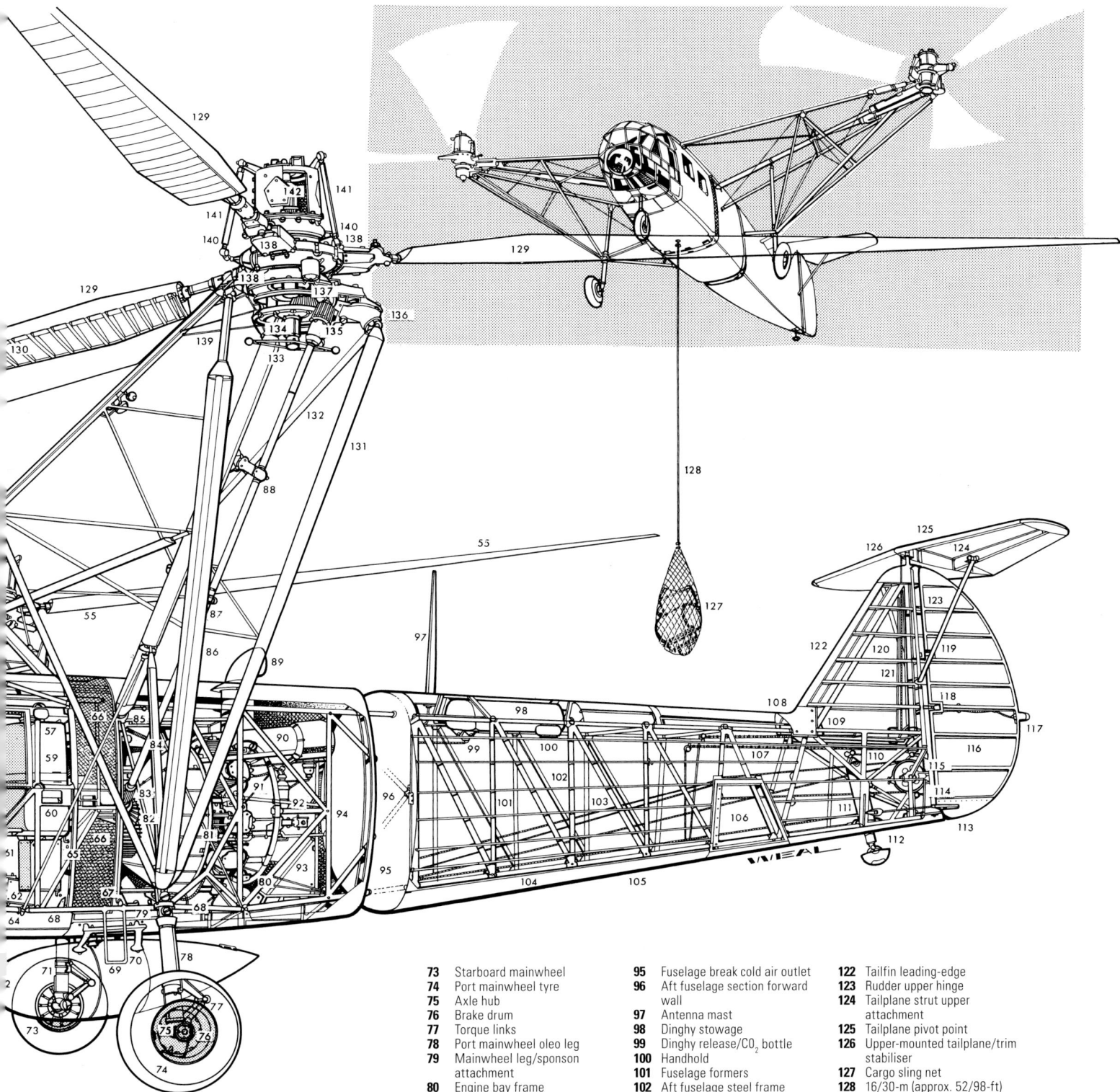

61 Oil tank (70-litre/15.4-Imp gal capacity)
62 Transformer
63 Load compartment lower frame
64 Strut/brace attachment
65 Load compartment aft bulkhead/firewall
66 Fuselage break cold air intake (mesh grille)
67 Frame lower attachment
68 Sponson/mainwheel brace struts
69 Sponson-mounted footrest
70 Auxiliary tank (ETC carrier) attachment
71 Starboard mainwheel leg
72 Ju 87-type auxiliary fuel tank (jettisonable)

Above: Though cumbersome, the Fa 223 was an effective helicopter, with a useful internal or external load-carrying ability. The type never reached service in the anti-submarine role, but was used in the transport and rescue roles. This is the V16, operating with the mountain warfare school at Mittenwald, near Innsbruck.

Above: D-OCEB was the Fa 266 V1 first prototype of the Hornisse original civil model, which made its first free flight in August 1940, after 100 hours of ground tests and tethered hovering.

that carried the two three-blade rotors and also provided the structural basis for the wide-track main units of the fixed tricycle landing gear. Constructed round a tubular steel spar with wooden ribs and a covering of plywood wrapped in fabric, each rotor blade was attached to its rotor hub by flap and drag hinges. Each rotor shaft was inclined inward by about 4.5 degrees and was also tilted slightly forward, and power was transmitted from the engine to the rotors via a friction clutch, gearbox, long transmission shafts and bevelled gears.

The second prototype, which was the first completed with the Fa 223 military designation, was the **Fa 223 V2** (D-OGAW) that first flew later in 1940 with a fully glazed cockpit and a machine-gun operated by the observer. It was soon destroyed in an Allied air raid, however. By the time the **Fa 223 V3** prototype appeared the Reichsluftfahrtministerium had abandoned the idea of different variants and settled on a multi-role Fa 223E, and the Fa 223 V3 reflected the fact, established the design features for all the models that followed, and incorporated dual controls and an electric winch. Only seven had been completed before the Delmenhorst factory, together with a number of incomplete helicopters, were destroyed by Allied bombing.

Delay follows delay

Operational trials began early in 1942, but by July of that year only two of the helicopters were available as a result of technical problems and constant production delays. Even so, the operational evaluation revealed the overall utility of the Fa 223, and the Reichsluftfahrtministerium ordered 100 examples of the **Fa 223E** production version, of which the first 30 were to be completed as **Fa 223E-0** pre-production and service test machines. Equipment varied according to role and included one 7.9-mm (0.31-in) MG 15 trainable machine-gun and two bombs or depth charges, a rescue winch and cable, a reconnaissance camera and a 300-litre (66-lmp gal) auxiliary fuel tank.

The Laupheim factory was destroyed by bombing in July 1944, and by this time only seven of the helicopters had flown. Another production facility was established at Berlin-Tempelhof, but only one more helicopter had been completed before the end of World War II in May 1945. It is thought that only 10 or possibly 11 of the helicopters actually flew during the war, three of them entering service with Lufttransportstaffel 40 in Austria. Of these, two were captured by the Allies, one making the first cross-Channel helicopter flight in September 1945. After the end of the war, two additional helicopters were assembled in Czechoslovakia from components for trials with the designation **VR-1**, and in France further development was undertaken by the Société Nationale de Constructions Aéronautiques du Sud-Est, which flew its sole **SE.3000.01** prototype in October 1948.

Focke-Achgelis Fa 223 Drache specification
Type: two-crew transport, rescue and reconnaissance helicopter
Powerplant: one BMW-Bramo 323Q-3 Fafnir (later BMW 301R) air-cooled nine-cylinder radial engine rated at 746 kW (1,000 hp) for take-off, 612 kW (820 hp) for 5 minutes, 515 kW (690 hp) for 30 minutes, and 462 kW (620 hp) for continuous running
Performance: maximum speed 175 km/h (109 mph) at sea level; cruising speed 120 km/h (75 mph) at optimum altitude; initial climb rate 336 m (1,100 ft per minute; service ceiling 4880 m (16,010 ft); range 700 km (435 miles) with auxiliary fuel
Weights: empty 3175 kg (7,000 lb); maximum take-off 4310 kg (9,502 lb)
Dimensions: rotor diameter, each 12.00 m (39 ft 4½ in); span over rotors 24.50 m (80 ft 4¾ in); length 12.25 m (40 ft 2¼ in); height 4.35 m (14 ft 3¼ in); total rotor disc area 226.19 m² (2,434.82 sq ft)
Payload: up to 1280 kg (2,820 lb) of freight

Among the many tasks in which the Fa 223 could have proved very useful was the rescue of downed aircrew or, as seen here, the recovery of major components of downed aircraft.

Focke-Achgelis Fa 225

Designed in an effort to provide the German airborne arm with an assault rotor glider offering a far greater capability than any standard winged assault glider to operate into small areas, the Fa 225 was a fascinating and largely successful technical exercise. The type did not enter production, however.

In the course of the first half of World War II, the assault glider was an instrument of major significance to the German airborne forces for the rapid and accurate landing of troops, and of the weapons and supplies on which they would have to rely before they were reached by conventional forces advancing on the ground. The Germans' initial capability led to some important tactical uses of *coup-de-main* undertakings to take and hold potential chokepoints, but use of assault gliders such as the DFS 230 was wholly dependent on the availability of a landing area of sufficient size on or adjacent to the target. In places where the landing area was restricted by natural or artificial obstacles, the glider's landing run could be shortened by braking rockets exhausting forward from the nose, although the landing approach remained unaltered unless another option, the brake chute, was used for a very steep approach.

The idea therefore arose of exploiting the almost vertical or very steep descent that could be provided by an auto-rotating rotary wing, and in 1942 Focke-Achgelis, a pioneer of rotary-wing flight, adapted a DFS 230B glider with the three-blade rotor of the Fa 223 helicopter on a pylon structure above the fuselage on the centre-of-gravity position. To cater for the increased landing load, fixed and braced tailwheel undercarriage replaced the DFS 230's skid. This **Fa 225** hybrid rotor glider was towed by a Junkers Ju 52/3m in tests, during 1943, and showed that it could land in 18 m (59 ft) or less.

The Fa 225 was not placed in production, however, prob-

Seen being towed behind a Ju 52/3m, the Fa 225 assault rotor-glider demonstrated its ability to land within a distance of only 14-18 m (46-59 ft). It was not, however, put into service.

ably as a result of changing operational requirements, and possibly because its advantages were offset by the fact that the towing speed was much lower than that of the standard DFS 230.

Focke-Achgelis Fa 225 specification
Type: assault rotor glider
Powerplant: none
Performance: maximum towed speed 190 km/h (118 mph)
Weights: maximum take-off 2000 kg (4,409 lb)
Dimensions: rotor diameter 12.00 m (39 ft 4 ½ in); disc area 113.10 sq m (1,217.41 sq ft)

The Fa 225 was based on the DFS 230B glider with its wing replaced by the three-blade rotor of the Fa 223 helicopter. The undercarriage was similar to that later used in DFS 230 Huckepack (pick-a-back) experiments. The guiding principle in the development of the rotor-glider was the desire to reduce the landing distance to a significant degree, allowing troops to be landed in confined spaces.

Focke-Achgelis Fa 330 Bachstelze

Designed as a gyro-kite to be towed as an aerial eye for surface-running, ocean-going U-boats, the Focke-Achgelis Fa 330 was workable as an aircraft, but the superiority enjoyed by Allied naval air power towards the end of the war meant that the concept was of limited use in operational terms.

Target location was always a difficult problem for a submarine operating on the surface, the range of vision from a U-boat's deck being about 8 km (5 miles). It was suggested in 1942 that an easily-assembled/disassembled small rotary-winged gyro-kite that could be launched, towed and retrieved by a submarine, could extend a submarine commander's range of vision by about five times. In 1942 Focke-Achgelis was requested to proceed with the design of such an aircraft, resulting in the **Focke-Achgelis Fa 330 Bachstelze** (Water Wagtail), which when assembled had a free-turning three-blade rotor pylon-mounted on a simple framework; this also carried an unprotected seat for the pilot/observer and a tail unit comprising a tailplane, fin and rudder at the end of a braced tubular boom.

Launch of the Bachstelze was accomplished when the submarine was running on the surface, the rotor which had been spun-up manually then autorotating in the wind, allowing the aircraft to be flown as a kite at the end of a cable, towed along by the U-boat. The pilot/observer had a telephone with which he could communicate with the submarine some 120 m (394 ft) below, and was normally winched down at the end of an observation sortie. However good the idea, U-boat commanders considered them an embarrassment, creating a new and difficult problem should an emergency dive be necessary and, as a result, they were used as little as possible, especially in the North and South Atlantic. Fa 330s were not built by Focke-Achgelis, but by Weser-Flugzeugbau that produced about 200 of these unusual aircraft. A considerable number survived the war.

Focke-Achgelis Fa 330 Bachstelze specification

Type: single-seat rotary-wing observation kite
Powerplant: none
Performance: operational airspeed between 27 and 40 km/h (17 and 25 mph)
Weight: without pilot 68 kg (150 lb)
Dimensions: rotor diameter 7.32 m (24 ft 0 in); length 4.42 m (14 ft 6 in); rotor disc area 42.00 m² (452.10 sq ft)

Above: Equipped with a basic two-wheeled undercarriage, some Fa 330s served with the flight school in Gelnhausen.

Below: U-boat commanders disliked the Fa 330, since it betrayed the location of the submarine, both visually and on radar. Only U-boats operating in the Indian Ocean deployed them with any regularity, since here the threat of Allied air power was reduced.

Below: A crew of four could assemble and disassemble the Fa 330 in three minutes. When not in use, the aircraft remained stowed in two watertight tubes in the U-boat's conning tower.

Below: The pilot/observer communicated his observations by a telephone line that ran along the tow cable. The Fa 330 was simple to fly, and an ingenious parachute system allowed the pilot to escape from the aircraft at relatively low altitudes.

Below: A rotary-wing kite, the Fa 330 allowed German submarines to locate targets in heavy seas. Towed aloft by Type IX U-boats to a maximum altitude of 220 m (722 ft), the pilot had a possible sighting distance of 53 km (15.5 miles), depending on weather.

Focke-Wulf Flugzeugbau GmbH

The Focke-Wulf company, created by an amalgamation with Albatros, was little known until the late 1930s. Then, with the benefit of Kurt Tank's design genius and a take-over by the huge AEG group, the company started to produce some classic aircraft types, including the classic Fw 190 fighter and Fw 200 transport that became one of Germany's most important maritime reconnaissance machines.

Until the late 1930s, the Focke-Wulf company was virtually unknown outside Germany, and its unpretentious products were frequently confused with those of the Dutch company bearing perhaps the best-known of names in aircraft manufacture between the wars, that of Anthony Fokker. This confusion was to be finally dispelled when such aircraft as the Fw 56 Stösser, Fw 58 Weihe and Fw 200 Condor, developed under the supervision of Dipl.-Ing. Kurt Waldemar Tank, had acquired a measure of international acclaim. Indeed, it was almost solely due to this singularly gifted, forceful personality, and the infusion of design and engineering talent that followed his appointment as technical director, that the small, obscure Focke-Wulf Flugzeugbau rose to prominence among international aircraft manufacturers and pre-eminence in the aircraft industry of Germany's Third Reich.

The Focke-Wulf Flugzeugbau AG was founded on 1 January 1924 by Heinrich Focke, George Wulf, and Dr. Werner Naumann, with a capital of RM 200,000. Focke and Wulf had collaborated in the construction of several aircraft before World War I, and had resumed this collaboration in 1921 to produce the A 7 Storch two-seat monoplane. The issue of a certificate of airworthiness for the aircraft by the Reichsverkehrsministerium in December 1922 prompted the creation of the Focke-Wulf Flugzeugbau, financial assistance being provided by Dr. Ludwig Roselius. Initially the new company shared a hangar with Deutsche Aero Lloyd at Bremen airport, its first product, the A 16 light transport monoplane, flying on 23 June 1924. Twenty-two A 16s were built over the next three years, the S 1 side-by-side two-seat training monoplane having made its debut in 1925, followed by a twin-engined training derivative of the A 16, the Gl 18,

Above: Heinrich Focke, born in Bremen on 8 October 1890, studied in Hanover, where he met Georg Wulf in 1911. Focke graduated in 1920 as Dipl.-Ing. (MS) with distinction, and continued in his aeronautical experimentation, which had begun with the construction of a glider in 1909.

Below: The Fw 190 V1 takes shape in Focke-Wulf's experimental shop at Bremen during early 1939. Note the ducted propeller intended to enhance the cooling of the radial engine.

Focke-Wulf Flugzeugbau GmbH

Above: Georg Wulf was the pilot for the first flight of the F 19 Ente, which took place on 2 September 1927. Wulf lost his life 27 days later when a control rod broke during a single-engined flight demonstration and the Ente spun into the ground.

These were the premises of the company which was founded as the Bremer Flugzeugbau AG but then almost immediately renamed as the Focke-Wulf Flugzeugbau AG.

in 1926. In that year the company acquired its own premises at Bremen, and in 1927 there appeared the A 17, the first of a series of single-engined transport monoplanes sharing the name Möwe (gull), together with the S 2 trainer.

The year 1927 was marred for the young Focke-Wulf company, however, by the death of Georg Wulf while testing the extremely novel F 19 Ente on 29 September, but despite this calamity and several financial crises, the concern survived, producing a variety of aircraft types during the late 1920s with varying degrees of success, including the A 20 Habicht light transport, the A 21 photographic monoplane, the W 4 float seaplane with cantilever biplane wings, and the S 24 Kiebitz sports and training biplane.

An amalgamated enterprise

Amalgamation with the Albatros-Flugzeugwerke GmbH of Berlin-Johannisthal in 1931 was a significant factor in the subsequent growth of the company, but even more significant was to prove the appointment on November 1st of that year of Dipl.-Ing. Kurt Tank as chief of design and flight testing. Despite comparative youth, the 33-year old Tank already possessed much experience. He had begun his career in 1924 with the Rohrbach Metallflugzeugbau, one of his first design tasks as a member of Ludwig Staiger's team being the hull of the Ro IIIa Rodra flying boat.

Tank had assumed steadily increasing responsibility in the design of the Ro V Rocco, the Ro VII Robbe II, and the Ro X Romar flying boats, and the Ro VIII Roland 10-passenger tri-motor aircraft, these large, all-metal monoplanes being assembled by Rohrbach's Danish subsidiary in Copenhagen. It was here in 1927 that the Ro IX Rofix single-seat all-metal fighter monoplane was flown, its design

having been primarily Tank's responsibility. With liquidation of the Rohrbach Metallflugzeugbau, Tank joined the Bayerische Flugzeugbau at Augsburg on 1 January 1930, being appointed chief of the project bureau, but after 18 months the BFW concern's financial difficulties resulted in Tank leaving Augsburg and joining the Focke-Wulf Flugzeugbau AG.

At this time, Focke-Wulf possessed 150 employees; had acquired a manufacturing licence for the Cierva Autogiro; was producing the A 32 Bussard and A 33 Sperber light transport aircraft in small numbers; and had the A 38 Möwe 10-passenger transport, A 43 Falke three-seat cabin monoplane, and A 44 (later Fw 44) Stieglitz two-seat training biplane under development. It was to be the last type that was to initiate a dramatic change in the fortunes of the Focke-Wulf organisation, being exported widely and eventually produced under licence in Argentina, Austria, Brazil, Bulgaria and Sweden. The Stieglitz's success was followed by the first Focke-Wulf aircraft designed under Tank's aegis, the Fw 56 Stösser, which was flown late in 1933, by which time Tank had been promoted to technical director. Eighteen months later the Fw 58 Weihe multi-purpose light twin followed, this eventually being licence-built by MIAG, Luther and the Gothaer Waggonfabrik, as well as in Brazil and Hungary.

In 1933, Focke-Wulf had begun production of 30 Cierva C 30 Autogiros, and from this point Professor Focke became increasingly engrossed in rotorcraft development. The company had by now been assigned contracts for the licensed manufacture of one of the first-line aircraft selected for the Luftwaffe, the He 45. A total of 219 of the Heinkel biplanes was eventually to be built by Focke-Wulf. This contract and the RLM decision to phase the company into the Bf 109 programme resulted in the need for immediate expansion. In turn, this led to the reorganisation as a limited company in June 1936, the new Focke-Wulf Flugzeugbau GmbH raising the necessary increase in capital that was to attain the figure of RM 2.5 million in 1938, with control of the company passing to the Allgemeine Elektrizitat Gesellschaft industrial conglomerate.

Focke-Wulf had now established a reputation with the Stieglitz, the Stösser and the Weihe, but less success had attended the company's developments in the field of combat aircraft, and thus licensed manufacture of Bf 109C fighters, begun in 1937, was followed by production of the Bf 110C, which continued until mid-1941. The latter was destined to be the last aircraft of 'foreign' design produced in quantity by the company.

Focke-Wulf had built two experimental Fw 61 helicopters in 1936, and had endeavoured to meet an RLM requirement for an air observation post and army co-operation aircraft with the Fw 186 autogyro, but Professor Focke had left the company in 1937 to devote all his time to rotorcraft development, establishing the Focke-Achgelis Flugzeugbau at Hoyenkamp, near Delmenhorst, and the Focke-Wulf company then confined itself to fixed-wing aircraft.

Something of Tank's extraordinary creative talent had meanwhile manifested itself in the Fw 187 fighter flown in 1937, and the Fw 189 tactical reconnaissance aircraft that had appeared in the following year, but it was the Fw 200 Condor commercial transport that did most to promote the name of the company abroad in the immediate pre-war years: it was the improvised military version of this aircraft that endowed the name 'Focke-Wulf' with a certain notoriety in so far as the British were concerned early in the conflict.

By the beginning of World War II, Focke-Wulf's facilities had expanded immensely. A branch factory had been established at Bremen-Hemlingen, and further factories were

"Fernbomber"

FOCKE-WULF FLUGZEUGBAU GMBH BREMEN

soon added to the Focke-Wulf complex at Bremen-Hastedt and Bremen-Neuenland, but no attempt had been made to conform with the RLM's dispersal directive of 1939. In the event, the Bremen factories were to be the first German aircraft plant complex to be dispersed, Tank being finally convinced of the need to move manufacturing facilities eastward, beyond the range of British-based bombers after RAF attacks had necessitated transfer of the Fw 200 assembly line to Dornier's Oberpfaffenhofen plant. He concluded that production operations should be divided among several plants in different cities, selecting Marienburg, Cottbus, Sorau and Posen-Kreising (Poland).

A classic fighter spurs further expansion

With the successful development of the Fw 190, and the constant increase in production orders for this fighter, further assembly and component plants were acquired at Tutow, Halberstadt, Gydnia-Rahmel, Neubrandenburg, Schwerin, Wismar, Einswarden, Warnemünde, Anklam, Erfurt-Nord, Lübeck and Hanover-Langenhagen, virtually all of which were engaged in component production or assembly for the Fw 190 and its derivatives, as were also AGO (otherwise Ago), Arado, Dornier, Fieseler and Heinkel facilities. Apart from 167 aircraft, all Fw 189 production was performed by the Focke-Wulf-controlled SNCA de Sud-Ouest at Bordeaux, and Aero at Prague, and by 1944, Focke-Wulf was one of the biggest employers of labour in the aircraft industry, having 11,920 direct and 17,040 indirect employees.

Tank himself assumed steadily increasing importance commensurate with that of the progeny of his drawing boards, becoming vice-president of the Akademie der Luftfahrtforschung in 1942, and receiving the title of professor from the Braunschweig technical school, but apart from developments of the Fw 190, none of Focke-Wulf's wartime designs was destined to see quantity production. The Tank-controlled design bureaux were prolific to the end, however, evolving numerous intriguing and novel projects.

Above: Originally conceived as an airliner, the Condor was adapted as a successful maritime reconnaissance bomber.

Above left: Fw 190 fighters proceed down a production line.

Right and below right: Designed by the inspirational Kurt Tank, the Fw 190 appeared in the skies over France during the summer of 1941. RAF intelligence simply could not credit the fact that this squat, angular fighter really had the measure of the sleek Spitfire Mk V. The 'Butcher Bird' came to dominate those skies for eight months, playing a particularly starring role combatting the disastrous Allied landing at Dieppe in August 1942. The Fw 190 remained one of the finest fighters operational over Europe until the end of the conflict in Europe.

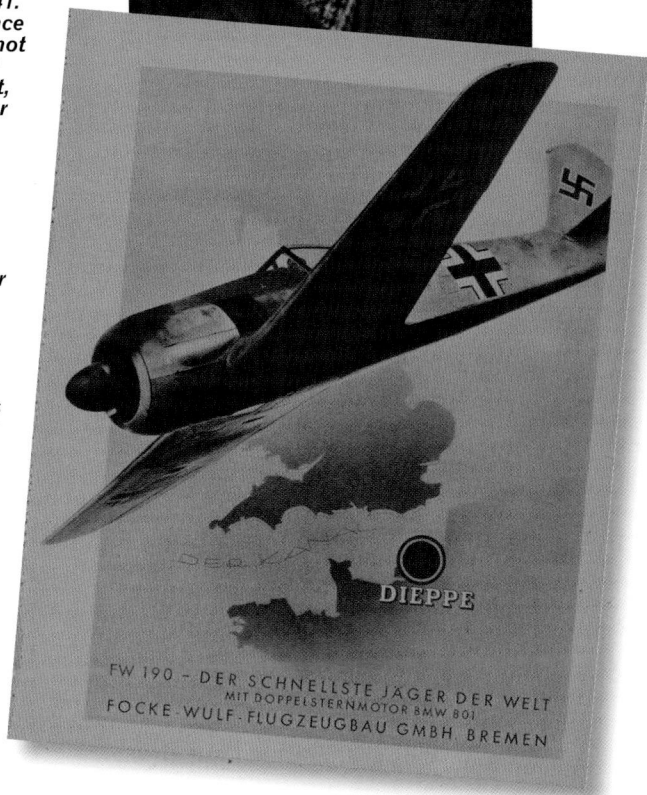

DIEPPE

FW 190 - DER SCHNELLSTE JÄGER DER WELT
MIT DOPPELSTERNMOTOR BMW 801
FOCKE-WULF-FLUGZEUGBAU GMBH BREMEN

Focke-Wulf F 19 Ente

A high-wing monoplane with an unusual canard layout and tricycle undercarriage, the Focke-Wulf F 19 Ente was designed as a light commercial transport, accommodating two passengers within an enclosed cabin. Only two prototypes were completed, and the aircraft was the first canard design to be certified for carriage of passengers.

Heinrich Focke's proposal for a radical twin-engine canard transport was submitted to the Deutsche Versuchsanstalt für Luftfahrt (DVL) in the mid-1920s and wind tunnel tests were conducted at Göttingen prior to work beginning on the construction of a prototype.

The **F 19 Ente** (Duck) was a shoulder-wing monoplane with a fabric-covered welded steel-

Above: Photographed in October 1930, the second Focke-Wulf Ente was at the time engaged on making a series of flights over Berlin, operating from the city's Tempelhof Airport.

tube fuselage that incorporated a small two-seat cabin in addition to the open cockpit for the two pilots. Conventional vertical tail surfaces were fitted but the horizontal surfaces took the form of a 5.20-m (17-ft ¾-in) span foreplane strut-mounted forward of the cockpit. Power was supplied by two 56-kW (75-hp) Siemens Sh.11 radials. Georg Wulf was the pilot for the maiden flight which took place on 2 September 1927, but he lost his life just 27 days later when a control rod broke during a single-engine flight demonstration and the Ente spun into the ground. A second aircraft, with Sh.14 engines, reduced-span wings and auxiliary winglets outboard of the engines, was flown by Cornelius Edzard late in 1930.

The second F 19 Ente introduced auxiliary winglets located under the wing, outboard of the Siemens Sh 14 engines. In 1931, this aircraft undertook a publicity tour of Western Europe.

Focke-Wulf F 19 Ente specification
Type: light transport
Powerplant: two 82-kW (110-hp) Siemens Sh.14 radial piston engines
Performance: maximum speed 142 km/h (88 mph); service ceiling 3000 m (9,842 ft)
Weights: empty 1175 kg (2,590 lb); maximum take-off 1650 kg (3,638 lb)
Dimensions: wingspan 10.00 m (32 ft 9 in); length 10.53 m (34 ft 6½ in); height 4.15 m (13 ft 7¼ in); wing area 29.50 m² (317.55 sq ft)

First flown in late 1930, the second F 19 was eventually put on display as part of the Deutsche Luftfahrtsammlung in Berlin-Moabit, where it was destroyed during an Allied air raid in 1944.

Below: Later in its career, the second F 19 acquired civil certification and ended its days as a test aircraft at the DVL's Berlin-Adlershof base. It flew on into 1939, carrying the registration D-1960.

Focke-Wulf Fw 44 Stieglitz

Kurt Tank's genius as a test pilot as well as a designer was first revealed in the Fw 44, a small training aircraft that, in its initial form, had revealed a number of major shortcomings. Tank then transformed this biplane into one of the most important and prolific primary trainers used by the Luftwaffe before and during World War II.

Second only to the Fw 190 as the most prolific Focke-Wulf design, the **A 44** (later designated **Fw 44**) **Stieglitz** (goldfinch) trainer appeared in 1932, the prototype making its first flight in the late summer of that year in the hands of Gerd Achgelis. Powered by a Siemens Sh.14a radial, the aircraft was a single-bay biplane with a fabric-covered welded steel-tube fuselage and wooden wings with fabric and plywood covering.

In its original form it had a number of unacceptable flight characteristics, but they were eradicated following an extensive test programme undertaken by Kurt Tank, who had joined the company in November 1931 from BFW and headed the design and flight test departments of Focke-Wulf when Heinrich Focke became pre-occupied with his rotary-wing activities. The Stieglitz became an outstanding aerobatic mount, particularly in the hands of skilled pilots such as Achgelis, Emil Kropf and Ernst Udet. The type won significant export orders from Bolivia, Chile, China, Czechoslovakia, Finland, Romania, Switzerland and Turkey; licence production was undertaken in Argentina, Austria, Brazil, Bulgaria and Sweden. Export aircraft carried the designation **Fw 44J**.

The Stieglitz was also built in substantial numbers for the Luftwaffe, serving as a trainer until the end of World War II, and

Kurt Tank lay behind the transformation of the Fw 44 into one of the world's best aerobatic aircraft of the pre-war era. The type has become sought-after in recent years for restorers and owners of vintage aircraft.

The Fw 44C was widely used for civil and military training in Germany and elsewhere, and had its reputation much enhanced by the aerobatic displays flown in the type by Germany's leading aerobatic pilots.

was also used by the pre-war Deutsche Verkehrsfliegerschule and the Deutsche Luftsportverband.

Focke-Wulf Fw 44C specification
Type: two-seat trainer
Powerplant: one 112-kW (150-hp) Siemens Sh.14a 7-cylinder radial piston engine
Performance: maximum speed 184 km/h (115 mph); cruising speed 172 km/h (107 mph); service ceiling 3900 m (12,795 ft); range 675 km (419 miles)
Weights: empty 525 kg (1,157 lb); maximum take-off 900 kg (1,985 lb)
Dimensions: wingspan 9.00 m (29 ft 6½ in); length 7.30 m (23 ft 11½ in); height 2.70 m (8 ft 10¼ in); wing area 20.00 m² (215.29 sq ft)

Focke-Wulf Fw 44 Stieglitz

The first production variant of the Stieglitz was the Fw 44B, of which only small numbers were built with the 89.5-kW (120-hp) Argus As 8 air-cooled four-cylinder inline engine.

Above: The Fw 44C's braced tail unit included a plain rudder and horn-balanced elevators. The fixed tailskid undercarriage was notably sturdy.

Located ahead of the engine firewall, the Fw 44C's two fuel tanks carried a total of 135 litres (29.7 Imp gal), the contents of the smaller, lower tank being used for inverted flying.

The Fw 44B had a trim appearance with its slender nose and staggered single-bay wing cellule, including a flat lower wing and dihedralled upper wing.

Left: This line-up of Fw 44C trainers is seen on the airfield of a German flying school during the 1930s. The type was used by both civil and military flying trainer establishments.

Above: The Fw 44's wing cellule had the normal arrangement of flying and landing wires, but needed no incidence-bracing wires as it had N-type interplane struts. The upper- and lower-wing ailerons were wire-connected.

Left: The Fw 44C was characterised by a radial engine, this 112-kW (150-hp) Siemens Sh.14A air-cooled seven-cylinder unit being installed at the front of the fuselage without any cowling.

Above: Fw 44C trainers of a Luftwaffe flying school are seen during formation training. Pupils progressed into this type after proving their potential in lower-powered machines, and then progressed to advanced flying and armament trainers.

Primary flying has always been attended by a high rate of mishaps, but the sturdy Fw 44C provided good protection for the pupil and instructor, and much of the airframe was often salvageable.

Focke-Wulf Fw 56 Stösser

The parasol-winged Fw 56 was the first Focke-Wulf design undertaken by Dipl.-Ing. Kurt Tank, and resulted from a requirement for a 'Home Defence Fighter' and advanced trainer with the As 10 engine. First flown in 1933, the Fw 56 remained in production until 1940 and served throughout the war with Luftwaffe training establishments.

Evolved to meet the demands of a requirement for a Heimatschutzjäger (home defence fighter), and the first Focke-Wulf design supervised by the forceful and talented Dipl.-Ing. Kurt Tank after his appointment in 1932 as the company's technical director, the **Fw 56 Stösser** was, years later, to be fallaciously credited with having influenced German development of the dive-bomber. While no claim to such distinction was founded on fact, the Stösser was, nevertheless, noteworthy enough. It offered exceptional structural integrity, was destined to play a vital role in the evolution of the Jagdflieger, and was to provide the backbone of the Jagdfliegerschulen throughout World War II.

In addition to the Focke-Wulf Flugzeugbau, the C-Amt of Göring's Luftfahrtkommissariat had invited the Arado, Heinkel and Henschel organisations to participate in the Heimatschutzjäger contest, competitive trials between contenders for production orders being scheduled for the spring and summer of 1935. The C-Amt envisaged the use of the chosen aircraft by both auxiliary target-defence formations and advanced fighter training schools, calling for a small and relatively light aircraft designed around the Argus As 10 air-cooled inverted V-8 engine, and mounting a single 7.9-mm (0.31-in) MG 17 machine-gun synchronised to fire through the propeller disc.

Revised specification

In the autumn of 1934, a year after the preparation of the original Heimatschutzjäger requirement, the specification was changed to provide for the installation of two MG 17s each with 250 rounds, plus an internal bay housing a magazine for three vertically-hung 10-kg (22-lb) bombs. The C-Amt did not specify the configuration to be adopted by the competing design teams, but evinced a marked preference for a monoplane, and the Focke-Wulf team, led by Oberingenieur R. Blaser and supervised by Tank, elected to adopt the parasol wing layout, of which experience been inherited through

In summer 1935 the Fw 56 was selected over the Ar 76 and He 74. Three Fw 56A-0 pre-production machines and about 900-1,000 Fw 56A-1 production aircraft followed up to 1940.

the company's purchase of the Albatros-Flugzeugwerke in September 1931.

Like its fellow competitors, the Focke-Wulf Flugzeugbau received a contract for three prototypes of its design for a combined light emergency fighter and Übungsflugzeug, (practice aircraft), this being allocated the official designation Fw 56. Considerable attention was paid to aerodynamic cleanliness in order to obtain the highest performance possible with the low-powered engine stipulated by the official specification, and the structure was entirely conventional. The fuselage was a rectangular-section welded steel-tube framework faired to an oval section, and covered forward with detachable light alloy panels and aft with fabric. The wing,

The decision by the Focke-Wulf design team to adopt a parasol wing configuration for the company's contribution to the Heimatschutzjäger requirement was influenced by Focke-Wulf's acquisition of the Albatros-Flugzeugwerke in 1931. Albatros ancestry was also revealed in the tailplane, which was mounted on the fin, with the elevators located forward of the rudder.

Focke-Wulf Fw 56 Stösser

Initially flown in November 1933, the Fw 56a first prototype received a commercial registration after they were introduced in Germany in 1934. Subsequently designated Fw 56 V1, the first prototype was registered D-ISOT, although the registration letters were initially applied incorrectly, as seen here, to read D-JSOT.

which was built in two sections joined on the centreline, featured three degrees of sweepback on the leading edge, stressed plywood skinning back to the rear spar, the remainder being fabric covered, and mass-balanced fabric-covered ailerons with steel-tube frames and light alloy ribs. The wing was carried above the fuselage by splayed N-struts connecting with the upper fuselage longerons, and sloping V-struts attached to the lower longerons. Alternative wing structures were designed and constructed, that of the **Fw 56a** first prototype comprising two spruce and plywood spars with spruce ribs, while that of the **Fw 56b** second prototype was of duralumin and steel tube.

The tail assembly revealed the Albatros ancestry of the aircraft, the plywood-covered wooden tailplane being superimposed on an abbreviated steel-tube fin built integrally with the fuselage, the elevators being forward of the rudder, and all movable surfaces being of wooden construction with fabric covering. The main undercarriage members comprised single cantilever oleo shock-absorber legs enclosed by slim metal fairings, the wheels and low-pressure tyres being carried by forks and covered by close-fitting streamlined spats.

The Fw 56a was completed and flown in November 1933 with an Argus As 10C Series I engine offering 179 kW (240 hp) for take-off. Initial flight trials proved generally satis-

factory, although the undercarriage was found to possess poor shock-absorption properties, and the raised fairing aft of the cockpit was removed at an early test stage as this was found to impede view aft. Completed shortly after the Fw 56a, the Fw 56b featured oleo legs of increased elasticity, and substantially enlarged main undercarriage fairings. This machine embodied the alternative metal wing structure, and more minor changes included the elimination of the curvature in the upper decking contour of the aft fuselage, and the redesign of the fillets enclosing the fuselage attachment points of the main V-struts.

Undercarriage modifications

Early in 1934, numerals had given place to letters for the registration of German commercial aircraft, and the Fw 56a, which was to be retroactively designated **Fw 56 V1**, was registered D-ISOT (although initially the registration letters D-JSOT were incorrectly applied to the aircraft), the Fw 56b (**Fw 56 V2**) becoming D-IIKA. In the meantime it had been discovered that the undercarriage of the Fw 56 infringed existing Messier patents, and as the initial flight trials had revealed the generally unsatisfactory nature of the existing undercarriage, a new unit had been designed, this being applied to the **Fw 56 V3** (D-ILAR) that was ready to join the flight

Above: The second prototype Stösser (D-IIKA), seen in its original form, was eventually used for a series of dive-bombing trials, one modification being the introduction of a vane-operated controllable-pitch propeller.

Above: Attached to the fusealge by a combination of N-struts and V-struts, the Fw 56's wing was built in two sections attached at the centreline, the construction being based upon a combination of stressed plywood skinning and fabric-covered surfaces.

The Fw 56 V3 entered flight testing in February 1934 and featured new undercarriage (the original infringed an existing patent), and a wooden wing similar to that of the first prototype.

Stösser D-IAQA is seen in flight in May 1936. Noteworthy is the main undercarriage, which combined legs enclosed by metal fairings, with large, unspatted high-pressure tyres.

The Fw 56 V4, which was the first of the pre-production Fw 56A-0 aircraft, incorporated a number of changes compared to the earlier machines. They included a revised exhaust arrangement to prevent noxious gases from entering the cockpit

test programme in February 1934. The new undercarriage, also of divided cantilever type, possessed legs each consisting of a steel tube anchored to upper and lower fuselage longerons, with a short, backwardly-hinged radius rod carrying the wheel axle and sprung by an oleo-spring unit attached at mid-point on the main leg. The legs were enclosed by metal fairings, but the larger wheels and high-pressure tyres adopted for the new undercarriage were left unspatted.

The Fw 56 V3 had a wooden wing similar to that of the first prototype, and was considered by Dipl.-Ing. Tank as the production prototype, a preliminary evaluation by the C-Amt of the competing Heimatschutzjäger designs having already favoured the Focke-Wulf and Arado contenders. Work was begun on a pre-production batch of three **Fw 56A-0** aircraft and, in conformity with the existing Focke-Wulf practice of naming the company's progeny after birds, the appellation Stösser (sparrowhawk) was allocated to the type.

The pre-production examples of the Stösser were also given Versuchs numbers, the first pre-production aircraft, the **Fw 56A-01**, thus also being the **Fw 56 V4** (D-ITAU). The Fw 56 V4 introduced some revision of the engine cowling panels, extended port exhaust stubs to eliminate a tendency

of the exhaust gases to blow into the cockpit under certain flight conditions, and a small dive brake immediately aft of the wing leading edge, over the fuselage centreline. The first prototype had crashed at Johannisthal during diving trials, Focke-Wulf test pilot Siewelcke losing his life, and as a minor structural failure in the wing was suspected as having caused the accident, the torsional strength of the wing had been increased by the introduction of profiled cables between the N-struts forward of the cockpit and the auxiliary struts between the main V-struts and the wing spars. This modification had been made on the Fw 56 V3, and accompanied by the dive brake introduced by the Fw 56 V4, the Stösser was found to possess exceptional diving capabilities, exceeding 485 km/h (301 mph) during trials, and easily pulling out of a terminal velocity dive begun at 1980 m (6,495 ft).

Full armament

The Fw 56 V4 was the first Stösser to carry full armament, two 7.9-mm MG 17 machine-guns being mounted in the upper decking of the forward fuselage and firing through troughs, and a magazine for three vertically-hung 10-kg bombs being fitted immediately behind the first fuselage frame, between the undercarriage legs. The second pre-production aircraft, the **Fw 56 V5** alias **Fw 56A-02** (D-IGEU), carried similar armament, but the third (D-IXYO) had the armament specified for the Übungsflugzeug, this consisting of only the starboard MG 17. Flight testing of the Stösser was undertaken at Johannisthal, Adlershof and Rechlin throughout 1934, and trials included the fitting of three prototype and pre-production examples with additional armament. Each Stösser was equipped with a pair of Bergmann sub-machine guns that were attached by brackets to V-struts and fired outside the propeller disc. However, these tests did not prove particularly successful, and the additional weapons were soon removed.

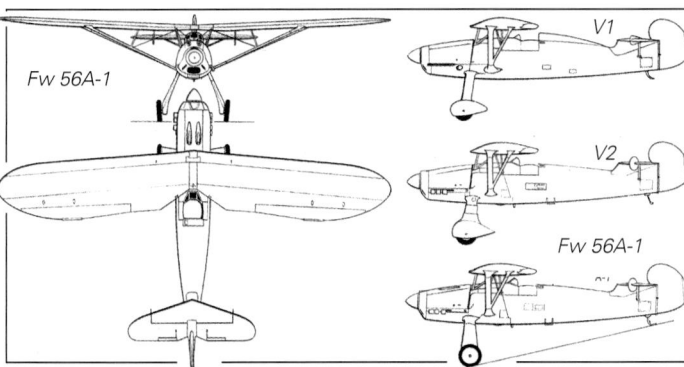

Above, left to right: The Stösser provided the highlight of many flying displays of the late 1930s on each side of the Atlantic. A very clean and outstandingly agile monoplane, the Fw 56 sported Focke-Wulf's stylised bird emblem, signifying a concern then enjoying a rapidly growing international reputation. D-IXYO (far left) was the Fw 56A-03 third pre-production Stösser.

Early Fw 56 Stössers await delivery to the Luftwaffe. For most of the war, the aircraft was used by schools for both fighter and dive-bomber pilots.

The final competitive evaluation trials were held in the summer of 1935, and although the Stösser was no novice's aircraft, and its aerobatic capabilities were marginally inferior to those of both the Arado Ar 76 and Heinkel He 74, it was adjudged the winning contender for production orders on the score of its structural strength reserves and the fact that its characteristics were most closely akin to those of the new fighter monoplanes under development for the Luftwaffe. Focke-Wulf was therefore ordered to proceed immediately with the series production of the Stösser as the **Fw 56A-1**.

The Fw 56A-1 differed in no major respect from the pre-production Stösser, retained the wooden wing featured by all earlier examples other than the second prototype, and was powered by the Argus As 10C offering 179 kW (240 hp) at 2,000 r.p.m. and 149 kW (200 hp) at 1,800 r.p.m., and driving a two-bladed fixed-pitch wooden Heine airscrew. All fuel was housed by a 100-litre (22-Imp gal) tank in the lower fuselage, and stressed to a load factor of 14, the Stösser had a disposable load of almost half its empty weight. It was by no means a docile aircraft, as many a fledgling fighter pilot was to learn to his cost, but once mastered it was a delightful machine from every aspect. In addition to the Jagdfliegerschulen of the

Luftwaffe, the Fw 56A-1 was also ordered for use by the para-military NSFK (Nationalsozialistischen Fliegerkorps, or National Socialist Flying Corps), these being delivered without armament but retaining provision for two guns.

Dive-bomber claims

The second prototype Stösser (D-IIKA) was retained by Focke-Wulf as a development machine, and it was the flight testing of this machine by Oberst Ernst Udet that was subsequently to result in entirely spurious claims that the Stösser had played a major role in German development of the dive-bomber by influencing the Luftwaffenführungsstab in favour of this radical weapon. Early in 1936, before service deliveries to the Luftwaffe of the Fw 56A-1 began, Udet, newly appointed as Inspector of Fighter and Dive-Bomber Pilots, visited Johannisthal where he flew a Stösser. Impressed by the diving characteristics of the aircraft and envisaging its possible suitability as a dive-bomber trainer, he requested that modifications be made to suit the Stösser for dive-bombing trials. Accordingly, the Fw 56 V2 was equipped with a vane-operated controllable-pitch propeller and improvised bomb racks beneath the wings, immediately outboard of the V-struts. Each rack carried three 1-kg (2.2-lb) smoke bombs, and dive-bombing trials were carried out by Flugkapitän Wolfgang Stein, who succeeded in placing an average of

Above: A pilot boards the Fw 56 V2 via the starboard-side step and the small hinged panel that was then raised and latched to constitute the starboard side of the cockpit.

Below: Fw 56A-1 D-IKNI was the mount of the aerobatic pilot Gerd Achgelis. The aircraft was fitted with an As 10E engine rated at 201 kW (270 hp) and driving a variable-pitch propeller.

Above: The Fw 56's parasol wing was supported over the fuselage by two sets of outward-canted N-struts, and braced on each side by a sturdy V-strut.

Above: The Fw 56 was notable not only for its agility, but also for its great structural strength. The main undercarriage units proved themselves well able to cope with hard landings.

40 per cent of the bombs within the target area. By this time, the dive-bombers competing in the second or definitive phase of the official Sturzbomber-Programm were already under test, and thus their development had been influenced in no way by dive-bombing trials conducted with the Stösser. Udet did perform further dive-bombing tests with the Stösser at Rechlin after replacing Oberst von Richthofen as chief of the Development Section of the RLM's Technisches Amt in June 1936, but the Fw 56A-1 subsequently served primarily as a fighter trainer.

Stösser demonstrations abroad

The internationally known German aerobatic pilot Gerd Achgelis became the leading exponent of the Stösser, and in 1938 his Fw 56A-1 (D-IKNI) was fitted with an As 10E engine which, with r.p.m. boosted to 2,100, offered 201 kW (270 hp), and drove an Argus variable-pitch propeller. Under the sponsorship of the Gilmore Oil Company, the modified Stösser was taken to the USA, where it was widely demonstrated by Achgelis. After its return to Germany, D-IKNI was flown until 1943 when it was crated and stored at Graudenz (now Grudziadz), Poland, but its subsequent fate is unknown. In 1937, the Stösser was released for export, the first foreign recipient being Austria's Luftstreitkräfte that purchased 12 Fw 56A-1s, although their service in Austrian colours was destined to be brief as, within a few months of their delivery, the Anschluss on 13 March 1938 resulted in the absorption of

the Luftstreitkräfte by the Luftwaffe. Hungary's air arm, the Magyar Királyi Légierö, also purchased the Stösser, a total of 18 being delivered during 1937-38.

The Stösser remained in production until as late as 1940, and although no record of the total quantity of aircraft of this type manufactured is known to have survived, some 900-1,000 were allegedly delivered. The Stösser served with the Jagdfliegerschulen throughout World War II, and participated in a number of experimental programmes. The aircraft was operated by Sonderkommando 9 at Königsberg as a tug for the Horten IV glider, and it was used by the DFS (Deutsche Forschungsanstalt für Segelflug) as the upper component of a Huckepack (pick-a-back) combination with a DFS 230 transport glider.

Focke-Wulf Fw 56A-1 Stösser specification
Type: single-seat fighter or advanced trainer
Powerplant: one Argus As 10C Series III air-cooled inverted V-8 engine rated at 179 kW (240 hp) for take-off
Performance: maximum speed 267 km/h (166 mph) at sea level, 257 km/h (160 mph) at 2000 m (6,560 ft), 233 km/h (145 mph) at 5000 m (16,405 ft); cruising speed (85% power) 245 km/h (152 mph) at sea level; initial climb rate 500 m (1,650 ft) per minute; climb to 1000 m (3,280 ft) in 2 minutes 24 seconds, to 2000 m (6,560 ft) in 5 minutes, to 3000 m (9,845 ft) 8 minutes 18 seconds; service ceiling 6200 m (20,340 ft); normal range 370 km (230 miles) at 245 km/h (152 mph)
Weights: empty 670 kg (1,477 lb); loaded 985 kg (2,171 lb)
Dimensions: wingspan 10.50 m (34 ft 5 ½ in); length 7.70 m (25 ft 3 in); height 3.55 m (11 ft 7¾ in); wing area 14.00 m² (150.70 sq ft)
Armament: one or two 7.9-mm (0.31-in) MG 17 machine-guns with 250 r.p.g., and provision for three 10-kg (22-lb) bombs

The Fw 56's tailplane was carried on a long-chord pylon that also served as a fixed fin, and was braced on each side by a single strut. This tailplane carried horn-balanced elevators each with an inset trim tab.

Below: Located largely to the rear of the elevators, the Fw 56's rudder was horn-balanced and fitted with a single trim tab. The rear element of the fixed undercarriage was a simple sprung skid. Like most of the Luftwaffe's smaller aircraft, the Fw 56 was at home on skis so that training could continue through the winter months.

Focke-Wulf Fw 57

In the first half of the 1930s Germany was one of several European nations that came to believe in the utility of the twin-engined multi-role heavy fighter. Among the several designs created and developed to prototype form was the Fw 57, which offered poor performance and handling.

By the time the embryo Führungsstab, the clandestine planning department of the RWM's Fliegerstab, had finalised its preparations for the initial equipment of the Luftwaffe that was to be revealed to the world less than two years later as a *fait accompli*, a wind of change was already rippling the surfaces of many fondly-cherished theories on aerial strategy; a stiff breeze generated by aerodynamic advances that, in the early 1930s, were following one on another. The aircraft ordered into production as first-generation equipment for Germany's new air arm were nothing if not conventional. They offered no design innovations nor advanced performance characteristics, but this was no reflection of any lack of foresight or awareness of the new structural techniques and changed air warfare concepts that were evolving abroad. It was tacit acknowledgment of the limitations in both experience and production capacity of Germany's aircraft industry at that time; the desire to provide as rapidly as possible the ring on which both the aircraft manufacturers and the fledgeling Luftwaffe were to cut their teeth.

In the summer of 1933, planning began, therefore, for the second phase of the future Luftwaffe's re-equipment; a phase involving the introduction of aircraft embodying the very latest design and constructional developments, and for which new combat tactics would be created. Studies were initiated with the objectives of forecasting future trends in aerial strategy and the long-term combat aircraft requirements of the Luftwaffe. Some dissension was inevitable as the Fliegerstab possessed its share of conventionalists to be convinced by the visionaries that tactics employed in any future aerial conflict would differ in many respects from those evolved during World War I, but one of the earliest results of its deliberations, which had been continued with the establishment of the Technical Department, or C-Amt, of Göring's newly-created Luftfahrtkommissariat, was the Kampfzerstörer concept.

The primary task foreseen for the Kampfzerstörer was that of clearing a path for bomber formations through the defensive fighter screens by which they were likely to be opposed, individual Kampfzerstörer groups approaching the target area in relays ahead of the bombers, their mission being to wear down the enemy defence. This scheme was opposed by the Generalstab, which, likening it to the medieval "verlorenen Haufen" or "lost crowd" tactic, considered it potentially ineffective and prohibitively costly. Other roles

The Fw 57 V1 began its flight test programme in the late spring of 1936. The dorsal turret was a mock-up of the electrically operated Mauser turret proposed for eventual installation.

foreseen for the Kampfzerstörer were bomber interception, the close escort of bomber formations, light bombing, reconnaissance and ground attack. Some factions in the C-Amt viewed the concept with disfavour for entirely different reasons to those of the Generalstab, believing that an aircraft of the size dictated by the multiplicity of roles that it was to fulfil, and labouring under the weight of the considerable armament proposed, must perforce be too slow and unwieldy to perform any mission effectively. They were overruled by Göring, however, who already foresaw the Kampfzerstörer as the spearhead of his Luftwaffe, issuing a directive that development should proceed with all possible speed.

Specification for a Kampfzerstörer

The Kampfzerstörer concept crystallised in the shape of a twin-engined all-metal three-seat monoplane with a heavy armament of flexibly-mounted cannon. The specification, which was finalised in the late autumn of 1934, and was issued to AGO, the Bayerische Flugzeugwerke, Dornier, Focke-Wulf, Heinkel, Henschel and the Gothaer Waggonfabrik, allowed project teams participating in the contest considerable latitude in their individual approaches to fulfilling the requirement, but specified the use of Daimler-Benz DB 600 engines, or, in the event of them being unavailable, Jumo 210s, and indicated that turret-mounted cannon armament was desirable. The desired performance characteristics, overall size and weights were stated in the broadest terms, and, thus, the importance attached to each of the conflicting capabilities demanded of a machine as versatile as that envisaged differed widely among the contestants.

AGO's submission, the Ao 225, placed accent on firepower, proposing the then unprecedentedly heavy armament of four 20-mm cannon; the Gothaer Waggonfabrik proffered the Projekt 3, a twin-boom study not dissimilar in concept to the Fokker G I that was to make its debut some two years later; both Focke-Wulf and Henschel proposed using the electrically-operated cannon turret under development by Mauser, while the Messerschmitt-designed submission from the Bayerische Flugzeugwerke ignored many of the requirements of the specification, and placed accent uncompromisingly on ultimate performance.

The two Fw 57 prototypes were essentially similar in external matters, but the second aircraft introduced modifications to the tail control surfaces, including a modified rudder balance and revised tabs on both the rudder and the elevators.

The Fw 57 V2 was essentially similar to the Fw 57 V1 in external matters, but introduced tail control surface modifications. All three prototypes suffered from excessive structural weight, and were underpowered and thus poor in performance terms.

Initial evaluation of the competing Kampfzerstörer projects was conducted in December 1934, and it was concluded that the proposals submitted by Focke-Wulf and Henschel conformed most closely with the demands of the specification. Although the Bayerische Flugzeugwerke submission possessed undeniable promise, the company was out of favour with the Luftfahrtkommissariat, and this fact, coupled with Messerschmitt's failure to adhere to several of the principal requirements of the specification, prevented it receiving serious consideration. At this juncture, Ernst Udet, whose own company, the Udet-Flugzeugbau, had been absorbed by the Bayerische Flugzeugwerke some 10 years earlier, and who had watched Willy Messerschmitt's work with keen interest, intervened with the Luftfahrtkommissariat. Although at that time possessing no official position, Udet enjoyed considerable influence in German aviation circles, and succeeded in gaining for the Bayerische Flugzeugwerke a development contract and an order for three prototypes of its Kampfzerstörer project which was allocated the official designation Bf 110. Similar contracts were placed with Focke-Wulf and Henschel whose projects were designated **Fw 57** and Hs 124, respectively.

Large fighter

The Fw 57 was by far the largest of the competing Kampfzerstörer, spanning no less than 25 m (82 ft), and detail design was the responsibility of Dipl.-Ing. Bansemir. The first all-metal aircraft of Focke-Wulf design, the Fw 57 was also the first to feature a monocoque fuselage. The wing comprised a main duralumin girder spar and auxiliary spar with light-alloy stressed skinning, and was built in three sections. Power was provided by two DB 600 12-cylinder liquid-cooled engines each offering 679 kW (910 hp) for take-off, and the main undercarriage members retracted aft into the engine nacelles, these each comprising triangulated units formed by a hinged fork, the legs of which were sprung by two oleo shock-absorbers, a hinged Vee-strut being mounted on a transverse tube, and the assembly being raised by an oleo-pneumatic screw-jack. Three-blade variable-pitch airscrews were fitted, and all fuel was housed in the wing centre section.

The proposed armament comprised two forward-firing gimbal-mounted 20-mm MG FF cannon that were intended to project from apertures in the extreme nose, and a third weapon of similar calibre mounted in an electrically-operated Mauser dorsal turret. The extreme nose was extensively glazed for the bombardier, whose task was also to load the forward-firing cannon which had limited traverse. Provision

was made in the fuselage for a small bomb-bay. No armament was installed when the first prototype, the **Fw 57 V1**, was completed in the late spring of 1936, a mock-up of the Mauser turret being installed in the dorsal position, but long before this aircraft made its first flight, the Führungsstab had reconsidered the wisdom of its Kampfzerstörer concept, and was in the process of drafting new specifications calling for more specialised aircraft. The Kampfzerstörer specification had, therefore, already been superseded when the Fw 57 began its rather dismal flight test programme.

It had already been ascertained that the Fw 57's structural weight had been seriously miscalculated – the wing structure alone was five times that originally calculated – and empty equipped weight without cannon armament and turret was 6800 kg (14,991 lb), 63 percent higher than that of the Hs 124. The Fw 57's handling characteristics proved unsatisfactory in virtually every respect. Teething troubles with the pre-production DB 600 engines limited flight testing, and the Fw 57 V1 made a forced landing on soft ground during the summer of 1936, and was written off. By this time, the second and third prototypes, the **Fw 57 V2** and **V3**, had been completed and had joined the flight test programme, which was continued in desultory fashion until the late autumn when it was finally abandoned.

Fw 57 V1 specification
Type: three-seat heavy fighter-bomber.
Powerplant: two Daimler-Benz DB 600 12-cylinder inverted-Vee liquid-cooled engines each rated at 679 kW (910 hp) for take-off.
Performance: maximum speed 404 km/h (251 mph) at 3000 m (9,850 ft); 365 km/h (227 mph) at sea level; maximum cruising speed 373 km/h (232 mph) at 3000 m (9,850 ft), 319 km/h (198 mph) at sea level; maximum ceiling 9100 m (29,855 ft)
Weights: empty equipped (without defensive armament) 6800 kg (14,991 lb); loaded 8300 kg (18,298 lb)
Dimensions: wingspan 25.00 m (82 ft 0 in); length 16.40 m (53 ft 9⅔ in); height 4.10 m (13 ft 5⅓ in); wing area 53.50 m² (791.15 sq ft)
Armament: (proposed) two 20-mm MG FF cannon on semi-flexible mountings in extreme nose and one 20-mm cannon in electrically-operated Mauser dorsal turret, plus six 100-kg (220-lb) bombs internally

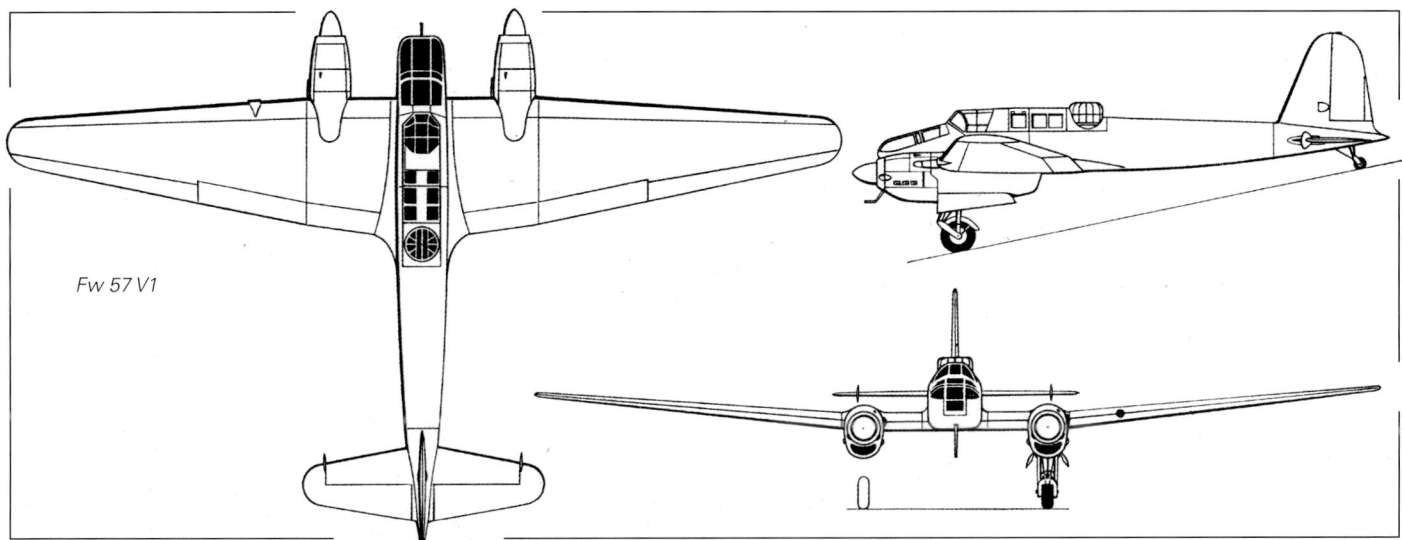

Fw 57 V1

Focke-Wulf Fw 58 Weihe

The Fw 58 Weihe was a pedestrian aircraft in performance terms, but was nonetheless vital to the development and operation of the Luftwaffe as a multi-role trainer and utility light transport. As the Leukoplast-Bomber, the Fw 58 was also an effective air ambulance popular to all elements of the German armed forces.

Destined to see extensive service with the Luftwaffe as a crew trainer, light transport and communications aircraft, the twin-engined **Fw 58 Weihe** (kite) was of typical Kurt Tank design for its period, and as such was a semi-cantilever monoplane of the low-wing type with a metal structure covered with light alloy and fabric, and tail-wheel undercarriage including main units which retracted into the engine nacelles.

The **Fw 58 V1** first prototype (D-ABEM) first flew in January 1935 with two Argus As 10C air-cooled inverted V-8 engines each rated at 179 kW (240 hp) and driving a two-blade propeller of the fixed-pitch type, and was outfitted for the instrument and radio training roles. There followed the **Fw 58 V2** and **Fw 58 V3** prototypes that differed mainly in being outfitted for the bombing and gunnery training role with racks for light bombs and single trainable machine-guns in open nose and dorsal positions. The Fw 58 was evaluated against the Arado Ar 77 and, being found superior in virtually every respect, was ordered into production.

Focke-Wulf had already started work on a pre-production and service trials batch of 10 **Fw 58A-0** aircraft, however, and they entered military service from 1936 as six-passenger light transports. The 14 **Fw 58A-1** production aircraft that followed the Fw 58A-0 pre-production aircraft were instrument and radio trainers intended primarily for civil use. The first full military variant was therefore the **Fw 58B** series for the bombing and gunnery training roles with a revised and fully enclosed nose carrying a single 7.9-mm (0.31-in) MG 15 trainable forward-firing machine gun in a rotating cone. The type was validated in a pre-production and service trials batch of six **Fw 58B-0** aircraft, and then came 50 examples of the **Fw 58B-1**. The 371 examples of the **Fw 58B-2** were generally similar to the Fw 58B-1 but manufactured by Fieseler (119), Gotha (165) and MIAG (87). Two of the

The main units of the Fw 58's tailwheel landing gear retracted rearward in bays in the underside of the two engine nacelles. After the main units had retracted, they were covered by doors that closed over them to reduce drag.

Fw 58B-2 aircraft were later adapted as twin-float seaplanes with the revised designation **Fw 58B-3**.

Air ambulance service

The **Fw 58C** series was the Fw 58B counterpart for radio and dual-control pilot training. Focke-Wulf led off with six pre-production and service trials examples of the **Fw 58C-0**, and followed with 34 examples of the **Fw 58C-1**. Also built to the extent of 81 aircraft by Focke-Wulf, the **Fw 58C-2** had enlarged fuel capacity, and another 432 aircraft were built by Fieseler (120), Gotha (155) and MIAG (157). One Fw 58C-2 was revised as the sole **Fw 58C-3** seaplane with twin-float alighting gear and the revised powerplant of two

The Fw 58B, with its revised nose of more streamlined appearance, looked a considerably more modern aircraft than the preceding Fw 58A series with its open nose gun position. However, there remained obsolescent features such as the strut bracing for the wing and tailplane.

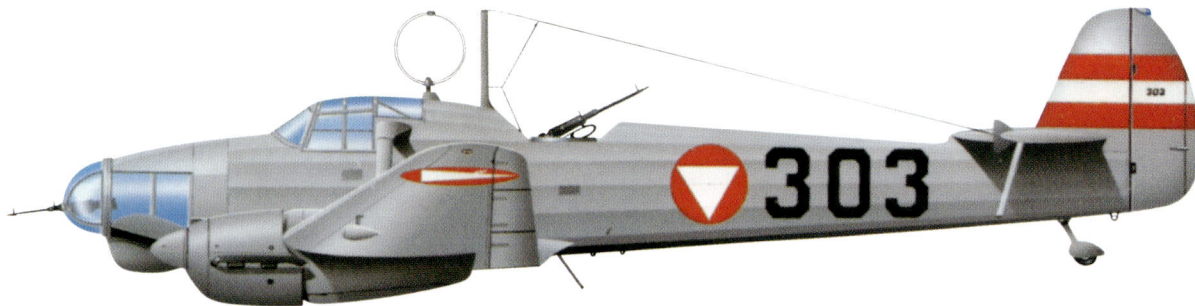

This Fw 58B was operated by with Bomberstaffel 1/B of the Bombergeschwader of Fliegerregiment 2 of the Österreichische Luftstreitkrafte (Austrian air force) during 1938.

Hirth HM 508D air-cooled inverted V-8 engines each rated at 209 kW (280 hp). The Fw 58C series aircraft saw very extensive use and were often pressed into service as air ambulances, which resulted in the nickname Leukoplast-Bomber (sticky tape bomber). One aircraft was sold to Gunnar Larsen of Denmark, and in November and December 1939 this machine (OY-DYS) was leased by DDL Danish Air Lines to operated a service between Copenhagen and Rønne on the island of Børnholm in the Baltic Sea.

The **Fw 58D-1** was a long-range variant of which three were produced for Zeiss, the optical equipment company, during 1939. **Fw 58E** was the core designation applied to the winterised version of the Fw 58B-2 with ski landing gear. The sole **Fw 58E-1** was the prototype conversion, while the **Fw 58E-2**, produced to the extent of 12 aircraft, was the

Above: With its open nose gun position and large radio antenna loop, the Fw 58 in its V2 and V3 prototype had something of an anachronistic appearance.

Above: The outer ends of the flat centre section, which was of constant thickness and chord, were braced to the upper fuselage on each side by a single strut.

Above: In its later forms, and especially with a 'solid' nose, the Fw 58 offered a much cleaner and more modern appearance. Smart cheat lines are worn by this liaison transport.

Above: The Fw 58 was a little sung but vitally important element of the Luftwaffe's capability to train air gunners, bomber pilots and radio operators.

The glazed nose of the Fw 58B incorporated a rotating cone portion in its front for a 7.9-mm (0.31-in) MG 15 trainable forward-firing machine-gun.

Luftwaffe ground crew work on an Fw 58. The almost triangular section of the engine nacelles stemmed from the fact that the engines were inverted Vee units.

Focke-Wulf Fw 58 Weihe

Above: Crew members embark on a multi-engine training sortie in their camouflaged Fw 58. In the background is the tail of a Heinkel He 111 bomber.

Above: The Fw 58 was a multi-role trainer based on an airframe that was simple and therefore cheap to build, and also easy to maintain even under adverse conditions.

Above: Without open gun positions and excescences such as the large radio antenna loop, the Fw 58 had a notably pleasing and workmanlike appearance in its staff transport role.

In the pilot training role, the Fw 58 had advantages such as twin control yokes, duplicated instruments and, on the centreline console, the engine throttles and undercarriage control levers.

definitive winterised model. **Fw 58F** was the core designation of Fw 58C-2 conversions for use as company or personal transports, and the seven aircraft were designated as the **Fw 58F-1** to **Fw 58F-7**. The Fw 58G was the family's dedicated air ambulance version, and production began with one **Fw 58G-1** manufactured by Focke-Wulf. The **Fw 58G-3** was the definitive model manufactured as 16 by Focke-Wulf and five by MIAG. The **Fw 58K** was the export model, which was also built under licence in Brazil (25 machines produced between 1939 and 1942 to supplement 10 imported aircraft) and Hungary (38 machines produced between 1943 and 1944 to supplement 229 imported aircraft).

Thus the German-built total of 1,987 aircraft including civil models for the domestic and export markets was complemented by a licence-built total of 63 aircraft, all for the military market. The Fw 58K also saw limited civil service, Lufthansa acquiring a total of eight aircraft in equal batches of four during 1938 and 1939. Some of these aircraft were fitted with the Argus As 10C powerplant, while others had Hirth HM 508D engines.

Focke-Wulf Fw 58B-1 specification
Type: light transport/gunnery trainer
Powerplant: two 240-hp (179-kW) Argus As 10C air-cooled inverted V-8 engines each rated at 179 kW (240 hp) for take-off
Performance: maximum speed 270 km/h (168 mph); service ceiling 5600 m (18,375 ft); range 800 km (497 miles)
Weights: empty 2400 kg (5,291 lb); maximum take-off 3600 kg (7,936 lb)
Dimensions: wingspan 21.00 m (68 ft 11 in); length 14.00 m (45 ft 11 in); height 3.90 m (12 ft 9½ in); wing area 47.00 m² (505.92 sq ft)
Armament: one 7.9-mm (0.31-in) MG 15 machine-gun in rear of cabin and one MG 15 in the nose glazing

Above: The Fw 58 V18 (D-OXLR) was used for trials with fixed tricycle landing gear, and on the ground was given an odd appearance by its nose-down attitude.

The Fw 58 was powered by air-cooled engines in close-fitting nacelles, and each engine drove a two-blade propeller whose hub was enclosed in a neat spinner.

Many Fw 58s were assigned to important military and industrial figures as personal transports. This machine was the first Fw 58A-0, retained by the manufacturer to ferry Kurt Tank, the company's chief designer. In 1942 it adopted these military codes and a smart Wellenmüster camouflage.

Left: An Fw 58G-1 Leukoplast-Bomber, is seen complete with red cross markings. The cabin could accommodate two stretcher cases as well as the seat for one medical attendant.

Below: Three Fw 58 aircraft are seen ready for export. The farthest machine was destined for Hungary, and the other two for Czechoslovakia.

Below: The Fw 58's wing was based on a flat centre section of constant thickness and chord, and carrying dihedralled outer panels that were tapered in thickness and chord.

Right: In common with all other training aircraft, the Fw 58 suffered from the hard and inexperienced handling to which it was subjected. Nose-over accidents were comparatively common.

Above, below and below right: The Fw 58B could be revised as the Fw 58BW seaplane with a side-by-side pair of metal floats in place of the standard wheeled main undercarriage units. Performance was severely affected by the greater weight and drag of the alighting gear.

Focke-Wulf Fw 61/Fa 61

The Fw 61 (later Fa 61) marked a turning point in the development of the helicopter as a practical flying machine. The type was rudimentary and of great overall width, but was reliable and fully controllable, set a large number of impressive world records, and paved the way for German helicopter development before and during World War II.

Heinrich Focke's rotary-wing experience was gained initially from licence production of Cierva C.19 and C.30 autogyros, leading to development of the **Fw 61** helicopter. The fuselage was similar to that of a light fixed-wing aircraft with a 119-kW (160-hp) Bramo Sh.14A radial engine mounted in the nose, the primary purpose of this powerplant being to drive two outrigger-mounted three-bladed counter-rotating rotors; it also turned a small-diameter conventional propeller for engine cooling purposes. The rotors were fully articulated and control was achieved by the use of cyclic pitch, differential pitch and differential collective pitch in the longitudinal, directional and lateral axes, respectively. Vertical control was achieved by varying rotor revolutions through the use of the throttle, in contrast to the present method of maintaining reasonably constant rotor speed and altering the pitch of the blades.

Following a maiden flight on 26 June 1936, one that is sometimes reported as lasting for 28 seconds, but which is recorded in Heinrich Focke's log book as 45 seconds, the Fw 61 prototype completed its initial development programme and then established a number of world rotorcraft records. On 25 June 1937 Ewald Rohlfs flew it to a height of 2440 m (8,000 ft) and remained airborne for 1 hour 20 minutes 49 seconds. Next day he set a straight line distance record of 16.40 km (10.19 miles), a closed-circuit speed record of 122.55 km/h (76.15 mph) and a closed-circuit distance record of 80.60 km (50.09 miles). Perhaps the most publicised flights were those made by Hanna Reitsch in the Deutschlandhalle during February 1938.

Such achievements encouraged Deutsche Lufthansa to order a passenger-carrying development of this helicopter, leading to the Fa 223 and Fa 266. By then Heinrich Focke had formed the new company Focke-Achgelis & Co. GmbH to concentrate on his interest in rotary-wing aircraft, this explaining the redesignation of the Fw 61 as the **Fa 61**.

Public displays of the Fw 61, often in tightly constrained locations and even inside large halls, gave the Nazi party good propaganda material, and also highlighted the helicopter's excellent controllability. This is the second prototype that flew in early 1937.

Focke-Wulf Fw 61 (as fully developed) specification
Type: single-seat experimental helicopter
Powerplant: one 119-kW (160-hp) Bramo Sh.14A 7-cylinder radial piston engine
Performance: maximum speed 112 km/h (76 mph) at sea level; cruising speed 100 km/h (62 mph); service ceiling 2620 m (8,600 ft); range 230 km (143 miles)
Weights: empty 800 kg (1,764 lb); maximum take-off 950 kg (2,094 lb)
Dimensions: rotor diameter, each 7.00 m (22 ft 11½ in); length 7.30 m (23 ft 11½ in); height 2.65 m (8 ft 8¼ in); rotor disc area, total 76.97 m² (828.51 sq ft)

The rotor system comprised a pair of counter-rotating rotors (each with three articulated and tapered blades) carried at the tips of large outrigger units and powered, via gearboxes and shafts, from the radial engine mounted in the nose. Each rotor included a cyclic pitch control system for longitudinal and directional control. Differential operation of the cyclic pitch arrangement provided lateral control.

Above: The Fw 61 was based on the powerplant, fuselage and tail unit of the Focke-Wulf Fw 44 Stieglitz trainer, in combination with revised undercarriage that included a nose unit to prevent nosing-over. The tailplane was relocated to the top of the fin, and braced by a strut on each side.

Right: The Fw 61 recorded its first flight on 26 June 1936 in the hands of Ewald Rohlfs, and in May of the following year made its first auto-rotative landing with the engine shut down. Successful as it was, however, the Fw 61 was only an experimental helicopter with no real practical application.

Below: The Fw 61's great overall width resulted from the adoption of a pair of side-by-side rotors carried by larger steel-tube outriggers. The rotors turned in opposite directions, each thereby cancelling the other's torque reaction. Power was transmitted to the rotors by long shafts.

Left: Seen in flight with the fabric covering removed from all but its control surfaces, the Fw 61 reveals the origin of its fuselage and empennage in the welded steel tube structure of the Fw 44 Stieglitz biplane trainer.

Above: The first prototype Fw 61 was tested with a number of undercarriage arrangements, initially with a small nosewheel as seen here. This gave way to a much larger nosewheel, which was also fitted to the V2. An extended tailwheel was also tested.

Right: The Fw 61 set many helicopter records, the last before World War II being the distance and altitude records of 230.45 km (143.05 miles) and 3427 m (11,240 ft) on 20 June 1938 and 29 January 1939, respectively. On both occasions it was piloted by Karl Bode.

Only two Fw 61s were built, **D-EKRA** being the second prototype. The two-blade propeller driven by the Sh.14A radial engine had only a small diameter as it was intended only to improve the cooling of the engine cylinders.

Focke-Wulf Fw 62

The Focke-Wulf Fw 62 biplane was a workmanlike attempt to create a shipborne reconnaissance floatplane for catapult launch from larger German warships, but was conceptually inferior to the rival Arado Ar 196 monoplane, and was therefore not ordered into production.

With the realisation that the Heinkel He 114 was unlikely to provide a suitable successor for the He 60 serving with the Bordfliegerstaffeln deploying catapult aircraft aboard Kriegsmarine surface vessels, the Technisches Amt of the RLM prepared a revised specification for a two-seat catapult floatplane. Issued in the autumn of 1936, the specification called for all submissions to offer alternative single- and twin-float arrangements, stipulated that the required performance should be attained on a total of 597-671 kW (800-900 hp), and indicated a preference for a single-engined configuration. Proposals were submitted by Arado, Dornier, Focke-Wulf, and the Gothaer Waggonfabrik, that of the last-mentioned concern, the Projekt 14-012, being the only submission envisaging a twin-engined configuration (two Argus As 410s). From the outset the Arado project was

The Fw 62 V2 differed from the Fw 62 V1 first prototype primarily in its alighting gear, which comprised a single centreline main float and two stabilising floats mounted on short struts under the outer parts of the lower wing. The tailplane, carrying horn-balanced elevators, was located forward of the fin, which carried a plain rudder.

favoured by the Technisches Amt, four prototypes being ordered under the designation Ar 196, the more conservative Focke-Wulf project being the runner-up, and two prototypes being ordered under the designation **Fw 62** as a back-up programme for the more advanced Arado design.

The alighting gear of the Fw 62 V1 first prototype comprised a side-by-side pair of single-step floats, the starboard unit fitted with a water rudder. An unusual feature of the alighting gear was the carriage of the floats on a sprung chassis designed to absorb some of the forces that would otherwise have been transmitted to the airframe during landings on choppy water. The outer wing panels were designed to fold rearward to facilitate shipboard stowage.

The Fw 62 V2 shows off its central main float and outrigger configuration. Unlike the Fw 62 V1, whose crew entered the aircraft by a step arrangement on the forward unit of the float chassis, the Fw 62 V2 had its steps incorporated into the rear unit of the main float chassis. Both versions of the Fw 62 performed adequately in trials, but neither was a match for the more up-to-date Ar 196 monoplane.

Both the Ar 196 and the Fw 62 employed the BMW 132 radial air-cooled engine, but whereas the former was a low-wing monoplane with enclosed cockpits, the latter was somewhat dated in concept, being a biplane with open cockpits. The Fw 62, the design of which was the responsibility of Ing. Arbeitlang, was conventional in every respect save one: it featured a sprung float chassis designed to cushion wave impact during take-off or landing. The equi-span wings were light alloy-covered two-spar metal structures, and carried metal-framed and fabric-covered ailerons and flaps. The upper wing was carried above the fuselage by splayed N-struts, and there were two sets of N-type interplane struts with double-wire cross-bracing in the plane of both spars. The fuselage was a rectangular-section steel-tube structure faired to an oval by former ribs, and covered forward by light alloy panels and aft by fabric. The two crew members were accommodated in tandem open cockpits, the pilot being seated above the observer and beneath a cut-out in the upper wing, and provision was made for a defensive armament of one 7.9-mm MG 15 machine-gun on a flexible mounting in the rear cockpit.

The first prototype, the **Fw 62 V1** (D-OFWF), was flown for the first time in the late spring of 1937, followed closely by the second prototype, the **Fw 62 V2** (D-OHGF). Both prototypes were powered by the BMW 132Dc rated at 656 kW (880 hp) for take-off and driving a two-blade controllable-pitch airscrew, but differed in that the V1 had twin single-step metal floats while the V2 had a single central main float with twin stabilising floats. The float chassis of both aircraft incorporated rubber-in-compression shock absorbers with oleo damping, and catapult points were provided.

The Fw 62 V1 and V2 were delivered to Travemünde during the summer of 1937 for official evaluation, but although the general characteristics of the floatplane were pronounced satisfactory and catapult trials were completed successfully, the more advanced characteristics of the Ar 196 were preferred, and development of the Focke-Wulf type was abandoned.

Fw 62 V1 specification
Type: two-seat shipboard reconnaissance and coastal patrol float seaplane.
Powerplant: one BMW 132Dc nine-cylinder radial air-cooled engine rated at 656 kW (880 hp) for take-off.
Performance: maximum speed 280 km/h (174 mph) at 1000 m (3,280 ft); cruising speed 251 km/h (156 mph); initial climb rate 380 m (1,247 ft) per minute; service ceiling 5900 m (19,360 ft)
Weights: empty 2300 kg (5,070 lb); loaded 2850 kg (6,283 lb)
Dimensions: wingspan 12.35 m (40 ft 6¼ in); length 11.15 m (36 ft 7 in); height 4.30 m (14 ft 1¼ in); wing area 36.10 m² (388.58 sq ft)
Armament: (proposed) one 7.9-mm MG 15 machine-gun on flexible mounting, plus four 50-kg (110-lb) SC 50 bombs on racks beneath lower wing

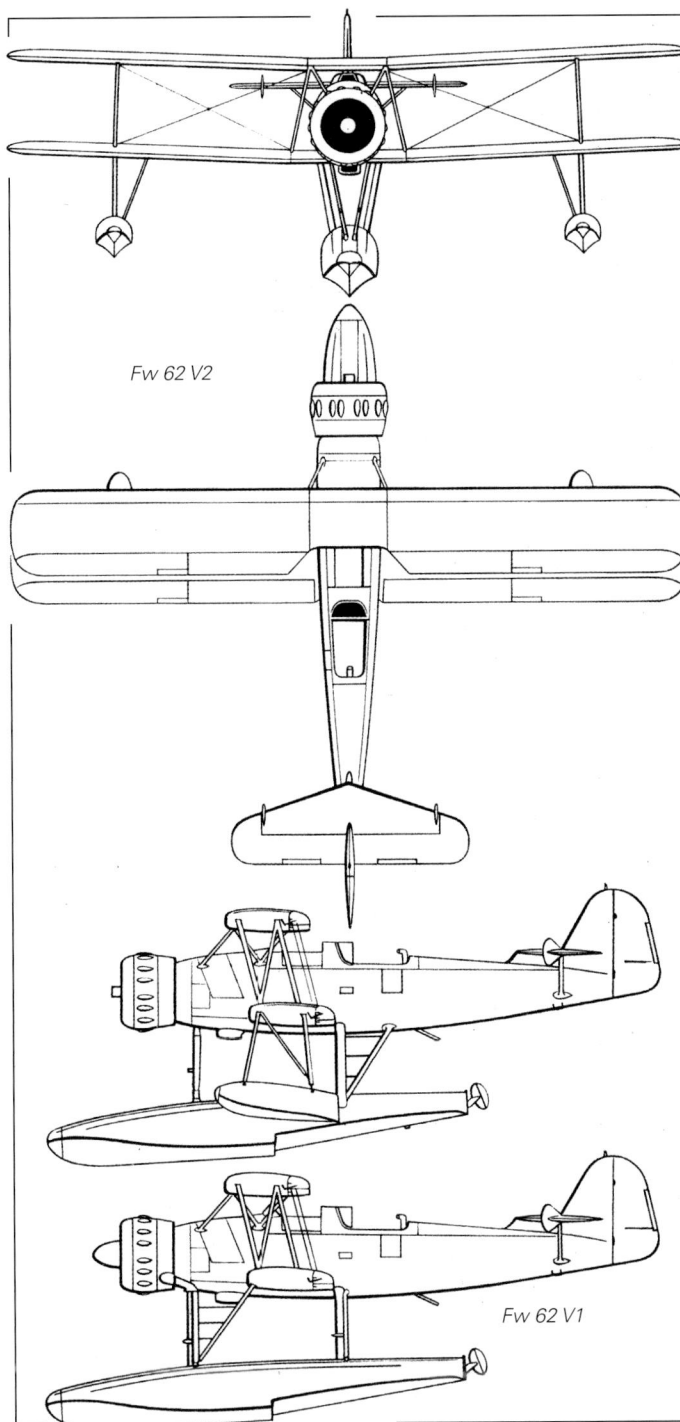

Fw 62 V2

Fw 62 V1

Focke-Wulf Fw 159

Though it possessed modern features such as retractable main undercarriage units and an enclosed cockpit, the Focke-Wulf Fw 159 was decidedly obsolescent in its use of a parasol wing with a number of drag-generating struts. In combination with problems of the undercarriage's actuation, this was sufficient to prevent production.

In military aircraft design the parasol monoplane with retractable undercarriage is among the true *rarae aves*. Indeed, the number of warplanes of this layout can be counted upon the fingers of one hand, and but three of them have been single-seat fighters. By the late 1930s any layout other than the low/mid-wing cantilever monoplane was considered *passé* for the land-based single-seat fighter, but early in 1934, when the Luftwaffenführungsstab finalised its single-seat all-metal fighter monoplane requirement, the parasol arrangement still had those who believed that the markedly superior field of vision it afforded the pilot was worth the loss of a few knots to the drag of the necessary bracing struts.

While few members of the Luftwaffenführungsstab suffered any serious doubt that the fighter of the future would be a low-wing cantilever monoplane, caution dictated evaluation of possible alternative configurations. Thus, in view of the exceptional promise being shown by Focke-Wulf's Fw 56 Stösser parasol monoplane, the Luftfahrtkommissariat's C-Amt suggested to the company's technical director, Dipl.-Ing. Tank, that the Focke-Wulf submission should utilise a similar wing arrangement in a scaled-up, more powerful Stösser, embodying state-of-the-art aerodynamic and structural refinements. Tank was made fully aware that all competing projects would be low-wing cantilever monoplanes, but the suggestion of the C-Amt presented him with the challenge of evolving a parasol monoplane that, by means of careful aerodynamic design, could offer a performance comparable with those of its low-wing competitors.

The manufacturers participating in the fighter programme were Arado (Ar 80), Bayerische Flugzeugwerke (Bf 109), Focke-Wulf (**Fw 159**) and Heinkel (He 112). Each was duly awarded a contract for three prototypes, and all had begun to cut metal before the end of 1934. Tank allocated primary design responsibility for the Fw 159 to Oberingenieur R. Blaser, and from the outset Focke-Wulf emphasised aerodynamic cleanliness in an attempt to compensate for the higher drag inherent in the chosen configuration. In so far as the basic parasol fighter monoplane configuration was

One of the very few single-seat fighter monoplanes of parasol configuration to feature retractable main undercarriage units, the Fw 159 was designed by Blaser and was of all-metal construction with a semi-monocoque fuselage of oval section incorporating an enclosed cockpit.

concerned, Blaser and his team found no shortage of design precedents, but only two such fighters embodying a retractable undercarriage were known to have flown, the Dayton-Wright XPS-1 and shipboard Curtiss XF13C-1, the latter having been tested initially as a biplane.

The Fw 159 was designed around the new Junkers Jumo 210 liquid-cooled inverted V-12 engine, as demanded by the specification, and incorporated an oval-section light metal semi-monocoque fuselage, The metal-skinned parallel-chord wing comprised a main box-spar and an auxiliary spar carrying the ailerons and flaps that occupied the entire trailing edge apart from the cut-out above the fuselage. Of modified NACA section, the wing was of relatively low thickness/chord ratio, and was carried above the fuselage by splayed N-struts, a single inclined aerofoil-section strut bracing the main spar to the lower fuselage longeron on each side. The pilot was seated beneath an aft-sliding hood, all fuel was housed in a single tank forward and below the cockpit, a releasable panel enabling the tank to be jettisoned in an

D-INGA was the registration of the Fw 159 V2 second prototype, which had an odd appearance as a result of its parasol wing and retractable undercarriage units. They were of narrow track and suffered from a number of intractable mechanical problems.

emergency. Particularly careful attention was given to ease of maintenance, almost the entire forward fuselage being covered by hinged panels providing ready access to power-plant, armament and ancillary equipment.

Retractable main units

Perhaps the most novel feature of the Fw 159 was its use of retractable main undercarriage units, but highly ingenious though the mechanism of this was, it was to prove the 'Achilles heel' of the Focke-Wulf fighter. The main legs were double-jointed, providing a form of levered suspension under compression, and each unit had an auxiliary oleo strut that, during the retraction process, compressed the lower main leg joint, the upper joint breaking and the entire unit being raised vertically through fairing doors barely larger than the wheel diameter. Although complex, the system was a model of ingenuity, and on test rigs the mechanism functioned flawlessly. The first of the three prototypes, the **Fw 159 V1**, completed in the spring of 1935, was mounted on blocks, and its undercarriage raised and lowered repeatedly. The legs retracted and extended with absolute precision, and after the successful completion of taxiing trials on the airfield at Bremen, preparations were made for initial flight trials.

The Fw 159 V1 was fitted with a Jumo 210A engine rated at 455 kW (610 hp) for take-off and driving a three-blade Schwarz wooden propeller of the fixed-pitch type. The aircraft took off on its first flight with Flugkapitän Wolfgang Stein at the controls. The undercarriage retracted perfectly, and Stein completed initial handling tests, made two moderately high-speed runs across the airfield, and entered the landing pattern. To the onlookers it appeared that the undercarriage had extended correctly, but Stein suddenly opened the throttle, raised the flaps and flew across the field with the undercarriage down. It was then seen that the main leg joints had only partly extended, Stein having been warned of the predicament by the undercarriage lights indicating that the legs had failed to lock. He circled the field time and time again, constantly operating the undercarriage mechanism in a fruitless attempt to lock the legs in position. The first prototype had not been fitted with fuel tank jettisoning equip-

Above: The Fw 159 V1 first prototype is seen before its sole flight.

Above: The Fw 159 V2 second prototype is seen after suffering undercarriage failure during a landing.

ment, and there was no alternative but to circuit the field until the fuel was exhausted and then risk a landing. Various suggestions were daubed in whitewash on the concrete hardstanding, the Fw 159 V1 having no R/T equipment, including the proposal that Stein should attempt a slow loop and work the hand pump during the final stage of the loop in the hope of utilising centrifugal force to lock the legs. Nothing proved of any avail.

Stein had taken off with full fuel, this being sufficient for two hours' flying and less than 30 minutes' flight testing had been undertaken when the undercarriage fault had been discovered. He was therefore forced to circuit the field for some 90 minutes before attempting to land. He finally approached the field in a long glide with the undercarriage partly extended, the legs immediately snapped off on making contact with the ground, and the aircraft somersaulted twice before coming to rest on its back. The Fw 159 V1 was a

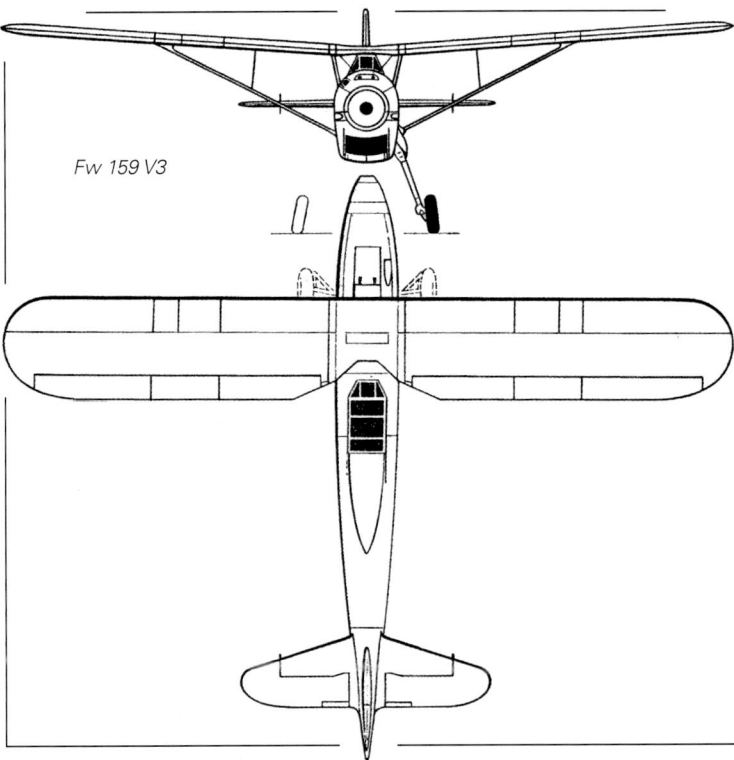

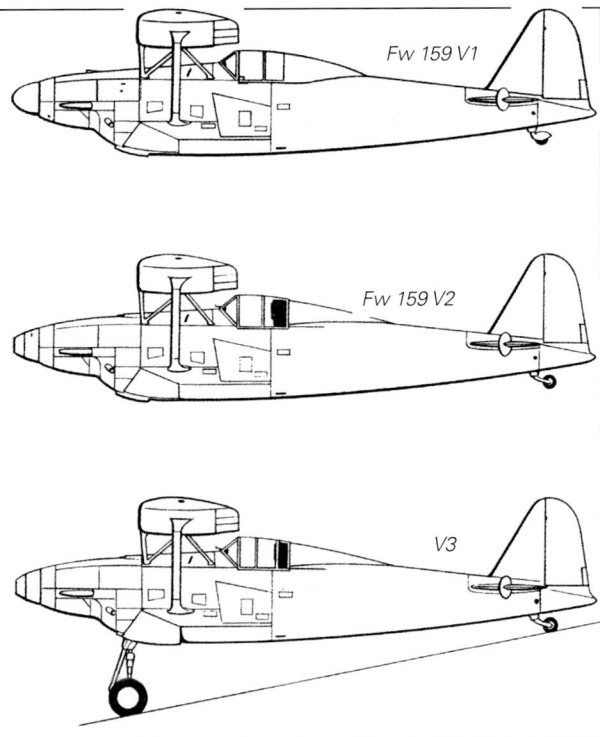

Fw 159 V3

Fw 159 V1

Fw 159 V2

V3

Focke-Wulf Fw 159

complete write-off but, miraculously, Stein suffered nothing more than superficial bruising.

It was subsequently ascertained that the engineers responsible for the design of the undercarriage had miscalculated its drag as it extended, and the oleo-hydraulic mechanism possessed insufficient power to counter the drag and lock the legs in position. Thus the second prototype, the **Fw 159 V2** (D-INGA), completed shortly after the abortive first test flight of the initial prototype, was fitted with substantially reinforced oleo-hydraulic undercarriage actuating mechanism. In other respects, apart from a lengthened tailwheel leg and unspatted tailwheel, it was identical to its predecessor, and flight testing began in earnest. The handling characteristics of the Fw 159 proved not dissimilar to those of the Fw 56 Stösser, but stalling speed was on the high side, climb rate was lower than had been calculated, and the turning circle was considered to be poor.

Addition of more power

The third prototype, the **Fw 159 V3** (D-IUPY), differed from the Fw 159 V1 and Fw 159 V2 in having a Jumo 210B engine which, rated at 447 kW (600 hp) for take-off, afforded 477 kW (640 hp) for five minutes at 2700 m (8,860 ft). The three-blade propeller of the previous prototypes was replaced by a two-blade Schwarz wooden propeller, also of the fixed-pitch type, armament was installed, and the cockpit canopy was revised, a three-panel glazed hood being introduced and the light metal fairing aft of the cockpit, previously attached

The Fw 159's performance was inferior to that of the rival Heinkel He 112 and Messerschmitt Bf 109 low-wing monoplanes, and development of the conceptually obsolescent Fw 159 was soon discontinued.

Left: The Fw 159 embodied a number of ingenious design features, but at an early stage it was realised that its configuration was anachronistic. Nevertheless, testing of the Fw 159 V3 (D-IUPY) continued into 1938.

Below: The design of the Fw 159 was optimised for ease of maintenance and, as revealed by this photograph of the Fw 159 V3 third prototype, virtually all equipment was readily accessible via hinged light metal inspection panels and hatches. With the Jumo 210G fuel-injected engine installed, the Fw 159 V3 attained a maximum speed of 405 km/h (252 mph).

to the hood, was fixed. The armament was two 7.9-mm (0.31-in) MG 17 machine-guns with 500 r.p.g. installed in the upper decking of the forward fuselage and synchronised to fire through the propeller disc. Provision was made for the installation of a 20-mm MG FF (Oerlikon) cannon to fire through the propeller hub, although this was never installed as the MG FF proved unsuitable for engine mounting.

During 1936 the Fw 159 V2 was fitted with the twin-gun armament, the fairing aft of the cockpit was fixed, and the two-panel glazed hood arranged to slide over the fairing, the three-blade fixed-pitch wooden propeller was replaced by a two-blade Junkers-Hamilton metal propeller of the variable-pitch type, and the Jumo 210Da engine with two-speed supercharger was installed, offering 507 kW (680 hp) for take-off and 500 kW (670 hp) for five minutes at 3900 m (12,795 ft). The Fw 159 V3 was also fitted with a two-blade metal propeller of the variable-pitch type and, eventually, a fuel-injected Jumo 210G engine rated at 522 kW (700 hp) for take-off and 544 kW (730 hp) at 1000 m (3,280 ft).

By this time in the late summer of 1937 the Reichsluftfahrtministerium had long since selected the Bf 109 for the re-equipment of the Jagdflieger. Both the Fw 159 V2 and Fw 159 V3 had been evaluated at the Erprobungsstelle Travemünde in the spring and early summer of 1936, but the preference of the Luftwaffenführungsstab for the low-wing cantilever monoplane evinced from the outset of the fighter programme had by now been strengthened as a result of the initial testing of the He 112 and Bf 109, coupled with developments abroad. The Focke-Wulf fighter was not given really serious consideration as a contestant, being viewed by the Erprobungsstelle Travemünde as some sort of half-way house between the fighter biplane, whose demise was now imminent, and the aerodynamically efficient low-wing fighter monoplane of the future: the Fw 159 lacked the agility of the former and the performance of the latter.

The Fw 159 had, in fact, little to commend it. In the form tested at Travemünde, the Fw 159 was barely lighter than the similarly powered He 112 yet possessed a substantially higher wing loading which, at 111.48 kg/m² (22.83 lb/sq ft), was only marginally lower than that of the 270-kg (595-lb) lighter Jumo 210-engined Bf 109. Despite the effort expended by Blaser's team to reduce aerodynamic drag, the Fw 159 could not seriously compete with its Heinkel and Bayerische Flugzeugwerke competitors in most aspects of performance, and it was improbable that the ingenuity displayed in the complex undercarriage design would find an appreciative audience among field maintenance personnel.

Although the Fw 159 was deleted from the fighter contest, flight testing and development continued into 1938 and, with the fuel-injection Jumo 210G engine, the Fw 159 V3 reached 405 km/h (252 mph) at 4500 m (14,765 ft), but the undercarriage retraction mechanism was never perfected, and the test programme was delayed on several occasions when one or other leg collapsed.

Focke-Wulf Fw 159 V2 specification
Type: single-seat fighter
Powerplant: one Junkers Jumo 210Da liquid-cooled inverted V-12 engine rated at 507 kW (680 hp) for take-off and 500 kW (670 hp) for five minutes at 3900 m (12,795 ft)
Performance: maximum speed 335 km/h (208 mph) at sea level, 370 km/h (230 mph) at 1500 m (4,920 ft), 385 km/h (239 mph) at 4000 m (13,125 ft); maximum cruising speed 365 km/h (227 mph) at 2700 m (8,860 ft); climb to 6000 m (19,685 ft) in 12 minutes 30 seconds; service ceiling 7200 m (23,620 ft); range 650 km (404 miles)
Weights: empty equipped 1875 kg (4,134 lb); loaded 2250 kg (4,960 lb)
Dimensions: wingspan 12.40 m (40 ft 8 in); length 10.00 m (32 ft 9½ in); height 3.75 m (12 ft 3⅔ in); wing area 20.20 m² (217.43 sq ft)
Armament: two 7.9-mm (0.31-in) MG 17 fixed forward-firing machine-guns with 500 r.p.g.

Focke-Wulf Fw 187 Falke

Kurt Tank's Fw 187 single-seat fighter proposal was evolved originally in 1936 as a private venture, based on two Daimler-Benz DB 600 engines, then under development. By the time the third prototype had been completed, the aircraft had been redesigned to meet the two-seat Zerstörer requirement, but no production order was forthcoming.

Born late in World War I, the twin-engined single-seat fighter never quite made the vogue until the mid-1940s. Desultory interest was displayed in the concept between the wars. The Boulton Paul P.31 Bittern appeared in 1927, and 10 years later, in 1937, work began on prototypes of the Westland P.9 Whirlwind. On the other side of the Atlantic, 1937 also saw work commence on the twin-boom Lockheed Model 22, destined to emerge as the XP-38 Lightning, and in the following year Grumman initiated construction of the G-34 Skyrocket. Elsewhere designers believed that there was a future for the twin-engined single-seater with an unorthodox arrangement of powerplants, one engine mounted as a tractor and the other as a pusher fore and aft of the pilot, a configuration created in 1917 for the Siemens-Schuckert DDr.I fighter, resurrected in 1931 by the Soviet designer Viktor Chernyshov for his ANT-23, and utilised again in 1938 by Fokker for the D.XXIII. The twin-engined single-seat fighter had few adherents, however, and of the aircraft in this category evolved prior to World War II, only Lockheed's P-38 was to enjoy substantial production.

High-performance fighter

Numbered among designers that *did* believe a place in the sun existed for the twin-engined single-seater was Focke-Wulf's Technical Director, Dipl.-Ing. Kurt Tank, who, in 1935, undertook a design study for a fighter in this category that he believed to offer a vastly superior performance to that of any fighter previously envisaged. No official requirement existed for such a warplane, but Tank relied on his performance calculations to convince the Technisches Amt of the desirability of developing such a fighter. His opportunity to reveal his project came early in 1936 when, under close security wraps, an exhibition of new weapons, prototypes and projects was held at the Henschel plant at Berlin-Schönefeld,

Above: The Luftwaffe threw away a winner when it rejected the Fw 187. By the time the pre-production aircraft were complete, the RLM had lost interest. Had the type been developed from the outset with the intended DB 600 engine, its performance could surely not have been ignored.

The Fw 187 V4 (D-OSNP) was the second two-seat prototype of Focke-Wulf's Falke, this joining the test programme in the late summer of 1938, being followed closely by the Fw 187 V5. The V4 was fitted with a blown single-piece windscreen, but lacked the radio mast of the V3.

Focke-Wulf Fw 187 Falke

its purpose being to apprise high-ranking party members, governmental officials and service personnel of the latest German developments in armament. Tank displayed drawings of his proposed fighter that, he claimed, would be capable of attaining 560 km/h (348 mph) if powered by two of the new Daimler-Benz DB 600 12-cylinder engines which, shortly before, had completed bench running at a rating of 641 kW (860 hp).

Above: Despite being designed for the new Daimler-Benz DB 600 engines, the Fw 187 V1 emerged with Junkers Jumo 210Ds as fitted to early Bf 109s and Ju 87s. The two rows of dark spots at the rear of the port engine cowl are the externally-mounted engine instruments. Also noteworthy are the hinged radiator intakes.

Above: The Fw 187 was characterisd by an extremely narrow fuselage, designed to reduce drag to a minimum. So cramped was its interior that certain cockpit instruments were fitted externally.

Above: The Fw 187 V1 is seen after installation of armament, which comprised two 7.9-mm (0.31-in) machine-guns flanking the cockpit. The same armament was provided for the Fw 187 V2.

Even the Führer, who attended the exhibition, was impressed, but Tank did not get the reaction that he had anticipated from representatives of the Technisches Amt. In their opinion it was pointless to utilise two engines for a fighter when one would suffice, and although Tank's project offered a greater radius of action than the new single-engined fighter monoplanes under test, the prevailing theory was that bombers of sufficient speed could be produced to dispense with any need for long-range fighter escort. Thus, the development of a twin-engined single-seat fighter was unnecessary. Tank then took his project direct to Oberst Wolfram von Richthofen, chief of the Development Section of the Technisches Amt. Von Richthofen subscribed to the view that an antidote would, sooner or later, be found for every new weapon; that the high-speed bomber would eventually be countered by interceptor fighters of even higher speed. He therefore gave Tank his support, and although his tenure of office as chief of the Development Section was destined to be brief, it was of sufficient duration for him to authorise a development contract for three prototypes of Tank's projected fighter, which was allocated the designation **Fw 187**.

The ultimate in speed

The specification accompanying the contract had been drawn up around Tank's own proposals, but with one significant change: the prototypes were to be fitted with Jumo 210 engines as all production of the more powerful DB 600 engine for at least two years ahead was earmarked for projects enjoying higher development priority. Design was entrusted to Oberingenieur Blaser who, undaunted by the lack of success attending his single-engined fighter, the Fw 159, was the most experienced member of Tank's team.

His brief was to strive for the ultimate in speed. In order to minimise drag, the light metal monocoque fuselage was, at its widest point, appreciably narrower than the fuselages of contemporary single-engined fighters. The cockpit, enclosed by a shallow, aft-sliding canopy, was literally tailored to accommodate a pilot of average build, and space was so limited that there was insufficient room on the instrument panel for all the necessary instrumentation, and rev counters, pressure gauges and other engine instruments had to be placed outside the cockpit, on the inboard sides of the engine cowlings.

The pilot was seated over the leading edge of the two-spar, metal-skinned wing that was built in three sections; the centre section, integral with the fuselage, featuring slight anhedral and accommodating fuel tanks, and the outer sections embodying marked dihedral and carrying the ailerons and flaps, wing aspect ratio being 7.7. Glazed panels were inserted in the lower portion of the extreme nose to improve the view for landing. Operated hydraulically, all three members of the undercarriage were fully retractable, the main units each having twin oleo legs and retracting aft into the engine nacelles.

The Fw 187 V1 (D-AANA) was fitted with Junkers-Hamilton airscrews for initial ground running. The aircraft subsequently received VDM propellers.

D-AANA was the initial prototype, the Fw 187 V1. The aircraft was completed in spring 1937 and was powered by two Jumo 210Da engines. Note the pressure-type pitot tube attached to the extreme nose, which verified the success of initial high-speed trials.

The first prototype, the **Fw 187 V1** (D-AANA), was rolled out in the spring of 1937 with two Jumo 210Da engines rated at 507 kW (680 hp) for take-off. They were provided with semi-retractable radiators and Junkers-Hamilton three-bladed variable-pitch airscrews. Initial flight testing was conducted by Focke-Wulf's new chief test pilot, Dipl.-Ing. Flugkapitän Hans Sander, who had left the Erprobungsstelle at Rechlin to join the company during March, and the prototype displayed an exceptional performance from its earliest test phase, clocking 525 km/h (326 mph) in level flight at 4000 m (13,120 ft) despite the relatively low output of its powerplants. The loaded weight of the Fw 187 V1 was 4600 kg (10,053 lb), more than twice that of the single-engined Bf 109B-2 single-engined fighter about to be phased into service with the Jagdflieger, and the Luftwaffenführungsstab refused to believe that the Focke-Wulf prototype had achieved a speed 80 km/h (50 mph) higher than that attained at the same altitude by its much vaunted Messerschmitt. It was suggested that Sander had been misled by faulty airspeed indicator readings. To prove that there had been no error, Oberingenieur Blaser had, at Sander's suggestion, a pressure-type pitot tube attached to the extreme nose of the Fw 187 V1 to provide absolutely accurate IAS figures, and further high-speed trials fully confirmed the earlier claim.

Pushing the limits

The wing loading of the Fw 187 V1 was considered, in the summer of 1937, impossibly high for a fighter, yet, for its size, the aircraft revealed surprisingly good levels of manoeuvrability, and its outstanding climb and dive characteristics led Tank to refer to the Fw 187 as his '**Falke**' (Falcon), using this in the sense of application rather than as an appellation. As flight testing progressed Sander steadily approached the calculated structural limitations of the Fw 187 V1, steepening dive angles on each flight. Calculations suggested that rudder flutter would not be experienced unless 1000 km/h (620 mph) was exceeded in a dive, but Blaser was personally of the opinion that the rudder would begin to flutter somewhere between 750 and 830 km/h (465 and 515 mph). At his insistence, therefore, an additional balance was fitted which, he assured Sander, would neutralise any flutter tendency provided the prototype did not exceed 740 km/h (460 mph), considered by Blaser to be the highest speed that Sander could attain in a dive with safety. Sander duly took off, climbed to around 7000 m (23,000 ft), and began his dive. The ASI was creeping towards 730 km/h (455 mph) when the tail of the aircraft began to vibrate violently. Getting no response from the controls, Sander was just preparing to bale out when he heard a loud bang in the rear fuselage and, simultaneously, the vibration ceased and full control returned. After landing

it was ascertained that the vibration had been caused by the additional balance weight, and that the audible bang had been the weight snapping off as a result of the oscillation.

Few changes were introduced on the Fw 187 V1, apart from a switch from Junkers-Hamilton to VDM airscrews, although a series of take-off and landings trials were conducted with double-wheel main undercarriage members, each wheel being fitted with a narrow, high-pressure tyre. This arrangement was found to offer no significant advantage over the original single-wheel member with low-pressure tyre to which the aircraft reverted. From the outset provision had been made for the installation of two 7.9-mm (0.31-in) MG 17 machine-guns flanking the cockpit, and they were fitted at an early flight test stage. Similar weapon provision was made for the **Fw 187 V2**, which joined the flight test programme during the summer of 1937. The second prototype was characterised by a narrower chord rudder with larger tab, balanced elevators with enlarged tabs, and a smaller, semi-retractable tailwheel. Furthermore, the Jumo 210Da engines

Above: The Fw 187 V1 suffered a failure of the starboard main undercarriage leg. The first prototype experienced its share of tribulations, including a loss of control response during high-speed trials, from which test pilot Hans Sander recovered.

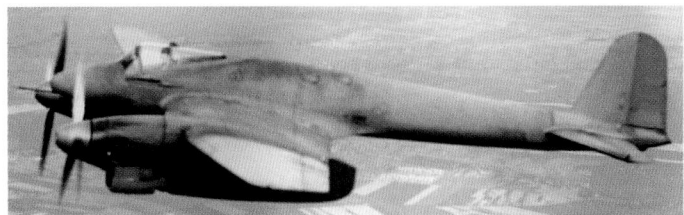

In addition to fuel-injected Jumo 210G engines with fixed intakes and ejector-type exhaust stubs, the Fw 187 V2 incorporated numerous minor improvements, including a narrower-chord rudder with a larger trim tail and a redesigned tailwheel.

Above: D-ORHP was the third prototype. Powered by Jumo 210G engines, the Fw 187 V3 first flew in spring 1938. The V3's subsequent accident, coupled with the fatal loss of the V1, did little to endear the Focke-Wulf fighter to the authorities.

Above: Seen here after a fire in the starboard engine necessitated a forced landing, the Fw 187 V3 displays the new canopy needed to accommodate a second crewman, and (just visible) the trough for one of the additional pair of dummy 20-mm cannon. Another minor change was the revised layout of the engine instruments.

The Fw 187 V4 was closely followed by the Fw 187 V5 (D-OTGN). The V5 was essentially similar to the V4. It also incorporated the modified windscreen, as did the V6.

gave place to fuel-injection Jumo 210Gs with fixed radiators and ejector-type exhaust stubs.

In June 1936, only a few months after authorising the construction of three Fw 187 prototypes, Oberst von Richthofen had been replaced as chief of the Development Section of the Technisches Amt by Ernst Udet. In some respects Udet was a visionary and in others a conventionalist. A highly experienced fighter pilot, he accepted the imminence of the biplane's demise with equanimity, subscribing to the view that the fighter had to maintain a performance advantage over its natural prey, the bomber, and could only do so by adopting a similar monoplane configuration. However, as did most of his colleagues, he believed that manoeuvrability remained of the utmost importance, and needed no convincing that, in this respect, a twin-engined aircraft could never compete on even terms with a single-engined machine. Thus, shortly after the Bf 109 had been committed to production, a fresh look had been taken by the Technisches Amt at the Fw 187, and it had been concluded that, as the Luftwaffenführungsstab could still envisage no requirement for a twin-engined single-seat interceptor fighter, the aircraft should be reconsidered as a Zerstörer, a category demanding at least two crewmembers and a heavy armament.

Several months before the Fw 187 V1 was rolled out for its initial flight trials, Tank had been instructed, therefore, to adapt the design as a two-seater, and an order for a further three prototypes was placed. While Tank considered the viewpoint of the Technisches Amt shortsighted, it was obvious that there was little likelihood of the Fw 187 being accepted for production as a single-seater, and bowing to the inevitable, Oberingenieur Blaser and his team immediately began work on the adaptation of the design to take a second crewmember. Work on the V1 and V2 was too far advanced to permit any radical changes in these prototypes, but the first metal had only just been cut on the V3, and the decision was taken to complete this as the first two-seat prototype.

Blaser was anxious to avoid any major increase in the overall dimensions of the fighter, and although a second

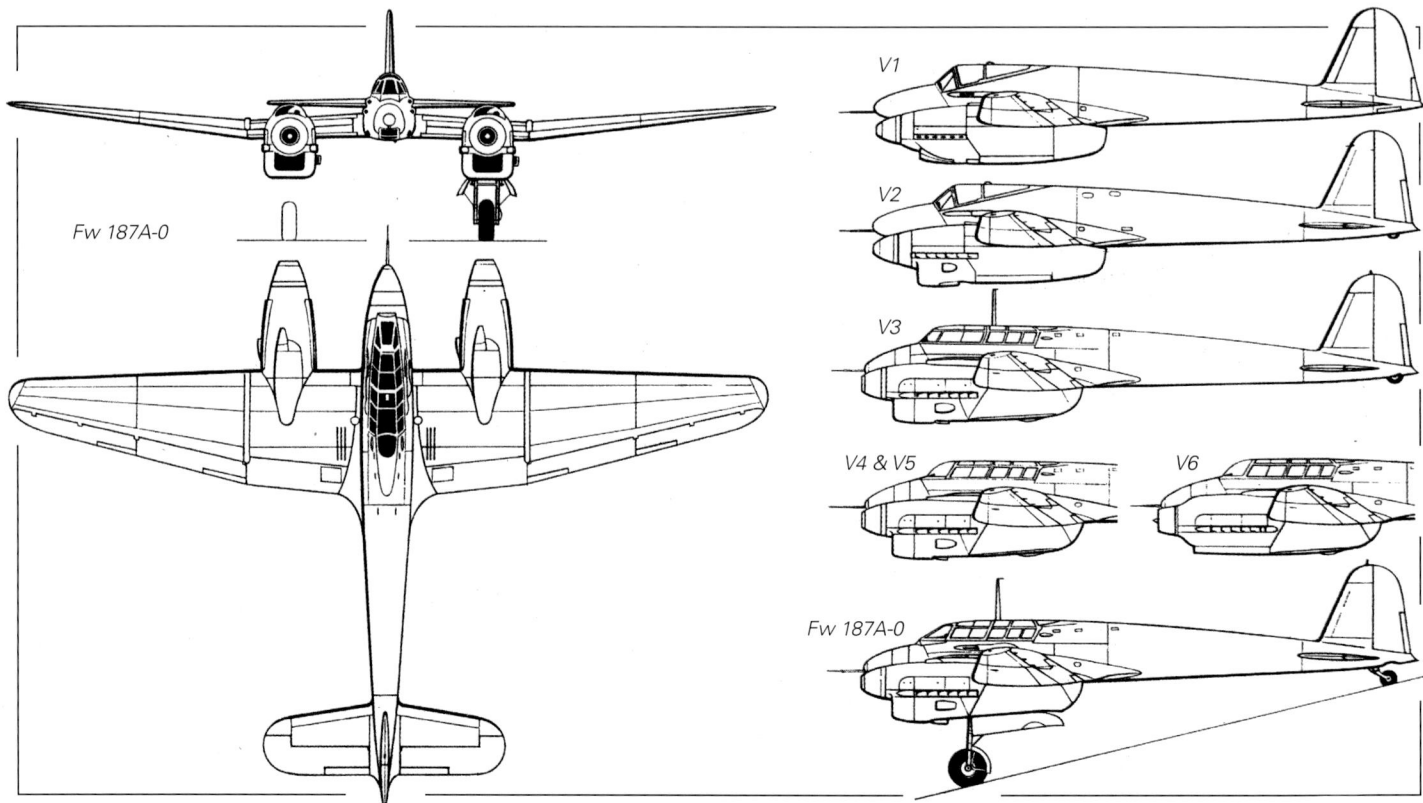

This Fw 187A-0 of the Focke-Wulf Industrie-Schutzstaffel, was used to defend the Bremen factory was in 1940. The A-0 aircraft were also used for propaganda.

cockpit was introduced to accommodate the radio operator, the fuselage was only fractionally lengthened. The insertion of the additional cockpit necessitated the repositioning of the fuselage fuel tank further aft, and to maintain the C of G position the engine bearers were lengthened. This change necessitated a redesign of the engine nacelles, the tails of which were reduced in length so that electrically-operated landing flaps could be added to the centre section trailing edge to cater for the increased landing weights. The two 7.9-mm MG 17 machine-guns were supplemented by a pair of 20-mm MG FF cannon in the lower fuselage (although only mock-ups of these weapons were, in fact, fitted), and a two-piece continuous 'greenhouse' type canopy enclosing both cockpits, the forward section hinging forward on its integral windscreen, and the rear section, complete with radio mast, hinging aft.

Powered by Jumo 210G engines, the **Fw 187 V3** (D-ORHP) was completed and flown in the early spring of 1938, but during one of the first test flights a fire in the starboard engine necessitated an emergency landing during which both main undercarriage members were ripped off. The fire was quickly extinguished, and apart from the undercarriage, the aircraft suffered only superficial damage. Some

weeks later, on 14 May 1938, misfortune again struck the test programme at Bremen, and the Fw 187 V1 was destroyed, its pilot, Bauer, losing his life. After completing his flight test schedule, Bauer had made a high-speed run across the airfield, pulled the nose of his aircraft up too sharply, stalled, and spun into the ground alongside the control tower. Although no blame for this tragic accident could be apportioned to the aircraft, coming so soon after the accident suffered by the Fw 187 V3 it did little to further the cause of the Focke-Wulf fighter with the RLM.

Prototype modifications
The **Fw 187 V4** (D-OSNP) and **V5** (D-OTGN) were completed during the late summer and autumn of 1938, and apart from some minor modifications, such as a fixed, duo-curve free-blown windscreen, were essentially similar to the V3. Evaluated at the Rechlin Erprobungsstelle, they received sufficiently favourable official flight test reports to warrant the placing of an order for yet a further three examples. In the meantime, Tank's pleas for permission to mount Daimler-Benz DB 600A engines in at least one prototype bore fruit, and permission was granted for such an installation to be made in the **Fw 187 V6**.

The Fw 187 V6 was the only aircraft to fly with the DB 600A engines for which the type was designed. With these powerplants fitted, the fighter was capable of exceeding 630 km/h (390 mph) in level flight.

Owing to the spindly fuselage and wings, the Fw 187 appeared to have engines far too large for the design. In truth, the Jumo 210s fitted to the pre-production aircraft were not powerful enough to realise the type's true potential.

A pre-production Fw 187A-0 is seen in flight. As the RAF offensive began to threaten Germany in early 1940, the Fw 187 was among the types organised into Industrie-Schutzstaffel, intended to defend the valuable aircraft production facilities. Pre-production Fw 187s formed an Industrie-Schutzstaffel to protect the Focke-Wulf plant at Bremen.

The extremely narrow fuselage and neatness of the armament installation can be seen in this view of one of the pre-production aircraft. Compared to the original single-seater, the fuselage of the two-seat Zerstörer was only marginally longer. However, the fuel tank needed to be repositioned, and consequent C of G considerations required other minor changes.

Above: The Fw 187A-0 was provided with a 'Zerstörer armament' of two 20-mm MG FF cannon and, seen here, pairs of 7.9-mm (0.31-in) MG 17 machine-guns mounted either side of the cockpit.

Above: The three Focke-Wulf Fw 187A-0 aircraft were given service markings and camouflage for genuine operational as well as propaganda purposes, and the aircraft gave convincing proof that the design had been unduly neglected. Note the machine-gun muzzles just below the pilot's cockpit.

Above: The addition of a second seat eliminated any rear view (and the radio operator could see nothing in that direction) but the clear undernose panel provided downwards view for landing.

Below: Even when converted from a single-seat fighter to a two-seat Zerstörer, the Fw 187 was extremely fast and manoeuvrable for a twin-engined aircraft. Fortunately for the Allies, the Luftwaffe stuck with the much less impressive Messerschmitt Bf 110.

Tank, like many other designers of high-speed aircraft, had become interested in the drag-reducing potential of surface evaporation cooling already demonstrated by Heinkel and under investigation by Messerschmitt. Tank elected, therefore, to embody this innovation in the Fw 187 V6 in order to wring the maximum performance possible from the aircraft. First flown early in 1939, the Fw 187 V6 (CI+NY) had 746 kW (1,000 hp) available from each engine for take-off, or nearly 43 per cent more power than was available to its Jumo 210G-engined predecessors, and a maximum of 1357 kW (1,820 hp) was to be had for brief periods at 4000 m (13,120 ft). Cooling problems were soon encountered with the evaporative system, accompanied by some skin buckling and distortion, but during a series of carefully timed and measured runs in October 1939, the Fw 187 V6 clocked 635 km/h (394.5 mph) in level flight.

Completed during the summer of 1939, the third trio of aircraft were designated as pre-production machines (**Fw 187A-01**, **-02** and **-03**), although the Luftwaffenführungsstab had already made it patently clear that, lacking rear defence, the two-seat Fw 187 did not fulfil its Zerstörer requirement, which, in any case, was being fulfilled adequately by the Bf 110. Retaining the Jumo 210G engines, the Fw 187A-0 carried full operational equipment. A heavy-gauge armour-glass windscreen was fitted, and the fixed forward-firing armament was augmented by a further pair of MG 17s in the fuselage flanks, the ammunition tanks being installed ahead of the radio operator's seat, this crew-member normally facing aft. By this time, wing loading had

Above: A close-up reveals the cramped conditions in the cockpit. Ammunition tanks were located between the pilot and radio operator, just visible behind the mid-cockpit bulkhead. The fuselage-side machine-guns were mounted very close to the radio operator.

Below: One of the three pre-production Fw 187A-0 fighters is shown in flight. These aircraft claimed a number of (doubtful) aerial victories during their sorties in defence of the Focke-Wulf factory in Bremen in 1940, before serving on an unofficial basis with 13.(Zerstörer) Staffel of JG 77 in Norway. A single pre-production aircraft was also employed by the Luftschiess-Schule (Air Gunnery School) in Denmark during 1942.

Focke-Wulf Fw 187 Falke

Luftwaffe aircrew 'scramble' to their waiting Fw 187 fighters. Despite propaganda to the contrary, the handful of aircraft completed were never officially issued to operational units.

With its narrow fuselage, short nose and powerful engines, the Fw 187 looked like a purposeful fighter. The radio operator faced aft to watch the rear hemisphere.

risen, and handling characteristics had suffered accordingly, but they were still good enough to warrant serious proposals for quantity production. However, the RLM was firm in its belief that the Bf 110 adequately fulfilled its Zerstörer requirement, and after official trials at Rechlin, the three Fw 187A-0 fighters were returned to Focke-Wulf.

As RAF intrusion of German airspace increased during the early months of 1940, several aircraft manufacturers formed their own 'Industrie-Schutzstaffel' intended for the aerial defence of the companies' facilities, manned by factory test pilots, and maintained by factory personnel. Such a unit was formed by Focke-Wulf at Bremen with the three Fw 187As, and Dipl.-Ing. Mehlhorn of the factory staff allegedly achieved several 'kills' while flying one of these aircraft. In what was presumably an endeavour to delude Allied intelligence into believing that the operational use of the Fw 187 was not merely limited to an Industrie-Schutzstaffel, with the conclusion of the French campaign the Propaganda Ministry began publicising the Focke-Wulf fighter as the new Zerstörer of the Luftwaffe. During the winter of 1940-41, the trio of Fw 187As was loaned to a Jagdstaffel based in Norway, and unofficially evaluated by service pilots, but the fate of this advanced fighter design had for long been sealed, and its career was to be confined to armament trials and equipment development tasks. In the summer of 1942, one Fw 187A-0 was temporarily attached to the Luftschiess-Schule at Vaerløse, Denmark, and in the following year a serious proposal was made to resurrect the aircraft for the night-fighting role, but discarded as impractical.

Given the availability of the intended DB 600 engines, the Fw 187 could have been a formidable fighter. In the event, the Jumo-engined model was still potent, but officials favoured the Bf 110.

Focke-Wulf Fw 187A-0 specification
Type: tandem two-seat heavy fighter
Powerplants: two Junkers Jumo 210Ga 12-cylinder liquid-cooled engines rated each at 522 kW (700 hp) for take-off and 544 kW (730 hp) at 1000 m (3,280 ft)
Performance: maximum speed 518 km/h (322 mph) at sea level, 530 km/h (329 mph) at 4200 m (13,780 ft); initial climb rate 1050 m (3,445 ft) per minute; climb to 2000 m (6,560 ft) in 1.9 minutes, to 6000 m (19,685 ft) in 5.8 minutes; service ceiling 10000 m (32,810 ft)
Weights: empty 3670 kg (8,157 lb); loaded 5000 kg (11,023 lb)
Dimensions: wingspan 15.30 m (50 ft 2¼ in); length 11.10 m (36 ft 5 in); height 3.85 m (12 ft 7½ in); wing area 30.40 m² (327.23 sq ft)
Armament: two 20-mm MG FF cannon and four 7.9-mm (0.31-in) MG 17 machine-guns

Extensive distribution of photographs of this aircraft type by the German Propaganda Ministry in the winter of 1940-41 was presumably intended to delude Allied intelligence concerning the actual status of what was referred to as the 'new Zerstörer of the Luftwaffe'.

Focke-Wulf Fw 189 Uhu

Possessing only modest performance but offering great agility and strength, the Fw 189 operated almost exclusively over the Eastern Front and provided the Luftwaffe with an exceptional tactical reconnaissance capability in support of the German army.

When, in 1941, the press department of the Reichsluftfahrtministerium (RLM) revealed the existence of the **Fw 189A** tactical reconnaissance and army co-operation monoplane, it bestowed the appropriate enough sobriquet of 'das Fliegende Auge' on this newcomer to the ranks of the Aufklärungsstaffeln (H), for, on the Eastern Front at least, the Fw 189A was destined to become literally 'The Flying Eye' of the German army. It

Above: Dispensing with the traditional concept that a tactical reconnaissance aircraft with all-round defensive cover should be a single-engined high-wing monoplane, the Fw 189 Uhu design surpassed all expectations in operational service.

Above: With its central nacelle possessing extensively glazed forward and rear sections, the Fw 189 offered its crew exceptional fields of vision for the reconnaissance task.

was to prove supremely versatile, universally popular with its pilots, and one of the most reliable aircraft ever to see Luftwaffe service, yet it was conceived at a time when few thought in terms of anything other than the classic single-engined high-wing monoplane formula as the best solution to satisfy the tasks for which the Fw 189 was conceived.

In February 1937, the first prototype of the Henschel Hs 126 was undergoing initial trials and bid fair to provide the Luftwaffe with the required replacement for the Heinkel He 46 in the Aufklärungsstaffeln (H), but the Technisches Amt of the RLM was already looking further ahead and, in that month, issued a completely new specification which demanded an aircraft appreciably more advanced than the Hs 146: a tactical reconnaissance platform carrying three crew members, offering all-round defensive cover and possessing a rather higher performance than anything previously envisaged for aircraft in this category.

From the drawing board of Dipl.-Ing. Kurt Tank, the Focke-Wulf concept of a twin-engined aircraft with twin tail booms and a central fuselage nacelle took the Technisches Amt somewhat by surprise as this organisation had envisaged a single-engined solution to its tactical reconnaissance requirement, though in fact the specification had merely suggested the desirable power and not stipulated that this should be derived from one engine. The merits of the Focke-Wulf proposal were soon apparent to the less bigoted personnel of the Technisches Amt, as were also the advantages inherent in a highly unorthodox suggestion appended by Tank to the submission, namely that interchangeable fuselage nacelles should be developed so that, while retaining the same power-plant, wing, undercarriage, tail booms and tail assembly, the same basic design could fulfil a number of roles, ranging from close support to crew training.

Like most such organisations, the Technisches Amt possessed its share of conventionalists as well as its visionaries, and the former viewed the twin-boom arrangement of the Focke-Wulf proposal with suspicion, protesting that

Supremely versatile and universally popular, the Fw 189 Uhu was essentially a low-altitude aircraft as dictated by its tactical reconnaissance role. The ride was extremely smooth, while the extensive glazing gave good visibility although, surprisingly, forward vision was impaired by refraction from the sloping panels. This example wears white distemper camouflage.

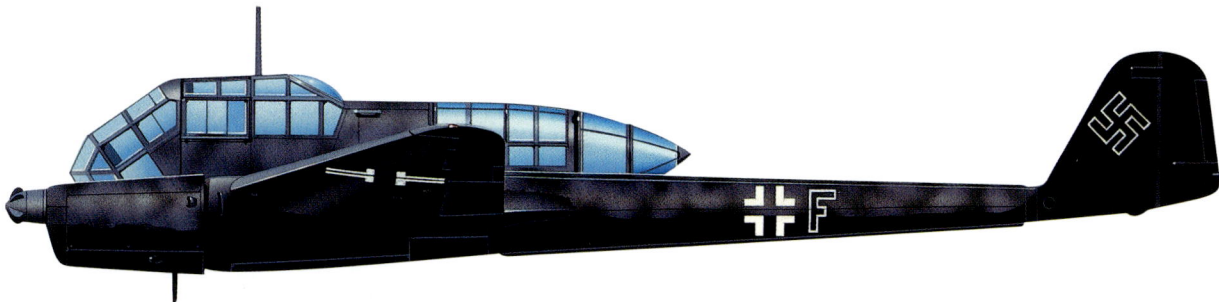

This Fw 189A-2 flew with Stab/NAGr. 15, which operated from German-occupied Poland during October 1944. Earlier, the Gruppe had parented a specialist Nachtkette for nocturnal operations.

The Fw 189's cockpit, where 'one was literally cocooned in glass', resembled the compound eye of an insect, and the propaganda department of the RLM nicknamed the type 'das Fliegende Auge' ('the flying eye').

this configuration must perforce be heavier than an orthodox fuselage, and that the open frame formed by the tail booms would be subject to distortion under the stresses of violent manoeuvres. Therefore, late in April 1937, contracts were awarded to both Arado for its more orthodox design proposal and Focke-Wulf for the construction of three prototypes of their respective projects, these being allocated the official RLM type numbers Ar 198 and Fw 189.

Prototype construction in the charge of Dipl.-Ing. E. Kosel began immediately, and the **Fw 189 V1** (D-OPVN) flew for the first time 15 months later, in July 1938, with Tank at the controls. The Fw 189 V1 was powered by two pre-production Argus As 410 air-cooled inverted V-12 engines each rated at 321 kW (430 hp) for take-off and driving a two-blade fixed-pitch propeller. It was joined by the second prototype, the **Fw 189 V2** (D-OVHD), in August and the third, the **Fw 189 V3** (D-ORMH), in September 1938. From the outset of the flight test programme the prototypes met the most sanguine expectations of the design team, and Tank promptly christened the aircraft **Eule** (owl), although this was destined to be supplanted by the popular onomatopoeic appellation **Uhu** in service.

Neatly conceived design

A low-wing cantilever monoplane, the Fw 189 was of all-metal construction. The three-spar stressed-skin wing comprised a flat, rectangular centre section between the tail booms supporting the crew nacelle on the centreline, the main and rear spars passing through the nacelle, and dihedralled, tapered outer panels attached to the centre section by bolts along the wing contour between the main and front spars, as well as at the main spar. Electrically operated fabric-covered split flaps were carried on the trailing edge between the ailerons and the booms, and across the entire centre section. The interchangeable oval-section booms carried the engine nacelles, housed the two 220-litre (48.4-Imp gal) fuel tanks, and terminated in stressed-skin vertical fins that supported

the tailplane between them. The rudders and elevators were metal-framed and fabric-covered. The hydraulically actuated main undercarriage members were raised aft into the engine nacelles and enclosed by hinged doors, and the tailwheel retracted laterally into the underside of the tailplane.

The Fw 189 V2 was essentially similar to the Fw 189 V1 but was equipped for armament trials. One 7.9-mm (0.31-in) MG 15 trainable machine-gun was mounted in the glazed nose and similar weapons fired from the dorsal step and the nacelle tail cone, two 7.9-mm (0.31-in) MG 17 fixed forward-firing machine-guns were mounted in the leading edges of the wing roots and four ETC racks, each able to lift one 50-kg (110-lb) bomb, were mounted beneath the outer wing panels. The Fw 189 V3 was not fitted with armament, but was the first prototype to be fitted with Argus automatic variable-pitch propellers and the so-called Einheitstriebwerk (standard unit) As 410 engine.

The successful outcome of initial trials with this trio of prototypes, and the generally unsatisfactory results achieved with the Ar 198 had meanwhile resulted in an order for four additional prototypes of the Fw 189. The first of them, the **Fw 189 V4** (D-OCHO), was intended as a production prototype for the planned **Fw 189A** series of short-range reconnaissance aircraft. Completed late in 1938, this prototype embodied minor changes such as revised engine cowlings; modified defensive armament that was now restricted to a pair of MG 15 machine-guns on trainable mountings; and revised undercarriage with semi-cowled main wheels and an enlarged tail wheel. After completing its factory trials, the Fw 189 V4 served as a test vehicle for various types of special equipment, including the Type S 125 smoke-screen apparatus, and spray containers for chemical warfare substances such as 'Lost' (the cover name for one of the 'Yellow Cross' group of chemicals, i.e. mustard gas compounds), which could be attached to the racks under the outer wing panels in place of the ETC bomb racks.

Fw 189B series

The second aircraft in the additional batch of four prototypes, the **Fw 189 V5**, was intended as the prototype for the planned **Fw 189B** series of trainers, and featured an entirely redesigned fuselage nacelle of refined aerodynamic shape with an

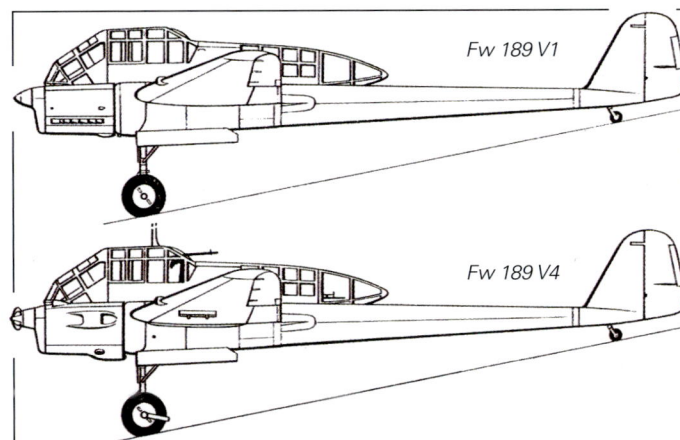

Fw 189 V1

Fw 189 V4

Focke-Wulf Fw 189 Uhu

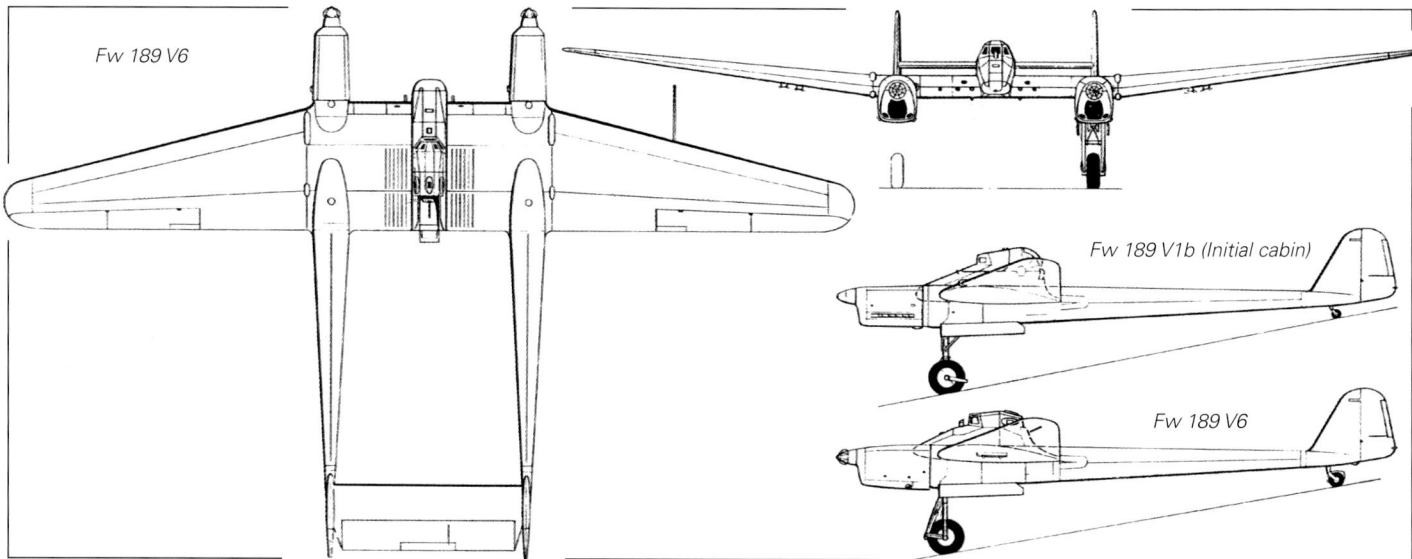

Fw 189 V6

Fw 189 V1b (Initial cabin)

Fw 189 V6

orthodox stepped windscreen. Dual controls were fitted and all armament was deleted, and the prototype of this variant first flew early in 1939. The order to start series production of the Fw 189A reconnaissance aircraft in the summer of 1939

With a completely redesigned fuselage nacelle, the Fw 189B was intended as a five-seat trainer. Delivery of 10 Fw 189B aircraft preceded Fw 189A production.

Below: The Fw 189B had a revised forward fuselage nacelle with a stepped cockpit offering side-by-side accommodation and dual controls for pilot conversion training.

did not materialise as the Oberkommando der Luftwaffe was perfectly satisfied with the Hs 126 with which it was still in the process of re-equipping the Aufklärungsstaffeln (H), but Focke-Wulf did receive instructions to proceed with a pre-production batch of three **Fw 189B-0** trainers and a production batch of **Fw 189B-1** service aircraft, delivering the pre-production machines and three of the Fw 189B-ls before the end of 1939. The remaining seven of these dual-control five-seaters were completed during January and February 1940, and subsequently delivered to the Luftwaffe.

Both landplane and twin-float seaplane variants of the trainer had originally been proposed, the float version being designated **Fw 189D**, the last of the additional batch of four prototypes, the **Fw 187 V7**, being ordered as a seaplane. The Fw 187 V7 was under construction late in 1938, employing an essentially similar airframe to that of the Fw 189 V5, but as a result of changes in seaplane procurement policy this aircraft was cancelled, the partly built airframe being completed as an Fw 189B-0.

Above: The Fw 189 V6 was completed as the first true Fw 189C prototype. It was essentially similar to the Fw 189 V1b, but incorporated variable-pitch propellers and fixed forward-firing armament in the form of two MG FF cannon and four MG 17 machine-guns. A pair of MG 81s protected the rear.

Left: The Fw 189 V1 first prototype took to the air in July 1938 with Kurt Tank at the controls. The aircraft (D-OPVN) differed little from the production aircraft that followed.

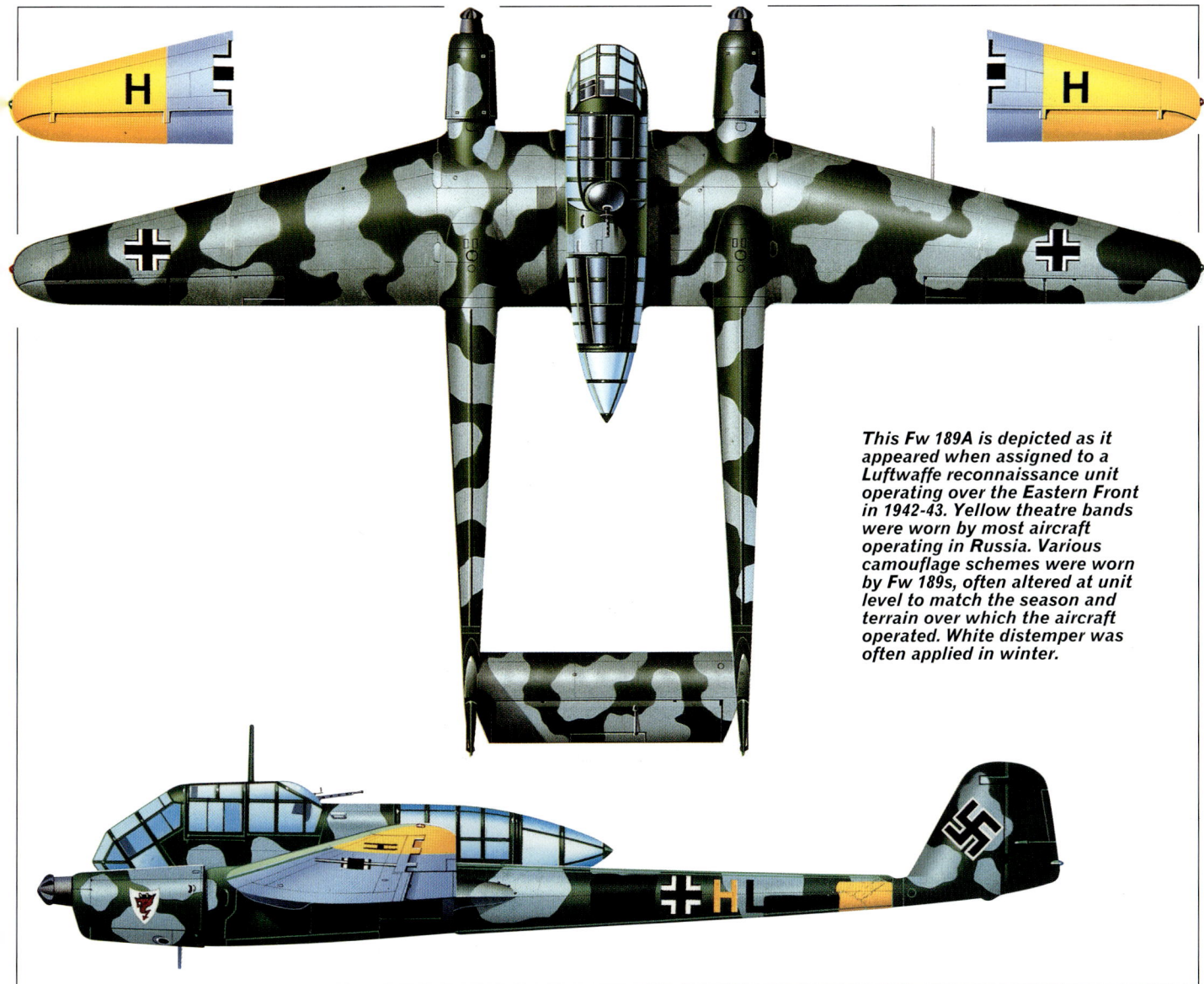

This Fw 189A is depicted as it appeared when assigned to a Luftwaffe reconnaissance unit operating over the Eastern Front in 1942-43. Yellow theatre bands were worn by most aircraft operating in Russia. Various camouflage schemes were worn by Fw 189s, often altered at unit level to match the season and terrain over which the aircraft operated. White distemper was often applied in winter.

Fw 189C series

The Fw 189 V1 was withdrawn from the flight test programme late in 1938 and returned to the Focke-Wulf company's experimental department for conversion for the assault or close-support role. The original fuselage nacelle was removed and replaced by an armoured nacelle of a size just sufficient to accommodate the pilot and a rear gunner seated back to back. The pilot peered through tiny armour-glass panels in an aft-hinged armoured hood, and the gunner was supposed to wield a single 7.9-mm (0.31-in) MG 15 trainable machine-gun through a small opening in an armoured visor.

With these changes and the designation **Fw 189 V1b**, the revised prototype resumed flight trials in the spring of 1939, but the results of these trials were sorely disappointing. The heavily armoured central nacelle changed the handling characteristics markedly for the worse, the performance was decidedly sluggish, and the test pilot reported that forward vision was totally inadequate, while the flight observer declared that from the aft seat a gunner would have difficulty in seeing an enemy fighter sitting on his tail. The Fw 189 V1b was therefore returned to the experimental department for further modification: the armour-glass panels in the pilot's hood were enlarged, and the gunner's visor was replaced by an armoured embrasure offering an improved aft field of vision and limited lateral fields of vision. Following these

further modifications, the Fw 189 V1b undertook comparative trials with the Henschel Hs 129 V2 and Hs 129 V3, which had been designed and built to meet the same assault aircraft requirement, but the results were inconclusive. While the Hs 129 was favoured on the score of size, the overall dimensions of this single-seater presenting a somewhat smaller target to ground defences, it offered its pilot an even poorer view than that enjoyed by the pilot of the competing Focke-Wulf aircraft, and while the flying characteristics of the Fw 189 V1b were poor, those of the Hs 129 were execrable. Shortly after the trials, the Fw 189 V1b was written off when, during a demonstration at Bremen, the pilot managed to avoid collision with a hangar, which he had not been able to see until the last moment, only by pancaking the aircraft very heavily.

However, the third of the additional four prototypes, the **Fw 189 V6**, had been ordered as a prototype for the **Fw 189C** assault model, and this machine was completed and test flown at the beginning of 1940. The armoured central nacelle was essentially similar to the definitive nacelle tested on the Fw 189 V1b, Argus As 410A-1 engines offering 347 kW (465 hp) for take-off and driving variable-pitch propellers supplanted the pre-production As 410 engines with their fixed-pitch propellers, a new undercarriage arrangement was introduced with twin oleo legs for the main members,

Focke-Wulf Fw 189 Uhu

The Fw 189A-1 equipped the majority of the Luftwaffe's numerous short-range tactical reconnaissance units in the USSR. Featuring the new Wellenmuster, or wave-mirror, pattern of camouflage, this aircraft served with 1.(H)/32 from the Petsamo base in December 1942 on the northern sector, in northern Finland.

and a new wing centre section was adopted. This centre section accommodated the fixed forward-firing armament of two 20-mm MG FF cannon and four 7.9-mm (0.31-in) MG 17 machine-guns. The rear gunner was provided with a pair of 7.9-mm (0.31-in) MG 81 machine-guns on a trainable mounting.

In the meantime, Henschel had begun construction of a pre-production batch of Hs 129A-0 assault aircraft, and by September 1940, when the Fw 189 V6 reached the Erprobungsstelle Rechlin, service suitability trials with them were already being undertaken by 5.(Schlacht)/Staffel of Lehrgeschwader 2 and, while the service pilots were very vociferous in their condemnation of the Henschel aircraft, the RLM concluded that the combination of various proposed improvements and a unit cost little more than two-thirds that of the competing Focke-Wulf design justified the selection of the Hs 129, and all proposals for production of the Fw 189C were abandoned.

Fw 189A series

Meanwhile, during the spring of 1940, Focke-Wulf had finally received production orders for the Fw 189A tactical reconnaissance aircraft, and a pre-production batch of 10 **Fw 189A-0** machines had been followed on the Bremen assembly line by the initial production version, the **Fw 189A-1**, 20 examples of which had been completed by the end of the year. By this time a full service evaluation was being undertaken by the Aufklärungsstaffeln (H). The favourable service reports, coupled with the OKL's somewhat tardy acceptance of the obsolescence of the Hs 126A, a fact underlined by combat attrition during the French campaign of May and June 1940, led to the allocation of a high priority to Fw 189A production, and a second assembly line was established at the former Aero plant at Prague in German-occupied Czechoslovakia.

Production tempo built up rapidly at Focke-Wulf's Bremen facility, but had begun to taper off during the early summer months as a consequence of the plant's more urgent commitment to the Fw 190 fighter programme, and thus, while the parent company delivered only 99 Fw 189As during the course of 1941, the Aero plant delivered 151, and towards

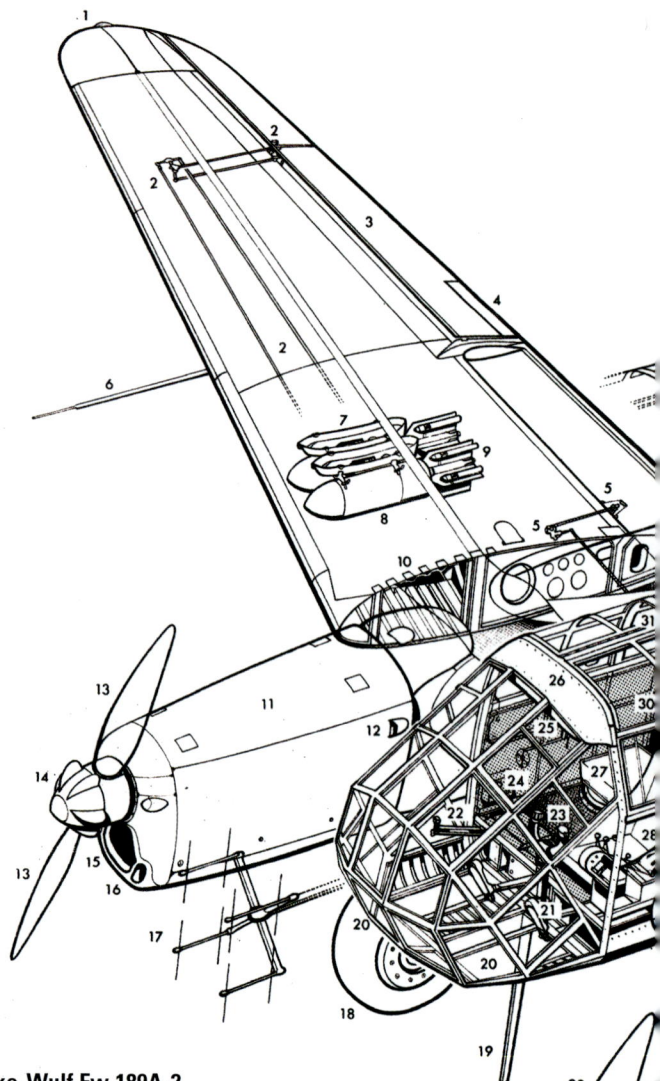

Relatively few Fw 189s were built at Bremen, most deliveries coming from the former Aero factory in Prague, Czechoslovakia, and French factories in the Bordeaux area.

Focke-Wulf Fw 189A-2 cutaway key

1 Starboard navigation light
2 Aileron control linkage (outer and inner)
3 Starboard aileron
4 Aileron tab
5 Starboard outer flap control linkage
6 Pilot tube
7 ETC 50/VIIId underwing rack fairings
8 Two 50-kg (110 lb) SC 50 bombs
9 Papier-maché 'screamers' attached to bomb fins
10 Wing centre/outer section join
11 Starboard engine nacelle
12 Air intake
13 Argus two-bladed controllable-pitch propeller
14 Pitch control vanes
15 Oil cooler intake
16 Engine air intake
17 FuG 212 Lichtenstein C-1 radar array (fitted to night-fighter adaptation)
18 Starboard mainwheel

Focke-Wulf Fw 189 Uhu

This Fw 189A-1 was allocated to 1.Aufklärungsstaffel (Heeres)/32, based at Petsamo in Finland during June 1942. The brown/green splinter camouflage was common in this theatre during the summer months.

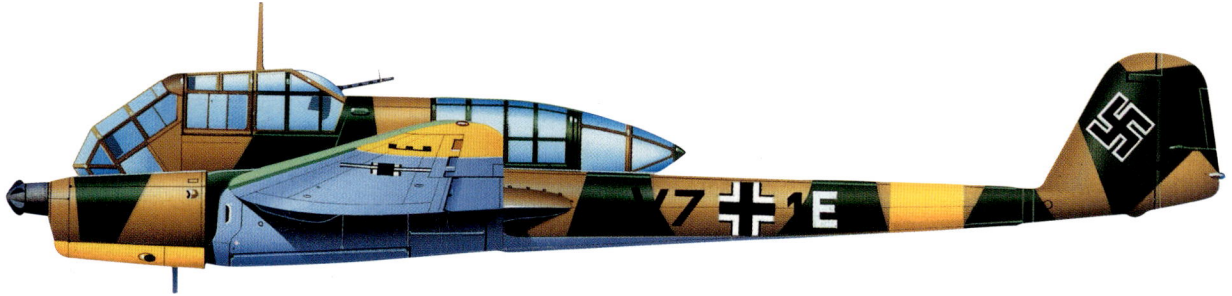

19 Ventral radio mast
20 Optically flat nose panels
21 Rudder pedals
22 GV219d bomb sight
23 Control column
24 Bomb switch panel
25 Pilot's ring-and-bead sight (for fixed wing-root machine-guns)
26 Padded overhead instrument panel
27 Navigator's swivel seat
28 Throttle levers
29 Pilot's seat
30 Mainspar carry-through
31 Centre-hinged two piece canopy hatch

32 Turnover bar with attached plasticised anti-glare curtain
33 Radio equipment

34 Shell collector box
35 Centre-section camera well (one Rb 20/30, Rb 50/30, Rb 21/18 or Rb 15/18 camera)
36 Canvas shell collection chute
37 Dorsal turret
38 MG 81Z twin 7.9-mm machine-gun
39 MG 151 (15-mm) fixed cannon in 'schräge Musik' installation (fitted to night-fighter adaptation)
40 Starboard tailboom
41 Rudder and elevator control cables

42 Ammunition stowage (dorsal position)
43 Entry handholds
44 Centre-section flap below crew nacelle
45 Wing-root gun access panel (raised)
46 Rear turret cone drive motor
47 Rear gunner's two-piece quilted pad

48 Ammunition stowage (rear position)
49 Rear canopy opening
50 MG 81Z twin 7.9-mm machine-guns (trunnion mounted)

51 Revolving Ikarin powered cone turret
52 Field of fire cut out
53 Aft glazing
54 Tailboom mid-section strengthening frame

55 Starboard tailfin
56 Starboard rudder
57 Rudder tab
58 Elevator construction
59 Tailplane forward spar
60 Elevator tab
61 Tatiplane construct
62 Tailwheel hinged (two piece) door
63 Tailwheel (swivelling)
64 Tail wheel retraction mechanism
65 Tailwheel well (offset to port)
66 Tailfin construction
67 Rudder tab

68 Rear navigation light
69 Tail bumper
70 Tailboom frames
71 Tailboom upper longeron
72 Mid-section strengthening frame
73 Tail surface control cables
74 External stiffening strake (upper and lower)
75 Master compass
76 Wing root fairing
77 Port outer flap construction
78 Aileron tab
79 Aileron construction

80 Port navigation light
81 Wing stringers (upper shell)
82 Lower shell wing inner skin stringers
83 Two-piece shaped wing ribs
84 Mainspar structure
85 Mainspar/boom attachment point
86 Rear spar/boom attachment point
87 Port fuel tank (110 litres/24.2 Imp gal)
88 Centre section one-piece flap
89 Wing walkway
90 Fixed 7.9-mm MG 17 machine-gun

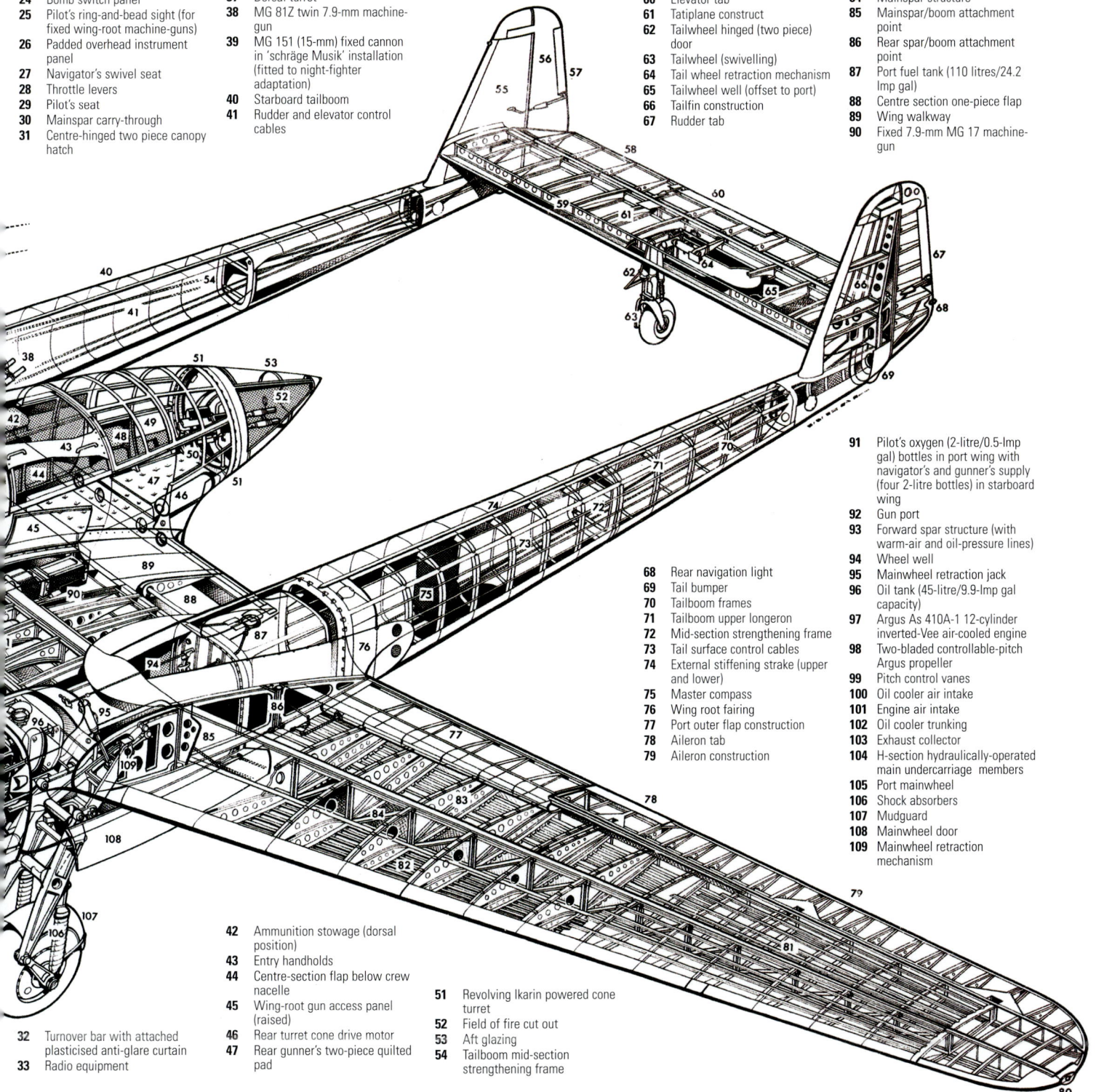

91 Pilot's oxygen (2-litre/0.5-Imp gal) bottles in port wing with navigator's and gunner's supply (four 2-litre bottles) in starboard wing
92 Gun port
93 Forward spar structure (with warm-air and oil-pressure lines)
94 Wheel well
95 Mainwheel retraction jack
96 Oil tank (45-litre/9.9-Imp gal capacity)
97 Argus As 410A-1 12-cylinder inverted-Vee air-cooled engine
98 Two-bladed controllable-pitch Argus propeller
99 Pitch control vanes
100 Oil cooler air intake
101 Engine air intake
102 Oil cooler trunking
103 Exhaust collector
104 H-section hydraulically-operated main undercarriage members
105 Port mainwheel
106 Shock absorbers
107 Mudguard
108 Mainwheel door
109 Mainwheel retraction mechanism

5.(H)/Aufklärungsgruppe 12 was operating this Fw 189A-1 (H1+EN) in the Poltava, Ukraine, region as part of Luftflotte IV during the summer of 1942. In March 1943 it was redesignated as 2.Staffel of Nahaufklärungsgruppe 2 as part of the reorganisation of reconnaissance units.

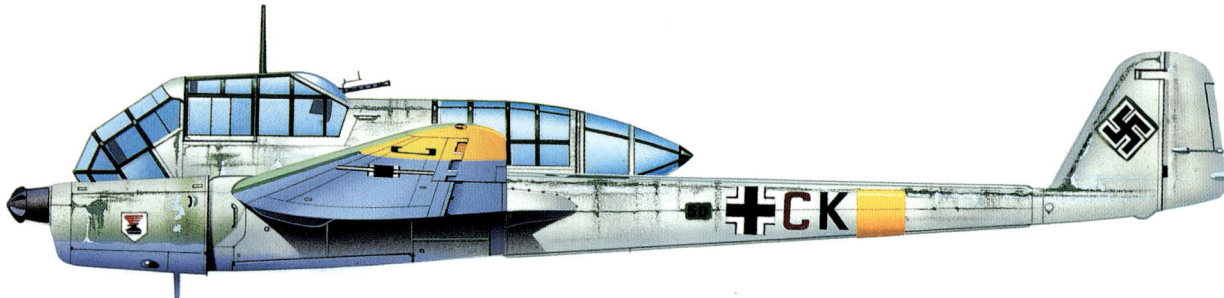

Covered with a white distemper for winter operations, this Fw 189A-2 (5D+CK) of 2.(H)/31 was based at Kursk, under the command of the Luftwaffekommando Don, during January 1943. This squadron was subsequently renumbered as 3./NAGr. 4.

Above: Stable horizontal flight and reasonably tight turns were possible at normal all-up weight at altitudes of up to 4500 m (14,765 ft), which was the single-engined service ceiling and at which the indicated speed was of the order of 160 km/h (99 mph), as compared with 180 km/h (112 mph) at ground level.

the end of the year the necessary jigs were delivered from Bremen to factories in the Bordeaux area for production of the Fw 189A to be started in France, where final assembly was carried out at Mérignac.

Refined production model

The Fw 189A-1 was basically similar to the Fw 189 V4, apart from some additional aerodynamic refinement of the engine cowlings, the use of As 410A-1 standard units, twin-leg main undercarriage members, and minor changes in operational equipment. The armament was standardised as two 7.9-mm (0.31-in) MG 17 fixed forward-firing machine-guns in the wing roots and two 7.9-mm (0.31-in) MG 15 machine-guns on trainable mountings, and four ETC 50/VIII racks were provided beneath the outboard wing panels for 50-kg (110-lb) SC 50 bombs. One Rb 20/30 camera was normally installed, but optional installations were the Rb 50/30, Rb 21/18 or Rb 15/18 cameras, and a hand-held HK 12.5 or HK 19 camera was usually carried. The crew comprised the pilot, navigator/radio operator who doubled as bombardier and dorsal gunner, and flight mechanic who doubled as rear gunner.

The Fw 189A-1 was succeeded on the assembly lines in mid-1941 by the **Fw 189A-2** that differed solely in having strengthened defensive armament, this comprising 7.9-mm (0.31-in) MG 81Z (twin MG 81) machine-gun installations in both the dorsal position and the cone of the fuselage nacelle. Manufactured in parallel was the **Fw 189A-3** dual-control pilot trainer, which was delivered to the Luftwaffe only in small numbers but supplemented by a number of Fw 189A-0 and Fw 189A-1 aircraft modified to a similar standard.

The first Fw 189A-0 aircraft had been delivered to a training Staffel, 9.(H)/LG 2, in the autumn of 1940, this unit earlier having received several of the Fw 189B trainers during the previous spring, but when the German 'Barbarossa' invasion of the USSR began on 22 June 1941, all the operational Aufklärungsstaffeln (H)

This Fw 189A-2 was operational with 1.(H)/31 at Demyansk during the summer of 1942. The emblem of 1.(H)/31, a sword superimposed by an eagle with forked lightning projecting from its claws, can be seen on the engine cowling.

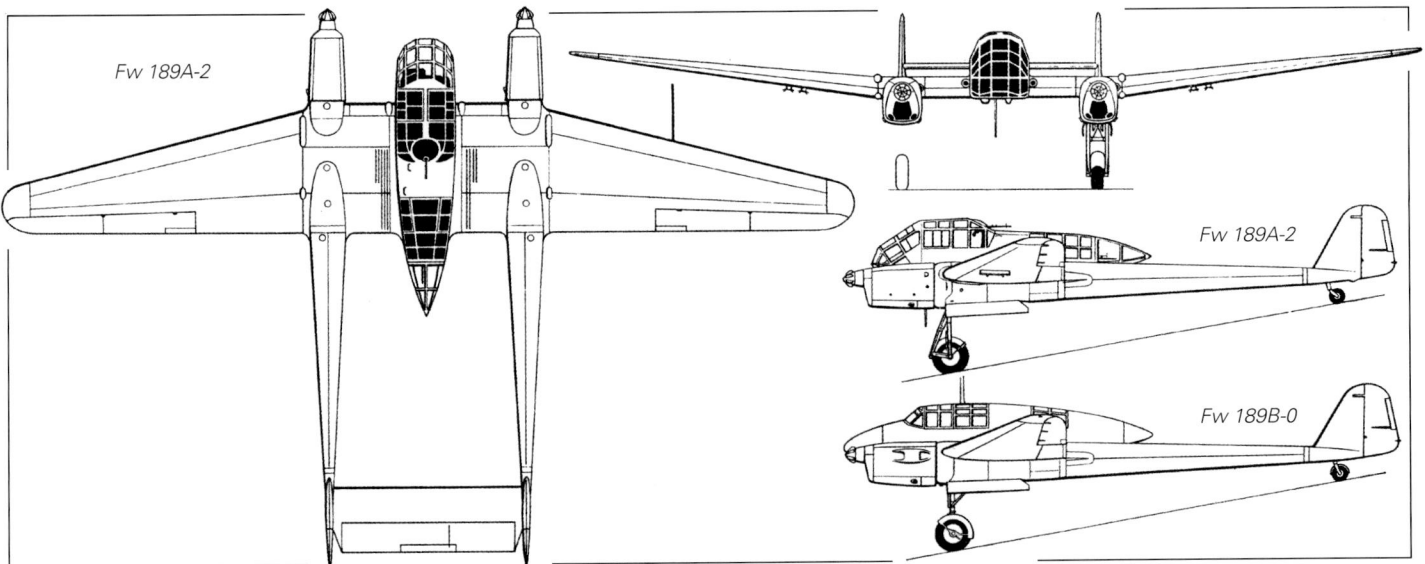

Fw 189A-2

Fw 189A-2

Fw 189B-0

were still equipped with the Hs 126. However, by the end of 1941, units were being progressively withdrawn for re-equipment, and in the spring of 1942 substantial numbers of Fw 189A-1 and Fw 189A-2 aircraft were appearing in the ranks of the Aufklärungsstaffeln (H) and their successors, the Nahaufklärungsgruppen, on the Eastern Front, where the type was to serve almost exclusively.

The year 1942 saw a marked increase in production deliveries of the Fw 189A, despite the fact that the manufacture of this type was steadily tapering off at the Bremen plant where only 57 machines were built. The Aero plant produced 183 machines, but the principal reason for the increased deliveries was the phasing in of the Bordeaux group of factories, which delivered 87 Fw 189A machines during the course of 1942, the Mérignac plant attaining an assembly rate of 20 machines per month in September of that year. By the spring of 1943, the French factories had become the sole source of Fw 189A supply, the Bremen and Prague factories finally phasing out production in the first two months of 1943 with 11 and three machines, respectively, while 194 examples left the Mérignac assembly line which, with a further 12 machines produced during the first weeks of 1944, brought total production of the Fw 189A to 828 aircraft, excluding prototypes.

During 1942, a batch of 14 Fw 189A-1 aircraft was supplied to the Slovak air force, and late in the year a quantity of Fw 189A-2 machines reached Hungary to equip the Hungarian 3/1 Short-Range Reconnaissance Squadron, which was deployed to the Eastern Front from March 1943, saw extensive use in the summer offensive around Kharkov, and continuously undertook reconnaissance and light bombing sorties in support of the Hungarian forces until March 1944. In Luftwaffe service the Fw 189A had virtually supplanted

completely the Hs 126A with the Nahaufklärungsgruppen on the Eastern Front by the end of 1942, and one Staffel with a mixture of Fw 189A and Bf 110C aircraft was operating in North Africa. In operational service, the Fw 189A surpassed all expectations, proving capable of undertaking sorties under the most adverse conditions and of absorbing considerable punishment yet still regaining its base. It was sufficiently agile to evade all but the most determined fighter attacks, and

Above: The Fw 189's chosen engine – and nobody ever regretted it – was the Argus As 410A-1, an air-cooled inverted V-12 unit. Very smooth at 3,100 rpm, and easy to start even in a Russian winter, this engine proved very reliable.

Left: Fw 189 was essentially a low-level aircraft and was very stable even in the bumpy air encountered close to the ground. The type also offered great agility and considerable strength.

Powerplant
The Fw 189 was powered by a pair of Argus As 410A-1 air-cooled inverted V-12 engines, each rated at 346 kW (465 hp) and driving a variable-pitch, two-blade Argus propeller.

2./NAGr. 16
This unit was formed in Russia in October 1942, serving in the southern sector. In 1944 it fell back with the retreating Wehrmacht through Bessarabia, being based at Kishinev (today Chisinau, the Moldovan capital) for much of the spring and summer. The subsequent retreat took the unit through Hungary and into Austria.

Configuration

The Luftwaffe's Technisches Amt visualised that its requirement for a new aircraft for the Aufklärungsstaffeln, to replace the ageing Heinkel He 46, would be met by a single-engined type, probably a high-winged monoplane. The competing Arado Ar 198 was just such a machine, but the Blohm und Voss BV 141 and the Focke-Wulf submission were more unconventional. The asymmetric BV 141 combined a glazed crew pod with a separate tail boom and single engine nacelle, while the Fw 189 featured two smaller engines, with interchangeable oval-section twin booms supporting the tail unit, and with a central crew nacelle. Of all-metal construction, the Fw 189 had a three-spar stressed-skin wing, with a rectangular centre-section supporting the crew nacelles and tail boom/engine nacelles, and with tapering outer panels. The fabric-covered split trailing-edge flaps were electrically operated, while the fabric-covered, metal-framed ailerons, rudders and elevator were manually operated.

Roles

Kurt Tank designed the Fw 189 to be a modular aircraft, with interchangeable fuselage nacelles to allow the basic design to fulfil a variety of roles. An Fw 189B was planned as a five-seat trainer, while the Fw 189C was designed with a small, heavily armoured nacelle housing pilot and gunner for the assault role. Neither version was selected for major production. The Fw 189A was intended as a reconnaissance type for the Aufklärungsstaffeln (H), with a crew of three consisting of a pilot sitting to port, with a navigator beside him on a swivelling seat that gave access to the glazed nose and to the twin defensive MG 81Z 7.9-mm (0.31-in) machine-guns mounted in the rear part of the main canopy. A dedicated gunner manned the Ikaria tailcone turret, with its second pair of MG 81Z machine-guns.

Production

Production of the Fw 189 at Bremen built up rapidly, but attrition of the Hs 126A in France was such that a second production line was set up at the former Aero factory in Prague. Production at Bremen tailed off during 1941, as a result of the plant's commitment to Fw 190 production, and jigs were transferred to Mérignac in France, which became the sole source of Fw 189 production during early 1943. A total of 828 production Fw 189s was produced, 293 of them from Mérignac and 337 from Prague.

Armament

Although intended for the reconnaissance role, the Fw 189 was surprisingly well armed. In addition to the two pairs of 7.9-mm (0.31-in) MG 81Z machine-guns in the crew nacelle (single MG 15s of the same calibre in the Fw 189A-1), the aircraft had a pair of 7.9-mm (0.31-in) MG 17 machine-guns in the wing roots and bomb racks for up to eight 50-kg (110-lb) SC 50 bombs. The final major production version, the Fw 189A-4, had increased armour protection and introduced 20-mm MG FF cannon in the wing roots.

Undercarriage

The Fw 189's tailplane retracted to port to lie within the tailplane, while the main undercarriage units retracted aft into the engine nacelle/tailboom junctions.

Focke-Wulf Fw 189A-2

2.Staffel, Nahaufklärungsgruppe 16
Graz-Thalerhof, 1945

This Fw 189A-2 of 2./NAGr. 16 is seen with Eastern Front tactical markings in yellow, as it was when captured by US forces at Graz in 1945. The slender wing, matchstick booms and small Argus engines of the Fw 189 did not give rise to much optimism when viewed for the first time, yet the type achieved an enviable reputation with its pilots. Superbly agile, the Uhu could escape most fighter attacks by tight turns, while the reliable engines and smooth ride made it a comfortable aeroplane in which to fly. Most served on the Eastern Front, wearing the theatre markings of yellow bands around the boom and wingtips. This is an Fw 189A-2, which introduced the MG 81Z twin machine-gun installation to both dorsal and tailcone positions.

Iain Wyllie

This Fw 189A-2 flew with 3/1 Ungarische Nahaufklärungsstaffel (Hungarian Short-range Reconnaissance Squadron) attached to Luftflotte IV, based at Zamocz in eastern Poland in March 1944.

provided it possessed a well co-ordinated crew, its defensive armament was effective enough to deter even these. On occasions it survived Soviet Taran (ramming) attacks, returning to base with half the vertical tail surfaces missing.

The final Fw 189A production model, which was introduced onto the assembly lines late in 1942, was the **Fw 189A-4** that was intended to fulfil both the tactical reconnaissance and close support tasks. Two 20-mm MG FF cannon replaced the 7.9-mm (0.31-in) MG 17 machine-guns in the wing roots, and light armour was added beneath the engine nacelles, fuel tanks and parts of the fuselage nacelle.

Consideration was given to producing a version of the Fw 189 powered by two Gnome-Rhône 14M 4/5 air-cooled 14-cylinder two-row radial engines each rated at 522 kW (700 hp) for take-off, and one Fw 189A-1 airframe was actually converted to take engines of this type after installation

Above: Everything about the Fw 189 was slender, especially the wing and tail booms. Despite this, the Uhu was an immensely strong aircraft, able to sustain large amounts of battle damage. The latter was a vital asset in the low-level, over-the-battlefield environment in which the Uhu operated.

Above: The Fw 189's cockpit layout was basically simple, and after ensuring that the canopy hatches were secured, the fuel safety cock levers checked, the main power supply switched on, and the temperature and pressure gauges working, the single cockpit switch automatically controlling the Argus two-blade vane-operated controllable-pitch propellers was set to start.

A view of the fuselage nacelle from the tail shows the rotating Ikaria powered cone turret. Together with the machine-gun(s) in the dorsal position, this gave the Fw 189 a useful tail 'sting' to ward off fighters seeking to attack from a position above and to the rear of the German reconnaissance aircraft. The type was considered agile, and proved quite a challenge for enemy fighters.

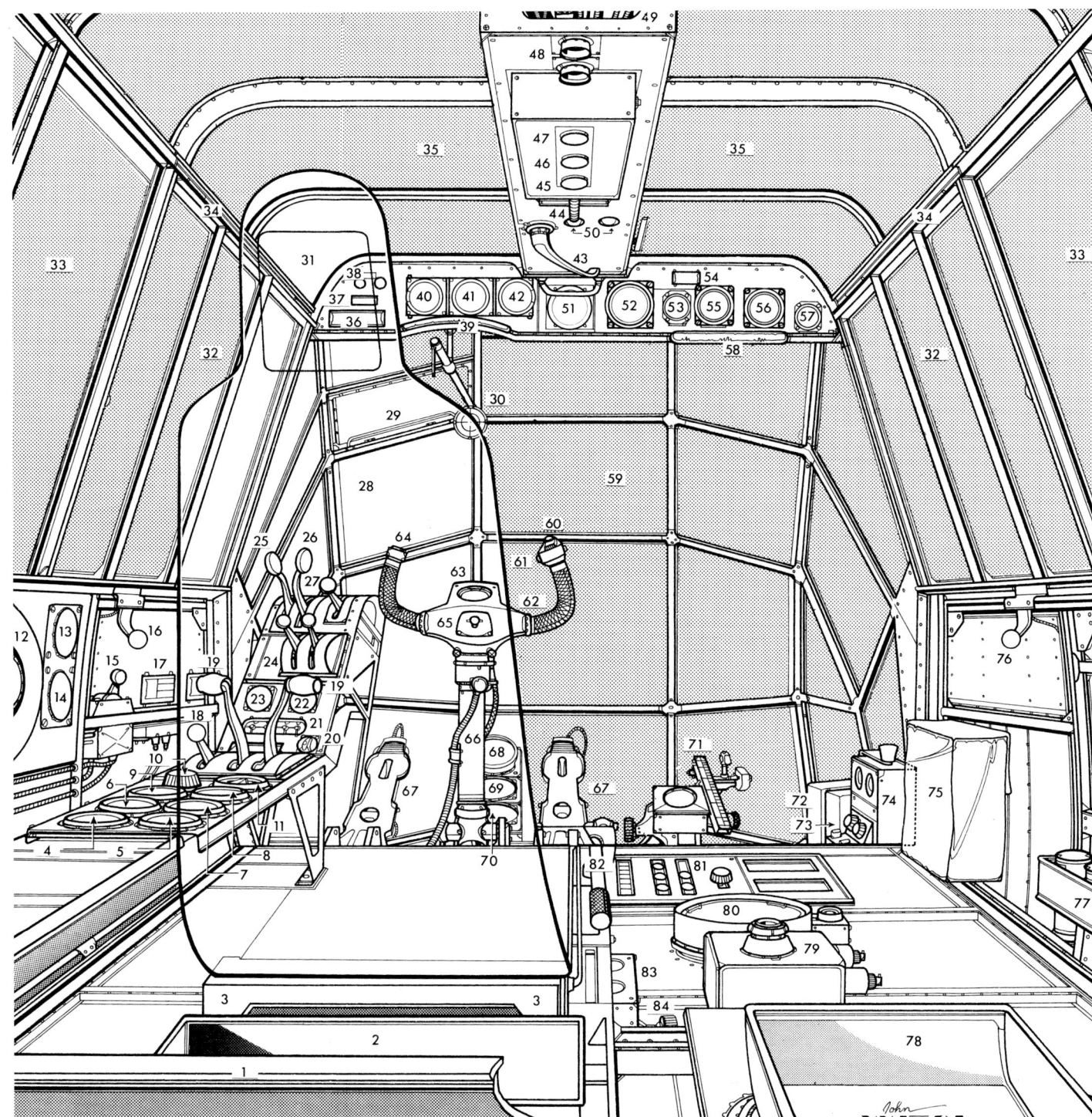

Focke-Wulf Fw 189A cockpit layout

1 Mainspar carry-through
2 Dorsal gun position shell-collector box
3 Seat support frame
4 Fuel contents gauge (port tank)
5 Fuel contents gauge (starboard tank)
6 Fuel and oil pressure gauge (port)
7 Fuel and oil pressure gauge (starboard)
8 Elevator trim indicator
9 Rudder trim indicator
10 Propeller setting switch
11 Flap positioning switch
12 Oxygen diaphragm
13 Oxygen pressure gauge
14 Oxygen monitor (pilot)
15 Landing lamp switch
16 Entry hatch locking mechanism (port)
17 Compass deviation cards
18 Fuel mixture control

19 Throttle levers
20 Master battery cut-out
21 Flap and undercarriage warning lamps
22 Oil temperature gauge (starboard)
23 Oil temperature gauge (port)
24 Ignition switches
25 Fuel safety cock lever (port)
26 Fuel safety cock lever (starboard)
27 Undercarriage lever
28 Pilot's seat
29 Hinged direct vision panel
30 Ring-and-bead gunsight
31 Pilot's armoured headrest
32 Hinged entry panels (lower section)
33 Fixed side panels
34 Hinge line
35 Hinged entry panels (upper section)
36 SKK 20-2

37 Pitot-tube heating indicator
38 Fuel contents warning lamps (port and statboard)
39 Pilot's leather crash pad
40 Airspeed indicator
41 Altimeter
42 Rate-of-climb indicator
43 Emergency canopy jettison handle
44 Grab handle
45 Instrument panel lighting switch
46 Navigation light automatic switch
47 Pilot-tube heating automatic switch
48 R/T headset sockets
49 Main instrument panel wiring conduit
50 Fire extinguisher buttons (port and starboard)
51 Turn-and-bank indicator
52 Artificial horizon
53 Radio-navigation indicator

54 Rudder trimming switch
55 Pilot's repeater compass
56 Manifold pressure gauge (port and starboard)
57 Cockpit illumination dimmer switch
58 Navigator's leather crash pad
59 Optically flat nose panels
60 Machine-gun firing button
61 Bomb release button
62 Charger switch (reverse face of control horn)
63 Clock
64 Elevator trimming switch
65 Cut-out switch
66 Control column
67 Rudder pedals (mounted on cantilever beams)
68 Direct-reading compass*
69 RPM indicator (port)*
70 RPM indicator (starboard)"
71 GV 219d bomb sight

72 FuG 25 radio control unit
73 G 4 D/F control unit
74 Remote-control unit and key
75 Navigator's map case
76 Entry hatch locking mechanism (starboard)
77 Flare cartridges (four)
78 Navigator's seat (rotating)
79 Picture-interval regulator
80 Picture-overlap control
81 Bomb release switch panel (with smokescreen apparatus)
82 Seat adjusting lover
83 Ignition switch box
84 Cockpit heating control

* mounted on canopy frame (forward of fuselage step)

Above: Fw 189A-1s are lined up fresh from the factory, awaiting armament. A very tough machine, the Fw 189 handled superbly and some reportedly returned minus one tail boom after undergoing ramming attacks by Soviet aircraft.

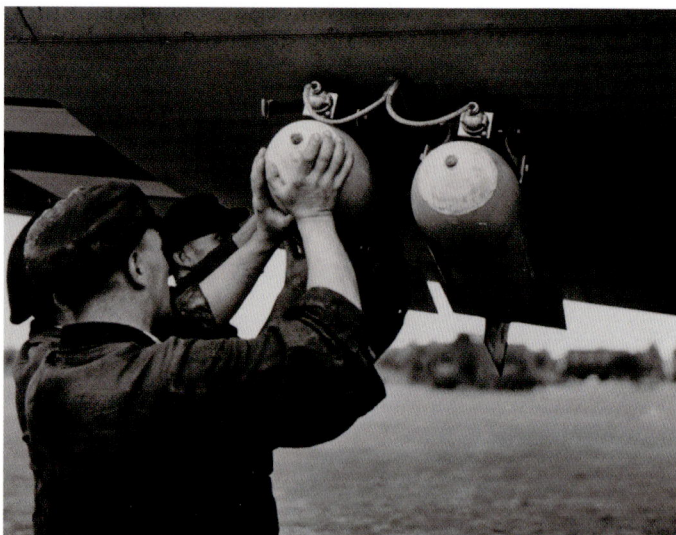

Above: An armourer completes the loading of an SC 50 bomb on an Fw 189's underwing bomb rack. Though small, such bombs provided a useful if limited close support capability.

Other underwing armament options for the Fw 189 were a pair of underwing containers for smoke or chemical warfare attacks.

drawings had been prepared by the SNCASO drawing office at Châtillon-sur-Seine. It was proposed that the version with the Gnome-Rhône powerplant should be manufactured as the **Fw 189E**, but the prototype crashed in the vicinity of Nancy while being ferried to Germany for evaluation, and the entire scheme was abandoned.

More power but little production

Another more powerful version of the basic design was the **Fw 189F-1** which, employing a basic Fw 189A-2 airframe, was powered by a pair of Argus As 411MA-1 engines. These powerplants were similar in general construction to the As 410A-1 but had a different gear ratio and increased r.p.m., offered 432 kW (580 hp) for take-off and 447 kW (600 hp) at 600 m (1,970 ft). When assembly finally came to a halt at Mérignac in 1944, the Fw 189F-1 had just been phased onto the production line, and only 17 examples of this version were delivered to the Luftwaffe. A more radically modified development, the **Fw 189G** with Argus As 402 engines each rated at 708 kW (950 hp), as well as a number of structural changes, was planned for production in 1942, but in the event the As 402 engine failed to attain production status, necessitating the abandonment of this project.

Focke-Wulf Fw 189A-2 specification
Type: three-seat tactical reconnaissance and army co-operation aircraft
Powerplant: two Argus As 410-1 air-cooled inverted V-12 engines each rated at 347 kW (465 hp) for take-off and 309 kW (415 hp) at 2400 m (7,875 ft)
Performance: [at 3950 kg (8,708 lb)] maximum speed 350 km/h (217 mph) at 2400 m (7,875 ft); maximum cruising speed 325 km/h (202 mph) at 2400 m (7,875 ft); economical cruising speed 305 km/h (190 mph) at optimum altitude; service ceiling 7300 m (23,950 ft); normal range 670 km (416 miles); endurance 2 hours 10 minutes
Weights: empty 2830 kg (6,239 lb); empty equipped 3245 kg (7,154 lb); normal loaded 3950 kg (8,708 lb); maximum take-off 4170 kg (9,193 lb)
Dimensions: wingspan 18.40 m (60 ft 4½ in); length 12.03 m (39 ft 5½ in); height 3.10 m (10 ft 2 in); wing area 38.00 m² (409.03 sq ft)
Armament: two 7.9-mm (0.31-in) MG 17 fixed forward-firing machine-guns in the wing roots, two 7.9-mm (0.31-in) MG 81 trainable rearward-firing machine-guns in the dorsal position, and two 7.9-mm (0.31-in) MG 81 trainable rearward-firing machine-guns in tail of the fuselage nacelle, plus four 50-kg (110-lb) SC 50 bombs on ETC 50/VIIId underwing racks

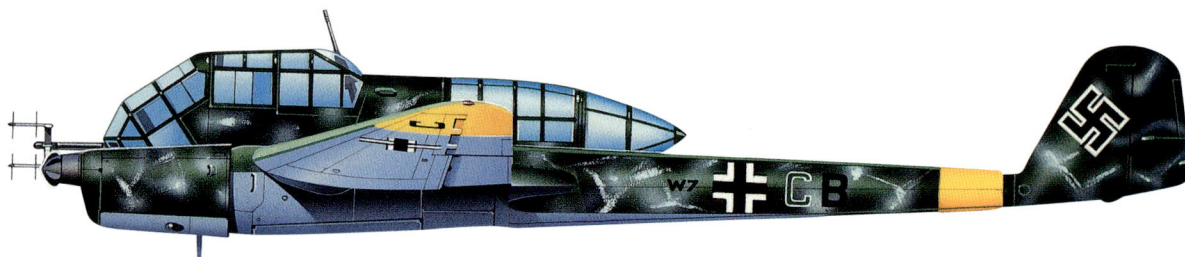

From March 1944 Fw 189As were equipped with radar and flown by NJG 100 in the extemporised night-fighter role. This aircraft carries the codes of Stab I/ NJG 100, which flew from various Polish and North German bases as German forces retreated. It ended the war at Lübeck.

Focke-Wulf Fw 190

Without doubt one of the premier combat aircraft of World War II, the Fw 190 was built in large numbers in several major production versions for fighter and fighter-bomber operations. Feared by the Allies, it became a centrally important tool in the German war machine between 1941 and the end of the war.

It is axiomatic that when a new combat aircraft is added to the inventory, its potential successor should have begun its passage across the drawing boards and, thus, in the early autumn of 1937, within a few months of the Bf 109B fighter reaching the Luftwaffe, the Technisches Amt of the RLM began to give active consideration to a successor. Little support was forthcoming from the Luftwaffenführungsstab. Indeed, certain elements within the Technisches Amt itself displayed anything but enthusiasm for the proposal, declaiming vociferously that the Messerschmitt was so far ahead in concept of any fighter extant that consideration of a successor was premature. Nevertheless, the further-sighted factions within the Technisches Amt persisted in their planning for a follow-on fighter.

By the spring of 1938, when some of the complacency of the Luftwaffenführungsstab had been dispelled by a combination of intelligence that other countries had not been asleep in so far as fighter development was concerned, and certain shortcomings revealed by the Bf 109 in Luftwaffe service, a specification for a new single-seat fighter was finalised. The Focke-Wulf Flugzeugbau, which was enjoying a growing

Right: This line-up of Fw 190F ground-attack aircraft belonging to II Gruppe/Schlachtgeschwader 1 was seen at Deblin-Irena in Poland. At the time of the picture, probably early 1943, this unit was transitioning onto the Fw 190F from the Bf 109, and was later to see action against Soviet forces.

The Fw 190 was a purposeful-looking design that was a great success in service, in both fighter and fighter-bomber roles. The Fw 190G shown here was captured by the Allies, and is seen in flight in the United States while under examination.

Focke-Wulf Fw 190

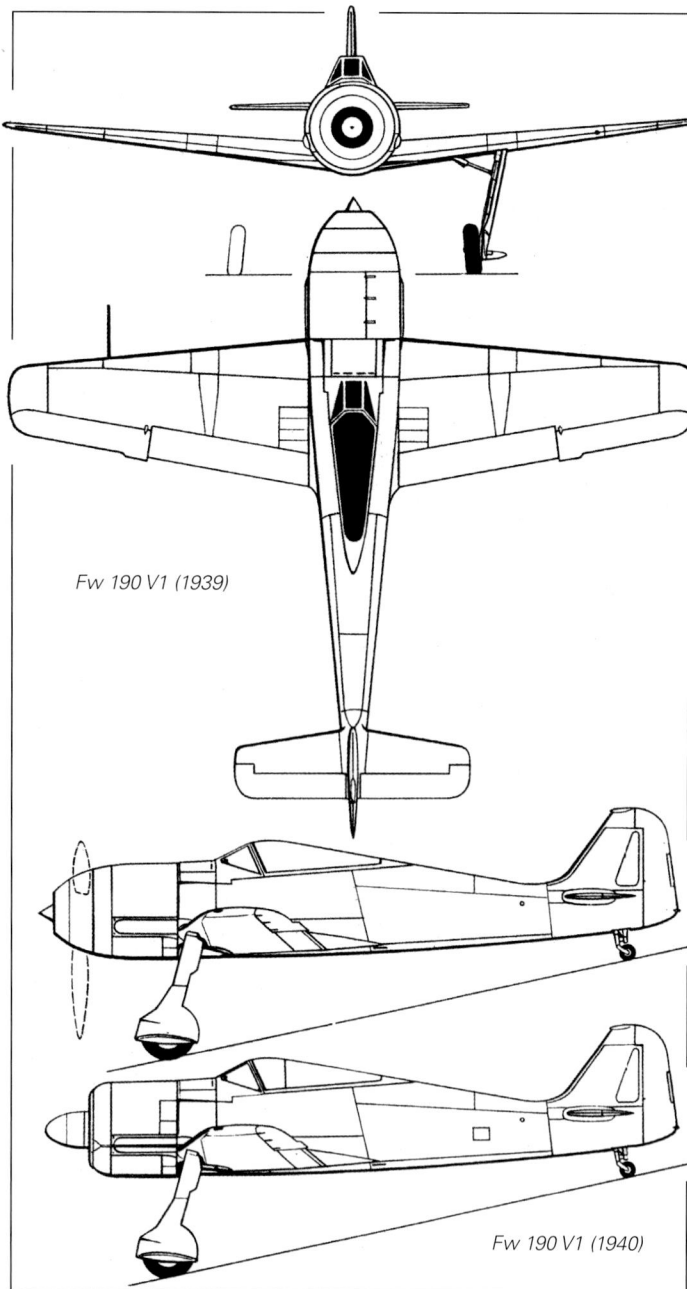

Fw 190 V1 (1939)

Fw 190 V1 (1940)

reputation with the RLM as a progressive company, possessed an experienced team and had design capacity available, was invited to submit its proposals for what the Technisches Amt still referred to as this "zweites Eisen im Feuer" – a second iron in the fire.

Dipl.-Ing. Kurt Tank submitted several alternative proposals to the RLM during the weeks that followed. For the most part they were based on the use of a liquid-cooled powerplant then considered *de rigeur* in Germany for fighters owing to its small frontal area and, in consequence, low drag. However, he diverged from what a consensus of RLM opinion considered the conventional in that he also submitted a proposal for a fighter using the powerful 18-cylinder two-row radial air-cooled engine then being bench-run by the Bayerische Motoren Werke, the BMW 139.

Radial advantages

Few in the Technisches Amt viewed with favour the idea of using a radial engine as a fighter powerplant owing to its drag and the restrictions that its bulk imposed upon forward view during take-off and landing. Tank finally succeeded, however, in convincing the Technisches Amt that there were two overriding considerations in favour of adopting the BMW 139 engine for the new fighter, apart from the fact that the air-cooled radial was less susceptible to battle damage than was its liquid-cooled counterpart. Firstly, in the years immediately ahead it seemed likely that the supply situation regarding high-powered liquid-cooled engines in Germany would be critical owing to the demands to be made on them by aircraft already ordered into production. Secondly, the BMW 139, in the form in which it was running on the test stands, already offered appreciably more power than could conceivably be available from either the DB 601 or the Jumo 211 for at least a further two years.

Swayed by the force of these arguments, the Technisches Amt awarded a contract for three prototypes of the radial-engined fighter which was allocated the designation **Fw 190**. Overall design responsibility for the new fighter, which was unofficially known to the company as **Würger** (Shrike) – a name much over-used subsequently in books but which was little used at the time – was delegated to Oberingenieur

The first prototype of the Fw 190, the Fw 190 V1 that was civil-registered as D-OPZE, first flew on 1 June 1939 with company test pilot Hans Sander at the controls.

This front view of the Fw 190 V1 was recorded at around the time of its first flight in June 1939. The distinctive full-width ducted spinner, together with an inner spinner, is especially evident.

Rudolf Blaser. As little urgency was initially attached to the development programme, Blaser's team, which included Oberingenieure Mittelhüber and Willy Käther, in charge of project and design offices, respectively, painstakingly developed a fighter in which an attempt was made to subordinate all details to a single coherent conception. While weight consciousness and simplicity were design keynotes, the underlying theory was the creation of a fighter that, offering greater structural integrity than any of its predecessors, demanded the minimum of field maintenance time and could be produced through the widespread use of dispersed factories and sub-contractors.

The result was an extremely compact, well-proportioned and attractive machine, the blending of the bulky radial engine into the overall contours being little short of a masterpiece of ingenuity. Overall dimensions were kept to the absolute minimum, and it was this effort to attain the ultimate in compactness that almost led to the fighter's undoing. In order to achieve minimal fuselage length the two-row radial was attached to the forward bulkhead and spar face by extremely short bearers, thus necessitating the positioning of the cockpit immediately aft of the bulkhead for centre-of-gravity reasons and, in consequence, in close proximity to the powerplant. Apart from risking excessively high cockpit temperatures, this arrangement ruled out the possibility of the primary armament being fuselage-mounted as favoured by the Luftwaffe. However, the alternative facing Oberingenieur Blaser's team had been an appreciably larger and heavier fighter.

Below: The Fw 190 V1 is seen in a part of the production facilities at Focke-Wulf's Bremen plant that was given over to prototype manufacture and development. The photo clearly shows the unusual ducted spinner, that was not used on production aircraft.

Right: A large series of pre-production Fw 190s, all BMW 801-powered, was built to develop the basic Fw 190 concept. One of these early aircraft is seen here, illustrating the large hinged opening panel ahead of the windscreen for armament access.

Above: The unarmed Focke-Wulf Fw 190 V1 with BMW 139 and ducted cooling spinner, is seen at the time of its first flight in June 1939. Numerous other differences from subsequent production versions are evident, including the small tail wheel, absence of fuselage mainwheel doors, and the hinged door covers on the main undercarriage to cover the main wheels.

Above: The Fw 190 V1 shows the attractive and compact lines of this well-designed aircraft. Apart from the change of engine, the basic layout remained constant throughout production – always a good sign of sound design.

Above: First of the 190 series to be powered by the BMW 801C-0 engine was the Fw 190 V5, built originally in small wing (V5k) and later, following an accident, in enlarged wing (V5g) configuration. The latter layout was chosen for production on account of its superior manoeuvrability.

Focke-Wulf Fw 190

One of the pre-production large-wing Fw 190A-0 development aircraft, numbered '25' on its cowling (Werk Nr 0025), is seen here on finals to Focke-Wulf's Bremen or Langenhagen facilities. An initial batch of no fewer than 40 Fw 190A-0 pre-production aircraft was produced, but there is evidence to suggest that approximately 60 such aircraft eventually existed.

Fortuitously, during the construction of the prototypes, the Bayerische Motoren Werke had been developing another and more advanced two-row radial engine, the BMW 801. Although this newer powerplant possessed a virtually identical overall diameter to the BMW 139, it was somewhat longer and appreciably heavier, but it offered considerably more development potential. Furthermore, the BMW 139 was not living up to its earlier promise, and the Bayerische Motoren Werke was anxious to abandon further work on this engine in order to concentrate its efforts on the BMW 801.

Discussions were held between the engine manufacturer, the Technisches Amt and Focke-Wulf during the spring of 1939 concerning the possibility of adapting the Fw 190 to take the BMW 801. The Focke-Wulf fighter had, of course, been tailored for the lighter BMW 139, and the proposed engine change necessitated a very extensive redesign of the airframe, resulting in a larger and heavier fighter than had been envisaged. Nevertheless, the decision to change to the new engine was finally taken at the beginning of June, some two weeks after the commencement of ground tests with the Fw 190 V1, and the Bayerische Motoren Werke's request to terminate BMW 139 development was granted.

It is possible that part of the motivation for this decision was provided by the initial ground trials with the Fw 190 V1. During these, excessive cockpit temperatures had been experienced and the necessity to extensively redesign the fighter for the new powerplant gave Oberingenieur Blaser's team an opportunity to resolve both this problem and certain shortcomings that were now to be seen in the basic concept of the aircraft. Thus, what could well have been a mediocre warplane was to be transformed into one of the truly outstanding fighters of World War II.

Above: The definitive BMW 801 radial replaced the BMW 139 of earlier aircraft in the Fw 190 V5. Here this important development aircraft is seen with the original short-span wings, before its crash and rebuild with longer wings.

Left: In this view of the prototype, D-OPZE, several features that did not find their way into the production Fw 190 are visible, including the ducted propeller and folding main undercarriage wheel covers.

Focke-Wulf Fw 190

In addition to the initial order for three prototypes, Focke-Wulf had, by this time, a supplementary order for a fourth or production prototype, and instructions to proceed with preparations for the construction of a pre-production batch of 40 aircraft. The Fw 190 V1 was already complete and the V2 had reached an advanced assembly stage, but the assembly of the V3 had still to begin and work on the V4 was only in the preparatory stage. It was therefore decided to discard both third and fourth prototypes and, instead, initiate work on a fifth prototype, the Fw 190 V5, intended from the outset to take the BMW 801 engine.

The shrike takes flight

The **Fw 190 V1** (Werk Nr 0001) had been rolled out in May, and had begun taxying trials at the hands of Dipl.-Ing. Flugkapitän Hans Sander, who was in charge of the flight test department. Powered by a BMW 139 18-cylinder two-row radial driving a three-bladed VDM variable-pitch airscrew with a large ducted spinner, the Fw 190 V1 featured an all-metal monocoque fuselage and a one-piece wing spanning 9.50 m (31 ft 2 in) and possessing a gross area of 14.93 m^2 (160.67 sq ft). Having 1156 kW (1,550 hp) available for take-off and weighing in at 2768 kg (6,103 lb) loaded, the Fw 190 V1 had wing and power loadings of 262 kPa (38 lb/sq ft) and 2.39 kg/kW (3.9 lb/hp), respectively. With the registration D-OPZE, it was flown for the first time on 1 June 1939.

From the outset, the Fw 190 V1 displayed beautifully balanced controls and an excellent turn of speed, but the 10-bladed cooling fan, driven from the airscrew reduction gear and intended to rotate inside the cowling at approximately three times airscrew speed, was not ready for installation, and the close proximity of the engine's inadequately-cooled rear cylinder row resulted in the cockpit temperature rising rapidly. As the canopy could not be opened in the air or even when the motor was being run up, the continuous use of an oxygen mask was necessary. During initial flights cockpit temperature actually rose as high as 55°C (131°F), and Sander felt, as he stated in his post-flight report, that he had his "Füsse im Feuer" (feet in the fire). A further source of discomfort was provided by exhaust fumes in the cockpit.

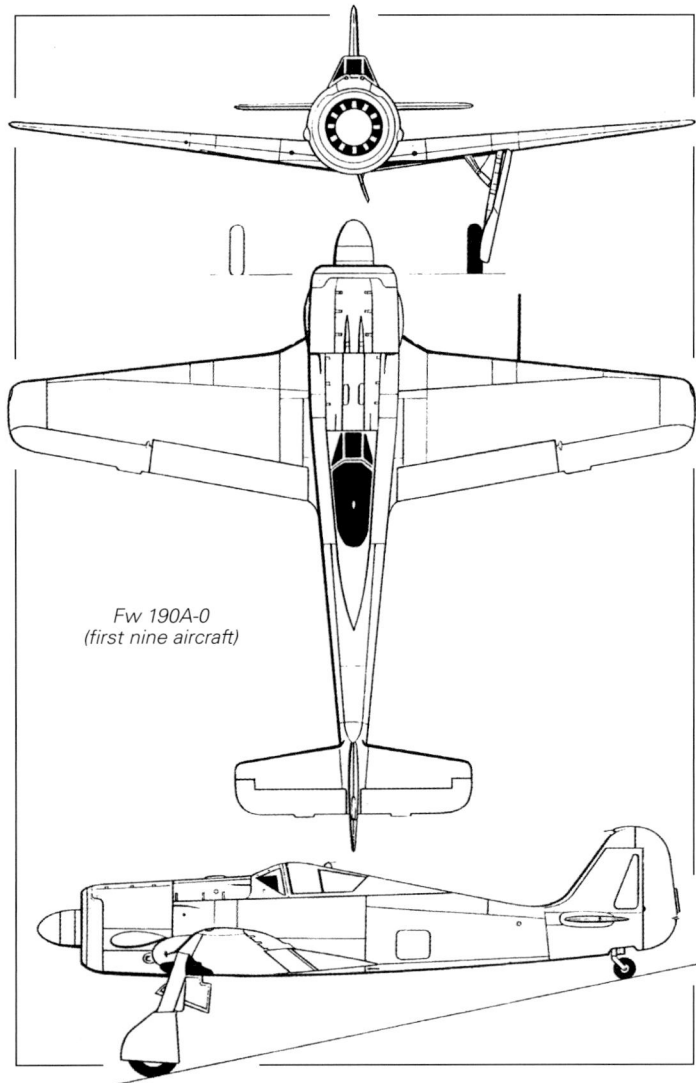

Fw 190A-0
(first nine aircraft)

Below: Several of the Fw 190A-0 pre-production aircraft were built with the small wing, whereas most of them had the production-standard large wing. The Fw 190 V5k is shown here.

Focke-Wulf Fw 190

*Above: Later in its career the first prototype of the Fw 190 series, **D-OPZE**, was taken off the German civil register and allocated factory codes (Stammkennzeichen) of **FO+LY**. It is seen here in the snow at Bremen, illustrating the cowling layout that was used for this aircraft after the curious ducted spinner was removed.*

Above: A line-up of pre-production Fw 190A-0 aircraft sits outside the factory. The basic design of the Fw 190 series that was to persist until the advent of the re-designed Fw 190D-9 is well illustrated in this view – the design layout remained constant throughout production of the Fw 190A fighter and F and G fighter-bomber series.

The compactness and neatness of the design is well evident in this picture of an early Fw 190 in flight. Particularly noticeable is the small frontal area, even with the BMW 801 radial engine fitted – it has always been a challenge to aircraft designers to neatly streamline a bulky radial engine with large frontal area compared to the comparative ease with which this can be achieved with an inline engine.

It was believed that engine cooling would be rectified with availability of the fan, and that exhaust fume seepage was a problem to be solved by adequate cockpit ventilation.

After only five flights with Sander at the controls, the Fw 190 V1 was ferried to the Erprobungsstelle Rechlin where it was flown by several of the Luftwaffe's most experienced test pilots, including Francke, Thones and Beauvais, who echoed Sander's praise for the handling characteristics of the aircraft. During the Rechlin trials a speed of 594 km/h (369 mph) was clocked in level flight, but the prototype was plagued continuously with engine overheating. Shortly after its arrival at Rechlin the civil registration was discarded, the aircraft becoming FO+LY. With the completion of handling trials, the Fw 190 V1 was returned to Focke-Wulf for installation of the engine cooling fan, the introduction of armament, and various minor changes.

In the meantime, the second prototype, the **Fw 190 V2** (Werk Nr 0002, FO + LZ), had been completed with a

10-bladed cooling fan and an armament of one 7.9-mm MG 17 machine-gun in each wing root. Flown for the first time on 31 October 1939, the Fw 190 V2 retained the ducted spinner of the V1 but, although engine cooling was markedly improved, the rear row of cylinders still tended to overheat. The Fw 190 V2 was flown for comparison purposes both with and without the cooling fan, and as tunnel tests with models suggested that the ducted spinner had only a marginal effect on drag, consideration was given to discarding this feature. Thus, the Fw 190 V1, which rejoined the test programme on 25 January 1940, was fitted with an orthodox spinner in an attempt to alleviate the cooling problem. Although testing proved that there was little to choose between the orthodox and ducted spinners when the fan was fitted, it was decided to adopt the former as standard for subsequent aircraft.

Prior to the departure of the Fw 190 V2 for firing trials at the Waffenprüfplatz at Tarnewitz, the prototype was demonstrated before Hermann Göring, who enthusiasti-

Above: The BMW 801 was very neatly integrated into the Fw 190 airframe, as shown by this BMW 801D in an operational Fw 190A. The large tubes behind the engine are exhaust pipes.

Above: The first prototype of the Fw 190 series, D-OPZE, lands during its initial test phase with the ducted spinner fitted and civil registration clearly marked.

Below: This aircraft, almost certainly the Fw 190 V5, shows off the small wing as fitted to the prototype machines and early A-0 development aircraft.

Above: The Fw 190 V1 is seen early in 1940 after the ducted spinner had been discarded.

Below: This early Fw 190 is undergoing what appears to be armament trials. Beginning with the Fw 190 V2, weapons development work was performed by several early Fw 190s.

Above: By early 1940 the Fw 190 V1 prototype had a conventional propeller and spinner and was coded FO+LY. The '01' on its tail was an abbreviated form of its Werk Nummer (construction number) 0001.

Left: Each cylinder of the BMW 801 radial engine had its own exhaust pipe in the Fw 190 installation – the oval projections at the front of the louvered panel. The louvres themselves were used to allow heated cooling air to escape from the engine compartment.

Below: One of the development aircraft shows off the Fw 190's distinctive gawky stance when parked on the ground. Extensive exhaust staining marks the fuselage aft of the rear of the cowling.

From early in the development of the Fw 190, the type was seen as having potential as a fighter-bomber, and experimental work with several types of ETC weapons racks was carried out to create a line of fighter-bombers alongside the pure fighter Fw 190 versions.

Above: This cockpit interior is of possibly a development or early production aircraft. In the top left are the armament switches and rounds counters for the guns/cannons, to the right of them the fitment for the Revi gunsight.

cally instructed Kurt Tank to turn out the Fw 190 "wie warme Semmel" (like hot rolls). The Reichsmarschall was not informed that Oberingenieur Blaser's team was wrestling with serious weight escalation in its attempts to adapt the fighter for its new powerplant. After firing trials at Tarnewitz, the Fw 190 V2 was returned to Rechlin for a further series of handling trials, completing some 50 flying hours before the crankshaft broke, the prototype crashing and being totally destroyed. Trials with the Fw 190 V1 (the code letters FO+LY having by now given place to the radio call sign RM+CA) continued, and in April 1940 it was joined in the test programme by the first BMW 801-powered prototype, the **Fw 190 V5** (Werk Nr 0005).

The BMW 801C of the Fw 190 V5 possessed a very similar diameter to that of the BMW 139 that it replaced, but it was both longer and some 159 kg (350 lb) heavier, the bare engine weighing 1053 kg (2,321 lb), and it was necessary to restress the entire airframe. Much of the structure was strengthened, and for CG reasons it was found necessary to move the cockpit further aft. This had the incidental advantages of alleviating the cockpit temperature problem and providing the space forward for the fuselage-mounted weapons requested by the Luftwaffe, although view from the relocated cockpit was poor for taxying. The cockpit itself was reduced in size, a 14-mm armour plate was introduced behind the pilot, and the canopy was modified, the moulded Plexiglas area being reduced. The rudder contours were changed, the inset fixed trim tab being replaced by an external tab; the main undercarriage members were beefed up, their attachment points repositioned and their rake increased; the wing leading-edge roots were extended forward to permit re-location of the wheel wells and simultaneously provide more space for gun bays; the hinged wheel half-doors were transferred from the main legs to the fuselage; and a larger tailwheel was introduced.

All these changes were made without increasing overall length by more than 10 cm (4 in), but normal loaded weight without armament had risen by some 25 per cent to 3425 kg (7,550 lb). The extended wing roots had increased gross area slightly to 15.03 m² (161.78 sq ft), and the BMW 801C engine offered 1194 kW (1,600 hp) for take-off, and thus wing and power loadings had risen to 321 kPa (46.6 lb/sq ft) and 2.87 kg/kW (4.7 lb/hp), respectively. As a consequence, climb rate and manoeuvrability suffered. The unwelcome effect on performance of the substantial weight increase had naturally been foreseen by the design team. It was well aware that the weight problem would be further aggravated by the installation of armament and full service equipment, gross weight escalating by something like a ton over that of the fighter originally envisaged. Work had already begun, therefore, on the design of a completely new wing of increased span and area.

Pre-production aircraft

Work on the pre-production batch of 40 **Fw 190A-0** fighters had been proceeding in parallel with the construction of the Fw 190 V5. When, in August 1940, this prototype collided with a tractor during a take-off, suffering extensive damage to the wing, it was decided to rebuild the aircraft to test the enlarged wing which, earlier, had been intended for one of the pre-production machines. The new wing employed a

Left: One of the Fw 190A-0 pre-production aircraft (Werk Nr 0020, KB+PV) shows off its mid-war grey colour scheme. The photograph was possibly taken at Rechlin, but more probably at Bremen.

Below: An Fw 190A-0 pre-production aircraft, KB+PR, illustrates a considerable amount of exhaust staining along its fuselage side. Some units adopted black markings to cover this area.

similar profile to that of the existing wing, and the structural arrangement was similar, comprising one main spar and one auxiliary spar with widely-spaced flanged plate former ribs, spanwise Z-section stringers and a stressed metal skin. The front spar, being continuous, passed through the fuselage, the wing being built in one piece. This complicated repair but saved some 136 kg (300 lb) in weight. Both leading- and trailing-edge taper were reduced, and thus, combined with an increase in overall span to 10.50 m (34 ft 5 in), this resulted in a 3.27-m² (35.2-sq ft) increase in gross wing area to 18.30 m² (196.98 sq ft).

The new wing, together with an enlarged tailplane, was fitted to the Fw 190 V5, the modified prototype being referred to as the **Fw 190 V5g**, the suffix letter indicating "grosser Flügel" (large wing). To differentiate between results gained with this rebuilt aircraft and earlier results obtained prior to reconstruction, the prototype in its original form was retrospectively designated **Fw 190 V5k** for record purposes, in this case the suffix letter indicating "kleiner Flügel" (small wing). Flight testing of the Fw 190 V5g revealed a loss of only 10 km/h (6 mph) in maximum speed as a result of the introduction of the larger wing, a marked improvement in climb, and a virtually complete restoration of the pleasant handling characteristics displayed by the first prototypes.

The aircraft could be rolled at fighting speed, and its diving speed was exceptionally high, but it was by no means faultless. The ailerons were finger-light but tended to vibrate in stalls, resulting in a rolling motion, and at high speeds they became ineffective over the mid-part of their range, lateral corrections necessitating full application of aileron control. Due to this ineffectiveness, the control column could be easily moved from side to side of the cockpit, resistance being felt only at the limit of movement. Another shortcoming was the over-effectiveness at high speeds of the elevator trim tab, while turning radius was unexceptional owing to the wing loading that remained rather high, despite the substantial increase in gross area. These faults were alleviated but never eradicated.

This front view is of a late pre-production or early production Fw 190A-series aircraft. Note the position of the pitot tube on the starboard wing leading edge.

Above: Several of the later pre-production Fw 190A-0 aircraft were fitted with the weapons fit as used in the Fw 190A-1 initial production series, as with this pre-production aircraft which had outer wing MG FF cannons fitted.

This production Fw 190A-1, TI+DQ, Werk Nr 067, shows the rearward-sliding cockpit canopy arrangement of the Fw 190 series, which included the decking behind the clear portion.

Above: One of the initial Fw 190A-1 production aircraft shows off its production configuration, with outer wing MG FF cannon and wing-root MG 17 machine-guns fitted.

Gunsight

The Revi C/12D reflector gunsight was fitted. Switch selection allowed the pilot to fire any pair of guns independently, or any combination thereof.

Cockpit

The cockpit of the Fw 190A-1 was covered by a one-piece, rearward sliding canopy, giving the pilot a marvellously unobstructed all-round view by the standards of w time. The rearward view was particularly noteworthy, despite being partly blocked by a heavily armoured headrest. This view, combined with the 'Butcher bird's' tremendous agility and good performance, made the type a Luftwaffe favourite and a deadly adversary in air-to-air combat.

Powerplant

Early Fw 190s were powered by the BMW 801C-1 engine, rated at 1193 kW (1,600 hp). These had been prone to overheating on pre-production aircraft and required much remedial work by Focke-Wulf and BMW engineers. In the Fw 190A-3, an uprated 1268-kW (1,700-hp) BMW 801D-2 was fitted.

Armament

As built, early production Fw 190A-1s were armed with four Rheinmetall Borsig MG 17 machine-guns mounted in the upper fuselage and wing roots and firing through the propeller arc. After an experimental installation in Fw 190 V8, some aircraft (including this machine) were retrofitted with a 20-mm MG FF cannon in each outer wing, the original weapon fit having proved inadequate.

II/JG 26 and Fw 190 conversion

Jagdgeschwader 26's II Gruppe had begun life as II/JG 234, itself formed from elements of JG 134 at Düsseldorf in March 1937 to fly Arado Ar 68s and early Messerschmitt Bf 109s. In November 1938 it became II/JG 132, and then renumbered as II/JG 26 on 1 May 1939. By then it was flying the Bf 109E, which the Gruppe took to Belgium and northern France in May 1940, this becoming the Gruppe's main area of operations until it was pushed back into Germany in late 1944. Conversion to the Fw 190A began in the second half of 1941, the Gruppe being tasked with testing the Fw 190 under operational conditions. The Gruppe's 6. Staffel became the first front-line unit to operate the Fw 190 when it received its initial Fw 190A-1s at Moorseele in Belgium. The rest of the Gruppe was fully converted by September, operating from Moorseele until the move to Wevelgem in October.

Focke-Wulf Fw 190A-1

6. Staffel/Jagdgeschwader 26

Equipped with some of the first production Fw 190A-1s, 6. Staffel/Jagdgeschwader 26 'Schlageter' was based at Wevelgem in Belgium during November 1941. This aircraft was flown by the Staffelkapitän, Oberleutnant Walter 'Jap' Schneider, who had scored 20 victories before being killed in December when his aircraft hit high ground in fog. JG 26's II Gruppe received successive variants of the Fw 190 as they were produced, and operated a fleet of A-1s, A-2s and A-3s until August 1942, when the last of the A-1s were withdrawn. The first of the A-4s arrived in September, soon becoming the Gruppe's standard mount, and were replaced as such by the A-5 from April 1943. Fw 190A-6s were delivered from June 1943, A-7s from January 1944, and A-8s from April 1944. The Gruppe ended the war at Flensburg with Fw 190Ds.

Undercarriage
The wide-track undercarriage of the Fw 190 made it more suitable than the Bf 109 for operations from rough or semi-prepared airstrips, a feature that was particularly exploited on the Russian front. The wide track also gave it more forgiving handling characteristics in the hands of inexperienced pilots.

Radio equipment
The FuG 7 radio was fitted to the Fw 190A-1, usually complemented by the FuG 25, an early IFF (identification, friend or foe) system.

Camouflage and markings
Standard Luftwaffe RLM 74/75 fighter camouflage adorns this aircraft, with RLM 76 undersides. JG 26 unit markings are not carried. On the aircraft's tail are kill markings for 19 of 'Jap' Schneider's air-to-air victories.

Illustrating the early production configuration of the Fw 190A-series, this aircraft is representative of the initial Fw 190A production machines that went into operational service in the late summer of 1941. The prominent 'teardrop' bulge on the side of the engine cowling covered internal pipework for air being directed to the BMW 801 engine's supercharger. On production Fw 190s, as shown here, this bulge had a straight upper edge, whereas on pre-production aircraft the bulge was a pronounced 'teardrop' shape.

The first two pre-production Fw 190A-0 airframes (Werk Nummern 0006 and 0007) were completed almost simultaneously with the commencement of Fw 190 V5g flight testing in October 1940, these being allocated Versuchs numbers as the **Fw 190 V6** and **V7**. Having similar fuselages to that of their immediate predecessor, they retained the smaller wing and horizontal tail surfaces. Whereas the Fw 190 V6 was initially flown without armament, and could be distinguished from later aircraft by its lack of the standard rudder balance, the Fw 190 V7 was the first BMW 801-powered aircraft to be fitted with armament, this comprising two Rheinmetall Borsig MG 17 machine-guns of 7.9-mm calibre in the upper decking of the forward fuselage immediately ahead of the pilot's windscreen, and two similar weapons in the wing

This Fw 190A-2 was the mount of Hauptmann Joachim Müncheberg, Gruppenkommandeur of II/JG 26 between September 1941 and July 1942. The Gruppe was based in northern France and Belgium in this period. By December 1941 Müncheberg had racked up 62 victories.

In the early days of the Fw 190 JG 26 marked its aircraft with the initial of the assigned pilot, who was Oberleutnant Wilfried Sieling in the case of this Fw 190A-2. However, it was also flown by the Geschwader-kommodore, Major Gerhard Schöpfel, who took over command from Adolf Galland in December 1941.

'Black 7' was one of the very first Fw 190A-3s to reach the front line. It was flown by Oberleutnant Karl Borris, Staffelkapitän of 8./JG 26, which operated from Wevelgem in early 1942. Borris was the only member of JG 26 to fly with the Geschwader throughout the war.

In May 1942 the Fw 190A was at the height of its supremacy over the Channel. Among the elite units was I/JG 26 at St Omer-Arques, whose Kommandeur, Hauptmann Johannes Seifert, flew this Fw 190A-3. He was killed the following year in a mid-air collision.

In mid-1942 C-in-C RAF Fighter Command, Air Chief Marshal Sir Sholto Douglas, wrote a strongly worded letter to the Under Secretary of State for Air, Lord Sherwood. Douglas complained that his force had lost the technical edge it had once had over the Luftwaffe and went on to say: "There is...no doubt in my mind, nor in the minds of my fighter pilots, that the Fw 190 is the best all-round fighter in the world today." This view shows several small- and large-wing Fw 190A-0 aircraft, probably at Rechlin under test during the summer of 1941.

roots, the pilot being provided with a Revi C/12C reflector sight. It had been the intention to mount the new 20-mm Mauser MG 151 cannon in the wing roots, but this excellent weapon had not previously been used with electric synchronisation gear, which was still under development.

The Fw 190 V7 was employed for firing trials at the Waffenprüfplatz at Tarnewitz, and a similar quartet of MG 17 machine-guns was mounted by the Fw 190A-0 fighters (commencing with Werk Nr 0008, KB+PD) that began to leave the assembly line in November 1940. The first two Fw 190A-0s were powered, like the prototypes, by the pre-production BMW 801C-0, but the third (Werk Nr 0010) and subsequent Fw 190A-0s received the production BMW 801C-l powerplant.

Among the earliest Fw 190s to get into action was this A-2 flown by the adjutant of II/JG 26, based at Moorseele in late 1941 and later at Wevelgem and, in early 1942, Abbeville. It covered the Channel dash by the warships on 12 February 1942 and saw fierce combat at the Dieppe landing in August.

The Fw 190A-3 began to arrive at JG 26's airfields in early 1942. II Gruppe received its first aircraft in March, to be followed in April by the Stab (illustrated), I and III Gruppen.

This Fw 190A-3 (Werk Nr 0538) of 4./JG 26 'Schlageter' operated throughout 1942 from Abbeville-Drucat. In September the II Gruppe of JG 26 began to re-equip with the Fw 190A-4. In the early months of 1943 a few Bf 109G-4s were assigned.

Fw 190A-3s supplanted in the front line by later variants found a new role in the fighter training organisation. This A-3 was still training pilots with IV/Ergänzungs-Jagdgeschwader 1 at Bad Aibling at the end of the war.

Focke-Wulf Fw 190

Fw 190A-1s line up for service fresh from the factory. Throughout the A-series the look of the Fw 190 differed little, although it was to see an amazing array of armament and roles.

Fw 190A series

The larger wing first flown on the Fw 190 V5g had shown its superiority from the earliest test phase, sufficient evidence being available for the Technisches Amt to opt for the new wing as standard, but the pre-production assembly line was too far advanced for the change to be introduced until the eighth Fw 190A-0 (Werk Nr 0015), completed at the beginning of 1941. Considerable pressure was now being brought to bear on Dipl.-Ing. Tank to hasten development tempo of the fighter with a view to service introduction by the late summer of 1941. Focke-Wulf had already received a contract for 100 **Fw 190A-1**s for which tooling was being prepared at Marienburg, while AGO and Arado had been instructed to prepare for production of the fighter at Oschersleben and

Warnemünde, respectively. A service test unit was being established at Rechlin-Roggentin, to which six Fw 190A-0 aircraft were delivered in March 1941.

Of the 40 Fw 190A-0 series airframes laid down, no fewer than 14 were subsequently to receive Versuchs numbers, and serve as development aircraft. The six delivered to the Erprobungsstaffel 190 at Rechlin-Roggentin between 22 February and 29 April 1941 (Werk Nummern 0013, 0014, 0018, 0019, 0021 and 0022) were subjected to an intensive working-up programme at the hands of both Rechlin and service personnel, aimed at wringing out the teething troubles and accelerating service acceptance of the new fighter. The service personnel had been selected from II Gruppe of Jagdgeschwader 26 'Schlageter', already designated as the first operational unit to receive the new fighter, and were led by Oberleutnant Otto Behrens.

Although the robust nature of the fighter and its excellent handling characteristics were quickly confirmed, the work-up programme was plagued with continuous powerplant difficulties. The BMW 801C-1 was, from several aspects, a very advanced engine of remarkably compact proportions. Provided with a single-stage centrifugal supercharger with two automatically-changing speeds, direct fuel injection and a centralisation of controls permitting the operation and control of boost pressure, engine speed, ignition timing and blower speed, the BMW 801C-1 utilised a 12-bladed cooling fan operating at 3.17 times airscrew speed, and a system of internal baffles. Positive air pressure built up in the cowling in front of the engine was used for cooling the cylinders, cylinder-heads, crankcase accessories and the oil, as well as for combustion. A VDM airscrew pitch-changing and constant-speed regulating device that, in normal operation, automatically maintained the selected speed by oleo-hydraulic means, added further complexity, and few of the teething troubles had been resolved when testing was transferred to Le Bourget in the northern suburbs of Paris.

At Le Bourget it was believed that the Fw 190A could be evaluated under realistic combat conditions by a detachment of personnel from II/JG 26, at that time based at Maldeghem in Belgium. The programme rapidly degenerated into what could only be described as a catastrophe, engines frequently overheating during running-up. Most take-offs proved abor-

This Fw 190A-3 of 9./JG 26 carries the number '1' to signify the aircraft of the Staffelkapitän, Oberleutnant Kurt Ruppert. The unit was based at Wevelgem for most of 1942, although it spent a short time at Beaumont-le-Roger late in the year.

'Black 8' was the Fw 190A-3 of Oberleutnant Wilhelm-Ferdinand 'Wutz' Galland, one of three brothers to serve with JG 26 (the best-known, Adolf, had been Kommandeur from August 1940 to December 1941). In June 1942 'Wutz' was at Abbeville-Drucat as the Kapitän of 5./JG 26.

The ace of hearts personal marking on this Fw 190A-3 identifies it as the aircraft of Hauptmann Josef 'Pips' Priller, as seen in August 1942 when he was Kommandeur of III/JG 26. He was appointed Geschwaderkommodore in January 1943.

tive, the engine seizing before take-off speed was attained, and when an aircraft did succeed in leaving the ground it invariably returned trailing smoke. The lowest cylinder of the rear row continuously seized as a result of inadequate cooling, oil and petrol leaks fractured, the heavily armoured oil cooling ring in front of the engine frequently split, and the airscrew's automatic setting mechanism constantly failed.

Teething troubles

Focke-Wulf blamed the powerplant for the fighter's troubles, and BMW blamed Focke-Wulf who, the engine manufacturer claimed, had paid insufficient attention to powerplant cooling in its basic design. So serious had the defects in the fighter become that an RLM Commission visiting Le Bourget recommended the cancellation of the entire Fw 190 programme. According to JG 26's Technical Officer, Ernst Battmer, the key to the problem lay in the collaboration between the airframe and powerplant manufacturers, but the RLM was persuaded to delay a final decision on the future of the fighter, and after some 50 modifications, the Fw 190A was finally accepted for service.

While trials were still under way at Le Bourget, the

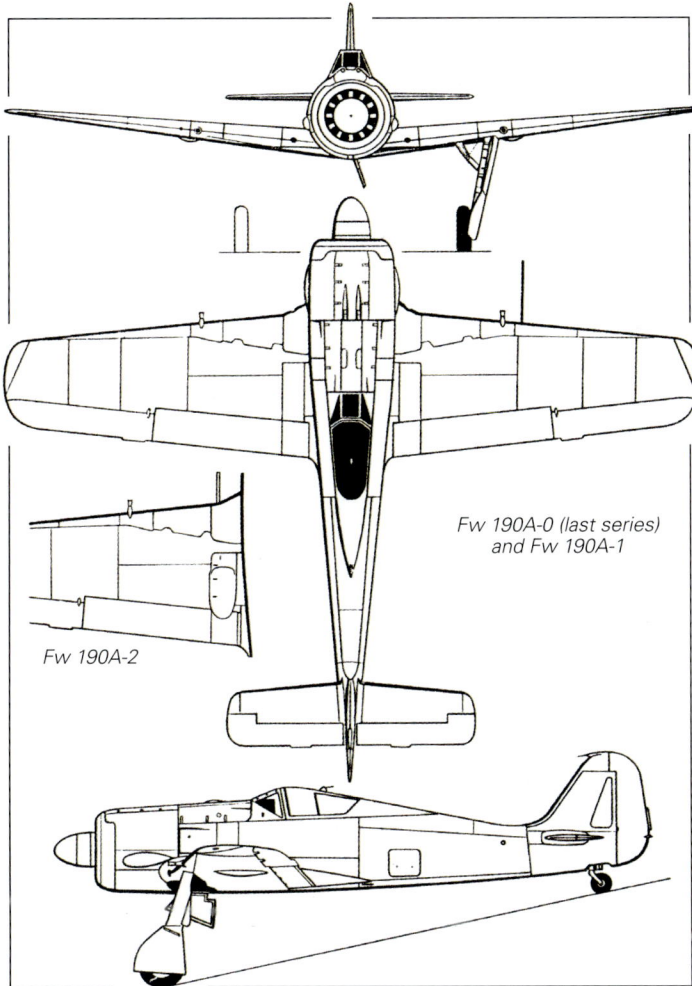

first production Fw 190A-1 fighters began to leave the Marienburg assembly line, the initial four being accepted by the Luftwaffe in June 1941, followed by 18 in July, all 100 (some company sources state 102) being completed by the end of October 1941, and the first **Fw 190A-2**s leaving the line in the following month. They were actually preceded by the first Fw 190A-2s from the Warnemünde and Oschersleben assembly lines that began deliveries in August and October, respectively, the three factories having delivered a combined total of 124 Fw 190A-2s by the end of 1941.

The Fw 190A-1 differed only in minor respects from the pre-production Fw 190A-0, changes being confined to assembly line modifications introduced as a result of first-phase testing at Rechlin-Roggentin. They included provision of heavier toggle latches locking the engine cowling in position, and a cartridge jettison system for the cockpit canopy that had refused to part company with the remainder of the aircraft at speeds exceeding 400 km/h (250 mph). Despite the inadequacy of their weight of fire, the four MG 17s were retained, and as a temporary measure, it was proposed to mount a pair of 20-mm MG FF (Oerlikon) cannon in the wings immediately outboard of the main undercarriage attachment points. A trial installation of the cannon armament was made on the eighth large-wing Fw 190A-0 (Werk Nr 0022), which thus became the **Fw 190 V8**, and a number of the production Fw 190A-1s were retrofitted in a similar fashion.

Fw 190A-0 (last series) and Fw 190A-1

Fw 190A-2

Above: The Fw 190 V8, Werk Nr 0022, seen here with eight SC 50 bombs, served for weapons development work.

The distinctive shape of the Fw 190 is well illustrated in this front view of a development or early production Fw 190A – note the MG FF cannon in each wing outboard of the main undercarriage attachment.

Focke-Wulf Fw 190

Flying from Cherbourg-Theville in July 1942, this Fw 190A-3 was assigned to III/JG 2. The elaborate eagle marking was applied to cover up the oil stains from the engine. The head portion on the cowling was later removed in favour of the cockerel badge.

At the end of July 1941, the first Fw 190A-1s began to arrive at Moorseele, northwest of Courtrai, Belgium, where 6./JG 26 began to convert from the Bf 109E-7. By the beginning of September, the entire II/JG 26 had re-equipped with the Fw 190A-1, and III/JG 26 at Liegescourt, north of Abbeville, had initiated conversion to the Fw 190A-1 from the Bf 109F while remaining operational.

Improved production model

The Fw 190A-2, considered by the Technisches Amt to be the first true production model of the fighter, was powered by the improved BMW 801C-2 engine and introduced the wing root-mounted 20-mm MG 151 cannon in place of the 7.9-mm MG 17 weapons of the Fw 190A-1, these necessitating the provision of shallow bulges on the inboard upper surfaces. The fuselage-mounted MG 17 guns were cocked and fired electro-pneumatically, and were provided with 1,000 rounds per gun in boxes located immediately aft of the engine, and the electrically-operated MG 151 cannon in the wing roots each had 200 rounds that were also housed in fuselage boxes. As weight of fire was still considered to be insufficient, most Fw 190A-2s were retrofitted with a pair of wing-mounted 20-mm MG FF cannon to supplement the standard armament, these each having 55 rounds.

The pilot was provided with a Revi C/12D reflector gunsight, and fire-selection equipment enabled any pair of guns or combination of pairs to be fired at will. The cockpit itself was small but of excellent layout, and provided a good view except for taxying. The armour-glass windscreen was set at the acute slope angle of 63° from the vertical, and the one-piece canopy, which could be jettisoned in an emergency by means of explosive cartridges, slid aft complete with the fairing. Equipment included FuG 7 radio, and armour protection for the pilot comprised a 14-mm plate attached to the canopy immediately aft of the pilot's head, an 8-mm shaped armour seat-back, and small 8-mm plates disposed above and below the seat-back and on each side.

The BMW 801C-2 possessed the same performance as the C-1, being rated at 1194 kW (1,600 hp) for take-off and emergency at sea level, and 1029 kW (1,380 hp) at 4600 m (15,100 ft), 1089 kW (1,460 hp) being available for climb. The engine mounting was of steel tubular welded construction and was of novel design in that the circular mounting ring, to which the motor was attached through 10 flexible rubber bushes, was hollow and formed an hydraulic fluid reservoir. No fuel was housed in the wings, two self-sealing fuselage tanks – one beneath the pilot's seat accommodating 232 litres (51 Imp gal) and the other being of 290-litre (64-Imp gal) capacity – being separated by a rear spar tie-through member.

The Fw 190A-2 weighed 3177 kg (7,005 lb) in empty-equipped condition, this being increased to 3245 kg (7,153 lb) with MG FF cannon installed, loaded weight ranging from

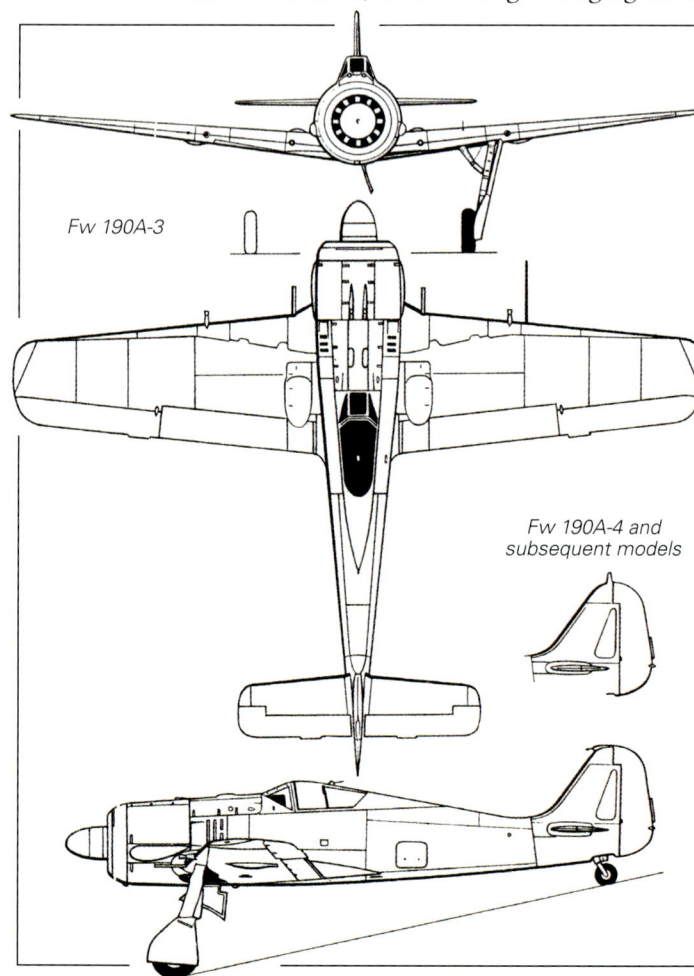

Above: An Fw 190 is seen from behind. Although the Fw 190 as a type enjoyed considerable success, as the war progressed this was an increasingly familiar view for Allied fighter pilots.

Early Fw 190As are prepared for flight. Note the MG FF cannon in the outer wing of the nearest aircraft, which also carries an external fuel tank beneath its fuselage.

Fw 190A-3

Fw 190A-4 and subsequent models

Focke-Wulf Fw 190

Oberleutnant Wilhelm Moritz, Staffelkapitän of 11./JG 1, flew this Fw 190A-3 in July 1942, when JG 1's IV Gruppe was based at Mönchen-Gladbach. The Gruppe moved to Deelen in the Netherlands before renumbering as I/JG 1.

In September 1942 Hauptmann Hans 'Assi' Hahn was Kommandeur of III/JG 2 at Poix, flying this Fw 190A-3. The Gruppe's aircraft wore Hahn's personal cockerel badge.

I/JG 51 converted to the Fw 190A-3 at Jesau in August/September 1942, prior to deploying to the Russian front. This aircraft was allocated to the Kommandeur, Hauptmann Heinrich Krafft, and has yet to receive yellow theatre bands.

During the winter months most Luftwaffe units applied white distemper over the standard camouflage. This Fw 190A-3 was the mount of 3./JG 51's commanding officer, Hauptmann Heinz Lange, and is depicted as it appeared at Vyazma-South in December 1942.

By January 1943 I/JG 51 was operating from the frozen surface of the Iwan-See (Lake Ivan). Hauptmann Rudolf Busch, who flew this Fw 190A-3, had taken over from Krafft as Kommandeur, although he was killed in late January in a take-off accident from the lake.

Having converted to the Fw 190A-3 from the Bf 109 in late 1942, JG 51's II Gruppe hastened back to Russia, and was operating from Orel in January 1943. This aircraft was flown by 7. Staffel's commander, Hauptmann Herbert Wehnelt.

Focke-Wulf Fw 190A-3 cutaway key

1 Rudder fixed tab
2 Tail navigation light
3 Leads
4 Rudder hinge/attachment
5 Tailwheel extension spring
6 Tailwheel shock-absorber leg retraction guide
7 Tailfin spar
8 Rudder post assembly
9 Rudder frame
10 Rudder upper hinge
11 Aerial attachment
12 Tailfin structure
13 Canted rib progression

14 Port elevator fixed tab
15 Port elevator
16 Mass balance
17 Port tailplane
18 Tailplane incidence motor unit
19 Tailwheel retraction pulley cables
20 Tailplane attachment
21 Starboard tailplane structure
22 Elevator fixed tab
23 Starboard elevator frame
24 Mass balance
25 Tailplane front spar
26 Semi-retracting tailwheel
27 Drag yoke
28 Tailwheel recess
29 Tailwheel locking linkage
30 Access panel
31 Actuating link
32 Push-pull rod
33 Rudder cables
34 Rudder control differential linkage
35 Fuselage/tail unit join
36 Elevator control differential
37 Fuselage lift tube
38 Elevator control cables
39 Bulkhead (No. 12) fabric panel (rear fuselage equipment dust protection)
40 Leather grommets
41 Rudder push-pull rods
42 Fuselage frame
43 Master compass
44 Flat-bottomed (equipment bay floor support) frame
45 First-aid kit
46 Optional camera (2 x Rb 12) installation (A-3/U4)
47 Control runs
48 Access hatch (port side)

49 Electrical leads
50 Distribution panel
51 Canopy channel slide cutouts
52 Canopy solid aft fairing
53 Aerial
54 Head armour support bracket
55 Aerial attachment/take-up pulley
56 Equipment/effects stowage
57 FuG 7a/FuG 25a radio equipment bay
58 Battery
59 Cockpit aft bulkhead
60 Control runs
61 Cockpit floor/centre-section main structure
62 Wingroot fillet
63 Underfloor aft fuel tank (291 litres/64 Imp gal)
64 Underfloor forward fuel tank (232 litres/51 Imp gal)
65 Cockpit sidewall control runs
66 Seat support brackets
67 Armoured bulkhead
68 Pilot's seat
69 Canopy operating handwheel
70 14-mm armoured backplate
71 Pilot's headrest
72 Canopy
73 Windscreen frame assembly
74 Armoured-glass windscreen
75 Revi gunsight
76 Instrument panel shroud
77 Throttle
78 Port control console (trim switches/buttons)
79 Control column
80 Seat pan
81 Starboard control console (circuit breakers)
82 Underfloor linkage
83 Electrical junction box
84 Rudder pedal assembly

85 Instrument panel sections
86 Screen support frame
87 Two 7.9-mm MG 17 machine-guns
88 Ammunition feed chute
89 Panel release catches
90 Fuselage armament ammunition boxes
91 Forward bulkhead
92 Inboard wing cannon ammunition boxes
93 Engine mounting lower attachment point
94 Cooling air exit louvres
95 Engine mounting upper attachment point
96 Oil pump assembly
97 Engine mounting ring
98 Fuselage MG 17 ammunition cooling pipes
99 Machine-gun front mounting brackets
100 Machine-gun breech blister fairings
101 Port split flap section
102 Flap actuating electric motor
103 Port outer 20-mm MG FF cannon
104 Aileron control linkage
105 Aileron fixed tab
106 Port aileron
107 Aileron hinge points
108 Port detachable wingtip
109 Port navigation light
110 Front spar
111 Wing lower shell

112 MG FF muzzle
113 Port mainwheel leg fairing
114 Aileron link assembly
115 Fuselage MG 17 muzzles
116 Muzzle troughs
117 Upper cowling panel
118 Fuselage MG 17 electrical synchronising unit
119 Exhaust pipes
120 Cowling panel ring
121 BMW 801D-2 radial engine
122 Former ring
123 Upper panel release catches
124 Forward cowling support ring
125 Oil tank armour
126 Oil tank (45.5 litres/10 Imp gal)
127 Annular oil cooler assembly
128 Cooler armoured ring
129 Engine 12-blade cooling fan
130 Three-blade propeller
131 Propeller boss
132 Oil cooler airflow track
133 Airflow duct fairing (to rear cylinders)
134 Lower panel release catches
135 Cowling lower panel section
136 Wingroot fairing
137 Centre-section wheel covers
138 Inboard 20-mm cannon muzzle
139 Wheel cover operating cable
140 Starboard wheel well

141 Mainwheel leg rib cut-out
142 Undercarriage retraction jack
143 Locking unit assembly
144 Inboard 20-mm cannon spent cartridge chute
145 Front spar inboard assembly
146 Ammunition feed chute
147 Fuselage/front spar attachment
148 Ammunition box bay
149 Starboard inboard 20-mm MG 151 cannon
150 Breech blister fairing
151 Fuselage/rear spar attachment
152 Rear spar
153 Starboard flap assembly
154 Inboard solid ribs
155 Rotating drive undercarriage retraction unit
156 Radius rod hinge
157 Outboard 20-mm cannon muzzle
158 Mainwheel leg strut mounting assembly
159 Undercarriage actuation drive motor
160 Starboard outboard 20-mm MG FF cannon
161 Front spar assembly
162 Ammunition drum
163 Rib cut-out
164 Aileron control linkage
165 Aileron fixed tab
166 Starboard aileron frame
167 Aileron hinge points
168 Rear spar

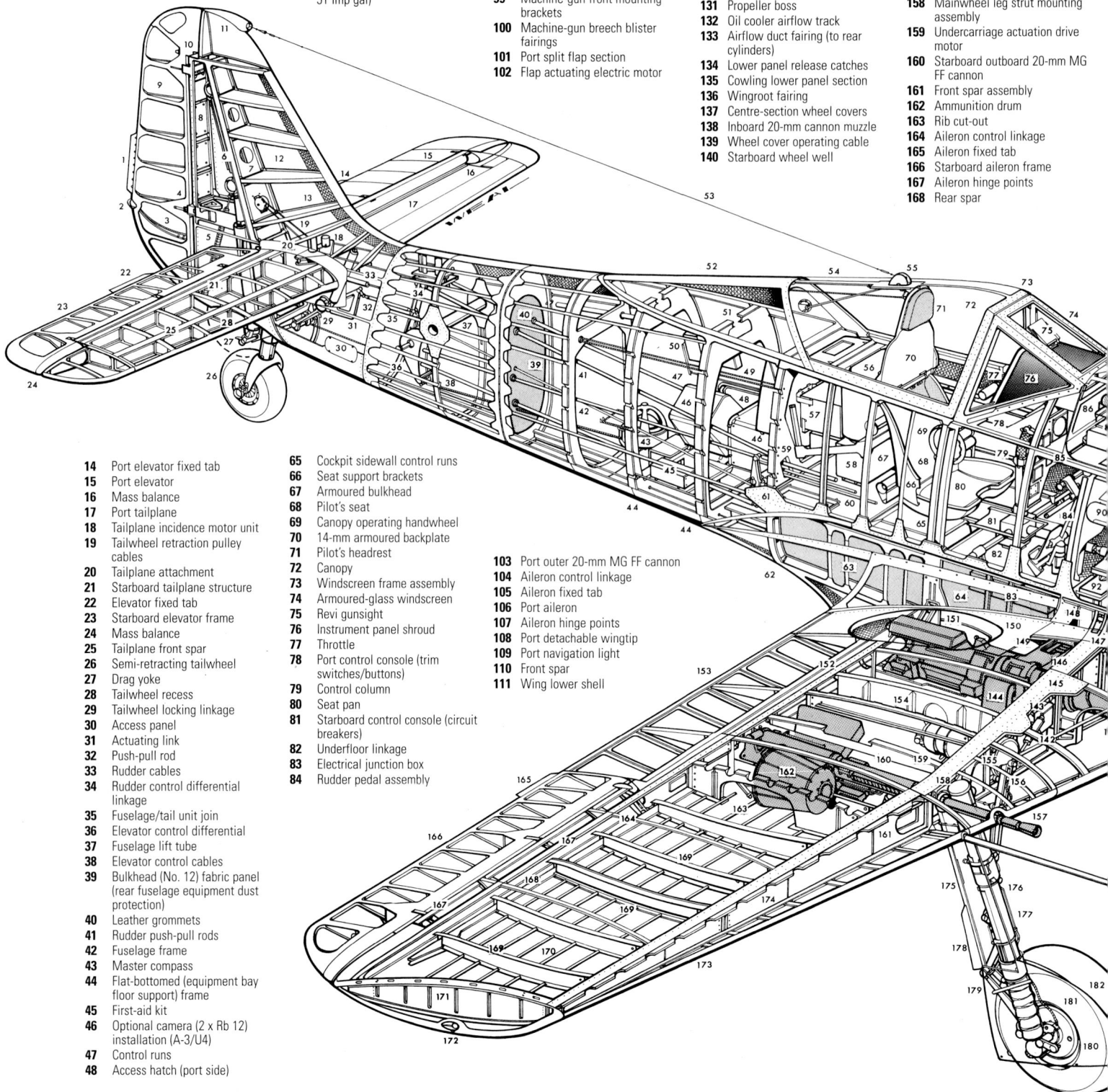

The centreline bomb rack and bomb insignia on the fuselage mark this Fw 190A-4 out as a dedicated Jabo machine. It was assigned to 10.(Jabo)/JG 26, flying from St Omer-Wizernes in the late summer of 1942. While flown by Feldwebel Karl Niesel, it was shot down on 17 October.

169 Wing lower shell outer 'floating ribs'
170 Wing undersurface inner skinning
171 Starboard detachable wingtip
172 Starboard navigation light
173 Leading-edge assembly
174 Nose rib attachment lips
175 Mainwheel leg fairing
176 Mainwheel leg
177 Brake lines
178 Fairing
179 Torque links
180 Axle hub assembly
181 Mainwheel fairing
182 Starboard mainwheel
183 Pitothead
184 Ventral bomb-rack aluminium aft fairing
185 Ventral bomb-rack carrier unit
186 ETC 500 ventral bomb-rack (A-3/U1)
187 SC 500 optional bomb load

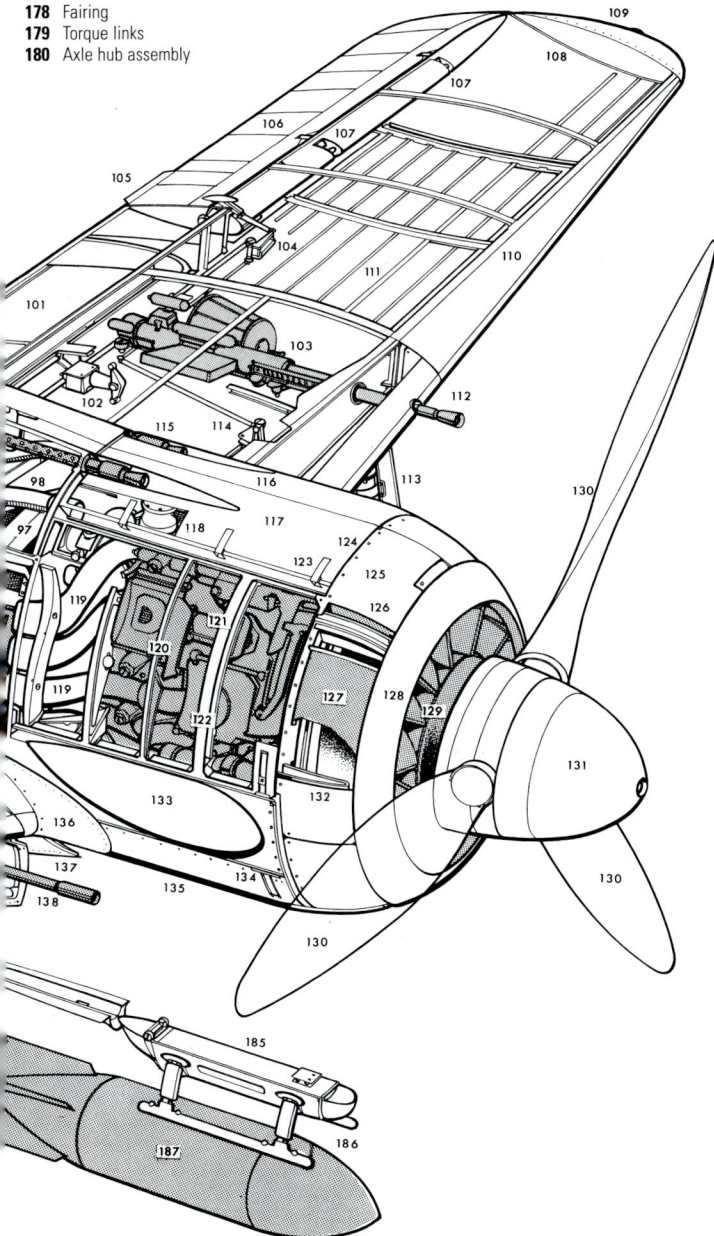

An early Fw 190 is seen from the rear. It can be distinguished as an early machine by its aerial attachment on the upper part of the fin, later aircraft having a 'pole' in this position.

3855 kg (8,499 lb) to 3978 kg (8,770 lb) with the supplementary cannon and ammunition. Essentially an air superiority fighter, the Fw 190A-2 established an immediate ascendancy over the Spitfire Mk V, and was a truly formidable fighter at altitudes between 5000 and 7500 m (16,400 and 24,600 ft), although speed fell off rapidly above and below this altitude band. Maximum speed in high supercharger gear at 5500 m (18,045 ft) was 626 km/h (389 mph), but in an emergency the throttle could be put "through the gate" and with override boost, which could be used for a maximum of one minute, a speed of 663 km/h (412 mph) could be attained at 6400 m (21,000 ft). At 1000 m (3,280 ft) maximum speed fell off to 518 km/h (322 mph), and normal range was 904 km (562 miles) at 444 km/h (276 mph).

Fw 190A-1 (Werk Nr 067, TI+DQ) is prepared for flight. The retractable footstep beneath the fuselage aft of the wing can be clearly seen.

Focke-Wulf Fw 190

Sleek, elegant and effective, the Fw 190 became one of the iconic aircraft of World War II, and was a major part of the Luftwaffe's war effort from 1941 onwards. This early production aircraft is representative of the early to mid-war Fw 190 series.

By the spring of 1942, deliveries of the improved BMW 801D-2 engine had begun, and this was introduced on the three Fw 190 assembly lines to result in the **Fw 190A-3**. Slightly more than 400 examples of the earlier Fw 190A-2 had been built, of which almost three-quarters had been produced by Arado and AGO. Externally, the Fw 190A-3 was identical to its predecessor on the assembly lines apart from modification of the engine cowling toggle latches and inspection panels, a revision of the supercharger air trunk fairing contours, and (after delivery of the initial production batches) the introduction of outlet louvres for motor cooling air. The BMW 801D-2 was generally similar to the BMW 801C-2 but compression ratio was increased from 6.5 to 7.22:1, and the high and low supercharger drive ratios were, respectively, changed from 7.46 to 8.31:1, and from 5.07 to 5.31:1. Take-off and emergency power was increased to 1268 kW (1,700 hp) at sea level, 1074 kW (1,440 hp) was provided at 5700 m (18,700 ft), and 1119 kW (1,500 hp) was available for climbing. Armament was standardised on the pair of fuselage-mounted MG 17 machine-guns, the two wing root-mounted MG 151s and the two MG FFs outboard of the undercarriage. Performance showed a marginal improve-

ment over that of the Fw 190A-2. The FuG 7a radio was supplemented by FuG 25a at an early production stage.

During the spring and summer of 1942, the Fw 190 V8, which, among several A-0 series airframes, had been re-engined with the BMW 801D-2 as a prototype Fw 190A-3, tested various wing and fuselage racks for bombs and drop tanks intended for proposed Jagdbomber (fighter-bomber) and Jagdbomber mit vergrösserter Reichweite (extended-range fighter-bomber) – usually abbreviated to Jabo and Jabo-Rei – conversions of the Fw 190A-3. From these tests was to stem the prodigious versatility for which the Focke-Wulf fighter was to gain distinction, and the first of the Umrüst-Bausätze (factory conversion sets) that, together with the series of Rüstsätzen (field conversion sets), turned this air superiority fighter into fighter-bomber, reconnaissance-fighter, night and bad-weather fighter, assault aircraft, torpedo-fighter and even two-seat trainer.

The Fw 190 V8 was flown with ETC 250 and 500 racks beneath the fuselage for 250-kg (551-lb) SC 250 and 500-kg (1,102-lb) SC 500 bombs, and racks beneath the wings for four 50-kg (110-lb) SC 50 bombs. It was also flown with a 300-litre (66-Imp gal) drop tank. By the late summer of 1942, provision for external racks was being made on the assembly line, resulting in the appearance in service of the **Fw 190A-3/U1** (the 'U' suffix indicating Umrüst-Bausätze) with an ETC 500 rack beneath the fuselage and the wing-mounted MG FF cannon deleted. The rack could take either a 250-kg or 500-kg bomb, or an adapter for four 50-kg bombs. Like those of all subsequent Jabo and Jabo-Rei models, the hinged wheel half-doors were deleted from the fuselage. The ETC rack and a 250-kg bomb reduced maximum speed by 45 km/h (28 mph) at sea level and 55 km/h (34 mph) at 6500 m (21,325 ft). The **Fw 190A-3/U3** was similar to the U1 but had an ETC 250 fuselage rack, some examples of this Jabo adaptation retaining their wing-mounted MG FF cannon and others having additional wing racks for SC 50

Experiments were made to determine the Fw 190's possible effectiveness as a long-range fighter-bomber (Jabo-Rei), including the configuration shown here with underwing drop tanks for additional fuel.

For a year from February 1942 Hauptmann Friedrich-Wilhelm Strakeljahn commanded 14.(Jabo)/JG 5, operating as part of the 'Eismeer' wing from Petsamo in northern Finland. This was his Jabo-equipped Fw 190A-3.

Focke-Wulf Fw 190

Oberstleutnant Walter Oesau was the Kommodore of JG 2 'Richthofen' from July 1941, and oversaw the Geschwader's conversion to the Fw 190. This was his A-4 when the Geschwaderstab was operating from Beaumont-le-Roger in February 1943.

Only a few Fw 190s reached North Africa, including when II/JG 2 went to Tunisia between November 1942 and March 1943. This is the Fw 190A-4 of the Gruppen-kommandeur, Oberleutnant Adolf Dickfeld, based at Kairouan.

With III/JG 2's cockerel badge on the nose, this Fw 190A-4 was flown by 9./JG 2's commander, Hauptmann Siegfried Schnell. His victory tally, and Knight's Cross and Oak Leaves, are meticulously recorded on the rudder.

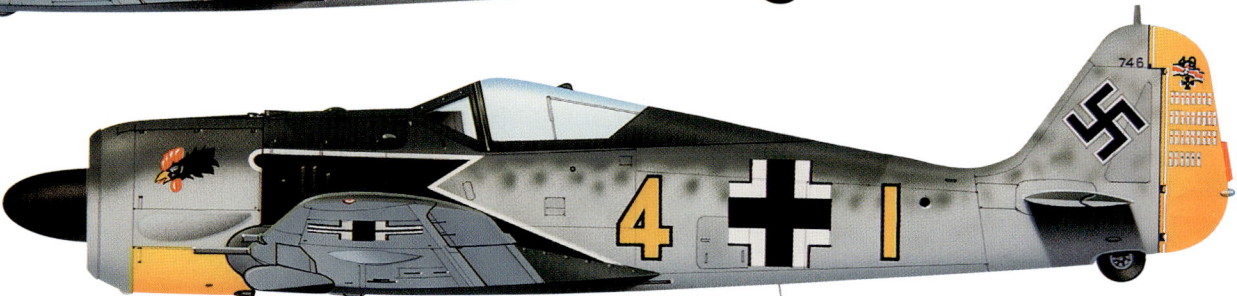

Wearing the stylised eagle's head marking that was adopted by JG 2 to cover up oil stains from the exhaust, this Fw 190A-4 was flown by Oberleutnant Horst Hannig, Staffel-kapitän of 2./JG 2 at St André and Tricqueville in May 1943.

This Fw 190A-4 was flown by the adjutant of Stab III/JG 2 'Richthofen', one of the top-scoring fighter wings of all time. The Gruppe began to receive the A-4 version in October 1942 while based at Poix in France.

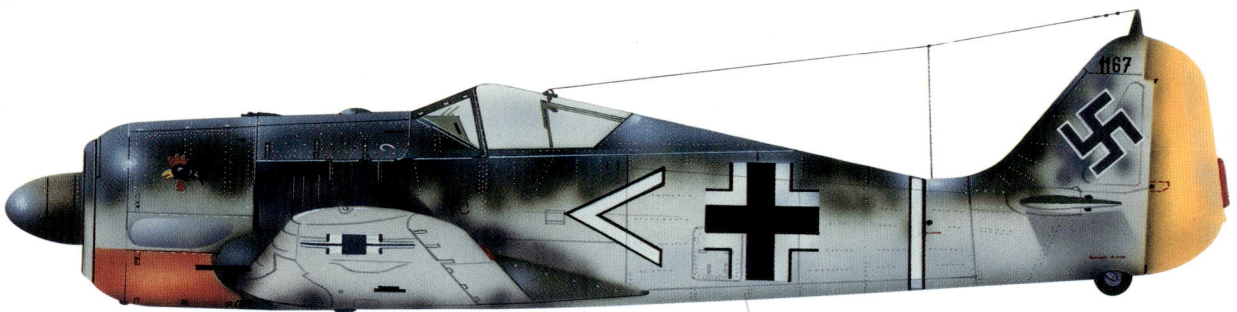

In early 1943 the II Gruppe of Schlachtgeschwader 1 withdrew to Deblin-Irena to convert to the Fw 190A for close support duties. A-models remained in service alongside the dedicated Fw 190F/G fighter-bombers until late 1944.

Focke-Wulf Fw 190

Oberstleutnant Johannes Trautloft commanded JG 54 for nearly three years, and introduced the famous 'Grünherz' symbol. On his Fw 190A-4 it was superimposed with badges for the Geschwader's three constituent Gruppen. The aircraft is depicted here as it appeared at Krasnogvardeisk in December 1942.

Among JG 54's rising 'stars' was Leutnant Walter Nowotny, who commanded 1. Staffel while at Krasnogvardeisk in November 1942. This was the month the Gruppe received its first Fw 190s.

Hauptmann Hans 'Fips' Philipp flew this Fw 190A-4 in January 1943. He commanded I/JG 54, and in March 1943 became the second Luftwaffe ace to pass the 200-victory mark. On the Russian front it was virtually unheard of for Experten to display their tallies on the aircraft for fear of retribution if shot down and captured.

In this Fw 190A-4 Feldwebel Karl 'Quax' Schnörrer regularly flew as wingman to Walter Nowotny, 1/JG 54's commander. The I Gruppe badge worn on the nose was the coat of arms of Nuremburg.

'Black 11' was a 2./JG 54 Fw 190A-4, assigned to Feldwebel Hans-Joachim Kroschinski in February 1943. JG 54's aircraft had the yellow fuselage band applied under the national insignia.

II/JG 54 began to convert to the Fw 190 in December 1942, taking its new aircraft from Ryelbitzi to Kalinin, and then to Orel by May. This A-4 was assigned to 6. Staffel's commander, Oberleutnant Hans Beisswenger, who flew it only briefly before being killed in early March 1943.

Focke-Wulf Fw 190

By the spring of 1943 I Gruppe of JG 54 was at Staraja-Russa with Fw 190A-4s, but the white distemper was being partially removed from the aircraft to reflect the terrain over which they flew. This aircraft was often flown by Walter Nowotny of 1./JG54.

This partly winter-camouflaged Fw 190A-4 was flown by Oberfeldwebel Anton 'Toni' Döbele, a member of Nowotny's flight in 1./JG 54. The I Gruppe badge has been painted out following an edict to remove all unit insignia, although the 'Grünherz' is retained.

During the late spring/summer of 1943 II/JG 54 was flying from Orel, its Fw 190A-4s wearing a new summer scheme of green and brown. This is the aircraft of Fähnrich Norbert Hannig of 5./JG 54.

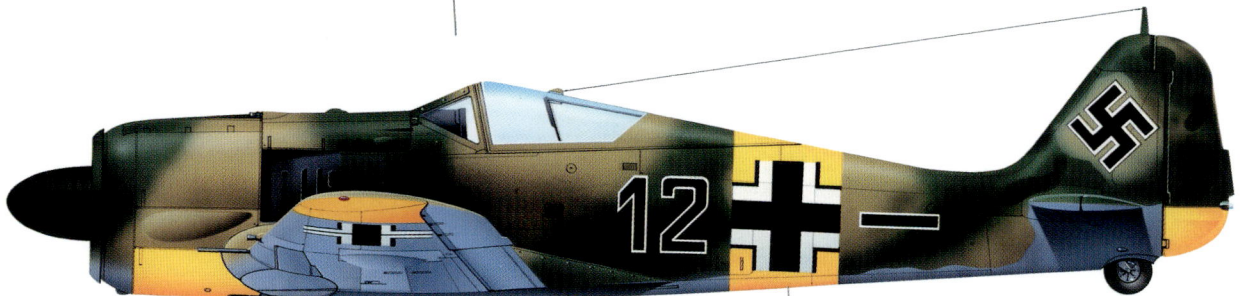

I Gruppe of JG 54 opted for a two-tone green summer splinter camouflage while based at Orel with Fw 190A-4s. Both I and II Gruppen were heavily committed during the battle at Kursk in July 1943.

Hauptmann Hans Götz was the Staffelkapitän of 2./JG 54, and flew this Fw 190A-4 in July 1943. By rights the aircraft's number should have been red, but the colour had been banned to avoid confusion with Soviet aircraft. Note that the 'Grünherz' has been painted out.

Dappled grey camouflages began to become more commonplace in mid-1943. In the second half of the year JG 54 was commanded by Major Hubertus von Bonin, who flew this Fw 190A-4 from Krasnogvardeisk.

Focke-Wulf Fw 190

'Yellow 1' was an Fw 190A-4 of 3./JG 51, based at Orel in August 1943 as part of Operation Zitadelle at Kursk. Although unit markings had gone, it was generally possible to tell JG 51 machines from those of JG 54 by the position of the fuselage theatre band.

This Fw 190A-4 of 3./JG 51 at Orel in June 1943 shows another variation of summer camouflage. The aircraft was the mount of Leutnant Josef Jennewein. The lucky numeral '5' had been his competition number when he won the 1940 world skiing championship combined alpine event.

Fw 190A-5s began to be delivered to II/JG 26 in March/April 1943, when the Gruppe was based at Vitry-en-Artois. This particular machine was allocated to the commander of 4. Staffel, Oberleutnant Otto Stammberger.

Josef 'Pips' Priller – Kommodore of JG 26 for two years from January 1943 – flew a succession of 'Black 13' aircraft, including this Fw 190A-5. It is shown as it appeared in June 1943 when the Geschwaderstab was operating from Lille-Vendeville.

5./JG 1's commander, Hauptmann Fritz Dietrich Wickop, flew this Fw 190A-5, which bears not only the Tatzelwurm badge of JG 1, but also a stylised seagull introduced by a former Staffelkapitän. It is shown as it appeared in April 1943, when 5./JG 1 was based at Woensdrecht.

This Fw 190A-5 was flown by Leutnant Rüdiger von Kirchmayr. As the markings suggest, he was the Technical Officer for II/JG 1, the spinner and Tatzelwurm being painted in green to represent the Gruppenstab colour. The aircraft has flame shields fitted, indicating its use by night on Wilde Sau missions.

Above: This Fw 190A-0 was employed as a test airframe for the Fw 190A-3/U3 fighter-bomber variant, the U3 factory modification providing an ETC 250 bomb rack for an SC 250 bomb.

A considerable amount of development work was carried out with the early Fw 190s to generate new armament options as the range of tasks that the Fw 190 was put to gradually expanded, including the possibility of greater internal wing armament.

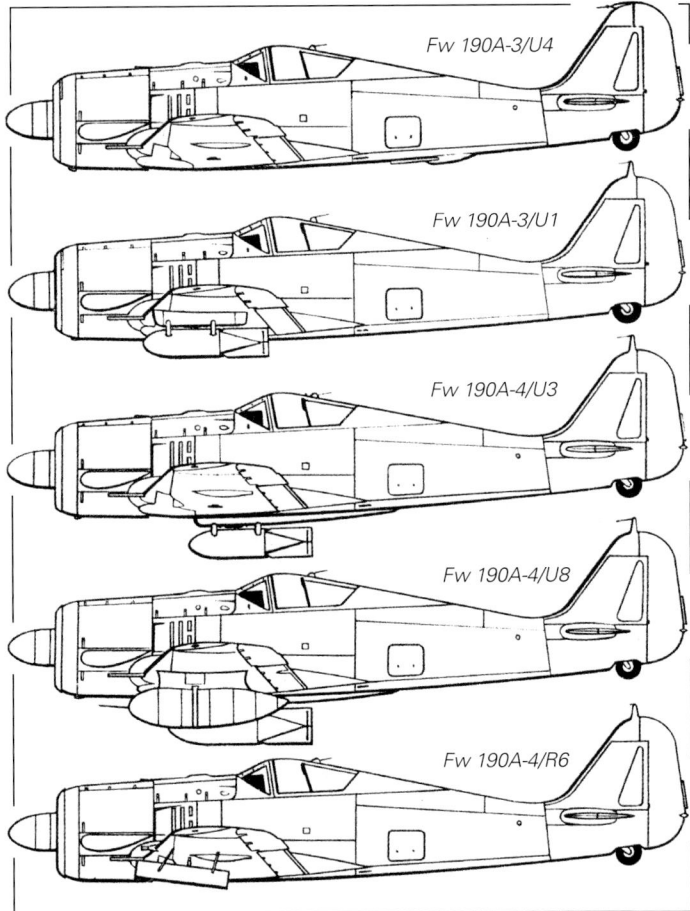

Fw 190A-3/U4
Fw 190A-3/U1
Fw 190A-4/U3
Fw 190A-4/U8
Fw 190A-4/R6

bombs. The **Fw 190A-3/U4** was an armed reconnaissance variant with two Rb 12 cameras mounted in the fuselage aft of the pilot and the MG FF cannon deleted.

Throughout 1942, Fw 190A production climbed steadily, the Fieseler plant at Kassel phasing into the programme in May, and a production peak being attained in July when 194 fighters were delivered. Whereas the Luftwaffe had accepted only 224 Fw 190As by the end of 1941, a further 1,878 had been accepted by the end of 1942, representing slightly more than 40 per cent of all single-engined fighter production in Germany.

During the course of 1942, production of the Fw 190A-3 had given place to the **Fw 190A-4**, the principal change introduced by this sub-type being the addition of an MW (Methanol-Water) 50 power boost system to obtain extra power below the rated altitude of the BMW 801D-2 engine, the mixture acting as an anti-detonant and enabling higher boost pressures to be used for short periods, although it had a disastrous effect on spark plug life. Another change was the replacement of the FuG 7a radio by FuG 16Z, the only external manifestation of this change being the introduction of a small vertical aerial pylon at the lip of the verti-

Focke-Wulf Fw 190A-4/U8 long-range fighter-bombers are seen on the flight line. One of the several armament/drop tank options available with this sub-type was a pair of 300-litre (66-Imp gal) tanks under the wings (seen here) with a 250-kg (551-lb) SC 250 bomb on the fuselage centreline. In this format, only the wing-root MG 151 cannon were retained as gun armament.

Focke-Wulf Fw 190

The two fighter wings on the Russian front began to receive Fw 190A-5s in March 1943. This machine was flown by Major Erich Leie, I/JG 51's commander, from Orel in May 1943.

Hauptmann Fritz Losigkeit took command of III/JG 51 in June 1943, just as the first Fw 190A-5s were arriving. He flew this machine while the unit was operating from Orel during the Kursk fighting.

JG 54's pilots scored heavily during the summer of 1943. In June 1./JG 54's Walter Nowotny passed the 100-kill mark. His aircraft at the time was this Fw 190A-5.

Wearing a two-tone green summer camouflage, this Fw 190A-5 was flown by Leutnant Robert 'Bazi' Weiss of 3./JG 54. The aircraft still carries its 'Grünherz' badge, which was something of a rarity at the time (June 1943, Orel).

Major Hubertus von Bonin took command of JG 54 in July 1943, flying a succession of Fw 190s, including this A-5. He was killed in action on 15 December over Vitebsk.

After Kursk II/JG 54 operated in the Ukraine, before moving north in early 1944 to Petserie in Estonia, with a brief detachment in the summer to the Finnish bases of Immola, Helsinki and Petajarvi. This Fw 190A-5 dates from that period, after which the Gruppe retreated into Latvia, and then to Germany.

Temporarily painted matt black, this is an Fw 190A-5/U8 Jabo-Rei aircraft with centreline bomb rack and wing drop-tanks, during the fighter-bomber attacks on southern England during the summer of 1943. It was operated by II/Schnellkampf-geschwader 10, based at Rennes-St Jacques in Brittany.

This Fw 190A-5 was the mount of Oberfeldwebel August Lambert of 5./Schlachtgeschwader 2, based at Bagerovo in late 1943. Lambert was by far the highest-scoring ace of the Schlachtflieger, with 116 victories.

This colourful Fw 190A-5 was flown by Major Hermann Graf while commander of the Ergänzungs-Jagdgruppe Ost in early 1943. This was a training unit headquartered at St Jean d'Angely but with several satellite bases in southern France.

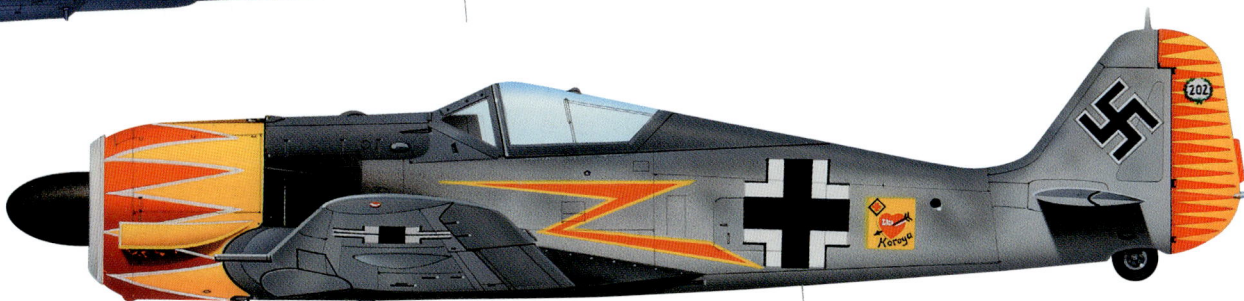

In July 1943 III/JG 2 began to receive the Fw 190A-6. Two months later this aircraft was being flown by Oberleutnant Josef 'Sepp' Wurmheller, the commander of 9./JG 2 at Vannes-Meucon.

Hauptmann Friedrich-Karl Müller was the most successful single-engined night fighter pilot. He used this Fw 190A-6 while acting as the Technical Officer of JG 300 in November 1943, based at Bonn-Hangelar.

JG 11 was formed in April 1943 to help defend Germany, and its III Gruppe was at Oldenburg for a year from June 1943. From October the Kommandeur was Major Anton 'Toni' Hackl, who used this Fw 190A-6. The white tail was sometimes applied to signify a unit leader.

Left: First of several planned torpedo-carrying versions of the Fw 190 was the A-5/U14, (Werk Nr 871), shown here carrying an LTF 5b torpedo. The rack fairing of this version was deeper than that on the U15, which carried an LT 950 (950-kg/2,090-lb) weapon. Note the considerably lengthened tailwheel assembly. Focke-Wulf wasted much time and money developing torpedo-configured Fw 190 versions that saw limited, if any, service.

The Fw 190A-5/U14 was adapted to carry an LTF 5b torpedo mounted on a modified underfuselage ETC 501/502 rack, in a proposed production configuration. The type had a lengthened tailwheel leg to allow ground clearance for the torpedo.

The 30-mm MK 103 long-barrel cannon installation is seen below the port wing of the Fw 190A-5/U11, prototype for the Fw 190A-8/R3 version.

cal fin. The application of Umrüst-Bausätze resulted in the **Fw 190A-4/U1** Jabo with two ETC 501 bomb racks and fixed armament restricted to the two wing root-mounted MG 151 cannon, which were harmonised at 200 m (656 ft) instead of the usual 450 m (1476 ft); the **Fw 190A-4/U3** Jabo with a single SC 250 bomb beneath the fuselage that could be replaced by a 300-litre drop tank, and additional armour protection for the engine and pilot, standard armament being retained (although, in practice, the MG FF cannon were usually removed); and the **Fw 190A-4/U8** Jabo-Rei that, with full gun armament, could carry a 300-litre ventral tank and four SC 50 bombs on wing racks, gross weight being 4450 kg (9,810 lb). With the MG FF cannon removed, the Fw 190A-4/U8 could carry two SC 250 bombs on wing racks in addition to the ventral tank, gross weight being 4752 kg (10,476 lb), and with only the wing root-mounted MG 151 cannon retained, a single 250-kg bomb could be carried beneath the fuselage and two 300-litre tanks beneath the wings on improvised racks.

This Fw 190A-8/trop test airframe has one SC 500 bomb beneath the fuselage and an SC 250 beneath each wing, in a weapons development configuration for the Fw 190F fighter-bomber series.

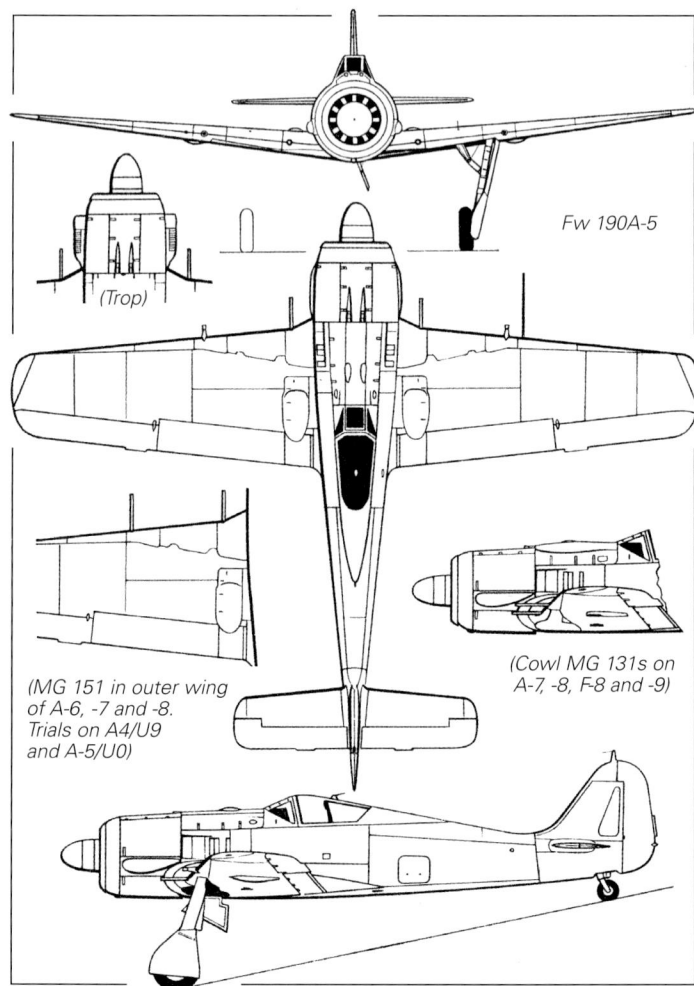

Fw 190A-5

(Trop)

(MG 151 in outer wing of A-6, -7 and -8. Trials on A4/U9 and A-5/U0)

(Cowl MG 131s on A-7, -8, F-8 and -9)

Below: The Fw 190A-5/U13 was a Jabo-Rei version featuring Focke-Wulf underwing racks for carrying either a bomb or tank.

Above: The Umrüst-Bausatz 8 (U8) factory modification changed an A-model fighter into a Jabo-Rei long-range fighter-bomber. Underwing 300-litre (66-Imp gal) fuel tanks and a centrally-mounted bomb were the main features. This is the A-5/U8 development aircraft (Werk Nr 636).

Fw 190A-3 specification

Type: single-seat fighter

Powerplant: one BMW 801D-2 14-cylinder radial air-cooled engine rated at 1268 kW (1,700 hp) for take-off and 1074 kW (1,440 hp) at 5700 m (18,700 ft)

Performance: maximum speed 502 km/h (312 mph) at sea level, 526 km/h (327 mph) at 1000 m (3,280 ft), 534 km/h (332 mph) at 1500 m (4,920 ft), 615 km/h (382 mph) at 6000 m (19,685 ft) (with override boost for one minute) 673 km/h (418 mph) at 6400 m (21,000 ft); normal cruising speed 447 km/h (278 mph); maximum range 800 km (497 miles); initial climb rate 862 m (2,830 ft) per minute; time to 8000 m (26,250 ft) 12 minutes; service ceiling 10600 m (34,775 ft)

Weights: empty 2900 kg (6,393 lb); empty equipped 3225 kg (7,110 lb); loaded 3978 kg (8,770 lb)

Dimensions: wingspan 10.50 m (34 ft 5½ in); length 8.80 m (28 ft 10½ in); height (over airscrew tip) 3.95 m (12 ft 11½ in); wing area 18.30 m² (196.98 sq ft)

Armament: two 7.9-mm MG 17 machine-guns in fuselage with 1,000 r.p.g., two 20-mm MG 151 cannon in wing roots with 200 r.p.g., and two 20-mm MG FF cannon in wings with 55 r.p.g.

Although relatively few Rüstsätze were applied to the Fw 190A-4, one of the first 'Pulk-Zerstörer' ('Pulk' being a Luftwaffe expression for a close formation of USAAF day bombers) was the **Fw 190A-4/R6** that made its debut in 1943 as one of several attempts to counter the 8th Air Force's massed formations, the suffix indicating the attachment of a pair of Werfergranate (W.Gr.) 21 mortars beneath the wings. The 21-cm (8.27-in) mortar shells were intended to break up the tight formations so that waves of interceptors following the mortar-equipped Fw 190s could get at the individual bombers. Tests with the Fw 190A-4/R6 were carried out at the Abt.F 7 at Rechlin where results indicated a +7-m (+23-ft) vertical deviation and a ±40-m (±130-ft) horizontal deviation over a distance of 1000 m (3,280 ft). The W.Gr. 21 was first used on a large scale over Schweinfurt on 14 October 1943, numbers of Fw 190A-4/R6 and -5/R6 fighters launching their 21-cm mortar shells outside the range of the bombers' defensive fire, and partly breaking up the formations of some 228 USAAF bombers. Sixty-two bombers were lost by the force during the action, 17 crashed after crossing the British coastline, and a further 121 were

damaged of which some 30 per cent proved total write-offs. Attrition was thus more than 50 per cent of the total bomber force, the Luftwaffe losing 38 fighters, a further 51 fighters being seriously damaged.

From April 1943, production of the Fw 190A-4 began to give place to the **Fw 190A-5**, the airframe of which differed from that of its predecessor significantly in having a modified engine mounting lengthened by 15 cm (5.91 in), this increasing overall length of the fighter from 8.80 m (28 ft 10½ in) to 10.95 m (29 ft 4.25 in). The Fw 190A-5 was intended from the outset to accept a wider variety of Umrüst-Bausätze. The principal of them were as follows:

A-5/U2: nocturnal Jabo-Rei with anti-glare shields, exhaust flame-dampers, an ETC 250 rack beneath the fuselage, and provision for two 300-litre (66-Imp gal) drop tanks. Gun armament was restricted to the wing root-mounted MG 151 cannon, and only two test and live operational examples were completed.

Fw 190A-5 (Werk Nr 151163, BG+KC) is seen prior to delivery. The subtype was designed specifically to accept a wider variety of factory conversion kits for different equipment and armament.

Major Hans-Günter von Kornatzki was the pioneer of the Sturm daylight defence concept, in which heavily armoured Fw 190s would press home attacks against USAAF bombers to very close range. This was the Fw 190A-6 'Sturmbock' he flew during the initial operations of Sturmstaffel 1, formed in late 1943 at Achmer and subsequently moving to Dortmund. The fuselage stripes differentiated the Sturm unit from the aircraft of I/JG 1 with which SS 1 operated.

411

Focke-Wulf Fw 190

Softly-spoken Major Erich Rudorffer led II/JG 54 from August 1943, ending the campaign with 222 kills. Most were gained in Fw 190s, like this A-6 seen as it appeared during the Gruppe's brief deployment to Immola in Finland in June/July 1944.

There is little to suggest that this Fw 190A-6 was flown by the top ace of JG 54, Otto Kittel, who was killed in February 1945 having scored 267 victories. This is how the machine appeared in August 1944 when 3./JG 54 was at Riga-Skulte in Latvia.

When Nowotny was promoted to lead I/JG 54, his successor as commander of 1. Staffel was Leutnant Helmut Wettstein. This was the Fw 190A-6 he flew while operating from Poltava in the late summer of 1943. The unit's first Fw 190A-6s had arrived in July.

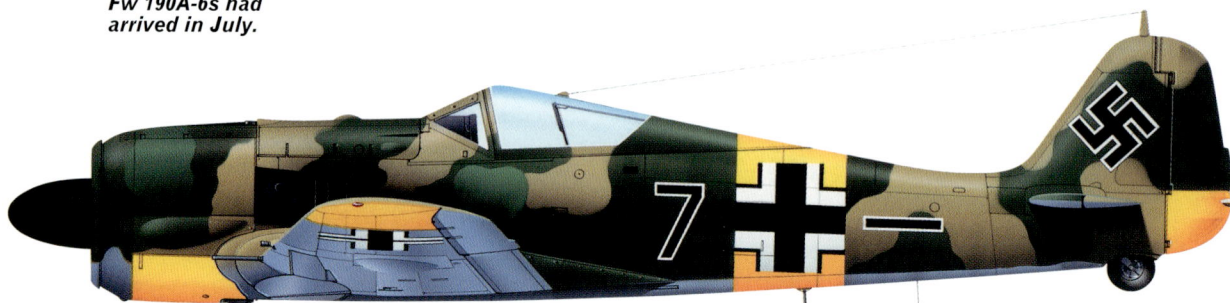

Exhibiting an unusual summer camouflage finish, this Fw 190A-6 was flown by Leutnant Emil 'Bully' Lang of 5./JG 54 in the summer of 1943. Lang was killed in September 1944 fighting P-47s, having scored 173 kills.

Walter Nowotny became commander of I/JG 54 in August 1943, and continued to rack up the kills. His 250th victory was achieved in this Fw 190A-6 on 14 October 1943, at which time the Gruppe was based at Vitebsk. Although the full Kommandeur markings are applied, the aircraft still carries Nowotny's lucky '13' below the canopy.

Major Anton Mader was the Kommodore of JG 54 for much of 1944, and flew this Fw 190A-6 from Dorpat, Estonia. The brown/green camouflage was found to be most effective over the terrain encountered on the northern sector of the Russian front.

412

Splinter camouflage

Luftwaffe aircraft generally had a two-tone splinter camouflage applied to the upper surfaces, with a sharp-edged demarcation between the two shades. The camouflage was applied by the factory, but was often tailored in the field to match the terrain and season. This was especially true on the Eastern Front, where there were marked differences between seasons, and between the northern, central and southern sectors.

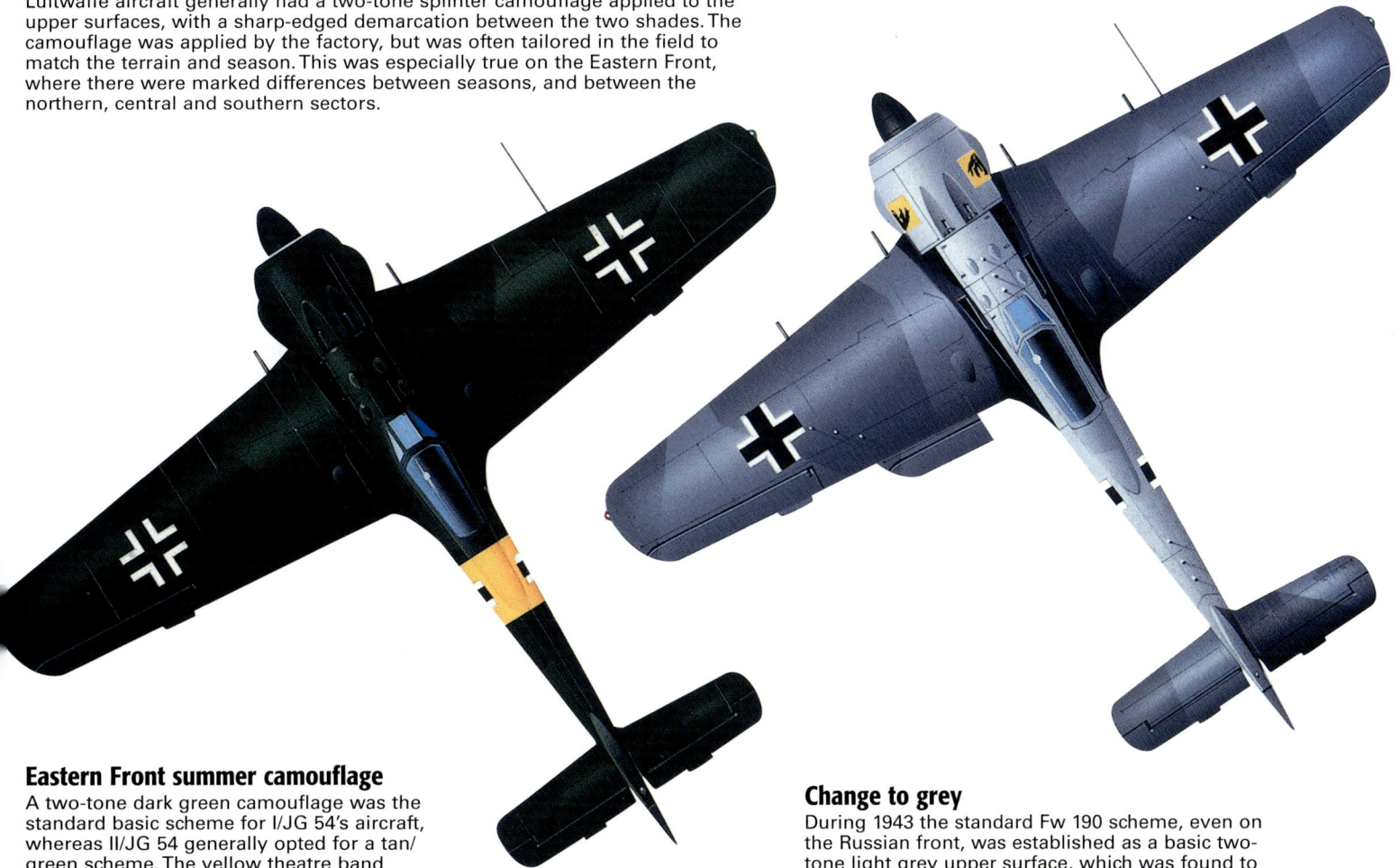

Eastern Front summer camouflage

A two-tone dark green camouflage was the standard basic scheme for I/JG 54's aircraft, whereas II/JG 54 generally opted for a tan/green scheme. The yellow theatre band provided an instant recognition aid during aerial battles.

Change to grey

During 1943 the standard Fw 190 scheme, even on the Russian front, was established as a basic two-tone light grey upper surface, which was found to offer the best compromise in terms of camouflaging the aircraft on the ground and in the air.

Two Fw 190A-5s were assigned as U12 Zerstörer development aircraft with a pair of MG 151 20-mm cannons in a large fairing under each wing. The normal outer wing MG FF cannon were deleted in this case. Seen here is BH+CC, Werk Nr 150813.

Focke-Wulf Fw 190

'White 11' was the Fw 190A-6 of Oberleutnant Hans Krause of 1./NJGr 10 at Werneuchen. It was one of a small number of aircraft fitted with FuG 216 Neptun V radar for Wilde Sau night-fighter duties, with a circular display screen in the top left of the instrument panel. As well as the antenna arrays, it had flame-dampers fitted.

A-5/U3: Jabo with fuselage and wing racks for maximum of 1000 kg (2,205 lb) of bombs and/or drop tanks. Total weight of armour increased to 405 kg (893 lb), and gun armament restricted to fuselage-mounted MG 17s.

A-5/U4: reconnaissance fighter with two Rb 12 cameras in

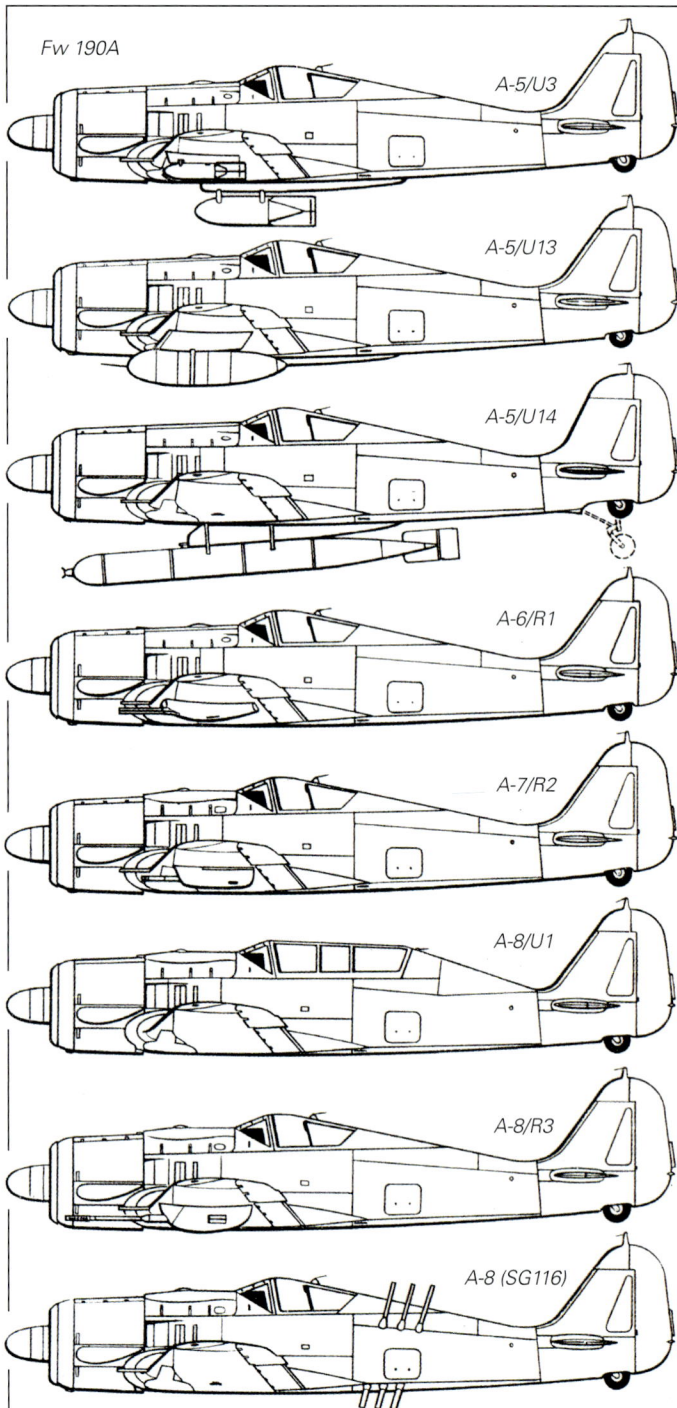

rear fuselage and wing-mounted MG FF cannon deleted.

A-5/U8: Jabo-Rei with SC 250 bomb beneath fuselage, two 300-litre (66-Imp gal) wing drop tanks and armament restricted to wing root-mounted MG 151s.

A-5/U9: Zerstörer with two 13-mm MG 131 machine-guns in fuselage, two 20-mm MG 151 cannon in the wing roots and two similar weapons outboard of the undercarriage attachment points. Two prototypes only (Werk Nummern 812 and 816).

A-5/U11: Schlachtflugzeug with 30-mm MK 103 cannon in place of MG FF cannon in wings. One development aircraft (Werk Nr 1303).

A-5/U12: Zerstörer with two 20-mm MG 151 cannon in tray beneath each wing in place of wing-mounted MG FF cannon. Two prototype aircraft (Werk Nummern 813 and 814).

A-5/U13: Jabo-Rei with fuselage ETC 501 rack and wing racks for two drop tanks. Gun armament restricted to wing root-mounted MG 151s. Two prototypes (Werk Nummern 817 and 825), one with Messerschmitt-designed wing racks and the other with Focke-Wulf designed wing racks.

A-5/U14: proposed torpedo-fighter with LTF 5b torpedo on adapted ETC 501 fuselage rack. Enlarged fin and lengthened tailwheel leg. Gun armament restricted to wing root-mounted MG 151s. Two prototypes (Werk Nummern 871 and 872).

A-5/U15: proposed torpedo-fighter similar to U14 but intended to carry Blohm und Voss LT 950 guided torpedo. One prototype.

A-5/U17: Schlachtflugzeug with ETC 50 wing racks. Development aircraft for F-series.

By the spring of 1943, the weight escalation that was accompanying the extension of the Fw 190A's operational tasks was giving cause for serious concern and, in an attempt to arrest its vicious spiral, Focke-Wulf undertook some rede-

From the Fw 190A-6 onwards, a 20-mm MG 151 cannon was mounted in the outer wing just outboard of the main undercarriage attachment. This very satisfactory arrangement was clearly visible due to the protruding blast tube for this weapon.

By February 1944 the Fw 190A-7 aircraft of I/JG 11 at Rotenburg had yellow Reichsverteidigung (RV, defence of the Reich) bands. This machine was flown by 3. Staffel's leader, Oberleutnant Hans-Heinrich König.

In February 1944 II/JG 26 was at Cambrai-Epinoy, continuing the cross-Channel fight. This Fw 190A-7 was allocated to 5. Staffel's Oberfeldwebel Adolf Glunz, the only NCO in JG 26 to be awarded the Knight's Cross.

Among the units ranged against the USAAF day bombers in April 1944 was I/JG 1 at Lippsspringe. 1. Staffel's commander, Hauptmann Alfred Grislawski, flew this Fw 190A-7, which wears the Geschwader's red RV band and a new Geschwader badge of a winged red '1'.

The white rudder and impressive tally signify that this was the Fw 190A-7 of an important pilot. It was the mount of Major Heinz 'Pritzl' Bär, Kommandeur of II/JG 1 while at Störmede in April-June 1944.

Although it was the aircraft above that was Heinz Bär's regular machine, he was flying this Fw 190A-7 when he achieved his 200th victory (of an eventual 220) on 22 April 1944. Bär had the outer cannon deleted from his aircraft as he preferred the agility over the extra firepower.

In April 1944 the first Fw 190A-8s were delivered to the Stab, I and II/JG 26. The Geschwader-kommodore, Josef 'Pips' Priller, flew this aircraft, complete with his ace of hearts marking and the name 'Jutta' (short for Johanna).

415

Focke-Wulf Fw 190

The 'blinkered' cockpit with extra armoured glass identifies this aircraft as an Fw 190A-8 'Sturmbock'. Special Sturm units were formed within the home defence units, this aircraft being that assigned to the commander of IV(Sturm)/JG 3 at Schongau in August 1944.

Although it lacks the extra canopy protection, this is another Fw 190A-8 'Sturmbock' of IV(Sturm)/JG 3. Its pilot, Unteroffizier Willi Maximowitz, undertook a number of successful ramming attacks on US 'heavies'.

Major Walther Dahl, Kommodore of JG 300, flew this Fw 190A-8 'Sturmbock' from Unterschlauersheim in June 1944. It is possible that it had formerly served with IV(Sturm)/JG 3, hence the white fuselage RV band.

This colourful Fw 190A-8 (not a 'Sturmbock') was flown by Unteroffizier Ernst Schröder of 5./JG 300 while based at Löbnitz in November 1944. The marking below the cockpit was the coat of arms of Cologne, with the city's carnival slogan.

The additional red markings on this Fw 190A-8 of 5./JG 300 marked it as the mount of the Staffelkapitän, Leutnant Klaus Bretschneider. The fuselage slogan was 'Rauhbautz (tough guy) VII'. The unit switched from Wilde Sau night operations to Sturm day tactics.

This 5./JG 300 Fw 190A-8 'Sturmbock', also from around November 1944 while based at Löbnitz, was flown by the 19-year old Matthäus Erhardt, and was given the name 'Pimpl' (youngster). JG 300's red RV band was subsequently changed to blue-white-blue to avoid confusion with JG 1.

Focke-Wulf Fw 190

One of the many attempts to up-gun the offensive capability of the Fw 190 was the installation of a WB 151-type gondola beneath each wing, each pod containing two MG 151 20-mm cannon. Two trials/development Fw 190s were converted as Fw 190A-5/U12s. One of them, Focke-Wulf-built Werk Nr 150813 BH+CC, is shown here. The configuration was later used as the Fw 190A-8/R1.

sign of the wing structure, the modified wing being tested on the **Fw 190A-5/U10** (Werk Nr 861) and adopted as standard for the next A-series production model, the **Fw 190A-6** that reached the assembly lines in June 1943. Intended primarily for operation on the Eastern Front, and for the application of Rüstsätze rather than Umrüst-Bausätze, the Fw 190A-6 standardised on a basic gun armament of two fuselage-mounted 7.9-mm MG 17 machine-guns and four wing-mounted 20-mm MG 151 cannon (two in the wing roots and two in the outer panels). Heavier armour was provided in strategic areas but, nevertheless, in its basic Zerstörer form, gross weight was held at 4140 kg (9,125 lb), wing loading thus being 319 kPa (46.3 lb/sq ft) and power loading being 3.22 kg/kW (5.3 lb/hp).

The initial version to reach the Eastern Front (during the winter of 1943-44) was the **Fw 190A-6/R1** Zerstörer that had the outboard MG 151 cannon deleted and a tray mounting a pair of MG 151s attached beneath each wing, thus providing a total armament of two MG 17s and six MG 151s. The external gun panniers resulted in a loss of 40 km/h (25 mph) in maximum speed and some 30 km (19 miles) in range but provided the fighter with an extremely effective weight of fire. The **Fw 190A-6/R2** Zerstörer had a 30-mm MK 108 cannon beneath each wing in place of the outboard MG 151s, but only one example (the **Fw 190 V51** Werk-Nr 53 0765) was tested. The **Fw 190A-6/R4** was another experimental aircraft (**Fw 190 V45** Werk-Nr 7347) that initially tested a GM 1 (nitrous-oxide injection) power boosting system and extended wing tips. It was later flown with a supercharged BMW 801TS engine. The **Fw 190A-6/R6** Pulk-Zerstörer carried a pair of W.Gr. 21 mortars for use against bomber formations, and the **Fw 190A-6/U3** was a frontline Jabo conversion with fuselage and wing bomb racks.

Late in 1943, the **Fw 190A-7** attained production, but

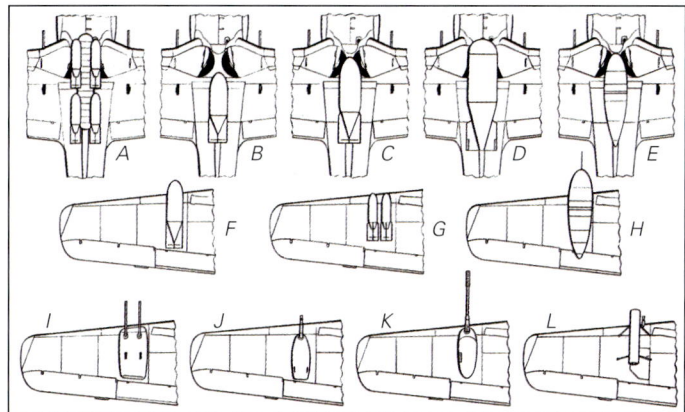

Fuselage loads: (A) four SC 50 bombs on ER-4 adapter; **(B)** one SC 250 bomb; **(C)** one SC 500 bomb; **(D)** one SC 1000 bomb; **(E)** one 300-litre (66-Imp gal) auxiliary tank.
Wing loads: (F) two SC 250 bombs; **(G)** four SC 50 bombs; **(H)** two 300-litre (66-Imp gal) auxiliary tanks.
Wing armament: (I) R1 comprising four MG 151s on A-6, A-7 and A-8; **(J)** R2 comprising two MK 108s on A-6, A-7 and A-8; **(K)** R3 comprising two MK 103s on A-8, F-3 and F-8; **(L)** R6 comprising two W.Gr. 21 mortars on A-4, A-5, A-6 and A-7

only some 80 examples of this sub-type were delivered, these differing from their production line predecessors in having simplified electrics, improved radio, a Revi 16B gun sight, and 13-mm MG 131 upper forward fuselage guns. At least half of them were completed (by Fieseler) as **Fw 190A-7/R2** Zerstörer with the outboard MG 151s replaced by externally-mounted 30-mm MK 108 cannon, and some were fitted with W.Gr. 21 mortars as **Fw 190A-7/R6** Pulk-Zerstörer.

During the latter part of 1942, two branches had sprung from the Fw 190A-series family tree, the F- and G-series,

In the aftermath of D-day II/JG 26 fell back through Belgium to northern Germany. By early September 1944 the Gruppe was at Brussels, from where this Fw 190A-8 was flown by the commanding officer of 7. Staffel, Oberleutnant Waldemar Radener.

417

Focke-Wulf Fw 190

Focke-Wulf Fw 190A-8 cutaway key

1 Pitot head
2 Starboard navigation light
3 Detachable wingtip
4 Pitot tube heater line
5 Wing lower shell floating rib
6 Aileron hinge points
7 Wing lower shell stringers
8 Leading-edge ribs
9 Front spar
10 Outermost solid rib
11 Wing upper shell stringers
12 Aileron trim tab
13 Aileron structure
14 Aileron activation control linkage

15 Ammunition box (125 rpg)
16 Starboard 20-mm MG 151/20 wing cannon (sideways mounted)
17 Ammunition box rear suspension arm
18 Flap structure
19 Wing flap under skinning
20 Flap setting indicator peephole
21 Rear spar

22 Inboard wing construction
23 Undercarriage indicator
24 Wing rib strengthening
25 Ammunition feed chute
26 Static and dynamic air pressure lines
27 Cannon barrel
28 Launch tube bracing struts
29 Launch tube carrier strut
30 Mortar launch tube (auxiliary underwing armament)
31 Launch tube internal guide rails
32 21-cm (W.Gr. 21) spin-stabilised Type 42 mortar shell
33 VDM three-bladed adjustable-pitch constant-speed propeller
34 Propeller boss
35 Propeller hub
36 Starboard undercarriage fairing
37 Starboard mainwheel
38 Oil warming chamber
39 Thermostat
40 Cooler armoured ring (6.5 mm/0.25-in)
41 Oil tank drain valve
42 Annular oil tank 55 litres (12.1 Imp gal)
43 Oil cooler
44 12-bladed engine cooling fan
45 Hydraulic-electric pitch control unit
46 Primer fuel line
47 Bosch magneto
48 Oil tank armour (5.5-mm/0.22-in)
49 Supercharger air pressure pipes
50 BMW 801D-2 14-cylinder radial engine
51 Cowling support ring
52 Cowling quick-release fasteners
53 Oil pump
54 Fuel pump (engine rear face)
55 Oil filter (starboard)
56 Wingroot cannon synchronisation gear

57 Gun troughs/cowling upper panel attachment
58 Engine mounting ring
59 Cockpit heating pipe
60 Exhaust pipes (cylinders 11-14)
61 MG 131 link and casing discard chute
62 Engine bearer assembly
63 MG 131 ammunition boxes (400 r.p.g.)
64 Fuel filter recess housing
65 MG 131 ammunition cooling pipes
66 MG 131 synchronisation gear
67 Ammunition feed chute
68 Twin fuselage 13-mm MG 131 machine-guns

69 Windscreen mounting frame
70 Emergency power fuse and distributor box
71 Rear hinged gun access panel
72 Engine bearer/ bulkhead attachment
73 Control column
74 Transformer
75 Aileron control torsion bar
76 Rudder pedals (EC pedal unit with hydraulic wheelbrake operation)
77 Fuselage/wing spar attachment

78 Adjustable rudder push rod
79 Fuel filler head
80 Cockpit floor support frame
81 Throttle lever
82 Pilot's seat back plate armour (8-mm/0.31-in thickness)
83 Seat guide rails
84 Side-section back armour (5-mm/0.19-in thickness)
85 Shoulder armour (5-mm/0.19-in)
86 Oxygen supply valve
87 Steel frame turnover pylon
88 Windscreen spray pipes
89 Instrument panel shroud
90 30-mm/1.18-in armoured glass quarterlights
91 50-mm/1.96-in armoured glass windscreen
92 Revi 16B reflector gunsight
93 Canopy
94 Aerial attachment
95 Headrest
96 Head armour (12-mm/0.47-in)
97 Head armour support strut
98 Explosive charge canopy emergency jettison unit

99 Canopy channel side
100 Auxiliary tank: fuel (115 litres/ 25.2 Imp gal) or GM 1 (85 litres/18.7 Imp gal)
101 FuG 16ZY transmitter-receiver unit

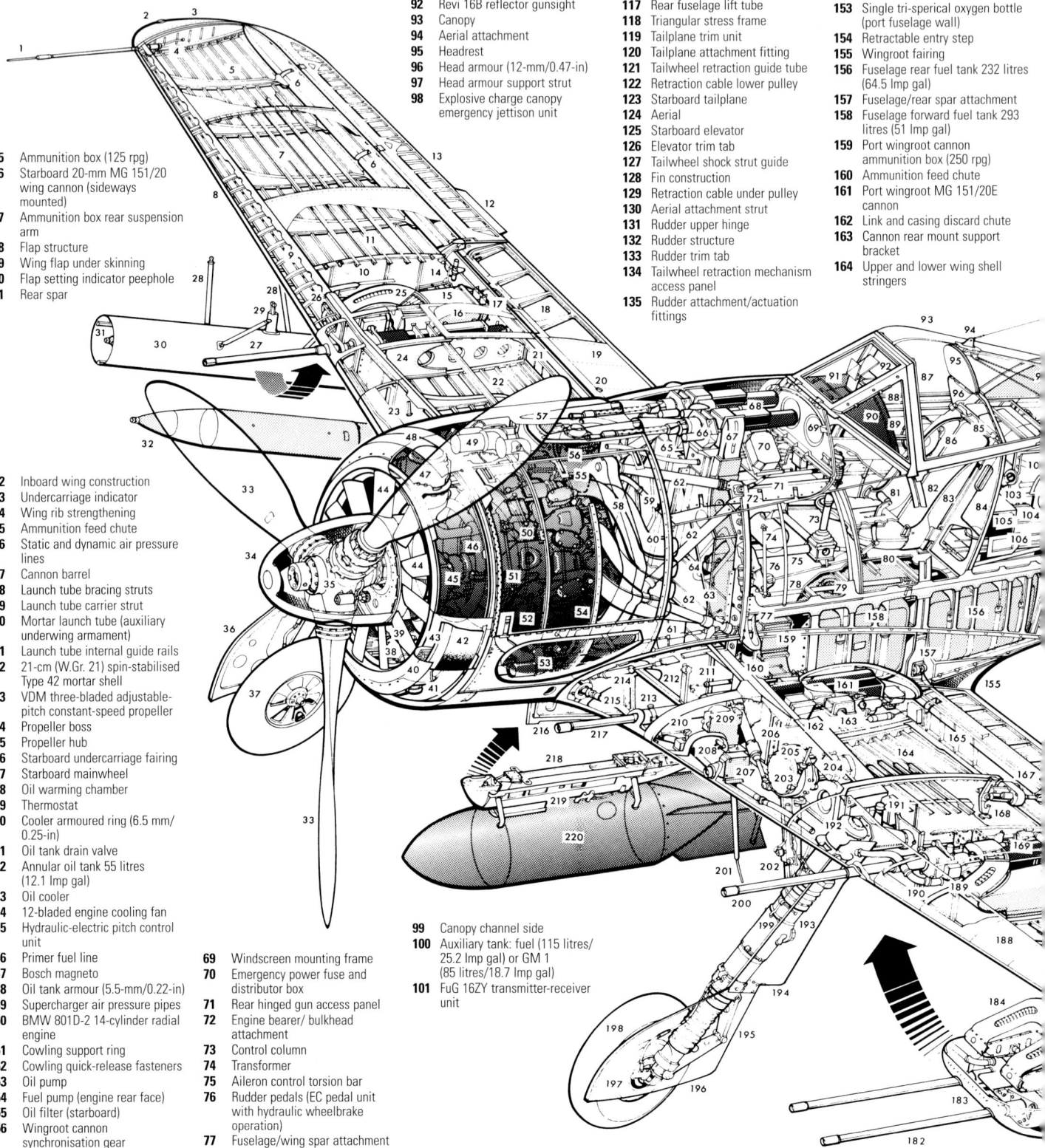

102 Handhold cover
103 Primer fuel filler cap
104 Autopilot steering unit (PKS 12)
105 FuG 16ZY power transformer
106 Entry step cover plate
107 Two tri-spherical oxygen bottles (starboard fuselage wall)
108 Auxiliary fuel tank filler point
109 FuG 25a transponder unit
110 Autopilot position integration unit
111 FuG 16ZY homer bearing converter
112 Elevator control cables
113 Rudder control DUZ flexible rods
114 Fabric panel (bulkhead 12)
115 Rudder differential unit
116 Aerial lead-in
117 Rear fuselage lift tube
118 Triangular stress frame
119 Tailplane trim unit
120 Tailplane attachment fitting
121 Tailwheel retraction guide tube
122 Retraction cable lower pulley
123 Starboard tailplane
124 Aerial
125 Starboard elevator
126 Elevator trim tab
127 Tailwheel shock strut guide
128 Fin construction
129 Retraction cable under pulley
130 Aerial attachment strut
131 Rudder upper hinge
132 Rudder structure
133 Rudder trim tab
134 Tailwheel retraction mechanism access panel
135 Rudder attachment/actuation fittings

136 Rear navigation light
137 Extension spring
138 Elevator trim tab
139 Port elevator structure
140 Tailplane construction
141 Semi-retracting tailwheel
142 Forked wheel housing
143 Drag yoke
144 Tailwheel shock strut
145 Tailwheel locking linkage
146 Elevator actuation lever linkage
147 Angled frame spar
148 Elevator differential bellcrank
149 FuG 25a ventral antenna
150 Master compass sensing unit
151 FuG 16ZY fixed loop homing antenna
152 Radio compartment access hatch
153 Single tri-sperical oxygen bottle (port fuselage wall)
154 Retractable entry step
155 Wingroot fairing
156 Fuselage rear fuel tank 232 litres (64.5 Imp gal)
157 Fuselage/rear spar attachment
158 Fuselage forward fuel tank 293 litres (51 Imp gal)
159 Port wingroot cannon ammunition box (250 rpg)
160 Ammunition feed chute
161 Port wingroot MG 151/20E cannon
162 Link and casing discard chute
163 Cannon rear mount support bracket
164 Upper and lower wing shell stringers

This Fw 190A-8 (Werk Nr 681382) belonged to the Gruppenstab of I/JG 26 'Schlageter' and was flown by the Kommandeur, Major Karl Borris, while at Grimberghen, near Brussels, in September 1944. Note the additional armour-glass plates bolted on to the sides of the sliding canopy.

165	Rear spar
166	Spar construction
167	Flap position indicator scale and peephole
168	Flap actuating electric motor
169	Port 20-mm MG 151/20E wing cannon (sideways mounted)
170	Aileron transverse linkage
171	Ammunition box (125 r.p.g.)
172	Ammunition box rear suspension arm
173	Aileron control linkage
174	Aileron control unit
175	Aileron trim tab
176	Port aileron structure
177	Port navigation light
178	Outboard wing stringers

189	Ammunition feed chute
190	Ammunition warming pipe
191	Aileron bellcrank
192	Mainwheel strut mounting assembly
193	EC-oleo shock strut
194	Mamwheel leg fairing
195	Scissors unit
196	Mainwheel fairing
197	Axle housing
198	Port mainwheel
199	Brake lines

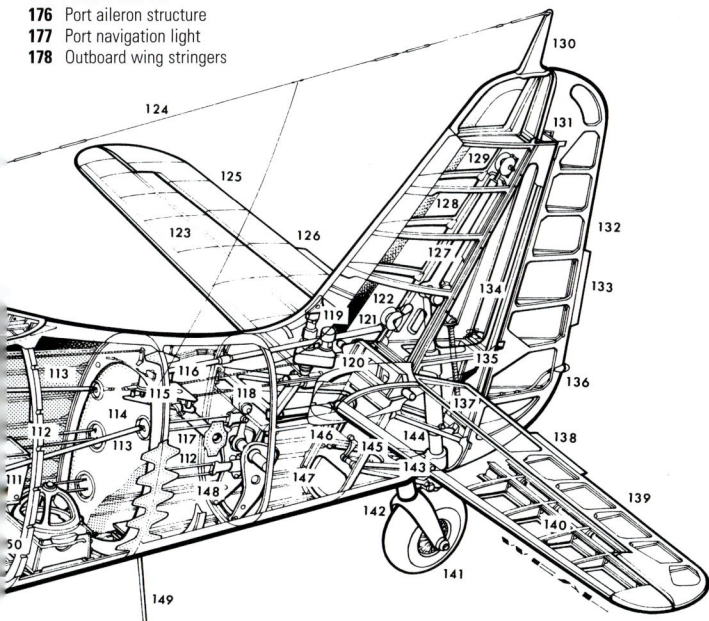

179	Detachable wingtip
180	A-8/R1 variant underwing gun pack (in place of outboard cannon)
181	Link and casing discard chute
182	Twin synchronised 20-mm MG 151/20E cannon
183	Light metal fairing (gondola)
184	Ammunition teed chutes
185	Ammunition boxes (125 r.p.g.)
186	Carrier frame restraining cord
187	Ammunition box rear suspension arms
188	Leading-edge skinning

200	Cannon barrel
201	FuG 16ZY Morane antenna
202	Radius rods
203	Rotating drive unit
204	Mainwheel retraction electric motor housing
205	Undercarriage indicator
206	Sealed air jack
207	BSK 16 gun camera
208	Retraction locking hooks
209	Undercarriage locking unit
210	Armament collimation tube
211	Camera wiring conduits
212	Wheel well
213	Cannon barrel blast tube
214	Wheel cover actuation strut
215	Ammunition hot air
216	Port inboard wheel cover
217	Wingroot cannon barrel
218	ETC 501 carrier unit
219	ETC 501 bomb rack
220	SC 500 bomb (500 kg/1,102 lb)

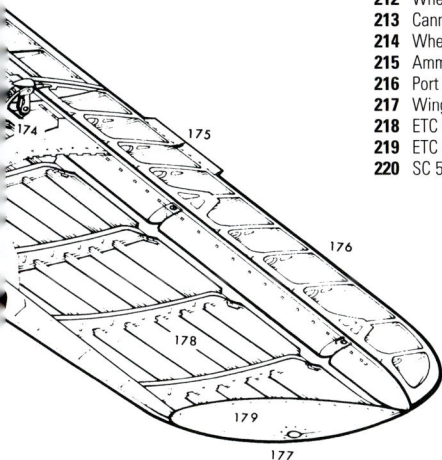

the former being a specialised close-support fighter-bomber, or Schlachtflugzeug, and the latter being a long-range fighter-bomber, or Jabo-Rei, production of these proceeding in parallel with the progressive derivatives of the basic A-series. Although the year 1943 had seen a 70 per cent increase in Fw 190 production, 3,208 (mostly A-series aircraft) being delivered, peak production being attained in July when 325 were accepted by the Luftwaffe, the proportion of total German single-seat fighter production represented by the Fw 190 had, in fact, fallen to 33 per cent.

Despite the Luftwaffe's constant demands for increased deliveries of the Fw 190, the German government had honoured an arms agreement negotiated with the Turkish government in 1941 by supplying 75 Fw 190A-3s (designated **Fw 190Aa-3**). The first of these fighters reached Turkey in February 1942, entering service in the following month and equipping the 3rd and 5th Squadrons of the Turkish Air Force's 5th Air Regiment at Bursa. The Fw 109A-3 was viewed with considerable enthusiasm and remained in Turkish service until 1948.

By contrast with the Fw 190A-7, the next and, in the event, last production A-series version of the fighter, the **Fw 190A-8**, was to be built in larger numbers than any other sub-type – sometimes claimed as 1,334, but more like 4,000 plus. Possessing an essentially similar airframe, power plant and basic armament to that of the A-7, the Fw 190A-8 embodied modifications permitting the installation of an MW 50 power boosting system, the cylindrical 114-litre (25-Imp gal) methanol-water tank for which was housed aft of the pilot, with provision for its replacement by an auxiliary fuel tank of similar capacity as required. To compensate for the weight of the MW 50 tank aft, the FuG 16ZY radio was moved forward and, when mounted, the ETC 501 rack was repositioned 20 cm (8 in) further forward. The MW 50 mixture was injected into the intake side of the supercharger, acting as an anti-detonant, providing charge cooling and

At least one Fw 190A was modified to test the Blohm und Voss Bv 246 Hagelkorn glider bomb. Poles beneath the Fw 190's wings flexed the bomb, so that it sprang away on release.

Focke-Wulf Fw 190

Tail unit
The tailplane was a variable-incidence unit, driven by a motor in the base of the fin. The elevators had small internal mass balances in a small 'horn' at each end. The sturdy fin had two spars, one vertical along the rear of the structure and one angled along the leading edge. The full-height rudder had a small 'horn' at the tip and a fixed tab. The rear fuselage structure was used to house various equipment, including the master compass and cameras in some variants. At bulkhead No. 12 was a fabric panel that acted as a dust barrier for the equipment. The large tailwheel was semi-retractable. A large shock-absorber strut reached up into the fin structure.

Fuselage and cockpit
The cockpit was well laid out and offered good visibility in flight. However, the broad nose and tail-down stance of the Fw 190 made ground visibility poor. The canopy, complete with fairing, slid back for ingress/egress, and could be jettisoned with explosive cartridges in emergency. Armour plate was provided behind and to the sides of the pilot. Fuel was held in two self-sealing tanks located under the pilot's seat, separated by a rear spar tie-through member. The forward tank held 193 litres (51 Imp gal), while the rear tank held 242 litres (64 Imp gal). Introduced on the Fw 190A-4, an FuG 16Z radio was installed in place of the FuG 7a equipment. A noticeable external difference was the small vertical mast for the wire aerial on the fin-tip. The aerial ran to an attaching pulley in the canopy, with a built-in take-up spring to maintain tension.

Main undercarriage
The stalky main wheel units retracted inwards to lie in the wingroots. The wide track made the aircraft stable on the ground, particularly useful when operating from the primitive airfields encountered by the Fw 190s on the Eastern Front. The small half-doors covering the bottom of the tyres when retracted were deleted from most bomb-carrying variants.

Powerplant
The Fw 190A-8 was powered by the BMW 801D-2 14-cylinder two-row air-cooled radial in the lengthened engine mount of the A-5. The air-cooled engine was rated at 1268 kW (1,700 hp) for take-off and 1074 kW (1,440 hp) at 5700 m (18,700 ft). Introduced from the Fw 190A-4 onwards was provision for MW 50 water-methanol boosting. This acted as an anti-detonant, allowing higher boost pressures to be used for short periods. The extra power gained was useful, but necessitated very regular spark plug changes, and required the installation of a cylindrical 114-litre (25-Imp gal) water-methanol tank behind the pilot. A 12-bladed cooling fan was mounted in front of the engine, facilitating a build-up of air pressure in the engine compartment. This provided more than adequate cooling for the front row of cylinders. Large ducts ran either side of the engine to take cooling air to the rear row. Cooling air was dumped through louvres on either side of the engine, downstream of the flush main exhaust outlets. The oil cooler was mounted in an annular arrangement around the front of the engine. The Fw 190 smashed the theory that only sleek, inline-engined fighters could achieve good performance. At the heart of the aircraft's performance was the beautifully designed low-drag cowling around the engine, which was armoured at the front.

Focke-Wulf Fw 190A-8

5. Staffel/Jagdgeschwader 300
Löbnitz

One of the major production versions of the Focke-Wulf Fw 190 was the A-8 'Sturmbock', shown here in its basic configuration with the ETC 501 centreline store rack moved forward 20 cm (7.9 in) and carrying a 300-litre (66-Imp gal) drop tank. Armed with four long-barrelled 20-mm MG 151/20 cannon in the wings and two MG 17 machine-guns in the nose, 'Red 19' was flown by Unteroffizier Ernst Schröder of 5. Staffel/Jagdgeschwader 300, in Defence of the Reich operations during October and November 1944. II Gruppe of JG 300 had been formed in November 1943 under Major Kurd Peters (awarded the Knight's Cross in October that year), and was one of the fighter units opposing the Western Allies during the invasion of Europe, flying by night on Wilde Sau missions, and then later by day on daring attacks against day bombers. In July 1944 the unit became II (Sturm)/JG 300, with Major Alfred Lindenberger as Gruppenkommandeur.

Canopy

This A-8 retains the original fighter-style canopy of the A-5, but some later production aircraft featured a new 'blown' canopy that had been developed to give pilots of ground-attack versions much better visibility.

Gun armament

In the upper decking of the fuselage were two 13-mm MG 131 machine-guns, as introduced first on the Fw 190A-7, with 475 rounds each. In each wingroot was an MG 151/20 20-mm cannon with 250 r.p.g., and a similar weapon outboard of the main undercarriage in each wing with 140 r.p.g.

Wing

As originally developed, the Fw 190 had been tested with two sizes of wing. The larger one was chosen for production, showing little degradation in speed performance but considerable advantages in other areas. The Fw 190 was very agile, particularly during rolling manoeuvres, but showed some lack of aileron control in high-speed dives. The wing was built around two spars, to which were attached a wingtip section, leading-edge sections and simple flaps and ailerons, the latter having fixed tabs. The through-spar construction made it very strong.

Focke-Wulf Fw 190

In July 1944 the Stabsstaffel and I Gruppe of JG 51 were falling back through Byelorussia. This Fw 190A-8 was on the strength of the Stabsstaffel, and carries the name 'Hanni'. Most of the unit's aircraft had names applied earlier in the year.

'Tanja' was another Stabsstaffel/JG 51 Fw 190A-8, assigned to Leutnant Günther Heym. This unit had formed in November 1942 from 6./JG 51 and stayed with the Fw 190 throughout the war, while the other Fw 190 elements of JG 51 (Stab, I and II Gruppe) converted to the Bf 109G in 1943/44.

enabling higher boost pressures to be used. The increased power could be used for a maximum of 10 minutes at a time, and at least five minutes had to elapse between successive periods of operation.

The **Fw 190A-8/R1** Zerstörer had a quartet of under-wing-mounted MG 151 cannon, the standard twin fuselage-mounted MG 131s introduced on the A-7 and wing root-mounted MG 151s, while the **Fw 190A-8/R2** differed only in having a pair of 30-mm MK 108 cannon in place of the paired MG 151s beneath the wings. The **Fw 190A-8/R3** was similar apart from replacing the MK 108s by longer-barrel 30-mm MK 103s that had a lower fire rate but a higher muzzle velocity. The **Fw 190A-8/R7** was a so-called 'Rammjäger', intended for ramming attacks against Allied bombers. Carrying standard armament, it was fitted with additional armour in order to increase its chances of penetrating the bomber formation's defensive screen, and the small numbers of this variant delivered were operated by special Sturmstaffeln. The **Fw 190A-8/R8** was an experimental close-fighting anti-bomber version with a pair of 30-mm MK 108 cannon beneath the wings, and the **Fw 190A-8/R11** and **R12** were all-weather fighters which it was proposed to fit with supercharged BMW 801TS engines. Equipped with the PKS 12 automatic pilot and heated cockpit canopies, these aircraft were intended to have either (R11) standard gun armament, or (R12) the outboard MG 151s replaced by MK 108s, but neither model was proceeded with.

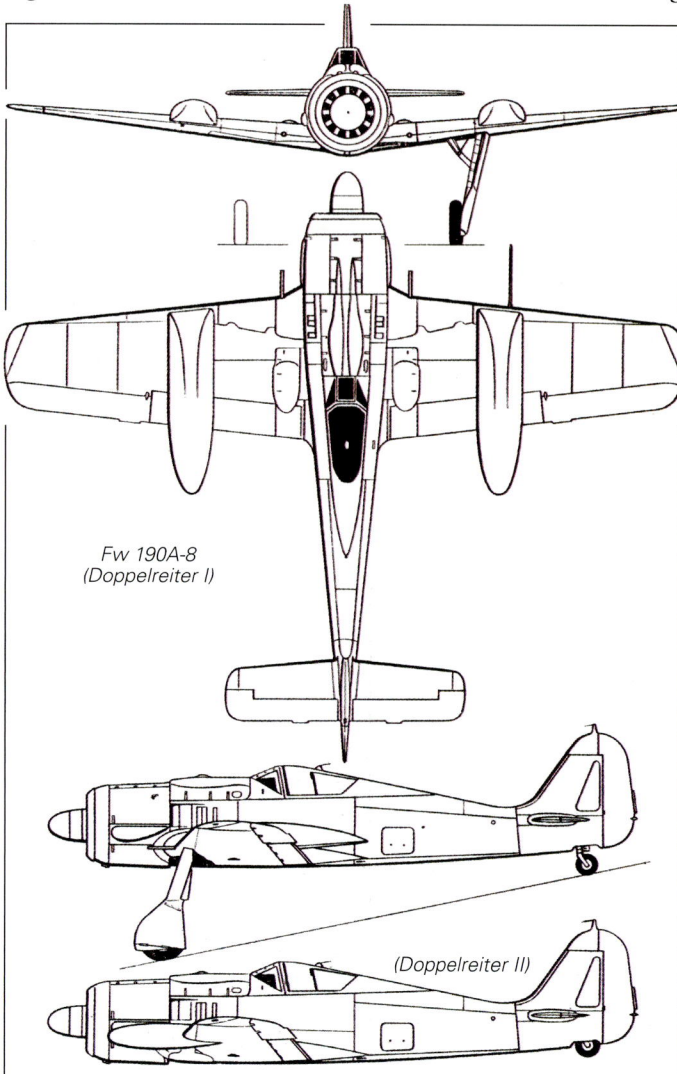

During 1943, work had begun on the design of a tandem two-seat fuselage to meet a Luftwaffe requirement for a conversion trainer for the re-training of former Ju 87 pilots. By October of that year, the Schlachtgeschwader were converting from the Ju 87 to the Fw 190 at the rate of a Gruppe every three weeks, and although the anticipated problems did not arise, three Fw 190A-8 airframes were converted as two-seaters, the intention being that they should serve as pattern aircraft for forward maintenance units to rebuild existing

Fw 190A-8
(Doppelreiter I)

(Doppelreiter II)

The potential firepower of the Fw 190A series was increased in this trial installation of a gun pod beneath each wing. Each pod contained a long-barrel MK 103 30-mm cannon. The development aircraft shown is an Fw 190A-5/U11, Werk Nr 151303.

Focke-Wulf Fw 190A-8 cockpit layout

1 Helmet R/T connection	
2 Primer fuel pump handle	
3 FuG 16ZY communications and homing switch and volume control	
4 FuG 16ZY receiver fine tuning	
5 FuG 16ZY homing range switch	
6 FuG 16ZY frequency selector switch	
7 Tailplane trim switch	
8 Undercarriage and landing flap actuation buttons	
9 Undercarriage and landing flap position indicators	
10 Throttle	
11 Throttle-mounted propeller pitch control thumbswitch	
12 Tailplane trim indicator	
13 Instrument panel lighting dimmer	
14 Pilot's seat	
15 Throttle friction knob	
16 Control column	
17 Bomb release button	
18 Rudder pedals	
19 Wing cannon firing button	
20 Fuel tank selector lever	
21 Engine starter brushes withdrawal button	
22 Stop cock control lever	
23 FuG 25a IFF control panel	
24 Undercarriage manual lowering handle	
25 Cockpit ventilation knob	
26 Altimeter	
27 Pitot tube heater light	
28 MG 131 'armed' indicator lights	
29 Ammunition counters	
30 SZKK 4 armament switch and control panel	
31 30-mm armoured glass quarterlights	
32 Windscreen spray pipes	
33 50-mm armoured glass windscreen	
34 Revi 16B reflector gunsight	
35 Padded coaming	
36 Gunsight padded mounting	
37 AFN 2 homing indicator (FuG 16ZY)	
38 Ultra-violet lights (port and starboard)	
39 Airspeed indicator	
40 Artificial horizon	
41 Rate of climb/descent indicator	
42 Repeater compass	
43 Supercharger pressure gauge	
44 Tachometer	
45 Ventral stores manual release	
46 Fuel and oil pressure gauge	
47 Oil temperature gauge	
48 Windscreen washer operating lever	
49 Engine ventilation flap control lever	
50 Fuel contents gauge	
51 Propeller pitch indicator	
52 Rear fuel tank switchover light (white)	
53 Fuel contents warning light (red)	
54 Fuel gauge selector switch	
55 Underwing rocket (W.Gr. 21) control panel	
56 Bomb fusing selector panel and (above) external stores indicator lights	
57 Oxygen flow indicator	
58 Flare pistol holder	
59 Oxygen pressure gauge	
60 Oxygen flow valve	
61 Canopy actuator drive	
62 Canopy jettison lever	
63 Circuit breaker panel cover	
64 Clock	
65 Map/chart holder	
66 Operations data card	
67 Flare box cover	
68 Starter switch	
69 Flare box cover plate release knob	
70 Fuel pump circuit breakers	
71 Compass deviation card	
72 Circuit breaker panel cover	
73 Armament circuit breakers	
74 Oxygen supply	

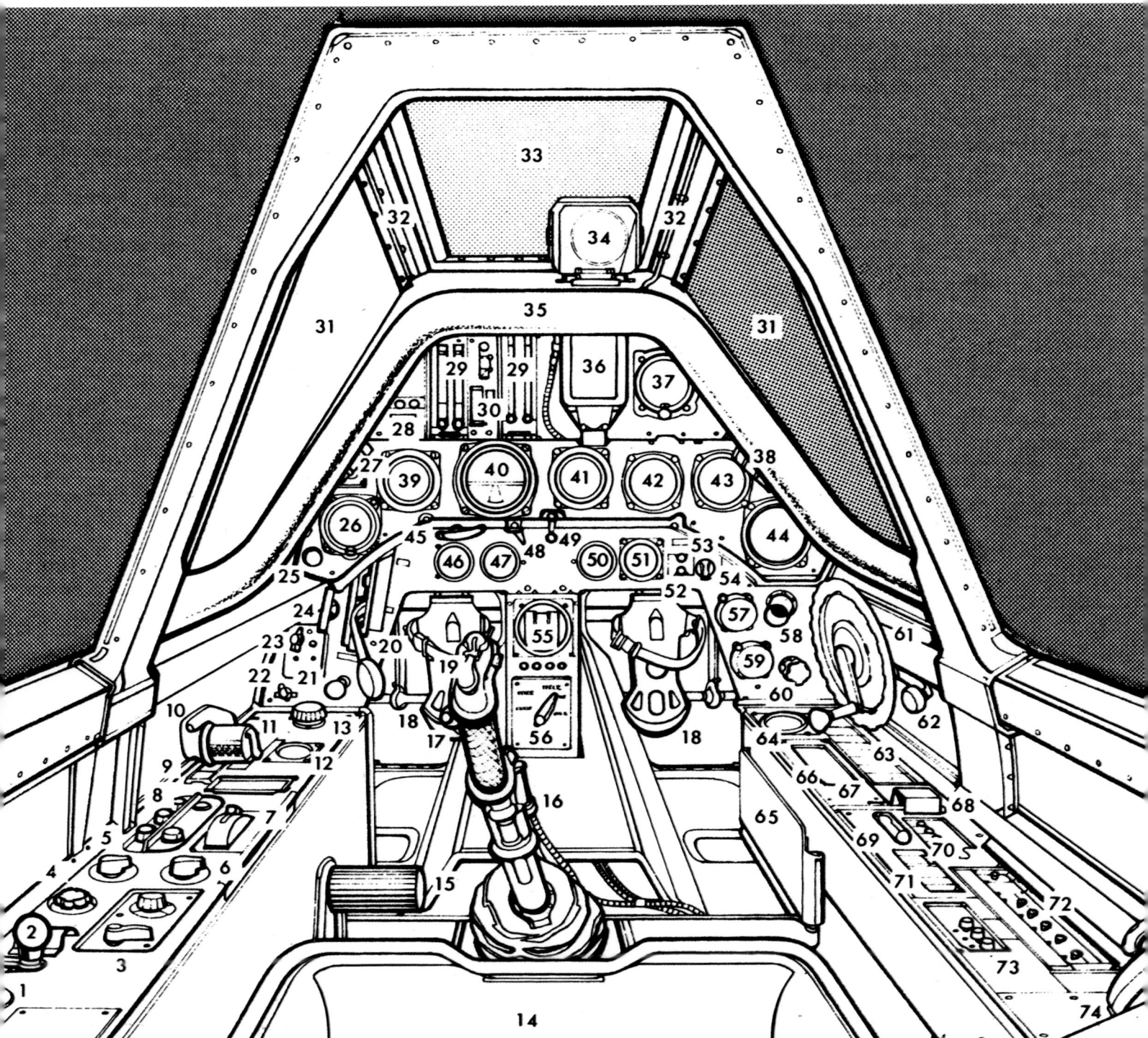

Focke-Wulf Fw 190

This Fw 190A-8 was assigned to Oberleutnant Karl Brill, Staffelkapitän of 10./JG 54 (13./JG 54 from August 1944), whose badge was an Indian head. IV Gruppe was formed for home defence duties, but was sent to the East instead. In the summer of 1944 the unit was operating in Poland.

Leutnant Heinz Wernicke, commander of 1./JG 54 flew this Fw 190A-8 from Riga-Skulte in September 1944. Both I and II Gruppe were in Latvia at the time, II Gruppe having returned from its Finnish adventure.

Oberleutnant Josef Heinzeller took over from Wernicke in charge of 1./JG 54, and flew this Fw 190A-8 from Schrunden as I Gruppe fought over the Courland front in late 1944.

This Fw 190A-8 was also involved in the Courland fighting, and was allocated to Hauptmann Franz Eisenach, Kommandeur of I/JG 54 while based at Schrunden in November 1944.

A new 7./JG 54 was formed in October 1944 within II Gruppe. This Fw 190A-8 was flown by the commander, Leutnant Gerd Thyben, while based at Liepäja (Libau to the Germans) in January 1945. At the time the unit was embroiled in the intense Courland battles.

A few late-production A-8s were fitted with the blown canopy. II Gruppe (this is a 6. Staffel machine) was still fighting from Liepäja over Courland until March 1945. This aircraft was flown by Hauptmann Helmut Wettstein, who had scored JG 54's 8,000th kill on 15 October 1944.

I/JG 1 spent Christmas 1944 at Twenthe in the Netherlands, equipped with the Fw 190A-8. In the new year a few Fw 190Ds were assigned, and then the Gruppe began conversion to the He 162 jet fighter.

aircraft as two-seaters under the designation **Fw 190S** (the 'S' suffix indicating Schulflugzeug). A second cockpit was inserted immediately aft of the standard cockpit, this occupying the space previously taken by the radio and other equipment. The rear fuselage decking was raised, and the two cockpits covered by a continuous canopy, the forward cockpit for the pupil being enclosed by a section hinging to starboard, and the aft cockpit for the instructor being covered by a section that slid rearwards. Rudimentary dual controls and instrumentation were provided in the rear cockpit, and as the **Fw 190A-8/U1**, the first of the three conversions was flown on 23 January 1944. The conversion was applicable to any A-series airframe, and apart from the three Fw 190A-8/U1 two-seaters, a so-far unidentified number of **Fw 190S-5** and **Fw 190S-8** trainers (respectively derived from Fw 190A-5 and -8 airframes, plus some F-8 models) were completed to serve with a number of conversion units and for high-speed liaison tasks.

Dispersed production

The immensity of the Fw 190 production programme by 1944 may be gauged from the number of factory complexes involved. The Focke-Wulf plant in Bremen had been the first major aircraft factory to be dispersed, the RAF bombing attacks of 1940 and 1941 on Bremen having convinced Dipl.-Ing. Tank of the importance of moving manufacturing facilities eastward, and distributing them among several plants, and he selected Marienburg, Posen, Cottbus and Sorau. Focke-Wulf followed the lead established by Junkers in building up a complex of 'shadow plants' and sub-contractors that fed the main assembly plants with components.

From 1942, licensees with direct contracts from the RLM for Fw 190 production established similar complexes, these including AGO at Oschersleben, Arado at Warnemünde, Fieseler at Kassel-Waldau and, from 1944, Dornier (Norddeutsche Dornier) at Wismar. Special committees had been established for each principal design to coordinate the complexes engaged in its production, and these committees were able to arrange the interchange of materials and components among the several manufacturers of the same type. For example, when, in May 1944, the Focke-Wulf Marienburg assembly line's sole source of Fw 190 tail assemblies at Posen was bombed out, the special committee for the Fw 190 immediately diverted enough identical assemblies from the reserves of the Arado and Fieseler licensee complexes to supply Marienburg while the Posen plant was being re-established in dispersed locations.

Production was also initiated in an underground plant operated by the SNCA du Centre at Cravant, near Auxerre, although, in the event, the first aircraft delivered from Cravant, an Fw 190A-5, did not fly until 16 March 1945. Production of both this and the Fw 190A-8 was subsequently continued for the Armée de l'Air under the designation NC 900, French manufacture terminating post-war in the spring of 1946 with the 64th aircraft. Some NC 900s were delivered to GC III/5 Normandie-Niémen, which operated the fighters for a brief period before they were finally grounded as a result of troubles with the BMW 801D-2 engines.

It is hardly surprising that, in view of its large-scale production, the Fw 190A-8 should participate in numerous experimental programmes. One Fw 190A-8 airframe (Werk Nr 530115), designated **Fw 190 V47**, was fitted with a new wing of increased area and higher aspect ratio designed by the Châtillon-sur-Seine drawing office of the SNCA du Sud-Ouest and, equipped with GM 1 boost, engaged in a series of high-altitude trials.

Another Fw 190A-8 (Werk Nr 380394) was used for a series of tests with so-called 'Doppelreiter' (Double-rider) auxiliary fuel tanks attached to the upper wing surfaces and extending aft of the trailing edges. These tanks, evolved

The Fw 190A-8/U1 (Fw 190S-8) was a two-seat conversion trainer, produced by adaptation of standard single-seat A-5 and A-8 fighters, plus some F-8 fighter-bombers, as illustrated by the preserved aircraft seen here.

Focke-Wulf Fw 190

By November 1944 the Stabsstaffel of JG 51 was flying its Fw 190A-8s from Memel, East Prussia (today Klaipeda in Lithuania). The city was besieged by the Red Army from October, and was finally overrun at the end of January.

This Fw 190A-8 was also flown by the Stabsstaffel of JG 51, while based at Neukuhren (later renamed Pionersky) in November 1944. The yellow markings of this and the aircraft above were probably applied in an attempt to prevent fire from German flak and ground troops, who by that stage of the war had become notoriously trigger-happy.

by the Forschungsanstalt (Research Establishment) Graf Zeppelin, were of 250-litre (55-Imp gal) capacity and could be jettisoned. Tests were undertaken at Parchim, Mecklenburg, by the Versuchs-Jagdgruppe 10 that, like its predecessor, the Erprobungskommando 25 at Achmer, also tested various experimental armament installations on the Fw 190A. Among the more unusual of these was the fanciful vertically-firing SG 116 Zellendusche salvo weapon comprising a series of 30-mm MK 103 barrels each containing a single shell, the shells being fired by a photo-electric cell, or Foto-Zellenfuhler. Known as the Magische Auge (Magic Eye), the cell was housed on the port side of the fuselage immediately forward of the battery of barrels, and was hoped to be activated by the shadow of the target bomber. There were several possible Zellendusche arrangements, one comprising three MK 103 barrels in line and installed in the port side of the fuselage immediately aft of the cockpit. They were mounted to afford one-and-a-half degrees of spread, and as fitted to an Fw 190A-8 for tests by VJG 10, the foremost barrel was set at an angle of 74°, the centre barrel at 73° and the rearmost barrel at 72.5°, the trio of shells being fired at

intervals of 0.03 seconds at a distance of approximately 50 m (165 ft) below the target.

Another far-fetched vertically-firing salvo weapon tested by an Fw 190A-8 (Werk Nr 733713) was the SG 117 Rohrblock, this comprising a cluster of seven 30-mm MK 108 barrels. Some tests were conducted with a single aft-firing 21-cm rocket tube mounted horizontally beneath an Fw 190A-8 with the aim of achieving surprise by a species of Parthian shot as the fighter pulled away from a bomber formation that it had already attacked with its forward-firing armament. Much less fanciful and far more advanced was the X 4 Ruhrstahl (DVL 344) wire-guided rocket missile, one intended to be being mounted beneath each wing.

The prolific A-series was ended with the **Fw 190A-9**, initially conceived as a Rammjäger with heavily armoured wing leading edges and a BMW 801F engine (similar in general construction to the BMW 801D-2 but having different supercharger gear ratios and offering 1492 kW/2,000 hp for take-off and emergency), but this concept failed to proceed further than the prototype stage. Production Fw 190A-9 aircraft, of unknown quantity, used the BMW 801TS/TH engine, nominally of 2,000 hp, which has sometimes been claimed to have been fitted with an exhaust-driven turbo-supercharger but this was not the case. The projected Fw 190A-10 and later A-numbered projects were not built.

No air force can fight without the skilled and dedicated work of its ground personnel. In the Luftwaffe, ground crews were often referred to as 'Black Men' due to their dark-coloured overalls, as seen here with an operational Fw 190.

Fw 190A-8 specification
Type: single-seat fighter and (U3) fighter-bomber
Powerplant: one BMW 801D-2 14-cylinder radial air-cooled engine rated at 1268 kW (1,700 hp) for take-off and 1074 kW (1,440 hp) at 5700 m (18,700 ft)
Performance: (without external stores) maximum speed 571 km/h (355 mph) at sea level, 647 km/h (402 mph) at 5500 m (18,045 ft), (with MW 50 boost) 657 km/h (408 mph) at 6300 m (20,670 ft); normal cruising speed 480 km/h (298 mph); initial climb rate 716 m (2,350 ft) per minute; time (with MW 50 boost) to 6000 m (19,685 ft), 9.9 minutes, to 8000 m (26,250 ft) 14.4 minutes, to 10000 m (32,800 ft) 17.2 minutes; service ceiling 10300 m (33,800 ft), (with MW 50 boost) 11400 m (37,400 ft); maximum range 800 km (497 miles) at 480 km/h (298 mph) at 7000 m (23,000 ft), (Fw 190A-8/U3 with two 300-litre/66-Imp gal) 1515 km (942 miles) at 440 km/h (274 mph) at 5800 m (19,000 ft)
Weights: empty equipped 3470 kg (7,652 lb); normal loaded 4382 kg (9,660 lb); maximum overload 4900 kg (10,800 lb)
Dimensions: wingspan 10.50 m (34 ft 5½ in); length 8.95 m (29 ft 4¼ in); height (over airscrew tip) 3.95 m (12 ft 11½ in); wing area 18.30 m² (196.98 sq ft)
Armament: two 13-mm (0.51-in) MG 131 machine-guns in fuselage, two 20-mm MG 151 cannon in wing roots and two 20-mm MG 151 cannon in outer wing panels. (Fw 190A-8/U3) ventral ETC 501 rack for single 250-kg (551-lb) SC 250 bomb or ER 4 adapter with four 50-kg (110-lb) SC 50 bombs, plus (optional) ETC 50 wing racks for four 50-kg (110-lb) SC 50 bombs

The red/yellow RV bands identify this Fw 190A-8 as being assigned to JG 301, in this instance 12. Staffel of III Gruppe. From October 1944 to January 1945 the Gruppe flew from Stendal, to the east of Berlin.

Displaying the black-white-black RV bands of Jagdgeschwader 4, this Fw 190A-8 flew with I Gruppe, based at Darmstadt during the winter of 1944-5. Painting of the Geschwader badge on the engine cowling was fairly rare at this late hectic stage of the war.

Still wearing RV bands, this Fw 190A-8 was the aircraft of II/JG 1's Kommandeur, Hauptmann Paul-Heinrich Dähne, operating from Garz on the island of Usedom in March 1945. Dähne was killed in April in a Heinkel He 162.

Wearing a much more subdued finish than Dähne's aircraft, this Fw 190A-8 was also on II/JG 1's books at Garz in March 1945. It was flown by 7. Staffel's commander, Major Bernd Gallowitsch.

III/JG 11's Kommandeur, Hauptmann Herbert Kutscha, flew this Fw 190A-8 in February 1945, when the Gruppe was operating from Strausberg to the east of Berlin, in the desperate defence of the capital.

Fw 190s continued to defend Berlin into the last days, this being an Fw 190A-8 of I/JG 11. A small detachment from this unit apparently operated from a city street until late April. Most of the Gruppe ended the war at Leck, surrendering to British forces.

Focke-Wulf 190F

II. Gruppe, Schlachtgeschwader 1

This Fw 190F-3 wears the Mickey Mouse nose markings of Schlachtgeschwader 1, with the red badge backing, codes and spinner of 5. Staffel. It is seen as it was in mid-1943, while staging through Deblin-Irena in Poland on its way to the front line. Because red markings were a source of confusion with Soviet aircraft, they would probably have been removed once in the operational area. Most of II/SchG 1 had converted to the Fw 190 in January, having previously operated a mix of Hs 123s and Hs 129s, before returning to the front with Fw 190A-4/U3s and A-5/U3s. Fw 190F-3s first arrived in May. By that time the Gruppe was fighting on the southern sector of the Russian front, having crossed the Kerch strait to reach Anapa, but in July it was redirected north to Varvarovka, on the lower edge of the Kursk salient. Both Fw 190-equipped Gruppen of SchG 1 were heavily involved in the intense fighting that followed.

Powerplant
The Fw 190 smashed the theory that only sleek inline-engined fighters could achieve good performance. The Fw 190F-2 was based on the Fw 190A-5 airframe, and featured the BMW 801D-2 powerplant. This engine developed 1268 kW (1,700 hp) for take-off and 1074 kW (1,440 hp) at 5700 m (18,700 ft). MW 50 water-methanol boosting was fitted as standard. Around the front of the engine was an annular oil cooler, and a 12-bladed cooling fan that built up pressure in the engine compartment. Cooling air was ejected at the rear of the cowling, downstream of the flush exhaust outlets

Fuel
Fuel was accommodated in two self-sealing tanks located beneath the pilot's seat. They were separated by the rear spar tie-through (the Fw 190 was built using a very strong through-spar construction). The forward tank held 232 litres (51 Imp gal) while the rear tank held 293 litres (64.5 Imp gal).

Armament
Gun armament consisted of a pair of 0.31-in (79-mm) MG 17 machine-guns in the upper fuselage decking, featuring a characteristic bulge over the breech block and each armed with 1,000 rounds. In each wingroot was a 20-mm MG 151/20 cannon with 200 rounds. A centreline ETC 250 bomb rack was used for a single 250-kg (551-lb) bomb. Two ETC 50 racks (for 50-kg/110-lb) bombs could be fitted under each wing. In addition to standard SC 250 and SC 50 bombs, the Fw 190F regularly carried the AB 250 Splitterbombe (cluster bomb) that could dispense a variety of sub-munitions. These included 224 SD 1, 144 SD 2, 30 SD 4 or 17 SD 10 anti-personnel/armour minelets, 184 B 1 incendiaries or 116 B 2 steel-nosed incendiaries. The widely-used SD 2 was the feared 'butterfly' bomb, which deployed small wings to slow its descent to earth.

Radio
The Fw 190F-2 used the FuG 16Z radio equipment, which had first been introduced to the family by the Fw 190A-4. The wire aerial stretched from a short mast on top of the fin to a spool mounted on the canopy. This was spring-loaded to take up the wire antenna when the canopy was slid backwards and to maintain tension in flight.

I Gruppe of Schlachtgeschwader 1 began to convert to Fw 190s in March 1943, receiving Fw 190A-5/U3s and Fw 190Fs. This F-2 was the mount of the Kommandeur, Hauptmann Georg Dörffel when the unit was based at Kharkov.

Oberleutnant Karl Kennel, CO of 5./SchG 1, flew this Fw 190F-2 or F-3 from Varvarovka during the Kursk battles in July 1943. SchG 1's black triangle marking had been deleted in favour of standard fighter unit markings. The aircraft was fitted with a dust filter.

Fw 190F series

At an early stage in its service career, the Fw 190 had displayed an extraordinary amenability to adaptation for operational roles other than that of the medium-altitude day fighter for which it had been conceived. Thus, in the late autumn of 1942, with growth in importance of the Schlachtflieger and the increasing unsuitability of the Ju 87 as a Schlachtflugzeug, a decision was taken to manufacture a version of the Focke-Wulf fighter optimised for the close-support or battlefield support role under the designation **Fw 190F**. Earlier it had been planned to produce a reconnaissance fighter based on the Fw 190A-4 airframe as the **Fw 190E-1**, but the requirement was adequately fulfilled by the application of the Umrüst-Bausatz 4 (U4) to Fw 190A-3 and -5 fighters, this comprising a single Rb 75/30,50/30 or 20/30 camera, or two Rb 12.5 cameras, and the adaptation being performed by forward maintenance units as required. Accordingly, the Fw 190E-1 proposal was abandoned.

In essence, the F-series was intended to standardise on the Umrüst-Bausatz 3 that consisted of an ETC 501 fuselage rack for a single 500-kg (1,102-lb) bomb, or an ER 4 adapter to enable four 50-kg (110-lb) SC 50 bombs to be carried, plus optional wing racks for a pair of 250-kg (551-lb) SC 250 bombs. Additional protective armour was provided for the engine, oil tank and pilot, and the undercarriage was modified with greater pressure in the shock strut to cater for

Left: Although designed primarily as a fighter, the Fw 190 proved easily capable of adaptation into the fighter-bomber role, carrying bombs beneath the fuselage and under the wings.

Below: An Fw 190A-3 (Werk Nr 447) carries four SC 50 bombs on an ER 4 adaptor beneath the fuselage, in a photograph dated 12 June 1942. Operations with Jabo and Jabo-Rei versions of the Fw 190A led to production of the dedicated Fw 190F and Fw 190G series.

Focke-Wulf Fw 190

Oberstleutnant Alfred Druschel was one of the key figures in the rise of the Schlachtflieger. As Kommodore of SchG 1 he flew this Fw 190F from Varvarovka during the Kursk battle.

8./SchG 1 was a semi-autonomous unit with Fw 190Fs and Hs 129s. This F-2 is seen as it appeared in September 1943, based at Poltava in the Ukraine.

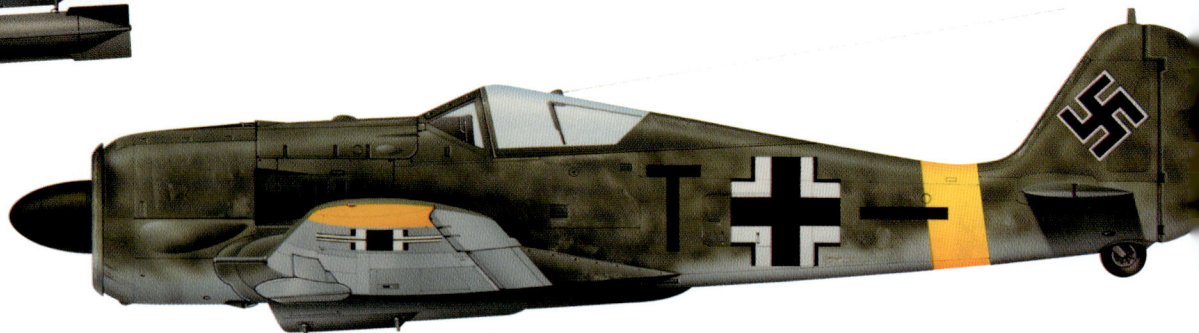

higher take-off weights. The initial version, the **Fw 190F-1**, was a somewhat rudimentary assembly line conversion of Fw 190A-4 airframes (equivalent to the A-4/U3), some 25-30 examples being delivered for service evaluation late in 1942. The outboard cannon were deleted, gun armament being restricted to the pair of fuselage-mounted 7.9-mm MG 17 machine-guns and the two 20-mm MG 151 cannon in the wing roots.

The first version built from the outset as a Schlachtflugzeug, the **Fw 190F-2** that appeared in the spring of 1943, was based on the Fw 190A-5 airframe (equivalent to the A-5/U3) and carried a similar combination of weapons and ordnance racks (usually restricted in practice to the fuselage-mounted ETC 501). By this time, the Fw 190A-4/U3 was being operated, alongside other types, in the close-support role by II Gruppe of Schlachtgeschwader 1 on the Eastern Front, detachments of these aircraft being deployed under both the Luftwaffenkommando Don and Luftflotte 4.

In the late spring/early summer of 1943, the **Fw 190F-3** variant appeared on Arado's Warnemünde assembly line. Manufactured in parallel with the Fw 190A-6, it embodied a similar revised and lightened wing structure. Armament was unchanged, but the ETC 501 rack beneath the fuselage gave place to an ETC 250 rack that could accommodate either a 250-kg (551-lb) SC 250 bomb or a 300-litre (66-Imp gal) auxiliary fuel tank. With four ETC 50 racks beneath the wings, the basic model became the **Fw 190F-3/R1**. With a pair of 30-mm MK 103 cannon beneath the wings, outboard of the main undercarriage attachment points, there was the **Fw 190F-3/R3**, but this

planned version was only built in very small numbers and was not satisfactory. Some 247 F-3s were built by Arado up to April 1944.

Fw 190F-3 specification

Type: single-seat close-support fighter
Powerplant: one BMW 801D-2 14-cylinder radial air-cooled engine rated at 1268 kW (1,700 hp) for take-off and 1074 kW (1,440 hp) at 5700 m (18,700 ft)
Performance: maximum speed (without external stores) 550 km/h (342 mph) at sea level, 634 km/h (394 mph) at 5500 m (18,045 ft), (with SC 250 bomb) 524 km/h (326 mph) at sea level, 592 km/h (368 mph) at 5500 m (18,045 ft); initial climb rate (without external stores) 643 m (2,110 ft) per minute; maximum range (without external stores) 750 km (466 miles) at 476 km/h (296 mph) at 7000 m (23,000 ft); range with SC 250 bomb 530 km (330 miles) at 534 km/h (332 mph) at 5500 m (18,045 ft)
Weights: empty equipped 3324 kg (7,328 lb); normal loaded 4400 kg (9,700 lb); maximum loaded 4920 kg (10,850 lb)
Dimensions: wingspan 10.50 m (34 ft 5½ in); length 8.80 m (28 ft 10½ in); height (over airscrew tip), 3.64 m (11 ft 11½ in); wing area 18.30 m² (196.98 sq ft)
Armament: two 7.9-mm MG 17 machine-guns in upper forward fuselage and two 20-mm MG 151 cannon in wing roots, plus ETC 250 fuselage rack for one 250-kg (551-lb) SC 250 bomb and (Fw 190F-3/R1) four ETC 50 wing racks for four 50-kg (110-lb) SC 50 bombs, or (Fw 190F-3/R3) two 30-mm MK 103 cannon

By late 1943 a change in operational priorities necessitated precedence being given to the G-series extended-range fighter-bomber, or Jabo-Rei, intended to supplant the Ju 87 in the Stukagruppen. The Stukagruppen were to be redesignated Schlachtgruppen in October 1943, by which time the Ju 87-equipped Gruppen were converting to the Fw 190G at the rate of some two Gruppen every six weeks.

The Fw 190F-4, -5, -6 and -7 had been planned as progressive developments of the Fw 190F-3, embodying various equipment and armament changes, but they were not proceeded with. F-series production moved in the spring of 1944 onto the **Fw 190F-8**, based on the highly-successful Fw 190A-8. Production of the F-8 was initiated by the Arado (in March) and Dornier (in April) plants at Warnemünde and Wismar, respectively, and during the early summer of 1944, the re-equipment of the remaining Ju 87 elements of the Schlachtflieger on the Eastern Front was accelerated.

In essence, the Fw 190F-8 differed from its predecessor, the F-3, in having 13-mm MG 131 machine-guns replacing

An Arado-built Fw 190F-8 (probably Werk Nr 580383, CM+WL) was used at the Tarnewitz weapons testing facility for various trials, and carries here a single ETC 503 stores rack beneath the starboard wing.

Above: This Fw 190F-8 was surrendered to US forces in southern Germany at the end of the war and was later transferred to the US. Here it is seen with the Foreign Equipment evaluation code T2-116.

the 7.9-mm calibre MG 17s in the upper forward fuselage, an improved bomb-release mechanism, and four ETC 50 racks beneath the wings as standard. It introduced a new blown cockpit canopy intended to satisfy some criticism voiced by the Schlachtflieger pilots of the view offered for the close-support task by the standard canopy. It was proposed to apply several Umrüst-Bausätze to the Fw 190F-8, although, in the event, few of these conversion sets were installed. The **Fw 190F-8/U1** was a proposed two-seat trainer, several examples of which were made as conversions (a preserved example exists to this day in England).

Bomb-torpedo tests

The **Fw 190F-8/U2** and **Fw 190F-8/U3** were to be fitted with the TSA 2A (Tiefsturzanlage, or low-diving equipment) for use with the new BT (Bomben-Torpedo) weapons, the former being intended to carry the 700-kg (1,543-lb) BT 700 and the latter the 1400-kg (3,086-lb) BT 1400. Primarily an anti-shipping weapon, the Bomben-Torpedo had the advantage that its trajectory did not deviate when it hit the water, thus reducing the likelihood of it missing the vessel at which it was aimed. The tactics evolved for launching the BT called for a shallow dive from about 1500 m (5,000 ft), the TSA 2A being used to indicate a point 30-40 m (100-130 ft) short of the target vessel. During the dive the pilot operated the BT release mechanism, keeping the vessel in the grid wires until, at 300 m (985 ft), the BT parted from the aircraft automatically. The TSA 2A compensated for the speed of the vessel and the time of fall of the BT, which was fused to explode when directly beneath its target.

One of the more bizarre weapons ideas that was tried out for the Fw 190 was the hugely optimistic SG 113A Förstersonde anti-tank contraption, mounting two downwards-firing 75/77-mm recoilless guns that were supposed to fire when the aircraft flew over a Soviet tank, fancifully triggered by the tank's magnetic field. Not surprisingly, they were not used operationally, but were tried out on this Fw 190F-8.

Both the Fw 190F-8/U2 and U3 were fitted with an elongated tailwheel leg which, together with the folding lower fin on the BT itself, provided sufficient ground clearance for take-off. The Fw 190F-8/U2 with its BT 700 and the Fw 190F-8/U3 with its BT 1400 were tested at the Waffenprüfplatz at Hexengrund (Gdynia) in August 1944 with considerable success, the weapons being dropped over

Major Heinz Frank was the Kommandeur of II/SG 2 for a brief period in July 1944, when the Gruppe had brought its assorted Fw 190s (including this F-3) back from the Crimea to Hungary.

The bulges forward of the windscreen identify this as an Fw 190F-8. It was assigned to Hauptmann Günther Bleckmann, the Staffelkapitän of 6./SG 2, and is shown as it was seen in May 1944 while at Bacau in Romania. This Staffel subsequently specialised in Panzerschreck and Panzerblitz operations.

Focke-Wulf Fw 190F-8

II Gruppe, Schlachtgeschwader 4

Schlachtgeschwader 4
This unit was formed as part of the major reorganisation of attack assets in October 1943. The Stab and I Gruppe came from SchG 2, while the II and III Gruppen came from SKG 10.

Formed from a Schnellkampfgruppe (II/SKG 10), II/SG 4 initially operated Fw 190Gs in Italy, but in July 1944 acquired Fw 190F-8s. It was then sent north to Riga, before being returned to fight off the Western allies along the Rhine in late 1944, and then back to the east in the last weeks of the war.

both water and soft soil, it being proposed that the BT should also be used against heavily-fortified land targets. Although production of the BT series of weapons was only in its initial stages, pilots from I/SG 5 were trained in the use of the 200-kg (441-lb) BT 200, the 400-kg (882-lb) BT 400 and the 700-kg (1,543-lb) BT 700, and, equipped with the Fw 190F-8, this unit was redesignated III/KG 200 in January 1945, although, on orders from Göring, remained under the General der Schlachtflieger. The III/KG 200 subsequently operated in the West, including a spell in Norway, on both daylight and nocturnal sorties, but there is no evidence to indicate the operational use of BT weapons by the unit's Fw 190F-8s. The Fw 190F-8/U2 and U3 were to have been manufactured by Blohm und Voss as the **Fw 190F-8/R16** and **R15**, respectively, but this plan was not put into effect. A similar fate befell a torpedo-fighter version, the **Fw 190F-8/U14** that, carrying a single LTF 5 torpedo and equivalent to the Fw 190A-5/U14, was to have been produced in quantity as the **Fw 190F-8/R14**.

Other Rüstsatz-equipped variants that failed to progress further than the experimental stage were the **Fw 190F-8/R3** and **R13**. The former differed from the standard aircraft in having a pair of 30-mm MK 103 cannon beneath the wings in place of the ETC 50 racks, and the latter was a Nacht-Schlachtflugzeug with exhaust flame dampers, ETC 503 wing racks for two 300-litre (66-Imp gal) drop tanks, FuG 16ZS D/F and communications equipment, and FuG

A large variety of munitions and sub-munitions could be carried on the centreline rack beneath the Fw 190, usually using an ETC 501 or equivalent rack, with the smaller munitions as here being mounted on an ER 4 adaptor.

25a IFF. Whereas the Fw 190F-8/R3 was abandoned after the completion of two prototypes by Dornier in November 1944, the Fw 190F-8/R13 would have been built by Blohm und Voss but for the increasingly disastrous course of the war.

Experimental weapons

The Fw 190F-8 served as a test-bed in numerous experimental weapons evaluation programmes, and an example of this type was used by Jagdgruppe 10 to test the SG 116 Zellendusche (previously tested as an anti-bomber weapon) as an anti-tank weapon, the trio of 30-mm MK 103 barrels being reversed to fire downward. Not surprisingly, a lack of success led to the early abandonment of this programme, and little more success was enjoyed by tests with several 15-mm MG HF/15 barrels beneath each wing, these being abandoned in favour of the Panzerschreck (Tank Terror) programme. The Panzerschreck was an 88-mm Wehrmacht rocket missile, and a trio of launching barrels was mounted beneath each wing. The first tests were carried out at Udetfeld by Major Eggers, and the Panzerschreck is believed to have been briefly used operationally on the Eastern Front in October 1944, but its poor ballistic characteristics led to its replacement in December by the Panzerblitz (Tank Lightning).

The Panzerblitz 1 (Pb 1) possessed twice the charge of the Panzerschreck and could be released some 200 m (220 yards) from the target, or about twice the distance necessary to achieve adequate penetration with the Panzerschreck. Eight Pb 1 rockets were carried beneath the wings of the Fw 190F-8 in two jettisonable wooden crates, but it was necessary to launch the missiles at speeds no higher than 490 km/h (305 mph), rendering the aircraft rather vulnerable to ground fire during the target approach. Thus, the Pb 1 gave place to the Pb 2, a modified 55-mm R4M air-to-air missile with a hollow-charge warhead and launched from a pair of underwing racks each carrying either six or eight rockets.

Yet another anti-tank weapon evaluated by the Fw 190F-8 was the Werfer-Granate 28/32 (W.Gr. 28/32), a 280-mm projectile carried singly or in pairs beneath each wing. This had been evolved from the earlier 210-mm W.Gr. 21 that had proved unsuitable as an anti-tank weapon on the Eastern Front. The Schlachtflieger tested the W.Gr. 28/32 operationally on their own initiative but results were somewhat disappointing. A more elaborate anti-tank weapon was the SG 113A Förstersonde which, as installed in an Fw 190F-8 (Werk Nr 582071, **Fw 190 V75**), comprised a pair of

AB 250 bomb
This Fw 190 is carrying an AB 250 Abwurfbehalter, a precursor of the modern cluster bomb. It was a container that opened in flight to dispense up to 144 SD 2 'butterfly bombs', or 30 of the larger SD 4 and 17 of the larger still SD 10 sub-munitions.

Rockets
Among the most effective of anti-tank weapons late in the war was the Panzerblitz rocket system, which consisted of seven 54-mm rockets beneath each wing. Each had a shaped charge warhead, and a full salvo could knock out the heaviest tank.

Cockpit
Well laid out and effectively armoured, the cockpit provided the pilot with good visibility in flight, but the broad nose and tail-down stance made ground visibility poor. Extra armour was incorporated to protect the pilot, oil tank and engine from groundfire. Introduced on late Fw 190Fs was a bulged canopy which dramatically improved the pilot's view of the world.

Schlachtgruppen
The Luftwaffe's close-support units had their origins in the Schlachtfliegergruppen of the pre-war period, although most of these units soon became Stukagruppen in the dive-bomber ranks. One, however, became II (Schlacht) LG 2 in November 1938, and this unit carried on the attack role until it formed the basis of a reborne attack organisation that was formed from January 1942 to answer growing close support needs. II (Schlacht)/LG 2 became the first Gruppe in a new Schlachtgeschwader (SchG 1), and from December 1942 a second Geschwader (SchG 2) was formed. On 18 October 1943 the Luftwaffe's entire attack fleet underwent a comprehensive reorganisation, drawing in the two Schlachtgeschwadern, all but one Stukagruppen, and the single Schnellkampfgeschwader. They emerged as a series of new Schlachtgeschwadern, with the simplified abbreviation 'SG'. At the same time, the Störkampfgruppen were reorganised as Nachtschlachtgruppen.

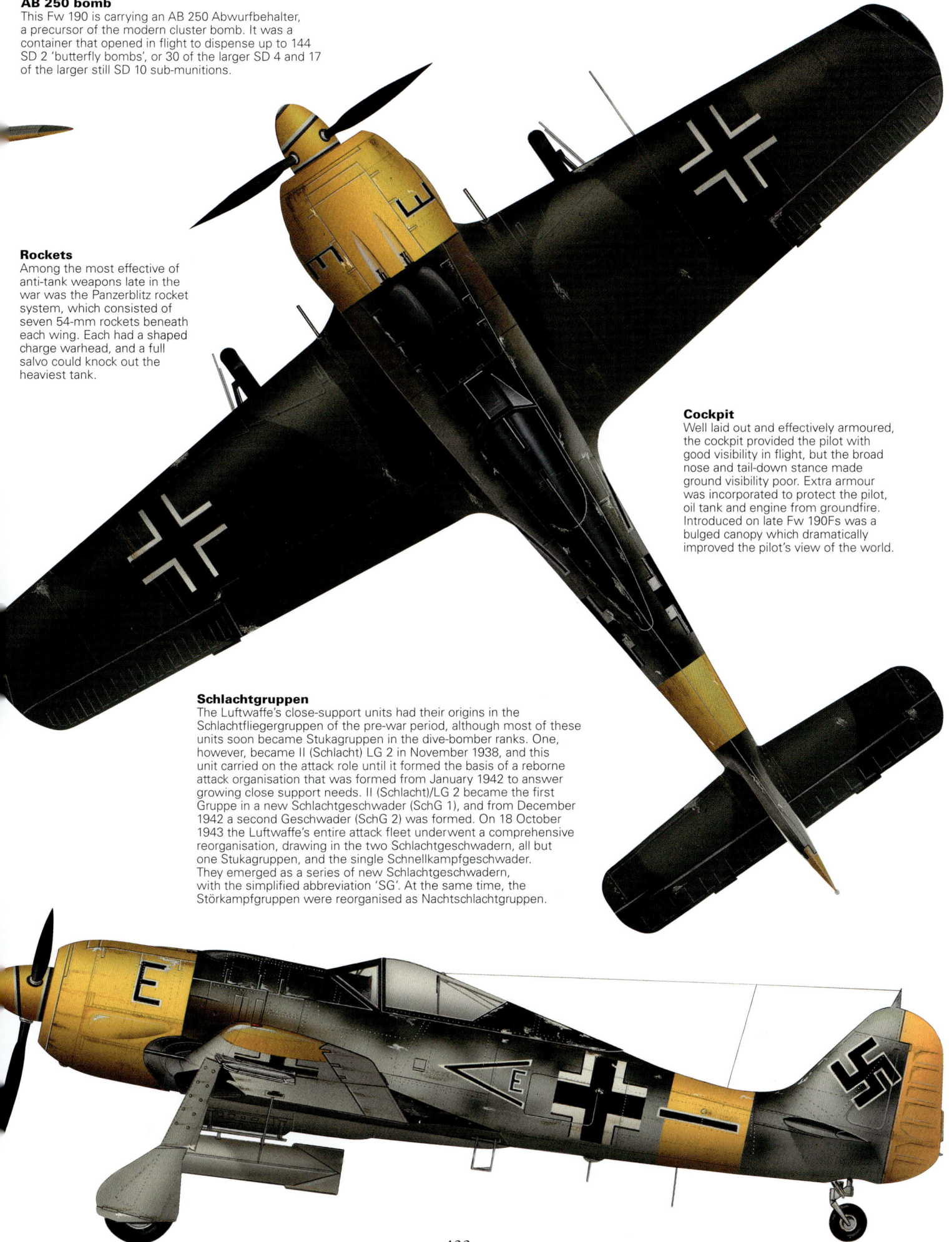

Camouflage

This F-8 wears a non-standard dark green base coat more akin to bomber aircraft, with a white/hellgrau (light blue-grey) meander pattern sprayed over the top, to disrupt the contours of the aircraft's shape. The yellow aft fuselage band and wingtip undersides were standard Eastern Front theatre markings.

Armament

The basic armament of the F-8 comprised a 20-mm MG 151 cannon in each wing root, with 250 rounds per gun. Then two 13-mm MG 131 machine guns in the upper fuselage decking, with 475 rounds per gun. These latter weapons replaced the 7.9-mm MG 17 gun of earlier F variants.

Canopy and fuselage bulges

Based on feedback from Schlacht pilots in combat, the F-8 was fitted with a bulged 'blown' canopy for increased visibility. This was also employed on late-model Fw 190As and Fw 190Gs. Being based on the Fw 190A-8 and retaining that variant's 0.51-in (13-mm) fuselage guns, the F-8 had the two bulges associated with these weapons ahead of its armoured windscreen.

Wing structure

The wing was built around two spars, to which were attached a wingtip section, leading-edge sections and simple flaps and ailerons, the latter having fixed tabs.

F series production

The F series was largely built by Arado and Dornier, production continuing from the F-3 straight onto the F-8, which was the equivalent of the A-8 fighter. Some had 'tropical' or dust filters as F-8/Tp or F-8(trop).

Weapon trials

Weapons trialled on the F-8 included the SG 113A Förstersonde installation of two downward-firing 77-mm recoiless anti-tank guns in each wing. They were intended to be triggered by the electromagnetic field of a tank as the aircraft flew over.

Focke-Wulf Fw 190

Undercarriage
The stalky mainwheel units retracted inward to lie in the wingroots. In turn this gave Fw 190 a very wide track, which made the aircraft very stable when operating from primitive airstrips prevalent on the Russian Front. During the spring and autumn months, when the airstrips could turn into bogs, the lower undercarriage doors were often removed to prevent the wheels clogging with mud.

External stores
A single SC 250 bomb on a centreline ETC 250 bomb rack, along with four SC 50 (50-kg/110-lb) bombs on ETC 50 racks under the wings was a fairly standard bomb load for the Fw 190F. Alternatively, an ER 4 adaptor could be added to the fuselage rack allowing, as here, the carriage of four SC 50s in this position.

Focke-Wulf Fw 190F-8

I Gruppe, Schlachtgeschwader 2 'Immelmann'

This machine was on the strength of 1./Schlachtgeschwader 2 'Immelmann', based at Görgenyaroszfalu, Hungary during the summer of 1944. I/SG 2 converted to the Fw 190F-8 from the Ju 87 at this base in July. At this time the Schlacht units of Luftflotte 4 were engaged in ferocious combat with Russian forces as the Germans retreated through Romania and Hungary, while USAAF P-51s, on long-range missions out of bases in Italy, were also just beginning to enter the fray. I/SG 2 fell back through Hungary into Austria and Slovakia, ending the war at Graz.

Bomb types
The F-8 was fitted with a centreline ETC 250 or ETC 501 rack and underwing ETC 50 racks as standard, although there were many variations. This aircraft is carrying eight SC 50 (50-kg/110-lb) bombs, including four on the centreline rack on an ER 4 adaptor.

Focke-Wulf Fw 190

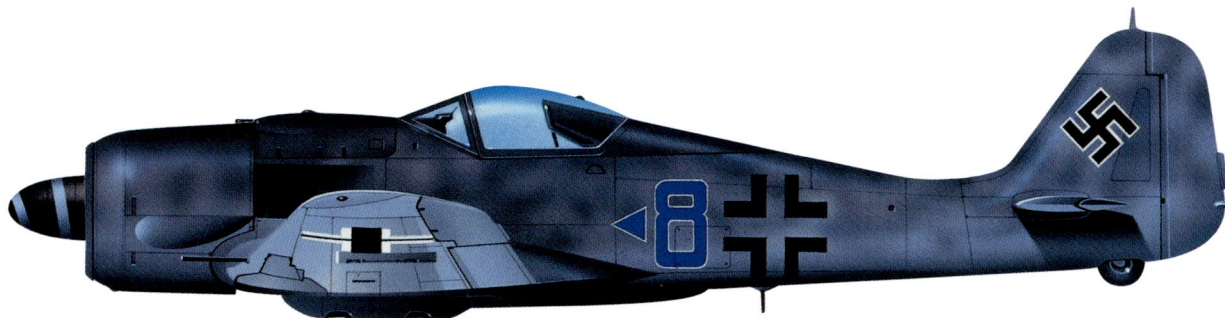

This late-production Fw 190F-8 was flown by Stab/SG 4 in January 194[ ] Based at Köln-Wahn, the unit was involved in the Bodenplatte raids on All[ ] airfields. On 1 January elements of SG 4 attacke[ ] St Trond in Belgium, losing the Geschwaderkommodore, Alfred Druschel, in the process.

77-mm recoilless guns firing vertically downwards from each wing, these very fancifully being supposedly triggered by the electromagnetic field created by a tank. Two further Fw 190F-8s were fitted with the SG 113A, the weapon successfully penetrating the armour of a captured T-34 tank during tests at Volkenrode. Wire-guided missiles tested by the Fw 190F-8 included the X 4 Ruhrstahl and the X 7 Rotkäppchen, neither of which attained operational status. Another weapon tested by an Fw 190F-8 was the Blohm und Voss Bv 246 Hagelkorn (Hailstone) glider bomb.

The Fw 190F-8 was succeeded on the Arado and Dornier assembly lines in September or October 1944 by the **Fw 190F-9**, which differed from the earlier model primarily in having a supercharged BMW 801TS offering 1492 kW (2,000 hp) for take-off and emergency, this being raised to 1693 kW (2,270 hp) with MW 50 injection and increased boost, and 1279 kW (1,715 hp) being available at 12190 m (40,000 ft). Some also had the Ta 152-type wide vertical tail unit. It was intended that this should be followed by the **Fw 190F-10** with the BMW 801F (TF) engine, but deliveries were not destined to commence before the end of the war. Other versions that were either produced as prototypes or were on the drawing boards, but failed to attain production were the **Fw 190F-15, –16** and **–17** that featured modified undercarriages with larger mainwheels and hydraulic rather than electric actuation, later radio equipment, the BMW 801TS or TH engine, an ETC 504 multi-purpose fuselage rack, and, in the case of the Fw 190F-16 or F-17, a TSA 2D sight.

Approximately 7,000 Fw 190Fs were built, but some of them were conversions or re-builds from earlier A-series airframes in Focke-Wulf's increasingly extensive 'recycling' scheme.

Fw 190G series

Evolved in parallel with the F-series Schlachtflugzeug, the G-series Jagdbomber mit vergrösserter Reichweite (Jabo-Rei), or extended-range fighter-bomber, for missions of longer-range than the radius of the battlefield support Fw 190F, utilised as standard the Umrüst-Bausatz 8 or 13 applied to the Fw 190A-4 or -5 fighters to convert them as fighter-bombers. The principal change introduced by the G-series was the deletion of the fuselage-mounted weapons, gun armament being restricted to the two 20-mm MG 151 cannon installed

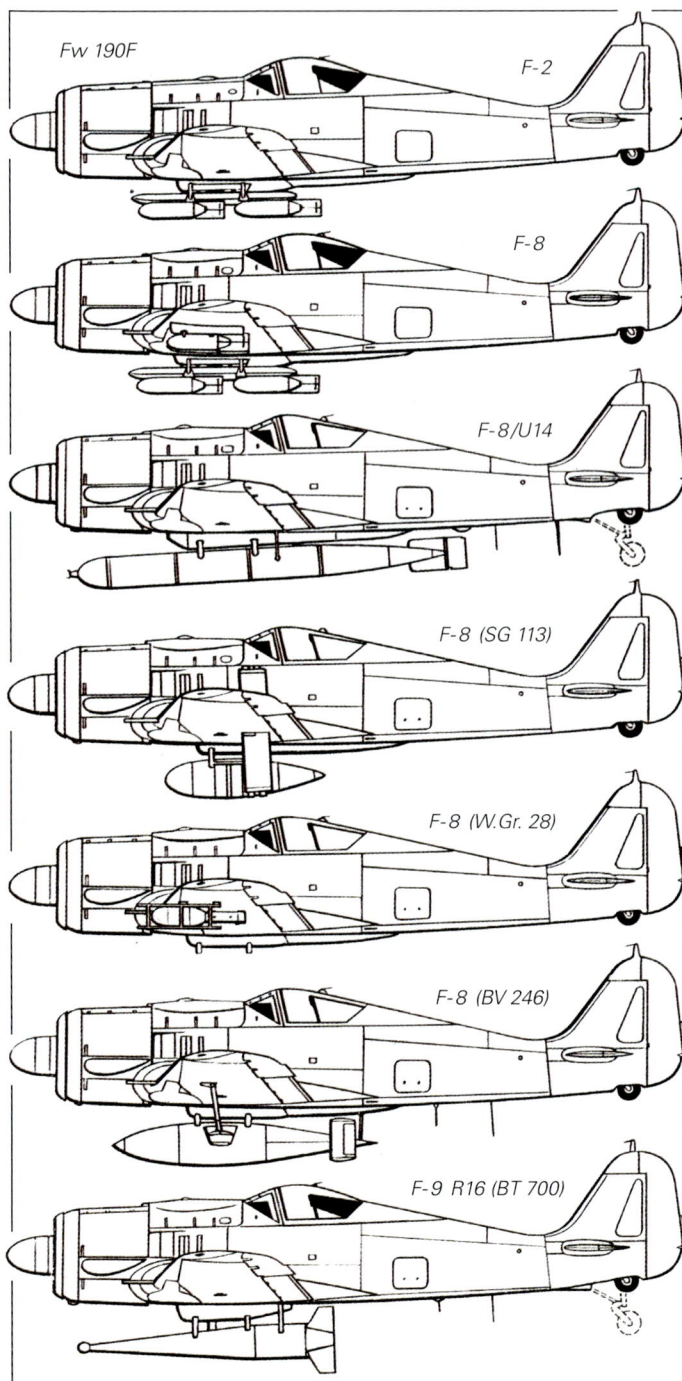

Fw 190F

F-2

F-8

F-8/U14

F-8 (SG 113)

F-8 (W.Gr. 28)

F-8 (BV 246)

F-9 R16 (BT 700)

An Fw 190F-series aircraft has two ETC 50 racks beneath each wing outboard of the main undercarriage; each rack could carry a 50-kg (110-lb) SC 50 bomb.

This Arado-built Fw 190F-8(trop) (probably Werk Nr 580383, CM+WL) was employed at the Tarnewitz weapons testing facility for various weapons trials and qualification. In this view it has an ER 4 adapter on its underfuselage rack, and two ETC 50 racks beneath each wing on each of which an SC 50 bomb is attached. This is a classic bombload as used on short-range fighter-bomber missions by Fw 190Fs.

in the wing roots. The initial model, the **Fw 190G-1** of which some 50 examples were produced, was based on the Fw 190A-4 (Fw 190A-4/U8) airframe and was fitted with an ETC 501 fuselage rack for a single SC 500 or SC 250 bomb, or ER 4 converter for four SC 50 bombs, plus wing racks (similar to the Ju 87 Stuka) for two 300-litre (66-Imp gal) fuel tanks. With two under-wing tanks, the Fw 190G-1 attained a range of some 1500 km (930 miles) at 386 km/h (240 mph), and with one tank on the central rack the range was 1040 km (645 miles) at 462 km/h (287 mph).

The first G-series Jabo-Rei to be built in substantial numbers, the **Fw 190G-2**, differed from the initial model only in being based on the slightly longer fuselage of the Fw 190A-5 (similar to the Fw 190A-5/U8), equipment and performance being virtually unchanged excepting, for example, simplified racks for the underwing fuel tanks. The **Fw 190G-3**, which began to leave the assembly lines in the late summer of 1943 and was similar to the A-6, introduced the PKS 11 autopilot as standard, modified Focke-Wulf underwing racks for fuel or bombs and, from October 1943, a petrol injection system for the BMW 801D-2 engine.

Provision was made for over-riding the boost control and the simultaneous injection of 96 octane fuel into the port air intake, the result being an increase from 1268 to 1395 kW (1,700 to 1,870 hp) for take-off, and an increase in sea level maximum speed without external stores from 547 to 573 km/h (340 to 356 mph). With dust filters and other equipment to suit it for use in the Mediterranean or Russian theatres it was designated **Fw 190G-3/Tp** (trop).

The next and final production G-series sub-type, the **Fw 190G-8**, was, in essence, the counterpart of the Fw 190A-8, and was manufactured between September 1943 and February 1944, production probably phasing out in the final days of February 1944. The Fw 190G-8 theoretically embodied all the modifications standardised by the A-8, such as repositioned radio and fuselage stores rack, and provision for an MW 50 tank (with which it became the **Fw 190G-8/R1**) or 114-litre (25-Imp gal) auxiliary fuel tank aft of the cockpit. It lacked the balloon cable-cutting device featured by the wing of some G-3s and, from January 1944, lacked the PKS 11 autopilot. It introduced into the G-series the new blown cockpit canopy as also fitted to the F-8 and some

Approximating to early Fw 190G standard, this Fw 190, GL+MY, has the installation for MG 17 machine-guns in its upper forward fuselage and an ETC 501 rack beneath its fuselage.

An early Jabo-Rei Fw 190 fighter-bomber shows off its undersurfaces for the camera. This view shows the attachment points for large fairings beneath the wings just inboard of the Balkenkreuz national insignia, which would carry long-range fuel tanks for the extended-range operations that the Fw 190G series of Jabo-Rei aircraft took part in.

Above: The classic Jabo-Rei configuration is demonstrated here by a Fw 190G-3. Under the centreline is a single SC 500 (500-kg/1,102-lb) bomb, with a pair of 300-litre (66-Imp gal) fuel tanks under the wings. When carrying larger bombs, the lower fins often had to be removed to allow ground clearance.

A-8s. In its initial production form, the Fw 190G-8 was fitted with an ETC 501 fuselage rack for a single SC 500 or SC 250 bomb, or a 300-litre drop tank, and the two wing racks could each accommodate either an SC 250 bomb or a 300-litre tank. A small number of aircraft were fitted with GM 1 (nitrous oxide injection) power boosting as the **Fw 190G-8/R4**, and some 146 late production machines were fitted with four ETC 50 wing racks instead of the ETC 503 as the **Fw 190G-8/R5**, these aircraft also having provision for two 114-litre (25 Imp gal) protected internal wing tanks.

G-series aircraft were tested with various experimental weapons, including the Bv 246 Hagelkorn glider bomb and the SB 800 RS Kurt rolling mine-bomb, tests with the latter being carried out at the Waffenprüfplatz at Leba in Pomerania during 1944. The Fw 190G saw limited service with 1000-kg (2,205-lb) SB 1000 and SC 1000 bombs, but the largest weapon to be delivered by G-series aircraft was the 1800-kg (3,968-lb) SC 1800 which, in February and March 1945, was carried by Fw 190G-1s of NSGr. 20 for use against bridge targets. Fitted with special tyres and with much standard equipment removed, the SC 1800-equipped Fw 190G-1s demanded a take-off run of at least 1200 m (3,900 ft). On 7 March, NSGr. 20 employed the SC 1800 in an attempt to destroy the vital Remagen Bridge. With the phasing out of Fw 190G production in February 1944, replacement aircraft were provided by modifying Fw 190F-8s or other suitable airframes, such as A-8 versions at forward maintenance units, as a part of the major 're-cycling' of Fw 190 airframes that took place later in the war.

Fw 190B and Fw 190C series

By the beginning of 1942, the Fw 190A was established in production and service, and most of the more serious shortcomings that had revealed themselves during the fighter's gestation had been ironed out. A solution had still to be found,

A dilapidated Fw 190 with weapons rack is examined by Allied troops. The codes, PL+GN, were known as Stammkennzeichen and were factory identification codes.

however, for the inadequacy of the altitude performance, and the first attempt to solve this problem was represented by the use of three standard but specially-converted Fw 190A aircraft as development airframes, including the Fw 190A-3 Werk Nummern 0528, 0531 and 0532. Initially they were fitted with new, larger volume supercharger air intakes on the side of their engine cowlings to increase airflow into the BMW 801D engine's supercharger, thus allowing for better engine output at higher altitudes. This initial study, conducted around September 1942 specifically with the BMW 801 and sometimes called Höhenjäger 1, proved disappointing.

Focke-Wulf was convinced that the desired performance could not be achieved with the BMW 801, and that this should be replaced by a liquid-cooled power plant. Dipl.-Ing. Tank favoured the DB 603, but this engine was viewed with disfavour by the RLM, having been developed by Daimler-Benz without official sanction. Tank was informed that the improved performance now being sought should be achieved with developments of the existing BMW 801 air-cooled radial or the Jumo 213 liquid-cooled inline engine that had just entered series production. Primarily as a concession to Tank, the Technisches Amt agreed to some design development of a DB 603-engined Fw 190 being undertaken, but it was made clear that such would be considered as a back-up programme with little likelihood of a series production order, as the production future of the DB 603 engine itself was still uncertain.

Of numerous alternative proposals made by Focke-Wulf for the high-performance or high-altitude fighter (Hochleistungsjäger), three were tacitly accepted by the Technisches Amt: a high-altitude fighter with pressure cabin, a turbo-supercharged BMW 801 engine and an 11 per cent increase in gross wing area that was assigned the designation **Fw 190B** (Höhenjäger 1); a similar high-altitude fighter powered by a DB 603 engine and designated **Fw 190C** (Höhenjäger 2); and a medium-altitude, stop-gap fighter essentially similar to the Fw 190A but having a Jumo 213A engine as the **Fw 190D** (also a part of Höhenjäger 2). The last-mentioned proposal had aroused the greatest interest in the RLM as, in view of the engine development situation and its close affinity with the existing airframe, it offered the

Fw 190 V13 (Werk Nr 0036, SK+JS), first flew in March 1942 as a part of the Höhenjäger 2 programme. It was powered by an early Daimler Benz DB 603A inline engine and was quite probably the first Fw 190-type aircraft to fly with DB 603 power. It was originally an early Fw 190A-0 pre-production development and trials airframe.

most immediate prospect of a fighter of superior performance without attendant disruption of existing assembly lines. Nevertheless, work on all three sub-series proceeded in parallel, a number of pre-production Fw 190A-0 airframes being assigned to the programme, together with 10 of 15 additional A-0 airframes (Werk Nummern 0046 to 0060) that had been laid down specifically for test and development purposes.

The **Fw 190 V12** (Werk Nr 0035) was intended to be the first real B-series airframe, fitted with a nitrous oxide injection or GM 1 system for use above the rated altitude of its BMW 801C-series engine. The nitrous oxide, which was retained under pressure in liquid form in a tank aft of the cockpit, provided additional oxygen for the engine, also acting as an anti-detonant. In the event, however, several late-build Fw 190A-0 airframes were used for the majority of Fw 190B development flying as B-0 airframes. These started with the **Fw 190B-0** Werk Nr 0046, which first flew on 20 January 1943 with Focke-Wulf test pilot Werner Bartsch in control. Coded TI+IK, it was the first of four prototype/ pre-production Fw 190B-0 aircraft: Werk Nummern 0046 to 0049, all originally from the Fw 190A-0 pre-production/ development aircraft allocations.

They were BMW 801D-powered, but lacked the necessary turbo-supercharger, with 0049 having GM 1 boost

As fitted to the Fw 190 V13, the annular radiator for the DB 603A-0 engine changed the previously clean forward profile of the type.

This aircraft, the Fw 190 V32 (Werk Nr 0057, GH+KV) was used for a variety of important trials and development projects. It is seen here in late 1943 or early 1944 in the configuration for the so-called 'Ta 153', with long-span wing and DB 603G engine fitted, but earlier in the war it was used in the Fw 190C programme with an earlier DB603 installed in a different trials configuration with a turbo-supercharger.

added. All had a pressure cabin, comprising sealing of the fireproof bulkhead, floor and sides, and a reinforced hot-air sandwich-type sliding canopy. They differed one from another in minor respects only with the exception of the

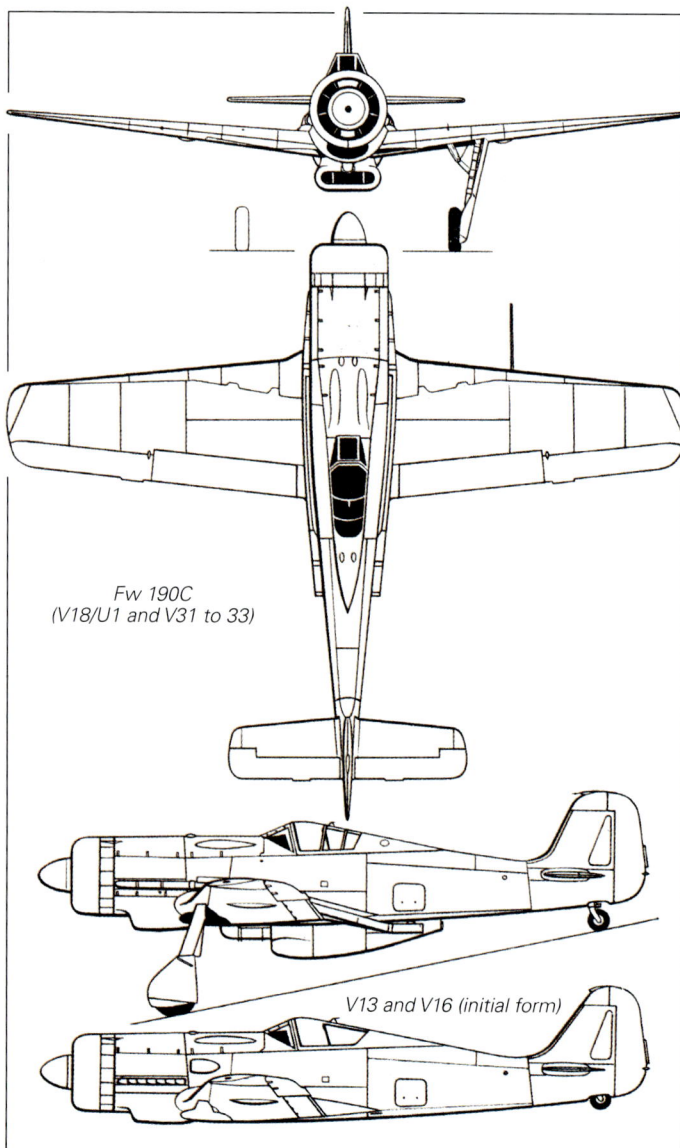

Fw 190C
(V18/U1 and V31 to 33)

V13 and V16 (initial form)

V24, which had the slightly enlarged wing (with span of 12.30 m/40 ft 4½ in and with a gross area of 20.30 m²/218.5 sq ft) that had originally been envisaged for both the B- and C-series. This wing had already been test flown by the **Fw 190 V15** (Werk Nr 0037, CF + OV), a pre-production Fw 190A-0 later fitted with a DB 603. There was also an **Fw 190B-1**, Werk Nr 0811, and the **Fw 190 V45** (Werk Nr 7347) and **V47** (Werk Nr 530115), which were BMW 801D-powered with GM 1 boost.

Disappointing trials

Nevertheless, flight testing of the BMW 801-powered Fw 190B-0 airframes proved generally disappointing. Effective combat altitude was boosted to some 7925 m (26,000 ft), but insufficient nitrous oxide could be carried to increase power for more than brief periods, difficulties were experienced in lagging the pipelines, and the weight of the system – with its compressed air cylinders and heavily-lagged GM 1 tank – was almost as much as the total gun armament of the standard fighter. However, the Focke-Wulf team had never considered the use of GM 1 boost in conjunction with the BMW 801 radial air-cooled engine as anything more than a possible temporary expedient, and design work was already well advanced on two of the other main developments of the basic design aimed at fulfilling the Technisches Amt demand for the Hochleistungsjäger.

One of the proposed B-series prototypes, the **Fw 190 V13**, had its BMW 801C-1 engine removed and replaced by a DB 603A-0 inline engine with annular radiator, the V13 thus becoming virtually a C-series prototype, though lacking exhaust-driven turbo-supercharger and pressure cabin. The liquid-cooled inline engine increased overall length by 0.67 m (2 ft 2½ in) to 9.47 m (31 ft 1 in), but the airframe remained essentially unchanged, and rearrangement of internal equipment restored the c.g. position, the Daimler-Benz engine being some 136 kg (300 lb) lighter than the BMW 801 that it replaced. The second B-series prototype, the **Fw 190 V16** (Werk Nr 0038, CF + OW), embodied similar changes to those applied to the V13, and neither aircraft featured cabin pressurisation or turbo-supercharger, the intention being to incorporate them at a later stage in the programme. They were followed by the first genuine C-series prototype, the **Fw 190 V18** (Werk Nr 0040, CF + OY), although this, too, initially lacked pressure cabin and turbo-supercharger.

High-altitude trials, which had been initiated at Bremen with the DB 603-powered V13 in March 1942, were transferred to Langenhagen where they were continued with the V16 and V18. Initially all three prototypes were powered by the DB 603A 12-cylinder inverted-Vee inline engine rated at 1305 kW (1,750 hp) for take-off, 1380 kW (1,850 hp) at 2100 m (6,900 ft), and 1212 kW (1,625 hp) at 5700 m (18,700 ft), but the V16, was transferred to the Daimler-Benz Erprobungsstelle at Echterdingen for engine and supercharger development tasks on 2 August 1942.

Prior to delivery to Echterdingen, the Fw 190 V16 had the ventral oil cooler intake suppressed, the oil cooler element being incorporated in the circular frontal radiator, and immediately on arrival the DB 603A engine was removed and replaced by a pre-series DB 603E, the DB 603E V83, with increased-diameter supercharger. The aircraft was tested with both MW 50 and GM 1 injection. Using the former the sea level maximum output of the engine was raised from 1343 to 1678 kW (1,800 to 2,250 hp), and from 1216 to 1417 kW (1,630 to 1,900 hp) at 5500 m (18,000 ft). GM 1 could be injected at the 'normal' rate of 3.54 kg (7.8 lb) per minute to provide a boosted output of 1119 kW (1,500 hp) at 8500 m (28,000 ft), or at an 'emergency' rate of 7.08 kg (15.6 lb) per minute to give 1111 kW (1,490 hp) at 9900 m (32,500 ft).

Fw 190 V16 flight trials

Flown by Flugkapitän Ellenrieder, the Fw 190 V16 attained 724 km/h (450 mph) at 7000 m (22,966 ft) during early trials at Echterdingen, and, using MW 50 injection, an initial climb rate of 1320 m (4,330 ft) per minute was clocked. On 10 October 1942 Ellenrieder claimed an altitude of 11000 m (36,090 ft), and 18 days later is believed to have reached 12000 m (39,370 ft). Soon, flights lasting as long as 90 minutes were being logged as a matter of course, despite the tremendous physical strain on the pilot. However, by this time the Technisches Amt was demanding operational altitudes of the order of 14000 m (46,000 ft), and it was obvious that such could not be attained without the application of exhaust-driven turbo-superchargers and pressure cabins.

Both the Deutsche Versuchsanstalt fur Luftfahrt (DVL) and Hirth-Motoren were developing exhaust-driven turbo-superchargers for use by the Fw 190C and other high-altitude aircraft. Constant teething troubles delayed their availability, but the DVL-developed TK 11 (Turbo-Kompressor 11), intended for altitudes of around 11000 m (36,000 ft), became available for installation late in 1942, and was first fitted to the original C-series prototype, which thus became the **Fw 190 V18/U1**. The TK 11 turbo-supercharger was mounted ventrally, and a DB 603G engine with increased-speed supercharger and increased compression ratio was fitted. Exhaust gases were led back over the wing roots by external pipes to drive the turbine, the compressed air from the blower being led forward, via an intercooler, to the supercharger.

Above: The Fw 190 V30/U1, originally one of the Fw 190C experimentals, was later rebuilt in the form shown as a Ta 152H prototype, with long-span wing and Jumo 213 powerplant.

The Fw 190 V16 (Werk Nr 0038, CF+OW) was one of the initial development aircraft for the DB 603-powered Höhenjäger 2/ Fw 190C high-altitude fighter programme.

The DB 603G drove an airscrew with four paddle blades, and was rated at 1417 kW (1,900 hp) for take-off and 1164 kW (1,560 hp) at 7375 m (24,200 ft), and with the TK 11 operating 1194 kW (1,600 hp) was available at 10670 m (35,000 ft). Other changes introduced by the Fw 190 V18/ U1 included a broader-chord fin and, some months later, a pressure cabin with similar specifications to that fitted in the Fw 190B-series prototypes. Pressure cabin trials were constantly delayed by failures of cockpit panels and valves, and the need to replace the rubber packing pieces sealing the canopy, coupled with difficulties in getting the necessary spares to Langenhagen. The Fw 190 V24 was briefly tested at Rechlin in May 1943, preliminary trials having been conducted at the Erprobungsstelle two months earlier with the Fw 190 V18/U1 which, at the time, lacked the pressure cabin but had a turbo-supercharger for its DB 603 engine.

Another of the prototypes in the Fw 190C series, the V30 (GH+KT) had a pressurised cockpit and turbo-supercharger, the latter fitted in the 'Kangaroo' fairing beneath the fuselage – there was nowhere else for the turbo to be fitted in the Fw 190's compact airframe.

Three views of the highly-important Fw 190 development aircraft, the Fw 190 V18 (Werk Nr 0040, CF+OY) display some of the modifications for the Fw 190C programme, including a pressurised cockpit with strengthened cockpit canopy, DB 603 engine with a four-bladed propeller, wide-chord vertical tail, and extensive external piping over the wing-roots to carry exhaust gases to the turbo-supercharger located beneath the fuselage in a large 'Kangaroo' fairing. This aircraft was also later used in the Ta 152H development effort.

Five further airframes had, in the meantime, been completed as C-series prototypes. These aircraft comprised the **V29** (Werk Nr 0054, GH+KS), **V30** (Werk Nr 0055, GH+KT), **V31** (Werk Nr 0056, GH+KU), **V32** (Werk Nr 0057, GH+KV) and **V33** (Werk Nr 0058, GH+KW). All were powered by the DB 603S(A) engine driving a four-bladed Schwarz wooden airscrew, and all had turbo-superchargers in distinctive ventral housings that resulted in them being known unofficially as 'Känguruhs' (Kangaroos). The V29 and V30 were transferred to Hirth-Motoren in the early summer of 1943 for installation of that company's Type 9-2281 turbo-supercharger, the V31, V32 and V33 having the DVL-devel-

Above and below: One of the Fw 190C development aircraft was the DB 603-powered Fw 190 V31 (Werk Nr 0056, GH+KU). On 28 May 1943, Focke-Wulf test pilot Werner Bartsch was flying the aircraft from Bremen to Langenhagen when the engine experienced difficulties. Bartsch succeeded in crash-landing it at Kaltenweide and survived.

oped TK 11 turbo-supercharger. All were either fitted with cabin pressurisation equipment from the outset of flight trials or received it during an early stage of their test programmes.

The Fw 190 V16, which had remained at Echterdingen as an engine test-bed, had had its DB 603E V83 replaced by a DB 603AA, which had a larger supercharger and the hydraulic supercharger gear pump from the DB 603E. With the new power plant, the Fw 190 V16 attained 719 km/h (447 mph) at 9000 m (29,530 ft) and 650 km/h (404 mph) at 12000 m (39,370 ft) at a loaded weight of 3700 kg (8,157 lb). Meanwhile, the Fw 190B-series prototypes, which were no longer considered likely to result in a serviceable high-altitude fighter, were confined primarily to pressure cabin development, and the test programme with the turbo-supercharged C-series prototypes dragged on. One of them, the Fw 190 V31, was written off on 28 May 1943 as a result of damage received in an emergency landing.

Teething troubles constantly plagued both DVL and Hirth-Motoren turbo-superchargers, the most constant source of failure being the inability of the pipes conducting the exhaust gases to withstand the extremely high temperatures generated. By the autumn of 1943, it was tacitly accepted that these turbo-superchargers still demanded much time-consuming development before they could attain sufficient reliability for service fighter installation. Accordingly, the Fw 190C was erased from the RLM's list of potential service aircraft, although the turbo-supercharger test programme continued. Eventually, with the demise of the Fw 190C-series programme, the various prototype/development aircraft that had been assigned as prototypes (the Fw 190 V29 to V33, excepting the V31, plus the V18/U1), were re-assigned and re-built as Ta 152H high-altitude development aircraft, as described in that section.

Priority had been allocated to the Fw 190D by the General-Luftzeugmeister Amt, despite the fact that, in the view of the Focke-Wulf team, the Daimler-Benz DB 603 was preferable as a fighter engine, offering superior altitude performance and greater development potential. Availability was the criterion, however, and quantity deliveries of the Jumo 213 were expected earlier than those of the Daimler-Benz engine.

Leutnant Theo Nibel's 'Black 12' of 10./JG 54 was downed by a partridge that holed his radiator near the British airfield of Grimbergen during Operation Bodenplatte. This aircraft was the first relatively intact D-9 to be captured, on 1 January 1945.

Operated by II/JG 26 from Nordhorn, this Fw 190D-9 took part in the attack on Brussels-Evere during the Bodenplatte operation. The D-9 with its powerful Jumo 213 engine restored some of the performance edge that had been lost to new Allied fighters.

Fw 190D series

The **Fw 190D** – the '**Langnasen-Dora**' as it has been popularly if somewhat incorrectly called ever since, or **Dora-9** as it was designated in its initial service version – was viewed by Dipl.-Ing. Kurt Tank as an interim development pending the availability of the definitive Ta 152. Nevertheless, it was found to be an extremely effective fighter in its own right. Indeed, from several aspects it was the most successful version of the Focke-Wulf fighter to attain service in quantity.

Development began in 1942 and three A-0 prototype/development airframes were assigned for conversion as D-series prototypes. The first of them (Werk Nr 0039, CF+OX) became the **Fw 190 V17** which, flown with a Jumo 213A-0 possibly during the summer of 1942 (the exact date is unconfirmed), was joined later in the year by at least two similarly-powered prototypes, the **V22** (Werk Nr 0044), and the **V23** (Werk Nr 0045). These D-series prototypes had similar wing and tail surfaces to those of the A-series, and the fuselage was unchanged apart from the introduction of an additional 50-cm (1-ft 7½-in) section immediately ahead of the tail assembly to compensate for the approximately 61-cm (2-ft) lengthening of the nose that had resulted from the replacement of the BMW 801 by the Jumo 213A – giving an overall length for production aircraft of 10.19 m (33 ft 5¼ in).

The D-series prototypes were equipped with a 20-mm MG 151 cannon in each wing root, the exact planned future format of weapons being initially undecided, and their test programme proceeded in parallel with that of the C-series aircraft. Late in 1943, a number of Fw 190A-8 airframes were adapted to take the Jumo 213A-1 engine for Luftwaffe evaluation (sometimes referred to as **Fw 190D-0** airframes), the first of them being the **Fw 190 V53** (Werk Nr 170003, DU+JC). Armament remained similar to that of the Fw 190A-8, including four wing-mounted MG 151s, but, in the meantime, the first D-series prototype, the Fw 190 V17, had been modified to the initial proposed production configuration as the **Fw 190 V17/U1** and prototype for the **Fw 190D-9** that attained production status in the early summer of 1944. The intended dedicated high-altitude pressurised **D-2**, and unpressurised **D-1**, were abandoned, leaving the D-9 as the first series-produced model.

The Fw 190D-9, the second prototype for which was the **Fw 190 V54** (Werk Nr 174024), differed from the pre-production D-0 and original prototypes in several respects. The chord of the tail fin was increased by moving the stern post aft by some 14 cm (5½ in), increasing the fin area by about 0.25 m² (2.5 sq ft) to eradicate some instability under certain conditions. The outboard MG 151 cannon were deleted from the wings, and the fuselage-mounted 13-mm MG 131s of the Fw 190A-8 were retained. Some minor structural changes were introduced, and the engine bearers were modified. If required, an ETC 504 rack was provided beneath the fuselage, with provision for two ETC 71 or ETC 503 racks beneath the wings, and a TSA 2D low-diving sight and an MW 50 methanol-water injection system could be installed – although ground-attack was never considered as a primary aim of the new fighter.

Initially, the Dora-9 was viewed with some suspicion by the Luftwaffe's fighter pilots, the Jumo 213 being considered essentially a bomber engine forced on the fighter manufacturers by the exigencies of the times, and Tank himself

One of the main Fw 190s used in the development of the Fw 190D series was the V53 (Werk Nr 170003, DU+JC) which shows off in this view the lengthened nose for the Jumo 213A inline engine.

The Fw 190D-9 was a very capable performer, and was of considerable interest to the Allies. This captured example is shown in the US after World War II, wearing the Foreign Equipment evaluation code FE-121. Sadly it was later scrapped, along with many of the other former Luftwaffe aircraft that were transported to the US after the war.

Focke-Wulf Fw 190

Gun armament
The D-9 was armed with a pair of MG 131 13-mm (0.51-in) machine guns in the upper forward fuselage, each with 475 rounds, and an MG 151/20 20-mm cannon in both wing roots, each with 250 rounds. Each weapon was synchronised to fire through the propeller arc. This armament remained constant throughout D-9 production.

Canopy
Early Fw 190Ds, including the prototypes, Fw 190D-0s and a few D-9s, featured the standard angular canopy inherited from the Fw 190A. Most production D-9s, however, were fitted with the 'blown' hood introduced by the Fw 190F-8, which provided better visibility and more room for the pilot to move his head.

Tank always regarded the Fw 190D as a stop-gap until the Ta 152 was ready, but it proved to be the best Luftwaffe fighter of the war, and a good match for any Allied machine.

Focke-Wulf Fw 190D-9

Jagdgeschwader 2 'Richthofen'

While II Gruppe/JG 2 remained with Bf 109s until almost the war's end, the Stab, I and III Gruppen converted to the Fw 190D-9 in December 1944. The staff flight was based at Merzhausen, from where this aircraft took part in sorties in support of the Ardennes counter-offensive. On 1 January 1945 it participated in Operation Bodenplatte against Allied airfields in Belgium. It was hit by US Army ground defences near Liège, the pilot being taken prisoner. Despite the fact that it carries staff markings, it was flown that day by Feldwebel Werner Hohenberg of 4./JG 2.

Markings
The chevron and double bars on the rear fuselage were applied for a 'Major beim Stab' (major of the staff flight). JG 2 was a Reichsverteidigung (Defence of the Reich) unit, and most of the aircraft wore RV bands forward of the tail, JG 2 being assigned yellow-white-yellow.

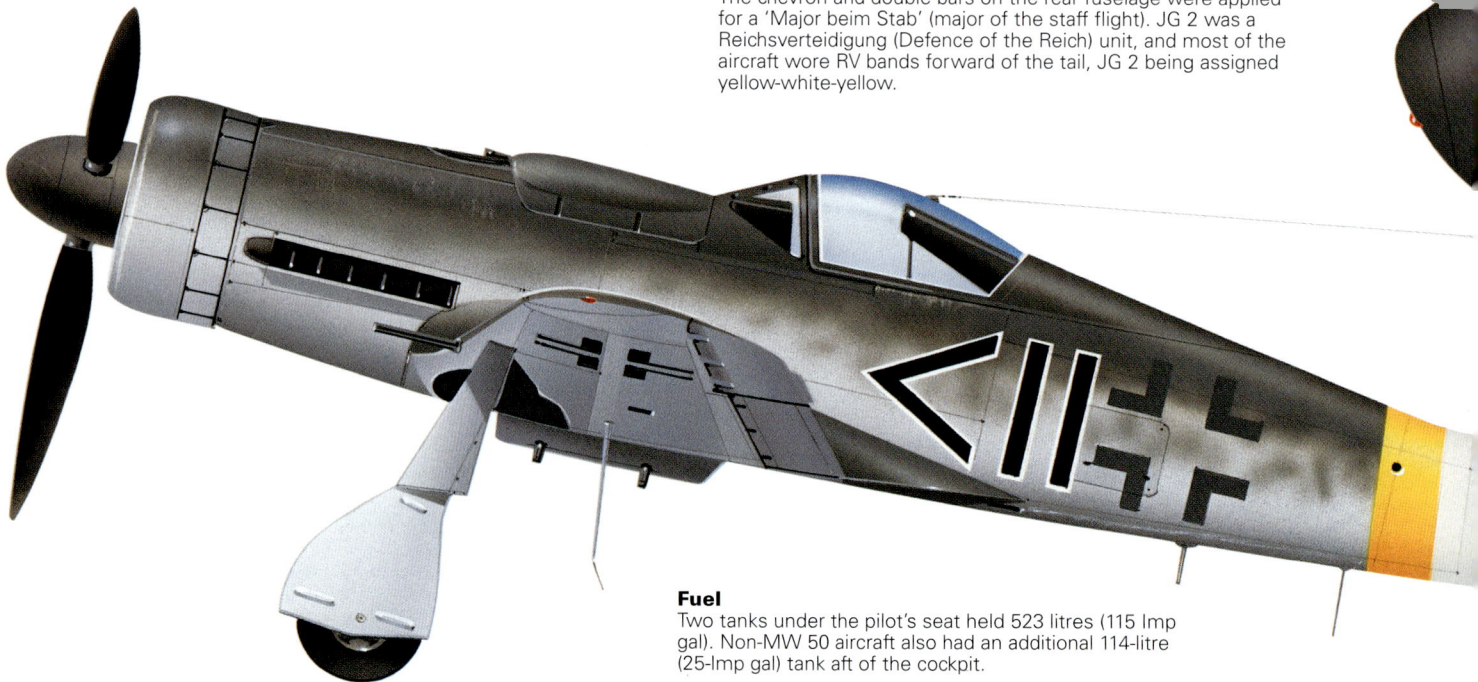

Fuel
Two tanks under the pilot's seat held 523 litres (115 Imp gal). Non-MW 50 aircraft also had an additional 114-litre (25-Imp gal) tank aft of the cockpit.

Offensive capability
In addition to the cannon, the Fw 190D-9 was provided with a centreline ETC 504 bomb rack which could carry a single SC 500 bomb. Provision was made for two ETC 71 or ETC 503 bombracks under the wings.

Powerplant
Powering the Fw 190D-9 was a Junkers Jumo 213A-1 12-cylinder engine, rated in standard form (without MW 50) at 1325 kW (1,770 hp) for take-off and 1195 kW (1,600 hp) at 5500 m (18,000 ft). The engine was installed as a complete 'power egg' attached to the forward fireproof bulkhead. Two semi-circular radiators surrounded the propeller shaft at the front in an annular arrangement, giving the engine the appearance of a radial. Behind the radiators were thermostat-controlled cooling gills. The three-bladed propeller was a VS 111 constant-speed unit.

Camouflage
Standard fighter camouflage of the period consisted of pale blue-grey undersides with medium-grey upper surfaces, the latter mottling into the former along the fuselage. The pale grey swastika was standard at this period of the war.

JG 2 and the Fw 190
As one of the two Jagdgeschwadern facing the RAF across the Channel in 1942, JG 2 was a natural choice for early deliveries of the Focke-Wulf fighter, and II Gruppe received its first Fw 190A-2s in March 1942. This Gruppe took the Fw 190 to North Africa at the end of 1942, but when it returned after a brief period of fighting in Tunisia it converted to Bf 109Gs. Meanwhile, at their French bases, the Stab, I and III Gruppen flew a succession of Fw 190A versions. The Geschwader also parented a dedicated France-based fighter-bomber unit, 10.(Jabo)/JG 2, which flew Fw 190As. This Staffel was reassigned to SKG 10 in April 1943. In September 1944 the Geschwader withdrew to Germany, taking part in the Bodenplatte offensive on 1 January 1945. By that time the Stab, I and III Gruppen were in the process of converting to the Fw 190D-9, the first of which had arrived with the Geschwaderstab in November 1944. All but sporadic defensive operations continued until March 1945, with II Gruppe having stayed faithful to the Bf 109 throughout.

Water/methanol injection
The 'Dora-9' had provision for the MW 50 system, which boosted power to 1671 kW (2,240 hp) at sea level, but this was fitted to only a few aircraft, the remainder having extra fuel in place of the MW 50 system. MW 50 could not be used for take-off, and was intended to give extra boost for a maximum of 10 minutes at a time up to 5030 m (16,500 ft). Enough water/methanol mixture was carried for 40 minutes' use.

Focke-Wulf Fw 190

From September 1944 to March 1945 the Stab, I and III Gruppen of JG 2 operated from airfields to the north of Frankfurt. III Gruppe, which flew this Fw 190D-9, was at Altenstadt.

did little to dispel these misgivings when, in October 1944, during a visit to the first Gruppe to convert to the Dora-9, III/JG 54 at Oldenburg, he commented that the Fw 190D-9 was but an "emergency solution" pending the availability of the Ta 152. Shortly afterwards, on 12 October, 9. and 10. Staffeln were transferred to Achmer and Hesepe, primarily to provide the Me 262s of JG 7 with top cover during take-offs and landings, when the jet fighters were extremely vulnerable. Once the pilots of JG 54 had thoroughly familiarised themselves with their new mount, their forebodings were seen to be unfounded, the Dora-9 being capable of out-climbing and out-diving its BMW 801-powered counterpart with ease. It also possessed an excellent turn of speed, and the pilots of the Jumo 213-powered Focke-Wulf were soon convinced that it was more than a match for the much vaunted P-51D Mustang.

The Fw 190D-9 was powered by a Jumo 213A-1 driving a three-bladed VS 111 constant-speed hydraulic airscrew, and was rated at 1320 kW (1,770 hp) for take-off and 1194 kW (1,600 hp) at 5500 m (18,000 ft). With methanol-water (MW 50) injection, power was boosted to 1671 kW (2,240 hp) at sea level, 1492 kW (2,000 hp) at 3400 m (11,150 ft), and 1402 kW (1,880 hp) at 4725 m (15,500 ft), although this was not fitted to all early aircraft, and was eventually made available as a field modification. The engine itself was installed as a complete power 'egg' (e.g. engine, bearers and cowling panels all in one supplied unit from Junkers) attached by four bolts at the fireproof bulkhead. Its two semi-circular radiators were mounted around the reduction gear casing at the front of the circular cowling, to the rear of which were annular gills automatically controlled by a thermostat mounted on top of the engine crankcase. Fuel was housed by two tanks beneath the cockpit, the front tank being of 232-litre (51-Imp gal) capacity and the rear tank of 291-litre (64-Imp gal) capacity. They could be supplemented by a 114-litre (25-Imp gal) tank aft of the cockpit as an alternative to the MW 50 installation. The latter could not be used for take-off but only in flight up to 5030 m (16,500 ft) for maximum periods of 10 minutes

at a time, boost pressure being increased by 27.6 kPa (4 lb/sq in), and sufficient MW 50 being carried for approximately 40 minutes' use.

The two MG 131 machine-guns in the upper forward fuselage were provided with up to 475 r.p.g., and the two MG 151 cannon (one in each wing root) each had 250 rounds. Armour comprised a 14-mm (0.55-in) plate for the pilot's head and shoulders, while the seat-back and surrounds were of 8-mm (0.31-in) plate. Protection for the engine consisted of two armour rings around the cowling, the forward ring being 11 mm (0.43 in) thick and the aft ring being 6 mm (0.24 in) thick. The parallel section added into the extreme rear fuselage was used to house eight oxygen bottles, these being located here to help counter-balance the additional weight forward.

Fw 190D-9 deliveries begin

Delivery of the Fw 190D-9 to the Luftwaffe began in August 1944 from Focke-Wulf at Cottbus, and Fieseler at Kassel-Waldau. The first two examples off the Cottbus line (Werk Nummern 210001 and 0002) were used for development work for the proposed but not series-produced **Fw 190D-10** with Jumo 213C engine (similar to the Jumo 213A but with provision for gun firing through the airscrew shaft) driving a VS 19 airscrew in place of the VS 111 (which did not permit an engine-mounted cannon), and an armament comprising a 30-mm MK 108 cannon firing through the airscrew hub and a single 20-mm MG 151 in the port wing root.

Several Fw 190A-8 airframes were earmarked for conversion as prototypes (**V55** to **V61** inclusive) of the **Fw 190D-11** fighter and Schlachtflugzeug. Apart from having additional protective armour, the Fw 190D-11 had revised armament, which comprised a pair of 20-mm MG 151 cannon in the wing roots and a pair of 30-mm MK 108 cannon mounted in the wings just outboard of the main undercarriage attachment points, and a Jumo 213E or F engine with a three-stage supercharger and revised air intake with no intercooler, MW 50 being injected before the third stage. **V56** Werk Nr 170924 is thought to have flown in August 1944, and some 17 of this variant are believed to have been built.

Relatively early in the production of the Fw 190D-9, the standard cockpit canopy had been replaced by a similar 'blown' canopy to that adopted for the later Fw 190A and F-series, and from early 1945 a small number were completed as **Fw 190D-9/R11** bad-weather fighters with PKS 12 auto-pilot and FuG 125 Hermine D/F navigational and blind-landing equipment. It was planned that, from early 1945, all new D-series aircraft would be suitable for the dual role of interceptor and Schlachtflugzeug. Three **Fw 190D-12** development aircraft (the **V63**, **V64** and **V65**) were planned for flight testing in early 1945, these having a Jumo 213F-1 engine in a new, more extensively armoured cowling, MW 50 injection, and an armament of one engine-mounted 30-mm MK 108 cannon and two 20-mm MG 151s in the wing roots. A number of sub-variants were planned, including the **Fw 190D-12/R5** with the increased compression-ratio Jumo 213EB engine and self-sealing wing tanks housing

The Fw 190D-9 was not only a good all-round fighter, but could also carry a limited air-to-ground load. This example has a stores rack beneath the fuselage for bombs of various sizes.

A tractor tows an Fw 190D-9, which carries a drop tank on its belly pylon. Generally regarded as the first kill that was achieved by the Junkers Jumo 213A-engined Fw 190D-9 was on 28 September 1944, when a III/JG 54 aircraft shot down an RAF Spitfire.

A long-nose Fw 190D-9 flies through a formation of American heavy bombers in this dramatic action photo. The bombers have just released their bombs (bottom right) and the Fw 190 has been captured by the bomber's strike camera as it makes its firing pass.

an additional 314 litres (69 Imp gal) of fuel, but the only sub-variant believed to have attained production status was the **Fw 190D-12/R11** bad weather fighter with PKS 12 and FuG 125 Hermine. Production start-up by Fieseler and Arado was planned for March 1945 but just how many were completed is unknown – possibly none.

It was proposed to replace the D-12 by the **Fw 190D-13**, the latter differing solely in having a 20-mm MG 151 in place of the 'engine-mounted' 30-mm MK 108, the centrally-mounted weapon having 220 rounds and the two wing root MG 151s having 250 r.p.g. Powered by the Jumo 213EB engine, it was, in its **Fw 190D-13/R5** form, to have had the TSA 2D sight and ETC 71 racks. Apart from two proto-type conversions (Werk Nummern 732053 and 732054), it now seems probable that at least 17 production examples were built by Roland from March 1945. A D-13 (Werk Nr 836017) flown by the Geschwaderkommodore of JG 26, Franz Götz, was surrendered to the British at Flensburg, northern Germany, in May 1945, and survives to this day.

Somewhat surprisingly, in the late autumn of 1944, the Technisches Amt, which had consistently supported the Jumo 213 engine in preference to the DB 603 for Fw 190 installation, reversed its earlier orders after a re-evaluation of the powerplant supply situation, issuing instructions for a changeover from the Junkers to the Daimler-Benz engine in the Fw 190D at the earliest possible opportunity. Therefore,

in October 1944, two early production Fw 190D-9s (Werk Nummern 210040 and 0043) were modified on Focke-Wulf's assembly line at Sorau to take the DB 603AE. During the course of that month, they were flown to the Daimler-Benz Erprobungsstelle at Echterdingen. The DB 603-engined Fw 190D had been named the **Haspel-Jäger**, as it had been Dr Haspel, the Director of Daimler-Benz, who had convinced the RLM of the advantages of re-engining the fighter. During trials at Echterdingen the converted aircraft clocked a maximum speed of 700 km/h (435 mph) and a service ceiling of 10000 m (32,800 ft).

Fw 190D-14/D-15

It was planned to manufacture the fighter in series with the DB 603E or DB 603LA engine as the **Fw 190D-14**, and with the DB 603EB or DB 603G as the **Fw 190D-15**, the latter actually preceding the former in being an assembly line conversion of the Fw 190D-9. Persistent reports exist that between 11-17 March 1945 an initial batch of some 15 Fw 190D-9s was flown to Echterdingen for conversion as Fw 190D-15s by fitting the DB 603G rated at 1417 kW (1,900 hp) for take-off and 1164 kW (1,560 hp) at 7375 m (24,200 ft). In the event, it appears that only one conversion had been completed and possibly flown when the Echterdingen test centre was occupied by US forces, but this final twist in the D-9 story remains somewhat shrouded in mystery.

Between 650 and 700 D-series fighters had been completed when all production finally terminated in 1945. In December 1944, Focke-Wulf's Marienburg plant, although appearing from the air to have been devastated by bombing, was alone producing eight Fw 190Ds daily. Luftwaffe acceptances of

The chevron-and-bar markings indicate the Geschwader IA (operations officer), while the black-white-black RV bands signify Jagdgeschwader 4. This Fw 190D-9 flew from Jüterbog-Damm early in 1945.

In February 1945 this Fw 190D-9 was flying with 1./Jagdgruppe 10 from Redlin, a satellite of Parchim. Like most units at the time, operations comprised daily engagements with foes ranging from the Yak-7s and La-7s of the Soviet V-VS, the daylight heavy bombers of the Allied strategic air forces, and the fighters of the 2nd TAF.

Focke-Wulf Fw 190

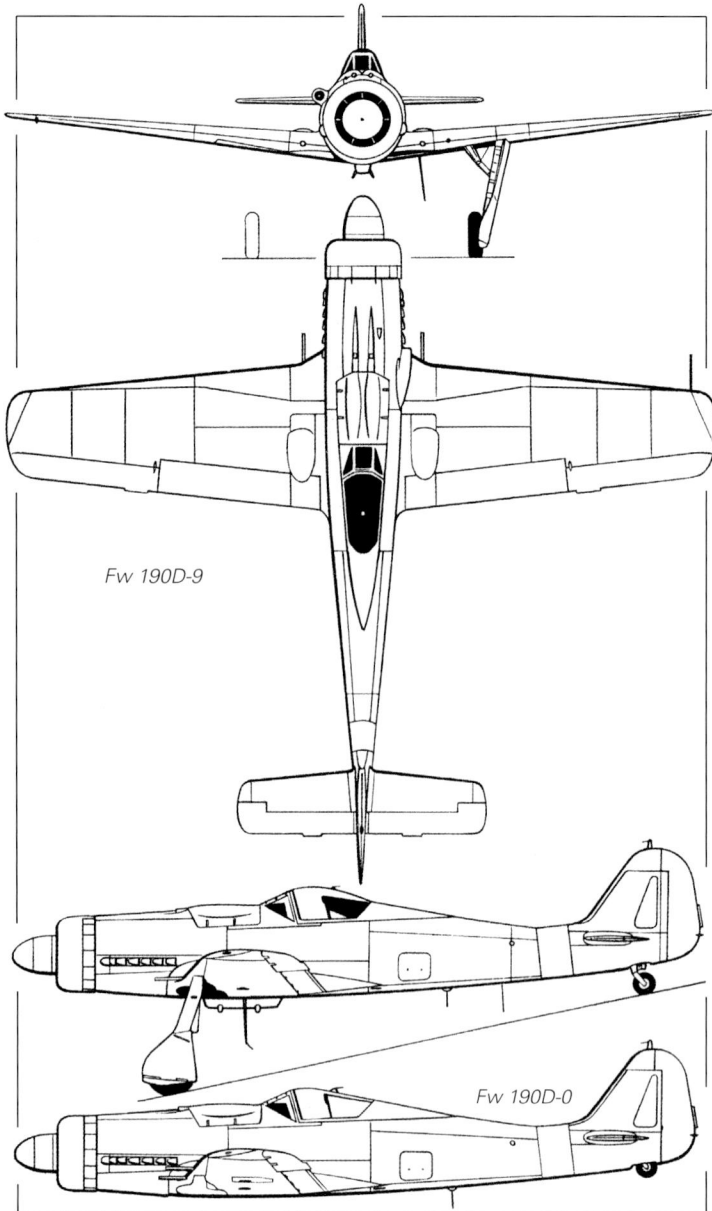

Fw 190D-9

Fw 190D-9

Fw 190D-0

Fw 190s of all types during 1944 had totalled 11,411 aircraft, representing a 375-per cent increase over the previous year and bringing to 16,724 the total number of examples of the Focke-Wulf fighter taken on Luftwaffe charge by the end of 1944. There is less certainty concerning output during 1945, official figures conflicting and in some cases being non-existent, and it is pure speculation to guess as to how many Fw 190s were produced during that period. It would not, however, have been the several thousand once thought likely.

Fw 190D-9 specification
Type: single-seat fighter and fighter-bomber
Powerplant: one Junkers Jumo 213A 12-cylinder liquid-cooled engine rated at 1320 kW (1,770 hp) for take-off and 1194 kW (1,600 hp) at 5500 m (18,000 ft), or with MW 50 injection 1671 kW (2,240 hp) at sea level and 1492 kW (2,000 hp) at 13400 m (1,150 ft)
Performance: (at 4350 kg/9,590 lb) maximum speed 575 km/h (357 mph) at sea level, 639 km/h (397 mph) at 3300 m (10,830 ft), 686 km/h (426 mph) at 6600 m (21,650 ft), 639 km/h (397 mph) at 10000 m (32,800 ft); maximum range (internal fuel) 837 km (520 miles) at 5640 m (18,500 ft); climb to 2000 m (6,560 ft) 2.1 minutes, to 4000 m (13,120 ft) 4.5 minutes, to 6000 m (19,685 ft) 7.1 minutes, to 10000 m (32,810 ft) 16.8 minutes
Weights: empty 3490 kg (7,694 lb); normal loaded 4300 kg (9,480 lb); maximum loaded 4840 kg (10,670 lb)
Dimensions: wingspan 10.50 m (34 ft 5½ in); length 10.19 m (33 ft 5¼ in); height 3.36 m (11 ft 0¼ in); wing area 18.30 m² (196.98 sq ft)
Armament: two 20-mm MG 151 cannon with 250 r.p.g. in wingroots, and two 13-mm MG 131 machine-guns with 475 r.p.g., plus (when required) one 500-kg (1,102-lb) SC 500 bomb on ETC 504 fuselage rack

Above: The Allies found abandoned in Germany large numbers of Fw 190s of all types at the end of the war, including this wrecked Jumo-engined example with guns in the outer wings.

The captured Fw 190D-9 coded by the Americans as FE-121 shows off its distinctive long fuselage in the US after the war. Although intended as a stop-gap, the Dora-9 proved to be a very good fighter for medium and low levels and was able to look after itself in combat against most Allied fighter types.

Oberstleutnant Gerhard Michalski assumed command of JG 4 in August 1944, flying initially on the Rhine front but later switching to the Oder theatre, hence the hasty overpainting of the RV bands. He flew this Fw 190D-9 in early 1945 from Jüterbog-Damm.

With 301 kills Gerhard Barkhorn was the Luftwaffe's second-ranking ace. This was the Fw 190D-9, named Christl after his wife, that he flew while Kommodore of JG 6 at Welzow.

This Focke-Wulf Fw 190D-9 with the early style of canopy was flown by Oberleutnant Oskar Romm, Kommandeur of IV/JG 3 while operating from Prenzlau in March 1945. Romm's wartime career ended in a crash on 24 April 1945, in which he was severely injured, his score at the time totalling 92 victories.

In the last weeks of the war IV/JG 51 converted to the Fw 190D-9, while based at Garz/Usedom. This example was flown by Leutnant Kurt Tanzer, Staffelkapitän of 13./JG 51.

Germany's most decorated soldier, Oberst Hans-Ulrich Rudel, flew this Fw 190D-9 as Kommodore of SG 2 while based at Grossenhain in March 1945. He also had a Ju 87G assigned, and it was in the Junkers aircraft that he flew his last wartime missions.

A mere handful of Fw 190D-13s reached the front line, this example being the aircraft assigned to Major Franz Götz, JG 26's last Kommodore. This is how it appeared at Flensburg in May 1945, when handed over to British forces.

Focke-Wulf Fw 190

Jagdgeschwader 6

JG 6 'Horst Wessel' was formed at Königsberg in July 1944 by the redesignation of the Stab, I and II Gruppen of ZG 26. Having previously flown the Me 410 in the Zerstörer role, the new JG 6 began life as a fighter unit, primarily equipped with Fw 190s. In October 1944 a third Gruppe was added, formerly I/JG 5 and flying the Bf 109G. By February 1945 all elements of the Geschwader were united at Welzow to the southeast of Berlin.

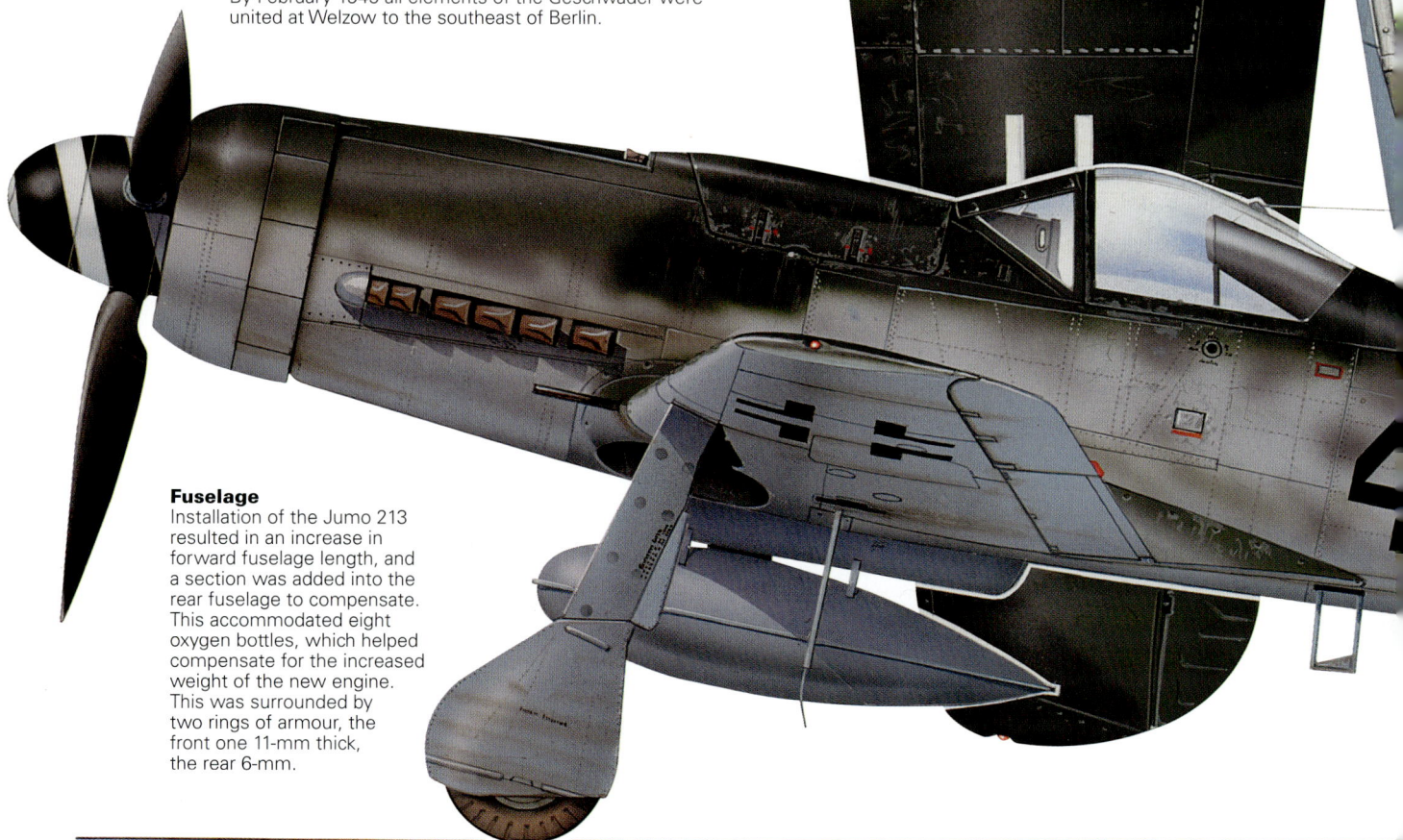

Fuselage

Installation of the Jumo 213 resulted in an increase in forward fuselage length, and a section was added into the rear fuselage to compensate. This accommodated eight oxygen bottles, which helped compensate for the increased weight of the new engine. This was surrounded by two rings of armour, the front one 11-mm thick, the rear 6-mm.

Focke-Wulf Fw 190D-9

III/JG 6, Welzow, March 1945

Although seen as an interim aircraft to fill in before the definitive Ta 152 could enter service, the Fw 190D was itself an excellent aircraft, blessed with good speed and climb performance. Many German pilots were sceptical of the new variant, but found it better than the BMW 801-powered Fw 190A in most respects, apart from roll rate.

'Dora Nine'

The Fw 190D-9 began rolling from the Cottbus and Langenhagen assembly lines during August and September 1944, and the first unit to re-equip with the new fighter, JG 54, achieved operational status in September/October 1944. By mid-December, D-9s equipped III/JG 54 at Varrelbusch, and I and III/JG 2. Despite its apparent parity with the latest Allied fighters, the D-9 suffered relatively heavy attrition. Many pilots were inexperienced and ill-trained, and the skies over Germany were simply too full of prowling USAAF and RAF fighters. Conversion of units to the new variant continued to the end of the war.

Undercarriage

The Fw 190 featured an outboard-mounted, inward-retracting main undercarriage layout. This design corrected one of the main faults of the Messerschmitt Bf 109 (and the Spitfire), namely tricky ground-handling characteristics of the narrow-track outward-retracting landing gear.

Unit

This particular aircraftt served with the III Gruppe of Jagdgeschwader 6 (III/JG 6) at Welzow in March 1945, one of a number of units to receive the type before the end of the war. The coloured fuselage bands signified aircraft assigned to home defence.

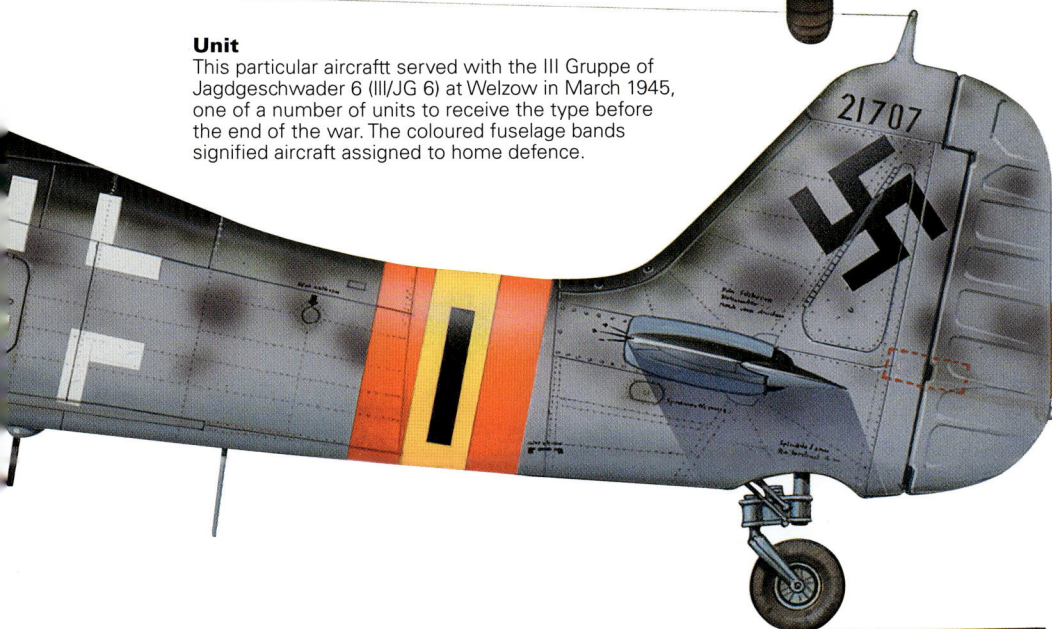

The 'Downstairs Maid'

This nickname was applied to the D-9 on account of its lack of cabin pressurisation and high-altitude potential. Intended only as an interim pending the fielding of the Ta 152, the Fw 190D-9 nevertheless performed exceptionally in the desperate defence of the Reich.

21707

Keith Fretwell

Above: An Fw 190A-0 development aircraft was modified for static ground ejection seat trials, inspired by test pilot Hans Sander, but they were comparatively unsuccessful. In this view the seat has just been fired: luckily its occupant was a dummy.

This is a line-up of Fw 190A-0 pre-production aircraft in early 1941, on the flight line at Bremen, during the period in which early production Fw 190A aircraft were being manufactured and prepared for combat. Particularly evident is the wide track of the Fw 190's main undercarriage, which was so useful in ground handling and operations from unprepared air strips – and was much appreciated by the pilots.

Fw 190 operational career

On 1 July 1941 II/JG 26 transferred from Maldeghem to Moorselle, north-west of Courtrai, where, at the end of the month, the first Fw 190A-1s arrived, the Gruppenkommandeur, Hauptmann Walter Adolph, taking up the first aircraft, and 6. Staffel being the first component of the Gruppe to officially convert to the Fw 190A-1 from the Messerschmitt Bf 109E-7, the Staffelkapitän being Oberleutnant Schneider. By 1 September the entire Gruppe had converted, and the first encounter between the Fw 190A-1 and RAF fighters took place shortly afterwards when a Schwarm (four aircraft) from 6./JG 26 patrolling over Dunkirk sighted a numerically superior force of Spitfire Mk Vs at some 4000 m (13,000 ft) over Gravelines. Enjoying the advantage of altitude, the quartet of Fw 190As attacked the Spitfires from out of the sun, shooting down three of the RAF fighters to provide the Focke-Wulf fighter with its first official kills.

Unfortunately for JG 26, the first Fw 190A-1 that the Jagdgeschwader was to lose to enemy action was flown by Hauptmann Adolph himself, a Ritterkreuzträger with 29 confirmed kills, including one in Spain with the Legion Condor. Adolph had taken-off from Moorselle on 18 September with seven other Fw 190As for a convoy escort patrol. Some 12 miles off Ostende the convoy was attacked by fighter-escorted Blenheims, and in the ensuing mêlée Adolph's Fw 190A was shot down, his body being washed ashore at Knocke three weeks later. At this time, British Intelligence was unsure of the status of the Fw 190, and the official communique relating to the action referred to the destruction of "a Curtiss Hawk (or Fw 190)".

During a second encounter between Fw 190As of II/JG 26 and RAF Spitfire Mk Vs, which took place on 27 September, the destruction of another example of the new German fighter was claimed, and commenting on the aerial activity during the previous week, The Aeroplane of 3 October remarked, '. . . among the RAF's victims last week was another enemy fighter with a radial engine'. One had been shot down the week before, and had been identified, a little doubtfully, as a Curtiss Hawk. In reporting the second, the Air Ministry made no attempt to name the type. Nor was it stated whether the machine was operating with a

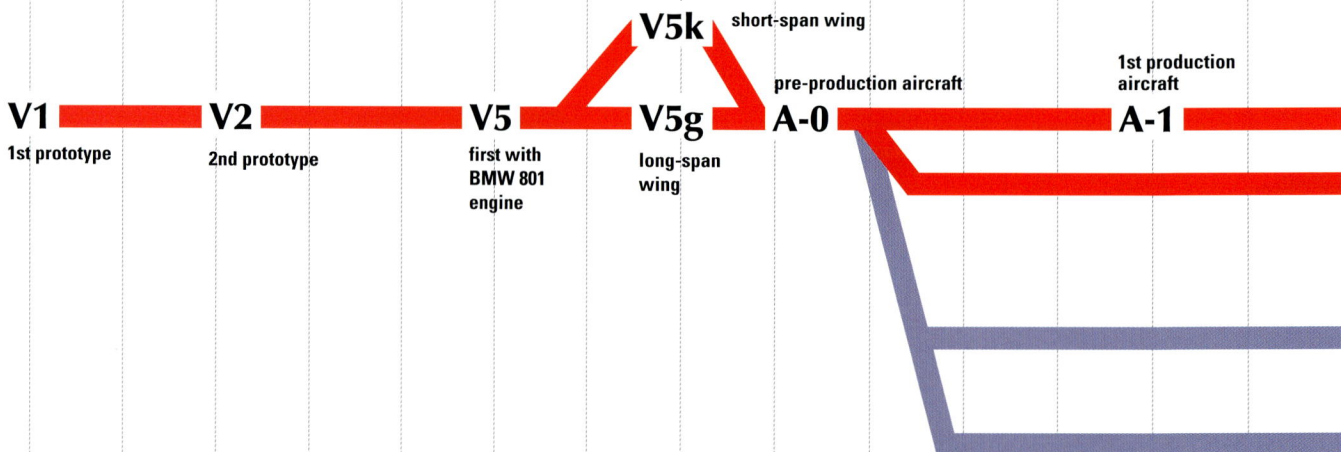

Focke-Wulf Fw 190 development
1939-August 1941

452

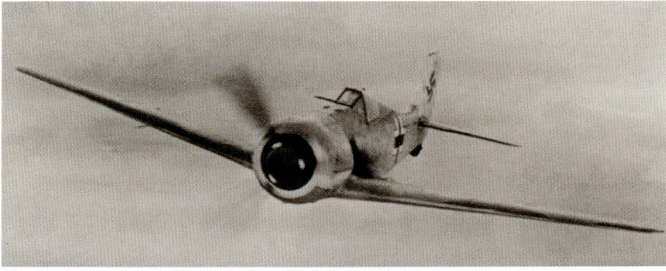

This view of an early Fw 190A shows the type's distinctive shape. In the first encounter with the new type RAF pilots thought that they may have been fighting the Curtiss Hawk, a few of which the Germans had inherited from the former Armée de l'Air.

Above: This view shows an early Fw 190A as seen from the rear glazing of an Fw 189 in a special sequence of photographs that was made by Focke-Wulf to publicise its products.

squadron or whether it was an odd one. Speculation about its identity may soon be settled but, in the meantime, the choice seems to lie between the Curtiss Hawk, late of the Armée de l'Air, and the Focke-Wulf Fw 190, fresh from a German factory'. However, any remaining British doubts concerning the operational debut of the Focke-Wulf fighter were soon to be dispelled.

Strength returns for JG 26 dated 25 October 1941 showed the Stab at Audembert with six Bf 109Fs, I Gruppe at St Omer-Clairmarais with 43 Bf 109Fs, II Gruppe at Wevelghem (to which base the unit had transferred on 15 October) with 45 Fw 190A-1 s of which 34 were serviceable, and III Gruppe at Coquelles (to where the unit had transferred from Liegescourt on 19 October), which was operational on 28 Bf 109Fs but was undergoing conversion to the Fw 190A, 38 examples of which had been delivered but only seven of them being serviceable.

Ascendancy over the Spitfire

The re-equipment of the Jagdgruppen with the Fw 190A proceeded initially at very low tempo but, nevertheless, despite the limited numbers of Fw 190s available for operational service during the closing months of 1941, the new type succeeded in establishing a marked ascendancy over its principal opponent, the Spitfire Mk V. While the Fw 190A could not compete with the Spitfire's superlative turning circle, it could outfly the British fighter on almost every other count,

What appears to be an Fw 190A-5 or equivalent has come to grief, apparently with an engine problem as evidenced by the large amount of staining along the fuselage side. The non-front-line code suggests assignment to a training unit.

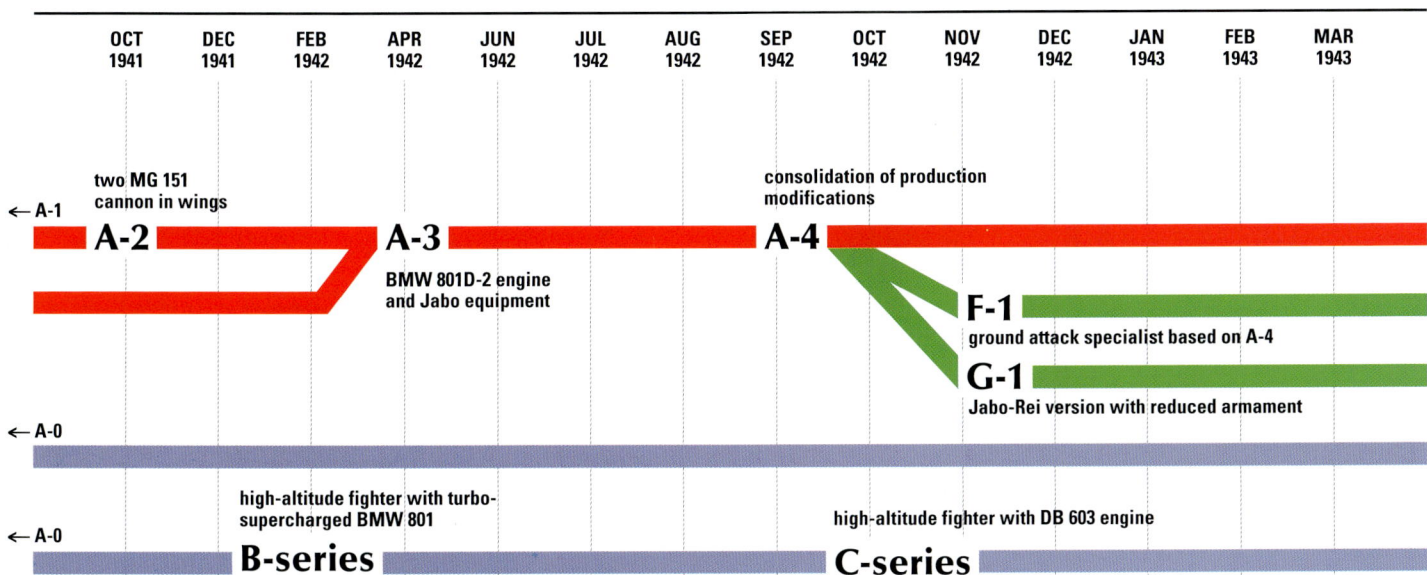

Focke-Wulf Fw 190 development
October 1941-March 1943

Above: In a staged photograph, an Fw 190A-2 closes in on an 'RAF bomber' (probably an Fw 189) over warships in the English Channel on 6 July 1942. One of the Fw 190's initial uses had been to cover the famous 'Channel Dash' by Kriegsmarine capital ships in February of that year.

Left: Two Fw 190As indulge in some mock dog-fighting. The Fw 190 was a comparatively easy aircraft to fly, particularly when compared to the Messerschmitt Bf 109 that was the other main fighter of the Luftwaffe in World War II.

and its superior speed enabled it to break off combat at will. Fortunately for the RAF, the troubles still being experienced with the BMW 801C engine kept the serviceability rate of the Fw 190A-equipped Staffeln of JG 26 relatively low, and the slow-firing MG FF cannon forming the main weapons of the Fw 190A-1 were anything but satisfactory.

The Focke-Wulf fighter was really blooded in action during Operation Cerberus or Donnerkeil, the hazardous dash through the Channel from the French port of Brest to safe anchorages in Kiel and Wilhelmshaven of the capital ships *Scharnhorst* and *Gneisenau*, and the cruiser *Prinz Eugen*, on 12 February 1942. The Bf 109Fs of JG 2 were primarily responsible for providing fighter cover during the first daylight stage of the passage, this Jadgeschwader being relieved by JG 26 off Cap Gris Nez, with 16 Fw 190A-2s of III/JG 26 arriving just as the first Swordfish torpedo-bombers attacked the German vessels. Subsequently, the Fw 190As of

An early Fw 190A in flight displays the radial-engined layout of the type to advantage. Also clearly visible is the installation of the two MG 17 machine-guns in the upper forward fuselage.

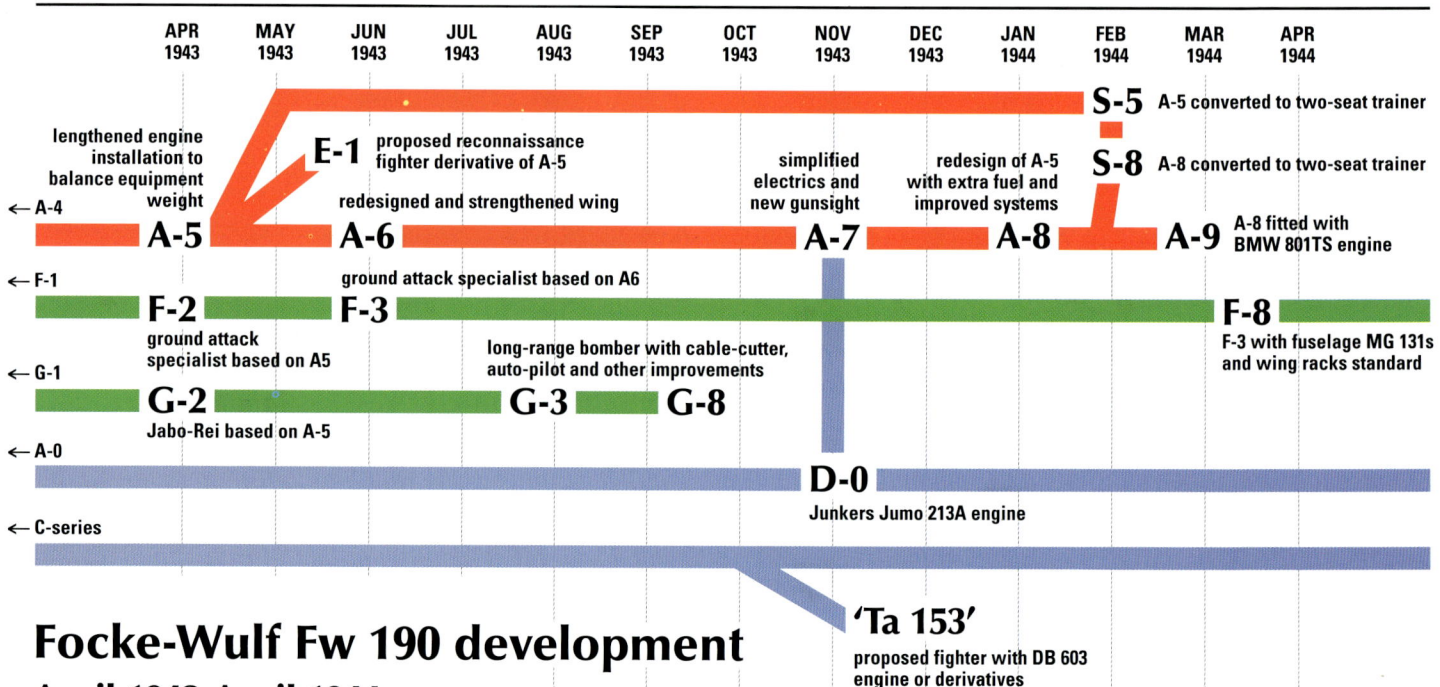

Focke-Wulf Fw 190 development
April 1943-April 1944

454

An early production Fw 190A shows off the functional lines of this highly-successful fighter. Initial operational Fw 190As entered combat in the late summer of 1941.

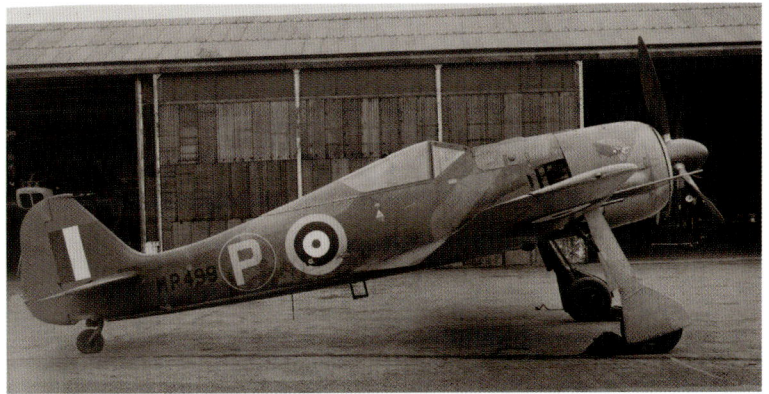

The force landing of an Fw 190A-3 in June 1942 presented Allied intelligence with a major coup. Allocated the code MP499, the aircraft was initially evaluated by the Royal Aircraft Establishment at Farnborough. It was then sent to the Air Fighting Development Unit at Duxford for tactical trials against Allied fighters.

II and III Gruppen and the Bf 190F-4s of I Gruppe of JG 26 provided continuous top cover until the weather deteriorated sufficiently to render fighter cover superfluous.

Shortly after participating in the 'Channel Dash', Jagdgeschwader 2 began conversion to the Fw 190A-2 and -3, the Luftwaffe monthly acceptance rate of the Focke-Wulf fighter having risen to 130-150 aircraft, and the strength returns for this unit for 28 April 1942 showed I and III Gruppen to have 36 and 38 Fw 190A-2s and -3s at Le Havre-Octeville and Cherbourg-Maupertus, respectively, with 6. Staffel having 11 Fw 190As at Beaumont-le-Roger. The Stab and I Gruppe of JG 26 had meanwhile also converted to the Fw 190A, but III Gruppe had reverted to the Bf 109F-4 and was destined to become the first recipient of the Bf 109G in the following month.

At the end of May, the Jagdflieger facing the RAF across the Channel under the control of Luftflotte 3 consisted primarily of Fw 190A-2s and -3s. Jagdgeschwader 26 possessed 89 Fw 190As (Stab, I and II Gruppen) of which 67 were serviceable, plus 38 Bf 109Gs (III Gruppe) and 16 Bf 109F-4/B fighter-bombers in 10.(Jabo) Staffel, while Jagdgeschwader 2 had 81 Fw 190As (Stab, II and III Gruppen) of which 66

were serviceable, plus 40 Bf 109Gs (Stab and I Gruppe) and 19 Bf 109F-4/B fighter-bombers in its 10.(Jabo) Staffel.

The latter Jagdgeschwader was to provide the RAF with an opportunity to evaluate the fighter that was causing the Spitfire Mk V squadrons so much concern, Oberleutnant Arnim Faber, adjutant of III/JG 2, inadvertently landing his Fw 190A-3 at the RAF base of Pembrey on 23 June. Faber, whose Staffel, 7./JG 2, had engaged Spitfires from the Exeter-based Polish Wing that had performed a strafing attack on the unit's Morlaix base, lost his bearings during the *mêlée*, mistook the Bristol Channel for the English Channel, and landed at Pembrey in the belief that it was a Luftwaffe base.

Allied prize

Faber's Fw 190A-3 was considered to be one of the most valuable prizes of the air war, and was promptly pitted in mock combat against the new Spitfire Mk IX that was taken on operations for the first time during the following month by No. 64 Squadron. Featuring a two-speed two-stage Merlin driving a four-bladed airscrew, the Spitfire Mk IX had been evolved as a matter of extreme urgency in an attempt to redress the fighter-versus-fighter situation that had arisen with the debut of the Fw 190A. The Spitfire Mk IX reduced but by no means eliminated the margin of ascendancy possessed by the Focke-Wulf, but the inability of Luftwaffe fighter pilots

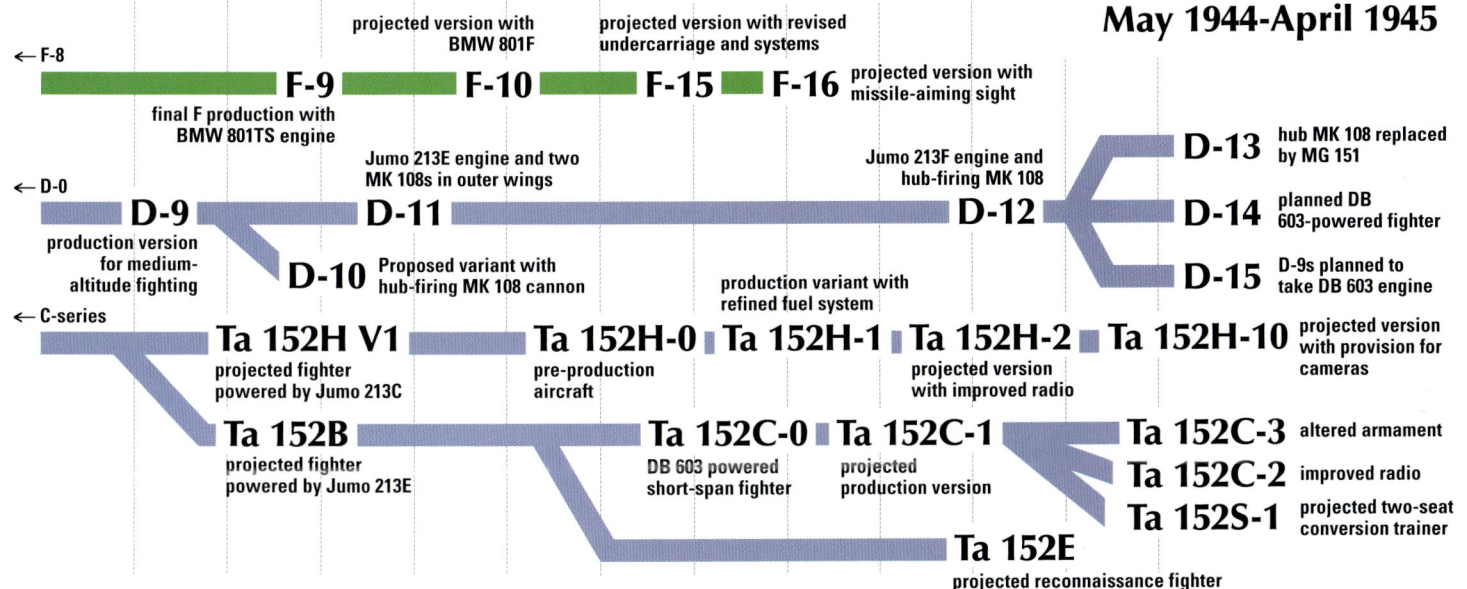

Focke-Wulf Fw 190 development
May 1944-April 1945

Focke-Wulf Fw 190

JG 26 and JG 2 were the main fighter units left in France during 1941, as others were sent east for the invasion of the Soviet Union. Operating from a grass strip in France during early 1942, these Fw 190A-2s form part of a schwarm being readied for one of the first combat missions. The aircraft are from 7./JG 2 'Richthofen'. Each of the unit's Staffeln had their own badge, which their aircraft proudly wore. The 'thumb pressing a top hat' emblem belonged to the seventh Staffel.

becoming operational on the Fw 190A before the end of the year (although II Gruppe's time with the Fw 190 was short, as it converted to the Bf 109G in December), while IV Gruppe was also operating the Fw 190A early in 1943.

Fw 190 in North Africa

The Fw 190 made only a fleeting appearance in the Mediterranean theatre. In November 1942 II/JG 2 left its French haunts for Bizerte in Tunisia, where it spent six weeks before heading south for Kairouan to meet the advancing Allies. Also in November 1942, the Luftwaffe sent a ground attack unit to North Africa. This was III/ZG 2, which arrived at Bizerte, although redesignated as III/SKG 10 shortly after. It operated throughout the Tunisian campaign from Sidi Ahmed, Kairouan and Gabès-West. Its headquarters withdrew to San Pietro in Sicily at the start of May 1943, but the Fw 190s continued to use Bizerte and Djedeida during daylight hours as the Allied net closed on Tunis and Bizerte, which both fell on the 7th. In June II/SKG 10 was briefly joined by the Stab, II and IV Gruppen as they attempted to repel the Allied attacks on Sicily and Italy.

The early months of 1943 saw a steady increase in the number and activities of the Fw 190A-equipped units. Strength returns for Luftflotte 3 in the West dated 10 January 1943 showed the Stab, I and III Gruppen of JG 2 with 101 Fw 190A-4s, and 10.(Jabo)/JG 2 with 10 Fw 190A-4/U3s; the Stab, I, II and III Gruppen of JG 26 with 130 Fw 190A-4s, and 10.(Jabo)/JG 54 (a temporary redesignation of 10.[Jabo]/JG 26) with 13 Fw 190A-4/U3s; 4.(F)/123 with a mix of reconnaissance Bf 109s and Fw 190A-3/U4 reconnaissance-fighters; 5.(F)/123 with nine Fw 190A-3/U4s, and Stab, 1. and 2. Staffeln of Nahaufklärungsgruppe 13 with 23 Fw 190A-3/U4s.

Strength returns for the Eastern Front for 31 January 1943 revealed an apparent paucity of Fw 190-equipped units, which were confined to one complete Jagdgruppe (I/JG 51 with 30 Fw 190As on the Central Sector under Luftwaffenkommando Ost), part of another Jagdgruppe (I/JG 54 that was operating both Fw 190As and Bf 109Gs in the Leningrad Region under Luftflotte 1), and one partially equipped Schlachtgruppe (II/SchG. 1 that was deploying detachments of Fw 190A-4/U3s under both Luftwaffenkommando Don and Luftflotte 4). In fact, fewer than 100 Fw 190s were immediately available on the Eastern Front at this time, other Gruppen being inoperational or undergoing conversion in Germany.

Operating as part of the Reich defence, the Luftwaffenbefehlshaber Mitte, in the German Bight area

to distinguish between the Spitfire Mk IX and the inferior Mk V at combat range endowed RAF pilots with some tactical advantage at first.

By the time of the abortive 'reconnaissance in force' by Canadian troops at Dieppe, on 19 August 1942, both 10.(Jabo)/JG 2 and 10.(Jabo)/JG 26 had converted from the Bf 109F-4/B to the Fw 190A-4/U1 fighter-bomber, and these Staffeln flew numerous sorties against the landing craft and support vessels, as well as against strong-points established by the invaders. All Gruppen of both Jagdgeschwader were in action throughout the day, accounting for the bulk of the RAF's admitted 106 losses. By September, the two Jabo-Staffeln were operating primarily with the Fw 190A-4/U3, and were performing small-scale, low-level fighter-bomber attacks over southern England, while another Jagdgeschwader, JG 1 based about the German Bight sector of northwest Germany and in the Netherlands, had begun to operate the Fw 190A, the Stab, II, III and IV Gruppen having converted before the end of 1942. The year also saw the appearance of the Fw 190A on the Eastern Front, I/JG 51 re-equipping at Jesau in September and becoming operatinal in the following month, II and III Gruppen also

A well-camouflaged Fw 190 with underfuselage stores rack is seen at a forward airfield. Ground-attack Fw 190s played a key role in campaigns, closely working with ground forces.

Fw 190F-8s of 1./SG 4 operated in Italy in the summer of 1944. Note that the swastika on the vertical tail surfaces has been overpainted and the insignia on the fuselage partly obscured.

Individual kills were usually recorded as bars, overlaid with the national insignia of the victim. If the pilot ran out of room for any more markings, a numeral was often applied, such as '100', and the bars continued from that number.

On the Western front Luftwaffe Experten recorded their victory tallies on the rudders of their Fw 190s, together with Knight's Cross awards. JG 2 and JG 26 used yellow rudders (right), and other units often had white rudders (above) for formation leaders. In the East victory markings were hardly ever carried.

were the Fw 190As of the Stab, II and IV/JG 1, and the specialised fast bomber Gruppe, III/SKG 10, which had been formed late in 1942 on the Fw 190A-4/U8, was brought up to full Geschwader strength in February 1943, comprising a Stab, I, II and III Gruppen to which a IV Gruppe was added in April, this being formed from 10.(Jabo)/JG 2 and 10.(Jabo)/JG 54. Schnellkampfgeschwader 10 had 127 Fw 190A-4/U8 fighter-bombers based in the Amiens area for attacks on southern England by the beginning of May 1943, its III Gruppe being based in Sicily for operations in the Mediterranean theatre. The II and IV Gruppen of SKG 10 were also despatched to Sicily in June, and were heavily engaged during the Allied invasion of the island in the following month. The three Gruppen suffered serious losses in heavy attacks on their airfields immediately prior to the landings, and had been decimated by the time they were withdrawn to Italy. Subsequently, in October, II and III/SKG 10 were redesignated II and III/SG 4, respectively, IV/SKG 10 becoming II/SG 10. I/SKG 10 remained in France to continue its fighter-bomber operations against southern England with Fw 190A-4/U8s.

Slow re-equipment

The re-equipment of the Schlachtflieger with the Fw 190F, although considered a matter of the utmost urgency, saw little progress during the course of 1943, owing to the more pressing claims of the Jagdflieger in the West, the constantly increasing combat attrition, and the failure of the aircraft industry to increase production tempo of the Focke-Wulf fighter as rapidly as had been planned. In fact, the Fw 190 was in short supply even for the Jagdflieger, and JG 2 and, to a lesser extent, JG 26, which were bearing much of the brunt of the conflict against the increasingly numerous USAAF day bomber formations, reverted to the Bf 109 during much of

Oberstleutnant Josef 'Pips' Priller, Kommodore of fighter wing JG 26, is helped from his Fw 190A at a base in France probably in the spring of 1944. Priller flew several Fw 190As, coded 'Black 13': this is probably an A-6.

the year. II/JG 2 was entirely Bf 109G-equipped from April 1944 until the end of the war.

Several fighter/training units were also operating Fw 190s from French bases during 1943, including the Jagdgruppen Ost, West and Süd with a mixture of Fw 190s and Bf 109Gs. A handful of Fw 190As saw service along the Atlantic and Biscay coasts in conjunction with Ar 196A float seaplanes as part of the Fliegerführer Atlantik's battle against RAF Coastal Command's anti-submarine patrols, the fighters being operated by 5./Bordfliegergruppe 196 which, in June 1943, was redesignated l./SAGr. 128.

In the Far North, Fw 190 strength was restricted to a few aircraft operated by I and IV/JG 5 in Norway, and by 14.(Jabo)/JG 5 in the Arctic Circle, but 1943 saw a gradual

An Fw 190F-8 of II/SG 2 taxis through the snow at a base in Hungary during the winter of 1944/45, its wheel covers having been removed to aid its progress. Often flown by the Gruppenkommandeur, Major Karl Kennel, the aircraft carries an AB 250 bomblet container.

'Black men' – as Luftwaffe ground crew were known throughout the service – prepare an Fw 190A-5 for gun calibration firing tests in the butts. The scene is France and the aircraft from JG 2.

Focke-Wulf Fw 190

An Fw 190A undergoes maintenance in this posed but nonetheless interesting photograph. The size of the aircraft is very evident in this picture, as are the wide paddle-type propeller blades.

Like many other German aircraft of the period, the Fw 190 was designed for easy access to all major internal equipment. Access to the engine was particularly good, with many large access panels.

build-up of Fw 190 strength for the defence of Germany proper under High Command Central, the Luftwaffenbefehlshaber Mitte. By early 1944, the major Fw 190 units concentrated for the defence of Germany included Stab, I, II and III/JG 1 and Stab, I, II and III/JG 11 that also operated Bf 109Gs, III/JG 54, Sturmstaffel 1, Stab, I, II and III/JG 300 and Stab, II and III/JG 301 that operated both Fw 190s and Bf 109Gs on Wilde Sau operations, and II and III/JG 302.

Fw 190Fs for the Russian front

With the rapid increase in Fw 190 production tempo that marked the early months of 1944, the re-equipment of the Schlachtflieger on the Eastern Front was resumed, and the conversion of some two Ju 87 Gruppen to the Fw 190F every six weeks resulted in only one Schlachtgruppe (III/SG 2) still being equipped with the Ju 87 for day operations by the autumn. By February 1944, the only Fw 190-equipped Schlachtgruppen attached to Luftflotte 2 in the Mediterranean area were I and II/SG 4 (formerly II/Schl.G. 2 and II/SKG 10, respectively) based at Viterbo in Italy, these units having operated against the Anzio beachheads. In the Arctic, under Luftflotte 5, the Fw 190 was being operated in the fighter-bomber role by 4./SG 5 (formerly 14.[Jabo]/JG 5), and in France, under Luftflotte 3, I/SKG 10 was still operating a dwindling complement of Fw 190 fighter-bombers, which, at the time of the Allied invasion in June 1944, were based at Dreux, the unit subsequently being redesignated III/KG 51 after virtual annihilation during the first days of the invasion.

The Jagdflieger in the West were ill-prepared to meet the Allied invasion, which necessitated the immediate redeploy-

Several Fw 190s rest in a blitzed hangar. Each has a cover over its engine and forward fuselage – special covers and tools were supplied with each aircraft by Focke-Wulf.

ment of part of the already overstretched fighter force, the Fw 190-equipped Jagdgeschwader bearing the brunt of the onslaught being the veteran JG 2 and JG 26 reinforced by III/JG 54. Few of the Jagdgruppen long survived the holocaust above Normandy as organised tactical units, and within two weeks of D-Day, Luftflotte 3 had been forced to restrict operations to a minimum owing to fuel shortages. The Schlachtflieger on the Eastern front were beset by a similar problem. Aircraft attrition in the Fw 190-equipped units had soared, but as by July 1944 the monthly Luftwaffe Fw 190 acceptances handsomely exceeded 1,000 aircraft, this was less a problem than the losses in aircrew, which were now of the order of 20 per cent monthly.

The Focke-Wulf fighter played a prominent part in Operation Bodenplatte, the Luftwaffe's last concerted offensive action of World War II, on 1 January 1945, this being a mass attack by 700-800 fighters on Allied airfields in France, Belgium, and the Netherlands. The force included Fw 190-equipped Gruppen from JGs 1, 2, 3, 4, 11, 26, 54 and SG 4, with I/JG 26 and III/JG 54 operating the new Langnasen-Dora, the Fw 190D-9. This version had joined operations with III/JG 54 in September 1944, all four Staffeln having been gathered together at Varrelbusch and subordinated to JG 26 on 25 December for Bodenplatte (this Gruppe being redesignated IV/JG 26 on 25 February 1945). The I Gruppe of JG 26 began converting to the Fw 190D-9 at the beginning of December, but some elements of II/JG 26, and III/JG 26, did not convert from the Fw 190A-8 and the Bf 109K-4 until after Bodenplatte. Some of III/JG 54's Fw 190D-9s were used for airfield protection cover for the Me 262 jet fighters of Kommando Nowotny shortly after becoming operational.

The Luftwaffe Quartermaster General's returns for 10 January 1945 listed the principal Fw 190-equipped units with the various Luftflotten as follows, the number of aircraft on strength being indicated in parentheses:

Luftflotte 1 in Courland and the Gulf of Riga area: Stab, I and II/JG 54 (80), and II/SG 3 (39).

Luftflotte 2 in northern Italy: NAGr. 11 (29) including a number of Bf 109Gs.

Luftflotte 3 on the Western Front: Stab, I, II and III/JG 1 (112); Stab, I, II and III/JG 2 (54); IV (Sturm)/JG 3 (35); Stab and II (Sturm)/JG 4 (27); Stab, I and III/JG 11 (72); Stab, I, II and III/JG 26 (183); III and IV/JG 54 (97); Stab, I, II and III/SG 4 (152), and NSGr. 20 (28).

Luftflotte 4 in Hungary and Yugoslavia: I and II/SG 2 (66) and Stab, I, II and III/SG 10 (69).

This is a pair of Fw 190Fs of II Gruppe, SG 1. The aircraft carry Russian front yellow theatre markings around the wingtips and cowling, and round the rear fuselage. Despite their assignment to the ground attack role, the Schlact Fw 190s scored numerous kills against Soviet fighters and ground attack aircraft.

Above: Groundcrew enjoy the sun in Italy in July 1943. The Fw 190 wears a white Mediterranean theatre band around the rear fuselage, and has white panels under the wing panels.

Above: The fairing visible underneath the fuselage numeral of this aircraft, and the lack of outer wing cannon, characterised the U4 reconnaissance version, in this case possibly an Fw 190A-5/U4. The unit could well be 5.(F)/123, which operated a mix of Bf 109s and Fw 190s on reconnaissance duties in France.

Below: Groundcrew prepare on Fw 190F of SG 3. This Geschwader converted from the Ju 87D in mid-1944 (retaining a single Ju 87D anti-tank Staffel), and fought mainly on the northern sector of the Russian front, with I Gruppe on the Courland front.

Above: Completely covered in white distemper, an Fw 190A of I/JG 54 taxis for a mission in the winter of 1942/43. The Gruppe was based at Krasnogvardeisk from late 1941 until February 1943, converting from Bf 109G-2s to the Fw 190 from November 1942. In mid-1943 it was embroiled in arguably the fiercest battle of the war, as the Wehrmacht and Red Army collided at Kursk.

Below: As Allied fighter-bombers roamed over France looking for targets around the time of the Normandy invasion in June 1944, the need for elaborate camouflaged dispersals became crucial.

Below: Clutching an SC 250 to its belly, an Fw 190F-8/R1 of II/SG 2 heads out for a mission in the winter of 1944/45. The unit had a few specialist Panzerblitz aircraft assigned.

Focke-Wulf Fw 190

A captured Fw 190G-3 is seen here undergoing evaluation by the USAAF. Based on the Fw 190A-4/U8 conversion, the G-3 was a fighter-bomber variant armed only with two MG 151 wing cannons.

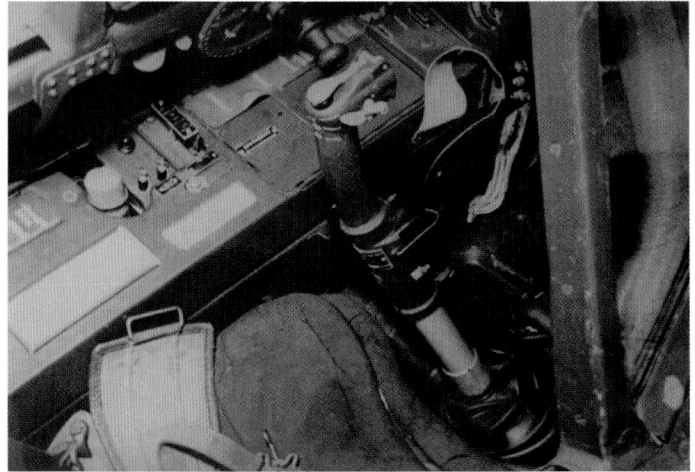

The Fw 190's cockpit was well designed and modern, with all the relevant controls within easy reach in a neat layout that included boxed-in side consoles. Also visible here is the control column.

Luftflotte 5 in Finland and Norway: III and IV/JG 5, both with a mixture of Fw 190s and Bf 109Gs.

Luftflotte 6 in east Prussia: Stab, II and III/SG 1 (82); Stab, I and II/SG 3 (90); Stab, I, II, III and 10.(Panzer)/SG 77 (141); NAGr. 2 (35) including some Bf 109Gs, and Stab/JG 52 (4).

Luftflotte Reich: II and IV (Sturm)/JG 300 (94); Stab, I, II and III/JG 301 (109); III/KG 200 (41).

Towards the end of February 1945, by which time some 30 per cent of all Fw 190 production facilities had been overrun by Soviet forces, much reorganisation of the operational formations of the Luftwaffe took place, this being followed by further reorganisation after the Allied crossing of the Rhine. Thus, on 9 April 1945, the principal Fw 190-equipped units were distributed as follows:

Luftwaffenkommando Kurland: Stab, I, II and III/JG 54 (127).

Luftflotte 4: 1/SG 2 (33) and Stab, I, II and III/SG 10 (83).

Luftflotte 6: Stab and IV/JG 3 (65); I and II/JG 6 (120); Stab, I and III/JG 11 (113); Stab, I, II and III/SG 1 (129); Stab and II/SG 2 (50); Stab and II/SG 3 (55); Stab, I, II and III/SG 4 (93); I (Panzer)/SG 9 (59), and Stab, I, II and III/SG 77 (123).

Demise of the hunter: the Fw 190 was very successful as a fighter in the mid- to late-war period, but was gradually outclassed and increasingly outnumbered as the war went on. The appearance of American fighters to escort heavy bomber raids, in particular, saw the increasing demise of the Luftwaffe's fighter force as 1944 wore on, with attrition among experienced pilots being particularly hard to make up. These Fw 190s are being very effectively shot up by Allied fighters in scenes that became more and more typical during 1944 and early 1945.

Mistel 2

II Gruppe
Kampfgeschwader 200
March 1945

Pilot
The ungainly Mistel combination was controlled by a single pilot in the upper component, either a Bf 109 or an Fw 190 fighter. Connections with the lower aircraft were by electric cables simply taped to the support struts and plugged into sockets in the underside of the fighter

Warhead
The 3.8-tonne shaped-charge high explosive warhead of the Mistel proved able to penetrate up to 20 m (65 ft) of concrete in tests

Fuse
The impact fuse was carried on a long proboscis, so that the shaped-charge warhead would explode fractionally before the bomber impacted the target.

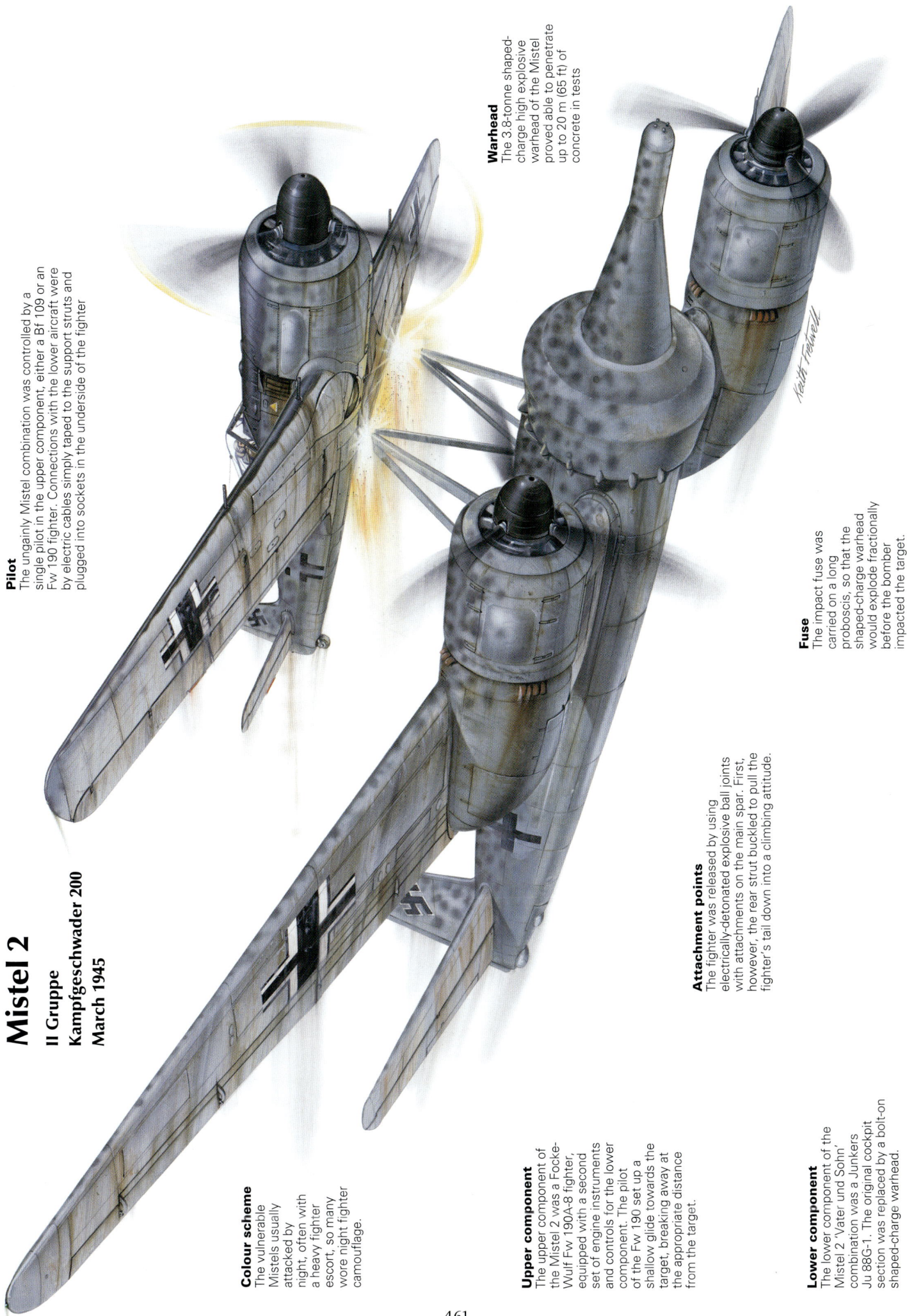

Attachment points
The fighter was released by using electrically-detonated explosive ball joints with attachments on the main spar. First, however, the rear strut buckled to pull the fighter's tail down into a climbing attitude.

Colour scheme
The vulnerable Mistels usually attacked by night, often with a heavy fighter escort, so many wore night fighter camouflage.

Upper component
The upper component of the Mistel 2 was a Focke-Wulf Fw 190A-8 fighter, equipped with a second set of engine instruments and controls for the lower component. The pilot of the Fw 190 set up a shallow glide towards the target, breaking away at the appropriate distance from the target.

Lower component
The lower component of the Mistel 2 'Vater und Sohn' combination was a Junkers Ju 88G-1. The original cockpit section was replaced by a bolt-on shaped-charge warhead.

461

By the end of World War II the surviving Luftwaffe Fw 190s were scrapped, except for those which were of interest to the Allies for evaluation or as war prizes.

German wartime publications often featured the Fw 190. The type became an iconic part of the German war machine, and at the time it was one of the German aircraft industry's most famous and successful products.

ries. The top-scoring attack Fw 190 pilot was Oberleutnant August Lambert of SG 2 and SG 77, who scored 116 aerial victories in the east before being shot down and killed by US fighters in April 1945. Often regarded as the pilot with the most aerial victories achieved in the Fw 190 is Oberleutnant Otto Kittel of JG 54, the vast majority of whose 267 aerial victories in the east were achieved in the Fw 190.

End of the Reich

With the splitting of Germany in two by the linking of US and Soviet forces at Torgau on the Elbe on 25 April, the surviving Fw 190 elements were, for the most part, divided between Luftflotte Reich controlling all flying units in the northern half, and Luftflotte 6 controlling flying units remaining in the southern half, but by then the Luftwaffe's remaining stocks of fuel were almost exhausted, and operations were strictly curtailed, many of the surviving Fw 190 Staffeln being grounded with empty tanks and thus unable to play any role in the final stages of the collapse of the Third Reich.

Nevertheless, some of the ground-attack units including SG 2 continued in service until the end of the war, with elements from this and other units fleeing the advancing Russians from their bases in the former Czechoslovakia at the time of the German surrender and landing at Allied-held air bases in southern Germany. Little-known operations included the Fw 190D-9s and D-11s assigned to the airfield protection flight (sometimes called the Würgerstaffel) of JV 44 at München-Reim, which flew airfield protection cover for JV 44's Me 262 jet fighters in the war's final weeks. At least two D-11s served with the Verbandsführerschule General der Jagdflieger (Training School for Unit Leaders) at Bad Wörishofen.

Luftflottenkommando Ost-Preussen: I/SG 3 (27) and Stab/JG 51 (20).
Luftflotte Reich: Stab, I, II and III/JG 2 (25); Stab and II/JG 4 (56); Stab, I, II and III/JG 26 (140); JGr. 10 (15); I and II/JG 301 (67); NSGr. 20 (27), and III/KG 200 (31).

A multitude of pilots scored significant numbers of air-to-air victories in the Fw 190, and the type became the preferred mount of many of the Luftwaffe's top Experten (aces). Such well-known pilots as Walter Nowotny, Heinz Bär, Josef Priller, Hannes Trautloft, and Walter Oesau – to name but a few – were among the many who flew the Fw 190 successfully in combat. Even some of the pilots of the low-level attack Fw 190s were able to create impressive tallies of aerial victo-

The Fw 190A became an important part of the Mistel programme of crude, guided missile operations late in the war. The Mistel combinations, like the one shown here, were little used and were very vulnerable to fighter attack. With an Fw 190A-8 upper component the combination was known as a Mistel 2 (operational) or Mistel S2 (training). As seen here, the Mistel S2's lower compartment retained its standard bomber nose.

Focke-Wulf Fw 191

The Fw 191 was planned in response to a requirement for a high-altitude strategic bomber. The requirement was notably ambitious and, as events were to prove, beyond the capabilities of the German aviation industry of the time. Even so, the Fw 191 did reach prototype form, and included a number of notably advanced features.

By July 1939 the German aircraft industry's experience with pressure cabins for flight at extreme altitudes was deemed sufficient for the Technisches Amt to issue the specification for a pressurised high-altitude bomber. This 'Bomber B' specification demanded very high performance, defensive armament in remotely controlled barbettes, and the powerplant of two Junkers Jumo 222 or Daimler-Benz DB 604 engines, both being liquid-cooled 24-cylinder units at an early stage of development. The most important requirement was the pressurised accommodation for the crew of three or four, and the specification was issued to Arado, Dornier, Focke-Wulf and Junkers, who submitted their final proposals in July 1940. The subsequent evaluation placed the Junkers Ju 288 and **Fw 191** as the winning contenders, the Arado Ar 340 being eliminated and the Dornier Do 317 being shelved as a possible later back-up programme.

A Focke-Wulf team led by Dipl.-Ing. Kösel immediately began detail design of the Fw 191 and, as the intended Jumo 222 engines (selected in preference to the DB 604 which was in fact abandoned in 1942) were obviously not going to be ready in time for installation in the first prototypes, it was agreed with the Technisches Amt that they should be completed with BMW 801 air-cooled radial engines that were then the most powerful units available and were of generally similar size to the Junkers engine.

Clean aerodynamic design

Construction of the **Fw 191 V1** and **Fw 191 V2** first two prototypes began late in 1940, the Fw 191 V1 starting its flight test programme early in 1942 with Dipl.-Ing. Mehlhorn at the controls, and the Fw 191 V2 joined the test programme shortly after this. The two aircraft were essentially identical apart from slight differences in the cockpit glazing. In overall terms, the Fw 191 was an extremely clean shoulder-wing monoplane of all-metal construction, and followed standard German practice in having all four members of the crew grouped together in the fuselage nose, which it was intended to pressurise in the production model. All the fuel was housed by two cells in the wing centre section and a series of five

The first two Fw 191 prototypes were completed, as an interim measure, with BMW 801 radial engines. The aircraft were almost dangerously underpowered with these engines.

cells in the fuselage above the bomb bay, and both prototypes were fitted with mock-ups of the remotely controlled defensive barbettes. They comprised a chin barbette intended to accommodate a pair of 7.9-mm (0.31-in) MG 81 machine-guns and directed by the bombardier-navigator, two barbettes containing similar armament in the tails of the engine nacelles, and a dorsal barbette with a single 20-mm MG 151 cannon and two MG 81s, all of which were to be directed by the radio operator. Lastly, there was a central barbette with one MG 151 and two MG 81s directed by the flight engineer.

One of the most unusual features of the Fw 191 was the use of electrics for all systems. Every safety device or trimming control, in fact, every item normally actuated mechanically or hydraulically was powered by an electric motor. Indeed, so numerous were the small electric motors that the aircraft was promptly dubbed 'das fliegende Kraftwerk' (flying power station). This extensive use of electrics had been made at the behest of the research department of the RLM, the Forschungsabteilung, despite protests from Focke-Wulf that such a concept was impracticable, involving an immense 'electrical weight' and rendering the aircraft extremely vulnerable in combat – one bullet passing through

The Fw 191 prototypes were completed with the bomb bay intended to provide the production models with the ability to carry a large and diverse internal weapons load, including air-launched torpedoes. Forward of the bomb bay, a bulge below the fuselage accommodated the remotely controlled barbette for the forward-firing defensive armament.

463

Focke-Wulf Fw 191

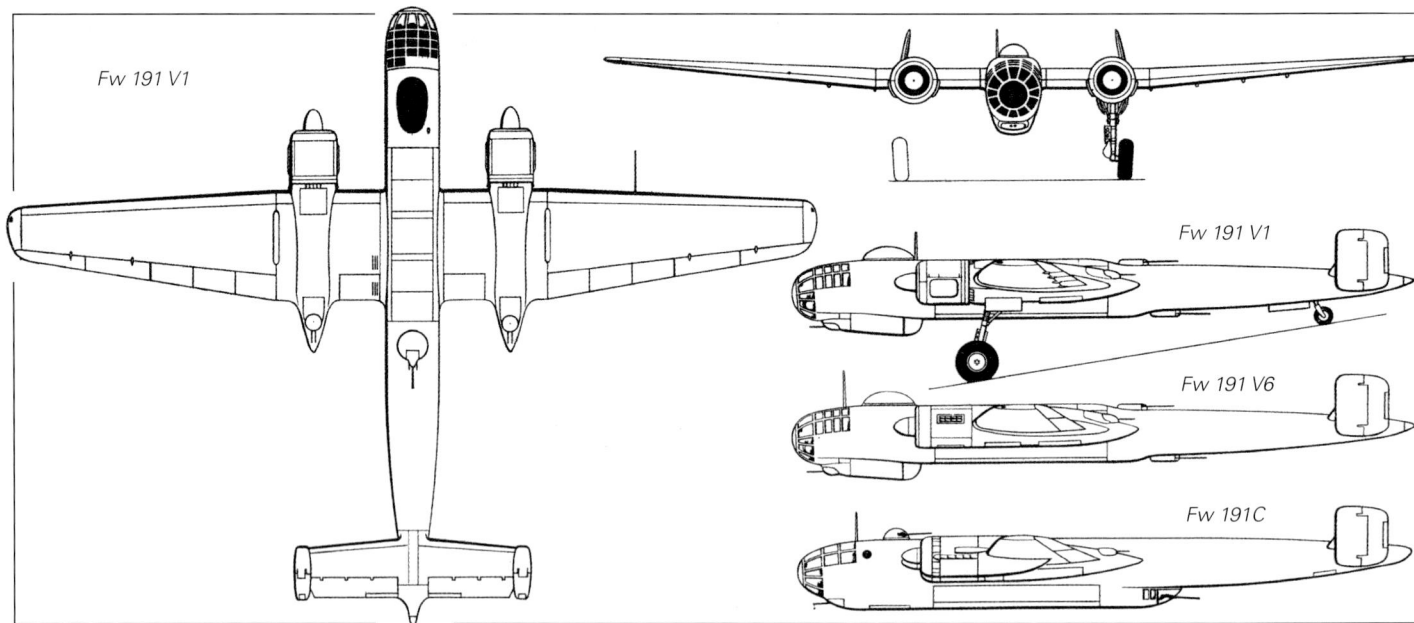

Fw 191 V1

Fw 191 V1

Fw 191 V6

Fw 191C

the right place being sufficient to put the main systems and all communications out of action. As was anticipated, from the outset of flight testing the electrical systems proved a constant source of trouble, a flight test rarely being completed without one of the systems failing. Another source of trouble, but one less expected, was the ingenious Multhopp-Klappe, a combined landing flap and dive brake fitted in four sections to the wing trailing edges: when extended, they presented a severe flutter problem. These troubles were compounded by the fact that the aircraft were dangerously underpowered, its two BMW 801MA air-cooled 14-cylinder two-row radial engines each offering only 1029 kW (1,380 hp) at 4600 m (15,090 ft), and this for aircraft weighing upwards of 20400 kg (44,975 lb) in test condition.

The Fw 191 V1 had completed a series of 10 flights when it was joined in the test programme by the Fw 191

Above: The remotely controlled ventral barbette, behind the bomb bay, was fitted with two 20-mm cannon. Located slightly father forward, the dorsal barbette carried the same armament.

All of the empennage's control surfaces were balanced and carried inset trim tabs. The use of endplate vertical surfaces enhanced the dorsal and ventral barbettes' fields of fire.

V2, but progress was disappointing as a result of the numerous teething troubles and, after the completion of 10 hours' flying by the two prototypes, the flight test programme was halted. Simultaneously, further prototype construction was shelved pending the development of the electrical systems to an acceptable stage of reliability and the availability of more powerful engines.

Three more prototypes

By this time three additional prototypes had been ordered and, together with the Fw 191 V3, two of these airframes had reached an advanced stage of assembly. From the outset it had been intended that the production **Fw 191A** would receive the Junkers Jumo 222, and trial installations were planned for the **Fw 191 V3**, **Fw 191 V4** and **Fw 191 V5**, but it had soon become obvious that this engine would demand an appreciably longer gestatory period than had been envisaged when the 'Bomber B' programme had been formulated. In fact, as a result of persistent and apparently insoluble teething troubles, doubts were being expressed in some quarters that the Jumo 222 would ever achieve production status. Thus, by the end of 1941, proposals had been made to supplant the Jumo in the Fw 191A with either the DB 606 or the DB 610, these each comprising a pair of DB 601 and DB 605 V-12 engines, respectively, the pairs being mounted side by side and driving a single propeller through a common reduction gear. Although the Daimler-Benz engines were substantially larger and heavier than the Jumo 222, they were appreciably more advanced in development, and were looked upon as an interim solution pending availability of the Junkers engine.

Kösel had made repeated applications to the RLM for permission to replace the more troublesome electrical systems in the Fw 191 by hydraulic systems, and late in 1942, with the decision to install a pair of flight-cleared pre-production Jumo 222 engines in an Fw 191 for evaluation, permission was granted to introduce hydraulics in place of electrics. The **Fw 191 V6** prototype, which was least advanced when the construction programme had been shelved, was selected for completion with hydraulic systems and Jumo 222 engines, and flew with these in the spring of 1943 with Focke-Wulf's chief test pilot, Flugkapitän Hans Sander, at the controls. The Jumo 222 engines each offered 1640 kW (2,200 hp) for take-off, but flight test results with the Fw 191 V6 were still far from satisfactory.

The Fw 191 V1 is seen with the rear half of the Fw 191 V2 in the foreground. The development of this advanced warplane was beyond German industry's practical capabilities of the period.

Advanced defensive armament

At this time it was proposed that the aircraft should be produced as the **Fw 191B** with either two DB 606 or DB 610 coupled powerplants. The defensive armament had been revised to comprise a single 20-mm MG 151 cannon in the chin barbette, twin MG 151 cannon in the dorsal and ventral barbettes, and a remotely controlled MG 151 cannon or two 13-mm (0.51-in) MG 131 machine-guns in the extreme tail, the engine nacelle barbettes having been deleted. The internal load could comprise either four 500-kg (1,102-lb) bombs or two 1500-kg (3,307-lb) LT 1500 torpedoes, and this could be supplemented by two 500-kg bombs, two LT 1500 torpedoes, or two LMA III parachute sea mines on underwing racks between the fuselage and the engine nacelles. Parallel proposals were made for what was, in effect, a simplified version of the basic design with pressure cabin and the complex system of remotely controlled gun barbettes deleted in favour of manually operated guns and manned hydraulically operated gun turrets. Known as the **Fw 191C**, this was to have had four separate Jumo 211F, DB 601E, DB 605 or DB 628 V-12 engines, a deeper bomb bay and more minor changes. However, after limited flight testing at Delmenhorst, the Fw 191 V6 had been transferred to Wenzendorf where it arrived simultaneously with the RLM's announcement of its decision to abandon the entire 'Bomber B' programme. Thus, before the end of 1943, all work on the Fw 191 terminated, and neither the Fw 191B nor Fw 191C left the drawing board.

Focke-Wulf Fw 191B specification

(This specification is based on manufacturer's estimates for the proposed production model with the DB 610 and, in square brackets, the DB 606.)
Type: four-seat medium bomber
Powerplant: two Daimler-Benz DB 610A/B [DB 606] liquid-cooled 24-cylinder engines each rated at 2140 kW (2,870 hp) [2013 kW (2,700 hp)] for take-off and 1909 kW (2,560 hp) at 7620 m (25,000 ft) [1976 kW (2,650 hp) at 4815 m (15,800 ft)]
Performance: maximum speed 565 km/h (351 mph) at 3950 m (12,965 ft) [560 km/h (348 mph) at 4180 m (13,715 ft)], 632 km/h (393 mph) at 9450 m (31,005 ft) [605 km/h (376 mph) at 9400 m (30,840 ft)]; initial climb rate at 23860 kg (52,601 lb) 460 m (1,510 ft) per minute [at 23585 kg (51,995 lb) 400 m (1,315 ft) per minute]; service ceiling at 23135 kg (51,005 lb) 8780 m (28,805 ft) [at 23040 kg (50,794 lb) 8290 m (27,200 ft)]; range with 3930 litres (864 Imp gal) of fuel 1800 km (1,118 miles) at 500 km/h (311 mph [1900 km (1,181 miles) at 470 km/h (292 mph)], with 7570 litres (1,665 Imp gal) 3860 km (2,399 miles) at 490 km/h (304 mph) [4010 km (2,492 miles) at 430 km/h (267 mph)]
Weights: normal loaded 25490 kg (56,195 lb) [23585 kg (51,995 lb)]; maximum overload 25319 kg (55,798 lb) [24995 kg (55,104 lb)]
Dimensions: wingspan 26.00 m (85 ft 3½ in); length 19.63 m (64 ft 4¾ in); height 5.60 m (18 ft 4½ in); wing area 70.50 m² (758.86 sq ft)
Armament: (defensive) one 20-mm MG 151 cannon or two 13-mm (0.51-in) MG 131 machine-guns in remotely controlled nose barbette, two MG 151 cannon in each of dorsal and ventral barbettes, and either one MG 151 cannon or two MG 131 machine-guns in extreme tail; (offensive) eight 250-kg (551-lb) or four 500-kg (1,102-lb) bombs, or two 1500-kg (3,307-lb) LT 1500 torpedoes internally, plus (overload condition) two 500-kg bombs or two LT 1500 torpedoes externally

As was standard in most German bombers of the period, the four-man crew of the Fw 191 was grouped closely in the nose, which featured extensive glazing of the multi-panel type.

Above: The Fw 191 was designed with gun armament in the rear of the engine nacelles. All barbettes were very clean installations, and designed for the carriage of potent defensive weapons.

Above: Part of the Multopp-Klappe (combined dive brake/flap)is shown deployed on the trailing edge of the Fw 191 V1's port wing. In its extended position it caused serious flutter problems.

Above: An Fw 191 prototype approaches with its undercarriage (three fully retractable single-wheel units) lowered and the Multhopp-Klappe trailing-edge flaps/dive-brakes extended.

Above: If its many teething and technical problems had been overcome and a major production programme implemented, the Fw 191 could have been a very useful first-line bomber.

Focke-Wulf Fw 200 Condor

Conceived and first built as a long-range airliner, the Fw 200 was then developed as a maritime reconnaissance bomber. Never produced in large numbers, and always beset in structural terms by its civil origins, the Condor roamed deep into the Atlantic to find and attack Allied convoys, and later to vector in U-boat packs.

Forced on Germany by circumstances against which her leaders had gambled, the **Fw 200 Condor** maritime reconnaissance bomber was an improvisation, having been designed solely as a commercial transport, but such was its success as a commerce raider that it was named by Winston Churchill as the 'scourge of the Atlantic'. The outcome of short-sighted thinking by the Oberkommando der Luftwaffe (OKL) and the Oberbefehlshaber der Luftwaffe, Hermann Göring, the Condor was an expedient, but one that nonetheless demanded a huge Allied effort before its threat was nullified, and by that time it had been responsible for sinking an immense tonnage of Allied shipping.

Commercial origins

The Condor stemmed from discussions in the spring of 1936 between Focke-Wulf's technical director, Prof. Dipl.-Ing. Kurt Tank, and Deutsche Lufthansa's director, Dr. Stüssel, during which Tank laid out his concept of a four-engined airliner based on a wing of relatively high aspect ratio and capable of transatlantic operation. Design and the construction of a fuselage mock-up continued throughout the early summer months, and in mid-July DLH placed a development contract with Focke-Wulf for what had by now become the Fw 200 Condor. The RLM-allocated type number was considerably higher than those being applied to new aircraft types at that time, but believed by Tank to be ideal for publicity purposes.

Some indication of Tank's certainty of the basic soundness of the Condor's design is revealed by the fact that construction of three prototypes began in the autumn of 1936 in parallel with preparations for a pre-production batch of nine aircraft. The first prototype, the **Fw 200 V1**, subsequently registered D-AERE and named *Saarland*, flew on 27 July 1937, a mere 12 months and 11 days from the date on which DLH had signed the contract.

Powered by four Pratt & Whitney Hornet S1E-G air-cooled nine-cylinder radial engines each rated at 652 kW (875 hp) for take-off, the Fw 200 V1 demanded only some minor redesign of the vertical tail surfaces as a result of initial flight trials, and was quickly joined in the development

Above: The Focke-Wulf Fw 200C-3/U2 was identifiable by the bulge in its gondola for the Lofte 7D bombsight. Fitting this device necessitated a reorganisation of the ventral armament.

Above: The Fw 200 V1 made its initial flight on 27 July 1937. Soon after, it received the registration D-AERE.

Ground crew work on an Fw 200 of KG 40. Based in western France, the unit's Condors flew far out over the Atlantic in search of the convoys on which the UK was dependent for much of its food, fuel and raw materials.

*The Fw 200 V1 first prototype was originally **D-AERE** Saarland, but was repainted as shown for the record flight to New York, with long-range tanks and redesignated as the Fw 200S-1. This flight, in August 1938, was beyond any other civil transport flying in the world at that time.*

programme by the **Fw 200 V2** (D-AETA *Westfalen*) and the **Fw 200 V3** (D-2600 *Immelmann III*), the latter being designated the official Führermaschine for the personal use of Adolf Hitler, and one of two Condors ordered by the Reichsluftfahrtministerium (RLM) for governmental use. The second and third aircraft were essentially similar to the first apart from having BMW 132G-1 (licence-built Pratt & Whitney Hornet) engines each having a normal rating of 537 kW (720 hp).

Subsequent aircraft, which began to leave Focke-Wulf's Bremen assembly line in the spring of 1937, were designated as **Fw 200A-0** pre-production machines, although the majority of them were also to be allocated Versuchs numbers. For example, the **Fw 200A-01** (Werk Nr 2893) D-ADHR

Saarland (a name transferred from the Fw 200 V1 when that aircraft was renamed *Brandenburg* in the summer of 1938) was also designated **Fw 200 V4**, while the **Fw 200A-03** (D-AMHC *Nordmark*) was the **Fw 200 V5**. The second A-series pre-production aircraft, the **Fw 200A-02** (Werk Nr 2894) had in the meantime been purchased by Det Danske Luftfartselskab (DDL), which began operating commercial services with this machine (as OY-DAM *Dania*) in July 1938. This Danish airline later acquired the **Fw 200A-05** (Werk Nr 2993) as OY-DEM *Jutlandia*.

The **Fw 200A-04** (coded D-ACVH *Grenzmark*) and **Fw 200A-06** (D-ARHW *Friesland*) with BMW 132Ls were also known as the **Fw 200 V6** and **Fw 200 V7**, respectively, while the **Fw 200A-07**, initially flown as D-ASBK,

*Left: The Fw 200 V1 Werk Nr 2000 sports the special registration **D-ACON** with which it made an epoch-marking Berlin-New York-Berlin flight in August 1938, following this in November with a flight from Berlin to Tokyo.*

Left: The Fw 200 V3 embodied a number of special features, including an armoured seat for the Führer which, with built-in parachute, was mounted over a jettisonable hatch in the floor.

Left: The Fw 200 V3 carried three different variations on the '2600' theme, this being the interim code. It later became 26+00.

*Above: This image depicts the Fw 200 V1 after being allocated its initial registration **D-AERE** but before the application of taper on the leading edge of the wing's outer panels.*

*Brandenburg, as the V1 (**D-ACON**) was renamed, is surrounded by a throng of public and press at Berlin's Tempelhof airport following its epic transatlantic crossings in August 1938.*

Focke-Wulf Fw 200 Condor

Powerplant
The original specification called for the Condor to be powered by four examples of the 720-hp (536-kW) BMW 132G-1 air-cooled nine-cylinder radial engine, a German licence-built derivative of the US Pratt & Whitney Hornet unit. US-built engines powered the first prototype, but subsequent aircraft had BMW-built engines.

Range
The Condor's main fuel tanks were in the wing centre section behind the main spar, each engine having its own separate tanks. The normal fuel load was 2300 litres (506 Imp gal), although considerably more could be carried. This gave a range of about 3220 km (2,000 miles).

Wing
The Condor's wing was made up of three sections, with a girder-like main spar in the centre, and auxiliary spars for the outer sections.

SPECIFICATION
Focke-Wulf Fw 200A Condor
TYPE: four-crew medium/long-range airliner
POWERPLANT: four BMW 132G-1 air-cooled nine-cylinder radial engines each rated at 537 kW (720 hp)
PERFORMANCE: cruising speed 335 km/h (208 mph); operational range 1450 km (901 miles)
WEIGHT: maximum take-off 14600 kg (32,187 lb)
DIMENSIONS: wingspan 32.84 m (107 ft 8.9 in) ; length 23.85 m (78 ft 3 in)
PAYLOAD: 26 passengers or freight

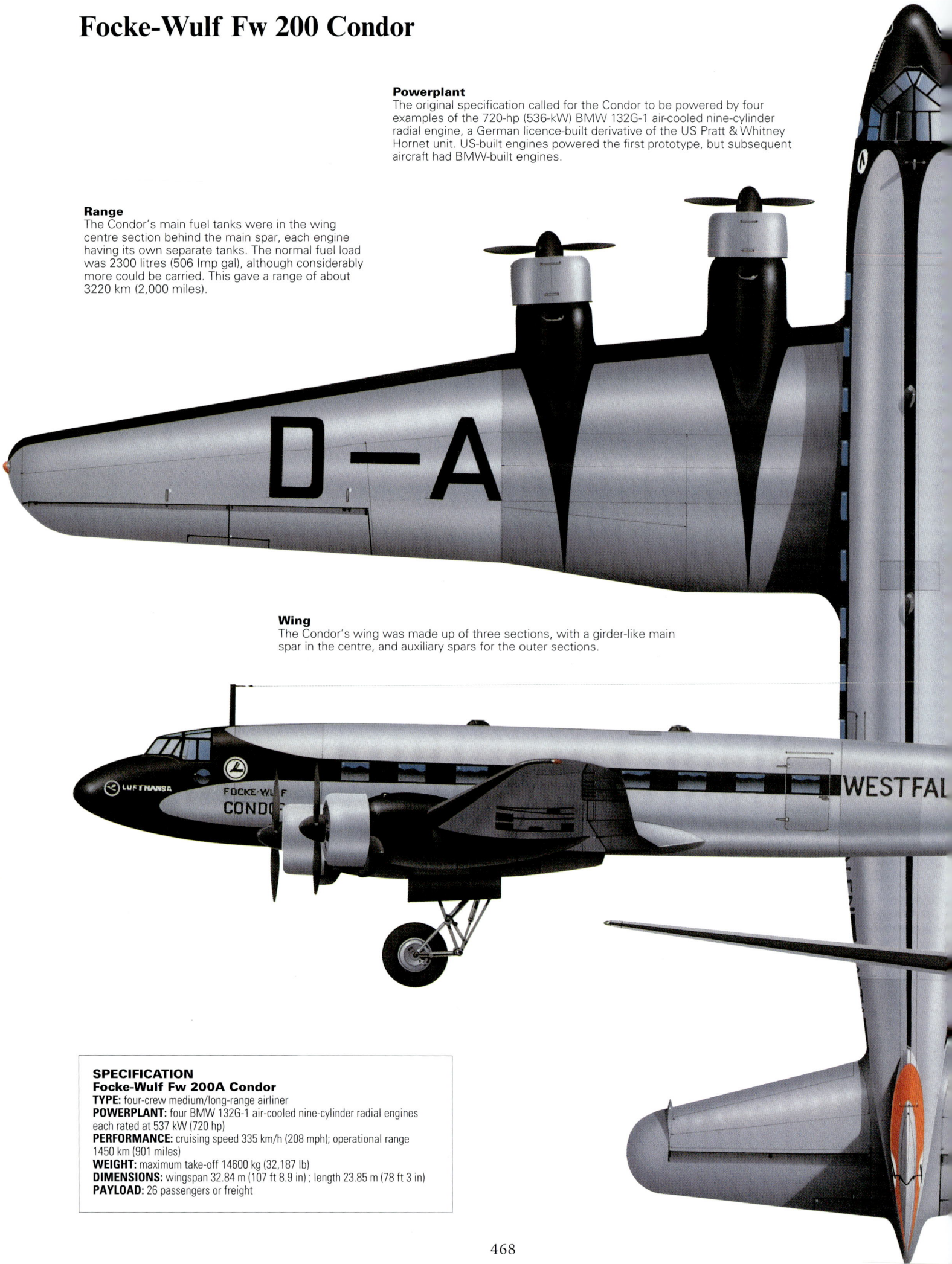

Focke-Wulf Fw 200 V2 Condor D-AETA *Westfalen*

Westfalen was the second prototype Condor, and first flew in 1937. The Condor had been built to fulfil a Deutsche Lufthansa requirement for an advanced land-based passenger aircraft. Delivered to the airline in early 1938, *Westfalen* bore most of the burden of the flight test and certification programme. Apart from a brief period in early 1939 when eight were on strength, the airline never operated more than four Condors, and by 1941 the fleet was down to two. One of the aircraft served almost to the end of the conflict, flying the airline's last wartime service to Barcelona in April 1945.

Crew
The flight deck of the Fw 200 seated two pilots side by side, with a radio operator on the starboard side behind the second pilot. Radio equipment was mounted in the nose under a non-conducting plastic nosecone

Main cabin
The main cabin accommodated 16 or 17 passengers in three-abreast seating, one to starboard and two to port of the aisle. At the rear of the cabin was a toilet. Access to the main baggage compartment was through a hatch in the starboard side.

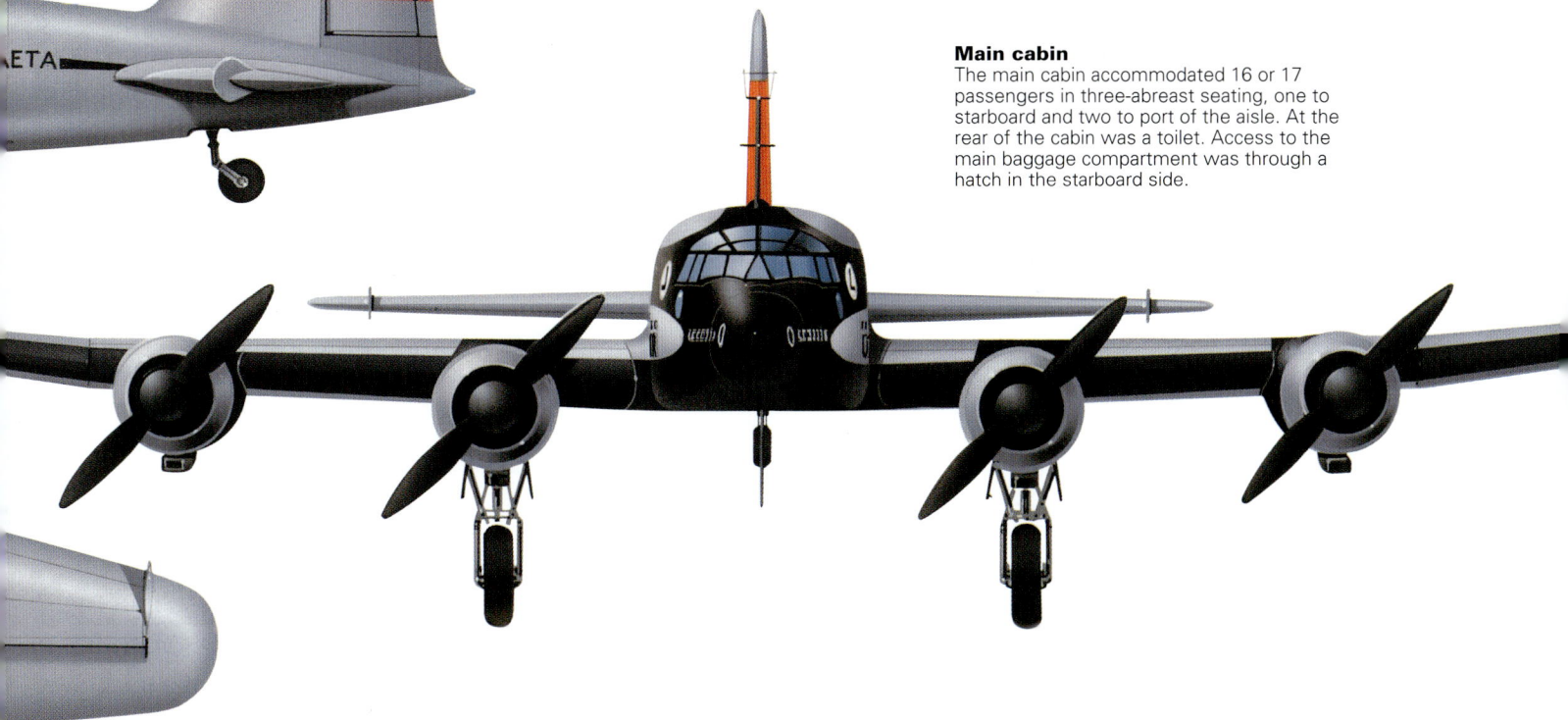

Focke-Wulf Fw 200 Condor

was delivered to the Brazilian Sindicato Condor Limitada (as PP-CBJ *Arumani*), together with the **Fw 200A-08** (PP-CBI *Abaitara*), and the final A-series Condor, the **Fw 200A-09** (alias **Fw 200 V9**) was delivered to DLH in the summer of 1939 as D-AXFO *Pommern*.

While production of the airliner was being established, the Condor had undertaken a series of long-distance publicity flights, the first of them, from Berlin to Cairo with one stop at Salonica, being flown by the Fw 200 V4 (D-ADHR) on 27 June 1938. Another long-distance flight began on 10 August 1938, when the Fw 200 V1 took off for a non-stop flight from Berlin to New York. For this flight the Fw 200 V1 was redesignated **Fw 200S-1** (the suffix letter indicating Sonder or 'special'), renamed *Brandenburg* and allocated the special registration D-ACON. The aircraft covered the

Above: The Fw 200 Condor promised a new age in civil aviation, allowing Germany to offer the possibility of long-range commercial flights across the world's greatest oceans. Here the Fw 200S is seen at Floyd Bennett Field in New York after its epic non-stop North Atlantic crossing from Berlin.

6560 km (4,075 miles) against strong headwinds in 24 hours 55 minutes at an average of 264 km/h (164 mph). The return journey was effected in 19 hours 47 minutes at an average of 330 km/h (205 mph) over a slightly more southerly route.

On 28 November 1938, the Fw 200S-1 took-off for Tokyo, stopping at Basra, Karachi and Hanoi for refuelling, and arriving at the Japanese capital in an elapsed time of slightly less than 48 hours, of which 42 hours 18 minutes were spent in the air. On the return flight, however, a fuel shortage resulted in the aircraft being ditched off Manila.

Focke-Wulf
Fw 200A-0 Condor
cutaway key

1. Electrically-operated rudder trim tabs
2. Rudder construction (fabric skinned)
3. Upper rudder hinge
4. Rudder post
5. Tailfin construction (metal skinned)
6. Electrically-operated elevator tab (port only)
7. Elevator hinge balance
8. Elevator tab
9. Tail cone
10. Rear navigation light
11. Elevator tab
12. Starboard elevator (fabric skinned)
13. Tailplane spar
14. Forward-retracting tailwheel (hydraulically actuated)
15. Tailwheel position (retracted)
16. Access hatch to tail cone
17. Aft main cargo hold (8.3-m³/293-cu ft capacity)
18. Cargo loading hatch
19. Crew's wardrobe space
20. Toilet ventilation
21. Toilet
22. Mail bay
23. Steward's occasional seat
24. First-aid cabinet
25. Main passenger door (port)
26. Main passenger cabin ventilation
27. Fuselage construction
28. Window cut-outs
29. Main passenger cabin (16 seats)
30. Coat rack
31. Bulkhead spar step-over
32. Mainspar carry-through
33. Bulkhead
34. Forward passenger cabin ventilation
35. Forward passenger cabin (nine seats)
36. Fuel filler covers
37. Twin fixed aerials
38. Three-part flaps
39. Centre wing construction
40. Aileron trim tabs
41. Port aileron (fabric skinned)
42. Electrically-operated aileron tab
43. Mainspar outer section
44. Centre wing/outer panel attachment
45. Nacelle panels
46. Two-blade Hamilton metal airscrew
47. Aerial mast
48. Hydraulics tank (undercarriage and flap actuation)
49. Forward baggage compartment
50. Flight deck door
51. Forward bulkhead
52. Radio operator's swivelling seat
53. Pilot's seat
54. Windscreen
55. Plastic-covered nose cone
56. Air conditioning intake
57. Trunking to flight deck/cabins
58. Twin D/F loops
59. Instrument panel
60. Control column
61. Downward vision port
62. Co-pilot's seat
63. Radio operator's table
64. Port main wheel
65. Ventral loading hatch
66. Equipment bay
67. Underfloor construction
68. Leading-edge cable runs
69. Wing/engine bearer construction

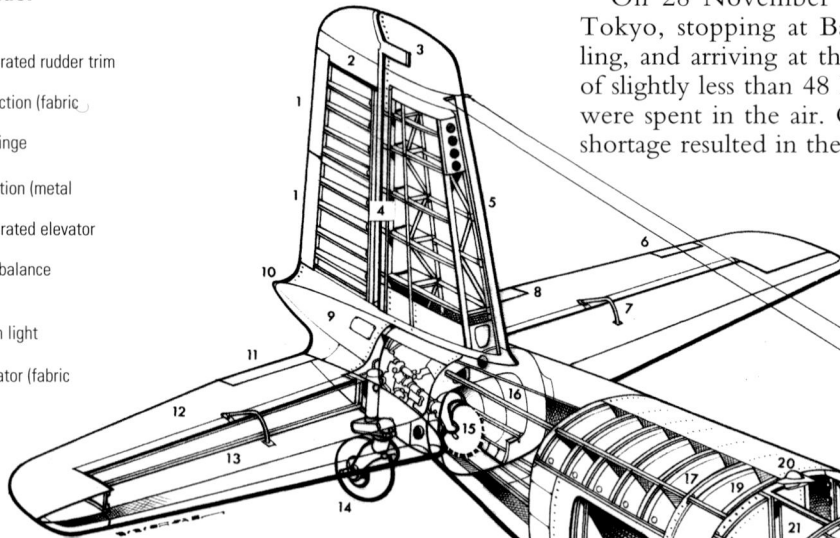

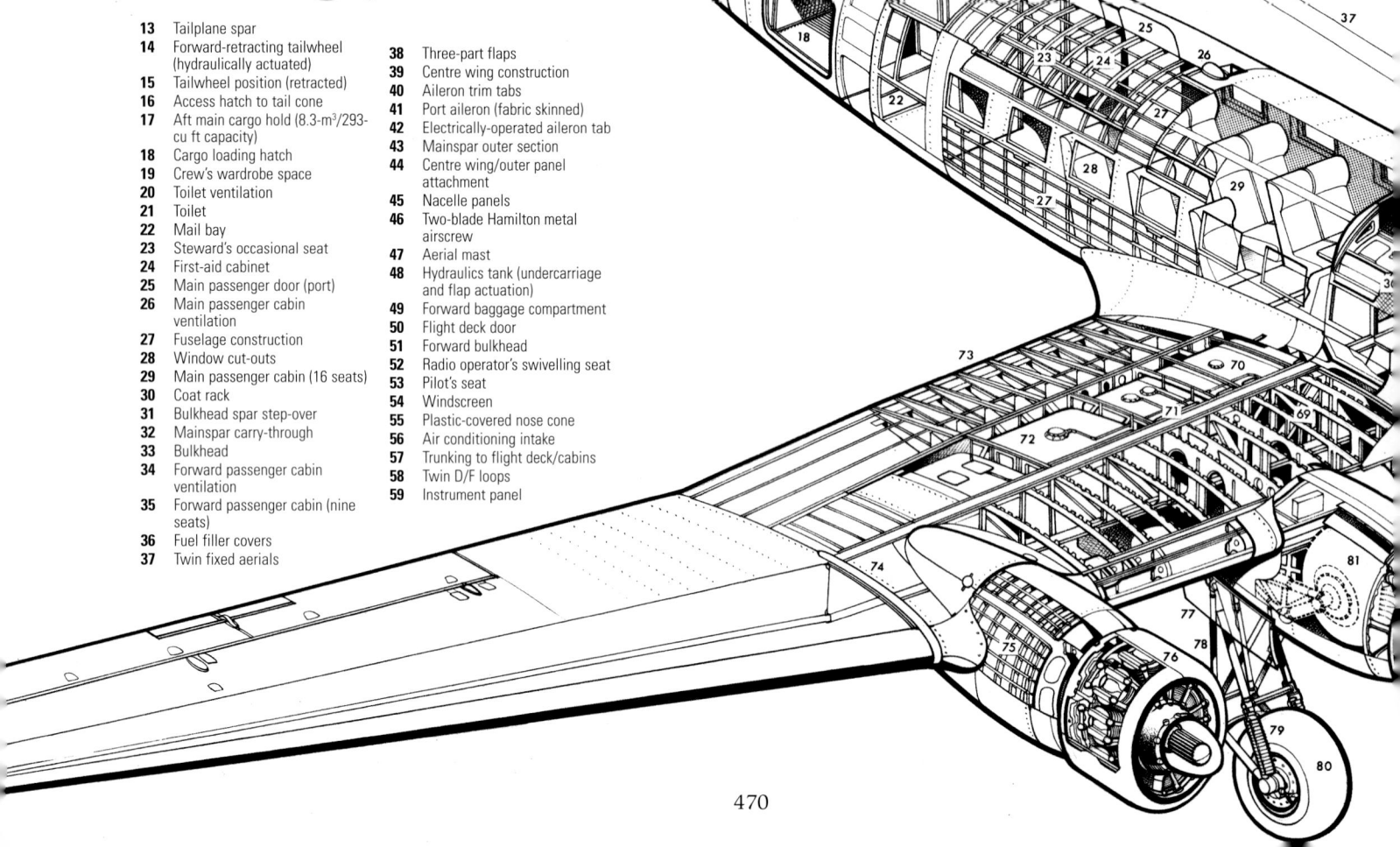

The Fw 200 V3 was taken on Luftwaffe strength as D-2600, the Führermaschine for the use of Hitler and other senior Nazis. It went through three changes of livery before receiving wartime camouflage. Its base was Berlin-Tempelhof.

By the autumn of 1938, work had begun on the initial production model, the **Fw 200B** that, with minor structural modifications, was proposed in two versions: the **Fw 200B-1** with BMW 132Dc engines each rated at 634 kW (850 hp) at 2500 m (8,200 ft), and the **Fw 200B-2** with BMW 132H engines each rated at 619 kW (830 hp) at 1100 m (3,610 ft). By comparison with the Fw 200A-0, the Fw 200B-1 had empty and normal loaded weights increased from 9780 kg (21,561 lb) and 14570 kg (32,121 lb) to 11275 kg (24,857 lb) and 17465 kg (38,503 lb), respectively. Structurally similar, the Fw 200B-2 possessed the slightly higher empty weight of 11300 kg (24,912 lb), but the normal loaded weight was lower at 17000 kg (37,479 lb).

Japanese interest in the Condor had been aroused by D-ACON's visit, and early in 1939 the Dai Nippon Kabushiki Kaisha (Japan-Manchuria Aviation Company) signed a

In its Fw 200 V2 civil form, the Condor was an attractive low wing monoplane powered by four BMW 132G-1 radial engines, each driving a two-blade propeller.

contract for five Fw 200Bs, this order being rapidly followed by a contract from the Finnish airline, Aero O/Y, for two Fw 200Bs. The Japanese contract for five transports was accompanied by a supplementary contract. Placed on behalf of the Imperial Japanese navy, this received no publicity as it called for a single Fw 200B adapted for long-range maritime reconnaissance. The prototype B-series airframe, the **Fw 200 V10**, was already under construction, and Tank elected to adapt this aircraft to fulfil the Japanese reconnaissance requirement. The Fw 200 V10 was therefore preceded into the air by several of the Fw 200Bs being built for the Japanese and Finnish contracts.

The Fw 200 V2 (D-AETA Westfalen) was employed on development trials from 1937. It went on to become one of only nine Condors delivered to DLH.

70 Starboard inner fuel tank
71 Starboard starter fuel tank
72 Starboard outer fuel tank
73 Flap construction
74 Centre wing/outer panel attachment point
75 Nacelle construction
76 BMW 132G-1 nine-cylinder radial air-cooled engine
77 Mainwheel door
78 Mainwheel retraction frame
79 Shock absorber struts
80 Starboard mainwheel
81 Mainwheel position (retracted)
82 Oil tank
83 Engine bearers

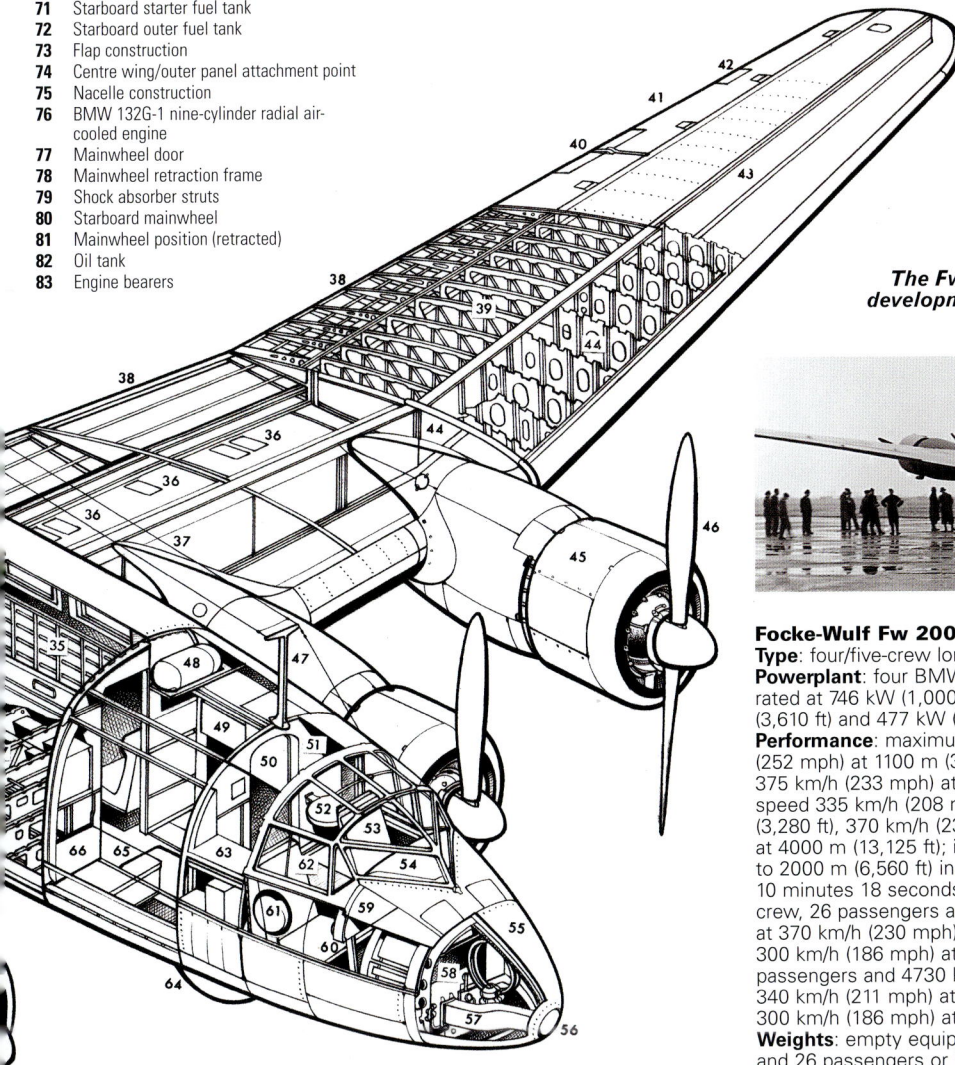

Focke-Wulf Fw 200B-2 Condor specification
Type: four/five-crew long-range airliner
Powerplant: four BMW 132H air-cooled nine-cylinder radial engines each rated at 746 kW (1,000 hp) for take-off and 619 kW (830 hp) at 1100 m (3,610 ft) and 477 kW (640 hp) for continuous cruise
Performance: maximum speed 385 km/h (239 mph) at sea level, 405 km/h (252 mph) at 1100 m (3,610 ft), 395 km/h (245 mph) at 3000 m (9,845 ft), 375 km/h (233 mph) at 5000 m (16,405 ft); maximum continuous cruising speed 335 km/h (208 mph) at sea level, 350 km/h (217 mph) at 1000 m (3,280 ft), 370 km/h (230 mph) at 2500 m (8,200 ft), 355 km/h (220 mph) at 4000 m (13,125 ft); initial climb rate 480 m (1,575 ft) per minute; climb to 2000 m (6,560 ft) in 4 minutes 18 seconds, to 4000 m (13,125 ft) in 10 minutes 18 seconds; service ceiling 7500 m (24,605 ft); range with four crew, 26 passengers and 2600 kg (5,732 lb) of fuel 1770 km (1,100 miles) at 370 km/h (230 mph) at 2500 m (8,200 ft), 2300 km (1,430 miles) at 300 km/h (186 mph) at 2000 m (6,560 ft; range with five crew, nine passengers and 4730 kg (10,428 lb) of fuel 3700 km (2,299 miles) at 340 km/h (211 mph) at 2500 m (8,200 ft), 4500 km (2,796 miles) at 300 km/h (186 mph) at 2500 m (8,200 ft)
Weights: empty equipped 10925 kg (24,085 lb) with four crew and 26 passengers or 19950 kg (24,150 lb) with five crew and nine passengers); maximum take-off 17000 kg (34,479 lb) with four crew and 26 passengers or 17500 kg (38,581 lb) with five crew and nine passengers)
Dimensions: wingspan 32.84 m (107 ft 8¾ in); length 23.85 m (78 ft 3 in); height 6.20 m (20 ft 4 in); wing area 118.00 m² (1,270 14 sq ft)

Above: D-ACVH Grenzmark was acquired by the German air ministry. Joachim Ribbentrop flew in it to the historic meeting with Vyacheslav Molotov in August 1939.

The Fw 200 V5 (D-AMHC Nordmark) sits on the tarmac at Tempelhof airport. It operated DLH services to places such as Barcelona until being destroyed in 1943.

Above: The sole Fw 200B-1 (D-ASBR Holstein) was taken over by the Luftwaffe and issued to KGr.z.b.V. 105.

Below: Werk Nr 021 (NA+WN) was the first of four unarmed Fw 200C-0 transports taken over by the Luftwaffe. Originally completed in January 1940 as D-ASVX 'Thüringen' for DLH, the aircraft was allocated to K.Gr.z.b.V. 105, which formed in March 1940 for operations to Norway. In June, with the campaign ended, the unit was partially disbanded and the Fw 200s reassigned.

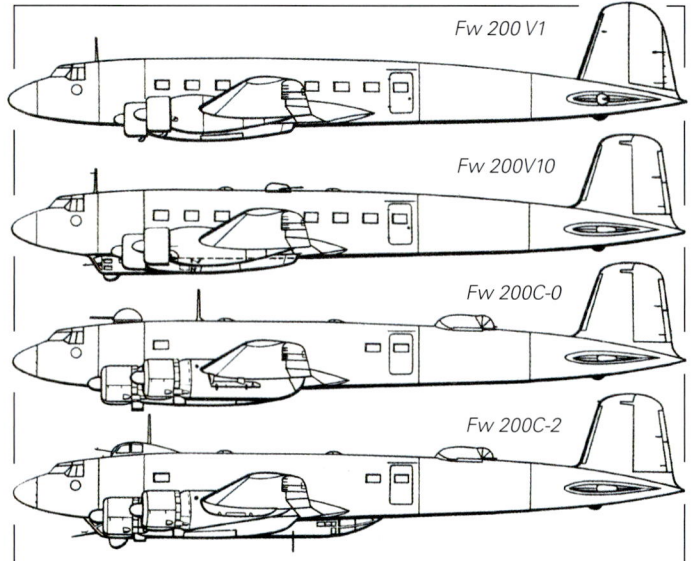

Fw 200 V1

Fw 200V10

Fw 200C-0

Fw 200C-2

In the event, the last Condors to be exported were the two Fw 200A-0 aircraft for Brazil delivered in August 1939, as by the time the first B-series aircraft were ready for delivery hostilities had begun in Europe and permission for their export was withheld, several of the aircraft being added to Lufthansa's fleet, the sole Fw 200B-1 becoming D-ASBR Holstein, and a trio of Fw 200B-2s becoming D-ABOD Kurmark, D-AMHL Pommern (as a replacement for D-AXFO, which had been written off), and D-ASHH Hessen.

Limited German commercial operations

The Condor's service with DLH was very limited, and at no time were more than four aircraft of this type included in the airline's strength. When World War II began, DLH was operating the Fw 200 V4 (D-ADHR), Fw 200 V5 (D-AMHC). Fw 200 V7 (D-ARHW) and Fw 200 V9 (D-AXFO). The Fw 200 V6 (D-ACVH), which had been used by Joachim Ribbentrop, the foreign minister, when he flew to meet

Josef Stalin in Moscow during the summer of 1939, and the Fw 200 V3 were held in the transport reserve pool at Berlin-Tempelhof, these being the only two Condors on Luftwaffe strength when World War II began.

During the winter of 1939-40, DLH's Condor fleet was briefly supplemented by the four Fw 200Bs, but in the following spring was once more depleted when most of the Condors were taken over by the Luftwaffe as part of the equipment of a special purposes transport unit, KGr.z.b.V. 105, which, in April 1940, was based at Kiel-Holtenau for the logistic support of German forces engaged in the 'Weserübung' invasion of Norway. Subsequently, two of the Fw 200Bs were returned to DLH, which operated them alongside the Fw 200 V4 (D-ADHR) and Fw 200 V5 (D-AMHC) until 1941, when the Fw 200 V4 was written off together with one of the Fw 200Bs (D-ABOD), reducing the airline's Condor fleet to two aircraft. In 1943, the loss of the Fw 200 V5 reduced the fleet to one Condor, and this, the Fw 200B-2 D-ASHH, operated DLH's last wartime scheduled flight on 14 April 1945, flying from Barcelona to Berlin.

D-ASHH was lost a week later when, on 21 April, it was hastily loaded with the baggage of the Berlin headquarters staff, and took-off for Barcelona, via Munich. The pilot, Flugkapitän Künstle, was confident that he could evade

Wearing white distemper and Eastern Front theatre bands, this Fw 200C-0 was one of the six delivered with defensive armament. The X8 codes identified the Flugbereitschaft RLM Staaken.

Allied fighters in the prevailing bad weather. The Condor reached Munich safely, took-off again and disappeared. Enquiries in Germany, Switzerland and Spain continued for a number of years, but it was not until 1954 that the mystery was finally solved when evidence was found near Piesenkofen in Mühlberg, Bavaria, that the heavily loaded Condor had crashed and burned, leaving no survivors. Only one commercial German-registered Condor survived until the end of the war, this being the Fw 200B-2 (D-AMHL *Pommern*) which, originally built against the Japanese order, had been operated by the so-called viermotorigen Transportstaffel and its successor, Lufttransportstaffel 290, under the direct command of the Lufttransport-Chef Berlin.

Fw 200C series

Work on adapting the Fw 200 V10 to meet the Japanese maritime reconnaissance requirement was still in progress when hostilities began in Europe. The airframe was little changed from that of the standard Fw 200B transport, but a single 7.9-mm (0.31-in) MG 15 trainable machine-gun was mounted in a dorsal turret positioned slightly forward of the wing's trailing edge, and a short ventral gondola, offset to starboard, was mounted beneath the forward fuselage, this housing the observer's station and single MG 15 trainable machine-guns firing fore and aft. Much of the fuselage was occupied by fuel tanks, and two vertical cameras were attached to the floor of the central fuselage with the camera operator seated aft.

The Oberkommando der Luftwaffe had gambled on having the Heinkel He 177 available for the long-range reconnaissance and anti-shipping roles, and only on the start of hostilities belatedly awoke to the Luftwaffe's total lack of an aircraft possessing range sufficient to allow it to harass British shipping far out in the Atlantic. The He 177 was still very much an unknown quantity as prototype trials had still to start, and the RLM was urgently requested to investigate the possibility of adapting the Condor for interim Luftwaffe use as a maritime reconnaissance bomber pending production of the He 177. As a four-engined commercial transport carrying four crew members and 26 passengers, the Condor employed a relatively light structure hardly suited for the military role now envisaged, but drawing upon its experience in adapting the Fw 200 V10 to meet Japanese requirements, the Focke-Wulf team drew up a proposal for a modified version, the **Fw 200C**, which was promptly accepted by the RLM and preparations initiated for an assembly line.

In essence, the airframe of the Fw 200C remained unchanged from that of the Fw 200B, apart from some minor local strengthening. The BMW 132H engines of the Fw 200B-2 were retained, but some refinement of the engine nacelles was accompanied by the introduction of long-chord engine cowlings. To cope with the higher weights at which the military model was intended to operate, the single mainwheels were replaced by twin-wheel units. A pre-production batch of 10 **Fw 200C-0** aircraft was ordered in September 1939 from the Bremen plant for delivery while the factory was tooling for the initial production **Fw 200C-1**,

Above: *BS+AJ was the fifth Fw 200C-1. Early production Fw 200Cs had a fixed cupola just aft of the flight deck for upper defence in the forward hemisphere, although later variants returned to a turret design. The first two Fw 200C-1s only had bomb racks under the outer engine nacelles, the remainder adding further racks immediately outboard of the engines.*

Above: *This Fw 200C-1 served with 3.Staffel of Kampfgeschwader 40, which operated from Bordeaux-Mérignac between June 1940 and March 1942, when it moved to Trondheim in Norway.*

Above: *The second production Fw 200C-1 (Werk Nr 002, BS+AG) is seen at Bremen shortly after completion early in 1940.*

and these pre-production aircraft were, in fact, Fw 200B airframes already on the assembly line when war began. The first four airframes were too advanced to be adapted for the maritime reconnaissance role and were therefore completed as transports without defensive armament, although the new twin-wheel main undercarriage members, modified engine nacelles, long-chord cowlings and three-blade variable-pitch

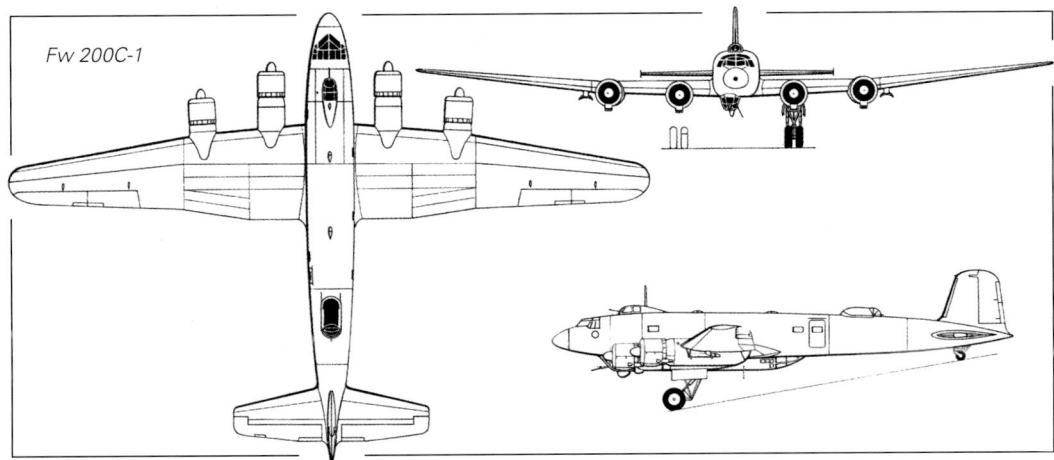

Fw 200C-1

Focke-Wulf Fw 200 Condor

Above: The Fw 200C-1 was the first Condor variant to enter service with KG 40, though it suffered serious structural problems. During the latter half of 1940 there were only six to eight servieable aircraft at any one time.

Right: The ventral gondola of the Fw 200 in its maritime reconnaissance bomber form offered an excellent bombardier station as well as gun positions.

Above: The hydraulically operated HDL 151 turret, with one 15-mm MG 151 cannon, offered considerable drag and degraded performance.

Right: The hydraulically operated Fw 19 forward upper turret (A-Stand) mounting a single 7.9-mm (0.31-in) MG 15 machine-gun was introduced on the Fw 200C-3, and replaced the fixed raised fairing featured by earlier sub-types.

Below: The electrically operated Fw 19 turret was a low-drag unit, but carried only one 7.9-mm (0.31-in) machine-gun.

Right: The pilot's position on the flight deck of an Fw 200 maritime reconnaissance bomber. The Condor flew well for an aircraft of its size.

Left: To cope with the greater weights associated with long-range maritime operations, the Fw 200C introduced twin-wheel main undercarriage units. Note the bomb racks outboard of the outer engine nacelle.

Displaying the lines of its graceful airliner parentage, this Fw 200C-1 was on the strength of Major Edgar Petersen's I/KG 40, based at Bordeaux-Mérignac, under Luftflotte 3 in the autumn of 1940. Despite accidents resulting from the overstressing of the airframe, by February 1941 I/KG 40's patrols were bringing in rich dividends.

propellers were fitted. The first of the four Fw 200C-0 transports (Werk Nr 021) was completed in January 1940 as D-ASVX *Thüringen*, and it was intended to deliver this aircraft to Lufthansa. However, before it could be taken over by the airline, the aircraft was impressed by the Luftwaffe (as NA+WN) and, together with the three following aircraft, was delivered to K.Gr.z.b.V. 105 for transport operations during the Norwegian campaign.

The remaining six Fw 200C-0 machines were completed with defensive armament and bomb racks for anti-shipping operations and, during the early spring of 1940, were delivered to 1.Staffel of the newly formed I Gruppe of Kampfgeschwader 40, which began attacks on British shipping from Aalborg-West in April. By 11 May 1940, only two of the Fw 200C-0s of 1./KG 40 were serviceable, and by the end of June, 1.Staffel had been withdrawn from operations for re-equipment with the Fw 200C-1 and transferred to Bordeaux-Mérignac, where it was attached to the IV Fliegerkorps under Luftflotte 3 for operations in support of the attack on the British Isles. Flying out across the Bay of Biscay and following an arc around the Atlantic coast of Ireland, attacking targets of opportunity, and landing at Trondheim-Vaernes or Stavanger-Sola in Norway, I/KG 40 enjoyed some success although it also suffered losses, one Condor being shot down over the English

Channel on 13 July and another north of Ireland on 20 July. By September 1940, before which the unit had undertaken some nocturnal bombing in the Liverpool-Birkenhead area, Condor strength had risen to 15 aircraft, and a Geschwader-Stab had been established, although this possessed only one Condor. During August and September, I/KG 40 accounted for more than 90,000 tons of Allied shipping, and one of its most spectacular successes was the discovery and bombing of the 42,348-ton Canadian Pacific liner *Empress of Britain* some 115 km (71½ miles) north-west of Donegal Bay on 26 October, the crippled liner being taken in tow but torpedoed and sunk two days later by the *U-32*.

Armament layout

The Fw 200C-0 possessed a defensive armament of one 7.9-mm (0.31-in) MG 15 machine-gun in an hydraulically operated upper turret immediately aft of the flight deck, a similar weapon on a trainable mounting firing from a raised aft dorsal position, and a third MG 15 firing aft and downward through a ventral hatch. The production Fw 200C-1 introduced a long ventral gondola offset to starboard, the nose of which accommodated a 20-mm MG FF (Oerlikon) cannon on a trainable mounting. The tail of the gondola mounted an MG 15 in place of the weapon fired through the

Below: The weight of the equipment added to an airframe designed for lighter-loaded civil operations meant structural problems for the maritime Condor. This is an Fw 200C-3/U1.

Above: Fw 200 Condor reconnaissance bombers with HDL 151 turrets are seen prior to delivery to KG 40. Serviceability was always a problem of great concern to the unit.

Left: The twin-wheel main undercarriage units retracted forward and upward into covered bays in the undersides of the nacelles for the inboard engines.

Right: The 20-mm MG FF trainable cannon in the forward part of the gondola of some Fw 200Cs was used primarily to suppress light AA fire as the Condor made a low-level bombing run.

475

Focke-Wulf Fw 200 Condor

Above: The Fw 200's rear dorsal position accommodated a gunner and one 7.9-mm (0.31-in) MG 15 or, later, 13-mm (0.51-in) MG 131 trainable rearward-firing machine-gun

The Fw 200C's long ventral gondola was offset to starboard and provided accommodation for one 250-kg (551-lb) cement bomb or 12 50-kg (110-lb) HE bombs.

Below: This photograph of the interior of an uncompleted Fw 200C reveals the frame and stringer interior structure inside the stressed-skin semi-monocoque fuselage.

ventral hatch. A further change was provided by the deletion of the hydraulically operated forward turret and its replacement by a fixed raised cupola which, also accommodating a single MG 15 on a trainable mounting, was, unlike the ventral gondola, centred on the fuselage.

The offensive load for armed reconnaissance missions was similar for both the Fw 200C-0 and Fw 200C-1, this comprising a single 250-kg (551-lb) bomb under each of the extended outboard engine nacelles, and a further 250-kg (551-lb) bomb on each of two underwing racks immediately outboard of the engines, but the ventral gondola of the Fw 200C-1 included provision for the stowage of a single 250-kg (551-lb) cement bomb that was used as a marker for checking the accuracy of bombsight readings and for assisting final adjustments before the four HE bombs were dropped 'for effect'.

The Fw 200C featured a semi-monocoque fuselage with an all-metal two-spar wing built in three sections, metal covered to the rear spar and fabric covered aft. Two-piece ailerons extended along two-thirds of the outer section trailing edges, and split flaps were mounted inboard of the ailerons. The Fw 200C-1 normally carried a crew of five which comprised pilot, co-pilot, navigator/radio operator/gunner, engineer/gunner and rear dorsal gunner. As the Condor was intended primarily for low-altitude attack, the navigator, who also fulfilled the function of bombardier, had to rely on a Revi sight. The basic fuel tankage totalled 8060

Above: As weights increased and the rigours of extended operations at low altitude made their effects felt, the Fw 200C suffered structural problems with the rear spar and fuselage.

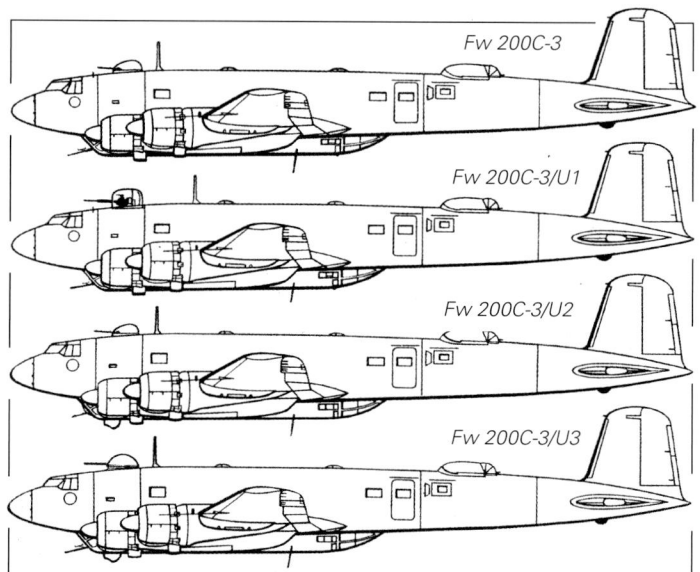

Fw 200C-3

Fw 200C-3/U1

Fw 200C-3/U2

Fw 200C-3/U3

A close-up view of an Fw 200C-3/U2 shows details of the redesigned engine nacelles made necessary by the variant's new BMW-Bramo Fafnir engines, the Fw 19 forward turret reintroduced in this variant and the Condor's complex main undercarriage. Also visible is the ventral gondola which, in the Fw 200C-3/U2, housed a Lotfe ID bomb sight and (though omitted from this particular aircraft) an MG 131 13-mm (0.51-in) machine-gun.

litres (1,773 Imp gal), but an overload of 900 litres (198 Imp gal) could be carried in an armoured auxiliary tank in the ventral gondola, and on occasions this overload was increased even further for maximum-endurance unarmed-reconnaissance missions by the addition of two or three 300-litre (66-Imp gal) drums that were stowed in the fuselage and used to refill the tanks in flight.

Need for accelerated production

Twenty-six Fw 200C-1 Condors had left the Bremen assembly line by the end of 1940, and Gruppe strength was gradually built up, although attrition was relatively high as a result of the aircraft's commercial transport heritage rather than combat. Only the first pilot enjoyed any armour protection and, all fuel connections to the engines being on the aircraft's underside, the Condor was extremely vulnerable to light anti-aircraft fire. However, the inadequate anti-aircraft armament of Allied merchant vessels at this stage of the war, coupled with insufficient escort vessels and almost complete lack of long-range aircraft and escort carriers, rendered I/KG 40's task relatively simple. The 'Achilles heel' of the unit's Condors was the haste with which they had been adapted for their task. Embodying virtually no structural strengthening they soon proved inadequate to meet the strain of continuous operational flying at low altitudes for long periods, and the violent manoeuvres that were sometimes called for when taking evasive action. There were numerous instances of the rear spar failing and the fuselage breaking its back immediately aft of the wing on landing, and during the latter half of 1940 rarely more than six to eight Condors were available for operations at any one time.

Despite its shortcomings, however, the Condor contin-

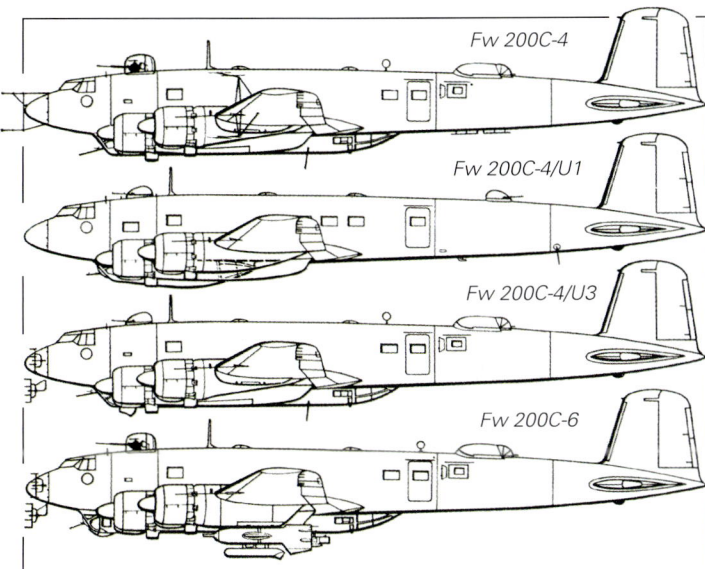

Fw 200C-4

Fw 200C-4/U1

Fw 200C-4/U3

Fw 200C-6

ued to enjoy auspicious success, and between 1 August 1940 and February 1941, I/KG 40 accounted for 85 Allied vessels totalling some 363,000 tons. By March 1941, when the increasing importance of the sea war led to the establishment of the Fliegerführer Atlantik, I/KG 40 had become a full three-Staffel Gruppe with an operational strength of 36 Condors, although the average Gruppe serviceability rate rarely exceeded 25 percent of total strength. The Fw 200C-1 had been supplanted on the assembly line at Cottbus by the **Fw 200C-2**, which was considered an interim model pending the introduction of the more extensively modified **Fw 200C-3**. Like its production predecessor, the Fw 200C-2 was powered by the BMW 132H engine, but differed in having new scalloped outboard engine nacelles that offered some drag reduction when their racks were loaded with either a 250-kg (551-lb) bomb or 300-litre (66-Imp gal) auxiliary fuel tank. New faired wing racks were also introduced, but these changes did not reduce the essential vulnerability of the Condor, and by the late summer of 1941 the offensive operations of the Condor had to be curtailed by the Fliegerführer Atlantik as a result of rising combat attrition.

The effectiveness of the anti-aircraft defences of Allied merchant vessels had been steadily increased and catapult-launched fighters had made their debut. Thus, Condor crews received orders not to initiate any attack and to seek cloud cover when attacked, offering fight only if absolutely necessary. Further, they had orders to return immediately to base even if only slightly damaged rather than continue to operate and jeopardise the safety of a valuable aircraft, their task being largely confined to shadowing Allied convoys. On sighting the convoy the Condor's crew informed its base, the aircraft's captain giving his opinion as to whether the convoy could best be attacked by U-boats or bombers. If it was decided to attack the convoy with U-boats, the Condor sometimes acted as the U-boats' Fühlungshalter, or contact plane, by sending out continuous D/F signals, its tactics being controlled by the Befehlshaber der U-Boote (commander of U-boats), no direct communication taking place between the aircraft and the U-boats it was responsible for directing.

Structural strengthening

By the summer of 1941, the improved Fw 200C-3 began to reach KG 40, this embodying major structural strengthening

The Fw 200C-3, the improved and structurally strengthened version of the Fw 200C-2, was delivered mid-1941, but still suffered some of the structural problems that had beset its predecessors. Other changes were uprated engines and an Fw 19 low-drag upper turret.

of both the rear spar and the fuselage. Even so, the Condor still suffered structural failures, and the Focke-Wulf concern never succeeded in entirely eradicating the problem. In order to maintain the performance of the Condor despite the substantially increased structural and equipment weights, the Fw 200C-3 received four BMW-Bramo 323R-2 Fafnir air-cooled nine-cylinder radial engines which, rated at 746 kW (1,000 hp) at sea level, offered 895 kW (1,200 hp) for take-off by means of methanol-water injection. Loaded weight had

risen to 21000 kg (46,297 lb), an additional crew member was carried, and the maximum bomb load was increased to 2100 kg (4,630 lb) in the form of one 500-kg (1,102-lb) bomb beneath each outboard engine nacelle, one 250-kg (551-lb) bomb on each of the two underwing racks, and 12 50-kg (110-lb) bombs in the ventral gondola. Such a load was never carried for the offensive reconnaissance mission, for which bomb load was usually four 250-kg (551-lb) bombs.

A hydraulically operated low-drag Fw 19 turret with a

Focke-Wulf Fw 200C-4/U-3 cutaway key

1 Starboard navigation light
2 Wing skinning
3 Starboard aileron
4 Aileron trim tabs
5 Outboard mainspar
6 Aileron control run
7 Wing ribs (centre section)
8 Wing ribs (forward section)
9 Wing dihedral break point
10 Starboard flap (outer section)
11 Starboard flap (centre section)
12 Starboard flap (inner section)
13 Wing fuel tank covers
14 Inboard mainspar structure
15 Starboard outer oil tank
16 Multiple exhaust stubs
17 Cooling gills
18 Starboard outer nacelle (angled)
19 Three-blade VDM controllable-pitch metal-bladed propeller
20 Propeller boss
21 Carburettor air intake
22 Auxiliary fuel tank 300-litre/66-Imp gal capacity)
23 Starboard inner nacelle
24 FuG 200 Hohentwiel search radar array (port antenna omitted for clarity)
25 Nose D/F loop
26 Nose bulkhead
27 Rudder pedals
28 Hand-held 13-mm (0.51-in) MG 131 machine-gun (D-Stand)
29 Lotfe 7D bomb sight fairing
30 Ventral gondola side windows (gondola offset to starboard)
31 Rear dorsal gunner's take-off seat
32 Pilot's circular vision port
33 First pilot's seat
34 Sliding windscreen panel
35 Co-pilot's seat (co-pilot also served as bomb-aimer)
36 Flight deck entry
37 Arc-of-fire interrupter gate
38 Cabin air inlet (starboard side only)
39 Hydraulically-operated Fw 19 turret mounting single 7.9-mm (0.31-in) MG 15 machine-gun (A-Stand)
40 Gunner's seat
41 Ammunition racks (A-Stand)
42 Bulkhead
43 Radio operator's rectangular vision port
44 Ventral gondola entry hatch
45 Radio operator's station (A-Stand gunner's station)
46 Ammunition racks (D-Stand)
47 Ammunition racks (D-Stand)
48 Ventral gondola centre section (with maximum capacity of one 900-litre/198-Imp gal armoured fuel tank or 12 50-kg/110-lb bombs)
49 Underfloor control runs
50 Cabin window stations (staggered two to port and three to starboard)
51 Underfloor structure
52 Fuselage oil tank
53 De-icing fluid reservoir
54 Aerial mast
55 Five main fuselage fuel tanks (canted)
56 Mainspar fuselage carry-through structure
57 Rear ventral gunner's take-off seat
58 Upper fuselage longeron
59 Mainframe
60 Cabin ventilators/air extractors
61 Fuselage side walls
62 Ammunition racks (C-Stand)
63 Second radio operator's take-off seat
64 Strengthened fuselage frame
65 Dorsal D/F loop
66 Starboard 7.9-mm (0.31-in) MG 15 machine-gun (F-Stand)
67 Beam gunners' take-off seats
68 Bulkhead
69 Dorsal aft gunner's position (B-Stand)
70 Dorsal glazing
71 Ammunition racks (B-Stand)
72 Hinged canopy
73 MG 15 machine-gun
74 Rear fuselage frames
75 Starboard tailplane structure
76 Endplate-fin balance section
77 Starboard elevator
78 Elevator hinge
79 Elevator tab
80 Tailfin front spar
81 Tailfin structure
82 Rudder balance
83 Rudder construction
84 Electrically-operated rudder trim tab (upper section)
85 Electrically-operated rudder trim tab (lower section)

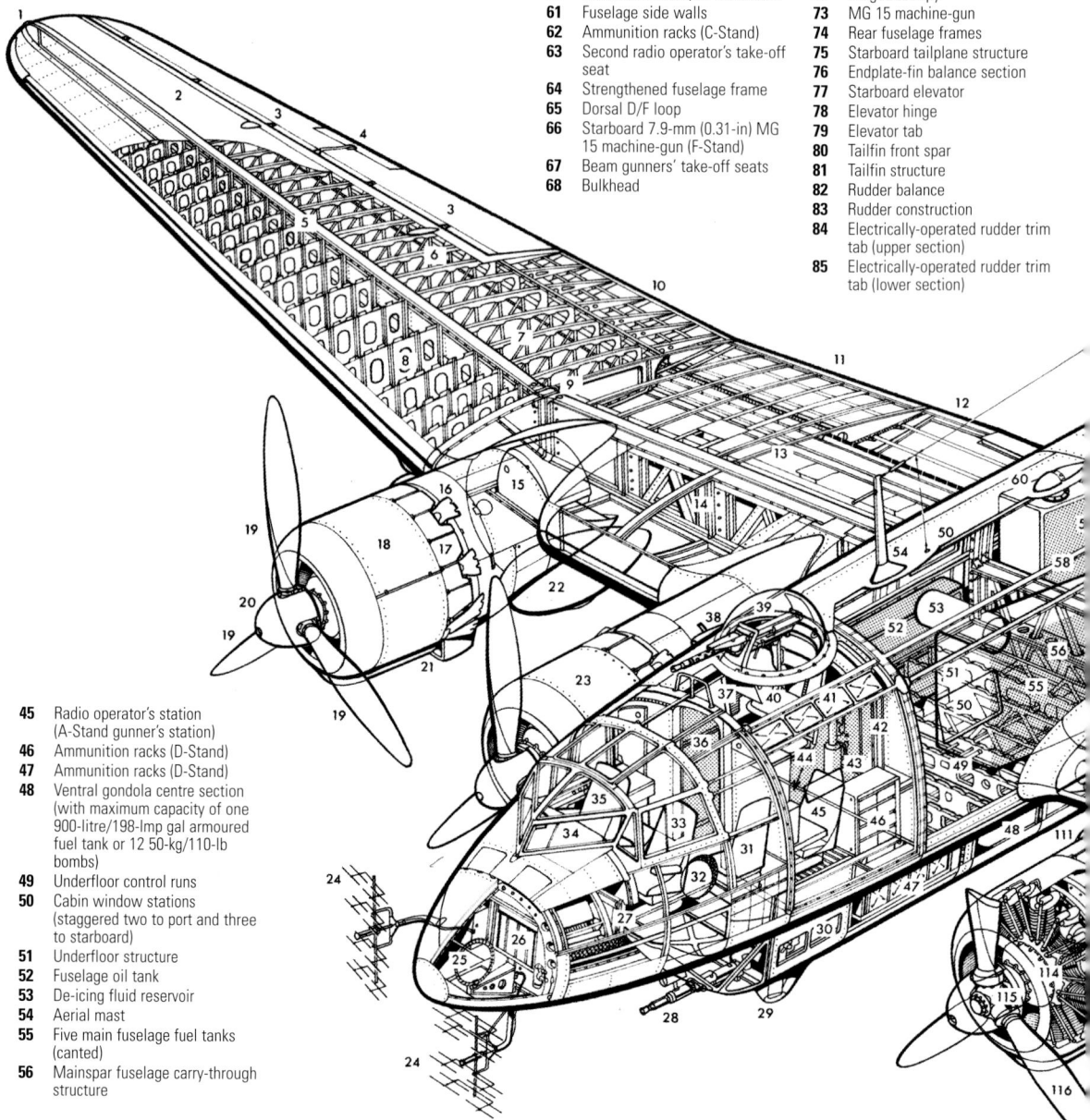

A sight much feared by Allied sailors deep in the Atlantic, the appearance overhead of an Fw 200C presaged a bombing attack or, later in the war, the subsequent arrival of a U-boat pack.

86 Rudderpost
87 Tail wheel mechanism access panel
88 Tail cone
89 Aft navigation light
90 Elevator tab
91 Port elevator
92 Electrically-operated elevator tab (port only)
93 Endplate-fin balance
94 Port tailplane
95 Elevator hinge
96 Tailplane
97 Forward retracting tailwheel
98 Tailwheel retraction mechanism

99 Control runs
100 Oxygen bottles
101 Aft bulkhead
102 Chute for Schwan D/F buoys, Lux light-buoys or flares
103 Port 7.9-mm (0.31-in) MG 15 beam gun (F-Stand)

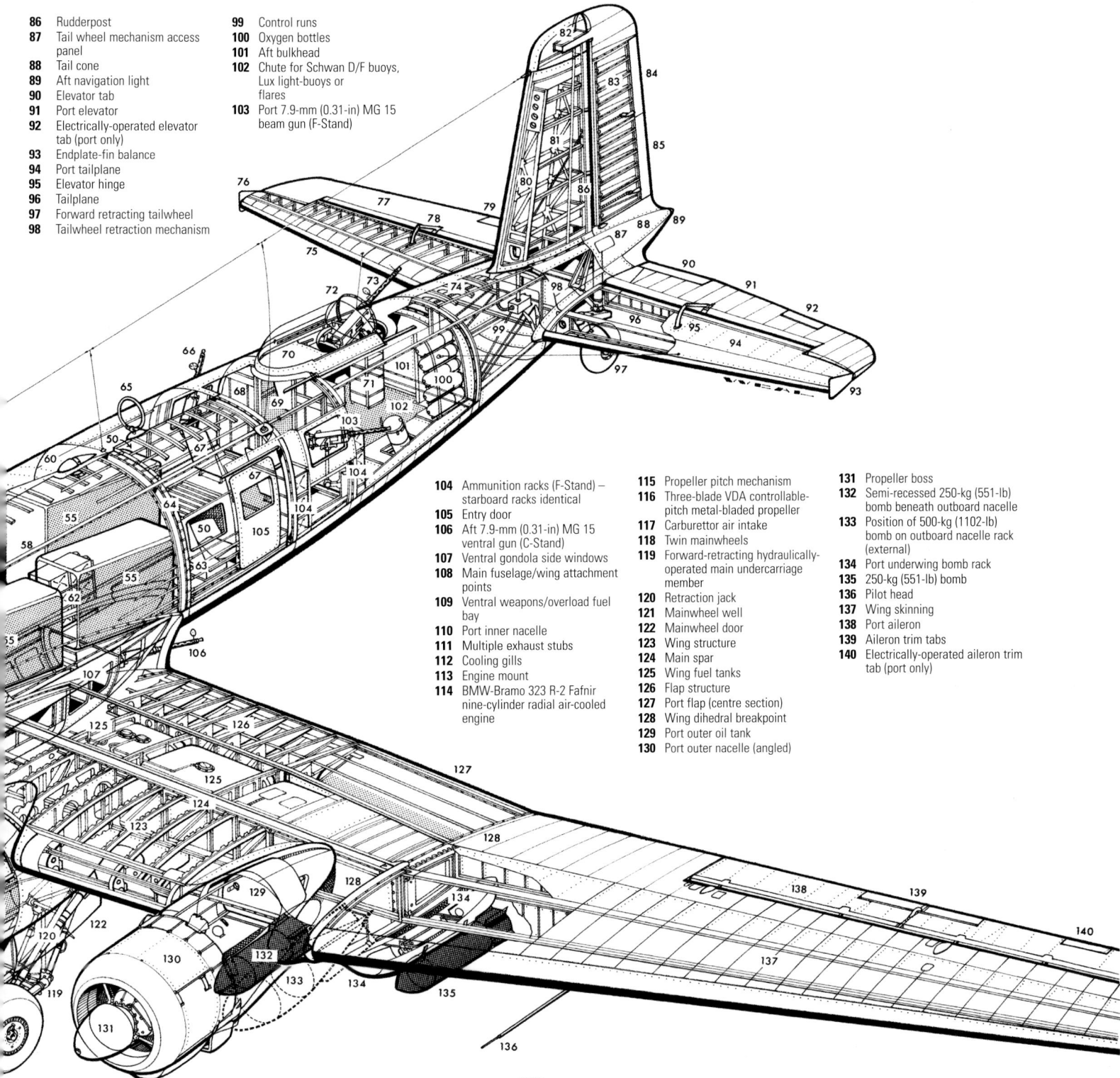

104 Ammunition racks (F-Stand) – starboard racks identical
105 Entry door
106 Aft 7.9-mm (0.31-in) MG 15 ventral gun (C-Stand)
107 Ventral gondola side windows
108 Main fuselage/wing attachment points
109 Ventral weapons/overload fuel bay
110 Port inner nacelle
111 Multiple exhaust stubs
112 Cooling gills
113 Engine mount
114 BMW-Bramo 323 R-2 Fafnir nine-cylinder radial air-cooled engine

115 Propeller pitch mechanism
116 Three-blade VDA controllable-pitch metal-bladed propeller
117 Carburettor air intake
118 Twin mainwheels
119 Forward-retracting hydraulically-operated main undercarriage member
120 Retraction jack
121 Mainwheel well
122 Mainwheel door
123 Wing structure
124 Main spar
125 Wing fuel tanks
126 Flap structure
127 Port flap (centre section)
128 Wing dihedral breakpoint
129 Port outer oil tank
130 Port outer nacelle (angled)

131 Propeller boss
132 Semi-recessed 250-kg (551-lb) bomb beneath outboard nacelle
133 Position of 500-kg (1102-lb) bomb on outboard nacelle rack (external)
134 Port underwing bomb rack
135 250-kg (551-lb) bomb
136 Pilot head
137 Wing skinning
138 Port aileron
139 Aileron trim tabs
140 Electrically-operated aileron trim tab (port only)

Focke-Wulf Fw 200 Condor

Above: Werk Nr 256 was an Fw 200C-8 with the FuG 200 Hohentwiel radar and equipment for launching Hs 293 missiles. The Fw 200C-8 was the last Condor sub-type to be built.

Below: The combination of the Fw 200C to locate and report, and the U-boat then to attack, provided the Germans with a powerful weapon against Allied convoys up to 1943-44.

Above: As well as its maritime duties, the Fw 200 had an important career in the Luftwaffe as a transport. A few were used for clandestine missions by KG 200.

Below: The 'office' of the Fw 200C shows the pilot's and co-pilot's seats to port and starboard with instruments ahead of them and the engine, flap and undercarriage controls between them.

single 7.9-mm (0.31-in) MG 15 machine-gun replaced the central raised fairing immediately aft of the flight deck, and two additional MG 15s were mounted behind sliding beam panels. The **Fw 200C-3/U1** differed in having a large hydraulically operated HDL 151 forward turret housing a single 15-mm MG 151 cannon with a 500-round belt and a spare 300-round belt, and a 20-mm MG 151 cannon with a 300-round belt in the nose of the ventral gondola in place of the obsolescent MG FF. Although the HDL 151 turret provided an appreciably more effective defence than the Fw 19 turret, its drag was not inconsiderable, reducing maximum speed by 25-30 km/h (16-18 mph), and the **Fw 200C-3/U2** reverted to the Fw 19 forward turret. The primary change in the Fw 200C-3/U2 was the introduction of the Lotfe 7D bomb sight that necessitated the replacement of the 20-mm MG 151 cannon in the nose of the ventral gondola by a 13-mm (0.51-in) MG 131 machine-gun, as the breach of the cannon interfered with the bomb sight's stowage. The Lotfe 7D substantially improved the Condor's bombing accuracy, and it was claimed that

the average error was only 20-30 m (22-33 yards) from a release altitude of 3000-4000 m (9,845-13,125 ft). The **Fw 200C-3/U3** had an EDL 131 forward turret with a 13-mm (0.51-in) MG 131 machine-gun and carried a similar weapon on a trainable mounting in the aft dorsal position, while the **Fw 200C-3/U4**, which carried an additional gunner to bring the crew complement to seven, and increased fuel capacity which boosted maximum loaded weight to 22700 kg (50,044 lb), retained the Fw 19 forward turret but mounted 13-mm (0.51-in) MG 131 weapons in place of the 7.9-mm (0.31-in) MG 15s in the beam positions.

Total Condor production during 1941 was only 58 machines, despite increased demand as a result of delays in the introduction of the He 177. Bomb damage to the Bremen facility was partially responsible for delivery delays, this having necessitated the transfer of much final assembly work on the Condor to Blohm und Voss, and creation of a second line at Cottbus. Indeed, deliveries could barely keep pace with I/KG 40's demands, and although the re-equipment of III/KG 40 with the Condor was considered a matter of urgency, only a few of these aircraft had reached this Gruppe by the end of 1941, and immediately an aircraft came off the line a KG 40 crew was specially sent to Cottbus to collect it. The shortage was further aggravated by the diversion of aircraft for special transport duties with the Reichskurierstaffel.

In February 1942, the Fw 200C-3 was replaced

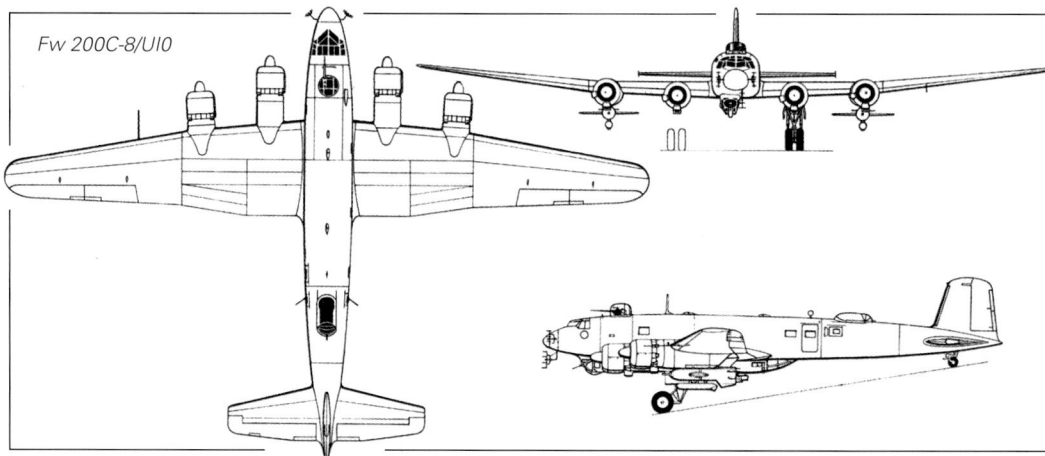

Fw 200C-8/U10

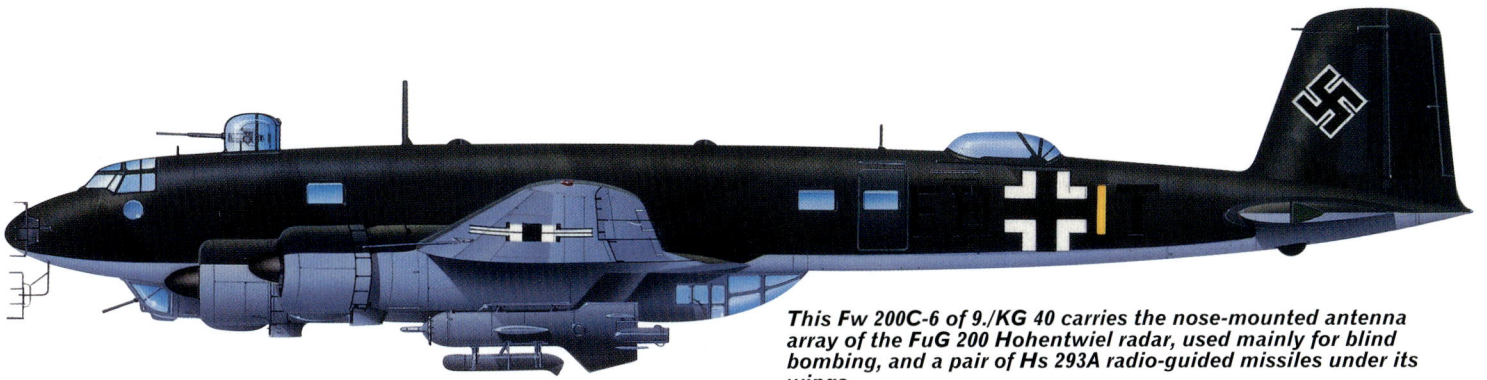

This Fw 200C-6 of 9./KG 40 carries the nose-mounted antenna array of the FuG 200 Hohentwiel radar, used mainly for blind bombing, and a pair of Hs 293A radio-guided missiles under its wings.

in production by the **Fw 200C-4**, a model manufactured in larger numbers than any other Condor variant. The Fw 200C-3 and Fw 200C-4 were basically similar, the principal differences being confined to those associated with search radar and communications radio.

Early production Fw 200C-4 machines were fitted with FuG Rostock search radar with antennas on the fuselage nose, and above and below the outboard wing panels, but Condors soon standardised on the later FuG 200 Hohentwiel that was used in conjunction with a blind bombing procedure, the Rostock serving solely for shipping search. A few of the aircraft of Stab III/KG 40 were later fitted with both Hohentwiel and Rostock, the double installation being necessitated by the fact that the latter, although having a wider search angle and a greater range than the former, would not provide readings at a range of less than 5000 m (5,470 yards) and was thus unsuitable for blind bombing, the Hohentwiel being accurate down to a range of less than 1500 m (1,640 yards). The large HDL 151 turret was restored on the Fw 200C-4, and either a 13-mm (0.51-in) MG 131 or 20-mm MG 151 was mounted in the nose of the ventral gondola, according to whether the Lotfe 7D bomb sight was carried, all other defensive positions mounting 7.9-mm (0.3-in) MG 15 machine-guns. The rated altitude of the Fw 200C-4 was 4800 m (15,750 ft), and the service ceiling was officially 5800 m (19,030 ft), but at this altitude the airframe was subject to violent vibration. The standard tankage provided a normal endurance of 14 hours at economical cruise with normal safety reserves, but endurance could be stretched to 18 hours. with overload fuel.

Closing the Atlantic Gap

The Allies, who had begun to take the measure of the Condor with the introduction of CAM-ships, enjoyed further success with the appearance of escort-carriers and Consolidated Liberator very long-range aircraft in Royal Navy and RAF Coastal Command service, respectively. This effectively closed the 'Atlantic Gap'. Several Condors of KG 40 were lost in December 1941 to Grumman Wildcat fighters from *Audacity*, one of the first escort carriers to see operational service. In March 1942, I/KG 40 was transferred to Trondheim-Vaernes in Norway to engage Russian-bound shipping under Luftflotte 5, but III/KG 40 continued to operate primarily from Bordeaux-Mérignac from where, towards the end of the year, 9.Staffel was detached to the Mediterranean for transport tasks, at first flying from Crete to Tobruk, and then from Lecce in southern Italy to Tunisia.

During 1942 some 84 Fw 200C-3 and Fw 200C-4 aircraft were produced, a few of them being delivered to the Ju 88-equipped 1.(F/120 based in Norway, and the similarly equipped 1.(F)/122 based in Sardinia, but most new Condors were allocated to KG 40 as they became available. However, at the beginning of 1943, Condor activity over the Atlantic fell sharply, 2./KG 40 remaining at Trondheim-Vaernes but 1. and 3./KG 40 being despatched to the Eastern Front for emergency transport operations. The two Staffeln,

with an operational strength totalling 18 aircraft, began ferrying supplies into the beleaguered German garrison at Stalingrad, and were known as the Sonder-Unternehmung Stalingrad, or K.Gr.z.b.V.200. Initially the Condors landed supplies on an airfield on the outskirts of Stalingrad, but as the German perimeter shrank they were forced to drop supplies by parachute, each aircraft carrying four supply containers on its bomb racks. On 18 January 1943, the Condors of K.Gr.z.b.V.200 were transferred from Stalino to Zaparozhye, from where they continued their supply-dropping activities for a month before it was decided that this transport undertaking was too costly. For five days the Condors then confined their activities to bombing railway communications in the Stalingrad area, after which the survivors were withdrawn to Berlin-Staaken where they became 8./KG 40. New 1. and 3. Staffeln had meanwhile been formed on the He 177. 8./KG 40 then transferred to Bordeaux-Mérignac for a resumption of activities over the Bay of Biscay. In the meantime, 1.Staffel, which had also been sent to Italy on a transport assignment, and 9.Staffel had returned to France, being

Above: The glazed position at the rear of the ventral gondola accommodated a gunner and one 7.9-mm (0.31-in) MG 15 trainable rearward-firing machine-gun.

Ready to taxi out for take-off, this Fw 200C-6 or Fw 200C-8 is outfitted for the stand-off anti-ship role with FuG-200 Hohentwiel radar, the HDL 151 forward dorsal turret and, at the front of the ventral gondola, the FuG 203b Kehl command transmitter associated with the Hs 293A air-to-surface missile.

Crew
The addition of an extra gunner in the Fw 200C-3/U4 and subsequent versions brought the crew complement to seven, having been raised from five in the Fw 200C-1 and C-2 to six in the C-3. The basic five-man crew consisted of a pilot and co-pilot, with a flight engineer/gunner, a navigator/bombardier (who also doubled as radio operator/gunner) and a rear dorsal gunner.

Anti-shipping operations
By late 1943, the main role of the Condor was to interdict Allied convoys from Gibraltar, whose departure was usually reported by German agents in Spain. The aircraft would usually take off in fours, flying out to an initial point at sea level and in close formation. They would then split up, fan out and fly parallel tracks some 40 km (25 miles) apart, periodically climbing to 300 metres (1,000 ft) and making a broad circuit while they searched for shipping with Hohentwiel radar. When contact was made the aircraft would contact the others and all would climb to make their attacks, which were undertaken from a minimum altitude of 2700 m (9,000 ft).

Focke-Wulf Fw 200 Condor

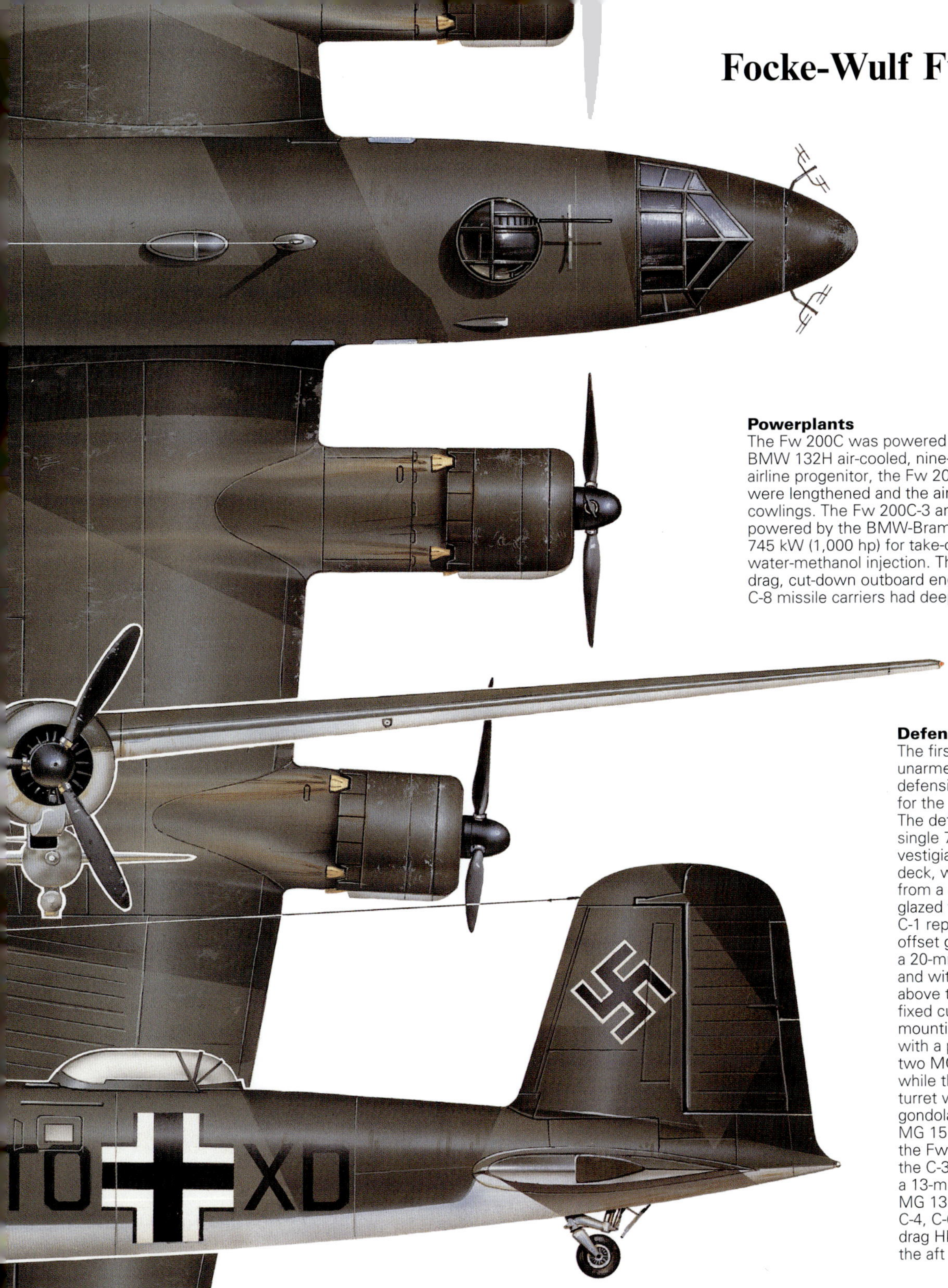

Radar
Early Fw 200C-4s had FuG Rostock search radar, served by antennas on the nose and outer wings, but this was soon replaced by FuG 200, with the nose antenna arrays seen here. A few aircraft had both Rostock and Hohentwiel, the Rostock having greater range and wider search angle but longer minimum range.

Powerplants
The Fw 200C was powered by the same 620-kW (830-hp) BMW 132H air-cooled, nine-cylinder piston engines as its airline progenitor, the Fw 200B-2, although the nacelles were lengthened and the aircraft received long-chord cowlings. The Fw 200C-3 and subsequent versions were powered by the BMW-Bramo 323R-2 Fafnir, rated at 745 kW (1,000 hp) for take-off, or 894 kW (1,200 hp) with water-methanol injection. The Fw 200C-2 introduced low drag, cut-down outboard engine nacelles, although C-6 and C-8 missile carriers had deeper outboard nacelles.

Defensive armament
The first four basic Fw 200C-0s were unarmed transports, but the next six had defensive armament and bomb racks for the maritime reconnaissance role. The defensive armament consisted of a single 7.9-mm MG 15 machine-gun in the vestigial turret above and behind the flight deck, with two similar weapons firing from a downward hatch and from the glazed fairing above the rear fuselage. The C-1 replaced the ventral MG 15 with an offset gondola, in the nose of which was a 20-mm MG FF on a flexible mounting, and with an MG 15 in its tail. The turret above the fuselage was replaced by a fixed cupola with an MG 15 on a flexible mounting. The C-3 replaced the cupola with a powered turret, and introduced two MG 15s behind sliding beam panels, while the C-3/U1 introduced an HDL 151 turret with a 15-mm MG 151 cannon. The gondola's MG FF was replaced by another MG 151. The C-3/U2 and U4 reintroduced the Fw 19 forward upper turret, while the C-3/U3 had an EDL 131 turret with a 13-mm MG 131, and with another MG 131 in the aft dorsal position. The C-4, C-6 and C-8 reintroduced the high drag HDL 151 turret and had MG 131s in the aft dorsal and beam positions.

Focke-Wulf Fw 200C-8/U-10 Condor

Kampfgeschwader 40, France, 1944

The last of the Condor sub-variants, the Fw 200C-8/U10 was a dedicated missile-carrier, with pylons under the outboard engine nacelles for a pair of Henschel Hs 293A anti-ship missiles. This example, one of the final handful delivered in January-February 1944, is shown still in four-letter factory codes, which would usually be replaced by a Luftwaffe letter/number code some time after allocation to KG 40. The obvious features of this late version include the big HDL 151 forward turret, the enlarged ventral gondola and FuG 200 Hohentwiel search radar. By 1944, the Fw 200 was far from being the 'scourge of the Atlantic' described by Winston Churchill, but was a lumbering leviathan, vulnerable to patrolling fighters or even to Allied maritime reconnaissance aircraft. When KG 40 mounted its first operation with the new Hs 293A missile, it was cut short when the missile-carrying Condor was forced down by an RAF Sunderland. When the invasion of France closed its bases, KG 40 got rid of most of its aircraft, one Staffel surviving and transferring to Norway and another withdrawing to Germany. Most of the unit's surviving Condors were simply passed to transport units, where attrition proved astonishingly rapid.

Focke-Wulf Fw 200 Condor

Above: Though of smaller calibre than the 20-mm MG FF cannon it often replaced, the 15-mm MG 151 belt-fed cannon had a higher muzzle velocity and greater range.

Above: Crews of I Gruppe of KG 40 parade for inspection in front of their Fw 200C-3 Condors. This Gruppe was the only exponent of the Condor over the Atlantic during its heyday.

Above: KG 40's aircraft often wore the unit's circled globe badge, which harked back to the days of peacetime when the Fw 200 promised to revolutionise air transport.

Above: In addition to its maritime role, the Fw 200 also undertook limited transport service in the military emergencies during the middle and final periods of the war.

based at Cognac and Bordeaux-Mérignac, respectively, and once again the Condor began to appear in numbers.

Production of the Condor continued throughout 1943, 76 aircraft being delivered in that year. This total included a number of **Fw 200C-8** machines built specifically as carriers for the Henschel Hs 293A missile. Before the delivery of the Fw 200C-8s late in 1943, a small number of Fw 200C-3/U1 and Fw 200C-3/U2 machines had been adapted to carry the Hs 293A, these being known after modification as **Fw 200C-6** aircraft. Equipped with the FuG 203b Kehl III transmitter for use with the FuG 230b Strassburg receiver of the Hs 293, the Fw 200C-6 carried a pair of these missiles on special carriers beneath the outboard engine nacelles. The Fw 200C-6 was used operationally by III/KG 40 for the first time on 28 December 1943, when one of four of the Gruppe's Condors, engaged in a search for British naval units, carried two Hs 293A missiles. In the event, the operation was abortive, as the Hs 293-carrying Condor encountered a patrolling Short Sunderland before it could make contact with the British vessels, and was forced down with the missiles still unlaunched.

The last few production Condors were Fw 200C-8s, those examples intended specifically for the Hs 293-launching role having deeper outboard engine nacelles and a forward-extended ventral gondola. The last eight aircraft were completed in January and February 1944, but by that time the Condor's days as an anti-shipping aircraft were numbered, and with the loss of KG 40's bases on the Biscay coast one of the surviving III/KG 40 Staffeln was transferred to Norway and the other withdrawn to Germany.

From mid-1944, the Fw 200 was employed increasingly and not inappropriately in the transport role role for which it had been originally designed. Two special transport versions of the Condor had, in fact, been built in 1942, these being the **Fw 200C-4/U1** (Werk Nr 137) and **Fw 200C-4/U2** (Werk Nr 138) featuring an abbreviated ventral gondola, an Fw 19 forward upper turret and a generally similar Fw 20

Below: The FuG 200 Hohentwiel radar provided the Fw 200C with a limited maritime search and blind-bombing capability, but the drag of the antenna array had an adverse effect on performance.

Above: Operating in the more turbulent lower regions of the atmosphere, and at times having to undertake violent manoeuvres, the Fw 200C's airframe suffered fatiguing stresses.

The first Fw 200s to be see front-line service were the Fw 200Bs taken over in March 1940 to serve with KGr.z.b.V. 105. This unit employed Condors for the duration of the campaign in Norway to ferry troops and supplies.

Focke-Wulf Fw 200 Condor

Right: Posed in front of 'their' Condor, which already has its propellers turning, these KG 40 crewmen review their charts before leaving Bordeaux-Mérignac on another long maritime patrol.

aft dorsal turret, both mounting a single 7.9-mm (0.31-in) MG 15 machine-gun, and similar weapons in the nose and tail of the gondola. The two aircraft differed solely in seating arrangements, the Fw 200C-4/U1 providing accommodation for 11 passengers and the Fw 200C-4/U2 accommodating 14. After the disbanding of KG 40 in the autumn of 1944, 8./KG 40 was redesignated Transportstaffel Condor in October, flying from Gardermoen in Norway until the end of the war. Three ex-KG 40 Condors were passed to Transportstaffel 5 in 1944, this unit subsequently being absorbed into 14./Transportgeschwader 4.

Operational methods

Reference has already been made to the vulnerability of the Condor owing to its lack of armour and the fact that all fuel lines were on the aircraft's underside and, as the danger of interception by Bristol Beaufighter and de Havilland Mosquito long-range fighters increased, the most northerly point to which Biscay-based Condors flew was 40 degrees N, there thus being no longer any link between the Biscay area and the northern waters patrolled by the Norwegian-based Condor Gruppe by 1942. There were two main areas of armed reconnaissance patrol operated by III/KG 40 Condors

based at Cognac and Bordeaux-Mérignac, one known as the kleine Aufklärung (limited reconnaissance) and the other as the grosse Aufklärung (extended reconnaissance). The dividing line between the two reconnaissance areas was approximately 45 degrees, the smaller extending to the limit already mentioned, and the larger to approximately 34 degrees N. The westerly limit of both areas was normally 19 degrees W, although on special reconnaissance missions Condors reached as far as 25 degrees W.

When approaching the northerly reconnaissance area, the Condors normally flew in formation at sea level for mutual protection, breaking up and proceeding singly on their shipping search at 11 degrees W. Sometimes Condors en route to this area had to make a detour as far south as Cap Ortegal to avoid patrolling fighters. One method of shipping search frequently adopted was known as the Fächer (fan). A typical search of this type in a southerly direction, starting from 15 degrees W, was to fly due west for 3 degrees, due south for 30 miles, due east for 3 degrees, due south for 50 km (31 miles), and so on until the allotted area had been covered.

With the Condors' return from emergency transport operations in the USSR and Italy in the spring of 1943, III/KG 40 operating from Cognac and Bordeaux-Mérignac discon-

Above: The Fw 200C-3/U2 introduced the Lotfe 7D bomb sight in the nose of the ventral gondola.

Above: Seen on the compass-swinging turntable, this was an Fw 200C-3, which introduced some structural strengthening.

The Fw 200's final armed version was intended for the anti-ship role with two Hs 293A rocket-boosted air-to-surface missiles carried under the outboard engine nacelles.

Condors were not particularly agile or sturdy, and were easy targets for the Allied fighters that prowled over the Bay of Biscay and Western Approaches during the later stages of the war.

Focke-Wulf Fw 200 Condor

Above: The Fw 200C seldom carried its maximum bomb load, but a typical fit included two pairs of 250-kg (551-lb) SC 250 bombs under and alongside the nacelles for the outboard engines.

Left: Though the weight of military equipment reduced the Condor's range, the aircraft nonetheless retained good over-water endurance. Shown here is an Fw 200C-3.

Left below: With the encircled globe emblem of I/KG 40 under the flight deck, this Fw 200C is being refuelled from an airfield bowser in preparation for another long-endurance mission.

Left and below: This was the fate that befell a number of Condors after months of punishing low-level flying and violent manoeuvres when avoiding Flak and/or fighters. The type's airframe was never adequately strengthened, an 'Achilles heel' becoming apparent in the rear spar of the mainplane. This proved liable to catastrophic failure, resulting in broken back (left) or a wing failure (below) on landing.

Above: This Fw 200C-3/U1, with a heater unfreezing its starboard inner engine, has been 'bombed up' with SC 250 bombs. This was probably during the two-month Stalingrad operation in early 1943.

Right: Part of the Fw 200C's structural problem stemmed not just from the addition of armament, but also of the weight of the electrical and electronic gear it had to carry.

Right below: The pilot of an Fw 200C signals from the flight deck. The availability of a co-pilot to back the pilot was essential on long-endurance missions where one pilot might become very fatigued and lose vital concentration.

Above left: The Fw 200 proved its worth in the transport role, with crews from 1. and 3./KG 40 transferring from France to the Eastern Front to support the beleaguered garrison at Stalingrad during January/February 1943, operating under the unit designation K.Gr.z.b.V.200. The Gruppe had 21 aircraft allocated, around half from I/KG 40 and the remainder from IV(Erg.)/KG 40, the Geschwader's Châteaudun-based training organisation.

This Fw 200C-1 (F8+AH) of I/KG 40, IV Fliegerkorps, Luftflotte 3, was based at Bordeaux-Mérignac, France, in 1940. This particular aircraft was flown by Major Edgar Petersen, Gruppenkommandeur of I/KG 40 and architect of much of the Condor's considerable success against British shipping during its first months of maritime operations. In April 1941 Petersen was promoted to command the entire Geschwader.

tinued its previous practice of flying routine reconnaissance in search of shipping targets; these duties were taken over by Ju 290As of FaGr. 5 at Mont-de-Marsan. In concert with the He 177s of II/KG 40 and the similarly-equipped 1. and 3. Staffeln of I/KG 40, the Fw 200s became solely concerned with shipping attack, being sent on a sortie only when a definite target had been sighted and its position reported.

The departures of Allied convoys from Gibraltar were regularly reported from Spain, and the time of arrival of the convoy in KG 40's sphere of operations could therefore be calculated, and it only remained for FAGr. 5 to establish the exact position of the convoy and weather conditions in the area before the Condors and He 177s took off. The only exception to this new policy was when the total effort of all aircraft in the Biscay area was demanded by the Fliegerführer Atlantik, such as when German blockade runners were attempting to make port. On such occasions the Condors reverted to armed reconnaissance to report the presence of any Allied warships in the area.

When Allied shipping was reported, a minimum of four Condors would take off to attack, the aircraft usually flying at sea level in close formation to a point such as Cap Ortegal before fanning out and flying on parallel courses at intervals of 40-50 km (25-30 miles). Each would periodically climb to 450 m (1,475 m) in a wide circle, making a search with its Hohentwiel, after which the original course was resumed. The first Condor to sight the shipping would then make R/T contact with the other aircraft. Low-level attack in conditions

of clear visibility was expressly forbidden, a minimum attacking altitude of 2750 m (9,020 ft) being prescribed.

Whereas the aircraft based in the Biscay area were concerned with shipping attack, the Condors based at Trondheim-Vaernes were engaged almost entirely on unarmed reconnaissance, shipping sightings merely being reported back to base, and bombing attacks were not normally performed by Condors in northern waters. A typical patrol called for a direct course to the north-east coast of Iceland and Jan Mayen Island before returning to base, or to the northern coast of Iceland and thence to a point some 65 km (40 miles) from the coast of Greenland before returning. The normal daily effort from Trondheim-Vaernes was only one aircraft.

As a warplane the Condor was not a particularly outstanding machine, but in view of the relatively small number of Condors available for operations at any one time it established a formidable record in the two years during which it could truly be referred to as the 'scourge of the Atlantic'.

Below: The rudder of an Fw 200C carries KG 40's equivalent of fighter 'ace' markings. The symbols indicated the Allied vessels (and their tonnages) that the aircraft had sunk.

Focke-Wulf Fw 200C-3/U4 specification

Type: seven-seat long-range maritime reconnaissance bomber
Powerplant: four BMW-Bramo 323R-2 Fafnir air-cooled nine-cylinder radial engines each rated at 895 kW (1,200 hp) for take-off with methanol-water injection, 746 kW (1,000 hp) at sea level and 701 kW (940 hp) at 4000 m (13,125 ft)
Performance: maximum speed 360 km/h (224 mph) at 4800 m (15,750 ft), 305 km/h (190 mph) at sea level; maximum cruising speed 335 km/h (208 mph) at 4000 m (13,125 ft), 275 km/h (171 mph) at sea level; economical cruising speed 255 km/h (158 mph) at optimum altitude; service ceiling 5800 m (19,030 ft); range at economical cruising speed with 7880 litres (1,733 Imp gals) of fuel 3555 km (2,209 miles), or with 9955 litres (2,190 Imp gal) of fuel 4440 km (2,760 miles)
Weights: empty 12950 kg (28,550 lb); maximum loaded 22700 kg (50,044 lb)
Dimensions: wingspan 32.85 m (107 ft 9½ in); length 23.45 m (76 ft 11½ in); height 6.30 m (20 ft 8 in); wing area 119.85 m² (1,290.10 sq ft)
Armament: (defensive) one 7.9-mm (0.31-in) MG 15 machine-gun with 1,000 rounds in hydraulically operated Fw 19 forward dorsal turret, one 13-mm (0.51-in) MG 131 trainable machine-gun with 500 rounds in aft dorsal position, two 13-mm (0.51-in) MG 131 machine-guns with 300 r.p.g. firing from aft beam hatches, one 20-mm trainable MG 151 cannon with 500 rounds in forward ventral position, and one 7.9-mm (0.31-in) MG 15 trainable machine-gun with 1,000 rounds in aft ventral position; (offensive) maximum bomb load 2100 kg (4,630 lb) comprising two 500-kg (1,102-lb), two 250-kg (551-lb) and 12 50-kg (110-lb) bombs

Focke-Wulf Ta 152

Germany's aircraft industry lagged far behind the Allies in developing a viable high-altitude fighter, too much emphasis originally being laid on offensive, low- to medium-level operations. Attempts to put this right led, too late in the day, to one of the finest of Germany's fighters, the high-altitude Ta 152H series.

Development of a viable high-altitude fighter for the Luftwaffe only became a high priority when Allied bombing missions from high level over the Third Reich (RAF by night and US Air Force by day) began to assume significant proportions – despite the protestations of many in the German aircraft industry, including Kurt Tank, that more resources and urgency should have been placed earlier into creating viable high-altitude fighters.

The story of the **Ta 152** started during 1942, when Focke-Wulf's designers were looking at many ways to increase the Fw 190's performance at higher altitudes. A number of possible ideas arose, the most important of them being designated by the company between **Ra-1** and **Ra-6**. Some of these proposals were for comparatively straightforward developments of the Fw 190 layout with different powerplants, but significantly there were also concepts in which the Fw 190 was only the basis on which a considerable amount of new design work was arranged.

This included the possibility of a completely new, long-span wing of high aspect ratio that would tackle the aerodynamics required for a high-altitude Fw 190 derivative. Focke-Wulf presented a number of these proposals to the RLM's Technisches Amt in May 1943. It was soon recognised that these concepts would form the basis of what was essentially a new aircraft type, and the sum of the Focke-Wulf recommendations received the RLM's numbering **8-152** during August 1943, with Tank's name being brought into the designation to give Ta 152. Eventually the Ta 152 designation came to include several distinct types – the **Ta 152A** and **Ta 152B** fighters, the **Ta 152C** fighter-bomber, and the **Ta 152H** high-altitude fighter, in addition to several more related developments.

Above: The Ta 152C series was powered by the DB 603, with supercharger intake on the port side, as seen here. The Ta 152H had the Jumo 213, with the intake on the opposite side.

The fifth pre-production Ta 152H-0 was Werk Nr 150005 (CW+CE), seen here having its compass 'swung' at Cottbus where it was built. Well over sixty years after the end of World War II it is still not clear exactly how many pre-production/production Ta 152Hs were actually built. So far 43 Werk Nummern have been identified, and no evidence has come to light to increase this total.

Ta 152A and B-series

Two distinct models of the fighter/heavy fighter Ta 152 for low- to medium-level operations were planned, the Ta 152A fighter and the Ta 152B heavy fighter (particularly in its **Ta 152B-5** version). The Ta 152A would have been a standard fighter for low-level to medium-level operations but with enhanced features over the Fw 190D-9 series then also being developed. Otherwise, the Ta 152A was to have been a comparatively straightforward adaptation of the Fw 190A airframe, but with the installation of a Junkers Jumo 213C inline engine (with GM 1 nitrous-oxide to provide additional engine boost at higher levels), and the adoption of an MK 108 30-mm cannon centrally mounted to fire through the propeller hub with 85 or 90 rounds. Two MG 151/20 20-mm cannons were to be fitted in the upper fuselage over the engine with 150 rounds each, plus one of these weapons in each wing root, with 175 rounds each.

There was also to be hydraulic actuation for the undercarriage and flaps instead of the production Fw 190's electric system, with the main undercarriage repositioned slightly further outboard. The fuselage length was increased due to the new engine, the wing was slightly repositioned, and a necessary increase in the rear fuselage length to maintain the centre of gravity was introduced, together with an increased-area vertical tail, making the fuselage length of the Ta 152A 10.78 m (35 ft 4½ in ft). The existing wing span of the Fw 190A series of 10.50 m (34 ft 5½ in) was increased by the installation of a 50-cm (19.7-in) extra section in the centre of the wing assembly, increasing the wing span of the planned Ta 152A to 11.00 m (36 ft 1 in).

Three prototypes were converted from early Fw 190A-0 pre-production development aircraft as the **Fw 190 V19**, **Fw 190 V20**, and **Fw 190 V21**. Conversion work was carried out at Focke-Wulf's Adelheide experimental facility near to the company's main plant at Bremen. The first to fly was the Fw 190 V19, Werk Nr 0041, on 7 July 1943. A rival to the Ta 152A was the Messerschmitt Me 209, but the RLM's hesitation and bad decision-making eventually led to the Ta 152A (and Me 209) being dropped.

The Ta 152B would have been similar in concept to the Ta 152A but powered by the Jumo 213E inline engine, and in its Ta 152B-5 form it could have formed the basis for a Zerstörer replacement for the Messerschmitt Me 410. Some development work on the armament for the Ta 152B series was carried out with the **Fw 190 V53** (Werk Nr 170003, DU+JC), including 30-mm MK 103 cannons in the wing roots, but the Ta 152B, too, was dropped by the RLM.

Kurt Tank poses in the cockpit of an Fw 190. Tank was a talented designer and engineer but was also a highly competent pilot. He often flew examples of Focke-Wulf aircraft, including the Ta 152. As a mark of respect to Tank, the German authorities allowed the Ta 152 to bear his initials in its designation, even though he remained a Focke-Wulf employee throughout the war.

Ta 152C series

The medium-level Ta 152C fighter-bomber was to have many of the changes that were pioneered and incorporated into the Ta 152A and Ta 152B – including the fuselage extension work, increased wing span, main undercarriage modifications and increased-area fin, and hydraulic undercarriage and flap actuation. It was planned to construct the wing as a two-piece structure, separated along the centreline and with large flanges attached above and below the forward wing spar to hold the structure together, rather than the Fw 190's one-piece wing main assembly.

To begin with, the Ta 152C-series was intended to be powered by the DB 603E of some 1,750 hp (1305 kW) for take-off, but it was hoped to introduce the DB 603LA during Ta 152C-1 manufacture. This engine would have MW 50 boost (which was actually used for cooling hot air from the DB 603LA's two-stage supercharger – it must be stressed that there was no intention to fit an exhaust-driven turbo-supercharger, the DB 603L-series were normally aspirated liquid-cooled engines with superchargers that used air).

Later it was hoped that the war situation would allow the DB 603L to be introduced into Ta 152C production, this engine differing from the DB 603LA by having a special cooler (intercooler) for the heated supercharger air and therefore not requiring the MW 50 system for cooling the air that

At the heart of the Ta 152 lay the basic structure of the proven Fw 190, but it had been so radically modified that it was essentially a new machine. The wings were new, the fuselage was lengthened and the tail surfaces modified. In its Ta 152H form, as seen here, the aircraft was potentially a match for the P-51D Mustang escorts that 'ruled the roost' at the high altitudes at which the USAAF heavy bombers routinely operated. However, the few Ta 152Hs that saw service only rarely tackled the bomber streams.

One of the best known of all the Ta 152 aircraft was the much-photographed Ta 152 V7 Werk Nr 110007 (CI+XM). This aircraft was one of the development prototypes for the planned Ta 152C series, in a configuration roughly equating to the bad-weather Ta 152C-0/R11. It first flew in January 1945 and was a new-build aircraft rather than a conversion of an Fw 190 airframe.

passed through the supercharger; the MW 50 could therefore be used purely for power boost of the engine's output, for example at take-off or in combat situations.

The DB 603L could develop 1,870 hp (1394 kW) for take-off, but with MW 50 boost it was estimated that this could be increased to 2,250 hp (1678 kW). The DB 603L-series engines were capable of being fitted with a centrally-firing 30-mm cannon in the so-called 'engine-mounted' configura-

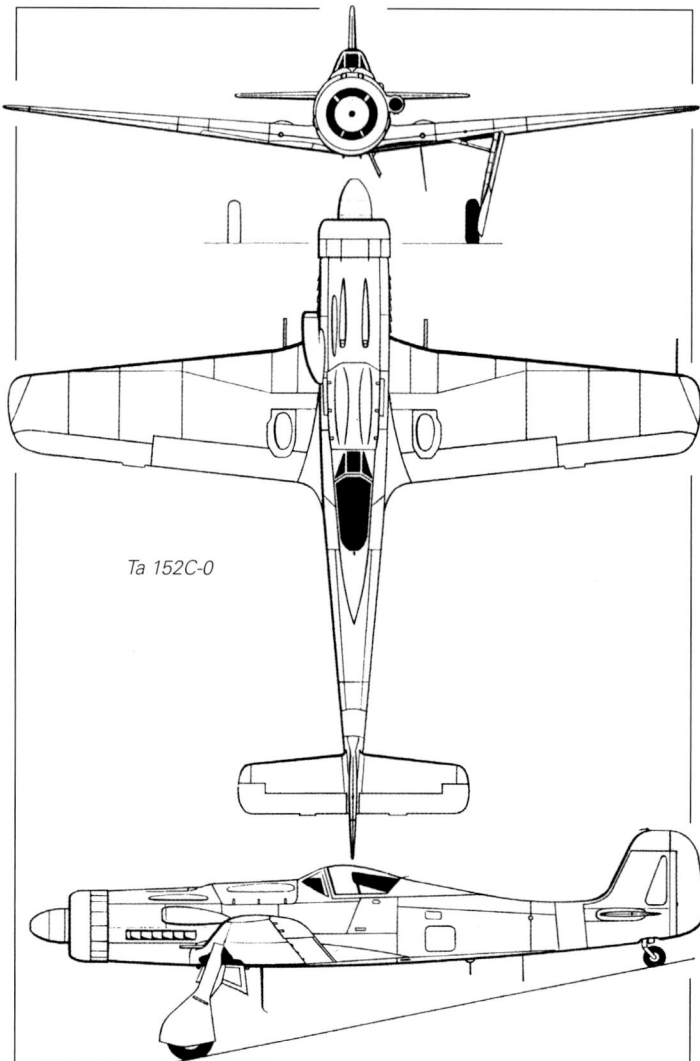

Ta 152C-0

tion. The **Ta 152C-0** pre-production, the **Ta 152C-1** early production aircraft, and the **Ta 152C-2** were planned to have an MK 108 30-mm cannon centrally-mounted to fire through the propeller shaft with 90 rounds, two MG 151/20 20-mm cannon in the upper fuselage over the engine with 150 rounds each, plus one of these weapons in each wing root with 175 rounds each. An ETC 503 weapons rack could also be fitted beneath the fuselage centreline of the Ta 152C series, able to carry bombs of up to 500 kg (1,102 lb), or a 300-litre (66-Imp gal) external fuel tank on a modified mounting.

Various equipment levels were planned for the Ta 152C family. Of these, the most important was the R11 or Rüstsatz 11, which was aimed at giving the Ta 152C a 'bad weather' capability. It included additional equipment such as a heated cockpit canopy, a FuG 125 'Hermine' ground-beacon receiver, which worked in conjunction with a FuG 16ZY radio to give the pilot direction-finding and homing information, and an LGW K23 or PKS 12 autopilot, and was intended to be included from the Ta 152C-0 onwards. The FuG 125/FuG 16ZY combination worked in conjunction with the 'Y' service network to give accurate location of the aircraft by ground-based controllers, who could then provide guidance information to the pilot, for example to find his airfield in bad weather conditions.

Several prototype/development aircraft were intended to pioneer the Ta 152C series. The first of them was one of the trials aircraft that had originally been used for development of the Ta 152A, the Fw 190 V21. Originally an Fw 190A-0 pre-production development aircraft, the Fw 190 V21 (Werk Nr 0043, TI+IH), had first flown on 13 March 1944 in Ta 152A trials configuration after being converted from its original Fw 190 layout. For the Ta 152C programme, it was now intended to be used to pioneer the installation of the DB 603 inline engine in the Ta 152 airframe. For this purpose it was re-built again, where it was initially fitted with a DB 603E engine. It was therefore the first Ta 152-comparable aircraft to have this power plant installed. In its new guise it was re-designated as the **Fw 190 V21/U1**.

On 3 November 1944 Bernhard Märschel took the Fw 190 V21/U1 up on its maiden flight under DB 603E power. As for new-build development aircraft for the Ta 152C series, Focke-Wulf intended no fewer than 16 prototype aircraft to be built at Sorau. They were to be part of a consignment of 26 Ta 152 development aircraft that were planned in the

The Ta 152 V7 was built at Sorau and was the second of three Ta 152C development aircraft to fly. Despite plans for the large-scale production of this version, the numerous problems faced by the German industry at the beginning of 1945, particularly the supply of DB 603L engines, prevented any from being completed.

summer of 1944. Eventually, most of the planned Ta 152C prototype/development aircraft were cancelled or were not completed. Nevertheless, three of the planned Sorau-built aircraft did fly. They were the **Ta 152 V6**, **V7** and **V8**, while several others, including the **Ta 152 V16**, **V17**, **V19**, **V20** and the **V21**, appear not to have been completed before the Sorau plant was taken out of the war due to the advance of Soviet forces.

Ta 152 V6 (Werk Nr 110006, VH+EY) was the first to fly, with test pilot Bernhard Märschel at the controls, on 12 December 1944. The aircraft was powered by a DB 603EC development engine, and successfully carried out some of the initial performance and system testing for the Ta 152C series. It was armed with MG 151/20 cannon in the upper forward fuselage and wing roots, and roughly approximated to the planned Ta 152C-0 pre-production series. A creditable maximum speed of 687 km/h (427 mph) was achieved at approximately 7620 m (25,000 ft) with MW 50 boost.

Next to fly was the Ta 152 V7 (Werk Nr 110007, CI+XM), which took to the air in the hands of Märschel in January 1945. It approximated to **Ta 152C-0/R11** standard due to its fit of 'bad weather' equipment under the R11 label, was armed like the Ta 152 V6, and was similarly powered by a DB 603EC engine. The final example of the three new-build Ta 152C development aircraft to fly was the Ta 152 V8 (Werk Nr 110008, GW+QA), on 15 January 1945. Also powered by a DB 603EC engine and armed in similar fashion to the Ta 152 V6 and V7, it was equipped with an advanced lead-computing EZ 42 gunsight.

With the DB 603-series engine installed, the Ta 152C in development or production form would have had a fuselage length of 10.80 m (35 ft 5¼ in), and the same wing span as the planned Ta 152A and Ta 152B series of 11.00 m (36 ft 1 in)

The Ta 152 V7 Werk Nr 110007 (CI+XM) runs up its engine in the snow of early 1945. Note the heavy exhaust staining on the left-hand fuselage, while the flaking of the light blue-grey paint on the lower engine cowling is also very visible. This aircraft approximated to Ta 152C-0/R11 standard due to its fit of 'bad weather' equipment, and was powered by a DB 603E-series development inline engine.

span, and area of 19.50 m² (209.89 sq ft). The projected combat take-off weight for fighter-bomber missions of the initial Ta 152C production aircraft was up to 5500 kg (12,125 lb), although this could have been increased with MW 50 boost. A maximum altitude of some 12200 m (40,000 ft) was hoped for, but most of the type's missions would have been flown at considerably less than that height. The Ta 152C series was unpressurised due to its planned mission profiles, but the type was intended to have a considerable amount of armour fitted for engine, radiator and pilot.

Unlike the Ta 152A, there was never any doubt about the production potential of the Ta 152C. It was an aircraft that the Luftwaffe badly wanted, and the RLM was intending for production to go ahead in the early months of 1945. Several production plants and various companies were earmarked to manufacture the Ta 152C, in what would have been a major manufacturing effort if the war had continued into

Intended for the fighter-bomber role, the Ta 152C embodied a number of major improvements over the Fw 190. Although at first glance the wing appeared similar, it was, in fact, slightly extended in span and repositioned. The characteristic lengthened rear fuselage was introduced to maintain the centre of gravity.

Focke-Wulf Ta 152

Above and left: The Fw 190 V30, Werk Nr 0055 (GH+KT), was rebuilt as the Fw 190 V30/U1 with the long-span wing configuration intended for the Ta 152H-series. It was actually the second Ta 152H-like aircraft to fly, but it crashed on 23 August 1944, killing Focke-Wulf test pilot Alfred Thomas. Focke-Wulf modified five Fw 190s to this standard, with Jumo 213E engines and most of the Ta 152 modifications, but lacking GM 1 boost.

1946. The general war situation, however, precluded any of these companies from participating in Ta 152C construction. A further problem was the difficulty that Daimler Benz encountered in developing and clearing for production the DB 603L-series engines that would have powered production aircraft, particularly the DB 603LA.

Advancing Allied forces discovered a treasure trove of Luftwaffe equipment and still-functioning aircraft factories as they pushed into Germany during the closing stages of the war. At the time it appeared that one of the German aircraft types that had been discovered in production form by the Allies was the Ta 152C. However, there remains to this day much controversy as to whether the Ta 152C ever really entered production. As for military service, the Ta 152 V8 was seconded to Rechlin for preliminary military testing in February 1945. There it appears to have been delegated to the 'Jagdstaffel Roggentin' and could be the only Ta 152C-type aircraft to see any kind of front-line military service. Indeed, it might well have been one of the test aircraft that found their way into the inventory of the Stab (headquarters) unit of the fighter wing JG 11 at Neustadt-Glewe in the closing weeks or days of the war.

Ta 152C-1/R11 specification (manufacturer's estimate)
Type: single-seat medium-altitude fighter and fighter-bomber
Powerplant: one Daimler-Benz DB 603LA 12-cylinder liquid-cooled engine rated at 1567 kW (2,100 hp), or 1716 kW (2,300 hp) with MW 50 for take-off, and 1305 kW (1,750 hp) at 9000 m (29,530 ft), or 1417 kW (1,900 hp) at 8400 m (27,560 ft) with MW 50).
Performance: maximum speed 542 km/h (337 mph) at sea level or 573 km/h (356 mph) with MW 50, 702 km/h (436 mph) at 11500 m (37,730 ft) or 740 km/h (460 mph) at 10000 m (32,810 ft) with MW 50; initial climb rate 930 m (3,050 ft) per minute; service ceiling 12300 m (40,350 ft)
Weights: empty equipped 4014 kg (8,849 lb); normal loaded 4834 kg (10,658 lb); maximum 5322 kg (11,733 lb)
Dimensions: wingspan 11.00 m (36 ft 1 in); length 10.83 m (35 ft 6½ in); height 3.38 m (11 ft 1 in); wing area 19.50 m² (209.89 sq ft)
Armament: one engine-mounted 30-mm MK 108 cannon with 90 rounds, two fuselage-mounted 20-mm MG 151 cannon with 150 r.p.g., and two wing-mounted 20-mm MG 151 cannon with 175 r.p.g.

High-altitude fighter developments

Amongst the different proposed versions of Ta 152, the one that definitely did enter production – and front-line service – was the high-altitude Ta 152H. With the possibility of US heavy bombers attacking targets in Germany from upwards of 9000 m (29,528 ft) and escorted by growing numbers of fighters, it became increasingly obvious to Focke-Wulf that a radical solution was needed to turn the Fw 190 into a genuine high-altitude fighter.

Initially, in the Höhenjäger 1 concept, several converted Fw 190As were used as development airframes (including Fw 190A-3s Werk Nummern 0528, 0531 and 0532). These were originally standard, armed A-3s seconded to the Höhenjäger 1 programme, and modified, most noticeably, with a new, larger volume air intakes on the side of

Werk Nummer 150005 was one of a 20-aircraft pre-production Ta 152H-0 batch built at Cottbus. Some of them saw action with III/JG 301.

Jagdgeschwader 301 was the main front-line operator of the Ta 152H, the type initially serving with III Gruppe before being allocated to the Geschwaderstab. JG 301 wore yellow/red Defence of the Reich fuselage bands.

the engine cowlings to increase airflow into the BMW 801's supercharger, thus raising output at higher altitudes. However, BMW's attempts to make a viable high-altitude version of the BMW 801 proved largely fruitless, even though testing took place with these aircraft around September 1942. Focke-Wulf then developed derivatives of the Fw 190 for higher-altitude combat as the Fw 190B and Fw 190C. Parallel with these was a stop-gap programme that involved re-engining the Fw 190 with the inline Jumo 213. The series-produced and combat-proven medium to high-level Fw 190D-9 was a result of this line of development.

The Höhenjäger 2 programme, involving the use of the Jumo 213 and other inline engines, also eventually bore fruit in the high-altitude version of the Ta 152 series, designated the Ta 152H. As a part of the large Höhenjäger 2 concept, by the end of 1942 at least one Fw 190, the V17 (Werk Nr 0039, CF+OX), was flying with a Jumo 213 installed as the first prototype for the Jumo 213-engined Fw 190.

Ta 152H series

The Jumo 213-powered Ta 152H was a true high-altitude fighter, and was developed against the backdrop of another failed fighter project, the planned high-altitude Messerschmitt Bf 109H. Many of the changes that were pioneered and incorporated into the Ta 152A, Ta 152B and Ta 152C were also intended for the Ta 152H – including the fuselage extension work, main undercarriage modifications and increased-area vertical tail, and hydraulic undercarriage and flap actuation, referred to earlier. There was pressurisation in the cockpit for the pilot, necessitating a specially-built and sealed cockpit structure and glazing for this version.

The Ta 152H's wing was of increased span and high aspect ratio. The new wing spanned 14.44 m (47 ft 4½ in) and had an area of 23.30 m² (250.80 sq ft). This compared with the 11.00 m (36 ft 1 in) span and 19.50 m² (209.89 sq ft) wing of the Ta 152C, which itself was increased from the standard Fw 190A's wing. Due to its size and to allow it to be repaired comparatively easily if damaged, it had to be made in two sections, left-hand wing and right-hand wing, joined along the centreline. Early production wings were built without the provision for internal fuel tanks.

The production-standard Ta 152H, however, would have six fuel cells, three in each wing, of 470 litres. Basically an all-metal structure with fabric-covered ailerons, the wing was normally a two-spar structure with conventional wing ribs, but constructed in two halves (top and bottom) and then joined to make the complete but complex structure. The Ta 152H's Jumo 213E allowed increased power in comparison to the Jumo 213A. It could also be fitted with an 'engine-mounted' cannon firing through the propeller shaft, which the Jumo 213A could not. The Jumo 213E delivered 1,730 hp (1290 kW) for take-off but could be boosted by MW 50 for take-off and low to medium-level operations, and by GM 1 for high-altitude performance.

The supercharger employed air and was not an exhaust-driven turbo-supercharger – which was true for all production versions of the Fw 190 and Ta 152. A maximum speed of 755 km/h (469 mph) was envisaged with GM 1 boost at 12500 m (41,010 ft) by the production-standard Ta 152H-1. A Junkers VS 9 three-blade variable-pitch propeller unit of 3.60 m (11 ft 9¾ in) diameter was usually fitted. As with the Ta 152C, a number of equipment levels were planned for the Ta 152H. Again, the most important was the R11 or Rüstsatz 11 to give the Ta 152H a 'bad weather' capability. It included much of the equipment that would have made up the R11 equipment levels in the Ta 152C series, plus an EZ 42 gunsight, although it appears that most production Ta 152Hs were equipped with the older but well-known and reliable Revi 16B gunsight. An FuG 25a IFF set was also intended as standard.

This is the nose of the National Air and Space Museum's Ta 152H-0 in the United States, showing the neatly-cowled Junkers Jumo 213E inline engine installation with its annular radiator at the front that gave the impression that the aircraft type was radial-engined. Also visible are the prominent cooling gills at the rear of the engine cowling and the arrangement of the six exhaust outlets. Although at first glance the colouring and camouflage on this stored, museum aircraft appears to be authentic, in reality it was re-sprayed after capture and its current overall finish, particularly on the upper surfaces, is not authentic.

The open cowling of the NASM's Ta 152H-0 reveals the installation of the Junkers Jumo 213E inline engine. Particularly noteworthy are the engine bearer details and exhaust outlets. The large hinged engine cowling panels allowed generous access for the ground crews when opened.

STÉPÁNEK P.

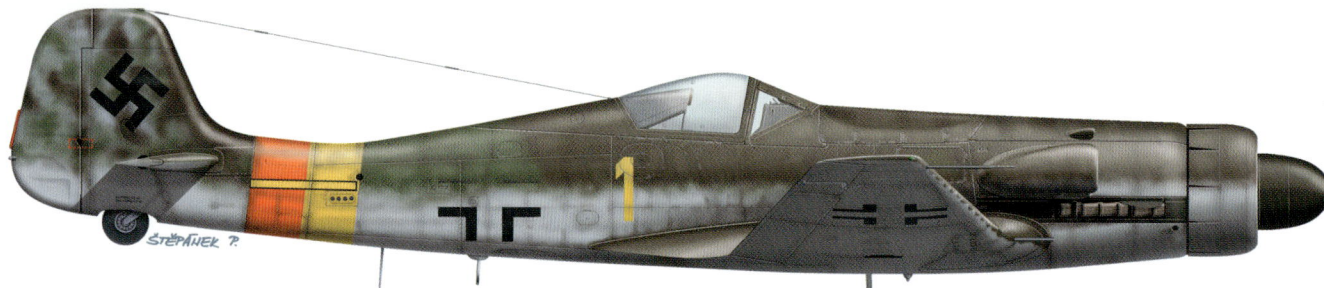

Focke-Wulf originally intended for a number of specially-built prototypes for the Ta 152H programme, which were to have been constructed at the Focke-Wulf plant at Sorau, but they were not built. Instead, Focke-Wulf converted a number of existing development aircraft to the developing Ta 152H layout. These were former Fw 190A-0 development and trials aircraft that had been converted to a variety of standards for the Höhenjäger 2 project. They were the **Fw 190 V18** (Werk Nr 0040, CF+OY), **Fw 190 V29** (Werk Nr 0054, GH+KS), **Fw 190 V30** (Werk Nr 0055, GH+KT), **Fw 190 V32** (Werk Nr 0057, GH+KV), and **Fw 190 V33** (Werk Nr 0058, GH+KW).

They all received some of the changes relating to the Ta 152A and Ta 152B described above. Such changes included the fuselage extension work, main undercarriage location modifications and increased-area fin. They were also fitted with the new long-span wing of 14.44 m (47 ft 4½ in) span planned for the Ta 152H. A pressurised cockpit was also

This Ta 152H served with the Stab/JG 301 from March 1945. The horizontal bar on the fuselage suggests allocation to the Geschwaderkommodore, Oberstleutnant Fritz Aufhammer.

installed, but they were unarmed and did not have the GM 1 boost system fitted. Two fuselage fuel tanks were to comprise 230 litres (50.6 Imp gal) forward and 292 litres (64.2 Imp gal) aft; they were situated in the lower fuselage partly beneath the cockpit as usual. The engine chosen was the Junkers Jumo 213E. The first of the converted trials aircraft to fly was the Fw 190 V33; newly converted at Adelheide and with the fresh designation **Fw 190 V33/U1**, it flew for the first time after conversion on 13 July 1944. This aircraft was therefore the first genuine Ta 152H prototype. Eventually, at least five of these converted 'prototype' aircraft flew, the final one in late January or early February 1945. The first meaningful testing at the Rechlin test centre for the planned Ta 152H took place in September 1944.

Manufacture of the **Ta 152H-0** pre-production aircraft commenced at Focke-Wulf's Cottbus facilities in eastern Germany in November 1944. This was well before proper testing had been completed for the H series. In the event, after

Ta 152H-0 Werk Nr 150003 is seen with a 300-litre (66-Imp gal) drop tank. This aircraft was tested at Rechlin by Erprobungskommando 152, and possibly went on to serve with the hastily assembled 'Jagdstaffel Ta 152' at nearby Roggentin airfield.

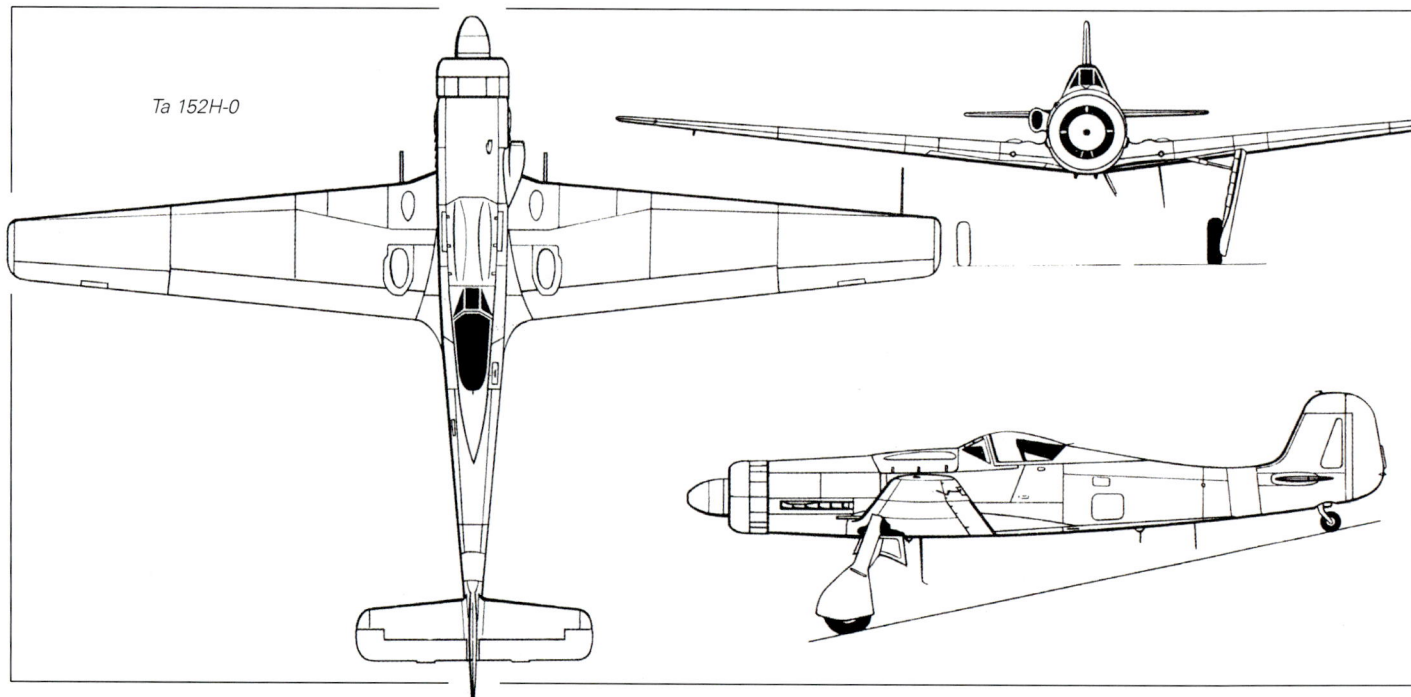

Ta 152H-0

Powerplant

The Ta 152H-1 was powered by the Jumo 213A engine. This version had a centrally mounted cannon, and could be boosted by the MW 50 water/methanol system at low altitude, or GM 1 nitrous oxide system at high altitude. Not all Ta 152H-1s were completed with these systems, however.

Focke-Wulf Ta 152H-1

Jagdgeschwader 301

It is likely that just 23 of the full production version of the high-altitude Ta 152H were built, and they served alongside pre-production Ta 152H-0s with JG 301 during the last desperate weeks of the Third Reich.

Camouflage

This Ta 152H is completed in a standard scheme comprising two-tone green (RLM 82 Lichtgrün and RLM 83 Dunkelgrün) splinter pattern upper surfaces and light blue (RLM 76 Lichtblau) undersides, with mottling blurring the demarcation between the two. At this very late stage of the war, schemes varied widely. RLM 75 Grauviolett (sometimes called Mittelgrau) could have been mixed with the two-tone greens. Similarly for undersides, a few aircraft had light grey, while others had some, or all of the underside left in natural metal.

Jagdgeschwader 301

JG 301 was formed in October 1943 as a home defence unit, initially equipped with the Bf 109G, which IV Gruppe flew until the war's end. In the second half of 1944 the three other Gruppen converted to the Fw 190A, with II and III Gruppe also receiving Fw 190Ds in early 1945. III Gruppe began the process of conversion to the Ta 152H in January 1945.

RV bands

At the end of 1944 17 of the Luftwaffe's Jagdgeschwadern were engaged on Reichsverteidigung (Defence of the Reich) duties. As a rapid means of providing visual identification during air battles aircraft were marked with Geschwader-specific fuselage bands, JG 301 using yellow and red.

Wings

The slender wings of the Ta 152H-1 were increased in span over those of the Fw 190 by around 4 m (13 ft), giving the type good performance and manoeuvrability at high altitude. Although based on a similar basic shape, they employed a new structure.

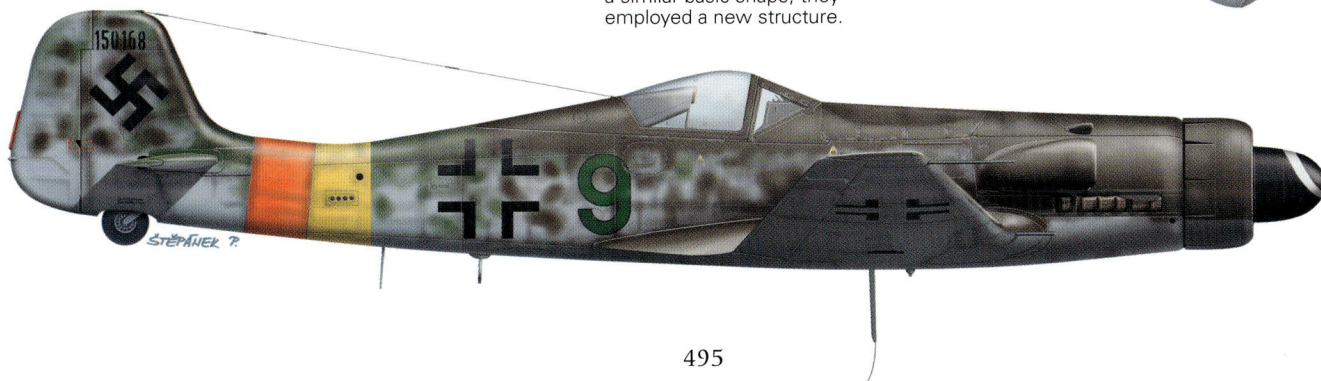

Focke-Wulf Ta 152

The port cockpit interior of the National Air and Space Museum (NASM) Ta 152H-0 shows the throttle lever with its characteristic yellow handle protruding upwards from the side console. Some restoration work was carried out on this aircraft in 1998, including work on the instrument panel and the addition of the wooden top decking to the side console just behind the throttle lever. The interior colour is predominantly black-grey

Focke-Wulf Ta 152H-1 cutaway key

1 Starboard navigation light
2 Pitot tube
3 Wing skinning
4 Aileron tab control linkage
5 Aileron tab
6 Starboard aileron
7 Aileron controls
8 Pitot tube heating
9 Wing lateral stringers
10 Flap controls
11 Flap panels
12 Flap actuating jack
13 Starboard wing fuel tanks (three bag-type)
14 Undercarriage indicator
15 Abbreviated steel front spar
16 Auxiliary intake
17 Supercharger air intake
18 Cooling louvres
19 Junkers three-blade wooden propeller
20 Spinner
21 Cannon port
22 Blast tube
23 Annular radiator
24 15-mm ring armour
25 Cooling gills
26 Starboard mainwheel
27 Exhaust stubs
28 Anti-vibration mounting pads
29 30-mm MK 108 cannon
30 Forged engine bearer
31 Engine accessories
32 Supercharger inlet trunk
33 Junkers Jumo 213E engine
34 Generator
35 No. 1 fuselage frame
36 Oil tank, capacity 72 litres (15.8 Imp gal)

37 Engine bearer/bulkhead attachment
38 Firewall
39 Engine bearer support member
40 Cannon shell ejector chute
41 Front spar carry-through
42 Front spar/fuselage attachment
43 Cannon ammunition box (90 rounds)
44 Cockpit forward pressure bulkhead (No. 1A fuselage frame)
45 Cannon retardation/ resistance mechanism
46 Instrument panel
47 Gunsight mounting
48 Control column
49 Rudder pedals

50 Underfloor control linkage
51 Floor support members
52 Cockpit floor (armoured)
53 Seat harness attachment
54 Pilot's seat (armoured)
55 Instrument panel shroud
56 Revi 16B gunsight
57 Armoured-glass windscreen
58 Starboard instrument console
59 Canopy rubber-tube pressurization
60 Rearward-sliding cockpit canopy
61 Headrest
62 20-mm head-armour
63 Turn-over bar and shroud
64 5-mm shoulder-armour (two-piece)
65 8-mm back-armour (two-piece)
66 Lead storage battery

67 Cut-out box
68 Dynamo
69 Cockpit rear pressure bulkhead (No. 8 fuselage frame)
70 FuG 125 navigation equipment (only in H-1/R11 all-weather variant)
71 Distributor
72 GM 1 tank, capacity 85 litres (18.7 Imp gal)
73 Tank armour (attached to No. 9 fuselage frame)
74 Radio bay access hatch
75 LGW-Siemens K 23 autopilot
76 FuG 16ZY radio transmitter receiver
77 No. 10 fuselage frame
78 Rudder control rod
79 Compressed air line
80 Master compass
81 Elevator control cables
82 No. 12 fuselage frame
83 Fuselage construction
84 AZA 10 signal cartridges (port and starboard)
85 Lift-hoist tube
86 Rudder rod/cable transition
87 Aerial lead-in and adaptor
88 Aerial
89 Cylindrical fuselage extension (frame Nos 14-1b)
90 Oxygen cylinder stowage shelf
91 Compressed air bottle for cannon operation, capacity 5

litres (1.1 Imp gal)
92 Elevator control quadrant
93 Fuselage/fin joint
94 Starboard tailplane
95 Elevator balance
96 Starboard elevator
97 Elevator tab
98 Fin construction

99 Tailwheel retraction cable
100 Rudder upper hinge
101 Rudder construction
102 Tailwheel leg retraction guide
103 Rudder hinge control
104 Rudder tab
105 Rear navigation light
106 Electric lead
107 Elevator torque tube
108 Tailwheel shock-absorber
109 Elevator tab
110 Elevator balance
111 Elevator construction
112 Semi-retractable tailwheel (380 x 150-mm)
113 Fin spar attachment
114 Antenna
115 DF loop
116 Retractable entry step
117 Spring-loaded hand/foothold
118 Rear fuselage fuel tank (protected), capacity 362 litres (80 Imp gal)
119 Rear spar/fuselage attachment
120 Forward fuselage fuel tank (protected), capacity 233 litres (51 Imp gal)
121 Wing gun breech fairing
122 Port MG 151/20 wing gun

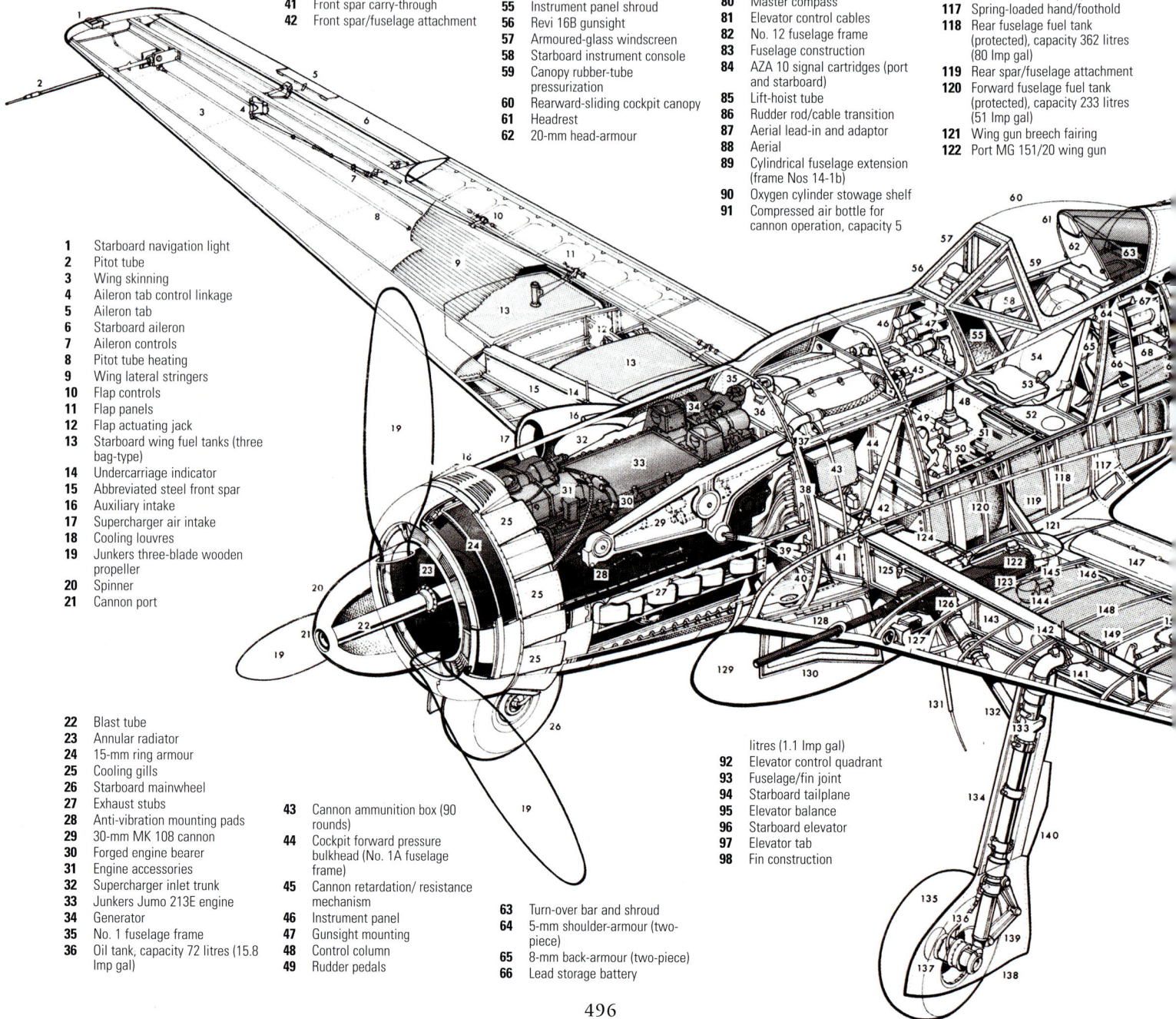

Focke-Wulf Ta 152

The third Ta 152H-0 pre-production aircraft was Werk Nr 150003 (CW+CC), and it is seen here at Cottbus (where it was built) just after completion. Note the wide-chord vertical tail, a distinctive recognition feature of the Ta 152 series, but one which was also used on some Fw 190D-9s and indeed on other late marks of Fw 190 as well. This particular aircraft initially flew on 3 December 1944 and was the first to be delivered to the Rechlin test centre for service trials. The trials were undertaken with some haste by Erprobungskommando Ta 152, commanded by Hauptmann Bruno Stolle, formerly the acting Gruppenkommandeur of I/JG 11.

123 Shell ejector chute
124 Port ammunition box (175 rounds)
125 Undercarriage retraction guide track
128 Gun barrel

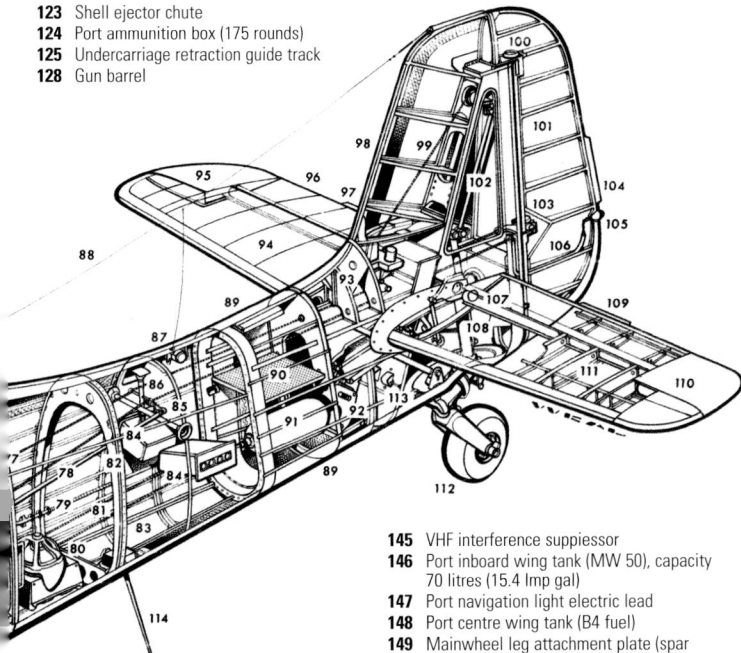

145 VHF interference suppiessor
146 Port inboard wing tank (MW 50), capacity 70 litres (15.4 Imp gal)
147 Port navigation light electric lead
148 Port centre wing tank (B4 fuel)
149 Mainwheel leg attachment plate (spar rear face)
150 Flap actuating jack
151 Port outboard wing tank (B4 fuel)
152 Flap structure
153 Wing lateral stringers
154 Wing rib stations
155 Wing skinning
156 Aileron tab control linkage
157 Aileron tab
158 Port aileron
159 Full span rear spar
160 Port navigation light

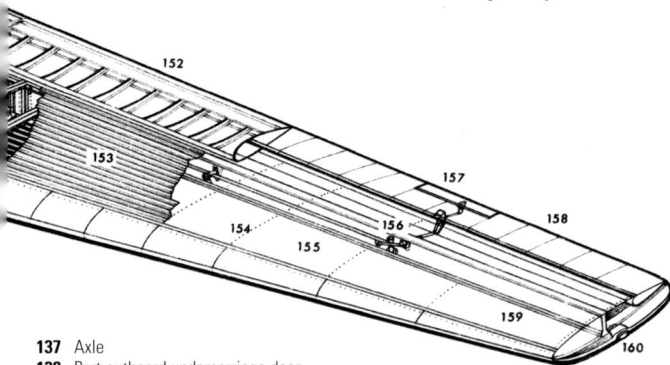

129 Auxiliary drop tank, capacity 300 litres (66 Imp gal)
130 Port inboard undercarriage floor
131 Ventral antenna
132 Undercarriage retraction strut
133 Towing lug (port and starboard legs)
134 Undercarriage leg
135 Port mainwheel (740 x 210-mm)
136 Brake cable

137 Axle
138 Port outboard undercarriage door
139 Shock-absorbers
140 Mainwheel leg fairing
141 Mainwheel leg pivot point
142 Undercarriage indicator
143 Abbreviated steel front spar
144 Fiml pump

all the delayed development work and lack of proper testing, production was carried out at Cottbus of only 43 known Ta 152H aircraft. They were Werk Nummern 150001-150020, and 150167-150169. This meagre total apparently comprised 20 Ta 152H-0 pre-production models and 23 **Ta 152H-1** production examples. It is possible that there were more, but no documentary proof has yet been found to substantiate this. It was intended that the Ta 152H-1 would have both GM 1 and MW 50 boost systems installed, but just how many of the 43 completed aircraft from the Cottbus assembly line had these systems fitted is impossible to verify. The Ta 152H-1 initial production version's armament comprised a synchronised 20-mm Mauser MG 151/20 cannon in each wing root with 175 rounds, and a 30-mm Rheinmetall-Borsig MK 108 cannon with 90 rounds 'engine-mounted' to fire centrally through the propeller spinner.

The first production aircraft to fly was Werk Nr 150001 (CW+CA), which flew at Cottbus with Hans Sander at the controls on 24 November 1944. Unfortunately, the quality of workmanship in the Focke-Wulf factories and at sub-contractors by that time was not of high standard, and production actually had to be halted for a time to sort out quality control issues. Several equipment levels were intended for the future production Ta 152Hs. The **Ta 152H-1/R21** was supposed to have the MW 50 boost system installed. Instability problems apparently precluded the use of the GM 1 high-altitude boost system until the **Ta 152H-1/R31** was introduced, which was apparently intended to be the first definite production version with both forms of boosting installed. Several factories were supposed to begin construction of the Ta 152H during 1945 in addition to Focke-Wulf's Cottbus facility, including Erla at Leipzig, but there is no evidence that any of them was able to start up production.

Reconnaissance and training roles

There was a planned photographic reconnaissance version of the Ta 152. Two separate roles were envisaged, namely high-level photography and low-level tactical photography. The latter would have been a replacement for the reconnaissance versions of the Bf 109 then still in service, including the tactical Bf 109G-8. This version would have been designated **Ta 152E-1**, powered by the Jumo 213E engine and based on the planned Ta 152B or powered by the DB 603L engine and based on the Ta 152C, with MW 50 boost available. Its wing span would have been 11.00 m (36 ft 1 in) like that of the Ta 152B and Ta 152C models. The high-altitude variant would have been the **Ta 152E-2**, later also referred to as the **Ta 152H-10**, based on the Ta 152H-1 airframe and general

Werk Nummer 150167 was the first of the production Ta 152H-1s, which began to enter service alongside Ta 152H-0s in late January 1945. The trickle of new production aircraft was flown straight from the Cottbus factory to JG 301's small operational fleet.

specification/armament with a pressurised cockpit and GM 1 boost system for high-altitude flight, plus an MW 50 tank in the wing (replacing the innermost fuel cell in the left-hand wing of this version) for additional performance boost at lower altitudes or at take-off. Several fuselage-mounted camera installations were envisaged, including an unwieldy fuselage projection that was tested on an Fw 190D-9 trials aircraft (Werk Nr 210002, TR+SB). The intended camera for this fitting would have been the Rb 50/18, mounted at an oblique angle within the housing. As far as is known, no Ta 152 photographic aircraft were series-produced, the termination of the war also ending this programme.

Other related schemes in the overall Ta 152 design effort that did not progress beyond the project or drawing office phase included the proposed two-seat training version of the Ta 152, referred to by Focke-Wulf as the **Ta 152S**. This training derivative would have resembled the layout of the trainer versions of the Fw 190, the Fw 190S-5 (based on the Fw 190A-5) and the Fw 190S-8 (based on the Fw 190A-8 and F-8), both of which were actually built and operated by the Luftwaffe (in conversion form from existing Fw 190s). The proposed seating arrangement for the Ta 152S was therefore for two crew members in tandem, with the instructor in the rear cockpit, both crew positions being covered by rather cumbersome multi-framed canopy panels. Based on the Ta 152C-1 with a DB 603 engine, the unarmed Ta 152S would have been a conversion programme from existing airframes. As far as is known, however, no two-seat Ta 152s were ever built.

Operational service

Preparations had moved ahead for the testing of the Ta 152H at the Rechlin test centre prior to the 'signing off' of the type for operational service, following the first flight of the initial

As a part of the programme for developing the Ta 152 series for use in photo-reconnaissance, a number of fuselage-mounted camera installations were envisaged for the planned reconnaissance Ta 152 variants. The most prominent was for the fitting of an oblique-looking Rb 50/18 camera in a special fairing that would have protruded from the left-hand fuselage side on the intended Ta 152E-1/R1 version. This installation was actually tried out on an Fw 190D-9 trials aircraft, Werk Nr 210002 (TR+SB), as shown here.

pre-production Ta 152H-0 (Werk Nr 150001). The initial Ta 152H-0 to arrive at Rechlin did so on 11 December 1944 (Werk Nr 150003), but it was hardly an ideal situation to be using new pre-production aircraft for this test work, for delays would inevitably result in the whole production process if any major problems were encountered. Only the Fw 190 V29 (Werk Nr 0054, GH+KS) had spent any meaningful time at Rechlin following its first flight in Ta 152H-like configuration on 24 September 1944. Indeed, this aircraft, during its initial service testing at Rechlin, had demonstrated one of the significant problems with the Ta 152 design, this being poor stability characteristics, particularly about the vertical axis. Supercharger surging with the Jumo 213E engine had also been encountered.

On 31 December, when four examples arrived, all 12 expected test aircraft were present. They were nominally assigned at Rechlin to a new evaluation organisation, Erprobungskommando 152 (EKdo 152). It was intended that this test phase would end on 1 April 1945, but the war situation was already seriously affecting work at Rechlin, and so this phase of the Ta 152H's career was necessarily brief. In fact, most of the examples of potentially front-line combat types that were present at Rechlin were absorbed into an *ad hoc* combat unit that was supposed to have front-line status.

To that end most, if not all, of the Ta 152H contingent was transferred from Rechlin to the nearby Roggentin airfield for 'front-line' defensive operations, with EKdo 152 being re-titled (on paper at least) Jagdstaffel Ta 152. On 8 February this temporary unit had eight Ta 152s on strength, mainly Ta 152Hs but possibly including the Ta 152C V8 (Werk Nr 110008, GW+QA). The third Ta 152H-0 was involved in trials there of a new wooden tail for the type. This mixed bag of test aircraft at these locations was thus pressed into service as improvised fighters to defend the research airfields, and there appears to have been a makeshift 'Jagdstaffel Roggentin' in existence for this purpose at that time.

The Ta 152H entered front-line Luftwaffe service in late January 1945. This took place, however, very early in the operational and manufacturer's testing of the type, reflecting how serious the situation had become for Germany by that point in the war. The first operational unit to fly the Ta 152H was fighter wing JG 301, which had to perform much of the necessary military testing and operational trials of the Ta 152H while 'on the job', and attempting to use the new fighter in whatever purposeful way it could.

On 27 January 1945 several pilots from III Gruppe of JG 301 were transported to Neuhausen to pick up their 11 new Ta 152Hs from the initial Cottbus production. This Gruppe had recently been relocated to the small airstrip at Alteno, to the north-east of Luckau. All 11 aircraft were subsequently flown back to Alteno. It was projected that up to 35 Ta 152Hs would eventually equip the Gruppe, but with production slowing to a virtual standstill at Cottbus the number of newly-built Ta 152Hs eventually dwindled to virtually nothing. At least some of III/JG 301's Ta 152Hs

were early pre-production Ta 152H-0 aircraft without the MW 50 and GM 1 boost systems installed.

A deteriorating war situation was a major feature of the Ta 152H's operational history right from the start. Not only was the manufacture of the type compromised by the loss of factories and the complete disruption of supplies and raw materials, but the Luftwaffe itself was increasingly in full retreat. A move had to be made by III/JG 301 westwards from Alteno to Sachau to the east of Wolfsburg on or around 19 February. Some piecemeal operations were flown with individual aircraft or in small numbers during this so-called 'work-up' phase, with one pilot claiming an American bomber on 21 February.

Disastrous debut

Finally, the Ta 152Hs and their pilots were considered combat-ready (or at least what passed for 'combat-ready' by that stage in the war), and on 2 March they flew against a US air raid on targets in the Böhlen, Chemnitz and Magdeburg areas. It was intended that the 12 or so Ta 152Hs would engage the American escort, while other fighters from the Geschwader would attack the heavy bombers. Unfortunately, the Ta 152s were accidentally attacked by Bf 109Gs from IV/JG 301. The whole operation was a complete disaster, and the Ta 152Hs do not appear to have got anywhere near to an American aircraft.

Few other interceptions of American bombers were attempted, even though this was the intended mission of the Ta 152H, and by the middle of March it was clear that no new Ta 152Hs were going to become available to allow III/JG 301 to build up to its intended strength of 35 Ta 152Hs. Instead, all the Ta 152Hs were transferred to JG 301's headquarters Geschwaderstab (Stab/JG 301). The Ta 152s were therefore moved from Sachau to Stendal to the west of Berlin, where the headquarters of JG 301 was stationed. Increasingly, most of the assets of JG 301 were used from mid-March onwards for ground-attack missions rather than defensive fighter work.

For this phase of the war, the Ta 152Hs were used as top cover for the fighters of II/JG 301 as they took off and landed from Stendal airfield, these being phases of flight that were particularly danger-ous with many marauding American fighters in the air. It has been claimed that the Ta 152Hs were used as fighter protection for Me 262 jet fighters on take-off and landing but this is incorrect, the small band of Ta 152Hs was hard enough pressed to cover its own shrinking

Above: Amongst the well-known images from the latter stages of World War Two is this line-up of Ta 152Hs of JG 301, in late January or early February 1945 at the airfield of Alteno near to Luckau, east of Berlin. The aircraft visible are probably from the early Ta 152H pre-production and production batches and could well be a mix of H-0 and H-1 versions, or H-0 with GM 1 boost provision. They carry JG 301's yellow and red rear fuselage Reichsverteidigung home defence coloured identification band. The aircraft at that time were a part of III/JG 301.

A detailed view of the rear fuselage of a Ta 152 shows part of the rear fuselage extension to the right of the picture. The access door is hinged open, and also visible is the small circular lifting point (which went right through the fuselage), the flare dispenser just below it, and aerials under the fuselage for the FuG 16ZY (the circular direction-finding loop) and the FuG 25a IFF (the rod near the flare dispenser).

Below: This historically important but inferior-quality photograph shows several Focke-Wulf fighters following the end of the war, awaiting scrapping. Nearest the camera is a former JG 301 Fw 190D-9, but the aircraft behind it is of great interest. It is the Ta 152H-1 Werk Nr 150167. This aircraft was discovered by US troops at Erfurt-North in good condition, but not long afterwards was photographed on this dump of wrecked German aircraft. The location of the dump is unconfirmed. It is possible that the front end of this aircraft was sent to the US, and much more recently was displayed at the Champlin Fighter Museum, although this too is unconfirmed.

Focke-Wulf Ta 152

'Green 4' is the only Ta 152 to have survived, and is now with the **US National Air & Space Museum**. It is a Ta 152H-0, most likely Werk Nr 150020 although this has not been positively confirmed. It was captured by the British at Aalborg in Denmark. It wore JG 301's RV bands, but they were painted over, along with other markings, by the British. The aircraft was subsequently turned over to 'Watson's Whizzers', the USAAF unit tasked with collecting German aircraft for evaluation. It was flown to France and then shipped to the US for evaluation at Wright Field, acquiring the registration FE-112 (later T2-112). It was turned over to the NASM in 1960.

area and its comrades in JG 301 during the final weeks of the war. On 10/11 April the Stab/JG 301 was forced to leave Stendal due to the imminent arrival of US troops, with a hasty move being made by the ground and air personnel to Neustadt-Glewe north-east of Ludwigslust.

The final limited sorties by the Stab/JG 301 Ta 152Hs were flown from Neustadt-Glewe. A number of successes were achieved against Allied aircraft. On 14 April three of the Stab Ta 152Hs intercepted several RAF Hawker Tempest fighter-bombers that were attacking railway installations at Ludwigslust, shooting down one of the Tempests. Due to the rapidly approaching Allied forces, in the following days Stab/JG 301 found itself flying against British, American and Russian fighters. One of the most successful combats for the small Ta 152H force occurred on 24 April, when approximately five Stab/JG 301 Ta 152Hs claimed four Russian fighters shot down while covering Bf 109s and Fw 190s of JG 301 as they carried out attacks on Soviet ground forces. Hasty arrangements were eventually made to evacuate to areas held by British forces rather than be captured by Soviet troops. Several of the Ta 152Hs were evacuated to Leck in Schleswig-Holstein and surrendered to the British.

Four or perhaps as many as six Ta 152s were also assigned to Stab/JG 11, possibly some, if not all, of the remaining test aircraft from the Rechlin contingent. It is very unlikely that Stab/JG 11 ever flew any of these Ta 152s in combat, for the unit only had a few days with the type and was only able to perform little more than familiarisation flights. As the end of the war drew near, attempts were made to fly these aircraft to Leck in order to escape from the advancing Russians. On the way, two appear to have been shot down by RAF Spitfires.

During its short operational career the Ta 152H proved to be a good combat aircraft, but it only briefly flew in its intended role of high-altitude fighter. The small number of operational Ta 152Hs were only committed to combat in piecemeal fashion in the chaotic final weeks of the war, frequently covering other German fighters on ground-attack sorties. On the few occasions that air combats took place the Ta 152H was found to be manoeuvrable at low level and to have sufficient firepower to score a number of victories – possibly as many as 13.

Ta 152H-1 specification
Type: single-seat high-altitude fighter
Powerplant: one Junkers Jumo 213E or E-1 12-cylinder liquid-cooled engine rated at 1290 kW (1,730 hp) for take-off (1530 kW/2,050 hp projected with MW 50) and 940 kW (1,260 hp) at 10700 m (35,105 ft) (1298 kW/1,740 hp) projected with GM 1)
Performance: maximum speed, at sea level (MW 50) 571 km/h (355 mph), at 9500 m/31,170 ft (MW 50) 732 km/h (455 mph), at 12500 m/41,010 ft (GM 1) 755 km/h (469 mph); initial climb rate 852 m (2,795 ft) per second to 10000 m (32,808 ft); service ceiling (GM 1) 14800 m (48,556 ft); range (clean) 1215 km (755 miles) at 605 km/h (376 mph) at 10000 m (32,808 ft)
Weights: empty 3920 kg (8,642 lb); maximum take-off, 5220 kg (11,508 lb)
Dimensions: wingspan 14.44 m (47 ft 4½ in); length 10.71 m (35 ft 1¾ in); tailplane span 3.65 m (11 ft 11¾ in); height 3.36 m (11 ft 0¼ in); wheel track/base 3.95 m (12 ft 11¾ in); wing area, 23.30 m² (250.8 sq ft); tailplane and elevator area 2.82 m² (30.4 sq ft); fin and rudder area 1.77 m² (19.1 sq ft)
Armament: two 20-mm Mauser MG 151/20 cannons in wing roots with 175 rpg; one 30-mm Rheinmetall-Borsig MK 108 cannon 'engine-mounted' firing through propeller spinner, with 90 rounds

Left: The Ta 152H that was sent to the US for evaluation had German insignia reapplied, but evidence of its former RAF roundels and fin-flash can still be clearly seen.

Right: Photographed at the RAE, Farnborough, in southern England in late 1945, this is the captured Ta 152H-1 Werk Nr 150168 that was taken to England after the end of the war. This photograph shows the aircraft being exhibited at the display of captured aircraft that was held at Farnborough in October and November 1945. W.Nr. 150168 was flown twice by the famous British test pilot Captain Eric Brown but it was not formally evaluated by the British and was later scrapped

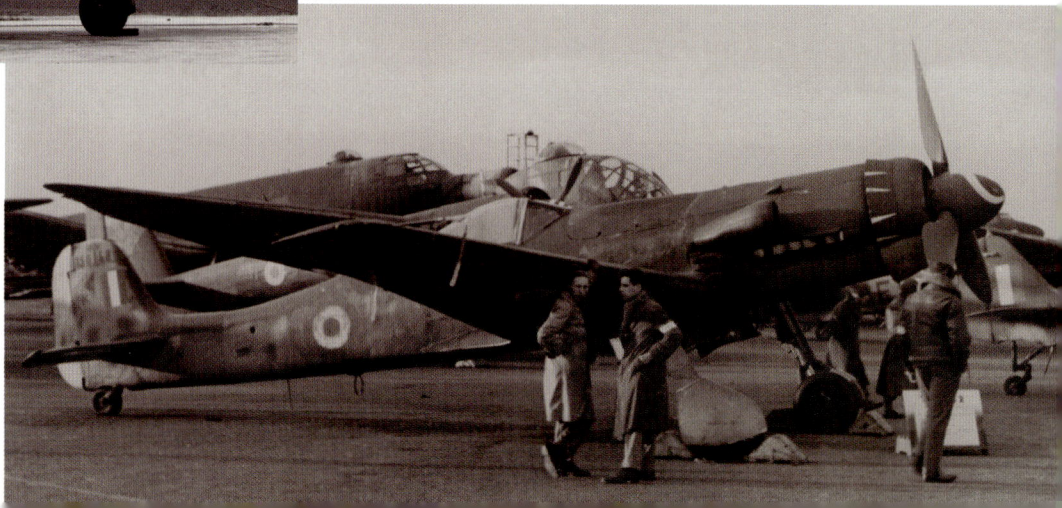

Focke-Wulf 'Ta 153'

The term Ta 153 is something of a 'red herring' as far as the overall Fw 190/Ta 152 programme is concerned. At one time it was widely thought that the Ta 153 existed as a major series of development aircraft, and also as a separate and distinct production version, but this has subsequently been proven to be erroneous.

The 'Ta 153' designation relates most closely to the development work that was carried out by Focke-Wulf on the **Fw 190 V32/U1** Werk Nr 0057 (GH+KV), which eventually became one of the Ta 152H development aircraft but which also existed in trials form with a Daimler-Benz DB 603 engine. Despite the Fw 190B and Fw 190C high-altitude fighter programmes having not progressed into production, Focke-Wulf nevertheless kept many lines of development open with regard to high-altitude fighter development, quite in addition to the changes that were made in the Ta 152 line that led to the Ta 152H high-altitude production aircraft. One of these development efforts was the re-engining of one of the development aircraft from the high-altitude programme with a later and potentially more powerful version of the DB 603-series engine, the DB 603S. Daimler-Benz was in the process of attempting to develop ever more powerful engines, some with turbo-supercharging, some useful for high-altitude flight, and the DB 627 was also considered for installation in an Fw 190 development airframe.

From these various lines of study several new ideas emerged. Recent discoveries of Focke-Wulf company documents suggest that a long-wingspan high-altitude fighter, tentatively named the Fw 190H, was on the agenda for Kurt Tank and his designers subsequent to a major July 1943 meeting between Focke-Wulf employees and Generalfeldmarschall Erhard Milch regarding new fighter development concepts. This aircraft would have had a wing area of slightly less than the Ta 152H and with prominently rounded wing-tips. Its proposed wing span was 14.80 m (48 ft 6¾ in). Power might have been supplied by either a Junkers Jumo 213E, Daimler Benz DB 603G, DB 627 or DB 632 engine, with turbo-supercharging an option for some of these engines with a DVL TK 15 turbo-supercharger. A planned armament similar

One of the less visible changes in the Fw 190 V32/U1 adaptation for possible high-altitude development was the widening of the track of the electrically operated main undercarriage units.

The Fw 190 V32/U1 is seen in the configuration in which it served as a test bed for features of a high-altitude fighter. The DB 603S engine drove a propeller with four wide-chord blades.

to that of the Ta 152H was intended. In the event this project did not go ahead, seemingly due to the planned development of the Ta 152H.

Development work was nevertheless carried out with the Fw 190 V32/U1, and at one stage this aircraft flew with a long-span wing and a DB 603S engine driving a four-bladed VDM propeller of 3.5-m (11-ft 5¾-in) diameter. Focke-Wulf test pilot Hans Kampmeier made the first flight with GH+KV after conversion to the DB 603S engine on 11 November 1943. This aircraft was a stop-gap configuration, with the DB 603S engine but no turbo-supercharger, and could have been a rapid solution to the problem of producing a viable high-altitude fighter in the quickest space of time. It is this combination that some writers after World War II have assumed was the 'Ta 153' layout, and it has often been said that the 'Ta 153' project was abandoned due to the development of Focke-Wulf's planned jet fighter, the Ta 183. This was not the case, the DB 603S/long-wing Fw 190 V32/U1 was one of Focke-Wulf's several lines of enquiry into the high-altitude fighter that eventually crystallised, very late in the war, as the Ta 152H.

Focke-Wulf Ta 154

In order to combat the nightly bombing raids against German cities by the RAF's Bomber Command, the RLM ordered the development of a two-seat night-fighter in summer 1942. The resulting Ta 154, designed by Dipl.-Ing. Kurt Tank, showed great promise in prototype form, but a series of accidents saw the project shelved.

During the years immediately preceding World War II, the Oberbefehlshaber der Luftwaffe, Göring, the Luftwaffenführungsstab, and the Oberkommando der Luftwaffe (OKL) were consistent in their unwillingness to think defensively; in their disinclination to give serious consideration to such distasteful possibilities as that of enemy aircraft making nocturnal incursions in strength over Germany. The attitude that defensive thinking was defeatist, and had no place in the Führer's short-term plan for victory, was to be maintained with but few concessions until mid-1942, one of these few concessions being the creation of a night-fighter arm in 1940 by Oberst (later Generalmajor) Josef Kammhuber on the instructions of Reichsmarschall Göring.

Systematically developed along preconceived lines, Kammhuber's night defence force, the Nachtjagd, enjoyed mounting success against a limited night offensive employing slow, poorly-defended bombers and uninspired routine tactics. The Luftwaffe's first General der Nachtjagd brought both energy and resourcefulness to the evolution of the nocturnal fighter arm, and it was the very success of the Nachtjagd with its improvised night-fighters that delayed development of the more effective interceptors for which Kammhuber constantly pleaded, and which, in view of the imminent debut in German night skies of more potent bombers, common prudence should have insisted upon.

Nachtjagd expansion

The doubt regarding the priority that should be allocated to the Nachtjagd coupled, from the summer of 1941, with the over-deployment of the Luftwaffe, resulted in determined resistance from the OKL to all attempts on the part of Generalmajor Kammhuber to achieve major expansion of the night-fighter arm, while Generalfeldmarschall Erhard Milch, the General-Luftzeugmeister, was a resolute opponent of any development of specialised night-fighters, averring that their task could be adequately fulfilled by existing warplanes.

The Ta 154 V15 was the eighth A-0 produced at Erfurt. First flown in June 1944, it was one of the first to be fitted with the 'Hirschgeweih' antenna array for FuG 220 Lichtenstein SN-2 radar.

With the escalation of the RAF night offensive in the spring of 1942, culminating in Operation Millennium on the night of 30-31 May, when the so-called 'Kammhuber Line' was swamped by 1,046 bombers despatched against Cologne, the writing that had for so long been on the wall was finally deciphered; the inadequacy of the improvised night-fighters for the task now facing them was made abundantly clear by their inability to account, together with anti-aircraft artillery, for more than a mere 3.8 per cent of the attacking force.

The Ta 154 V1 runs its engines during initial tests at Hannover-Langenhagen in July 1943. With no radar or armament, the first prototype recorded a speed of 700 km/h (435 mph) in level flight. The Ta 154 V1 was designed, built and flown within less than 10 months.

The Ta 154 possessed an excellent performance, and had it not been for the insufficient time available to resolve its constructional problems, it would undoubtedly have proved a highly successful fighter. This is the Ta 154 V7 (Werk Nr 0007, TE+FK), last of the Langenhagen-built prototypes.

Heinkel was already engaged in the development of the He 219 night-fighter evolved from an earlier Kampfzerstörer study at the behest of Generalmajor Kammhuber, who had succeeded in overruling the Technisches Amt previously opposing any such development and, after a series of hurried conferences, Dipl.-Ing. Kurt Tank of Focke-Wulf was invited to prepare a study for a specialised two-seat night- and bad-weather fighter. The requirement of the Technisches Amt stipulated a 2.75-hour endurance, a forward-firing armament of either four 30-mm cannon or a combination of 20-mm and 30-mm weapons, suitability for rapid quantity production, and, with a view to conserving steel and light alloys, a primarily wooden structure. Such was the urgency attached to the project that it was made plain to Dipl.-Ing. Tank that the award of a contract would presuppose the commencement of flight testing by mid-1943.

Work on the basic design study was begun in September 1942, this study being submitted to the Technisches Amt in the following month, promptly accepted, and allocated the official designation **Ta 211**. This was the first use of the 'Ta' prefix with an RLM type number, and was indicative of the prestige gained and increased responsibility assumed by Dipl.-Ing. Tank, who, by that time, had been appointed vice-president of the Akademie der Luftfahrtforschung (Academy of Aviation Research).

Wooden construction

The use of wood on so extensive a scale for the primary structure of a high-speed aircraft such as proposed by Tank met with disapproval from some factions within the RLM, despite the emphasis placed by the official requirement on the use of non-strategic materials. It was suggested that the necessary skills no longer existed in the wood-working industry, and that, although wood was the classic material for aircraft construction, the German aircraft industry had little experience of its use for a really high-performance aircraft such as was envisaged; that while the load acceptance limitations of metals could be calculated with certainty, a reversion to wood for the primary structure could well offer problems that would be time-consuming in their solution. However, the operational debut of the British Mosquito earlier in the year motivated against such strictures, and with the issue of the official contract to Focke-Wulf early in November, the highest priority was attached to the development of what German propagandists were to refer to as the Teutonic Moskito.

By this time, the RLM, which had adopted the practice of re-assigning type numbers included in blocks previously allo-

cated but not taken up by the manufacturers to which they had been originally assigned, acceded to Tank's request that Focke-Wulf be allocated the numbers 152-154 inclusive. He expressed his preference for the designation **Ta 154** for the new fighter, having earmarked the numbers 152 and 153 for derivatives of the Fw 190 already on the drawing boards, and this was duly adopted, the number 211 being subsequently assigned to Hütter for a derivative of the He 219.

Detail design of the Ta 154 was delegated to Oberingenieur Ernst Nipp, and the aircraft was basically a shoulder-wing cantilever monoplane featuring a wooden oval-section fuselage built in one piece from the front bulkhead to the axis of rotation of the rudder, and a one-piece two-spar wooden wing that was attached to the fuselage by four bolts. Apart from the forward fuselage and engine nacelles, which were covered by duralumin panels, and the elevators, which had fabric skinning, the entire aircraft was covered by laminated plywood. The ailerons, the variable-camber slotted flaps, the rudder and the elevators were of light metal construction, and hydraulically-operated tricycle undercarriage was provided.

Above: Powered by Jumo 211R engines, the first prototype, the Ta 154 V1 (TE+FE), made its maiden flight from Hannover-Langenhagen on 1 July 1943, piloted by Hans Sander.

In the absence of the Jumo 213, the first two prototypes were completed with Jumo 211R engines that were coupled with annular radiators, and which drove broad-bladed propellers.

Focke-Wulf Ta 154

The Ta 154 V7 was the last of seven examples of the Focke-Wulf fighter to be built at Langenhagen, before production switched to Erfurt.

The two crewmembers were seated in tandem ahead of the wing leading edge and beneath a one-piece jettisonable canopy hinging to starboard for entry and egress. Protection for the crew was provided by the 50-mm armour-glass windscreen, 30-mm armour-glass side panels in the canopy, a 12-mm armour plate attached to the forward bulkhead, and 8-mm armour panels set in the fuselage sides. All fuel was accommodated by two tanks with a total capacity of 1500 litres (330 Imp gal) immediately aft of the second cockpit, 116-litre (25.5-Imp gal) oil tanks being mounted in each engine nacelle. Provision was made for the installation of two 20-mm MG 151 cannon with 200 r.p.g. and two 30-mm MK 108 cannon with 110 r.p.g., these weapons being mounted in the fuselage sides below the leading edge of the wings, the ammunition boxes for the upper 20-mm guns being accommodated in the wing between the fuselage and the engine nacelles, and those for the lower 30-mm weapons being housed in the fuselage.

Strength tests

Detail design, prototype construction and the structural test programme had to proceed in parallel in order to meet the time schedule stipulated by the Technisches Amt. In view of this time factor, the test programme with the plywood monocoque fuselage and other wooden components was surprisingly thorough. The Luftfahrt-Forschungsstelle Graf Zeppelin had evolved a system of underwater drag-testing to determine the strength factor of aircraft structures. It had been ascertained that the dynamic pressure acting on a body moving at high velocity through air could be simulated with considerable accuracy at much lower speeds in the denser medium of water so, in the spring of 1943, Focke-Wulf began underwater drag-testing of a complete Ta 154 forward fuselage in the Alatsee, near Füssen, Bavaria. The forward fuselage was hung beneath a floating rig fitted with measuring instrumentation and hauled through the water at progressively higher speeds by power-driven cable winches.

In the meantime, construction of the first prototypes proceeded with remarkable rapidity, and the decision had been taken to switch from the Jumo 211N engine (rated at 1089 kW/1,460 hp for take-off and 1133 kW/1,520 hp at 1295 m/4,250 ft) to the more powerful Jumo 213. The latter was not available in time for installation in the first two prototypes, which were therefore completed with Jumo 211R engines with annular radiators, driving broad-bladed airscrews, and rated at 1007 kW (1,350 hp) for take-off and 1104 kW (1,480 hp) at 3000 m (9,850 ft). The first prototype, the **Ta 154 V1** (Werk Nr 0001, TE+FE), was flown for the first time from Hannover-Langenhagen on 1 July 1943, with Flugkapitän Hans Sander at the controls. Carrying no radar or armament, the Ta 154 V1 clocked 700 km/h (435 mph) in level flight during its initial test phase. The similarly-powered second prototype, the **Ta 154 V2** (Werk Nr 0002, TE+FF) completed shortly after the initial machine, differed only in having FuG 212 Lichtenstein C-1 with a four-pole antenna array of the so-called Matratze (mattress) type.

On 25 November 1943 the **Ta 154 V3** (Werk Nr 0003, TE+FG) joined the flight test programme. Also designated **Ta 154A-03/U1**, this was considered to be the first pre-production aircraft. The Ta 154 V3 was powered by two Jumo 213E engines with three-speed two-stage superchargers and rated at 1305 kW (1,750 hp) for take-off and 984 kW (1,320 hp) at 10000 m (32,810 ft), 1178 kW (1,580 hp) being available for climb and combat at sea level. The Ta 154 V3

A Ta 154 has its engines run up during ground testing. Plagued by a number of unfortunate accidents attributed to failure of the glue adhesive used in the manufacture of the wing in production aircraft, the RLM pulled the plug on the programme in August 1944.

was the first aircraft to carry full armament and, despite the not inconsiderable increase in power by comparison with the preceding machines, it suffered a 12 per cent reduction in maximum speed as a result of the combined drag of the gun ports, the Matratze array, and the necessary exhaust flame dampers. Nevertheless, performance was still sufficient to warrant the immediate placing of an initial production order for 250 **Ta 154A-1** fighters.

The initial Technisches Amt development contract had covered 15 pre-production aircraft with which all test programmes were to be conducted. Thus, these machines were allocated both Versuchs numbers and pre-production designations. For example, the **Ta 154 V4** (Werk Nr 0004, TE+FH), which flew on 19 January 1944, was also the **Ta 154A-04**, and the **Ta 154 V5** (Werk Nr 0005, TE+FI), which flew five weeks later, on 23 February, was also the **Ta 154A-05**. Only the first seven aircraft were completed at Langenhagen, the last of them, the **Ta 154 V7** (Werk Nr 0007, TE+FK), being flown in March, with the remainder of the pre-production batch being built at Erfurt. The pre-production machines differed one from another primarily in the form of radar antennas fitted. The Matratze array for the FuG 212 radar was replaced by a single centrally-mounted pole on some pre-production examples, while others featured the 'Hirschgeweih' (stag's antlers) array for FuG 220 Lichtenstein SN-2, and a housing above the cockpit for the rotating aerial of an FuG 350 Naxos Z H2S-emission receiver. Other equipment included a Revi 16B gunsight, FuG 10P HF communications set, FuG 16ZY VHF radio, FuG 25a IFF, FuG 101a radio altimeter, a FuBl 2 blind approach receiver, and a PeGe 6 radio compass.

Structural problems

An assembly line for the Ta 154A-1 had been set up at Posen (now Poznan), in Poland, but the first and second production examples (Werk Nummern 32 0001, KU+SN, and 32 0002, KU+SO) were completed at Erfurt, the latter flying on 13 June 1944, and crashing two weeks later, on 28 June, when the wing disintegrated in flight. Tank immediately issued instructions to halt the manufacture of wing assemblies pending a thorough examination of the wreckage of the second production aircraft to determine the cause

Above: The Ta 154 V3, also designated Ta 154A-03/U1, was the first prototype to have Jumo 213E engines and full armament, and was, in consequence, considered as the first pre-production aircraft.

The Ta 154 V1, the first prototype of the first German combat aircraft entirely of wooden construction since World War I, was, aerodynamically, of extremely clean design, but it failed to meet the more sanguine performance expectations of its design team.

of the accident. It was quickly ascertained that the Dynamit cold glue adhesive used in the manufacture of the wings of the production Ta 154A had rotted the plywood component joints. This problem had not been experienced with the pre-production aircraft which had used Goldmann Tego-Film glue, but the Goldmann factory in Wuppertal had been destroyed during an RAF attack shortly after production of the Ta 154A had begun, and the substitute glue had not been subjected to tests sufficiently protracted to reveal its effect on the plywood joints.

Tank, who by this time had been placed in charge of night- and bad-weather fighter development throughout the German aircraft industry, and had received the title of professor from the Braunschweig Technical School, was accused of

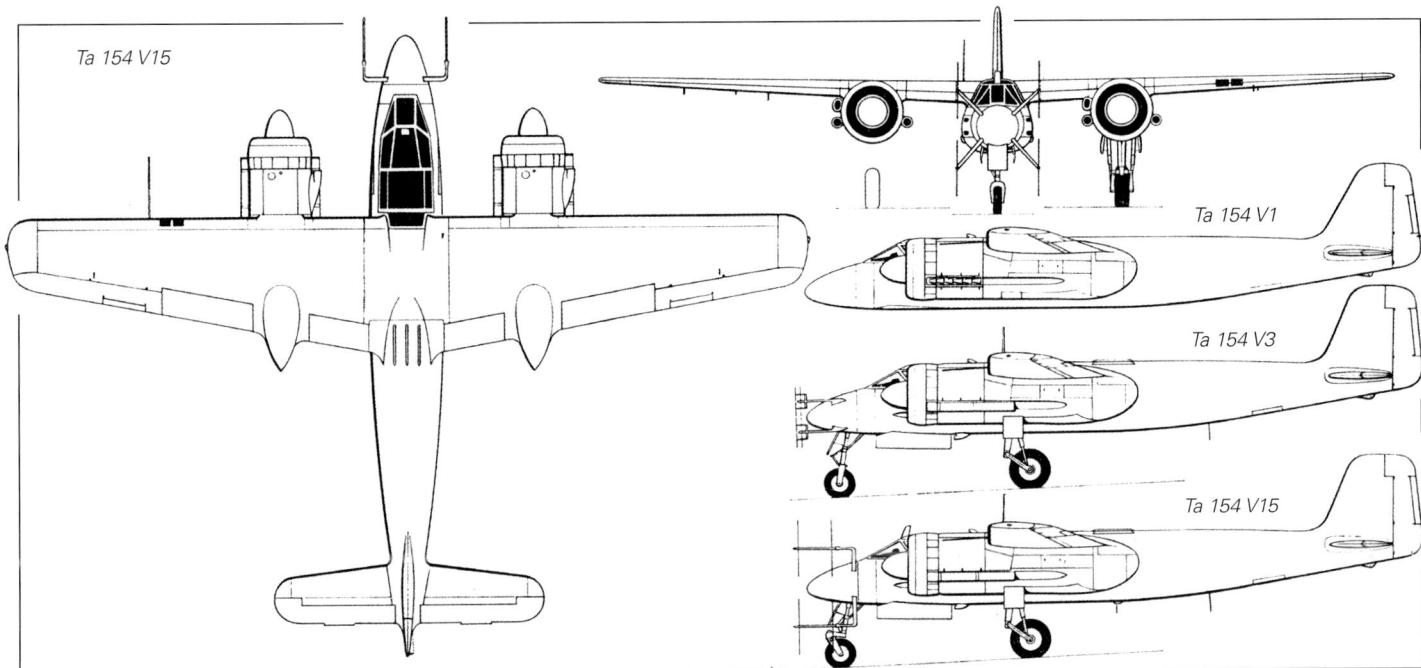

Ta 154 V15

Ta 154 V1

Ta 154 V3

Ta 154 V15

The Ta 154 V7 was the last of the prototypes. Intended primarily for handling and high-speed trials, it was not fitted with radar antennas. The power from the intended Jumo 213 engines and sleek design promised high performance, and there seems little doubt that the Ta 154 would have been a highly effective warplane had development continued successfully.

Focke-Wulf Ta 154A-1/A-4 cutaway key

1 Starboard navigation light
2 Wingtip fairing
3 Starboard aileron
4 Aileron hinge control
5 Aileron tab
6 Control rod linkages
7 Flap hinge control
8 Outboard double-acting split flap
9 FuG 218 radar aerials (Ta 154A-4)
10 Starboard engine oil tank access
11 Nacelle tail fairing

sabotage by Göring as a direct result of his decision to stop the manufacture of wing assemblies for the Ta 154. It transpired that the wings were being manufactured by a factory owned by the Gauleiter of Erfurt who had promptly complained directly to the Reichsmarschall, and that Göring did not even know the intended role of the Ta 154, let alone the difficulties that were being experienced with the glue.

Meanwhile, series production of the Ta 154A-1 had begun at Posen, the first example completed there (Werk Nr 32 0003, KU+SP) making its initial flight on 30 June, two days after the crash of the second production machine. During the landing approach the starboard wing flap failed and the aircraft was totally destroyed in the ensuing crash, but production continued at Posen, a further seven Ta 154A-1s having flown by 14 August 1944 when the RLM cancelled the entire programme. The Technisches Amt had begun to entertain serious doubts regarding the fighter when, shortly after the destruction of the second and third production machines, a Ta 154A-0 crashed as a result of an uncontrollable engine fire during single-engine climbing trials, and these doubts, coupled with the difficulties that were being experienced in arranging satisfactory subcontracting of wooden components, led to the decision to abandon all further development.

Above: The Ta 154 was referred to by German propagandists as the 'Moskito', on account of its primarily wooden construction.

The Ta 154 V15 was the eighth pre-production Ta 145A-0, later converted to represent the Ta 154A-4 with FuG 218 Neptun radar.

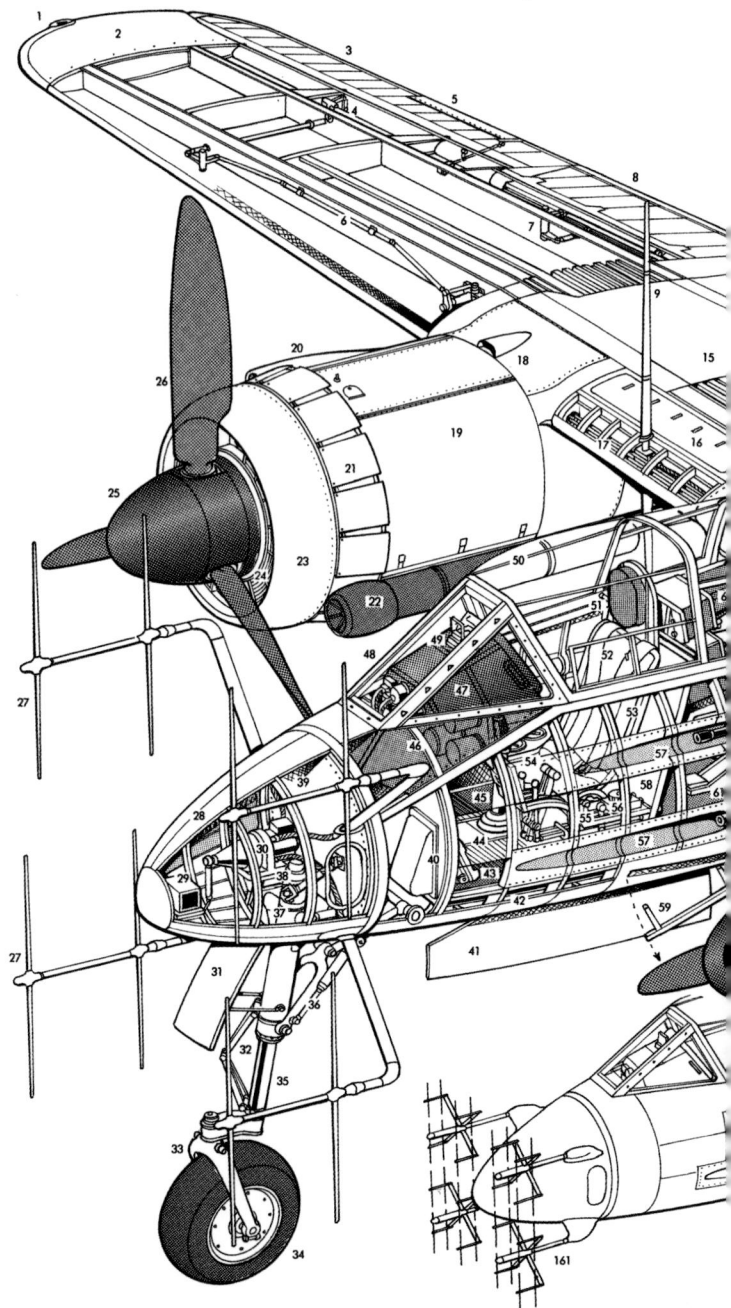

12 Inboard double-acting split flap segment
13 Aerial mast
14 Wing stringers
15 Glued plywood laminated skin panelling
16 Ammunition magazine access hatch
17 Engine control runs
18 Generator cooling air intake
19 Hinged cowling panels
20 Supercharger intake
21 Cooling air flaps
22 Exhaust flame suppressor
23 Cowling nose ring
24 Annular radiator
25 Propeller spinner
26 VS-9 three-bladed wooden propeller
27 FuG 220 Lichtenstein SN-2 radar antennas (Ta 154A-1)
28 Moulded plywood nose cone
29 Aerial tuner
30 FuG 220 transmitter
31 Nosewheel leg door
32 Torque scissor links
33 Nosewheel forks
34 Nosewheel (aft retracting and rotating)
35 Shock absorber leg strut
36 Retraction/breaker strut
37 Nosewheel leg pivot fixing
38 Leg rotating fixed link
39 Armoured bulkhead (12-mm plate)
40 Cockpit front bulkhead
41 Nosewheel door
42 Nose undercarriage wheel bay
43 Rudder pedals
44 Pilot's footboards

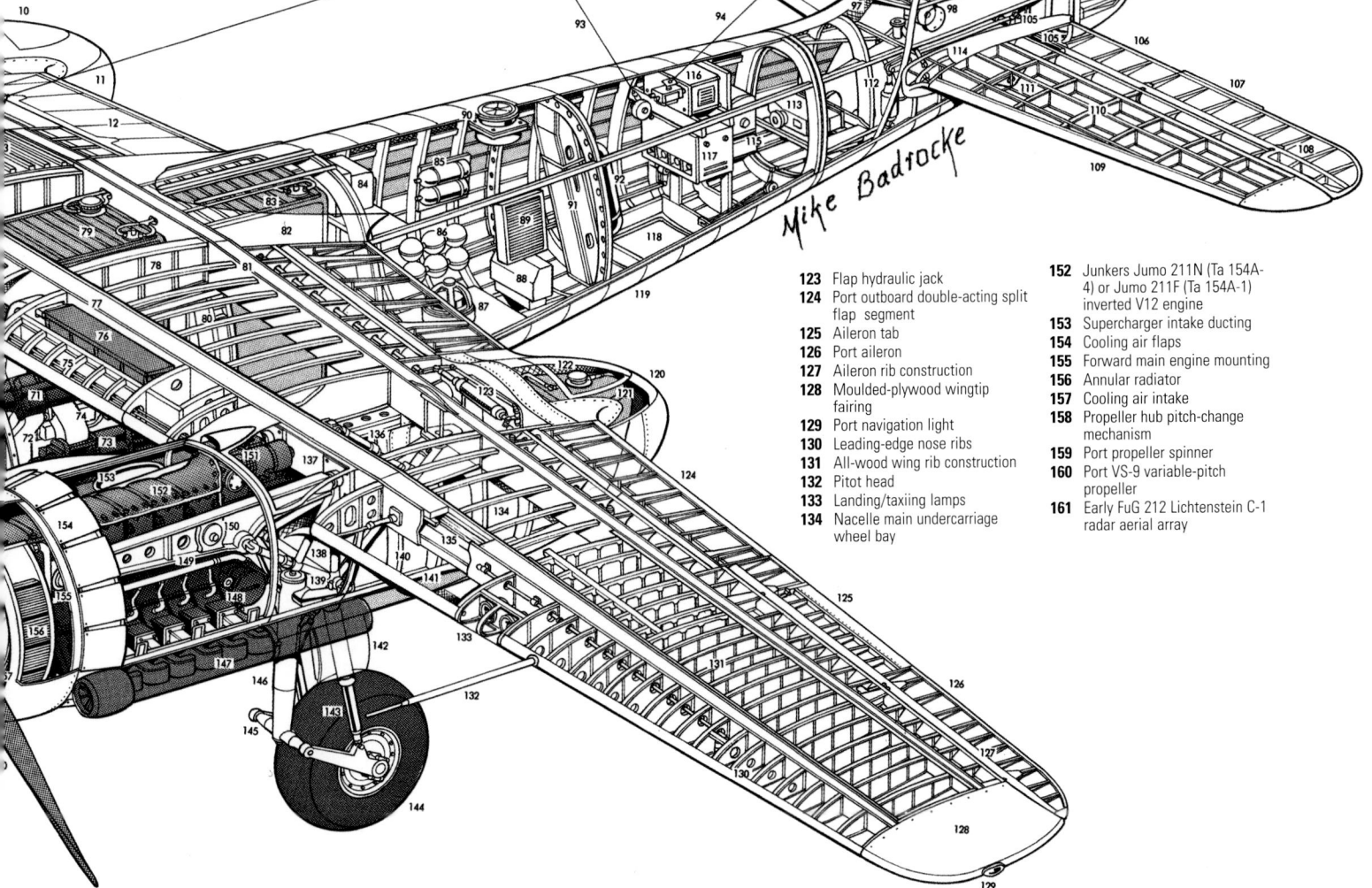

45 Control column
46 12-mm cockpit armour
47 Instrument panel shroud
48 50-mm armoured glass windscreen
49 Revi 16B reflector sight
50 One-piece cockpit canopy (hinged to starboard)
51 Armoured headrest
52 Direct vision sliding side window panel
53 Pilot's seat
54 Engine throttle and propeller pitch control levers
55 Fuel cocks and mixture controls
56 Trim control handwheels
57 Cannon muzzle blast troughs
58 Pilot's back armour
59 Retractable boarding ladder
60 Cockpit heater air intake
61 Rear seat footrest
62 Radar/radio operator's seat
63 Kick-in boarding steps
64 Radio equipment rack
65 Radar display and visor
66 Canopy handle
67 Control linkages
68 Ammunition feed chute
69 Radar/radio operator's armoured headrest
70 Central 30-mm ammunition magazine (110 rounds per gun)
71 MG 151 20-mm cannon (two)
72 Cartridge case and link ejector chutes
73 MK 108 30-mm cannon (two)
74 Lateral cannon bay, port and starboard

75 Leading-edge control runs
76 20-mm ammunition magazine (200 rounds per gun)
77 One-piece wing main spar
78 Wing attachment root rib
79 Forward main fuel tank (total fuel capacity 1500 litres/330 Imp gal)
80 Wing attachment fuselage main bulkhead
81 One-piece rear spar
82 Wing root trailing-edge fillet
83 Rear main fuel tank
84 Transformer-rectifier
85 Air bottles
86 Oxygen tanks
87 Master compass
88 Gyro unit
89 Electrical relay panel
90 Suppressed D/F loop aerial
91 Canted mounting strut
92 Compressed air bottle (cannon firing)
93 FuG 101 aerial lead-in
94 FuG 16ZY aerial cable
95 Starboard tailplane
96 Starboard elevator
97 Moulded-plywood fin root fairing
98 Aerial tuner
99 All-wood tailfin construction
100 Moulded-plywood fin-tip fairing
101 Rudder horn balance

102 Rudder trim tab
103 Rudder rib construction
104 Trim tab controls
105 Rudder and elevator hinge controls
106 Port elevator
107 Ground adjustable tab
108 Elevator rib construction
109 One-piece trimming tailplane
110 Tailplane rib construction
111 Ventral tail bumper
112 Tailplane sealing plate
113 Trim control jack and electric motor
114 EiV interphone
115 FuG 25a IFF transmitter/receiver
116 FuG 16ZY radio equipment
117 FuG 101 radio equipment
118 Ventral rear fuselage access hatch
119 Laminated-plywood fuselage skin panelling
120 Port nacelle tail fairing
121 Engine oil tank
122 Oil filler cap

135 Box section main spar construction
136 Main undercarriage hydraulic retraction jack
137 Engine bearer mountings
138 Main undercarriage leg mounting struts
139 Leg pivot fixing
140 Aluminium alloy nacelle rib construction
141 Exhaust duct fairing
142 Mainwheel leg door
143 Shock absorber strut
144 Port mainwheel (aft retracting)
145 Levered suspension axle beam
146 Main undercarriage leg strut
147 Exhaust flame suppressor
148 Magneto
149 Forged engine bearer
150 Rear engine mounting
151 Generators

123 Flap hydraulic jack
124 Port outboard double-acting split flap segment
125 Aileron tab
126 Port aileron
127 Aileron rib construction
128 Moulded-plywood wingtip fairing
129 Port navigation light
130 Leading-edge nose ribs
131 All-wood wing rib construction
132 Pitot head
133 Landing/taxiing lamps
134 Nacelle main undercarriage wheel bay

152 Junkers Jumo 211N (Ta 154A-4) or Jumo 211F (Ta 154A-1) inverted V12 engine
153 Supercharger intake ducting
154 Cooling air flaps
155 Forward main engine mounting
156 Annular radiator
157 Cooling air intake
158 Propeller hub pitch-change mechanism
159 Port propeller spinner
160 Port VS-9 variable-pitch propeller
161 Early FuG 212 Lichtenstein C-1 radar aerial array

Mike Badrocke

Focke-Wulf Ta 154

A Ta 154 undergoing pre-flight static testing illustrates the slim fuselage, which was narrower than the engine nacelles and their characteristic annular radiators.

At this time, several developments of the basic design were already on the Focke-Wulf drawing boards. The **Ta 154C** differed from the initial production model in having Jumo 213As rated at 1324 kW (1,776 hp) for take-off and 1193 kW (1,600 hp) at 5500 m (18,045 ft), a metal nose cone, a blown 'bubble'-type aft-sliding canopy, crew ejector seats, and twin 30-mm MK 108 cannon in a 'schräge Musik' installation. The **Ta 254** was a proposed high-altitude multi-purpose development with a 30 per cent increase in gross wing area, subtypes being the Jumo 213-powered **Ta 254A** and the DB 603-powered **Ta 254B**. Retaining the cannon armament of the Ta 154A-1, the **Ta 254A-1** and **A-3** were estimated to be capable of 680 km/h (424 mph) at 10590 m (34,750 ft) and 740 km/h (460 mph) at 10515 m (34,500 ft), respectively, the latter using MW 50 boost. The DB 603-powered **Ta 254B-3**, also using MW 50, was expected to attain 720km/h (448 mph) at 10360 m (34,000 ft), and with 2636 litres (580 Imp gal) total fuel the range was calculated at 1440 km (895 miles) at 590 km/h (366 mph). Tank was frustrated in his attempts to bring these projects to fruition, and the promulgation of the Jäger-Notprogramm (Fighter Emergency Programme) in November 1944 terminated once and for all any chance of the Ta 154 series being resurrected.

Exotic concepts

Around four of the completed fighters, identified as **Ta 154A-4**s when fitted with FuG 218 Neptun radar, were flown briefly by the Stab/NJG 3 from Stade during January 1945 and III/NJG 3 at Grove, and another three were modified as bad-weather fighters, apparently designated **Ta 154A-2/U4**. A handful are also thought to have been used in the training of jet pilots.

In the meantime, several ideas had been concieved to use the completed and semi-completed Ta 154As as expendable weapons against USAAF day bomber formations. During summer 1944, Focke-Wulf's Schöffel Bureau began preliminary studies of the possibility of adapting the Ta 154A as the lower component of a Huckepack combination with an Fw 190A-4. The **Ta 154A-2/U3** with a 2000-kg (4,410-lb) explosive charge in the forward fuselage was to be guided towards the bomber formation by the pilot of the Fw 190A-4 whose aircraft was to be attached to a superstructure similar to that used by the Ju 88 Mistel. It was proposed that the Ta 154A should be aimed at the bomber formation, the

Fw 190A pilot detaching his aircraft from the superstructure after aiming his charge which was then to be detonated by radio signal. Six Ta 154A-0 pre-production aircraft were, in fact, adapted for the Huckepack composite role, but after evaluation by various test pilots, including Horst Lux of Junkers, the scheme was abandoned as the size difference between the two components of the composite was considered insufficient to guarantee clean separation on release.

Another scheme considered for the adaptation of the Ta 154 as a 'Pulk-Zerstörer', or 'formation destroyer', was the use of one aircraft as a tug attached by a 6-m (20-ft) towbar to another aircraft carrying an explosive charge. On nearing the bomber formation, the Ta 154 tug was to enter a shallow climb, simultaneously releasing the towbar, the explosive-carrying Ta 154 then passing beneath the tug but the two aircraft remaining connected by control wires between the wingtips. In the immediate proximity of the formation, the Ta 154 tug was to be finally detached from its companion, the explosive charge of which would then be detonated. Although this highly original scheme for utilising the Ta 154 never progressed further than the drawing board, another idea for adapting this aircraft for the Pulk-Zerstörer role reached a more advanced stage.

Late in 1944, the Posen factory received instructions to rebuild six semi-completed Ta 154A-1 fighters as piloted explosive carriers. A rudimentary cockpit was to be inserted in the rear fuselage, aft of the wing trailing edge, and equipped with a downward-operating ejector seat. A 2000-kg explosive charge was to be inserted in the forward fuselage and fitted with three detonators: impact, time and acoustic. With pilot, explosive charge, and 1273 litres (280 Imp gal) of fuel, the Pulk-Zerstörer Ta 154A had a loaded weight of 9570 kg (21,100 lb). The pilot was intended to set the Ta 154A on a collision course with the bomber formation, and eject himself from the aircraft at a point at which he was reasonably sure that a hit was unavoidable. The six conversions were duly completed at Posen but none was flown.

The Ta 154 V3 made an initial 15-minute flight on 24 November 1943, and was then flown to Insterburg to participate in a demonstration for the Führer. The aircraft was initially flown with FuG 212 and a Matratze aerial array, as seen here.

Focke-Wulf Ta 154A-1 specification
Type: two-seat night- and bad-weather fighter
Powerplant: two Junkers Jumo 213E 12-cylinder inverted-Vee liquid-cooled engines each rated at 1305 kW (1,750 hp) for take-off and 984 kW (1,320 hp) at 10000 m (32,810 ft)
Performance: maximum speed 650 km/h (404 mph) at 7090 m (23,250 ft), 534 km/h (332 mph) at sea level; maximum range (internal fuel) 1365 km (848 miles) at 7000 m (22,965 ft), (with two 300-litre/66-Imp gal auxiliary tanks) 1860 km (1,156 miles); time to 8000 m (26,250 ft) 14.5 minutes; service ceiling 10900 m (35,760 ft)
Weights: loaded 8930 kg (19,687 lb); maximum 9550 kg (21,050 lb)
Dimensions: wingspan 16.00 m (52 ft 6 in); length 12.45 m (40 ft 10⅛ in) without antennae; height 3.50 m (11 ft 1½ in); wing area 32.40 m² (348.76 sq ft)
Armament: two 20-mm MG 151 cannon with 200 r.p.g. and two 30-mm MK 108 cannon with 110 r.p.g.

Index